BRAZILIAN CULTURE

BRAZILIAN CULTURE

AN INTRODUCTION TO THE
STUDY OF CULTURE IN BRAZIL

BY

FERNANDO DE AZEVEDO

Translated by WILLIAM REX CRAWFORD

Professor of Sociology, University of Pennsylvania,
and Former Cultural Relations Attaché,
American Embassy, Brazil

(Facsimile of the 1950 edition)

HAFNER PUBLISHING COMPANY
New York
1971

Published by
HAFNER PUBLISHING COMPANY, INC.
866 Third Avenue
New York, N.Y. 10022

Library of Congress Catalog Card Number: 76-151829

Printed in the United States of America

CONTENTS

PART II. CULTURE

CHAPTER ONE. RELIGIOUS INSTITUTIONS AND BELIEFS 139

The history of the missions and the history of Christian civilization—The Company of Jesus and the Reformation—The first mission of the Jesuits to Brazil—Catechism! José de Anchieta—The gospel in the jungle—The tempest of the Reformation and its repercussion in Brazil—The foundation in Rome (1622) of a permanent Congregation for the Propagation of the Faith—The expansion of missions—The missionaries against the abuses of the conquest—Antônio Vieira in his struggle against the slavery of the Indians—Culture in this period more or less the tributary of religion—Catholicism and the influence of Afro-Indian religions—The big house, the chapel and slave quarters—Churches and temples—The pulpit in Brazil—The training of priests—The orders and religious congregations—Their wealth and their flourishing—Masonry—The activities of the masonic lodges—The fusion of Church and State—The influence of the clergy—The great preachers—The religious question—Freedom of worship and of belief—Protestantism and its progress—Spiritualism and other forms of religion—Theosophy—Positivism—The "religion of humanity"—Religion and culture—The dominance of the Catholic religion.

CHAPTER TWO. THE INTELLECTUAL LIFE— THE LIBERAL PROFESSIONS 165

Intellectual formation essentially literary in character—Men of letters and scholars—The inheritance of scholasticism and of classic culture—Grammar and rhetoric—Slavery and the repugnance for crafts and activities based on manual and mechanical work—Tendency toward bureaucracy and professionalism—The foundation of courses of law—Juridical culture—Lawyers and jurists—The cultural function of law schools—Foci of ideas and political campaigns—The Escola Central—The two faculties of medicine—Doctors, engineers, and lawyers—The élite classes, cultural, political, and administrative, recruited from the professions—A politics of doctors and fazendeiros—The preponderance of jurists in politics—The school of mines in Ouro Preto—Osvaldo Cruz and Brazilian medicine—Professional associations—The prestige of those who hold diplomas—A culture markedly professional in character—The professions and letters—The effort to go outside the bounds of one's profession and through culture to dominate the profession—Book selling—Bookstores and libraries.

CHAPTER THREE. LITERARY LIFE 193

The beginnings of Brazilian literature—Portuguese literature written in Brazil—The first original manifestations—Gregório de Matos and satire—Social differentiation and linguistic differentiation—The coexistence of two vernaculars down to the eighteenth century—The theater of Antônio José da Silva—The two national poems—The poets of the Inconfidência—Revolutionaries in politics, conservatives in letters—Journalism and the struggles of independence and in the first Empire—Political literature—Romanticism in Brazil—The attraction of Indian themes—Gonçalves Dias, the poet of the Indians—José de Alencar and the Brazilian language—Castro Alves, the poet of the slaves—The evolution of the theater and its principal figures—Memórias de um sargento de milicias—The national thought of Tavares Bastos—Parliamentary eloquence during the Empire—Joaquim Nabuco and Rui Barbosa—Agitators of ideas—Tobias Barreto and Sílvio Romero—The splendor of journalism—Eduardo Prado—

The Brazilian Academy and the unity of the language—The great lyrical poets—History —The two aspects of the national spirit—Machado de Assis and Euclides da Cunha—Essayists, critics, and pamphlet writers—The movement of modern literature—The poetry of the younger writers—Novelists and short-story writers—The spread of printing—Literature and the public spirit.

The Dutch period—The retinue of Maurice of Nassau—The first foreign explorers—The colony and the home country—The darkness into which the home country plunged colonial Brazil—The installation of the Portuguese court in Brazil—Dom João VI and the first schools and institutions of science—The National Museum—Studies of botany and zoology—The journeys of foreign naturalists through the interior of Brazil—Geology—The paleontological research of Dr. Lund in Lagoa Santa—The physical sciences—From Bartolomeu de Gusmão to Santos Dumont—The National Observatory—The scant interest of the Brazilian in physical sciences—Dom Pedro II and the sciences—The School of Mines—Mathematics and its principal cultivator—Gomes de Sousa—Museums and libraries—The National Library—Nina Rodrigues and legal medicine—Osvaldo Cruz and the center of research at Manguinhos— Geography and history—The Historical Institutes—The scientific spirit enters historic and geographic studies—The Brazilian Institute of Geography and Statistics—Foreign cultural missions—The social sciences—Sociology and ethnology in Brazil—Science and philosophy— Positivism—The philosophy of Farias Brito.

Art in its various forms in the colonial period—During the Dutch domination in Pernambuco —Sacred architecture and the baroque—The early churches of Bahia and of Minas Gerais— The cloisters of the Northwest—The painting and decoration of the churches—Sculpture: Aleijadinho—Religious art and carving—An original Brazilian art—Master Valentim—Goldsmithing and the art of jewel cutting—The colonial house—Religious music and popular music—The first Brazilian composer: Father José Maurício—The mission of French artists (1816)—The Academy of Arts—Grandjean de Montigny, architect—The first expositions of painting—The rupture with the art of the colonial tradition—The awakening of Brazilian feeling in art—Painters of historical pictures—Vítor Meireles and Pedro Américo—Brazilian painting of manners: Almeida Júnior—The great landscape painters—Henrique Bernardelli and Batista da Costa—The fine arts and the industrial arts—Art enters journalism: caricature —Brazilian music—The Conservatory of Music—Carlos Gomes—The movement of modern art—Traditionalists and innovators—The sculpture of V. Brecheret—The minor arts—Painting and its dominant figures—Portinari—Architecture and the breaking of the bonds between the useful and the beautiful—Music: Villa-Lôbos—The public and the artist—Museums and picture galleries—Historians and critics of art.

PART III. THE TRANSMISSION OF CULTURE

The ecclesiastical origin of education in Brazil—The Jesuit Missions and catechism in the colonies—The first school master—Manuel da Nóbrega and Aspilcueta Navarro—Apostles and educators—José de Anchieta—In the patios of the colleges and in the villages of the catechumens—Schools of reading and writing—Popular literary education with a religious background—The expansion of the Portuguese language among the aborigines—The social landscape of the Colony—The patriarchal family—The situation of women—The three careers or directions followed by the sons—The chaplains and uncles who were priests—The ideals of the cultivated man in Portugal—Teaching and the Jesuits—The colleges of the Fathers—Bachelors and masters of arts—Higher studies in the home country—The role of the University of Coimbra in the training of the élite—Seminaries—The monopoly of teaching—Toward the training of clerics and men of letters—The system of teaching as an ally of the city against the country—The colleges of the Jesuits and the patriarchal regime of life— The process of urbanization of the élite—The work of the Jesuits and national unity—The Marques de Pombal and the expulsion of the Jesuits (1759)—The destruction of the colonial educational system—The reform of Pombal put into execution—The royal schools and the literary subsidy—The schoolmaster-priests and chaplains of the sugar mills—Colleges of the monastic orders—The period of decay and transition.

CHAPTER TWO.   THE ORIGINS OF SCHOLASTIC
INSTITUTIONS   365

The revival of culture in Brazil—The influence of the ideas of the encyclopedists—Azeredo Coutinho and the Seminary of Olinda—The work of Dom João VI: the founder of institutions —The first schools for higher vocational training—The foundation of law courses in the first Empire—The Additional Act (1834) and decentralization—The absence of organized basic teaching and of general university teaching—The Colégio Pedro II—The patriarchal economy and the corresponding type of culture—Education for civilization based on slavery—Exaggerated tendency in the direction of the liberal careers—The predominance of a culture of professional character—Popular education and the first normal schools—Secondary education of a classical type—The almost exclusive cultivation of belles lettres—The splendor and decay of private secondary education—The great educators—The cooperation of the religious orders in secondary education—The activity of Dom Pedro II—The influence of the higher institutions of culture—The reforms of the Viscount of Rio Branco—The School of Mines in Ouro Preto—The opinion of Rui Barbosa in 1882—Tendencies of pedagogical thought—The last speech from the throne—A fruit which was not yet ripe . . .

CHAPTER THREE.   DECENTRALIZATION AND THE
DUAL SYSTEM   409

The transformation of the social and economic structure—The first rise of industry and the abolition of slavery—The change in the political regime—The Republic and the triumph of the federative principle—The Military School and influence of Positivistic ideas—The reform of Benjamim Constant—The separation of Church and State—The competition of the Protestant Schools and the influence of American pedagogical theories—Decentralization and the dual system—The federal system made up of secondary and higher education—The Institute of Manguinhos as a center of scientific research—The successive reforms of secondary education—The parallel, irregular expansion of state systems—The development of primary and normal school education in the States—The progress of education in São Paulo, the new center of the economic life of the country—New higher schools for the liberal careers— Isolated movements in the field of technical and professional education—An analysis of the educational structure in process of formation—Duality in the vertical sense—The system of

ILLUSTRATIONS

Between pages 34–35

59. São João d'El Rei, in Minas Gerais. In the background, the Church of Carmel. Photo by Stille, in collection of the College of Philosophy of São Paulo.
60. São João d'El Rei, in Minas Gerais. Colonial street, and in the background the Church of Carmel. Photo by Stille, in collection of the College of Philosophy of São Paulo.

Between pages 66–67

61. São João d'El Rei, in Minas Gerais. Old bridge and a mansion of the Empire period. Photo by Stille, in collection of the College of Philosophy of São Paulo.
62. São João d'El Rei, in Minas Gerais. Mansion of the Empire period. Photo by Stille, in collection of the College of Philosophy of São Paulo.
63. Mansion of the Empire period, in Mariana, Minas Gerais. Photo by Stille, in collection of the College of Philosophy of São Paulo.
64. Rio de Janeiro. View of the colonial city, including the door of the Church of Carmel. Photo by Stille, in collection of the College of Philosophy of São Paulo.
65. Rio Bonito, state of Rio. The church dominating urban life. Photo by Stille, in collection of the College of Philosophy of São Paulo.
66. Rio de Janeiro. Rua Direita (Straight Street). Rugendas, *Voyage pittoresque au Brésil* (1835), Plate 3/13.
67. "Carioca Square, Rio de Janeiro," painting by Nicolau Taunay. Photo by Carlos.
68. "Hill of St. Anthony, Rio de Janeiro," oil painting by Nicolau Taunay. Photo by Carlos.
69. Ubatuba, general view. Photo by ENFA.
70. Manaus. An aspect of the city. Central collection of the National Council of Geography.
71. Salvador, Bahia. Castro Alves Square. Photo by Voltaire Fraga, in Brazilian Institute of Geography and Statistics.
72. Salvador, Bahia. Pedro II Square. Photo by Voltaire Fraga, in Brazilian Institute of of Geography and Statistics.
73. Rio de Janeiro. A view of the urban center. Photo by Rembrandt.
74. Rio de Janeiro. Paris Square. Photo by Rembrandt.
75. Rio de Janeiro. View of the Sugarloaf. Photo by Rembrandt.
76. Juiz de Fora, Minas Gerais. An aspect of the city. Photo by Postal, in central collection of the National Council of Geography.
77. São Paulo. A view of the city, with the Anhangabaú Park, the new Chá Viaduct, and in the background, the Municipal Theater.
78. São Paulo. View of the center of the city, with its principal group of new modern buildings and, in the background, the industrial district of Braz.
79. Port of Corumbá, Mato Grosso. Partial view. Photo by S.G.E.F., in central collection of the National Council of Geography.

Between pages 98–99

80. Fortress of Monte Serrat (dating from the period of the Dutch invasion), Salvador, Bahia. Photo by Voltaire Fraga, in Brazilian Institute of Geography and Statistics.
81. Fortress of St. Anthony (1772) in Salvador, Bahia. Photo by Voltaire Fraga, in Brazilian Institute of Geography and Statistics.
82. "Battle of Guararapes," oil painting by Vítor Meireles. Photo by Rembrandt.
83. "The Departure of the Gold Caravan," oil painting by Almeida Júnior. Photo by the Museu Paulista.
84. "Bandeirantes," oil painting by Henrique Bernadelli. Photo by Carlos.
85. The first inhabitants and Fernão Dias Pais Leme. Peristyle, left side, Museu Paulista. Photo by Museu Paulista.

86. Palace of Justice, dating from 1660, Salvador, Bahia. Photo by Voltaire Fraga, in Brazilian Institute of Geography and Statistics.
87. Ouro Preto. Tiradentes Square. Photo by Radio Inconfidência, Minas Gerais.
88. Pantheon of the Inconfidência conspiracy (the old penitentiary), Ouro Preto. Photo by Radio Inconfidência, Minas Gerais.
89. Former Palace of the Viceroys and Imperial Palace (now Department of Post Office and Telegraph). Photo by Stille, in collection of the College of Philosophy of São Paulo.
90. "Dom João VI," oil painting by anonymous artist, perhaps José Leandro de Carvalho, Church of the Rosary, Rio de Janeiro. Photo by Vosylius, in collection of the Census Bureau.
91. "Independence or Death," oil painting by Pedro Américo. Reproduction of the canvas preserved in the Main Hall of the Museu Paulista. Photo by Museu Paulista.
92. José Bonifácio de Andrada e Silva, the Father of Independence. Photo by Museu Paulista.
93. "Coronation of Pedro I," oil painting by J. B. Debret. Photo by Rembrandt.
94. Palace of the Acclamation in Salvador, Bahia. Photo by Voltaire Fraga, Urbo Salvador, in Brazilian Institute of Geography and Statistics.
95. Pedro II, before attaining his majority, in 1840.
96. "Pedro II, Emperor," oil painting by Pedro Américo. Photo by Rembrandt.
97. "Battle of Avaí," oil painting by Pedro Américo. Photo by Rembrandt.
98. "Naval Battle of Riachuelo," oil painting by Vítor Meireles. Photo by Rembrandt.
99. Duke of Caxias, the Pacifier (Luiz Alves de Lima e Silva, Rio de Janeiro, 1803–1880), who by his invaluable work as military leader and statesman, bringing peace to the provinces, saved and consolidated the union of the fatherland. Photo from the collection of the Companhia Melhoramentos of São Paulo.
100. General Manuel Luiz Osório, Marquis of Erval (born in Rio Grande do Sul, 1808, died at Rio de Janeiro, 1879), pride of the Brazilian army and one of the heroes of the Paraguayan War. Photo from the collection of the Companhia Melhoramentos of São Paulo.
101. Admiral Barroso (Francisco Manuel Barroso, Baron of Amazonas, born in Portugal, 1804, died in Uruguay, 1882), victorious in the battle of Riachuelo, "one of the greatest naval feats known to history." Photo from the collection of the Companhia Melhoramentos of São Paulo.
102. Admiral Marquis de Tamandaré (Joaquim Marques Lisboa, born in Rio Grande do Sul, 1807, died at Rio de Janeiro, 1897), one of the great figures of the Brazilian army. Photo from the collection of the Companhia Melhoramentos of São Paulo.
103. Cathedral of Petrópolis, in which lie the mortal remains of the Emperor Pedro II and the Empress. Photo by Preising, in *Travel in Brazil*, Vol. I, No. 3, p. 19.
104. Benjamim Constant Botelho de Magalhães, the founder of the Republic.
105. Counselor Rui Barbosa, the principal author of the Constitution of 1891. Photograph of the period of the Provisional Government, 1890.
106. Baron do Rio Branco (José Maria da Silva Paranhos, Rio de Janeiro, 1845–1912), well known historian, geographer, and diplomat, the "Deus Terminus" of Brazil, as Rui Barbosa called him. Photo from the collection of the Companhia Melhoramentos of São Paulo.
107. Counselor Rodrigues Alves, who presided over the transformation of the city of Rio de Janeiro, together with Mayor F. Pereira Passos, and over the extinction of yellow fever, with Osvaldo Cruz.
108. "Head of an Indian," mural by Cândido Portinari. Photo by Vosylius, property of Sr. Mário de Andrade.

Between pages 194–195

grammar of the Tupi language. Published in Coimbra in 1595. Photocopy from the Department of Ethnography of the College of Philosophy of São Paulo.

298. Title page of the *Vocabulário na lingua brasilica,* one of the greatest repositories of Tupi terminology in the seventeenth century. The author is unknown; it bears the date 1621. It was published in 1938. Photocopy from the Department of Ethnography of the College of Philosophy of São Paulo.

299. Last page of the *Vocabulário na lingua brasilica,* of 1621, anonymous, written in Piratininga and published by Plínio Airosa in 1938. Photocopy from the Department of Ethnography of the College of Philosophy of São Paulo.

300. Front page of the first edition of the *Arte da lingua brasilica* of Father Luiz Figueira, 1576(?)–1643, a real contribution to the study of the Tupi spoken in the north of Brazil. Probably published in 1621. The copy in the National Library of Lisbon is unique in the whole world (cf. Serafim Leite). Photocopy from the Department of Ethnography of the College of Philosophy of São Paulo.

301. Church of the old College of the Jesuits, Salvador, Bahia. Photo by Voltaire Fraga, in Brazilian Institute of Geography and Statistics.

302. College of St. Ignatius in São Paulo, in the eighteenth century. In *Revista do Serviço do Patrimônio Histórico e Artístico Nacional,* no. 4, 1940.

303. "Old Mother Church and College of St. Michael of the Jesuits, in Santos," painting by Benedito Calixto.

304. Old College of Our Lady of the Rosary, of the Jesuits, in Paranaguá. Photo by Hess, from the Archives of the Serviço do Patrimônio Histórico e Artístico Nacional.

305. College of Our Lady of the Rosary, of the Jesuits, in Paranaguá. Arches of the cloister. Photo by Hess, from the Archives of the Serviço do Patrimônio Histórico e Artístico Nacional.

306. College of Our Lady of the Rosary, of the Jesuits, in Paranaguá. Cloister patio, seen from one of the archways. Photo supplied by Dr. Daví Carneiro, historian and director of the Colonel Daví Carneiro Museum, Curitiba, Paraná.

307. Church of St. Francis, Recife, built in 1606. Photo by Stille, in collection of the College of Philosophy of São Paulo.

308. Church of St. Francis, Recife. Sacristy. Photo by Stille, in collection of the College of Philosophy of São Paulo.

309. Church of St. Francis, Recife. A view of the interior. Photo by Stille, in collection of the College of Philosophy of São Paulo.

310. Church of St. Peter, Recife. Principal façade. Photo by Stille, in collection of the College of Philosophy of São Paulo.

311. Convent of St. Francis, Olinda. View of the cloister patio. Photo by Stille, in collection of the College of Philosophy of São Paulo.

312. Convent of St. Francis, Olinda. The building as a whole. Photo by Stille, in collection of the College of Philosophy of São Paulo.

313. Convent of St. Francis, Olinda. View of the sacristy. Photo by Stille, in collection of the College of Philosophy of São Paulo.

314. Church of St. Francis of Assisi, São João d'El Rei. Photo by Stille, in collection of the College of Philosophy of São Paulo.

315. University of Coimbra, in Portugal, which played so important a part in the education of the Brazilian élite. North façade. Photo by Rasteiro. In *História de Portugal,* by Damião Peres, p. 605.

316. Seminary of Olinda, created by the Bishop Azeredo Coutinho and installed in 1800 in the old building of the College of the Jesuits.

333. Abílio César Borges, Baron of Macaúbas (Bahia, 1824–1896), physician and great educator, who gave more than forty years' service to Brazilian education.

334. João Pedro de Aquino, engineer, founder of the Aquino Day School (1867), through which, during more than half a century, there passed thousands of students. This school inspired Rui Barbosa, and furnished data for his reform proposal in 1882.

335. Anchieta Academy, founded by Jesuit fathers in 1886 at Nova Friburgo, in the state of Rio, one of the most important secondary schools of the country.

336. Pedro II, who always showed an extraordinary interest in intellectual matters and was a great encourager of education and culture in general. A little known official portrait.

337. The Imperial (later known as National) Museum, founded by Dom João VI as the Royal Museum. Here, beginning in 1876, scientific courses and public lectures were given at the initiative of Ladislau Neto, who was its director from 1874 to 1893. Photograph of the building in which the Royal Museum was originally located, and which was occupied in 1892 by the National Archives, with the transference of the National Museum to the Imperial Palace of the Quinta da Boa Vista, Rio de Janeiro. Photographic copy from the National Archives.

338. Facsimiles of the signatures of King João VI, the founder of institutions, of Pedro I, creator of law courses in Brazil, and of Pedro II, whose name is linked to all the scientific movements of the past century.

339. Viscount Rio Branco, under whose ministry (1871–1876) was established in 1875 the School of Mines of Ouro Preto, and reforms and movements took place that were of the greatest importance to Brazilian civilization.

340. Henri Gorceix (1842–1919), a Frenchman, who organized and was the first director of the School of Mines of Ouro Preto.

341. Joaquim Cândido da Costa Sena (1852–1919), mineralogist and third director of the School of Mines of Ouro Preto.

342. Counselor Rui Barbosa, author of the famous opinion no. 64, with which he supported, as reporter for the commission appointed on September 12, 1882, the plan for reform presented by Counselor Dantas, in the Chamber of Deputies. Photograph of the year 1918.

343. Counselor Leôncio de Carvalho, minister of the Empire, the innovator, author of reforms in 1878 of radical character based on liberal ideas.

344. Benjamim Constant Botelho de Magalhães, famous professor in the Military School, Minister of Instruction, Posts and Telegraphs, whose school reforms, undertaken between 1890 and 1892, all show to a greater or lesser degree the influence of positivist ideas.

345. A. Caetano de Campos, eminent physician and educator, one of the leaders of the reform movement of São Paulo, 1891–1895, a movement limited to primary and normal-school education, and strongly influenced by American pedagogical tendencies.

346. Colégio Granbery, at Juiz de Fora in Minas Gerais, created in 1889, one of many schools founded by Protestants in the last quarter of the nineteenth century. Such schools aided materially to spread American educational ideas in Brazil.

347. Cesário Mota, Secretary in the State Government, who, with the support of Caetano de Campos and Gabriel Prestes, promoted in São Paulo between 1891 and 1895 the most fruitful reform movement of the first decade of the Republic.

348. A view of the library of the oldest Normal School of São Paulo, still located in the building constructed in 1894 and enlarged in 1936–1938.

349. Another view of the library of the old Normal School, now known as Caetano de Campos Normal School

Between pages 482–483

350. The Polytechnic School of São Paulo, founded in 1893, three years before the Engineering School of Mackenzie College. Photo by Liberman.

351. The School of Manguinhos, created in 1901, which took the title in 1907 of Osvaldo Cruz Institute of Experimental Pathology, honoring its founder, who cleaned up Rio de Janeiro. Photo by Walter Sales, in *Travel in Brazil*, Vol. II, no. 2, p. 12.

352. The Institute of Manguinhos, which played an important part in the victory and spread of the scientific, experimental spirit. Reading room and library. Photo by the Photographic Section of the Osvaldo Cruz Institute.

353. The Institute of Manguinhos. Third floor gallery. Photo by the Photographic Section of the Osvaldo Cruz Institute.

354. Epitácio Pessoa, minister in the government of Campos Sales and author of the Educational Code of 1901, in force to 1910.

355. Rivadávia Correia, who was responsible for the "organic educational law" (decree of April 5, 1911). With its sectarian radicalism it reflected the positivist attitude then dominant in Rio Grande do Sul.

356. The Agronomical Institute of Campinas, which, created in 1887 by the Imperial Government, was transferred in 1892 to the State of São Paulo, and had Franz W. Dafert as its first director, 1887–1897. Old building (1920).

357. Luiz de Queiroz Higher School of Agriculture, at Piracicaba, created in 1901. Part of the grounds, with the principal building in the background.

358. Luiz de Queiroz Higher School of Agriculture. Laboratory, Department of Genetics, recently added to the equipment of the school.

359. Alvares Penteado School of Commerce, founded in 1902, one of the first commercial schools created in Brazil.

360. Nilo Peçanha, during whose government (1909–1910) schools for apprentices were created in the state capitals.

361. Paulo de Frontin Vocational School, in the Federal District, for domestic science and girls' vocational education, in its new quarters built during the administration of Antônio Prado Júnior (1926–1930).

362. Heitor Lira, a great idealist, who in 1924 founded the Brazilian Education Association. This has played a notable part in promoting and stimulating movements for the spread of culture and the improvement of schools in the country.

363. The United States School, in the Federal District, in traditional Brazilian style. One of the side views. Photo by Nicolas.

364. Uruguay School, in the Federal District, erected in various blocks between 1928 and 1930—one of the largest built during the administration of Antônio Prado Júnior. Side view from the patio of the school.

365. School for physically weak children, in the Quinta da Boa Vista (Federal District, 1926–1930). Gallery and fountain of one of the patios. Photo by Nicolas.

366. Father Correia de Almeida Consolidated School, at Belo Horizonte in Minas Gerais, where the new movement in education was especially strong under Francisco Campos and Mário Casassanta (1927–1930). Principal façade.

367. Pedro II Consolidated School, at Belo Horizonte, one of the most important school buildings erected during the administration of Francisco Campos, Secretary of State of Minas Gerais. Galleries and internal courtyard.

368. The Normal School of the Federal District. Building erected between 1928 and 1930, during the administration of Antônio Prado Júnior. Drawing by Cortez & Bruhns, architects.

369. The Normal School of the Federal District, which in 1933 was reorganized and named Institute of Education. A view of the courtyard. Drawing by Cortez & Bruhns, architects.

370. The new Normal School of the Federal District, reorganized by the reform movements of 1928 and 1933, and located in its new buildings constructed during the administration of Antônio Prado Júnior, 1926–1930. General view. Aerial photograph by S. H. Holland, Rio de Janeiro, 1930.

371. The new Normal School of the Federal District, known since its second reorganization in 1933 as Institute of Education, in its new buildings finished in 1930. Central court seen from a gallery of the ground floor. Photo by Nicolas, Rio, 1930.

372. Normal School of the Federal District, now Institute of Education. Gymnasium, magnificently equipped with apparatus, baths, dressing rooms, and galleries. Photo by Nicolas, Rio, 1930.

373. Francisco Luís da Silva Campos, one of the leaders of the 1930 revolution, and first Minister of Education and Health, author of the most important reform of secondary and higher education in the republican regime (1931).

374. The Biological Institute of São Paulo, created in 1928 as a result of the efforts of Artur Neiva, former assistant chief of the Osvaldo Cruz Institute, and reorganized by Professor Rocha Lima, its present director, who was also one of the colleagues of Osvaldo Cruz. General view.

375. The Biological Institute of São Paulo, for study and research in the pathology of all forms of life, animal and vegetable, and especially those that are of the greatest interest to man. Principal façade.

376. The Biological Institute of São Paulo. One of its experimental farms.

377. The Biological Institute of São Paulo, one of the greatest research centers in America—like the Osvaldo Cruz Institute, famed throughout the world. View of one of the laboratories.

378. The Agronomical Institute of Campinas, in the state of São Paulo, today one of the most important centers in Brazil for the investigation of plant life. One of the new buildings erected beside the old building.

379. The Agronomical Institute of Campinas. View of a greenhouse.

380. The Astronomical Observatory of São Paulo, in its new and excellent quarters. General view of the buildings. Photo by ENFA.

381. The College of Philosophy, Science, and Letters of the University of São Paulo—the first to be founded by government in Brazil. A view of one of its buildings, showing the greenhouses of the Botany Department. Photo by Liberman, São Paulo, 1942.

382. The first College of Philosophy, Science, and Letters—that of the University of São Paulo, created in Brazil by the decree of January 25, 1934. A view of the Mineralogy Museum of the Department of Mineralogy and Petrography. Photo by Liberman, São Paulo, 1942.

383. College of Philosophy, Science, and Letters of the University of São Paulo, in which, under the guidance of foreign and Brazilian professors, a group of first-rate research men has been formed. One of the biology laboratories. Photo by Liberman, São Paulo, 1942.

384. Principal façade of the Institute of Education of the University of São Paulo, which graduated in 1937 the first class of secondary-school teachers in Brazil. They had previously taken courses in the College of Philosophy.

385. Institute of Education of the University of São Paulo, which was created in 1933, and no longer existed in 1938. A view of the Ethnographic Museum of the Department of Educational Sociology.

386. The new and magnificent building of the São Paulo Public Library, to which was added

INTRODUCTION

What is meant by "culture"—The variety of meanings given to the word—The anthropological conception of culture—The inclusion under this term of both material and nonmaterial elements of civilization—The French concept of culture—The limitation of culture to nonmaterial elements—Nationalistic and universal concepts of culture—Civilization and culture—The point of view adopted by the author for the study of culture in Brazil—The factors of culture, physical, racial, technological and economic, social and historical—The concept of Brazilian civilization—Education, the transmission of culture—A work of synthesis—Difficulties of a work of this nature—"An hour of synthesis presupposes years of analysis"—Lack or insufficiency of specialized monographs—The usefulness of a comprehensive view, as perfect as possible.

WORDS TRAVEL, too. They migrate from one people to another, and even when they do not cross the frontiers of a State or the limits of the language in which they were formed, they pass from one class or social group to another, taking on "distinct tonalities which fasten upon them and end by adhering to them," and which come either from the particular mentality of groups existing side by side within a given society, or from the genius of the people to whose language they have been transferred. Thus, while the general activity of a society tends to standardize language, shaping it in its own image, the action of subgroups tends to make for differentiation, at least in so far as the vocabulary is concerned. "Every science, art, or trade in composing its terminology marks with its character words in common use." [1] The vocabulary of a science, then, is made up in part of neologisms, that is, words created especially to designate new ideas and notions, and in part of expressions introduced from the vernacular, in which their sense is more or less fixed. But, as Meillet notes, the meaning of a word in common use "is defined by the ensemble of ideas with which the word has been associated, and its associations obviously vary according to the group in which it is used"; [2] therefore terms such as "civilization" and "culture," both of recent creation and use, when introduced by scientists into a special vocabulary trying to give them a precise meaning, resist that effort with the wealth of ideas which they evoke and the variety of meanings which cling to them in common speech. Thence come the various more or less arbitrary meanings, sometimes restricted, sometimes amplified, and the varied shades of thought with which they appear in works of a scientific nature. The word "civilization," the use of which in French would seem to go back to the year 1766, and which signified a state contrary to barbarism, establishing a distinction between peoples with orderly government and savage peoples, came to designate, in ethnological language in French, as the term "culture" does in

[1] Michel Bréal, *Essai de sémantique (science des significations).* (Paris: Hachette), 3rd ed., p. 285.

[2] A. Meillet, "Comment les mots changent de sens," *L'Année sociologique,* Vol. 9 (1905–1906), pp.13-19.

1

English, "the ensemble of characteristics which the collective life of a human group presents to the eye of the observer," whether that group be primitive or civilized. Both terms, "civilization" and "culture," [3] in the ethnological and sociological vocabulary which they entered, served to designate two different ideas, which are opposed to each other and dispute for first place.

In fact, for Clark Wissler, who has undertaken to establish "a comprehensive system of the processes of human civilization and of the factors which contribute to it," [4] culture is the mode of social life, that part of human behavior which, coming from the external environment, material, intellectual, and historical, "makes of individuals what they become." The concept of culture in the Anglo-American sense has acquired a broad meaning like that of civilization in French, coming to embrace not only the spiritual elements but all modes of life, and even the material characteristics of life and of the organization of different peoples. If in the broad sense are included under the same term the products of mental, moral, artistic, and scientific activity, as well as the material bases of social evolution, all peoples, from primitive societies of embryonic organization to the most highly evolved societies, certainly possess a culture in the anthropological sense adopted by Wissler and other American anthropologists and ethnologists. This conception, which extends the term "culture" to the material bases of society and its technology and has acquired wide acceptance among American scholars, has its origin in England in the work of E. B. Tylor, and in that of the long series of his followers. The English anthropologist, fifteen years before the American, understood by the culture of a people "a complex which includes the knowledge, beliefs and arts, the morality, laws, customs and any capabilities and habits acquired by man as a member of society." It may seem that this definition includes no reference, or at least no very clear one, to the material factor; but if we consider that "customs, arts, and habits" certainly include material elements it will be easy to recognize that the word assumes in the work of Tylor, from whom the Americans derive their terminology, the same broad sense of their anthropological concept of culture.

Thus, the two admirable institutions, the anthropological section of the Oxford University Museum—a notable fruit of the efforts of Tylor and Henry Balfour—and

[3] In the Portuguese language the common meanings which the dictionaries record for these two words are the same that are given by French dictionaries. The *Vocabulário Português e Latino* of R. Bluteau (Coimbra, 1712) and the *Elucidário* of Viterbo (2nd ed., 1865) do not give the word "civilization." The *Dicionário* of Antônio Morais da Silva (8th ed., 1890), in which the term does occur, defines it as follows: "the advance, progress, and development of the state of society, as shown by the perfection of the laws, the mildness of customs, the great public works, and the intellectual culture as represented in the sciences, letters, and arts." The definition of Caldas Aulete (2nd ed., brought up to date, 1925) is almost identical, and is obviously based on that of Morais. In the *Novo Dicionário da Língua Portuguêsa*, Cândido de Figueiredo, by trying to achieve conciseness, became vague and obscure. "A people," adds Morais, "can be called civilized if it has forsaken barbarous ways, and is governed by law"—which is repeated word for word by Father Domingos Vieira (*Grande Dicionário Português*, 1873), who records the two terms "civilization" and "culture." As for "culture," aside from its concrete meanings (cultivation of the earth, of plants, breeding of animals, etc.), all these lexicographers, except Viterbo, bring out the figurative, abstract, intellectual meaning: "the cultivation of letters, science, the fine arts; instruction and education; the state of one who is intellectually highly developed." Bluteau, in 1712, already recorded it in its metaphorical sense, "the culture of talent, of arts and science."

[4] Clark Wissler, *Man and Culture* (New York: Crowell, 1923).

later that of the American Museum of Natural History, with Clark Wissler, succeeded after much research and debate in establishing a general agreement and at the same time a "deeper analysis of the idea of civilization and its content." Both groups, that of the school of cultural anthropology of Oxford and that of the American Museum of Natural History, include under culture the whole "social mode of life," the mode of life of a people as a whole,[5] giving the term the broadest extension of which it is capable. To be sure, the anthropological concepts of culture, according to these English and American scholars, differ on certain points; but they have in common the decision to include both material and spiritual elements. The anthropological definition of "culture," which, as we saw, goes back to the work of the first British anthropologists, Tylor and others, and which is accepted in the United States by eminent anthropologists such as Lowie, Kroeber, Goldenweiser, and Wissler, is clearly characterized by the fact that there are included in the term not only the habits and products of the mental activity of a people but also material elements. But if Tylor tended rather to limit culture to nonmaterial elements, which at least are preponderant in his total system of culture, Wissler on the other hand excludes language from culture, now treating it as a constituent part of the cultural system, now placing it apart; Wissler, then, includes under one term all social phenomena except morphological facts, or all that according to Durkheim are considered as social morphology, and that he considers as belonging to "man" and the "geographic environment." Marcel Mauss is justified, then, in criticizing the opposition Wissler establishes between man and culture and his division between language, society, and culture, as equally false and capable of giving rise to confusion rather than clarifying our understanding of the phenomena of culture and civilization.

French sociologists since Durkheim, comments Mauss, "consider all social phenomena as a whole and cannot even conceive of these divisions. For sociology this duality—*man* and *culture*—is nothing but a way of describing *homo duplex*, the social being and the psychophysiological being that man is. Any process of abstraction which would separate the social and the human being would be dangerous. We cannot conceive man without his culture. He would not be a man. 'Culture,' thus understood, is only another word to designate society, which is as much a part of *homo sapiens* as nature. And finally, there is no reason to distinguish and separate the different elements of social physiology from each other, law, for instance, from religion or from morphology." To the criticisms which Mauss makes of the not always consistent abstractions and divisions on which Wissler founds his theory—in many respects so fecund and suggestive—we may add those related to the difficulty of his fundamental attempt to subsume under the single rubric of "culture" the spiritual and material elements of society. It is impossible to deny the existence of relations between culture, properly so called, and the material bases of society and its technology; nor can one deny the interest there is in investigating the material, technical, and economic behavior of societies, and the material bases of this behavior. However, without denying the role played by material factors in the evolution of human groups and the usefulness of these studies which can furnish us points of departure for getting to know important aspects of social reality, it seems to some of us arbitrary and illegitimate to include under the same term the material bases of society

[5] "This round of life in its entire sweep of individual activities is the basic phenomenon . . . culture" (Wissler, *Man and Culture*, p. 2).

and its truly cultural activity (arts, letters, and science). Moreover, we run the risk of distorting the idea of culture in its restricted sense and giving support to a material, if not materialistic, interpretation of social evolution and the history of human thought.

While the term "culture" in the anthropological sense, Paul Arbousse-Bastide reminds us, "achieved recognition in the language of England and America, it met a decided resistance in France where already it had a deeply rooted and very spiritual meaning. In Germany its meaning varied in tormented indecision between the classic, impersonal significance and the national one, which was closely bound to the anthropological meaning." However, once the word had been adopted in this general sense, there came into use, along with the term in its inordinately broad meaning, the expressions "culture areas," "cultural levels," "cultural diffusion," "culture conflicts," and others such as the ideas of culture complexes and traits. Some of these, including "cultural levels" (*Kulturschichten*) and "culture areas" (*Kulturkreise*), had already been used by Graebner, the assistant of Willy Foy, director of the Ethnographic Museum of Cologne, in his work on the method of ethnology,[6] in which ethnology is presented, according to his much discussed definition, as "the science of the strata and areas of civilization."

As Mauss remarks, Wissler is one of the Americans who, under the influence of German ethnologists, and especially of Graebner, extended even further the use of the principle of culture areas, of centers of invention and routes of diffusion, as well as the concepts of complexes and traits. The success achieved by these ideas, in which the anthropological attitude toward culture was developed, is bound up on the one hand with the fact that thus material objects, being "more easily perceived, measured, and classified," become more susceptible of scientific description, and on the other hand with the fact that material elements and anthropological factors furnish "inexpugnable points of departure, much safer than collective representations, beliefs, traditions, social organization," which, to be sure, can be analyzed and treated objectively, but are "capable of tendentious interpretations and even of being simply made to order." Progress in the direction of objectivity, "observable in all sciences, especially those of more recent development, which are anxious to assert their scientific character" (we are still quoting Arbousse-Bastide), "favors this tendency to use material facts as a point of departure; they can be known exactly and surely." But in France the anthropological definition of "culture," with the wide meaning which the word acquired, embracing immaterial products of the human spirit as well as life habits, utensils, apparatus, and instruments, seemed to do violence to its current and traditional meaning, and to represent a debasing of a term employed to designate the highest creations of the human mind.

To be sure, the use of the term in the broad sense corresponds, as Samuel H. Lowrie points out, to a specific need of anthropology and ethnology, "the need of a term to signify all the achievements, material and nonmaterial, of a human group, without regard to its stage of social evolution." Faced with a choice between creating a new term and giving a new meaning to a word that exists in various languages, anthropologists preferred the latter solution, and gave the term "culture" this amply comprehensive meaning. They were within their rights and did no more than add to the term one more meaning over and above the various, widely different ones which it had in the languages

---

[6] Fritz Graebner, *Methode der Ethnologie* (Kulturgeschichtliche Bibliothek, ed. W. Foy), (Heidelberg: C. Winter, 1910).

in which it was found; [7] but this new meaning goes so much against the current from a past laden with spiritual connotations that, in accepting it in its anthropological sense, we must always keep in mind the sense in which we use the word, if the nature of the book or monograph is not sufficient to make it absolutely clear. The fact is that the word "culture" in the sense with which it passed over into the terminology of sociology in other countries, and in France above all, as Arbousse-Bastide bears witness, "continues to be the refinement of intelligence, the concern for the fine arts. It is held usually that it should be disinterested, that is, should not have immediate or narrowly utilitarian ends." It is a certain development of intellect, the taste for and interest in the arts and the progress of science, that characterizes culture, in which it is not difficult to recognize these essential elements: (1) a personal and collective effort to free man's spirit; (2) disinterestedness—that is, however close may be the relation between the useful and the beautiful, between the useful and the true, culture does not aim directly at utilitarian ends; (3) the sense of human tradition, which consciously or unconsciously, seeks as its supreme ideal whatever may be the richness of the sap which feeds its roots deep down in the national humus. By conserving and creating values, far from being indistinguishable from material life, technology, and economics, it is "an effort of intelligence and will to dominate and direct them" and to rise to the gods, that is, "to the impersonal and eternal values which are above men and some day may come to unite them." [8]

If, however, in this abstract or intellectualistic sense, it can be said that there is only one human culture, valid for all the societies that have attained a certain level of development, culture, even in this restricted sense, is always bound to national traditions and tends to take on different aspects and forms depending on its environment. It will be more authentic and original if the sap which rises from its roots deep down in the national humus is rich and substantial; but it cannot come into bloom as a true flower of civilization unless it opens, at the height of its growth, for all times and all peoples. This "union of culture and civilization, baptized among Latin peoples with the name 'humanism,'" according to Arbousse-Bastide, is what gives the word "culture" "its most complete, most human, and most fecund meaning." Concepts of culture can vary from one nation to another; national cultures can be, and actually are, made up in varying proportions, depending on the period and the people, of elements from the national tradition and from the tradition of humanity; but the universalist conception is not opposed by a nationalistic idea of culture except when, instead of a fusion or harmony of their elements, there is established on the contrary an antagonism of values, or there grows up the idea of the superiority of certain nationalistic elements to human and universal values. This is what happened to the meaning which the word "Kultur" acquired in Germany as early as the beginning of the nineteenth century under the influence of the

[7] This same meaning is to be met in the definition of "culture" according to Thurnwald, for whom culture is "the systematization and harmonization of all knowledge and skills, of the civilizing equipment and the traditional individuality of a people, their social and mental constitution, coming down through time. We call culture," adds the German ethnologist, "a system of attitudes, ways of acting, of customs and value judgments, institutions and organizations of a society." Richard Thurnwald, *Die menschliche Gesellschaft* (Berlin, 5 vols., 1931–1935), Vol. 4, p. xvi. Cf. Herbert Baldus and Emilio Willems, *Dicionário de etnologia e sociologia* (São Paulo: Editora Nacional, 1939).

[8] Paul Arbousse-Bastide, "Cultura e matéria: Que é cultura," *Estado de São Paulo*, July 21, 1935.

romantics; and the war only emphasized the phenomenon. The word emigrated from the French language and, with the loss of the humanistic sense that the classics gave it, came to be applied, as Tonnelat reminds us, to "a culture-type, the better example, the fitter to serve as a model to other national cultures, the more strongly it is supported by the power of the State and of religion." [9] In fact, says Tonnelat, "for the writers of the classic period the word 'Kultur' meant above all progress, both in the material and in the intellectual and moral senses, and this progress is an achievement of humanity considered as a whole. For later writers, on the contrary, it means an ensemble of intellectual achievements viewed as one's own property, sometimes even as the exclusive property of a limited community, which is thought of as a State or nationality." [10]

But, in spite of the complexity of the relation between civilization and culture, arising in large part from the variety of meanings given to these two terms in France and Germany, the distinction seems to us acceptable which Wilhelm Humboldt established when he defined "civilization" "as everything which in the material realm, in the development of customs and social organization, has the effect of rendering peoples more humane in their institutions and their mentality, considered in relation to those institutions," and reserves *Kultur* to designate a shade of refinement, marked by the disinterested study of science and art. "Civilization" has for Humboldt a wider meaning, embracing in its conceptual content not only technology and the applications of science to material life—certainly important matters—but also certain qualities of mind that emphasize its moral and intellectual aspects. The idea of politeness, of refinement and of culture is for Latin peoples so bound up with that of civilization (*civilis*, polished, refined) that the word always evokes in their minds the idea of decorum, that is, a certain equilibrium between intellectual and moral development and social organization. This same Latin meaning is found in German authors such as Humboldt, and more recently Burckhardt, for whom *Kultur* is in a way "the flower of history which lends its brilliance to the customs and institutions of a particular epoch." Culture, according to Arbousse-Bastide, "can mean

---

[9] Emile Tonnelat, "Kultur: Histoire du mot, évolution du sens," in *Civilisation: Le Mot et l'idée.* (Paris: La Renaissance du Livre, 1930).

[10] The word *Kultur*, borrowed from the French *culture*, "appeared only belatedly in the German language; and it was only in the second half of the eighteenth century that its use became common." At the end of that century, Tonnelat states, it had three principal meanings: (1) a state contrary to barbarism; (2) the modern freedom of the mind or emancipation from prejudices; (3) distinction and refinement of manners. These are the three meanings which "are to be met most of the time in the writing of authors of the classic period, although with varying shades of thought." Thus Herder, Kant, and Schiller consider culture "as the common property of all peoples, or at least as something which can become common property." For Humboldt, who in defining the terms *Civilisation, Kultur, Bildung* endeavors to give exactness to *Kultur*, that word "indicates that men have been able to rise above simple considerations of social utility and have undertaken the disinterested study of science and the arts." Goethe, however, has a different conception; he gives this meaning to *Bildung*, and considers *Kultur* as an ensemble of knowledge, customs, and traditions characterizing a certain people. (Cf. the anthropological meaning of "culture.") In any case, in the meaning they give to *Kultur*, the classic writers, says Tonnelat, "never associate with that word the idea of the superiority of one people to another." That idea arose with the generation of the romantics, to acquire strength with Fichte and his followers, for whom culture tends to be confused with the state or a nationality, and who attribute to their country or their people a cultural mission, proclaiming the superiority of German culture—the "culture-type" which is most qualified to serve as a model for other national cultures. (Tonnelat, *op. cit.*)

only a certain flowering of intelligence, by virtue of which man becomes more humane, that is, more inclined to understand and love other men. Culture is the part of intelligence in civilization." In the broader sense, which subsumes under the generic term "civilization" [11] material organization, economic, political, and social life, customs, and the spiritual life of a people, and "culture," a specific term with a limited sense, designates the vital impulse of letters, science, and arts, which by ennobling our institutions, continually enrich civilization and render it more fertile.

The point of view which we adopt in this work is, then, that given by the classic, French and German notion of culture, as clearly enunciated by W. Humboldt when he established the distinction between culture and civilization. With Humboldt, we understand by culture that moral, intellectual, and artistic state "in which men have managed to rise above simple considerations of social utility and have achieved the disinterested study of the sciences and arts." Social life, to be sure, can be reduced to a system of functions which aim at the satisfaction of men's fundamental needs, among which the economic function serves our material needs and the political function (to give only two examples) has as its object "to defend the existence of the society taken as a whole and also as the union of special groups," regulating the relations of individuals and groups to one another and to the whole—the state or nation. But a society, if it wishes to preserve itself and to assure its progress, far from being content with satisfying the requirements of its material life, strives to satisfy its spiritual needs by means of a constantly renewed élite, consisting of individuals, scholars, thinkers, and artists, who constitute a special social stratum, above social classes and outside them. Thus, "to create that spiritual atmosphere without which society cannot breathe, the spiritual bonds without which it would not be a unit, the treasury of spiritual goods without which it could not live," says Arnošt Bláha, "precisely this is the function of the intellectual." This function is, consequently, a function of production, of circulation, and of organization in the spiritual realm: creator of values and spiritual goods, by which it gives rise to a realm which is a fatherland and refuge for all, the mind not only distributes them and endeavors to make them accessible to the greatest possible number, but also undertakes the organization of society from a spiritual point of view, "attaining its highest expression when it undertakes to

[11] In his excellent study of civilizations, their elements and forms, Mauss endeavors to define the ensemble or system of facts which constitute a civilization. "The phenomena of civilization are by definition," says he, "social phenomena, but not all social phenomena are phenomena of civilization. There are some which are the exclusive property of a society, which give it its separate and isolated character. . . . There are others which have an important characteristic: that of being common to a larger or smaller number of societies and the more or less extensive past of these societies. To these we may reserve the use of the name civilization." Some, adds Mauss, are unfit to travel, while others naturally lend themselves to diffusion; of themselves they go beyond the boundaries of a given society, boundaries which for that matter it is often difficult to establish with accuracy. Thus the phenomena of civilization are essentially international, or extranational (Latin civilization, with its variants, the French, Italian, etc.), and civilizations are *limited* by their power of lending and expanding (positive phenomena) as well as by the resistance of the societies which compose them to the process of borrowing. And, finally, Mauss shows that the international character of the facts of civilization grows (science which is universal in its nature and uses a language that is necessarily human, technology, cinema, radio, etc.), and that "the number of common traits tends to increase, and each of the nations and civilizations tends to become more like the others by constant adding to the common base, in number, weight and quality." (Marcel Mauss, "Les Civilisations: Eléments et formes," in *Civilisation: Le Mot et l'idée*. Paris: La Renaissance du Livre, 1930).

organize moral life." Culture, then, in this restricted sense, and in all its manifestations, philosophical and scientific, artistic and literary, being a work of creation, criticism and improvement, as well as of diffusion and realization of ideals and spirtual values, constitutes the noblest and most fecund function of society, the highest and purest expression of civilization.[12]

Thus, having limited the sense in which we shall use the word "culture," that is, having taken it in its classic meaning, we shall direct our study to the production, conservation, and progress of intellectual values, of ideas, of science and the arts, of all, in short, which constitutes man's effort to dominate the conditions of material life and to free his spirit. As the social and spiritual level of intellectuals, scholars, thinkers, and artists is due not only to certain biopsychological superiorities intimately bound up with the nature of the individual, but also to the greater or lesser intensity of the action of civilizing influences, and as in consequence there cannot be spiritual creation where stimuli to the life of the spirit are lacking or spiritual values are insufficiently appreciated, the study of culture in all the variety of its forms, in its diffusion and intensity, is in itself a light that illumines the nature, power, and degree of development of a civilization. This study, which forms as it were the kernel or backbone of our work, is preceded by an analysis of the factors of all kinds which condition the production of cultural, scientific, and esthetic phenomena, and therefore serve to help explain them; it is followed by a description of Brazilian educational institutions, of general education and specialized training, of all that has as its object the methodical (or systematic) transmission of the culture in all its aspects. This, as will be observed, is an order of presentation that is at the same time logical, psychological, and genetic; for if culture presupposes and implies a complex of conditions which establish a social and historical climate favorable to the flourishing of letters, science, and the arts, the study of which is not only useful but quite indispensable to the understanding of cultural phenomena, the educational system which in every people aims to conserve and transmit the cultural heritage, constantly renewed and enriched as it is in the course of being handed down through successive generations, tends to develop and become more complicated in proportion as the creations of the spirit in the various realms of culture and civilization increase. In order to understand and explain the culture of a nation one must place it in a geographic, social, and historical framework, follow it through the different stages of its evolution, study its basic attitudes and tendencies, in order to indicate which of the institutions were organized with the object of transmitting the now systematized culture from generation to generation, thus insuring its continuity in time, its unity, its diffusion, and its progress.

And so, before beginning the study of culture as such which constitutes the central part of the book, it has seemed to us necessary to analyze the major influences that have been at work affecting the production of cultural phenomena, whether they be the physical environment and ethnic composition (the country, race), the economic, social, and political environment, urban environment (various types, the life of the cities), or the peculiar mentality of the people—this latter in its turn determined by all the elements which have conditioned its formation. These various orders of phenomena may all, in

[12] Arnošt Bláha, "Le Problème de l'intellectuel," in *Revue internationale de sociologie*, Vol. 44, pp. 361-372 (July-Aug., 1936).

varying proportions, have a definite relation to cultural facts, not only in that they furnish culture with subject matter, but above all because they provoke and guide, acting upon culture as causes or factors; it is quite possible, as far as certain kinds of phenomena are concerned (economic, urban, collective mentality), that they may undergo counterblows or reactions from culture, may receive from culture a definite stimulus. It is for this reason that instead of holding them to be true causes, we prefer to consider them as a complex of factors or conditions, substituting for the concept of cause that of correlation between the phenomena which constitute the principal object of our study and those which condition them and contribute to explaining them. The legitimate doubt which always prevents our jumping to hurried and oversimple conclusions in the study of social phenomena would not permit us to give allegiance to any of the so-called "geometric" theories, which have recourse to a *single causative factor* (geographic environment, race, economic factors, etc.),[13] theories which, as Alfredo Nicéforo justly points out, "may all have their interest and importance, but which, taken separately, cannot be more than a sort of monosyllabic interpretation of the complex phenomenon under discussion." However that may be, to analyze on the one hand those factors (geographic, racial, economic, historical, etc.) which not only vary from one people to another but form combinations in various proportions, and on the other hand the very life and evolution of a society under the pressure of those factors, and the influence of the society on the individual to whom it furnishes a frame of reference, the organization and structure of his mind—this is to explain how, in a given country, the phenomena of culture arose, the particular forms which they took, the direction and rhythm of their evolution.

Among the factors which contribute most powerfully toward the production of *cultural phenomena,* the development of cities [14] is one of the most important; its function is to intensify collective energy and to raise to the highest possible level of development the capacities that lie latent and dispersed in the population. Cities in fact are powerful instruments of social selection, whether, as Hansen sees them, they do nothing other than attract, by a kind of mechanical selection, the best elements of the country, serving to select them, without making any contribution to their value; or whether, as

[13] Although we would not neglect the influence of telluric, racial, and economic factors upon the behavior of individuals, and consequently upon social facts, we consider as arbitrary and unilateral any doctrine which attributes prime importance to the influence of the natural environment, race, or economic structure, "according to that vague idea of *homo geographicus* which might lead geographers to commit the same errors which the idea of *homo economicus* induced among economic theorists for more than a century." Neither the doctrine of geographic determinism nor that of economic determinism seems to us acceptable. The assertions of Ratzel about the territorial forms of States and the political evolution which they involve, "are there to keep us reminded," observes Lossier, "of the dangers there are in seeking in natural conditions the cause of given social structures which are far too complex to permit of a unilateral explanation." Ratzel's concept of society, as it is an excessively *passive* concept, attaches too much importance to the influence of nature upon man, neglecting the action of man on his natural environment—a factor which is perhaps more important. Lossier asks, "Is not the growing homogeneity of cultures and of tastes one of the most visible results of civilization, and is this tendency not an obstacle to the free play of natural laws?" (Jean G. Lossier, "De quelques théories géographiques au point du vue sociologique," in *Revue internationale de sociologie,* Vol. 47, Nos. 1-2, Jan.-Feb., 1939).

[14] Weber, Adna Ferrin, *The Growth of Cities in the Nineteenth Century: A Study in Statistics* (New York: Macmillan, 1899).

Weber holds, on the contrary they have the power of giving *reality* to qualities which would otherwise be only virtual, calling into existence forces which without that stimulant would remain inactive and dormant, and producing this effect of excitation by the mere fact of concentration. Thence the study, which seems to us highly interesting, of the development of great cities and of the concentration of population in urban areas. If the term "civilization," as Lenoir points out,[15] "refers to the ensemble of activities by means of which human beings pass from animality to humanity, it may seem paradoxical to apply it to the societies we call primitive. Do they not appear to have as their principal characteristic that of not being citizens and of not knowing the cities in which behavior and knowledge take on definite form and are transmitted?" There is, in fact, so close a connection between civilization and urban life that to designate the former phenomenon recourse was had to the term *civilis* (from *civis,* citizen; *homo civilis, zoon politikon,* of Aristotle), as the source of the word "civilization," used in various languages, and in itself implying the contrast, which goes back to ancient times, between the city (*civitas, polis*) and the country (*rus, silva*). Not without reason do we use the terms *civilitas, urbanitas,* civility, urbanity, when we wish to express refinement of manners, reciprocal benevolence in human relations, and on the other hand use the words *rusticus, silvaticus* (countryman, woodsman, rustic, uncultivated man) to designate precisely the opposite of civilized. In any case, even if the specific components of civilization are not always to be found in the characteristics of urban populations, are they not the "true objective indices of a superior civilization," as a result of the metamorphosis which cities produce in ideas and customs and of the powerful stimulus they offer for the flourishing of arts and letters and the creations of the spirit, the superexcitation produced by the phenomena of concentration?

To be sure, not all the transformations in ideas and customs which take place under the pressure of city life can be considered as evidence of an advance in civilization, at least from the moral point of view; nor must we confuse city life, which is characteristic of all civilizations, with the rapid growth of cities, which is a relatively new phenomenon. Certainly we shall not find in the great cities the purity, freshness, and innocence of country life, the charm and simplicity of the rural scene, nor the vigor and impulsiveness which is shown by the strong, instinctive life of the backlands. Besides, as internal migration is of the essence of the phenomenon, the progress of the great centers is frequently the result of migratory movements from country to city; cities, in modern civilizations, sometimes become veritable suction pumps applied to the rural populations that are within reach of the magnetic influence of urban communities. We all know with what impetuosity the younger generation throws itself into the pursuit of pleasure, in a kind of intoxication, when a small city, surrounded by a rural area, begins to undergo a transformation due to technology and the applications of science to material life, and its population grows and becomes denser, partly as a result of the incorporation into the old city of suburbs and neighboring districts, partly as a result of a population which comes from outside and is added to that which already has its roots there. But neither can it be denied that in the different forms through which urban life has passed from antiquity to our own times, the Greek and Roman cities, medieval and Renaissance and modern cities have played such an important part in the development of the arts, of

[15] Raymond Lenoir, "Les Sociétés humaines," *Revue de synthèse historique,* Dec., 1924.

literature and science that it is impossible to separate culture from city life. In fact, it is in the concentrated collective life of cities that we find developed an expansive force creating the energy of the individual genius; it is here that rich, original natures, if they do not exactly have their fount of inspiration, at least absorb energy and vigor through all their pores, benefiting by an air that is more intellectual, an atmosphere fuller of stimuli for the arts and sciences.

In any case, it is necessary to place Brazilian culture not only within the social, economic, and political framework of the history of the country, studying the factors and special environmental conditions that lie back of it, but also in the general movement of western civilization, of which our culture is only one of the special forms. Even before Mauss, Durkheim taught that, if there are social phenomena closely related to a certain social and political organism, to a people or nation, there are others which "transcend national boundaries and continue their development over a period of time longer than the history of a single society." [16] These facts or complex bodies of facts which, without being limited to a particular political organism, are nevertheless capable of being localized in time and space, constitute, Durkheim would teach us, the phenomena of civilization. If, then, a civilization—for instance, the Mediterranean—"constitutes a kind of moral environment in which a certain number of nations are immersed, and of which each national culture is only a particular form," it can be understood how important it is for our comprehension of the phenomenon in Brazil that we relate it constantly to its *fundamental source*—Iberic civilization, and more generally to western civilization—and then analyze the *special characteristics* which that civilization acquired in the interior of Brazil under the pressure of factors operating there and in conformity to the various conditions of our historical and social evolution. But the necessity we are under, in the direct study of cultural phenomena, of always remembering such relations, is even more obvious if we consider that among the social facts of civilization are to be found the fine arts, the forms and ideas of belles-lettres, and scientific knowledge. Thus, relating the history of Brazilian culture on the one hand to that of the ideas which had an influence upon it, and in general to the evolution of the great religious, political, and philosophical currents of the West, and on the other hand to the specific conditions of Brazilian social life, such as the country, racial factors, the forms of social, economic, and political structure, we shall be able to understand better the parallel evolution which took place in Europe and in Brazil, without wide separation from their common source; we shall understand more easily the special forms which culture took on among us, the ease with which certain currents of ideas spread, and the resistance which the society opposed to other manifestations and movements of western culture.

It is possible to observe in Brazil if we sum up the culture, after tracing the essential lines of the evolution of Brazilian society, a strongly marked phenomenon of *culture lag,* between culture and civilization. That civilization is present in Brazil in all its fundamental aspects, there cannot be the slightest doubt. Refinement of customs, respect for the human person, tolerance and hospitality, whether in relations between citizens or toward the foreigner, spirit of order and love of peace, constant improvement of juridical organization and of social techniques, and, more recently, the desire for comfort which

[16] Emile Durkheim and Marcel Mauss, "Civilisation et types de civilisations: Note sur la notion de civilisation," in *L'Année,* Vol. 12 (1909–1912), pp. 46-50 (Paris: Alcan, 1913).

has developed with the application of the sciences to material life, all these are a proof of the degree of civilization we have already attained, which, even when we compare ourselves with the most civilized peoples, can in many respects well offer us reason for pride. Among Latin peoples the word *civilis* has a moral significance—polite or refined; in this respect, in the matter of tolerance, of politeness, of a high distinction of manners, with just the right touch of reserve and respect for privacy, it may be said that the flower of civilization is in full bloom among us. And, given the intimate relations between civilization and culture, such that one cannot exist without the other, it is impossible to conceive of such a high degree of moral civilization as being compatible with neglect of culture or with the absence of that culture which has as its function to ennoble and strengthen civilization and to maintain society "on that level to which every advance in civilization raises it." Every part of our book in which we deal with culture shows that, in fact, it does exist, that it has already given evidence of itself in various typical works of literature or art, with a power and a spiritual delicacy that are quite worthy of our civilization. But it is not less certain that our culture has serious gaps, and that in quality as well as in quantity, especially from a philosophical and scientific point of view, it has not developed *pari passu* with our civilization, that it is noticeably backward in comparison with other countries that share our civilization, and is marked by superficiality and dilettantism, is artificial and "detached from the civilization in which it grew up." Still, to employ the language of Arbousse-Bastide, "besides maintaining the conquests of civilization, it is the duty of culture to guide and enlighten it, and that not merely with respect to the progress of technology." If by civilization man conquered things and material life, "by culture he must (especially in a period in which much importance is attached to material life) avoid allowing things to obtain their revenge and come to rule him."

Every people has, as it were, its own temperament and genius, the result of centuries, which are the products of the physical environment, of racial elements, and of their social evolution. These appear in their history and institutions, and in their language, literature, works of art and of philosophy. Culture in all its manifold manifestations, being the intellectual expression of a people, not only reflects the dominant ideas in each of the phases of its historic evolution and in the civilization of which it forms a part, but also penetrates into that dark and fecund realm in which the feeling of nationhood is born. However powerful may be the originality which the individual genius impresses upon his work of art or literature, this work also bears the stamp, more or less clearly outlined, of the spiritual and moral nature of the nation. But a society expresses its ideals, its collective character, and its tendencies—even better and more profoundly than in its philosophy, art and literature—through education, which not only is one of the most characteristic aspects of culture but is the very vehicle of culture and civilization. The study of education from its origins to its present state, in its structure, objectives, and procedures, cannot be omitted from a work which proposes to give a general view of the culture of Brazil. If, in fact, we remember that education in its essence is the transmission of a civilization, is pressure exerted by an older generation upon a younger one, with the purpose of making the latter accept and carry into practice the ideals of the older generation, we shall understand that "those ideals," as Paul Fauconnet says, "are perhaps most easily learned by observing the process of their transmission." In that which a generation does in order to create its successors, there is certainly an opportunity to surprise the secret of its soul and to get a picture of the whole society, seen through its system of education. It is for this reason, it is because of the elements which the study of education furnishes for the psychological and social analysis of the character of a people, that the French sociologist rightly considers the history of education as "one of the surest ways to penetrate the psychology of a people and the history of its past."

Thus, if education, which is a function of social life, varies in form and content from one society to another, and if every society tries by means of education to give actuality to its own unique ideal, "a practice or an institution cannot be diffused without showing profound evidences of the collective character." However, being directly dependent upon the general organization of society, education begins to show diversities related to social classes and the professions from the time when societies achieve a certain degree of differentiation, and continues to become more complicated in the course of its development, by reason of the greater complexity of social life. In proportion as the social organization and culture of a particular society become more complex, the techniques and knowledge that are transmitted to the younger generation grow and become complicated, and the changing educational system enriches itself by new and more specialized institutions. The quantity and the nature of the knowledge that is transmitted to the young, the variety of professional institutions that come into existence to meet a collective need for specialization, the poverty or complexity of the educational system, obviously vary with the social conditions of each human group and reflect their needs, their special mentality, their historic past, and the general tendencies of their evolution. If, then, we undertake an inquiry into the pedagogical institutions of a people, examining them in the course of their evolution and studying their structure, the objectives they pursue and the means they use to attain them—both of these social, for the nature of the objectives predetermines the nature of the methods [17]—it will be practicable to reconstitute not only their social evolution, their concept of life and of man, their hierarchy of values, the changes that have taken place in their ideas and in their particular mentality, but also the type, the kind, and the degree of culture which the people have attained, and which is always expressed in the institutions meant to maintain and transmit the culture from generation to generation. In a given people, interest in culture, in things of the spirit, manifests itself constantly and inevitably in the way society, working through the ensemble of its educational institutions, sets about educating its children, raising the cultural level, and extending to the greatest possible number the benefits of civilization.

It may with reason be objected that the necessary materials are insufficient, if not totally lacking, for a work of this nature, which aims at no less than giving a general view of Brazilian culture in its evolution, from its origins to its present state. A work of synthesis has, from its very nature, the double object of bringing together the fragmentary knowledge that until now has been scattered in detailed monographs, and of omitting all that is of secondary importance, non-essential or merely accessory, in order to seize upon the *essential* and trace the main line of development. A brief, practical,

---

[17] E. Durkheim, "Pédagogie et Sociologie," *Revue de métaphysique et de morale,* Jan., 1903, pp. 37-54.

schematic exposition runs the risk of losing itself in obscurity or of becoming superficial, unless it is preceded, during the course of its slow preparation, by a prolonged effort at analysis which seeks in every period, and with reference to each one of the cultural manifestations, to isolate the essential—that which survives, not only because of its intrinsic value, its authentic, original value, but because of its power to illumine and affect the whole culture. An hour of synthesis, it has been said, presupposes years of analysis; and the synthesis certainly gains vigor and exactitude in proportion as it penetrates deeply into events, going back to their causes and coming down to their consequences. The breadth of the cultural field which the author must illuminate, the variety of subject matters each of which would exhaust the ability of a specialist, and the complexity of the facts studied give some idea of the labor necessary in undertaking a work which is so extensive that only years of effort and the collaboration of many people could see it through. Of all the difficulties met in the preparation of this book, however, not the least was the insufficiency in some cases, the absolute lack in others, of specialized monographs. Such detailed studies by specialists, if they had been numerous, would have rendered an attempt at summary possible; and then the author need only have explored the data collected to arrive at a true picture, a profound understanding of the history of the culture of his country, in its evolution and in all its aspects.

Any one who has made the attempt to trace in broad lines the evolution of our literature, for example—or, within this limited field, that of one literary genre such as the theater or oratory—can testify to the difficulties which harass every effort to give a panorama of our culture in all its manifold manifestations. The action and interaction of social phenomena, the effect, so difficult to determine, of events on men and of men on events, the complexity of the evolutionary process, in which one must consider, along with the general tendencies observable in every evolutionary process, accidents and unexpected contingencies such as an invention or discovery—all these require a solid and broad base of special monographs, if in a work of this character the mind is not to waver on that vague boundary line which separates dream from waking, fantasy from reality, "the more or less" that is arrived at by intuition from the exact and precise which is achieved by systematic observation of facts. If one can already find, for some aspects of our culture, the materials that are indispensable in this essential task—materials certainly fragmentary, but within their limits truly instructive—the present state of our research and the poverty of our scientific equipment still render daring any effort to achieve clarity and order in the chaos of detail and to establish very distinct lines of demarcation between the various phases of our cultural evolution. In almost all the monographs, even in some of the best, in which penetrating, highly suggestive observations are not lacking, such scattered indications, however intelligent, scarcely conceal the absence of a direct attack upon the essential problems, of a systematic study of conflicts and repercussions. In addition to the fact that a large part of our source material is still unpublished and that there are few monographs that can be considered exhaustive, it is only recently, with João Ribeiro and Capistrano de Abreu, that our historical studies began to be pursued with a scientific spirit and consequently to show more rigor in their interpretation of facts.

But are we to conclude, from all the difficulties inherent in a work of this nature, that an attempt at summarizing Brazilian culture would be useless or fruitless? We think not. Above all, a bird's-eye view, however imperfect it might be, would have the advantage of bringing together in systematic form many acute observations, many sound data which, scattered through a large number of monographic studies, lose much of their power to explain and necessarily remain incomplete. However difficult it may be, it is possible, by utilizing known materials and the impressions formed in reflecting on the facts, to portray tentatively the history of culture in Brazil without caricaturing it to the delight of the pessimists who fail to place the Brazilian cultural effort in the framework of its social and historical climate, and at the same time without presenting a picture agreeable to our national vanity but of no value for opening our eyes to reality and leading us to further efforts to free our minds. Thus such a work would be essentially an examination of our own conscience, based on serious thinking and writing, backed by proofs; and, with all the defects that follow from the scarcity of sources upon which to rely, it would fulfill its purpose if it succeeded in creating new interest in the subject and leading some day to a masterly summary which will become possible only with the development of the necessary preliminary works of erudition and research. Already João Ribeiro, Pandiá Calógeras, and Pedro Calmon, among others, have written works from a general point of view, embracing the whole history of the country; and these works, without being definitive, are a sort of panorama in their different styles—one, of elegant sobriety, another, of energy and aridity, and the last, of highly colored poetry—through which their writers have given us a new vision of the history of our country and have made a great effort to penetrate to the very heart of the mechanism of our social, political and economic institutions.

The object of this work, limited to the study of culture, is much more restricted; and, if a general view of our whole historic and social evolution has already proved feasible, we may be permitted to attempt to present a similar view of our cultural evolution. It is this aim, in addition to the conviction that the work would be useful to Brazil, that inspired us to write this book, taking upon our shoulders the task which was laid there, a task so difficult and arduous that it might well have been laid on stronger shoulders. Certainly there must be some one to whom it can be proposed that he write a synthesis with a wide historical horizon, with a strong sense of the great problems, with a profound awareness of the complexity and interdependence of social phenomena, and likewise of the intimate relation of specifically cultural facts and activity with other social phenomena of different categories. The various manifestations of culture, of which we should have a false idea if we studied them as microcosms isolated within the social whole, have in this work been brought constantly into relation with the evolution of the main political, economic, and religious currents, which at various periods of western and Brazilian history have led the whole country in a single direction or arrayed some of its parts in conflict. We have always preferred the complex human fact to any rigid formula in which one might endeavor to imprison the many-sided living reality; rejecting all dogmatisms likely to falsify our understanding of the facts, our thought aims at an interpretation of cultural, esthetic, and scientific facts, an interpretation that is often sure and safe in view of the source material collected, and at other times hypothetical but we hope none the less suggestive. The spirit of synthesis and general ideas dominate the whole work, leaving in the shade or in the background to which their minor importance or influence relegate them, names, facts, and works without profound cultural signifi-

cance, which would have their place rather in an analytical work or in one that specialized in major and minor historic scenes. "Posterity abbreviates," as Emile Faguet put it
in his admirable way; "and it is within its rights, for we write for it; and it is also posterity's duty, and, however unlikely this may appear, a pious duty, since it abbreviates
only in order not to lose everything."

PART I

THE FACTORS OF CULTURE

CHAPTER ONE

LAND AND RACE

The physical environment—Topography and territorial extension of the country—The opposition of the two continental slopes—The two great hydrographic basins—Distances and the diversity of natural settings—Geomorphic and climatic environment—Flora and fauna—Mineral resources—Ocean and coast—Regions of dense and sparse population—The São Francisco, river of national unity—Origins and make-up of Brazilian population—The three races which contributed to the formation of the population of Brazil—Anthropological data—Distribution of the population in north and south—Natural increase of the population—Internal migration—Immigration—Race mixture—Social selection and classification—Static and dynamic density—The distribution of the population by age, sex, and race—The Brazilian.

I F WE EXAMINE the physical map of South America carefully, the dominant impression we get of this continent as a whole is that of an immense land mass which flows down like a volcanic eruption from the Andes to disappear into the Atlantic. The great wall of the Andes extends from north to south, a proud barrier of peaks and plateaus which rise to gigantic heights and fall abruptly, and from which not a single river flows into the Pacific, while on the eastern slope enormous masses of water, the Amazon in the north and the Plata in the south, and the waters of the São Francisco and Parnaíba between the other two great hydrographic basins, roll slowly or impetuously toward the Atlantic Ocean. On the Pacific slope an aggressive, vertical line predominates, with the roofs and peaks of the Andes raising their heads to the clouds, contrasting violently with the eastern terrain of high land, plateaus great and small, mountains rolling toward the east with an average height of less than three thousand feet, rising to about nine thousand only in the mountains of the coastal chain (Itatiaia, in Mantiqueira and the Pico da Bandeira in the Serra do Caparaó, in Minas), and toward the south lie lazily in the endless vastness of fields and plains. On the Pacific side the coast is smooth, poor in indentations and articulations, in contrast to the bays, gulfs, and coastal islands, slightly cut up but hospitable, bathed by the Atlantic. But if we turn our attention to the continent that faces us across the South Atlantic, the two coasts, African and Brazilian, will not fail to appear so alike in their general lines that we can without difficulty imagine the two present continents as the result of a cutting apart of a single former block. America constitutes, in fact—in so far as the present state of science permits us to judge—the remnant of an immense ancient continent which fell apart into Australia, surrounded by the Pacific, the Indies, separated by the Indian Ocean, and Africa and the South American continent, separated by the Atlantic Ocean. It was at the beginning of the period known in geological history as Cenozoic that valleys clothed themselves with earth, lowlands were inundated, the Andes, like the Alps and Himalayas, rose from sea level to beyond their present heights, and the earth took on the configuration which in its principal features and outlines it has today.

Analyzing this likeness of the coasts of the South Atlantic, Wegener,[1] as well as Pickering, was led to admit the existence of an old land connection between Brazil and Africa, and to suppose that these coasts are the edges of a widened fracture, America having suffered a movement equal to the width of the Atlantic. These two continents, actually united until the Cretacean era, must have drifted toward the west, pulled by solar attraction acting upon viscous bodies on the earth's surface. South America, in the opinion of the author of the theory of continental drift, "must have been contiguous with Africa, to the point of constituting with it a single continental block. This block was separated during the Cretaceous era into two parts, which in the course of time separated like two pieces of ice that break in the water. The outlines of these two lands are even today noticeably similar. Not only is there the great rectangular projection of the elbow which the Brazilian coast shows at the Cape St. Roque, which is reproduced in reverse by the idented elbow of the African coast in Cameroons; but in addition, for the regions situated to the south of these two points, for every projection of the Brazilian coast there is a corresponding indentation of similar shape on the African coast, and to every bay on the Brazilian side there corresponds a projection on the African side. At the time of the drift of these continental masses [2] toward the west, the anterior edge of the two Americas became extremely rugged as a result of the frontal resistance to its advance presented by the abysmal depths of the Pacific, a resistance explainable by the fact that the Pacific, having existed as it was since the most remote geological epochs, had had time to grow very cold and become more resistant. Thence resulted the gigantic chain of the Andes which runs from Alaska to the Antarctic.

The America which resulted from the ruin of this ancient world can be divided geographically into two great sections: on the west, Andean America, looking down on the Pacific; and on the east, Atlantic America: on the one hand, Brazilian, Amazonian, Caribbean, tropical America; and on the other the region of the pampas, temperate America. Now Brazil with its eight and a half million square kilometers—a vast country barred from the Pacific by the great wall of the Andes, and sloping entirely in the direction of the Atlantic—occupies in South America or Latin America an area only a little smaller than that of all of Europe or of the United States. Rising in the north in the plateaus of the Guianas to curve down into the Amazonian plain—"an immense trough through which empty the gutters of this side of the Andes"—this vast territory rises again to the south of the Amazonian lowland, in the enormous central plateau, "falling off gradually toward the north and east," in the words of Afrânio Peixoto, "rising at times almost to a peak in the southeast, ending at the Atlantic coast in a narrow border of low-

---

[1] Alfred Wegener, *Die Entstehung der Kontinente und Ozeane* (1st ed., 1915, 4th ed., 1929), transl. by Armand Lerner, Nizet, and Bastard as *La Genèse des continents et des océans: Théorie des translations continentales*, (Paris, 1937). Cf. A. Betim Pais Leme, "O depoimento do Brasil na discussão da teoria do deslize dos continentes segundo Wegener," *Boletim do Museu Nacional, Rio*, Vol. 5, p. 41, and "La Théorie de Wegener en présence de quelques observations géologiques concernant le Brésil," *C. R. Acad. des Sciences*, Vol. 186, p. 802.

[2] That theory of the great horizontal movements of the continents, by which Wegener explains the movements toward the west which gave rise, among other phenomena, by means of fragmentation and slipping, to the American continental block, not only does not reject, but actually implies the *theory of isostasy*. According to this idea, "the earth's crust floats in a state of equilibrium on a denser and more viscous support"—a state which can be disturbed by various factors (overloading of the earth's crust by a glacier, accumulation of sediment, etc.)

lands." The coastal mountain chain which now falls abruptly to the sea as if it were emerging from the bosom of the waters, and now descends toward the interior, forming along the coast a narrow strip of plain, appears to dominate the landscape, "like an immense wall following the coast and defending the interior." South of Mato Grosso the plains of Alto Paraguay, continuing those of Argentina and of the Grand Chaco, give this region an aspect of its own which markedly differentiates it from all other physiographic regions of the country. The opposition of the two continental slopes which define the backbone of the Andes—that of the Pacific, from which the chain of the Andes separates us, and that of the Atlantic, whose waters bathe the eastern part of the country from north to south—gives special importance to the side that faces the Atlantic, to the whole Atlantic system, which, as Calógeras says, "tends and naturally will tend to surpass socially and economically the fringe of the Pacific."

It was by way of the Atlantic that the colonizers made their entry, that international commerce was established; it is there that the major part of domestic commerce goes on, and that all the currents of civilization cross. The lungs of Brazil certainly breathe the air of the sea, of the Atlantic, and it is by means of the oxygen that it absorbs from the intensity of its sea-borne trade that the national organism will regain the vitality necessary to continue the exploits of the period of discovery and of the *bandeirantes,* by conquering the west for civilization. It is quite certain that the sea helps to form the intellectual and moral temperament of the people who live by it, extending their political horizon, stimulating their creative energies and making them foci of civilization. But without challenging the historic role played by the sea at all times, as Ratzel demonstrated,[3] or the notable contribution of the Atlantic to the history of Brazilian civilization, we must consider, on the one hand, that all maritime power depends on the nature and form of the lands which touch the sea and give access to it, and, on the other hand, that, if maritime power is developed on the water, it is on the continent that it has its point of departure and base of action. Capistrano de Abreu had already noted, as Afrânio Peixoto reminds us, that, "being without indentations, the immense seacoast of Brazil did not lend itself to navigation, and so the primitive inhabitants of the country remained isolated and backward. Even today coastwise navigation is so difficult that various near-by parts of the country live quite separated." Add the fact that, however great may be the action of the sea on the mind of men, the sea in itself is nothing more than a road open to humanity. It is, in the words of Durkheim, "a free field which calls for life to develop, but it is not a source of life. A purely maritime power is impossible; it must have support on land, and its continental bases must always be proportional to the importance of its maritime expansion. If the equilibrium is broken, the State, without a solid base, exposes itself to being swept away by the slightest disturbance." The very extent of the coast, which offers as many facilities to commerce as to invasions, emphasizing our role as a maritime State, renders the problems of national defense more serious and demonstrates that in order to dominate the Atlantic, the continental bases on which the nation is to rely must be solid and extensive.

The absence of valleys at right angles to the coast, which extends from one end of

[3] Friedrich Ratzel, *Das Meer als Quelle der Völkergrösse.* Munich: Oldenbourg, 1900. Cf. Hans Helmolt, *Weltgeschichte,* Vol. IV, *Die Randländer des Mittelmeers,* Leipzig: Bibliographisches Institut, 1900.

Brazil to the other with its beaches of white sand "between the dark green wall and the dark blue sea," marking its eastern boundary, and the magnificent Serra do Mar [4] which rises like a bastion parallel to the Atlantic coast line, but also like an obstacle to the conquest of the plateau, constitute, along with the immense length of the coast line, fundamental aspects of the geographic character of the country, and also constitute problems which nature has presented as challenges to the energy of man if he would rule the sea. Along the west, Brazil has 14,500 kilometers of land boundary from south to north bringing it into contact with practically all the Hispanic-American peoples; in contrast to this, on the east, it has almost 8,000 kilometers of seacoast bathed by the Atlantic. It is easy to understand why the colonizers began with the coast, "digging into the sand like crabs," in order later to surmount the cordillera and reach the plateau, whence exploring bands set out to make this the greatest center of Brazilian civilization. But the physical picture of the country, in bold outline from east to west, is that of the two continental slopes of the Pacific and Atlantic—the true *mare nostrum;* this fact takes on its full meaning and importance only if we consider the immense territories to be penetrated which have the coast as their base and are limited on the south by the valley of the Plata and on the north by that of the Amazon. The Brazil of the Amazon region, says Mário Travassos, "leads most directly to the ocean because it has the Amazon River as a natural highway, and it is most easily penetrable, for the Amazonian valley is the greatest receptive center of that tremendous amphitheater which curves from Caracas to La Paz. The Brazil of the Plata region, although it needs artificial aids to link it to the ocean, has on its coast ports with considerable ability to attract and also has the stimulus of two countries to the south which naturally react against the centripetal force of the Plata: the south of Mato Grosso, an extension of the states of São Paulo and Paraná, indicates its power to penetrate."

The immense volume of water which descends from the Andes collects in the limit-

---

[4] The geographical configuration of the south of Brazil is marked by two great traits which distinguish its physiognomy: higher toward the sea, the land descends toward the great depression of Paraná, where the lowest levels of the continent are reached, which would seem to be a prolongation of the geosyncline that existed at the end of the Paleozoic era, and connected with the fosse of the Andes. On the one hand, therefore, the escarpment of the Serra do Mar, and on the other the alluvial depression, the greatest known (the Chaco Boreal). These two geographic factors go back, perhaps, in their geological origins, to the Carboniferous or neo-Paleozoic: at that time the thaw moved in the direction of the basin of the Paraná, and in proportion as the Chaco gained in depth and filled up with sediment, by isostatic compensation, the land along the Atlantic rose. The waters of the Tietê, which probably flowed directly to the ocean, and which later, with the uplift at the beginning of the Quaternary, in large part ceased to move and became an extensive lake around the capital of São Paulo, in the gneiss of the Serra do Mar, separated from the Paraíba and finally emptied toward the west in the direction of the basin of the Paraná. Thus the Tietê, which had its source twenty-five kilometers from the ocean at an altitude of some 1100 meters, cut off from its old higher course, which at present belongs to the Paraíba, had time, before the land rose, to turn toward the west, "and to keep the way open by means of erosion." The crossing of the Serra do Mar was necessarily the first step in the conquest of the plateau, isolated from the ocean by that barrier, and from the interior by the floods of the middle course of the Paraná and the Paraguay: the serra was scaled by the first colonists, following the paths of the Indians, trodden later by the slaves, on whose shoulders coffee was transported until cable traction on the inclined planes of the São Paulo Railway was established. The lifting of the coast, however, which made the rivers run toward the interior, toward the Paraná, if it formed a barrier to communication with the ocean, permitted and favored travel (exploring, slave-making, and prospecting bands) to the sertão, along the rivers that flowed toward the interior.

less trough and overflows into a labyrinth of swampy forest and narrow waterways under the verdant tunnel of the prodigious equatorial forest; the destructive, erosive action of the torrent in its course, corroding mountains, tearing down banks and sweeping away parts of forests which float downstream, "like monstrous unmasted boats," in short, all that savage, tumultuous nature of Amazonia has already found its incomparable delineator in Euclides da Cunha, who in his pages on the "land without history" gave us the most superb picture of these overwhelming landscapes. For him, "man there is still an impertinent intruder. He arrived, unexpected, unwanted, when nature was still setting in order its most vast and luxurious salon. He met opulent disorder." And face to face with the spectacle of all the things torn apart and carried off by the muddy waters, man sees in the Amazon "the unknown journey of a territory on the move, the marvelous effect of a kind of migration of the lands: the land is abandoning man; it is in search of other latitudes." The amazing sight of this wonderful movement of land and water, this stupendous phenomenon of nature in process of evolution, leads Euclides da Cunha to accept the only geological theory which fits the picture and to see in Amazonia, along with Alfred Russel Wallace and Charles Frederick Hartt, perhaps the youngest land in the world, born of the last geological convulsion which raised the chain of the Andes. This is the same conception which he adopted in *Os Sertões*, when he studied the geological formation of the central part of Brazil; it served also as point of departure for Liais in his hypothesis of the origins and structure of these backlands.[5] According to this conception, in opposition to Wegener's theory, up to the Tertiary period South America was divided into two great islands by a Cretaceous ocean across its center which linked the Atlantic to the Pacific. But when the mountain range emerged from the waters and the rocky masses of the plateaus of the Guianas rose "this inland sea between the plateaus of the north and the mountains of the south closes on the west, grows narrower, is compressed, breaks up into isthmuses, and ends by being reduced to the channel of the Amazon."

Between the two hydrographic basins which characterize the Brazil of the Amazonian and Plata regions, communicating directly with the ocean through their network of rivers and making these regions two "more or less eccentric" worlds, there extend from north to south the northern subequatorial and the eastern slope of the plateaus, which are called upon, as it were, to link together those two enormous regions. The long line of convex coast which stretches from Guanabara to the Gulf of São Luiz, corresponds like a kind of cord, says Travassos, "to the terrestrial line marked by the upper and lower valley of the São Francisco and the Parnaíba." Or, in other words, "on the outside by sea, and on the inside by land, the function of these regions is to link, to make homogeneous, and to bind together the two Brazils that are essential from a continental point of view,

[5] According to this hypothesis of Emmanuel Liais (1826-1900), the French astronomer who came to be director of the Observatory of Rio de Janeiro, this stretch of the interior of Bahia "rises like a flat pile of worn-down mountains," in consequence of the convulsion which caused the rise of the Andes and raised the high plains of the Guianas, "sweeping all the land into a slow rotation around an axis" which he imagined as being "between the heights of Barbacena and Bolivia." The northern lands of Bahia bulk higher, continually rising, and the highest regions are dotted with lakes, while the lowlands continue to be immersed. See Emmanuel Liais, *Explorations scientifiques au Brésil* (1865), *Traité d'astronomie appliquée à la géologie et à la navigation* (1867). Cr. Euclides da Cunha, *À Margem da história* (3rd ed., Porto, 1922); José Maria Belo, *Inteligência do Brasil* (3rd ed., Editora Nacional, 1938), pp. 162-165, the essay on Euclides da Cunha.

that of the Plata and that of the Amazon." The line of the valley of the São Francisco would give us the string of this bow, the extremities of which are made up of the two regions of the Amazon and the Plata; the tighter we make the bow and the closer its ends come together, the farther and stronger will be the course of the arrow of civilization shot from the plateaus to the western region. This rapprochement between the end zones, with a decisive influence on both internal and continental politics, is the great task to be accomplished by a national policy in the fields of production, transportation, and communication—on the one hand made extremely difficult by the great distances, but on the other hand facilitated by the very fact that Amazonian and Plata Brazil represent "two regions that converge with reference to the real geographic center of the continent (the Bolivian plateau), either by artificial means (the port of Santos, the network of São Paulo railways, the Northwest), or by more natural highways such as the rivers of the Amazonian basin." The general movement of civilization toward the west, which has been called the "march to the west," is obviously related to this double movement on its flanks, a movement toward the Bolivian highland, which besides the advantage of bringing together the two ends of Brazil has another advantage, that of linking two oceans, uniting the Pacific—that great isolator of peoples—with the Atlantic, the waters of which seem to be rocking the cradle of a new civilization.

In this connection there is an observation by André Siegfried which does not strike us as being so true as it might appear at first sight. Siegfried [6] asserts that, depending on whether the destiny of the continent is more influenced by the geographic factor or by the historical factor, the Latin American democracies will move toward Pan-American unity or will maintain for many years to come those cultural ties with Europe which have bound Latin America to the old world since the period of colonization. Latin America, in other words, in the process of its rapid industrialization, will move as it has moved in the past, now about the vertical axis (the United States), now about the horizontal axis (Europe). But these oscillating movements, besides being determined more by economic, political, and cultural factors than by the geographic one, prove that Latin America continues to gravitate like a satellite around two great nuclei of civilization. As long as our continent does not create its own civilization for itself, renewing the culture which it drank at the same peninsular, Iberian spring, and does not establish a closer contact not only between Andean America on the one hand and the America of the tropics and the pampas on the other, but also between Latin America and Anglo-Saxon America, there will not be a sufficient material and cultural basis to dislocate the axis to the vertical, and to bring about the rotation on themselves, and from north to south, of the two continents, which are very different because of the marked contrast between the Iberic and the Anglo-Saxon. It is fruitless to seek in geographic conditions or in racial composition within Latin America a unity which comes instead from the "atmosphere of civilization." But the unity that exists, not as a definitive reality but as an on-going process, comes from the community of origins (Spain-Portugal), of the nations making up this continental block, most of them facing the Pacific, others the Atlantic, with the exception of the two isolated countries (Paraguay and Bolivia), which live to this day in a state of separation, economically and culturally, as a result of the very geographic opposition of the two slopes. The great latitudinal spread of Brazil, and in consequence its enormous distances, its

6 André Siegfried, *Amérique latine* (Paris, 1934). Cf. "Los Problemas de la América latina," in *La Nación*, Buenos Aires, July 11, 1937.

great variety of physical settings and differences in climate, would have split the country into two stagnant blocks, if historical factors such as internal and other migrations had not intervened to fuse into a single nationality regions so disparate, far distant from each other, and at times opposed in their geographic, climatic, and economic aspects.

If, in fact, the great natural regions into which Brazil can be divided are, according to the classification of Delgado de Carvalho, the Amazonian region, the subequatorial Northeast, the eastern slope of the plateaus, and the region of the Plata, each of these zones has natural, clearly differentiated subregions with peculiar physiognomies and distinct characteristics. The northern part of Amazonian Brazil, which rises in the region of the sierra composed of the granitic highlands of the Guianas and falls into the great trough of the Amazon and its tributaries, includes, in addition to these two regions, the *hiléia* or zone of tropical forests. This is the region of the great plains, forests, and rivers which remind us of the beginnings of the world. Not smaller nor any less differentiated is southern Brazil, which offers a contrast to the basin of the Amazon, and, including the coast and the slope away from the ocean between the Atlantic and the Serra do Mar, extends to the region of the mountain chain and to that of the plateau, where prairie and forest alternate—"the region that supports the eastern tributaries of the Paraná River"— and to that of the savannas of Rio Grande do Sul and the lowlands of Mato Grosso. Between these two immense regions which strikingly distinguish Brazil, from north to south, there stretch the subequatorial Northeast, including the Gulf of Maranhão (a sort of transition from the Amazon), the basin of the Parnaíba, the forest and plains of the northeastern slope, the coast, the forest and agricultural land of Pernambuco; and the eastern slope of the plateaus, including the coast of Bahia and Espírito Santo, with the basins of the Paraguassú, Jequitinhonha, and Doce, the region of the plains (a high zone), the valley of the São Francisco, the south of Minas and the valley of the Paraíba which extends through the States of Rio and São Paulo. This geographical synthesis, in which Delgado de Carvalho attempts to encompass and define the great natural divisions, the most typical regions and subregions which make up the vast territory of Brazil, embraces—comparable (perhaps inferior) in the diversity of its scenery to the marvelous natural resources of the United States alone—the most fantastic variety of physical settings yet gathered under a single flag as the habitat of a single people, having the same origins, speaking the same language, practicing the same religion, and possessing all the marks of a single civilization.

Immense forests like those of the Amazon, and regions stripped of vegetation like those of the Northeast which occupy one-tenth of the territory of the country; high plains and the watered low plains, rich in humus, that lie along the rivers, and arid, sterile, desolate lands; mountains and chains which rise abruptly to heights of almost nine thousand feet, and undulating hills and wide plateaus; swamps and lowlands with their chains of lakes and pasture lands extending beyond our vision; immensities of water, like those of the great pelagic river which, not yet confined within banks, wander bearing masses of silt, and rivers which pour through deep valleys, squeeze through gorges and rush from the heights, plunging down in cataracts like that of Paulo Alfonso, 180 feet high, to descend to the sea; short stretches of cut-up coast line, with their breaks and indentations, or smooth ones with their vast beaches extending in a straight line almost like a racecourse, closed in by rocky walls rising almost straight up from the shore where the waves of the ocean break, or opening into hospitable bays and coves dotted with picturesque islands. Who could take in all these aspects in their endless variety, reduce them to a synthesis and give us the physical portrait of Brazil, without losing a characteristic trait or an essential line of the whole? The diversity of landscapes and the juxtaposition of contrasts which is presented by just one city—Rio de Janeiro—set in one of the most stupendous geographical frames that ever surrounded an urban scene, led Monteiro Lobato to define the Capital in a provocative phrase as a "museum of landscapes." It is as if—in that microcosm reflecting the whole complexity of Brazilian life—there had been concentrated in a superb showcase for the pleasure and amazement of our eyes the most lovely and varied aspects of nature. There is not, however, any image which can give an idea of the vast territory, so extensive and so diverse, from the tumultuous Amazon to the hospitable hills of the highlands, from the arid zones with their burning suns to regions flourishing under torrential rains, from highlands to plains, from marvelous forests to prairies with limitless horizons. An English scholar, Buckle, as Afrânio Peixoto reminds us, "even thought that in such a luxuriant natural scene there was no place for man"; a more practical German, Humboldt, "estimated that the valley of the Amazon by itself could provide food for all humanity."

It is not to be wondered at, says Afrânio Peixoto, that, "with so vast a territory and such varying local conditions of altitude, proximity to or distance from the sea, soil bare or covered by vegetation, Brazil has various climates, in fact almost all the climates of the earth." Her enormous territorial extension, estimated at 8,500,000 square kilometers, covering thirty-nine degrees of latitude, and as many of longitude; the situation of her mountains and the differences in altitude between the strip along the coast, the valleys of the great rivers, and the highlands of the interior; the distribution of rainfall, which is abundant in most of the country (from 39 to 98 inches annually) and insufficient in the Northeast; and lastly the geological structure of some regions of the north and the center —all these would be enough to explain the diversity of climates of the country, located between the Tropic of Capricorn and the equator, and prove, says Afrânio Peixoto, "how difficult it would be to mark out on the map of the country definite, limited climatic zones." In any case we may distinguish, following the classifications of Morize, Delgado de Carvalho, and Afrânio Peixoto, which are substantially the same, the three great zones we call equatorial, tropical, and temperate. Of these the first, extending from the equator to the tenth parallel of latitude, includes all the northern States, and part of Goiaz, Mato Grosso, and Bahia; the second, between the tenth parallel and the Tropic of Capricorn, extends south from Bahia and Sergipe, including almost all of Mato Grosso and part of the west of São Paulo; and the third, the temperate zone, between the Tropic of Capricorn and the southern boundary of the country, occupies all the region extending from the south of São Paulo to the Rio Grande do Sul.[7] Barometric pressure, temperature, rain-

---

[7] The first zone, of equatorial or subequatorial climates, which Morize calls also by the name of the torrid tropics, shows an average temperature of 79° to 81° F.; in the zone of tropical or subtropical climate, the temperature, averaging from 73° to 79° F., varies in the highest regions between 55° and 70° F.; and in the third zone the average temperature is from 66° along the coast to 61° on the plateau. These zones may, according to the climatologists, be divided further into as many subregions as there are different climates resulting from meteorological phenomena. Thus the equatorial zone is divided into three subregions, the superhumid and the semiarid (Northeast region) in addition to the continental humid region; the tropical zone includes two subdivisions, the semihumid maritime and the semihumid continental; and the temperate zone is subdivided into

fall—all varying with the distance from the equator, and with the distribution of land and water, altitude, and dominant winds—lead to a great variety of climates, from the most delightful, such as that on the western slope of the Serra do Mar, to the most inclement, such as that of the Northeast, which is subject to the scourge of prolonged droughts. In almost all the interior highland the climate is pleasant and healthful, generally varying little in temperature; and, aside from the fact that among our climates extremes are lacking, because of our situation a little below the thermic equator and far from frigid regions, even the "slandered climate" par excellence [8]—that of Amazonia—shows limited variations, as may be observed at Manaus, where the greatest heat attained was 99.5° and the minimum 65.8°, while the average temperature in this city built in the very heart of the Amazon region is 79.75°.

But if on the climate depends the vegetable world—"intermediary between the principal spheres of geographic phenomena, those of the inanimate world and of the animate" [9]—Brazilian vegetation, like the soil and the climate, is characterized by extreme diversity. To get an idea of the variety of forms and species which would be sufficient, if fully developed, to meet all the needs of life, we have only to remember that, of 22,767 species classified by Martius, 19,619 are Brazilian, divided between flora in general and that of Amazonia, which in itself accounts for 40 per cent of Brazilian flora. The principal formation is the *mata*, with the fantastic exuberance of tropical growth and with all the mysterious and wild characteristics of the virgin forest: *matas* on terra firma and on flooded lowlands of Amazonia and forests of the Serra do Mar that extend along the coast and the great rivers, occupying, according to calculations made by Gonzaga de Campos, about five million square kilometers, or more than half of the total area of the country.[10] Species of trees are especially numerous in the Amazon region; and with the trees and the combinations of species we also find variety in the aspects of nature dominated by them; here are the Brazilian chestnut, the rubber tree, palms, orchids and, in the lakes and swampy forest, the marvelous victoria regia with its leaves opening out as much as six feet in diameter; in the northern zone of Maranhão and Piauí, the babassu trees, the groves of carnaubas and buritis, and in the south on the higher land, the pines and araucarias that rise, solitary, like sentinels, or stand in groves near the flat lands of the plateau. These fields, bare of vegetation or fenced in, marked by palm trees and sown with pines, flowering fields without trees, endless natural pasture lands, the desolate caatingas of the Northeast and the wild undergrowth of the Amazon region, rise with

---

three types of climates—the superhumid of the coast, the semihumid of the interior, and the semihumid of the highlands. See *Brazil, 1938: A New Survey of Brazilian Life* (Rio: Instituto Brasileiro de Geografia e Estatística, 1939).

[8] See Euclides da Cunha, "Um Clima caluniado," in *À Margem da história* (Pôrto: Chardron, 3rd ed., 1922), pp. 47-64.

[9] Paul Vidal de la Blache, "La Géographie politique," in *Annales de géographie*, Vol. 7, p. 102.

[10] According to the forest map of Gonzaga de Campos, the forested areas cover 4,956,723 square kilometers, while the rest of the country in open fields or under cultivation, which occupies an area of 3,554,466 square kilometers. Now, by these estimates, taking into account the total area of Brazil, which is 8,511,189 square kilometers, no room would be left for the unproductive area estimated at 1,800,000 square kilometers (21 per cent of the total area), of which the part covered by water alone is 1,110,000. The estimates of forested area and open fields are evidently excessive and must be corrected, in order to be in proper relation to the unproductive area as estimated by the Land and Production Statistics. Cf. Afrânio Peixoto, *Clima e saúde* (1939), pp. 92, 120.

their characteristic vegetation, covering from north to south a total area of 3,500,000 square kilometers of our national territory. Not in the *hileia* of Amazonia with its luxuriant flora, or in the dense forests and the open fields, or in the *matas* or the *sertão*, does the fauna peculiar to each of these regions, in spite of its variety, offer any of the great wild game that infests other continents. The wild animals, such as the jaguar, tapir, and boar, do not really constitute a menace to man; in Brazil only certain mosquitoes and some venomous reptiles—the coral snake, the jararaca, and the cascavel—are major dangers in the jungle, but even these do not offer a serious obstacle to the conquest of the tropics. An incalculable profusion of insects and a surprising variety of birds of variegated and brilliant plumage give life to the landscape and fill with their sounds and singing the forests that have been tamed by man and the wet, endless jungles.[11]

All this diversity of vegetation and animal life which, with its multiplicity of species and its exuberance, characterizes the pulsating life of hot countries, is conditioned by the diversity of soil, which in various regions is of a perennial fertility, due in the north to the Amazonian deposits, in Pernambuco, Bahia, and Campos (State of Rio) to the decomposed Cretaceous stratum (*massapê*), and in the south, to the purple earth, "a modification of the diabase and porphyritic earth which, in a vast sheet of lava, covered the Permian layer of Rio and São Paulo." A mountainous country, without being after all a country of high mountains, situated for the most part in the Torrid Zone between the equator and the Tropic of Capricorn, Brazil belongs to the oldest periods of the earth and reflects, in its complexity of relief and in its structure, the earth's geological vicissitudes. The oldest part is made up of crystalline mountain groups, like the one which extends in a long coastwise strip from Ceará to Santa Catarina—the Serra do Mar with its crystalline rocks, igneous or sedimentary—and that which occupies all the basin of the Rio Doce, and the Serra do Espinhaço with its magnificent deposits of iron, manganese, and gold. All the geological eras, from the igneous or Archean to the Cenozoic, with the two periods between, the Paleozoic and Mesozoic, are represented in Brazil by various groups strongly brought out in the general lines of the geomorphology and the structure of our mountains and in the fossils which go back to the most remote geological epochs. It is certain that the soil and subsoil of Brazil contain reserves of mineral wealth, such as copper, lead, silver, platinum, diamonds, both the amorphous black and the crystalline, besides other precious stones of incomparable beauty, and above all gold, which, as Roberto Simonsen notes, was enough to draw the attention of the economy of the whole world. But of the five minerals which most directly contribute to modern industry—coal, essential in metallurgical industry, chemistry, and transportation, oil, iron, the phosphates, and the salts of potassium—the only one which we possess in quantity is iron; it may be said that from the point of view of quality as well as abundance of this ore

11 Among insects, Bates collected 770 different species of butterflies alone in the neighborhood of Belem. Melo Leitão speaks of 850 species of birds in Brazil as compared with 450 in Argentina, and it is this remarkable variety that led Hudson to speak of South America as the "continent of birds." Ornithological species are numerous in Amazonas, on the interior plateau and in the south, where one of the most beautiful sights is the variety of aquatic birds with which the lakes of Rio Grande do Sul and the swamps of Mato Grosso are crowded. As to fish, which abound both along the coast and in the network of rivers, Agassiz estimated the number of species in the Amazon basin alone at almost 2,000, which would give Amazonas "almost twice the number of varieties that live in the Mediterranean, and a figure higher than that of all the species which the Atlantic nourishes from one pole to the other" (Louis and Elizabeth Cary Agassiz, *A Journey in Brazil*).

(especially in the center of Minas Gerais) Brazil is one of the countries which contain the largest deposits in the world. Coal, in the Carboniferous strata of the south, is inferior because of the admixture of schist; important deposits of phosphate ores have been discovered in the State of Maranhão. If signs of the existence of oil have been found in Amazonia and Alagoas, and indisputable proof in the drilling of the Lobato wells in Bahia, all the geological researches of half a century or more have as yet failed to reveal layers of potassium salts, which are of such great importance in intensive agriculture.

The extreme variety of the physical setting, and the consequent diversity of climate and resources, together constitute the beauty of the Brazilian landscape and make for the contrast of one region with another; and together they determine the types of human activity, assuring the multiplicity of cultures and of kinds of life. Brazilian civilization is a result of this infinite variety of human groups in the infinite variety of geographic scenes. Originating in western Europe, from which it crossed the Atlantic by caravel, it had to begin, as in fact it did, by establishing itself at various points on the coast (Ilhéus, São Vicente, Recife, and Rio), points which offered a secure anchorage to its fleets, and from which the colonists could later cross the barrier of the Serra do Mar in the direction of the plateau, where it gathered new strength for expansion, spreading great distances in the immense natural scene and spotting it with scenes of human activity. The vastness of the ocean, offering none of the ease of communication of the Mediterranean,[12] the general configuration of the coast, immense and little cut up, the variety of the regions over which we spread, and the enormous extent of highlands, of plateaus and sandy tablelands, restricting colonization to the conquest of the coast, and isolating rather than uniting population groups, did not make possible the phenomenon of concentrating urban societies. On the contrary, these geographic conditions persisted in keeping them separate, disconnected and distant from one another. Maritime expansion, along the coast, required land bases where maritime power could be built up, and upon which its action could be based. Hence the long period during which Brazilian civilization maintained itself by "digging in the sandy beach," according to the picturesque expression which reflects, on one hand, the difficulties of its march along the coast, moving "crabwise," and, on the other hand, the resistance which the mountains paralleling the coast opposed to its advance toward the interior and the conquest of the plateau. The waters of the Atlantic contributed more toward uniting Brazil and Europe than toward connecting the different zones of settlement, established far apart on the coast; and this connection had to be accomplished rather through the interior, by the migrations along the São Francisco val-

---

[12] If we compare a coast like the Brazilian, which extends from north to south and whose ends are far apart, dipping into the ocean like the ends of a parabola, with a basin in which the shores are close together and all the land near the coast, we can appreciate the *isolating function* of the former type of coast and the *unifying role*, for example, of the Mediterranean coast. The basin of the Mediterranean has, in fact, from the geographic point of view, as Helmolt remarks, an almost perfect unity: the same climate, the same rainfall, the same vegetation, the same living conditions, are, in short, imposed upon its coastal populations. Mountains come near the coast, except where there are great open valleys, like those of the Rhone, the Nile, and the Po. Life is concentrated on the lower slopes; islands are numerous, the shore line is cut up, and it is possible to make long sea voyages by short daily sails. The sea, then, does not separate people. The histories of various peoples are mixed and their civilizations enter into one another. The world of the Mediterranean forms an historic unity. Hans F. Helmolt, *Weltgeschichte*, Vol. 4, *Die Randländer des Mittelmeers* (Leipzig: Bibliographisches Institut, 1900).

ley, at the time when the rivers that penetrated the interior, like the Tietê, and the march of herds were opening the way to the taming of the Sertão. And in less than three centuries, by water and land, running all the risks of sea and river navigation, all the perils of interminable marches, the great task of exploration and conquest had been accomplished, and that of exploiting natural resources had been begun.

The grandeur of the geographic environment, magnificent in every respect, has more than once suggested the idea of the pettiness of man living in it, who seemed to many to be dwarfed by his natural setting. But when one considers the vastness of the territory, the variety of its aspects, the possibilities which it suggested and the difficulties which it presented to human labor, then one can appreciate the full importance and meaning of those "little islands of culture" which, as early as the end of the colonial period, stood out here and there, at enormous distances in every direction, and recorded in the landscape the constant effort of mankind to possess his environment and to utilize the forces of nature. If, moreover, we remember that this effort lasted for generations and was put forth by scanty populations scattered over an immense territory, and that everything in nature conspired to prevent their advance and force them to retreat, then we shall have a more vivid idea of the dramatic greatness of the human labor which was accomplished; and, instead of being dwarfed by his environment, man will appear only the greater in the face of his geographic setting. The very rivers, far from being highways, are frequently obstacles to civilization. If there are navigable rivers like the Amazon and its tributaries in the north, the São Francisco on the plateau, the Paraná and the Paraguay in the south, among many others (the greatest known network of rivers belongs to South America, with its sixty thousand kilometers of navigable rivers), the mountain ranges, the rapids and enormous waterfalls of the rivers which come down from the plateau did not permit them to serve man for their entire length. The waterfalls and cataracts, although of extraordinary scenic beauty and of incalculable wealth for the future when turned into electric power, by making the rivers impossible to traverse deprived man of those highways which nature seemed to prepare for him in her magnificent riverways. To be sure, rivers great and small served, some of them exceptionally well, to facilitate the mobility and expansion of the population; of all the riverways penetrating into the country none played a role so important as the São Francisco, which cut through the heart of central Brazil from south to north and thus connected the two parts into which the nation is divided. The São Francisco—"river of national unity," whose valley Capistrano de Abreu has called the "condenser of people"—favored the contact of the populations of the north and the south and thus played a role similar to that in North America of the Mississippi, "the father of waters," which linked the East to the West in spite of the separation imposed by the Allegheny Mountains, the plains of the Middle West, and the Rocky Mountains. But, generally speaking, we may say with Gilberto Freyre that, "without constancy of volume, or regularity of course, and varying widely in conditions of navigability and usefulness, the great rivers have been unreliable partners": these enormous masses of water, if they conferred spectacular greatness on the country, covered as it was by thick forests, "only partly, and never completely lent themselves to the civilizing function of communication."

It was on this immense, confusing stage, in a country with a hot climate, "where life was apparently easy," but where in reality physical conditions were adverse, that the colonizing effort of our Portuguese progenitors was exercised; from them in the first colonists came the seed that formed the essential nucleus of the Brazilian people. The thirteen ships which in 1500 left the Iberian Peninsula and plowed through the waters of the Atlantic on the way to the Indies, going far off their course and finally arriving at the American continent and the land of the brazilwood, did not merely discover new land for the Portuguese empire: they marked the beginning of a great colonial enterprise and of the drama of a new nation. This people that with Vasco da Gama found the route to the Indies and with Pedro Álvares Cabral discovered Brazil, that circumnavigated the globe with Fernão de Magalhães (Magellan), after these exploits by which in the sixteenth century it organized a great commercial empire surpassed in all history only by the British Empire, was for the first time to test its colonizing genius and its capacity to consolidate its conquests. The vastness of these dominions, of which only the fringe of the coast line was touched, the scanty population of the mother country, which at the moment of the discovery amounted to only 1,200,000 inhabitants, and the distances, at the time so enormous, which separated Portugal from her lands beyond the seas would suffice to give the measure of the difficulties faced by the governmental élite in order to make its colonizing effort equal to its maritime enterprise and to the glory of its discoveries. The white wave which was to spread through the country in successive movements of immigration, did not, therefore, reach 3,000 colonists in 1550; this meant that the domination of the civilizing colonists over the aboriginal population was at best sketchy. The Portuguese strain which slowly established itself in Brazil was not what one could call a race, in the biological sense, but was itself the result of the mixture of the primitive inhabitants of the peninsula—the early Iberians—and races and peoples which mingled in constant migrations across that peninsula, such as the Celts, the Greeks, the Phoenicians, the Romans, the Visigoths, and the Arabs, not to mention the Jews, of whom at a single time it received fifty thousand families, moved thither by order of Hadrian. The product of a long process of miscegenation, the Portuguese people, which maintained its position as the solid, primitive, dominant nucleus of the Brazilian people, would have to mix its blood in the colony with those of the two subject races—the American Indian, of Asiatic origin, and the Negro imported from Africa—and give to both of them a new tongue and a new civilization.

In the field of biology, as Roy Nash observes, "the Brazilian drama unrolls a theme of great importance for the race": the three races, white, red, and black mingled especially in the first centuries on a large scale, and a notable variety of types resulting from the crossing of white with Indians and Negroes, and on a smaller scale of the Brazilian indigenous inhabitant with the African Negro. Among these three races, however, which from the beginning came together to form the population of Brazil in unequal proportions that varied with the diverse regions of the country, that of the white conquerors became the fundamental element, although it had been small if one may judge from the calculations which gave Brazil in 1789, almost three centuries after the discovery, 1,500,000 Negro slaves out of a total of 2,300,000 inhabitants without including primitive societies. The savage peoples,[13] agricultural, hunting peoples, who must have been numerous in 1500, but whose numbers even today it would be difficult if not impossible

[13] Although information about the Indians at the time of the discovery is insufficient and ethnological statistics on the existing tribes have not been collected, it can be said, generally speaking, that the Brazilian savage was characterized by short stature, copper-colored skin, black, straight hair, a broad, flat face, depressed nose, Mongoloid eyes (far apart and small) dark chestnut in color,

to estimate with any assurance for lack of data, came in the great variety of their tribes and family groups from four principal groups: the Tupi, the Tapuya, the Arawak, and the Carib. Of these the most important group, that of the Tupis, was spread over the coast line from Rio Grande do Sul to Pará, and from Pará through the swampy forests of the Amazon as far as the river Madeira. Of the crossings between Indians and Portuguese, Roy Nash reminds us, "perhaps nine in every ten were with the women of this extraordinary forest people," the Tupis, whose language became the general language, and whose culture was the most widely disseminated in Portuguese America. The scarcity of white women contributed to encourage relations with the women of the country and to stimulate the mixture of whites and Indians, to whose offspring, the mamelucos, a great many families of the north central plateau owe their origin, and the vitality and the expansive force of the adventurous nomadism of the bandeirantes can be traced. José de Alencar's romance, *Iracema*, writes Afrânio Peixoto, "is symbolic of the love which the daughters of the country had for the white adventurer; I discovered that it is an anagram for America: might it be the intention of the author to describe the nuptials of the virgin land with the civilizing colonist?" But greater still was the contribution which was brought by the extensive wave of African immigrants—perhaps 3,300,000 according to the estimates of Simonsen—collected from a great number of different nations and imported on a large scale, almost without interruption, until the source was dried up in 1850 with the abolition of the traffic in slaves. The superiority of the Negro culture to that of the Indians, the intimacy of the contact which the slave regime was not slow in establishing between the two races, and the utilization of Negroes for domestic services opened a large field to this new form of race mixture, favoring everywhere, in the expression of Gilberto Freyre, "those loves of the master and the slave which the patriarchal colonial system permitted itself."

If, as one sees, the origins of the Brazilian people are clearly tied up with the mixture of the three races or with the progressive assimilation, in the early centuries, of the red and black races by the European whites in a great blood transfusion, there still remain to be entirely clarified questions relative to the various ethnic types, Portuguese and Negro, which flowed toward Brazil, to their respective anthropological characteristics, to the geographic distribution of the Negroes and the Indians, and to the proportions in which

---

and prominent cheek-bones. The social organization and culture of the American Indians, usually of a rudimentary character, varied widely of course as between the agricultural tribes in the forests of the Amazon and the communities of the woods that extended from Rio Grande do Sul to the Chaco and even perhaps to the broad lands of Mato Grosso, "whose culture centered around the herds of guanacos and flocks of rheas" as well as between these tribes and those of the eastern plateau of Brazil who lived by hunting. The pampas Indians of the far south, the Indians of the central plain who were mixed with the population of Goiaz and the northern part of Mato Grosso, and the natives of Amazon basin, whose culture extended from the Amazon "along the seacoast as far as their fragile canoes could carry them," all had, however, common traits in their material culture, such as the bow and arrow, firewood, the art of weaving baskets, stonework, which show their common origin in a remote period. Their "constitutional aversion to heat," in the words of Bates, seems to confirm the hypothesis of the Asiatic origin of the red savage who lived like an alien and an immigrant in these hot regions, "to which climate his original constitution was not adapted, and has not yet become perfectly adapted." (H. W. Bates, *The Naturalist on the River Amazons*.) The communistic conception of property is, according to Roy Nash, "a fundamental trait which unites all the American Indian peoples, whether agricultural or hunting."

the crossings with the white colonists went on.[14] It seems to us that one can now conclude with J. F. de Almeida Prado, in his exhaustive work on the early inhabitants of Brazil, that the white sources from which the mestizos were derived were very varied; and both Nina Rodrigues and Gilberto Freyre, in their studies of the African slave trade, have demonstrated the variety of "nations" and of culture areas from which the Negro slaves were transported, ranging from the most savage tribes of the Kaffirs to the Sudanese Negroes of advanced culture who predominated in the development of Bahia. The Africans of Brazil—authentic Negroes like the Hottentots and the Bushmen, and Fulahs, who are sometimes called "white Negroes," and mixtures like the slaves drawn from Senegambia or Portuguese Guinea, who are "considered by some to be superior to the rest from the anthropological point of view"—settled in diverse regions of the country, but in proportions which it is now impossible to determine because of the absence or destruction of documents and customs statistics on the entrance of slaves. The light which historic documents throw on this question, already amply investigated by Nina Rodrigues, Gilberto Freyre, Artur Ramos, J. F. de Almeida Prado and others, is not sufficient to clear it up, except perhaps in a general way and in some of its essential aspects, namely the question of the origin of the Brazilian people. The studies of these writers both from the physical and from the cultural point of view would, one might say, be condemned for lack of anthropological and historic data to remain in the field of conjecture whenever we enter upon details as to the first European colonists and the coming together and distribution of Negro slaves. Not fewer, or less deep, are the shadows which surround on all sides the questions as to the various American Indian peoples of the Amazon basin, of the plateau, and of the southern coast of Brazil. Among these peoples the marked differences of physical characteristics were not sufficient to hide a community of origin, which is shown in the principal traits of their structure, in the color of hair, eyes, and skin, and in the teeth which are in the form of a shovel, concave, and in the considerable breadth of the face in relation to the cranial dimensions.[15]

[14] The miscegenation which was practiced on a large scale in Brazil, according to Gilberto Freyre, was a corrective for "the social distance which otherwise would have remained enormous between the big house and the slave quarters." It reduced it, undoubtedly. But in the ethnic and social stratification the Africans, the Brazilian Negroes, and in general the mixed bloods of African origin, continued to find their place in the lower social levels, even when the Negro slaves showed higher culture than that of the Indians or even of the whites. If it was common, even frequent, to find a Brazilian who was descended from Indians, boasting of his origin, speaking with pride of his "caboclo blood," and feeling more Brazilian because there ran in his veins the blood of the autochthonous race, mixed with that of the white, the same thing did not occur with the mulatto, who sought, as he still does, to conceal his African origin rather than boast of it. The three races, white, red, and black, are distributed in the ethnic stratification, in superimposed levels with rank order. Racial prejudices, if they never reached the point of creating conflicts and opposition, always existed among us, too, as principles of social classification.

[15] The difficulty in determining the anthropological structure of the elements (white, red, and black) that entered into the make-up of the people, and the influence of each of them in the constitution of the national type, comes not only from the variety of types of each of these races, but from the geographic distribution of the elements and the different proportions in which they were mingled in different regions. There was not only, in our ethnic origin, a mixing of three radically different races. The two alien races, white and Negro, when they arrived had already been subjected to repeated crossings; on top of this they mixed with the American Indians in a true melting pot. The white colonists from Portugal came from an ethnic group that was extremely complex in its make-up. In the peninsular population, says Oliveira Viana, there were two fundamental groups:

Certainly, as far as the mixture of the white and the Indian is concerned, it was not on a large scale, unless perhaps in the first century; and it was progressively reduced, in part by the extermination of the savages and in part with their retirement en masse, driven back from the coast into the interior and the forests.[16] For three hundred years, the Negro element continued to grow with the uninterrupted importation of slaves from various parts of Africa, who crossed among themselves and with the whites, mixed bloods multiplying as a result of this type of crossing. If we stop to consider that at the beginning of the nineteenth century the number of slaves reached 1,500,000 out of a population of 3,500,000 Brazilians, including whites and race mixtures, and that from then on 1,250,000 more Negroes were introduced into Brazil up to the time of the abolition of the slave traffic in 1850, it will be easy to estimate the disproportion between the Negro nucleus and the dominant white race, and the enormous contribution that the continual importation of slaves made to the mixture of peoples, especially in the lowest social strata. According to the census of 1872, the first which was made in Brazil, out of a population initially put at 9,930,479 inhabitants, of which it was estimated 1,510,806 were slaves, there were 3,787,289 whites and 3,801,782 mulattoes and mestizos of various degrees, of whom about 2,000,000 (exactly 1,954,452) were of the African race and 386,955 of American Indian race, these latter, however, constituting one-fifth of the mestizos listed by the census. The race mixture with the American Indian predominated in the extreme north, in the zones of the Northeast and in the central States of Goiaz and Mato Grosso, while that of the white and African was much more intense on the coast, and from Recife to Rio de Janeiro and in Minas Gerais or, in general, in certain regions of the plateau

---

"a tall blond dolichocephalic, with the habits of the nomad and the conqueror; another darker in color, small in stature, dolichocephalic or brachycephalic, of sedentary and pacific habits." In the conquest and discovery and emigration to the new world, Oliveira Viana thinks, it was the blond long-headed type (*Homo europeus, of Lapouge*) that took the lead; this type was preponderant in the aristocratic class and was given to migration: on the other hand, the brachycephalic, short man (*Homo alpinus, of Linnaeus*), who formed the basis of the middle and lower classes, came later in a great stream of colonists, especially after the discovery of the mines. This hypothesis, however, does not have sufficient evidence to support it, and has not been confirmed by later studies and researches. The variety of types in the two subject races adds even more troublesome difficulties to the problem: the aboriginal population, in which there are subsumed under the common name *Homo americanus* at least two groups (Tupis and Tapuyas), subdivided into a great variety of savage tribes, is, in spite of its complexity, much less rich in anthropological types than the Negro race, in the masses of imported slaves. These African groups, coming from a great variety of tribes and "nations," vary not only in their culture (three, at least, according to Artur Ramos, who relates all the Negroes who came to Brazil to Sudanese and Sudanese-Mahommedan culture and to the Bantus), but also in distinctive somatic traits and psychological characteristics. We still have to explain, if we ever can, almost all the problems posed for pure anthropology by the diversity of peninsular types, Negro and American types, which came together and were mixed in the great melting pot in the first three centuries after the discovery.

16 "The percentage of autochthonous blood," writes Humberto de Campos, "is, in our veins, more important than we suppose or proclaim to the world. The story that the Indian preferred disappearance in large part to union with the invader comes from the confusion of the mestizos with the Portuguese after the second or third generation. The mulatto is unmistakable; the mameluco, on the other hand, can pass unperceived, even in the first generation. Examine attentively the 22,000,000 Brazilians who inhabit the north of the country and the States of the center, and you will see how much of the American ancestor is latent in them, in physical type and mental constitution." Humberto de Campos, *Crítica*, 1st series (Rio de Janeiro: Marisa, 2nd ed., 1933), p. 256.

1. Paraná Curiaú (Rio Negro). Thick forest along the river; islands with lagoons and lakes. Alexander Hamilton Rice, *Exploration en Guyane Brésilienne*, Plate XV.

2. Dense vegetation, characteristic of the islands of the lower Rio Negro. Rice, *Exploration en Guyane Brésilienne*, Plate XXIII.

3. Lower Rio Negro. Trunks and branches that have fallen as a result of
erosion by the water.
Rice, *Exploration en Guyane Brésilienne*, Plate XXV.

4. Maloca Shiriana, in the narrow waterway Linepenone (Uraricuera).
Rice, *Exploration en Guyane Brésilienne*, Plate LXXIII.

5. View from above of the gorge of Kulaihia, looking southwest. Rice, *Exploration en Guyane Brésilienne*, Plate XC.

6. Stretch of the Amazon River, near Faro. Photo by Rembrandt.

7. Stretch of the Amazon River, near Faro. Photo by Rembrandt.

8. Stretch of the Amazon River, near Faro. Photo by Rembrandt.

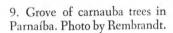

9. Grove of carnauba trees in Parnaíba. Photo by Rembrandt.

10. Two juazeiro trees—trees which resist the longest droughts. Landscape in Piauí. Photo by O. Domingues, in *Travel in Brazil*, Vol. II, No. 2, p. 20.

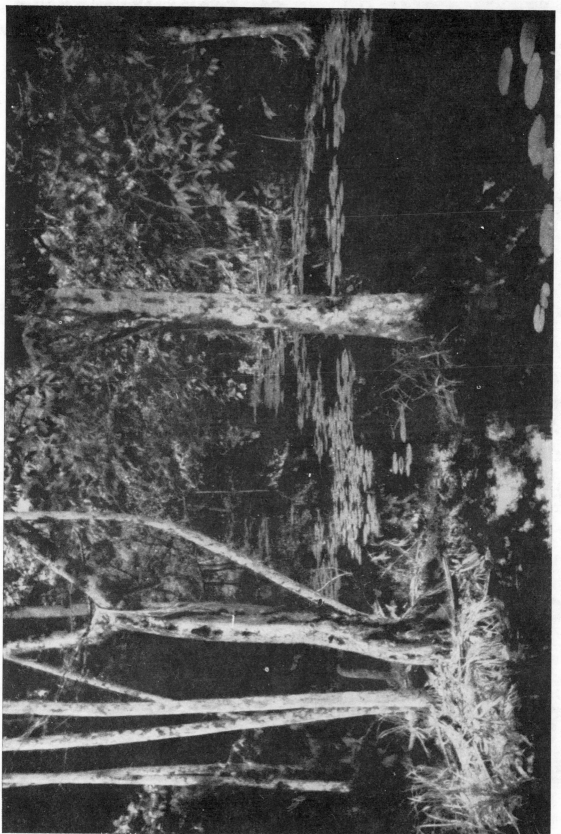

11. Canal of Iuna, near Belém, Pará. A narrow waterway. Photo by Rembrandt.

12. Grove of carnauba trees. Photo by Rembrandt.

13. Cactus, plant characteristic of the region of the Northeast. Photo by the Department of Agriculture, Brazil, in *Travel in Brazil*, Vol. II, No. 2, p. 19.

14. Black sand beach, in Natal. Photo by Rembrandt.

15. The peak of Jaraguá, in the state of São Paulo.

16. Mountains dividing São Paulo from Minas. São Bento do Sapucaí. Photo by ENFA.

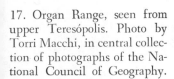

17. Organ Range, seen from upper Teresópolis. Photo by Torri Macchi, in central collection of photographs of the National Council of Geography.

18. River Paraíba, near Taubaté, state of São Paulo. Photo by ENFA.

19. Point Juréia. Iguape, state of São Paulo.
Photo by ENFA.

20. Iguassú, or Santa Maria Falls. Iguassú River.
Photo by Touring Club, in central collection of photographs
of the National Council of Geography

21. Mayongong Indian, hunting. Rice, *Exploration en Guyane Brésilienne,* Plate CXV.

22. Young Mayongong Kujumá Indian, armed with bow and arrows. Rice, *Exploration en Guyane Brésilienne,* Plate CXIV.

23. Tucan chief of the region of the Rio Negro. Photo by Ethnography Department of the College of Philosophy of São Paulo.

24. Cabin of Makú Indians in Tokixima.
Rice, *Exploration en Guyane Brésilienne,* Plate CXXX.

25. Parintintim Indian of the Madeira River.
Photo from Ethnography Department of the College of Philosophy of São Paulo.

26. "Mestizo," oil painting by Cândido Portinari. Property of the Pinacoteca of São Paulo.

27. "Big house" of the Magaípe sugar plantation, built in the seventeenth century.
Drawing by Manuel Bandeira.

28. "Manioc Mill," oil painting by Eugênio Brocos.
Photo by Rembrandt.

29. Old plantation, Itaboraí, state of Rio.
Photo by Stille, in collection of College of Philosophy of São Paulo.

30. Old agricultural machines.
From the Museu Paulista. Photo by Museu Paulista.

31. The caravan stops to rest (early nineteenth century).
J. M. Rugendas, *Voyage pittoresque au Brésil* (1835), Plate 3/19.

32. Litter for traveling. J. B. Debret, *Voyage pittoresque et historique au Brésil* (1834), Vol. II, Plate 16.

33. Washing for gold, near Itacolomí (early nineteenth century). Rugendas, *Voyage pittoresque au Brésil*, Plate 3/22.

34. Gold washers, Mato Grosso. Photo by Rembrandt.

35. Gold washers, Mato Grosso. Photo by Rembrandt.

36. Woman spinning. Photo from chair of Brazilian Geography of the College of Philosophy of São Paulo.

37. Woman of the interior working at the oven. Photo from chair of Brazilian Geography of the College of Philosophy of São Paulo.

38. Basket weaver.
Photo from chair of Brazilian Geography of the College of Philosophy of São Paulo.

39. Jangadas and sailors, on the beach of Cabedelo, Paraíba.
Photo by Panair, in central collection of photographs of the National Council of Geography.

40. Sailboats, in São Luiz, Maranhão. Photo by Panair, in central collection of the National Council of Geography.

41. Open-air market, in the port called Água de Meninos, Bahia. Photo by Kahan, in *Travel in Brazil*, Vol. II, No. 2, p. 3.

42. Market in Salvador, Bahia. Photo by Voltaire Fraga, Urbo Salvador, in Brazilian Institute of Geography and Statistics.

Visconde de Mauá

43. Viscount Mauá, outstanding figure who, between 1850 and 1870, endeavored by all possible means to develop among Brazilians an industrial spirit, promoting the building of railroads, ports, factories, and shipyards.
Photo from the collection of Companhia Melhoramentos of São Paulo.

44. Viaduct of the railroad between São Paulo and Santos. *Travel in Brazil*, Vol. I, No. 3, p. 10.

45. Top of the Sierra, Santo André, state of São Paulo. Photo by ENFA.

46. New dam of the Light and Power Company, state of São Paulo. Photo by ENFA.

47. View of a coffee drying field, state of São Paulo.
Travel in Brazil, Vol. I, No. 3, p. 7.

48. Plantation Santa Clara, in Dourados, state of São Paulo.
Photo by ENFA, in central collection of the National Council of Geography.

49. Monte Alegre factory, Piracicaba, state of São Paulo. Photo by ENFA.

50. Tamoio factory, Araraquara, state of São Paulo. Photo by ENFA.

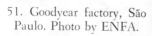

51. Goodyear factory, São Paulo. Photo by ENFA.

52. Jute factory, Taubaté, state of São Paulo. Photo by ENFA.

53. A beautiful view of the main highway between Rio and Petrópolis. Photo by Preising, in *Travel in Brazil*, Vol. I, No. 3, p. 16.

54. Recife—a view of the old city.
Photo by Stille, in collection of the College of Philosophy of São Paulo.

55. Colonial house in Carlos Gomes street. National monument, Salvador, Bahia.
Photo by Voltaire Fraga, in Archives of the Brazilian Institute of Geography and Statistics.

56. Old hillside of Our Lady of the Conception of the Beach, Salvador, Bahia. Photo by Voltaire Fraga, in Archives of the Brazilian Institute of Geography and Statistics.

57. Ouro Preto. Tiradentes Square. Photo by Radio Inconfidência, Minas Gerais.

58. Ouro Preto. View of a part of the city.
Photo by Radio Inconfidência, Minas Gerais.

59. São João d'El Rei, in Minas Gerais. In the background, the Church of Carmel.
Photo by Stille, in collection of the College of Philosophy of São Paulo.

60. São João d'El Rei, in Minas Gerais. Colonial street, and in the background the Church of Carmel.
Photo by Stille, in collection of the College of Philosophy of São Paulo.

closer to the coast line, to the ports of entry, and to the distribution of slaves—that is, in the region in which there was a dominance of large agricultural property with its slave-owning economy, and in the zone of mine exploitation. From this same census of 1872 we learn that the populations of the north and the south were distributed in equal parts, of about 5,000,000 inhabitants each, concentrated especially in Pernambuco, Ceará, Bahia, Minas Gerais, Rio de Janeiro, and São Paulo, which, with Rio Grande do Sul, then with nearly 450,000 inhabitants, even today constitute the chief centers of culture and of production of the country.[17] But this growth of population, and what subsequently took place even down to the census of 1920—if we consider the 300,000 foreigners, for the most part Portuguese, who were discovered in the first census, and if we keep in view that from 1872 to 1920 there entered only 3,200,000 foreigners, white immigrants—we may be sure that there must earlier have been a notable genetic development, with a growing predominance of the whites, of the diverse elements which entered into the composition of the Brazilian people.

To this fact of great importance in the formation of the nation, that the number of foreigners remained relatively small in proportion to the original nucleus, it is necessary, for understanding the phenomenon of Brazil, to add the mobility of the population; its movement, acting as an instrument of assimilation, contributed to the interpenetration and assimilation of different races and cultures. In addition to the slow infiltrations which, by being repeated, often produce as much effect as mass migrations, and the movement of the small farmers in our own century (toward the northwest in São Paulo) when the fertility of the soil they occupied was exhausted, there contributed toward the mixture of populations in the three first centuries, the migratory movements which tended toward an end established in advance: the movements connected with breeding and trading in cattle, following the pasturage along the valleys, chiefly the valley of the São Francisco; the movements caused by invasions as in the case of the Dutch war; and especially the movements of the expeditions to explore the Sertão. "To conquer the land," writes Euclides da Cunha, "we even had to produce the man capable of fighting it—bred in its image with its crudity and its energy in revolt—so as to evolve, in the entirely new mestizo type of the bandeirante, the exceptional figure of the man who became a barbarian in order to make roads across the desert, opening the first paths to progress." We all know the capital importance of these human migrations, the general theory of which

[17] In 1940, according to the *Sinopse preliminar dos resultados demográficos*, the population of Brazil was 41,565,083 inhabitants, of whom 16,005,992 were in the north (a region of 4,864,467 square kilometers running from the Territory of Acre to Bahia), and 25,559,091 in the southern States, which have a smaller area, estimated at 3,646,722 square kilometers. As the average density of the population of Brazil is 4.88 inhabitants per square kilometer, the density in this northern region, comprising the block of northern States, is a fraction more than 3, and in the southern States it reaches a bit more than 7 inhabitants per square kilometer. Virtual equality between the populations of the two great geographic regions, according to the Census of 1872, the definitive results of which gave, for the north, a population of 5,040,998 inhabitants, and for the south, one of 5,071,063, was followed, as we see, from a demographic point of view, by a break in the equality of the two blocks, with the southern States reaching more than 25,500,000 against little more than 16,000,000 in the northern part of the country; European immigration, of Mediterranean or Germanic origin, coming into the southern States, and internal migration from north to south contributed not only to change the earlier make-up of the population of Brazil, but to lead to this lack of equality or difference of 10,000,000 inhabitants in the population growth of the two regions.

was worked out by Ratzel,[18] and which are nothing other than the sum of movements by virtue of which human societies have come to group themselves and distribute themselves over the land at each moment of history. The maps of the movement of cattle and of the cattle-raising population made by Simonsen, and the general map of the exploring expeditions which we owe to Afonso Taunay, show quite clearly that the nature of the soil and the lay of the land contributed to determine the manner in which these masses of men moved over the territory in the colonial period, linking the north to the south and extending the colonial frontiers. The great rivers were, *par excellence,* as Gilberto Freyre justly observes, "the rivers of the bandeirante and of the missionary who went up them, conquering the difficulties of waterfalls and of irregular course." They scattered the colonizers, permitting the bandeirante to "become, as early as the end of the sixteenth century, a founder of subcolonies," penetrating toward the west by the waters of the Tietê or going up the valley of the São Francisco, which the bands of catechizers entered, and the civilization of cattle and hides was formed, and the expeditions from São Paulo, Pernambuco, and Bahia met one another.

These internal migrations, which by scattering and mixing groups among themselves contributed to accelerate the formation of our society—in its composition a hybrid of the Indian and later of the Negro—may have had their origins in the colonial tendency of the Portuguese to "spread out rather than condense"; but they were certainly favored and stimulated by economic interests (hunting Indians, the search for and the extraction of mineral wealth) and by the very extent of the space occupied. It presupposes, indeed, societies of little density with vast spaces at their disposal. It is a fundamental tendency of all societies to extend their geographic base; they are thirsty for space. Doubtless, as Ratzel observes, limited space plays a useful role; often limited spaces are the foci in which, thanks to an energetic concentration, high forms of civilization are developed. But as soon as these have been formed, they necessarily tend to spread out beyond their initial boundaries. The expeditions through which the nomadism of the bandeirantes—for the most part mestizos, of white and Indian blood—expanded thus constituted one of the most vigorous activities of a new society in formation. Thus, when early in the nineteenth century, a little before the abolition of slavery, an intensified immigration of Mediterranean and Teutonic origin began (Portuguese, Italians, Spaniards, Germans, and others), even this early the national nucleus was already formed and was sufficiently solid to digest and assimilate the mass of immigrants who came in annual, successive floods, at times in as great volume as those who were registered from 1888 to 1897 and from 1906 to 1914 and were repeated later in the ten-year period from 1920 to 1930 with other great influxes of immigrants. Besides, with the growth of white immigration after the abolition of the slave traffic the population of Brazil was just touching 7,000,000, to attain more than 14,000,000 in 1890, and to rise from 7,677,800 in 1854 to 37,000,000 in 1935, while in the same period the total number of European immigrants did not surpass 4,400,000. The gradual, progressive absorption of the immigrants by the original national nucleus went on as a regular process because of the presence of essential conditions without which this assimilation could not take place: the existence of a strong, original nucleus as a basis

---

[18] Friedrich Ratzel, *Anthropogeographie,* Vol. I. *Grundzüge der Anwendung der Erdkunde auf die Geschichte* (Stuttgart: Engelhorn, 1899).

for community of race, around which there was formed an ethnic community in consequence of continual miscegenation; the relatively low proportion of foreigners to
the original nucleus; and finally the distribution and nobility of the immigrant population, going from country to city, from agriculture to industry, and becoming more
easily assimilable in consequence of these changes which contributed to break the bonds
of their origin and to melt the foreign elements in the world of the Brazilian.[19]

It is due to this crossing—the biological process of natural selection facilitated in
part by movements of populations and by the absence of racial prejudice—that in Brazil
there was a fusion of the races, white, African, and American Indian, and that progressively the Brazilian people was formed from various ethnic elements, indigenous
and foreign, assimilated by the whites. That this people is an amalgam of various races,
themselves crossed and recrossed like the Portuguese which through its reproductive
activity, its mobility, and its adaptability to the tropical climate became the very center
of the national formation, and that this incessant melting process made the country,
in the expression of Mendes Correia, one of the major fields of ethnic and social assimilation which had ever existed—of neither of these facts is there the shadow of a doubt.
But on the one hand it is not less certain that "all the peoples that stand at the forefront of civilization," as Jean Finot reminds us, "possess a blood that is richer in heterogeneous elements, and all these peoples whose origins have been studied display the
same richness of ethnic elements which, by crossing, have contributed to form their
national unity." And, if Schneider's hypothesis is true, it is always five or six hundred
years after an intense racial mixture that the high points of civilization are produced,
generally foretold by a great poet—a theory apparently supported in China by the classic
epoch of Lao-tzu and Confucius (600–480 B.C.) five centuries after the conquest of
the Chou dynasty (1122 B.C.); in Greece by the birth of Aeschylus, six centuries after

[19] This mobility of the immigrant population existed everywhere, except among the Germans
of Santa Catarina and Rio Grande do Sul, and the Japanese in São Paulo and Amazonas. The
foreign groups in São Paulo, where they concentrated, and in other States had to be assimilated,
frequently divided as they were by moving. The German colonists, on the contrary, who had settled beginning in 1836 to the north of the Lagoa dos Patos on small agricultural properties, and
in Santa Catarina, reenforced by new arrivals, were able to maintain insulated colonies, with the
European type of rural life: the isolation of these colonists, today about 500,000, left to themselves
in the interior of the State, which was already isolated from the rest of the nation, permitted, as
Lambert remarks, the establishment of homogeneous German colonization, for a long time cut off
from relations with the really Brazilian elements of the country (J. Lambert, "As Colônias alemãs
no Rio Grande do Sul," I-II, in *O Estado de São Paulo*, June, 1939). The assimilation of the Japanese, although crosses between Japanese and Brazilians have been recorded, met an obstacle in
the tendency of these immigrants to concentrate in certain regions, and then to isolate themselves
in their colonies like cysts in the national organism. In any case, as the number of immigrants of
that nationality who entered through the port of Santos since foreign immigration began in 1808,
was 176,775 in all, the number of those who settled in the State of São Paulo was 163,929, the
Japanese, distributed through various regions, are lost in the total population of 7,000,000 inhabitants. The problem arose in 1936, with reference to the Amazon basin, when, according to a
contract between Amazonas and the Japanese, it was planned to spread over 10,000 square kilometers
of the State of Amazonas 300,000 Japanese. It was not only a problem of mass, but of distribution:
"300,000 Japanese spread over 8,000,000 square kilometers of Brazil would not be a danger,"
rightly remarks H. Hauser. "The same 300,000 over 10,000 square kilometers of the soil of the
State of Amazonas would undeniably constitute a danger." (H. Hauser, "A Imigração no Brasil e
o problema japonês," in *La Prensa*, Lima, Peru, Sept. 9-11, 1937.)

the invasion of the Dorians; in France by the flowering of the poetry of the troubadours at the beginning of the twelfth century, equidistant in time from the invasion of the Burgundians in the fifth century; or in Italy by the appearance of Dante, preceded six hundred years by the Lombard conquest of the north. Thus, in Brazil, a new country in rapid growth and, for that very reason, with its natural wealth and immense territory a great center of attraction for immigrants, this melting pot and mixture of races from the dawn of its life may have been preparing the biological humus in which a new civilization is to flourish. On the other hand, the analysis of the anthropological composition of our population as estimated from 1835 to 1935 demonstrates that the proportion of mestizos and Negroes, 69.6 (separately, 18.2 and 51.4) per cent in 1835, compared with 24.4 per cent white came down to 40 (Negroes separately, only 8) per cent in contrast with 60 per cent whites in the total population. The Negro and Indian races are disappearing, absorbed by the white, or to use the picturesque expression of Afrânio Peixoto, "there is, in increasing degree, a white albumen to refine the national sugar cane." If we Brazilians lacked the racial integrity of the types that formed us, and if we had race mixture (white and Negro) in excess, other physical and social elements such as the factor of the environment, the vitality of the primitive Iberian nucleus, the rapid fusion of races, the community of language and of customs and traditions, would have sufficed to form in Brazil a national type, that tremendous force, which in the United States, as M. Sampaio Ferraz writes, "formed and absorbed the currents that arose, transforming them rapidly into a type *sui generis* and unmistakably American." [20]

[20] The tendency to explain the special qualities of national character by climatic and racial differences encounters the strongest counterargument in the very process of the evolution of societies, whose transformations of social and economic structure are accompanied by changes in mentality, in the various phases of their development. True, both climate and physical environment in general, and race understood as the sum of hereditary factors, which are, for that matter, extremely complex—too complex for us to be very exact about them in the case of mixed peoples—exercise an influence upon the formation of the temperament and character of nations. But one cannot draw a portrait of a nation's mentality nor predict the future of a human society merely as a function of its ethnic composition. This is affirmed clearly by N. Colajanni (*Latins et anglo-saxons*, transl. by J. Dubois, Paris, Felix Alcan, 1905); and J. Finot (*Le Préjugé des races*, Paris, Alcan, 1935). "The phenomena which takes place in society," observes H. Hubert, "phenomena of growth and decomposition, religious and moral phenomena, etc., are social phenomena, and not racial phenomena. Moreover, the groups we can observe are so made up that it is not scientific to try to distinguish in their social and mental life the contribution made by the original aptitudes of their component parts." The study of races as component parts of human groups—a study of pure anthropology—must be completed and rounded out by the study of societies, in their structure and changes, which is the object of sociology. In fact, to use the expression of Thurnwald, created to distinguish social from biological selection, the different national types are "screened," that is, selected and formed, according to the ideals that are dominant in a certain period, in a given society. What is above all important is to know the conditions of screening (social selection) in a society, that is, to know the cultural values and the order according to which this selection goes on. The anthropologist, explains Baldus, commenting on the theories of Thurnwald and his disciple W. Muhlmann, "only takes into account the *objects* of screening and selection, that is, hereditary predispositions, or men as the carriers of these predispositions. The *subject* of screening and selection is the physical and social environment which forms the cultural horizon of a people. If you do not know this horizon, you cannot judge the effects of screening and selection." (Cf. E. E. Muntz, *Race Contact*, New York, Century, 1928; Frank H. Hankins, *The Racial Basis of Civilization*, Part II, "The Concept and Social Role of Race," New York, Knopf, rev. ed., 1931.)

In an environment like ours that from the beginning was made up of elements of varied origins, native especially during the first century, African for three centuries, and European, besides Semite, Arab, Syrian, and Japanese, the latter in small proportions, the mixing or fusing of heterogeneous races not antagonistic to one another, is a normal fact, not only useful but indispensable to the ethnic evolution of the Brazilian people. It is not a problem but rather the natural solution, this crossing of various races and nationalities which entered into the ethnic composition of the people, and which, regarded in this way, would constitute problems only when they showed themselves to be unassimilable, forming, or tending to form, compact colonies that turned in upon their origins, like cysts in the national organism. Truly, "when the facts are taken in a broad way, that is to say, over long periods," writes Hauser in *La Prensa*, "it may be admitted that from 1820, the eve of independence, to 1930 Brazil received about 4,000,000 immigrants. The stock of Portuguese origin grew to be about 30 per cent of this total, and if we add the Spaniards (12.2 per cent) we get a total of 42 per cent Iberians, while the Italians reached 34.1 per cent. The Germans, who were concentrated principally in the south, represent in the total only 3.5 per cent, and those of different origins 19.8 per cent—first among them being the French and the Belgians and more recently the Poles." Except in the cases just cited, however, we do not find, in the matter of immigration any problem of masses or of distribution. On the contrary, the whole Brazilian problem is to be found, as Hauser has already observed, in its population figures (41,565,083 inhabitants in 1940) and in its area (8,511,189 square kilometers) or, still more simply, in the figure of its density—"a density which is almost that of a desert." The Brazilian population is then, as we see, slightly greater than that of France in a territory fifteen and a half times as great, which would permit Brazil without being overpopulated to have about 400,000,000 inhabitants, not counting its semiarid zones, its swamps, or parts of the national territory that are difficult of access. The Amazonian forest, the thick woods and forests of Mato Grosso and Goiaz, constitute in the strict sense "solitudes in which the airplane—the only possible means of transportation in these regions—finds only scattered groups of habitations."[21] But, if

[21] This figure, the average density (4.88), is extremely low, as can be seen by comparing it with the density of some European countries in which the average number of persons who live on a unit area, in a given territory, attains 276 per square kilometer in Belgium; 192 in Great Britain and Northern Ireland; 141 in Germany; 139 in Italy, and finally 76 in France. In Japan, in 1934, the average density was 179, which places that country immediately next to Germany in population density. The average density of the population of Brazil, 3.59 in 1920, rose, according to the *Sinopse* previously cited, to 4.88 inhabitants per square kilometer in 1940; but this density varies greatly from one region to another, attaining 43.93 in Rio de Janeiro, 33.52 in Alagoas, 29.28 in São Paulo, 27.15 in Pernambuco, 25.62 in Paraíba, 25.33 in Sergipe (the States with the most dense population), to fall to less than one inhabitant per square kilometer in Pará, Territory of Acre, Amazonas, and Mato Grosso. According to data collected by the 1920 Census, out of 1,000 inhabitants 504 are males and 496 females, the number of males being noticeably higher in the States of the south because of immigration, and in Amazonia, Goiaz and Mato Grosso—regions of exploitation of forests and mines—while women predominate in the northern States, because of the exodus of rural workers to the south. In each 1,000 inhabitants this census finds 572 under twenty years of age, 400 from twenty to sixty, and 30 over sixty. The proportions of the generations, lowest among the oldest, the grandparents, then the generation in the prime of life, the parents, and highest among the children, show by the small number of the aged (30 over sixty years of age, compared to 75 in England, 80 in Germany, 82 in Bulgaria, 87 in Japan, and 128 in France), the

to this demographic situation created by scanty static density we add the low dynamic density, that is to say, the very small degree of economic and cultural exchange of these extremely rarefied populations, it will be easy to understand that the Brazilian problem is one of population, of penetration, of communication, of transportation, and that the key to the problem will rather be a rational plan of immigration in small numbers and of the distribution and assimilation of the chance currents, working toward the progressive incorporation of the immense semideserts of Amazonia, Mato Grosso, and Goiaz into the national civilization. The fact that the Brazilian is directing all his qualities of audacity, tenacity, and resistance toward this work of penetrating and conquering the lands to be populated, proves not only the enormous expansion which took place from the sixteenth century with the expeditions into the interior but, in our own day, the heroic undertaking of the conquest of the Territory of Acre and the victory of man over nature—that of the Amazon region, "a hidden mixture of waters and land completely leveled in its own greatness." The tribes that people this land, as Euclides da Cunha reminds us in his incomparable language, "are cut out for wild life. They do not cultivate the land nor beautify it, they tame it. The inhabitants of Ceará, of Paraíba, the backwoodsmen of the north in general, take their stand there, accomplishing without knowing it one of the major enterprises of our times. They are taming the desert." The society so presented of "titanic frontiersmen who are there building a land," and the firmness and the vigor with which the Paulistas advance through their back land, carrying civilization on their cowcatchers and in a decade bringing to maturity cities sprung from the soil, these things show the temper of the man of Brazil, perfectly acclimated to his new environment, grown strong in the hard struggle against hostile nature and limitless space. Certainly, if we cannot exactly determine the elements whose mixture in each of these regions produced the Brazilian people, and discern clearly in our population all the ethnic differences, still we can distinguish in the Brazilian—a Mediterranean of mixed blood with a variety of subtypes—a single national type on which the primitive groupings impressed their own strongly marked characteristics founded on material relationships and developed by long living together in the same territory, by community of language, and by common beliefs which have continuously characterized our civilization. It was André Siegfried that declared that, "if some day white civilization retrogrades, the indigenous civilization in Latin America, always ready to resume the direction of its own tradition, will endure." But the indigenous race which raised its bulwarks in the Andes and in some Central American countries, there to remain impervious to white infiltration, did not except in the first two centuries contribute in any appreciable manner to the formation of the Brazilian people, whose mestizos of Indian origin, like the native races still existing hidden away in their forests, would not be in condition nor have the capacity to resist an avalanche of white people. If we admit that Negroes and Indians are continuing to disappear, both in the successive dilutions of white blood and in the constant process of biological and social selection, and that immigration, especially that of a Mediterranean origin, is not at a standstill, the white man will not only have in Brazil

numerical superiority of the young, do not appear to have contributed to decrease noticeably the influence of the older generation, whose authority began to break down as a result of the revolutions after 1930, and the consequent rise of younger men to power and the renewal of political and cultural circles.

his major field of life and culture in the tropics, but be able to take from old Europe—
citadel of the white race—before it passes to other hands, the torch of western civilization to which the Brazilians will give a new and intense light—that of the atmosphere
of their own civilization.

BIBLIOGRAPHY

Agassiz, Louis and Elizabeth Cary, *A Journey in Brazil* (Boston, 1868); transl. as *Viagem ao
   Brasil (1865-1866)* (São Paulo: Comp. Editora Nacional, 1938—Brasiliana, Vol. 95).
Araújo Lima, José Francisco de, *A Amazônia: A Terra e o homem* (Rio: Editorial Alba,
   1933).
Carvalho, Orlando M., *O Rio da unidade nacional—o São Francisco* (São Paulo: Comp.
   Editora Nacional—Brasiliana, Vol. 91).
Cruls, Gastão, *A Amazônia que eu vi, Óbidos-Tumucumaque* (São Paulo: Comp. Editora
   Nacional, 1938—Brasiliana, Vol. 113).
Cunha, Euclides da, *A Margem da história*, Pt. I, "Terra sem história (Amazônia)," pp. 5–135
   (Pôrto: Chardron, 3rd ed., 1922).
Fróis de Abreu, S., *A Riqueza mineral do Brasil* (São Paulo: Comp. Editora Nacional,
   1937—Brasiliana, Vol. 102).
Hoehne, F. C., "A Flora do Brasil," in *Recenseamento do Brasil* (Sept. 1, 1920), Vol. 1,
   Introdução, pp. 97–230 (Rio: Tip. da Estatística, 1922).
Licínio Cardoso, V., *À Margem da história do Brasil* (São Paulo: Comp. Editora Nacional,
   1933—Brasiliana, Vol. 13), pp. 47–78, "O Rio São Francisco, base física da unidade
   do império."
Magalhães Basílio de, *Expansão geográfica do Brasil colonial* (São Paulo: Comp. Editora
   Nacional, 2nd ed., 1935—Brasiliana, Vol. 45).
Maull, Otto, *Vom Itatiaya zum Paraguay: Ergebnisse und Erlebnisse einer Forschungsreise
   durch Mittelbrasilien* (Leipzig: Hiersemann, 1930).
Melo Leitão, C. de, *Zoo-geografia do Brasil* (São Paulo: Comp. Editora Nacional, 1937—
   Brasiliana, Vol. 77).
Miranda, Agenor A. de, *O Rio São Francisco* (São Paulo: Comp. Editora Nacional, 1936—
   Brasiliana, Vol. 62).
Miranda Ribeiro, A. de, "Esboço geral da fauna brasileira," in *Recenseamento do Brasil*
   (Sept. 1, 1920), Vol. 1, *Introdução* (Rio: Tip. da Estatística, 1922), pp. 233–275.
Morais, Raimundo, *Na planície amazônica* (São Paulo: Comp. Editora Nacional, 4th ed.,
   1936—Brasiliana, Vol. 63).
Morize, Henrique, *Contribuição ao estudo do clima do Brasil* (Rio: Tip. do Serviço de
   Informações do Ministério da Agricultura, 2nd ed., 1927).
Peixoto, Afrânio, *Clima e saúde: Introdução bio-geográfica à civilização brasileira* (São
   Paulo: Comp. Editora Nacional, 1938—Brasiliana, Vol. 129).
Rangel, A., *Rumos e perspectivas*, especially pp. 139–251, "Aspectos gerais do Brasil" (São
   Paulo: Comp. Editora Nacional, 2nd ed., 1934—Brasiliana, Vol. 26).
Saint-Hilaire, A. de, *Voyage aux sources du Rio de S. Francisco et dans la province de Goyaz*
   (Paris, 1847–1948). Portuguese transl. in Brasiliana, Vols. 68 and 78 (São Paulo:
   Comp. Editora Nacional, 1936–1937).
Sampaio Ferraz, J. de, *Meteorologia brasileira* (São Paulo: Comp. Editora Nacional, 1934—
   Brasiliana, Vol. 33).
Soares de Sousa, Gabriel, *Tratado descriptivo do Brasil em 1587* (São Paulo: Comp. Editora
   Nacional, 3rd rev. ed. with notes by F. Adolfo de Varnhagen, 1938—Brasiliana,
   Vol. 117).

Spix, J. B. von, *Através da Baía* (excerpts transl. from the work *Reise in Brasilien*) (São Paulo: Comp. Editora Nacional, 3rd ed., 1938—Brasiliana, Vol. 118).

Steinen, Karl von den, *Durch Central-Brasilien* (Leipzig: Brockhaus, 1886).

Tavares Bastos, A. C., *O Vale do Amazonas* (São Paulo: Comp. Editora Nacional, 2nd ed., 1937—Brasiliana, Vol. 106).

Travassos, Mário, *Projeção continental do Brasil,* with Preface by Pandiá Calógeras (São Paulo: Comp. Editora Nacional, 2nd ed., 1935—Brasiliana, Vol. 50).

Wallace, Alfred Russel, *A Narrative of Travels on the Amazon and Rio Negro* (London, 1853); transl. as *Viagens pelo Amazonas e Rio Negro* (São Paulo: Comp. Editora Nacional, 1939—Brasiliana, Vol. 156).

II

Almeida Prado, J. F. de, *Primeiros povoadores do Brasil, 1500–1530* (São Paulo: Comp. Editora Nacional, 1935—Brasiliana, Vol. 37).

Baldus, H., *Ensaios de etnologia brasileira,* with Preface by Afonso E. Taunay (São Paulo: Comp. Editora Nacional, 1937—Brasiliana, Vol. 101).

Ellis Júnior, Alfredo, "Os Primeiros Troncos paulistas e o cruzamento euro-americano," in *Revista do Instituto Historico e Geografico de São Paulo,* Vol. 29 (1932), pp. 93–142. Reissued in book form under same title in Brasiliana series, Vol. 59 (São Paulo: Comp. Editora Nacional).

———, *Populações paulistas* (São Paulo: Comp. Editora Nacional, 1934—Brasiliana, Vol. 27).

Freyre, Gilberto, *Casa grande e senzala,* especially Chap. 4, "O Escravo negro na vida sexual e de familia do brasileiro," pp. 303–437 (Rio: Maia & Schmidt, 1933). Transl. by Samuel Putnam as *The Masters and the Slaves: A Study in the Development of Brazilian Civilization* (New York: Knopf, 1946).

Leite Filho, Solidônio, *Os Judeus no Brasil* (Rio, 1923).

Nash, Roy, *The Conquest of Brazil* (New York: Harcourt, 1926). Transl. as *A Conquista do Brasil* (São Paulo: Comp. Editora Nacional, 1939—Brasiliana, Vol. 150).

Nina Rodrigues, Raimundo, *Os Africanos no Brasil* (São Paulo: Comp. Editora Nacional, 1932—Brasiliana, Vol. 9).

Oliveira Viana, F. J., "O Povo brasileiro e sua evolução," Pt. 2, "Evolução da raca," in *Recenseamento do Brasil,* Vol. 1, *Introdução* (Rio: Tip. da Estatística, 1922), pp. 311–344.

———, *Populações meridionais do Brasil* (São Paulo: Comp. Editora Nacional, 1933).

———, *Raça e assimilação* (São Paulo: Comp. Editora Nacional, 2nd ed., 1934—Brasiliana, Vol. 4).

Pinto, Estêvão, *Os Indígenas do Nordeste* (São Paulo: Comp. Editora Nacional, 1935—Brasiliana, Vols. 44 and 112).

Ramos, Artur, *As Culturas negras no novo mundo* (Rio: Civilização Brasileira Editora, 1937).

Rodrigues Pereira, Astrogildo, "Imigração e colonização" (especially on Japanese immigration), in *Geografia,* journal of the Associação de geógrafos brasileiros, Vol. 1, No. 4, pp. 25–49 (São Paulo, 1935).

Roquete Pinto, E., *Ensaios de antropologia brasiliana* (São Paulo: Comp. Editora Nacional, 1935—Brasiliana, Vol. 37).

Teschauer, Carlos, "Estudos etnológicos," in *Boletim do Museu do Rio de Janeiro,* Vol. 1, No. 4 (May, 1924), pp. 247–253.

Brazil, 1938: A New Survey of Brazilian Life (Rio: Instituto Brasileiro de Geografia e Estatística, 1939).

Recenseamento Geral de 1940: Sinopse Preliminar dos Resultados Demográficos (Rio, 1941),

CHAPTER TWO

THE WORK OF MAN

The rosewood monopoly—Agriculture and rural life—The Sugar mills—Slavery regulated, an elementary technique and cheap labor—The discovery of gold and the penetration of the back country—Mining in Minas and Mato Grosso—The hunting of the Indian—The pasturage of Piauí, Goiaz and Rio Grande—Old and new ways—The greatness of human effort —Geographic limits and economic frontiers—The American interior and the Brazilian interior: similarities and differences—The coffee plantation—Once more, a single crop economy with a slave-owning basis—The concentration of wealth in the hands of the great owners—Economic life and social classes—Industrial workers in the Colony and in the Empire—Cultivation on a large and a small scale—Ports and coastwise navigation—Transportation and commerce—The tax system—The high point of industry and the phenomena of concentration—The variety and inequality among economic and cultural centers—The extractive industries—The exploitation of the subsoil.

ON THE IMMENSE STAGE of the discovered lands, open along the coast to the vastness of the sea and enclosed toward the interior by a limitless solitude, for almost half a century after the discovery the white conqueror added nothing to the natural landscape. Everything conspired to retard the occupation of the geographic environment by the white man, who left traces of his passage only in a spot here and there along the interminable coast: the enormous distances which separated Portugal from the new world; the vastness of the territory, together with all the poetry of mystery and all the dangers of the unknown; and the difficulties faced by a small country with a scant population in populating new territories. While the Portuguese, wavering between the glories of his adventures and his plans for colonization, was preparing to settle in the new geographic surroundings, one could see, in the natural landscapes that remained untouched and protected from the domination of the white man, only the humble clearings of Indian villages and lodges, in the heart of forests or along the banks of rivers, and the constant sorties to the shore of wandering tribes who left their ephemeral remains upon the sands of the beaches. The action of man as a geographic agent modifying the landscape was inevitably slow in a country whose territorial extension was to be "the pride of future Brazilians, but also their weakness," and of which, four centuries later, there still remained approximately 4,800,000 square kilometers out of a total area of 8,500,000 with a density like that of a desert, or less than one inhabitant per square kilometer.[1] Everything in this land of apparently easy life was "disequilibrium," writes Gilberto Freyre. "Great excesses and great lacks, those of a new country. The soil, with

[1] These 4,800,000, or more exactly 4,814,031, square kilometers constitute the total area of the States of Pará, Territory of Acre, Mato Grosso, and Amazonas, the densities of which are respectively 0.70, 0.55, 0.29, and 0.25 inhabitants per square kilometer, according to the "Sinopse Preliminar dos Resultados Demográficos" of the Census of 1940.

the exception of spots of exceptionally fertile black or purple land, was far from being so good that you could plant anything you desired in it, as the first chronicler enthusiastically described it. It was in large part rebellious to agricultural improvement, hard, intractable, impermeable. The rivers were other enemies of regularity of effort and of the stability of family life. Death-bringing floods and sterilizing droughts, such was the regime of her waters. And through the land and the thick forests so difficult to bring under control, and along the rivers that it was almost impossible to make economically useful in farm tillage, in industry and in the regular transportation of farm products—were nurseries of larvae, multitudes of insects and vermin harmful to man."

So, before establishing bases of colonization, the first plan which soon failed consisted in the division of the land of Santa Cruz into captaincies of thirty to sixty leagues along the coast, and in the giving of these enormous latifundia to nobles of the mother country; the Portuguese limited his activities to explorations along the coast which made of it one immense quay for loading and unloading his fleet. Besides the transportation of the native cotton and seeds, of animals and of Indians taken in little incursions into the country, the trade in the various kinds of brazilwood constituted the principal source of revenue of Portugal and of the contractors whose ships remained only long enough to chop down trees, transport and load the famous wood which was abundant in the forest along the coast.[2] The trade in this wood, which had many uses in cabinetwork and in textile industries, was not slow in becoming a crown monopoly, rented out to merchants and groups of capitalists, probably new Christians, among whom there stands out, as Afonso Arinos reminds us, "the Jew Fernando de Loronha, the principal contractor of brazilwood of early times, whose name, slightly altered, still persists as that of an island of the northeast region of Brazil." The cutting, loading, and placing of the red wood, if they continued to constitute part of Portuguese business during the first three centuries, took place on a large scale only in the sixteenth century and in the beginning of the seventeenth, and had a preponderant role only in the first half of the sixteenth century, before colonization—which came, properly speaking, with the cultivation of sugar cane. It was in fact in the precolonial period that this destructive economy attained its maximum development, which in its very nature did not contribute to fix man on the land or to initiate the organization of labor but, by the rapid placing of the wood in the most important market of Europe, did open to the mother country a vast field for exploitation and one of its sources of wealth. According to Fernão Cardim and Gabriel Soares, if we are to believe this, the captaincies of Paraíba and Pernambuco alone sent to Lisbon at the end of the sixteenth century and the beginning of the following century more than one hundred ships loaded with brazilwood,

---

[2] Brazilwood, from which came the name that stuck to the country originally called Land of the Holy Cross, was a tree native to America, of which there were various species in the woods along the coast. Imported first into Europe from Asia as early as the thirteenth century, its wood became known and appreciated for industrial uses. The scarlet dye which was extracted from it was employed to color textiles (hence the expression of João de Barros, "cloth-dyeing wood"). Used on a large scale, for this and other purposes, the wood received in the western world the name *lignum brasile* (*bresillum*) from the High German *blas*, torch or flame, or from the old Germanic *brasa* (M. Lubke, Rew. 1276; Diez, Dic. 63; A. Nascentes, *Dic. Etim. da lingua portuguesa*, 123) and from Linnaeus, who classified it with the scientific name of *Caesalpinea sappan*, taken from the Asiatic word *sapang* or *chappan* (red color), by which the Asiatic species were called. The Brazilian Indians called this wood *ibira-pitanga* (red wood).

so that the monopoly of this business gave to the crown 60,000 cruzados a year, or about 6,000,000 cruzeiros of Brazilian money. Although based on an industry that was purely extractive, the traffic in brazilwood, on account of its volume and its commercial value, awakened the envy of the French and so was a factor in inciting Portugal to combat them by means of creating nuclei of permanent settlements along the coast.

The establishment of the first sugar mill,[3] in São Vicente between 1532 and 1533, by Martim Afonso de Sousa, who had been awarded a captaincy and who associated with himself some foreigners, Italian and Flemish, "who knew this branch of agricultural mechanics," opened Brazil's first economic cycle and offered great vistas for colonization. Portugal, when she discovered Brazil, was already the mistress of the international sugar trade; and when the sugar cane was transported from St. Thomas in western Africa, and perhaps also from the island of Madeira, to São Vicente the trade spread rapidly all along the coast from south to north, including along the strip of the shore, the captaincies of Rio de Janeiro, Espírito Santo, Bahia, and Pernambuco. In the middle of the sixteenth century the production of sugar in Portuguese America was already ahead of that in Spanish America; it attained 300,000 arrobas a year at the end of the century, doubling that at the beginning of the seventeenth century, with a total value of 300,000 cruzados, or in present-day money 30,000,000 cruzeiros. The white, chalky, clayey *massapê*, resulting from the decomposition of the Cretaceous deposit of Santo Amaro in Bahia, of Pernambuco, and of Campos in the State of Rio, furnished the soil most favorable for the cultivation of sugar cane and, in the white spots that indicated alluvial deposits, outlined the first centers of civilization. The cultivable regions are still real oases, and naturally the first colonists began to group themselves in these little cultivable divisions, marked on the geological map by the decomposition of Cretaceous basins and by the presence of little rivers. In fact, these rivers—the smaller but nevertheless more regular rivers—"neatly offered to grind the sugar cane, to water the lowlands, to make the sugar fields turn green, to transport sugar, to serve the interests and needs of fixed populations, both human and animal, settled on their banks; there the great cultivation flourished," writes Gilberto Freyre, "the agriculture of the great estates prospered, cattle raising spread. Rivers of the type of the Mamanguape, the Una, the Pitanga, the Paraná-Mirim, the Serinhaém, the Iguassú, the Cotindiba, the Pira-

[3] Sugar cane, originally an Asiatic plant, was imported into Brazil and exploited for the first time in the Governor's Plantation, founded by Martim Afonso de Sousa at whose order "was brought from the Island of Madeira the plant of sweet canes" (Brother Gaspar da Madre de Deus, *Memórias para a história da capitania de São Vicente*). The captaincy of São Vicente, writes Brother Vicente do Salvador in 1627 (*História do Brasil*), "was the first land where sugar was made, and from which plants of sugar cane were carried to other captaincies." This text—the first to mention sugar cane in Brazil—according to which the first mill for crushing sugar cane and running sugar was situated in the captaincy of Martim Afonso, is supported by historians like the Viscount of Pôrto Seguro (*História do Brasil*, Vol. I, p. 204; vol. III), Hermann Wätjen (*Das holländische Kolonialreich in Brasilien*—Portuguese transl., *O Domínio colonial holandês no Brasil*) who located the first planting of cane from Madeira in the south of Brazil, and perhaps the greatest authority on the history of sugar, Edmund von Lippman (*Geschichte des Zuckers*, 1929 ed.), who affirms, citing Handelmann, that sugar was transported "for the first time to São Vicente, situated in the south, where the grantee Afonso de Sousa had two mills set up." Simonsen is of this opinion; for him the real beginning of growing sugar cane was undertaken by Martim Afonso in 1533, with the foundation in São Vicente of the "Governor's Plantation" (*A História econômica do Brasil*, Vol. I, São Paulo, 1937).

pama, the Ipojuca, the Mundaú, the Paraíba, regular, without the interruptions and floods of the great rivers, were valiant collaborators in the organization of our agrarian economy and of the slaveholding society which grew up in its shadow."

But if the colonist found along the shore, in the *massapê*, rich in humus, the fertile land bathed by these small rivers whose important civilizing role Gilberto Freyre has brought out with vigor and color, he lacked a worker to tame the land, to plant the sugar cane, to make the sugar, and to transport it on his shoulders to the merchant fleets. That worker was the Negro slave, who entered with the shoots of sweet cane and grew up with them. "By the heat of his blood"—the words are those of Soares Cabelo —"the land indefinitely kept its fatness, and, impelled by his strength, the mills functioned tirelessly for centuries and centuries. The Negro slave. Seven years of relentless work, and then worse than an old ox: an animal carcass to be thrown on the junk heap of the slave quarters. . . . He, the Negro, was and is, for sugar cane, what the sugar cane was for this country. Certain it is that without him it would never have been the principal means by which Brazil grew rich and noble." The introduction of Negro slavery, regulated and imposed by the necessity for cheap labor, like the sugar-cane fields and the cotton plantations in North America, led to the importation of slave labor and was one of the most important aspects and a fact of the greatest ethnic and cultural consequences in the agrarian and industrial economy which "for the first time permitted the country to regulate and pay its functionaries without being a charge upon the treasury of the mother country." Into the construction and development of the colonial economy based upon sugar and upon slave labor, there entered in equal parts the green cane, the white land of the *massapê*, the Negro slave; the plants from Asia, the land from America, the man from Africa, all utilized and exploited by the power of organization and discipline of the European colonizer—the Portuguese, who at that time ruled world commerce and saw the four continents associated symbolically in the most fruitful of his colonizing efforts. It is certainly due on the one hand to the colonizing capacity of the Portuguese and their Brazilian descendants, and on the other to the capacity for work and for submission of those 1,500,000 slaves imported for the sugar-cane fields and sugar mills, that these nuclei of production multiplied to the number of 238 a century after the establishment of the first mill in Brazil, and that Brazil held first place in the production of sugar in the whole world as early as the seventeenth century, producing a sufficient amount to supply all Europe, with a value in the three centuries in which Brazil was a colony, according to Roberto Simonsen, estimated at £300,000,000 sterling. Sugar, the most important article of international commerce, played the role at that time which coal assumed later in an industrial civilization, when it established the greatness of England—whose total exportation annually, in the middle of the seventeenth century, did not approach the £3,000,000 yearly of production and exportation of Brazilian sugar.

However, great as may have been the economic value of sugar cane and the sugar industry in Brazil,[4] this is not the most important aspect of the patriarchal type of econ-

[4] The production of sugar, so vigorously initiated in the sixteenth century, began to decline in the eighteenth, as a result of the competition of the sugar which France imported from its plantations in Guadeloupe, Martinique, and Santo Domingo, to export it again, thus attacking Brazil's supremacy in the world market. The replacement of cane sugar by beet sugar, using the process discovered by Delessert in 1810; the increase in production of beet sugar, by virtue of the improve-

omy which had the most profound influences upon the social and historic formation of the Brazilian people. It was with the sugar cycle that colonization really began. The sugar mill was, in truth, observes Barbosa Lima Sobrinho, "the first power capable of attracting and keeping the foreign immigrant. In it we had our first fortress against the attack of the pagan. A permanent element in civilization, it created in the still savage land those nuclei of intense social life to which the chroniclers of the sixteenth century were already referring with expressions of enthusiasm and surprise." It is with the patriarchal form of society and the slaveholding economy that the conquistador is transformed from a trader into a colonizer, managing to tame his geographic environment and rises, if still only along the coast, as a modifier of the landscape, violating nature in order to superimpose on natural regions a cultural landscape strongly characterized by the "big house" (the house reveals the man), by the slave quarters, by the sugar mills, and by the cane fields, and all that magnificent flowering of colonial architecture in the fortresses, churches, and convents.[5] The mark of man on the soil is a thing that he left even in the devastation which the land suffered through his destructive action, and of which, in the words of Gilberto Freyre, "it still keeps scars, when they are not open wounds, still bleeding from the devastating regime of agrarian exploitation"—the fire, the cutting down, the burning of the brush, "the parasitic exploitation of nature" in the phrase of Monteiro Baena, referring to Brazil. That whole picture corresponded to a social and economic structure of which Gilberto Freyre, in *Casa grande e senzala*,

---

ment of industrial techniques for its production, and finally the use of steam engines in the mills in the nineteenth century at last gave the European mills the first place in the production of this article, which for almost two centuries, constituted our main source of wealth. The exportation of tobacco (*herba. santa*), already known and used by the Indians in their ceremonies, although it dominated the world market for tobacco, did not, according to Roberto Simonsen, exceed £12,000,-000 sterling during the colonial period, as compared with £300,000,000 for the exportation of sugar, in that period.

[5] The rural residence of the lords of the mill and plantation is the "big house," and the expression is typical of the patriarchal regime and of single-crop agriculture based on slaveholding. Of a rustic simplicity, built of stone and plaster, with a roof of straw or tile, and a veranda of Alemtejo or Arabic type, the first big houses looked like camp structures and "remained enclosed in their Tupi stockades, in locations that were high and easily defended against the constant attacks of the savages." Later, from the second century of our national life, without losing their fortresslike appearance, these walled buildings rose with an imposing aspect which is the result of their taking on the proportions of mansions, with their roofs with turned up points, their hospitable verandas and their *copiares*—covered porches, perhaps of native origin—their carved doors and their mattings, used in the north to cover the window openings. These lordly houses, vast and solid, which from above dominated the plantations, were at the same time residence, fortress, religious center, factory, and bank; they generally had a chapel where the family dead were buried, and under the wide boards of their floors or their great stones the jewels and treasures of the family were hidden. And, as everything is concentrated and everything is produced in these great realms, which are organized in an autarchy and are self-sufficient, it was in the interior of the women's quarters that the household worked, under the stern direction of the ladies of the house, spinning, weaving, and dyeing cotton. In the slave quarters, depending on the big house, the numerous slaves of the plantation are crowded. Big house, chapel, and slave quarters, lord, slave, and religion, constitute the three structures or the three fundamental powers on which from the beginning the work and industry of the plantation rested. Cf. Gilberto Freyre, *Casa grande e senzala* (Rio: Schmidt & Maia, 1933); Pedro Calmon, *Espírito da sociedade colonial*, especially Part I, "A Sociedade" (Rio: Comp. Editora Nacional, 1935—Brasiliana, Vol. 40).

studying the sugar region of the Northeast, has given us a penetrating and illuminating analysis, not only with regard to the technique of production and of work—the single-crop system and slavery—but also with regard to customs, ideas, the moral code, the character of the religion of that aristocratic, slaveholding, rural society which grew up in it in the shade of the sugar mills. Certainly as each of those sugar regions, distant from the others, on the coast near Rio, Bahia, and Pernambuco, constituted an isolated unity, that geographic division of the arable land would have contributed to a political division, if at the same time on the coast the economic solidarity of all those productive centers, scattered but bound together both by the Portuguese monopoly of the trade and also by unity of culture and techniques of work, had not conspired to promote political unity. The obstinate, bloody struggles against the Dutch invader, who had settled at Pernambuco attracted by its sugar industry, had been only an index of that unity, but also a powerful means to consolidate it by uniting against the common enemy whites, blacks, Indians, and mestizos, and by bringing together for the first time on the very field of battle, men of Rio and of São Paulo, of Bahia and Pernambuco.

The agriculture which developed in these three centuries remained in the eyes of Brazilians the principal occupation and principal source of revenue, and the conditions of life on those great agricultural properties, on which most of the articles of consumption were manufactured, and which could be self-sufficient, served merely to maintain and to develop individualism, that is, one of the most marked characteristics of the Brazilian character. The new cycle of mining, which followed upon that of sugar without driving it out, for other reasons and in other circumstances, contributed only to accentuate this individualism and to mix the populations through one of the greatest movements of internal migration that have taken place in our history. Even in the early letters granting captaincies, the road to the interior was pointed out when these immense properties were limited to thirty to sixty leagues along the coast, with whatever islands might be found to ten leagues out to sea, and "through the back lands as far as they may reach." The coast, as it presented itself at the beginning, writes Alberto Rangel, "was a miserable bench with its fishing, coconut palms and brazilwood principally for anyone who came foretasting the incommensurable, fabulous riches." Everything conspired to incite men to go into the back country: the fascinating idea of the mines of gold and precious stones, which tormented the adventurous spirit of the colonists and stimulated their imaginations; the news which reechoed from the sounding board of the young towns on the threshold of the back country, taking on legendary proportions; the hunger for gold and the need for labor, urging them on to the capture of the savage, and in addition to the prospects of minerals and of red-skinned slaves, the rivers that ran inland, like natural ways of penetration, and the mountains which "served to sharpen desire by disclosing the horizon." All the attempts and expeditions in which the dreams and hopes of the conquistadores disappeared over almost two centuries, did nothing more than stimulate the spirit of adventure, spurred on without result by the constant appeals of the crown, until the bandeirantes of São Paulo, mestizo sons of white and Indian parents, bold and tenacious in the final twilight of the seventeenth century, tamed the land of the "general mines" (*minas gerais*) determining the zone of gold mining in central Brazil and opening the fields to successive discoveries of mines. These admirable deeds of the discoveries of the interior, opening up the immense riches of the "general mines," inaugurated the new economic cycle which moved masses of immigrants and adventurers, from all parts of the country, to the work in the extraction and refining of the mineral, joining in the hallucinatory search for gold and green stone (amazonite), in the gold washings of Minas and Bahia and in the extractive industry of Goiaz and Mato Grosso.

Gold mining, carried on by primitive methods and still dependent upon Negro labor, developed in such a way that during the half-century of greatest production in the "general mines" (1710–1760) "Brazil extracted in the most inaccessible regions, and transported to the coast with enormous difficulty, and exported to old Europe, according to the estimates of Roberto Simonsen, an amount of gold equivalent to 50 per cent of all the gold produced in the world in the three preceding centuries and equal to the total production mined in America from 1493 to 1850!" The miners and the Negro slaves, by the thousands, bent with their sieves over the beds of the rivers, in whose sands among the pebbles rolled the gold leaf, or dug at the feet of mountains, moving and breaking stones or opening galleries with their strong, muscular arms, so as to extract the metal from the rock in which nature was guarding it. But to all that wealth, made up especially of the surface gold retained in the sand of the alluvial streams, there was added from 1730 on, in the period in which the exploitation of mines attained its greatest intensity,[6] the wealth of diamond deposits rented out at the beginning to contractors who accumulated fabulous fortunes, and afterward exploited directly by the crown, which took over the monopoly of extraction. If the exportation of gold in three centuries, estimated at £200,000,000 sterling, had a great importance in the international economy and finance, that of diamonds was so great that, according to João Lúcio de Azevedo, "international prices of the stone were upset," during this period of less than a century in which production, according to the estimate of Calógeras, exceeded 1,300 pounds with a value higher than £10,000,000 sterling. The discovery and exploitation of the gold mines from the dawn of the eighteenth century, and that of the diamond deposits when the age of gold had begun to decline, contributed notably to the conquest of central Brazil and to the settlement of the interior, multiplying in the back-land farms and cities—of which more than half of those now in the Brazilian interior owe their origins, according to Luiz Camilo, to mining. In the period which then began— one of opulence and of the fever of creation, manifested in the splendor of Vila Rica, with the immense fortunes of the contractors, with their magnificent works and a church standing guard on every hill, which still recall by the luxuriance of their baroque style the most beautiful examples of religious architecture—the political center of the country moved from Bahia to Rio, and intellectual culture in Brazil reached a level never before attained. From the coast on which it flourished along with the sugar industry, the center of culture and of freedom of thought moved to the region of the "general mines, where, in the conflicts with the mother country, the dream expanded and the first arms of freedom were forged; and that region became in colonial history, under the influence of a gold civilization, the center of the most intense intellectual influence, and of the greatest diversity and richness in the arts and in letters.

[6] The royal letter of March 29, 1617, which commanded that the gold mines should be handed over to the vassals who discovered and exploited them was, as Alberto Rangel (*Rumos a perspectivas*, 2nd ed., 1934, p. 18) says, "the greatest stimulus to the zeal of the bandeirantes. The crown held out hope with this freedom and legalization of possession, although it added the tax of the fifth, cutting it out of the back, as it were, of the gold-hunters."

But, coming into existence with the sugar-cane civilization of which it was a part, and preceding gold mining and expanding in the course of and after that economic cycle, cattle raising,[7] limited at first to the necessities of the sugar mills and to the feeding of their populations, extended slowly from the middle of the sixteenth century through Brazil from the south to the north, Bahia and Pernambuco, and from Bahia, where it attained its greatest intensity, to zones ever more distant in the interior. Frequently it was along the cattle roads that the bandeiras marched, and when old Minas was swept by the bandeirantes the cattle raisers had already opened the roads to the zones nearest the mining centers. The herds preceded the bandeirantes, who not seldom settled down, becoming cattle raisers and making the desert fruitful; in their steps on the discovery of the "mines" came the gold washers and the prospectors for diamonds, and with the towns and cities which sprang up civilization marched through the back land. The two economic cycles of cattle and of gold crossed, at times intermingling in such a way that the territorial expansion of cattle facilitated the entrance of the bandeiras into the back country along old roads made by herds and cattle, and the bandeiras in their turn, by breaking new roads in all directions, favored the advance and the increase of the herds. So it was that in the ancient cities of the mining back land, like Vila Rica clinging to the flank of the hill, or Mariana lulled by the waters of the Carmel (Carmo) River, beside its famous churches full of treasures wrested from the gold-bearing sands by the gold washers and diamond hunters, there arose in humility for the refreshment of the herds public fountains "topped by coats of arms and crosses, with the edges of their basins worn by the rubbing of the animals' necks." Certainly that period, which Capistrano de Abreu named "cycle of hides," and which from its beginning in the sixteenth century expanded ever more and more until it included other economic cycles and gradually conquered, by way of the natural pasturage, the Brazilian back lands, had an importance that is truly notable from an economic point

[7] Cattle raising was introduced into Brazil as early as the first half of the sixteenth century, probably in the Captaincy of São Vicente, and was afterward extended to Bahia and other captaincies of the north. According to the teaching of Aurélio Pôrto, Brazilian cattle of São Vicente, extending to the south, were the origin of cattle raising in Paraguay, where it was introduced in 1555, from whose herds came all the cattle that reached from Uraguay to the banks of the Rio de la Plata, where Portugal founded the colony of Sacramento. "Toward the west, corrals of cattle," writes Afonso Arinos de Melo Franco, "reached Goiás and Mato Grosso, while the future territory of the 'general mines,' before the days of mining, was opened up by the cattle breeders of São Vicente." In the north, pastoral industry spread from Maranhão to Pernambuco, advancing through the whole Northeast, and reaching its highest development in Bahia, along the São Francisco River. It was to this region that the territory of Garcia d'Avila spread; he was a companion and friend of Tomé de Sousa, founder of the famous Casa da Tôrre, the greatest cattle ranch in Brazil, whose cattle—in such number that the potentate himself did not know how many they were—spread over leagues and leagues of pasture, whose area extended seven or eight leagues along the coast and 1,500 kilometers along the rivers into the interior. Erected on a hill from which, over the wide horizon, one could see the plains of Itapoã and the coast almost to Sergipe, the Casa da Tôrre, in Tatuapara, was an immense feudal property, with a vast collection of dwellings, defense walls and bulwarks for standing guard, and with its fields for raising cattle and mares and "some ten corrals inland," according to the testimony of Gabriel Soares (1584). Pedro Calmon in his *História da Casa da Tôrre* (Rio: José Olímpio, 1939) states that the Casa da Tôrre, between Bahia and Sergipe, served as an outpost and center of military action during the wars with foreigners, and rendered outstanding services in the long campaign against the Dutch. It was there that various expeditions into the interior were outfitted, not only to combat the Indian but also to hunt for silver mines.

of view, an importance doubtless growing and never dominant. It is not properly and rigorously a cycle: the ascending curve never fell, and never in any epoch showed a tendency to close the circle. There was no zenith with absolute dominion in national economy, as in the case of sugar, gold, and later coffee, and it never knew violent fluctuations or abrupt decline. If at the outset of the eighteenth century, when the mining cycle began, soon to attain its zenith, the total of the herds was estimated at a million and a half head, by the time of independence, when the decline of the gold era was already notable, it must have surpassed five million head.

That socioeconomic phenomenon, pastoral activity—called the "civilization of hides" because the hide was the only article for exportation derived from cattle—nevertheless gained its importance in colonial history less from the economic value of its exports (110,000 hides per year from the whole country at the beginning of the eighteenth century, increasing to 400,000 from Rio Grande do Sul alone in 1816) than from its influence as a factor for national unity and as a preponderant element in our development. The requirement of pasturage and of abundant territory for the fazendas or ranches for cattle raising and therefore its compulsory location in the interior, the multiplication of herds and the enormous drives through the back land, for internal commerce in meat, brought on an enormous development of internal migration and the taming of immense regions which without cattle would long have remained solitary and desolate. Along the cattle roads, followed also by the missionaries in the conversion of the Indians and by the back-country cowboys, and near the winter grazing land, ranches, and corrals in the interior of Piauí, Ceará, Rio Grande do Norte and Paraíba, as in Bahia and farther south in Goiaz, Minas, Mato Grosso, and Rio Grande do Sul, rest shelters, towns, and villages multiplied, some of which, grown into cities, have preserved in their names (Campo Grande, Campinas, Curral d'El-Rei, Campos, Vacaria, etc.) their origins which were bound up with the territorial expansion of cattle. That decisive influence of the pastoral element in our civilization did not pass unperceived by Capistrano de Abreu, Eugênio de Castro, Roberto Simonsen, and others who stressed the historic role of cattle in the penetration of the interior and in the settlement of its population, as well as in the formation of national unity, by bringing together the Brazilians of the north and the south, a thing which was facilitated by the internal migrations attendant upon the breeding, transporting, and dealing in cattle. In fact, writes Manuel Bonfim, it is in the vast interior that there arise "those vigorous currents in which peoples wander over hundreds of leagues, climbing mountains and crossing valleys, bringing together the fields of Guarapuava with those of Rio Branco. . . . Even now, the Amazonian lands are not completely known and the peoples of the land, following herds of cattle over the plains and caatingas, develop a wide range which, stemming from the river São Francisco, spreads customs, interests, and ideas from the Rio das Velhas even beyond the Parnaíba. In the south, taking part at the same time in the movement in the back lands (since there were more than a hundred Paulistas with cattle fazendas on the upper São Francisco), the activity of the bandeirantes along the Tietê and the São Francisco, the two great natural ways of penetration, creates the great movement which spreads through all the valleys, uniting them into a single population."

When one thinks of the obstacles of every kind which the back-country people had to conquer at the head of their herds and cattle, and the bandeirantes in their expeditions through the back country hunting the Indian or seeking gold fields, one cannot fail to recognize in this stupendous movement of territorial expansion the robust foundations upon which, in the interior, there began to rise the structure of the nation. The conquest, by man, of the geographic environment covered by virgin forest, walled in by mountains, rolled back by the peaks, sunk in swamps, cut by enormous rivers which radiated and crossed one another in practically all directions toward the sea and inland, is a wild epic in which there erupted with all the greatness of human effort, and in the immense framework of labor, pain, and sacrifice, "one of the vivid and authentic affirmations of Brazilian blood in hard lands" which led to pasturage and to cities, to the coast and to mining centers, in the continual movement to and fro of the waves of interior population. Certainly, in the background of the scene swarmed the Negro slaves, in the mining lands, over the broad beds of rivers, or at the foot of the mountains, or there moved about the mass of forest savages who, enslaved in every one of the expeditions, came down thousands at a time to be distributed or sold at a low price, in the cities and towns of the coast. But the origins of all peoples are sad and bloody (even Auguste Comte used to speak of the "ferocity of primitive countries"), and the trials and sufferings of the races that the white conqueror and the tamers of the back country found it necessary to enslave, and that sometimes offered stubborn resistance and sometimes yielded to the harsh imposition, must not make us forget the sufferings and the misadventures of the sertanejos and the bandeirantes, who had native blood in their own veins, and who, leading their cattle or marching in expeditions, fording rivers, scaling mountain heights and going deep into the forests, extended the frontiers of the country and conquered the interior for civilization. This phenomenon to which Turner gave the name "movement of frontiers" [8] to indicate the economic, territorial expansion of the country within its own political limits, and which is still going on in Brazil, was as J. F. Normano observes, the movement that truly formed the nation. Not half of the existing territory was as yet part of the economic life of the country, and the economic frontiers remained very far from the political frontiers. [9] The economic frontiers some-

[8] F. J. Turner, *The Frontier in American History*, p. II (New York, 1926).

[9] The political frontiers of Portuguese America were limited at the dawn of the sixteenth century almost to a strip along the coast, in which the ports and the first cities, with the cane fields and sugar mills, marked the extent of conquest and exploitation of the land by the Portuguese colonist. Internal colonization of the country really began with the sugar industry, which moved the limits of economic expansion beyond the coast line. The cowboys, "driving the Tapuyas away from the river banks that the cattle invaded" and advancing through the back lands in the search for new pasturage, contributed effectively to expand them. Cattle-raising was an invasion. The herd, writes Pedro Calmon, "grew on the march." The expeditions through the interior, opening by force of arms the road along which the bandeiras and later cattle and troops continued to advance, taming the interior, extended the political limits of the country and brought with them the possibility of economic development. But, while the geographic frontiers at the end of the eighteenth century had been laid down by the second boundary treaty of 1777, and the Brazilian territory by that time extended as far as the limits of the Spanish colonies, and only the territory of Acre was later added, the economic frontiers barely touched huge regions, solitary and almost totally unexplored; these were the lands of Pará, Amazonas, Goiaz, and Mato Grosso. The bandeiras were rather a phenomenon of geographic expansion than of use of the political territory or the incorporation of the newly conquered land into the economic life of the country. The discoveries and the exploitation of mines and the constant territorial expansion of the cattle industry, while they expanded the frontiers, were unable to maintain an economic frontier equally advanced; the economic

times advanced in different directions, sometimes retreated from the geographic limits, but it was without doubt due to the expeditions into the interior and to the tremendous expansion by the bandeirantes that Brazil "from the middle of the eighteenth century already included," as Simonsen reminds us, "an area practically equal to that which it occupies today, while the United States then did not occupy even a sixth part of its present territory."

This is precisely the fundamental difference already pointed out by Roy Nash, between the territorial expansion in North America, regular, orderly, continuous, in a single direction, accompanied practically always by progressive colonization of the interior, and the geographic expansion in Brazil, irregular, disorderly, carried out in practically all directions, without a parallel, simultaneous economic development. Doubtless, the sertão (whose morphology according to the usual interpretation came, as Alberto Rangel shows, from *desertão*, the first syllable being cut off) was in North America, as well as in Brazil, "the lure and the mirage of the early settlers and the great, exciting force of national energy." The gospel missionaries with their catechism, the cowboy with his herds, the bandeirante with his harquebus, and the miners with their pans, in turn played their separate parts in civilizing the country, opening roads by which the internal migrations continued to advance in various directions: in the notable work of Christianizing the Indians, in the incessant search for natural pastures, and also in the capture of the aborigines and the discovery and exploitation of mines. In the United States, "the zone of the sertão was mainly composed," writes Roy Nash, "of a line where there took place the struggle of the wave of humanity that was advancing from the colonized regions, bound for the west, within the period of time which was prolonged for three hundred years. This line (he adds) showed a regular, orderly advance, with no break in continuity, through the period until 1849 when the gold rush in California suddenly, in a single tremendous jump, brought the limit of the human wave to the shores of the Pacific, long before the initial phase of colonization of the Great Plains and the Rocky Mountains had taken place. But, in Brazil, as early as 1700, the discovery of gold (and earlier, we might add, the discovery of new pasturage fields) had split into thousands of fragments that frontier zone—between the colonized part and the unknown sertão—pushing the population out over an immense territory as if by a great aerial bombardment." This phenomenon of dispersion which resulted from the fact that the sertão of Brazil, extending "to a depth proportional to the unlimited line that faces the ocean," opened three directions, north, south, and west, to the expeditions while in the United States the human wave rolled practically always to the west, brought about the greatest geographic expansion that history records as carried out by a small group of human beings. But it did not permit colonization or economic development of the interior zone, and maintained until the beginning of the twentieth century, side by side with a narrow fringe of civilization along the coast and over the plateau in the regions nearest the coast, the immensity of forest belt, of forests and sertão, with their terrible economic and social problems.

But if in all the lands tamed by man none, unless it be the region of the "general mines," attained a thoroughness of exploration and economic development to match the

---

frontier showed in its forward and backward movements, and changes of direction, the fluctuations produced by the discovery of new territory and new mines and the gradual exhaustion of old pasture lands and mining zones.

political consequences of territorial expansion, the mine diggings and galleries, especially in Minas, and the transformation of the landscape by the cutting down and the burning of the forest are an unmistakable demonstration of the human effort that was directed toward the conquest and utilization of natural wealth. Not that the exploitation of brazilwood and internal colonization, begun with the planting of sugar cane, had forced back the forest cover from a great part of its primitive extent, estimated at 4,000,000 square kilometers: mountains continued to serve, as they still do, as a place of attraction on the plateaus, beside the unhealthful plain and the land invaded by swamps or by hostile forests, in the northern region of Mato Grosso, in Goiaz, and in Amazonia. But as the forest, without which the earth would have been almost uninhabitable by man, was always in the beginning a great enemy of colonization the struggle against it carried out by cutting and by fire had a modifying effect on the forest landscape, for which a cultural landscape was substituted that extended over the plains, climbed the slopes of the hills, and with the indigenous *sapé* of Brazil or the hay of African origin covered the fields between great old trunks abandoned on the ground. The diffusion of this molasses grass, observes Pierre Monbeig, "accompanied the destruction of the forest by fire, the great primitive, agricultural technique (*coivara*, as the Indians called it) the essential tool of the back countryman, as A. de Saint-Hilaire had already noted, showing the evolution of vegetation, after the cutting down and the burning of the forest. The plant landscape that is most frequent in the interior of Brazil is the *cerrado*, which appears natural but is not; it is not hard to conceive that in Brazil, as in the Sudan or Madagascar, such countrysides are the products of fire." The total replacement of the forest landscape by a humanized landscape was to begin with a new economic cycle, that of coffee growing, [10] on which the whole economic structure of the Empire came to rest, and to a great extent that of the Republic, too, thanks to which the city of São Paulo, "from the small town that it was at the end of the Empire, came to be one of the most important urban centers of the world." Herds and slavery, and later spades and highways and the ax of the woodsman opened the way for a new culture, and in place of age-old forests, which disappeared before the devastating invasion of the ax and of fire, there spread the "green wave of coffee," clambering up the mountain slopes of the coast, and extending rapidly along the valley of the Paraíbo do Sul, between Rio de Janeiro and the city of São Paulo.

[10] The coffee tree, indigenous in Abyssinia, got its present name (cafe) from Kaffa, one of the provinces in Ethiopia which constituted its original habitat. Carried by the Arabs to their country, it spread as early as the sixth century widely over Arabia, which for a long time was the exclusive producer, using it as the national beverage—a state of affairs favored by Mohammedan restrictions laid on the use of alcoholic drinks; from there it was exported to the west by Mocha (hence the name of one variety). From Europe, where even in the seventeenth century there were houses intended for the use of coffee, it was transplanted to America in 1720 by an officer of the French navy, Gabriel Mathieu de Clieu, who, on a voyage to Martinique in the Antilles, planted on that island the first specimens of the coffee tree. Although a little later, in 1727, coffee had entered Brazil, brought from Cayenne by Francisco de Melo Palheta, a Brazilian officer of the Portuguese colonial troops, coffee, cultivated in primitive fashion in Pará, only began to be commercially exploited a century later; and it was not until the second half of the eighteenth century that, transplanted to Rio de Janeiro, it found "the point of departure for its great development." Cf. Afonso E. Taunay, *História do café*; Basílio de Magalhães, *O Café na história, no folclore e nas belas-artes* (São Paulo: Comp. Editora Nacional, 2nd ed., enlarged and improved, 1939—Brasiliana, Vol. 174); William H. Ukers, *All About Coffee* (New York, 2nd rev. ed., 1935).

The cultivation of coffee, the dawn of which at the beginning of the eighteenth century coincided with the twilight of mining, reached in fact such a height that Rio de Janeiro exported 100,000 bags of it even in 1820 and 400,000 in 1830. This exportation—the product of plantations near Rio—was the point of departure for the new economic cycle which was to attain in São Paulo its principal center of production. It was with branches from the coffee tree that Dom Pedro I trimmed the hats of his officials and the guns of his soldiers; and the Empire which he founded recognized the closeness of its connection with coffee, as Afonso Arinos Sobrinho reminds us, later when "it placed a branch of the coffee plant on its coat of arms as a symbol of the national economy." From Rio de Janeiro that culture, built like that of sugar "on the burned-over remains of the great tropical forests," spread through the interior of São Paulo and Minas, especially along the banks of the Paraíba do Sul, in the valley of which it predominated until the decade of 1880 to 1890, maintaining the primacy of the port of Rio de Janeiro in Brazilian commerce. Among us, writes Alberto Rangel, "water not only quenched thirst, but guided men and enriched them; in the sands of rivers, among the tiny pebbles were found the flake of gold and the stone of the diamond. Three surprising elements of profit for the establishment and the movement of adventurers." The Paraíba do Sul River, which bathes a large part of the State (formerly Province) of São Paulo, and crosses the whole length of the State of Rio de Janeiro, thus performs in the cultivation of coffee the function which was performed by the Beberibe, Una, Serinháem, and other rivers in the sugar cycle; by the São Francisco and the Parnaíba in the center and in the north, the Paraná and the Paraguay in the west, and the Uruguay in the south in the breeding of cattle; and by the Rio das Velhas and the Ribeirão do Carmo in Minas, and the Rio das Garças in Mato Grosso, in the most intense phase of mining activity. Coffee followed the sound of flowing water, like sugar cane, cattle herding, and the extraction of metals and stones, either from the river beds or with the help of waters turned out of their courses. The coffee cultivation which developed in the Provinces of São Paulo, Minas, and Rio de Janeiro, "the most important part in the total coffee production of the Empire," included thus, as Afonso Arinos has justly observed, "a great geographic unity conditioned by a river system and divided politically by the territories of three provinces." But, if the base of the economic structure led from the sugar-raising Northeast to the region of "general mines" and afterward to São Paulo and Rio de Janeiro, and from sugar cane to gold and later to coffee, even in this last phase there was maintained the unity of production (the single-crop system) and the same instrument of exploitation: slave labor.

It was with coffee growing, on a latifundarian base and under a slave regime, that there emerged in the basin of the Paraíba a new rural aristocracy, the political support of the Empire, and that there was inaugurated in the south of Brazil, but still near the coast, a period of great prosperity and civilization. Wealth was concentrated in the hands of the great proprietors, whose fortune, based upon the slave quarters, counted in coffee groves, and built upon the lands and constructions destined for the improvement of coffee, was exhibited in their life of ostentation and pleasure, in the luxuriousness of their lordly residences in the country and in the greatness of their mansions in the city, such as the palaces of Catete and of Itamaraté, today sumptuous public buildings. Under the influence of coffee growing, which became one of the major types of agricultural exploitation in the world,[11] there was constructed to serve the coffee zone, through the initiative of the Baron of Mauá, the first railroad, the Central Railroad of Brazil, which, begun in 1853, reached the capital of São Paulo in 1877; Mauá developed the railroad system which in 1885 was composed of 57 railroads, some great and some small, with about 7,000 kilometers of track; there were begun the first highways, like the "Union and Industry" leading from Rio to Minas; there appeared, after 1860, the first large favorable trade balances; the urban landscape of Rio de Janeiro was transformed and enriched, which maintained itself as the great port of the country until 1894; the population grew; means of transportation were perfected; and in the pleasure of spending, in the emulation of luxury and in neglect of economy, there was developed an intense social life, and with the concentration of population there was inaugurated one of the periods of greatest intellectual effervescence and of the most brilliant culture in our civilization. But the decline of production of the lands touched by the Paraíba River and its tributaries, the political and social crisis which resulted from the abolition of slavery in 1888, and the new vigor shown in European immigration finally transferred the center of this economic activity to the plateau of São Paulo, which became the major producer of coffee. The slaveholding plantation system based upon the social institution of slavery and practiced according to empirical methods gave way to a capitalistic system of agricultural exploitation, based on free work and doubly developed by the application of new techniques to coffee cultivation and by the improvement of communications and transport. The discovery in São Paulo and in Paraná of purple earth—a splendid earth that results from the breaking down of igneous rock (diabase and porphyrite) and as good for the production of coffee as the *massapê* in the north was for that of sugar; the development of our major lines of penetration by land, the railroads of Mogiana and Sorocabana and the Paulista Railway, and finally the vigorous impulse which was given to immigration, attracted by the temperate climate of the plateau and the high return of labor, so that cultivation multiplied—all this caused the green ocean of the coffee plantation to move toward the interior, especially toward the west of São Paulo. The expansion of coffee production, writes Simonsen, which took place in the valley of the Paraíba and on a smaller scale on the plateau of São Paulo (which made Santos the world's greatest exporting port), "constitutes one of the greatest events in agriculture of all times, and is an honor to a people and to a nation."

[11] The exportation of coffee, which in 1820 barely reached 100,000 bags per year, in 1840 already exceeded 1,000,000 bags annually; and it rose to more than 2,000,000 bags in 1860-1870 and to 4,500,000 in 1880, the movement taking place through the Bay of Guanabara, which remained in first place in Brazilian commerce. In little more than half a century the production became 45 times as great as in 1820, almost multiplying tenfold in each decade. But after 1890, with the new phase of coffee cultivation on the plateau of São Paulo, the figures showed an incomparably greater development of production: from the 5,500,000 bags which flowed through the port of Santos in 1900, exportation rose in 1909, or only ten years, to 14,000,000 bags through the same port, besides the 3,000,000 which were exported from Rio de Janeiro. From 1933 to 1938, the highest production was attained in Brazil, with 29,000,000 bags out of a world production which oscillated between 25,000,000 and 38,000,000: in other words, there was an almost absolute domination by the Brazilian product in international markets. It is estimated that there are 3,017,000,000 coffee trees in Brazil, covering an area of four million hectares under cultivation, and of these almost half, or about 1,500,000,000 plants, are to be found in the State of São Paulo.

In this long period which extends for more than three and a half centuries from the Colony to the end of the Empire, all economic activity with the exception of cattle breeding was developed under an essentially patriarchal regime, in two great types of cultivation (sugar and coffee), between which were the extractive industries of gold and of diamonds, resting like the others on slave labor. The classes which this society superimposed in its stratification tended clearly to differentiate themselves by their occupation and level and style of life, running the gamut from the real aristocracy of the great houses and the plantations through the bourgeoisie of the cities made up of merchants, bankers, and exporters, and from two societies, rural and urban, to the complex and tumultuous mass of free workers, cowboys, and herdsmen in the sertão, gold washers of Minas and Mato Grosso, fishermen and rubber gatherers of the Amazon, peons and carters of the pampas. The exploitation of sugar cane, which as early as the middle of the seventeenth century brought in the north the beginnings of a first aristocracy—that of the lords of the sugar mill—and the plantations of the coffee region, in the shade of which there arose in the south, in the nineteenth century, a new slave-holding aristocracy, nourished on the seacoast a civilization in which the cities tributary to coffee production participated, while there still lived in their far distant villages, in their plantations and solitary properties, the population of the back lands, the free workers, mestizos, bodyguards, half-breeds and backwoodsmen, who had no advantage over the mass of the slaves except that of nature in the raw and of an atmosphere of freedom. The white man of the coast, closing the cycle of the bandeiras and the mines, grew ever more isolated from the life of the interior. Agricultural activities as well as those of mining and of cattle breeding, however, absorbed all the capital and all the labor that were available, not permitting in the colonial period anything but domestic industry, which resulted from the lack of relations with the rest of the world on account of physical isolation, an industry complementing agriculture, like that of the sugar mills, and the small industries, self-sufficient and widely scattered, in cities along the coast, in addition to shipyards in which were constructed numerous wooden boats, and which under the Empire were to make great progress. The extremely scattered population in the Colony even along the seacoast; the lack of dense nuclei of population; the difficulties of transportation, which was reduced to a matter of herds and oxcarts; the enormous distances; the regime of slavery and of plantations as a means of exploiting the land, and the really narrow policy followed by the mother country which in 1766 prohibited the trade of goldsmith, and by a royal letter of 1785 prohibited all manufacture of thread, cloth, and embroidered goods in Brazil—these constituted, as Simonsen observes, just so many obstacles to the rise of any kind of manufacture of value in the colonial period.

This situation was prolonged without any considerable alteration through the first and second Empires, in which all the elements were lacking for an autonomous industry that might be concentrated and mechanized, and that always seeks proximity of sources of energy, raw materials and a market, transportation, and above all labor—the principal factor, according to Blanchard [12]—still through all this period absorbed in the cultivation of coffee in the States of Rio, Minas, and São Paulo. The cultivation of coffee itself, to which immigration from Europe was directed in the last quarter of the nineteenth century, did not by its very nature facilitate mechanical work. "The productive life of the

[12] Raoul Blanchard, *La Géographie de l'industrie* (Montreal: Beauchemin, 1934), p. 174.

coffee tree, a plant of perennial character, extends," as Simonsen reminds us, "even in intermediate regions, for more than forty years, and its planting is done by preference on the slopes of hills." The growing of coffee, like that of sugar with its sugar mills, did not therefore produce in São Paulo anything but an industry of complementary nature, that of machines for its improvement and treatment; and in the making of these, more of wood than of iron, "the consumption of metal was not of a kind to justify the development of a metallurgical industry." Although industry in the Colony and the Empire was still incipient and elementary, we can nevertheless ask whether the slave absorbed all the industrial skills, or whether he left a place, and if so what place, to the free worker in city and country. Certainly, as happened in other countries and other civilizations,[13] servile labor employed in tasks of the most diverse character, prodigally employed and wasted, dominated in the domestic labor situation, in mining, as well as in the primitive transportation industry. All domestic work was done by slaves, and inside the great agricultural properties slave labor made "a majority of the articles of consumption, by manual processes or with rudimentary instruments." But to the slave labor which had so large a place in domestic economy there was opposed always free labor which had a great place in industry, not only in the direction but in the execution of tasks, and never ceased to develop, to extend, and slowly to improve its condition, and there were multiplied, recruited especially from among freed men, rural workmen, artisans in the cities, small artificers, independent stable workmen, or dependent salaried ones, carrying on small shops or industrial activities.[14] Although in the case of slave labor the expenses of purchase and of transportation as well as of maintenance correspond to the salaries paid to free labor, and although slavery contributed, at least in slaveholding centers, to influence the level of wages, there was nevertheless, a preference for slave labor, which for this reason offered a free labor a terrible competition, rendering useless and extremely rare a strike caused by a claim for a rise in wages.

But agriculture, which was preponderant from the Colony to the Empire, in the last days of which, in 1880, there occurred the first high production in industry, not only expanded under the republican regime, with the coffee cultivation reaching proportions never earlier attained, but also was modified by the gradual replacement of the single-crop system, by the cultivation of many crops in Pernambuco, Minas, Rio Grande do Sul, and especially in São Paulo, in which there were mixed in various proportions the different forms of human labor. At the beginning, so uniformly marked both in Pernambuco and in the State of Rio by sugar-cane plantations with the big

[13] Paul Guiraud, *La Main d'œuvre industrielle dans la Grèce antique* (Paris, 1900).

[14] Neither in the Colony nor in the Empire, as we see, did industry to satisfy domestic needs or industry complementary to agriculture, distinguished by Blanchard, who stresses their importance, play a very large role. We know that both in the former and in the complementary type (sugar-refining, for example), slave labor was employed, and that during this period slave and free labor existed side by side in independent industries. But in what proportions slaves and salaried workers engaged in these small industries; what was the nature of the industries in which slaves worked and those in which free labor was preferred; wage rates and their high points and variations and the influence of slavery upon such rates; the relations between employer and employee; the competition between the two economic classes, of slaves and free workers; the conditions of life which cannot have been very different as between slave and wage-earner; the crafts and trades which offered easiest access to freed slaves, these are all questions on which it is hard to find an answer, in part because of the scarcity of sources and statistics, in part for lack of monographs in which these questions have been studied thoroughly and exactly.

house, the slave quarters, and the sugar mill, and in the south in the States of Rio and Minas and especially in São Paulo by thousands of coffee trees which extended beyond the power of the eye to see, at times in a single, solid block, in closed file, the cultural landscape already presents us with a division of cultivable land and a multiplication of types of cultivation, with a great diversity of aspect corresponding to the multiple aspects of agricultural activities. The successive crises of coffee, the production of which threatened to surpass, and later actually did surpass the necessities of world consumption, the limitations imposed on the planting of coffee trees, the breaking up of great properties, contributed to spread the small-farm system, breaking the solid uniformity of the old rural landscape. "What was in fact, in its ensemble," asked Monbeig, "the Paulista landscape at the beginning of the century? That ocean of coffee trees planted uniformly and houses of workers in a row—a whole landscape which reflected the economic and social structure, the single-crop system and the plantation. And what does a photograph taken from a plane show us, along the railroad entering the forest near the town of Presidente Venceslau? Little properties and various types of crops. Behind the pioneer zone in which there are immense plantations of cotton, one sees the many orange groves of Sorocaba, the orchards of St. Roque, the grazing lands and coffee-shelling plants of Paraíba. Property tends to divide up, and a new form of habitat is being organized with the share-croppers in the cotton fields. In these landscapes which are sketched before our eyes there is reflected along with the many-sided types of cultivation, the more complex social and economic structure of the São Paulo of 1939." In the meantime, in these two phases of agricultural civilization, at the basis of whose organization resided the single-crop system, slavery and the big plantation, as in the capitalist regime of coffee raising, based on free labor, or in the nascent, many-sided type of cultivation which is now openly being developed, what impresses is less the effort made by man to dominate nature than his incessant struggles to maintain the conquest he has already made. In a country of torrential rain and burning sun, of parasitic vegetation and abundant fauna, the soil which is allowed to remain uncultivated grows worse, and the lands under cultivation would lose value and civilization would retreat at an instant's neglect of the multiple activities of cultivation.

But all this agricultural production of sugar and of cocoa in the north, of coffee and other products in the south, as well as the enormous production of the extractive industries, of gold and diamonds in the Colony, and of rubber in the Republic, necessarily had to lead to a system of communication and transportation, seeking the coast line, and in accordance with the technical possibilities of the time and the specific conditions of the environment. It is a study still to be made among us and one of the most interesting possible, that of the economic, political, and social history of the relations between the great types of cultivation and the development of the ports, between the network of communication of the country and the national evolution.[15] The

[15] Cf. Franco Borlandi, "Il Problema delle communicazioni nel secolo XVIII nei suoi rapporti col Risorgimento italiano," *Collana di Scienze politiche diritta dal Prof. Pietro Vacarri*, Series B, Vol. III) (Pavia, Torino, Treccani, Tuminelli, 1932); J. W. Gregory, *Story of the Road* (London: MacLehose, 1931), a brief and meaty study of roads through history; Yves Le Trocquer, *Les Routes et leurs techniques* (Paris: Alcan, 1931); Pierre Vilar, "Le Rail et la route, leur rôle dans le problème général des transports en Espagne," in *Annales d'histoire économique et sociale*, Vol. 6, No. 30, Nov., 1934 (Paris: Armand Collin).

formation of Brazilian unity, founded on the community of origins, of language, of customs, and of religion, is not only bound up with the affirmation of a rural aristocracy based upon the plantation and upon the same instrument of work—the slave in the Colony and the Empire: all that economically productive society needed, for the development of the production which it directed, an important network of transportation, and a whole system of well equipped ports. Thus it is that the organization of this economic equipment, although primitive in the Colony and so limited even under the Empire, constitutes one of the most curious technical aspects of the growth of the nation, because of its double origin linked, in the direction of the coast line, to the exploitation of the Colony by the mother country and, in the direction of the hinterland, to pastoral nomadism and the expansion of the bandeiras. Doubtless, in a country which has 7,000 kilometers of coast and about 44,000 kilometers of navigable rivers, the sea and the arterial rivers constitute a principal network of transportation; and it is not surprising that, as Roy Nash observes, "fourteen of the twenty-one capitals of Brazilian States are located on the edge of the liquid highway," and that of its seven greatest cities, five (Pôrto Alegre, Rio de Janeiro, Salvador, Recife, and Belém) are located at the edge of the principal artery of traffic and transportation, and only two (Belo Horizonte and São Paulo—the latter the second of the country but with its seaport in Santos) rise on the plateau. If we consider the movement that during half a century the exploitation of gold mines acquired, and for almost a hundred years that of coffee in the center south, we shall understand why Rio de Janeiro and Santos became the ports of the greatest movement in Brazil,[16] and why the density of the roads and the value of the ports have been very much less in the north than in the south, although the only road which links the south to the north from Vitória to Manaus, and from the capital of Amazonas to the frontier of Peru "continues to be today as in the times of Vasco da Gama, the vast ocean and the gigantic, watery spider web of the hinterland."

In spite of the fact that the country possesses one of the most extensive water networks in the world, and that interior navigation is the only means of binding together nearly two-thirds of Brazilian territory, river navigation, barred by rapids and waterfalls, even today is not regularly carried on except up to the edge of unexplored and deserted land and by boats of old type and little draft. Primitive pirogues—canoes dug out as a single piece from a tree trunk, of great weight and flat bottom in order to sweep over the rapids, continue to go, loaded, up and down the numerous waterways, especially the tributaries of the Amazon as far as the limit of steam navigation; and in the São Francisco and some of its tributaries, like the Paracatú, we meet still the old boats

[16] Thus, along the Atlantic coast, which is the only possible means of communication between the northern and southern shores for transportation on a large scale of passengers and cargo, there ply various navigation lines, for 3,500 miles, from Rio Grande do Sul, 160 miles from Pôrto Alegre, on Lagoa dos Patos, to Belém do Pará, situated about a thousand miles this side of Manaus on the lower Amazon. This distance from Pôrto Alegre to Manaus cannot be covered in less than 25 days by coastwise vessels. Besides Rio de Janeiro, a port unequaled in depth and space for anchorage, and the most beautiful in the world, where vessels of any draft can dock, and Santos, with a depth sufficient for steamers with a draft of 29 feet, we have, in respective importance as shown by gross tonnage, the ports of Recife, São Salvador (the second port, with respect to greatest depth), Belém do Pará, Rio Grande do Sul, and Paranaguá, and finally, in the north, Manaus which may be considered as the terminus on the Amazon for navigation coming from the Atlantic.

of the Douro River of Portugal, which were introduced by colonists at the beginning of the nineteenth century. Steam navigation, on rivers of sufficient volume and depth, was developed in the meantime but slowly, and has acquired considerable importance on the network of river transportation, made up especially of navigation in Amazonas, for the Amazon can be navigated by transatlantic steamers as far as Iquitos on the frontier of Peru; on the Paraguay River from Asunción to Cuiabá and São Luiz de Cáceres; on the São Francisco River as far as the port of Piranhas and above the falls of Paulo Afonso to Pirapora in Minas Gerais; on the Paraná [17] as far as the Seven Falls, and above them to Jupiá; and on other smaller rivers where in 1921 there were running almost 356 boats large and small, depending upon the draft of the river, and with a total tonnage of only 73,387 tons. But, besides the river communications, observes Roy Nash, "the network of paths constituted the vein system through which flowed the economic blood of the country, maintaining the unity of the Empire." The trails of the herdsmen which spread out from all the urban nuclei great and small—towns, villas, and cities—connecting the Brazilian population, in fact, exercised in the colonial system of communication a role as important perhaps as that of the rivers of penetration. Old roads—tapir trails, narrow paths cut by the Indians, trodden by the missionary in the catechism of the Indians—or more recent roads opened by the bandeirante, "that violator of the sertão and planter of cities," were progressively widened by the Portuguese with his load, by the cowboy with his herd, by the colonists with their oxcarts, and later by the businessman, the traveling salesman, the collector and the peddler, the advance guard of civilization. Our greatest lines of penetration, observes Euclides da Cunha, "from the Mogiana making for Goiaz over the old trails of Anhanguera to the Sorocabana,[18] adjusting themselves to the first thrust of the long journey of Antônio Raposo and the conquistadores of Guaíra," have been recognized for centuries and recall the exceptional figure of the man, the bandeirante, "who made himself a barbarian to make roads through the desert, opening the first paths of progress."

[17] The distance that can be navigated on the rivers of Brazil that are known and explored, is estimated at too high a figure by Roy Nash (70,000 kilometers); it does not appear to exceed 44,000 kilometers or, more exactly according to official data, 43,955 kilometers. The Amazon, by itself, with a depth accommodating vessels of 20-foot draft, offers 25,446 kilometers of navigable waters, or 57.89 per cent of the total for the country. The navigation of this great northern river was opened in July, 1867, to foreign countries, and in August of that year the first vessel to navigate the course of the São Francisco left Penedo for the port of Piranhas. See *Brazil, 1938: A New Survey of Brazilian Life* (Serviço Gráfico do Instituto Brasileiro de Geografia e Estatística, 1939).

[18] Of the four main railway lines which leave Rio de Janeiro, at least two—that which goes to Minas, through Juiz de Fora, Barbacena, Sabará, and along the valley of the Rio das Velhas, to Pirapora, and that which strikes toward São Paulo through the valley of the Paraíbo—follow the old roads of Minas and São Paulo. It is also by the old road, through the valley of the Paraguassu, that the engineer laid out the tracks of the railroad that starts from São Feliz, in Bahia; and it is by a traditional road that the trains which run from Salvador to Juazeiro on the banks of the São Francisco make their way. The first highway which scaled the plateau from Santos to São Paulo had no other line than that of the old road of the Serra do Mar. Those who live today in the great cities, know the picturesque history, and those who toil in the interior still have the rude experience of the hard journeys which lasted for months on end—the longest five months—by canoe with paddles or long oars or on donkey back along these hard or muddy roads, on which, with the exception of an occasional carriage going a short distance, one met no vehicle but the oxcart, breaking the solitude of the plains with its squeaks.

The great migration to the temperate regions of the south in the last quarter of the nineteenth century and the extraordinary development of coffee growing which absorbed the available capital and labor, were not slow in leading to the replacement in the coffee-growing region of the plateau (Minas and São Paulo) of the early means of communication by railways, the construction of which was timidly begun in 1854 with the first fourteen kilometers, and which in 1890 had already attained 9,973 kilometers, almost tripling in a decade (1880-1890) the extension of the steel rails.[19] The Central Railroad of Brazil, which as early as 1877 had reached São Paulo and was advancing through Minas toward the bank of the Rio das Velhas, the Leopoldina Railroad in the northeasterly direction toward Vitória and Rio Doce in Espírito Santo, the Inglêsa, which was begun in 1867 linking Jundiaí to the port of Santos, the Mogiana in the direction of Goiaz, and the Sorocabana, which ran along the banks of the Paraná to join later on with the Northwest, and the Paulista—one of the best railways in Brazil—came to constitute the railway system serving three states: Rio de Janeiro, Minas, and São Paulo. The coffee-growing zone of São Paulo was already beginning at the turn of the twentieth century to be crossed by excellent railroads which spread and irradiated, making a vast network of branches and so enriching the railroad system that in 1937 the State of São Paulo already had some 8,635 kilometers of railroads, or almost a quarter of the total in all Brazil (33,521), besides 15,000 kilometers of highways going out in all directions. But the remarkable development at the beginning of this century of means of transportation by the construction of railways and highways in the southern region of the plateau, the overproduction of coffee and the consequent return of farmers to the city, the phenomena of condensation of immigrants and urban concentration, and the formation of an internal market of some importance for industrial products constituted together with the construction of great electric energy plants, as Simonsen observes, the factors essential to the industrial evolution which went on faster after 1905, to acquire later and in consequence of the European war, new life and new directions. Brazil, in which coffee cultivation continued to be the basis of

[19] A simple inspection of a map of Brazil on which are marked the railroads existing in 1937 (cf. the map of the chief Brazilian railroads in 1922, in Roy Nash, *The Conquest of Brazil*) will show that the zone best served by railroads is that of the plateau included in São Paulo, Minas, and Rio de Janeiro, with its two projections to the north, as far as Vitória in Espírito Santo, and to the south, as far as Curitiba, linked to Paranaguá in the State of Paraná. In addition to a strip cut by railways in the southern part of Rio Grande do Sul, which already possesses about 3,212 kilometers of railroads, and another that stretches in the north from Fortaleza to Maceió, passing through Recife, and in which there is a network of 1,368 kilometers (Ceará Railways), only a few marks indicate rare railways, constituting fragments or parts of a possible comprehensive system of communication. From São Salvador in Bahia railways go out in four directions, of which the two most important are those that push as far as the banks of the São Francisco, one along the coast, and the other to Juazeiro in the interior (the Great Western, with 1,741 kilometers). If in the north we find other railroads like those from Petrolina to Teresina in Piauí, and from São Luiz in Maranhão to Teresina we find in the western region only the road Madeira-Mamore, with 366 kilometers, from Santo Antônio to Guajará-Mirim, and in the southwest zone, the one from Campo Grande to Corumbá in Mato Grosso. The total railroad mileage probably does not serve a seventh part of the territory of Brazil; the railroads (for, as Euclides da Cunha wrote, "they result, above all, from our progress") were most developed in the regions of sugar and cocoa in the north (Pernambuco and Bahia), of coffee in the south (Rio, São Paulo, and Minas) and in those regions of the hide and meat trade (Rio Grande do Sul) which are at the same time the chief economic centers of the country and its leading cultural centers.

the economic structure, was already on the road toward a new regime which was to find the more mobile forms the central axis of its economic activity, directing its efforts with the expansion of wealth, toward industrial production. The very evolution of industry in São Paulo, whose production now amounts to more than 43 per cent of the production of the nation and did not exceed 16 per cent in 1907, 20 per cent in 1914, and 33 per cent in 1920, shows, however, that the industrial phenomenon growing in this State after the war of 1914, had appeared in other regions of the country like the Federal District, Minas, Rio Grande do Sul, and, in the north, Bahia and Pernambuco.

Thus, the industry of the nation which under the Empire only began to become significant after 1885, in spite of various earlier efforts to implant industries in Brazil, had no great growth until the twentieth century, when it was favored by a combination of factors, some of them related to the rise of coffee on the plateau, and others resulting from the repercussions of the war of 1914 in the Brazilian market. Certainly the nineteenth century, in which, according to Vicente Licínio, there took place a most violent economic change with the replacement of the "gold and slave" team by the more energetic team of "machine and coal," was the century of the steam engine, of coal and of steel, and so of the industrial revolution. From the beginning of the nineteenth century, between 1808 and 1821, when Dom João VI made an effort to develop the metal industry and brought foreign technicians to study the possibility of organizing the industry in Brazil, down to the Viscount of Mauá, who between 1850 and 1870 tried in every way to stimulate an industrial spirit in the Brazilian environment, "smelting, forging, arming, constructing," promoting the construction of railways, of ports, of factories, of shipyards, all the efforts that were made to develop the industrial production of the Empire turned out badly. But the obstacles by which the foresight of Dom João VI was nullified and the iron energy of that singular figure the Viscount of Mauá was broken were less in the agricultural mentality of the time, in the absence of an imperial policy of protection for industry, in the tariff regime which was strictly fiscal in character, than in the lack of fuel, in the difficulty of access to iron mines, in the scarcity of labor, in the great distances and the extreme insufficiency of means of transportation. Industries do not develop except near the centers of production of fuel and in the vicinity of raw materials and in regions in which labor, transportation, and a consuming market favor their growth. It was the joint action of these factors which led to the rise of industry in certain regions of Brazil in the twentieth century: the construction of plants generating electric energy, which in our industrial centers had a role similar to that of the coal centers in England and the United States; raw materials above all for the textile industries and for the product of the food industries, which in 1920 already made up 67.8 per cent of the production of the nation; labor, which overproduction in coffee put at the service of industry; railways, the extension of which from 17,242 kilometers in 1906 attained almost double that (33,521) in 1936; and finally the market, which was expanded under the influence of the immigration from Europe, of new necessities, and of the growing insistence of the internal demand, and of the phenomena of concentration of population. The number of industrial establishments in the country was estimated at more than 60,000. They were distributed through São Paulo, which since 1910 has occupied first place, with 10,000 factories, and the Federal District, with about 20 per cent of the total production, and Rio Grande do Sul, Minas Gerais, the State of Rio de Janeiro, and Pernambuco.[20]

The growing of coffee, which extended over the vast plain of Tertiary deposits west of the Serra do Mar and through the whole interior until they received the spray and deposit of the tide of European colonists which spread out over the plateau, furnished the first substantial capital and, with the overproduction of coffee, the labor available for the progress of the industrial change which took place in the country. The old province of São Paulo which, worn out by the constant and periodical struggles of the bandeiras, had groped along for a hundred years in poverty and was gravitating in the orbit of mining, was then transformed into a prosperous State which, after 1886, came to be the major producer of coffee in Brazil and, after 1910, the major industrial center of Brazilian territory and today of the South American continent. The axis of economic activity, already in the eighteenth century turned away from the north to Minas Gerais with the discovery and exploitation of the veins of gold, moved this time to São Paulo, whose capital, in an excellent geographic situation, served by a first-class seaport for the flow of its production, became the principal railway center of the country and one of the great urban centers of the world. What the industry of São Paulo could not obtain from coal-bearing deposits such as those beside which arose the more compact industrial organizations of England, Germany, and the United States, was put at its disposal by plants generating electrical energy; this, for the industry of Brazil, took the place of the metallurgical coke of the other countries. "The formation of great lakes in the Serra do Mar by the damming up of rivers which flowed into the interior and the spilling of this volume of water over the slopes of Cubatão—an enormous work which is an honor to the foreign technicians who conceived it and carried it out—furnishes to São Paulo," observes Simonsen, "the possibility of obtaining sufficient energy to triple its actual industrial establishment and opens a wide horizon to many other undertakings." But with the extraordinary industrial revolution of São Paulo there rose another fact of the highest importance for the organization of the nation: the industrial division of labor, with a multiple diversification, brought on by the war of 1914, in the making of new products and with the specialization of industries in accordance with the peculiar advantages of the different States of the Federation. "Notwithstanding the regional character of the majority of our industries"—the words are Simonsen's—"there is a healthy interweaving of the various economic regions of the country." The numerous industrial products of São Paulo find a market all over the country, the industries of São Paulo import, in their turn, rubber, fibers, and cocoa from the north, "tobacco from Rio Grande do Sul, wood from Paraná, and pig iron

[20] It was after 1920 that the greatest industrial evolution took place in Brazil, especially in São Paulo. One can get an idea of the growth of manufacturing between 1919 and 1938 from the following statistics. Industrial production in paper money almost quadrupled in Brazil; quintupled in São Paulo. The number of workers, which had attained 275,512 according to the census of 1920, rose in 1938 to more than 950,000. Factories using electric power, estimated at 350, rose to 1,200 in 1938, with a production almost four times as great as in the base year. Not less significant is the shipping in the ports of Brazil, in which the number of ships entering and leaving, with a cargo of more than 17,500,000 tons, rose from 23,126 and 23,170 in 1919, to 34,088 and 34,063 in 1937, with about 50,000,000 tons, for transatlantic and coastwise commerce. (*Brazil, 1938: A New Survey of Brazilian Life.* Serviço Gráfico do Instituto Brasileiro de Geografia e Estatística, 1939.)

from Minas Gerais," so that products of industry in which they have specialized are exchanged between one State and another, and with the progress of the means of transportation, of lines of shipping, of railways, and of highways, and with growing diversification, there comes into existence an interdependence and an economic circulation of the highest interest for the life and unity of the nation.

Certainly, although the industrial production of the country has developed so much that even in 1936, attaining 8,000,000,000 cruzeiros, it surpassed by a wide margin agricultural production valued at 6,200,000,000 cruzeiros, one cannot see in this notable development any more than the dawn of an industrial civilization. In the picture of the distribution of the materials of the greatest industrial center of Brazil, Simonsen has already noted the predominance of articles for immediate consumption, which constitutes in itself alone in São Paulo almost half (46 per cent) and in Brazil more than half (67.8 per cent) of the total production. The economic situation which Osvaldo de Andrade defined with a picturesque expression, calling Brazil "the country of desserts" because its whole economy was founded on sugar, tobacco, and coffee, in the period that was preponderantly or almost exclusively agricultural, has not changed radically in the industrial phase, in which the majority of the products of its industries are foods and textiles. The absence of heavy and basic industries in the make-up of our economic equipment is doubtless one of our greatest obstacles to industrial evolution, the progress of which must be bound up, as it is everywhere, with the existence of fuel (coal) and rich iron deposits. But in the first place, if there exist in Minas Gerais the world's greatest known deposits of iron, the deposits of coal, an indispensable element for metallurgy, are not easy of access—being mostly in Santa Catarina and Rio Grande do Sul—nor do they present, with their high ratio of ash, the qualities required of coal for heavy industry. The smelting of iron which went on, in the colonial period, in primitive forges and by direct processes brought by the African Negroes, and was attempted by Dom João VI, who tried to install in the country between 1808 and 1821 the first blast furnaces, and was carried on industrially after 1818 at Ipanema in the State of São Paulo, was developed, however, in the twentieth century with the aid of vegetable coal, in high blast furnaces and others, the total production of which in 1936 attained 78,000 tons of pig iron and more than 77,000 tons of steel. The great distances, the lack of an internal market that might be called important and concentrated, and above all the absence of metallurgical coke have retarded until today the development of heavy industry, which requires enormous capital, and whose progress, depending upon fuel or electric energy, may come, as Simonsen says, simultaneously or successively from the application of the hydraulic energy available on the central south plateau, from a better industrial utilization of the poor coal of the Carboniferous basins of the Rio Grande, and from the exploitation of petroleum. Only then, with the production of iron on a large scale and the exploitation of the deposits of ore, whose existence appears to have been verified, in the *recôncavo* district of Bahia, will industrial evolution enter upon its most fruitful phase, and human labor, which except for the extraction of gold in the mines of Morro Velho has scarcely scratched the surface, come to explore the subsoil, extracting from it all the petroleum, which will furnish it, together with the hydroelectric power which is so easily transportable, the solid bases for the great economic and industrial revolution of Brazil.

Latin America in the nineteenth century was, writes André Siegfried, the greatest exporting center of unfinished and raw materials to Europe. The old continent was the factory, we, the country; it, the chimney; we, agriculture. However, among the South American countries with a strongly developing will to industrialize, Brazil, which down to the end of the past century, and as far as heavy industry is concerned down to this day, had remained tributary to the United States and the European countries, is tending ever more to shake off the old colonial shell and renew its economic equipment from the bottom up and begin a new cycle of exploitation. Industry, which in Europe and the United States even during the seventeenth and eighteenth centuries was frequently located in forest zones and later, in the century of coal, moved from the surface forests to the hidden forests of the mines and, in the age of petroleum, to the unstable fields of petroleum and mineral oil, was still feeding its furnaces and its means of transportation in Brazil with imported mineral coal, or with the fuel which its forests furnished. Coal, however, in Rio Grande do Sul, which has the best mines, although even their product is of poor quality, is beginning to take the place of wood under our boilers; and in the Federal District and in São Paulo the shift to electric power from the waterfalls multiplies the power of industry, bringing it closer to the sources of mechanical energy with which Brazil has been equipped by the incalculable wealth of the hydrographic basins of its cataracts. And when the sea gives us new forces whether through the utilization of the tides, through tidal basins, or through the utilization of temperature of the water according to the process of Georges Claude, one can imagine the sum of energies which will be added by the utilization of the ocean's calories to the hydraulic force which results from waterfalls. But it is not a question only of the struggle to transform material by industry in factory and plant, but of a struggle against distance and with space against time to bring about the progressive increase of the velocity of transportation—a struggle which in a country of such great geographic extension is a vital question, bound up in its very nature with the progress of the exploitation of centers producing fuel, coal, oil, and electric energy in which waterfalls and perhaps the tides of the ocean would be transformed. Railways which are electrified on the plateau or extend, penetrating the interior slowly; highways which spread out from the principal centers of population, providing for automobile traffic; and the progress of the merchant marine as well as of air transportation, whose civil and military lines in operation multiplied tenfold in less than ten years (1928-1937) are tending to reduce distance and to bring together the economic centers of the country, facilitating along with the circulation of people and of merchandise, the circulation of a national consciousness, of human culture and thought.

BIBLIOGRAPHY

Brito Lemos, João de, *Pontos de partida para a história econômica do Brasil* (Rio de Janeiro, 1923).

Capistrano de Abreu, J., *Caminhos antigos e povoamento do Brasil* (Rio: *Briguiet,* 1930— Edição da Sociedade Capistrano de Abreu).

Cunha, Euclides da, *Os Sertões (Campanha de Canudos)* (Rio: 3rd ed., 1905). Transl. by Samuel Putnam as *Rebellion in the Backlands* (Chicago, 1944).

————, *A Margem da história* (Pôrto: Chardron, 2nd ed., 1922), especially "Transacreana," "Viação sul–americana," pp. 115–135, 138–163.

61. São João d'El Rei, in Minas Gerais. Old bridge and a mansion of the Empire period.
Photo by Stille, in collection of the College of Philosophy of São Paulo.

62. São João d'El Rei, in Minas Gerais. Mansion of the Empire period.
Photo by Stille, in collection of the College of Philosophy of São Paulo.

63. Mansion of the Empire period, in Mariana, Minas Gerais.
Photo by Stille, in collection of the College of Philosophy of São Paulo.

64. Rio de Janeiro. View of the colonial city, including the door of the Church of Carmel.
Photo by Stille, in collection of the College of Philosophy of São Paulo.

65. Rio Bonito, state of Rio. The church dominating urban life.
Photo by Stille, in collection of the College of Philosophy of São Paulo.

66. Rio de Janeiro. Rua Direita (Straight Street).
Rugendas, *Voyage pittoresque au Brésil* (1835), Plate 3/13.

67. "Carioca Square, Rio de Janeiro," painting by Nicolau Taunay. Photo by Carlos.

68. "Hill of St. Anthony, Rio de Janeiro," oil painting by Nicolau Taunay. Photo by Carlos.

69. Ubatuba, general view. Photo by ENFA.

70. Manaus. An aspect of the city.
Central collection of the National Council of Geography.

71. Salvador, Bahia. Castro Alves Square. Photo by Voltaire Fraga,
in Brazilian Institute of Geography and Statistics.

72. Salvador, Bahia. Pedro II Square. Photo by Voltaire Fraga,
in Brazilian Institute of Geography and Statistics.

73. Rio de Janeiro. A view of the urban center. Photo by Rembrandt.

74. Rio de Janeiro. Paris Square. Photo by Rembrandt.

75. Rio de Janeiro. View of the Sugarloaf. Photo by Rembrandt.

76. Juiz de Fora, Minas Gerais. An aspect of the city.
Photo by Postal, in central collection of the National Council of Geography.

77. São Paulo. A view of the city, with the Anhangabaú Park, the new Chá Viaduct, and in the background, the Municipal Theater.

78. São Paulo. View of the center of the city, with its principal group of new modern buildings and, in the background, the industrial district of Braz.

79. Port of Corumbá, Mato Grosso. Partial view.
Photo by S.G.E.F., in central collection of the National Council of Geography.

De Carli, Gileno, *Geografia econômica e social da cana de açúcar no Brasil* (Ed. de Brasil Açucareiro, 1938).

Faria, Alberto, *Mauá* (Rio, 1926).

Felício dos Santos, J., *Memórias do distrito diamantino da comarca do Sêrro Fria (Província de Minas Gerais)* (Rio: Castilho, new ed., 1924).

Freyre, Gilberto, *Casa grande e senzala: Formação da família brasileira sob o regime da economia patriarcal* (Rio: Maia & Schmidt, 1933). Transl. by Samuel Putnam as *The Masters and the Slaves: A Study in the Development of Brazilian Civilization* (New York, 1946).

Licínio Cardoso, V., *A Margem da história do Brasil* (São Paulo: Comp. Editora Nacional, 1933—Brasiliana, Vol. 13).

Machado, Alcântara, *Vida e morte do bandeirante* (São Paulo, 1929).

Melo Franco, A. Arinos, *Síntese da história econômica do Brasil* (Rio, Serviço gráfico do Ministerio da Educação e Saúde, 1938).

Milliet, Sérgio, *Roteiro do café: Estudo histórico–demográfico* (São Paulo: Ed. da Escola livre de sociologia, 1938).

Nash, Roy, *The Conquest of Brazil* (New York, 1926). Transl. as *A Conquista do Brasil* (São Paulo: Comp. Editora Nacional, 1939—Brasiliana, Vol. 150).

Normano, J. F., *Brazil: A Study of Economic Types* (Chapel Hill: University of North Carolina Press, 1935). Transl. as *Evolução econômica do Brasil* (São Paulo: Comp. Editora Nacional, 1939—Brasiliana, Vol. 152).

Noronha, Santos, *Os Transportes antigos; meios de transportes no Rio de Janeiro.*

Oliveira Lima, Manuel de, *D. João VI no Brasil* (Rio, 2 vols., 1908).

———, *O Império brasileiro (1822–1889)* (São Paulo, 1927).

Oliveiro, Eusébio de, "Geologia estratigráfica e econômica," in *Recenseamento do Brasil* (Sept. 1, 1920), Vol. 1, *Introdução* (Rio: Tip. da Estatística, 1922), pp. 35–94.

Pandiá Calógeras, J., *As Minas do Brasil e sua legislação (Geologia econômica do Brasil)*, Vol. 3 (São Paulo: Comp. Editora Nacional, 2nd ed., 1938—Brasiliana, Vol. 134).

Rangel, A., *Rumos e perspectivas* (São Paulo: Comp. Editora Nacional, 2nd ed., 1934—Brasiliana, Vol. 26), especially "Os Sertões brasileiros," p. 39.

Simonsen, Roberto, *A História econômica do Brasil*, Vols. 1–2 (São Paulo: Comp. Editora Nacional, 1937—Brasiliana, Vol. 100).

———, *A Evolução industrial do Brasil* (São Paulo: Federação das industrias do Estado de São Paulo, 1939).

Taunay, A. E. de, *História geral das Bandeiras Paulistas,* Vols. 1–6 (São Paulo, 1924–1930).

CHAPTER THREE

THE DEVELOPMENT OF URBAN LIFE

The system of settlement on the margin—The early settlements, depositories of maritime commerce—The face of urban civilization turned toward the Atlantic—Fortified cities—Foreign invasions—The contrast between rural splendor and urban misery—The profit of the sugar mills—Freedom, the condition of the city inhabitants—The action of urban bourgeoisie on feudal society—Wars and native explosions—The cities on the plateau—The Villa of Piratininga, at the mouth of the sertão—The constant danger of attack by Indians—The bandeiras and the loss of population by the cities—Vila Rica and the route of gold—The centers of cattle trading—The splendor and decadence of the colonial cities—Before attaining the age of maturity . . .—The dispersion and isolation of urban settlements—The coast and the back country—The tranquillity and poverty of the cities of the Empire—Life in the cities—Industry and the growth of urban centers—The cities as political capitals—Foci of progress and of civilization.

A<small>LL OF HISTORY</small>, from the Colony to the Republic, as we have seen, is, in the words of Oliveira Viana, "the history of an agricultural people, of a society of agriculturists and shepherds. It is in the rural districts that our race was formed, it is there that the inner forces of our civilization were built up. The dynamism of our history in the colonial period comes from the country; and it is from the country that we get the bases on which the admirable stability of our society rests in the imperial period." But while "urbanism" may be a very recent condition of our social evolution, the study of the development of urban life presents a double interest, arising from the particular form of the Brazilian cities and from the special character which their genesis and evolution reveal, as well as from the relations that existed between culture and the development of urban centers. In all civilization, cities exercise as centers of concentration a role of major importance in the formation of the culture in its intellectual sense. They are powerful instruments of social selection, not only attracting to themselves, as Hansen thinks, by a selection which one might almost call mechanical, the best elements of the country, but also in addition to selecting them, contributing to make their value, as Weber observes,[1] making real the merits which otherwise would only be virtual and "overexciting forces which, without this stimulus, might remain inactive and dormant." They will be doubtless many times great destroyers of human life, but this consumption of social forces appears to Weber to be necessary in order to permit the cities to play their role, which is that of "intensifying collective energy, raising the latent and scattered capacities of the population to the highest point of possible development. The civilization of which they are foci, cannot, writes Durk-

---

[1] Adna Ferrin Weber, *The Growth of the Cities in the Nineteenth Century: A Study in Statistics* (New York: Macmillan, 1899). Cf. Carl Stephenson, *Borough and Town: A Study of Urban Origins in England* (Cambridge, Mass.: Mediaeval Academy, 1933).

heim, be obtained for any other price, and the cities which lead to this superexcitation of energy by the mere fact of concentration do not therefore consume without producing: "what they cost society is amply compensated by what they contribute." If, however, in addition to the conception of the role of cities in the development of culture, we consider the intense light which is thrown on the cultural phenomena by the analysis of the evolution and decadence of our cities in the Colony and in the Empire, we shall better understand the scope which the study of urban life has for us in Brazil. The position of these cities generally established on the seacoast, and their growth and decadence, with the successive dislocations of the axis of our national economy, contribute in fact to explain not only the significance of our culture, turned toward the Atlantic, but also the origins and fluctuations of cultural centers, obeying the rhythm of progress of urban settlements.

The enormous extension of the coast and the necessity of establishing on it for its defense the first nuclei of settlement, and above all the objective of Portugal, which cared more to exploit than to colonize, imposed on the conquerors of the land a system of marginal settlements and led them to sow the immense seacoast with towns and colonies, in the coves and anchorages which might offer security to their ships, galleons and caravels. The old settlements and factories before the division of Brazil into hereditary captaincies like Olinda and Iguarassú in Pernambuco, Santa Cruz in Bahia, Cabo Frio and Rio de Janeiro (Vila Velha), and the early primitive villas like São Vicente established by Martim Afonso in 1533, and Olinda by Duarte Coelho, in the regime of the hereditary captaincies, have no other origin, and they show clearly enough in the crises which they passed through, and to which some of them succumbed, the extreme difficulties attending their formation. The only colonial nucleus farther away from the sea is the town of Piratininga founded on the plateau by Martim Afonso, in which there lived the famous João Ramalho, with his mamelucos, his sons and his relatives. In the captaincies, which all started at the coast to go toward the west until they collided with the Spanish colonies, what was most important was defense against the attacks of the heathen and of the pirates who were putting pressure upon the incipient colonization, which was already imperiled on the narrow strip of land between the vastness of the ocean and the back country populated by numerous savage tribes. The evolution of feudalism in the direction of the absolutism of the crown, with the failure of the system of gifts of land and the consequent creation of central government, if it brought a great impulse to colonization, could not change in itself and did not change the difficult situation of these urban centers, embryonic and scattered, of a character more or less official, exposed to the envy of foreign ships and the attacks of the Indians.[2] There rose in this period, however, the first cities, Salvador which Tomé

[2] The idea of defense appears to have guided the location of the majority of early settlements, which were established on the coast or sought out places of difficult access, like the settlement of Piratininga, on the plateau. A city, essentially a grouping of wealth, must therefore be protected against the dangers which may arise from the pirate vessels that infested the sea, and from the savage tribes which rose from the heart of the forests to attack the white man. The forts built in strategic places, like São Cristóvão in 1589, near the Sergipe River, and the one ordered built in 1611 near the Ceará, were thus the germs of cities, São Cristóvão in Sergipe and Fortaleza in Ceará; and other colonial nuclei founded on the coast at this period, Natal in Rio Grande do Norte (1599), and Our Lady of Belém in Pará (1615), on the initiative of frontiersmen, were also centers of settlement and defense with which the "line of resistance," reduced in 1600 to a strip of land,

de Sousa made the first capital of Brazil; São Sebastião do Rio de Janeiro which Estácio de Sá founded in 1566 beside the Sugarloaf, and which Mem de Sá moved to the Morro do Castelo in 1567 after his victory over the French. There rose to the category of town the little settlement of Santo André da Borda do Campo and Piratininga which much later, with the bandeiras, was to have a preponderant role in the conquest of the back country, and which consolidated its position on the plateau during the struggle against the confederation of the Tamoya Indians. Depots of maritime commerce before anything else, these towns which had already formed regular populated places along the coast, like São Vicente, Rio de Janeiro, Vitória, Bahia, and Olinda, and from which sailed ships loaded with brazilwood and spices, were still little fortified cities with walls on a hill, like Rio de Janeiro, Vitória, and Bahia, all of them provided for defense against invasion, which became a serious threat with the attacks of the French in the sixteenth century (1555-1594), with the assaults of the English pirates, and with the Dutch war and occupation in the seventeenth century.

We cannot, then, think of these settlements and cities along the coast without paying attention both to their eminently commercial function as seaports and to their military function, which came less from their topographical peculiarities or the natural points of support which they had than from edifices constructed by the hand of man, like the crown of walls with which Mem de Sá surrounded his citadel of São Sebastião beside the old city of Vila Velha, or the fortress of Bertioga in São Vicente, which was constructed according to the orders of the first governor general in the captaincy of Martim Afonso. The colonists, however, obliged to exploit the land, brought to these towns on the coast and on the São Paulo plateau their traditional types of agriculture and others including grain and wine, corn and manioc, employing Negro and Indian slaves—the latter more than the former in the early cultivation, before African slaves in irons began to be deposited in great numbers on the beaches of the continent to do the fatiguing work of grinding sugar cane. Some of these colonies were already beginning to prosper when the cultivation of sugar cane, with its complementary industries—which, practiced on a large scale, came to constitute the basis of agricultural wealth in the colonial period—took away from the growing towns to the country the center of human work, offering on the sugar-cane plantations and in the mills the greatest field of activity and of exploitation. But the cultivation of the cane, whether because of the facilities of transportation to the seaports or because of its industrial nature with an extensive and complicated system of improvements, or indeed in order to maintain itself against the raids of savages, developed only along the coast, on which it contributed therefore to fix the colonization of the country. Maritime commerce and the defense of the coast joined from now on to the very cultivation of the cane which

---

from the bar of Paranaguá in the south to the mouth of the Potengi River in the north, was extended northward past the mouth of the Amazon. But as cities, in their origin and development, are always connected with communication, and try to centralize the exchange which is frequently their raison d'être, all the early settlements, situated on the best bays, took on from the beginning a markedly commercial character. The colony which had no city in the center of its territory, except possibly the settlement of Piratininga and that of Santo André da Borda do Campo on the plateau of São Paulo, was dotted along the immense line of the coast by a series of little centers of barter or of the import trade, or above all of export trade.

developed on the *massapé* lands near the coast in Pernambuco, in Bahia, and in the State of Rio and, far from turning toward the backland, contributed to maintaining the prestige of the coast, increasing behind it and at a little distance from the maritime cities. The old cities, those of the sixteenth century and the beginning of the seventeenth, still in the period of formation—weakened urban organisms, mediocre and at times badly situated, like Olinda which would not be slow in losing the primacy to Recife, and São Vicente which grew weak and yielded in favor of Santos, founded by the colonist Braz Cubas—became in the sugar zone "dependencies of the sugar mill, family towns where the lords came to pass the holidays, meeting for celebrations and banquets." Certainly it is the commercial people of the coast, as Oliveira Viana reminds us, "who then fill the role of bankers. It is they who advance to the smaller landowners the necessary funds to set up a 'factory.'" It is they who give the money to buy instruments, iron, steel, ropes, tar, sails, and other products on credit, says Antonil; and this obliges the landowners to be impeccably punctual with respect to the merchants because "if at the time of the fleet they fail to pay what they owe they will not have the wherewithal to equip themselves for the next harvest."

The greatest cities of the sixteenth century and the beginning of the seventeenth, Bahia, Olinda, Recife, Rio de Janeiro, and São Paulo, were, however, badly constructed, rude towns left to themselves, growing without any preconceived plan and obeying, at least in the primitive period of their history, only the general laws which rule over the development of any community. In these city communities made up of functionaries, merchants, and officers who were mechanics, Portuguese from the home country mingled with those born in Brazil (*mazombos*) and with mestizos, Indians, and Africans, associating together still in the manner of a camp, in a real tumult of races and groups, living parasitically under the shade and influence of the great lords of the sugar mills. What could then be called a "town" was not, in the expression of Gilberto Freyre, any more than an agglomeration of independent mestizos, together with some mechanics and "peddlers" of European origin; and if we calculate on the basis of the total population of Brazil at this time, estimated at 50,000, they could not have made up more than a scanty population in each of these urban nuclei. The poverty of these primitive cities, heterogeneous and therefore very picturesque, restless, and turbulent, was in contrast with the splendor of rural society, the wealth of which overflowed into the city houses of the lords of the sugar mills, in the reckless spending of feasts and banquets and in tourneys and other celebrations. And it is a fact that, with the development of the cultivation of sugar, the major part of the population was concentrated on the plantations, where there were formed little societies, complex, heterogeneous, too, but built on a solid basis. Without any relation to each other, "true, autonomous nuclei," says Oliveira Viana, "each having its own economy, its own life, its own organization," or "real towns" in the expression of Simão de Vasconcelos. The solidity of their social structure, on which were superimposed in a rigid hierarchy the three classes—that of the lords, that of free men living on their income, and that of the slaves who were the rural workers—assured the plantations of an overwhelming predominance over urban societies, both from the social point of view and from the economic. The necessity of condensing in these vast dominions a numerous population, the great distances which separated one from another, and the concentration of all the little industries on the sugar plantations, now numerous, which possessed everything and made everything,[3] not only gave colonial society, as Oliveira Viana correctly observes, "a gangliated and scattered aspect of extreme rarefaction" but strangled at their very beginning the urban populations which came to gravitate in the orbit of the great landed proprietors and to live in dependency on them. The city was a place to which one went to flee from the tedium and fatigue of work in the country, to expand in the tumult of potentates one's instinct for power and for the easy ostentation of opulence and of luxury which the wealth accumulated on their plantations permitted to the nobility of the country, that is, to the sugar lords.

But, remarks Gilberto Freyre, in the captaincy of Pernambuco as later in Minas in consequence of gold exploitation, "there was a foretaste of urban life—at the same time industrial and commercial, which was contrary to the privileges [of the rural aristocracy]. In Pernambuco this foretaste took place as a consequence of the Dutch dominion," in which, thanks to the presence and the activity of Maurice of Nassau, "Recife, a simple town of fishermen, built around a little church with the whole feudal and ecclesiastical shadow of Olinda to overwhelm it, had developed into the best city of the colony, perhaps of the continent." The transformation of the old town of Recife (1637-1644), in which the prince, surrounded by architects and painters, artists and intellectuals, ordered the erection of palaces and temples, bridges and canals, shops and warehouses, workshops and industries, not only accelerated the decadence of Olinda which had begun before the dominion of the Dutch, but brought to the colonists "the taste for cities with their own life, independent of the great landed proprietors." The differentiation, nevertheless, between the large proprietorship—rural economic unit—able to suffice for itself and the cities of the coast which were increasing "from simple points of storage and embarcation of the products of the land to autonomous populations with the lords of the mansions of the town talking big to those of the big houses of the interior," grew ever stronger under the influence of an ensemble of factors, economic, political, and social, which promoted the emancipation of the cities and their increase in strength. The very feudal conditions of agricultural colonization based upon a single crop and upon slavery, the growing debts of the lords of the sugar plantations, now attracted to the orbit and put into a position of dependents of the intermediaries and merchants, and finally, beginning with the eighteenth century, the new policy of the mother country—that is, the alliance of Portuguese imperialism with the merchants and with the common people of the cities against the rural magnates, and the spirit of commercial adventure which gave the Jews a new impulse— all tended to shift toward the colonial cities the center of gravity of the country both

[3] It was not only the size of these domains, latifundia in character, but the growing number of sugar mills and plantations, large and small, with their mills which, by absorbing a large part of the productive population of the country, forced urban life into the background. In the sixteenth century, in which sugar production had already reached 3,000,000 arrobas, the number of mills distributed through the various captaincies was estimated at 150 (São Vicente, Ilhéus, Bahia, and Pernambuco); almost half of these, Jônatas Serrano tells us, were in the captaincy of Pernambuco. And if we consider the proportion of sugar mills to population in each of these captaincies (76 mills to a population of almost 3,000 families in the captaincy of Bahia, and 60 in that of Pernambuco, which had no more than 2,000 inhabitants), we shall understand better the degree of concentration of population in the country, and the way in which the cultivation of sugar cane on these vast properties, insulated and far from one another, stood in the way of the growth of cities.

in a social and political sense; and as a result the cities continued to become richer and to increase in prestige. Freedom, from the beginning, was a condition of the inhabitants of the cities imposed by the very kind of life they led, and this could not fail to develop the heterogeneous society made up of foreigners, Jews, merchants, and peddlers, whites and mestizos, who, being neither lords nor slaves, lived in a constant state of effervescence and stood, as it were, as a wall against all privilege. It was a new mentality, restless and democratic to the point of demagogy, which was brought into opposition to the conservative and arrogant mentality of the rural aristocracy. The conflicts between Olinda, an ecclesiastical city and center of aristocracy, and Recife, a commercial port, which in 1710 had obtained the title of town and in which the Portuguese, nicknamed "peddlers," were dominant, cannot have been merely an explosion of the nativistic reaction (Brazilians against Portuguese), but was principally, writes Gilberto Freyre, "a collision that the political antagonisms, and confusedly those of race still more dramatized between rural and town interests." [4]

In proportion, however, as the conquest of the Atlantic coast was slowly extended, dotting it with settlements and towns dependent on the centers of agricultural production and on the external market, in the sixteenth century and above all in the following centuries, the expeditions which left the coast for the interior, the pastoral nomadism, the religious missions in the extreme north and the south, and the bandeiras with their enormous movement of expansion, crisscrossed the land and peopled the deepest corners of the Brazilian back country. The settlers penetrating the land and the missionaries with their civilizing action in the Amazon region gathered the heathen "of gentle nature and pacific habits" into numerous villages [5] to which, says

[4] In pp. 29-56 of his book *Sobrados e mocambos,* Freyre gives a brilliant analysis of the rise of the colonial cities in the seventeenth century and the consequent antagonism between them and the isolated big houses of cattle ranches and sugar plantations. For him Recife, transformed in the period of the Flemings, "constituted the first sketch of a people and of a bourgeoisie that there was among us, and the movement of 1710, known as the 'war of the peddlers' can be interpreted as a distinctly aristocratic movement, a bit antimonarchical, rural and antiurban—the national interest being ostensibly identified with those of the agrarian nobility." The old practice of spending the holidays in the cities—Olinda, for example—changed in the eighteenth century and the nineteenth, the author of *Sobrados e mocambos* tells us, to passing them "in country homes and plantations, which became in a sense picturesque dependencies of the bourgeois town houses. Country homes and plantations were kept by the owners not as the basis of their economic life, but for pleasure and recreation, and also as a kind of social decoration."

[5] The *aldeamentos,* that is, the gathering of Indians into villages, whether by grouping dispersed tribes in a single place or by the control of an already existing village, constituted both in Paraguay and Amazonas the point of departure or initial nucleus for numerous settlements and towns. These groups of savages, similar to the "missions" founded by the Jesuits in the south, were organized in Amazonas by other religious orders with the object of converting the heathen and facilitating the trade in spices. In São Paulo, where they also arose, at the initiative of the Jesuits, the *aldeamentos* rarely grew to become cities; the cities for the most part came from the settlements of the first whites, shipwrecked sailors, adventurers, and colonists (São Vicente, Cananéia, Santo André), from resting places of bandeiras or herds of cattle, and from military colonies (Lajes, Castro, Sacramento, Iguatemí). The chapel which presupposes a nucleus of settlement served on the plateau, as for that matter throughout Brazilian territory, "as a point of fixation for a population more or less scattered. It was around the chapel," writes Rubens Borba de Morais, "that the town was created. The life of the region centered on it. Around it were established commerce, the center of consumption—the city." The grant of land from which the plantation came, and with it the

Oliveira Viana, many cities and towns of today look for their origin, and which show by their very names (Viana, Soure, Aveiros, Amarante, Bragança, Santarém, Viseu), as do the towns that owe their origin to forts along the margins of rivers, "the preponderance of the white element, a Portuguese element, at the beginning of their colonization." All these towns and settlements which from north to south were being sowed over the immensity of the territory, situated at enormous distances from one another with extremely small populations, without a life of their own, were no more than little nuclei of settlements in which, only much later, in the nineteenth and twentieth centuries, urban centers of importance and value would come to be formed. Of the towns of the plateau of the center south, one above all—the oldest, founded by Martim Afonso in 1533—assumed at the edge of the sertão a capital importance, not only because of its topographic condition but because it constituted, like São Vicente on the coast, "one of the two initial foci of the spread of Paulista influence, and because Taubaté, Itú, and Sorocaba, three other great foci of conquest, expansion, and population, had their origin in it. Situated at the edge of the sertão and on the bank of the Tietê, which is a road of penetration made by nature, and 60 kilometers from its seaport and later at the crossroads which extend in practically all directions toward Paraná and Mato Grosso, Goiaz, Minas and Rio, Piratininga is the place on the plateau where the roads to the sea and the roads to the land begin, routes which relate its existence intimately to the circulation of merchandise. On the destiny of this town at the time of the bandeiras, of this city later in the age of coffee, as in its industrial phase, the influence of the roads was stronger than any other, the roads that lead from it or lead to it, with all their creative power, from the origins of Piratininga—the road of the Indian by the Serra do Mar—to the most brilliant period of its present civilization. But, like the coast center of São Vicente, which was becoming exhausted, not only nourishing the centers up on the serra, but also spreading its colonizing influence along the coast to the north and the south, São Paulo de Piratininga, on the plateau, did not develop except to drive all of its living strength toward the sertão of the north, the west, and the south, in the hunt for the Indian and the search for gold and, in its pastoral activity, seeking new fields for cattle breeding.

In general, the circle of influence of the cities varies with their importance; and the distance between the points of departure and arrival, or what might be called "the amplitude of the wave of immigration," is relatively as great as the urban center. The amplitude of the wave of expansion of those migrations which tamed the wilderness taking as their point of departure São Paulo de Piratininga, and after it Taubaté, Itú, and Sorocaba, and which lorded over all central and southern Brazil, has not, nevertheless, any relation with the importance or the volume of this urban center, the colonizing energy of which depends rather on the astonishing, dynamic activity of the race of mestizos which was formed on the plateau and on the really fruitful economic forces (the Indian, gold, and cattle) which drove the bandeirantes into the sertões. What these populating currents gained in extension or in area, reaching out over land and rivers prodigious distances from their initial starting point, urban life, which was still in a nascent state, lost in profundity—that life upon which they feed

chapel, the thing in which we should seek the origin of some cities, had nevertheless, as Borba de Morais himself recognizes with regard to the plateau, "greater meaning for the settlement of rural and scantily populated districts than for the concentration of population in the form of cities."

and to which they return to restore their colonizing forces with new resources and with new men. The Paulista bandeiras, extracted in fact from a vigorous race, one with young blood—the race and the blood of the mamelucos, the inhabitants of Piratininga—an overflowing excess of strength which the frequent, almost periodic struggles of the expeditions barely moderated for about a century of expansion of the back country. Founders of corrals, hunters of slaves, discoverers of gold, the Paulistas pricked on by the spirit of adventure, by envy, or by the necessity of expansion of their cattle scattered over all of the country, opening up the sertões, making roads, and establishing in the north, in the south and in the west nuclei of settlement and of civilization. The little town of Piratininga depopulated itself only to populate, but did not even succeed in growing rich: [6] the Paulistas, lords of the mines that had been discovered, were stripped of their land and repelled in 1709 by the Portuguese and sertanejos of Bahia who struggled to nullify by force the privileges of the bandeirantes; and like a symbol, Fernão Dias died in 1781, beside the Rio das Velhas, clutching against his breast the green stones which he supposed to be emeralds. . . . These successive struggles in its population, the enormous rise in prices between 1690 and 1709 led to a clamor of the people "oppressed by necessity," and in general the economic disturbances in the old populated zone of São Paulo, in consequence of internal migration, did not permit urban phenomena on the Paulista plateau, in the seventeenth and eighteenth centuries, to attain the slightest intensity, because urban life is in its nature a phenomenon of concentration to which the bandeiras, with their dispersive and expansionist character, opposed for almost two centuries an insuperable obstacle in themselves and in their consequences.

The place where we are going to see the phenomenon of concentration in cities most intensely produced is in the mining regions. These mines were discovered by the Paulista tamers of the wilderness in their formidable incursions into the back country; but the urban phenomenon must not be confounded with that of primary settlement, made by a great variety of systems and by stages, for it took place only

[6] Even at the beginning of the seventeenth century, the rustic simplicity and poverty of the interiors of houses showed how the urban life in the regions of the plateau differed from the city life of the sugar regions. In São Paulo, the houses of *pau-a-pique* or of stucco and wood, of stone and plaster, covered at first by a straw roof and later by tiles, when this type of roofing had spread along the coast, were generally of one story, and when in the eighteenth century they became higher they were only two stories. The furniture was simple and scanty. In place of a bed, there was the hammock used by the frontiersman of the plateau. In 1620, there was only one bed in São Paulo, which on the occasion of the corregidor's visit to the city was requisitioned for him, much against the will of the owner. It would seem that in the most active period of the bandeiras the urban scene in the little town was not very different, nor had living conditions changed noticeably, except perhaps in the case of a group of outfitters, who in the words of Afonso E. Taunay, constituted the "organization of the rearguard" of these expeditions. Among them, however, only one name became famous for wealth, that of Father Guilherme Pompeu, of the Leme family, "who grew rich," says Taunay, "without ever having seen the mining country, limiting himself to outfitting the miners, to whom he furnished herd after herd, taking them victuals, tools, cloth, arms, powder, chemical products, droves of oxen and swine." Such was his fortune, inherited from his parents and built up by the business of supplying bandeiras that, in his house, luxury reached the point of maintaining for guests "a hundred beds, each with its curtains and fine Breton sheets, and a silver basin under each of them." The silverware which came down from Peru, across the Andes, constituted the principal wealth of the houses of the bandeirantes.

through many difficulties, and in the beginning was a struggle against the two factors of dispersion and mobility of the back-country population, attracted from all points toward the "general mines" by the seductive illusion of rapid and easy wealth in the exploitation of gold. On the news of the success of the bandeiras there arrived from the home country and from the colony, from the towns of Portugal and from the little towns of Brazil, and from the most remote parts of the back country, a multitude of immigrants—white, black, Indians and mestizos, Portuguese adventurers, and inlanders from Bahia, who came to join the Paulistas, lords by royal grant of the discovered territory. Hamlets, settlements, and towns multiplied in the region of the mines; and the first mining centers, Cataguazes and Sabará, Vila Rica and Mariana (the last three raised in rank to towns in 1711), Caeté and Queluz, "were in turn the original foci of innumerable towns, villages, and hamlets, which spread over the valleys of the Rio das Velhas, the Paraopeba, and the São Francisco and on the tops of the hills." The growing population of foreigners attracted from distant lands by the obsession of gold, instead of concentrating in a few towns, was dispersed, broken up, and as it were "pulverized" in an extraordinary number of hamlets and settlements, which, developing above all along the valley of the Rio das Velhas, extended to the basin of the Jequitinhonha, where there arose, founded also by Paulistas, the towns of Diamantina, Grão-Mogol, and Minas Novas. This phenomenon of dispersion, which is explained by the march inward to the back country, always in search of new mines, and by the struggles between the Portuguese and the Paulistas, who, dislodged from their land, continued to penetrate the back country through Mato Grosso and Goiaz to a point where even the cupidity of the intrusive Portuguese did not reach, impelled by the restlessness which reigned in the captaincies because of the extortions of the treasury,[7] and was further accentuated by the very nature of the exploitation of alluvial gold which was deposited in the rivers and along the banks of rivers. The facility with which the mining operations changed their place of operation favored not only the development of a spirit of insubmission which fermented in the mines, but also the dispersion of this heterogeneous and fluctuating population, moving constantly in search or at the first rumor of the little grain which shines in the river or is hidden in the slopes of the hills. It was only later, after 1720, as Barros Latif observes, that the heavy work

[7] The taxes imposed upon the extraction of gold and the concentration of the mining industry in the hands of very few, like a real monopoly, and the draining off to Lisbon of the major part of the fabulous product, threw the population of the mines into servitude and misery. The indignation of the people, aggravated by the enormous rise in prices and the oppressive measures of the mother country, broke out in the successive uprisings of Pitanguí and Vila Rica in 1720, in which there stood out the singular figure of Filipe dos Santos, "a Spartan soul," condemned to death and, after being hanged, dragged behind a horse over the stones of Vila Rica. In the period of greatest production, which extended from 1710 to 1760, most of the population continued to drag out a miserable existence, in violent contrast with the wealth of the mine operators, between whom and the mother country the production was divided. It was in this social and political climate that all the germs of revolt fermented; the rebellion finally broke out, upon the demands of the Treasury, with the conspiracy of the Inconfidentes, plotted in all the heat of liberal ideas by a handful of priests, students, and poets and even of officers of the famous regiment of dragoons of Vila Rica, who united around the figure of Tiradentes, "the most ardent martyr among the preachers of liberty in the colonial period." The collection that had been ordered of the fifths that were in arrears only furnished the occasion for a rebellion of those who dreamed of independence and cherished republican ideals.

required for the gold of the mountain gave man roots in the land, and that the concentration of the miners due to the stability of work made the population lose its nomadic and adventurous character, contributed to fix it, and led the lords of the mines to construct their houses side by side with their mining operations.

So it is, then, that if the seventeenth century, the century of the bandeiras, was a century of territorial expansion, of conquest and of settlement, the century of gold, the eighteenth, was with the decline of rural patriarchalism in the north, and the movement of the bandeiras in the south, the century that saw the development of cities, in which there was formed and gained body a new bourgeois class anxious to dominate and already sufficiently strong to face the exclusivism of the families of landowners. Of all the different colonial areas, Pernambuco, Bahia, Rio, São Paulo, and Minas Gerais, it is in the last that a differentiation in this urban sense took place most early. In Minas, the eighteenth century is one of intense differentiation, writes Gilberto Freyre, at times frankly conflicting with the tendencies toward an integration in the rural, Catholic, Portuguese direction; and in Minas, under the influence of gold and of the city bourgeoisie dominated by the great mine owners,[8] there developed with a vigorous nativistic spirit, the most brilliant phase of civilization in the colonial period. Cities were concerned now with education; interest in the things of the spirit grew, and the lords of mines and the townsmen who were most prosperous sent their sons to Coimbra or Montpellier to finish their studies. "There came up by the hard way," Barros Latif tells us, "now and then a nail, and later, at the beginning of the century, wearing out a good many mules, the first pianos arrived." Social life acquired intensity and importance with the development of commerce, expanded in luxury, flowered in culture and in the arts, and reached a high point of dreams and of power; and after breaking out aggressively in bold revolt it hid its face in the conspiracies of independence, while the urban landscape was being radically transformed by the construction of temples, noble houses, and mansions. If the gold which came out of the mines permitted Dom João V the oriental luxury of his court and gave to Portugal Queluz and Mafra, enough remained in the colony to provide for the splendor of Mariana, of São João d'El-Rei, and above all, of the tortuous Vila Rica, clinging to the side of the hills, in the churches of which, shining with wealth, there is exhibited all the luxury of baroque art, and there is brilliant beaten gold on the edges of the altar, and there rise statues and pulpits of sandstone worked by Aleijadinho. But it is not only the cities of the region of the "general mines" that developed, producing in consequence of the mining operation the highest point of the urban life of the colonial period; when the political center of the country moved from Bahia to Rio de

---

[8] It was between 1710 and 1760, almost half a century, that the production of the "general mines" attained its peak, declining then to the beginning of the nineteenth century, when it was obviously decadent. The development of intellectual culture, as usually happens—for it is not parallel or simultaneous but rather successive in its relation to these periods of great economic activity —acquired its greatest intensity in the second half of the eighteenth century, with the leisure and tranquillity which middle-sized fortunes, better distributed than in the periods of great productivity, afforded. None of the gold-mining magnates attained, however, the fortune accumulated by some diamond contractors, like the famous João Fernandez de Oliveira, who, to show his power, had temples and palaces constructed, and had in his lordly residence a theater and exotic gardens, and whose wealth, becoming legendary, remained the most picturesque expression of the luxury and arrogant ostentation of these adventurers who grew rich in the mines.

Janeiro in 1763 this city—which kept the opulent production of the mines moving and was now the capital of Brazil—acquired such an impulse that in the fifty years from 1750 to 1800 its population multiplied, increasing from 25,000 to 100,000 inhabitants. Its economic importance also grew notably, and, if its appearance did not properly improve nor its social life gain brilliance, it did present a considerable extension and the proportions of a capital, with the intensity of its movement and the number and value of its public buildings. Its incomparable natural situation, the movement of the port which transformed it into the greatest center of exportation, the system of communication by land and by sea which linked it to all the captaincies, and the movement from north to south of the economic frontiers, all contributed to raise to a higher degree of intensity the urban life of this city, to which there was to be transferred, with the cycle of gold, the political center, and, with the decadence of the mining industry, which had retained it in "general mines," the very cultural center of the country.

No economic activity had, as we see, greater influence in the creation and development of the cities of the interior and therefore in the production of the urban phenomenon than the mining industry, both in the region of the "general mines" and in its repercussions on the political and commercial center which it moved to Rio de Janeiro and contributed to develop and differentiate in the urban sense. Certainly "in the work of colonizing our back-country interior there is no agent," says Oliveira Viana, "more powerful and efficient than pastoral industry. It is the vanguard of our agricultural expansion. The corral precedes the ranch and the sugar mill. After the cowboy comes the plowman. Cattle are the prelude to sugar plantations and grain growing." Cowboys, herdsmen and cattle raisers, Paulistas, Bahians and Pernambucans, driving their flocks of cattle, bring population to the deepest regions of our back country, from north to south, sowing the northern region with settlements, the basin of the São Francisco, the fields and plains of Mato Grosso, and pushing to the south as far as the hills and savannas of the Rio Grande the work of pastoral colonization. The migrations of cattle, led by bold back-countrymen into all of the rural corners and even the recesses of the high country, pushed back farther and farther "that living, mobile wall which the Indians formed with their wild confederations, making the penetration of the interior difficult." And it is by means of herds and by the movement of mule trains that the occupation of vast regions of the country was consolidated, regions where in every part many settlements and cities had their origins in pastoral activities, as is brought out even today by the bucolic and picturesque variety of their names (Vacaria, Curral, Campo Grande, Campos, Campinas, Pouso Sêco, Pouso Alto), expressing so clearly the influence of cattle on colonization. But if the pastoral economy exercised a prime function in widening the economic frontiers and was evidently one of the systems which led to the settlement of the country, marking the "first settlement" of a still empty region, it constituted a kind of primary settlement of a prodigious mobility and with a great power of expansion. The cattle economy, justly observes Afrânio Peixoto, "enjoys the peculiar faculty of occupying large areas with small population. It is, *par excellence,* an extensive industry." Factor of occupation and of settlement, of the first order, of dispersion and not of concentration, it is nowhere a force capable of contributing to intensify the urban phenomenon. The settlements founded by shepherds and cattle raisers near their resting places, in the fairs and cattle ranches, are urban formations which crystallize, develop, and differentiate slowly under the influence of the production of cattle and the trade in cattle, which, not requiring anything except enormous pasturage and fazendas for the herds, do not make the cities foci of attraction for the human masses and, until they emancipate themselves from the cattle trade, do not permit them to develop conditions of life of their own, nor require of them, on account of the "rusticity" inherent in this commerce, the climate and temper of life of cities that are so profoundly differentiated from the country.

It is, then, on the wide strip of the coast that the intensity of economic movement, born of the export trade and favored by it, tended to establish urban population and to resolve itself finally in a slow rise of the commercial and industrial class, made up of artisans and of exploiters of small industries. This rise above all of the townsmen, merchants and bankers, is so much the more observable in the cities near the agricultural plantations as it corresponds to a gradual impoverishment of the aristocratic class, easily seen in the habitual failure to balance their budgets, in the expedients to which these lords of the manor have recourse in maintaining their train of life, and in the chronic deficit they must face, which tends to transfer the economic and political axis from the "big houses" to the town mansions. But the very colonial cities which succeeded in developing and prematurely attained a certain grade of intensity and social brilliance, like Recife even under the dominion of the Dutch, and Vila Rica in the eighteenth century under the sign of the diamond and of gold, grew and entered into a period of decadence before they reached maturity and before they knew all the vigor of expansion of urban centers. Certainly, there were already beginning to appear everywhere symptoms of a new class eager to dominate, of townsmen and rich merchants in whose hands as creditors, one might say, you hear crack at times the bones of the old rural aristocracy, arrogant but sunk in debt, and who were manipulating the resources of a new technique—a bourgeois industrial technique—in its rudimentary and hesitating period of formation. Urban settlements, however—and the oldest and most flourishing are no more than large villages—had not only, to hinder their evolution, the distance and the isolation in which they lived: the movement and dispersion of the social mass which was accentuated with the expansion of the bandeiras, and the movement of the economic frontiers which now advanced and now receded, and with the oscillation and change of products, contributed to prevent the formation of great foci of urban concentration on the coast and on the plateau. A new country in formation, populated or remaining to be populated, its settlements do not present anywhere that strong attraction to the birthplace which belongs to people who have attained maturity, and who do not tend to emigrate even when they are living a life on a low material plane; they are characterized, on the contrary, by a taste for danger, for migration, and for an adventurous career. The necessity of new pasturage, the multiplication of sugar plantations and cattle ranches, the expansion of the bandeiras, and the discovery of the mines, keep in constant movement a large part of the population of different regions of the country—a mobile, wandering population which shows clearly in its movement back and forth the history of the pastoral economy, of expeditions into the sertão, and of mining, both in their rise and in their decline.

But when this movement and this dispersion of the social mass ceased, in large degree, and when the phenomena of internal migration from the coast toward the interior and from the plateau to the sertão in all directions diminished notably in intensity, there began in the country a profound dissociation, and with it a differentiation which various social and economic factors made ever greater between the shore and the back country. This fragmentation, from which resulted the formation of two mentalities that, when they could be differentiated, ended by opposing each other, constitutes one of the most interesting aspects of our social and historical formation, fecundated by internal migrations and afterward paralyzed at least in the interior by the isolation of the zones that were populated or occupied in the Brazilian back country. In their march to the west in search of wild Indians or fabulous mines—this is the way Humberto de Campos set down the phenomenon—"the Portuguese and Brazilians of the seventeenth and eighteenth centuries kept sowing fazendas, sugar plantations, and villages in which some of them established themselves, facing all the dangers of the immense green desert. When the chase of the aborigines ceased and the illusion of gold and precious stones was broken down, the bandeiras were rolled back and returned to the coast. The bandeirantes who had established themselves in the land remained, nevertheless, on their solitary properties. Marriages assuring the conservation of the race were made between relatives. Neighbors thirty or forty leagues apart became enemies when the boundary lines between properties were marked out. With the opening of the ports at the dawn of the nineteenth century, an act which contributed to the intensification of commerce, to the prejudice of agriculture and the pastoral industry, the populations near the coast turned entirely toward the sea, and thus the isolation of the white man of the extreme interior became more profound." In time the settlements, and even the rare cities of tiny proportions strewn through the interior, came to count upon their own resources, turning back many times into an obscure life and presenting the rudimentary aspects of human agglomerations, resigned and strong, whose almost savage energy is tempered in resistance to nature and to isolation. The life of these cities is diluted and absorbed in the life of everything of which they make a part, and which constitutes in a word the sertão. The high moral function of the sertão is to be, from now on, in the expression of Alberto Rangel, that of "an insulator against the trepidations of the coastal strip," the muscular center of the country, "a conservator of our most profound ethnic traits," "a hindrance to the easy denaturalization of the coast," of the cities of the coast which the illustrious writer compares to medullary points, "sensitive and motor centers receiving the first impressions of universal culture and of the interests, both high and low, of national policy and the reflection of which will be equilibrated and measured in the resistant fibers of the entrails of our land."

The very cities of the coast and those of the plateau until the middle of the nineteenth century were nothing more than villages, retarded and dirty, congested in narrow lanes and streets, with picturesque names, and spreading out on the periphery in their ranches and roads for herds, in their small estates and country houses which marked the transition between urban life and the all-encompassing solitude of the fields, of the plateaus and of the hills. Urban life, sleepy and obscure, limited by bureaucratic and parasitic functionalism and by a commerce that was "distrustful and niggardly," dragged out its life in the monotony of its streets and roads, the silence of which was hardly broken at long intervals by the squeaking of the oxcarts, by troops of horses and loaded mules, and by the songs of Africans and of herdsmen. It was all primitive in its rustic simplicity, this life of our cities: Negro women washing clothes at the fountains in the center, loaded mules beside the shops and animals running loose through the tortuous, narrow streets, where from the end of the eighteenth century in Rio, Olinda, and Recife "there already began to roll carriages, bumping over the stones and holes." The legislatures only later in the nineteenth century decided that the laundresses, says Gilberto Freyre, "should go to the stream outside the gate; for some cities, like Recife, had their arched gateways, outside which you were, as in medieval times, outside the gates." At night, at this time, "the street was ceasing to be a dark corridor which private people crossed with a slave going in front of them lantern in hand, and was coming to be illuminated by fish-oil lamps hung from high melancholy posts." Gangs of merry young men, serenades under quiet windows, the gliding past of the shade of a mantilla, under the mournful light of the lamp, it is to this that the nocturnal life of these colonial towns was reduced. . . . In the city of São Paulo, small and retarded, running down its muddy slopes where the herds of burros trotted, a collection of houses huddled inside the triangle formed by the churches of Carmel, of St. Francis, and of St. Benedict. In 1827 it was still so small [9] that with its houses, all of earth, and with adobe walls, "half of the city" could be contained, according to the testimony of Toledo Rendon, in the fenced land or garden of the Convent of St. Francis. The cities of the mining region like Vila Rica looked at this same time, as it were, like "a stage where a show has just been finished." No building, observes Barros Latif, no change inherent to new activity came to disturb the quiet atmosphere of the eighteenth century and the beautiful, sculptured façades of the churches grew old surrounded by the authentic houses of the period, as if a cosmic phenomenon had fossilized them."

But the life of the cities of the coast like Recife, Bahia, and above all Rio de Janeiro began to be profoundly transformed in the nineteenth century, in part because of factors of transformation in the agrarian economy which had been contributing since the eighteenth century to replace the prestige of the lords of the big houses by the prestige of the businessmen with their town mansions.[10] The progressive decay of

[9] Lieut. Gen. José Arouche de Toledo Rendon, first director of the Academy of Law, thus expressed himself to the Imperial Minister José Clemente Pereira, on the Convent of St. Francis, which he chose as the place for the law courses: "It [the convent enclosure] is so large that I consider it half the city." Bernardo Pereira de Vasconcelos, combating in the Constitutional Assembly the creation of law courses in São Paulo, alleged that "if 50 or 60 students should come to the Academy, they would have nowhere to live in São Paulo." So small did the old plateau city seem to him.

[10] The mansion—the urban type of residence—was in the colonial period and under the Empire the dwelling of the nobles. The height of these mansions rarely exceeded one floor in São Paulo, varied between two and three stories in Rio de Janeiro, three and four in Bahia, attaining six in Recife, where one finds the tallest, introduced during the rule of the Dutch. It is a big house of stone and plaster, "citified" into a mansion, with its roof of Roman tiles, turned up at the points and with wide eaves in Chinese style, with Florentine loggias and balconies and porches or verandas, an inner patio, colored tiles in the vestibule and grated Moorish balconies which came from the Arabs, as those other elements did from Chinese ports and the Italian peninsula by way of the Portuguese type of dwelling. Everything in these vast and solid houses, varying in height, wealth, and type from north to south, and turned from their original style by the necessity of adaptation to the environment, showed, as I have already had occasion to write, "the prudence and hospitality of the old families with their patriarchal life, whose religious spirit is registered in ornamental crosses, oratories, and chapels. The rich ceilings of worked or carved wood, the door trim, and the panels of tiles, and the internal patio on which open, in oriental style, the verandas and dining rooms, lend a note of gaiety to the interior of the big houses and the mansions of the nobles, with

rural aristocracy, from which, however, there still came the nobility of the Empire and the political chieftains of the provinces and of the townships, and the new policy of the mother country which, "neglecting a little bit colonial agriculture, gave all its best favors to cities and to men of commerce and even to workmen," contributed effectively to the development of cities, which were already beginning to exercise a great power of attraction over the country population. The opening of Brazilian ports to foreign commerce inspired by Viscount de Cairú in his advice to Dom João VI, and the installation of the court in Rio de Janeiro in 1808, accelerated still more the progress of this city, which besides being the capital of Brazil for almost half a century, now became suddenly the seat of the Portuguese monarchy. It is easy to understand the social and political influence which was exercised on the "big village," which Rio de Janeiro still was, by the unexpected arrival of Dom João VI with his retinue and the moving of the court to Brazil for a long period of thirteen years, followed closely by the movement of independence and the foundation of the Empire. The life of the court with all its requirements and all the prestige of royalty, with noblemen coming from the home country and artists brought from France like Lebreton, Debret, and Taunay, and the initiative of Dom João VI, which created the Royal Press, founded the Public Library, inaugurated the School of Fine Arts, established the Bank of Brazil, sketched the Botanical Garden, and erected factories, schools, and hospitals, could not fail to establish a strong current of renovation, which, reaching the very social structure, passed over the urban landscape of the old colonial city lightly and modified it.[11] It was not only the active presence of Dom João VI and the brilliance of the life of the court, the prestige which came from being the capital of the Empire, and the growth of its population, which assured the preponderance of the seat of the monarchy, afterward the imperial city: the multiplication of newspapers and printing presses, the prosperity of its schools, the movement of its commerce, all contributed to make Rio de Janeiro the greatest urban center of the country and to make the opinion of the cariocas (natives of the city) one of the most important forces of the nation. In the streets, so badly illuminated that when there was a fire at night "every resident of the streets through which the firemen passed was obliged to light their way from his windows," gas lamps began as early as 1854 to replace the fish-oil lights;

their splendid balconies and their vestibules, from which in one or two easy flights the imposing stairway attains the upper floor." The mansion conferred class distinction and, by distinguishing, isolated and separated the domestic life from the life of the street, the poor from the rich, the people of the huts from those of the mansion. It was eminently a "class" dwelling. The shades and shutters with which the windows, sometimes with glass, were provided, through which the sun's light filtered, the gratings and the "eyes" with iron crosses or narrow apertures, through which one could see the street without being seen, define in this type of dwelling the character of patriarchal life in all its austerity and reserve, and even isolation. The walls of its gardens, covered with broken glass or consisting of iron bars ending in sharp points, show moreover the desire to isolate and defend oneself against the street and its dangers.

[11] ". . . a great village of 45,000 souls," writes Euclides da Cunha, "dotted with swampy sections, invaded by the tides which swell its lakes, and badly and carelessly built, on the slope of the hills, filling the swampy valleys with its narrow winding streets, lined with woven window blinds, along which wound the miserable royal train of old sedan chairs with leather curtains, like the last rags of a vanished opulence." Cf. Euclides da Cunha, *À Margem da história*, Pt. 3, "Esbôço da história política: Da Independência a República," p. 222 (Pôrto: Chardron, 3rd ed., 1922).

and in the paved and policed city which was spreading out to the new districts of Catete, Laranjeiras, and Botafogo built on the lands of old country villas, there was allied to the picturesque the concern for an urbanism which was constantly to transform the old landscape. The younger generation, educated in Europe, in São Paulo, or in Recife, in the law courses founded in 1827, or in the schools of the capital, rarely returned, observes Gilberto Freyre, to the fazendas and to the sugar plantations of their fathers after graduating: "with their talent and their knowledge they came to enrich the court and to give brilliance to the city; diplomacy, politics, the liberal professions, and at times high industry absorbed them."

The germ of a new life, different from rural life, was thus constituted; and for this new life morphological formations of a new kind, the cities, were taking on their own appearance, commercial at first because of the great importance which maritime commerce acquired and later, in the twentieth century, industry, as a result of the development which took place chiefly in Rio and São Paulo. In the whole nineteenth century the role of industry was in this respect secondary; it was commerce that made the cities, and it was, above all, for commerce that our greatest urban centers grew up. Cities here, as in so many other civilizations, were born because from the body of the rural population there separated out a whole class of men who sought their subsistence by selling and buying, that is, commerce.[12] The renewal of the means of transportation with the organization of our railroad system, begun in 1854, the currents of immigration which moved toward the south attracted by the coffee plantations, the important rural exodus which followed the abolition of slavery in 1888 when the former slaves moved toward the coffee zone of the south and toward the cities, were so many other forces transforming the cities, whose principal function continued to be commerce—now not only local, with the neighboring country, but with other cities variously placed on the new lines of communication. The abolition of slavery and the consequent crisis during which the sugar plantations, concentrated for the most part in the Northeast, were completely disorganized formed the point of departure for a new evolution of urban life. Among the movements which led to the dispersion of the social mass at the end of the Empire and in the first three decades of the Republic, the centripetal one was provided, as Oliveira Viana rightly observes, "by the movement of rural population to the great cities of the coast and of the plateau and by the formation of great foci of urban life in the interior. This movement, peculiar to the republican period, is a consequence of the abolition of servile labor in 1888." The wealth wrought by coffee growing, the intensification of immigration after the abolition of slavery, the movement toward the city of the excess of immigrants because of the overproduction of coffee, the progress of commerce which brought afterward that of industry, and the improvement of the railway system—radiating from Rio de Janeiro toward Minas and São Paulo and from São Paulo all over the plateau—and finally the important industrial movement furnished the germs of urban civilization with all the conditions favorable to their full development.

With the powerful influence of coffee, of immigration, and of industry, it is not only the city on Guanabara Bay that has been radically transformed to take on the proportions and appearance of a great metropolis, in constant evolution. The old colonial

[12] Henri Pirenne, *Histoire da la Belgique: Des origines au commencement du XIV siècle* (Brussels: Henri Lamertin, 1900).

city, cleaned up by Osvaldo Cruz and remodeled by Pereira Passos (1902–1906), who laid out the Avenida Rio Branco and, with his reforming initiative, opened new perspectives to urban progress, acquired an extraordinary development in area, extending to the south through magnificent residential districts along the beaches of Copacabana and Ipanema, which communicate by means of tunnels with the center of the city, to begin, after 1930, growing rapidly in a vertical direction, by the multiplication of skyscrapers. The city of São Paulo, which even in 1867 was connected with its seaport, Santos, by the São Paulo Railway, and in 1877 with Rio de Janeiro by the Central Railway of Brazil, jumped from 70,000 inhabitants in 1886 to 1,200,000 in less than fifty years. Rebuilt at the initiative of Antônio Prado in 1910, the oldest city of the plateau, now the nexus of six roads and railroad center of a network that extends to Rio, Minas, Goiaz, Mato Grosso, and Paraná, cutting the State in almost all directions, did not stop developing about its old central nucleus, which has been broadened and transformed to include on the periphery a splendid crown of factories and garden cities. No city is closer to the progress of São Paulo than Santos, which tributary to the coffee and industrial region of the country, has become the most important Brazilian center of exportation, and one of its major urban centers. In all the regions of the central plateau, made up by the two States of Minas and São Paulo, in Rio Grande do Sul, and in Pernambuco, in which there has been manifest in varying degrees, above all since 1920, the most vigorous industrial development which our history records,[13] cities like Campinas, Sorocaba, and Ribeirão Preto in São Paulo, Juiz de Fora, Belo Horizonte, and Itajubá in Minas Gerais, Pelotas and Pôrto Alegre in Rio Grande do Sul, and Recife in Pernambuco, among others, had a great development marked by rapid progress in industry and commerce. And, as it is principally due to roads that cities grow or fail to grow and become nuclei of concentration or of distribution of agricultural or industrial products, and as even today the creative power of roads, far from vanishing, tends to be augmented with the new transportation techniques (steam engines and automobiles), new, small cities are arising which have been formed and have grown at the principal centers of railways, at the junction points and the crossings of highways and railways.

Certainly, the place where population condenses, attaining its highest degree of concentration and intensity of urban life, is in the cities, political capitals, the role of which and the development of which are explained in large part by the routes of communication which they command, as maritime or river ports, and centers of railway systems. All these cities from Pôrto Alegre to Manaus, passing through Florianópolis, Santos, Vitória, Bahia, Fortaleza, Recife, Paraíba, São Luiz do Maranhão, and Belém

---

[13] But even on the plateau of São Paulo, where industry gave a notable stimulus to urban civilization leading to the development of magnificent centers, closer together, urban life and rural life remain sharply different, separated by empty space that is uncultivated and has all the appearance of primitive landscape. When one leaves the city it is not for cultivated fields (truck gardens, farms, ranches) or landscapes arranged by the hand of man, but for woods and plains, hills and plateaus, a whole uncultivated region scarcely tamed by the frontier explorer. There is nothing that looks like the urban and rural landscape blending into each other, as they do in England, so that one barely notices anywhere the distinction between the two types of landscape, so typically differentiated with us, even in the most cultivated part of the plateau of São Paulo: the English countryside which Karel Capek compared to an "English garden," to express the extent to which that landscape had been worked over by man, presents, "with its shaded roads, its cottages hidden behind trees and meadows, a landscape that admirably expresses a civilization."

do Pará on the coast, and those which cling to the central plateau, like Curitiba, São Paulo, Belo Horizonte, and Cuiabá, were developed unequally, less under the influence of their geographic condition than under the impulse given by the economic, agricultural, commercial, and industrial growth of these various regions. In reality, remarks Lucien Febvre, "it is the State that creates the capital. Its prosperity creates the prosperity of the capital, its decadence involves that of the city which it chose as its head," as we can see ourselves by the striking example of Manaus, which developed notably with the production and the high-water mark of rubber in the Amazon region, to become stagnant for a long time with the depression of this industry. Of the five cities that are political capitals on the central plateau, São Paulo, Belo Horizonte, Curitiba, Cuiabá, and Goiânia—the newest of all, still being constructed—Belo Horizonte had an original formation which still stands out in the geometric beauty of its lines, straight or curved, and the magnificent vastness of its streets, squares, and avenues and in the luminous extension of its parks and gardens. An old aspiration of the *inconfidentes* who were already dreaming in Vila Rica of a change of the capital of Minas to São João d'El-Rei, "because the latter was a better situated town," the idea of changing the capital—discussed for ten years after independence, attempted in 1843 by General Andréia, Baron de Caçapava, who was then president of the province, discussed again in 1852 when Minas was governed by Dr. José Ricardo de Sá Rêgo, defended ardently by Father Paraíso in the Legislative Assembly—finally triumphed in 1893 after a campaign with which are linked the names of Alexandre Stockler and João Pinheiro, with law number 3 in amendment to the constitution of the State. And in less than four years, commenced in 1893 and inaugurated on the 12th of December, 1897, there rose a new city on the open land between the Contagem and Curral ridges, land with wide horizons to which it owes its name, and looking off on one side to the Pico da Piedade—"the old landmark of the early bandeirantes." In little more than forty years a new city to which the capital of Minas has been moved from the legendary Ouro Preto, and which preserves intact the intellectual traditions of Vila Rica, has expanded, grown rich, grown in perfection and beauty, passing with its 200,000 inhabitants beyond the circular wall in which the pleiad of its constructors expected to inclose it. This was the group to which, in the words of Aarão Reis, one of them and the chief of all, had been confided "the almost magical mission of endowing the State with a city—a true fairy tale."

That we are still very far from a typical urban civilization, even on the plateau of the central south, there is not the slightest doubt. To prove this we have the fact that, of all the capital cities of the coast and of the interior, only two have far exceeded 1,000,000 inhabitants and show the new and distinctive characteristics of a modern metropolis. These cities which have become cosmopolitan, and in which industry has passed to the foreground, are Rio and São Paulo, great manufacturing centers: Rio de Janeiro, which has become the most important city of the country, because it is the center not only of an intense economic life but of a vast administration; and São Paulo because, being the major producer of coffee since 1886, it has become as a result the most important industrial center of Brazil, with the advantage of having at its service, less than sixty kilometers away, the seaport Santos. Still more, if the city is in its origin a product of the differentiation between the labor which cultivates the land and a group of artisans, commercial men, and industrial leaders, established in the center of this area with commercial relations extending later and entering into contact with different cities, out of this approximation and out of this contact there result new forms of specialization. Now, compact concentrations of industry [14] have not been formed as yet, except in São Paulo; moreover we do not yet have more than a sketch of industrial division of labor in our process of specialization or differentiation of the principal manufacturing cities. The disproportion in number and importance of the great cities on the coast to the larger ones of the interior, which are as a matter of fact still close to the coast, like Belo Horizonte bound up to Rio, and São Paulo to Santos, and Curitiba to Paranaguá, shows that we still face toward the Atlantic and remain subject to all of the external influences upon our national civilization. But there is no country which has been born of itself, or which, in being born, growing, and forming itself, has been able to get along without external influences. "The shock comes from outside," writes Vidal de la Blache. "No civilized country is the exclusive product of its own civilization; or at least it cannot engender anything but a limited civilization, like a clock, which after running for a time, stops by itself. It is necessary, in order that it may rise to a higher degree of development, that its life shall be in communion with that of a region more vast which will enrich it with its own substance and infilter into it new ferments." This circulation of sap and of the current of life and renovation is through the great cities which, being essentially centers of exchange, along with their commercial exchange, are the indisputable foci of progress; it is in them, as Durkheim considers, that "the moderating influence of the age is brought down to a minimum, tradition has less control over men's minds, and it is in them that ideas, fashions, customs, and new necessities are elaborated to spread out afterward through all the rest of the country."

[14] Euclides da Cunha, relying on Hermilo Alves's monograph *Problema da Viação Férrea para Mato Grosso*, thinks that "the land between the two waterfalls, Urubupungá on the Paraná and Itapura on the Tieté, a league apart, is the future basis of the most important of industrial centers in South America, having at its disposal the incalculable mechanical energy of those cataracts, which added to that derived from the falls of Avanhandava and transformed into electric energy, will not only satisfy all the needs of industries but provide traction for the railways which pass there. Thus one can locate ideally, with sure foresight, in these out-of-the-way places, where today [about 1908] one can hardly distinguish, stifled in the wild brush, the ruins of a military colony that failed— *a very rich city of the future*. Above all, if we note that it will be one of the busiest ports of call of the greatest interoceanic traffic of this continent; for the intercontinental destiny of the Northwest is inevitable and extraordinary." (Cunha, *À Margem da história*, 3rd ed., 1922, p. 160.)

BIBLIOGRAPHY

Agache, Alfredo, *A Cidade do Rio de Janeiro: Extensão, remodelação, embelezamento— organizações projetadas na administração Prado Junior* (Paris, 1930). Cf. Agache, "Un Exemple de sociologie appliquée: l'urbanisme," *Les Etudes sociales*, 55th yr., Ser. 10, Vol. 5, pp. 107–125 (Apr., 1935).

Barros Latif, Miran M. de, 'As *"Minas gerais"* (Rio: A Noite, 1940).

Borba de Morais, Rubens, "Contribuições para a história do povoamento em São Baulo até fins do século XVIII," in *Geografia* (journal of the Associação dos Geógrafos Brasileiros, São Paulo), Vol. 1, No. 1, pp. 69–87 (1935).

Calmon, Pedro, *História social do Brasil*, Vol. 1, *Espírito da sociedade colonial*, and Vol. 2, *Espírito da sociedade imperial* (São Paulo: Comp. Editora Nacional, 1935, 1937— Brasiliana, Vols. 40, 83).

Costa, Luiz Edmundo, *O Rio de Janeiro no tempo dos Vice-Reis (1763–1808)* (Rio: Imprensa Nacional, 1932).

Freyre, Gilberto, *Sobrados e mocambos: Decadencia do patriarcado rural no Brasil* (São Paulo: Comp. Editora Nacional, 1936—Brasiliana, Vol. 64).

———, *Olinda: 2nd guia prático, histórico e sentimental da cidade brasileira* (Recife: Drechsler, 1940).

Leite, Serafim, *Páginas de história do Brasil* (São Paulo: Comp. Editora Nacional, 1937—Brasiliana, Vol. 93), especially Chap. V, "A Fundação de São Paulo," and Chap. XIV, "Conquista e fundação do Rio de Janeiro," pp. 81–97, 217–218.

Lubambo, Manuel, "Olinda: Sua evolução urbana no século XVI," in *Fronteiras*, Vol. 6, No. 22 (Feb.–Mar., 1937), pp. 3–8.

Melo Franco, Afonos Arinos de, *Roteiro lírico de Ouro Preto* (Rio: Sociedade Felipe d'Oliveira, 1937).

Oliveira Lima, Manuel de, *Sur l'évolution de Rio de Janeiro* (Antwerp, 1909).

Oliveira Viana, F. J., "A Evolução da sociedade," in *Recenseamento do Brasil* (1920), Vol. 1, *Introdução* (Rio: Tip. da Estatística, 1922), pp. 281–310.

Rangel, Alberto, *Rumos e perspectives* (São Paulo: Comp. Editora Nacional, 2nd ed., 1934 —Brasiliana, Vol. 26), especially "Os Sertões brasileiros" and "A Sociedade brasileira no primeiro reinado," pp. 7–39, 43–71.

Rodrigues, J. Onorio, and Joaquim Ribeiro, *Civilização holandesa no Brasil* (São Paulo: Comp. Editora Nacional, 1940—Brasiliana, Vol. 180), especially Chaps. XVI–XVII, "Meio urbano," "Meio rural," pp. 205–259.

Saint–Hilaire, A. de, *Segunda viagem do Rio de Janeiro a Minas Gerais e a São Paulo*, transl. Afonso E. Taunay (São Paulo: Comp. Editora Nacional, 1932—Brasiliana, Vol. 5).

CHAPTER FOUR

SOCIAL AND POLITICAL EVOLUTION

The colonization of Brazil, its forms and objectives—(a) The fixation of man on the land—The feudal experience—The shock of three races and cultures—Colonial society—The reign of sugar—The splendor of rural life—(b) The penetration and conquest of the land—Internal migration and the entry into the back country—The bandeiras—Mass phenomena—The dislocation of the frontier—The reign of metals—The formation of the mind and of the national unity—(c) The independence of the land—The patriarchal economic regime—Nobility and rural aristocracy—The bourgeoisie of the cities—Individualism and the precursors of democratic ideology—The second Empire and political unification—Politics and romanticism—The abolition of slavery—(d) The democratization by land—The persistence of the social and economic structure—The Republic—The regional spirit—The federative system and political parties—Political professionalism—Immigration and the single-crop cultivation of coffee—Small property cutting up the plantations—The rise of industry—The evolution of contemporary society.

I<small>T MAY SEEM AUDACIOUS</small> to attempt to reduce to a brief synthesis a picture of the origins and evolution of the forms of social and political structure which Brazilian society has assumed from the time it began to be formed in the first century and down to our days. But, difficult as a task of this kind may be, and although it is in its nature one always open to corrections as a consequence of later researches, the local studies and monographic investigations which have already been made permit us to bring together the elements at our disposal in order to obtain a broad vision of the whole. Moreover, if we consider the importance of the function which physical, demological, economic, and urban factors exercise in the process of social and political evolution, the major lines of this synthesis, so useful and in fact necessary to the study of our cultural evolution, already stand out with such clarity that it will not be necessary to do more than detach them from the facts studied and accompany them in their development and present them with as great precision, rigor, and detachment as possible. The difficulty of a synthesis, which is only the result of the documentation furnished by specialized monographs and analytical work, is not only the insufficiency of work of this order, of research and investigation, but the temptation to which so many are accustomed to yield, through taste or excessive care not to neglect any detail, embarrassing themselves with a multitude of "little facts." Now, whatever may be the determining role of the little facts, they should not make us forget general tendencies, explicable themselves by general causes. "To discern in the whole of historic events dominating general facts, which furnish as it were an armature or skeleton, to show how to these general facts of the first order there are subordinated others, and to go on thus until one arrives at the detailed facts which can offer a dramatic interest and pique our curiosity but not our philosophical curiosity"—thus Cournot defined the object of his *Considerations,* which constitute the most vigorous effort by a philosopher to apply to modern history the great leading ideas: ideas of chance and the irrational, of order and of reason, which he drew from the practice of the sciences and experimented with, applying them to all the disciplines.[1] This also is our objective, when we attempt to define in its general lines and its principal causes the movement of our civilization.

In the vast territory that had been discovered and occupied only in part, along its coastwise strip, exploited by the mother country and for the mother country, peopled by a great majority of aboriginal inhabitants, and by a scanty minority of whites, the Portuguese hardly laid claim in the thirty years following discovery to anything except the extraction and commerce of dyewoods, of which they reserved a monopoly for themselves. But the very business of brazilwood, which was found in abundance near the coast, and the incursions of the French pirates, who, taking advantage of the abandonment of the lands newly discovered, pillaged the villages of Indians and disputed with the Portuguese their exploitation and their dominion, finally led the mother country to turn its attention toward Brazil and to enter frankly upon the path of colonization. The immensity of the territory, the distance which separated it from Portugal, and the elementary stage of the culture of the primitive inhabitants—wild savages who wandered through the American forest or were scattered through an infinity of lodges and villages—constituted, nevertheless, almost insuperable obstacles to the establishment of colonies and the foundation of an empire. Colonization, which therefore had to take on new forms and follow new objectives, truly began with the expedition of Martim Afonso de Sousa, in 1530, and the giving away of hereditary captaincies, which marked the period of the fixation of man on the land, in which up to that time the first explorers had limited their activities to traffic in brazilwood and to reconnaissance of the coast. The division of Brazil into fifteen hereditary captaincies and giving each one of these to a captain-general, worthy through excellence of lineage or through individual prestige, and with discretionary powers,[2] constituted in the last analysis a feudal experiment clearly marked by the essential element of that regime, which was characterized in European feudalism by the distribution and holding of land as a means of fixing man, arousing him to its defense, and giving him an interest in colonization. It is only thus, writes Ronald de Carvalho, "confiding that portion of uncultivated land to the energy of men of good will, that the crown could keep without major expense the prize that was so coveted by many highwaymen." Certainly, there being no already constituted social structure, there could not occur, and actually there did not occur, in Brazil with

---

[1] A. A. Cournot, *Considérations sur la marche des idées et des événements dans les temps modernes,* with introduction by Félix Mentré, republished in Bibliotèque de Philosophie (Paris: Boivin, 1934). Cf. *Souvenirs de Cournot (1760–1860)* (Paris: Hachette, 1913—published by Bottinelli); Félix Mentré, *Cournot et la Renaissance du probabilisme au XIXe siècle,* 1908.

[2] "Above the captains-governors there was, to be sure, the king," writes Tavares de Lira, "with those powers which he had not yielded nor delegated, and there were the ordinances and general laws of the realm 'with respect to whatever had not been the object of some special determination in letters making grants or laying down regulations.' This, however, made little difference, seeing that in reality the rights of the free colonists and the harsh duties of the slave laborers took form in the will and acts of the grantee—military chief and industrial leader, lord of lands and justice, distributor of farms and of punishments, constructor of towns and undertaker of wars against the Indians." Cf. A. Tavares de Lira, *Organização política e administrativa do Brasil: Colônia, Império e República* (São Paulo: Comp. Editora Nacional).

this system the superposition of one class by economic and political dominion of the feudal lords over the primitive inhabitants, and the formation between one and the other of relations of dependency resulting from the ownership of the soil. But if there does not exist a parallelism between the economic and political organization in Brazil and the economy of medieval Europe, it is incontestable that the organization that was instituted by the giving of captaincies with the end of binding man to the earth and arousing him to defend it, thus assuring to the mother country the dominion of the colony, followed principles that were essentially feudal.

This first measure of the highest interest for colonization was insufficient, in spite of its proved advantages, to accomplish the ends which were proposed, and it was not long until it required steps to complete it: the creation in 1549 of a general government having in view especially the formation of a center of unity and consequently the better defense of the land. The abandonment by some donees of the lands that had fallen to them, the failure of others in the enterprise of colonization, the falling out among themselves of the lords of captaincies who were independent of one another, and the difficulties in which they all found themselves when it came to defending their lot against aggression by Indians or foreigners, made people feel almost immediately the need for a central government with a jurisdiction over the totality of the land occupied and divided. The struggle which was to last through centuries down to modern times, between regional tendencies and unifying tendencies, between centralization and decentralization, already stood out at this period in the two measures which followed each other, that of the feudal system of giving land away and that of the general government, proposed to correct the inconveniences of the former by means of a centralization of political power.[3] The captaincies, which from that time, with the appointment of Tomé de Sousa, remained under the control of the central government with its seat at Bahia, "in the course of time passed one after another, by acquisition of the public treasury, under the yoke of the mother country." But if, with the transmission from private individuals to public ownership of the last hereditary captaincies and the submission of all to a single government, one might consider the feudal experiment closed, can it not also be said that there is rooted in the primitive regime and the permanence of geographic, economic, and political conditions which determined it, and in the other social factors, "a spirit of domination," which persisted for a long time in the political life of the country, developed with regional oligarchy, and often assimilated to the administration of

[3] Still to achieve organization, as yet heterogeneous and adventurous, the colonial society made up at that time of Portuguese from the home country and born in Brazil, of Indians, mestizos, and Negroes, could not feel as "an external imposition," from without inwards, the political institutions implanted in the country. The relations of production, elementary as they were, could not give rise to other than very simple social relations nor produce in this incipient society other necessities than those of its own defense and security against the attacks of Indians and the invasions of pirate ships. There had not yet been formed the consciousness of a distinction between a new nationality or even a new society and that of the distant mother country, from which people barely claimed more direct and efficient aid. The fatherland was only one: Portugal. "The homes of the richest lords," writes Jônatas Serrano, "had no comforts; one felt that the settlement of the alien nobility in Brazil was provisional and that everyone wanted to return home as soon as possible." (*Historia do Brasil,* p. 134—Rio, Briguiet, 1931). The political institutions planned in the mother country and transplanted to the colony, serving the simple interests of the local society in an embryonic stage of development, were really serving the interests of the mother country which created them. The two were at that time one.

the fazendas, of the factories, the government of the provinces and of states? It is not less important for an understanding of our social and political evolution in the first three centuries to note the fact that political institutions founded by the mother country preceded any forms whatever of social organization in the colony, in which in the first half of the sixteenth century a society in formation was barely sketched. Before the cultivation of sugar, in the middle of the first and second centuries, furnished the growing colonial society with the elements necessary and the background for a solid and stable social structure, there was already established a whole political mechanism based on the system of the captaincies, tempered and corrected by the central government, which was destined to promote the fixing of man on the land, its defense, and its colonization.

Nowhere along the coast, dotted with human groups, or on the plateau on which there had already been established the town of Piratininga, did the growing society meet conditions favorable for its organization. Scattered in little nuclei that were sparse and at a great distance from one another, made up originally of two races, the white and the red, in the most diverse stages of culture, crowded between the coast and the plateau, between the attacks of pirates and the assaults of savages, it lost its old social structure that had come from the mother country without elaborating a structure proper to itself, and it continued with its colonists, its exiles and its Indians, as a phenomenon that one might call presocial, a "state of society in suspense," amorphous and fluctuating, seeking new forms. Its extremely scanty population, the heterogeneity of its initial composition, which was complicated by the importation of African slaves, the perils which blocked it on all sides and the shocks of three races and cultures, necessarily helped to retard the progress of social organization and led it to concentrate its elementary forces in an instinctive effort at concentration and defense. Between the Portuguese who had already attained a high degree of civilization and whose capitalism was in the commercial phase, exploiting agricultural products, and the Indian who remained in a primitive stage, that of gathering, hunting, and fishing, and could not pass abruptly to the agricultural stage, there was an enormous social distance which not only made impossible the assimilation of Indians in the rural economy, but persisted as a source generating social conflict. The Portuguese colonists entered immediately into contact with the Indians, whether enslaving them by force or trading with them pacifically in the interchange of products; and, if at times they were received in friendly fashion by the primitive peoples, thanks above all to the incomparable activities of the missionaries, they were repelled frequently by other savage tribes whose attacks they could not escape except by great efforts. The ethnic melting pot, fusing the whites and Indians on a large scale because of the scarcity of white women, the seduction which the dominating race exercised over the Indian women, and the pacific action of the Jesuits "transforming the harsh instinct of the savage into an instrument that helped colonization," contributed to diminish to a certain point the antagonisms of the two races and to promote the assimilation and adaptation of their cultures. The culture of the African Negroes, who unlike the Indians had already reached an agricultural state, and the smaller difference between the social structure of the African tribes and the patriarchal family of the Portuguese colonizers, not only rendered possible, as Roger Bastide observes, the assimilation of Negroes to the Brazilian economy, although under an abnormal and pathological form—that of slavery —but also with the miscegenation that was largely practiced, for lack of white women, corrected "the social distance which otherwise would have been very great between the masters and slaves."

It was with the exploitation of sugar cane that the patriarchal system of the Portuguese, based on slave labor, gave a vigorous impulse to colonization and furnished colonial society in the massapê lands, from the recôncavo district in Bahia to part of Maranhão, with the framework of a closed social organization, the formation of which had begun in the middle of the first century, to attain in the second the maximum of its development. In a society notably lacking in equality, like the primitive colonial society, in which the demographic difference accentuated the social, and later the political inequality, and the first social classification (Portuguese, Indians, mestizos) was based upon pigment, the distinction of classes established on an economic base met in the distinction of races a material and visible sign of differentiation. Lords and slaves, whites and Negroes. The races, white and African, formed an ethnic stratification, the layers of which corresponded exactly, as you see, to social stratification, to the two classes which the plantation system of monoculture and the slave system separated and superimposed, raising the lords of the sugar plantations to the category of nobility, and degrading to the lowest level the masses of slaves. "Color meant nobility," Pedro Calmon reminds us, citing Martius; [4] "there was one common origin of plebeianism—the African trunk; in the elaboration of a subrace capable of passing for white consisted the elevation and the rehabilitation of man." On one hand the richness of the soil, which, in the words of Gilberto Freyre, permitted generations of lords of the sugar plantations "to succeed one another in the same plantation, to grow stronger and to put down roots in houses of stone and stucco," and on the other hand endogamy, frequently practiced, with cousins marrying cousins, and uncles nieces, contributed powerfully to give the dominant class, in this society that formed a solid hierarchy, the structure of an aristocracy which, without historic tradition and without nobility of blood, was graduated and estimated its titles by the extent of its plantations, by the number of its slaves, by leisure and by ostentatious luxury. Later, other factors were to intervene to fortify this society, formed into classes, profoundly distinct and differentiated. The law which forbade the execution of the lords of the sugar plantations for debts, creditors not being able to take from them more than a single crop, and the law of the family which gave to the first born the whole succession, forbidding the division of the patrimony, added to the custom of not selling their slaves, who were included without division in their hereditary property, "were to consolidate," writes Pedro Calmon, "this emerging aristocracy, corrupted by the institution of slavery, exploited by commerce, immobilized and demoralized by the ignorance, the sensuality, and the mysticism which throve from their inactivity."

The sugar lord who solely because of his economic situation considered himself raised to the nobility, sovereign and father with an authority practically without restriction in the patriarchal family, seeing in work a slave occupation,[5] was a little king in

---

[4] In J. B. von Spix, *Através da Baía* (excerpts transl. with notes by Piraja dá Silva from the work *Reise in Brasilien*) (São Paulo: Comp. Editora Nacional, 3rd ed., 1938—Brasiliana, Vol. 118).

[5] There seems to be related to the inactivity of the lords of the mills and later of the ranchers of the center south—which was considered as a "sign of membership in the upper class"—the repugnance of the Brazilian for manual or mechanical labor, which was the occupation of slaves during the long period of slavery; such work was the mark of the slave's status. The regime of production and work which created the very type of aristocrat and of big house and the very type of slave and

his almost unlimited territory, with the right of life and death, although it was not expressly established by law, "over those who depended upon him, working on the land or serving on the plantations." The church, if on the one hand it softened the rigors of the exercise of this power, contributed on the other with its model discipline to maintain in equilibrium the relations between lords and slaves, strengthening the authority of the former and developing the spirit of obedience, conformity, and submission in the latter. The reduction of the social body or the fragmentation of society into these complex organisms, these immense, self-sufficient properties which distance isolated from one another, showed itself in a new tendency toward feudalism, that is toward the disintegration of the whole into independent parts with a tendency to weaken the higher central levels, and preparing in the sugar plantations, in which authority of the lords was concentrated, unexpected forms of individualism. In contrast, however, with the feudal regime, in which there are common psychological traits in the noble and the peasant and a dominating mentality which colors all social life, in the Brazilian society of the second century the differences of race and culture and the special conditions created by slavery, which not only made a hierarchy but set in opposition the two˙extreme classes, at the beginning permitted not the least development of common feeling between the lords of the sugar mills and the masses of slaves. But the psychology of the dominant class under the patriarchal regime, in which the big house and the chapel helped each other reciprocally, imposed itself in such a way and so strongly on society that it ended by giving a tone to the whole social life, subjecting to its influence not only slaves assimilated to the whites, but the free population of rural workers.[6] Besides, as Gilberto Freyre has emphasized, "what the plantation, monoculture, and slavery accomplished in the direction of making an aristocracy, setting apart the extremes of Brazilian society, lords and slaves, with a scanty and insignificant filling of free people 'sandwiched' between the antagonistic extremes, was in large part canceled out by the effect of miscegenation." These crossings which contributed so much to social democ-

---

slave quarters, developed among the lords of the sugar plantations, says Gilberto Freyre, "the same taste for the sofa, for the rocking chair, for cuisine, for women, for horses, for gambling." Montesquieu (*Persian Letters,* Letter 78), referring to the inhabitants of the Peninsula, had expressed the opinion that "he who remains seated ten hours a day gains twice the esteem of him who sits no more than five hours, for man acquires nobility by taking his ease in a chair." In Minas Gerais, as Southey asserts and as Pedro Calmon (*Formação brasileira*) reminds us, no one had ever seen a white man take an agricultural implement in his hands.

[6] The organization of the sugar plantation with its mill, at once factory and fortress, not only furnished our first product and our first money (sugar), the most powerful agency of colonization and the mainstay of our social organization, but also contributed notably to the defense of the land along the coast. Factory and fortress, with its numerous population of slaves and rural workers, it was the big house of the plantations that opposed the most tenacious resistance to the Batavian invasion, so closely connected with the history of sugar cultivation, which laid the first basis of our civilization. The massapê lands supported near the coast the plantations in whose big houses, walled and built like fortresses in order to resist the attacks of Indian tribes, there were forged discipline and organization, the arms for the defense of the colony against pirate raids and the Dutch invasions. The very geographic unity of the country is, in part, at least as far as the strip along the coast is concerned, a product of the patriarchal economic regime in which the rural aristocracy of the lords of the sugar mills was formed, and later, in the nineteenth century, that of the great leaders of politics and of the Empire.

ratization and furnished, with the mestizos, the first elements of reaction against the lords of the manor, the social rise of the ablest of the negroid element, the growing hostility between country and city and between agriculturists and merchants, and finally the development of the urban bourgeoisie ended by sapping at the base the solidity and prestige of the rural aristocracy of the lords of the big houses, who represented in Brazilian history "the tendency that was most characteristically Portuguese, that is, traditionally minded, in the sense of patriarchal stability." The social structural rigidity which was formed and maintained for almost three centuries, based upon sugar (plantation) and the Negro (slave quarters) and multiplied near the coast in vast enterprises directed by white masters and cultivated by an army of Negroes, had, besides its social and economic function of the first importance, a role of a primary order in the struggles with aborigines and later with the French pirates and the Dutch invaders.

But, in proportion as the organizations of the sugar mills multiplied, concentrating the Negro population around the big houses and giving rise to the rural aristocracy based on monoculture and slave labor, there developed under the influence of the sugar reign, and in the shade of the splendor of rural life, the bourgeoisie of the cities. There were two societies, both heterogeneous and complex—one solidly constructed, the other equalitarian, one prosperous and rich, the other sunk in urban misery—and they were not slow in confronting each other and entering into conflict, with their opposed tendencies and mentalities. The little cities of the coast with their rustic, village aspect, with their small trade, their drygoods shops, and their wine taverns, developed in their free population of Portuguese, generally of Jewish race, a new, more malleable and dynamic society, in which were found conditions favorable to the expansion of "the Semitic tendencies of the Portuguese adventurer toward merchandising and business." When in the seventeenth century the civilization still was purely agricultural, there were already present symptoms of the struggle which was to open in the following century and explode in the "War of the Peddlers," between the rural nobility already deeply sunk in debt and the urban bourgeoisie, in which the mercantilism of the Portuguese immigrant was slowly raising its strength above the ruin of the lords of the sugar mill. The social structure of the cities, before the defeat of the aristocrats of Olinda in 1710 by the merchants of Recife, had already been organized on the model of the patriarchal and the slave-owning system of the colony. To the mansions of the rural aristocracy corresponded, beginning with the seventeenth century, the mansions of rich Portuguese whose clientele swarmed on the ground floor, as in the shade of the big house collected the mass of slaves in the slave quarters. "The mansion reproduced deliberately," as Pedro Calmon points out, "a social hierarchy. On the noble floor lived the master, and on the ground floor downstairs, his slaves, and many families had sixty or seventy or more persons who were not necessary." In contrast, however, with the lordly organizations of the sugar plantations, this social hierarchy, graduated by the distinction between masters and slaves, rose above the mass of the free population of small merchants, peddlers, and artisans, who were neither masters nor slaves, and who constituted by their preponderant majority, their mercantile activity, and by the mixture of races and cultures, a dynamic reality which developed in time as a force for equality. But, if they tended to differentiate themselves even to the state of creating opposition between these two societies, rural and urban, which were formed on the coast and its vicinity, more profoundly different from them was the society which developed in the interior of the country—that of the shepherds and cattle raisers of the sertão.

Colonial society, divided on the coast between the sugar plantations and the cities, between the rural aristocracy and the urban bourgeoisie, was divided again under geographic and economic pressure between these societies of the coast strip and those of the interior which grew up as distinct branches, "not understanding each other and without any contact." While, in fact, on the coast by the patriarchal economy accomplished a singularly notable colonization enterprise, and while there arose with the organization of the sugar plantations a second line of resistance and defense of the colony, the march of the cattle and the armed expeditions into the interior, impelled by economic factors, were undertaking the task of penetrating and conquering the land. What is generally pointed out in these phenomena of dislocation of the masses that we call the bandeiras and the internal migrations, induced by pastoral life with its geographic and social function, is no more than its economic consequences and the expansion of the territorial domain. Certainly the eighteenth century, thanks to this double movement of herds driven by cowboys searching for fields and natural pasturage [7] and of the bandeirantes chasing Indians and searching for gold and precious stones, was the century of conquest and integration of the nation, which was being formed in the immensity of the territory. The requirements of labor, the thirst for gold, and the necessity for raising herds began and finished in two centuries a political and demographic task of the greatest importance recorded in our history, through which Brazilian territory was expanded, conquered, reconnoitered, and marked by nuclei of settlements. "Forcing back the frontier beyond the conventional meridian of Tordesillas," says André Carrazzoni, "the tamers of the sertões, the beaters of the forest, the animators of

[7] In the Northeast, "in proportion as the sugar plantations grew, the pastoral area and the virgin forest kept shrinking rapidly," says Gilberto Freyre. The single-crop system of sugar drove the cattle into the interior. The settlement of the interior, from north to south, and moving westward, was largely, as we have already pointed out, a natural function of that economic agent of our primitive rural organization. But one must make a distinction, with Aurélio Pôrto ("A Funcão socio-geográfica do gado rio-grandense," *Jornal do Comércio*, Nov. 10, 1935). "In the north, in the center south," he writes, "it was the man driving his herds of cattle into the hinterland, settling there with the admirable organization of the corrals that opened the way to the peopling of the land. The São Francisco was the wonderful route of the first penetration. Soon after, the curve ascended to the north, along the great rivers, and brought to the extreme Northeast the possibility of making a good living on the plains." In the extreme south, in Rio Grande, the contrary is to be seen. "It was the ox that called man. It was the economic wealth already in existence (cattle and natural pasturage) and the very special conditions of the environment, fitted as it was for all parts of the process of breeding, that attracted the Portuguese and the Spaniard. And, as neither conquered the other, they divided the territory, fixing the boundary line with long bloody marks. Both, with the magnificent resources to be found there, were to be amply provided with meat and hides. At the beginning the activity of the Portuguese was simply that of a herdsman. The movement of cattle reached Laguna, which at the beginning of the eighteenth century became the great cattle center of Rio Grande. The Minuan Indians soon allied themselves with the Portuguese and became the drivers of pampa herds to the colony of Sacramento. Later, cattle forced the settlement of man on the soil, and the first ranches came into existence in the vicinity of Viamão. Later they spread through the neighboring plains. But man in defense of his lands became warlike, and inevitably his interests collided with those of his neighbors who were settling beyond the Plata River."

the deserts, all those men who created the heroism of the bandeiras, were pioneers of the territorial greatness of the Brazil of today." And if the fixing of the limit of the territory, or the exercise of the powers of the Empire constituted a frontier, which for Ratzel "is a peripheric organism which advances or retreats, measuring the force or the weakness of the society which it limits," the expansion of this territory to its present-day frontiers gives us the measure and the most vigorous expression of the immense expansionist force of this society which carried it out. But not less important are the social effects of this movement of population and this dislocation of frontiers: the society to which they gave place, the profound differences which they established between the coast and the interior, and the social types which they created and which reflect the nature of their relations, their dispersive activities, and the origins of their formation. These two facts of the extreme mobility of the population of the interior, which begins with the movement of herding and has as its major expression the adventurous nomadism of the bandeirantes, and their marked heterogeneity due to the coexistence of three fundamental elements (white, Indian, and mestizo) contributed notably to develop the individualistic feeling and equalitarian and democratic ideas which characterized the society of the plateau and of the interior.

To be sure, in colonial society as in ancient society and in the feudal order, people do not have the idea of humanity in general, as is demonstrated by their sentiments with regard to the African and the Indian, nor that of the individual, as is revealed by the distinctions of classes, the regime of slavery, and the pressure which society exerts on the individual. But these distinctions and these pressures are incomparably less in the societies of the plateau and the interior, made up for the most part of mestizos, part white and part Indian, and whose social life "without big houses but also without slave quarters," based almost exclusively on cattle and scattered by the mobility of population, created in the pastoral zone "a type of civilization opposed to the sugar civilization." It was especially with the movement of populations, resulting from the incessant exchange of influence, as with the genetic mixture of races, that the classes and their differences grew less, as much through the assimilation of the individuals which they separated as through the differentiation of the individuals which they included. The activities of the bandeirantes and of cattle breeding completed by their modes of life the work of liberating the individual: living almost according to the law of nature, a great part of the time far from home, and separated by thousands of kilometers from the civilization of the coast. This race of mamelucos, arrogant and brave, accustomed to counting upon themselves, formed, in the free atmosphere of the interior, the social material most favorable to the constitution of a law that was in a way more individualistic and more equalitarian. In the cattle-breeding zones the direct contacts which the system of labor established between workers, generally few, and the boss, placing them on a plane of equality or at least comradeship ("even today the peon on the cattle-raising ranch in the central south has the symbolic name of comrade"), the chief exigencies of a technical nature which follow from the activity of peon and cowboy, and the fact that the workers of the pastoral zone as a rule are free considerably reduced the social distance between the cattle breeders and their workmen. It was exactly contrary to the situation in the sugar zone, where the workers were slaves and the technique of production, if not more elementary, was more limited and more routine, and the boss, as A. A. de Melo Franco says, "could remain as he did fortified in his big houses, directing the Negro group of the sugar-cane fields and mills through stewards, foremen, and factors." More gregarious than the sertanejo, the agriculturist of the forest "did not pass out of the family phase of his evolution," writes Pedro Calmon, "and the proprietors were united for certain ceremonies and for the tie of marriage which fixed their little aristocracy," in these fragmentary, scattered societies, the customs of which, weakened by the instability of the social organization, were softened as much by their democratic character as by the greater accessibility to heterogeneous elements and by their more lively consciousness of common peril that came from isolation and from distance.

The social physiognomy was not much modified on the plateau, when the cycle of gold was established with the discovery and exploitation of the gold mines: in the towns and cities which the bandeirantes founded, or which have their origin in mining work, there grew up a new society without great class differences, retired and suspicious, composed in great part of miners and slaves, merchants and peddlers, farmers and cattle raisers. No society was formed in Brazil under such diverse ethnic and cultural influences as this which was born in the tumult of the bandeiras and in the struggles between the Portuguese and the mestizos, and which grew with the extractive industry of gold and the exploitation of diamonds. Founded by Paulistas, who discovered the mines and ended by being driven out of their own property after the final combat of Rio das Velhas in 1709, it suffered on the one hand the successive invasions of the bandeiras made of whites, mestizos, and Indians, and on the other the assaults of the Portuguese coming from Portugal and from various captaincies and of the sertanejos of Bahia—the "emboabas" who disputed the control of the mining region and seized it from the discoverers. To these mixed and crossed races were added the Negro slaves brought in large droves for working the mines. In these new societies formed by the rapid action of heterogeneous elements, usually separated from their families and their races, as in the Greek colonies cited for example by C. Bouglé, "it is not groups but individuals that we find (hence their individualistic character); and among these individuals who are organizing their life competition, less restrained by custom, is more fruitful, wealth is more mobile, and distinctions are more rapidly attenuated." Hence their equalitarian character. The reign of the metals which was installed in the mountains of the central south was certainly so important from the economic point of view that it supplanted the reign of sugar, transferring to the south the center of economic and political life of the colony; but from the social point of view it did not give rise to a new structural system, nor did it change noticeably in its essential line that which was already sketched on the plateau. The movement of the mines, the richness of the surface soil, the mobility of wealth, the ease with which money could be made, the very fluctuations of the extractive industry, and the rapidity of evolution of this economic cycle did not give the mine owners, who rivaled the sugar planters in opulence and luxury, either the time or the conditions that were favorable to stratification of a social hierarchy with the tranquil solidity of the aristocratic patriarchal system of Pernambuco. It was in these societies of the plateau, unstable and heterogeneous, adventurous and democratic, that there developed the spirit of liberty and political emancipation to which the mother country, squeezing them through the tax collector [8] and the oppressive measures of the Royal Letter of 1719, furnished the spark for the explosion in the revolts of Pitanguí and of Vila-Rica in 1720; and it was in them that there were forged in conflicts with the mother country, from Filipe dos Santos to Tiradentes in 1789, the first arms of the republican idea and the first forms of the national consciousness.

The singularly notable work of the missionaries, who from the earliest period of colonial life had traversed Brazil from north to south, planting Catholicism in the heart of our land, and making it really "the cement of our unity," and the wars with the French and the Dutch, especially the latter, for whose expulsion there united in defense of the soil and the faith, whites, Indians, and Negroes, Paulistas, men of Rio, Pernambuco, and Bahia, had already established the bases for the formation of the spirit and unity of the nation. But the tremendous conquest and geographical expansion accomplished by the exploration of the Amazon basin and the development of the pastoral industry and, above all, in the seventeenth century, by the epic of the bandeirantes who attained the Andes and pushed on with Manuel Prieto to the Pacific, thus forcing the change from the dividing line of Tordesillas to the present limits of our territory, created by this movement of frontiers a population of scattered nuclei extremely distant from one another. From this point of view, through their expansionist power, the bandeirantes were a dissociative phenomenon, tending to break up the population, scattering it over the vastness of the territory. The dispersion of the colonial population, continually more and more rarefied as the frontiers were pushed back, and as the centers of population multiplied in the discovered territory, and the differences of types of economy and of social organization, of ethnic character, of cultural level, and of political tendency, between the coast and the interior, almost entirely separated from each other, attenuated and dissolved the unity and the collective consciousness that was growing up. The bandeiras, nevertheless, on one hand, pulverized society into small groups, making it jump like sparks all over, and contributed on the other hand to assimilating and to fusing them, leading by the intensity and frequency of contact in their internal migrations to the greatest interchange of influences which has

[8] Undoubtedly, the excesses of the treasury in its tax-collecting program touched the lordly domains of the aristocratic families, too, those families which grew up in the sugar civilization; but the new feudal lord, with all due regard to proportion and the differences of regime, did not lack resources for meeting the blows of the mother country and the appetite of the tax collector. Moreover, the solidity of the social structure of the sugar plantations, the richness of their deep soil, the extension of their vast domains, isolated and transmitted intact from father to eldest son, and the laws which prohibited attaching their lands for debt, gave great stability to the fortunes accumulated by the landed aristocracy. All the moves of the treasury, which were such blows to the inhabitants of Minas, failed against the power and authority of the lord of the sugar plantation, when he could not deal directly with the mother country. Sugar was not only a product which we exploited; it was also, as has been pointed out, our first money. It was in the hands of his city creditor, to whom his own improvidence had brought him, that the sugar aristocrat who lived in sumptuous and spendthrift fashion was fated to end. Hence the struggle which grew up and ended with the victory of the merchants of Recife in 1710, a struggle between that city, in which the Portuguese dominated, and Olinda, the center of the aristocracy, seat of the bishopric and of the government of Pernambuco. The conflict between the urban bourgeoisie and the rural nobility later took on the aspect of a reaction against the mother country, with opposition to the governor who was supported by Recife, and finally in the bandeira unleashed by Bernardo Vieira de Melo of the Republic of Olinda, an aristocratic republic patterned after the Republic of Venice.

80. Fortress of Monte Serrat (dating from the period of the Dutch invasion), Salvador, Bahia.
Photo by Voltaire Fraga, in Brazilian Institute of Geography and Statistics.

81. Fortress of St. Anthony (1772) in Salvador, Bahia.
Photo by Voltaire Fraga, in Brazilian Institute of Geography and Statistics.

82. "Battle of Guararapes," oil painting by Vítor Meireles.
Photo by Rembrandt.

83. "The Departure of the Gold Caravan," oil painting by Almeida Júnior.
Photo by the Museu Paulista.

84. "Bandeirantes," oil painting by Henrique Bernadelli.
Photo by Carlos.

85. The first inhabitants and Fernão Dias Pais Leme.
Peristyle, left side, Museu Paulista. Photo by Museu Paulista.

86. Palace of Justice, dating from 1660, Salvador, Bahia.
Photo by Voltaire Fraga, in Brazilian Institute of Geography and Statistics.

87. Ouro Preto. Tiradentes Square.
Photo by Radio Inconfidência, Minas Gerais.

88. Pantheon of the Inconfidência conspiracy (the old penitentiary), Ouro Preto.
Photo by Radio Inconfidência, Minas Gerais.

89. Former Palace of the Viceroys and Imperial Palace (now Department of Post Office and Telegraph).
Photo by Stille, in collection of the College of Philosophy of São Paulo.

90. "Dom João VI," oil painting by anonymous artist, perhaps José Leandro de Carvalho, Church of the Rosary, Rio de Janeiro.
Photo by Vosylius, in collection of the Census Bureau.

91. "Independence or Death," oil painting by Pedro Américo.
Reproduction of the canvas preserved in the Main Hall of the Museu Paulista.
Photo by Museu Paulista.

92. José Bonifácio de Andrada e Silva, the Father of Independence.
Photo by Museu Paulista.

93. "Coronation of Pedro I," oil painting by J. B. Debret.
Photo by Rembrandt.

94. Palace of the Acclamation in Salvador, Bahia.
Photo by Voltaire Fraga, Urbo Salvador, in Brazilian Institute of Geography and Statistics.

95. Pedro II, before attaining his majority, in 1840.

96. "Pedro II, Emperor," oil painting by Pedro Américo.
Photo by Rembrandt.

97. "Battle of Avaí," oil painting by Pedro Américo.
Photo by Rembrandt.

98. "Naval Battle of Riachuelo," oil painting by Vítor Meireles. Photo by Rembrandt.

99. Duke of Caxias, the Pacifier (Luiz Alves de Lima e Silva, Rio de Janeiro, 1803–1880),
who by his invaluable work as military leader and statesman, bringing peace to the provinces,
saved and consolidated the union of the fatherland.
Photo from the collection of the Companhia Melhoramentos of São Paulo.

100. General Manuel Luiz Osório, Marquis of Erval (born in Rio Grande do Sul, 1808, died at Rio de Janeiro, 1879), pride of the Brazilian army and one of the heroes of the Paraguayan War.
Photo from the collection of the Companhia Melhoramentos of São Paulo.

Barão do Amazonas

101. Admiral Barroso (Francisco Manuel Barroso, Baron of Amazonas, born in Portugal, 1804, died in Uruguay, 1882), victorious in the battle of Riachuelo, "one of the greatest naval feats known to history."
Photo from the collection of the Companhia Melhoramentos of São Paulo.

102. Admiral Marquis de Tamandaré (Joaquim Marques Lisboa, born in Rio Grande do Sul, 1807, died at Rio de Janeiro, 1897), one of the great figures of the Brazilian army.
Photo from the collection of the Companhia Melhoramentos of São Paulo.

103. Cathedral of Petrópolis, in which lie the mortal remains of the Emperor Pedro II and the Empress.
Photo by Preising, in *Travel in Brazil*, Vol. I, No. 3, p. 19.

104. Benjamim Constant Botelho de Magalhães,
the founder of the Republic.

105. Counselor Rui Barbosa, the principal author
of the Constitution of 1891. Photograph of the
period of the Provisional Government, 1890.

106. Baron do Rio Branco (José Maria da Silva Paranhos, Rio de Janeiro, 1845–1912),
well known historian, geographer, and diplomat, the "Deus Terminus" of Brazil, as Rui
Barbosa called him.
Photo from the collection of the Companhia Melhoramentos of São Paulo.

107. Counselor Rodrigues Alves, who presided over the transformation of the city of Rio de Janeiro, together with Mayor F. Pereira Passos, and over the extinction of yellow fever, with Osvaldo Cruz.

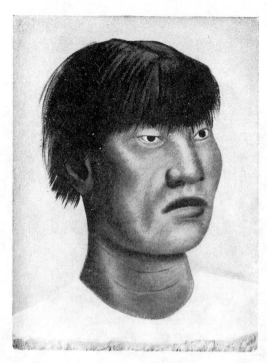

108. "Head of an Indian," mural by Cândido Portinari.
Photo by Vosylius, property of Sr. Mário de Andrade.

109. "Indians," study for one of the murals of the Ministry of Education and Health.
Photo by Vosylius.

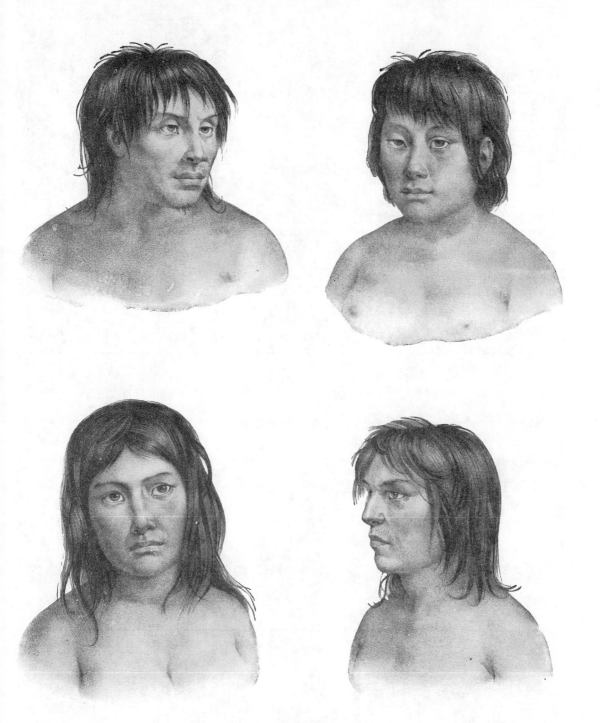

110. Machacari and Camaca Indians.
Rugendas, *Voyage pittoresque au Brésil* (1835), Plate 2/3.

111. Hunter.
Collection of the Municipal Library of São Paulo. Rugendas, *Voyage pittoresque au Brésil*,
Plate s/n.

112. "Negro," oil painting by Cândido Portinari.
Photo by Vosylius, property of Sr. Carlos Drummond de Andrade.

113. "Fernão Dias Pais Leme," statue by Luiz Brizzolara.
Photo by Museu Paulista.

ever been carried on on the plateau and in the interior. Peoples were mixed, and with the discovery of the mines they met anew in mountain mining camps, as well as in the plains of Pernambuco, in the Dutch War, whites, Negroes, Indians, and mestizos, peoples of the north and south, instigated by the desire for gain and attracted by the covetousness of gold. Of the two languages which were spoken—the Portuguese which children were learning in school, and the Indian which was spoken in the family, according to the testimony of Antônio Vieira—the Portuguese language, affirms Aires do Casal, only then, in 1755, began to predominate and become the general language. Ethnic and cultural differences between the peoples of the coast and of the north, among whom Portuguese, Negroes, and mixtures of white and Negro mixture predominated, and those of the plateau of São Paulo, made up of Portuguese and Spaniards, mamelucos, and Indians, whose families lived intimately connected one with another, began to grow weaker with the fusion of peoples and races, as a result of the continual movement of populations in the Brazilian hinterland. The intense activity of the bandeirante, descendant of Indians and searcher for mines of gold and silver, joined the slower but none the less efficacious work of the trade carried on by herdsmen, intermediaries between the sertão and the coast, "who did not limit themselves," writes Pedro Calmon, "to guiding animals of burden, but were also the messengers, the mailmen, the ambulatory businessmen, spreading along their way the ideas and novelties acquired in the cities."

So then, when mining declined at the end of the eighteenth century, the sentiment of national unity and the idea of emancipation were not only latent but alive. This is the century not only of territorial expansion, which attained its plenitude with the treaties of Madrid (1750) and of Santo Ildefonso (1777), but also of the nativistic reactions—the War of the Peddlers in Recife in 1709, and of the emboabas in Minas in 1710, the two conspiracies of Vila-Rica, that of 1720 which had its martyr in Filipe dos Santos, and that of 1789, in which the heroic figure of Tiradentes was the polarizing nucleus of that mystic fluid which was irradiated by the ideas of liberty, of students, poets, priests, and magistrates. On the plateau the Paulistas and Mineiros—like the people of the north in the second century in the campaign against the Dutch—had had, from the beginning of the third century, their baptism of fire, to construct the unity and independence of the nation, dreamed of in the conspiracy and in the trenches, whose foundation had been cemented with the blood of martyrs. The community of dangers incurred, and later the remembrance of the great actions accomplished in common—"this is the ordinary means," observes Lucien Febvre, "by which the national feeling is confirmed and exalted." It was in the face of the enemy—made up in the beginning of foreigners and afterward by the mother country with its tax policy and oppression—that Brazilians began to recognize themselves as a single people. In the time of Dom João VI, when the movement which resulted in the independence of the land was in progress, proclaimed in 1822 by Dom Pedro I, one may say that Brazil was already unified and made one. The moral factor of religion, the work of penetrating and peopling the territory, the contact and mixture of peoples to which it gave rise, the fundamental unity of customs and traditions, the unity of language which became established, and the conflicts with the mother country, had in fact formed, on the conquered soil possessed in common, all those elements which constitute, by binding together different environments and social types,[9] the organic and moral solidarity of a nation. But, although less intense, the forces which were working to break up the society and the country attained, before the first Empire was installed, an acute phase, whether with the separatist ferments which were burning the most prosperous provinces of Brazil, or with the mad policies of the mother country, which, despairing, declared the independence of the provinces in order to weaken the bonds which tied them to the central power, leaving without effect the institution of the tribunals of justice of Rio, and trying to make the Prince Regent return to Portugal. Sedition with nativistic tendencies and republican character, which in 1817 broke out in Pernambuco, was rapidly put down in the government of Dom João VI, by the energy of Count dos Arcos, Governor of Bahia; but the spirit of disorder and secession was propagated, with the lack of equality in culture and economics of one region as compared with another, with the differences of political reaction on the part of different environments and social types, whose lack of understanding and opposition were aggravated by distance and by isolation, and with the shock between natives and Portuguese, the antagonism between nativists and reactionaries, and the conflict between the aspirations of liberty and conservative tendencies.

All the indecisions and perplexities, advances and retreats, which characterized the political life of the first half of the nineteenth century from the rise of Brazil to a kingdom and the campaign for independence, and which can be attributed to the irresolute spirit of Dom João VI and the impulsive temperament of Dom Pedro I, come

[9] The very different societies into which the old colonial society was divided, and to which there correspond three distinct mentalities—that of the country, that of the cities of the coast, and that of the plateau—gave rise to "social types" which were formed and developed in social climates that were notably diverse but isolated from one another. Hence the at times radical differences in political attitudes and reactions in the face of the same situation. The lord of the sugar plantation in the north; the lord of the city mansion—a type of wealthy bourgeois—of the coast cities, who afterwards multiplied through the interior; the cattleman and the peddler; the bandeirante, hunter of half-breeds and tamer of the frontier; the owner of the cattle-breeding fazendas, the cowboy and the bandit, frontier types, and the gaucho (cowboy of the south), who developed in the cattle-breeding regions, constitute so many different social types, to which, under the Empire, there would later be added the coffee grower, corresponding in the south to the aristocracy of sugar, and a product of the same single-crop system with large plantations and slave labor; the drummer, an intermediary between the interior population and that of the coast, with a civilizing role, and the farmer of the pampas, in Rio Grande. The origins of each of these and other social types, how and when they arose, their essential function and the complementary functions which customs and necessity added, their characteristics and habits of life and the social role they played, all has been clarified in the works of social history or live again for us in the vivid pages of fiction. The differences between these social types are not, however, determined only by differences of economic and productive systems (cultivation of sugar cane, pastoral industry): the geographic conditions of the cattle-breeding regions, so diverse in the extreme south and in the sertões, gave rise to different types of cowboys—the cowboy of the north (vaquero) and the cowboy of the south (gaucho); the latter was different from the former in dress, language, customs coming from the habitat of the Indian horseman of the south, and by his adventurous and bellicose spirit. Both were strong and fearless, but the gaucho was "more agile," writes Aurélio Pôrto (*loc. cit.*), "and more flexible, for he had in front of him the green savanna, almost endless, to fly over on horseback, throwing his bolas, his lasso and couching his lance, while there [in the north], clad in leather, pricked by the spines of the bushes, man felt, even when pursuing fleeing game, the overwhelming hostility of nature."

rather from an antagonism of interest which split the society into extreme factions, and from the divorce which up to this time had isolated one from another the various groupings into which the country was divided, taking away its unity and holding up before its eyes the phantom of its dismemberment. The conflict between the federative spirit which had its roots in the local regionalism of the hereditary captaincies, and the unifying tendencies of the monarchical regime, exploding in revolt and seditions in the provinces, raised barriers between the latter and the central government and made an agreement between the political forces in action ever more difficult. The weakness of Dom João VI and the instability of Pedro of Bragança gave meanwhile to both, as later his spirit of moderation and equilibrium gave Dom Pedro that plasticity which Euclides da Cunha noted with relation to the Prince Regent, which enabled him "to adjust himself to the incoherency of the protean society in which he arose," and which was maintained all through the first reign and the Empire. The most solid thing from a social point of view in this tumultuous and anarchical society was still the rural aristocracy of the lords of the sugar plantations, at times reactionary and always conservative, which withdrew, distrustful, while the political struggles lacerated the bourgeoisie of the city, setting against one another the most diverse factions. The single-crop system, the plantation, and slavery, which in the words of Gilberto Freyre "conditioned so decisively the social development of Brazil," were to furnish to the nascent Empire, once order had been assured, its great political lords—the barons of the massapê land in the north and the aristocrats of the coffee fazendas in the south—in the second half of the nineteenth century. It was, in fact, upon the regime of patriarchal economy and the rural aristocracy to which it gave rise that the monarchy relied to resist the difficulties of political struggles going on in the center, or breaking out at a distance in the provinces. The shocks between the monarchical and democratic currents, the federalists and the unitarians, the absolutists and the liberals, and the different political reactions of the provinces, isolated among themselves, being reflected in the violent debates of the legislature and in the bitter polemics of the press, in street riots and local rebellions,[10] were creating an atmosphere charged with the electricity of storms, and were pushing the maintenance of order to the front among the preoccupations of the government and the Empire. In this heterogeneous, inconsistent, and unstable society, split by in-

[10] These local revolts during the whole first half of the nineteenth century resulted not only from the conflicts between the federalists and unitarians, absolutists and liberals. During the whole period, nativistic feeling continued very strong and led to periodic explosions in the greatest centers of Portuguese power. Reactions against the Portuguese, naturally more violent in colonial Brazil, broke out again at the time of independence, especially in the war of independence in Bahia—"that transatlantic piece of Portugal," in the phrase of Humberto de Campos. But in the coast rebellion of liberal and social character that broke out in the province of Pernambuco in 1848 and 1849, with socialistic claims, nativistic feeling exploded with surprising violence. "The simple fact that on June 26, 1848, a Liceu student was wounded by a Portuguese," Figueira de Melo tells us, "gave rise to the carnage and fighting of that day and the next, on which to the accompaniment of cries of 'Kill the sailor' various Portuguese who were pacifically going about their business were killed." There was then drawn up a petition to the provincial legislature which demanded, besides the calling of a constitutional assembly to take up a program of social reform in harmony with liberal progress, "the exclusion of aliens from retail trade, and the exclusion of all unmarried Portuguese within fifteen days, as implacable enemies of Brazil." Cf. J. M. Figueira de Melo, *Crônica da Rebelião Praieira em 1848 e 1849* (Rio: Tipografia do Brasil, J. J. da Rocha, 1850).

ternal dissensions and by offenses directed against the national unity and against the state, only those could remain in power who had the courage to renounce doctrinal ideas, to adjust themselves to a multiple and complex reality, extremely changeable, and to whom principles served only as opportunistic tactics, varying according to events.

The great men through this tormented epoch were the architects of the social and political order, like that notable figure José Bonifácio, who occupied the ruins of a storm which he himself had helped to unleash, and whose ministry, menaced by the liberal movement, soon after independence was proclaimed, "saved the revolution," writes Euclides da Cunha, "following the terrible policy of Saturn crushing the revolutionaries." Not other was the function after the 7th of April of the Regency, which was set up "as a moderator of national agitation, as an escape measure for the potential revolt." In the period of the Regency, the three greatest men of the time could in fact do nothing else than restore order in political chaos, gluing together those forces without cohesion and fusing them into two parties which were to fill the history of the Empire. Evaristo da Veiga served the monarchical principle, "one identified with the unity of the country"; under the iron fist of Father Diogo Antônio Feijó, who restored civil authority, demagogic anarchy was tamed and put down, and Bernardo Pereira de Vasconcelos rose from the liberal ranks with all the force of his indomitable energy to lead a campaign against disorder. "I was a liberal," he explained his new attitude later on; "then liberty was new in the country and was in the minds of all, not in the laws, not in practical ideas. Power was everything; I was a liberal. Today, however, the aspect of things is different: democratic principles have won everything, and have put much in danger. Society which then ran risk through power now runs risk through disorganization and anarchy." The republican idea which even in the colonial period had in 1789 found its most beautiful expression in the Inconfidência of Minas, and had inspired the two vigorous movements of Pernambuco in 1817 and in 1824, suffered a profound blow with the monarchical reaction which led to the Regency, but only to break out again with unmeasured violence before this period was over in the war of the *farrapos*. In this campaign which lasted ten years, from 1835 to 1845, limited to Rio Grande,[11] and which was fought for "political independence under the auspices

[11] The mistakes in the administration of the province, the excessive taxes and recruiting were the fuse laid to give the spark to the movement which, although with strong separatist tendencies in its defiance to the central government, leaned, as Celso Vieira writes, with the support of the text of Aug. 29, 1838, "toward a remote Brazilian confederation" ("Evolução do pensamento republicano no Brasil," in *A Margem da história da República*, pp. 35-55). But federalist and republican ideas met in the land and social landscape of Rio Grande an environment truly favorable to their development. The land, with its low hills and pampas, with their limitless horizons, "which level things and people," and the pastoral activity which in its very nature places on a level of equality peons and ranchers, cowboys and bosses, had produced in the south an original type, cavalier and warlike, vigorously individualistic and with equalitarian tendencies. It was not distinguished from other social types in Brazil especially by its language, with Spanish inflections, above all on the frontier and by its characteristic customs which cause us always to think of the gaucho with his barbecue, his maté, and his wide riding trousers. Social life as it was created by pastoral life, had given the gaucho ways of being, feeling, and acting which, while shared with the pastoral types of the north, had taken on, as we have seen, a special stamp on the plains of the south. "The farm hand, the peon, here or there in the north, the center, or the south," says Ildefonso Simões Lopes, "is rather a companion in the day's work than an obscure servant. We

of the republican system," in the Republic of Piratini, there developed in episodes of dramatic intensity the most robust demonstration of strength of federalist and republican ideas recorded by our history. But even before the farrapo revolution was suffocated and the province was pacified by Caxias, who had been waging war for three years for the regime and for national unity, the democratic principle had entered upon its decline and all the political forces, channelized in two strongly organized groups, were beginning to equip themselves for the struggle which was to last almost half a century, for the whole period of the second Empire. After 1836, the political history of Brazil can be summed up in fact, as Baron de Rio Branco observes, "in the struggle of two parties—the conservative and the liberal."

The wave of republicanism flowed back little by little, and the rest of the radical, democratic party betook itself to the ranks of the liberals for the defense of public liberty within the monarchical regime. From 1845 on, the provincial revolts being crushed one by one, the Empire continued to consolidate itself by the free play of the constitutional mechanism, which was now possible from the struggle and utilization of those organized forces between which there was an equilibrium, and which alternated in power and in opposition. Political tempests, unleashed by the passions of factions, grew less, and in spite of the temporary, unlimited interventions imposed by circumstances or necessities of the moment a continuous and permanent action of the two parties permitting an equilibrium assured the monarchy a period of splendor between 1855 and 1864, to which Dom Pedro II contributed something with his liberal temperament and spirit of moderation. But while political unification was being accomplished by the Empire, which centralized authority and moved to the court the center of gravity of public life, the social state remained without noticeable transformation over the whole extent of the territory. The very dispersion and lack of continuity of a scanty society which had spread irregularly over the country, broken up into nuclei like little islands of a vast archipelago, to use the lucid image of Nestor Duarte, and broken like an "unfastened thread, tenuous and long, without any tentacles to bring it together and promote community." The same disparity between the area of social expansion and the area of political efficiency, to which Oliveira Viana refers, was a cultural lag which since the first century had occurred "between the territorial march of society and the territorial march of power, a sort of discordance between two perimeters, the social and the political, the latter being always incomparably smaller than the former." And because of this antagonism of the desert and of distances, the very disequilibrium was not a growing disequilibrium between the men of the sertão and those of the coast, between a cultural élite educated in the European fashion and capable of rising to the height of a political system that had been born in England, and the mass of slaves and free population, rude and uncultivated, scattered and lost in the profoundest recesses of the sertão, or lost in the isolation of the plain.[12] In this social

---

often sleep with him in the damp open air. We share with him the frugal meal from our saddlebags on long trips through forest and over the plains. He is as excited as we when in the roundups of good years the number of animals with the mark of the boss has increased. Our families are not above having social relations with his."

[12] "Well versed in the writings of European publicists, glibly handling themes which had no relation with their environment, the most brilliant statesman," writes Gilberto Amado, "were certainly not always the most useful. Their political activity consisted in embroidery on questions

and political state which was characterized by the inexistence of an enlightened society, politically organized, and from which one could not get an electoral body capable
and responsible, the élite groups, small in number and in quality, with some figures
of the first importance, were and continued to be in the republic, as I wrote in 1936,
"a fragile shell of refinement applied to enormous geographic bodies, still elementary
or chaotic, little cultivated aristocracies, the main human support of which was only a
primitive, amorphous, badly cut block." [13]

But diverse factors of an economic and social order were working to bring about
a change in the structure of the country and were threatening to take away from the
Empire, with the decadence of the territorial aristocracy and the tendency toward abolition, its principal base of maintenance and resistance; namely, the lords and the slaves.
The urban centers of the coast and the plateau served doubtless as points of support
for a strong administrative system which had extended to the whole country, preserved without extinguishing it what remained of the federative system, and consolidated to the same extent the power of the Emperor, while Rio de Janeiro became the
center of a vast administration. The numerous bureaucracy to which it gave rise, and
which was to grow out of all proportion later, during the whole republican period, was
a kind of collectivism, as Gilberto Amado correctly observes, supported by the public
treasury, the elements of which were recruited among "lawyers, doctors and engineers,
former lords whose families had been ruined, sons of slaves, of mestizos and mulattoes,
distributed through public functions and liberal careers." It was slavery that, making
the work on the land seem abject, obliged the sons of free men to betake themselves to
State employment when they could not be lords and did not wish to accept the status
of slaves. Because work (rural or mechanical) was an "occupation of Negroes, mestizos
and whites believed that it would dishonor them." Urban centers like Rio and São
Paulo, meanwhile, without losing their political and administrative character, were beginning to be transformed under the influence of the economic factors, of a better system of communication and transportation, of Mediterranean immigration, and of the
changes in the distribution of population, with the profound effects upon social and
political organization. The second half of the nineteenth century—in which there
began a period of excitement and of economic initiatives, banks, factories, enterprises,
railroads, and navigation companies, the entry of immigrants and of foreign capital
although on a small scale, credit facilities, the accessibility of capital now far more
abundant, and accomplishments of every kind—tended in fact to transform the old-
world structure of the country, still depending upon slavery and the urban picture
dominated by bureaucracy. The crises of 1851, 1857, and 1864—crises of growth as
Vítor Viana calls them—resulted from the technical and economic transformation

---

of the day—foreign loans, reforms of criminal or civil law, budgetary questions, matters of parties
or elections—splendid, eloquent speeches which as far as subject matter goes might have figured
in the parliamentary annals of France or England. In those who were considered to be less cultured, that is, in a Paraná, an Itaboraí, later at Cotegipe, one could feel the experience which familiarity with business gives, the care in observing, the abundant factual background which gave
to their speeches the hard texture of reality." Cf. Amado, "As Instituicões políticas e o meio social
no Brasil," in *A Margem da história da República* (Rio: Anuário do Brasil), pp. 57-79.

[13] Lecture series "Educação e seus problemas"—"Política e educação," first lecture on Oct. 23,
1936, at the University of São Paulo.

which was going on and from the facility of producing in order to increase the circulation of wealth and to favor these transformations. Preceded by F. Caldeira Brandt at the dawn of the nineteenth century in Bahia and by J. Ramos de Oliveira in Pernambuco,[14] prepared and aided afterward by Tavares Bastos, Capanema, Teófilo Otoni, Mariano Procópio, and Teixeira Leite, and with its vigorous action supported by Viscount de Mauá—a great pioneer of technological progress who drew into his orbit intelligent satellites of the first order in business—this period marked the critical point of the little industrial revolution, which was aborted, because of special conditions which were still extremely unfavorable in our national environment.

In spite of the enterprise of the pioneers of industrial technique, this realistic policy, oriented toward the great practical problems of the national economy, could not in fact find a receptive environment either in the landed aristocracy, with its old way of the agricultural production depending upon slave labor, or in the urban bourgeoisie, with its rudimentary commerce and industry pulverized in small enterprises; either among conservatives or among liberals. Once experience had proved the advantages of free labor and of great industrial and agricultural enterprises, the system had to become general as a grave threat to the conservatives, who were in the main proprietors of land and of slaves with a low power of production. The liberals for their part, dominated by a romantic conception of politics, did not see in abolition, of which they looked at only the moral and human aspect, anything else than a stage in the march of liberal ideas toward the victory of the democratic principle. It was impossible to establish harmony between the technical and economical transformations on the one hand and the social and political changes on the other, in the face of the tremendous gulf which juridical mentality had created between the economic and the social. On the advent of the liberals to power, favored by the Emperor, there began a "policy of dynastic suicide," on which Dom Pedro II had embarked without understanding perhaps that the throne rested on the landed aristocracy and that to weaken this aristocracy would be to weaken the throne. The situation of balance which the imperial policy had attained in 1862, expressed, as Gilberto Amado observes, "the fullness of the high tide. There had meanwhile commenced the conservative outgoing tide, and a strong democratic current was about to come to the fore. An unexpected event held it back, however. This was the Paraguayan War." After the long campaign (1864–1870) carried on in the south, which contributed so much to tightening the bonds that held together Brazilians of practically all provinces, whites, mestizos and Negroes, fusing the populations on the field of battle, political passions were rekindled, and there broke out with a new intensity in the parliament and in public meetings a struggle for the federative principle, taken up with vigor in the Republican Manifesto of 1870, for the abolition of slavery, and in general for liberal ideas. The growing differentiation and complication of urban societies, broken up into a great number of groups, the progressive march of liberal ideas, and the very centralization which, unopposed to social complication and far from being contrary to it, was preparing for democracy, had prepared the way for the strengthening republican current. It was, nevertheless, from the abolition of slavery that the decisive blow came. The replacement of the regime of slave labor by that of free labor, sapping the very bases of the agrarian economy and

[14] Cf. Vítor Viana, *O Banco do Brasil*, p. 362, and V. Correia Filho, "A Iniciativa do Caldeira Brandt," in *Jornal do Comércio*, Oct. 3, 1937.

the rural aristocracy, and therefore the economic foundations of the Empire, produced such an effect that a little over a year later the throne finally fell; the religious question and the military question had already deprived it of two other supports represented by the conservative forces of the church and the army.

The Empire represented in our political evolution an effort at unification, sufficient for the Republic to begin without the two perils of fragmentation and of caudillism. The monarchy, by the centripetal force which dynastic institutions developed, had a historic role in the formation of nationality. It was the first force which intervened to restore order in social chaos and to derive from this tumult political effects; and, whether putting down local rebellion and revolts in the provinces, or maintaining balance between the two forces organized in parties, it was able to achieve the unity of the country, passing on intact to the Republic the territorial inheritance which was handed down from our ancestors. But both the Empire, which was not able to escape the clutches of the liberal block, and the federative Republic which followed it were superstructures set up in imitation of theoretical models by an élite without a people and without the organization of public opinion, undermined by partisan struggles of a political-military nature, and hamstrung by the professional bureaucracy, which made laborious its adaptation to the forms and conditions of social life. This double movement of ideas and of things in its long history through the Empire, and the success of the individualistic philosophy, with a religious and political basis, aided by the abolition of slavery, by immigration and by the rise in industry, ended by demolishing the framework of political life which was also the framework of social life. The almost exclusive predominance of the sugar plantation owners in the north and the coffee fazendeiros in the south—a governing class to which were generally reserved the high functions of the central government as well as those of local administration—could not long continue after the destruction at its base of the wealth and preponderance of the sugar zones and the coffee cultivation, which rested, both of them, on slave labor. Abolition wiped out and ruined large properties, where lords and fazendeiros had established with slave labor their vast systems of cultivation. The abandonment of the old agricultural properties, the transmission by purchase, to the urban bourgeoisie or to the public treasury, of palaces and aristocratic residences in the south, and the decadence of the lordly domains, demonstrate clearly the degree of disorganization to which the agricultural economy had been brought by the law of the 13th of May extinguishing slavery. The social and economic structure nevertheless remained almost the same, based upon a single-crop plantation system which retarded the division of large properties, and therefore the democratization of the land; and the system even expanded in São Paulo, which was able to preserve its landed aristocracy, thanks to the inflow of immigration and foreign capital. The middle class, which never forms within a nation a compact body and a very distinct part of the whole, which always belongs a little to other classes and at certain points is confused with them—this class expanded and grew richer without being organized, as a result of the rapid movement which abrupt changes bring about in the social scale of professions and wealth during periods of transition.

But if the implantation of the republican regime was a victory of the middle class, rising against slavery, monarchy, and aristocracy and aided in the struggle by deserters from the rural nobility, the political power that had been royal or aristocratic did not become popular except in theory, and the old economic power and the new political power in reality remained closely associated. The fact is that when the Republic was proclaimed industrial capitalism, and a considerable proletariat, had not yet developed. Capitalism at this time was still in its commercial phase, and consequently depended on the exploitation of native agricultural products. The new élite which came into existence in the urban bourgeoisie, composed in general of learned men, doctors, engineers, and above all lawyers, had to find one of its points of support in the landed aristocracy, which in São Paulo was rising again with the capitalization of its agriculture, directed by fazendeiros and carried on by armies of farm hands, and was being restored in the north with the rapid assimilation of the freed Negro into the new capitalistic economy, and by the reconstruction of wealth in the sugar zones. The national policy, once the military crisis had been dominated and civil order reestablished, with Prudente de Morais, would come to gravitate round the axis constituted by São Paulo and Minas under fazendeiros and cattle raisers, which was reinforced on one side by Pernambuco and Bahia in the north, and on the other by Rio Grande, with its already powerful pastoral industry. The union of Minas and São Paulo not only permitted a balance between the north and the south, represented respectively by the northern bloc and by the great frontier states, distant and isolated, but drew into its orbit the smaller states as satellites of a political system. The gravest national crises either were solved by the force of cohesion of these two states of the central plateau which held in their hands the great levers of command, or were unleashed in civil struggles and commotions, every time the alliance broke down, and the center of gravity of national policy was moved to the north or to the south. If in the make-up of this system the center of movement of political life varied from one region to another and at times, as in the *civilista* campaign headed by Rui Barbosa, with such force that it touched all the springs of action, the major nucleus of resistance of forces of conservatism in the Republic was in the central State and especially in São Paulo, where there was formed a new landed aristocracy. We cannot say that the democratic ideal had been systematically mocked by the landholding class, newly risen to the rank of governing class, either directly by the possession of power or by utilizing political power and putting it at the service of economic power. If in fact this landed aristocracy deepened the distance between classes and converted democratic institutions into a mantle hiding a new despotism—an oligarchical despotism which it favored and sustained—it is certain that this unification of republican policy around the single-crop system of the landowners, fazendeiros, cattle raisers, and lords of sugar plantations was, within the federative system, a corrective of the first order to the decentralizing tendencies.

Certainly, given the progressive expansion of the federative principle which had its roots in tradition and drew all its force of character from isolation and from the autonomous differentiation of the provinces, built in a general way around the old captaincies, it cannot surprise us that the unity of the imperial regime gives place to the victorious federalism of 1889, with the coup d'état which destroyed the throne and began the republican regime. Federalism seemed to all the best form and the only one susceptible of maintaining national unity, in a people of heterogeneous ethnic formation and social structure, the unity of which, constituted by the provinces of the Empire, separated by great distances, in very different physical and climatic surroundings, had developed into a regime of administrative autonomy and of economic regionalism. But, if the Republic was not able to take any other form than the federative one and could only consolidate itself by the guarantee and coordination of regional freedoms, federalism without the essential complement of national parties brought in its bosom germs which were to endanger the vitality of the regime and provoke a reaction against the prerogatives of the State. Decentralization carried to an extreme hindered the work of national reorganization and, promoting the substitution of local parties for national parties and the formation of real oligarchies like those "aristocratic patriarchies" of the Empire to which Saint-Hilaire referred, permitted the monopolization of political power by the dominant regional parties directed by the great families. These parties which at the beginning, in the two first decades of the Republic, still fought for ideas, came to represent only unprecise programs, the main point of which appears to reduce itself to setting up an electoral machine and to the conquest and exploitation of political power. They are, in brief words, to employ the expression of Ostrogorski,[15] "great factories of opinion which endeavor to mechanize everything and tend to substitute for a government of responsible men, a mere government of the machine." Social, economic, and pedagogic reforms whether by the central government or by local governments, when they were not reduced to mere pretexts, gave an opportunity for the placing of protégés, and the very influx of foreign capital rendered easier the proliferation of public offices, "resulting from a superabundance of money in the treasury which," writes Gilberto Amado, "men who had no obligation to render accounts to public opinion that did not exist with regard to their deeds either good or bad did not know how to use." [16] The political conventions, in which all the interests except the general interest were represented, were in the manipulating hands of professional men, to whom Ostrogorski refers, and who employ all means in order to make the views on which they had previously fixed prevail. Unleashing a struggle by any kind of method, distributing according to services rendered or the hostility which a person has shown the party recompenses and punishments of all kinds, they arrive at the stage of incontestable power in their efforts to establish passive unanimity, to annul personalities in order to subject them to the disciplines of the party and to

[15] M. Ostrogorski, *La Démocratie et l'organisation des parties politiques* (Paris: Calmann Lévy, 1903).

[16] The parties thus became true "placement agencies," handling state employees like an electoral clientele and putting the administration at the service of an aggressive personalism and of domestic policies. Looking out for the family (*afilhadismo*) or nepotism—expressions which at first indicated the transmission from fathers to sons or from uncles to nephews of public or elective office, and then came to express, more generally, protection dispensed to individuals out of a personal or partisan interest—contributed to stratify political bodies and tended to make of administration and politics as were closed classes, like castes, ruled by a group of "political monopolists" who ran the machinery of the State. The "turning out" which in the more violent struggles marked the victory of an organized party, or of one transitory group over another, constituted the process of purging functionalism and the political chambers of the chief persons tied up with the defeated factions. But this political structure with its rigid hierarchy, based on a professional bureaucracy and supported by landholders and "doctors" (bachelors of law and physicians), was connected at the top with the political power that was in the hands of party men and at the base was tied in with the popular orders: the henchman and the heeler are characteristic types which grew up as consequences of the enlargement of political groups and the necessity of connecting the leaders, by means of intermediaries, with the inconstant and fluctuating electoral body.

continue in their policy of eliminating those values which formed the moral and intellectual basis of civilization.

Thus "begun to assure on the one hand the functioning of an ever more complex government and on the other the free expression of the opinion of ever more numerous citizens," according to the observation of Ostrogorski,[17] parties became ever more incapable of serving as the instruments of government and did nothing except to stifle, under fictitious opinions maintained by external conformism imposed on the majority, any real movement whatever of opinion. The great public powers fallen under their control became weak; administration met obstacles, the authority of leaders was diminished, absorbed as they were in the necessities and cares of elections; and, as public men were not responsible to the public, what preoccupied them was not the true interests of the public. As to opinion, "it appeared to be rather distorted than reflected by this whole system. Yet, to tell the truth, sometimes it revolted and broke the machine. It maintained its repressive power but lost its preventive power. Manipulated by parties or crushed by them, it did not succeed in doing anything more than create an atmosphere of general weakness." The policy of the governing class, the organization of a militarized police like little armies capable of standing up against the central government, the frequent appeal to force and to lack of discipline and the military crises produced by the political exploitation of the barracks, showed not only the weakness of the state in its struggle with such violent forces but "the absence of a public sentiment on which political institutions could rest and could gain in their turn another ascendancy in collective sentiments and ideals." The fact that democratic ideals were not in tune with the existing cultural pattern is proved not only by the prolonged struggles which were undergone to implant them but by the crises and revolutions which could imperil more than once the very institutions and forces that had developed in order to conserve them; "sufficiently strong to undermine the old political order," writes S. Lowrie, "they showed themselves too inconsistent to become the effective

[17] The conclusions reached by Ostrogorski in his penetrating analysis of the organization of political parties (*op. cit.*), although based on observations of parties in England and especially in North America, throw a brilliant light on the parties formed in Brazil during the Empire and the Republic, which were not sufficiently studied in their genesis, in the various phases of their development, and with regard to their methods of action. There certainly are common tendencies, as Ostrogorski tries to bring out, in the social analysis of these political forms that are revealed or appear to be revealed wherever democracy is organized party-wise or where parties come to constitute the essential springs of the mechanism of political life. But we must not lose sight of the differences in social formation, national characteristics, and historic background. These organizations, natural, useful and in any case inevitable in a democratic regime, evidently have in the particular conditions of every environment and in their social and political growth the explanation of the forms they take on, their special tendencies, and their processes of action, as well as of the services they render or the risks they cause democracy to run. For example, in Brazil, because our industrial organization only began to grow vigorously in 1920, they did not have the great influence which they had in North America; we had fewer of those alliance of "sinister interests" in which political monopolists were associated with economic monopolists, armed, because of their immense fortunes, with an inconceivably great power; but, among us, the fragmentation of opinion into "local parties," in the regime of the Republic, developing to a high degree the personalism of leaders, the regional spirit and tendencies of domination, and therefore of exploitation of political causes, still more endangered the vitality and solidity of democratic institutions. Cf. A. Tôrres, *A Organização nacional* (São Paulo: Comp. Editora Nacional—Brasiliana, Vol. 27); Oliveira Viana, *O Idealismo na constituição* (Rio, 1927).

base of a new political order." Great, then, as was the value of some eminent figures that acted upon the political scene during this period—like Prudente de Morais, Campos Sales, and Rodrigues Alves, parliamentary orators who were really notable like Rui Barbosa, and diplomats of great perspicacity such as was Rio Branco, the Deus Terminus, fixer of our frontiers—they did not succeed and could not succeed by their personal prestige and personal action in doing more than shed a brilliant light at times on democratic institutions which were wavering on the precarious and fluctuating basis of a population as yet incapable of exercising its political rights and assuring the solidity of the representative system. In the collision between the idealism of Rui Barbosa, who in his purity was the incarnation of democratic ideals and placed all his incomparable eloquence at their service, and the realism of Pinheiro Machado, who had risen with all his caudillo energy, with the authoritarian force of discipline and coordination, the latter current had necessarily to prevail, playing with its political machine, getting along without appeals to the people and to public opinion and counting upon the great indifferent and amorphous majority which existed in the Republic in order to dominate—like a "prolongation of the colony forming the *caput mortuum* of the great national organism."

But the great movement of Mediterranean immigration which began, the prosperity which installed itself in the south with the single-crop system based upon free labor and permitted the investment of Brazilian capital in industry, the influx of foreign capital on a large scale, and the very crises of coffee, from which there came other effects, the overflowing from the fields toward the city of the excess of farm workers—all these contributed vigorously to lead after 1920 to the greatest industrial development which our economic history has recorded. The social physiognomy of Rio de Janeiro was transformed, and also that of the great centers of the plateau and of some regions of the north and south as well as of Pernambuco and Rio Grande; and the development of industry and the progress of new means of transportation, and the phenomena of urban concentration, not only acted directly upon habits of life, mentality, and the very morality of groups, but produced the effect of a powerful economic current generating a spirit of association, of which the growth of larger and more active urban communities was only one of the multiple manifestations. But at the same time that this spirit of organization grew division of labor with all its effects, brought on by the growing complexity of the social system, was preparing in our urban centers in which it was installed unexpected forms of individualism. And if we consider that these phenomena of technical and industrial transformation and of concentration of population were produced in a few scattered points of the land along the coast, acquiring the greatest intensity in São Paulo, we will understand how, instead of serving as instruments of assimilation of the population, they began by accentuating the causes of economic differences, which made them unequal on different planes of prosperity and were linked in great part to diversity of physical, climatic, and demographic conditions. "Located between the intransigently Portuguese north and the slightly Spanish extreme south, São Paulo," wrote Humberto de Campos in 1919, "is a slice of bologna separating in a sandwich the halves of the same geographic piece of bread. Its immediate neighbors, the people who are undergoing little by little the effect of its civilizing influence, do not perceive this difference on account of the suavity of the transition. The northerner, principally he who comes from the interior region, is the one who can see on simple contact the radical change of the scene and of the human drama." The high degree attained by agriculture and human culture and by industrial techniques, especially in São Paulo, was in fact moving toward this State the predominance in both realms of production and increasing its capacity to create, to renovate, and to produce and therefore its civilizing power; it necessarily had to conserve it, while liberal in its political reform, in the rear guard of reaction as far as social and economic reforms were concerned.

The plantation system of landholding was still in existence at the beginning of this industrial rise, remaining the base of our economy, both in the south with the green richness of the coffee plantation, and in the north in which with the advent of power machinery in the sugar mills the old plantation grew up again. "The lord of the land moved," writes Duarte Lima, "giving place to the lord of industry who from afar, in his city office, administered the enormous machine which multiplied production." In the south, parallel with the development of industry, the fazendas were extended with their modern equipment and their lordly houses, and farm production attained proportions never before seen and appeared once again to take its position as the chief support of the national economy. The lack of labor for farm work with the diminution of immigration and of resources to pay it, and above all the depression of 1929, with its financial difficulties, made a contribution, nevertheless, to the breaking up of the old Paulista estates and to the dissemination on a large scale of small properties which had grown rapidly because of breaking up the land into lots, in zones of exhausted land and in regions in which insect enemies had produced great devastation. If the number of agricultural properties from 1930 to 1934 grew in São Paulo by 110,975 reaching a total of 274,740, while the official statistics recorded 163,765 in 1930, this difference was certainly not due merely to the breaking up of estates that existed in 1931, but to that of small and medium-sized properties scattered all through the interior of the state. But, although reduced to proper proportions,[18] we cannot deny that democratization by means of land was beginning to be seen in the central south,

---

[18] In a country of such great territorial extent and such sparse population, the large plantation is a normal fact which has a role of the greatest importance not only in economic life, but also in the conquering for civilization of unpopulated or almost desert regions. It is by the latifundium that settlement begins, and its progressive breakup is only the terminal point of a long process of evolution, accelerated by economic and demographic causes. The fact that the large estate still exists even in the very State in which property was most broken up is sufficiently demonstrated by the fact that, as there are 2,100 owners of properties greater than 500 alqueires in São Paulo, the total area of these properties (3,073,359) is almost equivalent to the total area occupied by the 22,749 owners whose lands vary from 50 to 500 alqueires, and greater than the total area occupied by the 249,990 small proprietors of 5 to 50 alqueires. If we consider a farm of less than 50 alqueires as small, one from 50 to 200 as medium, and one of more than 200 alqueires as large, we find that in São Paulo, in 1934, there were 249,990 small farms, 18,819 middle-sized ones, and 5,931 large properties with a total area of 8,726,335 alqueires. Of this total area, 2,492,852 alqueires were divided into small farms, that is, among the 249,990 owners; 1,886,124 alqueires among middle-sized properties, that is, among 18,819 owners; and 4,347,378 among large estates, that is, 5,931 owners. But the 2,001 masters of more than 500 alqueires alone cover a total area greater than the whole area divided among the 249,990 small owners. Of these, 106,572 own less than 5 alqueires, 70,400 from 5 to 10 alqueires, 49,253 from 10 to 25, and 23,765 from 25 to 50. See the *Estatística agrícola-zooténica*, published by the Secretariat of Agriculture, 1933; the agricultural and animal census, carried out in São Paulo in 1934; cf. Aguinaldo Costa, "O Latifúndio em São Paulo," in the review *Problemas*, São Paulo, 1936.

because of the double fact of the breaking up of the large properties and the subdivision of the small and medium-sized properties, so that the ownership and exploitation of cultivated land was shared by a large number of rural proprietors, while previously it had been almost completely monopolized by a small minority of the great lords of the land. This double phenomenon from which there resulted the progressive substitution of a many-crop type of cultivation for the single crop, grew more intense, as we see, as a result of the effect of the coffee crisis in 1929, which was so fruitful in economic, social, and political consequences. It was by means of it as an effect that the road to the revolution in 1930 was smoothed—a plan for liberal revolution which, when it was aborted, became a counterrevolution. The political machine of the State was broken down with the economic failure, and the dominion of the great families was brought to a close. A new economic power moved into the hands of one class of men and the old political power to another. In this breakup of agriculture, and in the dissociation between economics and politics which resulted from it, there was present the germ of a revolutionary process, the true causes of which were hidden by a mass of rapidly changing political factors, and which was necessarily to find its solution retarded by a series of internal and external factors.

The revolution of 1930 swept away the old political framework, attempting to find outside it new forces on which to rely; and in the antagonisms of economic interests, in the collisions of new political currents and of elements of the old regime which were endeavoring to survive as extinct institutions, in conflicts between civil authority and military force, a rude trial was given to the resistance of democratic ideas, which were not slow in surrendering to the assaults of authoritarian tendencies. Beliefs with relation to power, undergoing change everywhere, and the necessities of economic life tended to modify political power, which changed hands and nature through entering in 1934 upon a new democratic experiment, which came to a close three years later in the open political crisis of the decomposition of constitutional liberalism. All this period which extends from 1931 to 1937, a period of political agitation, of lack of confidence with regard to the old formulas, and of hesitation on the margins of new solutions, did not constitute politically either progress or total regress, but was "a phase of incubation." Industry on the one hand, acquiring a new importance and becoming diversified in accordance with the regional environment, in types of specialization which complete one another mutually, tended to become one of the instruments most capable of assuring a true national unity by the interrelation of economic interest. But the democratic movement appeared to be in inverse ratio to the development of large industry. Distances, on the one hand, although far from being eliminated, were considerably reduced by the rapidity of means of locomotion, by the development of commercial and military aviation, and above all by the radio, which, permitting a direct contact between men in a central situation and the people at a distance, was able to assimilate great countries to the city-state of classic civilization, developing the prestige of the chief and the leader, and reducing the importance of representatives and of parliaments, who were no longer effective intermediaries between their electors and the government. Centralization was once more deemed the only means of safeguarding moral and political unity and of solving the antinomies which exist in the play of economic forces in the national life. The new regime, installed with the support of armed forces, by the revolutionary coup of the 10th of

November, 1937, in which the crisis of liberalism broke down in the bosom of Brazilian society, accentuated the tendencies to give greater power to the President, restored central authority, dissolved parliament and political parties—those machines which it appeared practically impossible to take to pieces—assumed the control of power and of the nation, and, limiting regional prerogatives, marked the retreat of federalism to centralization. It was a new phase that was inaugurated in which the principles of order, of unity, and of national defense were once more imposed with all their force as in the period of the regency; and society now centralized—since all centralized societies are equalitarian—moved toward equalitarianism driven by great social and economic reforms,[19] while there was accomplished one of the greatest efforts of unification and reconstruction in a spirit and on a base that were eminently national.

[19] Societies evolve in the direction of equality, and after civil and political equality, they always claim economic equality; but, as has been stated, all centralized societies are equalitarian, and the most equalitarian are the most centralized. Moreover, it would seem that "if democracy exists everywhere and is on the point of existing everywhere, it is because true aristocracies," writes E. Faguet, "cannot stand centralization with its suppression of social distance." Legislators or revolutionists who promise at the same time equality and liberty can give us only one of the two, Goethe said: they are either visionaries or charlatans. Centralization doubtless favors evolution toward equalitarianism and prepares the way for democracy which can, without losing its essential qualities, take on new forms and presupposes, by the very nature of the regime, a public opinion as enlightened as it is organized, if not in the whole area of social life, at least in the whole territory reached by the march of political power.

BIBLIOGRAPHY

Amado, Gilberto, "As Instituicões políticas e o meío social no Brasil," in *A Margem da história da República* (Rio, 1923), pp. 57–58. An inquiry by writers of the generation born under the Republic.

Azevedo, Aroldo de, "Goiânia: A 'Made' City," in *Revista Brasileira de Geografia*, Vol. 3, No. 1 (Jan.–Mar., 1941), pp. 1–19.

Bonfim, Manuel, *O Brasil na América: Caracterização da formação brasileira* (Rio: Francisco Alves, 1929; 2nd ed., São Paulo: Comp. Editora Nacional—Brasiliana, Vol. 47).

Calmon, Pedro, *História social do Brasil*, Vol. 1, *Espírito da sociedade colonial,* and Vol. 2, *Espírito da sociedade imperial* (São Paulo: Comp. Editora Nacional, 1935, 1937—Brasiliana, Vols. 40, 83).

Calógeras, J. Pandiá, *Formação histórica do Brasil* (São Paulo: Comp. Editora Nacional, 2nd ed., 1935—Brasiliana).

———, *Estudos históricos e políticos (Res nostra)* (São Paulo: Comp. Editora Nacional, 2nd ed., 1936—Brasiliana, Vol. 74).

Cunha, Euclides da, *A Margem da história* (Pôrto: Chardron, 3rd ed., 1922), especially pp. 213–309, "Da Independência à República (esboço político)."

Deffontaines, Pierre, "The Origin and Growth of the Brazilian Network of Towns," *Geographical Review*, Vol. 28 (1938), pp. 379–399.

Duarte, Nestor, *A Ordem privada e a organização política nacional* (São Paulo: Comp. Editora Nacional, 1939—Brasiliana, Vol. 172).

Figueiredo, J. Lima, *Cidades e sertões* (Rio: Bloch, 1941—Biblioteca Militar, Vol. 40). Pages from the history and geography of Brazil.

Freyre, Gilberto, *Casa grande e senzala* (Rio: Schmidt, 1933). Transl. by Samuel Putnam as *The Masters and the Slaves* (New York, 1946).

Freyre, Gilberto, *Sobrados e mocambos: Decadência do patriarcado rural no Brasil* (São Paulo: Comp. Editora Nacional, 1935—Brasiliana, Vol. 64).

———, *O Nordeste* (Rio: Olímpio, 1937).

Holanda, Sérgio B., *Raízes do Brasil* (Rio: Olímpio, 1936—Coleção "Documentos Brasileiros").

Licínio Cardoso, Vicente, *A Margem da história do Brasil* (São Paulo: Comp. Editora Nacional, 1933—Brasiliana, Vol. 13).

Lira Heitor, *História de D. Pedro II*, Vols. 1 (1825–1870) and 2 (1870–1880) (São Paulo: Comp. Editora Nacional, 1938—Brasiliana, Vols. 133, 133A).

Magalhães, Basílio de, *Expansão geográfica do Brasil colonial* (São Paulo: Comp. Editora Nacional, 2nd ed., enlarged, 1935—Brasiliana, Vol. 45).

Monbeig, Pierre, "O Estudo geográfico das cidades," in *Revista do Arquivo Municipal*, 7th yr., Vol. 73, pp. 5–38 (São Paulo, Jan., 1941).

———, *Algumas observações sobre Marília, cidade pioneira*, offprint of the *Revista do Arquivo Municipal*, No. 78, pp. 221–230 (São Paulo: Departamento de Cultura, 1941).

Monteiro, Tobias, *História do Império* (Rio, 1927).

Nabuco, Joaquim, *Um Estadista do Império* (Paris, 3 vols., 1898–1900).

Normano, J. F., *Brazil: A Study of Economic Types* (Chapel Hill: University of North Carolina Press, 1935).

Oliveira Lima, Manuel de, *Formation historique de la nationalité brésilienne* (Paris), or *Formação histórica do Brasil* (São Paulo: Comp. Editora Nacional—Brasiliana).

Prado Júnior, Caio, *A Evolução política do Brasil: Ensaio de interpretação materialista da história* (São Paulo, 1934).

———, "Nova contribuição para o estudo geográfico da cidade de São Paulo," in *Estudos Brasileiros*, 3rd yr., Vol. 7, Nos. 19–21 (July–Dec., 1941), pp. 195–221.

Rangel, Godofredo, *Rumos e perspectivas* (São Paulo: Comp. Editora Nacional, 2nd ed., 1934—Brasiliana, Vol. 26), especially pp. 43–71, "A Sociedade brasileira no primeiro reinado."

Saint–Hilaire, A. de, *Segunda viagem do Rio de Janeiro a Minas Gerais e a São Paulo (1822)* and *Segunda viagem ao interior do Brasil* (São Paulo: Comp. Editora Nacional—Brasiliana, Vols. 5, 72).

Simonsen, Roberto, *A História econômica do Brasil*, Vols. 1–2 (São Paulo: Comp. Editora Nacional, 1937—Brasiliana, Vol. 100).

Soares Quintas, Amaro, *A Gênese do espírito republicano em Pernambuco e a revolução de 1817* (Recife: Imprensa industrial, 1939).

Tavares de Lira, A., *Organização política e administrativa do Brasil (Colônia, Império, República)* (São Paulo: Comp. Editora Nacional).

Vieira, Celso, "A Evolução do pensamento republicano no Brasil," in *A Margem da história da República* (Rio: Anuário do Brasil, 1923), pp. 35–55.

Werneck Sodré, Nélson, *Panorama do segundo Império* (São Paulo: Comp. Editora Nacional, 1939—Brasiliana, Vol. 170).

CHAPTER FIVE

THE PSYCHOLOGY OF THE BRAZILIAN PEOPLE

Analysis of the collective character—The interpenetration of Afro-Indian and Iberic cultures —The white enslaver and miscegenation—The result of the contact of the three initial cultures—The harmony and incompatibility of certain original traits—Some fundamental traits— The domination of the effective, the irrational, and the mystical—Attitude toward life— Fatalistic resignation—Tolerance and hospitality—Instinct of reaction of defense: reserve and irreverence—Brazilian humor—Plasticity in adaptation to new situations—Lack of economic interests—Lack of foresight and spendthrift habits—Delicate and highly excitable sensibility —Lively and superficial intelligence—Lack of the positive spirit of objectivity and exactness— Explosive will—Capacity for great effort—Action made up of impulses without constancy and without spirit of continuity—Value attributed to the human person—Anarchic individualism —Individualism hindering political concentration—Absence of the spirit of cooperation—A people of pioneers—Personal prestige and the social hierarchy—The man of the coast and the man of the interior—North and south—Diversity of regional types and fundamental unity —Transformations of mentality and their internal and external causes.

I

T IS NOT only in the peculiar characteristics of their life, their customs, their language, and their institutions that a people, or more generally a human group, is distinguished from others. It is also by its temperament and collective character. A product of a great variety of factors, geographic, ethnic, economic, and social, in which the first two play an important part but not a preponderant one in its formation, the collective character is a synthesis of the most diverse elements harmonizing and resistant, which combine or tend to combine, constituting the original physiognomy of a people or a nation. "A temperament, collective or individual," emphasizes Durkheim, "is an eminently complex matter and cannot be reduced to a simple formula. Character in groups as in individuals is the very system of all of the mental elements; it is what makes their unity. But this unity is not tied up simply to the preponderance of one or another particular tendency, more or less marked." It is not, then, by generalizing our observation of individuals, but by analyzing the natural environment, and more than that the human environment, the institutions, and the historic and social evolution of each people, that it becomes possible to reconstitute, at least in its main lines, their character—"explicable in itself, not by any single geographic or racial cause, but by the combination of multiple influences." The great natural forces like the physical environment, the climate, and the race shape, in fact, a people profoundly at the moment when its soul is still virgin; and prolonging their action through their history, observes Boutmy,[1] these factors are capable by modifying the human environment of perpetuating hereditary traits which were imprinted from the beginning on the first generations.

[1] E. Boutmy, *Essai d'une psychologie politique du peuple anglais au XIXe siècle* (Paris: Colin, 1901).

115

But, in proportion as civilization develops, social forces have more influence on the character of nations than do the natural forces, which had a role of prime importance in their origins and their formation. If, then, the soul of a people is not "an eternal essence," something immutable and definitive; if the characteristics which compose it are in a state of perpetual transformation, the analysis of the collective character, so complex in its nature, subject to such diverse influences and for that reason changeable with the modification of the system of institutions within each people, must pay attention to the research for mental habits and tendencies that are "sufficiently persistent and sufficiently general."

The complexity of a collective character, the variety of influences which join to shape it, and this fact, that it also is susceptible of change, would be enough to demonstrate the difficulties which arise before one who proposes, I do not say to sketch a systematic picture which would explain the Brazilian character, but to set down a certain number of traits, collected in observations and studies from which one can gain an impression of the whole. A reading of the authors who have studied the psychology of peoples leads us to recognize how difficult it is in this subject to achieve precision. But in the analysis of the psychology of the Brazilian people the study of the collective ethos meets difficulties so much the greater as the traits which characterize the people are presented to us with the lack of precision that is natural in young peoples, who, not having as yet attained their maturity, have not succeeded in affirming their distinctive characteristics and achieving the harmonious fusion of the different mental elements which have entered into their composition. That we already have a character of our own, a particular cut of our own, a personality that is living and in some respects marked, there is not any doubt. But, besides some basic elements more easily definable, there is here so much that is vague and imprecise, fluctuating and variable, that it renders this psychology in many points, if not unapproachable, at least resistant to a sure and penetrating analysis. The monographs and studies that have been made before, resulting from the work of various authors, thinkers, and sociologists, do not furnish us with sufficient elements for a political and social psychology of the Brazilian people, whether in the traits by which they endeavor to define it—transitory, because they are tied up with diverse phases of our evolution and tend to disappear with social change—or in their explanation, which is almost always tied up with geographic conditions and the three races which at the beginning joined to make up the Brazilian people. But great as has been the pressure of the environment upon race, at the time when practically no social product was interposed between one and the other, between the race and the environment, can we explain many things in the history of a people, asks C. Bouglé, by this primitive pressure? And great as has been, at certain points of the national territory, the mixture of whites and Indians, or whites and Negroes, or the influence of their respective cultures, especially in the first three centuries, can we accept these explanations through atavism, in relation to elements which owe less to the Indians and Negroes than to the forms of social life, and can we take as general and persistent traits, traits that are peculiar to certain groups, or linked to various stages of our evolution?

To be sure, Indians and Negroes not only contributed notably to the colonization and conquest of Brazil, but also were fused, mixing with the Portuguese more intensely in the first two centuries, and in varying proportions in different regions of the territory. If the aborigines collaborated to an important degree in the work of opening up and conquering the interior, if they constituted, together with the mamelucos, according to Gilberto Freyre, "a great moving world of flesh, which kept enlarging toward the west the colonial frontiers of Brazil," it was "the clay of the black people which fertilized the sugar-cane plantation and the coffee plantation and softened the hard earth," exercising a civilizing function from the point of view of agriculture and economics.[2] The mixture of whites and Negroes, of whites and Indians, as also more rarely that of Indians and Negroes, strewed the white population with mestizos of all types and shades. This population, in the north, at least, was to be 50 per cent of indigenous blood, and it is only on the plateau and in the south that the white population acquired once more its predominance, restoring itself in its primitive sources with the influx of immigration of Mediterranean and Germanic origin. We cannot, then, either from the racial point of view or from the economic point of view, underestimate the importance of these contributions to the ethnic composition and the mental formation of the Brazilian people. Physical and mental habits, conceptions of life, and techniques of work necessarily had to change with the contacts and interpenetration of the three cultures, and under the pressure of these phenomena "resulting from the direct and continuous contact of groups of individuals of different cultures with the consequent changes in the original cultural pattern of one or of both groups." But in the first place the fusion of the three cultures never became complete, and the assimilation of Indians and Negroes by Iberian culture always remained superficial, and the Iberian culture predominant at every point, so that the profound discord was preserved, which was only covered over by various compromises, and the Indians and the Negroes stood on the margin of two cultures—that of their own origin, which they forgot and of which they lost the characteristics, and that of the dominant culture in which they were never completely integrated. In addition to this, certain traits which are supposed to form part of our collective character, like sadness, relaxation, sensuality, are as little traceable to the Negro as dissipation or detachment from the soil and the spirit of adventure, which people attempt to explain by atavism, as an inheritance from the American Indian, are to the aborigine. What was pernicious about the influence of the Negro in the life and formation of the society of the Brazilian people, was due less to race than to the conditions of slavery, as Joaquim Nabuco had already observed when he affirmed that it was not the Negro race that was a bad element in the population, but "that race reduced to slavery." This same "cold, vile sadness" which Ronald de Carvalho considers one of the results of "two immense melancholies, that of the

---

[2] "We are a people still in its infancy," comments Humberto de Campos, "a subrace that is now receiving the elements for its characterization. And which of these elements will prevail? Will Portugal manage to preserve in the gold of the new coin the stamp which it was the first to impress, or will the new peoples of Europe triumph in their attempt to complete in the south of Brazil the epic of colonization? To discover is not to colonize," adds the illustrious critic. "The fundamental Brazilian race will be that which has most weight in the definitive formation of the nation, establishing its genius, its type, its language, its traditions. What gives a name to a land is not its soil, not the calcareous or schistous compounds of which it is composed, but the planting done in it, the useful vegetation, the green wealth which has made it rich. What yesterday was waste land, prairie, purple land, lost that name when it was tamed to take that of sugar-cane land, truck garden, coffee plantation. It is the growth of vegetables and man that baptizes the land." Cf. *Crítica*, 1st series, Marisa, 2nd ed., 1933.

Negro and that of the Indian, both enslaved," and which in his opinion would weigh so heavily upon the character of the people, does not have its roots in the Africans, who rather communicated to our domestic life a note of joy, and whose extraordinary reserves of happiness and of robustness permitted them to endure well, writes Gilberto Freyre, "the sad drudgery of the work of the sugar cane which was too much for the Indian."

In his book *Retrato do Brasil*—an essay on Brazilian sadness according to the author's own classification, and "the ugliest portrait which Brazil could hope to receive from one of her sons"—Paulo Prado indicates that two of the principal characteristics of the Brazilian are sensuality and envy. They are, in his opinion, traits which characterized us in the time of our ancestors, and from them, from the sexual passion which wore out the Portuguese and the Indian, and from the hunger for gold in which their soul was crystallized in the eighteenth century, there resulted "the sadness of the new race to which the African brought his sickly collaboration as an exile and a slave." The Brazilian people, Humberto de Campos nevertheless observes in a page of great brilliancy, "is not at all a sad people, nor does it have any source from which to derive this evil. The Portuguese is jovial, fond of good times, communicative. The joyfulness of his villages proves it and so do his country parties, at which the national dances predominate. And our Indian was no less so. His feasts were noisy, tumultuous, and lasted days, at times weeks." Our native inhabitant, taken by himself, adds the illustrious author, was, to be sure, taciturn. But to be taciturn is not to be sad. Taciturnity is one of the characteristics of hunting peoples and becomes a habit from the exigencies of the occupation. Silence, quiet, do not mean, then, sadness, which can only come from disgust with life. Our savages lived satisfied with their conditions. And, considering themselves instinctively happy, they lived joyfully, just because sadness as we define it can only come from confronting destiny and from a certain feeling of inferiority that one derives from this confrontation." The five different psychological traits with which, for himself, A. A. de Melo Franco characterizes Brazilian civilization, marking it forever with their influence, are not general and persistent, but are also, as the author of *Conceito de civilização brasileira* classifies them, residues that are typically Afro-Indian, that is, elements making up inferior cultures assimilated by the white race. Lack of foresight and dissipation, lack of appreciation of the land, salvation through chance, love of ostentation, and disrespect for the legal order, which he attributes to our forefathers, Tupi-Guaranis or Negroes—an inheritance which has remained in our blood and our souls—are rather, as Miranda Reis correctly observes, characteristics of a certain stage of the evolution of a people, like the lack of appreciation of the land or the mental retardedness of popular masses, or mysticism in its various forms, above all in the forms which it takes on in the lower social strata, of a love for chance, for gambling and every kind of superstition.[3]

[3] Thus, defects or traits of character, such as sadness, improvidence, or lack of interest in the land, intimately connected with certain stages in our evolution, and destined to disappear or change with modifications of the social structure, are mistakenly attributed to the influence of the Indian or the Negro and considered as typical racial aspects of our civilization. Indians and Negroes are, as Miranda Reis calls them, "the scapegoats" (in *Boletim do Ariel*, Vol. 6, No. 4, Jan., 1937). Now that sadness which for Paulo Prado is one of the traits of our civilization, and which is laid at the door of these racial elements, comes from neither. "The chroniclers of the sixteenth and seventeenth centuries," writes Humberto de Campos with reference to the Indians, "are unanimous in proclaiming their waggery, love of horseplay, jokes, loud laughter, and noisy

Certainly we have still to study (if indeed we ever come to study them), with greater scientific rigor, the result of the meeting of the three initial cultures and of the fusion of the three races, the white, the red, and the black who entered into the early composition of the Brazilian people. Race cannot fail to be an important factor. These numerous crossings which have taken place, above all during the first three centuries, between the racial elements that make up our population, were capable of conveying to the Brazilian soul some of the characteristics of these peoples, modifying as they modified that of the white conqueror and colonizer. The transformation of racial origins varied from one region of the land to another, depending on the greater or smaller percentage of Indian or African blood which was mixed with the white blood; but they stand out strongly in the very harmony or incompatibility which exists between this or that trait of character, between this or that character or institution, and in the peculiar characteristics which distinguish the peoples of the north and of the south in their tendencies, their tastes, their way of living and reacting, and therefore the forms and types of their behavior. It is for this reason and not only because of the diversity of landscape and climate that the very homogeneity of the Brazilian people is in contrast with the variety of forms which their civilization presents, depending upon the social environment. But above all the contact and mixture with aboriginal races, as Sérgio de Holanda has brought out in a vigorous essay, did not change profoundly the inheritance which we received from the Iberian Peninsula and did not make us so different from our grandfathers beyond the sea, as we should like to be. "From Portugal came the present form of our culture: the rest was plastic material which was subjected, for good or ill, to this form." The Portuguese clay, thrown on the mold of the American world, then all to be colonized, came out, evidently, transformed. It is a powerful breath, but an entirely new one, that animated the old statue. It does not seem to us (and this is another indispensable, preliminary consideration) that one can clarify the character or predict the future of a human group on the basis of its ethnic composition. The phenomena which take place in it, as H. Hubert observed, phenomena of growth, of decomposition in the economic, religious, and moral sense, are social phenomena and not phenomena peculiar to race. Besides this, the

---

games when they were in groups, as may be seen, to cite an example, in Léry, in that visit to the village of Euramiri, in which the cannibals passed the night in shouting and grimacing with the sole object of amusing the stranger." (*Crítica*, 1st series, Marisa, 2nd ed., 1933). The improvidence and lack of attachment to the soil come, in some indigenous tribes, from their nomadism, which in turn is a result of their type of life (hunting and fishing) and only disappears with the transition from that to an agricultural regime and the progress of agriculture. The problem, in this case, too, cannot be stated in terms of race, but in economic and social terms. In whatever way it shows up, gross elementary mysticism (belief in unknown magical forces, feeling for chance, fatalism, gambling, and superstitions in general) is not a survival from the Indian and the Negro but, as Miranda Reis observes, "a universal fact, to be found in the lower levels of any country; it has nothing to do with race and blood but is a result of the dominance of the affective over the rational, where science does not give the latter means of defending itself. Being characteristic of mental backwardness in the masses, it may properly be considered as a survival when it occurs among the educated, but it is a survival of the backwardness." Love of ostentation, which is pointed to as a trait in the national character, is also not inherited from Africans or Indians, but is one of the most typical manifestations of an early attitude, "always the enemy of simplicity," according to the very words of Melo Franco in *Conceito de civilização brasileira* (São Paulo: Comp. Editora Nacional, 1936–Brasiliana, Vol. 70).

observable groups are so made up that it is not scientific to try to distinguish in their social and mental life the contribution of the original aptitudes of their different elements, so much the more so as they were mixed in extremely unequal proportions from one region to another, presenting a great variety of types and subtypes of race which do not permit us to establish from an ethnic point of view "the legitimate, authentic, true Brazilian."

Among the dominant traits, one of the strongest, sometimes considered as the very key of Brazilian character, is the domination in his structure of the emotional, the irrational, and the mystical, which penetrates every spiritual being, either softening or arousing his will, depending upon the situation, and giving his intelligence an aspect that is essentially emotional and freighted with imagination. Certainly all human groups, as Ribot [4] has taught us, are formed and maintained by a community of beliefs, of opinions, and of prejudices, and it is the logic of sentiments that serves to create and defend these beliefs. This sentimental logic, complex and confused, of which the scholar is ignorant and from which his scientific and rational logic turned away, varying as it does with social conditions, played and still plays a considerable role in the life of groups. Moreover, if this sentimental logic would not be possible except through the fact that the individual consciousness lends itself to it—as Ribot demonstrates, decomposing the psychic mechanism which renders possible this reasoning *sui generis,* of which sentiments, emotive states form the essential reality—it is not less certain that mental states constituting the material of these operations are essentially collective. They are beliefs, ideas, or conclusions relative to future life or residing at the basis of magic and divination, which take on different forms in different societies and within the same society in different social layers or classes. But in the Brazilian, sensibility, imagination, and religiosity have such intensity and force that culture rarely covers them over, only contributing to raise the effective and the mystical from their primitive gross forms to higher and more delicate forms. This constant interference of sentiment in our judgment and opinion, the forms of emotional reasoning so frequent in all social classes, the facilities with which we believe and propagate everything that is strange and miraculous, our lack of interest in objective considerations—are they not shown in fact by the affective and mystical background which appears in the tendency to put and to solve in personal terms of "friend" and "enemy" the most concrete problems, and in the very conception of authority, founded on the sentimental faith of men in the superiority of a chieftain or of a social group? It is necessary, in order to understand these traits, not to forget either the origins of the Brazilian, stemming from the Iberian Peninsula, and more especially of the Portuguese in all his dominions, or the environment in which he was formed and in which his activity developed and in which it is easy to find, in the survival of the state of mind of the first colonist and in the apostolic work of the missionaries prolonged through generations, an explanation of the persistence and vitality of the religious sentiment.

But this religious sentiment which presents in the north a more mystical character, more closely related to dogma or inclined to superstitions and fanaticism in the popular strata and in the interior, took on in general a different direction, more formalistic, concentrating in ceremonies, practices, and religious rites. Religion developed freely,

[4] Théodule Ribot, *La Logique des sentiments* (Paris: Alcan, 1905).

adapting itself here as everywhere to the necessities of this new society of lords of the manor, of sertanejos and pioneers and therefore to the kind of life which the exploitation of an immense land imposed upon the descendants of the first immigrants and of the new immigrants. In contrast, then, to the United States, where the religious sentiment seems to us not to be closely related to dogma, nor to allow itself mystic dreams, and where the clergy have been occupied chiefly with "removing the rigidity and the clouds from theology" in order to retain everything which motivates action—as Boutmy observes in his penetrating analysis of the psychology of the American people [5]—religion in Brazil did not assume this essentially ethical and practical appearance which was impressed upon it in the northern country on the one hand by the aesthetic severity and the rigidity of customs of the Puritans, its first colonists, and on the other by the mobility and the intense activity of the work of colonization. There is in every system of colonial life, writes Gilberto Freyre, "a mild domestic religion of relations, practically of a family sort, between saints and men that—from the patriarchal chapels of the big houses, the temples always occupied in celebrations, baptisms, marriages, saints' feasts, confirmations, novenas—presided over the social development of Brazil." This religion, "so domestic, lyrical, and festive, with saints who are the friends of men, with an Our Lady who was the godmother of little children," this fraternization in values and sentiments of the land and heaven, would not have occurred here if, as Gilberto Freyre says, there had dominated over our social formation another type of Christianity, "a type more clerical, more ascetic, more orthodox, Calvinist or rigidly Catholic." The tendency of the Brazilian to dissolve all social hierarchies touched his religious feelings too, modifying and enriching them with ingenuity and spontaneity, with the closeness of living, almost living together with the gods who appeared, as in the Greek age, walking over the earth, humanized, taking part in the domestic intimacies of believers. Whether by the force of this religious sentiment, with its rich spontaneity and human sympathy, or through the action of tropical nature, depressing and crushing man, the Brazilian is not a man in revolt, for he is resigned, docile, and submissive to physical and moral fatalities which he has learned to endure with courage and to subordinate himself to them without bitterness, when he recognizes that they are superior to his resources of defense and action. His attitude in the face of life—a mixture of indulgence, piety, and irony—is a kind of resigned capitulation to the assault of the forces of a hostile nature, difficult to dominate, the violence of which he knows by his own experience, and which he has learned to confront, almost always without support, counting only upon himself, in his adventurous entries into the country, in his expeditions to tame the land, and in his incursions through the interior.

Of all the distinctive traits of the Brazilian, perhaps one of the most general and constant, which constitutes his strength and his weakness at the same time, the most attractive and communicative, and the one which stands out most upon first contact and is most marked when you live with him, is, then, his kindness which appears to burgeon from the soul of the people, from their native temperament. Their sensitivity to the suffering of others, the ease with which they forget and forgive offenses received, a certain shamefacedness about showing their own egoism, the absence of any racial pride, a repugnance to radical solutions, tolerance, hospitality, liberality and gen-

[5] *Eléments d'une psychologie politique du peuple américain: La Nation, la patrie, l'Etat, la religion* (Paris: Colin, 1902).

erosity in hospitality, these are so many manifestations of this emotional element that is so strongly marked in the national character. It is not a question of "politeness," which is always and everywhere the product of the refinement of civilization, a quality rather acquired than natural, refined in living with men, in frequency of contacts with the sources of culture, in the civilizing action of travel, and above all, more than in experience, in a taste for social life with all its niceties and artifices. It is a delicacy without calculation and disinterested, frank, ingenuous and of a primitive simplicity, at times rustic, but frequently penetrated with tenderness and held back by timidity and discretion. Moreover, if strangers feel among us almost as if they were at home, and if they are so easily assimilated to the original nucleus of the nation, it is because our land is the most maternal, sweetest, most receptive, most human, capable of exerting the soft pressure of its arm around the waist of all races and of all peoples.[6] This kindness, which like an equalitarian feeling is heedless of distinctions of classes and differences of races, which withdraws as if offended before violence and brutality, which diminishes repression, individual or collective, and renders the Brazilian so easy to be led when you appeal to his reason and above all to his sentiment, and so difficult to move by force, has its origins in the profoundly Christian formation of our people, in the common possession of sentiments and values, and in social democratization, toward which great contributions have been made on the one hand by religion and on the other hand by the race mixture so widely practiced among the three initial races, and later with the other races brought to the south by currents of immigration. The contact of the Negro must also have contributed, according to Gilberto Freyre, to refining the treasures of sentiment which religion and the fusion of races had built up. "He gave us a revelation of a kindness greater than that of the whites, of a tenderness such as Christians do not know, of a warm voluptuous mysticism with which he has enriched our sensibility, our imagination, and our religiosity." What had, however, a notable influence upon the development of this cult of hospitality, in which there grew like a flower of civilization the sentimental delicacy of the Brazilians, was the enormous distances which separated the nuclei of population one from another

---

[6] This essential principle of cordiality toward the most diverse peoples and races was certainly favored in its origin and development by the very process of the initial formation of our people, with the contributions of the three races, white, red, and black. In a country which had its origin in the fusion of these races, and in whose formation, still of recent date, the phenomena of race mixture stand out prominently, tolerance flowered naturally as a spontaneous sentiment, fed at its roots in the tradition and lively awareness of these contacts and mixtures of different peoples and cultures. But the principle and the sentiment of catholicity, one cannot deny, are related also to our religious background and the Christian sentiments which in this connection entered deeply into our minds, exalting and refining the charity, sympathy, and fraternity which are stronger and more obvious the closer we get to the oldest parts of our population. The feeling of cordiality and hospitality, in fact, put down such deep roots in the social mind that in no period, not even the most agitated of our history, was the Brazilian disposed to give up the old tradition and heritage of human sympathy in favor of any other attitude, which would, indeed, seem to him a heresy, involving brutality and violence toward other peoples and cultures. The old Roman expression—*hospes, hostis*—always seemed to us to have no meaning. All the manifestations of Jacobinism or of violent reactions against foreigners were mere episodes in our history: provoked by attacks, real or imagined, on our national dignity, they lasted only long enough to achieve satisfaction and did not succeed in turning that admirable attitude of hospitality, tolerance, and human sympathy away from the line of its natural development.

and the isolation in which they lived, scattered and separated: the arrival of strangers, of travelers, whether of their own nation or foreign, at these communities—fazendas, settlements, and towns—insulated in the interior, was always a festal note which in renewing contact with the coast and the external world and reestablishing the sensibility and the taste for social life, broke for hours or days the sadness and monotony of the solitude. A messenger from the cities, a bearer of news—a present from the gods in this territorial immensity dotted by little nuclei—the stranger, to whom arms and sometimes hearts were opened, brought enthusiasm to the family, nostalgic for other surroundings, awoke their curiosity, and, tracing in their spirit wider horizons, left them looking at the mirage of distant lands . . .

But this hospitality, far from being open and without reserve, is almost always accompanied by vigilant attention and at times by severe discretion. In the study of individual characters, moralists are accustomed to describing a great variety of types, depending upon the predominance of such and such defects or qualities, which, rigorously speaking, are only abstractions or inventions of their minds. Seen in this light, the novelist who presents his personages whole, endowed with virtues and laden with defects or vices, and caught in the life, in full activity, gives us a more concrete reality than that which, under the name of moralist, is given to us by the analysis of a virtue, a vice or defect. And the same thing happens in the analysis of a collective character. There are groups, just as there are persons, who have one or another or various of these defects; but they have also an existence which influences them, and in which they play their part. Their existence or their mode of life modifies their defects, just as the latter modify one another by the fact of their coexistence.[7] Thus this trait of hospitality so characteristic of the Brazilian, coexisting with others, such as a natural reserve and distrust, was modified under the influence of the latter, and took on a peculiar character only explicable in terms of the specific conditions of our formation. Great as may be their hospitality, the Brazilians, even those of the north, who are more ready in speech and more communicative, do not open themselves easily or totally. "The recesses of their consciousness as of their homes," writes Tristão de Ataíde, "remain closed for a long time to the man who does not slowly win the confidence of the son of the land." This distrust and reserve, which constitutes one of the traits of our character, can be one of its defects. But if we follow the social evolution of the Brazilian people it is easy to recognize in it one of its most notable defense reactions. In a new country of heterogenous formation, subject to the influence of different races which are slowly being assimilated to the primitive core, and of an extremely scanty population, man, exposed in his solitude to the extortions of the treasury, to the encirclement of adventurers and the gain of merchants, had to live on the alert in a perpetual distrust which, even when he opened the gates of his house, would lead him to close those of his intimacy and of his heart. The social atmosphere which isolation and distance created, just as it contributed to develop the cult of hospitality, contributed also to fortify the family sentiment—as the family was the nucleus which offered the most support—and to maintain in an atmosphere of reserve the relative felicity which they enjoyed, and which was exposed to dangers and to the seduction of strangers, travelers, and foreigners.

[7] Ch. Fiessinger, *Les Défauts, réactions de défense.*

There is not, however, in this attitude of distrust anything that is either aggressive or out·of tune with the hospitable spirit; and, if it is constant like a reaction of defense, it assumes, combined with other qualities or defects, different aspects and a series of nuances which go from reserve in speech and dissimulation to that apparent incontinence in language which permits one to speak a great deal without saying anything, or at least without opening one's heart. It is more notable in the central south among Paulistas and Mineiros, and above all among the latter, the inhabitants of Minas, whose formation was conditioned by certain peculiar factors depending upon the nature of their work and their life in the mining regions. Miran Latif describes the inhabitant of Minas by saying that he is always attentive, always on the watch to pick up possibilities that are shining furtively, the grain that shines in the sand of the river; he is always on the lookout. Trying to win by perspicacity, confiding more in his good star than in work, the Mineiro, as a result of being so distrustful, ends by turning a bit hypocritical. He becomes imaginative and full of suspicion. His language shows the mentality of one who is always standing behind, and he adopts the indeterminate tense of the verb in which the action is continued and may be avoided. "Does this river give good gold? It is giving some, replies the gold washer. It is giving, but tomorrow perhaps it will not give. It is the reply of one who makes no promises. . . . The abuse of the gerund reflects the lack of frankness of one who wants to be able to say that he asserted nothing, or perhaps the scruple of one who does not dare to affirm." This special aspect which grew stronger among the inhabitants of Minas because of the atmosphere of lack of tranquillity in which they lived—developing from the isolation of their captaincy from the rest of the colony, the exigencies of the treasury, the facilities for moving mines, and the contact with the commerce of the town—and which made them men in appearance affable and diplomatic, but fundamentally reserved and full of suspicion, is a psychological trait of the people of the interior, of the caboclo, and in general of the Brazilian, although less notable on the coast and in the great centers of population. The heterogeneity of the ethnic composition of the people, their contact with different cultures, the isolation of the captaincies, the fiscal policies of the home country, economic fluctuations, and the deceptive invitation of nature, apparently so easy and opulent but really so avaricious and inconstant in the distribution of its wealth, show how an unfavorable environment, exciting individuals to react, was able to contribute to the formation of the Brazilian character and imprint upon it the trace of that indulgent skepticism which shows, under a singular plasticity of adaptation to new situations, a great prudence and malice of the mind. The Brazilian, under the pressure of these causes, learned to react and to defend himself by distrust, doubt, and irreverence, maintaining an attitude of expectation and observation. But it is truly admirable that this skepticism which shows in an attitude of complacency and good humor, of piety and of irony in the face of life—the flower of the wisdom in which mature and refined civilizations grow—should have arisen as one of the most lively traits of its character in a simple and young people, still in process of formation.

Of a primitive simplicity, easy to content in his material necessities, living and being satisfied with little, the Brazilian has the sobriety of the inhabitants of countries which do not offer anything but a poor surface of cultivable land and whose farm lands cannot conserve their value except by continuous occupation and incessant effort. In a mountainous country of a tropical nature, hard and savage, in which the slopes, the prolonged droughts, and the torrential rains constitute obstacles to cultivation, man had necessarily to habituate himself to frugality in food and to saving in his expenses. The Brazilian is not, in fact, and never was tortured by the thirst for gold, as Paulo Prado believes, and as we might be led to believe by the expeditions carried out by the Paulistas to the interior, driven by a spirit of adventure and stimulated by the sovereign power, for the discovery and exploration of mines. The parsimony of the miner—this also, as we have seen, is not so much a manifestation of avariciousness as a desire to continue to enjoy the little to which one has become habituated. "In proportion as the new possibilities [in the exploitation of mines] begin to disappear," writes Barros Latif, "people save ever more in the bottom of their trunks. This love for money, however, is not an itch to gain it. There is felt only the fear of losing it." This avidity for gain, this preoccupation with the future, is not certainly characteristic of the Brazilian. Calculation is not the essence of this people. What is beyond the present hardly exists for any of them. The present is what counts, and therefore he neither has the cult of work nor disdains all those light and fugitive pleasures which make the charm of life. But if this lack of love for work cultivated under the long regime of slavery is in the middle class a whole moral tradition of the home country nobility, to whom "a worthy leisure always appeared more excellent and even capable of conferring nobility than the insensate struggle for daily bread," does not the discontented indolence of the people in general come rather from the habit of living with little more than nothing and from the consciousness of the disproportion between the gain which is always scanty and the hard labor of acquiring it, between the effort expended on the work and the result really obtained? The foundation of Brazilian character, as Mílton Rodrigues brilliantly wrote, "is a rustic simplicity; the environment which created him, in his first period, did not give even to the rich comfort, even when it conceded to him luxury. Accustomed to this, he does not have the necessities of the European; and when opulence comes, it surrounds him without getting into him, and he does not know how to use it, passing abruptly from lack to exhibitionism and disintegration."

It is not, then, from the Indian that the Brazilian inherited lack of foresight and dissipation of goods; bound up, on the other hand, with the constant instability of our social life, they accompany as characteristics proper to it those periods of economic fluctuation which, wiping out old fortunes and causing new ones to rise, invite people to dissipate wealth and tend to substitute for confidence in the continuity of work a hope for miracles and for sudden turns of fortune. This economic and social instability, the fragmentary process of our formation by nuclei, scattered, unrelated one to another, the discontinuity of economic and cultural contact, and the extreme scantiness of our population, which is so harmful to the intensity of spiritual life, explain also the attitude of the Brazilian toward culture, generally considered among us not as a practical necessity or moral value, but as a sign of class or distinction. Not that the Brazilian lacked interest in things of the mind: his delicate and excitable sensibility, his keen intelligence, the ease with which he adapted himself to a minimum of material life, and his very religious traditions, not only awoke in him a lively notion of the subordination of material values to moral values, but gave him a strong inclination toward things of the spirit. But our culture is generally a literary and superficial culture, made up, as Mílton Rodrigues observes, "to fill the leisure hours of unoccupied people, a culture which does not involve sentiments nor lead to strong convictions." It is not only the age-old tradition of a scholastic, verbalistic, and dogmatic discipline and of Iberic influence that kept the Brazilian so far away from the positive spirit of objectivity and of exactitude, with so little interest in ideas, and so easily impressionable and subject to the charm of form, to the apparatus of language and the pomp of erudition. The delicacy and force of his sensibility, if they prevented his yielding to a morality without generosity and arts without refinement and literature without beauty and inspiration, contributed, together with everything that his intelligence had that was vivacious and keen, to separating him from philosophical speculation and from scientific investigation, which require severe technique and a strong discipline of one's thought. What characterizes him is not penetration, nor vigor, nor profundity, but facility, grace, and brilliancy; it is rapidity in assimilating, a total absence of exactitude and precision, a talent for indirection and for seizing upon those aspects of things which touch intelligence less than sensibility. Moreover, in this mobile and dispersed world, dominated by immediate material necessity, philosophy and science have no time to put down roots. And do not all the defects of this verbalistic, scholastic, and dogmatic culture which we inherited from the Portuguese, and which penetrated us so deeply in the teaching of all grades, reveal less a weak intelligence than an intelligence badly educated and therefore capable, as has already been proved, of attaining distinction under a new form of guidance in all fields of literature and the arts as well as of technique, science, and pure thought?

Intelligence and sensibility have between them an alternating play which is our mental and moral life; and it is necessary that sensibility should not excite it too much, so that intelligence may develop in all its fullness and be capable of influencing sensibility, controlling it or favoring it. Partly by the influence of the three races who entered into the composition of our people, and partly by the action of the physical environment and the climate, and in addition through the very conditions of our social formation, there appears in the Brazilian a strongly marked domination of sensibility over intelligence. Hence, out of these defects of emotional domination come certain aspects of our intellectual life, through which sensibility passes a constant current of vibration, agitating its surface. One might perhaps be able to trace a more systematic and explanatory picture of the Brazilian character if one sought the key not in intelligence but rather in sensibility, which exercises a great influence also upon our will, imposing upon it in an irregular rhythm, out of beat, made up of depressions and sudden starts, of indolence and impetuosity. All the explosive quality of our will, this aptitude for maintaining under an appearance of laziness, lassitude, and indifference reserves of energy which are let loose under the imperative of necessity or on the shock of emotion—do they not show a marked preponderance of sensibility over intelligence or, to employ the technical terms of physiology, of the neuroglandular systematic system with all its impulses, instincts, and defects over the brain with its capacity to compare, to judge, and to conclude? The activity of the Brazilian, in a general way, has nothing in it that is premeditated or reflective. It is made up of impulses, at times violent, but passing and without continuity. Peoples, however, like individuals, do not carry on the struggle for life only with their good qualities, but also with their defects, which they employ to defend themselves, and which after having served them become precious and habitual, until they form our individual or collective character. It is an illusion to see in the air of indifference and lack of worry of the Brazilian a principle of weakness, for the indolence in him represents rather an "economy" of forces, a "defense reaction" against the climate and the physical and social conditions of the environment. It is certain that doubt, when it has taken its position and maintained itself within him, obliges him to retreat and to preserve himself inactive, even to a state of laziness, and indifference that amounts to detachment. Not always, however, is attack the best form of defense. It may be and it will be many times expectation, a capacity for waiting, and watching for the moment when one is to enter into action. This gift of responding to external stimuli, this aptitude for reacting, this capacity for making great effort, although discontinuous, is so strongly marked in the Brazilian that, at an emotional shock, all his forces are immediately mobilized, and unleashed, and then they surprise us always even to the point of astonishment by the violence of their combative power, which was hidden and economized under a neglectful inaction in which he appeared to take delight.[8]

In that strange mixture of virtues and defects which in various proportions make up Brazilian character, and on which the rude commands of life impinge as principles of order, one of the most active elements is doubtless individualism. It comes from the Iberian peoples. It grew to the point of aggressiveness under the favorable conditions which life in the interior offered it, and later the frontiers of the south, and it acquired for the Brazilian all the efficacy of an instrument of defense. It is always, at the same time, destructive of all restrictions which tend to make society prevail over the individual, and is a great disciplining agent wherever the prestige of the law and the authority of institutions do not make themselves felt efficiently or are endangered. This individualism of Iberian origin is not, however, creative as is Anglo-Saxon individualism; nor does it possess the same social significance or content. It is, on the contrary, up to a certain point, negative. Although abundantly nourished in the sertões, without limits and without restraint, which with their vast extent offer an easy refuge, as in the frontier regions near the boundary line, individualism, which

[8] This trait of character marked "by the impressive rhythmic alternation of extreme impulsiveness and long periods of apathy," which conceals under an attitude of indolence and fatigue a remarkable power of reaction, is exceptionally marked in the frontiersman. Everywhere, however, the activity of the Brazilian shows discontinuity and violence in contrasts; intermittent or sporadic, it goes from relaxation to enthusiasm, from the languor of indifference to rude or chivalric types of reaction. In a page of *Os Sertões* that is admirable in its clarity and vigor, Euclides da Cunha after describing the type of the frontiersman shows how deceiving in this permanently tired man is "all that appearance of fatigue. Nothing is more surprising than to see the sertanejo's listlessness disappear all of a sudden. In this weakened organism complete transformations are effected in a few seconds. All that is needed is some incident that demands the release of slumbering energies. The fellow is transfigured. He straightens up, becomes a new man, with new lines in his posture and bearing; his head held high now, above his massive shoulders; his gaze straightforward and unflinching. Through an instantaneous discharge of nervous energy, he at once corrects all the faults that come from the habitual relaxation of his organs; and the awkward rustic unexpectedly assumes the dominating aspect of a powerful, copper-hued Titan, an amazingly different being, capable of extraordinary feats of strength and agility." (From p. 90 of Samuel Putnam's translation, *Rebellion in the Backlands,* Chicago, 1944. Published by The University of Chicago Press.)

in the unpopulated interior is a necessary condition for one's own protection and defense, found in Brazil new sources of exaltation in the patriarchal and slaveholding regime of agriculture in the north and on the plateau. The whole tendency of the interior with its immense territory outside the reach of the law, and with all of the dangers which place highest among the social virtues physical courage, self-confidence, astuteness, and power of pretending, was to create "a type of man rebellious to any form whatever of social organization," and to stimulate the development of classes which were not only social but antisocial, whose aggressive individualism had necessarily to take the place of the law and of protection by the state. The nomadic life imposed by the pastoral regime, in the limitless land in which one breathed an atmosphere of unshackled freedom, contributed to accentuating the individualistic character of the man who was formed in this atmosphere of isolation, of boldness, and of adventures. But the power acquired by the sugar lords on the coast of the north or by the owners of the great coffee plantations in the basin of the Paraíba and in general on the whole plateau of the central south, the relative isolation in which they lived, and the regime of autarchy on the plantations, the proprietors of which were proud of acquiring almost nothing outside their own land, could not fail, on the one hand, to aggravate under this or some other form the sullen individualism which had been generated in the interior. It is not only in the mining region or in the grazing region, but also under the pressure of other causes in the patriarchal centers of the great agricultural properties, that there developed this rebellious individualism which at times grows more serious, aggressive, or arrogant, becoming pride of life or of strength in the zones of the interior as well as in the nobility. It is the individual that counts; and if this rude individualism implies an extremely lively feeling of personality, it does not among us always involve a respect for life proportional to the importance which we give to the independence of each man with regard to his fellow and to the value of the human person. Stimulating individual sentiments of boldness, courage, and arrogance, it assures doubtless its flowering; but, imposing on life the principle of individualistic competition, it nourishes at the same time, together with dispersion and lack of discipline, the sources of rivalry and conflict.

If to this individualism, not always aggressive but destructive and anarchic, we add regionalistic tendencies, developed by the political breakup of the colonies into collective individualities (the captaincies), that were distant and isolated from one another, and into a multitude of little cells, we shall find in these two phenomena a great centrifugal power, the explanation both of a lack of social cohesion and of a constant active or passive resistance to the centralization of political power in the country. The essential character of Brazilian history for a long period of more than three centuries, continued vigorously through the Empire and the Republic, is this double fact of individualism and of regionalism resulting from the juxtaposition of small and large States, without contact with one another and subject to diverse influences geographic and social in their growth. Hence the absence of a spirit of cooperation in the Brazilian. "Initiative," writes Sérgio de Holanda, "even when it was constructive, was continually in the sense of separating men and never of uniting them." On the land "for all our barons, there was no durable collective agreement possible, unless it was imposed by an external force that was respected and feared." Certainly the common enemy, represented it may be by the Indian in his incursions or by the foreigner in his attempts to conquer and occupy, constituted a unifying element, tending to reduce individualism and regionalism and to stimulate the union of individuals and collective unities in our isolation. Against this hostile environment, peopled by enemies, "one cannot struggle alone," observes Mílton Rodrigues. "One struggles in bands organized, as it were, on a military basis, whether it is a question of the entry into the interior and bandeiras, or agricultural exploitation or pastoral life in the region already conquered. Work in common is the rule, work which requires of all the same rude qualities and the type of work which is equalizing, and which demands, nevertheless, the indisputable authority, the limitless authority of a chieftain, who only by his position is distinguished from those under his command." It is true that this fact, which at first sight might show a spirit of cooperation, only shows the lack of cohesion in Brazilian society, and it is a phenomenon with sound roots.[9] This cohesion maintained besides by the authority of a chieftain, of a power without limits, dominated, so to speak, the surface of society in these groups united by the bonds of a common danger; but at the center the society remained essentially individualistic. These formations in bands constituted rather an *accidental* phase in the attempts at organization in which a pioneer people was engaged in fighting for the conquest and exploitation of the land, than an expression of any tendency toward the development of groups. They were social formations, sporadic and transitory in nature, which were organized for limited ends under the imperative of necessity, and they were later dissolved, without leaving any vestige in the social structure in the form of permanent institutions or associations.

Whoever has not lost sight of these fundamental elements in the process of our formation, so strongly influenced as it was by individualistic and regional tendencies,

[9] Of all the social institutions, it is the family that shows greatest solidity and cohesion, for individuals join together and unite in domestic society, finding in it a refuge and a defense against all the disintegrating influences of the environment. There what counts is generally not the individual, but the institution: the family. Founded on Christian bases; stimulated in its development both by the influence of Catholicism, in Brazil as everywhere, and by the combined action of all the causes which tended to *insulate* every group of families, that institution became a point of support and a system of protection for the individual, and especially, for women, subjected as they were to a system of reclusion everywhere that the power of the law and the presence of the State made themselves felt only weakly. The patriarchal nucleus offered the greatest support, as happens in growing societies. In the castlelike houses of the sugar plantations or ranches located in the back country, and even among the sertanejos scattered all over the interior, the family acquired in social life an authority and a strength that were greater in proportion as the political power was retarded. In this way there grew up a domestic particularism which burst out so often in the interior in long family feuds over boundary questions or personal quarrels that became conflicts between clans, and which had a great influence on political life, preyed upon as it was by family partisanship (nepotism, *filhotismo*) and monopolized by the great families. Thence the characteristic of moral solidarity and cooperation exhibited by the Brazilian family while it was still in the patriarchal stage, in which the rigid control of the chief did not involve either absence of conjugal intimacy of the Arab family—in which the spouses remain widely separated—or the crude, abstract type of domestic discipline found among the Jews. The necessity of union in the face of common dangers, isolation, and great distances contributed to making the ties of solidarity and affection closer in the bosom of the family, and to make the slogan "One for all and all for one" the fundamental principle of protection and defense by itself of the institution and the individuals who composed it.

cannot, as one sees, be surprised by the function of democracy and the effect in Brazil of the equalitarian movement. Certainly, as Sérgio de Holanda has observed, life was incomparably more gentle, more receptive of social, racial, and even religious differences, and everything conspired to emphasize the tendency to dissolve all social hierarchies. The contact of different races, the miscegenation practiced on a large scale, varying according to latitude and social class, internal migrations, the nomadism of pastoral life, the freedom of life in the sertões and in general in the interior of the country, the spirit of independence which distance and isolation had generated, all contributed to developing to a high degree democratic feeling and equalitarian tendencies.[10] Hence, perhaps, the eminently popular character and the great force of expansion felt in the Brazilian carnival, in which Almir de Andrade sees, as it were, "a protest—a gigantic protest of delirious, mad multitudes against the formulas which separated them from each other, against all of the artifices which the social order requires for the preservation of itself." It seems that in that anonymity of all, in the identification with the mass, "all the walls which divided men into classes and into individuals were one by one broken down, dissolved and diluted; all the social conventions are destroyed; all the parts are fused into a single unitary whole, where everything is homogeneous and uniform." [11] But if the democratic tendency in Brazil is so spontaneous and vigorous it is necessary, for a comprehension of the functioning of democracy, to see behind institutions, the customs, and the men that are acting and that are the "forces" of political life, and to surprise them in their methods of action and in their movement. The individualism and libertarian spirit and the traditional influences of local feeling lead men to group themselves about persons and not ideas. They make parties ever less capable of serving as the instruments of public interest and, little by little, transform county spirit, the principal inspirer of life in the Republic, into an instrument of servitude. All its struggles tend to take on by force of individualism a personal character; and even when we believe that we are applauding or combating ideas, what we really are idolizing or refusing, are the individuals who incarnate them, and the Brazilian is generally incapable of separating them from their ideas, not only in the realm of politics but, agitated by passion, in the very intellectual realm in which divergencies of doctrine involve almost always separation and conflict of persons.

[10] The democratic feeling which is so strong in the Brazilian, and is one of his characteristic traits, is especially developed in the inhabitant of Minas, as a result of the special conditions of his type of work and way of living. The owner of the mines, Barros Latif tells us (in *As "Minas gerais"*), depended on many people and, discussing with all kinds of traders the acquisition of merchandise which the monopoly of Portugal offered at exorbitant prices, he necessarily had to become democratic. In continual arguments over the counter of business houses about the purchase of barrels of dried fish or pieces of dried meat, he was forced to play the part of householder in order to escape ruin. "Baron or viscount let him be, and everything would be more expensive. To bargain with a quiet conscience, he had to become humble, and the rich were content to be on equal terms with the poor." The permanent contact with the commerce of the towns led the mine operator to equalitarian tendencies. His environment plus a certain amount of Semitic blood (according to Barros Latif, large numbers of the Jewish race came to the mines) made the mineiro a champion of democracy in Brazil.

[11] Almir de Andrade, *Aspectos da cultura brasileira: A Alma brasileira e o carnival* (Rio: Schmidt, 1939–Pensadores brasileiros, Vol. 3).

In a country in which personal prestige is everything, independent of inherited name, and the union of individuals and groups had to be made consequently about chieftains or personalities with prestige, the principle of cohesion and of social hierarchy could not be strong; nor could the tendency toward centralization be dominant. All our social and political history shows, as we have already emphasized, how strong was the resistance opposed by the provinces to centralizing movements which, above these territorial governments and regional governments, raised a common and unitary organization which surrounded them, reducing regional autonomy as well as the instinctive reaction of individualism against hierarchies or any and every form of social life which might become an obstacle to the autonomy of the individual. Individualism on the one hand, and regional tendencies resulting from the process of our growth on the other, lie at the base of this traditional personalism, deeply rooted in the Brazilian and intimately connected with the life of parties and their mechanisms of action. The type of social organization most solidly formed into a hierarchy which is recorded by our historical formation was that of agricultural society based upon plantations and slaveholding. But the phenomenon of urbanism, the development of commerce, the transformation of urban structures in the democratic direction, the extension of intellectual culture, and growing individualism ended by breaking down the rigid groupings of rural society, even before they were attacked at their very bases by abolition. What remained of them, as it were a residue transferred to political life, was the morality of bosses and farm laborers, of lords and slaves, formed and developed in the social regime of slavery. This moral system it was—made up of two principles, that of the sovereign authority of the chief, the heir of the lord, and that of the unconditional fidelity of the servant—that gave a social content to personalism by way of the rule that was so complacent and gentle for the submissive, so arrogant and bold with relation to any restrictions whatever upon their dominion and expansion. "Even today," reflects Mílton Rodrigues, "if we should analyze the component elements of that conflict which is here denominated 'prestige,' perhaps we should find them in that type of relation between the protégé and the proprietor which characterized our formation by semi-feudal, isolated, agricultural nuclei. That trait which an intense individualism imprinted upon our political character, and from which most of the sentiment of common interest and the spirit of cooperation are far distant, was still more emphasized with the development of bureaucracy, to which social and economic conditions in the country drew the urban bourgeoisie from the time of the Empire; together with the habit of appealing to the government with regard to anything whatever which interested more than two people, according to the correct observation of Roy Nash, and with the constant absorption of all social functions by the State."

While, as Boutmy observes, in North America the State arose as a conscious creation of individuals, and the citizens show themselves little desirous of seeing it intervene in their relations,[12] in Brazil the state appears as a providence which comes before individuals, and to which they run for defense and protection. What one sees, behind the structure of the state, is not the collective interest of which it is or should be the supreme expression, but an objective will which is developed and reenforces that of individuals, so that the latter can be completely realized. It is not a society organ-

[12] E. Boutmy, *Eléments d'une psychologie politique du peuple américain* (Paris: Colin, 1902).

ized politically, which like a magic mirror transmits to the individual with its image a new power. It is, above all, living forces, personalities which act and hold in their hands the levers of command. It is not institutions, it is not an authority which is respected, whoever may be the individual in whom it is incarnate, but the people who hold power or who act upon the political scene, surrounding themselves with an aureole of prestige. This respect and this attraction for outstanding individualities do not present, however, the mystical character of devotion to the point of sacrifice which great chieftains and leaders of masses are accustomed to imposing upon individuals attracted by their magnetism. Suspicious and irreverent, enamored of events and of sensations, the Brazilian shows in his attitude rather an almost spectacular interest in the active force of representative types and a constant effort to strip off from the real human physiognomy to which it is often attached the fascinating mask of the pre-destined. Territorial extension and the innumerable succession of geographic settings in which the panorama of the country unfolds, and the very dispersion of groups, tend to extinguish in man the visible image of the State on account of the distances at which the governors keep themselves. Besides, the discord already noted between the territorial progress of society and that of power, between the area of social expansion and that of political efficiency, and the fact of not being forced constantly to defend individuals and to reconquer an assurance against external enemies did not give time or means to the State, nor impose upon it for a long period the necessity for fortifying itself on account of the fear of war, and of putting its force to work, bringing together the relations of individuals among themselves and of the individuals with the State. If, however, some trace of mysticism is met in the attitude of the Brazilian toward the State, it is a certain fetishism of formulas and of regimes, which is expressed in an almost ingenuous confidence in the efficacy of *a priori* constructions of perfect social and political institutions, and must come as much from the lack of a long political tradition as from a revolutionary spirit still surviving from the eighteenth century, which believed that reason had the power to interrupt historical continuity and regulate the course of events.

Patriotism in Brazil, as in the United States, is also more utilitarian than mystical, and it rests upon individualism, far from acting contrary to it. Although it is nourished here as everywhere upon the belief that the nation represents a great tradition and is the embodiment of an ideal which it is necessary to defend, it is turned more toward the future than toward the past, with historical perspectives that are brilliant but not long. If it takes on rarely the mystical form to which the people of the West are habituated, the reason is that in fact it lacks a past. American peoples in general, as Boutmy observes in relation to the United States, cannot love their nation as a venerable past, since they see it forming under their eyes and, so to speak, are shaping it with their own hands. It is only little by little that, brought closer together every day and united one to another, groups acquire a true collective consciousness. Their imagination then asks of the future those long perspectives which the past refuses in a new people of recent formation. But all the struggles in which the Brazilian fought show the force and vitality of this national sentiment which grew up without the stimulating frequency of hostile contact, and which tends to develop ever more in proportion as the population becomes denser and as interchange of an economic and cultural nature is multiplied between its regions. What strikes us at the first glance in this singular fact of the existence of a collective spirit already so deep rooted, is that this feeling has been formed and has acquired such vitality in a country in which there did not contribute to develop it, either territorial extension or density of population or the powerful stimulus of external enemy. The national sentiment is, in fact, one of those which grow by opposition and come to take on a religious character, an almost fanatical one, of idolatry, of sacrifice, and of immolation under the pressure of external aggression or of the invasion of its territory. Experience shows the existence of "an effective bond and a law of concomitant progression between the density of population and the strength of national feeling." We can understand, also, that in small States patriotism tends to acquire greater intensity, as in ancient Greece, in which, according to the observation of Jardé, "this sentiment, if not engendered, was at least developed by the small extent of the State." The national territory was, in fact, for the Greek "a concrete and living reality. The citizen knew it in all its aspects and all its corners. He could many times, from the top of his Acropolis, embrace in a single glance the whole city-state up to the frontiers which were marked upon the horizon by a circle of mountains." [13] Now, in spite of the great territorial extent and the scanty population of the country which could only help to weaken it, and in spite of the fact that it has lacked tempering by those great dramatic struggles with which the collective spirit grows strong and noble, the sentiment of patriotism is one of the living forces of the Brazilian and is barely hidden under his gentleness, humanity, and tolerance toward other countries.

But if these constitute some of the common traits of the psychology of the Brazilian the fundamental unity in the national character which they show was not formed nor attended by any damage to the great diversity of regional types which renders the social landscape in Brazil one of the most rich and picturesque. It can be said certainly in a general way that the Brazilian is altruistic, sentimental and generous, capable of impulsive passions, violent but only slightly tenacious, loving life more than order, pacific, hospitable, suspicious, tolerant by temperament and by lack of concern. This much with respect to sensibility. A hard worker, endowed with the vigorous individualism which characterizes pioneer peoples, but without the spirit of cooperation, and holding under a displeasing attitude of indolence and of relaxation extraordinary reserves of energy. So much with regard to his will, which, acting impulsively and therefore without continuity, appears to tend constantly to concentrate, economizing its strength for great periodic reactions, either individual or social. Of an acute sensibility, of a rare intellectual vivacity, and of an imagination rich in fictions which predispose him more to letters and the arts than to the sciences, the Brazilian is not less interesting with respect to his intelligence, almost primitive in its facility of "catching in the air" and in his intuition, nourished on sensibility and his instincts of direction. But if this appears to be in its general lines and most important traits the portrait of the Brazilian, the easily distinguishable common type develops in an admirable variety of subtypes both psychological and social, differentiated in their traits from one region to another. It is not a question of differences or divisions which are not specific and peculiar to Brazil, but which everywhere separate the city and the country, the coast and the interior, setting off the respective populations with marked characteristics which arise from their

[13] A. Jardé, *La Formation du peuple grec* (Paris: La Renaissance du livre, 1923).

particular mentality, from their mode of life, their customs, and their tendencies. Here, as in all countries, there are in opposition the restless and brilliant atmosphere of the great cities and the tranquil and restful atmosphere of the provincial cities; rustic simplicity, the reserve and traditionalistic spirit of social groups which live isolated in mountains or separated by great distances, and therefore keep themselves more closed and homogeneous, and the accessibility to new ideas, the tendency to progress, the love for adventure and the thirst for gain of the great cities, of heterogeneous make-up and cosmopolitan in nature. It is not without reason, writes Bouglé, that we attribute to mountains "a conservative influence. The coast, on the other hand, on which the most heterogeneous elements brought by the waves can enter into contact, make societies more mobile in a way and less traditional."

The most characteristic differences bound up with a diversity of ethnic make-up, with the variety of physical surroundings, and with the specific conditions of social formation are those which can be found between the populations of the north and those of the south, and are sufficiently marked to be perceived in spite of the great unity of spirit and feeling. It is necessary to take into account as one of the factors which have contributed most notably to distinguish the people of the south and those of the north, what might be called the favorable social influence of environments that are naturally unfavorable, to which some authors attribute a great importance. In fact, in no region of the country does external nature present itself in so barbarous and disorderly a fashion, so terribly confusing in the strength and variety of its landscape, as in the land of the north in which, offering to men voluptuous impressions and varied sensations, it seems to invite sensibility to fasten upon things, and intelligence to be invaded by enthusiasm and exultation. The man of the north is, actually, more movable, more lyric and dramatic; the man of the south, more measured, more positivistic and realistic; in the former, the preponderance of sensibility over reason, the love of eloquence, gestures, and enthusiastic attitudes; in the latter, a greater dominion over the nerves, sobriety to the point of reserve, equilibrium and moderation. The north, writes Jorge Amado, giving his opinion on the two populations, "seems to me more lyrical and mysterious; the south, more rapidly changeable and progressive." But in this human landscape in which there appear two types so clearly differentiated—the one expansive, inflammable, categorical in its affirmation; and the other retiring, prudent and conciliatory—there stand out also other differences not only in the populations of the central south but also between these and those of the extreme south, where there has developed one of the most characteristic types of our historic and social formation. Although they are so close together, the Paulista, whose discretion is almost hostile, so reserved it is, with his tendency to action, enterprising and tenacious, the inhabitant of Minas, distrustful to the point of hypocrisy, prudent to the point of pessimism, with a great power of adaptation, with clear good sense and exemplary habits, and the Carioca, with his good humor reaching the point of irreverence, his sense of the ridiculous and his taste for good living and the pleasures of life, are so different that these traits which separate them do not pass unperceived by even superficial observation. Of all these social types there stands out, however, the inhabitant of Rio Grande, the gaucho properly so called, who is romantic and cavalier, in whom a vigorous individualism, passionate enthusiasm, and combative ardor are mixed with an emotional sensibility and a natural generosity to form an original type with a harsh and rebellious accent, proceeding by contrasts of violence and conciliation, of an authoritative enthusiasm and melting sentimentality, and loving arrogance of gestures as much as nobility of attitude.[14]

Meanwhile, if these differentiating traits show the fragmentary process of our formation which favored the flowering in a variety of geographic settings of the picturesque diversity of the humanity, the traits of similarity, so general and persistent, show that Brazil has become a historic unity, a system of civilization in which common ideas circulate and in which there appear the tendencies of this civilization to its present-day expansion. All these groups of societies differentiated under the primitive pressure of race, environment, and of regimes of production and labor, having participated in a common life, have formed a more or less coherent society with its own customs, traditions, and characteristics. But some of these regional differences have grown weaker, as certain traits or tendencies, which as a whole constitute Brazilian character, are tending to be transformed by internal and external causes which are producing modifications in the social and economic structure and consequently in our very national mentality. From the transformations which have already been produced on the plateau of São Paulo, there has already resulted the fact that what constituted its primary base is hidden from our glance, not only by the mixture and assimilation of European peoples to the primitive core of the population, but also by the mass of new institutions which have been superimposed and which has altered the base by the simple fact of this superposition. Some traits are still to be observed in their purity and original force, certainly in larger or smaller size communities strewn through the interior, which maintain their ancient character, while those of the coast line and of the plateau have been transformed, since it is upon them that the light of industrial civilization has shone more intensely since the beginning of this century. In the same country in which natural conditions remain the same, all life is being modified, since peoples are changing as they are on the plateau; and to the extent that civilization is developed, as we have seen, social forces have more influence upon the character of nations than do

[14] Reviewing Castilhos Goycochêa's book *O Gaúcho na vida política brasileira,* Coaraci points out that "there are two types of inhabitant of Rio Grande, two kinds of characteristic individualities." The one to which we refer is undoubtedly the more frequent: "the popular and well known type of gaucho, sentimental and generous, swashbuckling and given to theatrical gestures and resounding phrases, chilvaric and disposed to make speeches, who shouts when he talks and loves to tell tall tales." But there are also "the cold and impenetrable men, we might almost say unfeeling, never carried away in explosive emotions, averse to boasting, who rarely reveal their purposes, but rarely are deterred from carrying out the courses they have secretly determined upon." Besides this distinction, says Coaraci, we find the existence in Rio Grande do Sul, "of two distinct attitudes, permanently antagonistic and frequently in open conflict. They are the *frontier spirit* and what the author calls the *city spirit.* The whole history of Rio Grande do Sul becomes clear in the light of this distinction. Castilhos Goycochêa shows us that the long duration of the beggars' insurrection was due to the predominance of the frontier spirit; that the antagonism between the two attitudes never ceased to exist; that these attitudes are not limited to party circles, but penetrate and invade branches of all factions and continue to exist in close contact within them; that the periods of peace and tranquillity in the south are those in which the city spirit was dominant; that at the time of Júlio de Castilhos the *pica-paus* (republicans) were dominated by the city spirit, while the *maragatos* (federalists) were inspired by the frontier spirit. It was the former that won out and directed the policies of Rio Grande, in its characteristic isolation from 1894, the date of the defeat of the federalists, down to 1923, when the Treaty of Pedras Altas was signed." (Vivaldo Coaraci, article in *O Estado de São Paulo,* Sept., 1935.)

natural forces. With the contact and more frequent communication between the coast and the interior, the north and the south, thanks to mechanical means of transportation (the automobile and airplane), with the assimilating force of the radio, with the changes in social and economic structure in a single direction, and with the transformation of the demographic situation we may associate the recent transformation of the psychology of the Brazilian people. These changes go on still within certain limits and in the direction of the fundamental traditions and tendencies with which the temperament of each people affirms its character. However much modern nations may strive to be complete and to secure success in economics and industry, politics and military life, literature and art, they conserve certain characteristic peculiarities, and they are notable for the emphasis laid on this or that national quality, furnishing with this very differentiation a principle of wealth and strength for the civilization of which they are part and to which they make their contribution with their progress in different fields.

BIBLIOGRAPHY

Baldus, Herbert, *Ensaios de etnologia brasileira* (São Paulo: Comp. Editora Nacional, 1937—Brasiliana).

Barros Latif, Miran M. de, As *"Minas gerais"* (Rio: A Noite, 1940).

Buarque de Holanda, Sérgio, *Raízes do Brasil* (Rio: Olímpio, 1936).

Garcia, Rodolfo, and others, *Os Judeus na história do Brasil* (Rio: Uri Zwerling, 1936).

Goulart, Jorge Salis, *A Formação do Rio Grande do Sul* (Pôrto Alegre, 1929).

Leite Filho, Solidônio, *Os Judeus no Brasil* (Rio, 1923).

Machado, J. de Alcântara, *Vida e morte do bandeirante* (Sao Paulo, 1929).

Melo Franco, Afonso Arinos de, *Conceito de civilização brasileira* (São Paulo: Comp. Editora Nacional, 1936—Brasiliana, Vol. 70).

Oliveira Lima, *Pernambuco: Seu desenvolvimento histórico* (Leipzig, 1895).

Prado, Paulo, *Retrato do Brasil: Ensaio sôbre a tristeza brasileira* (São Paulo, 1928; 2nd ed., Rio, 1931).

Ramos, Artur, *As Culturas negras no Novo Mundo* (Rio: Civilização Brasileira, 1937).

Rugendas, Johann Moriz, *Viagem pitoresca através do Brasil*, transl. by Sérgio Milliet (São Paulo: Martins, 1940).

Siegfried, André, *L'Amérique Latine* (Paris, 1934). Transl. as *Impressions of South America* (New York, 1933).

Silva Rodrigues, Mílton, *Educação comparada* (São Paulo: Comp. Editora Nacional, 1938), pp. 233–245, "O Brasil: O Povo e a sua índole."

Tristão de Ataíde, "Traços da psicologia do povo brasileiro," In *A Ordem* (Rio), Feb., 1934.

PART II

CULTURE

CHAPTER ONE

RELIGIOUS INSTITUTIONS AND BELIEFS

The history of the missions and the history of Christian civilization—The Company of Jesus and the Reformation—The first mission of the Jesuits to Brazil—Catechism: José de Anchieta —The gospel in the jungle—The tempest of the Reformation and its repercussion in Brazil— The foundation in Rome (1622) of a permanent Congregation for the Propagation of the Faith—The expansion of missions—The missionaries against the abuses of the conquest— Antônio Vieira in his struggle against the slavery of the Indians—Culture in this period more or less the tributary of religion—Catholicism and the influence of Afro-Indian religions —The big house, the chapel and slave quarters—Churches and temples—The pulpit in Brazil—The training of priests—The orders and religious congregations—Their wealth and their flourishing—Masonry—The activities of the masonic lodges—The fusion of church and State—The influence of the clergy—The great preachers—The religious question— Freedom of worship and of belief—Protestantism and its progress—Spiritualism and other forms of religion—Theosophy—Positivism—The "religion of humanity"—Religion and culture—The dominance of the Catholic religion.

IT MAY SEEM STRANGE at first sight that when we approach the analysis of the culture in the more restricted sense, and in its fundamental aspects, we should begin by studying religious beliefs and institutions. Certainly, taking the term "culture" in its broadest significance, as it is common in the field of cultural anthropology, religious beliefs and institutions are an integral part of the spiritual culture of a people. Seen in this light, it would be one of the conditions and factors of culture in the more limited sense of intellectual, literary, artistic, or scientific development. But so intimate and constant are the relations between the development of religion in Brazil and that of intellectual life in our first three centuries, that one cannot for that long period separate one from the other. In that phase of our social formation, it was indeed out of religious aims, forms, and essentials that practically the whole culture was developed in this part of the continent. Religion had an influence in the colonial period that was without doubt preponderant and practically exclusive in the organization of the system of culture, which, as much in its content as in its forms and institutions, shows vividly those relations of close dependence between culture and religion. It is not only points of contact that were established between them, zones of influence and of interpenetration, but true bonds which tied them together from their beginning, interweaving their roots and obliging us to relate our cultural history to events, institutions, and influences in the field of religion. Tributary to religion, on whose sap it was nourished for a long time, culture only later, especially in the nineteenth century, became detached from the church, without ceasing to the Christian in its spirit and in its manifestations, in order to tie itself up with professional life and institutions designed for the preparation for the liberal professions. Thus, of ecclesiastical initiative and religious content at the beginning, growing up in the shade of convents, seminaries, and the colleges of the priests, and later of a utilitarian character, promoted in higher schools for professional training, culture cannot be understood or explained in its evolution, if we neglect to set forth first of all the religious and professional activities to which it was tied, and above all those of the Catholic religion which with its beliefs, its morals and its rites rocked the cradle and sealed the tomb of successive generations.

Brazil, we can say with Serafim Leite, was born Christian. It was born Christian above all through the faith which burned in the breast of the discoverers and their king, and which had been transported with their customs and usages, their merchandise, and their arms, in the holds of the caravels. The great cross of native wood borne in procession by the Portuguese and Indians and planted beside the altar erected under the open sky at which Brother Henrique de Coimbra said Mass the 1st of May on terra firma was, in the official act of taking possession of Brazil which was celebrated in Pôrto Seguro, the august symbol of the conquest of the newly discovered lands for Christian civilization. The name Island of the True Cross (Ilha de Vera Cruz), with which the first historian, Pero Vaz de Caminha, had baptized these lands, had come as an inspiration of the religious sentiment which animated the discoverers, and which was to be transferred from the little peninsula country to the vast territory which was now open to the propagation of the faith and to the colonizing effort of the Portuguese. The Catholic religion at the time of the discovery had already penetrated the entire length and breadth of the Portuguese realm, from the little cities to the towns and villages and settlements, and so deeply that four centuries later Antero de Figueiredo, in his expedition to Portugal, could still feel it in all its purity and rustic simplicity, "in the white shrines of the crossways, with their red roofs and little lamps, their animism and their paternosters; in the black cross at the edge of the road; in the crucifix of the village squares—symbols which lend a religious air to the roads, to the corners, to the rocks and hills, spiritualizing the land and the air by the feeling of devotion." [1] In that country, with a population so scarce that at this time it did not exceed probably a million inhabitants, scattered over valleys and hills or grouped in rare cities with narrow, congested streets, religion had been disseminated through all social classes, and the cross which rose on top of churches was carried in processions and in pilgrimages to miracle-working chapels in the country, rose on the ships, adorned the hilt of swords and hung over the breast of layman and priest, of peasant and of nobleman. It was an atmosphere of religiosity and of faith that was breathed in Portugal, and if it was perhaps warmer and more laden with mysticism in the convents and sanctuaries, it spread everywhere, in the evangelical word which descended from the pulpits and in the vibrations of the bronze bells which tolled slowly from the towers of the Christian churches. In the fleet of Pedro Alvares Cabral there went toward India, which was its destination when it left Belém, certain Franciscan missionaries: the cross of the caravels that served for the lands of the heathen or for the maritime adventures of the discoverers opened its arms for the evangelization of barbarous tribes and the conquest of souls. But, to carry out this work of the extension of the Kingdom of God in this part of the new world, there had to be developed as in India a whole general staff of select men, the Jesuits.

Now from the time of the voyages of St. Paul down to our own days the history of missions is bound up with that of Christian civilization, and missionary annals continue

[1] Antero de Figueiredo, *Jornadas em Portugal* (Paris-Lisbon and Rio, 1918).

through the centuries the acts of the Apostles.[2] The propagation of the faith, in the meanwhile, encountered in the sixteenth century apparently invincible obstacles. On the one hand, the discipline of the clergy and of the church which had been contaminated by the sensual life of the Renaissance and by a rather idolatrous admiration for the ancient world, and impregnated with pagan orientalism, was tending to break down in the abuses of the Popes and the great ecclesiastics; and, on the other hand, there was breaking out in the very bosom of Catholicism, as a consequence of these abuses, and under the pressure of reformatory ideas, the greatest schism which had yet disturbed its spiritual unity and the preaching of the Gospel. The hour was grave. Catholicism "had suffered the formidable attacks of a Luther, a Zwingli, and a Calvin. Half of Europe was broken up into Protestant sects. Politics caused disorders of the great countries, dividing them to weaken them; and the earth was still ·soaked in the blood of the massacre of St. Bartholomew's Day and of the tremendous killings of Anabaptists and Huguenots." It was at this time of struggles and religious dissensions that there arose the Company of Jesus, founded in 1534 by St. Ignatius of Loyola. From this company, even before it had been erected in 1540 into a religious order by Paul III, there arose one of its most eminent sons, St. Francis Xavier, to carry the gospel to India. To use the expression of Pope Pius XI, God in this way was making the century of the Reformation "the century of the Council of Trent, of the renascence of the old religious orders, of the rich flowering of new religious orders, the century of the gold of sanctity." In fact, the evangelical movement took on again its ascending curve, and among the great dates of the missionary calendar there figure in this century those of the successes of the Apostle of India and of Father José Anchieta, the apostle of America. In 1549, about fifty years after the discovery, and when the Society of Jesus was nine years old, there arrived in Brazil with the first governor general, Tomé de Sousa, the first mission of Jesuits, directed by Father Manuel da Nóbrega, a religious leader of great knowledge and virtues, "the greatest politician of Brazil" as Southey called him, and the founder and organizer of missions to the Indians. This mission four years later, in 1553, was reenforced with another handful of missionaries, among whom was a young Jesuit, nineteen years old and of a weak constitution—Father José de Anchieta, who came from Tenerife in the Canary Islands and was to become famous as a result of the sanctity of his life, his spirit of sacrifice, and his apostolic zeal in the propagation of the gospel in the jungles and the sertões.

The activity of these admirable men in the defense and conversion of the heathen and in the penetration of the back country, amid dangers and tasks of every order, cannot be estimated except by measuring it against the extent of the geographic and social area in which it was carried on and by the variety of services in which it was divided, which entered into all fields. Certainly, it was in Christianizing the land that the efforts of the Jesuits were concentrated, and it is in the service of this fundamentally Catholic point of view that the surprising activities of the missionaries were developed, extended, and multiplied. There is not the slightest doubt that the tireless and fecund action of these missionaries surpassed the mere field of the spiritual. They formed with their rigid discipline, in the incoherent and fragmentary colonial society, a compact, homogeneous whole, capable of resisting dissolving influences and of establishing a

---

[2] Florian Delhorbe, "Les Missions catholiques dans le monde," in *Le Mois* (Paris), Mar. 1 to Apr. 1, 1939.

minimum of moral and spiritual unity between the Portuguese colonists and the primitive peoples, assimilated to the new civilization. The Society of Jesus did not limit itself to indoctrinating all with the word of Christ, edifying them by the sacraments and the example of their virtues; nor did it employ only religious means to spread the gospel and to assure a moral cohesion in the fidelity of the tribes that were catechized. It attacked despotism and the abuses of the colonies. It led an offensive against dissoluteness in customs, with which social stability, given the accessibility of Indian women and the scarcity of white women, was being broken down in its fundamentals. They opened schools for reading and writing and even built with their own hands colleges like that of the city of Salvador—the first in Brazil—that of São Vicente, and in 1554 that of São Paulo in the fields of Piratininga.[3] They concentrated the Indians in settlements in which, in the shade of the church and the school, the land was cultivated and all the necessary industries were practiced. There began "with the slow tread of the missionary" —to employ the expression of Euclides da Cunha—that amazing colonizing penetration which only later was to obtain its maximum of intensity, "spreading through three points of the compass, following the swift route of the bandeiras." The first schoolmaster of Brazil, understanding the importance of that truly efficient instrument for infiltration that is comprised by the elementary school, the Jesuit created schools and erected colleges everywhere; he was accompanied by his medicine, his school dispensary —"a general depository of everybody"—and with his industries, his farming and his cattle breeding, he became one of the most powerful agents of colonization in these parts. The authority and prestige the Jesuits acquired among Indians and colonists gave these religious leaders, in the sixteenth century, a position of the first importance in colonial political life, in which they played a part as counselors, and to which they sometimes succeeded, by their decisive influence, in giving a new direction, assuring the success of Portuguese arms.

The activity of Father Manuel da Nóbrega in colonial politics was in fact of the first importance. It was he that led the governor, Mem de Sá, to adopt a new system for the subjection of the Indians and induced the King of Portugal to expel the French from Rio de Janeiro and encouraged Estácio de Sá in the struggle against the invader allied with the Tamoya Indians. Until then "the Portuguese," writes Serafim Leite, "were following the Roman system of dividing in order to conquer. They promoted the division of the Indian chiefs among themselves and took advantage of this division."

[3] What the life of the first Jesuits in Piratininga was, Father José de Anchieta tells us in one of his letters, written in an edifying spirit of piety and resignation and with much picturesque realism, rich in details. "Here they made," he writes, "a little house of straw, with a door of interwoven sugar cane, and here the brothers lived for some time, crowded together; but the crowding was a help in standing the cold which in that region is great, and there it often freezes. The beds were hammocks, such as the Indians are wont to make; for covers they had the fire for which the brothers, when they had finished their afternoon lessons, went to the woods to get firewood, and brought it home on their backs so they could pass the night, and their clothing was little and poor, without nether garments nor shoes, and was of cotton cloth. For the table they used for a time wide leaves of trees instead of napkins: towels could be dispensed with where victuals to eat were lacking, and they had nowhere to get food except from the Indians, who gave them alms of flour and sometimes (but rarely) some little fish from the river or game from the forest. Many a time they were sorely famished and cold: nevertheless, they continued their study with fervor, at times reading their lesson outside in the cold, which was more tolerable than the smoke inside the house." (Simão de Vasconcelos, *Crônica da Companhia de Jesús*, p. 83, No. 151).

For Father Manuel da Nóbrega, "this was not the correct system; the better system was that of the strong hand." The peace imposed by firmness and by force would not only render the conversion of the Indians easier, as in fact it did when they became incorporated within civilization, but also give more solid guarantees to the life of the colonists and to the colonizing effort which was being developed until this time under the permanent pressure of attacks by rebellious tribes. The activity of the Jesuits, including the campaign of Mem de Sá against the French, besides being inspired above all by religious motives, had a political purpose which can never be too much emphasized. It contributed to reestablishing a union between Indians whom the French were dividing and arousing against the Portuguese, to prevent Portuguese America from being cut in two parts, and moreover, to preserve unity of religion against the dangers that were menacing it. Others, to be sure, see the proceedings of Father Nóbrega in a different light. We see behind this conduct, not only the solicitude of his apostolic zeal, but also the keen vision of a great statesman. In 1557, a year and four months after crossing the Bay of Guanabara with his ships, Villegagnon brought to Rio de Janeiro an expedition organized at Honfleur in Normandy, of which a committee of fourteen Huguenots, chosen by Calvin and by the church of Geneva, formed a part. This was the first mission of the Reformed Church which trod the land of Brazil; and it was to spread in the Portuguese colonies "the terrible tempest of the Reformation which was to drag away from the heart of the church so many peoples." The discord which broke out between the Calvinists and Villegagnon; the return of the major part of them to Europe in 1558, the sacrifice of four others who signed the admirable Calvinist "profession of faith" written by Jean de Bourdel, and fell victims to the bloody vengeance of the French governor himself, reduced doubtless the chances of diffusion of the Protestant sect in Brazil. But whatever may be the point of view in which the impartial historian places himself, it is impossible not to recognize the importance of the attitude of the Jesuits in the face of the peril of the transporting of religious struggles which were lacerating Europe to the little colonial society still in the process of formation, scattered and heterogeneous and already split by grave internal dissensions.

Without the energy of Mem de Sá, seconded by the tireless activity of Nóbrega, not only, as Southey says, "would this city which is today the capital of Brazil have been French," but a large part of the southern region would also have been French and the Portuguese colonization with its triple unity of language, religion, and territory would have been gravely compromised. Of all of the episodes in which the vast plan of Nóbrega for the expulsion of the French unfolded itself, none, however, was so famous as the mission which the illustrious Jesuit carried out, accompanied by Anchieta, visiting the Indians to negotiate peace and offering himself as a hostage with the risk of losing his life. The celebrated expedition from which resulted the armistice of Iperoig (1563), agreed upon between the Tamoyas and the Portuguese as a result of the mission of Nóbrega and Anchieta—the most perilous embassy with which anyone was ever charged, as Southey called it—is doubtless one of the most beautiful pages of the missionary annals of the Company of Jesus, and of its patient and humane work of colonization. What is surprising in all this civilizing enterprise initiated by the Jesuits fifteen days after they had disembarked and multiplied in a variety of services over almost three centuries, is that they carried it out alone for about thirty years and only after 1580 had help in their apostolic task from missionaries of other orders such as the Benedictines,

Franciscans and Carmelites. The apostolic activities were to acquire everywhere a new impulse on the 6th of January, 1622, when Gregory XV founded a permanent Congregation for the Propagation of the Faith; and during that century Catholic missions spread, only to enter upon a new decline in Europe and in distant countries toward the end of the eighteenth century, as a consequence of the French Revolution and the Napoleonic Wars. But even after the entry of the monastic orders in the seventeenth century, it was the Jesuits that initiated almost alone another campaign—the most memorable of all in which they took part—in defense of the freedom of the Indian, opposing the wall of their own breasts, consecrated by the cross and the fire of their burning word to the traffic and exploitation of American tribes. The attacks of the mamelucos, the most terrible enemies of the Indians, upon the settlements and towns of the inhabitants; the incursions of the bandeiras organized with the express object of capturing Indians; the destructive invasions in the south, against the mission of Guaira and the reductions of Paraguay, Uruguay and Tape; [4] the persecutions which they suffered in the north in Pará and Maranhão, from which they were twice expelled, in 1661 and 1684, and the tremendous offensive of accusations and slanders showed the intensity which the obstinate struggle of the Jesuits against the slaveholding colonists attained, and their unshakable decision not to sacrifice, in obedience to the powerful, the ideas of respect for the human person and freedom of the Indians which they held. In this struggle against the captivity of the aborigines, there stands out in the north the incomparable figure of Father Antônio Vieira, an evangelizer in the penetration of the sertão, a cunning diplomat and notable orator whose eloquence in defense of the oppressed race broke out with the irrepressible force of an explosion and is only comparable to that of Rui Barbosa two centuries later, in his campaign for the freedom of the Negro slaves.

[4] In the task of converting the Indians, the Jesuits showed great psychological tact which permitted them to carry the light of the gospel farther than any other missionaries. They immediately made an attempt to learn the Tupí-Guaraní language, which they acquired with a success matched by few, and in their classes, in which they mixed white and Indian (*columis*) children, they made "each learn the language of the other: the Indians, Portuguese; the Portuguese, Brazilian." In winning souls, while they did not neglect adults, they directed their serious attention to the realm of childhood, and, "as they knew that there is nothing like children to attract children," they set about importing orphan children from Lisbon, who arrived in 1550, in the second expedition of the Jesuits, and were to become, writes Serafim Leite, "agents to effect a connection with the Indian boys of Brazil." They managed to put up with certain customs of the Indians, in order to attract and win them. But all this apostolic activity, remarkable from so many points of view, was not without errors of technique and vision. It seems to me that one of them was the stress laid upon the intellectual side in the education of the colonists and, above all, in the training of the Indians: the Franciscans, as Gilberto Freyre has pointed out, were concerned above all to make craftsmen and technicians of the Indians, while the first Jesuits were almost ashamed, we read in their chronicles, that it was necessary for them to perform mechanical offices. The greatest mistake, however, practiced doubtless with the high object of the defense of the Indians, was the "segregation" of the natives in large villages. However well organized they were—and the settlements known by the name of reductions in Paraguay became little cities, prosperous and peaceful—their effect was to create for the Indians a social environment that was artificial, putting an obstacle, from many points of view, in the way of the transition from savage life to civilization, besides constituting real ethnic and cultural cysts in colonial society, for they lived quite apart from it under the jurisdiction of the Jesuits. Giving up the culture from which they came, under the guidance of the missionaries, the Indians did not succeed in integrating themselves in a new situation, not ideal, but real, and remained halfway between two types or styles of culture, of very different levels and character.

In the face of an action of such large scope on the religious, social, and political plane, in which missionaries of all orders were able to maintain among the colonists an authorized superiority, as much by their sacerdotal ministry as by the culture and dignity of their life, one can estimate the degree of penetration which the work of propagating the faith attained among the Indians and colonists. Christianization, properly so called, of the natives and of a great number of the mixed breeds, "although superficial and on the crust," in the severe judgment of Gilberto Freyre, was undeniably, as he himself recognizes, almost exclusively the work of the fathers of the Jesuit Society who contributed more than all the others to make Catholicism really the cement of our unity. In proportion as the gospel spread out through the sertões and the forests in an immense effort at conversion, it insinuated itself into the dark region of the slave quarters, bringing along with faith to that race dishonored by the piracy of slavery a word of comfort and some energy, and promoting the mass conversion of the Negro population caught in the clutches of the slave traffic. The missionaries, so ardent in the defense of the freedom of the aborigines, were obliged to put up with Negro slavery, established by sack consecrated into a legal institution, just as in India they were forced to compromise with the separation of castes, so deep-rooted was it in the blood (especially in the south of India), attacking evangelization by the easier conversion of the outcast (pariah), who saw in the missionary a protector against his exploiters. Since it was not possible for them to destroy Negro slavery (and we all know the campaign that was necessary for almost a century to achieve its abolition), they endeavored to render the servile condition less hard and to lend every possible assistance, moral and religious, to the victims of slavery. But the monks, and especially the Jesuits, established their most solid points of support for this vigorous missionary expansion in the schools and colleges which they founded, and with which for almost three centuries the history of culture in Brazil became intimately tied up with the history of missions. The church and the school appeared, in colonial life, so close together that there are no villages of Indians, no towns or cities, within the sphere of action of the missionaries, in which beside the Catholic temple—church, hermitage or chapel—one does not find at least a school in which boys can learn to read and write. At the beginning, elementary education, and later, education in the humanities, in the colleges of Rio de Janeiro and Pernambuco, and in that of Bahia, in which, reorganized in 1557, higher education was provided, degrees of master of arts were given in 1578, and in this course of art (philosophy) there had already matriculated in 1598 forty students. While the college of Bahia was being established, writes Serafim Leite, also by the initiative of the Jesuits, "others were simultaneously or successively founded in the principal Portuguese towns of Brazil, which during the sixteenth century had no other teacher."

It was in these colleges and the houses of the Jesuits that the first libraries of the country were installed, and for a long time they were the only centers for spreading culture on the coast and on the plateau. In them were educated during the sixteenth century, among others, Benito Teixeira, the author of *Prosopopéia*, Brother Vicente de Salvador, to whom we owe the first history of Brazil, and Jerônimo Albuquerque Maranhão; in the seventeenth century, Antônio Vieira, Eusébio and Gregório de Matos; and in the eighteenth century, the poets Santa Rita Durão, Basílio da Gama, and Alvarenga Peixoto were pupils of the Jesuits, "all or almost all," said the Baron of Rio Branco, "those who had some name in letters, sciences, arts, or politics in colonial Brazil."

In these three centuries which the colonial regime includes, teaching, given over entirely to the clergy, was the exclusive charge of the Jesuits in the first century of our formation, and in the later centuries was given above all by the religious leaders of the company and of the Benedictines, Capuchins, Carmelites, and in a general way the priests, either regular or secular, in their colleges, convents, and seminaries. "Pioneers of our civilization," writes Vilhena de Morais with respect to the Jesuits, "at the same time that they dedicated themselves to their spiritual ministries . . . like the sons of St. Ignatius of Loyola that they were, they did not forget the cultivation of sciences and letters. It is they, really, that created and almost exclusively maintained for two hundred years, public instruction among us. It is they that gave to poetry, to chronicles, to history, to philosophy and eloquence their oldest representatives in a country still sunk in the darkness of barbarism. They are the only ones who studied the language of the savages. . . . They finally are those who had the glory of presiding over the intellectual formation of our most notable writers of the seventeenth and eighteenth centuries." One may then say without any undue emphasis that the culture of Brazil, developed by the church through our colonial history, was tributary to religion. Certainly, because it did not have a suitable environment, it did not succeed in developing except within certain limits even among the ecclesiastics—the best educated men of the time, whose knowledge did not exceed that of Latin and theology—and the individual who had mastered Latin and French continued to be so rare, says Armitage, "that he was looked upon as a genius so transcendent that people came from long distances to consult him." But although dominated by the predominant or almost exclusive influence of religion, and shaped especially to provide a professional education for priests, this culture of a literary and scholastic character was up to a certain point disinterested, without utilitarian preoccupation, and was characterized by its organic unity, linked as it was to a certain conception of life that at this time was dominant in the mother country and in its only university center.[5]

Thus with all its defects, which were those of the teaching of the time, excessively literary, abstract; and dogmatic, this culture, if to be sure it created an artificial élite superimposed upon the ignorant mass of the colony, had the advantage of bringing about, even if it were from above, through its uniform character, a profounder assimilation of the Brazilians of the north and of the south, of the coast and of the plateau. The students of the colleges of the fathers were, as Gilberto Freyre has pointed out, "once they were graduated, elements of urbanization and of universalization, and in an environment powerfully influenced by the autocrats of the big houses in the direction of rural stagnation and of extreme regional differentiation. In their way of dressing, in

[5] No better intellectual result was to be expected in the colony, when in Lisbon, the capital of the mother country, ignorance was general and profound in the sixteenth century, and only two persons, according to the affirmation of R. Oliveira, were occcupied in teaching reading to little girls. In the seventeenth and eighteenth centuries the situation in the mother country, in this respect, did not change noticeably until the time of the Marquis de Pombal, and the mass of the illiterate throughout the country was enormous. The clergy held in its hands a monopoly of education. The only university that functioned in the overseas country—Coimbra, founded in 1290 in Lisbon and moved in 1537 to Coimbra—was also under the direct influence of the clergy and especially of the Society of Jesus which took control of it in 1555, and it constituted with its limited and bookish courses, of additions, glosses, and commentaries, rather an apparatus for mental sterilization than a factor in intellectual and scientific progress.

their style of life, they represented a tendency for the dominion of the European spirit and that of the city over the country, or the turbulently rural, incarnated many times by their own fathers or grandfathers." The sugar plantation was opposed to the city; and if it be true that the lord of the plantation—an almost feudal lord—having the government of his property and the policing of his region, was the lord of his plantation, of his slaves and of his chapel, still religion mounted guard over the patriarchal family with its chaplains and its uncles who were padres, whose moral and cultural influence reached all the big houses. These priests, generally of the secular clergy, not only exercised the functions of chaplains; they were assistants, advisers, and often the first teachers of sons of well-to-do families, who from them went on afterward to Europe for higher studies. The number of illustrious men of the colonial epoch and of the first years of the Empire who received their primary and secondary education in the colleges of the fathers exceeds, writes Gilberto Freyre,[6] that of those educated at home with chaplains and uncles who were former padres. Chaplains and fathers although more subordinate to the fathers of the family than to the church, nevertheless did not fail to represent under the roof of the big patriarchal houses something subtly urban, ecclesiastical, and universal—the church, Latin, the classics and Europe, the feeling of another life beyond that dominated by the glance of the lord from the top of his big house. But the chaplains of the big houses in addition to assisting the patriarchal family, were there to Christianize the slave quarters and to lend their aid to the lords in the policy of assimilating slaves: like the missionaries in their schools and churches, in the villages of the heathen, the chaplains with their chapels beside the slave quarters, constituted outposts on the coast and in the sertão, not only for the preaching of the gospel, but also to maintain the unity of religion and to preserve the religiosity of the colonists against indigenous fetishism and the animism of the African which were tending to corrupt Catholic belief and doctrine.

The religious life of the colonists, threatened both in the city and on the plateau, was in fact by virtue of its contact with two different cultures, that of the Negroes and that of the Indians, so much the more exposed to these influences as the communication with the two ethnic and cultural groups grew in profundity and in proportion to the ignorance of the mass which facilitated the assaults of primitive mysticism. Religion, considers Gilberto Freyre, "became the point of contact and of fraternization between the two cultures, that of the masters and that of the Negro, and never an insuperable and hard barrier." It was this policy of adaptation and compromise that it was proper to adopt; and the church actually did adopt it, in order to Christianize the Indians and slaves. But the gradual, progressive assimilation of the latter into the mass of the colonists could not be without the risk of exposing Catholic beliefs and rendering them permeable to these cultures of the aborigines and of Africa, and to their beliefs, rites, and superstitions. The Christian religion which, inherited from Portugal, was contaminated with all these Afro-Indian impurities, above all in the lower social strata of colonial society, reached an acute phase in the seventeenth and eighteenth centuries in which religious life on the one hand and sexual passion and the dissoluteness of custom on the other came, according to the observation of Pedro Calmon, "to menace with extinction the white race in a colony infested by Africans." No one went without his rosary

[6] Gilberto Freyre, *Sobrados e mocambos: Decadência do patriarcado rural do Brasil* (São Paulo: Comp. Editora Nacional, 1936—Brasiliana, Vol. 54), p. 100.

in his hand or his beads about his neck; all punctually knelt in the streets upon the sounding of the Angelus; and in the governmental palace of Bahia, according to the testimony of La Barbinnais, people prayed in the corners.[7] While the first son in patriarchal families succeeded the lord of the manor, according to the law which gave to the first-born the entire succession, and the second went to study in Europe, the third entered the church, taking his vows at fifteen years. "The vocation will come later with the habit, the tonsure, and vow." Rich girls, in a society where the number of men was always superior to that of women, went to take their vows in Portugal and afterwards in Brazilian convents, and their movement to the cloisters reached such a point, that scarcely had the convent of St. Clare been founded in Bahia in 1669, when the number of marriages in that year went down to five in the capital of Brazil. Churches were multiplied everywhere, and beginning with the seventeenth century Brazil was a country of churches and of convents,[8] and the charm which the churches exercised over the multitudes was indeed extraordinary. Some, like the Convent of Carmel in Bahia, and those of Vila-Rica Mariana in the eighteenth century and those of Rio de Janeiro, became celebrated for the tranquil solidity of their construction, the harmony of their architectonic lines, the beauty of their interiors, for their balustrades and arches, their altars and their pulpits, their chapels and sacristies, and for the precious things and objects of art upon which you could not possibly gaze without hearing a voice out of the past that spoke through the richness of their historic memories.

The Catholic religion, impregnated with mysticism, like a leafy tree had already sunk its roots deep into the land, and, sheltering colonial society under its vast shade,

[7] La Barbinnais, *Nouveau voyage*, Vol. 3, p. 206.

[8] In the Church of Carmel at Bahia there still stands, in the midst of all its riches, at the left of the Chapel of the Most Holy, the old wooden pulpit in which Brother Eusébio da Soledade, a Carmelite, the brother of Gregório de Matos and the disciple of Antônio Vieira, used to preach; he was even considered in his time a rival of Father Vieira in sacred oratory. Among other treasures which make this church one of the richest of Brazil, it contains a sumptuous main chapel, with a carved and gilded altar; magnificent balustrades of jacaranda wood, carved with native designs; the great crucifix of Santo Cristo do Monte, three centuries old; the reliquary of the time of the Dutch, "doubly precious on account of the high value of its carving and because it was given by the defender of the island of Itaparica, the brother of Father Antônio Vieira"; and three candelabra of gilded bronze, sold with the real crown of Portugal and brought with him in his flight by Dom João VI, being hastily snatched from the palace (Costa Rêgo, in *Correio da Manhã*, Rio, June 15, 1940). The Church of St. Francis of Assisi, the masterpiece of Antônio Francisco Lisboa, called Aleijadinho (little cripple), and that of Our Lady of the Rosary, among others in Ouro Preto, and that of St. Francis in São Jõao d'El-Rei not only recall, in the wealth of their gold and the splendor of their decoration, the brilliance of the period of the mines, but exhibit the original art of that mestizo genius, sculptor, and architect who bequeathed us marvels in his wooden figures, such as those of Christ, of Mary Magdalene, and of an Apostle in the sanctuary of the Good Lord Jesus of Congonhas, and in his incomparable work cut in soapstone. His churches, which in the words of Manuel Bandeira represent "a cunning solution of the adaptation of the baroque to the environment of eighteenth century Minas, do not create that atmosphere of an almost sickly mysticism which we find in many others." The Church of St. Francis of Assisi, built according to a plan of Aleijadinho, and the Church of the Rosary, in which curves predominate, constitute the most original monuments of our colonial religious architecture, which is so rich in Rio de Janeiro, Minas Gerais, Recife, and especially Bahia, with the sumptuous church of the Monastery of St. Francis in Salvador, and the Church of Grace, which goes back to 1582, and being even more ancient than that of the Aid (Ajuda), was the first seat of a bishop. Cf. *Guia de Ouro Preto* (Serviço do patrimônio histórico a artístico, 1939); Simão de Vasconcelos, *Mariana e seus templos* (1938).

was dissolving in the unity of faith the regional, social, and cultural differences of the Brazilian people in the course of their formation. An active, combative force and a fortress for resistance, it served also as a dike against the invasion of the French and afterward against that of the Dutch, for whose expulsion the word of the preachers in their pulpits was associated with the warlike action of the convents themselves, there being mixed, as in the Church of Carmel of Bahia, "the smell of incense in the religious ceremonies with the smell of powder which that convent had vomited forth in its struggle against the rule of the Dutch." It was from the pulpit that there thundered the incomparable eloquence of Father Antônio Vieira, in favor of the freedom of the Indians against the slave-owning colonists, in Pará and Maranhão, as well as in defense of the soil and the faith in Bahia in 1640, in his famous sermon for the success of the arms of Portugal against those of Holland, when the latter had been expelled from Bahia and concentrated in Pernambuco.[9] It was from the tribune consecrated by the priestly insignia and covered by the immunity of the church that resistance many times exploded, after being cultivated in convents and seminaries, as in that of Olinda, "a true nest of liberals and revolutionaries" against the insolent despotism of the lords, the usurpations of public power, and the assault of the foreign invader. It was also by preaching in the pulpits, as well as by teaching in the colleges, that the power of national unity became stronger through the generations, first established by unity of language, for the priests spoke it with the most purity and spread the taste and interest for studies of the vernacular. The training of priests, to which the first Jesuit institution for higher learning was destined in Bahia as early as the end of the sixteenth century—made up of the three faculties of dogmatic theology, moral theology, and arts (Philosophy)—was provided in fact with diligent care not only in the society and in the convents of the principal religious orders, as among others in the seminaries of St. Peter and St. Joseph, created in Rio at the beginning of the eighteenth century, in that of Mariana (Minas), which dates from 1750, and in that of Olinda, founded in 1800 by Bishop Azeredo Coutinho, in a former Jesuit college. It was in these courses designed to prepare students for the priesthood, either the regular or the secular clergy, that the future educators of youth were formed, for they were almost all clerics; and since many of the youths who entered the convents gave up the career, some with their studies completed or about to be concluded,[10] most of our men of letters were recruited among the students of the colleges of the fathers or those who had left the convents and the seminaries. If it had not been for the important contribution of these institutions and of the religious congregations, with the expulsion of the Jesuits settled upon in 1759 by the Marquis de Pombal, the pedagogical and cultural system of the country would have been completely stripped; for it was the work in large part of the Jesuits, who, deported as prisoners

[9] "As a catechist," wrote the Count of Laet, "he [Vieira] went into the interior, winning many tribes of the Brazilian heathen to Christianity; as a politician, he was the right arm of his sovereign, and proposed measures and obtained resources for the expulsion of the Dutch who had seized the north of Brazil; as a preacher, he eclipsed the most famous, and by the delicacy of his conceits as well as by the boldness of his style, rose to such a height that no one approached him; an excellent prose writer, it can be said of him that he fixed the syntax of our speech, as Camões had fixed the vocabulary of Portuguese." (Carlos, Count de Laet, "O Frade estrangeiro," lecture given May 22, 1903, in the Círculo Católico.)

[10] Henry Coster (Koster), *Voyages dans la partie septentrionale du Brésil, depuis 1809 jusqu'en 1815*, transl. from the English (Paris: Lelamag, 1818), Vol. I, p. 59.

to Portugal, not only saw their goods confiscated, but all their books and manuscripts destroyed—"those highly valuable treasures of rare erudition." [11]

But if the Jesuits, apostles and teachers, conquered an indisputable place in the evangelization of the Indians and the education of youth, contributing more than all others toward the intellectual formation of Brazil in the time of the colony, religious leaders of other orders were preparing themselves in the silence of the cloisters for the activities of teaching and, at the end of the eighteenth century, for research in the natural sciences. In botany, the most eminent figure of the eighteenth century is Brother Mariana de Conceição Veloso of the Capuchin order, author of *Flora Flumi-nense* and creator of sixty-six genuses and four hundred species of plants belonging to Brazilian flora. His manuscripts were found in 1825 by Antônio de Arrabida; his inherit-ance was continued in his specialty by Brother Leandro do Sacramento, a Carmelite in Pernambuco, who traversed practically all of Brazil during a period of six years and left twenty-three works written, and provided the scientific organization for the botanical garden, and later by Alves Serrão, better known by the name of Brother Custodian, also a Carmelite, who, "in spite of the scarcity of his resources," writes Artur Neiva, "accom-plished a considerable piece of work in a brief space of time in the direction of the Botanical Garden." It is also from the Carmelite order and the Franciscan that there came to honor the episcopal throne some of the greatest figures of the Brazilian church. And after the Jesuit, Antônio Vieira, in the seventeenth century, the sacred tribune only acquired a new brilliance in the nineteenth century with the three great Franciscans, all preachers of renown, São Carlos, Jesús Sampaio and Mont'Alverne, who ascended the pulpit of the royal chapel in the time of Dom João VI and with their eloquence dominated half a century of religious life down to the beginning of the second Empire, when for the last time, after eighteen years of silence, on the invitation of the Emperor, Pedro II, the word of Mont'Alverne was heard in a famous sermon. In the political struggles in Recife there died, "shot beside the gallows, because there was no criminal who would serve to garrote him, the patriot Brother Joaquim do Amor Divino Caneca, a republican of 1817 and one of the most representative figures of the Confederation of the Equator." [12] Seeing once more these venerated shades, Father Roma and Brother Caneca in the sublimity of their sacrifice, Father José Maria Brayner in the epic of Pirajá, Father Miguelinho, and others, Costa Rêgo began to think, and not without reason as he visited the Convent of Carmel in Bahia, "of the utility of reinstalling the spirit of the Carmelite in Brazil. Because, he writes, we are unfortunately forgetful of the profound lesson with which the Carmelite taught us to be strong and at the same time to be Brazilian." [13] The fact is that the Carmelite order in Brazil, where the first group of Portuguese monks arrived in the fleet of Frutuoso Barbosa, eighty years

[11] "The expulsion of the Jesuits," writes Eduardo Prado, "was another Alcazar-Kebir for the overseas empire of Portugal, like that of the sixteeenth century for the kingdom. With the expulsion of the Jesuits in the past century, civilization retreated hundreds of leagues from the center of the African continent and of Brazil. The prosperous settlements of Paraná and Rio Grande fell into ruins; the Indians returned to savage life; the villages of Amazonas were depopulated, and down to the present day solitude and the desert reign where there was once human society."

[12] Inscription on the monument set up by the Instituto Histórico e Geográfico de Pernambuco, July 2, 1917, in the square of Five Points in Recife, where the heroic republican friar fell, shot to death.

[13] Costa Rêgo, in *Correio da Manhã*, Rio, June 15, 1940.

after its discovery, has been connected with the history of our struggles for liberty, with the bravery and the sacrifice of some of its sons.

The diffusion of the monastic orders, of the Carmelite, Benedictine, and Franciscan types, after their entry into Brazil at the beginning of 1580, was rapid along the whole coast, especially at Rio, Bahia, and Pernambuco. No obstacle hindered the development of this collectivity—church or monastery. The religious crises let loose by the acts of the government of Maurice of Nassau (1637–1644), who banished the friars of Pernambuco and prohibited the construction of new churches, did not last long enough nor were they carried on with sufficient intensity to prevent the material and spiritual restoration of the monastic order. Goods flowed into them. The property of the monasteries increased and grew richer; some of them even possessed great properties, fazendas, buildings, and slaves and were able to live, not relying upon the faithful, but upon the income of their endowments.[14] Spreading the useful arts, giving an incentive to the progress of letters, organizing libraries and archives and cultivating the soil, the monasteries, with which schools were practically always associated, exercised a highly moralizing and civilizing function from the time of the colony and throughout the period of the Empire. In the old city of São Paulo, erected in the shade of the Jesuit college, its initial nucleus, the triangle formed by the secular monasteries of St. Benedict, of Carmel, and of St. Francis, in the halls of which, opened to the patio of the cloister, the faculty of law had functioned since 1827, represent as in a symbol the domination of religious life and the preponderant influence which monastic establishments exercised over the history of colonial times. In the nineteenth century other religious congregations came to join these monastic orders, already rich in tradition; and the Lazarites and the Dominicans, among others, became active, in addition to those who wore the robe of the Society of Jesus, who wrapped themselves in the coarse gown and the cord of the poor man of Assisi, or who wore the wide tunic of St. Benedict.[15] The Lazarites founded in 1821, with fourteen pupils, in the mountains in Minas

14 The Prince of Wied Neuwied, in his journey through Brazil between 1815 and 1817, had occasion to stop in one of the monasteries of the order of St. Benedict, in the town of São Salvador, near Cabo Frio. Situated on the plain of Goitacazes, near Rio de Janeiro, to whose abbey it belongs, this convent is not one of the most important of the Benedictine order, but it "possesses valuable lands and property." "The building is vast," the famous German naturalist tells us; "it has a pretty church, two patios, and a little inner garden, with garden plots surrounded by stones and planted with balsaminaceous plants, tuberoses, etc. In one of the inner patios there rise tall coconut palms laden with fruit. The convent has fifty slaves, living in huts near a wide square in the middle of which there rises from a pedestal a great crucifix. Besides, there is a great sugar mill and many other works. This rich convent also possesses many horses and oxen and several corrals and ranches in the neighborhood. It receives 'tithes of sugar from various properties in the neighborhood' " (Maximiliano, Prince of Wied Neuwied, *Viagem ao Brasil*, transl. by Edgar Süssekind de Mendonça and Flávio Poppe de Figueiredo, revised and annotated by Oliverio Pinto (São Paulo: Comp. Editora Nacional, 1940—Brasiliana, Vol. I), p. 96).

15 The Benedictine monks who came to settle in the colony in 1580, with the Franciscans and Carmelites, first installed themselves in the captaincy of São Vicente in 1586, in Rio de Janeiro in 1589, and in Olinda in 1597, and there erected their first monasteries. The prohibition not to receive new monks, laid upon the convents by the Marquis de Pombal in the eighteenth century, and again in 1855 under the Empire, by the government of Prime Minister Nabuco de Gouveia, led to a serious monastic crisis which attacked the order of St. Benedict, threatening to wipe out its cloisters. All the other religious orders in the country established themselves in Brazil in the nineteenth century, in which there arrived the fathers of the Congregation of St. Vincent de Paul,

Gerais, the lonely college of Caraça, in which for almost half a century of the national life there was given a type of teaching marked, like that of the Jesuit, by the same preoccupation with the study of rhetoric and of Latin, and which became, thanks to the severity of its discipline and the rigor of its work, as Gilberto Freyre writes, "something sinister in the social landscape of Brazil in the early days of the Empire, snatching away children from the sugar mills . . . from the interior cattle-raising fazendas, from country houses, and from city mansions." Religion continued to be a vital element in society. There was established a permanent interchange between the church and the world; there emerged liberal and revolutionary priests in the Revolution of 1817, in which there appeared thirty-two representatives of the clergy, and in other episodes so expressive of the community in which political society and religious society mingled. Monks became bishops, and bishops and priests, statesmen, and the two types of clergy, the regular and the diocesan, who were the principal factors in the intellectual life of the country, with this interpenetration of the religious and the profane, actively participated in all the manifestations of political and social life.

This mixture of the religious and the secular, favored as much by the regime of patriarchal economy and by the penetration of temporal interests in the convents, in consequence of their wealth in real estate, as by the dominance of the clerical element in the social élite of the country, was to become even more marked with the interference of a new institution and with the union of Church and state from the time of the first Empire. It is in fact with the development of Freemasonry that the church and the world were mingled more closely and that there grew up a crisis from which there resulted the major conflict of our history, between the religious and the political. Freemasonry, begun in its modern aspect in 1717 in London, spread through the world, reaching France in 1725 and later Portugal. There in 1735 the first Masonic lodge was founded and thence it spread to Brazil at the end of the eighteenth century and the beginning of the following one. Because of its obscure origins, which were alleged to go back to Hiram, the architect of Solomon's temple, to the mysterious initiations of the ancient Order of the Temple, and also to the working men's corporations which constructed the Gothic cathedrals; and because of the prestige which its sacred character gave it, the mystery of its formulas, and the sumptuosity of its hierarchy; and because of its moral and political ends, this national and international association of men who professed principles of fraternity and recognized each other by emblems (the right angle, the compass, and the apron) was not slow in showing vigorous life and in spreading throughout Brazil, entering all its social levels and classes. A social and

---

of the College of Caraça, the French Dominicans of the province of Toulouse in 1881, and the Salesians in 1883, by direct order of Don Bosco. The three first preaching friars of the Dominican order settled in Uberaba, where they had the beautiful church of St. Dominic built and founded the convent of the Dominican Sisters, and whence they pushed on to Goiaz in 1897, to devote themselves to the conversion of the Indians in Conceição do Araguaia. The Salesian Fathers, coming from Uraguay, on the invitation of Bishop Dom Pedro Maria de Lacerda, and by the decision of Don Bosco, settled first in Niteroi, where they founded, in the very year of their arrival, the college of Santa Rosa, and then in 1885 in São Paulo, where they created the School of Arts and Crafts of the Sacred Heart of Jesus. The missionary fathers of the Heart of Mary settled in Rio de Janeiro in the present century in 1907, and from that city—the point of departure of their missionary activity and the place in which they built the church of Meier—they expanded into São Paulo and other States of the Union.

humanitarian institution designed to serve the welfare of humanity and social progress, although it was condemned by various Popes, beginning with Clement XII in 1738 and coming down to Leo XIII in 1884, it attracted Catholics and not a small number of high representatives of the regular and secular clergy by showing that it did not care to what religion its candidates belonged. This attitude of religious tolerance and the political aims which the Masonic societies had in mind, since they were founded to struggle for the independence of Brazil, the destruction of the monarchy, and for republican ideas, permitted Freemasonry [16] to win over to its secret societies, along with civilians and the military, also churchmen and friars, including some of the most illustrious of the different monastic orders. There enlisted in Masonic lodges, fighting under one or another Orient, prominent figures of the diocesan clergy and of the regular clergy, like Canon Januário da Cunha Barbosa, in the period of independence, and Father Diogo Antônio Feijó, Count de Irajá, Bishop of Rio de Janeiro, who anointed and crowned Pedro II, Brother Santa Teresa de Jesús Sampaio and Brother Mont'Alverne, Franciscan friars, and the greatest sacred orators at the time of the Empire, all thirty-third degree Masons. There was no Masonic lodge in which there did not figure side by side with civilians, fighting for the same ideals and participating in their rights and activities, some liberal wearers of the cassock.

[16] Contrary to the thought of A. J. de Melo Morais (*História do Brasil Reino e do Brasil Império*, I, p. 5), who would trace the origin of Masonry in Brazil to the time of the Minas Conspiracy (1786-1789), the first Masonic lodge appears to have been that which, under the name of the Areopagos of Itambe, was founded in 1799 by a former Carmelite friar, Arruda Câmara, in Pernambuco. It had as its principal object to set up a republican government and did not last more than three years. With the lodges which arose in São Salvador in 1807, 1808, and 1813, the Great Orient of Brazil was founded; its work, like that of the lodges, came to an end as a result of political commotions and the abortive revolution of 1817 in Pernambuco. In 1800 a lodge was started in Rio de Janeiro, and another in 1808 in Pernambuco, with political objects. It was, however, with the three lodges founded, one in Niteroi in 1812 and the other two in Rio in 1815, with the object of achieving the independence of Brazil, that finally the Great Orient of Brazil was founded, independent of the Great Lusitanian Orient. These secret societies to which belonged some of the most eminent men of the time, from civil, military, and ecclesiastical circles, had a decisive part in the campaign of independence. It was from their political activities that they derived the authority and power which they attained among us, and which they kept up for almost a century. After the abdication of Pedro I, a grand master of Masonry from the time he was prince regent, there was established on Nov. 23, 1831, the Brazilian National Great Orient, and a severe struggle between it and the Great Orient of Brazil, which had been restored under its first grand master, José Bonifácio, broke out. Various crises followed in Masonry; and there resulted from a new schism in the Great Orient of Brazil, or the Vale do Lavradio, in 1864, the foundation in Rio de Janeiro of another, the Great United Orient, or Valley of the Benedictines, the former having been recognized by sister institutions in France and Portugal as the only representative of Brazilian Masonry. In 1882, however, the union of the two Great Orients was marked by a treaty; the first, as the older and certainly the more powerful, predominated. In the last phase of breakup and decentralization of Masonry, new Great Orients arose, in 1884 that of the north, which aimed at the independence of the north and did not last more than five years; that of São Paulo and that of Rio Grande do Sul in 1893; that of Minas in 1894, and finally, in 1900, that of Bahia. Besides the high services which it rendered to the independence of Brazil, Masonry, now widespread through the country, took an active part in the propaganda for the abolition of slavery and for the republican regime. At present, in a period of obvious decadence, Masonic lodges, in so far as they still exist, have lost their early character and their political power, and function as philanthropic and humanitarian associations, in a sphere of influence and action that is constantly being more limited.

The union of church and state, when it was established by the Constitution of 1824, was already, so to speak, consecrated by tradition. The Catholic religion was, in fact, the official religion. In a country colonized and civilized in the shade of the Cross, its life, not only its religious life, but its moral, intellectual, and even political life, for about three centuries developed largely, if not through the initiative, at least with the constant participation of the clergy. The church had in the city a role of the first importance; and worship was maintained under its arches in sumptuous ceremonies and solemnities and was carried out into the streets by its processions with the magnificence of their retinues among the multitudes that knelt at the passage of the Host under the august canopy held up by priests. Evangelizing missions and pastoral visits enlarged ever more the frontiers of religion, spreading and fortifying its rule as far as the towns of the interior and the most remote corners of the sertão. The social position of the Fathers, notes Rugendas, at the beginning of the nineteenth century, "is one of the finest and most characteristic traits of the moral spirit of the colonists of Brazil: they are counselors, friends of the family, comforters, protectors of the oppressed, mediators in dissensions and enmities." [17] It was, moreover, the church which presided through its clergy and especially its religious orders over the education of youth in convents and the colleges of the Fathers. And if in general, writes Viriato Correia, "perhaps there is no other country which has had its life so closely connected with cassocks and monks' robes as Brazil," there is also not one of our revolutions "which has not had a Father or a friar fighting for the ideal of liberty." [18] The priests implicated in the conspiracy of Minas, those who in large numbers joined the civilians in the revolution of 1817, and whether or not forming part of the Masonic rite took part in the struggle for independence, were following, in the political movements of our history, the national tradition of Catholicism, which, encouraging through the energy of the Jesuits the reaction of Estácio de Sá, in the sixteenth century cut the wings of the dream of an antarctic France and helped to shake off the Batavian yoke together with the armies which in 1640 were struggling at the same time for the faith and for the integrity of our territory. But this notable influence of the clergy, from whose ranks there also came in the eighteenth century a physicist of the importance of Father Bartolomeu de Gusmão, the discoverer of the aerostat, and, at the beginning of the nation, a botanist of the authority of Brother Conceição Veloso, a composer like Father José Maurício and a statesman of the mettle of Diogo Feijó—this influence, we see, had attained its culminating point in the first half of the nineteenth century. There were also great preachers, Canon Januário da Cunha Barbosa and Father Sousa Caldas among the seculars, and Brother Francisco de São Carlos, Brother Santa Teresa de Jesús Sampaio, and Brother Mont'Alverne among the Franciscans, who with their eloquence added a new brilliance to the influence of the church and the intellectual authority of the clergy.

If, however, the light that was shed by the church had many dark points, not all was light in the influence of religion, beneficial and helpful in so many respects, nor was everything really useful to our formation. The predominance, if not the entire exclusiveness of the clerical element in the civilizing work, and the academic and bookish orientation of the teaching which was given in monasteries and seminaries, for a long time had a harmful effect on Brazilian culture, many characteristics of which, such

[17] Johann Moriz Rugendas, *Viagem pitoresca através do Brasil* (São Paulo: Martins, 1940).
[18] Viriato Correia, "Batinas liberais," in *Correio da Manhã*, Rio, 1920.

as its inclination for purely literary and rhetorical studies and its love for the bachelor's diploma, instilled by the Jesuits, beginning with the sixteenth century, are connected with this half-secular education of a religious type. All of the generations which followed in the colony and in the Empire show in the qualities and defects of their culture "this regime of monastic domesticity," in which they were brought up. The domination of fathers and friars in our cultural élite also was not without some consequences which were damaging to religion itself. Solicited as the result of the scarcity of cultivated men and under the pressure of social and economic causes, our ecclesiastics—the literati of the time—were not slow in leaving their own natural field of action to enter worldly activities alien to their ministry. Thus, on the one hand, weakening their character in political struggles, inside and out of the Masonic lodges, becoming recruiters for this or that party, they ended even in Brazil by losing their prestige and compromising the authority of the church and in moving in the direction of persecution. Politics, on the other hand, favored by the regime of the union of church and state, tended to interpose in affairs of a spiritual order, disturbing the harmony between the two powers and weakening the power of the bishops, whose control over the mass of priests and the faithful had become ever less efficacious. It was against this state of affairs that the great voice of the Bishop of Olinda, Dom Vital, a young Capuchin friar, was raised, seconded by Dom Antônio Macedo Costa, Bishop of Pará, when Masonry, in reply to the attitude of the Bishop of Rio de Janeiro suspending a Masonic priest from his orders in 1872, appealed to all the lodges of Brazil to break out with an offensive against the episcopate. The ever growing authority of Masonry, which had attracted Catholics and priests, and regalism—"the preeminence of civil authority over ecclesiastic, as contained in germinal form in the Constitution of 1824"—were the causes of the religious conflict. Bishops Dom Vital and Dom Macedo Costa exhorted priests to leave Masonic organizations; and after they had issued an interdict against the orders which should refuse to eliminate from their membership those who belonged to the Masonic sect, the fraternities had recourse to the crown, which raised the interdiction. The illustrious prelates of the church refused to obey the order of the Viscount of Rio Branco, the first minister of the government and a master of Masonry, and tried and convicted as rebellious functionaries, they were condemned and were imprisoned in the Fortress of São João and on the Island das Cobras.

It was certainly not religious intolerance which led to the tenacious resistance of the two prelates in the issue between the bishops and Masonry, which marked, like the dividing of the waters, a culminating and critical point of the regime of union of state and church, and one more stage in the development of the progressive idea of liberty of thought and belief. What the Brazilian bishops were defending was their legitimate authority, in matters purely spiritual, over the clergy and the orders subordinate to the ecclesiastical authority, and threatened at once by the moral and political influences of the Masonic lodges and by the activity of the civil authority which considered the clergy as a class of civil functionaries. In this struggle, which lasted for three years (1872–1875) and shook the public opinion of the country, there was established a line of demarcation between the church and the Masonic bodies, and between the ecclesiastical authority and the civil power which tended to absorb it in its constant incursions into the spiritual realm, resting its authority upon the Constitution of the Empire. The Catholic Church was the official religion, and although doubts over its dogmas issued in writing constituted on the part of the press crimes punishable by law, it was liberty of conscience which triumphed in the Constituent Assembly, "with the restrictions which the special position of Catholicism imposed upon it," observes Plínio Barreto. It was a priest, Father Muniz Tavares, who in the Constituent Assembly of 1823 had defended intrepidly freedom of thought and of opinion, fulminating with fiery words against the intolerant and declaring emphatically in one of the points of his oration that he recognized in religious liberty "one of the most sacred rights which man may have in society; a sacred right, because conscience is a sanctuary where no human power has the right to penetrate." From another Father, José Martiniano de Alencar, there were also heard in the same Constituent Assembly, as Plínio Barreto reminds us,[19] "the most sensible words over the eternal problem of freedom of the press." During the Empire, other voices of priests and preachers, like Mont'Alverne, were heard in defense of freedom of conscience; and the best proof of religious tolerance during the nineteenth century in Brazil is to be found precisely in the contemporizing attitude of the church, face to face with Masonry, to which there belonged many Catholics, priests, and even friars, and against which it reacted energetically only when that institution of philanthropic and political character undertook open opposition to the bishops. The religious question, showing all the disadvantages of the union of church and state, prepared the way, then, for the separation of the two powers, temporal and spiritual, a separation which the Republic was to achieve in its fundamental law of 1891, in which there triumphed without restriction the principle already established in the Constitution of 1824, that of freedom of worship and of belief.

It was in this period that Protestantism was implanted in Brazil, spreading out like Catholicism from the coast to the plateau and in a century reaching, in its sphere of action, practically all the provinces of the country. The seed sown in the sixteenth century by the Calvinists who came in 1557 did not germinate; of the fourteen Huguenots who composed the mission chosen by Calvin and of which the historian Jean de Léry was part, most returned to Geneva in order to escape Villegagnon, four were executed by his order in Guanabara Bay and Jacques de la Balleur, who came in 1559 to the captaincy of São Vicente to join three other French Calvinists, ended his life in 1567, hung as a heretic by order of Mem de Sá, in Rio de Janeiro after eight years of confinement in Bahia in jail and in irons. He was a theologian and an eloquent preacher, versed in Spanish, Latin, Greek, and Hebrew. The new attack, a more vigorous and prolonged one, in the seventeenth century and under conditions that were singularly favorable, failed with the expulsion of the Dutch. From 1630 to the retirement of the Flemings in 1654, missionaries worked actively and fruitfully, and they stood out so in their work of conversion that "many were the Indians," according to the testimony of the Jesuit, André de Barros, "who were as Calvinistic and Lutheran as if they had been born in England and in Germany," and were so full of the new ideas that "they called the church *moanga*, that its to say, 'false,' and the doctrines *morandubas abares*, that is, the 'lies of the Fathers.' " The fight between the two Christian religions, the Catholic and the Protestant, was so much the more bitter in proportion as the Dutch mission proved its efficacy, supported as it was for the long period of foreign domination by the Company of the West Indies and by Count Maurice of Nassau, an excellent adminis-

[19] Plínio Barreto, *A Cultura jurídica no Brasil* (1822–1922) (São Paulo: Biblioteca do Estado de São Paulo, 1922), No. 2.

trator, who stimulated the work of conversion, provided for the coming of new missionaries, and created schools and hospitals. The reaction against the Dutch and the anti-Catholic measures taken by the Calvinist consistory in Recife, and the expansion of the Flemings after a desperate struggle, uprooted in the Northeast the Reformed Church, which had been propagated by the activity of the evangelical ministers of the Netherlands and by the pastoral work of the colonial churches. The circumstance that the Catholic faith and patriotism found themselves on the same side facilitated extraordinarily the struggle against the Dutch, a struggle in which the Jesuits took part with great efficiency and in which J. Fernandes Vieira, with his victory over the Dutch arms, won the title, conferred by Pope Innocent X, of "the restorer of Catholicism in Portuguese America." It was, however, only in the nineteenth century, in which religious freedom was assured, although with limitations, in the Constituent Assembly of 1823 and in the Constitution of 1824, that finally evangelical churches took root in Brazil, with their form of worship carried on in houses with the appearance of residences and without the external form of a church.

The first church which was founded then was the Anglican, which in 1819 laid the cornerstone of its chapel in Rio de Janeiro,[20] and there was to come to accompany it in its evangelizing effort, the Methodist church, in 1836, with a little nucleus of the faithful. There followed in the course of the century the founding of other churches; the Lutheran in 1845, the Congregational in 1858, the Presbyterian in 1862, the Baptist in 1882, and the Episcopal in 1890, all with the exception of the Baptist, which began its work in Bahia, being organized in Rio de Janeiro. It was in the latter city that Protestantism was installed in the nineteenth century and that it secured support as a center of irradiation, to extend to all the country with the Republican regime and its unrestricted liberty of worship and belief. The first phase of the attempt in the colonial epoch was followed by the cycle of establishment or definite founding which coincided with the Empire, and to which there followed in the Republic the period of expansion. If the work of evangelization carried on by these churches—and it is the Baptist, Lutheran, Presbyterian, and Methodist which developed most—shows a notable power of expansion with their 4,000 preachers divided between the lay preachers (3,000) and ministers, the cultural work of Protestantism is not less important. Passionately interested in liberty and making of the reading of a book a means of spiritual development, Protestantism tended to accompany the movement of the propagation of the faith and of Christian ideas by an intellectual movement. The American schools, introduced into the country in the early days of the Republic at a time when public instruction was still very retarded, made a notable contribution in São Paulo, not only to changes in methods but also to intensify teaching. The Protestants founded great colleges like Mackenzie in São Paulo, Granbery Institute in Juíz de Fora, Gamon Institute, also in Minas, and the Evangelical high schools of Bahia and Pernambuco. They gave a stimulus to didactic literature which was enriched by works of the first order at that

[20] Before religious freedom was assured by the Constitution of 1824, England, in the last years of the colonial period, in 1810, had signed with Portugal a commercial treaty in which it was stipulated, in Article XII, that Portugal would give English subjects in her territories freedom of worship, "in private churches and chapels," and that the building of houses of worship would be permitted with the condition that on the exterior they should look like residences. By this treaty between Dom João VI and England, Protestants, although they would not be allowed to make converts, would have special cemeteries and their funeral rites would be respected.

time, such as the grammars of Julio Ribeiro and Eduardo Carlos Pereira, the arithmetic and algebra of Trajano, and the work of Otoniel Mota and the readers of Erasmo Braga, and they made an efficient contribution to the spread of popular education through the system of Sunday schools, the number of which in 1934 amounted to 3,912, spread with their approximately 15,000 official teachers over the large field of action within the reach of the churches.[21] In proportion as its numbers multiplied as a result of pastoral work, in which there stand out important figures like Alvaro Reis (1896–1925) and Erasmo Braga (1877–1930), Protestantism developed and enlarged its social activity, creating hospitals, day nurseries, and orphanages. Broken up for more than a century but unified by means of the confederation which officially represents Protestantism in Brazil, the missionary work of its churches, concentrated in the principal urban centers, is expanding, especially in the states of the south (Santa Catarina and Rio Grande), thanks to the influence of foreign colonies and, as it is easy to understand, with more vigor in the new zone than in the old cities, which are traditionally Catholic.

The two churches, the Catholic and those of the Reform movement, more recently arrived in Brazil, at least in their permanent form, thus collaborate in maintaining the Christian character of the civilization of the country; and if Protestantism, with its indisputable progress, is far from taking away the primacy of the Roman church in an environment that is traditionally Catholic, its proselytizing force and its power of cultural and social action do not fail to act as a factor of rivalry. The theological and ecclesiastical differences which separate the two religions, both Christian and both founded upon the gospel, necessarily lead them to fight and to try to find in their institutions of learning and of culture and in their activities of a social character points of

[21] There is not the slightest doubt that the sphere of Protestantism has grown and its work multiplied, not only its religious activity but also the educational and social side. This development is the more remarkable in view of the fact that it has always met on the part of a Catholicism that is more than four centuries old in Brazil, and from the Catholic traditions of the Brazilian people, a decided and constant opposition. In 1935 there were already about 1,500,000 persons under the sway of the evangelical churches; and, as compared with 2,876 parishes, 76 curates, 30 chapels under the care of clergy in the Catholic church, according to official data of 1934, there existed in 1935, 1,231 Protestant churches and 645 ministers, not counting the churches and ministers of communities of colonists. Great Protestant churches, like the Presbyterian Church of Rio, the former House of Prayer, rebuilt in Gothic style and reputed "the most handsome and majestic evangelical church in Brazil," arose; there were others in Rio, in São Paulo (Campinas, Rio Claro, Araraquara, Botucatú), in Paraná and in Rio Grande do Sul. It is estimated that ten million copies of the Scriptures, in whole or in part, were distributed down to 1936 in Brazil. Not less important is the educational work which is carried on in large high schools and in Sunday schools, the latter with a total matriculation of 180,991 pupils in 1934, and that of the Y.M.C.A., an institution that is evangelical in nature and of American missionary origin; these associations make a contribution of great value with their educational activities in their three centers, that of Rio de Janeiro—the first to be founded in Brazil, in 1893, and now with a property worth $250,000—that of Pelotas in Rio Grande do Sul and that of São Paulo. The contribution of Protestantism in hospital and orphanage work, although it is more recent, can show hospitals like the Evangelical Hospital of Rio de Janeiro, the Samaritan of São Paulo, the Vila Samaritana in São José dos Campos, the Ebenezer Sanitarium in Campos do Jordão, and various orphanages in Rio, in Minas, and São Paulo. The expansive power of Protestantism can be appreciated by examining the value of the property held, estimated at $25,000,000, according to Domingos Ribeiro, who includes in this total, churches, pastors' residences, seminaries, schools, hospitals and orphanages. Cf. Domingos Ribeiro, *Origens do evangelismo brasileiro* (Rio, 1937); Erasmo Braga and Kenneth G. Grubb, *The Republic of Brazil: A Survey of the Religious Situation* (World Dominion Press, 1932).

support for the conquest of souls and for religious domination. While all this power of irradiation is enriched and renewed in the sources of culture and tends ever more to rely upon centers of cultural activities, the expansion of spiritualism, in which devout mysticism becomes intoxicated, began in the bosom of the lowest and least cultivated classes, had its origins in the naïveté and ignorance of the public and the attraction which mysteries and phenomena which are considered supernatural and communications by means of mediums between the visible and invisible world, between the living and the dead, everywhere exercise. The very expansion of spiritualism among people of lower mentality—a movement much greater moreover than would appear at the first examination—was an evident proof that spiritualism (modern spiritualism, 1842) had not yet passed over to a really scientific phase and that it, in general, keeps the character of a religious sect with its mediums and its seances in which, side by side with visions and hallucinations, there are produced certain obscure and little known facts. Science doubtless has neither affirmed nor denied the existence of some of these facts, for the explanation of which spiritualism constantly has recourse to the supernatural, but it also has proved nothing and has not been able to come to any conclusion in spite of all of its efforts. In any case, whether these realities were true or problematical, in what respect would they be superhuman? From the fact that the science of these phenomena (metaphysics) has not yet been formed, it does not follow that they are divine. Different from spiritualism, theosophy professes that "man is a spirit who has fallen from a divine order and who, obscured by matter, is trying to climb up through successive stages of transformation to his original state." This religious philosophy which in its various sects and tendencies, despising reason and faith as a means of knowing the divine nature, claims to reach it by a kind of illumination, a special intuition of the divine, is represented in Brazil by various societies created for its propagation, and their influence, limited to a very special public, does not appear to have made any contribution to the religious culture or the intellectual formation of the country.[22]

Although also limited to a restricted circle of adherents, Positivism, however, was not slow in developing influence and in playing as a doctrine an important role in the

[22] According to official data of 1930, besides the Catholic religion, which is that of the great majority of the Brazilian people, and the different Protestant churches, there also exist the Orthodox church, with eight churches and eight priests, and the Israelite church with nine synagogues. During the whole colonial period, what barred the entry of the foreigner in our ports was heterodoxy, or, as Gilberto Freyre writes, "the spot of heresy in the soul. . . . The danger was not the stranger nor the dysgenic individual, but the heretic." That was the reason for the obstinate reaction against the two chief attempts at implanting Protestantism in the sixteenth century in Rio de Janeiro, and in the following century, in Pernambuco. The adventurous spirit of the Semitic people, the religious persecutions in Portugal, and later, the wealth of the mines led to a great movement to Brazil of persons of the Jewish race who concentrated above all in São Paulo, in Pernambuco, in Bahia, and in Minas Gerais, achieving distinction as merchants and sugar-mill owners, and both in the cultivation of letters and in the liberal professions. But most of them were "new Christians" who, menaced in Portugal with the fires of the Inquisition, sought refuge and a place of exile in Brazil and to whom the Society of Jesus gave such protection that it actually led to conflicts between that religious order and the Holy Office. Except for the period of Dutch rule, in Pernambuco and in the conquered captaincies, the Jews did not publicly profess the religion of Moses. The Israelite church was not, then, able to establish itself until the end of the nineteenth century and, like the Orthodox church, only for an extremely limited circle of the faithful. After Catholicism, followed in decidedly second place by Protestantism, in spite of its extraordinary spread, it is spiritualism

intellectual and political life of Brazil, at the end of the Empire and in the Republican period. The general movement of Positivism among us began with a group of young Brazilians who were studying at the University of Brussels in 1860, and among whom there were two Paulistas, Luiz Pereira Barreto and Joaquim Alberto Ribeiro de Mendonça and Antônio Brandão Júnior, who came from Maranhão. Thanks to the influence of a young French woman, Mlle. Ribbentrop, who as a girl had been present at the lectures of the philosopher in the Palais Royal, these Brazilian students, writes Hermes Lima, "were initiated into Positivism of which they were to be, later in their own country, the true forerunners." After the death of Auguste Comte, which occurred about this time (1857), Positivism was divided into two schools, one of which, under the direction of Pierre Lafitte, was the one which gained most territory in foreign countries and especially in Brazil, where it succeeded in bringing together a team of workers. For those who were bound up with this faction of Positivism, the theories which E. Littré, the chief of the other branch, regarded as the product of the mental illness of Auguste Comte, were perhaps the most precious things that the French thinker had left behind him. It was this current, that of orthodox Comtism, as Euclides da Cunha called it, which in the south of the country acquired the larger number of adherents among us, precisely for those theories of Comte which were rejected by Littré and which were concerned with the political and religious organization of society. These social and religious ideas of the master, and among them the preponderance of the family in the system, represented in our Positivism, through the charm which they exercised, a role such as was exercised in the propagation of Protestantism, beside its essentially Christian character, by the ideal of individual liberty, the constant ideal of developing the human personality and the importance attached to morality and therefore to everything capable of developing in our hearts the feeling of responsibility and of justice. The moral and political ideas of Comte penetrated the military school; and republican propagandists and reformers, and the sect or "religion of humanity," which found its adherents only in the higher classes, had its teaching given by such admirable figures as Miguel Lemos and Teixeira Mendes, and its churches and its worship, which consist essentially of sacraments, celebrations, and pilgrimages. But if in the evolution of Brazilian thought it had at a certain time a real influence, not as a method of investigation but as a social and political doctrine, Positivism, the religious sect, accessible to a handful of men, has remained, to employ the expression of Euclides da Cunha, "changeless, crystallized in the profoundly religious and incorruptible soul of Teixeira Mendes."

The decree which after November 15 separated the church from the state did not, however, have its origin in the development of sectarian Positivism. It was rather a victory of the lay movement with which the principle of neutrality of the state with regard to the religious problem was restored, and there was assured to the Catholic church itself in Brazil, as the pastoral letter of March 19, 1890, recognizes, "a certain sum of liberties which she never succeeded in getting in the time of the monarchy."

---

which down to the present has had the greatest development in quantitative terms, with about four million members, distributed through various spiritualist centers (there are more than 400 in São Paulo alone), forming a federation but without any influence in the field of culture. A Metapsychical Society of São Paulo, which is more a society for study than a religious center, is attempting to give a scientific slant to the investigation of the phenomena called *spiritualistic* and considered supernatural.

The new regime was indisputably—the words are those of Father Júlio Maria—"liberty restored to the church after a long, sad period of slavery." It was not sectarianism which triumphed, but the principle of liberty of worship and belief, which, if it permitted a normal activity and expansion to other churches, brought to the Catholic church freedom from its regime of dependency and from the oppression exercised by the state. In the monarchical period the prestige of the clergy had in fact suffered; the activities of the church had diminished, and the monastic orders were attacked at their living source by the prohibition of receiving novices; [23] the power of the crown and the power to create livings tended to transform the clergy into a parasitic superstructure, nourished by a regime of privileges and subsidies with which oppression was masked, and to reduce the church, with the weakening of the episcopal power, to being a simple instrument of political power. No one understood better the perspectives open to the church in the new regime than Father Júlio Maria, that notable sacred orator who, as Jônatas Serrano writes, "in a career of preaching which is unique in our history, in its manner and in its breadth," made a constant appeal to the clergy to promote political and religious pacification, to broaden their sacerdotal mission by a deeper comprehension of the social function of religion and "frankly to invite democracy, without political hypocrisy or religious cowardice, to come to the social banquet of the gospel." The cloud of difficulties with which the atmosphere had been laden from 1889 to 1891, disturbing the new relations between the church and the state in the new regime, was finally dissipated in 1905 by the diplomatic action of the Baron of Rio Branco at the Holy See, and the consequent naming by the Pope of the first Cardinal of Brazil and of all Latin America, Dom Joaquim Arcoverde de Albuquerque Cavalcante, Archbishop of Rio de Janeiro. But the clergy, both secular and regular, with their scanty ranks, took refuge in the sanctuaries, "from afar looking at the people with whom they formerly had been so intimately connected," and while in the colonial period and until the first half of the nineteenth century, intellectual, social, and political life had been characterized by the connection of the church and the world, in the Republic, the church, with the lines cut which had bound it to the state, appeared to hesitate to take to the open for an action of large scope in an atmosphere of full liberty of thought. The Brazilian church passed through a crisis of lassitude from which it was to arouse itself in the twentieth century, especially after the Great War, in spite of serious obstacles, in order to undertake new initiatives in various fields of religious, social, and cultural activity.

[23] The movement of Pombal against legacies and the monastic orders, forbidding the orders to receive novices, was certainly disproportionate to the ends he had in view: it was extremist, like the realistic policy which took the form of a similar decree of the imperial government in 1855, in that it attempted to correct an abuse that was in our customs, with another, that of a blow directed at freedom of conscience. It was, undoubtedly, necessary to react against "the inveterate speculation which was practiced with the daughters of the best Brazilian families expatriated from here under the pretext of educating them, only to condemn them to convent life in the mother country." Not less important was the other abuse which Pombal endeavored to restrain, "of the legacies to religious establishments, a general monomania which attacked families, favoring idleness and fanaticism." But with the same blow that was directed at these abuses that had grown up in an atmosphere laden with mysticism, freedom of conscience suffered, and those who wished to do so were forbidden to follow their own vocation. The convents entered upon a period of decline and, with their Brazilian reserves exhausted, there fatally occurred what happened in the Republic: they fell into the hands of foreign friars, summoned to repopulate the convents which were weakened by the prohibition against receiving novices.

In this whole period, religion was neither a stimulant nor an adversary of thought: hence a mutual indifference between culture and religion. The future clerics were no longer recruited, as in the colony, from the best Brazilian families and in the same establishments, seminaries, and colleges of the Fathers in which the new generation of colonial society was being prepared with a unity of mind and direction. To that community of ideas and sentiments which then had developed between the clergy and the nation—a community manifest in all of the activities of colonial life and in the constant participation of priests in the inconfidencias and revolutions down to the end of the first Empire, and so much the stronger as the clergy had an eminently national character—there followed reciprocal indifference, if not practically a dissociation between the church and the world, between religion and the living forces of society. On the one hand, vocations for the priesthood, which had become more and more rare, found in the bosom of the Brazilian family, were isolated and shut up in seminaries and no longer participated in the life of other students. The clergy, on the other hand, was slowly being denationalized whether by the entry in the twentieth century of monastic orders coming from France, Belgium, and Italy, or by the progressive infiltration of foreigners in the secular clergy, or by the handing over to German friars of the traditional monasteries of St. Benedict, with their rich endowments. This growing "denationalization" of the regular and secular clergy, ever more mingled with foreign elements, not only weakened the old bonds which had united, as in a single body, religion and society, the church and the people, but tended, according to some, to transform the clergy into a closed class with interests of its own and to impress upon it the appearance, either external or dissimulated, of being a "foreign political party." It was at this moment, surrounded by difficulties and grave menaces to the prestige of the church, that there began the most vigorous Catholic movement of our history, important for the amplitude of its social activity, for its new interpenetration of church and the world, for the renaissance of the religious and national spirit at the same time, and for the combative attitude, not always marked by an ecumenical spirit, a Catholic spirit, or a great breadth of vision. The forces, "that have taken refuge in the sanctuaries," according to the expression of Father Júlio Maria, came out from the convents and churches to take positions in the trenches: for the trench is everywhere, in the parliament and in the houses of government, in the press and in the radio, in the schools and associations in which the embattled soul of youth is being prepared for the struggle, and in which elements of the advance guard are being prepared to open a way for the tranquil and secure advance of the church and the clergy.

The role played by eminent intellectuals like Jackson de Figueiredo, who began the spiritual Catholic movement, and Alceu Amoroso Lima, who carried on his inheritance and followed him in the leadership; the appeal to academic youth and to working classes who organized into associations with a religious character; the active participation of illustrious Catholics in campaigns which the church undertook against divorce and in favor of religious education in the schools, and the recourse to modern techniques of propaganda showed to what point in Brazil the Roman church has mobilized its forces and renewed its processes, to confront the religious and social problems and the difficulties which prevent their solution. This religious renaissance is not more than twenty-five years old. The pen of the journalists in the daily press and, recently, propaganda by radio, if they have not replaced the words spoken in the pulpit, in which even under

114. "Antônio Raposo Tavares," statue by Luiz Brizzolara.
Photo by Museu Paulista.

115. Dinner.
Debret, *Voyage pittoresque et historique au Brésil* (1834), Vol. II, Plate 7.

116. A Brazilian lady at home.
Debret, *Voyage pittoresque et historique au Brésil*, Vol. II, Plate 6.

117. Plantation family, beginning of the nineteenth century.
Rugendas, *Voyage pittoresque au Brésil*, Plate 3/16.

118. Lady going to mass, carried in a sedan chair (beginning of the nineteenth century).
Debret, *Voyage pittoresque et historique au Brésil,* Vol. III, Plate 5.

119. Morning of Ash Wednesday at church.
Debret, *Voyage pittoresque et historique au Brésil,* Vol. III, Plate 31.

120. Flower seller at the door of a church.
Debret, *Voyage pittoresque et historique au Brésil,* Vol. III, Plate 6.

121. Government functionary, leaving his home accompanied by his family.
Debret, *Voyage pittoresque et historique au Brésil,* Vol. II, Plate 5.

122. Inhabitants of Minas, beginning of the nineteenth century. Rugendas, *Voyage pittoresque au Brésil*, Plate 2/18.

123. São Paulo costumes.
Rugendas, *Voyage pittoresque au Brésil*, Plate 2/17.

124. Plantation family.

Rugendas, Voyage pittoresque au Brésil, Plate 3/17

125. Jangada men.
Archives of the Brazilian Institute of Geography and Statistics.

126. Cowboy of Marajó.
Archives of the Brazilian Institute of
Geography and Statistics.

127. Cowboy of the Northeast.
Archives of the Brazilian Institute of
Geography and Statistics.

128. Cowboys of Goiaz (Inhabitants of Goiaz).
Rugendas. *Voyage pittoresque au Brésil.* Plate 2/19.

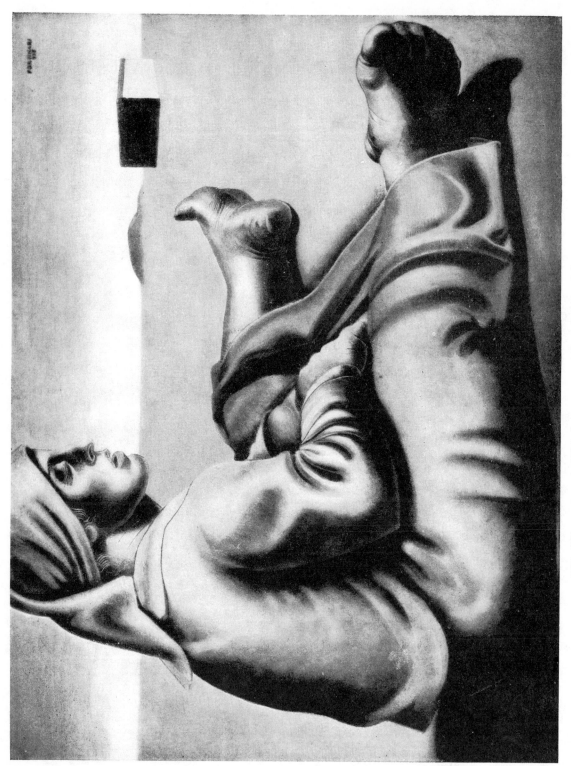

129. "Sharecropper's Wife," tempera painting by Cândido Portinari. Photo by Rembrandt, property of Sr. Mário de Andrade.

130. Gaucho type. Archives of the Brazilian Institute of Geography and Statistics.

131. Gaucho type. Archives of the Brazilian Institute of Geography and Statistics.

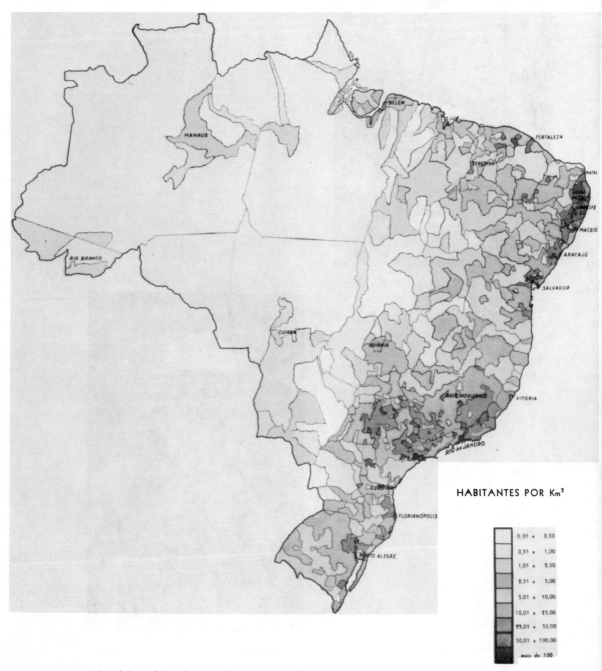

HABITANTES POR Km²

	0,01 a 0,50
	0,31 a 1,00
	1,01 a 2,50
	2,51 a 5,00
	5,01 a 10,00
	10,01 a 25,00
	25,01 a 50,00
	50,01 a 100,00
	mais de 100

132. Map of the density of population of Brazil, by townships, in September, 1940.

133. Father José de Anchieta, S.J. (born in Canary Islands, March 19, 1534, died in Espírito Santo, Brazil, June 9, 1597). Reproduction belonging to the Ethnography Department of the College of Philosophy of São Paulo.

134. "The First Mass in Brazil," oil painting by Vítor Meireles. Photo by Rembrandt.

135. Mother church and residence of the Jesuits, in Rerigtiba, now called Anchieta,
Espírito Santo.
(The original house restored, containing the old cell of the great missionary.)

136. Father Manuel da Nóbrega, S.J. According to a conventional sculpture by Francisco Franco, published by Seraphim Leite.
Drawing by Giselda Lopes da Silva.

the Republic there were raised the magnificent voices of Father Júlio Maria, of Monsignor Paula Rodrigues, of Father Chico and Father João Gualberto in São Paulo, acquired through their effectiveness greater prestige, eclipsing the eloquence which retired, its old brilliance lost, to the mystic and tranquil atmosphere of the churches. A literature, Catholic in spirit, attained an intellectual level and a volume of publication which Brazil had not yet known, being enriched by works of the first order, like those of the Jesuit, Father Leonel Franca, one of the highest figures if not the most important in the national clergy and in Catholic thought. Church institutions of learning, lyceums and gymnasiums, for boys and colleges for girls,[24] orphanages and training schools maintained by various congregations of nuns grew in number; higher schools were founded, like those of Agriculture and Veterinary Science in Olinda in 1913, and also by the Benedictine monks in São Paulo, the Faculty of Philosophy of St. Benedict; in 1935 there were created near São Paulo, through the efforts of the League of Catholic Women, a Boys' Town; and while everywhere human sympathy, illuminated by faith and incarnated in sisters of charity, was at the side of those who suffered in hospitals, caring tenderly for them, the church spread out to the interior its apostolic activities, catechizing Indians by means of the Dominicans in Conceição do Araguaia, by the Benedictines in Rio Branco, and the Salesians in Mato Grosso and Rio Negro. Faithful to its traditions, the Catholic church is being renewed, adapting itself to conditions of present-day life and with its fifty-four dioceses, seventeen archdioceses and twenty-three prelatures, under the direction of the Brazilian cardinal, and its numerous orders and congregations in constant activity, it maintains an indisputable domination among the religious institutions of the country, contributing to develop, with its insistence on the primacy of spiritual values over the values of life and matter, a sense of Christian humanity which goes back to the historic and religious origins of the civilization of our country.

[24] Although the number of lay schools, either public or private, for the education of girls has constantly increased, there is a marked preference on the part of well-to-do families for schools conducted by religious orders. Among them there stand out the colleges, almost all of them boarding schools, of Our Lady of Zion, of the Sisters of the Sacred Heart of Jesus, of the Marceline Sisters, and of St. Augustine. The order of St. Augustine, founded by (St.) Pierre Fourier (1565–1640), has had ever since its arrival in Brazil in 1907 a school in São Paulo (Colégio des Oiseaux), to the high-school part of which was added in 1933 a higher faculty of letters and sciences under the name of the Institute "Sedes Sapientiae," and another, with a kindergarten, created later on, in Santos, in the State of São Paulo. The Marceline Sisters, who arrived in 1911, conduct in Brazil six schools for girls, and among them that of Botucatú (State of São Paulo), the first opened by this order. The schools of Zio, of São Paulo, of Campanha (in the south of Minas), of Petrópolis, and of Rio de Janeiro are among the most flourishing religious schools for the education of young females.

BIBLIOGRAPHY

Badaró, F., *L'Eglise au Brésil pendant l'Empire et pendant la République* (Rome: Bontempelli, 1895).

Braga, Erasmo, and Kenneth G. Grubb, *The Republic of Brazil: A Survey of the Religious Situation* (London: World Dominion Press, 1932).

Dornas Filho, J., *A Padroado e a igreja brasileira* (São Paulo: Comp. Editora Nacional—Brasiliana, Vol. 125).

Furtado de Meneses, *Clero mineiro* (Rio, 1933).

Franca, Father Leonel, *Catolicismo e protestantismo* (Rio: Schmidt, 2nd ed., 1931).

Júlio Maria, Father, *Memória histórica* (Rio, 1900). 1st vol. of *Livro do Centenario.*

Lehman, *O Brasil católico* (latest ed.).

Leopoldo e Silva, D. Duarte, *O Clero nacional e a Independencia* (Rio: Centra D. Vital, 1922).

Leite, Father Serafim, *Páginas de história do Brasil* (São Paulo: Comp. Editora Nacional, 1937—Brasiliana, Vol. 93), Chap. I, "Influência religiosa na formação do Brasil," pp. 11–33.

————, *História da Companhia de Jesús no Brasil*, 1st and 2nd vols. (Lisbon, 1938, 1939).

Luiz Alves, José, *Os Claustros e o clero no Brasil*, 1st vol., Vol. 57 of *Rev. do Inst. Hist.* (Rio: Companhia Tipográfica do Brasil, 1895).

Madureira, M. de, *A Liberdade dos índios: A Companhia de Jesús—Sua pedagogia e seus resultados* (2 vols., Imprensa Nacional, 1927–1929). Presented to the Congresso internacional de história da América, 1922.

Magalhães, Basílio de, *Estudos de história do Brasil* (São Paulo: Comp. Editora Nacional, 1940—Brasiliana, Vol. 171), Chap. II, "Dom Pedro II e a Igreja Católica," pp. 89–162.

Morais, Benjamim, *Subsídio para a história da Igreja Presbiteriana, no Rio de Janeiro.*

Pereira Caldas Júnior, Antônio, "Maçonaria no Brasil," in *A Maçonaria no Centenário*, ed. Antônio Giusti (São Paulo: A Maçonaria no Estado de São Paulo, 1922), pp. 17–44.

Ribeiro, Domingos, *Origens do evangelismo brasileiro* (Rio: Gráfico Apolo, 1937).

Ribeiro, Leonídio, and Murilo de Campos, *O Espiritismo no Brasil: Contribuição ao seu estudo clínico e médico-legal* (São Paulo: Comp. Editora Nacional, 1931), especially pp. 155–188, "Um Inquérito entre especialistas brasileiros."

Rodrigues, José Carlos, *Religiões acatólicas.*

Serrano, Jônatas, "O Clero e a República," in *A Margem da história da República* (Rio: Anuário do Brasil).

————, article on the church in Brazil and its cultural influence, in *Dicionário de geografia e história eclesiástica,* published by Letouzey in France.

Trindade, Canon Raimundo, *Arquidiocese de Mariana: Subsídios para a sua história* (São Paulo, 1928).

Vilhena de Morais, E., *Qual a influência dos jesuitas em nossas letras?* (special vol. of *Revista do Instituto Histórica*, Vol. 5, for the Congresso de história nacional of 1914.)

————, "O Patriotismo e o clero no Brasil," in *Jornal do Comércio*, special number devoted to the Holy Year (Rio, 1925), pp. 181–197.

Brazil, 1938: A New Survey of Brazilian Life (Rio: Serviço Gráfico do Instituto brasileiro de geografia e estatística, 1939), pp. 396–397, "Cults."

CHAPTER TWO

THE INTELLECTUAL LIFE—THE LIBERAL PROFESSIONS

Intellectual formation essentially literary in character—Men of letters and scholars—The inheritance of scholasticism and of classic culture—Grammar and rhetoric—Slavery and the repugnance for crafts and activities based on manual and mechanical work—Tendency toward bureaucracy and professionalism—The foundation of courses of law—Juridical culture —Lawyers and jurists—The cultural function of law schools—Foci of ideas and political campaigns—The Escola Central—The two faculties of medicine—Doctors, engineers, and lawyers —The élite classes, cultural, political, and administrative, recruited from the professions—A politics of doctors and fazendeiros—The preponderance of jurists in politics—The school of mines in Ouro Preto—Osvaldo Cruz and Brazilian medicine—Professional associations—The prestige of those who hold diplomas—A culture markedly professional in character—The professions and letters—The effort to go outside the bounds of one's profession and through culture to dominate the profession—Book selling—Bookstores and libraries.

T HE FIRST LEADERS of colonial society were recruited among the nobility, sugar-mill lords and priests; and in addition to nobility and ownership of land, what determined access to the social ladder was instruction, which was exclusively in the hands of the clergy and especially of the Jesuits. The possession of great rural properties served in the colony to perpetuate on a large scale the distinction of classes, on the one hand, the aristocracy represented by Portuguese nobility in transition—more or less unstable— and that originating in the land, composed of the lords of the sugar mills, and on the other hand the regular clergy who became, especially with the Jesuits, "the great colonial producers" whose authority, social and economic, was gradually fortified with agriculture and the cattle-raising fazendas. But in the center of colonial society, heterogeneous, dispersed and without cultivation, there soon arose a new social category, due to the instruction offered by the Jesuits—that of the intellectuals who, having completed their studies and become masters in the colleges of the Fathers, went to take their degrees at Coimbra, to acquire with the title of "licenciados" and of doctor, an easy access to the noble class through government office. It was an old custom in well-to-do families whose first born, inheriting the land, followed the career of his father, to send the second son to Europe to study, while the third they reserved to the Church, and he took his vows in one of the convents, generally of his own country. One son a learned man and another a priest or friar were a reason for pride for the old families. Meanwhile, the intellectual formation which they received, essentially literary in character, directed not toward technique and action but toward form, training in eloquence, and exercise in the dialectic functions of the mind, could not make of these masters of arts and licenciados anything but men of letters, imitators and scholars whose main intellectual pleasure consisted in contact with the old Latin authors. A force of conservatism

165

rather than an instrument for freeing the mind, this upper-class teaching, dogmatic and rhetorical, which shaped all according to the same pattern of culture, made scanty minorities of lettered men who, foreign and superimposed upon the social environment, fluctuated like an imported intellectual élite. Here was nothing alive and truly new and fecund, nothing of observation of nature and the cult of the *genius loci*, to awaken the creative power and the critical sense in this coherent and uniform culture on its universalist base, crystallized in the Latin humanities, like a nucleus around which, in proportion as one went up in the hierarchy of learning and of functions, the mass of religious materials grew denser (apologetics, theology, ethics), with the object of preparing for the priesthood.

The classics, almost exclusively Latin—since Greek was not included among the subjects of higher learning until later by the friars of St. Francis—constituted in fact the base upon which the whole instruction offered in the colleges of the Jesuits and in the seminaries reposed. Grammar, rhetoric, and philosophy, frequently studied in the Latin authors themselves, who had received the inheritance of the Greeks and rendered it easier to assimilate, possessed, in addition to the interest which followed from its especial objects, in this teaching impregnated with the humanities, that of being true instruments to develop Latin culture, which was situated at the very heart of instruction. The inheritance of scholasticism and of classic culture with the dominance of Latin, grammar, and rhetoric [1] was transmitted, without being enriched or transformed, through generations of scholars to the end of the eighteenth century, when the Franciscan friars by virtue of a royal order of 1772, established in Rio de Janeiro a course of higher studies, in which for the first time there figured, in addition to Greek and Latin, the official teaching of two modern languages. Only at the beginning of 1800 did Azeredo Coutinho, the bishop and governor, who exercised an extraordinary influence over the mentality of the country and without whom "there would never have arisen the idealistic generation of 1817," according to the judgment of Capistrano de Abreu,[2] break with the old colonial tradition of Jesuitic teaching by founding the seminary of Olinda on the new model and with a broader point of view; offering the teaching of drawing, of physical sciences and mathematics, of chemistry, of botany and of mineralogy side by side with the old subjects of the Jesuit colleges. This seminary in effect "transformed the conditions of teaching and therefore the intellectual conditions of the captaincy" of Pernambuco.[3] Down to this period the teaching of the colleges of the Fathers, writes Gilberto Freyre, leaving the intellectual landscape around men empty

---

[1] As Gilberto Freyre recalls, rhetoric "was studied in Latin authors—reading Quintilian, reciting Horace, memorizing the orations of Cicero. Logic and philosophy, too: once more it was the orations of Cicero that constituted the principal objects of study. The philosophy was that of orators and priests. Verbosity, and the tone always that of the apologists, which corrupts the dignity of analysis and breaks down the intellectual honesty of criticism. Hence the tendency toward oratory which remained with the Brazilian, disturbing his effort to think and to analyze things. Even when he is concerned with matters which demand the greatest verbal sobriety, exactitude rather than literary effect, a conversational tone rather than speechifying, the greatest possible purity of objectivity, the Brazilian without noticing it raises his voice and rounds out his phrases. This is the result of much friar's Latin; of much priest's rhetoric" (*Sobrados e mocambos* [1st ed. São Paulo, 1936], p. 269).

[2] Capistrano de Abreu, *Um Visitador do Santo Ofício*, p. 14.

[3] Oliveira Lima, *História da Revolução de Pernambuco em 1817* (Recife, Memorial ed., 1917).

in order to allow only orthodox Catholic ideas to grow in the individual, had broken in the Brazilian, especially the educated class, not only his lyrical relations between man and nature . . . but also the curiosity to learn, the desire and the taste for knowing, the joy in adventures of the intelligence, of sensibility and of scientific exploration, adventures in the discovery of the things of this world. If, however, this standardizing teaching of the Fathers of the society stifled intellectual spontaneity, deprived people of a taste for analysis, and for centuries damaged the critical spirit of the Brazilian in colonial society, it was certainly, as Gilberto Freyre recognizes, "most useful to the social integration of Brazil," creating and spreading throughout the country a system of culture which not only contributed to consolidate the Christian religion—one of the living forces of spiritual unity in the colony—but made a contribution to the assimilation of the Brazilian élite from north to south, fusing into a unity of culture all the regional differences of a social, economic, and political nature.

Although this teaching, entirely literary and ecclesiastical, may have contributed largely toward the disdain for useful sciences, lack of interest in nature and a horror at manual labor, it cannot be considered responsible for this lack of love for work with the earth and for mechanical arts which remained one of the characteristic traits of the Brazilian. A product of the time and of conditions of social life in the home country, it was transferred to the colony, together with the customs, usages, religion, and mentality of the nobility, for which freedom had become synonymous with leisure and work something equivalent to slavery. This mentality grew stronger with the lascivious laziness of a hot climate in which men had few necessities and where their vital necessities were relatively easy to satisfy, and in a social environment in which the distinction of classes and the regime of slavery relegated to an inferior plane the mechanic arts and the manual skills as signs of inferiority of social class. Besides, the disdain for manual work, here as everywhere where there are classes, was always a distinctive trait of the nobility, who thought they were degraded by servile work and whose superiority in a social hierarchy was marked by their being able to have themselves served and by the number of slaves or servants capable of assuring them a maximum of comfort with a minimum of effort. If profession gives "class" and classes determine it, influencing the choice of professions, what was held to be an occupation of slaves could not attract or give "class," but rather any activity of an intellectual sort which raising people to noble occupations might be capable of taking the place of land ownership and the privileges of birth. The Jesuitic system of teaching, entirely literary and rhetorical, did no more than to give value to letters and to accentuate, with the distance between the intellectual élite and the mass, the horror felt for manual and mechanical labor which came from "that Portuguese inclination to live on slaves," to which there had been successive contributions by the Sephardic culture and in the colony by the social regime of slavery. "Side by side with the Moorish tradition," writes Gilberto Freyre, "there was the influence of the friars, great agriculturists, who in Portugal had been on the opposite side from the Jews," enemies of manual labor and from remote times inclined to a regime of slave labor. "If later [he adds] parasitism invaded even the convents, the reason is that not even the enormous energy of the monks was able to row against the tide." The monasteries, which in Portugal "besides being houses of prayer and of study had become centers and schools of industrial activity, laborious agricultural colonies," according to the observation of Esteves Pereira, ended also in Brazil, under the regime of slavery, by relying upon slave labor, utilizing numerous field slaves in their great, active properties.

The almost complete absence of industries, the routine of the single-crop system, and the elementary character of commercial activities, not creating any necessity for professional specialization, nor requiring technological effort of a high level, contributed together with other factors to discredit manual or mechanical functions exercised by artisans, slaves, and freed men. What interested this society of elementary structure was, in fact, a type of culture which would favor the access of the intellectual élite, if not to nobility, at least to the so-called "noble" occupations, creating a new aristocracy —that of college graduates and doctors. For these noble functions, such as that of being a magistrate or a canon, which required a minimum of intellectual specialization, it was sufficient to have a literary and abstract culture, such as was given by the colleges of the Fathers, by methods which were based, not upon action and the concrete, but upon reading, commentary, and speculation. The spiritual arms which made up the arsenal of the master of arts, "that colonial equivalent of the college graduate of today," included no more than the Latin humanities and some general notions which lay at the basis of philosophy and theology and which were appropriate to trained preachers, men of letters, and scholars. Thus there came into existence the intellectual and literary tendency which was developed during more than three centuries in the direction of the cult of the college graduate, bureaucracy, and the liberal professions. If the intellectual traditions of the Jews must have made a contribution to this—and Gilberto Freyre attributes to their influence our taste for the bachelor's or doctor's ring with its ruby or emerald and the mania for glasses and the pince-nez, "an Oriental reminiscence of Jewish flavor"—it is certain that no influence in this direction in the home country or the colony was greater than the educational system and the culture which resulted from it. The role which a culture shaped by this type of teaching exercised was so preponderant that not even the Dutch scientific and technical missions in the period of the occupation of Pernambuco, nor later on the isolated reactions of the seminary of Olinda in the eighteenth century, and of the colleges of the French and English that were established here in the nineteenth century "to the great indignation of the Fathers," succeeded in opening a wider breach in the purely literary, intellectualistic tradition of the old colonial teaching of the Jesuits. The fact is that the conditions of social and economic life after the expulsion of the Fathers of the Company in 1759, and down to the end of the nineteenth century, were characterized by the same regime of slavery and the same economic organization; and the slow progress in the field of industry was not sufficient to give much value to practical and technological work and maintained professional types on a low level and kept the hierarchy of industrial functions in an extremely simple state. The title of bachelor and of doctor continued to be a sign of class and the callosities of hard work remained repugnant to the hands of the sons of the sugar-mill owner and the bourgeois of the city mansions.

But the rise of the college graduate and of the cleric, which dates from the seventeenth century, with those first values of Brazil, Gregório and Eusébio de Matos and Antônio Vieira, this last Portuguese by birth, but all educated in Bahia by the Jesuits, a rise which was emphasized in the following centuries with the college graduates of Rio and of Minas Gerais (Vila Rica), had no doubt a great importance in the social and political life during the last period of the colony. If, on the one hand, this stand-

ardized culture which those who studied with the Fathers of the Company and went
to take their degrees in Coimbra received tended to bring together the élite from the
north and the south of the country, creating relations between Pernambucanos, Bahianos,
the inhabitants of Rio and Paulistas,[4] the values incarnated by the college graduate,
white or mulatto, "came to constitute an element of differentiation within a rural and
patriarchal society which was trying to integrate itself and achieve balance." Sons of
the sugar lords and fazendeiros, they brought back from Coimbra, from Montpellier or
from Paris, along with new ideas and new styles of living, the germ of reaction against
the customs of the big patriarchal houses from which they had come. Boys of the new
bourgeoisie of the cities, sons or grandsons of "peddlers," "to whom European education
had given new value," observes Gilberto Freyre, "returned the social equals of sons of
the oldest and most powerful families of landowners." These new college graduates
and clerics, with their growing prestige in the colonial society and their new mentality,
romantic and revolutionary, marked the political triumph not only of the city man over
the country people but that of the colony over that of the home country, that of republican ideas over the monarchical tendencies of the Portuguese and the landholders.
The Inconfidência of Minas, according to Gilberto Freyre, "was a revolution of college
graduates just as the two revolutions of Pernambuco, prepared by men of the eighteenth
century, that of 1817 and that of 1824, were to be revolutions of bachelors of arts, or
at least of clerics who were bachelors in priests' robes, some educated in Olinda in the
liberal seminary of Azeredo Coutinho." The voyages to the old world to complete one's
studies in universities offered to Brazilian youths from diverse regions the contacts
which the isolation of population and the absence of communication between the captaincies did not permit them in Brazil. It was not only new ideas, new mysticisms, and
new customs which these boys educated in Europe brought back, but a feeling for
the country, as a result of their more lively consciousness of the differences which ever
more separated the colony from the home country. In Coimbra, where they became
friends, achieved understanding and agreement "for the first time," Pedro Calmon tells
us, "students perceived the existence of a home country, enormous and primitive, which

[4] Most of the young Brazilians who went to Europe to study, chose Coimbra; others went to
Montpellier and Paris, and more rarely, to Germany and England, where, at twenty years or a
little more, they graduated in philosophy, medicine, and especially in law. Among the "inconfidentes," Cláudio Manuel da Costa, of Minas (Ribeirão do Carmo) and Inácio José de Alvarenga
of Rio de Janeiro took doctor's degrees at Coimbra; Domingos Vidal Barbosa of Minas, and from
the State of Rio, José Mariano Leal and José Joaquim da Maia, who in 1786 had an interview in
Nîmes with Jefferson, the ambassador of the United States in Paris, and died in Lisbon on his
way home, studied medicine in Montpellier; and José Alvares Maçiel, in England, where he took
his doctorate in natural sciences and philosophy. From the north—from Pernambuco and Bahia—
with the wealth created by the cultivation of sugar cane, and later, in the eighteenth century, from
"general mines," with the wealth derived from the exploitation of the gold mines, Brazilians set
sail in greater numbers to study in European universities. Recife, Bahia, and Vila Rica were, consequently, the greatest centers of intellectual life in the colony. Few were the Paulistas, little more
than twenty, who graduated at Coimbra, with its opportunities for advanced study; and, among
them, the two Gusmãos, of Santos, Bartolomeu Lourenço, inventor of the aerostat, canon and professor of mathematics in the University of Coimbra, and Alexandre, a diplomat, who also completed in Coimbra studies he had begun in the Jesuit school; the three Andradas, José Bonifácio,
Antônio Carlos and Martim Francisco, also of Santos, as well as Fernandes Pinheiro, Viscount of
São Leopoldo, and from São Paulo, the two Toledo Rendons, Francisco Leandro and José Arouche,
who was the first dean of the Law School of São Paulo.

belonged to them. The national idea arose thus. There was formed on the banks of the Mondego a youth that renewed itself annually, going from the sugar mills and later from the cattle-raising fazendas and the mining communities to study laws and canons in the university."

Meanwhile, with the expulsion of the Jesuits in 1759 by the Marquis de Pombal, without the complementary measure of substituting for their schools others, there fell to pieces for more than fifty years the whole cultural system resting upon the colonial structure of Jesuit teaching, to flourish once again under the Empire, allied to another more liberal type of culture bound up now with the idea of preparation for the professions, the training of military men, lawyers, doctors, and engineers. A culture that had been tributary to religion became thus tributary to the liberal professions, without being stripped of its old humanistic and ecclesiastical content, at least until the second half of the nineteenth century, and during that century the seminaries and the colleges of the Fathers remained in large part the basis of the schools for training for the professions. In any case, it was a culture that was not free and disinterested but strongly marked by its professional object and application. There was not, rigorously speaking, a rupture of tradition, but rather a breakdown of "the unity of culture," when to the culture of clerical origin, that had been fed by the colleges of the Jesuits and the seminaries, and refined in the University of Coimbra, there succeeded as a new phase in our cultural evolution a culture with a professional base, developed in institutes that were fragmentary and disbursed, looking in different directions in accordance with their specific objects. The great mass remained alien to the new institutions. The intellectual élite became more numerous and more refined by profiting by these courses. The prestige of the title of bachelor and of doctor grew, only to decay later on with the increased number of college graduates; and the new courses, because they had not taken in their development an eminently practical and professional turn, and because of the lack of institutions destined for the study of philosophy, science, and disinterested studies, became centers of intellectual unrest and nurseries of journalists and politicians, men of letters and scholars. Thus when higher learning was taken away from the domination of the clergy to be reestablished under the sign of the professions, the intellectualistic and literary tendency which had come down from the colony continued to follow the line of its normal development as a class distinction, indulgence in studies with a professional object, rather than because its ornamental character, as a result of the growing application of letters to political journalism and to eloquence in public meetings, on the bench and especially in parliament. It is not in these schools and professional courses created at the beginning of the nineteenth century that "the professional man" took vengeance on the man of letters, the scholar, and the orator—other intellectual types which continued to flourish throughout the Empire in the shade of the academies, and to exercise all their aristocratic power with the double additional prestige of the title of bachelor and doctor and the power of attraction of eloquence and letters.

If as early as the reign of Dom João VI there were instituted, with studies of natural history and arts, the first professional courses of medicine and of the navy, it is only in 1827 with the creation of juridical courses in Olinda and São Paulo that there were formed finally the two major nuclei of higher learning and of juridical culture in the country. Intellectual life in the north, after a period of isolation and segregation, acquired once more its ancient prestige with the foundation in Olinda of the juridical course, moved later on in 1854, to Recife, while with the first school of law there was inaugurated in São Paulo one of the most lively centers of intellectual culture. Both of these courses of juridical and social science in Olinda and in São Paulo, created on August 11, 1827, were installed in old convents, the latter in the former convent of the sons of St. Francis, the former in the traditional monastery of São Bento, like a symbol of the superposition of two cultures, the religious and the professional which followed it, replacing the ecclesiastical spirit by the juridical spirit and religious conservative dogmatism by a revolutionary and critical intellectualism. It is through them, in fact, that there penetrated into Brazil the influence of the English and French philosophers, and later in Recife that of the Germans, with Tobias Barreto. It is in them that there were forged and tempered the political arms for the struggles for right and the liberal campaigns. It is out of them that there rose on the wings of poetry and eloquence, to be spread everywhere, the seeds of revolutionary ideas, while there was being formed in the retirement of studies and of teaching, an élite of makers of the law to give support to the juridical and political structure of the state. "Yielding probably to the intuition that in it [in the juridical culture] there is the axis of all Christian civilization, the imperial regime almost immediately after our achievement of independence," writes Rui Barbosa,[5] "consecrated to the study of law two faculties, one in the north and the other in the south, with polar situations dominating the movement of our moral world." However, without destroying the greatness of Olinda, the pearl of the north, weakened perhaps but never deprived of its life, one cannot seriously doubt that the teaching of São Paulo always exercised its national mission on a higher level, with a more powerful influence and a wider amplitude. Bologna, once famous among educational cities, with its *universitas scholarium* and its *doctores legentes* was called par excellence at one time, "the learned and the free" joining together on its ancient coins with the solemn legend of its rights, *libertas*, the slogan par excellence of teaching, *Bononia docet*. São Paulo, indisputably, has a right to the two titles on the same coat of arms: "It professes liberty and teaches justice."

It is with these schools—the first set up in Brazil—that our culture was emancipated from that of Portugal, breaking with the University of Coimbra, for three centuries the cradle of Brazilian culture, and rising progressively from the poverty of juridical letters manifest in the Constituent Assembly of 1823 to the level of being one of the greatest juridical cultures, if not the greatest, of the American continent. The paucity of jurists and of juridical knowledge were, in fact, such that in that assembly, to which the greatest notabilities of the time came, only three or four deputies, writes Plínio Barreto, "revealed some familiarity with the juridical institutions of other peoples," and people even suggested the idea of securing by contract jurisconsults in Portugal to take charge of the law classes. . . . But in all the fields of this knowledge and in the various branches of juridical activity, it was not long until there arose figures like Pimenta Bueno, Teixeira de Freitas, and Lafayette Rodrigues Pereira in the Empire, and in the Republic, Carlos de Carvalho, the civilist leader who was equal in rank to the two last; Rui Barbosa, Carvalho de Mendonça, the two João Mendes, João Monteiro, Clovis Bevilaqua, and Pedro Lessa, lawyers, judges, and builders of the law who would honor the juridical culture, the magistrates' bench, and the profession of lawyer in the most

[5] Rui Barbosa, speech in São Paulo, Dec. 17, 1909.

civilized country. In 1830 there came the Criminal Code, the organization of which had been determined upon by the Constitution of 1824. In 1850 there was promulgated the Commercial Code, which was followed immediately afterward by that marvelous masterpiece of legislation which is Rule 737, which we owe to the pen of Carvalho Moreira, Baron of Penedo, and to the juridical knowledge of the editor Nabuco, of José Clemente and of Caetano Alberto and to the cunning experience of the Baron of Mauá. Out of the task, which was given to Teixeira de Freitas in 1855, of reorganizing the classification of the laws of the country, "there was born that magnificent *Consolidação das Leis Civís,* whose light crossed the frontiers of the country and illuminated the legislation of other peoples." This magnificent work of synthesis, in the authoritative judgment of Plínio Barreto, is "the greatest scientific monument which the Empire bequeathed us." The discussion of the Brazilian Civil Code, which only entered into force on January 1, 1917, almost a century after the Constitution of 1824, which had determined upon its organization, "will also remain," observes Plínio Barreto, "a brilliant chapter of juridical culture. The spirit of Rui Barbosa dominated it with all the splendor of his unlimited knowledge, endowing it with an imperishable brilliance." The drawing up of this Code had been confided, in 1858, to Teixeira de Freitas, who was not able to finish it, and successively thereafter to Nabuco, Felício dos Santos and Coelho Rodrigues, but it is from the hands of Clovis Bevilaqua that the final project issued for its legal consecration. The gains for liberalism, the combination of the juridical and the political spirit, the urbanization of a judicial apparatus, the prestige of the magistrature and the vigorously juridical conception of international relations so effectively put into force in the diplomatic action of the Barao do Rio Branco in the solution of frontier questions and so brilliantly proclaimed by the voice of Rui Barbosa, the champion of right and justice in the Conference of the Hague in 1907, show with incomparable vigor the place which juridical culture and faith in the principles of justice, in legal order, and in strength of right had won in our land.

But it was not only in the development of the juridical life of the country that these and other schools founded later in Rio de Janeiro (1891), in Belo Horizonte (1892), in Curitiba, in Bahia, and in Manaus played a preponderant role in addition to their special mission. Under the Empire and in the Republic down to 1934, when there was created in São Paulo the first school of philosophy, sciences, and letters, the schools of law exercised a supplementary cultural function, stimulating general culture in their theoretical courses and opening out to their students perspectives for other studies. In the preference of the sons of poor and well-to-do families for the study of law, we must not, then, see only a taste for the title of bachelor of law, which is tied up with the whole tradition of the colonial prestige of college graduates, nor merely a growing number of vocations for juridical studies which spread throughout the country, but also an aspiration toward a general, disinterested culture on the part of youth who could not acquire it except in these courses which were full of the spirit of philosophy and of letters. No institution of higher learning was more called upon than the law schools to exercise this supplementary function, not only by the more philosophical character of their studies and by the greater application of letters to the activities of the career, but also because of all the faculties of all the professional schools, it is those of law which, by the very nature of their courses, found their very *raison d'être* by preference in the cultural element, and not in the economic and technical element, and developed a more robust faith in spiritual power, in the unifying virtue of intelligence, and in moral values. The law schools [6] were, then, in the nurseries of an élite of culture and urbanity, from which large numbers went into administration and politics, journalism, letters, and teaching (and even into the theater), which were full of college graduates, deserters from the professional groups of which they kept, together with their education, only the degree and the ruby ring on their fingers as signs of their class and their prestige. Moreover, from the earliest years of such education, the political world and the academic world were mutually related; and in no other centers of studies did the agitations of political life have so intense an effect as in the law schools, and to political life youth gave with the participation of its generous enthusiasm the contagious strength of great movements of opinion. There was, in fact, not a single liberal campaign with the movement of which the atmosphere of academic life, intoxicating in its temperature, was not laden, and to the development of which professors and students did not give a new movement, joining the necessarily slow work of intelligence to the more rapid and impetuous force of feeling. Centers of ideas and of political campaigns, these schools, in whose buildings generations of jurisconsults, lawyers, and statesmen were nourished upon the science of justice, became, moreover, centers of democratization and of the fusing of national unity. In them there were to be found, arriving at an understanding among themselves, Brazilians of all States and of all social classes, who were later to scatter after five years of living together, through the capitals and the interior, taking with them to all the corners of the country, along with the spirit of struggle and liberal reaction, the cult of justice and of right.

But these schools and the professional juridical culture which they originated, far from favoring the creation of a new mentality, contributed rather to accentuate the literary and rhetorical aspect of colonial culture, which through them acquired a new life with the extremely vital elements of their tradition. A tradition with its roots in the system of colonial teaching, it was humanistic and abstract and so persistent

---

[6] On the level of professional education, the number of law schools greatly exceeds that of the schools of medicine and engineering: in 1940, in comparison with ten engineering schools, eleven medical schools, fourteen of pharmacy and odontology, five of agronomy and veterinary science, there were twenty official or inspected law schools. To the two original law schools others were added, gradually extending over the country, in Rio de Janeiro, in Belo Horizonte, in Bahia, in Pôrto Alegre, in Florianópolis, in Curitiba, in Niteroi, in Vitória, in Maceió, in Fortaleza, in Teresina, in São Luíz do Maranhão, in Belém do Pará, in Manaus and in Goiânia, so that there are States, outside the Federal District, where two are in operation, such as São Paulo (the old Law School and the Paulista School), the State of Rio de Janeiro (the Niteroi School and that of Campos), and Rio Grande do Sul (the school of Pôrto Alegre and that of Pelotas). It is in Minas that we find the largest number of schools of engineering: the School of Mines, in Ouro Preto, the schools of engineering in Belo Horizonte and in Juíz de Fora and the Electrotechnical Institute of Itajuba (four in all), while São Paulo has only two: the Polytechnic School and Mackenzie, both in the capital of the State. The States of Amazonas, Maranhão, Piauí, Ceará, Alagoas, Espírito Santo, Santa Catarina, and Goiaz have only a single institute of higher learning: the law school. In the north, from Espírito Santo, for nine law schools there are no more than three of engineering, the Polytechnic of Bahia and the Polytechnic and Engineering Schools of Pernambuco. The Polytechnic School of Pernambuco, in Benfica Street, Recife, a private school founded in 1912, recognized as possessing public utility in 1917 (Legislative Decree No. 3435, Dec. 27, 1917), which has at present only one course, that for industrial engineers, graduated only 84 engineers from 1912 to 1940, or an average of three per year. Cf. *Expressão cultural e social da Escola Politécnica de Pernambuco* (Recife: Diário da Manhã, 1940).

that the technical schools, like the academies of medicine and surgery, the military school, and the agricultural school founded in the time of Dom João VI (1808–1821), did not lead to any notable transformation of this mentality, directing it to science and to its application to technical or industrial activities. In this respect the action of Dom João VI was openly reconstructive and almost revolutionary when he established in his court in the city of Rio de Janeiro a Royal Military Academy "to give a complete course of mathematical sciences and of the sciences of observation and of the military sciences in all their breadth," so that (the expressions are still those of the royal decree) "in these same courses of study there will be trained skillful officers of artillery, engineering, and even officers of a class of engineers who would be geographers and topographers, who will have also the useful job of directing, administratively, mines, roads, ports, canals, bridges, and road building. While, however, the faculties of law begun in the first Empire had begun to participate and to influence strongly the social and intellectual life of the country and to favor in a large degree the national agitations of a social and political nature, all those scientific and technical foundations begun by Dom João VI, who hoped to create an interest in economic problems and develop the metal industries of the country, did not exercise an effective influence in the direction of giving our culture a new spirit, improving the economic conditions of society, and breaking up the groups to which it had been habituated, of college graduates, men of letters, and scholars. All the long, generous effort of Dom João VI in creating schools and institutions of a technical nature and establishing courses of economics, veterinary medicine, and agriculture, and organizing and reforming the military and naval academies, was an open offensive against the tendencies and characteristics of colonial instruction which left society unequipped with personnel capable of promoting its reconstruction on an economic basis. But this series of attempts did not succeed in attracting and galvanizing more than a small group of wills, insufficient in their number and strength to break down old prejudices and to arouse the national economy from the apathy in which it was vegetating. If one of the principal causes, if not the greatest, of the lack of success of this new policy and culture resided in an agricultural economy based upon slave labor and the lack of industrial activity in the country, it is certain that the discursive and dialectical propensities of the Brazilian mind contributed toward this result, since that mind was more inclined to letters than to sciences, more to the liberal professions than to the "useful professions," which are connected with technique and activities of a manual and mechanical order.[7]

[7] In one of the pages of his diary, the engineer L. L. Vauthier, commenting on the celebrations in Recife in Homage to Pedro II (Dec. 2, 1840), records, like a perspicacious observer, but with acrimony and a certain aggressiveness, the Brazilian tendency to rhetoric and to dislike of any kind of field work, of manual or mechanical character. "What people! They do not refrain from any expression, however exaggerated, for the most ardent love and overwhelming enthusiasm. They do not really think, I am convinced, a quarter of the things they write." And later: "When they speak of a country, everything bad that happens to it they attribute to lack of patriotism. . . . I should like to see some one ask one of these idlers who talk so much about patriotism to carry a surveyor's level and help take a level. He would say right away that he is not a *servant* or a *slave,* that he is a freeman and was not born to carry things." Cf. *Diário íntimo do engenheiro Vauthier (1840–1846),* with Preface and notes by Gilberto Freyre (Rio: Publications of the Serviço do Patrimônio Histórico e Artístico Nacional, 4, Serviço Gráfico do Ministério da Educação e Saúde, 1940).

The vicissitudes through which preparation for civil engineering passed, with its courses reduced to courses for topographical engineers from 1810, and those of bridges and roads from 1832, and connected with the courses of officers and military engineers, until the creation in 1858 of the Central School into which the Military School was transformed [8] and which was the only one of its kind in the whole country until 1876, show how much effort it cost in Brazil to have the profession of civil engineer develop and acquire importance and autonomy. In São Paulo the school of "road engineers" desired by the plan of the Topographic Cabinet, created in 1835 by Rafael Tobias de Aguiar, functioned for only two years (1836–1838), reopened in 1842 with twenty-three pupils, and went out of existence in 1849 as a result of the budgetary law of that year. Only later, forty-three years after this attempt, was there created in May of 1893, in São Paulo, an engineering school, which did not succeed in opening its doors, as also a higher school of mathematics and of sciences applied to arts and industries, which did not begin, although it was created in August of 1893, with the name of Polytechnic Institute. Attempts and reforms followed one another in the field of technical education down to 1874, in which year there was founded, based on the old Escola Central, the Polytechnic School of Rio de Janeiro—the last phase of a long process of formation—followed closely by the School of Mines, founded in 1876 in Ouro Preto, and after a long interval, by the Polytechnic School of São Paulo, now in the republican regime. Nor were the attempts made in the realm of practice any more successful, for as Euclides da Cunha observes, "the most imperious measures were born aborted." The idea of fighting distance and cutting down the enormity of the land by means of railroads (an idea already cherished by Diogo Feijó, when in October of 1835 he signed the first law on railroads), had arisen again in 1840 in the case of the franchise given to a pertinacious foreigner, Thomas Cochrane. But the brilliant professional struggled in vain in the midst of a weakened society until the complete failure of his progressive thought. The technical mission of Frenchmen hired in Paris in 1840 by Francisco do Rêgo Barros, afterward Baron and Count of Boa Vista, proved with its presence in Pernambuco not only the lack of professional men in the country and the low level

---

[8] In fact, in the Royal Military Academy, founded in 1810, after 1832, and by virtue of the decree which added to it the Marine School, military and civil engineers (of bridges and roads) and naval engineers were graduated. In 1833 the Naval Academy was separated from the Royal Military Academy, in which the military course and that for engineer officers were broadened. The situation did not change materially in 1839, in which year the Military Academy took the name of Military School, with the same objectives. It was with the reform of the Military School in 1842 that there arose, side by side with the military courses, of cavalry, infantry, and artillery, a seven-year engineering course. The process of differentiation, however, did not begin till 1858, when the Military School took the name of Central School, and the School of Application, created in 1855, that of Military School; the courses of officers and military engineers were given in the Military School and that of civil engineers in the Central School, in which, in addition to the civil engineering course (two years) there was established a basic course of mathematics and physical and natural sciences, common and required in whole or in part of the candidates for the courses in infantry, artillery, and General Staff, and in military or civil engineering. In 1874, finally, the two schools were separated, the Central School becoming the Politechnic School, with the three courses of civil engineering, now in three years, the course in mining, also of three years' duration, and the two-year course in arts and manufactures, with a basis of the general (two-year) course and the courses of physical and natural sciences or of physical sciences and mathematics, of three years.

even at that time of the profession of engineering, but also in the constant conflict with the environment, the shock of two cultures and two tendencies—the conservative and the innovative. From 1840 to 1846, this mission, which brought as its head the engineer Louis Léger Vauthier, and which was made up of a group of technicians, Boulitreau, Millet, Buessard, Morel, Portier, all Frenchmen, had to confront in patriarchal, slave-holding Brazil, in spite of the support of the president of the province, a most tremendous opposition. "The European personality," as Gilberto Freyre emphasizes in the preface to the *Diário íntimo* of the engineer Vauthier, "is what gives the drama of maladjustment a revolutionary note and the American environment is one of conservatism, of routine, and at times, one of inertia. The man of the old world is the one who, in this case, was the innovator."

This lack of understanding and the resistance in which attempts in the field of technical education and the practical order broke down show clearly enough the tremendous gulf which colonial teaching, of ecclesiastical origin, had created between the land and man, between culture and the work of colonization. It is on them that there broke down a series of attempts of Dom João VI, whose spirit, directed toward the technical and economic order, rose again thirty years later and this time with a new brilliance and real enthusiasm in the bold enterprises of Irineu Evangelista de Sousa, Baron of Mauá, to whom we owe, along with the seventeen kilometers of the line of the Grão Pará, and without any favors from the government, "the first steps in the majestic conquest of the plateaus." It is, moreover, in the routine and hostilities of the environment that the robust will of Mauá broke down, although several times triumphant, with an élite group of Brazilian engineers, and finally weakened under the weight of the obstacle which led him to renounce his great plans and to sacrifice to the hands of the English the builders of the present São Paulo Railway, inaugurated in 1867, the first railway concession in São Paulo. Under the tenacious influence of Mauá, who gave a new turn to things, impressing a direction opposed to the colonial mentality, and by virtue of the decree of June 26, 1852, which, "establishing a guaranteed interest rate gave a practical beginning to the railway industry," there were opened new perspectives to technical and economic activities and a larger field for Brazilian engineering. From 1867 to 1875, and therefore in a period of eight years, there were begun, almost all by São Paulo enterprise and São Paulo capital, the trunk lines of the great railways: from Santos to Jundiaí (1867), the Campanhia Paulista (1872), the Ituana (1873), and in 1875 the Sorocabana, the Mogiana, and the São Paulo-Rio, which carried its track as far as Mogí das Cruzes, completing in June of that year its line to Cachoeira, the terminal point of the Pedro II Railway. The Escola Central, which was transformed in 1874 into the Polytechnic School of Rio de Janeiro and to which there was added that of Mines in Ouro Preto in 1876, and only later in 1893 that of São Paulo, was then the only center for professional training of civil engineers in the whole country. Although recent in the history of our professional training, engineering, which only grew up in the second half of the nineteenth century and at the present time has ten schools divided between private and official ones, can show such brilliant figures as Teixeira Soares, the builder of the railway from Curitiba to Paranaguá—one of the most notable works of engineering in Brazil—C. B. Otoni,

Teófilo Otoni, André Rebouças, Pereira Passos,[9] rebuilder of the city of Rio de Janeiro, Paulo de Frontin, Arrojado Lisboa, Pandiá Calógeras and, in São Paulo, Antônio Francisco de Paula Sousa, the first director of the Polytechnic School, and Francisco Pais Leme de Monlevade, who conceived and began to execute in 1913 the plan for the electrification of the Paulista Railway Company.[10] Besides, if we consider that it was only in these schools and the medical schools that the teaching of mathematical sciences, physics and chemistry reached a higher level, although applied to certain professions, we will understand the role which engineering and medicine had in the culture of the country, either by awakening greater interest in concrete local problems or by developing our tastes for studies of an objective character.

In fact, at the same time that courses in military engineering were created, there were established the first schools in medicine and surgery in Bahia and in Rio de Janeiro in 1808, that is, in the same year in which Dom João VI and his court arrived in Brazil, expelled from Portugal by the armies of Napoleon. It was in one of those

[9] See Correia Filho, "André Rebouças," lecture given Jan. 13, 1938, at a formal meeting of the Engineering Club of Rio de Janeiro, in *Jornal do Comércio*, Rio, Jan. 16, 1938; Sampaio Correia, "Francisco Pereira Passos," lecture given Aug. 28, 1936, on the invitation of the Ministry of Education and Public Health, in commemoration of the centenary of the birth (1836) of the rebuilder of the city of Rio de Janeiro, in *Correio da Manhã*, Rio, Aug. 29, 1936.

[10] It was Euclides da Cunha who pointed out the contrast between the development of the railway system of Argentina and the growth of railroads in Brazil. While the former country, in 1907, already had 20,814 kilometers of railroads, it was estimated that Brazil had 17,242, although it should have had about 70,000 kilometers "if we admit that mileage should be proportional to the population of the two countries and the distances covered by the national territory." This difference which "suggested observations which are obviously unfavorable to us," are explained, however, by Euclides da Cunha, above all by the contrast between the two physical environments: that of Argentina, where the land submitted "from the first steps, without the defiant repulse of harsh, repellent peaks, giving herself wholly, in the low-lying humiliation of her plains," and that of Brazil in which mountains and swamps raised the greatest obstacle to the final conquest of the plateau and to the advance of the rails in all directions (*A Margem da história*, 3rd ed., 1922, pp. 140 and 141). It is for this reason that in the construction of the main lines into the country that Brazilian engineering encountered its hardest test, and that various leaders distinguished themselves, such as the Viscount of Mauá, who was not an engineer; André Reboucas, Mariano Procópio, C. B. Otoni, Pereira Passos, Assis Ribeiro, great administrators of the Central do Brasil, Paulo de Frontin, for laying the second track along the Serra do Mar, and Teixeira Soares, the builder of the railroad from Paranaguá to Curitiba, remarkable for its works of art undertaken by the railroad engineers. In port engineering, although the great plans have been those of foreigners, there are three great names, Francisco Bicalho, Sousa Bandeira, and Alfredo Lisboa, and in mining, Gonzaga de Campos and his school, Calógeras, Arrojado Lisboa and Costa Sena, the third director of the School of Mines in Ouro Preto. The great hydroelectric plants, like Ribeirão das Lajes, Ilha dos Pombos and Cubatão—the last one of the greatest undertakings completed in Brazil—are plans and work of foreign engineers, with the collaboration of Brazilians. In civil construction, Aarão Reis, who was director of the committee of engineers charged with building the city of Belo Horizonte, and Saturnino de Brito, the greatest name in sanitary engineering—a field in which we note General Jardim, Sampaio Correia, and Teodoro Ramos in Rio and in São Paulo as other names that honor Brazilian engineering. Cf. Euclides da Cunha, *A Margem da história* (3rd ed., 1922), "South American Transportation," pp. 139-163; Moacir Silva, in *Revista Brasileira de Geografia*; Alberto Rangel, *Rumos e perspectivas* (São Paulo, 2nd ed., 1934—Brasiliana, Vol. 26); José Luiz Batista, *O Suro ferroviário brasileiro no segundo reinado e o seu desenvolvimento*, offprint of Nos. 11 and 12, 1938, of the *Boletim* of the Inspetoria Federal das Estradas.

cities, in Bahia, that as early as the colonial epoch [11] the first center of medical culture in Brazil developed, thanks, observes Gilberto Freyre, to the coming to the city of Salvador as early as the seventeenth century "of Jews who were expert in the science of treating the sick and who prescribed pork in order to prevent any lover of tale-carrying from distrusting them. Medicine was always very much a field of specialization of the Sephardic Jews, their means of competing with the father-confessors and the chaplains in influence over the great families and the powerful people of the government. It certainly was they who brought medicine to Brazil in its most advanced form and developed it in Bahia and in Recife." [12] Until the time of Dom João VI, however, those rare Brazilians who desired to follow this profession had no other recourse than to go to study in Montpellier, in Paris, and above all in Coimbra, to which a major part of them went and where some of them succeeded in establishing themselves, like José Francisco Leal and José Correia Picanço, both included in 1772 by the Marquis de Pombal in the teaching body of the faculty of medicine of that university. These medical courses, begun in the early part of the nineteenth century, did not noticeably alter the situation. Only with the law of September 9, 1826, which authorized the two medical academies to give diplomas in surgery, and above all with the law of October 3, 1832, which transformed these schools into the National Medical Schools of Bahia and Rio de Janeiro, modeled on that of Paris, did the profession of clinical med-

---

[11] In the first and part of the second century of the colonial period, the colonists and especially the Indians knew no other "physickers" than the Jesuits, who, not being medical men by profession, writes Serafim Leite, "perforce had to keep within the bounds of empirical therapeutics and elementary prophylaxis. But they avoided doctoring through the humanistic culture they possessed, which was the highest of their time. Indeed, they had to be very much on their guard against it. The Indians, with the primitive mentality, demanded marvelous cures, as if life and death were in the hands of the Jesuits" (Serafim Leite, *Páginas de história do Brasil*, p. 195). The Indians called the fathers their *pocanga*, that is, "their true medicine." And, in fact, when professional medical men did not come, they were the doctors of the Indians, in the treatment of whose diseases they used largely medicinal herbs and the experience of the natives which they picked up in their contact with Indian medicine men, and in general with the culture of the primitive populations. In a country in which there were "neither physickers nor barbers," circumstances imposed on them the humanitarian duty of coming to the aid of bodily infirmities, as far as was possible, with the local resources and the school medicine chest. In each missionary, we may say, there lived a doctor. As for the professionally trained men, except in Salvador and Recife, at the end of the seventeenth century, they were always too few to suffice for the cities, and even at the end of the eighteenth century, the Viceroy Luiz de Vasconcelos e Sousa (1779–1790) was asking the mother country to take measures "so that there might be at least four physicians in the region, insufficient as to number and as to help." The two learned physicians who formed part of the Dutch mission, brought by Maurice of Nassau, and who returned to Europe, Wilhelm Piso and Georg Marggraf, left us a chapter of first-rate importance, *Medicina Brasiliensis*, the first part of *Historia naturalis Brasiliae* (1648), a remarkable work in every way. Among the new Christians—Jews who came from Amsterdam or Portugal and practiced medicine especially in Bahia—and among the Portuguese physicians themselves who came to carry on their profession and rarely settled permanently in Brazil, none accomplished anything nor started anything capable of exercising a long-term influence upon the development of medicine in the country. It was, however, a learned medical man of Bahia, Dr. Alexandre Rodrigues Ferreira, more naturalist than physician, sent in 1783 to study the natural riches of Brazil, to whom we owe the best observations on fevers in Mato Grosso and "the first and most exact description of beriberi in Brazil."

[12] Gilberto Freyre, *Sobrados e mocambos: Decadência do patriarcado rural do Brasil* (São Paulo, 1936), p. 271.

icine acquire a notable position in professional circles and there begin a period of more fruitful activities in the field of medical teaching. The two cities became important centers of European intellectual culture, not only that of a technical character, related to medicine, but through its intermediary, that of the natural sciences which lie at the base of the profession. In Bahia, a scientific center with a life of its own in the middle of the nineteenth century, there rose in the pathological studies of our country figures of the value of a Wucherer, the discoverer of the parasite which bears his name; of a Paterson, of a Silva Lima, "the discoverer of the clinical doctrines about beriberi," of an Almeida Couto or of a Nina Rodrigues, the creator of legal medicine, in whose school were educated Oscar Freire and Afrânio Peixoto; while in Rio de Janeiro there was developed a brilliant group of clinicians, surgeons, and professors who under the Empire attained the indisputable prestige of a Sales Tôrres Homem, an eminent clinician and teacher, of a Vicente Sabóia and Andrade Pertence, great surgeons, and who were followed in the Republic by a whole chain of important names like Miguel Couto, Miguel Pereira, Almeida Magalhães, and others, educated in the school of Francisco de Castro, "a charming and brilliant teacher," who gave a new brilliance to teaching and to clinical work and raised Brazilian medicine to the highest intellectual authority.

Certainly the upper classes by grouping and separating the professions had a powerful influence all through the period of the Empire and the Republic on the choice of liberal professions, which came to have an evident superiority as noble occupations over all those of a technical, manual, or mechanical character. In our élite, however, almost entirely made up of lawyers, doctors, and engineers, it was the bachelors and doctors who acquired the greatest authority and prestige in the hierarchy of the professions. The attraction exercised by these two types of schools, those of law and of medicine, more in harmony with our intellectual tendencies—even medical teaching remained for a long time more theoretical and speculative than experimental —were so intense that it was not long before there was established a great disproportion between the number of doctors or graduates of law school and those who were practicing their chosen profession which they had, in general, chosen prematurely at the age of eighteen, less for their individual tendencies or because they had a vocation for it than because of the social influence leading to these careers. In a country the greatness of which was, above all, political and juridical, and the juridical structure of which had begun before its social and economic structure rose, it could not be commerce, nor industry, nor technique in their rudimentary condition, but law which must attract to itself a large part of the living forces of the nation. The important thing to us was not the practice of business nor industrial technique, nor applied science, nor even scientific investigation, but such and such knowledge which individuals acquired by growing pale over their books and in which they found a point of support, above all, one ornamented by letters, for the expansion of their prestige as men of letters, scholars, jurisconsults, and political orators. The graduate of law school took, then, the first place in the professional and social scale and among the liberal professions; no other played a part more important in the intellectual and political life of the country. Then, if a second nature dominated him in a way, as it does any other professional man, medical or engineering, which makes him see things from a special angle—the juridical point of view—the breadth of knowledge which the profession of lawyer requires gives him a greater intellectual plasticity and leads him to face questions from various points of view, facilitating improvisation which ceases to be a defect and becomes a useful thing. The physician followed him closely: the influence which he tends to exercise in great families, the extension of endemic and epidemic diseases, and the large field open in Brazil to clinical activities armed the physician and in many cases the pharmacist—the poor man's doctor in the interior—with an enormous social prestige and even a political one, especially in the smaller urban centers. The engineer, on the other hand, obliged by his principal activities (field work) to live in a relative isolation, working not on human material—interests and sufferings—but on wood, stone, iron, and cement, without stimuli in his profession for an intellectual life or for great accomplishments in an agricultural economy and an elementary organization of labor, and with that practical and positive spirit which comes from a more frequent contact with the physical and mathematical sciences, never acquired the power of influence nor the social influence which opened up to the graduates of law school and learned men an access to all positions, political and academic, and to the highest posts in administration.

The large number of schools of higher learning and of professional type, and particularly of medical schools (eleven in 1940) and of law (twenty in that same year), in a country in which the well-to-do class is not relatively numerous, is an evident proof of the exaggerated tendency of that class to seek liberal careers. Penetrated in general throughout the nineteenth century by the old bookish and dialectic spirit, higher education was constantly creating a kind of new aristocracy, that of the men with diplomas, whether of those who remained in the professions for which they are prepared or those who deserted and overflowed the professional circle into letters, journalism, politics, and administration. All this teaching—which remained a satellite of European culture in its universalistic and theoretical character and rarely was able to undergo a transformation due to criticism, observation, and experimentation, even when it was directed toward a practical apprenticeship—and the diplomas which are signed and sealed, opened to youths, graduates of law school and doctors, positions and public functions in all the administrative and political circles of the country. The class of intellectuals of a professional type which incessantly had grown since the time of the Empire and especially in the Republic, and in which there were formed types of mentality enclosed within the narrow circle of their professions or open to larger horizons, is nothing more than a simple social category, or what may be called an intellectual élite of the country, which most of the time did not seek or did not believe that it could find means of subsistence except in governmental or administrative activities. That a large number of bachelors of law, of doctors and even of engineers went into public functions in order to ask of the government the means of life which the exclusive practice of their profession could offer only a few of them, is a fact which arises immediately from an examination of the administrative and political ladder from top to bottom and of the dominant elements in its make-up. But with the growing number of bachelors of law and of doctors who came out in crowds from these schools, the number of candidates for these positions and jobs in the state was multiplied. They came to constitute an even more numerous class of functionaries and men of letters, saturated, in the Republic as under the Empire, "by the European formulas which looked down upon the society from which they had come and cherishing vast ambitions." If the functionalism which developed so extraordinarily had its origin in slavery, which, degrading work on the land and belittling mechanical work, "obliged the sons of free men who could not become lords and would not descend to the level of slaves, to take the path looking toward employment by the state," it was certainly the cult of the bachelor of laws which contributed most to develop this inclination for public and political offices, in which it installed itself as if by right. "From it," writes Gilberto Amado, "was born that irresistible inclination to public office which the new regime could not fight but rather encouraged, because, not having created work or professional instruction, it could not avoid the fact that the youth, educated in academies, not being fit for work on the farm or in business or technical work, should turn to public employment." [13]

The governing classes of the country, made up for the most part of graduates of law school, "were characterized by great receptivity for novelties in the field of law," but with their minds very little open to observation or to science, to economic realities or technical problems, and they were bound to acquire all those characteristics and intellectual habits of language and action which professional culture and activity are accustomed to give to the lawyer. Nothing marks the man like his profession; and nothing was stamped in so lively a fashion upon the culture and politics of the country as the professional physiognomy and mentality characteristic of the bachelor of law. The direction of politics, shared between this professional aristocracy and the land-holding families, between the doctors and the fazendeiros, with the theoretical culture of the former and reactionary spirit of the latter, was entirely dominated by an élite which had not been prepared to solve technical problems or to order and govern the community with a vigorous spirit of reconstruction.[14] The class of the intellectuals, which persisted in its ignorance of the vital necessities of the country, continued, under the influence of men of state, "with all the habits peculiar to legalists, educated abstractly," to limit their activities to politics, to the liberal professions and to literature,

[13] Gilberto Amado, "As Instituições políticas e o meio social," in *A Margem da história da República* (Rio: *Anuário do Brasil*), p. 74.

[14] The political criterion which almost always ruled over the formation of governmental circles gave rise to a ruling class composed, in general, of bureaucrats and party members, like a new aristocracy provided with privileges. But every time the technical standard prevailed over the political in the choice of men, or the general interest over that of a group, problems of the greatest importance for the life of the nation were either settled or advanced toward solution. The history of yellow fever is one of the irrefutable and eloquent demonstrations of this fact. In the field of public hygiene it is possible to present another, of equal importance, although limited to one of the regions of the country: prophylaxis against leprosy. Yellow fever, from 1849 on, almost every year, in its periodic rise, took a great many victims and was a disgrace to the country. In 1859 Wucherer, Paterson, and Silva Lima in Bahia recognized the fact that yellow fever was the reigning epidemic in Salvador, and for more than fifty years the terrible disease devastated, in the summer, the coast cities, and at times reached the plateau. At the end of the past century the North American physician Finlay and the French expedition of Marchoux and Simond had discovered in Havana the mechanism of transmission of yellow fever by the striped mosquito (*Stegomyia fasciata*) that is born and develops in stagnant water. In São Paulo, Pereira Barreto, Emílio Ribas, and Adolfo Lutz began the new attack on the black vomit with their experiments in the Isolation Hospital, and as Arnaldo Vieira de Carvalho, the great surgeon, points out, they risked their lives "to demonstrate the new truth and to get authority to impose new methods of attack on the American plague, offering themselves as sacrifices on the altar of science." It was, however, during the government of Rodrigues Alves (1902–1906) that Osvaldo Cruz, chosen and given unlimited support as the man capable of solving the problem, led a sanitary campaign against the

while business, commerce, commercial and industrial enterprises, like pure science and applied science, research and investigation, appeared to be of interest only to foreigners. Men of abstract education, writes Gilberto Amado, referring to the politicians of the Empire, "all lacked the scientific education necessary to the understanding of a country which more than any other needed a constructive policy"; and "nearly all were led to concern themselves more with the external aspects than with the fundamentals of problems." And it is for this reason that the noblest figures of one or the other party under the Empire—and the same may be said of the statesmen of the Republic—"with respect to the concrete realities of the country accomplished nothing more than being decorative. Well versed in European publicists," Gilberto Amado observes, "writing on themes which had no relation with their environment, the most brilliant statesmen were certainly not the most useful." However, besides helping to attend to the necessities of political and cultural circles, in which he always was dominant with his plasticity of adaptation, the bachelor of laws, as Sampaio Correia noted, was the only professional man who was equal to the task which this world in process of formation required, and who faithfully fulfilled his social functions. Bringing with him everywhere the juridical spirit of respect for right, law, and justice, harmonizing human relations and giving a political structure to the Republic, the lawyer was not only an explorer and pioneer of civilization, but "a magician who succeeded in legalizing transmissions of land by the gentle and pacific processes of taking possession, and who obtained from a handful of men drawn toward adventure their recognition of the power and wisdom of law and with it the stability of the organic force of the State."

To this domination of the cult of the bachelor cultivated all through the Empire in the two law schools, and of the growing influence of political and cultural élites, there are related the notable preponderance which the juridical had in general over the economic, and the anxiety to give to society a juridical and political structure over the preoccupation with confronting and solving its technical problems. It is one of the most striking examples of the lack of interest in the study and solution of questions referring to the material and economic organization of the country that we found in the history of the foundation of the School of Mines. The greatest resource of colonial Brazil was certainly the exploitation of its great deposits of gold-bearing and diamond-bearing soil, accumulated on the surface of the earth and discovered by the bandeirantes on their expeditions through the sertões. But the exploitation of the mines, in proportion as the wealth of the superficial layers was exhausted and one passed from the simple work of gathering these riches to that of extracting the gold from subterranean layers, became ever more difficult and complex, requiring the substitution for routine and empirical methods of new techniques of research in the soil, of mine work and metal extraction. Hence, and as a result of the state of abandonment in which the

---

fever, and applying the new methods of direct attack on the foci of transmission, lowered the death rate of the disease from 948 cases in 1902 to 39 in 1906. Yellow fever was practically extinct in this part of the American continent. From 1909 on there was, in fact, no further trace of the disease. The problem of leprosy for its part, if it has not yet been solved in the country, can be considered solved in São Paulo, by means of a really model organization, started by Emílio Ribas and notably developed, with the colony system of isolation, by Sales Gomes and his first-class helpers, notable for their competence and spirit of self-sacrifice.

mines of Brazil were falling, arose the idea of creating a school of mines, an idea already cherished by Dom João VI when he was prince regent, when in the document of May 13, 1803, he spoke "of establishing mineralogical and metallurgical schools like those of Freyberg and Schemintz, from which there resulted for those countries such great and outstanding advantages." The question arose in more precise form in 1832 in the General Assembly, which voted the law of October 3 of that year, approved by the regency, creating in the Province of Minas Gerais a course of mineralogical studies. This law remained for forty-three years without being carried into execution. It was only in 1876 that there was installed in Ouro Preto, through the initiative of Pedro II, a School of Mines with the principal object of training mining engineers, geologists, mineralogists, and metallurgists. It was the second technical school of engineering that was started in Brazil, two years after the Polytechnical School into which the Central School of Rio de Janeiro had been transformed in 1874, again following French models. The School of Mines begun in Ouro Preto as a result of the decision of the emperor, who had invited the French engineer Claude Henri Gorceix to come to Brazil in order to prepare a plan for him and to take charge of its execution, was within our system of culture an original and solitary institution, faithful to the spirit which its founder and first director impressed upon it, anxious as he was from the very beginning to make of it not only an establishment for professional training but a center of research and of scientific work. Clinging to the mountains of Minas, far from the principal urban, industrial, and cultural centers of the country, that school in which there were trained professional men of the first order and in which eminent teachers were professors, men like Gorceix, Armand de Bovet, and Artur Thiré, who were hired in Paris, and Arquias Medrado, Costa Sena, Leônidas Damásio, Barbosa da Silva, and Rocha Lagoa, among others, was never able to acquire sufficiently active vitality in order to give to its precise and experimental teaching greater power of penetration and to influence effectively the transformation of mentality and the improvement of techniques.

Certainly if in the field of engineering this school did not, due to the isolation which limited its zone of influence, carry out the renovating function which the Institute of Maguinhos later exercised in the field of experimental medicine, it was equally dominated by the desire to give a new direction and to open up new perspectives to the engineering of Brazil and to solve Brazilian questions with Brazilian brains. The object which was proposed in its organization, the vast field which was opened for geological and mineralogical research around the very institution, and the scientific and experimental spirit which its illustrious founder transmitted to it and which was passed on to his best collaborators, led it to concentrate its attention to the mineral wealth of Brazil, investigations of the subsoil and the problems of the iron industry. The studies of Henri Gorceix on the rocks of the vicinity of Ouro Preto, the deposits of topaz and the tertiary basins of Gandarela and Fonseca; the contributions of a Costa Sena in the field of geology and mineralogy, and the activities in the field of investigation of Brazilian fossils carried out either under the inspiration of Gorceix or under the powerful influence of Orville Derby, showed in what direction the School of Mines was headed and up to what point it contributed to the spirit of investigation and to the progress of Brazilian engineering. It was, in the field of engineering, a role such as was played, although on a much larger scale and with greater influence, by the Institute of Manguinhos founded by Osvaldo Cruz, who cleaned up the city of

Rio de Janeiro and remodeled experimental medicine and was "the master of masters," who, creating this laboratory of investigation in the field of experimental pathology, equipped Brazilian medicine with an instrument of fruitful transformation. "In the history of Brazilian science, the name of Osvaldo Cruz," writes Oscar Freire, "marks a deciding phase. The desire to solve national problems with our own elements, producing in Brazil a science for Brazil—all was being lost in isolated or scattered efforts. It was necessary to found a nucleus where capable workers should be united and whence the light of the new orientation and new horizon should be spread to all Brazil. And this is the function that Osvaldo Cruz exercised admirably, so that one may say of him, as his major title of glory: Osvaldo Cruz gave a truly Brazilian form to medical science, establishing the principle that in Brazil one must study medicine and hygiene for Brazil." [15] The Institution of Manguinhos, already proclaimed "the greatest scientific glory of Brazil," which, in 1907, took the name of its founder, is, in fact, as a school of tropical medicine, according to Rui Barbosa, "the spring of which all Latin America came to drink."

Meanwhile, in spite of these great isolated and dispersed efforts to which Oscar Freire referred, and the systematic but limited activity of a school of mines or the greater amplitude and force of penetration found in the Institute of Manguinhos, what predominated in each one of the intellectual careers was the idea of professional application; and research itself, when any was done, was found to be directed toward the needs of the profession. Except perhaps in the law schools, in which, due to the excessive weight given to theoretical notions, the balance between theory and practice broke down and there was opened a larger field to general culture, preference was given in all of our institutions for professional training everywhere to a practical apprenticeship, which still occupies a place of importance, although there is growing more marked in our medical schools the tendency to a special scientific preparation and to the spirit of research and experimentation. In consequence, then, of the preponderant importance given to practical and professional life, the experimental sciences

[15] Not only in sanitation but also in the efforts made "to develop medicine and hygiene in and for Brazil" was Osvaldo Cruz supported and followed closely by first-class disciples and collaborators, such as Carlos Chagas, Artur Neiva, and Belisário Pena; the latter, persuaded thereto by Cruz, accompanied him in 1910 on his trip to the Madeira-Mamoré region in the Amazon. As early as 1907 Belisário Pena was commissioned, together with Carlos Chagas, to fight the epidemic of malaria in the north of the State of Minas; and when he finished his work on the commission organized by Osvaldo Cruz, which extinguished yellow fever in Pará (1910–1911), he took part in 1912, with Artur Neiva, in a scientific excursion to the north of Bahia, to the southwest of Pernambuco, to Piauí, and to the south and north of Goias (see the report published in the Memorias do Instituto Osvaldo Cruz, 1916). He was director of the Rural Prophylaxis Service, created by President Veneslau Bras (Decree 13,000 of May 1, 1918); he founded the Sanitary League of Brazil; he published, in addition to numerous articles and lectures, several works, among them *Saneamento do Brasil* (1st ed., 1918, 2nd ed., 1923); when he was Director of Rural Sanitation, in 1920; he promoted the setting up of rural prophylaxis in 15 States; he undertook the most vigorous campaign we have known to awaken the sanitary conscience of the people and to fight hookworm disease, worms, malaria, leprosy, and alcoholism; in 1927 and 1928 he traversed a large part of the State of Minas, as well as the States of Alagoas, Pernambuco, Paraíba, and Rio Grande do Norte, in a propaganda and educational campaign, and later, from 1928 to 1930, he traveled in Rio Grande do Sul on invitation of the governor. Promoted to be Inspector of Sanitary Propaganda and Education in 1928, he was finally appointed in 1930 Director of the National Department of Public Health (1930–1932).

were for a long time almost unknown outside the museums, like the National Museum, and the observatories and other institutes that were more penetrated by scientific spirit and method; and even today, in spite of the technical schools and the laboratories recently created, it is difficult for the investigator or the savant in Brazil to find any of those sinecures so numerous in Germany, in which he can, sheltered from necessity, continue his disinterested studies. Everywhere in all the institutions of higher learning may be found the same subordination of science to art, the same desire for the immediate and proximate application, the same utilitarian direction having in view the public function or the private career, the same inclination, in consequence, to view things from a special angle—the professional angle, even though questions are more general and complex and transcend the frontiers of a single profession. On the precarious basis of scientific culture and the almost total absence of the critical and philosophical spirit, it was natural that there should develop, as in fact there did develop, in generations of "deserters" from the professions, that culture of encyclopedic nature in which thought gains in extension and loses in profundity; and the creative spirit was always distant and its place was taken by erudition, and even this almost always among us more or less apparent and without substance, hiding an absolute lack of solidity of knowledge under a surface that is at times brilliant. Hence the reason why there has not been formed, even under the shelter of freedom, a cultivated élite, the influence of which upon the masses would have been notable and which one could not hope for as a result of an education of a strictly professional character, and certainly therefore prejudicial as much to the individual taken alone as to society viewed as a whole. The enormous disproportion between the number of purely scientific societies, which can almost be counted upon one's fingers, and the associations of lawyers, engineers, doctors, and pharmacists [16] that exist in the country is in itself a fact that illustrates forcibly the expansion of the professional spirit and the growing prestige of the diploma holders.

If, then, independence, as Pedro Calmon observed, "did not find already formed a mental aristocracy cut off from the clergy, and purely lay," what the Republic found and did not do more than develop was a new aristocracy of bachelors and doctors of law entirely nourished in the schools of professional training or made up of "deserters"

---

[16] Among the principal medical associations of the country, first place belongs to the oldest of all, the National Academy of Medicine, into which was transformed in 1889, taking that name, the Imperial Academy of Medicine, which in turn had resulted from the reorganization in 1835 of the Medical Society, founded in 1829 by J. C. Soares Meireles, J. M. Cruz Jobim, L. V. de Simoni, J. M. Faivre, and J. F. Sigaud, with the object of promoting "the progress and development of medical sciences and, in general, benefiting humanity by the study and application of the means favorable to the conservation and improvement of the public health." It has always enjoyed an active existence and great authority, as may be seen from the almost uninterrupted publication of the journal of the society, which as it accompanied the history of the organization took various names, and which today has more than 100 volumes, entitled *Boletins da Academia Nacional de Medicina*. Between 1845 and 1886, when the Society of Medicine and Surgery of Rio de Janeiro was founded under the presidency of Catta Preta—another important medical body —"many other associations were born and died in Brazil," as Antônio Austregésilo wrote, enumerating fourteen of these medical societies, including pharmaceutical and medicopharmaceutical ones. The Society of Medicine and Surgery of Bahia, which in 1894 succeeded the Medical Society, founded in 1888, published down to 1908 two volumes of annals, and since that time has kept up as organ of the Society the *Revista de Medicina*. Numerous other societies were founded later, in São Paulo, where we have the Society of Medicine and Surgery and the Paulista

from the professions. Just as ecclesiastical or clerical as was the culture which was developed in the colony within the shade of the colleges of Fathers and the seminaries, so great was the professional character of that culture which began to grow and expanded in the clarity of the schools and academies formed to train doctors, engineers, and lawyers. "The sacristies, the cells of the friars, the pulpit, and the vicaries polarized," writes Pedro Calmon, "the intellectual animation which appears in the ideological documents of that picture of revolution and national definition," and they had throughout the period of the colony, with the colleges and seminaries, the same role in the cultural formation of Brazil that was exercised during the Empire and the Republic by schools destined to prepare men for the liberal professions, marking with an emphatically professional character our culture which had barely freed itself from the circle of attraction of ecclesiastical influences. Of the three great traditions of Europe in which our culture was formed, the one which predominated in it was not, however, as one might judge by its religious origins, the profound feeling of an inner life and of a mission to accomplish characteristic of the Judaic-Christian tradition, nor the cult of pure intelligence inherited from the Greeks, but the tradition of rational law coming from the Romans. While in the north of the American continent, under the incentive of its immense mineral wealth and of the industrial exploitation of the subsoil, there was carried on a "unilateral development, almost exclusively based upon progress in material things," there burgeoned in Brazil, like a flower of civilization, juridical culture powerfully fed upon the moral and religious traditions of the nation. During more than a century, or for almost all of the period following National Independence, it was the voice of law that was heard loudest; and in the academies and in their shadow, intellectual life acquired its greatest intensity and its greatest power of influence. With the growing complexity of the social and economic system of the country, and the specialization of functions resulting from the process of the division of labor, the field of activities with professional applications doubtless expanded without corresponding to new necessities in the liberal careers, as in agriculture, in industry, and in commerce, and there arose in consequence specialized institutions and schools destined to meet the needs of the growing technical and professional circles or those that were in a full state of development. But the literary and juridical type of mentality outweighed all others, the scientific, the technical, and that of rational organization; and in the process of its evolution there was scarcely sketched an emancipation of culture, which is still found confined to life and to professional activities and without the conditions and the impulses that are necessary if it is to rise above the professions and to transform the élite of the country from "carriers" of culture to "creators" of a national culture expressing the spirit of a new civilization.

Medical Association, among the oldest; in Rio de Janeiro, where associations of a general character were founded, such as the Sindicato Médico or specialized associations such as the Brazilian Society of Neurology, Psychiatry, and legal Medicine, founded in 1907, in various capitals (Pôrto Alegre, Niteroi, and Manaus) and even in less important cities of the interior, in Minas and in São Paulo. If the development of organizations in the field of engineering, and of law did not show as great quantitative growth as in the medical field, the two professions can show associations like the Engineering Club of Rio, the Institute of Engineering in São Paulo, and the Order of Lawyers of São Paulo and Rio, besides professional groups and institutes of real influence in professional circles.

The tendency toward letters even in the professional field and the scattered work done by the disinterested cultivators of science reveal a truly notable effort among Brazilians to surpass and to dominate their professions by means of culture. This inclination does not, in fact, correspond merely to the eminently literary tradition of our culture, as a result of the influence of the colonial system of teaching, but also, from a love for professional culture, to a noble aspiration to perfect and free the spirit, which is the more sought after because literary prestige always was, among ourselves, capable of adding something to the authority and power of intellectual influence of our professional men. It is not only, one sees, that tradition which was developed and which grew stronger from the time of the Empire; it is, moreover, a reaction against the limitations of a culture of a professional type, a means of fleeing from the field of those specializations which tend to separate professional groups, isolating them from each other because of the differences of mentality of the various groups. Or, in other words, it is a "reaction" within tradition. On the literary plane, more than on the political plane, communications between professional men have been established and have grown close. So if letters, being an ornament to one's diploma and one's fortune, facilitated access to public life, it was not they, through the idealism which they are accustomed to stimulate, that were the most capable of allowing men who were placed at points of observation to see politics in a state of nudity, stripped of all fictions and all legends, without bitterness. To free themselves from the tyranny of the professions and to escape narrow specialization, there was no other recourse for the Brazilian than literature, which enlarged his horizon, gave him new intellectual arms, and furnished him with "that grain of fantasy and of dreams which could moderate the furor of the ordinary attention of man to practical ends." So then, if a few professional men owed all the prestige which they won exclusively to the exercise of their profession, most of those among them who attained intellectual eminence not only did not disdain letters but sought and at times found in them support and a more efficacious means to spread their authority beyond the bounds of the liberal professions. In some, letters ended by dominating over the profession; in others, there prevailed over letters, which did not succeed in absorbing them, the profession in which they had specialized; and in a rare few the profession and literary art, rising to a high level, were associated and were balanced in such a way that their specific professional culture became the substance of their letters, and their letters the most noble instrument of the profession.[17]

[17] This love of letters came to be so common that in Brazil no professional man seemed to think he was complete unless he doubled as a member of the literati. Bachelors of law, through the very nature of their studies and because skill in language is so useful to them in their profession, were most apt to feel the pull of this powerful attraction. There was hardly a student of law who did not pay his tribute to poetry and rhetoric or perpetrate in his youth some literary "sins"; and it was only when literature smiled upon them that the lawyers thought opportunity for an intellectual career was knocking at their door, so close were letters and the profession in their field. It was the epoch of poets, orators, chroniclers, scholars, grammarians, and literati. The grammarians were for the most part writers who failed and turned into "philologists": "those who can, do; those who can't, teach," wrote Bernard Shaw, not without reason. In none of the lawyers were law and letters so happily wedded as in Rui Barbosa, in whom there was a rivalry between the writer and orator, the journalist and scholar, the lawyer and jurisconsult, all on the same extremely high level. Although there may not be great affinity between letters and medicine, it was the doctors, after the example of the lawyers, who yielded most to the itch of the word and the temptation of literature and allowed themselves to be ruled by concern for language, tightening the cord to

But if letters contributed to humanize culture and to favor the effort to go beyond the profession, bringing a decisive contribution to the intellectual life, which otherwise would have remained reduced to professional circles, without brilliance and without vigor, letters had their serious inconveniences: making intelligences less utilitarian on the one hand and more subject on the other to the seduction of form, they took away the sense of reality and retarded the appearance of a critical and creative scientific and experimental spirit in the evolution of Brazilian thought.

Letters were not, in fact, in large measure anything more than a bridge thrown out to permit doctors, lawyers, and engineers (the only ones who received higher instruction in Brazil) to pass from one bank of professional culture to another bank of culture, under the archway of their own ideas and sentiments tied up with their classes and professions. Far from being, as in other countries, the intellectual crowning of a culture long nourished on social life and founded on philosophic and scientific thought, which had to be shared and which sought in them the variety and richness of resources for its expression, they did not generally go any further than an intellectual activity, practiced as an exercise and diversion of the mind, unsatisfied within the framework in which it was enclosed and driven to break its bonds and to make an opening in other directions. The engineer and above all the doctor and the lawyer, in a general way like the professional men and specialists, always found it simple and easy to "live outside their specialty (professional or intellectual) on the ideas of everybody, that is on a little baggage of ideas worn out like old money in circulation for a long time." The truth is that all this intellectual life, literary and political, for more than a century, gave at first view the impression of a magnificent tree which was extending its arms toward the sky. But examined more closely, one could not fail to discover the fact that it was condemned to perish, with its roots almost on the surface of the earth, without force to penetrate the more profound strata in which, spreading out, it might join and interlace itself with the roots of social and national life. Hence an artificial literature without substance and without convictions, without heat and without height, which was contented with an empty verbalism, with the illusion of knowing things only because one knew their names, and which, believing that speaking and writing were an excuse for doing neither, gave individuals the means of closing themselves in, sheltered away from the real, and gave them a pretext to turn their backs upon reality and action. Certainly of the two attractions of the two electric poles, the literary and the scientific,

---

the uttermost, to the point of preciosity, artifice, and love for archaic forms. Francisco de Castro started this group of literary doctors, great writers, some of them like Afrânio Peixoto, a group to which were added gradually Miguel Couto, Aloísio de Castro, Antônio Austregésilo, and Clementino Fraga, all of the Brazilian Academy of Letters. The relative isolation to which their profession condemned them and the closer contact with physical sciences and mathematics kept the engineer from this contagion, up to a certain point conferring immunity against the grammatical and literary virus which was in the air and was transmitted less by books than by the power of tradition. Garcia Redondo, of the first group of professors of the Polytechnic School of São Paulo, and Luiz Carlos da Fonseca, poet, railway engineer, are among those rare cases in which letters have been joined to engineering activity. Euclides da Cunha, a military engineer by accident, cannot be called upon to serve as an example: his thought always dwelt in higher spheres than his job and his professional environment; he was in full truth a writer, a vigorous and original master of prose and one of the greatest prose writers of American literature.

the one which exercised the most powerful influence on our national life was the literary pole, whose power of attraction, developed during the regime of colonial education, did not cease to increase during the Empire in the shade of the liberal professions and among the deserters from the professions, which within the conditions of the social environment offered to the mind only the perspectives of literature and the arts. But, effect and cause at the same time, this domination of letters, which goes back to the colonial traditions of education, if it resulted on the one hand from our lack of scientific education, on the other, by falsifying and impoverishing the image which it gave us of reality, substituting a conventional world for the real world with all the occupations and problems, doubtless contributed to turn us away from the path of science and to retard its progress. The attraction we feel for the charms of language and for external brilliance was what was cultivated by it, and with such intensity that professional men sought in literature not only indulgence but a means of interesting the public and of making their own profession "live."

We cannot, however, seek only in our unilateral, literary tradition the origins of our lack of interest in science and technique which, although cultivated in various fields by individual, isolated efforts, had been developed only with difficulties and have been very backward as compared with the state of events. Our cultural organization, set up in the period of the Empire with almost all of its essential parts, which maintained themselves during the Republic, was not fit to produce anything but a professional aristocracy, and it is to that that the aristocracy of the mind was reduced, cultivated as it was by schools of higher learning in which bachelors and doctors of law were turned out on a large scale. There were no other sources of training and recruitment of an élite, and these groups were consequently impoverished in authentic values. If "for each million Englishmen there are about two hundred and fifty eminent men, that is, men with a nationwide renown and fame," to judge by the data of Francis Galton, we cannot estimate for Brazil at more than thirty the number of notable personalities of the type of José de Alencar, Joaquim Nabuco, the Baron of Rio Branco, Osvaldo Cruz, and Euclides da Cunha, whereas Brazil could easily possess more than fifteen hundred eminent individuals according to the conclusions of Oliveira Viana, based upon calculations of the population and not counting the mass of the illiterate. The fact is, that in the meshing of the gears of our cultural and educational system, reduced, on the higher plane, to schools of professional training, there has evidently been lacking, observes Oliveira Viana, "some piece or other, an essential piece, that has the function of picking out these individuals and making them reach the élite group." This piece is one which is made up everywhere of an ensemble of institutions destined to develop scientific spirit and methods in the different realms of human knowledge and to apply them to direct and thorough investigation on all the planes of national reality, its natural resources, its necessities, and its spiritual, political, and economic problems. Besides, if the individual is bound to the society which surrounds him and from which he is nourished; if his very psychological and intellectual life is an exchange, a constant communication, and if communication nourishes us as much as difference "that by means of which man surpasses himself, creates, invents, and conceives," the Brazilian still lacked the intensity of intellectual exchange between men, groups, and institutions, between Brazilian culture and that of other nations [18] which would lead to genuine culture. The isolation in which we live was not only an isolation of Brazil with regard to other nations during the whole colonial period, but within the national unity, between different groups and institutions. Intellectual life, being isolated in different zones of production, in the north with the civilization of sugar, later on in Minas Gerais with the mining of gold and diamonds, and finally in the valley of the Paraiba with the cultivation of coffee, followed the rhythm and the evolution of these economic cycles. The élites which were formed in different regions and which remained isolated by the great distances could only communicate in the center of life of the country through their most illustrious figures, just as great trees which, planted at long intervals, can touch each other only by their highest branches.

This situation, so characteristic of the colonial period and of the Empire, lasted, although in less marked form, down into the Republic to the year 1920, in which the development of industry and commerce, the growth and multiplication of urban centers, and the progress of communication commenced to favor contacts which restored to the individual, together with a more profound awareness of his dependence on social life, his "fertility" and his means of intellectual expansion. But it was only after the Revolution of 1930 that these economic and cultural changes were intensified and new values created and new possibilities for literature were opened up, a literature which, instead of limiting itself to amusing the rich, was impregnated by social atmosphere, became aware of local problems, and thus came to correspond in a more lively fashion to the spiritual necessities of the country. Beside those circles, almost exclusively limited to the liberal professions, in which our old élites were recruited, there arose new centers of study with the faculties of philosophy, science, and letters, of sociology and politics, which opened their possibilities to the most varied individual

[18] It was the Northeast, wrote Gilberto Freyre, "with its civilization of the sugar mill, full of leisure for study, that gave Brazil its greatest orator—Father Vieira; its greatest satiric poet, Gregório de Matos; its greatest mathematician—Sousinha; its greatest philologist—Dr. Morais, transplanted from the sugar civilization of the south to Pernambuco, where he became a plantation owner." It was in the sugar cycle that there arose, in the Empire period, the greatest jurist, Teixeira de Freitas; a great politician, orator, and diplomat, Joaquim Nabuco; the greatest political orator, Rui Barbosa; a poet of genius, Castro Alves; the best scientific brain of Brazil, Nina Rodrigues; a man of the temper and distinction of Bishop Dom Vital; a historian like Oliveira Lima; innovators and polemical writers of the value of Tobias Barreto and Sílvio Romero, and a painter like Pedro Américo. The intellectual life which flourished in the mountains of Minas Gerais under the inrush of population associated with mining, and remained almost as insulated as that which developed with the sugar civilization, began with the poets Basílio da Gama and Santa Rita Durão, and broke forth, with generous idealism winning the crown of martyrdom, in the dream of national independence sung by the lyric poets of the Inconfidência, Tomaz Antônio Gonzaga, Cláudio Manuel da Costa, Silva Alvarenga and Alvarenga Peixoto. In São Paulo, which they left to study in Coimbra, the most remarkable personalities of the end and beginning of the past century, the two Gusmãos, Bartolomeu and Alexandre, the inventor and the diplomat, the writer Matias Aires, the engineer Lacerda de Almeida, and the three Andradas (all of Santos, with the exception of the engineer), there arose during the coffee cycle three of the most original figures of Brazilian medicine, Pereira Barreto, Miguel Pereira, and Osvaldo Cruz, the greatest of all, and a fine composer, Carlos Gomes, the greatest glory of Brazilian music. Growing up in different environments, alone and isolated, and made up of men in the most varied situations and with the most diverse mentalities, these élite groups, without relations with one another, followed one another and moved as the economic frontier moved and slowly mingled with the upper layers of society.

aptitudes, so that intellectual life took on an intensity and extension which the history of our culture had never known. Certainly this broadening of circles and this intensity of intellectual life could not be obtained except at the cost of a noticeable lowering of the level; but by stimulating the exchange between groups and institutions and broadening the field of search for gifted individuals, a contribution was doubtless made to the great movement of ideas in different directions and to arouse a public of greater receptivity, more capable of making literature, science, and all cultural movements "live." The truly notable development which the book industry and book trade acquired, and the new bookstores and libraries, which were installed everywhere, showed the great reach of this little intellectual revolution in which people began to give an attention at least equivalent to that which they had given to the professional, literary, and political, now to the scientific and technical, to the social and economic. Great libraries, national and state, which had formerly as their principal, if not their only, clients historians used to the methods and the disciplines of research, now sought out by students and intellectuals of all types, felt the necessity of being reorganized and enriching themselves in order to facilitate the work of the reader, to perfect the means of consultation and to become centers of investigation and scientific work. The new was not only created by the prolongation of an existing line, marked by literary traditions and the liberal professions; it was the flowering of a critical and creative spirit which, causing us to lose our attitude of superstition before written texts, invited us to escape from our bookish culture into the real world and drove us to the study of ourselves and our problems and to the investigation of reality in all fields.

BIBLIOGRAPHY

Almeida Nogueira, *Tradicões e reminiscéncias* (Lisbon: A. Editora, 7 vols., 1908–1912).

Austregésilo, Antônio, "Esboço histórico da medicina no Brasil," in *Medicina no Brasil*, ed. Leonídio Ribeiro (Rio: Imprensa Nacional, 1940), pp. 385–404.

Barreto, Plínio, *A Cultura jurídica no Brasil (1822–1922)* (São Paulo: Biblioteca do *Estado de São Paulo*, No. 2, 1922).

Bevilaqua, Clovis, *História da Faculdade de Direito do Recife* (Rio: Francisco Alves, 2 vols., 1927).

Calmon, Pedro, *História social do Brasil*, Vol. 1, *Espírito da sociedade colonial*, Vol. 2, *Espírito da sociedade imperial* (São Paulo: Comp. Editora Nacional, 1937—Brasiliana, Vols. 40, 83).

Freire, Oscar, "Evolução da medicina no Brasil," in special ed. of *O Estado de São Paulo*, Sept. 7, 1922.

Freyre, Gilberto, *Casa grande e senzala* (Rio: Maia & Schmidt, 1933). Transl. by Samuel Putnam as *The Masters and The Slaves* (New York: Knopf, 1946).

———, *Sobrados e mocambos: Decadência do patriarcado rural no Brasil* (São Paulo: Comp. Editora Nacional, 1936—Brasiliana, Vol. 64).

Leite, Father Serafim, *Páginas de história do Brasil* (São Paulo: Comp. Editora Nacional, 1937—Brasiliana, Vol. 93), Chap. XIII, "Os Jesuitas no Brasil e a medicina."

Magalhães, Fernando, *O Centenário da Faculdade de Medicina do Rio de Janeiro, 1832–1932* (Rio: Barthel, 1932).

Neiva, Artur, "Osvaldo Cruz," in *Medicina no Brasil*, ed. Leonídio Ribeiro (Rio: Imprensa Nacional, 1940), pp. 59–66.

Olinto, Antônio, "Memória histórica: História da fundação, instalação e organização da Escola de Minas," in *Anais da Escola de Minas*, Ouro Preto, No. 7 (1905), pp. 9–114.

Oliveira Lima, Manuel de, *D. João VI no Brasil (1808–1821)* (Rio: *Jornal do Comércio*, 2 vols., 1908), chap. "A Revolução pernambucana de 1817."

Pacífico Pereira, Antônio, *Memória sôbre a medicina na Bahia* (Imprensa Oficial do Estado, 1923). For the centenary of independence in Bahia.

Vampré, Spencer, *Memórias para a história da Academia de São Paulo* (São Paulo: Livraria Académica, 2 vols., 1924).

Vauthier, Louis Léger, *Diário íntimo (1840–1846)*, with Preface and notes by Gilberto Freyre (Rio: Serviço gráfico do Ministério do Educação e Saúde, 1940—Publications of the Serviço do patrimônio histórico e artístico nacional, No. 4).

Viana Dias, Mário, "Instituto Osvaldo Cruz," in *Medicina no Brasil*, ed. Leonídio Ribeiro (Rio: Imprensa Nacional, 1940), pp. 98–107.

CHAPTER THREE

LITERARY LIFE

The beginnings of Brazilian literature—Portuguese literature written in Brazil—The first original manifestations—Gregório de Matos and satire—Social differentiation and linguistic differentiation—The coexistence of two vernaculars down to the eighteenth century—The theater of Antônio José da Silva—The two national poems—The poets of the Inconfidência— Revolutionaries in politics, conservatives in letters—Journalism and the struggles of independence and in the first Empire—Political literature—Romanticism in Brazil—The attraction of Indian themes—Gonçalves Dias, the poet of the Indians—José de Alencar and the Brazilian language—Castro Alves, the poet of the slaves—The evolution of the theater and its principal figures—Memórias de um sargento de milicias—The national thought of Tavares Bastos— Parliamentary eloquence during the Empire—Joaquim Nabuco and Rui Barbosa—Agitators of ideas—Tobias Barreto and Sílvio Romero—The splendor of journalism—Eduardo Prado— The Brazilian Academy and the unity of the language—The great lyrical poets—History —The two aspects of the national spirit—Machado de Assis and Euclides da Cunha—Essayists, critics, and pamphlet writers—The movement of modern literature—The poetry of the younger writers—Novelists and short-story writers—The spread of printing—Literature and the public spirit.

LITERATURE is not only one of the elements of general culture; but as a result of the specific conditions of our almost exclusively literary formation, it was the first element and the most persistent, the strongest and the most expressive in our culture. If only in our own times the factors which condition intellectual life have combined and acquired the necessary intensity to create the "profession of writer" (and even today an author rarely lives on the result of his intellectual production), from a very early time in the second century there were enough of them to produce in the rural aristocracy and in the bourgeoisie, whether born in the old country or here, what might be called a "literary climate." At the beginning of every society, as Novicow observes,[1] what predominates—since it is necessary first of all to live—is economic activity; and intellectual life does not arise until much later, when the existence of individuals who are purely or principally intellectuals becomes possible with the formation of a wealthy class, so situated that it can directly or indirectly maintain them, and with the leisure which does not come without wealth and which opens wide opportunities to study. The intellectual élite grew up naturally among us, as everywhere, as a result of economic differentiation. Those who had the wealth and leisure for study—the Portuguese noblemen and after them the lords of the sugar mills and the great miners—either took a closer interest in intellectual things or—what happened most of the time—if they personally did not devote themselves to these studies called them forth in others, promoting the education of their sons, giving them opportunities to acquire culture, and supporting

---

[1] M. J. Novicow, *L'Élite intellectuelle et l'aristocratie.*

the producers of the literature that was capable of entertaining them in the long empty hours of the big houses and of the city mansions. But this intellectual élite which then arose brought with it in its entirety in successive generations a common character which the universalist culture of a European type, strictly literary and acquired in the colleges of the Fathers and developed at Coimbra, thrust upon it: it was an élite of bachelors of law and of literary people. It did not exercise nor could it exercise a real influence on colonial society, limited as it always was to the restricted circles in which a state of prosperity had been created by the sugar industry in the north and by the exploitation of the mines in the south. It was without roots in the land and in the social environment, the experience, necessities, and aspirations of which were not reflected in its culture; and it was subject to the economic fluctuations to which it owed its flourishing as well as its decline and which did not give it the necessary time to renew and perfect itself through generations and to become an aristocracy of the spirit with sufficiently deep roots and sufficiently recognized to have a profound effect upon the social consciousness.

At the beginning of the intellectual formation of Brazil, the preoccupations and ideas of a literary character, almost all of which came from Europe, were the privilege of a handful of people of the higher class, whose interests they served or at times even opposed: a culture which cultivated men neither wished nor thought of applying to reality, keeping it only for the recreation of their empty hours and to mark more clearly the difference between the small privileged class and the ignorant mass. As it was a purely precocious and artificial imitation of the home country, literature did not succeed in being more than "a sign of class," distinguishing the upper class like an "ornament for the drawing room of the immense colonial house which Brazil still was." Without paying attention to any end, without having any true function in the social picture, "pure activity of the spirit," explains Genolino Amado,[2] "could give pleasure, but never aroused respect and ended by being disdained as is everything which in spite of being amusing is useless and inactive. Seeing a literature that had no utility for its producer, since it was not enough to give him a profession and had no social and humanitarian sense for its reader, since it was far separated from reality, the people became accustomed to consider it as a simple, curious skill, a strange gift which nature gave to certain individuals, perhaps as a compensation, because it had denied them a capacity for more constructive and consistent activity." Hence, as a result of this artificial literature without substance and without relation to its environment, the attitude of the Brazilian toward men of intelligence and things of the spirit, and, according to Genolino Amado, a strange inclination "to be satisfied with the defeat of intelligence. The intellectual appeared to him to be likable and interesting only when he sank to venality of opinion and the Bohemian life of creation." [3] However that may be, literary work always con-

---

[2] Genolino Amado, *Um Olhar sôbre a vida* (Rio: Olímpio, 1939).

[3] Far from being peculiar to the Brazilians, this tendency is a universal one, which takes this or this form, declines or grows, depending upon the conditions of social life and the temperament of the nation. The Romans, with their scientific and utilitarian spirit, farmers and warriors, had the same attitude toward the things of the mind—poetry, science, and philosophy, and were not interested in literature except as a result of the influence of Greek culture and teachers, whom they called disdainfully *Graeculi*, but whom they later came to associate with, and then surrendered to their seductive power. Among modern peoples, do not the English, empiricists without knowing it, have the same attitude toward the pure savant, the intellectual who may be able to compel their esteem, but who will find it difficult to get their real sympathy? In the English language, which

CATECISMO
BRASILICO

Da Doutrina Christãa,

Com o Ceremonial dos Sacramentos,&
mais actos Parochiaes.

COMPOSTO

Por Padres Doutos da Companhia de
J E S U S,

Aperfeiçoado, & dado a luz

Pelo Padre ANTONIO DE ARAUJO
da mesma Companhia.

Emendado nesta segunda impressaõ

Pelo P. BERTHOLAMEU DE LEAM
da mesma Companhia.

LISBOA.

Na Officina de MIGUEL DESLANDES

M. DC. LXXXVI.

Com todas as licenças necessarias

137. Frontispiece of the 1686 edition of the Brazilian catechism of
Father Antônio de Araújo.
Photo by Rembrandt.

128. "The Last Tamoyo," painting by Rodolfo Amoêdo. Photo by Rembrandt.

139. Father Antônio Vieira (born at Lisbon, 1608, died at Bahia, 1697),
a Jesuit who served Brazil for fifty years, and the greatest preacher to use the
Portuguese language.

140. Sacristy of the Cathedral, Salvador, Bahia.
Photo by Voltaire Fraga, in Brazilian Institute of Geography and Statistics.

141. Cloister of the Convent of St. Francis, Salvador, Bahia. Photo by Voltaire Fraga, in Brazilian Institute of Geography and Statistics.

142. Church and Monastery of St. Benedict, Salvador, Bahia. Photo by Voltaire Fraga, Urbo Salvador, in Brazilian Institute of Geography and Statistics.

143. Church of the Rua dos Passos (eighteenth century), Salvador, Bahia.
Photo by Voltaire Fraga, in Brazilian Institute of Geography and Statistics.

144. Ouro Preto. An aspect of the city from the atrium of the Church of
São Francisco de Paula.
Photo by Radio Inconfidência of Minas Gerais.

145. São João d'El Rei. Church of St. Francis of Assisi.
Photo by Radio Inconfidência of Minas Gerais.

146. São João d'El Rei. Church of St. Francis of Assisi. Another view.
Photo by Radio Inconfidência of Minas Gerais.

147. Ouro Preto. Church of Our Lady of Carmel, side altars.
Photo by Radio Inconfidência of Minas Gerais.

148. Doorway of a church, São João d'El Rei.
Photo by Stille, in Collection of the College of Philosophy of São Paulo.

149. São João d'El Rei. The mother church.
Photo by Stille, in Collection of the College of Philosophy of São Paulo.

150. São João d'El Rei. Church of Carmel.
Photo by Stille, in Collection of the College of Philosophy of São Paulo.

151. Tiradentes. Mother church. Detail of the organ.
Photo by Radio Inconfidência of Minas Gerais.

152. Tiradentes. Mother church. Retable and ceiling of main altar.
Photo by Radio Inconfidência of Minas Gerais.

153. Mariana. Church of Carmel.
Photo by Stille, in Collection of the College of Philosophy of São Paulo.

154. Altar of the Church of the Happy Death, Rio de Janeiro.
Photo by Stille, in collection of the College of Philosophy of São Paulo.

155. Church of St. Francis of Paula, Rio de Janeiro.
Photo by Stille, in collection of the College of Philosophy of São Paulo.

156. Church of St. Benedict, Olinda. Photo by Stille, in collection of the College of Philosophy of São Paulo.

157. Collecting alms for a church festival. Debret, *Voyage pittoresque et historique au Brésil* (1834), Vol. III, Plate 29.

158. "Comfort," painting by Prisciliano Silva, of Bahia.
Photo by Voltaire Fraga, in Brazilian Institute of Geography and Statistics.

159. Cathedral of Olinda, Pernambuco.
Photo by Stille, in collection of the College of Philosophy of São Paulo.

160. Dom Fra Vital de
Oliveira, Bishop of Olinda.

161. Dom Antònio de Macedo
Costa, Bishop of Belém.

162. Union Church. Presbyterian Church of São Paulo. One of the beautiful Protestant churches in Brazil.

TEMPLO BETH-ISRAEL

163. Temple Beth-Israel. Artist's sketch of a synagogue in São Paulo, now completed.

164. The University of Coimbra, where during the colonial period those who studied with the fathers of the Society of Jesus went to take their degrees.

165. The Law School of São Paulo, formerly Convent of St. Francis. It was founded here in 1827.

166. São Paulo College of Law. The building has been restored in the traditional Brazilian style and on the same site on St. Francis Square, where the law course has been given ever since 1827.

167. Monastery of St. Benedict in Olinda, where the law course, founded in 1827, was originally given.

168. Recife College of Law. Rear façade and entrance to the library.

169. Teixeira de Freitas, whose consolidation of civil law is "the greatest juridical monument which the Empire bequeathed to us."

170. Lafayette Rodrigues Pereira (born in Minas, 1837, died at Rio, 1917), leader of the "civilian" campaign and one of the most learned jurisconsults of Brazil.

171. Rui Barbosa (born at Bahia, 1849, died at Petrópolis, 1923), a jurist of remarkable
erudition and one of the greatest lawyers of Brazil.
Photo from the collection of the Companhia Melhoramentos of São Paulo.

172. Clóvis Bevilaqua (died 1945), "from whose hands came the final draft of the Brazilian Civil Code, then enacted into law."

173. Pedro Lessa (born at Sérro, Minas, 1859, died at Rio, 1921), professor, judge, and writer on legal subjects.

174. João Mendes, lawyer, professor, and judge.

175. The Central School, which in 1874 changed its name to Polytechnic School and now is the National School of Engineering.

stitutes a kind of witness bearing. It is related to a period and shows its tendencies, and to a country and reveals its usages and mentality, and to a social species from which the writer has come and reveals its customs. Still, without human interest this literature of conformists—rarely of innovators—has great historic value which comes from the constant relation between the artist and the environment of which he is an expression whether he has adapted himself to it or revolted against it—since "to rebel against one's time is still to be part of it." The social atmosphere in which colonial literature was bathed was the same which in the peninsula surrounded the colonizing people and which had been transferred to this side of the Atlantic with its stewards, noblemen, and functionaries, merchants and adventurers, and above all by the élite, composed in the beginning of the priestly class, and which monopolized teaching in the colleges and seminaries. The only home country was Portugal, and so long as the differentiation which went on did not become sufficiently great to awaken the consciousness of a distinction between Brazilians and Portuguese, what was produced in the colony could not be anything but a Portuguese literature written in Brazil, as a dim reflection of the far-off mother country.

In the sixteenth century, the first of our history, the eminently Portuguese character of this literature stands out in such bold relief that if necessary it can be considered as "a colonial chapter of Portuguese literature." If, from some points of view, travel books, narratives of the chroniclers, and letters of missionaries are related to Brazilian literature, it is generally because they took Brazil as their object or were "dated" from the colony, in which, in addition to taking possession of the land and exploiting its wealth, what was preoccupying the home country was its rule and the conversion of the Indians. The hesitating policy of Portugal, for a long time neglectful of the nearly discovered land, the difficulties which stood in the way of colonization, and the failure of the regime of the captaincies, did not permit any noticeable development of early colonial society, scanty and dispersed, in which it was only in 1549 that there was introduced a ferment of culture with the first Jesuit missions, even before the planting of sugar cane on a large scale, which was to furnish an economic substructure for its civilization. Besides the famous letter of Pero Vaz de Caminha, a scribe at Calcutta who had come with the fleet of Cabral, and the log of the voyage (*Diário de navegação da Armada que foi à terra do Brasil em 1530*) of Pero Lopes de Sousa, there stand out in

---

has made up pejorative terms to designate the intellectual, "it is said that such and such a thing is high-brow in order to indicate that it belongs too much to the intellectual; and with a mixture of compassion and disdain, that so and so would be a good guy if he were not so brainy." The fact is that, in the last analysis, true intelligence is so uncommon among men and so disturbing to what is established, to the old order of things, that its existence and activity produce fear, caution, and hostility, as if there were a question of something magical, demoniacal, or superhuman. In the Brazilian this tendency, which is shown in a form—one that is decidedly Brazilian—of irreverence and neglect, is less the outgrowth of a practical and positive spirit than of a kind of instinct of defense. His attitude of distrust and skepticism, is it not rather a reaction of good sense against excessive intellectualism and the abuses of imagination in a literature without social and human sentiments and without contact with that reality which we all feel and whose expression we seek for in vain in the artists and thinkers, prose writers, and poets? The spirit of routine to which intelligence always constitutes a threat, the lack of relationship, from the time of the colony, between the masses and the élite, haughty and distant, and the vanity that is so hard for the élite to avoid, also contribute not a little among us to produce hostility and envy among the nonintellectual classes which form the great bulk of the nation.

this period among Portuguese documents of major historic interest as far as Brazil is concerned the *Tratado da terra do Brasil* and the *História da Província de Santa Cruz* (1576) of Pero Magalhães Gandavo, friend of Camões, and that work which Capistrano de Abreu calls monumental, the *Tratado descritivo do Brasil em 1587*, by Gabriel Soares de Sousa, who came to Brazil in 1567 and settled in Bahia as the lord of a sugar mill. All these were Portuguese—two of them functionaries of the kingdom who stayed only temporarily in the New World and remained for a short time—with the exception of Gabriel Soares, who settled in the colony, returned to Portugal in order to request a license to exploit the mines and, coming back to Brazil with the designation of captain-general and governor, perished in 1591 in an incursion into the back country. The thought as well as the language was also Portuguese, with a vernacular flavor and in that clear style which Camões praised in Gandavo in the elegy written for his book and in which one recognizes a trace of the classic spirit of the sixteenth century—that of the greatest splendor in Portuguese literature—and with that descriptive note, that taste for the picturesque, and that lyrical enchantment in the face of the landscape which ruled so powerfully over the mentality and literature of the country. But if these works do not belong to Brazilian literature except in the sense that they were written in Brazil and inspired by it, like that of the German, Hans Staden, who in 1556 told the story of his adventures, and those of the Frenchmen André Thévet, who wrote his *Singularidades da França Antártica* (1558), and Jean de Léry, author of the *História de uma viagem feita à terra do Brasil*, printed in 1578, the letters of Manuel da Nóbrega, José de Anchieta, poet and dramatist, and of other Jesuits, and the treatises of Father Fernão Cardim, they present a singular interest which is more than merely informative and documentary.[4] Through these pages there breathes the atmosphere of colonial society and a current of sympathy for the land and people of Brazil, whose confidants and directors the Jesuits were and to whom they brought, with their colleges and their lively interest in Indians and colonists, the first elements of culture and of civilization.

[4] Capistrano de Abreu and Vale Cabral published in four volumes under the title of *Cartas jesuíticas* various manuscripts of the National Library: I—*Informações e fragmentos históricos,* of Father José de Anchieta (1584–1586) (Rio, 1886), one vol. 84 pages; II—*Cartas,* of Father Manuel de Nóbrega (1549–1560) (Rio, 1886), one vol., 186 pages; III and IV—*Cartas avulsas* (1550–1568) (Rio, 1887), 326 pages. The whole writing of Anchieta, made up of poetry, *autos* and songs, in Portuguese, Spanish or Tupí, was always an instrument the apostle to the heathen and teacher of the sons of Portuguese used for the propagation of the faith: it is simple to the point of ingenuity and characterized by great spontaneity and freshness of feeling. The letters, full of information on the life and customs of the time, and his grammar of the Indian language are, however, more important than his Portuguese poetry or Latin verse and the little works for the religious theater which he wrote to amuse and edify the colonists. Father Fernão Cardim, a missionary to Brazil, where he arrived in 1584, was rector of the schools of Bahia and Rio, procurator and provincial of the Society of Jesus. If the merits implied by these titles are not enough, writes Afrânio Peixoto, "it would suffice that he was a link in that chain to which Anchieta and Vieira belonged, standing between the two, aiding the last years of one and receiving the other." His works, of real historic interest, *Clima e terra do Brasil,* a manuscript of Evora, published in 1885 by Capistrano de Abreu; *Do princípio e origens dos índios do Brasil,* published in 1881, also through the efforts of the historian, and *Narrativa epistolar de uma viagem à Bahia, Rio, Pernambuco, etc.,* published by A. Varnhagen in 1847, were brought together in a single volume, with notes by Rodolfo Garcia, under the title, *Tratado de terra e gente do Brasil* (Rio, 1925).

It is only in the seventeenth century that there arose in the north, with the sugar civilization, the first prose writers and poets born in Brazil but still Portuguese in their thought and in the form which they gave to their work, following the taste of the home country. It is the first generation of intellectuals entirely educated by the Jesuits according to molds imported from Portugal, whence new religious missions continued to arrive, bringing with them ideas and literary modes. For some time it was considered that the first literary document left by a Brazilian was the mediocre little poem called *Prosopopéia* of Bento Teixeira, which Rodolfo Garcia has identified, placing its Brazilian nationality in doubt, as the work of a converted Christian, a native of Pôrto, who testified in Olinda before the Holy Office. This poem, intoned in praise of Jorge de Albuquerque Coelho, the governor of Pernambuco, and published in Lisbon in 1601, and the *Diálogos das grandezas do Brasil* written in 1618—a work of greater value because of its wealth of information originally attributed to Bento Teixeira but really by an unknown author—are related to the same category of documents which have nothing in common with Brazilian literature except having been written in the colony or having as their object the Brazil of that time. In 1627, Brother Vicente do Salvador, a Bahiano, finished his *História do Brasil,* in which he criticizes the Portuguese and affirms his love of his native land; but as he is writing rather a book of stories than the history of Brazil, he bequeathed to us with this work rather a "history in bedroom slippers," in the picturesque expression of Capistrano. Father Simão de Vasconcelos, a Portuguese, who came as an adolescent to Brazil and took his vows at the age of nineteen in the Society of Jesus, published among other works the *Crônica da Companhia de Jesús* (1663) and the *Vida do venerável Pe. José de Anchieta* (1672). In eloquence overshadowing the Jesuit, Antônio de Sá, and the Carmelite, Brother Eusébio de Matos, with their sermons full of the subtleties and conceits in the taste of the times, there stands out the almost solitary figure, in so many respects notable and so intimately related with the history of Brazil, of Father Antônio Vieira, the greatest sacred orator of the Portuguese language in all times. The great preacher, Portuguese in origin, who passed fifty of the ninety years of his life in Brazil, serving in missions, in the pulpit, and in politics, and who confessed that he owed to Brazil "as a result of his second birth the duty of a son," was certainly, as Afrânio Peixoto writes, "the most Brazilian of the Portuguese classic writers, the greatest of the Brazilian classics, to such an extent is the best of his thought Brazilian, just as he was Brazilian in his style, which is gentle and fluent, without the labored and recherché qualities of the Portuguese of his time." Among the first original manifestations in which Brazilian literature appears, rather in content than in form, are the satires of Gregório de Matos Guerra (1633–1696) of Bahia—that terrible son of the Portuguese, with a viper's tongue, who was the greatest colonial poet who vituperated colonial society, with its taste for ostentation and luxury, its unruly customs, its nobility, and its mestizos. In the biting and violent satires which he drew from his implacable observation and in which he portrayed in crude colors the society of the colony, flagellating lords and prelates, Portuguese and Brazilians, whites, Negroes, and mulattoes, there do not appear, however, any refining changes in the Portuguese language, transplanted to Brazil and kept almost intact, without a regional note, by this Brazilian poet.

The form in which orators, chroniclers, and poets expressed themselves was, and continued to be for a long time, that of the cultivated language spoken in the home country, with all the purity of its vocabulary and syntax and with the virtues and vices of the style, varying according to individual taste and literary fashion. Both the sermons of Father Antônio Vieira, with his magnificent eloquence, and the satires of Gregório de Matos, called the "mouth of hell" because of his invectives and his censure of everything and everybody, were directed to a high-class public more prepared to understand them, like the élite public of Lisbon, Coimbra, or Pôrto. The fact is that the more cultivated classes were proud of speaking and writing the Portuguese of the home country—the official language which endeavored to preserve itself in every way from indigenous and African contamination, while Tupi, the so-called "general" language, competing with Portuguese in the proportion of three to one, according to the opinion of Teodoro Sampaio, was the language which was most used generally in common speech. The situation was like that which occurred in Asunción in Paraguay, where according to Southey's words, "they understood sermons in Guarani better than in Spanish, and there were women with Spanish names and Spanish origins, who did not understand the language of their own country," and the language of the natives, Humberto de Campos tells us, had become commoner in the towns and cities that were growing up than Portuguese.[5] Portuguese was not, in fact, more commonly spoken than Tupi, in which from the first years of the home country, Jesuits trained themselves in order to have greater facility in their mission and which even became so common among the colonists that in Maranhão and Pará the language of the Indian was exclusively used in the pulpit. Thus, when one desired to speak to the people, it was the language of the savage which was used most, Portuguese being reserved as an official language for the more cultivated social strata. Hence the conventional and mundane character of the literature of Portuguese thought, which was meant for the higher classes of colonial society, while in the lower classes there was going on a linguistic differentiation of the spoken language in the two countries—or rather in the colony and in the home country—and the formation of a popular language and literature in which there were mingled in different proportions, depending upon the region, indigenous [6] and African elements. Certainly "the fundamental unity of race and of language among the tribes which extended from the mouth of the Amazon to that of the Plata, was an important factor in the possibility of forming a purely Brazilian language." But the creation of an American language was opposed not only by the existence of Portuguese as an official language but especially by the fact that

[5] Humberto de Campos, *Crítica* (Rio: Marisa, 2nd ed., 1933), pp. 209-219.

[6] Gilberto Freyre, studying the role of the *columin* (Indian lad) in the making of the language of the country, recalls the testimony of Father Simão de Vasconcelos, when he affirms, in the biography of Father José de Anchieta, that the apostle to the heathen "was at the same time teacher and pupil" and that the *columins* "served him as pupils and teachers." It was that language, writes Gilberto Freyre, that grew out "of the collaboration of the *columin* with the priest, out of the first social and trade relations between the two races, and we may go so far as to say that the invading people adopted for daily need and use the speech of the conquered people, reserving their own language for limited and official use. When the Portuguese language—always the official one— later won over the Tupi, and became, side by side with it, a popular language, the colonizer was already impregnated with the rustic influence of the native; his Portuguese had already lost the odor and harshness of the speech of Portugal; it had been softened into a Portuguese without *rr* or *ss;* it had become almost infantile, children's speech, under the influence of the Jesuit teaching in collaboration with the *columins*" ("Formação da família brasileira sob o regime de economia patriarcal," *Casa grande e senzala,* 1st ed., pp. 172-180).

these two languages existed side by side in rivalry—Portuguese and Tupi, both popular languages which could not coexist without penetrating each other and being transformed as a result of internal process of evolution and by the pressure of reciprocal influences and the contacts of the language and culture of Africa. The cultivated language, penetrated to its very center by the spirit of the home country, under whose influence, direct or indirect, bachelors and doctors of law were trained, floated too high in the social scale to be aware of these transformations and to allow itself to be influenced or penetrated by them.

The opulent life which was developed with the flourishing of agriculture in the towns and cities of the coast, and which expanded to the plateau with the exploitation of the mines, contributed in fact to separate and isolate a small minority of functionaries, men of letters, and lords of sugar mills, raising them high above the level of the people. The last group, forming a kind of rural nobility like the feudal barons, the fuctionaries for the most part coming from Europe—a despotic aristocracy, arrogant in their manner of treating people—and the bourgeoisie, whether from the old country or American, which was occupied with commerce, mines, or the liberal professions, constituted this rich class apart, proud of its fortune and of its position. "The abundance of domestic slaves," observes Lúcio de Azevedo with regard to Rio de Janeiro at the end of the seventeenth century, "facilitated that easy life to which the atmosphere inclined people, and in the houses of the well-to-do it supplied with its industry much of what today is furnished by stores and workshops." The luxury and vanity at that time were so surprising that Father Fernão Cardim considered that they surpassed in the colony anything that he had observed in the Kingdom of Portugal itself. While the great mass of the population was sunk in ignorance and misery, the wealthy class grew refined in its pleasures and sought in a recherché culture recreation of their mind and a sign of distinction, educating their sons in Coimbra and maintaining in their big houses and city mansions, for their leisure hours, collections of books equal or superior to that of João Mendes da Silva, the father of Antônio José, whose collection of books at the end of the seventeenth century, "not insignificant for a colonial establishment," was composed of two hundred and fifty volumes, one hundred and fifty-odd of them, books of law. This was the social environment in which the literature of the colonial epoch flourished and in which lived that limited public for which it was meant. It was a literature without roots in the earth and without any other function than that of entertaining the rich who, like individuals of a superior category in general, were less connected with the colony than with the home country and, by means of it, with foreign countries in general. This literature could not fail to have a markedly Portuguese character, full of the recherché and artificial, which is marked in the Academies such as that of the Esquecidos (1724) and of the Felizes (1736) and the Seletos (1752) in Rio de Janeiro, and of the Renascidos (1759), all ephemeral in their duration and all impregnated, as their very names indicate, with a false and precious spirit coming from the literary associations of the other side of the sea, which served them as a model. Although the nativistic sentiments which were germinating in the sixteenth century had already entered upon a period of maturity in the eighteenth century, still it is not Brazil but rather Portugal which is the magnetic pole which exercised the greatest power of attraction upon us. In his *História da América portuguêsa* (1730) in a gongoristic and showy style like that of a man who is writing to produce "an effect," Rocha Pita barely allows a note of nativism to creep into his national emphasis, while the note of Lusitanism, stronger and more frequent, appears in the very title of the work—one of the most esteemed of the time. Of the Brazilians who went to study at Coimbra, those who achieved most distinction in science, politics, and the arts remained there in the home country: the two Gusmões of Santos, Bartolomeu, the inventor of balloons, and Alexandre, statesman and diplomat, secretary of Dom João V, settled in Portugal, as well as the moralist and classical scholar Matias Aires of São Paulo, who in 1752 published in Lisbon his *Reflexões sôbre a vaidade dos homens;* and the poet Santa Rita Durão of Minas Gerais, who, taken at nine years of age to Portugal, studied there, took his vows there, and died there; and before them, carried away in the weight of misfortune which ruined his family, Antônio José da Silva of Rio de Janeiro, bound to Brazil practically only by his origin and birth.

Antônio José, in fact, although born in Rio de Janeiro in 1705, the son of João Mendes da Silva, embarked in 1712 in his seventh year in company with his parents for Portugal, where he was educated, studied canon law at Coimbra and, accused of Judaism, died in 1739, burned by the Inquisition. Antônio José, the Jew; a lawyer like his father, "but in his free hours a poet and a writer of farces, or perhaps to speak more exactly, a lawyer in the hours which he had left from his occupation with the pen and the theater," was, after Gil Vicente, the greatest figure of the Portuguese theater, then in decadence, as in fact the theater of that time was everywhere. His theatrical works, composed between 1729 and 1737 and published in two volumes in 1744 with the license of the same inquisitor who had ordered the imprisonment of the author in 1737, appeared in the Theater of Bairro Alto in Lisbon as a vigorous popular expression of a rebellious spirit of sensibility and wit. With his satires, censures, and witticisms he "took his vengeance for his suffering, smiling insolently in the very faces of the powerful." But both in language and in thought the work of the notable comic author who gave us the highest measure of his comic verve, of his clear and precise style and his original technique, the piece—the best of them all—*Guerras do Alecrim e Magerona* (1737) belongs to Portuguese literature just as Antônio José owes to Portugal his whole intellectual formation, the source of his inspiration, his triumphs, and the lack of comprehension and the hostilities which culminated in his martyrdom. He was a great poet, carried away as a child from Brazil in the first storm which the Inquisition loosed upon his family and again now in Portugal at thirty-four in the second persecution which the Holy Office moved against him, condemning him to death, not for his writing, but because of a suspicion of Hebraism which had cost his mother the torment of the wooden horse, moral torture, and three years of imprisonment. If, then, we do not count in the first half of the eighteenth century its principal figures—Antônio José who, having moved to Portugal, exercised no influence in our letters, Rocha Pita, a sugar-mill lord in Bahia and author of a "history of high buskins" and Joãs Antônio Andreoni (Antonil), Italian by origin who came to Brazil at forty-nine years of age as a visitor of the Society of Jesus, and who gave us in his *Cultura e opulência do Brasil* (1711) a work full of precious colonial information, nothing very worthy will remain in the balance of the intellectual and literary life of the country. And yet, in the second half of the century there was assured throughout the territory the definitive victory of Portuguese over the Tupi language, a conclusion to which Pombal,[7] gave his help, since with his expulsion of the Jesuits in 1759 he gave "a death blow to the creation of a truly American language." It was in this period that there arose, reestablishing the tradition of Vieira, the three great classical scholars by temperament and education, the moralist Matias Aires of São Paulo, the poet Santa Rita Durão of Minas Gerais, who lived in Portugal, and the lexicographer Antônio de Morais Silva of Rio de Janeiro, a sugar lord in Pernambuco and the author of the *Dicionário de Língua Portuguêsa,* published in its first edition in 1789, "the best guide for classical usages." It was also in this century of nativistic reaction that the Inconfidência Mineira, the greatest of all, brought together for the first time politics and letters, attracted by the idea of national freedom.

The development of mining, moving the economic axis of the country from the north to the south, not only furthered the creation of new urban centers and with them new foci of culture in the "general mines," but also contributed to increase nativistic and republican feeling. The special nature of the business of gold and of diamonds, the intensity of economic exchange, the difficulties which the treasury put in the way of the accumulation of fortunes, and the growing tendency to break up wealth among a great number of miners contributed, on the one hand, to fuse the population attracted from all parts by the desire for wealth and by the spirit of adventure, and tended to level all classes so that as a result equalitarian and democratic ideas developed. On the other hand, the nativism, which had broken out in the war of the Portuguese in Minas Gerais (1709) at the beginning of the century and in the war of the peddlers (1710) in Pernambuco, acquired greater vigor and intensity in the sedi-

---

[7] The success attained by the Tupi language in the sixteenth and seventeenth centuries was not kept up in the eighteenth, as can be proved by comparing the bibliographies on the native language in the first two centuries and in the third, as well as by the changes which took place in Portuguese as spoken in Brazil, which could only come about as a result of growing contact between Portuguese and other languages (native and African) and by its ever greater penetration into all social levels. The language of the colonizer was not then just an official language, but was also a popular language, and spread so through all classes and social groups that the differences between the Portuguese spoken in the colony and in Portugal became more and more noticeable in prosody, in vocabulary and in syntax. The poet Domingos Caldas Barbosa, son of a Portuguese father and an African mother, born in Rio de Janeiro in 1740, was at that period able to take to the mother country, where he settled, the accents and rhythm of the Brazilian *modinhas,* based on the old forms of popular poetry among the Portuguese. It was this mulatto poet, facile and sentimental, as Manuel Bandeira recognizes, who was "the first Brazilian in whom we find a poetry that is entirely ours in feeling." The last representative of the Minas group, Silva Alvarenga (1749–1793), also a mulatto, the natural son of a poor musician, came from the people and from the people he got, as a counterbalance to Arcadian influences, the more Brazilian character of his poetry, a language that seems younger, softer and more flexible, and a keener awareness, a more ardent interest in things of this country. We cannot, then, admit, as Humberto de Campos, basing his opinion on Southey, believes, that "the happy fate of the Portuguese language in America was the work of Pombal." The minister of Dom José, expelling the Jesuits, the great scholars and propagators of the Tupi language, only contributed to extinguishing the last centers of the teaching of that language—the schools to which the fathers sent the younger brothers to learn Tupi—and to silence the language of the Indian in the work of conversion and preaching. Humberto de Campos writes: "Not knowing the native language, the clergy that came from Portugal to take the place of the Jesuits preferred to teach children the Portuguese language, rather than learn that of the savages themselves. The natives gradually accepted the change." (Humberto de Campos, *Crítica,* 1st series, 2nd ed., Marisa, 1933.)

tions of Vila Rica (1720) and in the conspiracy of Minas (1789) as a natural reaction against the extortions of the Portuguese treasury and the savage policy of oppression adopted by the home country. All of the great poets of the time are from Minas; nevertheless the two epic poets, Brother José de Santa Rita Durão (1720–1784), born in Cata Preta near Mariana, author of *Caramurú*, and José Basílio da Gama (1740–1795), a native of São José del Rei, now called Tiradentes, the author of *Uruguai*, lived, the former from infancy and the latter from his adolescence, in Portugal, to which they owed their education and where they made their permanent residence and died. *Uruguai*, written in free verse and published in 1769 in Lisbon, is a superior piece of work in its originality, in the grace of its style, which is flexible and eloquent, in the vivacity of its coloring, and in the warmth of its imagination, while *Caramurú*, in the oitava rhyme of Camoens, published twelve years later in 1781, is considered the most Brazilian poem which we possess. Through both of them there circulates a warm feeling for the American earth, in the exaltation of the Indian, in the dramatic evocation of episodes of our history, and in the painting of the natural beauties of the country.[8] However, the place at which the greatest lyric poets were concentrated, brought together as much by affinities in literary taste as by common ideas of national liberty, was in Vila Rica, an already legendary city, but as it were "confused," in the expression of J. A. Nogueira, "by the violent disorder which had been stamped upon it by the incursion of the bandeiras in their hand-to-hand struggle with the hillsides full of gold." These are the poets of the Inconfidência, more or less faithful disciples of the Arcadian school, all of them compromised in the revolt of Minas and all of them condemned to imprisonment and exile: Cláudio Manuel da Costa (1729–1789), of the old town of Ribeirão do Carmo, afterward the city of Mariana, a master of language and of the technique of verse, polishing his cold and at times ingenious strophes in his mediocre poem *Vila Rica* and in his sonnets laden with Portuguese Arcadianism, without force of thought or true inspiration; the two Alvarengas, Inácio José Alvarenga Peixoto, who was born in Rio de Janeiro in 1744, "a poet of little feeling but of facile and highly colored imagination," of whose works there remain to us beside the *Canto Genetlíaco*, twenty sonnets, three odes, and two poems of the kind called liras; and Manuel Inácio Silva Alvarenga (1749–1814) of Vila Rica, who left us, especially in *Glaura*, erotic poems, a poetry that is essentially Brazilian; and greatest among the Arcadians, Tomaz Antônio Gonzaga (1744–1792), author of *Marília de Dirceu*, the love poem that enjoys more esteem in the Portuguese language than any other, and in which there come

---

[8] The action of *Uruguai*, a poem in five cantos, is the war which Portugal, aided by Spain, waged against the seven Nations of the Missions of Uruguay, incited to rebellion by the Jesuits against the treaty of 1750, which transferred them from the rule of the Jesuits to that of the Portuguese. In spite of the fact that the matter is limited and mediocre for an epic, Basílio da Gama was able to weave out of it an original poem, full of warmth and feeling, with picturesque coloring and some dramatic episodes, like the death of Lindóia, in which his lyric inspiration is strongest. The subject matter of *Caramurú* is not broader in scope than that of *Uruguai*, but taking as the object of his poem the discovery of Bahia by Diogo Alvares Correia, or *Caramurú*, Santa Rita Durão gave it breadth by literary artifices, like that of the dream or vision of the Indian maiden *Paraguassú*, which permitted the imaginative treatment of episodes of our history taking place later than the principal action. The poem, which extends through ten cantos, already makes us feel the note of Americanism which later and with more intense feeling appears in the work of Gonçalves Dias, the great poet of the Indian.

together a communication of emotion, naturalness in painting, and elegancy of language without affectation. Portuguese by birth, he is, as Afrânio Peixoto writes, "Brazilian by his father and by the more than ten years that he lived here,[9] by the love which inspired him and chiefly by the martyrdom which he unjustly suffered among us."

But, although the influence of Arcadianism was marked in this group of poets and especially in Cláudio and Gonzaga, the Brazilian note is already so noticeable in some of them and so repeated in Silva Alvarenga that Ronald de Carvalho does not hesitate to consider him a forerunner of romanticism, or more exactly, "the link which binds the Arcadians and the romantics." The first accents of the romantic movement, the deeper roots of which are to be sought in the poem of Basílio da Gama and which extend through the odes and seven-syllable lines of Silva Alvarenga, were to continue to vibrate through the last members of the Arcadian school and the description of nature of the mystical poem *Assunção da Virgem* of Brother Francisco de São Carlos (1763–1829) and, above all, in the religious poetry of Father Sousa Caldas (1762–1814), sad and pessimistic, but truly inspired. If, in the lyrical poetry of Arcadian influence, whether love poetry or sacred poetry—and these two sacred poets both born in Rio are attached to this school—there is to be seen a slow evolution in the direction of the romanticism which marked in the nineteenth century the dawn of our intellectual independence, the poets of the Inconfidência, revolutionaries in politics, in general were conservative in literature. The fact is, that changes in ideas precede, and changes in form follow, a social metamorphosis. In not one of them, in fact, was there a rupture with the classic forms, nor a cry of revolt, unless it is in the *Cartas chilenas*—in its poetry, spontaneous or labored, serene and melancholy like a twilight in the mountains. It is not among the Inconfidentes that one meets a renovator of the technique of verse nor a poet of keen sensibility or restless spirit. The former preceded them with the poem *Uruguai,* the work of greatest originality during the colonial period; and the latter came later and was known as Sousa Caldas, a poet for whom pessimism and the struggles of the inner life were only the point of departure, a point of support from which the religious poet took off for the highest flights. In the meanwhile, the analysis of this group of poets which collected around Tiradentes does not reveal to us only the transition between the Arcadians and the romantics. All the poetry of the Arcadians of Vila Rica already shows in its restraint of sentiment and form the special characteristic of the intelligence of Minas and of that humor which is one of its charms and, as Mário de Andrade observes, "has no traditional way of showing itself but breaks out from a single type of intelligence and shows itself in many different manifestations." Between the satires of Gregório de Matos and the *Cartas chilenas* there is a gulf, in fact, "which is not made deep merely by the distance of a century, but especially by the intellectual passion with which the poet of Bahia laughs and by the reserve with which the Chilean Letters smiled." Beside this, in the shade of the

---

[9] It was, to be exact, sixteen years that Tomaz Antônio Gonzaga lived in liberty in Brazil: nine years of childhood and adolescence, between the age of eight, when he came to Brazil with his father, and seventeen, when he returned to Portugal to study at Coimbra, and seven years in the district of Vila Rica, to which he was dispatched in 1782 as judge and estate administrator and where he stayed until he was taken prisoner in 1789 and held on the Ilha das cobras (Snake Island). He left prison in 1792, to be exiled in Mozambique.

group of Minas, which, allowing its imagination to stroll among shepherds in a gentle bucolic poetry, managed to nourish the revolutionary idea of the independence of the country, there was born with this latter document political literature—which is the most abundant and characteristic of the national spirit. The Chilean Letters, which some attributed to Cláudio Manuel and others with greater reason to Tomaz Antônio Gonzaga—a terrible satire in verse against the governor, Luiz da Cunha Meneses and his favorites, and an important document for criticism of manners and customs—define exactly the characteristics of this literature to which the liberty of press and political struggles, especially after independence, had opened all the flood gates, inundating the country with satires, libels, and pamphlets.

The coming of Dom João VI with all his court at a period of decadence in colonial life due to a double crisis—one part of which was old, that of sugar cane in the north, and the other more recent, that of the exploitation of the mines—was certainly with its fruitful consequences a political event of the utmost importance for Brazil in every respect. It is not only the moving, in itself so important, of an entire court of about fifteen thousand persons, troops and households, and with all the wealth which the king and his retinue had hastened in their flight to ship to Rio de Janeiro, where the new seat of government was installed. The opening of the Brazilian ports to foreign navigation—the first farsighted act of Dom João VI, in 1808—the increase of commerce, now direct with England, and the first economic measures taken by the king imparted a notable stimulus to the mercantile activities of Rio de Janeiro and of the principal coast cities, producing a great rise in economic life and opening new horizons to the intellectual life of the country. The urban physiognomy of the great village of forty-five thousand souls which Rio de Janeiro then was, was profoundly transformed, and with the presence of the court, social and worldly life expanded and acquired the intensity and brilliance of foreign capitals. Circumstances, as Euclides da Cunha observes, "brought to our land the only statesman capable of transforming it." Dom João VI, the creator of institutions, founded among others, museums, schools, and libraries, began the royal press, and in other ways stimulated economic and intellectual production, transforming the old colonial town into the capital of the new Portuguese Empire and into our greatest center of culture, with its library which in 1826 was already considered one of the best in the world, and with its press, which after independence at this same time was made up of fifteen Brazilian newspapers and two foreign ones. If, however, it was with Dom João VI that the press arose in the colony with the *Gazeta do Rio,* the official organ, it was only in the struggles of Independence and afterward that there came the newspapers *Diário do Rio,* the *Revérbero Constitucional, Jornal do Comércio,* and the *Aurora Fluminense,* among others that enjoyed great public esteem from the time of the first Empire. Intellectual life in the period of Dom João VI and in the reign of Pedro I, if it was not exclusively concentrated, at least acquired an extraordinary intensity in the sacred and profane rostrum and in the press, which became the most powerful instrument for stirring up Brazilian agitations. While in the pulpits were heard the independent voices of Father Sousa Caldas and of Francisco de São Carlos, raised to the dignity of royal preacher by Dom João VI; of Brother Francisco de Sampaio, and of Brother Francisco Mont'Alverne (1784–1858), whose violent and emphatic eloquence had already reached the plenitude and height of its expression; the great journalists of the time, Hipólito da Costa,

Gonçalves Ledo and Januário da Cunha Barbosa in the *Revérbero Constitucional*, Brother Francisco de Sampaio in the *Correio do Rio,* who in 1822 drew up a petition to the prince requiring him to stay in Brazil, led in the press political campaigns which reached the maximum of vigor in the first Empire and during the whole period of the Regency. This was a period "necessarily critical and destructive," in which the ephemeral but efficacious literature of political journalism occupied the most important place. "The doctrine of agitation of Hipólito da Costa, which until then had lain dormant in the London presses of the *Correio Brasiliense* (1808–1822), with all the inconvenience of distance and of isolation, suddenly moved," writes Euclides da Cunha, "to the very center of national life."

The proclamation of political independence, the liberty of the press, established in the constitution, and the political struggles which broke out with extreme violence favored the rise of journalism in Brazil and gave it an extraordinary power of expansion. To the tenacious campaign conducted from London by Hipólito da Costa— the greatest journalist of the time—in favor of independence and the emancipation of the slaves, there succeeded polemics with wide effects upon public opinion, provoked by nativistic reactions, by debates in the Constituent Assembly (1823), and by party questions, and in these, among other writers, Bernardo Pereira de Vasconcelos, a notable politician, author, and journalist, took part, as well as J. J. Carneiro de Campos in the *Tamoio*, "organ of an unbridled radicalism," and above all Evaristo da Veiga, bookseller, journalist, and politician, who directed the *Aurora Fluminense* (1827–1835) with notable brilliance, incorruptible firmness, and manly courage. The press in 1830, "with vigor which it was never again to have in Brazil, led by the *Aurora Fluminense* of Evaristo da Veiga, had taken," writes Euclides da Cunha, "the leadership of the movement, rendering it irrepressible, spreading into the provinces with the *Observador Constitucional* of Líbero Badaró in São Paulo, with the *Universal* in Minas Gerais, and in the north, with the *Baiano* of Rebouças." It is, in fact, through the decisive action of the press that the political movement of 1830 and 1831 became sufficiently vigorous to force the abdication of Dom Pedro I and to put an end to the first Empire. The role of Evaristo da Veiga was in this episode as important as that of Hipólito da Costa in the struggle for independence. The press, which had preceded parliamentary eloquence in its influence on the public mind and was the bed, deep and many-branched like a river network, through which there rushed the impetuous torrent of passions, was traversing its period of greatest fame and influence. It was by the newspaper that political careers were begun or strengthened, and rare were the public men who succeeded in escaping the seduction of journalism. Among them there stood out from others who were of less importance, Lopes Gama (1791–1852), also a satirical poet, in the *Diário de Pernambuco;* Justiniano José da Rocha (1812–1862), Sales Tôrres Homem (1782–1876), physician and member of parliament, author of the *Libelo do provo,* signed by Timandro; Odorico Mendes (1799–1864), translator of the *Aeneid* and the *Iliad* and the greatest humanist of his time; and João Francisco Lisboa (1812–1863), lawyer and scholar, classical writer par excellence, who published in Maranhão various political newspapers and left us the *Jornal de Timon,* a collection of essays in two volumes which gives the best idea of the brilliance of his personal reflection and the richness of his culture, and in the *Vida do Pe. Antônio Vieira,* the most mature and the best documented of his investigations in the field of history. Journalism, the greatest weapon from the time of the struggles for independence and during the first Empire, was, however, to yield place to parliamentary eloquence, an aristocratic form of political thought which was already arising in this period of agitation with a brilliance and force capable of forcing into the background the action of newspapers in the second half of this century, with the coming of the second Empire, the reestablishment of internal order, economic stability, and the expansion of romanticism into all the manifestations of the literary and political life of the country.

We were in 1850 and the following year at that epoch of the nineteenth century in which in Europe science was already beginning to impose on all minds its ordered vision of the world. Religious discoveries demonstrated the superiority of its methods. They can all be summarized in this principle: submission to the object. It is the very negation of romanticism, the essence of which is a lyrical and imaginative exaltation of sensibility and a revolt against the real when it prevents this exaltation. But in Brazil, 1850 corresponds to 1830 in Europe, and we were at that time, about 1850, at the height of the romantic movement. Certainly, from 1835 to 1836, with the publication of the *Suspiros poéticos* of Gonçalves Magalhães, printed in Paris, and the poem *A voz natureza,* of Pôrto Alegre, there had already arisen, with these forerunners in Brazilian poetry, the spirit of reaction against classic forms, greater liberty of rhythm, a taste for the picturesque, and a feeling for nature which sang in all the verses of the romantic. We can date from this period the appearance of a new poetry, in which the romantic movement was beginning, still without warmth and without vibration, a movement which in the author of the *Suspiros poéticos* found its inspiration above all in patriotic and religious sentiment, and was animated by a more lively feeling for nature in the *Brasilianas* (1865) of Pôrto Alegre and in some excellent descriptive pictures of his poem *Colombo.* In the second half of the nineteenth century, from 1845 to 1875, there arose a magnificent group of poets from Gonçalves Dias to Castro Alves, who almost all died in the very prime of life, some of them like Fagundes Varela and the poet of the Indian, when they had scarcely attained maturity and were still in the first force, if not of their inspiration, at least of their intellectual life. It was Alvares de Azevedo (São Paulo, 1831–1852), "that child of genius who scarcely gave a sample of what he might have become" with his *Poesias* (1853), sad and tortured, in which there are mingled fantasy and reality and which show, in their doubt and irony, the restless quality of his mind. In the fantastic tales *A noite na taverna,* the artificial world in which he lived by his imagination wears a mask of horror and perversity and reveals at times something satanic in that dying of joy which fills the eyes with tears. There was Junqueira Freire (Bahia, 1832–1855), also a poet essentially subjective in nature, a free and rebellious spirit, who suffering the blow of a tragic awakening to life, added his mystic dreams to the rebellion of a deserter of the convent, and seemed to allow himself to fluctuate between earth and heaven in his *Inspirações do claustro* (1855). There was Casimiro de Abreu, of Rio de Janeiro, the author of *Primaveras* (1859), the gentle singer of saudade, whom neither the will of his father, nor exile in Portugal, nor illness could turn from his vocation, and who became, with his sentimental, ingenious, languid poetry and his impressions of nature and his love for his land, one of the most read poets of Brazil and the dearest to adolescents. There was also the poet of *Cantos e fantasias* (1865), of *Cantos do êrmo e da cidade* (1869), and of *Evangelho nas selvas* (1875)—Fagundes Varela, in whose poetry, which has felt the influence of all of these earlier writers, there are mingled in a singular fashion the feeling for nature and inner life, exaltation of the Indian, and the social note, a restless sensibility, and an ardent enthusiasm, and to whose inspiration a landscape, a bit of the sky, a "thing seen" or a presentiment, a doubt, a dream give a shock and an initial movement, causing one of the chords of his lyre to vibrate and ideas to pass into the field of imagination.

But, standing out among the greatest, Gonçalves Dias (1823–1864), of Maranhão, was a forerunner of all in the publication of his poems; and with him romantic lyricism, rather than taking the essentially subjective character of the poetry of Alvares de Azevedo, Junqueira Freire, or Casimiro de Abreu, appear strongly marked with its essential elements, not only in its cult of individualism, but with the seduction of nature and its religious tendencies. In his *Primeiros Cantos* (1846), *Segundos Cantos* (1848), and *Ultimos Cantos* (1850), all written in the period of youth between seventeen and twenty-seven years, the Brazilian poet, however, gave to his poetry a peculiar style, which is perhaps his most original note, joining the feeling of the picturesque, emotional power and the white heat of inspiration to an admirable, classic sense of sobriety and balance. While in other poets of the time, the word frequently precedes and is more important than the emotion and the thought, in this mestizo poet the constant effort to control his emotion, without stifling spontaneity and vigor, permit him to give his poetry, in its clarity and precision, one of the purest forms of the Portuguese language spoken in Brazil. The feeling for nature and the American landscape which were to lead him easily to the cult of the aborigines, the fruit of the land, although idealized by the imagination; the phenomena of race mixture of the white and the Indian all over the country, and above all in the north; and the still lively remembrance of savage ancestors and of primitive cultures brought about in him a surprising return to indigenous themes, attracting other romantic writers to his orbit. The interest in the aborigine, in the man of nature, an interest which came directly from an interest in the landscape and the earth, and was one of the strongest expressions of Brazilian nativism, was in reality the romantic note, struck with most persistence by Gonçalves Dias, the rhapsodist of the Indian epic in his *Timbiras,* in his *Canção do Tamoio* and in *I-Iuca-Pirama,* and by José de Alencar (1829–1877), of the State of Ceará, in his novel *Guaraní* and in his short stories *Iracema* and *Ubirajara*—true prose poems admirable for their descriptive pictures and for their movement. The author of *Timbiras* and of other epic romantic poems, a poet and an Indianista, who gave us in his *Vocabulário de língua geral* evidence of his knowledge of the Indian language, and the novelist of *Guaraní*—considered a masterpiece and which has gone through several editions—are central figures of literary romanticism in which the former was the master in poetry and the second in prose fiction. These works, notable for various reasons, in which the conflict between the races, between the man of nature and the man of civilization, was presented for the first time, have remained like fragments of the epic of the race and formed the basis of a poetic and romantic cycle of Brazilian literature. In the great national poet, as in the vigorous novelist and dramatist, there is the same gift of the picturesque, the same feeling for tropical nature, and the same lyrical breath of inspiration and idealism. But as to form, if the poet of the Indian, master of the secrets of the traditional language, remains faithful to the genius of Portuguese language, which he fixed in his works and of whose origins he showed his knowledge in the *Sextilhas de Frei Antão,* written in archaic Portuguese, José de Alencar is, on the other hand, the renovator who receives and imparts to his artistic prose the vocabulary, the expression, and the special terms of speech that result from the transformation of the spoken language in Brazil.

It is intensely interesting to follow and to bring out the different literary tendencies and currents of ideas which this many-sided and fecund writer, as it were, captured and received into his work, and those against which he came to react, like that of the abolition of slavery. If he was the beginner of Indianism in his prose fiction with his first novel *Guaraní,* in which he shows himself to be an observer of nature capable of admirable pictures of the life of the savage, transfigured by the eyes of romanticism, his restless attention was not fixed upon mysterious landscapes and upon the burning atmosphere which serve as a background for romantic adventures and conflicts between the indigenous race and that of the conquerors. He dives into the past, from the depths of which he brings back in his hand the *Minas de Prata* and the *Guerra dos Mascates;* and, to the emotion of historic memories, there is added in *O Gaúcho* and in *O Sertanejo* the joy of the traveler who discovers regional aspects and more varied horizons, from the savannahs of Rio Grande to the brushwood and forests of the sertões. In other novels such as *Cinco minutos,* in *A Pata da Gazela* and in *Tronco do Ipê,* or in the comedy *O Demônio Familiar,* he shows himself to be an excellent observer of patriarchal society, drawing a series of pictures of women, and throwing light upon the habits of Brazilian life and various aspects of the history of our customs. A keen observer, endowed with an impetuous imagination, his political activity and his more intimate contact with imperial society were to prepare him to perceive more clearly and to record more gravely those transformations through which the Portuguese language was passing, and to which Gonçalves Dias had been less sensitive, educated as he was in Coimbra (1838–1845) and more affected by his education and stay in Portugal, by the feeling for the forms of a language that was authentically Portuguese. In addition to romantic affinities, as marked in the poet as in the novelist, the critic cannot find in the work of Alencar those classic reminiscences which are easily recognized in the forms of Gonçalves Dias. "A conservative in politics (he was opposed to the emancipation of slaves), José de Alencar," writes Manuel Bandeira, "initiated in the literary and linguistic field a nationalistic reaction in favor of Brazilian forms in that he maintained a lively polemic with the brothers Castilhos and with our literary men who were faithful to the rules of Portuguese grammar." The great novelist not only believed in the existence or formation of a national language, but also, accepting without repugnance certain common forms which had come to characterize it, he did not disdain to employ them in his work, although with a prudence which the conditions of intellectual life and the domination in literature of the cultivated language over the spoken language imposed upon a man of taste. He was not a writer or a poet of a small sect who did not wish to touch any but the souls of the élite, but rather a novelist, essayist, and politician at the same time, who, not making a cult out of the élite, did not have to make a great effort to yield to the popular tendency and to refresh and improve in the living sources of the spoken language, his artistic, nervous, and changeable prose, already so strongly marked by the characteristics of Brazilian speech.

In the abolitionist movement, in which the first attempt at social reform in Brazil showed itself, another romantic writer—this one a lyric and epic poet—Castro Alves (1847–1871), found a current of ideas strong enough to transport him on its waves. Certainly, even before him, as I wrote in *Ensaios*,[10] the São Paulo poet José Bonifácio the younger (1850) had shown an interest in the life of the slaves and given to some of his poems those accents that are to be matched only later, in the great poet of Bahia. A contemporary and rival of Castro Alves, Tobias Barreto sought in this same abolitionist ideal material for his poetry. But in no poet before or since has poetry of a social inspiration breathed so much idealism, such overwhelming force of conviction, and such burning religious inspiration as make of Castro Alves the unsurpassable and masterly interpreter of this great aspiration. The poet of the slaves not only has an extraordinary verbal power but he has also, to warm his poetry and give it a current of life, a sentimental power which no one has surpassed among us. He became popular with his *Espumas Flutuantes* because he exchanged the order of thought for that of the heart and the feeling for nature for that of humanity, which made him enter enthusiastically into the tumult of social passions. So impetuous is his lyrical impulse that even in poems like *Sub tegmine fagi,* when one thinks that he is going to fold his wings to clothe these strophes with bucolic sweetness, he allows himself to be carried away to the cloudy heights of poetry by the strength of his inspiration. He is perhaps the greatest, although the least intellectual, of our poets, verbal and sonorous, but also full of strength and substance, like Victor Hugo, who even today is read "just as one breathes the mountain air and touches an admirable material." People who read either of them can only allow themselves to be penetrated and keep silence. The predominant tonality of his poetry is doubtless, with its ideals of liberty, the life of the slaves. His lyre, however, like that of the great poets, as I have already said, "has all the chords." The sensibility of his soul, open to all emotions from the most delicate to the most violent, does not permit him to fall into the monotony which might result from a note struck in a way that if not exclusive might at least be persistent. Recalling the anguish of a sad and repulsed race, he now wraps us, as in his *Cachoeira de Paulo Afonso,* in the lulling rhythm of a voluptuous grace or of a burning caress under which there penetrates the intimacy of the heart; and now attacks powerfully the popular vein spreading in the orchestral harmonies of *Vozes d'Africa* and of *Navio Negreiro,* the mysterious shudder of fate and of terror which runs over our skin like the shivering of fever. It is, then, because of the essence of his poetry, which is not sealed by perfection but is profoundly living, human, and Brazilian, that even today the light from the past shines like an aureole upon the youthful figure of this poet who, dying at twenty-four, had already won great popularity, the attribute of those who succeed in propagating a great passion.[11]

Social and political passions which were spread so intensely by the poetry of social inspiration and broke out in the debates of the press and of parliament did not, however, have a striking influence in the theater, which, closer to the soul of the people in its very nature, had become in other countries one of the most efficacious instruments to concentrate and spread these feelings. Poetry, with Gonçalves Dias in *Escrava,*

---

[10] Fernando de Azevedo, "A Poesia social no Brasil," *Ensaios* (São Paulo: Comp. Melhoramentos de São Paulo, 1929), pp. 90–102.

[11] De Azevedo, *op. cit.*

with Tobias Barreto, and above all Castro Alves; eloquence with Joaquim Nabuco and Rui Barbosa, and the novel with Bernardo Guimarães in *Escrava Isaura* did permit themselves to be penetrated by this living, human interest in the slave, to which romanticism, arousing imagination and sensibility, gave the dramatic character of collective passions in the poems of Castro Alves and in the orations of Rui Barbosa. No dramatic author succeeded in animating himself with this religious and social inspiration which made the greatness of classic drama nor tried to exploit successfully those dark shadows which lie between the two races or the richness of our historic traditions. The tastes and predilections of the public, which were fixed upon the novel, overcame in Brazil the taste for the theater, which everywhere had extended with the expansion of romanticism. Thus the theater, which rigorously speaking had its beginning in this period, did not succeed in knowing glory except through one great actor, João Caetano dos Santos (1808–1863), who had a notable power of interpretation and a singular force of dedication in the obstinate struggle to organize a Brazilian theater. Although the staging and the dignity of spectacles still left much to be desired, the figure of João Caetano, who rose with his surprising talent and worked indefatigably for twenty-four years, from the presentation of *Olgiato* (1839) by Magalhães down to his death, almost alone dominated the stage with his passionate warmth, with his highly developed dramatic sense, and with the sureness of his diction. He was a great actor in search of authors. Not that Brazilians lacked the disposition for the scenic form of literature; but the victorious competition of stock and of the foreign theater, the commercial character of enterprises which always preferred a piece that had proven successful to the unpublished work of an unknown author, and the small possibilities that Brazilian authors found to secure representation and to acquire practical knowledge of their job necessarily kept off the stage the productions of our writers. Meanwhile, in spite of this rivalry which made it difficult to get on the stage and in consequence without a stimulus for the production of Brazilian work, authors of theatrical pieces were not entirely lacking, beginning with Gonçalves de Magalhães, Pôrto Alegre and Gonçalves Dias, and other novelists and poets, who after a few mediocre attempts gave up the dramatic career. The greatest of them all, Luiz Carlos Martins Pena (1815–1848) of Rio de Janeiro, the creator of the Brazilian theater, left in his plays, and especially in the comedy of manners [12] like the *Juiz de Paz na Roça* (1838), the *Noviço* and *Quem casa quer casa*, a moral picture of a whole period, reflected also in some of its aspects with spontaneity and grace by Joaquim José da França Júnior

[12] The comedy of manners and character, which is the highest and noblest form of theatrical art, although it had writers who cultivated it in Brazil, such as Martins Pena, França Júnior and José de Alencar, did not attain in them great power in expression, dialogue, nor the study of character and the painting of manners. Their plays are, however, our best social satires, showing a comic vein in Martins Pena, who has a rare gift for provoking laughter and showing things in a ridiculous light, and the more direct observation of life in José de Alencar; from these authors we got the plays which seem most likely to live, and which, having made their own generation smile, did not fail to do the same with later generations. In the complex variety of theatrical types, it is they that show the strongest side of our Brazilian theater. The tragedies of Gonçalves Magalhães, *António José* (1839) and *Olgiato,* to which João Caetano when he put it on, lent all the glamour of his interpretive power, do not justify the enthusiasm of their contemporaries. The whole repertory made up of dramas of Joaquim Manuel de Macedo, José de Alencar, Franklin Távora, and others, occupying the stage from 1854 to 1875, has, to tell the truth, no more than a historic interest in the development of our dramatic literature.

(1838–1890) of Bahia, in his comedy *As Doutoras,* in three acts, and by José de Alencar in *Demônio Familiar* (1857), all of which show the promise of our literature in this special form and serve to define its tendencies.

It was, above all, by the novel, caught up, like poetry, by the torrential force of romanticism, that the taste of the public was satisfied, leaning toward works of a sentimental character rather than toward those which are penetrated by a sense of reality. First place necessarily belongs during this period to Joaquim Manuel de Macedo (1820–1882) of Rio de Janeiro, a novelist, writer of comedies, and poet who attained extraordinary popularity with *A Moreninha* (1844) and *Moço Louro* (1845), narratives of passion of a romantic character, published in many editions and still living in the memory of all; Bernardo Guimarães (1827–1885), with his *Garimpeiro* and *Escrava Isaura,* in which among a great deal that is fantastic there stands out a regional note; and José de Alencar who, remaining faithful to the romantic tradition in the admirable pages of *Guaraní* and of *Iracema,* does not hesitate before the reproduction of reality in his novels and comedies of manners. The feeling for nature from which there flowed their interest in the Indian, opened, however, to the imagination of the novelists another field of exploitation, the interior. But in natural landscapes, José de Alencar in *Minas de Prata* (1862) and Bernardo Guimarães in *O Ermitão de Muquém* and in *Lendas e romances* (1871) began and made fashionable the tendency to dwell upon the interior which was marked in Franklin Távora (1843–1888) and in Alfredo Taunay (1843–1899), who in *Inocência,* published in 1872, came to mark, as Manuel Bandeira observes, "progress in this kind of writing through his greater sense of reality in the description of the life of the interior and through his limitation of the element of idealizing sentimentality." But if with Alfredo Taunay, because of his sense of objectivity in the painting of types and the natural setting of the country, and because of the sober elegance of his style, we already find the beginning of a new literary tendency, the book in which the reaction against idealistic excesses became most vigorous is *Memórias de um Sargento de Milícias*—a novel which appeared eighteen years before *Inocência,* and in the full glory of the romantic period, with all the force and spontaneity of an original creation without influences and without models. The author of this novel, Manuel Antônio de Almeida (1830–1861), who, when he published it in 1854, was still a medical student, emerged like a "realist before realism," anticipating a current which was to exercise a marked influence in our literature only toward the end of the nineteenth century. What awakens a lively interest in the novel of this young writer who disappeared in the full flower of his talent is not exactly his art, but the reality seized with his keenness of observation; and the very emotion which at times caused him to feel intensely did not come to him from his sentiments but from sensations, or, in other words, it comes through the eyes.[13] This very original novel,

[13] In his study of Manuel de Almeida, written on the occasion of the centenary of the birth of this author of the second Empire and read at one of the sessions of the Brazilian Academy of Letters by Augusto de Lima, Xavier Marques points out the error of Ronald de Carvalho, when he considers the *Memórias* a safe guide for any one who wishes to know "the customs of the middle classes between 1850 and 1860." According to Xavier Marques, we do not have in the book a picture of the society of that time, but a remembering of "types and manners of a lower social level of carioca colonial society," brought to life "with such splendor that it has led people to disregard chronology. In reality, his almost photographic process, catching bare reality trait by trait, has all the appearance of the account of an eye-witness; and what is no more than recreation by memory

which passed almost unperceived and had no influence, represents in the field of letters, with all its faults and imperfections, the same realistic feeling which was revealed in the world of thought by the eminently Brazilian work of Tavares Bastos (1839–1875), who in his *Cartas do Solitário* (1863) and in the *Vale do Amazonas* and in *Província,* renewing himself by his contact with reality, preceded by almost a century and is the forerunner of the period in which the great struggle opened between idealism and realism in politics, and was to disappear in the arena of partisan struggles to continue in the only field—that of solid and objective studies—which is proper for the vital problems of a nation.

It was not, in fact, the social and economic studies begun with such assurance, such depth of view by Tavares Bastos, which could interest a country whose politics at this time was directed in accordance with an idealistic conception, and when liberal ideas and claims furnished the principal source for great public debates. The eloquence which in the colonial period could only show itself in the pulpit took on new life in the first Empire with the parliamentary regime, developing rapidly with the organization of the two parties and the stability of the second Empire. The influences of public life and of parliament in England, which served as a model to our political institutions, and the romanticism which contributed to accentuate our literary and idealistic tendencies, made of the word the weapon par excellence and the most efficacious instrument in the political field, raising parliamentary eloquence to great heights. This was the period of debaters, in which intellectual force expanded in the most varied forms, "scintillating in the sarcastic irony of a Bernardo de Vasconcelos, in the persuasive dialectic of a José Bonifácio the younger, in the imposing gravity of a Fernandes da Cunha, in the torrential impetuosity of a Ferreira Viana or of a Silveira Martins, and in the aristocratic eloquence of a Joaquim Nabuco, who from the first to the second kingdom shared among themselves and with others of the same stature the first place in political eloquence." [14] But parliamentary eloquence, in which intentionally or by suggestion problems of the environment, general and eternal themes were embraced, themes which always and everywhere were the very soul of poetry and the substance of eloquence, never achieved such a high point as in Joaquim Nabuco and Rui Barbosa, the former the champion of abolition, the latter the greatest of our orators of all

---

in the book, acquires in the mind of the reader the flavor of direct observation." It seems to me, however, that Antônio de Almeida, instead of giving us a historic reconstruction of a certain society of the time of Dom João VI, presents not a *retrospective picture* of colonial types and manners, but a direct picture of the manners and figures of his own time, which his keen analytical insight caught in these portraits, in which his personal observations are hidden under the form and coloring of historic reconstruction, although he actually gathered them in real life, between 1850 and 1860. "At that time . . ." he is always warning us, as Xavier Marques points out. But is not this an habitual trick of novelists, who in order to feel freer about faithfully reproducing reality, put the facts and manners they observe in a historical framework, as if it were reconstruction of the past? In any case, whatever point of view we take toward this aspect of his work, whether we consider it contemporary or historic picturing of the Brazilian scene, Manuel Antônio de Almeida is, without a doubt, the forerunner of realism in Brazilian literature, a title of merit for his taste for objectivity and exactness, and the clarity with which he portrays his types and the fidelity with which he describes society and manners.

[14] Fernando de Azevedo, "Pequena introdução ao estudo de algumas figuras contemporâneas de oradores políticos" (Short introduction to the study of some contemporary figures in the field of political oratory), *Ensaios* (São Paulo: Comp. Melhoramentos de São Paulo, 1929), pp. 67-79.

time. Balanced and harmonious, Joaquim Nabuco (1849–1910), politician and diplomat, who possessed the eloquence of a thinker, an eloquence disciplined by reason but animated by generous frankness and a wide and fruitful inspiration, stood head and shoulders above the multitude of orators of his time, using in the tribune that same natural and precise style and admirable clarity which is one of the charms of his work as a historian in *Um Estadista do Império* (1897–1899) and *Minha Formação* (1909). Both of them, the orator of Recife and he of Bahia, coming from the Empire, were about forty years old, practically of an age, when the Republic was proclaimed. While, however, political ostracism silenced the voice of Joaquim Nabuco, Rui Barbosa (1848–1923), an idealist and a romantic, after a short period of exile from which he sent us his *Cartas de Inglaterra* (1896) was, under the new regime which was begun, a brilliant projection of the old parliament. He was, if I may be permitted to repeat myself, "of the old times in his education, full of a broad and generous type of liberalism, with the tenacity of his evangelizing campaigns, which brought a note of messianic excitement, and in the delight which he felt in dominating assemblies and experiencing contact with multitudes. . . . In his golden language, purified of all refuse by the work of an artist and hammered out in the fire of volcanic inspiration, scintillated at every moment sparks of the genius of Latin eloquence, and with him there was extinguished the last and greatest torch which had been lit in the period of the Empire."

If it had not been for the eloquence of this orator, in which passion bubbles forth as from its own fountainhead, spreading about him the emotion which flowed from the orator to his audience and from the latter to the former, the parliament of the Republic would have fallen more rapidly from the height to which the great figures of the Empire had raised it. In that aristocracy of scholars and men of letters, Rui Barbosa had conquered, before he was forty, an indisputable position, not only by his juridical knowledge, by the wealth of his scholarship, by the force of his irresistible argumentation and by his power of expression in words, but also by his knowledge of all the secrets of the language. He had, equally, a feeling for the vernacular and a taste for artistic form; and in all his work, with its great variety and extension, he always found, as few have done either before or after him, the steel of style to produce the spark upon the stone of the old language buried in the treasure house of the classics. But all that eloquence, to which romanticism gave grandiose, almost spectacular, proportions and with which the parliament became, during the period of the Empire, "the forge of our letters," was being menaced, toward the end of the century, in its old prestige, by a current of philosophic and scientific ideas with which the romantic cycle came to a close, and there were opened perspectives for a new, realistic conception of life and of the world. The struggles about these ideas had as their theater in Brazil the city of Recife, in which Tobias Barreto (1839–1889), aided by Sílvio Romero (1851–1914) and by his disciples, became the predominant figure of the greatest movement of renovation in the intellectual history of the Empire. The center of intellectual life in the north was by the combativity of this many-sided writer of Sergipe transplanted from the field of political struggles to debate about doctrine under the retarded and successive influences of great creators of systems. Without being a philosopher or an original thinker, but rather an agitator in the field of ideas and a destroyer of routine, Tobias Barreto rendered the culture of his nation marked services, drawing people's attention to philosophical studies, popularizing the German authors, and contributing as no one else did to the renovation of juridical concepts in Brazil. His indomitable courage and his love of struggle, which carried him into polemics nearly always violent and wild like those of Sílvio Romero—another admirable debater in the field of ideas—if they deprived him of the serenity necessary for creative work, formed about his name an atmosphere of battle and permitted him to make a little intellectual revolution of freedom of the mind in an atmosphere laden with prejudices. But when the tempest of the innovators broke out in the north, almost entirely limited to that region and to the doctrinary field, these lively polemics in which they took positions vis-à-vis great currents of thought in France and in Germany had no greater effect upon the national life than the political debates which were going on in the south about the Republic, and with which a new phase of splendor in Brazilian journalism was begun. The prose writer with a nervous and magnificent style, Raul Pompéia (1860–1891), and a political and social essayist of the scope of Eduardo Prado (1863–1895) "entered fully into the political battle" and in opposite camps. The former, the novelist of *O Ateneu,* a fine artist of an extreme sensibility, fought with faith and the fearlessness of the revolutionary for republican idealism; the latter, born in São Paulo, a great mind that will remain among the most brilliant writers of the century and one profoundly impregnated with universal feelings, was a reactionary in politics who in *Fastos da ditadura militar* vigorously defended the Empire and tradition at the beginning of the new regime.

The fact that the echoes of the campaign of renovation, directed without diminution of energy by Tobias Barreto and Sílvio Romero, who embraced in the same worship and almost made no distinction in their aspirations between letters and science, should have died out too early is explainable as a result of the terrific force of our tradition. The markedly literary and scientific spirit never permitted people to cultivate simultaneously these two flowers of the human spirit. But what surprises us at first sight is the divorce that with the new regime was established between politics and letters and which has been studied with a rare perfection of analysis by Tristão de Ataíde in one of his critical essays.[15] The individualistic reaction with its explosions of rebellion, the taste for art as art or for art cultivated for its own sake and stripped of its social function, the lack of existence of the profession of writer, and the hostility and the dislike with which letters and politics came to look upon each other contributed notably to this separation and caused the class of intellectuals to oscillate between dispersing their energies in a literary bohemia and in associations and little gatherings and the reserve of an elegant pride which ended at times in complete isolation. Letters, to which the parliamentary regime in the Empire had given a notable importance and almost a practical value, utilizing them as one of the tools of political and social action, became in the Republic not only alien but suspect to politics, which was ruled by the spirit of immediate utility and was sunk in military questions and partisan agitations. Without a public sufficiently numerous to maintain it and furnish it the economic bases of its emancipation, and without a new intellectual environment which would have been, like the old parliament, a focus of attraction and of convergence for the most eminent figures of the time, the class of the intellectuals, of literati, not

---

[15] Tristão de Ataíde, "A Margem da história de República," *Política e letras* (Rio: Anuário do Brasil), pp. 237-292.

finding support anywhere, attempted to strike an attitude of affirmation, of opposition expressing itself not just by struggle but by all those forms of bohemian life in which the revolt of the mind is hidden. Hence came naturally enough the idea which in the literary meetings of the *Revista Brasileira* arose at a suggestion of Lúcio de Mendonça —that of the Brazilian Academy of Letters, founded in 1896 as a result of the initiative of that poet, of Joaquim Nabuco, and Machado de Assis, its first president. This institution, today admirably housed in the quarters which were a gift from France,[16] aiming to concentrate all the great names of Brazilian literature and to promote, along with the cult of letters that of the language of our country, would finally assume a function of an importance that is not merely literary but social and political, that of defense of the unity of the language of Brazil. If, in fact, we consider on the one hand to what vicissitudes a language transplanted to a new environment is subject and the multiplicity of factors which worked to produce its transformation and consequently the production of dialectical forms, and on the other hand, if we remember that community of language is the strongest basis for a civilization and of national unity, we will understand easily the role of institutions like this, destined to stimulate, to popularize, and to consecrate studies of language and the great works of the literature of the country.

The dissent between literature and politics and the creation of the Brazilian Academy of Letters constitute, together with the intensity which the reaction against romanticism acquired, the three most important facts of the literary life of the country in the twilight of the past century. The antiromantic movement, which goes back to 1860, and of which the reactionary doctrine of Tobias Barreto in the field of philosophy and science and the politico-social realism of Tavares Bastos are vigorous expressions, took shape with the introduction of the philosophical ideas of the nineteenth century and acquired notable vigor in prose and fiction with Aloísio de Azevedo (Maranhão, 1858–1913), author of *O Mulato* (1881), who began his career with *A Casa de Pensão, O Homem,* and *O Cortiço,* and above all with Raul Pompéia, who left us in *O Ateneu* a novel that is admirable in the minute exactitude of its observation, in the naturalness of its pictures, faithful, clear, and expressive, and also in the sobriety

[16] The Brazilian Academy of Letters, founded in Rio de Janeiro, Dec. 15, 1896, modeled after the French Academy, started with thirty academicians, who elected the other ten to complete the number established by the statutes of the Academy. Afrânio Peixoto writes: "At first in the *Revista Brasileira* of José Veríssimo, thanks to which it came into existence, then in its own quarters, and finally in the building which France gave it, the Academy without interruption continued its inconspicuous existence, the blessed existence of honorific institutions. But a Maecenas, the bookseller Francisco Alves, bequeathed it $250,000 to use as endowment and prizes. It thus lost something, that national good will which considers honors and property as superfluous." The Brazilian Academy, however, really won in this way material means which were not only to assure the continuity of its existence and progress, but the possibility of carrying out more completely the cultural functions which its founders had planned, and to which were to be added others, related to the defence of the language and literature of the country. The Academy has been accused of receiving to its bosom retired diplomats, tired orators and statesmen; but, being par excellence a conservative institution (and hence its opposition to literary novelties that have not been consecrated by glory), it tends to rely upon other great institutions, insuring the place and influence of literature by joining to it the sciences, politics, and religion. It seemed natural, if not entirely in the interest of literature, that, following the example of the French Academy which served as its model, the Brazilian Academy should receive eminent citizens as a reward for services they had rendered the country, as the Pritaneum did in ancient cities.

of his style, which is truly splendid in its simple, strong gravity. He is, like Aloísio de Azevedo, an excellent observer of manners, but in his way both of facing reality and of expressing it maintains with the force of his original personality a position of equilibrium within the school of which he adopted the processes without falling into any of its defects. Extreme in both respects, compared with the author of *O Ateneu*—a satire, limpid and lively, of the system of education in a private school of Rio—we find Júlio Ribeiro (1845–1890) of Minas Gerais, who in *A Carne* carried the naturalistic process to the crudest boldness, and Coelho Neto (1865–1934), almost a repentant naturalist, in whom there appears to have been, from the very beginning, the contrary of a true naturalist, a visionary whose imagination instinctively enlarged and amplified every object. It might be said that he is the last great romantic because of his faculty for embracing vast wholes and because of his burning imagination (with which more than once he carried idealization as far as symbolism) and the pomp of his language, which is frequently damaged by a bubbling flow of words which makes it difficult for him to express his emotion. In *O Sertão* (short novel) and *A Treva* (short stories), the fecund writer of Maranhão, who was also a restless observer of the life of cities in *Inverno em Flor, Tormenta,* and *A Conquista,* portrays in lively colors the environment and the customs of the interior, but without that feeling for the real and that objectivity in analysis that Afonso Arinos (1868–1916) had in his stories *Pelo Sertão* and *Lendas e Tradições,* or the firmness in the design of his characters which is possessed by Afrânio Peixoto in *Maria Bonita, Bugrinha,* and *Fruta do Mato.* But it is in poetry and not in the novel that one feels most profoundly and most broadly the antiromantic movement, in the school of Parnassianism, which in certain respects is a return to classicism in the sense that the important thing for the Parnassians, as with the classic writers, is rather to be than to appear moved; it is to govern one's emotion, to substitute for the luxuriousness which romanticism gives to verbal expression a classic concept of form which shall be clean and precise, and sobriety of images, submitted like one's whole language, to the discipline of art and reason. Therefore the Parnassians, like the classics, seem to us cold; and we consider as a defect exactly what they hold to be their most precious quality—reserve, measure, equilibrium.

The four great names of the Parnassian school are, in the judgment of practically all, Alberto de Oliveira, who, more than any of the rest, submitted to its rigid discipline; Raimundo Correia, Olavo Bilac, and Vicente de Carvalho. The first, Alberto de Oliveira (1857–1937), a native of the State of Rio, gives us in his work *Canções Românticas, Meridionais, Sonetos e Poemas, Versos e Rimas,* not only the document that most specifically expresses this reaction against the lachrymose sensibility of the romantic and evinces a respect for art in the highest degree, but also some of the most beautiful poems of Parnassian inspiration, remarkable for their descriptive vigor, the absolute rightness of their images, and the purity of their metrics and expression. If his sonnets and poems, with their intense coloration, their magnificent breadth, are in general almost exclusively plastic, in some of them, as in *Vida em Flor,* under the delicacy of the poem, now more simple and natural, there is barely hidden the vibration of a delicate sensibility. In Olavo Bilac (1865–1918), also of Rio (and one of the greatest poets of the country, with a flexible and elegant form), very finely chiseled intelligence no longer so firmly commands the heart, which trembles with joy of the senses even to the point of voluptuousness, and inspiration is fresher and more spontaneous in *Panóplias,* in *Via Látea,* and in *Sarças de Fogo,* and rises in his last book, *Tarde,* which is penetrated with mystical idealism and the grave and melancholy beauty of thought. The finest sensibility, the pessimistic, ironical, melancholy humor, the ability to communicate an emotion that is graver and more concentrated, and the naturalness of expression which is more musical constitute the charms of Raimundo Correia (1859–1911), who in *Primeiros Sonhos, Sinfonias, Versos e Versões,* and *Aleluias* presents us with pictures of a finished grace and of a frankness of execution that is unequaled, and of a great delicacy of sentiment. It is, however, perhaps in the *Poemas e Canções* of Vicente de Carvalho (1866–1924) of Santos that poetry acquired more tenderness and dramatic intensity in its marked evolution in the direction of the human, and there was reestablished in the chain which linked the past to the present a solid, brilliant link in which the voices of the sea and the songs of the earth, the sentiment of nature and of the human heart are fused in lyric poetry. But at the very heart of Parnassianism [17] arose symbolism, which was in France the reaction against the realistic school and appeared among us as a pure reflex of a distant reaction already almost in a state of decline. This reality, in the imitation of which the realists in poetry and in prose fiction have pretended to enclose art, the symbolists decided to interpret, to penetrate the mysteries covered with their appearance and discover its ideal meaning. All that this school wished to introduce into poetry, vague and fluid and secret as it was, no one could express better among us than Cruz e Sousa (Santa Catarina, 1863–1898), a Negro poet whose emotion, strong enough to dominate him, was reflected entirely in the verses of *Missal* and *Faróis,* with their irregular language but of great rhythmic beauty and with that obscurity which is a defect es-

[17] Since our object was only to trace in its general lines the evolution of literature in Brazil in a short essay which should contain the essentials and not be too dry, it was not possible to stop and analyze every one of the poets connected with the different schools that followed one another through the various phases of that evolution. Besides, the poets joined together in each of these groups, like the Parnassian school, were sufficiently alike to have a family resemblance. What it was important to do, then, was to bring out the culminating figures who gave new forms to poetry or in whom a given movement of ideas was expressed with the greatest intensity and inventive power. Nevertheless, it is well to remember that no school had more representatives in Brazil than Parnassianism, with its marked tendency to impart a sculptural quality to the art of words and to make the poetic form a refined means of expression. It was Gonçalves Crespo (Rio, 1847–1883), for whom two countries are rivals, that of his birth and that of his adoption, forerunner of the Parnassian school and one of the most perfect poets in the correctness and beauty of the form of his verse, "who allowed himself to be so sincerely and vividly inspired by family scenes of Brazilian life"; others are Luiz Guimarães (Rio, 1847–1898), polished and elegant in form: Luiz Murat (Rio, 1861–1929), a lyric poet with metaphysical tendencies; Guimarães Passos (Alagoas, 1867–1909), author of *Versos de um Simples* (1891) and of *Horas Mortas* (1901); Emílio de Meneses (Parana, 1867–1918), satiric poet and extreme Parnassian; Francisca Júlia da Silva (São Paulo, 1874–1920), a poetess who left us in *Mármores* (1895), later republished under the title of *Esfinges,* a work of sculptural beauty, but without great warmth of emotion; Augusto de Lima (Minas Gerais, 1859–1934), with his colorful verses rich in ideas; Mário de Alencar (Rio, 1872–1925), of delicate sensibility and with a classic sense of balance; and B. Lopes, who arose in 1881, a master in the art of evoking little pictures of rustic life that are admirable for the natural feeling and spontaneity. At the beginning of the twentieth century appeared a new force, Augusto dos Anjos (Paraíba, 1884–1913), contradictory and disillusioned, whose peculiar quality, in his poems *Eu* (1912), comes especially from his way of expressing himself that is original to the point of extravagance, his prodigality in metaphors, scientific in character, and his reflections, which frequently interfere with his lyricism and the expression of his temperament.

sential in symbolism. While this poet who spread the fame of the school among us was winning the enthusiastic adherence of disciples and sustaining the fires of the opposition to these new forms of poems, the austere isolation in which Alfonsus de Guimaraens (1870–1921) lived in Minas Gerais fecundated his somber, liturgical poetry, peopled with visions of death, although modified by religious sentiment.

If, then, we search at each of these moments for the cause of the transformation in the literary taste of the country, it is not difficult to find it in the action of a foreign literature, nearly always the French, and in the influence which the great intellectual currents of the time exercised upon our mentality and our institutions. This is what happened, also, in the evolution of historical studies, if not with regard to their amount, which is more related to internal causes, at least with regard to their attitudes and the methods which were gradually transforming them in accordance with new theories of history. Brazilian feeling tends naturally to express itself vigorously and has, ever since the dawn of our political liberty, in historical studies, which constitute one of the first literary manifestations and are to be explained "by the ardor that a people which has entered upon the possession of its liberty and independence naturally puts in the search for its family titles and in linking its future to its past." The political struggles of the first Empire and in the period of the Regency and the brilliance in the second Empire of parliamentary life, a center of attraction for intellectual activities, did not permit the nineteenth century to make an effort to throw an intense light on the past of the history of Brazil. The greatest historians of the first half of the nineteenth century are two foreigners, Robert Southey, who in his *History of Brazil* gave us in 1810 the first history of Brazil based on documentary proofs, and Ferdinand Denis, to whom we owe a résumé in French of the literary history of the country published in 1826. In the chair of history in the school of Pedro II, then the only official establishment of secondary education, there succeeded each other, down to the time when in 1883 it was occupied by a professional historian, three eminent men, one a notable poet, Gonçalves Dias, one a novelist of the great public, Joaquim Manuel de Macedo, and the Baron of Rio Branco, who knew the material profoundly but, as was revealed later, was above all a diplomat and statesman. In the second half of the nineteenth century, in which our historians were connected with the French theories of history of the romantic period, there arose, nevertheless, João Francisco Lisboa (Maranhão, 1812–1863), who in the last part of the *Jornal de Timon* (1852–1855), with his research on the history of Maranhão and the life of Father Vieira, gave us the proof that he was a research man of the first order, capable of using a vigorous and meaty style; Joaquim Caetano da Silva (1810–1873) of Rio Grande, author of the *Memória sôbre os limites do Brasil com a Guiana Francesa* and of the notable work *L'Oyapock et l'Amazone,* which Rio Branco utilized in order to win the victory in the question of boundary with France in Guiana; and the two great names among the leading historians of Brazil, Francisco Adolfo de Varnhagen (1816–1878), Viscount of Pôrto Seguro, and João Capistrano de Abreu, who succeeded the Baron of Rio Branco in the chair of history at Pedro II. The appearance in 1854 of the *História do Brasil* by Varnhagen, who had been preparing himself for this fundamental work by a long series of tasks and researches, was sufficient to win for the author the first place and to justify the title with which posterity has endowed him—"the father of our history." In almost half a century of scholarship and of research Capistrano de Abreu

(1853–1927) became the historian indicated by all as the only one capable of writing a masterly synthesis of our history, with his gift of penetration, with the rigor of his methods, and with his synthetic spirit in the exposition of facts.

That work of synthesis for which his qualities of historian and clear and sober writer predestined him was never written by Capistrano de Abreu. Commencing by specializing in research on the century of the discovery, he dissipated his energies later in various fragmentary works—models of historical monographs—in which he left us a witness of the vigor of his mind, of his brilliant intuitions, and his great scholarship. In his books *O Descobrimento do Brasil* (1883), *Capítulos de História Colonial* (1907), and *Caminhos Antigos e Povoamento do Brasil* as in prefaces, annotations, and summaries, a scattered but opulent work, this notable renovator of historic studies in Brazil, if he did not create a Brazilian school of history, did arouse a movement which was truly fecund in ideas and in research. The historiography of colonial Brazil under his leadership entered upon a phase of investigations and discoveries with which it has been throwing light upon the secret significance of our past. Among the contemporaries of Capistrano de Abreu, who continued the work of studying documents but in other fields of the history of the country, there stand out the names of Joaquim Nabuco, to whom the biography of his father and his autobiography in *Um Estadista do Império* and in *Minha Formação* furnished the opportunity for beautifully written pages, reconstituting the political life of the second Empire; Oliveira Lima (1867–1928), a native of Pernambuco, who collected from the archives an abundant documentation for his work, like the patient investigator he was; and João Ribeiro (1860–1934) of Sergipe, one of the most eminent and many-sided writers that Brazil has had, with the clarity of his ideas, the perspicacity of his analysis, the sureness of his erudition, the natural grace of his style, and who was the first to abandon in his textbook *História do Brasil* the purely chronological criterion "delineating happenings according to the principal foci from which culture was spread." The historical tendency which has been developing since the second half of the nineteenth century took on a new and vigorous life in the Republic, above all in the later years, under the influence of such notable researchers as Rodolfo Garcia, Tobias Monteiro, Afonso Taunay, the historian of the bandeiras; Pandiá Calógeras, Basílio de Magalhães, Vilhena de Morais, Jônatas Serrano, and Otávio Tarquínio de Souza, and of the new generation of brilliant historians in whose studies, as in those of Pedro Calmon, one can see the progressive penetration of the sociological attitude and methods. The history of Brazilian literature, which, to tell the truth, was founded by Sílvio Romero (Sergipe, 1851–1914), one of the greatest workers on the national literature, which for a long time was not able to count upon more than three writers, has acquired in the last twenty years an extraordinary development in work of broad vision and of detail. Its bases established by Sílvio Romero in his *História da Literatura Brasileira* (1888), his main work, and by José Veríssimo (Para, 1857–1916), the former ardent and impetuous, and the latter more serene and objective, but without the vigorous style and the breadth of view which distinguished the historian of Sergipe, and also by Araripe Júnior (Ceará, 1848–1911) in his critical essays, literary history, and criticism, of comparatively recent origin, took on a more disinterested phase of analysis and of penetration with Ronald de Carvalho, who gave them a new brilliance by the quickness of his intelligence and the sensitiveness of his literary taste. At the beginning, apologetic and emphatic, careless of facts and without penetration and analysis, but later solid in its documentation and in its desire for objectivity, not harmed by the warmth of its passion, as was fitting at a time in which the pen was a weapon and literature was a fight; rapid and light and later impregnated with psychological reflections, literary history, like history in general, allowed itself to be penetrated by general ideas and sociological notions, which are utilized by Nelson Werneck among others, in studying the facts of literary evolution in their relation with economic phenomena.

The reign of our literary past, already far enough away to arouse the pleasure of discovery and the charm of the unknown, and the high level which letters have attained, as much in the sense of universality as in a regional sense, explained this growing effort to become aware of our national literature. Literature had, in fact, attained its maturity, in Brazil, a maturity so marked and characteristic in the variety of its aspects that it necessarily would awaken an intense intellectual curiosity, leading us to examine it in every aspect. In the work of Machado de Assis (Rio, 1839–1908), who explored all the fields of literary activity, one of its tendencies culminated in a perfect art—that which was developed among us, as A. de Queiroz Filho observes, "under the impulse of the spirit of civilization and under the inspiration of occidental traditions and culture." The poet of *Ocidentais* (1879–1880), the novelist of *Memórias Póstumas de Braz Cubas* (1881), of *Quincas Borba* and of *Dom Casmurro*, the storyteller of *Papéis Avulsos* (1882), of *Histórias sem data* and of *Várias Histórias*, attained in his career, which was a constant rise, a unique position in the scale of aesthetic and human values of our civilization. Master of himself and of his art—the most lucid Brazilian expression of balance, measure and classic taste—skeptic on the surface through a kind of intellectual modesty, extremely delicate but serious, however, and more decisive than might appear, he barely conceals under his humorous tone of skepticism and irony, the background of human tenderness, "sentiments absorbed at the most living and purest sources of sensibility." Hence that pessimism that is entirely his own, without acidity and without irritation, and the delicate feeling of that elegant, pure poetry which his reserve and timidity marked at the very height of the romantic period with a subtle originality, triumphing effortlessly over all of the influences of the schools. His power of reflection, his rare ability of psychological analysis appear in his stories and novels, leaving their mark not only on the study of human types and character conflicts but also upon the retiring and serious expression which is worn by the mentality of this merciless observer of the inner life and of the landscape of the human soul. It is with Machado de Assis, in fact, that "the inner world, the psychological gallery, the universe of thought began to exist in Brazilian literature." But if the spirit of civilization flowers with such freshness in Machado de Assis, "who crystallized the universality of our thought," Euclides da Cunha (State of Rio, 1866–1909), a man who was American to his marrow, and in whom the spirit of conquest emerges "directed toward the fascination of the unknown horizon, the seduction of the virginal mysteries of the earth," fixed, as no one else has done, in his work the local color and the aspirations of the interior, and the particular physiognomy of our nationality. These writers reflect two phases of the national spirit,[18] the one turned

[18] "By virtue of special circumstances, and unique phenomena of our history, the formation of Brazil," writes A. de Queiroz Filho, "faced in different directions and was stimulated by two spirits, the effect of which is notable in various episodes of our history and works of our literature. They

toward the Atlantic, the other toward the interior. An eminently Brazilian writer, with his keen sense of the earth and of national life, jumping from reason and pure art to listen above it to the voice of the instinct of the race, he uses, to understand them, all his knowledge and sweeps them away in the impetuous current of his thought as the river which he describes sweeps away in its immense waters pieces of the forests. The powerful passion of the imagination which at times falsified his view also sharpened his gaze and gave him brilliant intuitions, and if here and there they were harmful to the observer, still they served the painter who was incomparable in his pictures of tropical nature. Euclides da Cunha owed his imagination both in *Os Sertões* (1902), his masterpiece, and in *Contrastes e confrontos* (1907) and in the magnificent essays of *A Margem da história* (1909) the boldness and vigor of his writing, the lightning flashes of his grandiose visions, and the almost epic force of his style, which is ardent, quick, dense, and vigorous.

In *Os Sertões*, in fact, as in his essay on the Amazon, *Terra sem história*, it is not so much reality that is extraordinary, as the light which this magnificent writer throws upon it. Nothing is false or fantastic in these geographic canvases of spectacular greatness. The singularity of all this—events and nature—which Euclides da Cunha reproduced with an intense liveliness and a picturesque power that had no equal, comes from the manner in which the artist puts them in relief, expressing without hesitation, swollen by his imagination in all its dramatic force, the image which he has received from our world. He possessed a writer's temperament that was truly original and to the highest degree that faculty of literary invention and of new artistic form that, while it imposes itself upon our admiration, has always refused to serve as a model. It is through this extraordinary strength of his style that the illustrious geographer, historian, and social observer was able to present the life of the interior in its primitive and brutal aspects, and to give as no one else has, the strange feeling of all that is great and powerful, contradictory and traitorous in the land and in tropical nature, which appears to have attained in his work the very paroxysm of expression. Without this vigor and without this vibrating style, but with a notable sense of reality in his observation of landscape and of the customs of the interior, Afonso Arinos, an admirable

---

are the spirits of conquest and of civilization. The latter, a result of the natural tendency toward conservatism and stability, attempts to build the nation in the light of the inspiration of western European traditions and culture. The former, marked by a feeling of movement, brimming with energy, the most powerful expression of which was the heroic movement of *bandeirismo*, drawn by the fascination of unknown horizons, by the seduction of the virginal mysteries of the earth. . . . The spirit of conquest awoke the creative sap of the new land, and it was the beginning, the moment of inauguration of a new life. The spirit of civilization was good sense, continuity, the idea of dependence, of prolongation and of adaptation; it brought to the new life of the colony the sap of cultural roots many centuries old. It was within this situation of twofold directions that we grew and essayed our first steps in the vacillating uncertainty of the early days of the country. In literature, the two goals created parallel routes. Machado de Assis and Euclides da Cunha are incarnations of their extreme expressions. One crystallized universality of thought. The other caught the local color, the feeling of the land, the peculiar character of our national being. Machado was a gentle voice, a product of a highly refined culture; he took from our spirit its universal part. Euclides sought the interior, bestrode and crossed the mountain range which separated Brazil into stagnant, closed, and impermeable realms, saw the "reverse of the medallion"; extended the horizons of intellectual nationalism, giving our culture a stronger love of the land." (A. de Queiroz Filho, "Duas faces do espírito nacional," in *O Estado de São Paulo*, Dec., 1937).

student of the sertão, an excellent storyteller, in his books of short stories *Pelo Sertão* (1917), *Histórias e Paisagens, Lendas e Tradições,* "spoke more and better about the things and the men of the Brazilian interior than a considerable number of scientific and historical works, painfully extracted from forgotten archives." [19] But the development of the cities was not to be slow in giving first place to the novel and in moving the interest of writers from the country to urban life, enriching the line of novelists which had culminated in the glory of Machado de Assis, with that first-rate novelist, Lima Barreto (Rio, 1881–1922), a penetrating observer with a marked sense of humor who, in the *Triste fim de Policarpo Quaresma* (1913) and other novels, fixed aspects and pictures of urban and suburban life of the capital. The fact is, as Genolino Amado reminds us, "that the novel is a phenomenon and a product of the city. All the great constructions of literature which represent life to us in its human element, take place in urban situations. . . . If the external action at times takes place in a rural setting, the internal action is still a reflection of the city because the personages take to the country their intimate problems, the troubles of their souls or their interests which can only exist when there exists a great urban life and which result from the very complexity of the metropolis." [20] The narrative of rural inspiration detaches itself from the soil on whose inexhaustible stuff it was nourished, to become transformed with Aloísio de Azevedo, Raul Pompéia, Machado de Assis, and Lima Barreto into the authentic novel and to spread, under the influence of urban life, until it contains everything and represents everything that characterizes narratives of the Indians and the sertão, gaining in objectivity, in penetration, and in human sense what it has lost in lyric interest, in descriptive taste, and in local color.

If, however, it was in Machado de Assis and Euclides da Cunha that there were asserted with great intensity on the one hand the universality of thought and the richness of its human contact, and on the other the attraction of the land and of the man of America, a whole series of essayists continues to be divided in these two directions. They are not afraid of general ideas nor the concrete problems of the complex Brazilian reality. There is opened to literary exploitation a field that is ever more vast; and, where there have been seen only solitary figures, an Araripe Júnior, an impressionist critic, subtle to the point of obscurity; a Carlos de Laet (Rio, 1847–1929), a conservative in politics and in religion, a terrible polemist with a biting irony, and an Alberto Tôrres, a vigorous political thinker of the type of Tavares Bastos, there appeared critics, essayists, and pamphleteers who in their chronicles and studies demonstrated a particular aptitude in analysis and in understanding the questions which occupy European thought or are of interest to the life of our own country. The fact is that with the Great War began one of those periods to which Talleyrand refers, when he describes the period of Louis XVI and in which "the general spirit of society undergoes a modification in every respect. People want to know everything, to plunge to the depth of everything, to judge everything. Sentiments were replaced by philosophic ideas, passions by analysis of the human heart, the desire to please by opinions, amusements by plans and projects." In the field of literary criticism, Ronald de Carvalho unites in his essays brilliance of thought and graces of style of highly colored, poetic nature. Antônio Tôrres, the breaker-down of prejudices, gives to his hard pamphleteer's

[19] Ronald de Carvalho, *Pequena História da Literatura Brasileira* (Rio: Briguiet, 1919).
[20] Genolino Amado, "O Romance, a cidade e o campo," in *O Jornal,* Rio, No. 5,892.

blows the firmness and precision which come from his mental discipline and from the strength of his style; Agripino Grieco brings criticism to public taste with the combativity of his bitter spirit, with the striking flavor of his expressions, which are insolent but unexpected, and have a kind of caricatural power, and with the brilliance of his imagination; and Humberto de Campos, poet and chronicler, a master of the language and of criticism, characterized by a thought that is more mature and an art that is more complete, annexes to his personal reflection, which is extremely brilliant, the whole vast field of his experience and of his reading. In the study and debate of religious questions, the major essayist and pamphleteer we have had on the Catholic side, Jackson de Figueiredo (Sergipe, 1891–1928), is followed by Tristão de Ataíde in whose essays, in the second phase of his career, moral and religious preoccupations predominate, taking some of the artistic qualities away from the brilliant, perspicacious critic that he was, for the profit of the moralizing desire of the fervent Christians. If both, identified since their profession of faith, in their cult for order, for discipline and hierarchy, represent that which is most conservative in Brazilian thinking, Tristão de Ataíde, nevertheless, replaces the order of the impulsive violence of the founder of the Centro D. Vital by an intellectual type of action that is more vigilant, but not less intransigent, and has greater power to convince. In social and political studies directed at the great questions the present-day world is debating and toward the imperativeness which our Brazilian problems have assumed, urging the study of the past as a key to the comprehension of the present, there stand out among others Gilberto Amado, a writer who is at the same time a thinker, who hides under the brilliance of his style, which is of a great precision; Vicente Licínio Cardoso, a humanist with a generous and deep spirit, more preoccupied with ideas than with forms; Oliveira Viana in his magnificent essays directed largely in the anthropological and racial direction and full of political realism, and Gilberto Freyre, to whom, as well as to Oliveira Viana, we shall have to return again in another chapter and who, by the rigor of his method and the brilliance of his conclusions initiated in his syntheses of sociological interpretation a truly fruitful movement for the direction of our social studies, if not a definitive one.

It must not surprise us, then, before this essentially critical movement of analysis and of dissection that has developed since the war of 1914, that it should share the same revolutionary spirit as the innovating current in the field of literature initiated in 1922 by court poets, critics, and novelists in the Week of Modern Art in São Paulo. The limpid but sonorous voices of the last generation of Parnassians was still echoing, as in the case of Amadeu Amaral (São Paulo, 1875–1929), author of *Névoa* and of *Espumas,* a poet of fine sensitivity and of grave and polished expression, and Raul de Leoni (Rio, 1895–1926), the enchanting and harmonious artist of *Luz Mediterrânea,* when there broke out the modernist current, led by a group of young men to whom Graça Aranha (Maranhão, 1868–1931), the brilliant novelist of *Canaã,* had from the beginning given his generous adherence, led on by the enthusiasm of the initiators of the movement. As early as in the poems of Ricardo Gonçalves and Afonso Schmidt, in which the social and human note would be struck with vigor,[21] attaining in the former a harsh accent of revolt, or in the lyric poetry of Hermes Fontes (Sergipe, 1890–

[21] Fernando de Azevedo, "A Poesia social no Brasil," *Ensaios* (São Paulo: Comp. Melhoramentos de São Paulo, 1929).

1930), touching in its mystic idealism, there passed a breath of reaction against the Parnassian school, if not the barely concealed desire in our São Paulo poets to cast down all of the idols. At this same time Monteiro Lobato, who has the gift of observation, was giving to the tales of *Urupês*—slices of life torn out of reality—the color, the tone, the aspect, and the movement of life itself; and although faithful to the genius of the language, he was able to extract from it new riches, giving it new youth with his vigorous and bare style, which is one of absolute clarity and exactness. The impetuousness, however, with which men threw themselves into the renovating adventure, among others a critic of art and literature like Mário de Andrade, a spirit of the vanguard, censorious and combative, or of the temper of Osvaldo de Andrade, and the three São Paulo poets of this generation, Guilherme de Almeida, Cassiano Ricardo, and Menotti del Picchia, transformed this movement, strengthened still more by the personal prestige of the author of *Viagem Maravilhosa*, into an agitation of revolutionary character, turned toward concerns with literary formulae, but really useful to the renovation of Brazilian literature by reason of the iconoclastic spirit it brought with it. If it produced nothing great and of final value, if it did not contribute, due to its lack of a new conception of life, to fertilize our consciences, it served doubtless to free them from the old things against which it arose: old techniques of verse, Parnassian eloquence, the taste for great themes, and our clinging to the traditional forms of the Portuguese language spoken in Brazil. This process of emancipation, begun by the movement of 1922, which was critical and destructive but without any truly creative force, took on new and more powerful life with the revolution of 1930, which, Almir de Andrade correctly observes, "by breaking the old political regime, exercised a psychological role of freeing restrained tendencies. Every victorious attempt against political power has a very marked disinhibiting capacity. It stimulates the expansion of new forces, it imposes an unconscious necessity to make new affirmations." [22] Brazilian literature, however, far from being led in a single direction, broke up into groups, as, it is true, happens everywhere, into a plurality of tendencies which come into conflict, unite, or achieve balance, depending on individual taste and the variety of foreign influences, among which we may say were those of the modernist movement, now weakened in its renovating drive; and the near classic reaction with its return to equilibrium and harmony between form and substance; and that of introspection and the sounding of the interior world and of objective observation of social reality; and finally, that of the spirit of Brazilian nationalism and the spirit of civilization which, developing as parallel tendencies in our intellectual evolution, present themselves under new forms.

But among so many names which arose in poetry and prose fiction and which at times shone for a little while only to disappear into oblivion, it is too early to separate those which will remain and to determine with precision which are the truly original contributions to the progress of our literature. Our proximity to these works which have followed each other tumultuously, without giving us time for reflection, and the abundance of the material to be examined do not permit definitive judgment on contemporary literary history. The successive vogues created around names, at times bringing to the foreground works of secondary merit, and ostracisms of equal disproportion,

[22] Almir de Andrade, reply to the questionnaire in the *Revista do Brasil* on present-day tendencies in Brazilian literature.

relegating superior ability to a kind of oblivion, impose upon us the necessity of reexamining our intellectual values, so that each one may find the place he deserves in an opinion that has been restored to truth without the excessive enthusiasm or without the secret hostility of contemporaries. However, among those who have won our admiration, we may remember in poetry Manuel Bandeira, of a delicate sensitivity, critical and sad; Augusto Schmidt, sensitive and strong at the same time, very personal in his tone and in his inspiration; Jorge de Lima, with his original poetry, simple even to the point of authentic ingenuity and with its popular flavor; Adalgisa Neri, an ardent who breathes life and expresses it with a kind of exasperated sincerity; and Cecília Meireles, who has retired into an inner world as into a kingdom of exile, whence she transmits to us a message in her poems, with their nostalgia for the infinite, with everything vague and fluid, and therefore charming in her symbolic thought, rich in suggestiveness. In the novel in which the most divergent tendencies cross, and especially those of James Joyce and of Marcel Proust, one may distinguish in a general way two great currents, that of the north, neonaturalistic, dominated by a taste for putting down on paper aspects of our social life, with José Américo de Almeida, José Lins do Rêgo, Graciliano Ramos, Jorge Amado, Amado Fontes, and Raquel de Queiroz; and that of the south, which rather takes delight in studies of the psychological, moral, and mental world, in which there stand out, to mention only a few, Plínio Salgado, Lúcio Cardoso, Cornélio Pena, Marques Rebêlo, Telmo Vergara, Erico Veríssimo and Otávio de Faria, passionately devoted to the inner life and to the art of analyzing states of mind and the movement of ideas and passions.[23] Although belonging to worlds that are entirely different, with their different conceptions of life and of man and with well marked individual characteristics, they are frequently alike in emphasis, in the picturesque style, and in the intensity of the process of reliving the past in all its aspects

[23] Our literature, which is more lyrical and thoughtful, has at all times found its strongest expression in poetry, in the descriptive novel, and in eloquence rather than in philosophy, the essay, and the theater or any other literary form which in its nature requires more analysis and reflection. Machado de Assis himself, who with his novels introduced into Brazilian literature interest in the inner life and became a master in the study of character, did not find in the theater a form well adjusted to the particular cast of his mind. The quite personal and essentially subjective talent of the great novelist seemed not to be congenial to the qualities of invention and the gift of life that are necessary to the successful work of the theater, which requires in drama a broad lyrical quality and forces the author to retire to the background in order to give life to the creatures of his imagination. At the time when, under the influence of Brazilian novelists, like Machado de Assis and Lima Barreto, and foreigners, like James Joyce and Aldous Huxley or Marcel Proust and André Gide, the psychological novel and the novel of manners experienced a new life, one might at first sight think that the development of our theater would have recorded real progress. But if we preserve a due sense of proportion and take the word in a relative sense, we see that no notable theatrical work was produced. Founded in reality by Martins Pena, in the first half of the nineteenth century, and exploited with relative success in the second half of that century by José de Alencar and França Júnior, and more recently by Artur Azevedo (Maranhão, 1851–1908), satiric poet and writer of comedies, with his delicious fantasies and biting wit, and by Paulo Barreto (Rio, 1881–1921), journalist and columnist, the comedy of manners is today represented by a little group of theatrical writers like Raimundo de Magalhães Júnior, Ernani Fornari, and Joracì de Camargo. There is not really a decadence of the Brazilian theater, which is still developing slowly, without being able to show figures capable of establishing a dramatic tradition among us, by means of a series of works with great intensity of life, vigor in the analysis of characters, and breadth of conception.

and in giving us the totality of events and their effect upon consciousness and the re-actions which they lead to in the individual. But already one can note in some, among the major figures of this period—which has been the most fruitful in the history of the Brazilian novel—a double effort in the direction of paying attention to the neces-sities which lie at the base of classic art and sacrificing details for the sake of great, significant facts, or of choosing characteristic traits, excluding secondary and parasitic traits and of extinguishing one's self before the things that one represents, giving to them only the care necessary to let them move us by simplicity and sincerity of ex-pression.

Thus, although this literary production may not always be of the highest quality, for it is meant rather to entertain and hold the attention of the reader, and although it may not be possible to point out more than one or two works that are truly original and strong, the very quantitative expansion of this literary movement is in itself an index of the growing interest of the public in Brazilian literature. If there is still a con-siderable business in French and English books in the country, still the field of influ-ence of Brazilian authors is constantly growing and some of them are already able, if not to live by their pen, at least to make the pure activity of the mind a principal occupation, whereas it had previously had no function in the social setting and had not succeeded in being a profession. This divergence between the pleasure of the author and the pleasure of the public, or in other words between the producer and consumer—in which Humberto de Campos rightly saw one of the causes of the mo-notony of literary life in Brazil [24]—is tending to disappear as a result of the greater concern of authors not to depart from reality and to satisfy the preferences of the pub-lic, which today as always is making what might be called a "literary climate." The state of the press, as a result of the circulation of a great number of daily papers; the space which the most important daily newspapers give to literary criticism and to in-formation about new books; the network of services of distribution which the pub-lishers are extending over the whole country through bookstores and agencies, and the

---

[24] In a country with old literary traditions, in which authors and public have found a sym-pathetic atmosphere, as can be seen from the spread of books and printing, cultural journals, espe-cially literary ones, have rarely enjoyed success and have been few in number and of brief life. The oldest of these reviews, in the present century, *A Ilustração Brasileira,* founded in 1909 in Rio de Janeiro by the company O Malho, had under the guidance of Medeiros e Albuquerque, and with the collaboration of the greatest poets and writers of the time, a brilliant period which came to an end in 1915. His publication was suspended in that year but resumed in 1920, to be once more interrupted in 1930, to be resurrected in 1935, with two lapses of five years each in an existence of little more than a quarter of a century. In 1916 there was founded in São Paulo and directed successively by Plínio Barreto and Monteiro Lobato the *Revista do Brasil,* which, twice discontinued, reappeared in Rio in 1937 in its third phase under the editorship of Otávio Tarquínio de Sousa. The *Boletim de Ariel,* an excellent monthly edited by Gastão Cruls and Agripino Grieco, lasted no more than seven years. *Inteligência* (a monthly of world opinion) founded by Samuel Ribeiro, in São Paulo, owes the reception which established its fame to its informative and popularizing character rather than to literature. In Rio de Janeiro there appeared, as a result of the efforts of Brício de Abreu, in newspaper form, the weekly *Dom Casmurro,* de-voted exclusively to literature. If we add, then, to these reviews and literary papers the *Anuário Brasileiro de Literatura* which first appeared in 1937, we shall have, in the history of our literature in the present century, the complete picture of the literary reviews of major interest and influence, among which we cannot list the periodicals that were without importance, were ephemeral, and exercised a limited influence upon a very small circle of readers.

176. André Rebouças, one of the greatest
figures in Brazilian engineering.

177. Paulo de Frontin, city planning and
railway expert, among whose accomplishments there stand out the carrying out of
the city planning improvements in Rio de
Janeiro and the laying of the second track
of the Central Railroad of Brazil, along the
Coast Range.

178. Francisco Pereira Passos, engineer, mayor, and remodeler of the city of Rio de Janeiro, which he began to transform, under the government of Rodrigues Alves, from an old colonial city into one of the greatest of modern metropolises.

180. Francisco Bicalho, outstanding in port engineering.

179. Saturnino de Brito, one of the most illustrious names in sanitary engineering in Brazil.

181. Teixeira Soares, who planned and brought into existence the railway between Curitiba and Paranaguá, so admirable esthetically and in its general plan.

182. Francisco Pais Leme de Monlevade, engineer, whose notable wisdom in conceiving and beginning in 1913 the plan for the electrification of the Companhia Paulista de Estradas de Ferro, made him "the pioneer and beginner of heavy electric traction in Brazil."

183. Medical College of Rio de Janeiro, in its new building on the Praia Vermelha.
Photo by Vosvlius, in collection of the Census Bureau.

184. Medical College of Bahia. Photo by Voltaire Fraga, Urbo Salvador, in Brazilian Institute of Geography and Statistics.

185. Medical College of Pôrto Alegre, in Rio Grande do Sul. Principal façade.

186. Francisco de Castro (born at Bahia, 1857, died at Rio, 1901), great physician and professor in the Medical College of Rio de Janeiro.

187. Arnaldo Vieira de Carvalho, surgeon, founder and first director of the Medical College of São Paulo.

188. Miguel Couto, physician and professor of clinical medicine in the Medical College of Rio de Janeiro.

189. Miguel Pereira, of the Medical College of Rio de Janeiro.

190. Osvaldo Cruz, public health expert who cleaned up Rio de Janeiro (1902–1906), and founder of the Institute of Manguinhos.

191. Facsimile of the title page of the "Sermon, preached by Father Antônio Vieira, on the interment of the bones of the hanged men," Lisbon, 1753.

SERMAM,

QUE PREGOU

O P. ANTONI.

VIEIRA,

AO ENTERRO DOS OSSOS

DOS

ENFORCADO

NA MISERICORDIA DA CIDADE DA BAHI
havendo guerras naquelles Eftados.

Reimpréffo á cufta

DE D. T. A.

F. do S. Officio.

LISBOA,

Com todas as licenças necessarias. Anno **1753.**

192. Pulpit of the Church of Succor in which Father Antônio Vieira preached, Salvador, Bahia. Photo by Voltaire Fraga, in Brazilian Institute of Geography and Statistics.

CARAMURÚ.
POEMA EPICO
DO
DESCUBRIMENTO
DA
BAHIA,
COMPOSTO
POR
.JOSÉ DE SANTA RITA
DURÃO,

Ordem dos Eremitas de Santo Agoſtinho , na-
tural da Cata-Preta nas Minas Geraes.

LISBOA
NA REGIA OFFICINA TYPOGRAFICA.
ANNO M. DCC. LXXXI.
Com licença da Real Meza Cenſoria.

193. Facsimile reproduction of the frontispiece of the poem *Caramurú* by Santa Rita Durão, Lisbon, 1781.

194. Facsimile of the frontispiece of *Uruguay,* poem by José Basílio da Gama, Lisbon, 1769.

O URAGUAY
POEMA
DE
JOSÉ BASILIO DA GAMA
NA ARCADIA DE ROMA
TERMINDO SIPILIO
DEDICADO
AO ILL.ᴹᴼ E EXC.ᴹᴼ SENHOR
FRANCISCO XAVIER
DE MENDONÇA FURTADO
SECRETARIO DE ESTADO
DE
S. MAGESTADE FIDELISSIMA
&c. &c. &c.

LISBOA
NA REGIA OFFICINA TYPOGRAFICA
ANNO MDCCLXIX
Com licença da Real Meza Cenſoria.

Frontespicio do poema dedicado ao irmão

195. Marília bridge, in Ouro Preto. Partial view.
Photo by Radio Inconfidência of Minas Gerais.

196. Gonçalves Dias (born in Maranhão, 1823, shipwrecked on the Maranhão coast, 1864), a great Brazilian poet. Drawing by J. Wash Rodrigues, State Archives of São Paulo.

197. Castro Alves (Bahia, 1847–1871). Drawing by J. Wash Rodrigues, State Archives of São Paulo.

198. José de Alencar (born in Ceará, 1829, died at Rio, 1877), dramatist, novelist, politician, and jurisconsult.
Photo from the collection of the Companhia Melhoramentos of São Paulo.

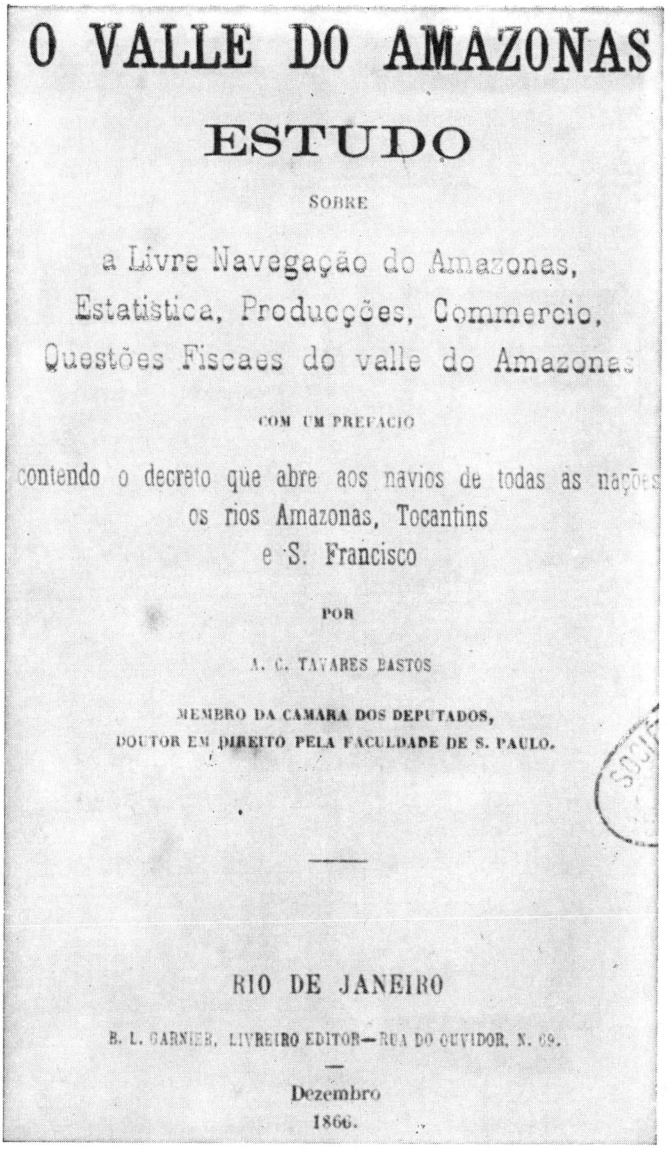

O VALLE DO AMAZONAS

ESTUDO

SOBRE

a Livre Navegação do Amazonas,
Estatistica, Producções, Commercio,
Questões Fiscaes do valle do Amazonas

COM UM PREFACIO

contendo o decreto que abre aos navios de todas as nações
os rios Amazonas, Tocantins
e S. Francisco

POR

A. C. TAVARES BASTOS

MEMBRO DA CAMARA DOS DEPUTADOS,
DOUTOR EM DIREITO PELA FACULDADE DE S. PAULO.

RIO DE JANEIRO

B. L. GARNIER, LIVREIRO EDITOR—RUA DO OUVIDOR, N. 69.

Dezembro
1866.

199. Facsimile reproduction of the front cover of *O Valle do Amazonas,* by
Tavares Bastos, 1866 edition.

200. Joaquim Nabuco (Joaquim Aurélio Nabuco de Araújo, born at Recife, 1849, died at Washington, 1910), politician, parliamentary orator, diplomat, and historian.

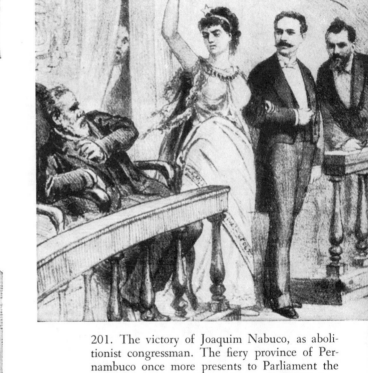

201. The victory of Joaquim Nabuco, as abolitionist congressman. The fiery province of Pernambuco once more presents to Parliament the rightful representative of its first and fifth districts, and gives a terrific lesson to the slaveholders of the Chamber, represented by their leader. Drawing by Angelo Agostini, in the *Revista Ilustrado*, June 13, 1885.

202. Counselor Rui Barbosa, editor in chief of the *Diário de Notícias*. Drawing by Ângelo Agostini, in the *Revista Ilustrada*, 1888.

203. The Brazilian Academy of Letters.
Photo by Vosylius, in collection of the Census Bureau.

204. Olavo Bilac (Olavo Braz Martins dos Guimarães Bilac, Rio, 1865–1918),
great lyric poet.
Photo from the collection of the Companhia Melhoramentos of São Paulo.

modern resources of publicity and propaganda are contributing notably to reduce, if not to eliminate, the divorce between artists and the public, and to increase that power of penetration which is already sufficiently great so that at times it crowns with bookstore success, works without real literary interest. . . . It is no longer true that literary schools have a monopoly of the judgment of literature, considering it as the privilege of a small class and conferring their favor upon one and rejecting another, with their prejudices or with their limited criteria. The numerical growth and the elevation of the cultural level of the public called upon to judge literary work removes from the tyranny of small groups the fate of works of literature that are now almost at the same time placed within the reach of socially different publics and of circles that are ever less restricted. If one may set down to the account of the expansion of this literary life, which has come closer to the preferences of the public, a certain lowering of the level which is accustomed to accompany movements characterized by great production, it is certain that these periods of intellectual effervescence, of activity, and of literary influence, by awakening vocations and fecundating consciousness, are preparing great movements of renewal and creation in the artistic field. But this high-frequency current that has been established between authors and the public and from which the literature of the country is getting its great power of reaching the public is not to be explained only by the flourishing of the novel—the popular form of literature —because of the greater wealth of social and human significance in works of fiction, by the more profound agreements between what is written and what people want to read, and by the pressure of publicity which, if at times it does not have this object, always has the effect of awakening the taste and habit of reading. At the roots of this mutual penetration between the public and authors, one meets also the Brazilian character of our literature, the manifestations of which are still marked by foreign influences and which, however, moving in the direction of spiritual freedom, presents a more marked ethnic flavor and possesses a climate of its own, through which it seeks a means of affirmation and sometimes succeeds in this aim of real originality of thought and of expression.

BIBLIOGRAPHY

Andrade, Almir de, *Aspectos da cultura brasileira* (Rio: Schmidt, 1939).

Andrade, Murici, *A Nova Literatura brasileira* (Pôrto Alegre: Globo, 1936). Critique and anthology.

Ataíde, Tristão, "Política e letras," in *A Margem da história da República* (Rio: Anuário do Brasil, n.d.), pp. 237–292.

Azevedo, Fernando de, *Ensaios* (São Paulo: Comp. Melhoramentos de São Paulo, 1929), especially "Pequena introdução ao estudo de algumas figuras contemporâneas de oradores políticos," pp. 67–80, "A Poesia social no Brasil," pp. 90–102, "A Raça na poesia brasileira," pp. 110–131, and studies of Coelho Neto, pp. 175–193, and Amadeu Amaral, pp. 164–175.

Bandeira, Manuel, *Antologia dos poetas brasileiros da fase romântica* (Rio: Imprensa Nacional, 1937—Publications of the Ministério da Educação).

———, *Antologia dos poetas brasileiros da fase parnasiana* (Rio: Ministerio da Educação e Saude, 2nd ed., 1940).

———, "A Autoria das *Cartas chilenas*," in *Revista do Brasil*, 3rd fase, Vol. 3, No. 22 (Apr., 1940), pp. 1–25.

Campos, Humberto de, *Crítica,* 1st series (2nd ed.) and 2nd series, 2 vols. (Rio: Marisa, 1933).

———, *Sepultando os meus mortos* (Rio: Olimpio, n.d.).

Carvalho, Ronald de, *Pequena história da literatura brasileira* (Rio: Briguiet, 1919; 4th ed., 1929), with Preface by Medeiros e Albuquerque.

Castro, Eugênio de, *Geografia linguística e cultura brasileira* (Rio: Gráfica Sauer, 1937). An essay.

Cunha, Euclides da, *A Margem da história* (Pôrto: Chardron, 3rd ed., 1922), especially Pt. 3, "Da Independência à República," pp. 213–309. A political sketch.

Denis, Ferdinand, *Résumé de l'histoire littéraire du Portugal et du Brésil* (Paris: Lecointe & Durey, 1826).

Grieco, Agripino, *Evolução da prosa brasileira* (Rio: Ariel, 1933).

———, *Evolução da poesia brasileira* (Rio: Areil, 1933).

Lafayette Silva, *História do teatro brasileiro.* Separate, from the memorial "João Caetano dos Santos," in *Revista do instituto histórico e geográfico do Rio de Janeiro* (José Leite, n.d.).

Licínio Cardosa, Vicente, *Pensamentos americanos* (Rio: Estabelecimento Gráfico, 1937), especially "Mauá: Um Homem e um livro," "Um Novo Livro de Oliveira Lima," "Alberto Tôrres," and "Tavares Bastos e Alberto Tôrres."

Lúcio de Azevedo, J., *Novas Epanaforas: Estudos de história e de literatura* (Lisbon: Classica Editóra, 1932), especially "O Poeta Antônio José da Silva e a Inquisição," pp. 138–143, and "Academia dos Renascidos," pp. 219–249.

Matos, Mário, *Machado de Assis: O Homem e a obra* (São Paulo: Comp. Editora Nacional, 1936—Brasiliana, Vol. 153).

Miguel Pereira, Lúcia, *Machados de Assis: Estudo crítico e biográfico* (São Paulo: Comp. Editora Nacional, 1936—Brasiliana, Vol. 73).

———, *A Vida de Gonçalves Dias* (Rio: Olímpio, 1943—Coleção "Documentos Brasileiros"). Containing the unpublished diary of the journey of Gonçalves Dias to the Rio Negro.

Mota, Artur, *História de literatura brasileira* (São Paulo: Comp. Editora Nacional, 1930). Period of formation, 16th and 17th centuries.

Neiva, Artur, *Estudos da língua nacional* (São Paulo: Comp. Editora Nacional, 1940—Brasiliana, Vol. 178).

Paixão, Múcio da, *Teatro no Brasil* (Rio: Editora Moderna, n.d.).

Peixoto, Afrânio, *Noções de história da literatura brasileira* (Rio: Francisco Alves, 1931).

———, *Panorama da literatura brasileira* (São Paulo: Comp. Editora Nacional, 1940).

Romero, Sílvio, *História da literatura brasileira* (Rio: Garnier, 1st ed., 1818, 2nd ed., 1902).

———, *Evolução da literatura brasileira* (Minas: Campanha, 1905).

Sanchez, Edgar, *Língua Brasileira,* Vol. 1 (São Paulo: Comp. Editora Nacional, 1940—Brasiliana, Vol. 179).

Serrano, Jônatas, *Homens e idéias* (Rio: Briguiet, 1930).

Süssekind de Mendonça, Carlos, *História do teatro brasileiro,* Vol. 1 (1564–1890) (Rio: Mendonça Machado & Co., 1926), chaps. "Idéias gerais," "Os Precursores," "A Formação cênica e literária."

Veríssimo, José, *História da literatura brasileira da Bento Teixeira (1601) a Machado de Assis (1908)* (Rio: Francisco Alves, 1916).

———, *Estudos da literatura brasileira* (Paris: Garnier, 6 vols., 1901–1907).

Werneck Sodré, Nélson, *História da literatura brasileira: Seus fundamentos econômicos* (São Paulo: Edições Cultura Brasileira, n.d.).

Wolff, Ferdinand, *Le Brésil littérairre: Histoire de la littérature brésilienne, suivie d'un choix de morceaux tirés des meilleurs auteurs brésiliens* (Berlin: A. Ascher, 1883), Chap. XVI.

CHAPTER FOUR

SCIENCE

The Dutch period—The retinue of Maurice of Nassau—The first foreign explorers—The colony and the home country—The darkness into which the home country plunged colonial Brazil—The installation of the Portuguese court in Brazil—Dom João VI and the first schools and institutions of science—The National Museum—Studies of botany and zoology—The journeys of foreign naturalists through the interior of Brazil—Geology—The paleontological research of Dr. Lund in Lagoa Santa—The physical sciences—From Bartolomeu de Gusmão to Santos Dumont—The National Observatory—The scant interest of the Brazilian in physical sciences—Dom Pedro II and the sciences—The School of Mines—Mathematics and its principal cultivator—Gomes de Sousa—Museums and libraries—The National Library—Nina Rodrigues and legal medicine—Osvaldo Cruz and the center of research at Manguinhos—Geography and history—The Historical Institutes—The scientific spirit enters historic and geographic studies—The Brazilian Institute of Geography and Statistics—Foreign cultural missions—The social sciences—Sociology and ethnology in Brazil—Science and philosophy—Positivism—The philosophy of Farias Brito

IN AN EXTREMELY BRIEF SUMMARY, through thirty crowded pages, we have watched the development of our literary history, its first manifestations in the colonial period, following the model of the Portuguese, although at times there is evidence of American thought; the lively flowering, unequal and without order during the nineteenth century, the more disciplined, rich, and fruitful production of the twentieth century. What immediately attracts our attention in the history of Brazilian literature is not only the continuity of the literary movement, through three centuries, the growing variety of talents of the first class in each one of these periods, but the vitality and strength with which the originality of our national literature asserts itself progressively in the different phases of its evolution, and especially beginning with the romantic movement. In no other activity of the mind has the intelligence of Brazil expanded with so much vigor, nor manifested so great a power of invention. We may even consider literature as the most characteristic Brazilian product, the least contestable witness of originality on the part of the national spirit. If we compare, however, the progress in this domain of activity with that of the sciences, what strikes us in this contrast, established even in the most summary analysis, is the disconcerting impression of the disproportion between literary progress and scientific development which, in a rigorous sense, began to take place only in the nineteenth century, and then with its attention turned only to the realm of the natural sciences and with extreme slowness. This preponderance of the literary spirit over the scientific spirit has been so marked and so persistent in the whole history of our culture that there have not been lacking critics who have attributed it, after a superficial examination, to a particular form of the mind related to ethnic and therefore biological factors, as if it were a question of a natural and irremovable lack of aptitude for scientific studies and research, for pure science and speculation. Certainly the Brazilian people, like any other, presents us with a complex of fundamental traits which characterize it and which reflect upon their institutions and tendencies, marking them with a special stamp. But whatever may be the traits or the salient facts which can be pointed out as peculiar to a race, they are susceptible of being modified with transformations of social life. The variations of mentality which they make up are related in the first place to social variations and given a constant relation between these two types of change, we cannot deliver a sentence on the lack of aptitude of a people for any branch whatever of human activity except in the face of its attitudes and reactions in a new social state created by the contacts of different cultures. Moreover, this slowness of scientific progress and our backward state in this field comes, it is easy to prove, from political, economic, and cultural factors which have contributed powerfully to create a social atmosphere that for a long time was unfavorable to the cultivation of science and which has driven our activity into other directions.

During the whole colonial period, from the discovery to the coming of Dom João VI to Brazil, there were in fact not recorded in the history of our culture anything but sporadic and isolated manifestations—of strangers who, seizing advantage of the opportunity of their stay in the colony, took the inhabitants and the natural wealth of the country as the object of their study; and of some exceptional figures of Brazilians who had lived outside the country, and in the home country and later in the colony devoted themselves to scientific activity. Neither the foreign savants who collected in American countries the material for their work nor the eminent Brazilians who, educated in Europe, accomplished work of scientific value abroad exercised any influence whatever upon the development of a scientific attitude and methods in Brazil. It is in the Dutch period, or more exactly, under the government of Maurice of Nassau (1637–1644)— "a brilliant parenthesis" opened by the arrival and closed by the departure of the Flemish prince—that there was inaugurated in colonial Brazil a period of scientific activity, carried on by a group of scientific men that the Count of Nassau brought to Pernambuco. This important mission, the first which he brought to Brazil, arrived in Recife in 1637, a century after the beginning of the populating of the newly discovered lands by the Portuguese. In this mission there was, among other men, Wilhelm Piso, a physician of Amsterdam and the founder, along with J. Bontius, of colonial medicine, and Georg Marggraf, a German naturalist. These authors left us in their *Historia Naturalis Brasiliae* (first edition, 1648; second edition, 1658) a work of the first importance for its wealth of data and observation, and the most notable that was published on medicine, and the flora and fauna of the country in the colonial period. If, as a result of his observations upon the chief diseases in northern Brazil and the therapeutic action of medicinal plants, Wilhelm Piso—the first physician who treated ancylostomiasis, who indicated the transmission of snake poison by the teeth of the serpent, and who made examination of tissues in Brazil—is justly considered the creator of the Brazilian study of disease, the glory of having laid the foundations of natural history goes to G. Marggraf, who collected, drew, and described all the plants and animals which he met in his numerous scientific explorations. So enormous was the bulk of the material collected in these expeditions, even into neighboring captaincies, that according to

Alfredo de Carvalho, "the study of the count, the museums of two universities, and various private collections (among them that of Sebasch, afterward so famous) were enriched with them and for more than a century science was nourished on this provision." The scientific activities of G. Marggraf were not, however, restricted to the field of natural sciences. In the observatory installed between the years of 1637 and 1644 by the Prince of Nassau—the oldest of the Southern Hemisphere—he carried on important meteorological and astronomical observations from which there have remained for us, preserved by Barleus,[1] only the calculations relating to the solar eclipse of November 12, 1640; and he wrote a topographical and meteorological treatise on Brazil, published in an appendix to the second edition (1658) of the great work in which there figures in eight books out of the twelve which make it up, the enormous scientific spoil collected by the German savant.

It is certain that Judaic-Dutch Recife became, in the period of the occupation, as Gilberto Freyre says, "the greatest center of intellectual differentiation in the colony, which the Catholic effort in the direction of integration was trying to preserve intact as against the new sciences and new languages. With Count Maurice of Nassau, there arose in the midst of the cashew trees the first astronomical observatory in America. A botanical garden and a zoological garden rose among the gitiranas and the mango trees, where formerly there had been only crab holes. There appeared Piso and Marggraf, the first scientific eyes to study the Indians, the trees, and the animals of Brazil; pastors of the religion of Calvin preaching new forms of Christianity; Franz Post painting plantation houses, the thatch-covered huts of Indians, the Negro shacks, cashew trees along the rivers, Negroes carrying dirty linen on their heads; Pieter Post, tracing the plans of a great city of high mansions and of deep canals through which one could pass in a canoe as in Holland." [2] But these little scattered foci, the last witnesses of the great flame of the spirit of culture which Maurice of Nassau left, were not slow in being extinguished, on the one hand by the short duration of the Dutch rule, which had been maintained by force, and on the other by the growing hostilities directed against the invaders, heretics, in whom the colonists came to see the enemies of their country and of religion. The spirit of integration in the Catholic and Portuguese direction was to end by dissolving differences, attracting the population of Pernambuco once more into the orbit of Iberian influence. Marggraf died in 1644, in the very year of the retirement of the Prince of Nassau to Holland, where four years afterward W. Piso published the first edition of a notable work in which the Flemish physician and the German naturalist had collaborated. The great agitation which followed the departure of Nassau in May, 1644; the wars against the Batavians, defeated in Europe by England and in America by the Brazilians, in the two battles of Guararapes, and finally, the capitulation in 1654 of the invaders, who gave up their conquest, left the whole civilization which the Flemish prince had tried to build on the soil of Portuguese America completely unarmed and on the point of breaking up entirely. "Of the work of the administrator nothing survived," writes Capistrano de Abreu; "his palaces and

---

[1] Gaspar Barleus, *História dos feitos recentement practicados durante oito anos no Brasil e noutras partes sob o govêrno do ilustríssimo João Maurício, Conde de Nassau, etc.*, translation and notes by Cláudio Brandão (Rio: Serviço Gráfico do Ministério da Educação, 1940).

[2] Gilberto Freyre, *Sobrados e mucambos* (São Paulo: Comp. Editora Nacional, 1936—Brasiliana, Vol. 64, p. 272).

gardens were consumed and devoured in the fire and blood of the following year; his artistic collections went to enrich various establishments in Europe, and the Americanists are studying them;" and the books of Barleus, Piso, and Marggraf which "because of their patronage attained a height which no Portuguese or Brazilian work can be compared with in colonial times, appear even to have been little read in Brazil in spite of being written in Latin, the universal language of the time, so insignificant are the remains which we find of them." [3]

Down to the nineteenth century, no other missions of foreign savants came to Brazil; and if among the visitors of colonial Brazil some showed an interest in the nature of our country, like the Frenchman Dampier (Bahia, 1704), La Barbinnais (1714), and Bougainville, who was in Santa Catarina in 1763 and in Rio in 1765, their observations did not in general involve anything more than that feeling for the picturesque expressed by travelers who are amazed by tropical landscapes. A taste for traveling, the spirit of adventure, the interest in the newly discovered land in America and in Asia stimulated these isolated undertakings of foreigners who left no vestige of their passage through the colony, whence passing naturalists, however—a Ph. Commerson (1767) and Joseph Banks (1768), who spent three weeks in Guanabara—sent respectively to the Museum of Natural History of Paris and to London herbariums collected in Rio de Janeiro. The colony continued to be alien to the scientific revolution which was going on in the old world and sunk in the thick obscurity in which the home country was, in this respect, wrapped, like the whole peninsula "outside the isothermic line of this revolution." Over the whole surface of the peninsula, considers Rui Barbosa, "scientific instruction did not exist. In the middle of this century (the eighteenth) there was not in Spain a practical chemist. More than a hundred and fifty years after Harvey, they were still ignorant there of the circulation of the blood. The University of Salamanca in 1771 had refused public entry, disdainfully and in no uncertain terms, to the discoveries of Newton, Gassendi, and Descartes, because they could not be harmonized with Aristotle. In Portugal, university studies were vegetating under theological routine, just as the colleges were monopolies of the religious orders and also the rare primary schools which were nothing more, we may say, than diocesan establishments under the direction of the clergy and the inspection of the bishops." [4] Teaching, subject to the administration of the clergy and transferred in 1555 to the hands of the Jesuits, without doubt the best humanists of the time, was characterized by the teaching of grammar, rhetoric, and scholasticism, and was reduced on the higher level to theological and juridical letters, beside the medicine of Galen, remaining almost completely closed for more than two centuries to the study of experimental science. It was a whole cultural system erected for the training of priests, men of letters, and scholars, and which, developing in its autonomous orbit, resisted the powerful attraction of the new methods and progressive tendencies which were agitating the civilized world. If to this cultural atmosphere, satisfied with the purely bookish and dogmatic forms and the controversies inspired by the old scholastic spirit, we add the policy of isolation adopted by Portugal with relation to the colony, which reached the point of depriving

[3] Capistrano de Abreu, *Capítulos da história colonial* (Rio, 1907), pp. 90-91.

[4] Rui Barbosa, *O Centenário do Marquês de Pombal*, speech given May 8, 1882, in the Imperial Theater of D. Pedro II.

it of all communication and commerce with the nations of Europe; [5] the regime oppressing liberty of thought and of criticism and the desperate tenacity with which the home country suffocated all the manifestations of living culture in the country and all the means of its propagation, we will have the sad picture of the almost invincible obstacles which rose in Brazil, preventing the penetration of the critical and scientific spirit and the spread of the study of the sciences of observation.

In this long period of obscurantism, interrupted only by the breach which was opened in it by the administration of the Flemish prince, the sterile discussions, precious to the point of the ridiculous, in which the intelligence of literary academies which followed one another in the colonies continued to split hairs, we do not meet any rigorous examination of ideas and of facts. Nature in the variety of its landscapes and aspects was rather a savage force, defying the boldness of adventurers and explorers, a spectacle with which poets and men of letters entertained themselves, or a springboard whence the mystic imagination threw itself into the infinite. Rarely did it appear to the eyes of the Brazilians as an inexhaustible field of observation awakening their scientific curiosity. For tens of literary academies which followed one another in the colony, one does not meet until 1770 even a single academy of sciences. The first of this kind, the Academia Científica, which was founded in 1771 in Rio de Janeiro, three years after the reform of the University of Coimbra by the Marquis de Pombal, had only an ephemeral duration (1771–1779), and with its activity reduced to the creation of a botanical garden on the Morro do Castelo and to some undertakings of a practical character and to interchange with foreign academies, it did not exercise any influence upon the evolution of Brazilian thought. Although it proposed to make studies of pure science and of applied science, uniting in the same society those who claimed to devote themselves to physics, as well as those who studied medicine, surgery, pharmacy, and agriculture, the Scientific Academy begun by the viceroy Marquis de Lavradio [6]—forerunner of a National Academy of Medicine and the Brazilian Academy of Sciences—did not meet in the variety of its objects nor in the amplitude of its plan of action sufficient means to assure the continuity of its existence and its

[5] This policy of segregation adopted by Portugal which "always sought to prevent the contact of foreigners with the people of Brazil," was never expressed with such severity as in that famous message sent June 2, 1800, by the government of the mother country to its representative in Para, only eight years before the arrival of the prince royal in Brazil, and in which the coming of the great Humboldt to the land of Brazil was prohibited. "It is not, then, to be wondered at," observed Juliano Moreira, "that the ideas which were current in the civilized world did not penetrate into Brazil. It was stated by Armitage, an English historian who lived here for two decades, that by the policy of Portugal one of the loveliest and most fertile regions of the globe had been deprived of all communication and trade with the other nations of Europe, to such an extent that the admission and residence of foreigners were forbidden there. If the ships of nations allied to Portugal were sometimes allowed to anchor in the ports, their passengers and crew were forbidden to set foot on shore except when accompanied by escorts of soldiers. The result of all this was 'vast general ignorance of what was going on in the world, except what Portugal wanted known.' There was not in all Brazil a single printing press. . . . The condition of the Brazilians," concludes the same historian, "was truly one worthy of sympathy as compared with that of Europeans." Juliano Moreira, "O progresso das ciências no Brasil," in *Anais da Biblioteca Nacional,* 1913, Vol. 35 (Rio: Oficinas Gráficas da Biblioteca Nacional, 1916).

[6] Varnhagen (Viscount of Pôrto Seguro), *História geral do Brasil (antes de sua separação e independência de Portugal)*, 3rd ed., unabridged (Companhia de Melhoramentos de São Paulo, n. d.).

progress. While still a student at Coimbra, Silva Alvarenga of Vila Rica, who had received in Portugal the impression of the current of new ideas, attacked in his satire *O desertor das letras,* the old methods of teaching while he was at the university before the reform of the Marquis de Pombal. Returning to Brazil, to which he brought his taste for science, he founded a scientific society which also had a short duration and was reborn later, in 1786, and restored by the poet with the approval of the Viceroy Luiz de Vasconcelos under the name of Literary Society of Rio de Janeiro. . . . In its broad outlines, stratified in rigid formulae, colonial culture maintained a climate entirely unfavorable to any movement showing an interest in the sciences; and it was not surprising when, even in the home country, in which the reforms of education promoted by the ministry of Dom José produced a true revolution, the natural sciences, looked upon askance as yet, "were like bastards to whom the generosity and clemency of Pombal had given a place to stay and a shelter in that arrogant, literary group of inheritors who made their home in Coimbra. They were sciences of plebeians and were almost unknown as being too recently arrived and lacking in genealogical coats of arms." [7] But a small group of Brazilians who were studying at Coimbra at this time, between 1760 and 1788, and breathed there the new cultural atmosphere, was the first to take advantage of the teaching in the university, reorganized in 1768 by Pombal, who added to the program of the courses, studied natural history and mathematics, established an observatory, created laboratories and museums, and "recognized the dignity of the teaching of science."

If at the dawn of the eighteenth century there stands out in Portugal the extraordinary figure of a Brazilian, Father Bartolomeu Lourenço, who rose above his environment to take part in the first experiments with the aerostat and to whom justice assures in the annals of scientific progress a place among the immortal forerunners of aviation, there arose after 1775, in the twilight of that century, a consummate geographer like Lacerda e Almeida, a Conceição Veloso, and an Alexandre Rodrigues Ferreira, great naturalists, and a mineralogist of the value of José Bonifácio de Andrada e Silva, "the greatest and the most cultivated of the Brazilians of his time." The first, Francisco José de Lacerda e Almeida (São Paulo, 1750), educated at Coimbra around 1776, plunged into the interior on his return to Brazil, "sweeping the territory from west to east, from a southern branch of the Amazon and across the water system of the Paraguay and Paraná," and fixing the coordinates of hundreds of localities. He embarked in 1790 for Lisbon with his notes and maps, which he was to present to the Royal Academy of Sciences, and left in 1796 on a geographic mission to the colonies of Portuguese Africa, where death found him in October, 1798, after he had passed the upper Zambesi, searching for the central region of the African continent. In his *Diário da viagem de Moçambique para os rios de Sena,* published only in 1936, he describes for us the great wealth of data and observation, the great enterprise in which he succumbed and which was attempted by the expedition of which he made a part, almost a century before the glorious exploration (1871) of Livingstone and Stanley to the upper sources of the river Nile. But "the greatest profit for Brazil in the reform of the Marquis de Pombal, beside the Andradas, was," according to Juliano Moreira, "the fact that it produced a naturalist, Alexandre Rodrigues Ferreira" (Bahia, 1756–Lisbon, 1815), a physician of Bahia

[7] In Juliano Moreira, "O progresso das ciências no Brasil," in *Anais da Biblioteca Nacional,* 1913, Vol. 35 (Rio, 1916).

who had come to Brazil charged with making an inventory of the natural wealth of the country, having disembarked in Belem in 1783, and who, by his scientific explorations in the Amazon and by his notable work, above all in the fields of botany and zoology, merited the name of "the Brazilian Humboldt." The author of *Viagem filosófica,* illustrated by colored drawings, and of more than a hundred books and memorials not published even today, he passed through the bitterness not only by knowing they would not be published, but also of seeing his originals and designs and precious collections of natural history requisitioned by General Junot in 1808 on the request of Geoffroy de Saint-Hilaire; they were transported from the Museum of Ajuda to that of Paris, and the French naturalist used them, relying in his research on the work of the great Brazilian naturalist. The spoil which under these official orders G. de Saint-Hilaire seized in Portugal on the occasion of the invasion of the French troops was not limited to the material collected by Alexandre Rodrigues Ferreira. On August 29, 1808, in the same two-wheeled carriage in which he rode to the Royal Press of Lisbon, he took with him 554 plates belonging to the notable *Flora Fluminense* of Brother José Mariano da Conceição Veloso (Minas, 1742–1811), a victim, like the naturalist of Bahia, "of a lack of comprehension of the community in which they lived," writes Artur Neiva, "and of the unheard of usurpation which scholars of such great value practiced upon them." [8] Of the Brazilians who studied at the University of Coimbra after its reform by the Marquis de Pombal, the greatest of all, José Bonifácio, a notable mineralogist, "the Portuguese Andrada" whom Bruhns mentions among savants of universal reputation, companions of Humboldt, carried on an intense scientific activity in European countries, published memoirs on the mines of Portugal, and occupied the chair of metallurgy at the University of Coimbra.[9] However, on his return to Brazil,

[8] See on the eminent Franciscan friar, Brother José Mariano da Conceição Veloso, the notice published in 1868 by José Saldanha da Gama in the *Revista* of the Instituto Histórico, and the excellent study of Tomaz Borgmeier, published under the title of "Frades Naturalistas," in *Vozes de Petrópolis,* 1919.

[9] The preference of José Bonifácio (Santos, 1767) for natural science was shown at once, at the University of Coimbra, to which his father sent him to study law: besides the law course, he attended classes in philosophy, taking his degree in both schools. The love of the experimental sciences had appeared early in the young Paulista. Scarcely had he finished his course when he entered the Academy of Sciences of Lisbon, and in 1790 undertook a study tour of the leading scientific centers of Europe, with the aim of attending courses given by the great teachers of the time. In Paris he listened, among others, to Chaptal and Fourcroy, followers of Lavoisier, and Haüy, the founder of mineralogy in France; and, in Freiburg, where he went on the advice of the School of Mines, of Paris, he studied with Abraham Werner, the "founder of systematic mineralogy, which he separated from general chemistry, as being a discipline worthy of special study." From Freiburg, José Bonifácio, a fellow student now of Humboldt's, in the famous Sâone school, went to visit the mines of Tyrol, of Styria, and Corinthia; in Pavia he attended the lectures of Volta, the inventor of the voltaic pile, and after studying the geological structure of the Euganian Mountains in Turin, he went to Great Britain, where he visited Priestley, the rival of Lavoisier, and then Scandinavia, putting himself into contact with the greatest workers in the field of chemistry and mineralogy. In the mineralogical investigations which he carried out in Sweden and Denmark, on the suggestion of Torbern Bergman, one of the great founders of mineralogy, whom he met in Upsala, he discovered four new species (the Petalite, the Spodumene, the Cryolite, and the Scapolite), "besides eight minerals which could be included as varieties in species already described by his predecessors or contemporaries." In his dazzling youth, writes Euclides da Cunha, "he was a kind of minister plenipotentiary of the mind and heart of our new nationality, accredited to all the capitals of the Old World." Returning from Portugal, after ten years of scientific

the agitated political life of the time drew him away from sciences, to the progress of which no one could have made a greater contribution, in order to make of him one of the great builders of the nation.

It is, however, with the installation of the Portuguese court in Brazil that, properly speaking, the history of our culture begins, for, until this time, one cannot find anything but sporadic manifestations of exceptional figures, educated in Portugal and under foreign influence in the eighteenth century and sent, some of them, to Brazil as foreign functionaries to carry on studies and observations of a scientific character. The first measure of a character not merely commercial and political, but cultural, taken by Dom João VI, was doubtless the opening of the ports of the colony to foreign nations. Under the inspiration of the Viscount de Cairú, whom he met in Bahia, the prince regent upon disembarking in Salvador signed the decree of February 28, 1808, opening the ports of Brazil to navigation and to foreign commerce, and in consequence, facilitating our intellectual relations with European countries and opening channels through which the influences of different cultures could penetrate and be felt. This act would be enough to clothe with importance even from the point of view of our own culture, the arrival of Dom João VI, who was to open new horizons to the life of the country in all respects. But it was not only this. It is also in the administration of Dom João VI (1808–1821) that there arose the first institutions of a cultural character, among others, the Royal Press, the Public Library, the Royal Garden, later, in 1819, to be called the Royal Botanical Garden, and the Royal Museum, in addition to the first higher schools destined for the training of surgeons and military engineers. To the King of Portugal there belongs the glory of having laid the corner stone of great institutions like the National Library and the National Museum, created under the title of the Royal Museum, by decree of June 6, 1818, and of the schools for higher professional training, with the foundation of the School of Surgery in Bahia, instituted by the Royal Letter of February 18, 1808, and transformed in 1815 into a college of medicine and surgery; of the Academy of Medicine and Surgery created by the decree of April 1, 1813, and of the Military Academy from which there resulted in 1858, as a result of successive transformations, the Central School of Rio de Janeiro. It cannot be said that Dom João VI, with all these magnificent initiatives, had begun in a calculating fashion a policy of cultural dislocation, bringing up into first place the teaching of the sciences hitherto almost entirely unknown and giving to economics and to technology primacy over literary teaching. What the King of Portugal was aiming at directly was above all, in creating these schools and institutions, to equip the colony in which the seat of the monarchy was installed not only with surgeons and engineers that were indispensable to a sanitary and military defense and who could no longer come

---

wanderings, he carried on research and wrote monographs on the mines of this country; and, turning from the field of pure science to its applications, he efficiently carried out important technical activities as general superintendent of the mines and metals of the realm, to which position he was appointed by a Royal Letter of May 18, 1801, and in the direction of the works of Mondego. First professor of the chair of metallurgy in the University of Coimbra, founder of chemical and mineral sciences in Lisbon, José Bonifácio resigned on August 2, 1816, at the age of forty-nine. His career in the sciences was, as one can see, a constant rise, and the gravity and solidity of his scientific work did not in the least detract from his social and political concerns and the charm of his imagination and style. Cf. Euclides da Cunha, *A Margem da história*, 3rd ed. (Pôrto: Chardron, 1922), pp. 235-236.

from the home country, but also with institutions which would be capable of transforming the great village of Rio de Janeiro into the new capital of the Portuguese Empire. But certainly he gave great encouragement, which might have been definitive but which turned out to be only transitory, under the pressure of various causes, among which not the least was the prolonged action of later events, forcing questions of order and of security upon the attention of the government, from the time of the struggles for national independence down to the beginning of the second Empire.

All these reforms undertaken by Dom João VI—the creator of institutions in Brazil —were not, in fact, sufficient to produce profound transformations in the colonial mentality of the country, which continued to live a life crystallized around old centers of culture. The instruction which was given in the colleges retained, in general, a strictly literary character; and the scanty network, the links of which were the making of the school system in process of formation, was constituted by institutions of middle education (colleges or aulas) almost all still directed by Fathers, and upon the coast and the plateau it did not collect more than a small number of candidates for the Military Academy, the medical and surgical schools, and later, after 1827, those of law. All education, built upon a basis of these courses in the colleges, the seminaries, and in the shade of the convent, was still a centripetal force which attracted men toward an all-absorbing center of interest—literature, eloquence, and erudition. The new institutions, isolated and dispersed, which in the time of Dom João VI came to constitute the superstructure of the cultural system, were unstable, without deep roots in that organization in which nothing was created to make basic reforms, nothing to draw us away from the preoccupations of our literary education and make our culture turn in the direction of philosophic and scientific studies. "There is nothing more illustrious than the Greek mathematicians," we could say with Cicero (*Tusculanian Discourses*, VIII, 6). "But we have limited our studies to the utility of measuring and of calculus. On the other hand, we devote ourselves too early to eloquence; for us a man is not a scholar in the first place and an orator in the second; science comes only in second place." This contrast between critical and disinterested thought and Latin rhetoric continues to dominate the whole history of our culture, over which at this time there still fell the dark shadow of the influence of the sixteenth century in the Iberian Peninsula, in which, according to Antero de Quental, "a generation of philosophers, learned men and creative artists, was followed by a vulgar crowd of scholars without criticism, of academicians, of imitators." For this reason, the instructions written by José Bonifácio had no influence whatever. These instructions were sent by the Junta of São Paulo on October 9, 1821, to the São Paulo representatives elected to the Congress of Lisbon, suggesting to them among other measures those of the reorganization of secondary and higher education, and the creation of a university in São Paulo, with the faculty of philosophy, in which the physical and natural sciences and pure and applied mathematics would begin to form an obligatory part of the curriculum in the national plan for education. The chair of physics was not created until 1832. In the medical faculties —the two centers in which that science began to be taught—in spite of the fact that the ports of Brazil were opened by Dom João VI in 1808 and books were allowed by Pedro I to come in, in 1821, the penetration of works of science went on slowly and very backwardly as compared with the rapid invasion of foreign letters imported especially from France. Romanticism was not to be slow in arousing even to the state of agitation an intellectual movement which neither scientific thought nor the critical spirit had ever produced to the same degree or in the same manner during the whole century. In place of a faculty of philosophy and of sciences in accordance with the old suggestions of José Bonifácio, the generation with the juridical spirit, educated in Coimbra, that had gone back to the traditions of the days before Pombal and was more concerned to give a political and juridical structure to the nation, created in 1827, with the Law Schools of São Paulo and Olinda, the two centers of jurisconsults and lawyers, orators and government men.

Meanwhile, the creation of the Royal Museum, of the Botanical Garden, and the medical schools was to stimulate the development of studies of botany and zoology. The tropical world with its extraordinary wealth in vegetable and animal species, opening like a vast field of observation, could not fail to attract the attention of the phytologists of the country and abroad. It was, in fact, through the natural sciences that our scientific culture began; in no other field did a larger number of research workers appear in Brazil; nowhere else did the contributions of Brazilians to the progress of scientific studies acquire greater importance. But to this end there must have contributed not only the immense wealth of our forests and fields in vegetable species and the great incentive of the numerous foreign naturalists who were attracted from everywhere by nature in Brazil and traveled over Brazil in all directions, stirring up interest by their research, but also the creation of the Royal Museum [10] and of the chairs of

---

[10] The Royal Museum, now the National Museum, was one of the things started by Dom João VI, who founded it by the decree of June 6, 1818, following the suggestion of Tomaz Antônio de Vila Nova Portugal. As early as the eighteenth century, Dom Luiz de Vasconcelos, twelfth viceroy of Brazil (1779–1790), had founded the House of Natural History, which became better known as the House of the Birds and was short lived. The Royal Museum was originally located in the building now occupied by the National Archives in Campo de Santana, with the materials given by Dom João VI, and made up of objets d'art, a collection of pictures and another of mineralogy, bought from Werner, the learned professor of Freiburg with whom José Bonifácio studied. Later, in 1823, the mineralogical collection of José Bonifácio was added to the National Museum, which was enriched in the years that followed by various collections in the field of zoology, gifts of foreign naturalists traveling in Brazil, like Langsdorff, Natterer, and von Sellow, to whom the minister of Dom Pedro I made an appeal for their aid to the struggling museum. In the middle of the nineteenth century, the National Museum, to which there had come by acquisition, exchange, and gift various mineral, botanical and zoological collections, was considered the most important in South America; and its library, founded during the administration of César Burlamaqui (1847–1866), had begun with about 3,000 volumes, to become at the end of the nineteenth century, one of the richest in works relating to the natural sciences. In charge of the museum there were men of value like Brother Custódio Alves Serrão (1825–1847), to whom is due the first important change in the museum, by the regulation of February 3, 1842; Brother Alemão (1866–1874), aided by Ladislau Neto, who succeeded him as director, and, more recently, Batista Lacerda (1895–1915), another important reformer, and Bruno Lôbo, Artur Neiva, and Roquete Pinto. In his long and fruitful administration (1874–1893), Ladislau Neto made important changes, such as the public lectures that were often honored by the presence of the emperor; the publication of the Archives of the National Museum, a review created by the decree of March 28, 1876, the fifth volume of which, in 1881, was devoted to *Flora Fluminense,* by Brother Conceição Veloso; and the founding of the Laboratory of Experimental Physiology, in which the first experiments in physiology in South America were made by Louis Country and Batista Lacerda. The building of the National Museum, which since 1892 has been located in the former imperial palace of the Quinta da Boa Vista, was remodeled and enlarged by the addition of three stories during the directorship of Roquete Pinto (1926–1935), who in 1931 was the source of the new

botany, and the very character of natural history, which, having as its first object the observation of living beings, describing and classifying them, is of all sciences the most accessible and the one which, although it imposes the same rigor of observation, the same exactitude in the analysis of the facts, does not require the same intellectual effort, the same power of reasoning, and the same capacity of the creative mind and of abstraction. "Natural history, principally in its systematic aspect," writes Miguel Osório de Almeida,[11] "requiring so little of the faculty of reasoning, is one of the sciences most within reach of those who, without having, through lack of vocation or general instruction, a high capacity to accompany abstract ideas, are endowed with a great love for science and a sincere desire to serve it." The tradition, initiated at the end of the eighteenth century by two eminent Brazilian naturalists, Brother José Mariano da Conceição Veloso of Minas and the physician Alexandre Rodrigues Ferreira of Bahia, and by Manuel de Arruda Câmara of Paraíba (1752–1810), author of *Centúrias Pernambucanas,* was continued by a group of first-class botanists, like Brother Leandro do Sacramento (1779–1829, a Pernambucan friar who introduced the teaching of botany into Brazil and gave a scientific organization to the Botanical Garden; Brother Custódio Alves Serrão, director of the Imperial Museum from 1828 to 1847; the councilor Francisco Freire Alemão, teacher of botany in the Medical School and "the greatest botanist of South America," who also directed the National Museum from 1866 to his death in 1874; and João Barbosa Rodrigues—the most remarkable botanist that Brazil possessed after Freire Alemão—director of the Botanical Garden from 1889 to his death in 1909, and the author of *Sertum Palmarum,* a monumental work in two volumes, in folio, to which he owes his scientific reputation, in studies of his specialty in the botanical field. If among Brazilians these were the outstanding figures in scientific investigation of our flora, in which field Freire Alemão and Barbosa Rodrigues attained an indisputable authority, many others stand out in Brazilian botany, such as, to cite only a few names of most importance, Joaquim Monteiro Caminhoá (Bahia, 1836–1896), author of the great *Botânica médica e geral* (1877); Saldanha da Gama (1839–1905); Kuhlmann, our greatest specialist in grasses; Adolfo Ducke; Alvaro da Silveira, who wrote *A Flora e as serras mineiras* (1908), and Brother Hoehne, director of the Osvaldo Cruz Gardens in Butatã and of the forest experimental station of the Alto da Serra in São Paulo, and with a total of contributions, as Artur Neiva reminds us, of more than one hundred new species described.

---

reforms by which the traditional institution "enlarged its field of activity in research, in the study and popularization of natural phenomena." It was then divided into nine technical departments, grouped into five sections: (1) Mineralogy and Geopetrography; Stratigraphy and Paleontology, under the direction of A. Betim Pais Leme; (2) Botany, with two divisions, under Prof. Alberto Sampaio; (3) Zoology (vertebrates and invertebrates), for which Miranda Ribeiro was responsible; (4) Anthropology and Ethnography, under the direction of Heloísa Tôrres, now director of the museum; and (5) that of Natural History, created by Roquete Pinto, who added to the scientific activities of the museum the function of education, equipping it to be a useful instrument of education. (Cf. Paulo Roquete, "O Museu Nacional e a educação brasileira," in *Jornal do Comércio,* Rio, July 10 and 11, 1933.)

[11] Miguel Osório de Almeida, "A Mentalidade científica no Brasil," lecture in the auditorium of the *Jornal do Comércio,* Rio de Janeiro, Aug. 26, 1920, printed in the *Folha Médica,* Rio, Sept. 1920.

In the field of zoology, if the progress was not as remarkable as in the equally vast field of botany, there were not lacking Brazilians who distinguished themselves with original research in almost all of its departments. In the first half of the past century, writes Artur Neiva, "among those who worked most on the botany and zoology of Brazil, particularly that of Pará and Maranhão, there figures Antônio Correia de Lacerda, author of a voluminous and important production which he left unpublished and the manuscripts of which are still, for the most part, preserved in the National Library." With him there begins a line of eminent investigators, among whom there stand out on our first examination Carlos Moreira, one of our greatest zoologists and our greatest specialist in crustaceans; Adolfo Lutz (1855–1940), who made important contributions both in the field of pure zoology and that of medical zoology, throwing light on problems relating to the systematic description of insects and to the biology of various groups; Rodolfo von Ihering, who published the *Fauna do Brasil* and the *Dicionário da Fauna do Brasil*—the only zoological dictionary which we possess; and more recently, C. de Melo Leitão, of the National Museum, with important original works on arachnids; and O. de Oliveira Pinto, ornithologist, now director of the Department of Zoology of São Paulo. Among the zoologists born in Brazil, perhaps the greatest of all, Alípio Miranda Ribeiro, a consummate ichthyologist and one of the companions of Rondon, "has done great work in practically all the fields of zoology, always with the same brilliance, and has covered practically the whole country in his scientific expeditions." [12] However, the part which foreign naturalists who lived among us had in the development of these studies has been really notable; and if any objection may be made to these research men who have rendered such great services to the cause of science, it is that they did not make an effort to create a school and to train disciples. Among the foreign collaborators who devoted themselves to the study of the flora and fauna of the country, there stand out for their original contributions Teodoro Peckolt (Pechern, 1822), who came to Brazil in 1847 and was decorated by Dom Pedro II for his services in the field of botany; C. A. Guilherme Schwacke (Alfeld, 1848–1904), who covered between 1873 and 1891 various states of the north and south, and was a professor of botany in the School of Pharmacy of Ouro Prêto beginning in 1891; Emílio Goeldi, founder of the Museum of Pará, now called the Goeldi Museum, and author of *Os maníferos do Brasil* (1893) and of the *Aves do Brasil*; Hermann von Ihering (Keil, 1850), founder of the Museu Paulista of which he was director from 1894 to 1915, and who, carrying on research in practically all the fields of zoology, became in his specialty (molluscs) "one of the greatest authorities of the world"; A. F. Marie Glaziou (France, 1833), who lived among us for thirty-four years (1861–1895), builder of the Garden of Acclimatization of the Quinta da Boa Vista, and of the Passeio Público, and botanist of the Cruls Committee of the plateau, of whose collection (22,770 examples of our flora) a part figures in the National Museum (the Glaziou Herbarium); Alberto Löfgren (Stockholm, 1854–1918), who came to Brazil in 1874, botanist for fifteen years of the Geographic and Geological Commission of São Paulo, and later of the Committee on the Drought, and one of the collaborators of Pacheco Leão; and above all for his competence, and for unrivaled services to science, Fritz

[12] See "Esbôço geral da fauna brasileira," by Alípio Miranda Ribeiro, in *Recenseamento do Brasil* (September 1, 1922), Vol 1, Introduction, (Rio: Statistical Printing Office, 1922), pp. 232-275.

Müller, the most notable observer of nature in our country,[13] "the prince of observers," in the opinion of Darwin, and certainly one of the greatest naturalists of the century.

The seeds sown in this field of studies germinated; and if we still lack great aquariums, gardens, and zoological stations, to which we have never known how to give adequate organization, we already do have botanical gardens and nurseries, besides museums equipped with splendid collections and growing more adapted to the function which is theirs as centers of research, of promoting the progress of the natural sciences. But in the history of the work carried on by Brazilians and foreigners resident in Brazil in order to acquire knowledge of the flora and fauna of the country, it is not possible to forget the extraordinary contribution which was made by foreign naturalists, especially Germans, Englishmen, and Frenchmen, who in isolation or in scientific expeditions replaced the missionary and the bandeirante in revealing the country and our natural wealth. "They were," writes Euclides da Cunha, "strange names—Mawe, Koster, Waterton—forerunners of others more illustrious, all of them nationalized among us by the affection with which they looked upon the portentous nature of our country." Among these elect figures who, according to Euclides da Cunha, "jumped from one point to another of the coast, and went to discover the wealth of a nature that was unequaled, an immense page of natural history which we have not been able to read," [14] the greatest of all, Martius (1794–1869), who came accompanied by Spix in the nuptial train of the Princess Leopoldina, arrived July 15, 1817, at the city of Rio de Janeiro. These two young Bavarian naturalists, Martius, a physician and botanist, and Spix, a zoologist, had been appointed by the King of Bavaria to form part of the scientific expedition which in Vienna joined the royal train of the archduchess, who had become engaged to Dom Pedro, the heir to the throne of Portugal, and later first Emperor of

[13] Of all the foreign naturalists who settled in Brazil, none, we can affirm, was superior to Fritz Müller in the rightness of methods of analysis, in almost instinctive power of observation of facts, and in creative interpretation. Coming to Brazil as a result of the movement of 1842, when he was barely thirty, the young physician and naturalist from Germany lived from 1852 on in the county of Blumenau (Santa Catarina), where he died in 1897, having lived forty-five years, or almost half a century in Brazil. A field naturalist of the National Museum, and one of the most illustrious of its staff as long as the monarchy lasted, he was dismissed from his position, which was only partially a salaried one, in 1890, immediately after the proclamation of the Republic, when he had given about thirty-eight years to the service of science and the country. The first important contributions in the field of Indian archaeology were brought from the Amazon Valley to the National Museum by Ferreira Pena and by the German scholar. Among his scientific contributions, one of the most important, if not the greatest, was the discovery—published in the fourth volume of the Archives of the National Museum, in 1881—of a crustacean "of tiny size, but curious form, *Elpidium bromeliarum,* described from examples collected from bromeliaceous or similar waters." The discoverer of the law that ontogeny recapitulates phylogeny, which Haeckel called the fundamental law of biogenetics, Fritz Müller defended the doctrine of Darwin in his famous book, *Für Darwin* (1864), with the material that he collected in Brazil in his researches on crustaceans. He published in 1879 another book which led to lively debates in the world of science: "On a remarkable case of mimicry among the Ituna and Thyridia butterflies," in which he, in part, attacked the theory of Bates on mimicry, a theory which the great English naturalist based on his studies of Amazonian butterflies. Darwin called him "the prince of naturalists," and Haeckel, who wrote his biography, considered him a hero of science, for his unselfishness and his spirit of sacrifice, which led him, through sheer moral nobility, to refuse the funds put at his disposal by a world-wide subscription opened by scientific societies with the object of supporting the great scholar.

[14] Euclides da Cunha, *À Margem da história,* 3rd ed. (Pôrto: Chardron, 1922).

Brazil. In about three years these two pioneers traversed practically the whole territory of the country, working over it from north to south to a distance of 4,000 kilometers, and from east to west to make a total of 6,500 kilometers traversed, and accomplishing one of the most notable tasks of study and research which is recorded by the history of scientific expeditions. The material which the great botanist collected in his long excursion over Brazil amounted to 300,000 examples, in which there figured a collection of 7,000 species and varieties of plants, with exact indications and accompanied by drawings made *in loco* by the two naturalists. Returning to his country when he was still little more than twenty-six years old, he planned the publication of a great work, of which he drew up the plans in 1825, on all of the flora of this part of the American continent. The founder of the *Flora brasiliensis,* a monumental work of which the first part came out in 1829, and which, replanned in 1840, required sixty-six years for publication of its 130 parts, was able to initiate and to advance the execution of this grandiose enterprise, in the collaboration of which it was necessary to obtain the assistance of sixty-seven botanists and of most of the civilized countries of the world. On the occasion of his death in 1868, there had already been printed forty-six parts of the present *Flora brasiliensis,* for the publication of which Dom Pedro de Alcântara, the son of Dona Leopoldina, made a contribution, and which was carried out by Eichler (1868–1887) and Urban (1887–1895), his successors in the bold enterprise. The fundamental work for the study of systematic botany, the *Flora* of Martius, "the greatest work yet published on botany," embraces in its 130 parts and 40 volumes *in folio,* illustrated with 3,000 engravings, 20,000 Brazilian species described, of which not less than 5,939 were new to science.

But before Martius and Spix, there had already been in Brazil, at the beginning of the nineteenth century, the savant Humboldt, and the German naturalist Prince of Wied-Neuwied (1782–1867), who, in the short period of two years (1815–1817) traversed the States of Rio, Espírito Santo, Bahia, and Minas Gerais, studying principally our birds and mammals. He offered part of his herbarium, composed of 650 specimens, to Martius, who arrived in our country in the same year in which the prince of zoology was returning to Europe after his long excursion. In the work of this illustrious naturalist, a passionate ornithologist, who wrote one of the most interesting travel books (*Reise nach Brasilien,* 1820), there stands out a notable work in six volumes (*Beiträge zur Naturgeschichte von Brasilien*), in which he treated in a strictly scientific fashion the animal forms which he had had an opportunity to observe. Later there came other Germans like Natterer, who covered the country during a period of eighteen years, gathering and collecting a great amount of material, which is to be found in the Museum of Vienna. No one among French naturalists is dearer to us, because of his constant attitude of sympathy toward Brazil, than A. de Saint-Hilaire (1779–1853), who, arriving in 1816, also before Martius, traversed for six years (1816–1822) almost 15,000 kilometers, exploring from the botanical point of view the states of the center and the south, collected abundant material (about 7,600 specimens) for the Museum of Natural History of Paris, and left in the volumes describing his expeditions one of the most precious documents and the richest in information and facts of scientific value and on the latest period of our colonial life. Among the English, of whom twenty-three names of botanists, herborizers, and authors of travel books are cited in the *Flora* of Martius— and five botanists contributed monographs toward this great work—the first to arrive in

Brazil at the beginning of the nineteenth century was the zoologist Swainson (1817–1818), who published later his book on the birds of Brazil; the botanist George Gardner (1812–1849), who covered Brazil from the south to the extreme north, making botanical studies from 1831 to 1846, and gave his short but fruitful existence of thirty-seven years to scientific investigation; and Charles Darwin, one of the greatest savants of the nineteenth century, who twice visited Brazil—1832 in the ship *Beagle,* anchored in the bay of Rio de Janeiro, where he remained for three months, and four years later (1836) in Recife, for seven days, when he was returning from his voyage of exploration. The most important group of British naturalists who visited us is, however, that of the "Amazonian cycle," as it was called by Adolfo Ducke, and made up of Alfred Russel Wallace and Bates, who came together to Brazil in 1848 in order to attempt to solve the problems related to the origin of species, and the botanist Richard Spruce (1817–1893), who arrived a year later than Wallace in 1849, and when he had finished his botanical works in the Amazonian Forest in 1855 went on to Ecuador and Peru, returning to England in 1864 by the Pacific. It was in Brazil that Wallace and Darwin began the marvelous series of studies which culminated in the intellectual revolution produced by the immortal book *Origin of Species* (1859) by Darwin, and that Bates discovered animal mimicry by studying the Amazonian butterflies. Of the immense material collected by these two naturalists in the Amazon and Rio Negro—and Bates alone collected 14,700 animal species (of which 8,000 were new) and 14,000 insects—the collections of Wallace were lost in the fire which took place on board the ship in which he was returning to his country.

This extraordinary movement of interest in Brazil, which from the beginning of the nineteenth century had awakened the curiosity of foreign naturalists [15] did not,

[15] The history of naturalists' journeys and scientific expeditions in Brazil and their contribution to the progress of the study of nature in our country in all its aspects is still to be written, and it is only recently that the main facts have become clear. Besides the general publications and specialized monographs which some of these enterprises took as their object, the principal thing that has made known the story of these trips and expeditions is the publication of the fundamental works of the foreign explorers in Brazilian editions. The limits of this work do not permit a detailed study nor even a complete listing of the names of those illustrious travelers who honored our country with their visits and, with their works, contributed not only to make Brazil better known in the civilized world, but also, and above all, to extend and enrich our knowledge in the vast field of the flora, fauna, and geology of the country. These works are already listed in catalogues, some of them specialized and limited, like that of Asher on works by Netherlanders, or Constatt's of German works, or J. Branner's on geology, mineralogy, and paleontology, the *Bibliografia mineral e geológica do Brasil,* published by Miguel Arrojado Lisboa, in the *Anis da Escola de Minas,* and the *Bibliografia geográfica* of Rodolfo Garcia, and others of a general character, of works on Brazil, incomplete or limited to a certain period. Among these, the *Dicionário* of Inocêncio Sacramento Blake is antiquated, and the *Biblioteca Brasiliense* of J. Carlos Rodrigues, which with its wealth of notes became, so to speak, a classic, consulted and quoted by European and American bibliographers, contains only works (about 2,600) pertaining to the colonial period. Of all the catalogues of works on Brazil, the most complete up to now is that which the Biblioteca Nacional organized and published in 1881, on the occasion of an exposition of Brazilian history, in which there were listed about 20,000 works, including books, pamphlets, and magazine articles. The most important catalogue of foreign works on Brazil is the *Biblioteca Exótico-Brasileira,* by Alfredo de Carvalho, the first volume of which was published in Rio de Janeiro (Emprêsa Gráfico-Editora, 1929). It is a volume of 400 pages which contains the *first part* of the catalogue of those works, listed by alphabetical order of the authors' names, embracing letters *A, B,* and *C* only and containing about a thousand works catalogued. The publication in this volume of the manuscript

however, remain limited to the field of flora and fauna. With the coming of Dom João VI and the opening of the ports to foreign commerce in 1808, with which the memorable cycle of voyages and scientific expeditions to Brazil began, there came to the country also in a not insignificant number, geographers, geologists, and paleontologists. The taste for travel, notably developed in the nineteenth century, the feeling for the exotic and the thirst for the unknown, attracting foreign scholars from all parts, made of this century one of the periods most fruitful in discoveries and scientific investigations of the natural wealth of Brazil. Geological studies of the soil of Brazil were begun between 1810 and 1820 by Feldner, Varnhagen, and Eschwege, German scholars in the service of the Portuguese government; the first important contribution was made by G. L. von Eschwege, with his three works on geology and mining, published between 1822 and 1833; these studies were taken up again by travelers who traversed Brazil from the period of Independence down to the middle of the second Empire. Among others, D'Orbigny (1823–1833) went to the upper part of Mato Grosso; in 1841, the Dane Peter Claussen, who resided among us for a long time, went to Minas Gerais; the Belgian Parigot to Santa Catarina and the Frenchman Pissis, "who drew our first geological map," to Bahia, Minas Gerais, São Paulo, and Rio; Castelnau (1843–1847) chose for his researches the region of the plateau; and Helmreichen (1846) among the Germans and Allport (1850) among the Englishmen, went, the former to Minas Gerais, the latter to Bahia, to prosecute studies on the geological structure of our land. It was at this time, between 1835 and 1844, that Peter Wilhelm Lund (1801–1880) began to bring together the material, now collected at the Museum of Copenhagen, to determine the geological nature of the plateau, and taking advantage of the vast field open for study of fossils in the valley of the Rio das Velhas, he carried on a memorable series of investigations of grottoes which were to make him one of the most eminent scholars in the domain of paleontology. The celebrated Dane who had been in Brazil before, at the end of 1805, and had then done some research on the flora and fauna of Rio de Janeiro (his first works were on birds without a gullet, the customs of ants, and the shells of eggs of mollusks), finally returned to our country, where he settled in Minas Gerais and never left us again, after having shaken the scientific world with his extraordinary discoveries. If his important work of the glorious ten-year period of his paleontological research effected little advance as far as the geological structure of the land is concerned, Peter Lund did manage to discover in his exploration of about eight hundred grottoes and caves, and among them those of Maquiné and Sumidouro, human bones of the very ancient race of Lagoa Santa, and remains of animals for the most part extinct and gigantic in size, embracing in his researches in general the study of 54 genuses and 114 species, the greater part of them new to science. On May 25, 1880, he passed away in his retirement at Lagoa Santa, where he lived for forty-seven years, one of the greatest scholars who has trodden our land and the first to reveal the secrets of the prehistoric Brazilian world and the founder of paleontology in Brazil, a subject "that is now a century old among us," thanks to his research and discoveries.

---

pages sold to the National Library is all that remains and could be salvaged with the aid of Eduardo Tavares from the immense amount of material collected by Alfredo de Carvalho, who listed, for his projected catalogue, about twelve thousand printed works in twenty-six different languages. (Cf. Heitor Lira, "Biblioteca exótico-brasileira," in *Jornal do Comércio*, Jan. 13, 1930).

In this long period (1822–1865) of scientific activities carried on in the field of mineralogy, zoology, and paleontology, by foreigners traveling through Brazil or residing in our country, like the Scandinavian scholar, the Brazilians and their government remained almost alien, like simple spectators before this immense scientific material which was flowing out of the ports of the country and this crossing and recrossing, from the coast to the interior, of travelers and expeditions. The explorers, attracted by the natural phenomena of our country, came and went without awakening in general, in the regions that they crossed, anything more than a movement of curiosity accompanied by the natural hospitality of the Brazilian. "Nobody perceived them," observed Euclides da Cunha bitterly, nor was disposed to follow their example. Among the Brazilians at this time, no one made a contribution to zoology except a Manuel de Sousa, who went into Amazona (1849–1850), and a Pereira Cabral, who in 1850 carried on a research in Rio Grande do Sul; and the only Brazilian expedition which was organized then, in 1857, on the proposal of the Historical Institute for the scientific exploration of the provinces of the north and of which G. Raja Gabaglia, Gonçalves Dias, Schuch Capanema, Freire Alemão, and César Burlamaqui formed a part, lasted only a short time and did not succeed in producing great results. The ethnographic material collected by Gonçalves Dias in Amazonas figures in the National Museum, and the collections and notes brought together for the geological section were lost in a shipwreck. The researches of Lund, which remained for a long time unknown, were only brought to popular attention and translated later by Leônidas Damásio and Henri Gorceix, the latter under contract in 1875 to organize and carry out the plan for a school of mines in Ouro Prêto. The expedition of Agassiz which the government resolved to help and which between 1865 and 1866 traversed a large part of Brazil, began finally, writes Juliano Moreira, "a new epoch in the study of geology among us." It was then that there were created by several provincial governments, the first geological commissions. The geologist Charles Frederick Hartt, who formed part of this expedition (Thayer Expedition), the cost of which was defrayed by Nathaniel Thayer, also an American, to study the ichthyological fauna of the Amazon basin, and led by the Swiss naturalist Louis Agassiz (1807–1873), was, however, the central figure of this movement of research and of geological studies in Brazil. Returning on his own account to our country in 1867, the American scholar completed the geological reconnaissance of the coast from Rio to Pernambuco; he published in 1870 his *Geology and Physical Geography of Brazil*, the most important work of the past century on Brazilian geology. He visited the Amazonian region in 1870 and 1871 and, charged in 1873 with organizing a general geological service, he succeeded in three years in giving a great stimulus to these studies, maintained after his death in 1876, thanks to Orville Derby and J. C. Branner, the two most illustrious among his disciples and companions in the organization of this service. Interrupted in 1878 by the government, which at that time reorganized the geological and mineralogical section of the National Museum, it was newly reorganized only in 1907 as the Geological and Mineralogical Service of Brazil and, as Juliano Moreira writes, it was confided, "to the highly competent direction of Orville Derby with a staff of indisputable worth, of which we need cite only the names of Francisco de Paula e Oliveira and Gonzaga de Campos, to whom we owe so many works, as may be seen in the magnificent *Bibliografia mineral e geológica do Brasil* published by Arrojado Lisboa in the Annals of the School of Mines of Ouro Prêto."

But if in the field of natural sciences, and especially that of botany and zoology, there is recorded in the past century an important contribution by Brazil, although inferior to the contribution of foreigners—which was certainly more important in all of these fields—when it comes to physics we did no more than transmit the science already known. Physics in Brazil, from the time the teaching of this science was begun in the Medical School as a result of the reform of October 3, 1832 "was only cultivated," according to the correct observation of Francisco Venâncio Filho, "as a subject of instruction, and there only appear now in some technical institutions the first researches mainly of a utilitarian character." There was no contribution of an experimental order, much less in the field of theory, "which required a long development of habits of abstract thought." Doubtless in the field of application there stand out in bold relief two great names "separated by two centuries from each other and united by the same glory"—that of Bartolomeu Lourenço de Gusmão (Santos, 1680–1724), the inventor of the balloon, and that of Alberto Santos-Dumont (Palmira, Minas Gerais, 1873–Santos, 1932), who discovered the dirigibility of the balloon and the airplane. To Bartolomeu Lourenço, the "flying Father," the first American inventor, there belongs, in fact, the glory of having proved, between August 5 and 8 and in October of 1709, with his experiments in Lisbon, the application of the principle of Archimedes to gases, that a body lighter or less dense than air can go up in space. Santos-Dumont, two centuries later, solved two great problems, that of the dirigibility of the balloon in 1898, in which he won, on September 18, the "Deutsch de la Meurthe" prize, directing his balloon (already in the form of a cylinder terminating in two cones at the extremities) from the park of the Aero Club at Saint-Cloud to the Eiffel Tower, which he went around, returning to his point of departure over a total course of 11 kilometers in 30 minutes; that of the "heavier than air" on October 23, 1906, in an indisputable flight which was accomplished in Paris in his little plane called the "14-bis" and which constituted according to Venâncio Filho, "the most memorable moment in the history of aviation." But both of them, Bartolomeu Lourenço who preceded the brothers Montgolfier by seventy-four years, causing a balloon to ascend with hot air (the ascension of the "lighter than air") and who has also the priority in the discovery of the balloon, undisputed after the work of Afonso Taunay on this inventor of genius; and Santos-Dumont, whom Edison called "the bandeirante of the air," and to whose credit there are two inventions—that of the dirigibility of the "lighter than air," and that of the ascension of the "heavier than air"—both lived, carried on their studies, and accomplished their memorable experiments outside of Brazil, the former in the home country, a victim of the scientific backwardness of his environment, and the latter in Paris, where he succeeded in attracting universal attention to his experiments. The Jesuit, the pioneer of the balloon, who in 1701, having just completed his sixteenth year, was sent to Lisbon to finish his studies, settled definitely in Portugal, after a short stay in 1705 in Bahia, and became an outstanding figure at the court of Dom João V and died poor and without resources in a hospital of Toledo. In 1891, also when very young, about eighteen years old, Santos-Dumont started for Europe and settled in Paris, beginning a series of studies and experiments which culminated in two great inventions, of 1898 and 1906, to return to Brazil only in 1922, when he was already universally famous for his discoveries. If—what we can affirm with pride—these two inventors are Brazilian and therefore the highest glories of Brazil and of the Western Hemisphere, not only were they not "products" of the national culture, but they also exercised no influence whatever on the progress of scientific thought in Brazil nor did they mark a phase of its evolution in the history of our culture.

The observations and scientific acivities in the field of astronomy did not begin in Brazil until the second half of the past century.[16] The French astronomer, Emmanuel Liais, who had broken his connection with the Observatory of Paris and had arrived in Rio de Janeiro in 1858, joined on the request of Dom Pedro II a scientific commission charged with observing in Paranaguá the total eclipse of the sun in 1858, and of which there formed part, among others, Cândido Batista de Oliveira and Antônio Manuel de Melo. From 1858 to 1871, Emmanuel Liais was engaged in intense activity: returning to Rio, he was connected with the commission for geographic and geodetic studies and explored the early provinces of Minas Gerais, Bahia, and Pernambuco. He studied the hydrography of the upper São Francisco and of the river Velhas and carried on in his portable observatory numerous observations on comets and on the origin and nature of zodiacal light, being finally, in 1871, named director of the Imperial Observatory, at that time not connected with the naval or military schools to which it had been

[16] On the subject of the first observatory in Brazil—built in Recife during the period of Dutch rule, between 1636 and 1644—we have nothing but the references in Barleus to astronomical observations carried on during that decade. It disappeared, like so many scientific institutions, with the reconquest of Pernambuco by the Portuguese. In 1827, almost two centuries later, there was created in the first Empire, by the decree of October 15 of that year, the first observatory of Rio de Janeiro, which, taking in 1846 the name of Imperial Observatory, continued to serve as a center of instruction for the students of the military and naval schools. It was only as a result of the decree of January 3, 1871, in the ministry of Araújo Lima, that this observatory, which had been publishing meteorological annals since 1851, emancipated itself from the naval and military schools to assume its own proper character, which it maintained from then on, although it was for a long time badly housed and equipped. Named director of the Imperial Observatory in that same year, Emmanuel Liais, who had been in Brazil since 1858, took up his duties in 1874 upon his return from a trip to Europe, where he had been charged by the government with the task of buying new instruments and superintending the construction of others for the observatory. It was as a result of the efforts of Emmanuel Liais that the first volume of the *Anais* of the observatory appeared in 1882; these annals were entirely the work of Louis Cruls, who in 1884 took over officially the duties of the French savant as director of this scientific establishment. It was Louis Cruls, its second director (1884–1908), who conceived the first *Anuário* of the observatory (1883) and founded in 1886 the *Revista* of the observatory, a monthly publication in the field of astronomy. In the third volume of the *Anais* we find an account of the work of the three missions sent to observe the passage of Venus over the sun. In 1909, when the observatory was under the direction of Henrique Morize, the separation of the meteorological and astronomical services took place; the eminent climatologist succeeded in setting up the first Brazilian meteorological service, endowing it "with excellent instrumental equipment and the best of methods." In 1910 there reappeared, with the *Anuário* of 1909–1910, the *Boletim Mensal of Observacoes* (the numbers of January to March, 1908). In the history of Brazilian meteorology, in which there stood out in the early days the names of L. Cruls, H. Morize, F. Draenert, O. Weber, and A. Lisboa, among others we note the figures of Américo Silvado, in the Naval Meteorological Service, and J. Sampaio Ferraz, onetime director of the Brazilian Meteorological Service and author of a fundamental work on Brazilian meteorology. In addition to the National Observatory, the only agency now active is the Observatory of São Paulo, directed in the early days by Belfort de Matos, which includes meteorological service but has no important discovery or astronomical work to show. (Cf. Delgado de Carvalho, *Météorologie du Brésil* [London, 1917]; Tancredo de Paiva, *Bibliografia do clima brasílico* [Rio, 1928]; J. de Sampaio Ferraz, *Meteorologia Brasileira* [São Paulo, 1934—Brasiliana, Vol 33].)

formerly annexed as an observatory for teaching. The decree of January 3, 1871, and the act of the government confiding to Emmanuel Liais the direction of the observatory "marked an important date in the history of astronomy in Brazil." In 1874 Emmanuel Liais returned from Europe with new instruments acquired or ordered for the building of the observatory, the direction of which he assumed, and there arrived in Brazil a young Belgian, twenty-six years old, a mathematician and geodesist, Louis Cruls (1848–1908), who, admitted to the observatory as assistant astronomer, soon became one of the most brilliant collaborators of that institution. His memoirs on Mars (the spots of the planet and the length of its rotation) and on the determination of the length of the rotation of the planet Jupiter, and his observations—which won him the Valz prize of the Academy of Sciences of Paris—on the comet discovered by Elleny on September 7, 1882, were not slow in raising L. Cruls to a foremost place in the field of scientific activity. In 1884 the Belgian astronomer was named as a worthy continuer of the French scholar, to succeed Emmanuel Liais, who had retired to Europe. The passage of Venus over the disc of the sun in 1882 was observed by three missions organized by L. Cruls: one headed by the Baron of Tefé and sent to the island of São Tomaz; another directed by Oliveira Locaille, also a Brazilian, which made interesting observations on the Elleny comet, and was sent to Olinda; and the third, the most important, which was established under the responsibility of L. Cruls himself in Punta Arenas on the Strait of Magellan. The illustrious Belgian scientist who published in addition, in 1890–1892, two memoirs on climatology, was followed, after his death in Paris in 1908, by Henrique Morize (1860–1930), born in France, who having arrived in Brazil in 1875, when he was still an adolescent, finished his studies in the Polytechnic School of which he was to be one of the great figures, and in 1891 was the first astronomer of the observatory. Professor of physics and meteorology from 1896, director beginning in 1908 of the National Observatory, and one of the founders of the Brazilian Academy of Sciences (1916), he succeeded in giving the observatory its new installation from the hill of São Januário. He secured in 1909 the separation between the services of meteorology and of astronomy and, among other works of high value such as *Nosso céu* and *Previsão do tempo*, he left a notable monograph, *O clima do Brasil,* which he wrote for the *Dicionário Histórico, Geográfico e Etnográfico,* organized in 1922 by the Historical Institute of Rio de Janeiro. The observations of Fernandes da Costa on double stars and the series of micrometic measurements taken between 1924 and 1926, continuing in the National Observatory the research begun by L. Cruls in 1878 and the work of Alix de Lemos on Tides and of Lélio Gama on variation of latitudes, constitute, in a period of decline of these scientific activities among us, one of the few and more interesting Brazilian contributions to the progress of astronomical studies.

This contrast between the scientific production of foreigners who traveled over the country or came to reside in it and the sparse and isolated contributions of Brazilians, and the strongly marked lack of equality between the literary studies and scientific studies, show very clearly the fact, so many times pointed out, of the lack of interest of the Brazilian in sciences in general, particularly in the physical sciences. There are not lacking persons who would conclude from this indifference, after a hasty examination, that there is a natural lack of aptitude on the part of the Brazilian for scientific work, or at least, and this is more exact, would blame his lively but superficial intelligence and his will, made up of impulses, for the disproportion between his activities and the results of his work in these fields. It seems actually that, although he is not lacking in an ardent curiosity, he is not accustomed to bring to work of this character the strength of reflection, the objective spirit, the patience and the tenacity which scientific research requires. Science, as Charles Richet wrote, "is not a young girl of easy habits whom a promise or a caress is sufficient to seduce; she is cold, pitiless, and it is necessary to sacrifice to her for a long time everything that one loves in order to obtain the most insignificant favors." But the truth is that the love of fact, the critical and investigating spirit and enthusiasm for experimental methods could be developed among us everywhere; and the principal cause of the lack of interest of the Brazilian in science, far from resulting from a natural lack of aptitude, is rather the type of teaching which is almost exclusively literary, bookish, and rhetorical, which has been implanted in Brazil since the time of the colony and down to the end of the Empire period. A culture that is excessively verbal and far removed from the concrete, too full of rhetoric and of poetry, too far removed from humble, earthly realities, without a counterbalance in science, "is it not on its way," asks Léon Flavien "to atrophy of character, to that form of impotence which is called dilettantism?" [17] This exactly was our culture—the culture which one might expect from a system of education entirely without scientific faculties or institutes for higher study—for which the art of writing is not the art of thinking; in which literature and science, far from obeying the same rhythm, for more than three centuries failed to harmonize, and which was characterized by a profound divorce, if not antagonism, that had grown up between the two branches which are meant to fortify each other mutually in the general and systematic plan of education.[18] If it is certain that "the sciences, without letters, become mechanical and brutish," according to the thought of Anatole France, who in some words in *La Vie en fleur* covers this question in all its aspects, "letters without science are empty, and so science is the substance of letters." When there broke out among us, developing during the period 1840 to 1870, the current of romanticism, which is in its essence a lyric exultation of sensitivity and a revolt against the real when it disturbs this exultation, it did not in individuals, without protection against themselves, appear to oppose against this tendency to subjectivism that habit of reflection and objectivity which the mathematical sciences are accustomed to develop, being the instrument of reasoning par excellence, and the physical sciences, the instrument par excellence of investigation. In the Brazilian intellectual world, in which letters

[17] Léon Flavien, "Les Sciences exactes et la culture générale," in *Enseignement scientifique,* Jan. and Feb., 1929 (Paris, Léon Eyroles).

[18] "We are a people of sophists and rhetoricians, fed on words, and the victim of their illusory prestige," wrote Rui Barbosa in 1882, "and we do not perceive that this perversion, the root of all our calamities, is the *result of our education* in school, at home, in college and professional school. Our education is limited to the mechanical cult of the phrase; thus we receive, ready-made, without verification, the opinions that we adopt; thus we come to neglect all mental activity of our own; thus we acquire the deep-rooted and pernicious habit of either not perceiving reality at all, or perceiving it only through those 'clouds,' capable of mingling in the most absurd manner and taking on the most arbitrary shapes, with which the comedy of Aristophanes symbolized the inanity and illusions of the sophistical schools of his time." (Rui Barbosa, speech given in the Liceu de Artes e Ofícios, Nov. 23, 1882, in "Orações do Apóstolo," published by the *Revista de Língua Portuguesa,* Rio, 1923.)

were practiced without the complement and counterweight of science, romanticism—
that powerful river of poetry which everywhere bore off a great deal of refuse in its
proud waves—had necessarily to accentuate the old colonial tendency to literature and
to subjectivism, sweeping away all values and devastating everything in its passage
like a mountain torrent. . . .

Hence the character of the evolution (if we may so call it) of science in Brazil,
developing by jumps, more through the strength of some exceptional spirits, self-made
men, than by the pressure of the cultural environment, which among us is always
hostile, if not to intelligence, at least to research in the field of pure science. Instead
of developing like a river which, having its source far away, is scattered through many
branches, receives many tributaries, and is divided in a great delta, made up in its
branches of the various sciences of observation, the cultivation of science has proceeded irregularly in advances and retreats, in movements without continuity and in
different directions, and by means of masters without disciples. The "Palestra Científica" Society, which followed the Velosiana Society of Natural Sciences founded by
Freire Alemão, and which had as its object "to be concerned with the study of the
physical and mathematical sciences, particularly with application to Brazil" (Decree
1820 of September 13, 1856), had a brief duration, and did not succeed in publishing
more than the first number of its archives with the stipend given by the emperor. The
review *Minerva*, which disappeared with its third number, did not last longer nor
have greater success than the review *Guanabara*—a review of science and letters also
founded earlier by Freire Alemão, whose name is to be found connected with practically all of the attempts at this time in the field of natural sciences. The emperor
Dom Pedro II, himself enamoured of higher studies, the "most devoted Maecenas the
nation ever possessed," according to Artur Neiva, and a sovereign who, according to
the astronomer Babinet, merited rather the title of savant than that of "crowned ama-
teur," and who tried so valiantly to promote the progress of the sciences in Brazil, had
his efforts broken by the passive resistance and barely concealed hostility of this intellectual and political environment, dominated by men of the rhetorical spirit and of
abstract education, in whom literature, juridical ideas and questions and political debates absorbed the whole thought of the nation.[19] For was it not Dom Pedro II, in 1882,

[19] There is not the slightest doubt that Dom Pedro II played an active part in encouraging
science, and was moreover himself a student of the sciences. In his long reign he was ever at the
forefront of scientific movements, stimulating them in every way possible and lending the prestige
of his presence to the meetings of scientific societies and institutes, like the Historical and Geographic Institute, at many of the sessions of which he presided, the meetings of the Palestra
Científica (Scientific Lecture) Society, and also the public lectures arranged in the Imperial Museum by Ladislau Neto (1874–1893), lectures which dealt with problems of botany and zoology,
physiology, geology, and anthropology. Striving to know everything, loving men of learning and
science, he showed the same curious and sympathetic attitude toward all branches and in relation
to all eminent men, whether philosophers, savants, or artists. A student of Hebrew and Sanscrit,
in which he was particularly interested, he cultivated some of the sciences, such as astronomy, in
which, according to the opinion of Babinet, in the preface to *O Espaço celeste*, he acquired a
really profound knowledge. On the night of a reception in the palace of São Cristóvão, catching
sight of Richard Burton, he called the English author to his study, engaging in conversation with
the famous explorer, "while," writes Oliveira Lima, "the diplomats were waiting for him to appear
and exchange the usual small talk." In Paris, where he sought the acquaintance of Victor Hugo,
making the first call himself, in the face of the reluctance of the great poet, a radical republican,

who was combated and ridiculed in the very session of the Congress, by intelligent and cultivated men like Ferreira Viana, who riddled the emperor with sarcasms because he had asked for a modest credit of 60 contos to facilitate scientific observation of the passage of the planet Venus over the disc of the sun? And was it not "on his quality as a learned man, as if that were harmful to the man who governed," that the attacks and the bold criticisms of the Chief of State insisted most strongly, of a great prince and a great Brazilian who governed us forty-nine years and was the ambassador of our culture in all the countries which he visited? If Dom Pedro II did not do for the progress of the sciences in the country as much as might be expected from his culture and experience and his interest in higher studies, it was certainly because, outside of a small and select group, he rarely found for his suggestions and plans an efficacious support in the dominant mentality which was more given to theoretical schematizations and to flights of oratory. Dom Pedro II, in this respect, repeats and explains José Bonifácio, the notable mineralogist, who had for ten years frequented the major centers of culture in Europe as the patriarch at the dawn of nationality, a solitary figure among those men who, as Gilberto Amado says, "constituted the only living reality of the country," and who, with their education, "based on the canon law and on all the vices of the juridical metaphysics of the period," remained in their closed exclusivism, alien and indifferent to the noble ambition of the learned Brazilian to lead Brazil to enter the movement for the progress of science and higher studies. In the second half of the nineteenth century, in the long reign of Pedro II, this cultural atmosphere had not been noticeably modified. Literary men, politicians, and orators still had the same disdain for concrete realities and experimental sciences, which have the merit of correcting what is too excessive in the spirit of system and doctrines, escaping the control of fact and observation. For these men, with their literary and abstract education, who constituted the élite of the period, nothing seemed stupider than a fact, according to the expression of that philosopher who had reason to become irritated against facts which did not agree with his theory. . . .

It was, however, enough that there should rise to power and remain in power five years (1871–1876) a man like the Viscount of Rio Branco, whose government came "like a long civilizing truce," in the expression of Euclides da Cunha, to inaugurate in this period a new cultural policy, planned and executed under the inspiration and by the joint action of the emperor and his first minister—one of our greatest statesmen. This policy had in its favor two circumstances: Rio Branco, an engineer, came from the Central School where he was professor of mechanics and director, and

---

to go to "the house of emperors," he showed a keen interest in the researches of Charcot in the School of the Salpêtrière; and, in the United States, when he visited the Centennial Exposition of Philadelphia in 1876, he was able to appreciate immediately the importance of the recent invention of the telephone by Alexander Graham Bell, although it was still in an experimental stage. Admired by the leading foreigners of his time, of a writer and diplomat like Count Gobineau, savants like Flammarion and Pasteur, poets of the stature of Victor Hugo, he became popular in Paris, and was more looked up to in its intellectual circles than any other sovereign; we get an idea of the interest he aroused, quite aside from the prestige of royalty, from the impression he produced on Friedrich Nietzsche when they met on a Swiss mountain, and the Brazilian emperor and the German philosopher, traveling together in a stage coach, without knowing each other, fell into conversation. (Oliveira Lima, "O Imperador e os sábios," in *Jornal do Comércio*, Rio, July 4, 1926.)

although he was connected with the conservative party, "he did not represent really," according to the correct observation of Euclides, "any of the monarchical parties." An engineer and professor of mechanics and later of political economy, he brought to politics a new spirit formed in the discipline of the physical sciences and mathematics and with which he had grown accustomed to seize the whole difference which separates true science—science founded on fact—from the pretense of science founded on verbal theories. More a diplomat than a politician and "appealing without distinction to the dissidence of his own party and to the good will of his adversaries, liberals or republicans," he had his hands free and unembarrassed for action of great scope, the widest and most profound of the whole policy of the Empire. It was thus that he was able to accomplish in all fields of activity and especially in the cultural realm, a series of things which, if they had continued at the same rate and in the same direction, would have given a strong turn and marked a course opposed to that of his predecessors; a course, moreover, which was that of the colonial tradition, which would once more come to prevail again for almost half a century. In 1872 Charles Frederick Hartt, who joined the expedition of Agassiz in 1865 and had finished visiting the Amazon region, was charged by the Brazilian government with the organization of a general geological service. The ministry of Rio Branco thus initiated the preparation of our road and geological map, "soon after abandoned by the government which followed them"; it succeeded in giving a great stimulation to geological studies in the country, at the front of which there remained until his death the American scholar, aided in carrying out these services and the development of these studies by Orville Derby and J. C. Branner, and promoted the census of 1872, the first which was conducted in Brazil. In the reforms of education which he undertook, he reorganized in 1874 the Central School, which came to be called the Polytechnic School, so that it was transformed not only into a great center of professional education but also into an institution capable of spreading "the highest theoretical knowledge of the exact sciences." He created special chairs like that of mathematical physics and experimental physics in this school and in the Military School which resulted from the division of the old Central School, and he founded in 1876 the School of Mines, installed in Ouro Prêto in 1877, in which, under the direction of Henri Gorceix, the creator of the school, there was educated a notable generation of specialists in mineralogy, geology, and mines. The academic instruction which in general even in 1882 was to be, according to Rui Barbosa,[20] "infinitely far from the scientific level of the age," with these reforms and creations, the most important since Dom João VI, took a vigorous new life, following the guidance of this admirable statesman. The School of Mines—as its *Anais* will testify, full as they are of valuable contributions—under the learned leadership of Henri Gorceix and with the stimuli of Orville Derby and of the petrographer Eugênio Hussak, among others, became in the last quarter of the nineteenth century one of the greatest, if not the greatest, centers of high culture, which, far from being reduced to the mere training of mining engineers, made a constant effort to apply and propagate scientific methods of research in the study of the geology, of the natural wealth and principal fossils of Brazil.

But these moves, like the earlier ones, had no life except through their initial

[20] Rui Barbosa, *Reforma do ensino primário* (Rio, 1882), p. 1.

propulsion and the tenacity of some eminent figures who were rare and solitary, and at times of a little group of workers to whom foreign scholars had managed to transmit the disinterested spirit of research and speculation. In a general sense, if we make an exception of a few centers of study and research like the Imperial Museum, the Polytechnic School, and the recent School of Mines, what was still to be seen everywhere was the same lack of interest in the investigations of pure science, the same resistance to the entry of scientific methods, and even to the notion, already common in the nineteenth century, of the utilitarian value of science which is accustomed to bring to the peoples who honor it, not only glory but also wealth, an ideal which we persisted in considering an eccentricity, or at the most a luxury. This persistent attitude in the face of science put in bold relief one of the gravest failures, if not the fundamental vice, of our traditional education, full as it was of a purely literary spirit, with its tendency to rhetoric, sophistry, and verbalism. In this intellectual atmosphere, fed by a system of education and of culture, destined almost exclusively to develop literary qualities and professional specialization, it certainly was not favorable to the progress of the experimental sciences, which contributed still less to awaken a taste for mathematics and to render us accessible to the attractions of those serene heights of theory in which everything is solved by the equations and formulae of algebra. Nevertheless, there arose in the middle of the nineteenth century an extraordinary figure who began the line of mathematicians of Brazil and who must have educated himself under the influence of his own calling for these studies and the force of his creative spirit and intuition. This is Joaquim Gomes de Sousa,[21] most vigorous and

[21] Joaquim Gomes de Sousa (1829–1863), born in Maranhão, the greatest mathematician of Brazil, was, as Carlos Pontes observed, so precocious as a child "that there is no precedent and no case to match him in the whole history of Brazilian thought." Sent by his parents to Rio de Janeiro in 1844 to enter upon a career in the army, he left the Military School in his first year, and at fifteen entered the Medical School, pursuing the course to the third year and then requested and obtained the right to take examinations in all the subjects of the old Military School, and passed the successive examinations with exceptional brilliance in the presence of the emperor and before a numerous audience, and on June 1, 1848, received his bachelor's degree and on October 14 of the same year his doctorate in physical and mathematical sciences. He was nineteen when he defended his thesis; appointed immediately afterward professor in the Military School, he betook himself to Europe and graduated in medicine in Paris. In 1855 he presented to the Academy of Sciences of Paris his scientific papers, published posthumously in 1882 by the Brazilian government (Joaquim Gomes de Sousa, *Mélanges de Calcul Intégral,* a posthumous work to which is added a memoir by the author, on the subject of sound, and a preface by Charles Henry. Leipzig: F. A. Brockhaus, 1882). In 1856 the mathematician Stokes presented to the Royal Society of London a note containing a résumé of the first paper, on the problem of the inversion of definite integrals. Having devoted himself to physics and the highest abstractions of higher mathematics, "he applied himself with even more zeal to studies of philosophy, history, economics, and the social sciences in general, not less than to those of literature properly speaking" (João Francisco Lisboa, *Jornal de Timon,* 2 vols., Maranhão, 1852–1854). Member of Congress in 1856, a jurist who had never studied a single year of law, he confronted in the Chamber Nabuco de Araújo, a great orator and one of the greatest cultivators of juridical writing. Taking part in the debates occasioned by the denunciation, he presented against the ex-minister of the crown for having dismissed two magistrates without due process (Carlos Pontes, *Nabuco de Araújo e Gomes de Sousa: O Caso da aposentadoria violenta dos magistrados* [The case of the unjustified dismissal of two magistrates], in *Jornal do Comércio,* June 24, 1934). Passing away prematurely, at thirty-four, in London, on his second trip to Europe, his short life, brilliant and fruitful, was, as Amoroso Costa says, "a model of thought and action."

the highest mathematical spirit that Brazil has produced, "an intellectual giant," according to Euclides da Cunha, "the most complete brain of the century, jurist, physician, and poet, leaving us pages on infinitesimal calculus which even today dominate all mathematics." [22] A professor at nineteen in the Military School, where he studied only the first year and attained in 1848 the degree of bachelor and of doctor in physical and mathematical sciences after varied and successive examinations in all these subjects, the young mathematician presented to the Academy of Sciences of Paris in 1855, three memoirs of the highest value: on the determination of unknown functions under the sign of a definite integral, on a theorem of mathematical analysis (integral calculus), and on sound, published later with other work at the instigation of the imperial government. A great mathematician who belonged, according to the judgment of Amoroso Costa, "to the class of geometers in whom intuition predominates," and who manipulated in a masterly way the instrument of algebra, his work, brought together after his death in a volume with the title *Mélanges de Calcul Intégral* (1882) and made up of seven memoirs and some fragments, is considered by Teodoro Ramos truly remarkable in the boldness and ingenuity of its conception. "A geometer," writes the scholar Charles Henry, who wrote the preface to this posthumous work, "he attacked the most difficult and urgent problem of science; a mathematician, impassioned for experiment and observation, he appreciated the charms of art; the brute necessity of the social problem and the sad complexities of the philosophical problem did not leave him indifferent. A child prodigy, an ideal nature, complex and sickly, he belongs to that family of intelligences which appears to have been created to show the fundamental identity of all the branches of knowledge, to those souls prematurely stolen away from their work, whom the poetry of antiquity called dear to the gods and who across the centuries and in different circumstances recall to us the melancholy figure of Pascal."

If even in the second half of the nineteenth century mathematical science in Brazil was honored by a Pereira Reis and a Licínio Cardoso, who, however, were specialists in other fields of study, it was only in 1879 that there appeared in the *Revista* of the Polytechnic School works by a young man, twenty-three years of age, which announced the appearance of a mathematician of the stature of Gomes de Sousa. Although he disappeared prematurely, like the scholar of Maranhão, who died at thirty-four, Oto de Alencar (Ceará, 1874–1912) left a remarkable amount of work, and as a professor of the Polytechnic School from 1902 to his death, he succeeded in that ten-year period in raising the level of mathematical studies to a height which they had attained in Brazil only with J. Gomes de Sousa, half a century before. The importance of his work and the value of his teaching in the various disciplines which he professed, beginning in 1902 as a substitute professor, gave him a right to the nomination as full professor in 1907 without competition, by the proposal of the faculty of the school in which he had studied and of which he became one of the leading figures. Holding the chair of experimental physics through the chance that he had occupied it as a substitute, Oto de Alencar, who had real experimental ability, was preoccupied, because he was essentially a specialist in algebra, with the mathematical aspect of physical phenomena. The collection of notes and memoirs published in 1906 under the title *Física e Eletrotécnica* dates from this period. In this there stand out his studies

---

[22] Euclides da Cunha, *À Margem da história: Da Independência a República* (esboço político) (Pôrto: Chardron, 3rd ed., 1922).

on thermodynamic potentials, "a forerunner of the theory of relativity of Einstein," according to the opinion of one important critic. Among other works published here and in Europe and accepted by Gomes Teixeira in the *Jornal de Ciências Matemáticas* of Pôrto, and by Darboux in the *Bulletin des Sciences Mathématiques,* we may note his memoirs on the theory of least surfaces, on the velocity of sound, developing the theory of Gomes de Sousa, whose methods and results he utilized, and on the geometrical application of the equation of Riccati—perhaps the most original of all—in addition to critical and scientific studies on some errors in mathematics of A. Comte, and with which, departing from the mathematical conceptions of the French philosopher, he marked in the school "the beginning of a reaction against Comtism." A disciple and successor of Oto de Alencar, who represents in the history of mathematical ideas in Brazil, according to Lélio Gama, "the union between the old Positivist school, whose anachronism he himself showed, and the modern school, the principles of which he was the first to fight for," M. Amoroso Costa (Federal District, 1885–1929) became a tireless fighter in the campaign begun by his master for the complete renovation of mathematical studies among us. "Not possessing," writes Teodoro Ramos, "the brilliant talent as an analyst that Oto de Alencar had, Amoroso Costa nevertheless proved to be a more profound thinker, a more balanced mind, and a more vigorous champion of pure and disinterested science." Perhaps the greatest cultivator among us of mathematical philosophy, following closely the lessons of Henri Poincaré, who exercised upon his mind a considerable influence, and delighting in contemplating the purely aesthetic side in mathematical science, this illustrious professor—the first in Brazil to occupy himself with non-Archimedean geometry—distinguished himself for his astronomical work, like the memoir on the evolution of double stars; or his mathematical ones, like his original investigations on the theory of divergent series; and especially by his essays in philosophical and scientific criticism. If to those three great names we add that of Teodoro Ramos (São Paulo, 1896–1936), the greatest mathematician of Brazil in his time, the Abelian who with such great profundity and originality treated of the functions of real variables (his doctor's thesis), of the definite integrals, of discontinuous functions (1926), and of vectorial calculus (1930), and fought so hard to raise the level of studies of mathematical analysis and of rational mechanics, and finally the name of Lélio Gama, who, in the Polytechnic School and the School of Sciences (1934–1938) of Rio de Janeiro, kept up brilliantly the tradition of mathematical studies, we will have the complete list of the scientific lineage which had its beginning in Gomes de Sousa and comes down to our day in a small but illustrious series of Brazilians who were really occupied with abstract matters far distant from their practical application.

But in this period in which the mathematical sciences took on new life, with Oto de Alencar and his successors, and the continuity between masters and their disciples was established, there entered into intense activity the Museu Paraense, founded by Emílio Goeldi in 1885. Herman von Ihering, called to direct the Museu Paulista begun in 1893, gives it a high scientific tone; Barbosa Rodrigues reorganized the Botanical Garden, starting a new phase of research; and Nina Rodrigues undertook in Bahia for the first time "the rigorously scientific study of that considerable part of our population made up of the Afro-American element." In addition to the National Museum, which in the history of our country has played a role of major importance in the development of the natural sciences and which passed through great transformations under the direction of Batista Lacerda (1895–1915), there began to collaborate in scientific activities in the country new institutions like the Museu Paraense, later to be called (1900) the Museu Goeldi in homage to its founder, and the Museu Paulista which had just been created by the government of São Paulo. The former, the Museu Goeldi, possessed the richest and most varied tropical collection of the world, and in addition to a zoological garden connected with it, a botanical garden and one of the most complete specialized libraries of the country, with 21,000 volumes. Its most fruitful period was under the direction of its founder, a naturalist of universal renown, who was followed later by Jacques Huber, a Swiss botanist, who died prematurely and who was one of the foreign naturalists who devoted most study to our country and its natural wealth. The latter, the Museu Paulista, founded on August 28, 1893, and organized by Decree No. 249 (July 26,1894), with the object of studying the natural history of South America and especially of Brazil, was not slow in imposing itself upon the scientific circles of the world, with its activities conducted on a high plane by Hermann von Ihering (1894–1915), a remarkable zoologist to whom the government confided its management on the suggestion of the eminent geologist, Orville Derby, then director of the Geographic and Geological Commission of the State. At the end of the nineteenth century, in 1890, the Botanical Garden,[23] was separated from the Instituto Fluminese de Agricultura, and J. Barbosa Rodrigues was named its director. Turning this old institution toward scientific objects, he carried out a series of

[23] This great institution, which has been developing for more than a century, has its origins in the old Royal Garden, a garden for exotic plants, created by Dom João VI in 1808 in the plantation of the Lake of Rodrigo de Freitas, and enlarged by the king himself and opened to the public in 1819 under the name of the Royal Botanical Garden. A garden for "acclimatization," at first aiming at introducing into Brazil the cultivation of spices from the East Indies, it was not slow to acquire excellent collections of plants, thanks, above all, to the measures taken by Dom João VI to support and stimulate "all who cared for the acclimatization and cultivation of exotic plants." The marvelous garden of Gavea, which still proudly displays, next to the bust of its founder, the royal palm planted by Dom João VI in 1808, did not lose, however, its original character as a garden of acclimatization, to take on that of a scientific institution, until the administration, so fruitful in results, of Brother Leandro do Sacramento (1824–1829), who gave it the new direction. During the second Empire, in which the Botanical Garden was for a long time under the direction of the Instituto Fluminense de Agricultura, various eminent men took part in its administration; among these leaders in the field of natural science were men like Brother Custódio Serrão, in the first half of the nineteenth century, and F. L. César Burlamaqui and P. G. Pais Leme, who introduced important changes of a technical and administrative character. It was only under the new regime in which the Botanical Garden, separated from the Instituto, entered upon the new phase of its history, and the most fruitful, with the appointment in 1890 of J. Barbosa Rodrigues, the botanist of the great *Sertum Palmarum,* a work in two folio volumes, who, returning to the ideas of Brother Leandro, restored the Botanical Garden to its research functions and gave new opportunities to scientific work. After the death of Barbosa Rodrigues, it entered upon a period of decline, to rise again with Antônio Pacheco Leão, professor of botany in the Medical School and disciple of Osvaldo Cruz, who introduced reforms, with the same general object, with the aid of Löfgren, Ducke, and Kuhlmann instituting measures of remarkably progressive character. The last two of these scientists were Brazilians; together these collaborators transformed it into a center of research on Brazilian flora. In 1938, with the reform of the Ministry of Agriculture, the Botanical Garden was made part of the Forest Service, which was reorganized at that time, when it became the Botanical Section of that service. The Garden, the area of which is estimated at 546,343 square meters (135,182 wild, and 322,099 cultivated), possesses seven thousand different species, besides thousands of ornamental plants cultivated in greenhouses, and belonging to some two hundred different families.

reforms of a technical character, and by enriching its herbariums and its living collections, creating its library, and intensifying its exchange with similar establishments abroad, he contributed brilliantly, in a manner only comparable to the later action of Antônio Pacheco Leão, to transform it into the richest park in the world and a center of botanical research. The eight volumes of the *Boletim* of the Museu Paraense, of which the first appeared in 1904; the twenty-three volumes of the *Revista* of the Museu Paulista, the thirty of the Archives of the National Museum, and the *Arquivos* of the Botanical Garden bear witness to scientific activity in Brazil in the various periods of the history of these institutions.

As for libraries, beginning with the National Library, the most important of all and the richest of South America, with its 500,000 volumes and numerous manuscripts, they were still not organized as centers of research and scientific work. Of their double function—that on the one hand of conserving the finest collections of the time, enriching and completing them, and on the other of receiving all contemporary production in the field of literature and history, science and journalism—they did not carry on efficaciously, because of the straitness of their resources, anything more than the first function, which, however, is of great importance due to the richness of their old deposits which historians, their principal clients, accustomed to the methods and discipline of research, considered precious treasures, true archives in which they came to gather their documentation.

Among the scientific activities which characterized this period of intellectual development (1890–1914), and which distinguish it as one of the most fruitful in the history of our culture, there stands out because of its value and its power of attraction, the work accomplished by Nina Rodrigues in the field of legal medicine and in anthropological and social studies on the Afro-American population. With the appointment in 1891 of Raimundo Nina Rodrigues to the chair of legal medicine of the Medical School of Bahia, there began a new phase in the scientific evolution of legal medicine in Brazil, to which Agostinho de Sousa Lima, beginning in 1877 as professor of the Medical School of Rio de Janeiro, had already made an important Brazilian contribution, limited, however, to the application of medicolegal knowledge to the interpretation of the laws of the country. The illustrious scholar of Maranhão, justly considered the creator of legal medicine in Brazil, undertook in fact during the fifteen years of his teaching (1891–1905) in the school of Bahia, a remarkable work of critical revision of foreign techniques and of actual creation, as a result of the practical and experimental studies of Brazilian medicolegal problems. His work on human races and on penal responsibility (1894), and measures with regard to legitimacy and on the legal condition of the mentally diseased (1901), as well as his studies of the psychopathology of the mutilation of cadavers, in which he established the distinction, today classic, between defensive and offensive mutilation, marked an epoch and created a school—the Bahian school of legal medicine—which, carried on by his disciples Oscar Freire and Afrânio Peixoto, has remained active down to the present, through the disciples of the latter in Bahia, in Rio, and in São Paulo. But his monograph with regard to the influence of racial factors upon criminal responsibility—a work in which he advocated a differential penal treatment according to race and with which he began to undertake to give a Brazilian form to legal medicine—is, at the same time, as Alcântara Machado observed, "the beginning of a series of studies on Brazilian mestizos and Negroes." His essays in social psychopathology, like that which the collective psychosis of Canudos inspired him to write, or that which has for its object the study of a Brazilian terrorist, Marcelino Bispo (who made an attempt against the life of Prudente de Morais), constitute important contributions in the series of direct scientific investigations on our own population which, begun by the substantial monograph of 1894, were to reach their peak in a work interrupted by death, *O Problema da raça negra na América portuguesa,* "a synthesis which was to crown these investigations." This work of Nina Rodrigues, considered as a whole, "fruitful as no other was," writes Alcântara Machado, "because it marked the birth of a school which gave us leaders of the value of Afrânio Peixoto, Oscar Freire, Diógenes Sampaio, and continues to enrich us with a Flamínio Fávero, a Leonídio Ribeiro, an Artur Ramos," and, we may add, an A. F. Almeida Júnior and one other contemporary name—this one that of an illustrious writer and jurist which anyone except Alcântara Machado might pronounce. Among the disciples and continuers of Nina Rodrigues in the field of legal medicine, we note Oscar Freire, with his important studies on the cadavers of the fauna of Brazil; Afrânio Peixoto, who carried out with Juliano Moreira interesting experiments on the psychology of evidence [24] and worked out a model regulation for microscopic medicolegal work, "praised without restriction both in Brazil and abroad"; Flamínio Fávero, a disciple of Oscar Freire, with a revision, in which he was aided by his assistants and collaborators, of medicolegal techniques, and Leonídio Ribeiro, especially because of the originality of his studies on the pathology of fingerprints, conducted with great brilliance.

It was not only in legal medicine and the studies of the Negro race that, thanks to the fruitful activity of Nina Rodrigues, that critical and experimental spirit was introduced into Brazil with which, in the civilized world, all the fields of knowledge and all the professions and activities based on the practical application of the new discoveries were renewed. Theories about fermentation, and the pathogenic role of microbes, based on the memorable experiment (1865–1881) of Pasteur, in whom according to Rui Barbosa, "the very genius of experimentation was incarnated," and whose name was linked to the new era, had been guilding in São Paulo the research of L. Pereira Barreto (1840–1923) on the production of beer, the making of wine, and the problem of the transmission of yellow fever, which had crept into the Brazilian territory. As early as 1887, this learned investigator, with his objective and practical spirit, who since 1876 had devoted himself to a series of experiments in São Paulo looking to the renovation of methods and the solution of the problems of agriculture and industry, succeeded, as a result of his researches, in catching a glimpse of the mechanism by which yellow fever was transmitted, a method which was later to be established precisely by the theory of Havana. Barely was the discovery announced that the spotted mosquito (*Stegomyia fasciata*) was the bearer of the disease, when he took part in the experiments of Adolfo Lutz and of Emílio Ribas, who to demonstrate the new truth did not hesitate to risk their own lives in the Isolation Hospital of São Paulo. To Emílio Ribas belongs the glory of having used for the first time in Brazil, in 1902, in the struggle against yellow fever, new processes which in the following year would be applied in a larger field in the great campaign of cleaning up Rio de Janeiro. At this time, in

[24] Juliano Moreira, *Psicologia do testemunho,* lecture given in 1926 in the auditorium of the Polytechnic School of Rio de Janeiro, in *Jornal do Comércio,* Jan. 29, 1935.

1899, there returned to Brazil a young Paulista, Osvaldo Cruz, who had been for three years, from 1896 to 1899, in Paris at the Institut Pasteur, in the very center which the creative genius of the new medicine "had enlivened with his personal contact and had left immortalized with the inheritance of his tradition." Appointed at twenty-eight years of age director of the Instituto Bacteriológico on the suggestion of Émile Roux, the helper and collaborator of Pasteur and then director of the Institute of Paris, of whom the government had asked that he suggest the name of a specialist, Osvaldo Cruz immediately revealed, along with his capacity as a man of science, an extraordinary power of organization in the victorious struggle against the plague of India, which had entered Santos in 1899 and was already spreading in 1900 in that city and in Rio de Janeiro. "Another happening," writes Rui Barbosa, "was to follow this, and one in which we had to oppose not the mere strength of an invasion, but to react against a completed conquest, the dominion of Brazil by yellow fever." During the presidency of Rodrigues Alves, Osvaldo Cruz, given in 1903 the function of the director of public health, accepted the mission which was imposed on him, and undertaking to extinguish yellow fever in Rio de Janeiro in three years, he managed to extirpate it within that time, after the most vigorous and intrepid campaign that was carried on among us, and in which he was guided by the experience of Cuba, corroborated by that of Panama. After cleaning up Rio de Janeiro, he turned toward the north, where he began and finished in six months, with a systematic persecution of the spotted mosquitoes, the extinction of the fever in Pará, and then confronting the problem of malaria in the region of the Madeira-Mamoré, he drew the general plan for the sanitation of the valley of the Amazon. But, great as were the services he rendered to Brazil— and they were remarkable in every respect—conquering the plague, yellow fever, and malaria, they were not superior in their scientific value and their practical consequences to the work which he undertook in nationalizing experimental medicine, "carrying on in Brazil, science for Brazil," and creating with the foundation of the Institute of Manguinhos in 1901, not only the greatest center of scientific research of the country but a whole brilliant school of scholars and experimenters in various branches of the sciences cultivated in that institution.

It is in this institution [25] that Osvaldo Cruz concentrated all his efforts and all his

[25] The Institute, created in 1901, at the end of Guanabara Bay, under the name of Federal Blood Therapy Institute, and through the efforts of the Baron of Pedro Afonso, was originally meant for the preparation of serum and vaccine against the plague, to be used in the fight against the bubonic plague, which had invaded the country. The official name, however, gave way to that of the Institute of Manguinhos, taken from the name of the property placed at the disposal of the Baron of Pedro Afonso by Mayor Cesário Alvim, where its first improvised buildings were located. Not more than six years had passed since the founding of the Institute when, in September, 1907, in the International Public Health and Population Congress in Berlin, Osvaldo Cruz received the greatest recognition he could hope for: the jury of the Exposition of that Congress, in which 2,525 professional men took part, singled out from among the 123 expositions of the most civilized countries, the work of the Institute of Manguinhos and conferred on Brazil the first prize, the gold medal of the empress. In 1908 the School of Manguinhos, which had grown and had greatly expanded the field of its operation, especially in medical zoology, and had been transformed by Decree 1812 of Dec. 12, 1907, into the Institute of Experimental Pathology, was given the name of Osvaldo Cruz Institute, in honor of its eminent founder, who with his school of tropical diseases brought in the most important and fruitful period in the history of medical science in Brazil. On the old grounds of the estate of Manguinhos, in the outbuildings of which

capacity as organizer, attracting and grouping for scientific research a team of young men who were not slow in earning by their labors a just fame and in constituting, in the chain of the traditions of the Institute of Manguinhos, a solid and brilliant link binding the master of masters with their own disciples. "A research man extraordinary in his activities and without rivals in technique, Osvaldo Cruz is revealed," according to Rui Barbosa, "as a matchless educator of learned men"; awakening their talent and creating a school, he possessed, more than anyone else, the art of inspiring a taste for science, of finding the raw material of talent and of training his disciples in the technique of research and of experimentation. From the very beginning there was formed, under the leadership and influence of this creator of modern medicine in Brazil, "that constellation of prize-winning young men who were themselves masters; in every one of whom there was mirrored the glorious image of their model": a Gaspar Viana, who died prematurely at twenty-nine, discoverer of the endocellular forms of the "Tripanozoma Cruzi" (the forms of Gaspar Viana); an Alcides Godói, who made in 1906 the first great discovery of Manguinhos, of a vaccine against symptomatic carbuncles; an Henrique Aragão, who carried out in 1907 the first of the great pieces of work on protozoology; a Cardoso Fontes, who in 1909 published his first studies on the filterable quality of the virus tuberculosis; an Ezequiel Dias, an Artur Neiva, a Rocha Lima, and a Carlos Chagas, who in 1909, won for the institute its greatest triumph with his work on the American tripanozome and its propagating agent (*Tripanozoma Cruzi*), and upon whom, for this discovery, "the Schaudin prize, conferred, as the result of the judgment of the Germans, the honor of being the most notable of the world's protozoologists." To this nucleus formed in Manguinhos, there came, attracted by Osvaldo Cruz in 1908, the savant Adolfo Lutz (1855–1940), who had established the bases of medical zoology in Brazil in his memorable work carried on in São Paulo. It is in this institute that there also worked entomologists like César Pinto and Costa Lima, an endocrinologist of the importance of Tales Martins—our greatest authority in questions of internal secretions—a Flávio da Fonseca, who specialized in protozoology and in venomous animals and a specialist in intestinal worms of the importance of Lauro Travassos, "one of the most productive investigators and leaders that Manguinhos has formed." It is from this center of research and of scientific work—the greatest American school of tropical medicine—that there spread over all the country the critical and experimental spirit displayed by such disciples of Osvaldo Cruz as Pacheco Leão, who remodeled the Botanical Garden of Rio de Janeiro; Artur Neiva, who created in São Paulo the Instituto Biológico; and J. Florêncío Gomes, who began in 1913 the scientific phase of the Instituto de Butantã,[26] vigorously carried on by Afrânio Amaral, his suc-

the first laboratories of experimental medicine in Brazil had been installed, there rose, still under Osvaldo Cruz and as a result of his work, the splendid central building, in Gothic style, of the Osvaldo Cruz Institute, which with its laboratories and a library of 75,000 volumes—today one of the most important in the world—besides two smaller buildings, a hospital, and various annexes, makes up the leading school of tropical medicine in South America. This institution is the great dream that Osvaldo Cruz (1872–1916), who died prematurely at forty-four, "dreamed in his youth and achieved in maturity."

26 It was, in fact, in the Institute of Manguinhos, where he had specialized, that J. Florêncio Gomes prepared himself for the studies, which he carried out in the years following 1913, on the systematic study of our snakes, in the Butantã Institute of São Paulo. That institution, founded in 1899, had begun its work under the direction of Vital Brasil (1899–1919), in the field of the

cessor and the greatest specialist in snakes in Brazil. It is with him that there began the new institutes of research which were founded in the country, like the Ezequiel Dias in Belo Horizonte, the Biológico in São Paulo, the Borges de Medeiros, in Pelotas, the Institute of Experimental Pathology in the North in Belém, Pará, so that we may say that practically all of the scientific research institutes of the country in the field of medical zoology were, if not created, improved or aided by research men educated at the school of Manguinhos. In the direction of this School of Experimental Medicine, Osvaldo Cruz was followed in 1917 by his disciple Carlos Chagas, who developed and completed the organization, and the latter was succeeded by Cardoso Fontes, its third director. We may be able to appreciate its capital importance by the more than 2,500 scientific works published since its beginning, the larger part of them in the *Memórias* of the Institute of Osvaldo Cruz, "the greatest South American repository of articles referring to microbiology and parasitology."

But Manguinhos, which has its beginning at the very height of the era of Pasteur, "could not escape," as Tales Martins well observes, "the microbiological approach and the application which monopolized the early activities of the institute, and very usefully too." If with the changes which were carried out on the instance of Carlos Chagas after 1917 there was created moreover, according to a plan made by Osvaldo Cruz himself, a section of physiology and new horizons were opened to scientific activities, "it is only with Álvaro and Miguel Osório that we finally saw physiology born healthy in our country, practically at the same time as Bernardo Houssay rose in Argentina." In his private laboratory, around 1915, Álvaro Osório de Almeida, the beginner of physiological research among us, won his first victory with his work on basal metabolism in the tropics; and in the Institute of Manguinhos, to which J. Carneiro Filipe, in spite of being an engineer, won the honor, because of his notable scientific accomplishments, of being called to direct the section of physical chemistry applied to biology and to begin the phase af therapeutic chemistry of that institute, Miguel Osório was charged in 1920 with the laboratory of physiology. Osório had already won fame by his important research in the physiology of the nervous system and respiration and

---

preparation of vaccine and serum against the bubonic plague. The really scientific phase of that institute, started by Vital Brasil, and his helpers, between 1901 and 1912, and further developed in 1913 by J. Florêncio Gomes, grew rapidly after 1910, thanks to the new leadership of Artur Neiva, of the School of Manguinhos, and then director of the Sanitary Service, and the fruitful activity of Afrânio Amaral, head of the snake section, who was called to succeed Florêncio Gomes in the direction of the institute in 1919. In 1918 the first numbers of the *Memórias de Butantã*, Vol. 1, were published, and also work on medicinal plants; between 1919 and 1921, the second number of Vol. 2 of the *Memórias*, or the first volume of the *Anexos de Ofidiologia*, in which Afrânio Amaral described the morphology and biology of the Jararaca of the island Queimada Grande, and three other new Brazilian species; and six volumes of the *Anexos de Botânica*, in which F. C. Hoehne expounded his systematic classification of our flora and Afrânio Amaral published his original work on the treatment of ulcers by dry serum. In 1931, by Decree 4941 of March, Butantã Institute was changed into a center for the study of experimental medicine and biology, applied to human pathology, in accordance with the plan of Afrânio Amaral, who having left the institute in 1921 had returned to assume its direction in 1928. It was at this time and after this change that, as the number of works published between 1935 and 1938 attests, the scientific work of the institute grew. Attracted by the new leadership (1928–1938), in addition to Brazilian experts, such as Tales Martins and Flávio da Fonseca from the School of Manguinhos, great foreign specialists from the German universities came to lend their aid.

later was to win the Einstein prize of the Academy of Sciences and the Sicard prize of the Medical School of Paris. It was with the new laboratories and the research that was undertaken in new fields of investigation, of a pure and disinterested character, that the scientific work of this institute was enlarged still more. The origins of the institute go back to a decisive struggle that Brazil was compelled to fight against the plague and yellow fever until these were exterminated. "When the government," writes Tales Martin, "resolved to attack the problem of yellow fever, a problem of life and death for the nation, it found the man—Osvaldo Cruz. Profiting by the consequent prestige to create Manguinhos, Osvaldo Cruz looked after our intellectual hygiene, making one of those enormous forward steps that are only possible in countries in the stage of formation; from practically nothing it came to possess one of the best institutes of experimental medicine in the world." But if this, our greatest cultural step, is a consequence of a plague that had become too rooted and devastating, besides humiliating, for the Brazilian to remain with his arms crossed before the terrible problem, it is certain that its development was extraordinarily favored not only by the marvelous activity of a man—Osvaldo Cruz—but also by the social atmosphere of restlessness and the intellectual and scientific effervescence which transformations in the economic structure and the political regime had produced in Brazil after 1890. It was at this same time in which the great work of Osvaldo Cruz established its bases and acquired momentum, that there appeared, between 1902 and 1909, *Os Sertões* and other works of Euclides da Cunha, explorer and geographer, all of these works marked by high scientific spirit; and that there developed on a wider plane, the exploring expeditions of General Cândido Rondon, charged in 1907 by the Minister Miguel Calmon with "crossing the unknown zone and studying the natural resources of the region traversed," that is, from Mato Grosso to the Amazon. This notable Brazilian, tamer and civilizer of the interior, "on revealing such a great unknown tract of our country, looked after scientific investigation so well, that in the authoritative judgment of Artur Neiva, his name as the proponent of the natural sciences in Brazil in the modern epoch comes immediately after that of Osvaldo Cruz." If we keep in view, in fact, what the 66 publications of the Commission of Strategic Telegraph Lines from Mato Grosso to Amazonas represent in botany (8,000 specimens, many collected by Rondon himself) as well as in zoology (6,000 specimens) we may conclude with Artur Neiva that "no Brazilian scientific expedition contributed so much to the development of natural history among us and none won us so much fame abroad."

Not less important, however, was the contribution to geographic and ethnological studies by the work of the commission headed by General Rondon, who having gotten his initiation in the work of taming the interior with Major Gomes Carneiro, began in 1892, as leader, that extraordinary series of expeditions with which, extending telegraphic lines or proceeding to examine frontiers, he was "to open to science an enormous field for verification and discovery." Of the race of beaters of the sertões, made up of Lacerda e Almeida (1750–1802) of São Paulo, an engineer and geographer who explored the Amazon, Pará, and Mato Grosso; of an Alexandre Rodrigues Ferreira, doctor and naturalist of Bahia (1756–1815), noted for his scientific expeditions in Amazonia; of a General Couto de Magalhães (1837–1898) of Minas, another great ethnographer and specialist of the sertão, author of *Viagem ao Araguaia* and *O Selva-*

gem; General Rondon accomplished during his thirty-eight years (1892–1930), with his travels and expeditions, one of the most fruitful pieces of work of the history of Brazil, not only from the point of view of territorial conquest but also from the geographic point of view. After *Os Sertões*—"the most notable piece of human geography which a bit of land has yet merited at the hand of a writer"—and other essays such as *Terra sem história,* in which Euclides da Cunha, a geographer abreast of the most modern theories, put the whole vigor of his style at the service of his scientific culture and his power of observation, there appeared in 1916, with the same new spirit and built upon a basis of original research, the *Rondônia* of Roquete Pinto, a narrative of the expedition of 1907 and a model of the ethnographic and an anthropological monograph on the indigenous tribes of Mato Grosso. Thus, led by Euclides da Cunha with his genius for describing the land and the people, and Roquete Pinto, who returned from the Ronon expedition with a work of the highest geographic and ethnological importance, there developed in various sectors of this vast field of geographic studies of Brazil, a theory of research men, with a Raimundo Lopes in geoarchaeology, with his studies of lake dwellings and shell piles; Alberto José Sampaio in geobotany, a Melo Leitão in zoogeography, and Sílvo Frois de Abreu in mineral and industrial geography; while Delgado de Carvalho and F. Raja Gabaglia, pioneers of modern geography in Brazil, struggled for improvements in the methods of teaching geography. Historical studies, stimulated for almost a century by the Brazilian Historic and Geographic Institute, founded in 1838, and more recently by other institutions of this same nature, like that of São Paulo, founded in 1894 and renovated by Capistrano de Abreu, who published in 1907 his *Capítulos da História colonial,* and by a João Ribeiro, with his masterly synthesis of the history of Brazil, also entered upon a new phase, which was characterized by the growing penetration of the scientific spirit both in the taste for analysis and in the synthetic spirit, and by research for facts and their interpretation. In São Paulo, beginning in 1917, Afonso Taunay, director of the São Paulo Museum, concentrated all his efforts to organize the section of Brazilian history, constantly enriching it. This organization had already been proposed in Decree No. 249 of 1894, and amplified in 1922 by Law No. 1911, under the government of Washington Luiz, with which it began a notable development, at the same time that there was founded in Rio de Janeiro the National Historical Museum, today one of the greatest and most important of the country.[27] The gigantic work, begun by Washington Luiz between 1916 and 1924, in the field of research, restoration, publication of documents in their primitive integrity, was to be continued only later under the government of Armando Sales, by the Historical Institute of São Paulo. But the movement in the field of geography and history had been started with such vigor that this magnificent series of works and studies of documents was not to be interrupted. In 1931 there be-

[27] The Paulista Museum, to which its first director H. von Ihering, a naturalist, had given chiefly the character of a museum of natural history, was gradually changed, with these reforms undertaken by Afonso Taunay, into a great historic museum (Afonso Taunay, *Guia da secção histórica do Museu Paulista* [São Paulo: Government Printing Office, 1937]). The National Historical Museum, founded in 1922, and located in an old colonial building, was one of the things which sprang from the new interest in historical studies, awakened by the commemorations of the Centenary of National Independence. Although it is recent, it already has collections of great variety and high historic value, divided into twenty halls, according to periods (First and Second Empire, Paraguayan War, the Republic) and according to type of material.

gan to come into existence with the Brasiliana, published by the Editora Nacional, the most vast and rich library of Brazilian studies, accompanied after more than a five-year period, by the collection *Documentos Brasileiros,* published by José Olímpio under the guidance of Gilberto Freyre and, ten years later, in 1940, by the *Biblioteca Histórica Brasileira,* created by the efforts of the Martins Publishing House of São Paulo, which confided its direction to Rubens Borba de Morais.

The effect of the Brasiliana, which attained in a ten-year period about two hundred titles and was certainly a victory for our national culture, was clearly symptomatic of the renaissance of historic, geographic, and social studies, which was to encounter, after the revolution of 1930, an intellectual atmosphere extremely favorable to its further progress. With this encyclopedia, which "is revealing Brazil to the very people who thought they knew it best," there began a series of movements, both public and private, all aiming at the exploitation and development, both in extension and in profundity, of Brazilian studies, with which Brazil might become more and more aware of itself. The revolution of 1930, leading to a fruitful agitation of ideas, like that which had occurred after 1889 as a consequence of a change in economic and political regime, accelerated the movement of intellectual and scientific fermentation which was already traversing the country under the growing pressure of external cultural influences. Meanwhile, as the greatest problems were no longer those of public health, threatened at the end of the last century by the plague and by yellow fever, but problems of another order, social, political, and economic, aggravated everywhere by the more intense application of new methods of industrial production, it was these that the revolution brought to the foreground, creating about them an eager, curious, and restless atmosphere, an atmosphere that was not only restless, but even one of battle, likely to stimulate studies of the social sciences, to divide intelligences, and to give intellectual activity a sectarian spirit. Hence the domination of a concern for reform over the desire for objectivity in the greater part of these works in which, through the constant mixture of the planes of theory and the normative, it is not always easy to disentangle philosophical ideas or simple and unilateral doctrines from the content due to scientific research, which is in general very limited. The thinker whose only ambition should be research upon facts and reflection upon them knows that the world does not belong to him except as an object of his study, and "even if he could he would perhaps find it so curious that he would not have the courage to reshape it." Characterized at the beginning by this practical and applied attitude, this intellectual movement was one of the most fruitful which has arisen among us, not only on account of its intensity, but also because of the variety of movements to which it gave rise in various sectors of study and in scientific work. It was at this time, in 1931, that the university problem was most intensely discussed and that there was an attempt made in the reform of Francisco Campos, to solve it. In 1932 in São Paulo, the School of Sociology and Politics was founded, and later, in 1935, a Faculty of Philosophy, Science, and Letters—the first officially supported one which arose in Brazil —followed soon after by the Faculty of Sciences of the Federal District and by the National Faculty of Philosophy. It was between 1934 and 1935 that there was organized in São Paulo the Municipal Department of Culture, the activities of which in the field of historical and social research we can see in the excellent *Revista do*

Arquivo Municipal, and there was founded the Society of Sociology and that of Ethnography and Folklore, and the Association of Brazilian Geographers, besides other institutions of the same nature in various States. It was at this same time that our statistical services in general took on a remarkable development, being founded by J. L. S. de Bulhões Carvalho, the illustrious director of the census of 1920, and that there was created in 1934 in Rio de Janeiro, as a result of the efforts of the Federal Government and thanks to the incomparable tenacity of Teixeira de Freitas, aided by men of the first rank, the Brazilian Institute of Geography and Statistics, one of the most important institutions and one of the most far-reaching in science, social, and political affairs founded since the Revolution.[28] The missions of foreign professors, contracted in 1934 for the University of São Paulo—the first which received the influence of this kind of culture—and for those of Rio de Janeiro and Pôrto Alegre, intensified research in the field of ideas and facts; initiating for the first time in Brazil scientific investigations in experimental physics, they contributed notably to the penetration of the scientific spirit and methods in all the fields of intellectual specialization.

In the field of sociological studies which developed under the influence of Brazilian and foreign professors, especially after the introduction of sociology into the program of university studies, there appeared side by side with the first systematizers of sociology, research men and social historians who tried to give the story of our growth as a nation clearly and precisely in the living light of documents. Among the former, professional sociologists, there continued the work of a Pontes de Miranda and of a Delgado de Carvalho, a Miranda Reis, a Fernando Pires and an Emílio Willems, to cite only the names of some who have contributed most to apply scientific methods to the study of social phenomena and to the progress of the comparative study

[28] The Brazilian Geographic and Statistic Institute, created by Decree-Law 24,609, of July 6, 1934, although it is a recent institution, is one of those which has shown the greatest vitality, in the three great sectors embraced by its services: statistics, geography, census. Among its chief activities we find the creation of uniformity in statistics in Brazil, the remarkable work to which Teixeira de Freitas has devoted his great abilities and spirit of sacrifice since 1921; the publication of the *Anuário Estatístico;* the organization of topographic maps and the development of Brazilian cartography, to which contributions of the greatest value had already been made by the Foreign Office and the War Department through the Commission on the General Map of Brazil, organized in 1900, and the Military Geographic Service, created later, which were brought together in 1932 under the name of the Army Geographic and Historical Service; the preparation of a new and up-to-date edition of the map of the Engineering Club, published in 1922; a national exposition of city maps, in 1940, including all the *municípios* of Brazil, to the number of 1,574; the preparation of studies of statistical terminology and of a bibliography of Brazilian geography; and most important of all, the task entrusted to it by the federal government, putting under its responsibility and direction, through the National Census Commission, under the presidency of Dr. Carneiro Filipe, the census of 1940, the broadest in scope yet undertaken in Brazil. Presided over by Dr. J. C. de Macedo Soares, diplomat, historian, and former minister, and having for its general secretary Dr. M. A. Teixeira de Freitas, this institute carries on active work in the field of research and operations in geography and statistics and maintains two quarterly publications, both models of their kind: the *Revista Brasileira de Geografia* and the *Revista Brasileira de Estatística.* (Cf. the 1939 Report of the president of the institute, Dr. José Carlos de Macedo Soares, to the President of the Republic [Rio: Printing Office of the Instituto Brasileiro de Geografia e Estatística, 1940]; *Legislação orgânica do Sistema Estatístico-Geográfico Brasileiro* [1934–1939], Vol. 1, Organização Nacional [Rio: Printing Office of the I.B.G.E., 1940].)

of human groups and their institutions.[29] Among the latter, the social historians Oliveira Viana, who preceded all of them with his *Populações Meridionais* and *Evolução do Povo Brasileiro,* and Gilberto Freyre, the greatest interpreter of our social history, have made with their work of social analysis not only a contribution of the first importance to the penetration of our past, but have given an example and a stimulus to the scientific study of societies. They contributed, in fact, to emphasize the utility of efforts made in the field of teaching and research, in the sense of maintaining the true scientific value of sociology apart from all doctrinary preferences and preoccupations with practical necessities. In *Casa grande e senzala* (1934), a work remarkable for its precision of analysis and one extraordinarily rich in observations, Gilberto Freyre gave us the most influential work which has been published in Brazil since *Os Sertões.* In this great book, dedicated to the study of rural patriarchal society in the colonial epoch, as in *Sobrados e mucambos* (1936), in which he treats of the decadence of the rural patriarchal society and the formation of the urban bourgeoisie, and in his regional monograph *Nordeste,* the eminent Brazilian sociologist, as Roger Bastide observes, "proceeding by the accumulation of small facts, by minute, almost infinitesimal analyses, coming back to certain important traits always with new light to throw upon them," succeeded in resuscitating, "through these hundreds of crowded, compact paragraphs, laden with details, an atmosphere and a climate that has disappeared, that of old Brazil." [30] His sociological work, which is characterized by the application of the historical-cultural method to the study of Brazilian growth and in which there is manifest a strong reaction against the racial thesis of Oliveira Viana, marks without doubt an extraordinarily fruitful and decisive phase in the scientific evolution of social studies in Brazil, renewing the methods of investigation and opening up new perspectives. In the three works *O Negro Brasileiro* (1934), the *Folclore Negro do Brasil,* and *As Culturas Negras no Novo Mundo,* Arthur Ramos, continuing the research of Nina Rodrigues, accomplished a series of studies of the greatest scientific interest on the origins of the Negroes imported to Brazil, their distribution through the different regions of the country, their customs and their primitive cultures. But if the work of Gilberto Freyre, who also studied the Negro "in the whole system of his social relations," and the work of Artur Ramos, in which he has studied him "in himself and independently of his social position," have led to a great interest in scientific Afro-Brazilian studies, succeeding in awakening in the North a literary movement which exalts the African, the studies of the indigenous tribes continued silently in the activities of museums and ethnographic explorations, isolated and dispersed, especially in Mato

---

[29] Cf. Pontes de Miranda, *Introdução à sociologia geral* (Rio: Pimenta de Melo, 1926); Delgado de Carvalho, *Sociologia.* 2 vols. (Rio: Francisco Alves, 1931); *Sociologia educacional* (São Paulo: Comp. Editora Nacional, 1933); *Sociologia experimental* (Rio: Sauer, 1934); Fernando de Azevedo, *Princípios de sociologia: Pequena introdução ao estudo de sociologia geral* (São Paulo: Comp. Editora Nacional, 1st ed., 1935; 2nd ed., 1939); *Sociologia Educacional: Introdução ao estudo dos fenômenos educacionais e de suas relações com os outros fenômenos socias* (São Paulo: Comp. Editora Nacional, 1940), Spanish ed., *Sociologia de la educación* (Mexico: Fondo de Cultura Económica, 1942).

[30] Roger Bastide, "État actuel des études afro-brésiliennes: Le Problème du contact des races," in *Revue internationale de sociologie,* Vol. 47, Nos. I-II, Jan., Feb., 1939, pp. 77-89 (Paris, 1939); cf. Paul Arbousse-Bastide, Preface to Gilberto Freyre's book *Um Engenheiro francês no Brasil,* Collection of Documentos Brasileiros (Rio: José Olímpio, 1940), pp. i-xxxv.

Grosso and in Maranhão. The Brazilian school of ethnology, traditions of which go back to Alexandre Rodrigues Ferreira, Gonçalves Dias,[31] and Couto de Magalhães, and which have been receiving the collaboration for more than a century of Martius, Von den Steinen (1888), Schmidt, and in the twentieth century, Colbacchini, Herbert Baldus, and Kurt Nimuendaju—the greatest of them all—acquired new life with Roquete Pinto, in his studies over the Parecis and the Nambiquaras, and Heloísa Tôrres, with her investigations on the ceramics of Marajó, to enter a new phase of interpretation and analysis of the structures of primitive society in which two foreign ethnologists stand out, Kurt Nimuendaju, with his notable monographs on the eastern Canelas (*Ramkökamekra*) and Lévi-Strauss, with his masterly pages, published in 1937 in the *Revista do Arquivo Municipal*, on the Bororós of the northern region of Mato Grosso.

This is, in its general lines, the story of the evolution of scientific culture in Brazil in a period which extends to a little over a century. In the whole history of our culture, remarkable in the scientific field for notable figures, that are, however, exceptional, there has always been lacking, to establish the equilibrium of our intellectual health, the habit of mathematical objectivity and that love of fact, that rigor of observation, that constant control of theory by our senses, and that critical and experimental spirit which only physics, chemistry, and the natural sciences could give us. The general attitude of the Brazilian face to face with science—an attitude of admiration for the conquest of science, but of indifference and lack of interest in scientific work—is determined exclusively by the cultural atmosphere in which he has been educated and by the conditions of social and economic life. If he has his roots in a type of education which is almost three centuries old, with the predominance, if not the exclusive domination of letters, it was not the less favored and stimulated by immediate, utilitarian needs, characteristic of young countries in which practical problems of a material and economic order necessarily must put in the second place, if not relegate to complete abandonment, preoccupations of a cultural nature. A young people, whose élite for more than three centuries of the colonial regime were shaped by the mechanism of a verbalistic and literary teaching, destined like no other to make man an isolated individual, incapable of action, defenseless against himself, Brazil, when she had barely awakened to liberty, had to confront arduous and complex problems which she was not prepared for nor capable of solving, and which, from the very dawn of the nation, blocked her on all sides. On the one hand there was the tendency to subjectivism which was developed with the exclusive cultivation of letters, forming a dogmatic spirit, increasing sensitivity and favoring extravagances of the imagination; and on

---

[31] Gonçalves Dias, as we have said, was a member of the Brazilian commission organized in 1857 for the scientific exploration of the provinces of the north; he was requested to study the Indians of Amazonas. The great poet of the Indian—and our greatest poet—who was also an Indian student of indisputable merit, author of the *Dicionário de Língua Tupi* (Leipzig, 1856), collected in two years abundant ethnographic material, which was deposited in the National Museum, disorderly and unclassified. The recent studies of Raimundo Lopes, completed thanks to the documentation brought together by Nogueira da Silva, have succeeded in large measure in restoring and classifying this valuable collection; the report which described it (a volume of the Exposition of 1861) was forgotten, and it was broken up and scattered and its remnants were not adequately interpreted. (See Chestmir Loukotka, "Línguas indígenas do Brasil: Distribuição e bibliografia, in *Revista do Arquivo Municipal*, fifth year, Vol. 54, Feb., 1939, São Paulo, pp. 147-174.)

the other hand, the boundless utilitarianism, to which the hard struggle for the conquest of a minimum of material life habituated us, were to remain for four centuries like traditional elements as unfavorable as possible to the progress of the sciences through the work of research, which is only possible and efficacious when there is present the habit of a severe technique which requires constant preparation and enforcement of discipline at every moment. But if between science and philosophy there is only a difference of point of view, to wit, that "the philosophic point of view is more general and presents itself always a little in the character of an adventure," a leap into the unknown without keeping constant points of support; if philosophy does not differ from science, which it presupposes and on which it is based, except by a greater generality of hypotheses,[32] it is easy to understand that science and philosophy, being intimately connected in their evolution, the latter could not have grown in a country of recent scientific culture, in which social and economic conditions were always as little favorable to scientific research as to philosophic speculation and therefore to the flowering of original ways of looking at life and the world. The afternoon is certainly, in the existence of individuals as in that of peoples, the hour of dreaming and of meditation. In young peoples who are still struggling to achieve unity and maintain their freedom, this dream, fed on an interest in transcendent problems and on meditation, when it comes to sweep away some pioneer spirits, is often interrupted and its wings are quickly broken and its inspiration is short-lived. The wide horizons are generally prohibited to it. What concerns it above all, for the problems which agitate it, are particular local and national solutions, not human solutions; and although we have found inspiration in contact with outside cultures, we have not been able to create anything more than a culture for domestic use, like certain wines which cannot be exported and have no flavor except in the very place in which they are made.

The evolution of philosophic thought among us is so closely connected during the first three centuries "with the ideological climate" of the peninsula under which our colonization developed, and in the nineteenth century with imported European currents of philosophic thought, that the history that philosophy has had in Brazil, as Cruz Costa observes, is no more than the history of that influence and of that continued importation. If the relations between Brazilian literature and European literature have a pendulumlike rhythm from the middle of the nineteenth century, since our literature has attempted now to affirm itself and to be itself, and now to return, in order to renew itself, to the great fountain of foreign literatures, the relations between philosophy in Brazil and the currents of western thought are on the contrary marked always by a character of pure imitation and subordination. Philosophy, being reduced in the colony to the rigid framework of the old philosophy which was bequeathed us by the Portuguese tradition, in the words of Euclides da Cunha, "parroted in the gross eclecticism of Father Mont'Alverne," and during the nineteenth century followed in all its changes the rhythm of different directions imposed by new philosophic currents, whether materialistic or positivistic. "What is immediately noted in the greater part of the Brazilian philosophical writing," writes Father Leonel Franca, "is lack of originality. We cannot yet claim, like the great civilized nations, a certain autonomy of thought, but what we can claim that is new and our own is very little and very slight. We reflect more or less passively the ideas of others. We navigate

---

[32] Abel Rey, *La Philosophie moderne* (Paris: Ernest Flammarion, 1911).

slowly and following in the wake opened by other ships. We reproduce, in the philosophic field, the struggles of other lands and we fight with borrowed weapons." In fact, no vigorous element of creation, no rebellion of critical thought, no deviation from the paths already opened and trodden. But if the analysis of the evolution of philosophic ideas in Brazil does not offer any research in the field of ideas or any production that is truly original and therefore no thinker sufficiently robust and profound so that we may give him the name of "philosopher," Brazilians were not indifferent to questions which concerned European thought from the beginning of the past century, and some of them, brilliant and persuasive essayists, made notable contributions to the spread among us of modern philosophic currents of thought, such as positivism and materialism in their various forms. They are agitators of ideas like Tobias Barreto, who reacted in the north against French imitation, but only to subordinate himself to German culture, dragging after him a whole generation of illustrious Brazilians into the orbit of the influence of the movement of ideas which he began in Recife, and which Carlos de Laet called ironically, the "Teuto-Sergipan school," bringing together in the very name the Germanism of the head of the school and the small province of his birth. A restless and combative spirit within whom there succeeded, depending upon the period, a spiritualist, a positivist, a metaphysician, and even a materialist, Tobias Barreto, like Sílvio Romero, was above all a sower of ideas and a demolisher of routines, and more than anyone he contributed with his works and his polemics, to spread systems and philosophic currents of thought. In both of them—and these are the greatest many-sided writers of the so-called "school of Refice"—as in their disciples in general, we find the same instability and incoherence of thought which led some of our essayists to go through various systems only to return at times to their point of departure; the same seduction by novelties, the same restlessness and lack of discipline of the mind, and instead of philosophic speculation which is serene and fecund, the public debate which is passionate and sterile and takes the form of wild polemics. No doctrine, however, after the scholastic one, had more effect among us nor exercised a more disciplinary role than that of the positivist school, which was introduced into Brazil in the second half of the nineteenth century [33] and was spread in the south especially under the leadership of L. Pereira Barreto, Miguel Lemos (1854–1916), and Teixeira Mendes (1855–1927), "that profoundly religious and

[33] The spread of the philosophy of Auguste Comte in Brazil dates from 1858, in which year A. F. Muniz de Aragão gave us in the introduction to his *Elementos de Matemáticas* (Bahia, 1858) the first résumé known of the positivist doctrine. About that time (1857–1863), some young Brazilians, students at the University of Brussels, like Luiz Pereira Barreto and Francisco Antônio Brandão Júnior, felt, while they were still abroad, the first influence of that current of thought which only after 1870 began to spread in the north of the country, in which the ideas of Auguste Comte were immediately counterbalanced and then dominated by the monism of Haeckel, and especially in the south, where positivism ruled until the end of the past century—which marked its decline. In various articles ("Teologia e teodicéia não são ciências"; "Moisés e Laplace"; "A Religão perante a psicologia") published in 1868, Tobias Barreto, until then an idealist, shows the positivist attitude to which he was for a time inclined. Among the group of students in Brussels, F. A. Brandão Júnior published in 1865, under the influence of positivist ideas, a book on *A Escravatura no Brasil*, and L. Pereira Barreto, then a loyal disciple of the school of Comte, gave us in 1874 the first volume of *As três filosofias*. It was not until 1877 that there appeared the *Primeiros ensaios positivistas*, by Miguel Lemos, who, together with Teixeira Mendes, was to have the greatest influence in the leadership of the positivist movement in Brazil.

incorruptible soul," in the words of Euclides da Cunha, a kind of spiritual director and austere priest of a new religion. Positivism, a philosophy which aborted and became a system of morality and religion in Brazil, from which there came ideas of social and political reform rather than methods, made a notable contribution through the mental and moral discipline of the men who received the impression of this current of thought, like Benjamim Constant, to the reaction against anarchy, the defense of order, and the consolidation of the new political regime.

If, however, we had a "professional philosopher," it was without doubt Farias Brito (Ceará, 1862–1917), who, getting his initiation under the German influence of the north, directed the spiritual reaction against the two currents, positivism and materialism, which were disputing between them the supremacy in Brazilian thought. Without being a profound and original thinker, the author of the *Base física do espírito* (1912) and the *Mundo interior* (1914) was doubly faithful to his ideal as a philosopher, giving himself entirely to problems of a speculative order, allowing himself to be so penetrated by his convictions that he really succeeded in living them, adjusting his own life of work and struggles to his work as a thinker. Certainly, although it was dominated by a mystical spirit and crossed by tragic visions of life, the work of the Brazilian thinker of the *Mundo interior,* in which there is brought out the cunning of his critical sense, and of the *Base física do espírito,* a methodical study of the evolution of psychology in the nineteenth century, shows as a whole an independence of judgment, a solidity of philosophical knowledge, although limited to the last three centuries, and such maturity of intelligence that they would be sufficient to raise him to a unique position in the history of philosophy in Brazil. But if his unlimited dedication to abstract studies, the intense pleasure which he felt in thinking, his sincerity more than his coherence, the harmony between the man and the thinker, and the dominant characteristic of his philosophy, which approaches Christian spiritualism without, however, attaining it in any of his books, constitute perhaps the principal secret of the position which he has acquired among all those who have been concerned with things of the spirit, and especially in Catholic circles. In the field of philosophical studies, no movement, however, has been comparable to that which arose in the field of experimental sciences, around that focus of research created in the Institute of Manguinhos and which led to the foundation in 1916 of the Brazilian Academy of Sciences, the first lasting movement in the direction of coordinating the efforts of Brazilian investigators in the different sectors of the vast field of scientific study. After Farias Brito, in the year 1918, there appeared the first history of philosophy worthy of that name, written in the Portuguese language in Brazil, that of Father Leonel Franca, a Jesuit philosopher and a historian of philosophy who, in his second edition enriched his excellent work of a didactic nature by a synthesis of the history of philosophy in Brazil, the most complete and the clearest which has been written in the whole period of our national life. The enormous backwardness in which philosophy in Brazil has remained has led some essayists like Tobias Barreto to attribute it to a "natural defect of the Brazilian intelligence." But when one thinks, on the one hand, of the fact that the first faculties of philosophy and sciences, preceded by some attempts in the same order, were only created from 1934 on, four centuries after the beginning of colonization in Brazil, and that on the other hand, during our whole history, the country has only known higher schools of a professional type destined to train people for the liberal careers, the country produced great scientific values in the midst of conditions that were generally unfavorable. One cannot fail to search for the cause of this fact in the value of the race which here flowered in the heart of nature. Where one must seek for the causes of our backwardness in the field of philosophy and science is, then, in the lack of higher studies of a methodical and profound nature under the direction of great teachers and—more than in this deficiency—in the whole system of education and of culture that was set up from the time of the colony to develop exclusively our literary and dialectical attitude and our taste for rhetoric and erudition. Brazil, emancipated from the oppression by the home country while still in its adolescent period, breathed deeply in the dawn which followed the intellectual night and felt at ease beside the bubbling fountain of letters, without dreaming that this crystalline water, fed by classic springs, concealed more than one snare for the freedom of our mind and that there was more than one illusion for our culture under these enchanting flowers.

BIBLIOGRAPHY

Amoroso Costa, M., *Conferência sôbre Oto de Alencar* (Rio: Casa Leuzinger, 1918).

Andrade, Almir, *Aspectos da cultura brasileira* (Rio: Schmidt, 1939), Chap. II, "Os Novos Estudos sociais no Brasil), pp. 35–83, and Chap. IV, "Aspectos da cultura científica," pp. 143–179.

Betim Pais Leme, A., "Etat des connaissances géologiques sur le Brésil: Rapports avec la théorie de Wegener sur la dérive des continents," *Bull. Soc. Geol. France,* 4th series, Vol. 29, pp. 35.

———, "La Théorie de Wegener en présence de quelques observations géologiques concernant le Brésil," *C. R. Acad. des Sciences,* Vol. 186, p. 802.

Cap, L., "A Astronomia no Brasil," in *Educação* (São Paulo), Vol. 11, No. 2 (May, 1930). Transl. from the *Gazette* of the Antwerp Astronomical Society, May, 1929.

Correia Filho, V., *Alexandre Rodrigues Ferreira: Vida e obra do grande naturalista brasileiro* (São Paulo: Comp. Editora Nacional, 1939—Brasiliana, Vol. 144).

Cruz Costa, João, "Alguns aspectos da filosofia no Brasil," in *Filosofia, Ciências e Letras,* Vol. 3, No. 6 (Apr., 1938), pp. 46–54.

Fávero, Flamínio, "Instituto Oscar Freire," in *Medicina no Brasil* (Rio: Imprensa Nacional, 1940), pp. 239–244.

Fonseca Filho, O. da, "Dados históricos sôbre as investigações de protozoologia, especialmente as de interêsse médico realizadas no Brasil," in *Medicina no Brasil* (Rio: Imprensa Nacional, 1940), pp. 108–128.

Franca, Father Leonel, *A Filosofia no Brasil* (Rio: Pimenta de Melo, 1928), Chap. III, "Noções de história da filosofia," pp. 233–307.

Francovich, Guillermo, *Filósofos brasileños* (Rio, 1939).

Freyre, Luíz, "A Obra matemática de Teodoro Ramos," in *Jornal do Comércio,* Rio, July 5, 1936.

Furtado Reis, T., *Os Brasileiros na história da navegação aérae: Dúvidas e controversias* (Rio, 1934).

Hoehne, F. C., "A Flora do Brasil," especially "Notas históricas sôbre o estudo da flora no Brasil," in *Recenseamento do Brasil* (Sept. 1, 1920) (Rio: Tip. da Estatística, 1922), Vol. 1, *Introdução,* pp. 103–126.

———, *Botânica e agricultura no Brasil no século XVI* (São Paulo: Comp. Editora Nacional, 1937—Brasiliana, Vol. 71).

Lima, Hermes, *Tobias Barreto: A Epoca e o homem* (São Paulo: Comp. Editora Nacional, 1939—Brasiliana, Vol. 140).

Lira, Heitor, *História de D. Pedro II* (São Paulo: Comp. Editora Nacional, 1938–1940—Brasiliana, Vols. 133, 133A, 133B).

Mamede, Eduardo, "Instituto Nina Rodrigues," in *Medicina no Brasil* (Rio: Imprensa Nacional, 1940), pp. 233–239.

Matos, Aníbal, *Peter Wilhelm Lund no Brasil: Problemas de paleontologia brasileira* (São Paulo: Comp. Editora Nacional, 1939—Brasiliana, Vol. 148).

Melo Leitão, C. de, *A Biologia no Brasil* (São Paulo: Comp. Editora Nacional, 1937—Brasiliana, Vol. 99).

——, *Zoogeografia do Brasil* (São Paulo: Comp. Editora Nacional, 1937—Brasiliana, Vol. 77).

——, História das expedições científicas no Brasil (São Paulo: Comp. Editora Nacional—Brasiliana).

Moreira, Juliano, "O Progresso das ciências no Brasil, in *Anais da Biblioteca Nacional do Rio de Janeiro*, Vol. 35 (1913), pp. 32–47.

Neiva, Artur, *Esboço histórico sôbre a botânica e a zoologia no Brasil* (São Paulo: Soc. Impressora Paulista, 1929). From Gabriel Soares de Sousa, 1587, to Sept. 7, 1922.

Osório de Almeida, M., "A Mentalidade científica no Brasil," in *Folha médica* (Rio, 1920), pp. 115–118. Lecture given Aug. 26, 1920, in the auditorium of the *Jornal do Comércio*, Rio.

Ramos, Teodoro, *Estudos: Ensino, ciências físicas e matemáticas* (São Paulo: Oficinas das Escolas Profissionais do Liceu Coração de Jesús, 1933), Pt. 1, Gomes de Sousa, Amoroso Costa, pp. 7–25.

Roquete Pinto, E., "Aborígenes e etnógrafos," in *Anais da Biblioteca Nacional de Rio de Janeiro*, Vol. 35 (1913), pp. 89–107.

——, "Rondônia," in *Arquivos do Museu Nacional*, Vol. 10 (1917). In book form, 3rd enlarged ed. (São Paulo: Comp. Editora Nacional, 1935—Brasiliana, Vol. 39).

——, *Ensaios de antropologia brasiliana* (São Paulo: Comp. Editora Nacional, 1933—Brasiliana, Vol. 22).

Sampaio, A. J., *Fitogeografia do Brasil* (São Paulo: Comp. Editora Nacional, 1934—Brasiliana, Vol. 35).

Sampaio Ferraz, J., *Meteorologia brasileira: Esboço elementar de seus principais problemas* (São Paulo: Comp. Editora Nacional, 1934—Brasiliana, Vol. 33), especially "Ligeira bosquejo histórico," pp. 19–35, "Pesquisas científicas," pp. 444–457, "O Ensino da meteorologia no Brasil," pp. 509–516.

Serrano, Jônatas, *Farias Brito: O Homem e a obra* (São Paulo: Comp. Editora Nacional, 1939—Brasiliana, Vol. 177).

Taunay, Afonso de E., *Visitantes do Brasil colonial (seculos XVI–XVIII)* (São Paulo: Comp. Editora Nacional, 1933—Brasiliana, Vol. 19).

——, *Bartolomeu de Gusmão e a sua prioridade aerostática* (São Paulo: Imprensa Oficial do Estado, 1938).

——, *A Vida gloriosa e trágica de Bartolomeu de Gusmão* (São Paulo: Imprensa Oficial do Estado, 1938).

Tales Martins, "Os Irmãos Osório e a evolução da fisiologia no Brasil," in *Medicina no Brasil* (Rio: Imprensa Nacional, 1940), pp. 323–331.

Viana Dias, Mário, "O Instituto Osvaldo Cruz," in *Medicina no Brasil* (Rio: Imprensa Nacional, 1940), pp. 98–107.

Wätjen, Hermann, *O Domínio colonial holandês no Brasil: Um Capítulo da história colonial do século XVII*, transl. by P. C. Uchoa Cavalcante (São Paulo: Comp. Editora Nacional, 1938—Brasiliana, Vol. 123).

CHAPTER FIVE

ART

Art in its various forms in the colonial period—During the Dutch domination in Pernambuco —Sacred architecture and the baroque—The early churches of Bahia and of Minas Gerais— The cloisters of the Northwest—The painting and decoration of the churches—Sculpture: Aleijadinho—Religious art and carving—An original Brazilian art—Master Valentim—Goldsmithing and the art of jewel cutting—The colonial house—Religious music and popular music—The first Brazilian composer: Father José Maurício—The mission of French artists (1816)—The Academy of Arts—Grandjean de Montigny, architect—The first expositions of painting—The rupture with the art of the colonial tradition—The awakening of Brazilian feeling in art—Painters of historical pictures—Vítor Meireles and Pedro Américo—Brazilian painting of manners: Almeida Júnior—The great landscape painters—Henrique Bernardelli and Batista da Costa—The fine arts and the industrial arts—Art enters journalism: caricature —Brazilian music—The Conservatory of Music—Carlos Gomes—The movement of modern art—Traditionalists and innovators—The sculpture of V. Brecheret—The minor arts—Painting and its dominant figures—Portinari—Architecture and the breaking of the bonds between the useful and the beautiful—Music: Villa-Lóbos—The public and the artist—Museums and picture galleries—Historians and critics of art

I N HIS REPLY to the investigation made by *Foi et Vie* on humanism, Romain Rolland, referring to the excessively narrow idea that university education has given us of the "literature" of a people, shows the necessity of widening the boundaries of this notion beyond the works called literary, which are not more than one story of the edifice of culture. "It is not, for example, knowing Germany (neither its thought nor its art), if we reduce it to its men of letters. . . . It is useful to remember the river Rhine with its great mystics Eckhart, Böhme. And culture, is it something assured by books? Would not the exercise of logical and constructive reason profit quite as much or more with the study of a great prelude, with a fugue of J. S. Bach, as with that of a poem or novel? And what poem, what novel of Germany goes farther in the analysis of the human heart than German sculpture of the fifteenth and sixteenth centuries? A great people does not express through its written language except in part, either its sensitivity or its experiences of life and its reason." [1] Great as may have been, then, the predominance of literary manifestations in our cultural history—and this preponderance reveals in itself less a trait of the national temperament than the character of the intellectual education which prevailed in the colony and the Empire—one could not claim to know Brazil without the study of its culture in other forms, plastic, pictorial, and rhythmic, which are as important for the comprehension of a people as the creation of literary genius. It is by art in all of its forms, and not only by the

[1] In *Pour un humanisme nouveau* (Cahiers de Foi et Vie, Paris), by Paul Arbousse-Bastide; preface by F. Strowski.

documents of cultivated or popular literature, that the characteristic original culture of a people manifests itself in fact, as the author of *Jean Christophe* reminds us. It is in statuary and painting, in architecture and in the decorative arts, in music, in the major and minor arts, that each people finds, as it were, the language, "a figurative writing," or means of expressing its thoughts, its necessities and aspirations. Certainly the history of art in Brazil reveals to us an extremely slow progress in art in almost all of its forms. But if we consider on the one hand all the social elements that are implied in aesthetic sentiments, "the profound effect of the social life upon the emotions of the individual," and all that life in society and social institutions bring to the development of art, and on the other hand the isolation in which the centers of culture in Brazil grew up in a sort of ganglionated society, with its centers initially separated from each other by vast distances and also separated from the centers of European culture, we cannot be surprised by the slow propagation of some forms of art in the colonial period and even during the period of the Empire. Moreover, the history of the arts is the history of leisure, which follows periods of economic prosperity; and in a people oppressed by immediate necessities and material life, the primordial necessities have necessarily to prevail for a long time over the necessities of luxury, which, being the expression of the development of a perfected life, are conditioned by the intensity and concentration of social life—both properties of urban civilization—and results of frequence of contact with different cultures. It is this subordination of art to a multitude of social necessities that are more urgent that explains our backwardness in the field of aesthetic activities. "At the banquet of humanity," said André Gide, "art is only called upon to finish the meal; its function is not that of nourishing but that of intoxicating." [2]

This hierarchy of importance between the different social functions, from the most urgent to the luxury functions which a society exercises through its artistic activity and which are destined in large measure to favor the former, could at first sight give us the explanation of the artistic movement which took place in Pernambuco during the rule of the Dutch. The occupation by the Flemings of the richest region of the country in the very heart of the sugar-cane cultivation, and the effort of creating a civilization of an urban type during the administration of Maurice of Nassau (1637–1644) might suggest the idea of the relation between artistic activities which were manifested in this period and the urban phenomena or the concentration of social life which followed the development of Recife, the construction of Olinda, and the foundation of a new city strewn with dikes and canals. The urban landscape of Recife was completely transformed by the constructive activity of the Dutch, and it became the most populous and cosmopolitan center of America, a city preferred by merchants, Jews, soldiers and workmen, and connected by a bridge to the island of Antônio Vaz, where there arose, according to the plans of Pieter Post, "in the fashion of Holland," the city Mauricéia (Mauritzstadt), the first that was built in Brazil according to plans laid down by an architect. Here arose the first city mansions; social life grew more intense; and Recife, which did not possess at the arrival of Nassau more than one hundred and fifty houses, could now boast, two years later, two thousand constructions; the city of the prince expanded with its palaces and gardens and there passed into its mansions and country houses wealthy bourgeoisie and lords of sugar mills. But

[2] Charles Lalo, *L'Art et la vie sociale* (Paris: Gaston Doin, 1921), pp. 94-97.

in this new Holland "the first attempt at urban colonization in Brazil," the flowering in which art broke out in its various forms, did not result as a product or consequence of these phenomena of urban concentration, of too short duration to have the power to provoke them. It was to such an extent the work of Dutch artists without effect upon their environment that it would be difficult to give it a place in the history of Brazilian art as the initial phase of its development. Of the six painters whom Maurice of Nassau brought with him and of whom only three are known, Albert Eeckhout, Zacharias Wagner, and Franz Post, the brother of Pieter Post, not one in fact was related to the country or trained disciples or marked in any way with his influence the first phase of the evolution of the arts in Brazil. In the colony directed by the Prince of Nassau, which was a Dutch cyst in America, the whole artistic movement, which was exclusively a foreign movement, remained insulated, without effect, within the limits of the three urban centers in which, under the government of Nassau, there were installed architects and mechanics, painters and sculptors, learned men and artists from Holland. The engravings, paintings, and color drawings which composed Dutch art and which even today have not been completely inventoried, were scattered through the museums of the Hague, Amsterdam, Munich, Prague, Vienna, and Copenhagen. Of the architecture imposed upon the tropical city there remained only, as Gilberto Freyre remarked, a reminiscence of Flemish roofs, some of them inclined almost straight up and down and conserved by tradition in the oldest mansions of Recife. It was, none the less, the Dutch who brought to the north of the country a feeling and a taste for urban life, and that, introducing into the American continent the spirit of the Renaissance, broke for the first time the unity of the Jesuitical culture; and it was with them that there arose in Brazil the first artistic manifestations, with Pieter Post planning cities which should reflect the Dutch countryside; with Franz Post,[3] greatest of the painters who came in the train of the Flemish prince, painting

[3] During their stay in Brazil, the Dutch painters studied and put down on their canvases and in their drawings all that was most characteristic in their new physical and social environment: landscape, aspects of life and of the agricultural technique of the sugar mills, local types, Negroes, Indians, and mestizos. Hence the originality and the historic and geographic interest of this art, based on the environment and full of the local color that the Flemings were the first to take to Europe in their pictures of the Brazilian scene. In almost all the pictures in which they painted the Brazilian natural scene, the landscapes are "humanized," serving as background for types of Indians or Negroes, aspects of city life, the technique of the sugar industry or the rural labor of the plantations. In some pictures, such as Wagner's painting, "The Residence of the Prince of Nassau in Recife," one might even criticize a rather exaggerated desire to attain a very lively effect with the movement of clients and slaves in the courtyard of the palace. The picturesqueness and coloring of the pictures bathed in tropical light, in which everything was portrayed that the human landscape offered to the eye of the artist, constituted, in the Renaissance of northern Europe, the most attractive side of Dutch painting based on Brazil's northeast. Finished portraits or sketches of racial types, "which here offered them the delight of the exotic," writes Gilberto Freyre, sometimes bear no signature, like the picture of the native dance in the Ethnographic Museum of Copenhagen, two portraits of Brazilian Negroes and, in the Zoobilion, pictures of a dance of Negroes, and a slave market in Pernambuco and a village of Brazilian Indians or Tupis. (See Paul Ehrenreich, "Sôbre alguns antigos retratos de índios sul-americanos," transl. by Oliveira Lima in *Revista* of the Archeological Institute of Pernambuco, No. 65). We have of Franz Post, the artist of the drawings which border the maps of Barleus's book, among other works, the engravings which picture the Palace of Bela Vista (1643), the summer residence of the governor in Mauricéia, a view of the city of Olinda, a chapel of Pernambuco, the ruins of which recall the

in his pictures, with their intense color, aspects of the tropical countryside and of the rural life of the sugar plantations, and with Wagner and Eeckhout, who left in their drawings and portraits of local types, Indians, Negroes, and mestizos, work of great ethnographic interest and documentary value. Of all the intellectual and artistic activities, the one which was least developed in the Nassau period dominated by the Renaissance was literature, in part owing to the cosmopolitan surroundings of Recife, which were more favorable to the flowering of the plastic arts than to that of literature, and in part because, as Honório Rodrigues rightly observes, besides the fact that there was no unity of language in the Dutch colony, the language of the invader never succeeded in imposing itself in a way which would create a "public" for literary production.

But this impulse which the Dutch gave to the arts, raising them in the Nassau period to the same level to which they raised the whole of culture, did not have any effect nor exercise any influence on the older and more stable strata of the population in the very captaincies that were conquered. Besides being ephemeral (since rigorously speaking it did not last with the same intensity more than eight years), it was superficial, and for this reason this contact of North European culture with the Portuguese culture had further to attenuate its effect, the profound differences which separated the two cultures in conflict—that of the invaders who came late and that of the first colonizers of the country, who had already built up in the whole territory "one single civilization." While the Dutchman, bourgeois and Calvinistic, was inaugurating in the Northeast a civilization of an urban type, promoting the development of civil architecture, giving a stimulus to sciences and art, "reducing by his iconoclasm the ornamentation of churches," and awakening the taste for city life and for the interior decoration of residences, the Portuguese, an agriculturist and Catholic, continued to mark with his essential characteristics the Brazilian culture that was in the process of formation, in the cultivation of letters which the Jesuits taught to youth, in the neglect of sciences, in the scant attention given to urban development, in the simplicity of his houses with their bare walls and in the ornamental luxury of the churches. In the one culture, coming from the north of Europe, the creative, artistic, critical, and experimental spirit, nourished by the two currents of the Renaissance and the Reformation which flowed together; in the other, of Iberic origin, the dialectic, literary, and religious spirit, almost medieval in character, which gave an impressive uniformity to the social and political landscape of our civilization. Not even the culture of Pernambuco itself, which suffered most closely and directly the influence of the Dutch culture "separated," writes Honório Rodrigues, "from Brazilian civilization, due to the influence of these other

---

Alentejo style of the Renaissance, and the first Brazilian landscapes. Besides the color drawings (1637) in which he set down the war dance of the Tapuyas, a native village, a sugar mill, the slave market in Mauricéia and four local types, Zacharias Wagner painted the residence of the prince in Recife and a negro slave woman, which last passes for one of his best works. As for Albert Eeckhout, brother of Gerbrandt Eeckhout, a pupil of Rembrandt, the two excellent crayon studies of Tapuya Indians, to be found in the Public Library of Berlin, would suffice to give him high rank among the painters of the Dutch artistic mission. (See reproductions of some of these pictures in J. Honório Rodrigues and Joaquim Ribeiro, *Civilização Holandesa no Brasil* [São Paulo: Comp. Editora Nacional, 1940–Brasiliana]; *Frans Post Exposition*, with an introduction by Ribeiro Couto and a catalogue of the pictures shown [Rio: National Museum of Fine Arts, Ministry of Education and Health, 1942].)

values. The contact was rapid and therefore there was only the superposition of cultural layers on the life of the Northeast." Portuguese, Catholic culture, older by a century in America, had already put down its roots and extended sufficiently to dissolve the cultural elements imported by the invaders, who were heretics, whose works were not to be long in disappearing in the destruction of war and in the loss of fires, and in whose points of view there were only seen centers of rebellion, suspect from the religious point of view, which under the spiritual domination of the Jesuits reached the point of mysticism in the Brazilian population. It is above all in the eighteenth century that there began in fact the history of the arts in Brazil, with religious architecture and the related arts put to the service of the interior decoration of churches, both inspired by baroque tendencies which were then dominant in Europe and transplanted to Brazil with all that that spirit meant of romanticism, sentimental opposition to the rational, or in other words, of reaction to the classic Renaissance. A phenomenon of a general character which had its origin in the art of the Counter Reformation of Italy (or of Spain, as others insist), the baroque movement had a profound effect in Brazil, because the Jesuits who adopted it were more preoccupied with the aesthetic problems of ornamenting the interiors of their churches than with their architectural aspects. The general idea of these works in the baroque style—temples, churches, and palaces, which are everywhere in Europe great, emphatic poems—was not embarrassed by any logic, even of architecture. It is all based upon the primordial necessity of a lyric interest. The spirit, or, if you wish, the style of the baroque in sculpture, in painting, and in architecture, and in the variety of forms and aspects which it assumed, depending upon the country, represented in Italy, in Spain, and especially in Austria, the triumph of the theatrical, of feeling over the intellectual. It "was the creation of a fabulous world, a world on a par with the potentates of the time, magnificent, almost deified, a world which does not rest upon the ground, but which lives in the absolute and its dreams." It was in this style, derived from a feeling of reaction against classic dogmatism in the peninsula, that the religious feeling of the country found its means of expression, utilizing it not only for the ornamental and essentially liturgical decoration of the interior of the churches of the Jesuits, but also for the architectonic conception of numerous temples; and if there is an art of Brazilian civilization in the colonial period, it was without doubt, as Augusto de Lima Júnior writes, the architectonic and decorative art that found its inspiration in the baroque, which, having been the style of the splendor of Portuguese civilization, once transplanted with it to Brazil, became the magnificent expression of the patriarchal, religious, sentimental, and mystical character of our period of formation.

It was not, however, the Jesuits who brought the baroque to its highest point when they utilized it—not as a plastic architectonic expression, but for the interior decoration of their temples, or, to employ the words of José Mariano Filho, for the development of the liturgical, ornamental part. Nor did religious architecture of baroque style transplanted from Portugal follow in the colony the same line of development as in the home country and a local evolution that was uniform in all regions. Of the churches and buildings of the Jesuits following classic Portuguese models, like the Colégio of Bahia, an edifice of Benedictine lines, only two, according to Augusto de Lima Júnior—the Cruz dos Militares in Rio and another in Recife—represent the authentic baroque as worked out by the Jesuits, who only in Maranhão, where they had great resources, left notable remains, but of heavy and monotonous façades, like that of the old church of Castelo in Rio, "with capitals at the corners of the front, reminiscent of Brunelleschi's Renaissance architecture, and the pine tower that is so very Portuguese." For Roger Bastide, who studied the evolution of the baroque in Brazil from the sociological point of view, the hypertrophy of the interior decoration in comparison to the architectonic part— one of the common characteristics of Brazilian baroque—had its explanation rather in the poverty of the country and its progressive enrichment, and therefore in the economic factor. "The church could only ornament itself in proportion as wealth increased, but as the exterior was already finished, the baroque could only triumph in the interior." In addition to the differences which separate the European baroque from the Brazilian baroque and which are related, as Roger Bastide says, to differences between European society, which is aristocratic, and colonial society which is patriarchal (hence the simplification of the Brazilian baroque through the influence not only of the economic element but through that of the simplicity of the social environment), the styles of baroque in the country become differentiated according to the region, taking on in the Northeast, in Rio, and Minas Gerais characteristics of their own that are purely defined.[4] What differentiates during the eighteenth century the religious architecture of the Northeast from that of Minas Gerais, where the prohibition of religious orders on the part of the government prevented the development of conventual architecture, which was replaced by the churches of societies, there are, among other elements, the contrast between their poor sacristies and the rich sacristies, "true drawing rooms of the Northeast," and the less important role played by tiles in the

---

[4] Religious architecture in Brazil, which sprang from the Portuguese church—the model of our churches—follows the evolution of ecclesiastical architecture in the home country, which arose from preromantic, took on a mixed character, at once religious and military, half cloister and half fortress, and underwent, in the seventeenth and eighteenth centuries, the influences of the baroque. Of the two styles that Portugal had, the romantic and the Manueline Gothic, it was the romantic which had the greater influence among us, so that we may consider the Brazilian church, as Augusto de Lima Júnior remarks, as preromantic contaminated by the Arabs and "going through a slow but continuous evolution from Renaissance motifs to the most recherché baroque." All the stages of this long evolution can be found in Brazilian territory in examples which go from the most rustic to the most sumptuous. But the variety of architectonic forms in Brazil comes not only from this "temporal" superimposition of forms, corresponding to different phases of the evolution of Portuguese architecture, but also from a kind of "differentiation" in space, or, in other words, from the special character which colonial religious architecture took on in its development, under the various influences of different parts of the country. These regional differences beween the baroque of the Northeast and that of Minas Gerais, between the architecture of the extremes (north and south), of the coast and the mountains, match the diversity of physical and social environments of an extremely scattered society, originally made up of nuclei of population separated by long distances and evolving in their long continued isolation to form very different social structures. The regional styles of the colonial period are, according to Robert C. Smith, who distinguishes at least four different kinds of building: (1) the Italian style, cold and severe, of the Jesuit establishments at the two ends of the country, Rio Grande do Sul and Amazonas; (2) the seventeenth century architecture of the north of Portugal, localized in Minas Gerais and Maranhão, where you find much of tropical Viseus and Bragas; (3) the style of the capital, later passing through complicated French and Italian influences, superimposed upon Portuguese models; (4) colonial architecture of the Northeast, with two different traditions, one tending to imitate the baroque style of rural Portuguese churches, and the other originating in the seventeenth century, based on the official court architecture of Lisbon or the temples of the Portuguese in Bahia and Pernambuco.

churches of Minas. "For the scattered society of the Northeast," explains Roger Bastide, "the church constituted the great social bond, the unifying cement of the patriarchal families, and the sacristy represented the Sunday aspect of this bond." The differences in decorative treatment with tiles were bound up with the differences in the recruiting of professional groups: "On the coast this recruiting took place among persons who immigrated from the south of Portugal and who brought with them, as Gilberto Freyre suggests, a little of the blood and the aesthetic taste of the Moors, while the recruitment in Minas Gerais took place chiefly among mestizos of Indians, Negroes, and whites." But with its common traits and its characteristics peculiar to regions, in both the architectural and decorative part, all of these great religious buildings upon which the spirit was impressed and which show, above all in their interior decoration, the pomp of the baroque, do not go back beyond the eighteenth century and are posterior therefore to the gold rush in Minas Gerais from 1698 on, which drew all of the attention of the home country to the extraction of mineral wealth, and by stimulating the opening of roads, the foundation of cities, and the current of immigration from the north to the south, contributed to form in a brief period "a dense strip of population through the interior of Bahia and Pernambuco to the center of Minas Gerais," whence there spread the greatest economic movement of the colonial period. Internal migrations, the arrival of groups of immigrants, attracted from Portugal by their hunger for gold, the presence in these groups of artists, sculptors, and architects, and the flourishing of an urban civilization necessarily has to produce those contacts and those "social frictions" which led to a movement of civilization and from which there was to result the development of culture in all of its aspects. From the point of view of architecture, the churches of Bahia were not slow to benefit by the cycle of mining; and later, by the route of the bandeirantes of Bahia—the so-called "road of the Portuguese"—and by the road from Rio to Vila Rica, there were opened routes for art which were at the same time the routes of slaves and of merchandise from the home kingdom, for the regions of the miners and gold washers in the mountains of the plateau.

Certainly this admirable rise of colonial art, from which there resulted the most beautiful religious monuments of the country, followed after a considerable period from the splendor of economic life which under the influence of the exploitation of gold and diamonds developed in Minas Gerais and in the interior of Bahia. It is not commercial activity but rather leisure which favors the arts in general.[5] That the technique of art should have a slower development than economic splendor is a fact generally observed and more than once verified in Minas Gerais, whose artistic high point does not correspond to the high point in economic development. "The extraction of gold," comments Roger Bastide, "attained its maximum between 1726 and 1750. Now, at this time the cities of Minas knew only humble habitations of stucco and modest chapels; it is only in the second half of the eighteenth century that there rose the great civil and religious monuments of which the region is so proud" and that, with the churches and the cloisters of the Northeast and especially of Bahia, constitute the major part of the artistic wealth of colonial Brazil. If in general the plans came from the home kingdom, sent from the seat of religious orders, and all, or nearly all, architects were imported, and if the architectural culture did not develop in the

[5] Lalo, *op. cit.*

colony, in which the teachers who were the authors of the sketches were almost always Portuguese, there did multiply in the Northeast, in Rio and in Minas Gerais, artists who had acquired from their teachers in the home country great ornamental ideas, the taste and the feeling for decoration, and who, having assimilated the foreign tech-niques, made these acquisitions their own, marking them at times with an original character resulting either from a different spirit or from the employment of new materials. The great painters of Bahia, of the value of Manuel da Costa Ataíde, and the best carvers of saints of the so-called "school of Bahia," like Manuel Meneses da Costa, rose after the fever of business; it was at this time, in which the artisan was barely distinguishable from the artist, that in the convent of St. Francis in Serinháem (1747) a sculptor of rude genius, writes Robert C. Smith, was able to create the angels, birds, and shells of the marvelous pulpit, and also the balusters of the monastic stairway with its sculptures, "works which came from the worship of some unknown Aleijadinho of the Northeast"; and both in Minas Gerais and on the coast there appeared a few of those painters, woodcutters, and sculptors who contributed to raise the baroque art of ornamentation to a high level and to create magnificent church interiors, re-splendent with the abundance of their carving, with sculptural work, and with all the beauty of the adornment of the madonnas and the images. But the greatest of all is without doubt the mestizo of Vila Rica, Antônio Francisco Lisboa, the Aleijadinho (little cripple) [6] who rose in the second half of the eighteenth century, when the

---

[6] Antônio Francisco Lisboa (1730–1814), Aleijadinho, a great artist, sculptor, and carver, born in Vila Rica, son of master Manuel Francisco Lisboa, is, without doubt, the dominant figure in the history of the arts in Brazil during the whole of the colonial period, and perhaps, according to José Mariano Filho, the greatest Brazilian artist. The nickname with which he passed into his-tory, and which has surrounded him with the aura of legend, came from deformities caused by leprosy, which attacked him in 1777, or when he was forty-seven, and which seems with its muti-lation to have deprived him of most of his fingers. He learned his trade with his father, a Portu-guese sculptor and architect, who had been taught by Batista Gomes, a pupil of the French engravers Antoine Menguin and Francis Martheau, and in architecture, aside from the paternal lessons, he benefitted by contact with António Pereira de Sousa Calheiros, José Pereira Arouca and José Antônio dos Santos, who made up the artistic triumvirate of Mariana and passed for the greatest masters of the time. He had a school of master carvers of saints, his disciples and aids, probably the artists who made many works which are attributed to him, the anatomical defects of which, in contrast with other works which are truly beautiful and correct, have been explained as due to his illness or to intentional deformation of the figures. Although he was from childhood destined to the career of wood cutter and sculptor, he appears to have been as much an architect as a carver of statues, and he certainly was an architect if, as Rodrigo de Freitas and Diogo de Vasconcelos claim, the plans for the churches of São Francisco de Assís and of Our Lady of the Rosary are his, for the latter has been called "the most beautiful sacred monument of Minas Gerais and one of the most important of the country." José Mariano Filho, however, disputes the theory that the mestizo genius was the maker of the plans of those churches, constructed in the second half of the eighteenth century, under the artistic direction of Aleijadinho, who according to this critic only helped out in the ornamental or sculptural part of these churches with their elliptical ground plan and round towers. According to José Mariano Filho, however, to Aleijadinho belongs the glory of having given national form to the new architecture of Borrominic character, introduc-ing changes and details, "not anticipated in the original European plans of the church of Our Lady of the Rosary," in the plans for the church of St. Francis of Assisi of Ouro Preto and of São João d'El-Rei. (Cf. Rodrigo J. Ferreira Bretas, *Traços biográficos relativos ao finado Antônio Francisco Lisboa*, 1858; Renato Alves Guimarães, *Antônio Francisco Lisboa*, São Paulo, 1931; Gastão Penalva, *O Aleijadinho de Vila Rica*, Rio, 1933; Diogo de Vasconcelos, *A Arte de Ouro*

diamond-bearing districts were already in a period of decadence, and succeeded in dominating by his genius the art of the great carvers of Bahia and Pernambuco, who had prepared various generations of makers of saints and carvers for the service of religious buildings, and who renewed and purified their art. Educated in the art of carving by his father and by various other masters from the home country, like João Batista Gomes, in whose school of arts in Vila Rica there were trained a Joaquim Carneiro da Silva, a Portuguese, famed afterwards in Rome as one of the greatest artists of his time, and an Antônio Fernandes Rodrigues, a mestizo of Mariana, and the maker later on of notable works in Portugal (1758) and in Italy—Antônio Francisco Lisboa became more celebrated than his masters and merited by the creation of his genius that there should be given to the eighteenth century—the third century of the colonial period, the name of "the century of Aleijadinho." A carver, he enriched the interiors and frontispieces of churches with numerous works of carving, both in wood and in pumice stone, working on pulpits, tribunes, altars, stairways and doorways and upon the completion of the liturgical furniture, as a sculptor the greatest classic artist of Brazil, he was the creator of the ornamental decorations of the facade, the statuary of the three central figures of the Passion of the Sanctuary of Congonhas, —true works of art, the modeler of images in sandstone—the stone of Aleijadinho, which was to become so famous, writes Augusto de Lima Júnior, carved by the deformed hands of this genius who was a mestizo. As an architect, finally, when there emerged in Ouro Preto the influence of the baroque of Borromini, with the church of Nossa Senhor do Rosário, with its elliptical ground plan and its round towers, he was able to create with his two replicas of São Francisco de Assís, of Ouro Preto and of Sao João d'El-Rei, the Brazilian baroque, introducing essential modifications in the facade, adding rectilinear sections, uniting the traditional rectangular form of the old churches, drawn according to the plan of the Church of Jesus in Rome, to the new curve of the style of Borromini, and thus breaking the uniformity of the imported baroque with his original conception.

The commercial relations with the home country developed under the influence of the discoveries and the exploitation of mines, and the more frequent contact through Portugal with more advanced civilization played in the middle of the eighteenth century a role, the importance of which cannot be denied, in this movement of forms of art and this sequence of exchanges, which was to reach the point in Vila Rica of the invention of types and of motifs. What led to this phenomenon of renovation of the old Portuguese models influenced by the Jesuits, and permitted Aleijadinho to create an original art with his Brazilian baroque, was the new element which came with the unexpected introduction of the baroque of Borromini in the church of Nossa Senhora do Rosário, constructed according to a plan noted down and coming, as it is supposed from Italy, and consequently the action and reaction of Portuguese architectonic form and of foreign influences meeting and modifying each other. It was above all with the creations of this mestico that carving and statuary and religious architecture attained a relative degree of perfection in Minas Gerais, and it was with

Preto, Bi-centenary edition, 1934; José Mariano Filho, *"Considerações acerca do templo de Nossa Senhora do Rosário e de São Francisco de Assís, de Ouro Preto,"* in "Estudos brasileiros," Ano II, Vol. 4, no. 10, Rio, 1940; and the bibliography of Aleijadinho, prepared by Judite Martins. "Revista" of the National Service of Historic and Artistic Property, 1939).

them that the phenomenon, of so great an importance in the life of the country, of the social rise of the mulatto was hastened, at first a rise that took place through the plastic arts, music and letters, and later through the clergy and politics in the period of the Empire. Art is, in fact, a means of forming social classes; and the man of color, the Negro or the mestizo,—a plastic artist of the importance of Aleijadinho, a Valentim da Fonseca e Silva,—the great Master Valentim, designer and carver,[7] whose works constitute proof of a remarkable plastic sense and the finest decorative taste, or a José Maurício, the greatest figure of our sacred music,—took vengeance on the white, although following his example, and scaled the barriers that had been raised by racial prejudice, rising in the social scale through their artistic and intellectual activities. In this respect, as in others, the history of the arts in Brazil offers an immediate interest for the understanding of our social history. But, in addition to the development of the art of carving, of such vast and varied application in the religious field, in the internal ornamentation of temples and of religious architecture, which attained its splendor during the twilight of the colonial regime, real artistic interest in this period is not presented except by the art of goldsmithing of which even the slaves took advantage. In the land of precious stones,—the greatest center in the world for the production of gold in the first half of the eighteenth century, goldsmithing, although it did not have the development which might have been expected from the abundance of precious metal which served the artist as raw material, was one of the arts which flourished, in spite of all of the restrictions opposed to it in the home country, which was exclusively preoccupied with the collection of gold and the stamping of money. All the measures, some of them extremely severe, taken after 1698 against goldsmiths and which culminated in the prohibition of goldsmithing and of the art of engraving in the Royal Letter of July 30, 1766, did not succeed in reducing, except temporarily, the number and activities of the goldsmiths in Rio de Janeiro and in various captaincies.

[7] Valentim da Fonseca e Silva, a Brazilian mulatto, educated in the home country under the great teachers of the time, was, at the end of the eighteenth century, the great figure in decoration, in Rio de Janeiro. Upon returning from Portugal, where he had the best technical instruction according to José Mariano Filho, he began to work with artists of reputation, who contracted out the carving, but it was not long before the superiority of his work ensured him tasks of greater importance and artistic value. Prepared to do the work of carving and engraving, and at the same time a master at casting, Valentim da Fonseca e Silva "seems to have learned to cast bronze in Portugal, perhaps under Bartolomeu da Costa, the royal bronze-caster, maker of the statue of the Marquês de Pombal and of the magnificent cannons that are in the Historical Museum. All those marvellous pedestals and the cartridges that beautify these cannon with their inscriptions, prove the hand of the master foundryman." A remarkable draughtsman, who became better than the Portuguese artists of his time, a founder, carver, sculptor and architect, Master Valentim, writes José Mariano Filho, "furnished well thought out designs and details, afterwards executed not only in wood and silver, but also in white chalk stone," like the washstand of the sacristy of the church of Our Lady of Carmel, in Rio de Janeiro, which was executed in Portugal after his drawing. The twelfth Viceroy, Luíz de Vasconcelos e Sousa (1779–1790) entrusted him with tasks of the greatest importance and artistic interest, for he could find in the colony no Portuguese artist capable of doing the work that Valentim did. He was superior to all, in fact, in carving, both in the intelligence of his ideas and in the neatness of their material execution, following the pattern of Portuguese art. At the very end of his life, between 1810 and 1811 (Valentim died in 1813) he did the altar of the Church of Our Lady of Delivery, which had burned in 1789 and which he had restored, making the things that were most urgently needed. (José Mariano Filho, in "Estudos Brasileiros," Ano II, Vol. 4, no. 12, pp. 656-658, Rio de Janeiro May-June, 1940.)

By virtue of the Royal Letter, there were closed, according to the information of F. Marques dos Santos, 142 goldsmiths' shops, with their forges demolished and the instruments of their art taken away. But when the thirteenth Viceroy, the Count of Resende (1790–1801) arrived in Rio, he saw with surprise whole streets full of goldsmiths, with many shops and places of work in which there were plying their trade "375 masters and 1500 workmen." The great number of silversmiths and of goldsmiths, jewel cutters, gravers, and foundry workers in the captaincies of Pernambuco, Bahia and Minas Gerais, and especially Rio de Janeiro, shows not only that the persecution of the goldsmith "never amounted to so much as is supposed," but also that the reaction of the crown was aiming above all at safeguarding money (gold coins), repressing smuggling, and perhaps of restraining the luxury which was being developed "with the prosperity which had been reached in colonial goldsmithing through the skill of its artists and the perfection of its work." For Marques dos Santos, who made the most important contribution to the history of goldsmithing in Brazil,[8] the archives of the brotherhoods and the collections of the old churches, when they are sufficiently investigated, will have much to say about the abundance of jewels and their manufacture in colonial Brazil, which took on a new importance in the reign of the Prince Regent, Dom João, when he removed the restrictions upon the work of the goldsmith and from then on, in the first and second Empire.

A luxurious art, of an eminently secular or worldly character, colonial goldsmithing was destined not only to favor the ostentation of the families of the lords of the sugar mills and the miners and of the wealthy bourgeoisie, but to adorn the images of saints in the great days of religious feasts. "In the churches down to the second reign, whether they were churches of Campos dos Goitacazes, of the city of Cunha, of Sabará or Olinda,"—writes Marques dos Santos—"they would have sets of jewels of every kind for every image. With what grace the devout ladies clothed the images on the days of the feast! They put on them a new dress, earrings, brooches, knots, bracelets, stomachers, necklaces of beautiful rosaries, everything with diamonds, chrysolites, rubies and colored stones." One of the richest and most beautiful collection of antique jewels, of chrysolites and diamonds which we have seen, adds Marques dos Santos, was sold to a goldsmith of the street Luiz de Camões by the church da Boa Morte in Rio de Janeiro. "Many of them were tiny emeralds making a delicious contrast to the diamonds." This preponderance of the religious sentiment, which our formation under the spiritual domination of the Jesuits and of the monastic orders raised to the first plane in the whole colonial period, to the point of making the very art of goldsmithing tributary to the church and putting it at its service, would be sufficient to explain the inferiority of civil architecture, of residences and public buildings in comparison to the sumptuous architecture of cloisters and churches with their magnificent interiors. The ecclesiastical monuments in this society, not worldly but profoundly religious, constituted a characteristic trait of colonial Brazil. Everywhere in the midst of a scattered population, there rose the monastery or the church with its antique structure, raising its quadrangular, massive towers above the city, poor in civil construction with its few mansions and big lordly houses constructed according to Portuguese

---

[8] Francisco Marques dos Santos, *A ourivesaria no Brasil antigo*. Lecture given at the Institute of Brazilian Studies, May 24, 1940. In "Estudos Brasileiros," Ano II, Vol. 4, no. 12, pp. 625-647, May-June, 1940.

models. Civil architecture did not develop except in Minas Gerais. In the Northeast, observes Robert Smith, it had "neither the relative originality nor the wealth of religious architecture. Its cities never had the splendid public buildings of Minas Gerais, the grand military constructions of Para. The very house of the governors of Bahia (1663–1890) was a reproduction of some house or other of the Portuguese congress of some provincial city. It lacked the towers and the portals of the edifices of Ouro Preto and the elegant lines of those of Mariana. The preeminently rural life of the region, the quiet existence in the midst of the sugar cane fields, the almost total isolation of the lords of the manors during the major part of the year, made necessary little ostentation in the public life of the city. The early lords of the sugar mills did not make a cult of the *urbs*." [9] We may say then in a general way that in this period, the residence —the big house of the sugar mill or the mansion of the city—was a contrast in the rude solidity of its construction and the severe simplicity of its lines, to the sumptuosity of architecture and the exuberance of internal decoration of the religious temples. There is not, in fact, a governor's house, a municipal palace or a nobleman's estate, which shows through its baroque form, the intensity of life and of movement, the splendor of social life and the taste for luxury of the aristocratic society in which the baroque in Italy and in Austria developed so vigorously and in such great wealth of forms. But the works of art, if we would appreciate them and feel them, must be seen as Degas claimed, where they were born, in the face of and in the light of the central character of the civilization of which they were a part and which is made up of the conjunction of various elements. The architectonic austerity of the colonial mansion, in which the simplicity of the colonial environment is so faithfully expressed, corresponds to their interior, made up of ample and hospitable living rooms, bare walls and heavy furniture, which give to the whole that sober character, reaching the point of severity, and that tranquil stability on which the regime of the patriarchal family reposes. In the old colonial house, the walls of which were rarely ornamented by artistic pictures,—which surprised the Dutch,—the luxurious furniture carved in jacarandá or in cedar,[10] even in the eighteenth century when the style of Dom João V

[9] Certainly, on the one hand, the growing up in the Northeast, come the cultivation of sugar cane, of a rural society, scattered over the sugar plantations with their big houses, and on the other, the concentrated societies of Minas Gerais, where there flourished in the eighteenth century with its extractive industry and trade in gold, an urban civilization, constitute the principal reason why civil architecture was less brilliant in the Northeast than in Minas Gerais. This is the reason that Robert Smith gives us in the study alluded to, in which he examines the characteristics of colonial architecture in the Northeast. (In "Estudos Brasileiros," ano II, Vol. 4, no. 10, pp. 419-430, Rio de Janeiro, February, 1940.) Roger Bastide, while he accepts this explanation, introduces, however, another element which helps to explain the difference. "It may also be," he writes, "because the Northeast was more closely connected with the mother country, being on the coast rather than in the interior, and therefore there was less necessity for a display of Portuguese power, while the region of Minas Gerais, far in the interior, less in contact with the mother country, and inhabited by descendants of Paulistas with their stronger nativistic feelings needed buildings which would make them feel the absolute power of the home country; so we see that baroque civil architecture is always connected with the idea of absolutism." (See *Estudos da estética sociológica brasileira*. Article V. In "Estado de São Paulo," Sept.-Oct., 1940.)

[10] The luxurious furniture, both civil and religious, in Minas Gerais, imported in the early days from Bahia, as one can see from the styles of the sixteenth and seventeenth centuries, in which the great pieces were designed, later came to be made in the workshops of Minas itself. After 1730, writes Augusto de Lima Júnior, "the cabinet-makers and wood carvers of our cap-

with its French influence began to dominate, maintains the excessive robustness of the carpentry and vigorous ornamentation required by the architectonic solidity of the urban habitations, with their powerful construction, in which an agricultural economy and the social scene have caused great simple forms to prevail and in which the wood-work was more important than the decoration.

All this first phase of art in Brazil—corresponding to the colonial period, was one of religious architecture, painting and statuary. Down to the time of Dom João VI, art had taken refuge in churches and convents. Religious arts offered the first manifestation of Brazilian musical art, and if everywhere, as Mário de Andrade writes, "sound was always a factor in religious edification," here also through the domination of Catholicism from the beginning of our social formation, music was born mixed with religion. The songs and sung solemnities which the priest taught or composed to be taught the Indian children constituted, from the time of the first missions of the Jesuits, an important instrument in the work of conversion; and according to Simão de Vasconcelos, the very songs of the Indians which contained Christian doctrine were set to the organ to serve for the propagation of the faith in American tribes. Certainly, while in the chapels and churches in which on feast days there were celebrated sung masses, Gregorian music flourished, and there were spread among the Indians and Africans, religious songs and songs of the three kings (pastoral dances, such as the nau catarineta), popular music grew slowly in the sugar mills and in the cities under the influence of the primitive music of the slave quarters, of the Indian villages and of the Portuguese towns. All the people, the Portuguese and Spanish, Amerindians and Africans, who contributed to our formation in the first three centuries, brought with their languages and cultures, their songs and their dances, which were mingled in our still unstudied musical folklore, composing it and enriching it.[11] Although in the present

---

taincy followed the artistic development which took place in Portugal, in the time of Dom João V, where oriental and Hispanic-Arabic themes, introduced into Flanders and the north of France returned raised to a higher level by the influence of the French furniture makers." The fundamental plans and designs of these pieces of furniture, in which at the end of the century certain typical manifestations of originality can be seen, as Augusto de Lima Júnior points out, were imported from Portugal, whence they came inspired by new art forms and lured by high prices. According to José Mariano Filho, the influence among us of the Louis Quinze style, nationalized in Portugal under the name of Dom João V, was especially felt in the seventeenth century in civil furnishing, and then was extended later to sacred decoration, "until then under the thumb of the ornate baroque favored by the Jesuits." From primitive furniture, crudely made in accordance with classic models, to furniture that found its inspiration in the Dom João V style, evolution went on through the intermediate forms of Manueline Jesuit and the sumptuous Louis XV style, the influence of which was felt "in sacred decoration, through the strong treatment of moldings and the depth of carving." (Cf. Augusto de Lima Júnior, *A Capitania das "Minas Gerais": Suas origens e formação*, pp. 114-118. Lisbon, 1940. José Mariano Filho, *Evolução do mobiliário e da ornamentação litúrgica sob a influência dos jesuitas e de Dom João V*. In "Revista do Brasil," Ano III, 3rd phase, no. 22, pp. 41-44, April, 1940.)

[11] Cf. Roquete Pinto, *Rondônia*, 3rd edition. The music of the principal Pareci songs, taken down by phonograph. Pp. 128, 134-137, 143, 252. Series Brasiliana, Vol. 39, Comp. Editora Nacional, São Paulo, 1935; Elsie Houston—Peret, *Chants populaires du Brésil*, first series. Introduction by Philippe Stern. Librairie Orientaliste, Paul Genthner, Paris, 6e, 1932; José Siqueira, *A música brasileira no ciclo da cana de açúcar*. In "Revista da Semana," Rio de Janeiro, September 9, 1939; Mário de Andrade, *Compêndio da História da Música*, 3rd ed. Chapter XII; Música popular brasileira, pp. 167-177. L. G. Miranda, São Paulo, 1936; *Música do Sargento de Milícias*.

state of folklore studies it is impossible to know in what measure the African, indigenous and Portuguese elements influenced these songs and music of a popular nature, on which we have almost no documentation, it is the Portuguese influence which appears to have dominated, for this was "the most vast of all," and the principal source of melodies of our really beautiful folk music, in the opinion of Mário de Andrade, was that of the Negro slaves, in contact with whom our rhythm "attained the variety which it has—one of our musical riches." The penetration of the African dances, religious or warlike, and their survival in the popular dances of Brazil, in the whole series of batuques, sambas, candomblés, maracatus and cana verdes, accompanied by various instruments among which those of percussion predominate (ganza, puita, atabaque), show, in fact, how decisive the African influence was in the formation of our popular music and that it was superior doubtless to that of the aborigines from whom there came the caterete and the catira—a Guaraní dance which Anchieta used to catechize the savages, and various instruments like the chocalho (an adaptation of the maraca) and perhaps the puita, which, generally considered to be of African origin and known in the diamond region by the name of *N'gomma Puita,* is considered by some to have come from the Indian drum. If, then, in the whole colonial period, the Africans who found in music "the principal solace in their exile in America," flooded Brazil with their nostalgic dances and their monotonous singing, the Portuguese made a contribution no less notable with their dances, their songs and their European instruments. It is from them that there came our cradle songs (acalantos) and other poetic and lyrical forms, like the moda and the fado which appear to have been originated in Brazil, and which Mário de Andrade,—one of our greatest musical folklorists, considering it a "Brazilian form of the lundum of Angora," judges correctly to have been the property of the Brazilians before it became, in the middle of the nineteenth century (after 1840 or 1849) a sung dance, Portuguese par excellence.

But if popular music and songs which were to result from the fusion of the songs and dances of the colonists, the aborigines and the Negro slaves, had taken form at the end of the eighteenth century, it was religious music which had, under the pressure of social circumstances, the greatest social and historical importance in the three centuries of the colony. There was still almost half a century to run for the first creations of popular music and of traditional songs to acquire original character and expression and hence influence and power of irradiation. In them there met with a predominance of this or that exotic element and with a great wealth of forms, "the discursive rhythm constant in the Indians, the rhythmic moving to and fro of the African, according to the picturesque expression of Mário de Andrade, and the melodic arabesques of Portugal, now pure and now contaminated." The religious music which dominated them had already attained such historic strength and had penetrated so far the various social strata that even in the popular songs of Brazil, according to the observation of the illustrious musical critic, "there appear phrases from oratories, in free rhythm and bearing a remarkable resemblance to plain song in their melodic design." The influence of religious music was profound in Brazil, not only in what Sumner Maine calls the "trituration" of society. It not only contributed to fuse into a unity the patriarchal

In "O Estado de São Paulo," December 8, 1940; Artur Ramos, *O negro brasileiro,* 1st vol. *Etnografia religiosa.* 2nd ed. Chapter VII: *A dansa e a música dos candomblés.* Pp. 223-243. Series Brasiliana, Vol. 188. Comp. Editora Nacional, São Paulo, 1940.)

family and to mingle from north to south all social groups in an intense process of spiritual unification,—the basis of political unity, but it also played an important part in all the cultural and artistic manifestations of the country. It is, then, also under a religious or sacred form that music was expressed with most intensity, being widely cultivated and used for magnificent celebrations in the chapels and churches of the colony. In this environment of musical religiosity which attained with the coming of Dom João VI and his court its period of greatest splendor and lasted down to the middle of the nineteenth century, there arose the first artistic manifestation of Brazilian music: Father José Maurício. Educated probably under masters who had been trained in the extinct school of the Jesuits in Santa Cruz and ordained a priest at twenty-five in 1792, his extraordinary musical ability met from a very early date in the social environment itself and in the liturgical solemnities, not only a stimulus but a source of inspiration for creation. If the artist, at the same time that he is an artist, is a man subject to all of the common influences, what he tends to express spontaneously in his works are the feelings and ideas which the surrounding activities, economic, juridical, moral and religious inspire together in the public and in him. His initial training in contact with the musical Fathers from whom he received his first lessons; his participation in the choir of the church; the influence on his mind of the pomp of ecclesiastical solemnities, and the priestly career which he embraced, naturally were to lead him to make use of sacred music to give artistic expression to his emotions.[12] A musician

[12] José Maurício Nunes Garcia (Rio, 1767–1830), son of mulatto parents, was able, in spite of his lowly origin, to take courses in Latin grammar and philosophy, to become a priest, in 1792, and reach, in his ecclesiastical career, the post of royal preacher. About his musical education, begun while he was only a child and carried on under the direction of musical priests, like Silva Reis, the great organist of the time, we know so little for certain, that L. H. Correia de Azevedo prefers to consider him self-taught—the product of his own talent and efforts. That he was not a pupil of the Jesuits and did not attend the class in music which they maintained for Negro slaves, on the fazenda of Santa Cruz, becomes obvious if we simply compare dates: the Jesuits had been expelled from Brazil in 1759, eight years before the birth of José Maurício, and their property in Santa Cruz, confiscated at that time, had passed to the Crown. It is probable, however, that the Carioca mestizo was educated in the still extant traditions of Santa Cruz, and with teachers trained in the Jesuit school. In 1798 he obtained a license to preach and was appointed Kapelmeister of the Cathedral in Rio de Janeiro, the musical services of which soon became famous under his direction. "He himself, with practice," writes Correia de Azevedo, "became an excellent organist; the singers trained and rehearsed under his baton did marvels and caused lively astonishment in the court when it came here in 1808." José Maurício was appointed in that very year, by the Prince Regent Dom João, inspector of the Music of the Royal Chapel, and later royal preacher; the composer-priest worked hard, and composed down to 1811 almost two hundred works for the use of the Royal Chapel, beside others which he wrote "for various orders and other churches and some few profane works." With the arrival in Brazil in 1811 of Marcos Portugal, the notable Portuguese composer whom Dom João VI had sent for, in order to impart more brilliance to his musical parties in the Royal Chapel and Royal Theatre of São João, the official prestige of José Maurício suffered; he was looked upon askance by the Portuguese composer and treated in hostile fashion, while the latter was named professor to the royal family and director of the musical events in the Chapel and the Paço. The famous Sigismund von Neukomm of Salzburg (1778–1858), pupil of Haydn, the great German pianist and composer, had come in 1816, on the artistic mission led by J. Lebreton, and who had to struggle against the power of Marcos Portugal, did justice to José Maurício, lamenting that while he was alive the Brazilians did not have sense enough to appreciate the artist they possessed, "so much the more precious as he was the product of their own resources." Returning to Portugal, Dom João VI, who called him a "new

of rare ability and culture who knew and played the great German and Italian classics such as Bach, Haydn and Mozart, Rossini and Palestrina; a very fertile composer who up to the age of forty-four had already composed for the Royal Chapel alone nearly two hundred works, for the most part forgotten and lying in manuscript, Father José Maurício left notable works, and among them a Mass in G minor and a Requiem Mass, one of his masterpieces, and also "a masterpiece of religious music in Brazil," comparable according to Mário de Andrade, "in its melodic invention, its serenity, its pure clarity, to what was being done in this kind of work by the Italians of the time." His religious conviction dominated almost all of his musical work, in which there is reflected along with the spirit of the time "the image of a calm society organized into a hierarchy accepted by all," and which stands out in its most representative character, not only in the sincerity which is manifest in the clarity of accent, in the purity of melodic line, and in great spontaneity of inspiration, but also in the quality of style that is purely harmonic and which seems to proceed from Haydn and Mozart, who were his favorite composers.

Of all the arts—architecture, painting, sculpture and music, which were cultivated in the colonial period, in the religious form or under religious inspiration, the one which was slowest to acquire truly artistic character and expression was then sacred music, with Father José Maurício, who marks the transition between the two periods,—that of art permeated by the religious spirit and that of new sources of inspiration. It was with the creations of this talented mestizo that religious music culminated in a period,—the beginning of the nineteenth century—, in which the various manifestations of colonial art which flourished in the shadow of churches and cloisters had already entered into their decline. Although the domination of religious music was to last down to the middle of the nineteenth century, it knew its period of greatest splendor in Brazil with Father José Maurício, but there is already observable in the time of Dom João VI, the lay movement in music, with the development of urban life and the brilliance of musical parties, and with the arrival in 1811 of Marcos Portugal, a composer already famed for various operas which figured in the repertory of Italian theaters, and of Sigismund von Neukomm, German pianist and composer, who came in 1816 with the mission of French artists. Of the disciples of Father José Maurício, none persevered in the path of the master and the greatest of them all, Francisco Manuel da Silva, who also associated with Sigismund von Neukomm, is one of the greatest figures which Brazil has yet produced. The finest thing that he left us was the national hymn to which he owes his fame in the history of Brazilian music. But this process of secularization of the arts already being developed under the pressure of social, economic and political causes was to be accelerated by the activities of an artistic mission which came to Brazil in 1816 on the suggestion of the Count da Barca, a minister of Dom João VI

Marcos," lamented in a letter to Father José Maurício, in his own handwriting, not having taken him along to Portugal to take charge of musical events in the Royal Chapel of Lisbon. Father José Maurício died in 1830, a few days after Marcos Portugal. In 1856, Manuel de Araújo Pôrto Alegre wrote his biography; the biographer had in his youth known José Maurício in his last years. (M. A. Pôrto Alegre, *Iconografia brasileira. Apontamentos sôbre a vida do Pe. José Maurício Nunes Garcia.* In "Revista" of the Brazilian Historical Institute, Vol. 19. Pp. 349-369; Viscount de Taunay, *Traços biográficos do Pe. José Maurício.* In "Revista Musical," ano II, 1880, nos. 7 to 13, 15, 17 and 20; Manuel Antônio Moreira de Azevedo, *Biografia do Pe. José Maurício Nunes Garcia.* In "Revista" of the Brazilian Historical Institute, Vol. 39, 2nd part, p. 293.)

in Rio de Janeiro. The French mission which had as its leader Joaquim Lebreton, of the Institute of France, was made up of J. B. Debret, historical painter, the brothers Nicolas Antoine Taunay, a painter of landscapes, and Auguste Marie Taunay, a sculptor; of Grandjean de Montigny, architect; of the engraver Charles Simon Pradier; of the brothers Ferrez, besides other auxiliary artists and craftsmen, all of them French with the exception of Neukomm, the German composer, former pianist attached to the house of Talleyrand. This heterogeneous group of artists, in which there were prominent figures, victims of political persecution in the home country, was to constitute in their land of exile the principal nucleus of the future Academy of Fine Arts, created under the temporary name of the Royal School of Sciences, Arts and Crafts, by the decree of August 12, 1816, and installed ten years later in 1826 with certain modifications of structure and its definitive name,—the Academy of the Arts—, which the decree of November 20, 1820, had given to the new institution. The history of this artistic mission, which is mingled in the first twenty years with that of the Academy of Arts, and of the role which it played, is the history of the conflicts of two cultures of different aspects and levels, and of the natural actions of the environment to which the group of artists contracted in Paris was transported. The French mission became the central event of the epoch and, with its first activities, marked the breaking up under the influences of a new conception, of the art of the colonial tradition and Portuguese origin, and the conflict between a liturgical art and French secularism imported by the mission. However, the diversity of elements which composed it, prize-winning artists, masters and artisans,—hence the first idea of the Count da Barca of the creation of a school of arts and crafts; [13] the death in 1819 of J. Lebreton, the head of the mis-

---

[13] The Royal School of Sciences, Arts and Crafts, created August 12, 1816, in the same year in which the mission of French artists disembarked in Rio de Janeiro, was changed by decree on October 1, 1820, into the Royal Academy of Drawing, Painting, Sculpture, and Civil Architecture, and named, according to another decree of the same year (November 23, 1820), Academy of the Arts, in which capacity it came really to exist or operate only in 1826, under the first Empire. The Academy of Fine Arts, which had for its first director the Portuguese painter Henrique Jose da Silva (1826–1834) was later directed (1834–1854) by Félix Emílio Taunay, son of Nicolas Antoine Taunay and his pupil, and later Baron of Taunay, and between 1854 and 1857, by Manuel de Araújo Pôrto Alegre (Rio Grande do Sul, 1806–1879), a former pupil and professor of the Academy, painter and poet, who conceived one of the most important changes in the Academy, creating courses in applied mathematics, anatomy for artists, archaeology, aesthetics and history of the fine arts, and founding the gallery—the first to be organized in Brazil. In 1845, by the decree of December 19, there was created the prize of a trip to Europe, the length of which was changed from three years to five in 1852. Reorganized for the first time on May 14, 1855, under the leadership of Pôrto Alegre, its director, the Academy of Fine Arts passed through other changes under the Empire: that of May 14, 1859, which created day and night courses, and that of May 16, 1871; and in 1890 it took the name of National School of Fine Art, by a decree of November 8 of that year, which once more reorganized it. During the Republic, the National School of Fine Arts passed through successive reforms, in 1901, through the efforts of the Minister of Justice, Epitácio Pessoa, in 1911, as a result of the fundamental law on teaching, and in 1915, with the Carlos Maximiliano law; in 1931, after radical changes, it was added to the University of Rio de Janeiro. Two years later, decree 22,897, of July 6, 1933, now in force, introduced changes in the teaching of the School, reorganizing the courses in architecture, painting, sculpture and engraving. In January, 1937, the galleries of painting, sculpture and engraving were separated from the School of Fine Arts to constitute the present National Museum of Fine Arts. Directed by Augusto Bracet, the School of Fine Arts, into which with the Republic the Academy of Fine Arts was transformed, with its origins going back to the Royal School of Sciences, Arts

sion, and the return to his home country of Charles Simon Pradier in 1818, and Nicolas Antoine Taunay in 1821; the hostility of the social environment, which was naturally reactionary, in which old Brazilian artists of the colonial epoch and Portuguese artists who had arrived in the time of Dom João VI and the artists who had arrived from France met. The conflict between cultures that were so different and the consequent nativistic reaction from which it resulted that the direction of the Academy of Arts was given to the Portuguese painter, Henrique José da Silva, were so many other contretemps and obstacles to the plans of the mission engaged by the Marques de Marialva which ended by scattering, breaking up into the isolated individual influences of some of its dominant figures.

In fact, when the Academy of Arts was installed in 1826, the French mission had already suffered the loss not only of its chief, a man of thought and action, but of some of its best members, among them the two Taunays, Nicolas Antoine, perhaps the most notable figure, who retired to Europe in 1821 and gave an exposition in the summer of 1822 in Paris of some excellent landscapes almost all done in Brazil, and Auguste Marie Taunay, the sculptor, who died in 1824 in his residence in Tijuca in Rio de Janeiro. Colonial society, transformed by the presence of Dom João VI and his court and agitated by political tempests, became, in the campaign for independence in the first reign, the theater of the struggle between artists of diverse origins and tendencies. The foreign artists, already resident in the country, like the painter Pallière and the architect Pezerat, and above all those who remained from the mission headed by Lebreton, met a strong opposition on the part of Portuguese artists who had come at the end of the colonial epoch and the old Brazilian artists "almost all mestizos and of humble origin, whose rudimentary culture," observes José Mariano Filho, "had been secured at the cost of enormous effort, without the remunerative protection which was now freely dispensed to persecuted foreigners." This was an agitated period in which three distinct currents crossed and came into conflict, and the academic doctrines of French art were superimposed upon the colonial tradition which resisted, side by side with the culture of Portugal, the new ideas and the imported techniques. Nonetheless, the mirage of a joint action and of the unrestricted domination of the mission in an environment that was tumultuous and anarchic, full of prejudices and fixed ideas was not long in being dissipated. In this environment French, Brazilians and Portuguese disputed the first place and surrounded the cradle of the Academy of Arts. The Portuguese were almost always attracted and joined the Brazilians in a single front of battle and of resistance to the action of the foreign artists. But, if there was not an awakening of the national feeling in art, as there was in the field of politics,—the foreign elements who made their way into Brazilian life, although they were not numerous, did not permit either the triumphs of the old colonial spirit nor the artistic predominance of Portuguese elements.[14] The French mission which José Mariano Filho called "a pretty

and Crafts, (1816), has seen successive directors such as the sculptors Rodolfo Bernardelli and Correia Lima, a critic and art historian of the value of José Mariano Filho, painters such as Batista da Costa and Lucílio Albuquerque and the architects Lúcio Costa and Arquimedes Memória, whose names are linked to the history of Brazilian art both by their works and their services.

[14] Among the artists coming from various parts of the world who at this time were in Rio de Janeiro, forming a true artistic melting pot, F. Marques dos Santos recalls various Brazilians, from the colonial period, such as Manuel Dias de Oliveira, professor of design; José Leandro de Carvalho, the portrait painter of Dom João and his court, and Francisco Pedro do Amaral, decorator

205. Vicente de Carvalho (São Paulo, 1866–1924), one of the greatest lyric poets of Brazil.

206. João Capistrano de Abreu (born in Ceará, 1853, died at Rio, 1927).

207. Sílvio Romero (Sílvio Vasconcelos da Silveira Ramos Romero, born in Sergipe, 1851, died at Rio, 1914), who made the greatest contribution to the development of the history of Brazilian literature.

Rio, 8 de Julho - 1922

Amigo Sr. Affonso Vizeu

Com muita saudade da sua companhia e do generoso trato com que sempre fui distinguido por todos os amigos, durante tres annos de esforçado e utilissimo trabalho, venho depor nas suas mãos, pedindo-lhe que a restitua aos demaes directores e socios da Liga de Depesa Nacional, a honra da investidura que recebi para servi-la, como seu Secretario Geral, posto em que sempre me senti apagado por haver nelle refulgido o genio de Olavo Bilac. Tenho um coração simples, um tanto quanto bravio, como a terra virgem do nosso Brasil, por isto, talvez, ingenuo na sua sinceridade. Como ao do Poeta as alegrias e as dores da Patria fazem-no vibrar a impetos. O acto, do qual se orgulharia qualquer Povo, praticado por esse pugillo de brasileiros, que se renderam heroicamente, á Morte, levando ao peito, á guiza de escamas de couraça, pedaços da nossa bandeira, vale por uma Epopéa e dá cópia sublime da valentia da nossa gente. O que eu nelles queria honrar, com um braçada de flores, não era a rebeldia, mas a Fé, a coragem levada até a ~~morte~~ abnegação, a exaltação e Dignidade, a belleza do gesto de Heroismo antigo. Era para taes grandezas d'Alma que eu pedia o culto que Antigone, insurgindo-se contra as proprias leis thebanas, e desafiando a morte, prestou ao corpo de Polynice, que tambem se rebellara contra a Patria, mas que era seu irmão. Negaram-mo. Irei cumpri-lo e, para que a peregrinação, em que vou, não acarrete difficuldades nem levante suspeição que possam comprometter a Liga, exonero-me do cargo que nella exerço. Não me incitam, nem jamais incitaram, outras vozes senão as da Patria e o que della ouço são palavras de justo orgulho por ser Mãe de taes heroes, e de lastima por os haver perdido, purificados de toda a culpa no proprio sangue, quando sahiram do fórte na destemida arrancada, com a bandeira ao peito e que, por ser uma só, foi por elles dividida em tantos pedaços quantos eram os que commungavam os fragmentos do augusto symbolo, como se fossem particulas de uma hostia que a todos servisse de viatico.

Creia-me, meu caro Sr. Affonso Vizeu, seu sincero e devotado amigo, em quem manda com direito absoluto de amizade,

Coelho Netto

208. Facsimile of a letter of Coelho Neto.
Archives of the Coelho Neto family.

209. The Museu Paulista, the greatest center for sources and for research in the history of Brazil and especially of São Paulo. Ipiranga Park, São Paulo. Photo by the Museu Paulista.

210. Machado de Assís (Joaquim Maria Machado de Assís) at 25.

211. Machado de Assís. Drawing by J.
Wash Rodrigues, in State Archives of São
Paulo.

212. Euclides da Cunha (born in State of
Rio, 1866, died at Rio, 1909).

213. Bust of Euclides da Cunha in São José do Rio Pardo, state of São Paulo.

214. View of park on the Pardo River, in São José do Rio Pardo, state of São Paulo, including a view of the bust of Euclides da Cunha and the rustic shelter in which he wrote *Os Sertões*.

215. Humberto de Campos (Maranhão), poet and chronicler, master of the language and of the art of criticism.

216. Facsimile of frontispiece of *Historia Naturalis Brasiliae,* by Piso and Margraf.

217. Bartolomeu Lourenço de Gusmão, the "Flying Father," whose experiments with the balloon assure him a place among the immortal forerunners of aviation. Bartolomeu de Gusmão Room in the Museu Paulista; in the center, the portrait of the Brazilian inventor. Photo by the Museu Paulista.

José Bonifácio de Andrada e Silva.

218. José Bonifácio de Andrada e Silva (born at Santos, 1763, died at Rio, 1838), first professor of metallurgy in the University of Coimbra, an important mineralogist and "the greatest and most learned Brazilian of his time."
Photo from the collection of the Companhia Melhoramentos of São Paulo.

219. Counselor Francisco Freire Alemão, a noteworthy botanist, teacher of botany in the Medical School and Director of the National Museum (1866–1874).

220. J. Barbosa Rodrigues, "the most outstanding botanist of Brazil after Freire Alemão," Director of the Botanical Garden (1889–1909) and author of the *Sertum Palmarum*.

221. Alípio Miranda Ribeiro, a great ichthyologist and perhaps the greatest zoologist born in Brazil.

222. Alípio Miranda Ribeiro, in his research laboratory, in the National Museum.

223. Emílio Goeldi, founder of the Museu Paraense, now known as the Museu Goeldi, and author of *Os Mamíferos do Brasil* (1893) and *Aves do Brasil.*

224. Jacques Huber, Swiss botanist, who worked in the Museu Paulista, one of the foreign naturalists who have devoted themselves most wholeheartedly to our country and the study of its natural resources.

225. Hermann von Ihering, founder and Director from 1894 to 1915 of the Museu Paulista, and one of the world's greatest authorities on the Mollusca.

226. Fritz Müller, "the prince of observers" according to Darwin, and one of the greatest naturalists of the century. He lived forty-five years in Brazil, serving science and the country.

227. Peter Wilhelm Lund (born in Denmark, 1801, died at Lagoa Santa, Minas Gerais, 1880), one of the most eminent scholars in paleontology, famous for his researches on fossils in the valley of the Rio das Velhas.

228. Louis Agassiz (1807–1873), Swiss naturalist who led the Thayer Expedition in 1865–1866 and began "a new era in the study of geology among us."

229. Charles Frederick Hartt (1840–1878), American scholar who took part in the Thayer Expedition, completed in 1867 the geological survey of the coast (from Rio to Pernambuco), and published in 1870 the most important work of the past century on Brazilian geology.

230. Orville A. Derby (1851–1915), colleague of Charles Frederick Hartt and continuer of his work, in organizing the general
geological service 1873–1878, to whose competent hands was entrusted the direction of
the geological and mineralogical service of
Brazil, reorganized in 1907.

231. Luiz Felipe Gonzaga de Campos
(1856–1925), Brazilian geologist, colleague
of Orville Derby from 1907 to 1915 and
author of important works.

232. John C. Branner (1850–1922), a disciple and colleague of C. Frederick Hartt in
the organization of the geological services
and the development of geological studies in
Brazil.

233. A. Betim Pais Leme, geologist of the
National Museum and author of excellent
monographs on Wegener's theory of the slipping of continents, which he studied in its
bearing on Brazil.

234. Pedro II, inspirer and cultivator of the sciences, who during his long reign (1831–1889)
was at the forefront of all movements for scientific progress in Brazil.
Photo from the collection of the Companhia Melhoramentos of São Paulo.

235. Hall commemorating Santos-Dumont.
Room B-9 in the Museu Paulista. Photo by the Museu Paulista.

236. Santos-Dumont (born in Minas, 1873, died at Santos, 1932), whom Edison called "the prospector of the air," and who distinguished himself in two fields of invention—the dirigibility of aircraft lighter than air, and the ascent of machines heavier than air.

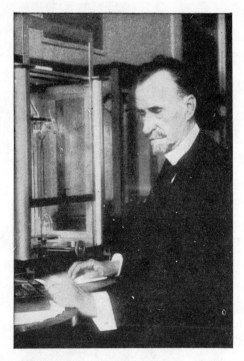

237. Louis Cruls (1848–1908), Belgian astronomer, Director (1884–1908) of the Imperial Observatory of Rio de Janeiro, which was founded by the French scholar Emmanuel Liais in 1874.

238. Henrique Morize (1860–1930), professor of physics and meteorology, and Director of the National Observatory after 1908, who was responsible for the first meteorological organization of Brazil and wrote a distinguished monograph on *The Climate of Brazil*.

239. Viscount Rio Branco, under whose ministry the most important movements and reforms in the scientific field during the period of the Empire took place.

adventure," established itself finally, making disciples and creating schools, and art in Brazil was modified as a result of contact with it. It is to its remaining members that the progress of the Academy of Fine Arts in the first reign and up to 1840 is due; and no influence, to be sure, was equal in this period to that of J. B. Debret, historical painter, disciple of David, and professor of historical painting down to 1837,—the admirable artist who left in his *Viagem Pitoresca ao Brasil* a precious collection of drawings of high documentary value; of Grandjean de Montigny, disciple of Percier and Fontaine, and "an architect of genius," in the excessively kind judgment of Euclides da Cunha, but certainly a great artist, who left no disciples equal to his extraordinary merit and whose passage through Brazil was marked by various projects of monuments with artistic and architectonic value and by the majestic edifice of the Academy of Arts, by the fountain of the Carioca square, and by four or five residences like that of the Viscount of Rio Comprido and that of Félix Emílio Taunay, the son of Nicolas Antoine, and his disciple, professor of landscape, author of designs which G. P. Ronmy used in order to paint the Panorama which was exhibited with success in Paris in 1824, and second director of the Academy of Fine Arts, in which position he succeeded Henrique José da Silva, the most obstinate adversary of the famous mission. The two public expositions of 1829 and 1830,—the first which had been carried out in Brazil due to the initiative and efforts of Debret and Montigny, showed with the progress of their disciples the influence which these two great artists had; if they were not identified with their environment, they were at least entirely devoted to the progress of the Academy of Arts and to the development of art in Brazil.

---

of the National Library and of the house of the Marquesa de Santos. Of the Portuguese who came in the time of the Prince Regent and King, we note in the first reign Antonio de Carmo Pinto de Figueiredo and João Jose de Sousa, known for their drawings and etchings; Manuel da Costa, architect of imperial and national buildings; Joaquim Cândido Guillobel, who did drawings and water colors, of whose artistic value we still have a proof in the watercolor *Tropeiro em viagem*, among other works; and Henrique José da Silva, also active in line drawings and painting, painter of oil portraits of Dom Pedro I and first director of the Academy of Arts. The figures of greatest importance among the foreign artists residing in Brazil, and those who had the greatest influence, were two immigrants from France, who came, it seems, for political reasons: the engineer captain Armand Jullien Pallière, painter and teacher of design in the Royal Military Academy, and Pedro José Pezerat, an architect whom Pedro I took into his service in place of Manuel da Costa, and who, in this office, restored the Imperial Palace of São Cristóvão. The painter Armand Pallière, who married a daughter of Grandjean de Montigny in Rio, left us, beside drawings of uniforms, Brazilian personages and customs, the design for the Imperial Order of the Cross, and a magnificent self-portrait. About this time there were in Rio, but only temporarily, various other foreign artists, like Henry Chamberlain, English consul during the first reign, painter and watercolorist, and Johann Moriz Rugendas, a great German artist who, leaving the Langsdorff mission, stayed in Brazil until 1825 and when he returned to Europe took with him an enormous collection of drawings published in part in his *Viagem pitoresca através do Brasil*, a book of the highest historical interest as well as artistic merit, on account of the text, and above all, the handsome pictures, and, as Sérgio Milliet writes, "one of the most curious and honest documents about old Brazil." It was in this little circle of artists, heterogeneous and of unequal merit, with groups of artists with contradictory tendencies, that the French mission had to work, encountering all kinds of difficulties, but in the long run exercising an influence upon it, since the mission was the most powerful cultural nucleus. (See Francisco Marques dos Santos, *Artistas do Rio de Janeiro colonial*. In "Estudos Brasileiros," Vol. 3, pp. 26-33; *As belas artes no primeiro reinado* (1822–1831). In "Estudos Brasileiros," ano II, Vol. 4, no. 11, pp. 471-509, March-April.)

It is in this period that there occurred for various reasons and under the influence of French culture, the rupture with the tradition of colonial art; and although the new artistic manifestations were still formless, they already showed an open process of the secularization of art in the search for new objects and new sources of inspiration. The old arts did not docilely accept these foreign movements. In painting as in sculpture what was observed was rather change than progress; and if in architecture the new classic style did not establish itself, in spite of all the efforts of Grandjean de Montigny, no attempt to return to the past was successful. In any case it would have been useless to attempt to return to the forms of colonial architecture which now could not be restored, and no movement in favor of the Brazilian forms of the baroque, which had attained its splendor in the Northeast and especially in Ouro Preto, took place. The Palace of Itamaratí, the work of Jacinto Rabelo, one of the disciples of the French architect, "was conceived," writes J. Mariano Filho, "as if in opposition to the thought of the master, and the Santa Casa de Misericordia is not properly a neoclassic composition, but is essentially classic and finds its inspiration in Vignola." The fact is that the old arts were neither sufficiently rich to repel the foreign influence nor sufficiently powerful to transform their borrowings into new creations of a beauty marked by the genius of the race. It was not a question in general in this period of doing anything more than copying foreign models, without the slightest creative imagination. It was, however, the new world which arose, revealing promises of the future even in its first most characteristic works in spite of their ingenuity. The great period arrived with Dom Pedro I (1822–1831) "the period of the oil portrait, of historical painting, of landscapes and of genre." In 1840, expositions of painting became common and in 1845, the prize of a trip to Europe was begun. The duration of this European prize, three years, was raised to five years in 1852 when the Academy of Arts was still under the direction of Felix Emílio Taunay. The French mission, awakening our taste for art and creating a tradition, had accomplished its civilizing mission, which was to be completed from now on by the prizes granting a trip to Europe where the best artist educated by the Academy would go to finish his studies. The French mission, then, did not break up without forming a school and leaving some disciples. Among those who received the direct influence of the artists of this mission, it is not necessary to point to more than Augusto Müller (1815), German by birth, who had all his artistic education in Brazil, the most notable artist of his generation and the successor of Felix Emílio Taunay in the chair of landscape and the painter of an excellent portrait of Grandjean de Montigny; an Agostinho José da Mota (1828–1875) one of the greatest if not the greatest landscape painters of his time; a J. Correia Lima (1814–1857), disciple of J. B. Debret, whom he followed in the chair of historic painting as substitute professor, and Manuel de Araújo Pôrto Alegre (Rio Grande do Sul, 1806–1879) afterwards Baron de Santo Angelo. The disciple and friend of Debret, with whom he travelled to Europe in order to meet the masters of the time and whom he succeeded in the chair of painting in 1837; poet and painter, historian and critic of art, Pôrto Alegre, who did not become notable in any of these fields, was nonetheless the most enthusiastic partisan of the mission and had no equal for his interest in art in Brazil. He helped in the foundation of the Conservatory of Music and the National Academy of Music and Opera, wrote the first biography of Father José Maurício and contributed, as few have done, to the progress of the Academy of Arts of which he was one of the first students and when he came to be professor (1837) and third director (1854–57), one of the most useful and brilliant men in the initial troubled phase of the history of that institution. None of them, however, made any new contribution to the art of his country; and a long time was to pass before the Brazilian artist could finish his artistic education and become master of his technique and his ideals, and be capable of transforming what he took from strangers into something original and more beautiful.

But the art which was being secularized and tended to leave the exclusive service of the gods to consecrate itself to that of men, commenced to look for inspiration in national life, military or patriotic, without losing its interests in religious matters. It became more human, it was man which interested it, but above all the great personage, the heroic man. All which was merely anecdotal or contingent, all which constituted the warp and woof of material and daily fact, retained it little and rarely took its attention. It proceeded by preference by means of allegory and symbol. What began then and continued for about fifty years from the period of independence, was the epoch of the allegorical picture, of oil portraits of personages of importance, and of historical paintings, or in other words, a whole art which feared the ugly and the common, the ephemeral and little facts and whose conception of beauty was closely related to the greatness of events. The political emancipation of the country; the interest which the new awareness of the life of the nation awoke in our history; the development of this national consciousness; the influence of the French school of battle painting; the romantic movement in the first half of the nineteenth century, and finally the war of Paraguay in 1865–1870, calling attention to heroic episodes, led artists to explore this still intact vein of the great national events. They did not appear satisfied except when they were undertaking large Biblical and historical compositions. It was in the choice of subject that the national feeling in art began to manifest itself under the influence of romanticism; [15] and within the spirit of this painting devoted to his-

15 The love of travel and of the exotic and the spirit of adventure constitute one of the characteristic aspects of the romantic movement which resulted, on the one hand, from revolutions, wars, emigration and exile, and on the other, from the progress of history and philology, "which seek tradition and the mixture of themes from folklore, of images common to the imagination of all men." Everywhere there arose, coming from Europe, scholars, thinkers and artists who, attracted by new fields of observation and work, carried influences between this or that European nation and the countries of America. This is one of the facts which, together with the desire to get rich and the spirit of adventure, explain the large number of scholars and artists from abroad who from beginning to end of the nineteenth century, appeared in Rio de Janeiro and other regions of the country, where many of them finally settled, identifying themselves with the new and promising environment. Among the artists, certain names stand out, in the middle of the nineteenth century: to cite only the chief ones, Jules le Chevrel, a Frenchman, who as a rival of Pedro Américo for the chair of design, which he later occupied, was the first to recognize the superiority of his rival and the right of the latter to win the competition; J. Baptiste Borely, also French, painter of a beautiful pastel portrait of Councillor Tomaz Gomes dos Santos; Nicolau Facchinetti, an Italian painter, a landscapist, who lived in Rio from 1849 on; Ferdinand Krumholz, a Dutch artist who lived in Rio between 1845 and 1855 and left in his portrait of Pôrto Alegre an excellent work; Henri Nicolas Vinet, pupil of Corot and a landscapist, who came to Brazil in 1856 and was a faithful interpreter of nature in Brazil; Angelo de Martino who, on arriving in Brazil in 1868 went to the theatre of the war in Paraguay, where he was attached to the headquarters of Caxias and on board warships, and left us some admirably conceived canvasses, in which he set down historical episodes of our navy, like *A Abordagem dos couraçados, A passagem de Humaitá* and *O Combate de Riachuelo;* Tomás Driendle (Bavaria, 1846), a painter of figures

tory, landscape itself, in a period in which landscapists still refused to look at nature, only entered a "collaboration" and was no more than a background of hills, of a corner of woods or of a curve in the river which served as accessories to a bit of sacred, or classical, or national history. The horror of the real, the taste for the grandiose, and the love for academic themes constituted a characteristic trait of the idealism in which Brazilian art delighted in almost the whole of the nineteenth century, and which acquired, between 1861 and 1886, its greatest power of expression in the two famous painters of historical painting, Vítor Meireles and Pedro Américo, painters of canvasses that found their inspiration in heroic motifs of our history and whose art is far from being reduced, as Luiz Martins thinks, to a "transplantation in opera style of all the Horace Vernet battle painters." Both of them studied in the Academy of Fine Arts and, supported by Dom Pedro II, went to Europe where they took lessons, the former with Minardi and Consoni in Italy and with Delaroche in Paris, the latter, Pedro Américo, with Ingres, Horace Vernet and others in Paris, attending also certain university courses. A master of design and a great painter, considered the founder of Brazilian painting, Vítor Meireles (Santa Catarina, 1832–1903) left beside numerous portraits of personages of the time, the *First Mass in Brazil* and the magnificent battle pictures, *The Passage of Humaitá, The Battle of Guararapes* (1869) and *The Battle of Riachuelo* (1872), pictures which he received an order to paint and which stand out in a notable manner from the artistic production of the time on account of the firmness of the drawing, the poetic feeling and the vigor and technique of their execution. The major work of art which Brazil possesses in this field, however, is the *Battle of Avaí* by Pedro Américo (Paraíba, 1843–1905), one of the greatest Brazilian painters, who acquired his fame not by his canvasses inspired by Biblical subjects which he himself preferred (*David, Judas, Sorrowful Virgin, Jacobean*) but by his paintings of battles and other historical episodes like the *Fight of Campo Grande* and the *Proclamation of Independence,* in which he was able to give life and movement and in which there come together to give them a high degree of plastic power, clarity of coloring, art of composition in the details, and depth of aerial perspective and a broad grasp of composition.

The work of artists contemporary with these or following them, or who were their disciples, still showed a marked fondness for Biblical and historical subjects. Landscapes and painting devoted to family scenes and to common life were still infrequent in expositions of painting, nor could they compete in number or quality with the historical canvasses or those inspired by Biblical motifs, or with the pastel and oil portraits. Décio Vilares (Rio, 1851), disciple of Pedro Américo, composed his two *Jeromes* (*Saint Jerome at prayer* and *Saint Jerome translating the Hebrew books*) and the *Flight into Egypt,*—pictures in which we may admire the purity of the drawing, the harmony of the coloring and the intelligence of the composition; but it is in portraits of women and children that his art flowers in full maturity, with his attempt to seize and to repro-

---

and portraits, whose canvas *Uma cena de família na Baviera* is justly considered a masterpiece; and, finally, Georg Grimm (Bavaria, 1846), professor of landscape painting, to the teaching of which he gave a new direction, becoming one of the most influential teachers of the Academy of Arts. All made important contributions and some very valuable ones, to the development of art in Brazil; the intellectual growth of the arts and artistic culture was in the nineteenth century intimately connected with foreign cultures.

duce the most difficult thing in physiognomy, the expression. A disciple of Vítor Meireles, Rodolfo Amoêdo, who was also the winner of a prize of the Academy of Arts in Paris, after seeking inspiration in sacred history (*The departure of Jacob, Jesus at Capernaum*) turned toward native subjects, leaving us *Marabá*, sunk in her romantic melancholy, and *The last Tamoyo*, the best of his pictures because of its originality of conception and vigor of execution. It was also in historical paintings that Aurélio de Figueiredo (Paraíba, 1854–1916), brother and disciple of Pedro Américo, took most pleasure, as is revealed by his sketch, *Discovery of America, Osório* and the picture which represents the ball on Treasury Island in November, 1889, beside the *Meeting of Paulo and Francesca da Rimini*, considered the most perfect of his work.[16] But it is with Almeida Júnior (Itú, São Paulo, 1850–1899), the most original and personal of all of our artists of the nineteenth century, that Brazilian painting was really founded and the division occurs between the followers of European tendencies who insist on the conservation of foreign techniques, and the nativists, who turn to the search for the Brazilian, the regional, the new, both in subject matter and in technique, and is most marked by the search for the accidental, the individual and the evolution from idealism to realism. The great artist who, with a pension given by the Emperor, was in Paris when the struggle for the renewal of pictorial technique was at its height and the history of impressionism was attaining its culminating point with Camille Pissarro, Auguste Renoir, Edouard Manet, Edgar Degas and others, "passed untouched through the artistic battle," as Sérgio Milliet observes, "and returned as Brazilian as before." It can be said that the Paulista painter gave a proof of his originality, frankly attacking the present and the living in scenes, customs and local types—, after having tried with success, historical painting in his *The Departure of the Caravan*, a magnificent canvas, and the *Flight into Egypt*, which is one of the best pieces of work inspired by the Biblical story. He was finally convinced that he would find, and in fact he did find, the

---

[16] These are not, however, the only representatives of historical painting, which, begun under the influence of the French mission, is incipient in the pictures of Pôrto Alegre and other, and continued to develop through almost the whole of the nineteenth century, exercising until the twilight of romanticism an influence which even the most original artists could not escape. In the art work of Zeferino da Costa (Rio de Janeiro, 1840–1915), the bulk, if not all of the work, consists of historical and religious pictures and decorative panels, some of which were done for the Candelaria church. Benedito Colixto (São Paulo, 1853), who studied with Vítor Meireles, immortalized the glory of São Vicente and the conquest of the plateau with his pictures *Pôrto das naus* (São Vicente) *Partida da frota de Estácio de Sá* and *Em caminho de Piratininga*— episodes of colonial history in São Paulo. Another famous painter who worked in practically all the genres, Antônio Parreiras, a native of the State of Rio, brings to life on the canvas the founding of Niteroi, of São Paulo and of Rio de Janeiro, giving us in *Morte de Estácio de Sá* (Founding of Rio de Janeiro) one of his most beautiful pictures, remarkable for the historic fidelity with which he restores the period and for imaginative power. The colonial history of São Paulo furnishes material to Oscar Pereira da Silva (State of Rio, 1867), who was a pupil of Vítor Meireles, and to Henrique Bernardelli: the former, painter of the *Fundação de São Paulo*, and the latter of *Os bandeirantes*, in which he reproduces a scene from the march of a bandeira of São Paulo through the forest, beside the two pictures *Aleijadinho* and *José Maurício na Corte de Dom João*, in which he pictures the great colonial artist and the first Brazilian composer. A native of Rio Grande, Augusto Luiz de Freitas, who was a pupil of Bernardelli, in the School of Fine Arts (1895–1898), strong and vigorous in temperament, takes as the subjects of some of his pictures episodes from gaucho history, admirably recreated in *A chegada dos açoreanos* and *A Batalha de Azenha*, which form part of the collection of the State, in Pôrto Alegre.

elements of his production around himself in the very life around him, in the things of every day, in the goings and comings of familiar persons in the rural environment of São Paulo. He is, in fact,—to employ the expression of Luiz Martins—, "the painter of the dawn of our agricultural prosperity and the fixer of our rural life at the beginning of the era of the greatness of coffee." In his pictures *The Countryman stalking game, The Countryman picking tobacco, The violinist, Boredom interrupted, On the watch, Country people, Saudades, Mandinga, The hunter, Country scene* and others, in which the science of the painter and the sincerity of the observer are united, there is without doubt "a mind that is unequivocably Brazilian, something unconsciously barbarous and fertile—a necessary consequence to young land—which no foreign artist was able to translate. He is the first classic of our painters.[17] Along with Vítor Meireles, whose disciple he was and much more than Pedro Américo, Sérgio Milliet writes, "Almeida Júnior had the importance of a dividing line for Brazilian painting. With him our artistic freedom is asserted and with him we win a place in the history of contemporary art."

But, of this man who was the greatest of our painters of the past century and always equal to himself whatever the motif out of the present or the past that was proposed to his brushes, we cannot say with Luiz Martins that he was "a beautiful, sterile spectacle," a single and solitary figure in the history of our painting. He was, on the contrary, not the beginning but the indication of a natural evolution which was going on from the historical painters "down to the generation of Santa Rosa and of Portinari," a movement from idealism to realism, from an art in which the concern for the beautiful and the great predominated, to an art that was naturalistic, an art of observation and of truth, that found its inspiration in the geographic and social land-scape of the country. The place that he occupies in the evolution of Brazilian painting, as the painter who is typically Brazilian, is the highest and most important which any artist of the past century attained. But the evolution which he marked in an exceptionally notable way is also indicated in his time, at least with regard to the anecdotic concern with the subject, by a Pedro Weingartner (Pôrto Alegre, 1858), a landscapist and a painter of gaucho scenes, types and customs, and Belmiro de Almeida (Minas Gerais, 1858), who selected by preference as the subject of his canvasses, aspects and figures from ordinary life, principally in the higher social strata. Returning in 1882 to São Paulo and drawn out of the orbit of academic and urban influences to a small, deserted and dark city—the center of an active agricultural life,—what met the eyes of the São Paulo painter was this rural life of the plantations and of the coffee farms in all its dominant aspects, customs and types. The formula of light, not the impressionist one, "but that of Cabanel, which is more primary," he brought home from Europe for his pictures with their clear and burning colors. The country life of Rio Grande with its typical landscapes and customs found its first painter in Pedro Weingartner, who painted with a partial analysis and without boldness of technique, but with the truth and sincerity of Almeida Júnior; and like the great painter of São Paulo, he also who had been in Paris, paid no attention to the impressionists, and according to the observation of Ângelo Guido, "remained somehow outside the innovations of his time."

[17] Cf. Monteiro Lobato, *Almeida Júnior.* In "Revista do Brasil." Ano II, p. 35, São Paulo, January 13, 1917; Sérgio Milliet, *Almeida Júnior.* In "Ensaios," pp. 142-151, São Paulo, 1938; Luiz Martins, *Almeida Júnior.* In "Revista" do Arquivo Municipal, Ano VI, Vol. 66, pp. 5-22, April-May, 1940, São Paulo.

The painter of Minas, Belmiro de Almeida, who came to stay in Rio de Janeiro, was heedful of the suggestions of another set of surroundings and became the painter of urban life, revealing in *Falls, Bit of garden, Picture* and in other canvasses, a profound and touching feeling for intimacy and something voluptuous in his search for elegant line, in his preferences for veiled atmosphere, and in his delicacy of feeling. With the painting of regional customs, which has its source in realism and of which Almeida Júnior is one of the forerunners and the most representative figure of the nineteenth century, there developed at the same time, the painting of landscapes with Antônio Parreiras, born in the State of Rio, one of our most fertile artists and one of great skill in practically all of the types of work which he explored: João Batista Castagneto, Italian by birth, who obtained his artistic education in Brazil and whose excellent marine paintings won him the grand gold medal in the Exposition of 1884, and some others, almost all disciples of Georg Grimm, a German landscapist, who, contracted to take the chair of landscape at the Academy, profoundly changed the teaching, leading his pupils to see and observe nature and scattering them over the beaches and through the mountains. The Brazilian landscape "which French artists could not comprehend," writes José Mariano Filho, "was only revealed to us afterward, when Henrique Bernardelli felt its splendid and truculent quality." But it is not with the vigorous work of Bernardelli (Mexico, 1858), Brazilian after 1878 by his own choice, that the most brilliant phase in the evolution of contemporary landscape painting was begun. The greatest of our landscapists was without doubt João Batista da Costa (State of Rio 1865–1926), professor of painting (1906) and director of the School of Fine Arts (1915), whose production bears witness to the most complete and powerful personality which we have yet had in the interpretation of Brazilian landscapes. The technique of his pictures is such that it amazes specialists and as to the charm which one feels in the finished work, there is no one who can escape it. Among his numerous pictures which are particularly notable in their vigor of observation, their delicacy of coloring, which is always correct, and in the sincerity of the feeling, *Tranquillity, Lent, The beloved corner, The road to the corral, Morning* (Alto da Serra, Petrópolis), *The Prisoner, The flowering field, After the rain, Repose, Rustic idyll,* and *No hurry* touch us still by the ideal of peace and purity which they suggest, by the poetic feeling of the bucolic life as much as by the transparency and correctness of his tonality and the harmony of his line.

The history of Brazilian art which had been before that of schools or of local or regional flowering, became, as we see, in the nineteenth century, one of great teachers who imposed upon others their aesthetic vision, attracted disciples and spread their influence in time and space. The coming of Dom João VI and his court, the French mission, the founding of the Academy of Arts, which drained from the provinces to Rio de Janeiro a great number of talents, were not slow in making the capital of the Empire the greatest center of art in the country. An academic tradition was created under the influence of the French school which furnished a new technique to our painters and sculptors, as well as to our composers, who underwent at the same time Italian influences, while with respect to civil and religious architecture, progress was slower, "the best that we had," as José Maria Belo remarked, "was still the old, colonial Portuguese tradition." The slowness of changes in the urban landscape which still in Rio de Janeiro, as in the capital of the provinces, had its old colonial aspect during most of the nineteenth century, did not permit a greater development of civil architecture, which always and everywhere had been connected with the progress of great cities. The artists, above all the painters and musicians, traveled and consequently their horizon was enlarged. The coming of realism which led the artist to search about him in his own environment, in the individual and in the accidental the makings of his production, contributed to free Brazilian art and, in the painting of Almeida Júnior, H. Bernardelli and Batista da Costa, there began a nationalistic reaction in the direction of a freer interpretation of life, of customs and of the Brazilian landscape. If differences of schools, so marked at the beginning of the nineteenth century, when colonial artists, Portuguese and foreigners met, tended to dissolve in the middle of the century, when all of the artists had in their resemblance to each other a family air, more of these differences began to be marked again in a greater variety of tendencies opening new perspectives of work and struggles which were to be fruitful. The position which the Academy, now traditional, occupied in the history of the arts during the second Empire, with the artists who got their education in it, was due, nevertheless, not only to the influences of the French mission and of the school to which it transmitted its cultural inheritance and to the public, now made up of a small élite in Rio de Janeiro and stimulated by expositions of painting (since all art necessarily presupposes a public) and also the vigilant protection which the Emperor gave to artists, facilitating or paying for their travel for purposes of study. The same zeal with which Dom Pedro II encouraged scientific enterprise may be noted in his support of the arts, and if his love of science led the chief of the state to exchange letters with the notable physiologist Du Bois-Reymond, about the foundation of a great institute of physiology in Rio de Janeiro, his interest in the arts arrived at the point of nourishing his dream, as impossible to realize as the former, of giving to Richard Wagner the permanent direction of the theater in our capital . . . When it was not possible for him to go to see the exposition of an artist, as happened in the case of Pedro Weingartner when it was held in Rio de Janeiro, some years after he had received a pension which Dom Pedro II gave him, the Emperor requested him to bring some of his paintings to the Palace at São Cristóvão so that he might enjoy them. But if it was in Rio de Janeiro that in any case the major center of artistic influence was kindled in Brazil, in the old cities of the north, Belém, Recife, and especially in Bahia—whose school of painting (the so-called Bahiana school) goes back to the end of the eighteenth century and in which there was founded under the Empire, as a result of private initiative, an Academy of Fine Arts (1877),—a whole legion of artists were at work, amateurs and professionals, who modestly and practically without stimuli were carrying on their work within the narrow framework which tradition and convention imposed upon them. In these meteoric formations—milky ways of regional culture, from which no star of the first magnitude detached itself—, there was nevertheless sketched an artistic movement which in the following century, with the development of large cities, took on major proportions and a deeper meaning, leading to the creation of new centers of aesthetic culture in the old cities of the north as well as those of the south, in Pôrto Alegre, Belo Horizonte, Curitiba and above all in São Paulo.

The major part of these productions in the marginal zones of artistic culture which developed in Brazil, which had the capital of the Empire as its center, not only show us the average level of Brazilian art in the nineteenth century, but the great differences of level and of the aspects of artistic life in the center of the country and in the cities, in which artists frequently were still working in the manner of the eighteenth century under the influences of the colonial Portuguese tradition. If we follow closely the evolution of art in the old cities of the north (in those of the south the artistic movement was still extremely limited), we would scarcely see a change. The transformation under the influence of great teachers in Rio de Janeiro was slow and gradual and developed in proportion as these urban centers gained in density of population and in intensity of economic and social life. One did not observe even in the center of the art life of the country any interaction of poets and artists, no influence of creative thought on plastic or pictorial invention, nor of the artist on the poet. Art, which was still limited to painting and sculpture, the flat image and the plastic representation, and which was manifested on a larger scale with more vigor in painting, did not give and could not give signs of coming down "from that Olympian region inaccessible to common people in which (according to Rui Barbosa) an error canonized by the centuries kept it clasped to the heart of all, as an integral part of common education." If with the object of promoting extraordinary individuality in the various branches of the fine arts, an Academy was founded and traveling scholarships were offered—scholarships given to those who distinguished themselves—and individual or collective expositions were arranged, it was only later, in 1856, that there was created through the efforts of Bethencourt da Silva, disciple of Grandjean de Montigny, the School of Arts and Crafts with the object of developing industrial arts and of making art a part of all industries and of diffusing among the masses, a taste for applied art. But in a country with elementary industry and a low standard of living, without the necessary technical conditions for the development of industries of taste and still without an artistically educated public, it was not possible for art to expand in alliance with industrial culture, applied to the object of daily use upon which the artist impresses a seal of beauty and with which he reaches his highest privilege—that of beautifying and purifying life and making the attractions of art come within the reach of all. Hence, from the very conditions imposed upon the industrial environment, the odyssey of that admirable institution of Bethencourt da Silva which "born in disdain, wandered, struggled and begged for many years," as Rui Barbosa writes, and which having been an "oasis in the desert," only many years later was copied in other places like the Schools of Arts and Crafts of São Paulo and of Recife, created with the same object of promoting popular education through art, and of enlarging the field of application of art to industry. The penetration of art into the various social strata which was going on in the meanwhile, slowly, not only as a result of general expositions but also as a result of efforts made to diffuse tastes and the sciences of decorative art, and as a result of the progress of the graphic arts, to which Henrique Fleiuss contributed in a brilliant and efficacious manner by founding the Imperial Artistic Institute and the reviews *Semana Ilustrada* and *Ilustração Brasileira,* and by giving, especially to the first of these publications in 1860 and 1876 the important collaboration of his own drawings. Caricature and humorous drawing began at this time and by extending the public which they amused, and bringing together in the same sentiment of pleasure both the elite and the masses, they have been factors in the popular struggle of art and constitute the first real collaboration between the arts and literature. The first caricaturists Angelo Agostini, who directed the *Revista Ilustrada* and *Dom Quixote,* and Bordalo Pinheiro, a remarkable Portuguese artist who lived for some years in Rio de Janeiro, contributed in this way to our artistic movement, putting their art at the service of politics and inaugurating the specialty from which there came to distinguish themselves in the twentieth century, artists like Raul Pederneiras, Calixto Cordeiro, Carlos Lenoir (Gil) and more recently, between 1910 and 1930, J. Carlos in Rio de Janeiro and Voltolino in São Paulo, and in whom the censorious spirit of our artists, their moral and social sense, and the qualities of their drawing, were to permit us to establish a tradition in this kind of work and give to caricature a higher place in the hierarchy of the arts.[18]

But this enrichment and enlargement of art over the primitive colonial scheme of things did not happen merely in relation to the plastic arts, and especially historical painting which was in Brazil the great art of the second Empire. Painting, like literature, which is the product of individualistic peoples, acquired in the second half of the nineteenth century a development that was only comparable to what has happened in these recent years. No artist down to the present has had more power to make us see the intimacy of regional life and customs than Almeida Júnior, who disappeared tragically in 1899. What we call "the painting of customs" was born with him. Also to music, which took on a secular character, new perspectives were opened in the second Empire, which, according to Mário de Andrade, was "perhaps the period of greatest external brilliance in Brazilian musical life." Spix and Martius who arrived in Rio de

---

[18] There is a great difference between caricature and humorous drawing: while the former has its source in the realism which is the foundation of new art, and is a drawing all the elements of which are due to observation of physical and moral character (there is "character" in caricature), humorous drawing "is not closely related to pure drawing. It conceives of the drawing not in complete liberty, but under the sign of the imagination. The quality of the drawing is not to be the interpretation at all costs of the real, but the expression of the artist's mind." Both categories, however, like all the manifestations of the comic, are always followed with close interest by the public, which is made up of all social classes. Humorous drawing, and, above all, caricature tend to produce a leveling of classes, bringing them together in a common pleasure, and contribute to the artistic education of the mass of the population; they are specialties which, by their very nature and their social and political function, are directed to, and interest the great public. Before Henrique Fleiuss—one of the pioneers of caricature in Brazil—this genre was already exploited, although with little value as art, by various artists of earlier generations. It was after him that it acquired, however, new life, which Bordalo Pinheiro directed. Caricature is a genre which is especially suited to the critical attitude of our artists, to their moralistic tendencies and their love of the comic and grotesque, which satiric observation obtains by dint of deforming reality intentionally, while preserving its essential characteristics. The greatest of these artists in the past century, Ângelo Agostini, and those who came after him Raul Pederneiras, Calixto Cordeiro, J. Carlos, Bastos Tigre, Voltolino, Di Cavalcanti, Belmonte and others, all with their own original traits, are caricaturists, at times excellent ones, who once they are on the trail of the comic and the ridiculous, use all that they can find, using their art especially to improve politics and in satirizing customs. But few of them, except in an occasional piece of work, bridged the distance which separates the caricaturist from the humorist, and which separates the moralist from the poet. Later, Carlos Lenoir, who, under the pen name of Gil, published many *portraits-charge* and fantasies in ink, and recently, Di Cavalcanti, are those who most often reached the level of humorous drawing, the graphic value of which "is a function of an attitude of mind and a poetic atmosphere." The humor of *Gil* seems natural at times; and if he had an extraordinary talent for caricature, it was caricature in his own manner, expressing less what he saw than what he felt, and bathing in joy, good humor and English *humor* his vision of men and events. But, to tell the truth, there is here a whole book that remains to be written on the evolution of caricature, in its broad lines, and of the contribution made by each of these artists to its progress in a little less than a century.

Janeiro in 1817, observed that music was then "cultivated in Brazil in preference to all the other arts, particularly in Rio de Janeiro," concluding that this art would certainly be the first in which Brazilians would attain early a high degree of perfection.[19] For Freycinet, who was in Brazil soon afterwards, "of all the arts cultivated by the Brazilians and Portuguese, music is the one which has the major attraction for them, and it is in it that they are most successful." [20] However, the impulse which Father José Maurício had given to church music came to an end. His Masses, like those of Marcos Portugal and of Sigismund von Neukomm, "the latter written in the style of the most celebrated German composers," marked in the time of Dom João VI the high water mark of sacred music in Brazil. Its decline commenced in the first Empire. "Religious music," writes Mário de Andrade, "still much appreciated and written, was losing little by little the dominating importance which it had first had." After a long period of weakness, artistic music was born again more varied in its manifestations and more dispersed over the country; and there spread in such a manner the fashion of playing the piano, that in Pernambuco there was a workshop for these instruments, and Wetherell was astonished to find them "a hundred leagues in the interior, transported on the shoulders of Negroes," just as Castelnau,[21] who visited Rio in 1843, was astonished to see them and hear them in practically all of the houses of Rio, even in the most modest. Rio was nicknamed by Pôrto Alegre (1856) "the city of pianos." This was the period of bands and orchestras, which were organized everywhere; of concerts by native and foreign virtuosi; of opera companies which, composed of the most celebrated artists sang in Italian in Rio de Janeiro practically every winter, the number of their spectacles given in a season in the capital of the Empire sometimes rising to sixty. It was also the period in which the first musical institutions and societies were founded, such as in 1841 the Conservatory of Music, [22] and, in addition to the Brazilian Philharmonic

---

[19] See Spix and Martius, *Reise in Brasilien*, Vol. I, p. 106.

[20] Freycinet, *Voyage autour du monde sur les corvettes L'Uraine et la Physicienne*. Paris, 1825, Vol. 1, p. 216.

[21] Castelnau, *Expéditions dans les parties centrales de L'Amérique du Sud*, etc. Paris, 1850, Vol. 1, p. 61.

[22] The origin of the present National School of Music goes back to the Conservatory of Music which Francisco Manuel da Silva, composer of the National Hymn, was authorized to found by legislative decree 238, November 23, 1841. During the century since that decree, we may distinguish three phases in the history of the traditional institution, "perhaps the oldest establishment for musical education" in this part of the American continent. In the first phase (1841–1855), the Conservatory which Francisco Manuel was authorized to found and which began to operate only on August 13, 1848, in a branch of the Imperial Museum and in conformity with decree 496 of January 21, 1847, preserved the character of a private institution, recognized and aided by the government. The second phase (1855–1890) began with the reform of 1855, by which the Conservatory was entirely reorganized, changing from a private to a public institution, forming part of the Imperial Academy of Fine Arts, of which it was the fifth section. The Imperial Conservatory of Music which continued to be directed by Francisco Manuel da Silva until his death (1865), was installed in 1872 in the street of Luiz de Camões, in a new building, the cornerstone of which was laid in 1863, as a result of the efforts of its founder and first director— the famous author of the National Hymn. After the proclamation of the Republic, the old conservatory, cut off from the Academy of Fine Arts, became the National Institute of Music, with a new organization based on ideas of the reform commission which included Alfredo Bevilacqua, José Rodrigues Barbosa and Leopoldo Miguez, and which was appointed by Aristides Lôbo, Minister of the Interior of the Provisional Government. The National Institute of Music, which in

Orchestra, an instrumental society (1841), the Imperial Academy of Music and the National Opera, founded in 1857, also as a result of the efforts of Francisco Manuel and which had, according to Mário de Andrade, "a period of extraordinary national brilliance, having four operas sung in the language of the country and also an important amount of Brazilian musical production." It is also in the second Empire that, as the illustrious musical critic reminds us, there moved to Brazil the two founders of Brazilian pianistic virtuosity, Artur Napoleão, who in 1878 founded, together with Leopoldo Miguez, an establishment for pianos and music, and whose "crisp manner became traditional in Rio de Janeiro," and Luiz Chiafarelli, the founder of the Paulista school of piano music; and instrumental societies were multiplied in the later days of the regime, among others the Beethoven Club (1882) in Rio de Janeiro, the Haydn Club (1883) in São Paulo, under the direction of Alexandre Levy, and the Popular Concerts, begun in 1887 by Carlos Mesquita, in Rio de Janeiro.

In this atmosphere full of interest in music, which had its roots in the liking of the Brazilians for music and was constantly stimulated by opera companies and societies of concerts, it is natural that there should arise, even at the end of the nineteenth century, the first flowering of Brazilian musicians and composers. Between Father José Maurício who died in 1830 and with whom the period of sacred music came to a close, and Carlos Gomes, the creator of Brazilian music, we do not find more than one composer of great merit. That was Francisco Manuel (1795–1865), who was a disciple of Sigismund von Neukomm and Marcos Portugal, and became famous as the author of the National Hymn, and founder of the two greatest and most important musical institutions of the Empire. He was, in the chain of Brazilian composers, the link which bound the period of sacred music with that of profane music which attained its splendor at the end of the second Empire. For Mário de Andrade, who considers art, even in this phase of its evolution "fundamentally European, even among the nationalists who took an interest in the musical representation of Brazilian life," the nationalistic concern was reflected in Carlos Gomes (1836–1896), Alexandre Levy 1864–1892) and Alberto Nepomuceno (Fortaleza, 1864–1920),—"the most national of them all",—while among the less characteristic figures "too much bound to European tradition," there appear Leopoldo Miguez (Niteroi, 1850–1902), Henrique Oswald (1852–1931), Francisco Braga (1871–1945), Barroso Neto and others. All of them, however, whether with nationalistic tendencies or more under the influence of Europe,

---

1890 was again reformed (decree 934, October 24), continued, however, to operate in its old building until 1910, when it moved to the building which had served as the National Library, in Passeio Street; here in 1913 a new class-room building was opened, and in 1922 an auditorium for concerts. In 1931, with a new structure, based on the reform of Francisco Campos (decree 19,852, April 11, 1931), it was made part of the University of Rio de Janeiro, and the name was changed to National School of Music, by law 452, of July 5, 1937, which created the University of Brazil. In this last period (1890–1940), the most brilliant and fruitful of all in the history of the institution, its directors were: Leopoldo Miguez (1890–1902); Alberto Nepomuceno (1902–1903) (1906–1916); Henrique Oswald (1903–1906); Abdon Milanez (1916–1922); Alfredo Fertim de Vasconcelos (1922–1930); Luciano Gallet (1930–1931); Guilherme Fontainha (1931–1938) and Antônio de Sá Pereira, who was appointed in 1938 and still remains at the head of the establishment. (See *Otávio Bevilacqua, Leopoldo Miguez e o Instituto Nacional de Música*. In "Revista Brasileira de Música," Vol. 7, 1st part, 1940, pp. 6-18; José Rodrigues Barbosa, *Alberto Nepomeceno*. In "Revista Brasileira de Música," Vol. 7, 1st part, 1940, pp. 19-39.

are expressions of that musical romanticism which at the time was dominant and in which there stood out as figures of the greatest importance in Brazilian music down to the present time, Henrique Oswald, the most completely equipped musician of his generation in the judgment of Mário de Andrade, and before him and greater than all, Carlos Gomes, a native of Campinas in São Paulo, and one of the most powerful artists that Brazil has yet produced. Between the two attitudes in the composition of opera at that time,—that which came to us from Italy as an inheritance from Verdi and other composers of the peninsula represented by Mascagni, Leoncavallo, Puccini, and the other which has its origin in Wagner and Strauss, and in which program music in which the orchestra has a principal part prevailed,—it was the former, the Italian approach, which exercised the greatest influence on our composers of operas. If the German tendency is represented by Leopoldo Miguez, who reveals himself in his lyric drama *Saldunes* as one of our rare Wagnerians, sincere in his faith but without great power of musical invention, the other approach more generally followed had its highest representative in Carlos Gomes, almost all of whose work was strongly marked by Italian influence. Having studied in Milan where many of his compositions were written, such as *Fosca* (1872), *Salvador Rosa* (1874), *Maria Tudor* (1878), Italian in their inspiration and character, his style is that of the contemporaries of Verdi in almost all of his work with the exception of *O Guaraní*, the most famous and perhaps the most original, and the one which especially by its overture, which has become part of the repertory of popular bands, contributed most to make him known in Brazil and abroad. The author of numerous operas among which we may note beside *Guaraní*, *Fosca* "the most knowing and the most complicated" of them all, and *Lo Schiavo* (1898), and of compositions for voice and piano, Carlos Gomes was certainly one of the great melodists of the nineteenth century and a technician of the first order within the limits of his style, which owes however very little to American sources. If the Brazilian composer lacks that lively feeling for the stage which seems to be innate in Verdi, and if his inspiration, although broad and spontaneous, did not always obey his will in the search for new forms, his work of unequal merit is doubtless one of the most beautiful and robust in the musical production of Brazil on account of its lyric warmth, the melody which is almost always abundant, a certain firmness of design, and a very strongly marked boldness of development, and also by the strength of creative sentiment which rarely loses any of its richness, its freshness and its power of communication to others.[23]

[23] The opera *O Guaraní,* based on the novel by José de Alencar, was sung in the Scala of Milan in 1870 with great success; and the public which heard it later, on almost all the opera stages of Europe, was not mistaken when it yielded to the charm of this music, with its clear, clean melodic line that awakens the mind and holds the attention. In Brazil it was sung for the first time in 1871, in Rio de Janeiro, through the efforts of the Brazilian Philharmonic Society, which celebrated the forty-fifth birthday of Dom Pedro II with the first performance of *O Guaraní.* It was on that occasion that Carlos Gomes made the acquaintance of André Rebouças; the great engineer sought him out at the fourth performance, driven by an enthusiasm which was only equalled by the solicitude with which from then on he followed the life and musical activity of the São Paulo composer. He met him again, two years later, in Turin and Milan, and wrote brilliant articles glorifying him, and when he met the returning composer in 1880, he published the article *Carlos Gomes e a emancipação,* in which he studied the relations between the work of Carlos Gomes and the campaign for the freeing of the slaves. The close friendship which united André Rebouças and

But with the Republic, as Mário de Andrade observed, "the decline of the external brilliance of music became gradually more marked," after it attained its major intensity at the end of the second Empire. And not only that of music, but that of painting among the plastic arts. This decline, which is visible in all artistic manifestations and which became more and more pronounced down to the European war (1914), seems to have been brought about by a complex of causes, of which not the least was the maintenance of the system of individual protection and of pensions to artists which had earlier been centralized and directed by the Emperor himself, and so by those very directive mechanisms which assured the cohesion, the homogeneity and the external brilliance of political institutions. In fact, during the Empire the number of young men who came to Rio or were sent to Europe to finish their studies at the expense of Dom Pedro was very great, for the Emperor always preferred to the "system of Dom João VI"—that of hiring artistic and cultural missions to come to Brazil—the system of sending artists to finish their studies abroad. There was even created with this system "an artificial, sterile movement," since, according to the just observation of Eduardo Prado, "it is not by sending to Europe youngsters who are more or less infant prodigies and geniuses, more or less misunderstood, that one will succeed in encouraging Brazilian art," the progress of which is less bound up with certain exceptional artists than with the development by all possible means of the artistic education of the country. Besides, of the two factors of art as a manifestation of national life, wealth and education, neither had acquired the intensity capable of raising the development of the arts to a high level, or of maintaining them in the state in which they began. Brazil was a democracy in which, as Eduardo Prado then wrote, there was not to be found a real aristocracy, rich and powerful, such as is necessary to the development of luxury and the arts; and teaching, whether the general instruction of the nation, which in the last analysis depends upon its civilization and its wealth, or artistic professional training, did not constitute then, as they do not even today in spite of all their progress, a system that was sufficiently developed in height and in breadth to produce great results. The Brazilian artist could not then and cannot for a long time be anything but "an exception, brilliant perhaps, but without great utility for the advance of art in general in this country." For the development of the more modest forms of art, as for painting, sculpture and architecture, what was lacking above all in Brazil was technical and professional teaching which at that time was limited to two schools of arts and crafts, that of Rio de Janeiro, founded in 1856 by Bethencourt da Silva, and that of São Paulo. On the plane of higher artistic teaching, the government of the Republic seemed to be content, like that of the Empire, with the Academy of Fine Arts founded in the time of Dom João VI. Meanwhile, with the victory of federalism, there occurred, although it progressed slowly in the field of the arts, as an accompaniment to the phenomenon of political decentralization, a movement of spreading out, of which the earliest manifestations are new, artistic, professional schools, which arose in the States through private initiative, like the School of Design and Painting in Curitiba, the Institute of Fine Arts at Pôrto Alegre (1908) where in 1929 there took place the first

---

the Viscount of Taunay had its roots in their common interest in art and their admiration for the musical genius of Carlos Gomes; Taunay was another enthusiast for the great and noble artist who, in the performances of 1871, was the living personification of his country and the symbol of its glory in the field of the arts.

Salon of Fine Arts, the Academy of Fine Arts in Manaus, founded by Joaquim Franco, that of Belém in Pará (1918), that of Belo Horizonte, the School of Arts and Crafts of Recife,[24] and the School of the Fine Arts of São Paulo (1925), which had gradually been transformed since the end of the nineteenth century into the principal center of artistic culture after Rio de Janeiro. The Academy of Fine Arts of Bahia, a private institution which came down from the Empire (1877), reestablished in 1899, took on a new life. Musical institutions were multiplied all over the country and side by side with the National Institute of Music of Rio—the oldest of these establishments—there began to play a part the Conservatory of Music of Recife, that of Pôrto Alegre, reorganized in 1910, the Dramatic and Musical Conservatory of São Paulo, founded in 1906, the Society of Symphonic Concerts (1921) and the Society of Artistic Culture, which was founded also at this time in São Paulo and which has already led to about five hundred artistic events or recitals. This movement of artistic expansion which took place, although without great strength except in the capital of São Paulo, was not without its consequences for the evolution of arts in Brazil. With its centrifugalism it broke up the uniform approach of the old official equipment, giving greater opportunities to the expansion of forces and to the development of different currents and spreading the field of artistic activity more and more over the territory of the nation.

[24] None of the institutions of Arts and Crafts which were created then made any effort to restore popular or native arts and to save the scanty artistic heritage of the little regional industries which, without any doubt, belong to art "on account of the ornamental character of their products." Those that survived continued to develop for a long time almost entirely outside the schools. The lace and embroidery with which linen was profusely decorated, and which was widely used in liturgical garments (alfaias and paramentos), constituted one of the most interesting traditional home industries of the country. Although their patterns were not very varied, they were work "full of character, approaching in their design, the oriental embroidery which the Portuguese inherited from the Moors." The lace and embroidery of certain provinces of the North, like Ceará and Pernambuco, the principal centers of productions, became famous. In the old province of Rio Grande do Sul, the customs of pastoral life which were dominant in the region as well as in the valleys of Minas Gerais led to the development of the industry of saddle-making which was characterized by extraordinary wealth of ornamentation. But this industry of harness, richly worked with appliqued leather and silver ornaments soon entered upon a period of decay, to disappear entirely in the present century: "today," Eduardo Prado wrote in 1889, and it is from him that our information is derived, "customs are not the same; long trips on horseback have been replaced by travel by rail, and the picturesque equipment of the horses has yielded to less rich, but more practical products, of European industry." One might list certain goldsmithing products, also of regional character (Santa Catarina and Rio Grande do Sul), as well as the work done on *cuias* made of half of a coconut or native gourd, trimmed with silver, and with a pedestal and handles also of wrought silver, used for drinking mate, and the industries that produce ornaments made with the brilliant plumage of certain birds and at times taking the form of wreaths of flowers—imaginative and admirably executed objects, which recall the native feather arts; the best reputed workshops for such things were in Rio de Janeiro. Of all the industries which had some ornamental or artistic character, the most important, however, if not for merit of style, at least for volume and variety of production, was certain that of clay vases, made of black or red clay, such as pots, vases and water jars of the types called *talhas, moringues,* and *bilhas, alguidares,* and *anforas,* much used in the home, in convents and churches. With very varied shapes, imported by the Portuguese, and showing Arabic or Hindu or Egyptian influence, these lustrous, varnished ceramics, sometimes painted over enamel, like the big *anforas* of Bahia, had their chief centers of production in Bahia, Pernambuco, and in Santa Catarina. (Cf. Eduardo da Silva Prado, *L'art.* In "Le Bresil en 1889." Edited by a group of Brazilian writers under the direction of M.F.J. de Santa-Anna Nery. Chapter XVIII, pp. 538-545).

The roads are different but the convergence may be toward the same points, the artistic capital of the country. The movement of modern art is one which starts from the States, from the periphery and moves toward the center. Its greatest center of expansion was in the capital of São Paulo, in which not only did there meet to favor the arts the wealth produced by coffee growing and by the industrial development and a more complete system of education, but there also helped to renovate the spirit and produce a variety of tendencies the meeting in that cosmopolitan city of different ethnic groups with their different cultures. The movement here as everywhere did not develop without struggles between traditionalists and innovators, between those who were resistant to the novelty of all progress and spirits who were in love with the new and the uncertain "faustians," to employ the expression of Spengler, revolutionaries in the arts, although as conservative and reactionary as the rest, in all other fields. The new aspirations which, under the influence of foreign schools, arose from groups heterogeneous in their composition and in the tendencies of their principal components, and which had nothing in common except the desire to destroy old values, so invaded the environment that not only did they manifest themselves in the renovating zones of the opposition but took up quarters in the very center of the conservative zone, like the Literary Academy and the Academies of Fine Arts. This was the pre-revolutionary period of which the tumultuous week of Modern Art in São Paulo in 1922 was a symptom. But, in this movement which does not involve to render it fruitful a new concept of life and art, and in which the "revolutionary spirit" had no profundity and did not go beyond a superficial renovation of technique, evolution was necessarily slow and the certainty of a comprehension of a modern art and the progress of its awareness did not assert themselves except as a result of internal conflict, of antagonisms of rival tendencies which struggle among our artists, fighting to mark them with their character and to acquire predominance. To the linear evolution of a doctrine or a tendency, there now followed the multiplicity of standards and divergent techniques which, in the struggle against reactionary rear guards, found a common field in which they could agree. If a whole group of really gifted young men were behind this artistic movement which has been continued down to the present day and if their productions were numerous, rare were those who manifested a deeper type of activity like a Brecheret in the field of sculpture, a Brazilian of Italian origin, the great sculptor of the Monument of the Bandeiras, and in whom a sculptural sense appears to be quite instinctive and in whom there are united to give him his exceptional position, his rare sensitivity, skill in translating it, his sense of the monumental and his gift for attaining fullness of activity without losing any of the freshness of his sensation. It was with him that sculptural art was restored in Brazil with a new spirit and a new form. The tradition of sculpture had been lost after Aleijadinho and Mestre Valentim, in the colonial period,[25] and the Brazilian sculptors of the nineteenth century, like Almeida Reis (Rio,

[25] Beside the makers of images and statues of saints, who worked in wood and soapstone, and with some of whom, like Aleijadinho, religious sculpture reached a high artistic level in Brazil, master carvers were very active in the colonial period, and have left us ornamental medallions and marvellous work in intaglio in the interior decoration of the old churches. It was in the art of carving in metal, ivory and especially in wood, that the master workmen of Bahia and Pernambuco became famous; so great was the development of these arts of carving under the influence of the Jesuits, that even before the rise of a school of art connected with Aleijadinho and Master

1840), Rodolfo Bernardelli (Mexico, 1852), and Correia Lima (1878), to cite only the principal figures, had not been able to continue its high value. Certainly these artists did not lack talent and although they may have lost themselves in a kind of academism and may have done damage to their art by their abundant production, like Bernardelli, since their work was made up of commissioned works (busts and monuments) which did not permit them to give expression to themselves in the full breadth of their gift, still some of their works of sculpture, harmonious and well finished, are worthy of figuring in our art galleries, even although they are without strength and spontaneity of invention. If, from some points of view, their names have been connected with the history of the arts, especially of culture in Brazil, it was rather through their technical instruction and the fervor they were able to inspire in their disciples toward the art of sculpture. But none of them made any original contribution to Brazilian sculpture, in which Brecheret achieved a position as a notable artist, giving a strange character of novelty and of audacity to his work, which is of great plastic value and does not impress us only by its external aspects, but also by unexpected intensity of expression and with a conciseness and economy and schematic simplicity that result from his vigorous power of synthesis and translate the progress of his mind toward a new type of classicism.

It is not, however, in sculpture that this new movement attained its greatest vitality or showed its greatest variety of tendencies. Although they are the arts of the oldest tradition and those which in the colonial period give us the most characteristic manifestations, sculpture and architecture did not entirely succeed in rising from the swamp in which they had stagnated in the first and second Empire. If, in fact, we were to make a detailed history of these three arts—painting, sculpture and architecture—and if we decided to follow it in all the steps of its slow evolution from the period of Independence, we could mark clearly the contrast between the evolution of each of these and the almost absolute domination of painting over the other two arts down to our day. Painting, the great art of the nineteenth century in Europe, was of all the arts the one which was most developed in the period of the Empire, as even today it is the one which includes the greatest creative effort of the Brazilians. For always many have devoted themselves to this art (and it would not be possible to name them all except in a specialized work); and even at the present time, the three phases of evolution are

Valentim, one can observe, José Mariano Filho tells us, "various regional schools of carving." This, as we have noted, was the period of splendor in decorative sculpture in the service of temples and churches. The carvers, who were the masters and true beginners of the plastic arts, enjoyed the highest esteem in the colony. Glyptics which uses hard and precious materials; the art of the engraver who executes the milling and matrices of coins, an art which acquired new life in the period of the Empire, with Augusto Girardet, maker of bas reliefs and medals, and with his disciples; and that of the goldsmith who engraves on gold and silver objects for religious rites, make up, together with work in wood and soapstone, the great bulk of our older sculpture. Clay, however, which always and everywhere was the chosen instrument of sculptors for small objects, was not, in general, used except for vases, in the original shapes of which the art of our terra-cotta artists was concentrated. It would seem that the art of sculptured objects and terra-cotta images was not brought to Brazil with that of painted ceramics, although it was an old domestic tradition cultivated with art in Portugal and had, in the middle of the eighteenth century, entered upon a renaissance, with the famous clay workers of the school of Mafra and the spread of the art through various centers of production, famous for their dolls and puppets—baroque in style—and for their figures of painted clay.

superimposed or opposed to each other—that of the older artists, that of the younger ones, and that of the moderns—brilliantly represented, the former phase by Pedro Alexandrino, an excellent painter of still lifes, and Benedito Calixto, whose landscapes have lost none of their interest which in their time they awoke. The second, that of the earlier generation, by an Edgar Parreiras, Paulo do Vale Júnior and Osvaldo Teixeira, among others, and that of modern painting by a Lasar Segall,[26] A. Volpi, Tarsila do Amaral, a pioneer in modern art in Brazil, Santa Rosa and Portinari—the greatest of them all. In spite of the tendencies, conquests and evolutions of art and of the different currents which it is constantly creating, one must, if one is to characterize an epoch, come to discuss the different physiognomies and the most marked personalities. Those who were the most successful and who gave the strongest expression to the period, either because they submitted or because they were opposed to it, survive their time and leave their companions behind and appear alone in all the majesty of their work, in the greatness of their production. The whole history of art is made up thus. In modern painting, which had its forerunners in Brazil, Paulo Rossi, Vitório Gobbis, Hugo Adami, Gastão Worms, Di Cavalcanti, and which is characterized by heterogeneity of groups, "in which there go hand in hand," as Sérgio Milliet writes, "impressionists of the first order like Volpi, expressionists like Segall, eclectics like Portinari, primitivists like Tarsila," there rises the dominating figure of Portinari, with his unequal production, varied and restless, but now with all the characteristics of a definitive work. Master of a marvelous technique which has permitted him in his portraits and genre painting to go from one school to another, from one period to another in the history of art, utilizing all the processes of painting, Cândido Portinari (State of São Paulo, 1903) appears finally to have found his road by going from experiment to experiment, to have mastered his technique and to have triumphed over all the disorder and incoherency, which moreover are very fruitful, and which are common in men endowed by an exuberant nature and with a real power of invention. No one among us has seen the spectacle of things with more ingenuous, but at the same time clearer and more penetrating eyes, nor had such a concentrated vision of the social landscape, a vision as concentrated as it is profound, nor so vigorous a power of accentuating reality deforming it and bringing out with surprising force of expression, in a work that is strange in aspect but powerful in thought, nationalistic in sentiment, but laden with truth and a richness of human content. Having an extraordinary *pris sur le vif* of types of scenes of rural life, the painter of São Paulo, born among Italian farm workers on a coffee plantation, reveals himself in his frescoes in the new building in the Ministry of Education and Health, a Diego de Rivera, with less power of imagination, less breadth of composition perhaps, but a more acute sensibility and a greater psychological power. What he paints in his magnificent murals is more what he feels than what he sees, or in other words, they are figures, scenes of manners and of human landscapes, as his sensibilities surprised them and as his extraordinary power of sympathy, an attribute of the greatest creators of pictures and of symbols, reconstituted them, restoring them as pieces of life.

It may seem strange at first sight, that, in contrast with painting, architecture did not in the Empire show any important activity and from the colonial period down to

---

[26] See Paul Fierens, *Lasar Segall*. Éditiones des Chroniques du Jour, Paris, 1938; Robert C. Smith, *Lasar Segall of São Paulo*. In "Bulletin of the Pan-American Union," May, 1940, pp. 382-388.

the Republic, did not make progress in any direction. Neither in the line of evolution within the colonial spirit, the tradition of which was lost, nor according to the new roots which Grandjean de Montigny tried to impress upon it with his sober classical architecture. To be sure, in the second Empire in which the best buildings were still the oldest, there arose, isolated and scattered, some first class construction. The building of the Portuguese library in the Manueline gothic style, palaces like that of the Count of Nova Friburgo (1862), the present palace of Catete, in white and rose colored marble, that of Itamaratí, that of Guanabara, the old residence of the Princess Isabel, entirely restored in 1908, and the country place of Mariano Procópio, constructed (1861) in Juiz de Fora by the German architect M. A. Gambs, in the green background of a magnificent park. But the break with tradition, without involving a complete giving up of colonial creations in favor of the classical formula, the domination of an agricultural economy, and the slow transformation of the urban landscape, frustrated all efforts to produce great works of civil, religious and military architecture, which entered upon a period of stagnation or decay all over the country. If we consider, moreover, that of the three arts—painting, sculpture and architecture—the last, if not more material than the other two, certainly is the most dependent upon material, it would be easy to understand that one could not expect a great rise of architecture where workmen paid no attention to the exigencies of French technique and where labor that was capable of following the new leadership of foreign architects was scarce. If the latter, great architects like Grandjean de Montigny, were not able to derive advantage from Brazilian material and labor which had permitted religious architecture to know a phase of splendor in the colony, Brazilian architects were no more than foremen or at the most "civil engineers, without special artistic knowledge." Under this apparent sleep in which the architect of Brazil had sunk, there was hidden however a slow and obscure necessity to prepare. It seemed that a climate favorable to a new rise of architecture had been created with the remodelling of the principal cities in the first quarter of the new century, and with a perfect fever of building the old cities which were being transformed and the new ones which were rising on the plateau, according to modern plans. But when, under the impulse of the rubber industry in the north and of coffee in the south, the ancient cities began to be rebuilt and Rio de Janeiro to strip itself of its old colonial aspect to acquire the splendid appearance of a great modern city, the accelerated pace at which the development of urban centers went on was rather an obstacle than a factor making for progress in architecture. In the rush of buildings which were multiplied, clamoring on every side for workmen and architects, the lack of labor and of specialized professional men opened an ever vaster field to improvisation in every sort of venture. "Middle-men promoted to be architects," as Nereu Sampaio rightly observes, "simple contractors almost illiterate became architects, and unscrupulous foreigners" found the field open for their greater activity without any restraint by public opinion in a social environment which lacked artistic education and was without leaders in the professions with ideas sufficiently clear and well defined to guide the extraordinary movement of urban building. Architecture then suffered under multiple influences; a period of servile copying of exotic styles and historic models began, and in the suburb avenues which were cut through—Rio Branco and Beira Mar, in Rio de Janeiro—as if at an international contest in extravagance, the classic, the ogive, Moorish art exhibited their flamboyancy in a picturesque variety of bizarre construction in the most varied styles. This was the triumph of bad taste and extravagance which Monteiro Lobato calls the "architectural carnival," and which did not lack, to mark the violence of the contrast in this incongruous succession of styles, the old colonial architecture, stripped of its ancient beauty and stifled in a mass of baroque luxury of decorative details.

It was at this time, around 1920,—a period of indecision and of feeling one's way in a more or less adventurous sense, that the movement for the renaissance of colonial architecture, still uncertain but already fruitful, got under way,—"the only one which speaks to us of our historic origin and which, involving a well defined racial character, corresponds from the point of view of private dwellings to the nature of the climate." What it hoped to do was to lead us to study carefully our ancient models, not to reproduce them, but "to take up again the thread of tradition and to face in a new social setting what our ancestors intuitively adjusted marvellously to the different nature of climate and materials." [27] This movement became more useful as, turning to the Brazilian type of dwelling, the architects had lost the notion of functional, rational architecture, or the awareness of the utilitarian value of the principal elements that entered into their architectural composition and which were employed, according to the observation of José Mariano Filho, as "mere ornaments," whereas they had a "function,"—that of defense against the climate,—in the colonial house, which was admirably adapted in its details to the conditions and necessities of the environment.[28] With the break of the bonds between the beautiful and the useful, between the utilitarian character and the artistic effect of the elements which the traditional architecture offered, there was a natural tendency to fall into excessive adornment and to consider as inspired in colonial architecture, the whole building to which one gave the seal of the baroque and which had in its facade architectonic details treated in profusion purely as decorative elements. . . . By dint of yielding to the taste for the picturesque and searching for effects, they ended by neglecting "the organic function" of these elements (porches, shaded balconies, tiles), the ornamental idea of which rather than their utilitarian value came to determine their structure and their application. But the campaign which has gone on in the last quarter century in favor of the study of colonial dwellings and the return to the forms of traditional architecture in which a brilliant part was played by Ricardo

27 Cf. Fernando de Azevedo, *Arquitetura colonial.* VIII. As conclusões de nosso inquérito. In "O Estado de São Paulo," April 29, 1926.

28 "In fact," I wrote in 1926, concluding the inquiry on the subject of colonial architecture, "were not the wide eaves, the verandas and windows, the terraces and the shaded balconies of these solid houses, arranged, like the inner patios, for the defense of the house against the action of the sun's rays? The thick walls of the colonial houses were not only forced upon us by the building materials of the time: wattle and logs. Even when they were of stone, they were huge, for they had to play a role in the house: to protect it against the surrounding high temperature. The very tiles, the meaning of which in the architectonic composition we have lost the tradition of, to such an extent that most architects just look upon them as purely decorative, were also part of these buildings for the purpose of defense against the climate. Of Arabic origin, the tile was used by the Portuguese in reception rooms, vestibules and at times in porches with the same object that the Arabs originally had in using them: to maintain the coolness of the interior of the house in the hot summer weather." (Fernando de Azevedo, *Arquitetura colonial.* VIII. In "O Estado de São Paulo," April 25, 1926.)

Severo,[29] José Mariano Filho and F. Nereu Sampaio, among others, did not occur without results nor did it develop without struggles with the current that was forming inside the general movement of renovation. The traditional current from which resulted studies, debates and investigations, in addition to buildings of value—residences and public buildings which found their inspiration in colonial architecture—was opposed by a frankly modern movement which was characterized by the rejection of all traditionalisms, by an appeal to reason and by a search for new forms. Represented by Cristiano das Neves, Lúcio Costa—one of our greatest architects—and more recently by Flávio de Carvalho, this current had in its favor in the reaction which it led against colonial forms, the great prestige of simplified form, the return to a conception of the work in view of what it is meant for, construction in reinforced concrete, the straight and vertical line and the spreading of a taste for modern architecture, so long combatted but now victorious in works of large proportions. On the plane of the private dwelling, an obstinate search for the new at any cost continued to drive architects to modify constantly their sources of inspiration and to renew the "repertory" of forms, which recalled frequently the massive constructions,—Assyrian and Arabic—, by their exclusive use of straight lines, of the equilibrium of masses, and by being covered with terraces. However it may be, both parties not only showed an appreciable effort to simplify forms (process of stripping off the superfluous) and adapting the structural elements more and more to their function and building for the purpose for which they were meant (rationalism), but also by directing themselves towards the search for a unity impressing the eye, succeeding in awaking a taste for homogeneous wholes, in which the house and the landscape and the interior details (decoration, furniture, rugs, curtains) should constitute a whole carefully planned. The art of gardens, which "in a hot climate and one of rich vegetation should be more than ever a complement of architecture," as Edruado Prado had already noted in 1889, and which was rarely practised in the nineteenth century, in which few houses offered themselves the luxury of a garden,[30] acquired, with the development of architecture, a notable life not only in the public gardens but in great private gardens, especially in those of São Paulo, which became famous on account of the beauty of their planning and the charm of their vegetation, and at times were prolonged into the interior of the buildings. One feels everywhere the ever more marked influence of English gardens and of French landscaping, to which

[29] Ricardo Severo, *A tradição*. Lecture given October 25, 1911, in the Institute of History and Geography of São Paulo; *A arte tradicional no Brasil*. Lecture given in the Society for Artistic Culture of São Paulo; *A Arte tradicional*. Lecture in the Polytechnic Club of São Paulo; *De arquitetura colonial no Brasil*. In "O Estado de São Paulo." Edition commemorating the Centenary of Independence, September 7, 1922; *A Propósito da arquitetura colonial* (interview). In "O Estado de São Paulo," April 15, 1926.

[30] "In the cities," Miss Maria Graham wrote in 1821, "few houses possess the luxury of a garden. These gardens seem like real vases of oriental flowers, but they appear to be well suited to the climate. Plants from the gardens of Europe grow side by side with the gayer plants and the bushes of the country. . . . Sometimes you find fountains or benches under the trees, forming very cool and delicious shelters in this hot climate." (*Journal of a Voyage to Brazil*. 1 Vol., London, 1824, p. 162). "The Portuguese gardens a century ago," wrote Eduardo Prado in 1889, "were and continued to be for the most part private gardens, in Brazil, but they were imitations on a small scale of Le Nôtre's style, with straight lines, symmetrical flowerbeds, and plots framed by hedges of box, sometimes replaced by tiles, bottoms of bottles or rows of shells." (*L'art*, Chapter XVIII. In "Le Brésil en 1889," pp. 519-562, Paris.)

Rio de Janeiro owes some of its most beautiful gardens, that of the Praça Paris among the newest, and among the oldest those which were designed and planted by Glaziou in the second Empire.

But if, in the last quarter century, the influence of modern ideas was so powerful in all plastic arts, giving us in sculpture a Brecheret and in painting a Portinari, and opening for architecture new possibilities, it was not less intense in music to which it opened one of its most brilliant and fruitful periods. Forming part of this general movement of modern art which had such an effect in all of the artistic manifestations of the country, music in Brazil tended not only to free itself from the other arts and to become "pure suggestions," and ever more musical, but also to penetrate more deeply into popular music and songs to find there, in their native sources, the elements of its own renovation. In the period of Carlos Gomes, as Mário de Andrade writes, "what makes the essential base of national music, popular work, still has not given us a song of our own," and there only appeared at the end of the nineteenth century and from then on (these are his words) "that amalgam of Ibero-American tendencies which today characterizes the music of the nation." [31] If, however, one can say with Pereira de Melo that at the beginning of the Republican period there started, in the history of our music, a "period of nativism" still weak and hesitating, and only later, in the last twenty years—

[31] Popular Brazilian music, which resulted from the fusion of the different elements, and in which the influence of the Negroes was surpassed only by that of the Portuguese, arose, in fact, in its characteristic forms, only at the end of the nineteenth century, after a long period of preparation. If, however, the peculiarities and tendencies which mark it, within the tradition and the fundamental components from which it came, are sufficiently clear, still it is not, and perhaps will not be possible to indicate exactly what was the influence of each of them upon the great variety of forms in which the musical ability of the nation finds expression. What can be attributed to American Indian sources begins to be revealed by the study of the material collected in the National Museum, which today, thanks above all to the research of Roquete Pinto, has at its disposal an excellent collection of recorded music of the Indians and of frontier songs. A more profound study of Negro musical folklore remains to be made; this music reveals, side by side with instrumental music, essentially rhythmical in character, "a vocal music with simple melodic phrases," the study of which will be the more interesting because it is certain that the African too, as Mário de Andrade observes, played a very important part in the formation of Brazilian popular songs. But if what constitutes popular music or poetry is also the unfaithful tradition of works of composers who might have been professional composers, what is the part played by the old colonial composers, and those of the Empire—inventors of *modinhas* or composers of dances and songs, whose work was in part preserved, and became for the most part anonymous, impersonal, a part of the treasury of popular music? Just recently Roger Bastide referred to one of the most important sources of dances and popular melodies, "for the most part old art forms of the salon and the court which, having long fallen out of favor in the aristocratic circles that started them, have survived in distant provinces." It was thus, explains Roger Bastide, that the form of the *mote* with its "turns," of the 1780's, a learned form, became popular in the nineteenth century, when the modinha was in the mouth of the people. The people are not creative, but conservative; the elite can, doubtless, "take popular themes and make them recherché, but it is a case of reconquest, by the learned, of something that once belonged to them, and that they had forgotten." The resemblance between Brazilian and Russian songs, noted by Mário de Andrade, shows us to what a slight extent popular music and poetry are local: they are really less so than art music or cultivated poetry. However, although it is derived from Portuguese sources for the most part and contaminated by the addition of the most diverse elements, there does exist in Brazilian music, as a result of Afro-American influences, a popular, native vein, something original, which does not come from the Peninsula and is strongly marked by the Brazilian character.

and not only in the ten year period after 1930 as Luiz Heitor insists–, that we see that nativism that began at the end of the nineteenth century, with popular music neither indigenous, nor African, nor Portuguese, arriving at a definite period of development and at its peak. It was a music which was worked out by society and came to have all the spontaneity and freshness "of the amalgam of our Ibero-American tendencies." Between Carlos Gomes and Henrique Oswald, who are the "most characteristic representatives of our musical romanticism," and modern music, inspired by folklore and art, which has in Villa-Lôbos its high exponent, there figures as in a phase of transition Glauco Velasquez (1884-1914), a romantic in essence, influenced by Wagner, and a fertile composer, of a refined sensibility and real creative power, whose music develops, as Renato de Almeida writes, "between symbolism and impressionism, in half images which are completed in our own minds thanks to their intense emotion." In the modern current which seeks in Brazilian folklore its source of inspiration, there stands out the important figure of Heitor de Villa-Lôbos (1890), whose concern, different from that of other folklore composers, is not however,–considers Frankenstein,–that of conserving and embalming native material, but rather that of expressing the energy contained in its elements. His lyrical pieces, like the five suites to which he gave the name of *Bachianas brasileiras,* led on by his enthusiasm for the spirit of Bach, and which constitute "a curious fusion of the style of Bach and the folklore music," his *Choros,* among which Number 8 is remarkable, "for its enormous, rhythmic vitality, its complication, the primitive vehemence and lyricism of the earth;" his great orchestrations of folklore music and of original material based on the forms of popular music, his symphonic poems, fantasies and variations, reveal such a wealth of ideas, such a prodigious spontaneity and such great exuberance and vitality in its rhythm, that they were not long in placing him, in the judgment of the most authoritative critics, among the first composers of the two Americas. If Villa-Lôbos is not, as Alfred Frankenstein has emphatically said, "one of the greatest prodigies which this century has produced in the field of music," he is certainly a generously gifted composer, as fertile a self-taught musician, "perhaps the most talented to appear after Mussorgsky," in the words of Paul Rosenfeld, who is amazed at his extraordinary, involuntary power and his fertility of imagination; a Rabelais of music as Irving Schwerke called him, on account of "the gigantic in his taste and spirit, the element of humor, irony and fineness and greatness of style which composed his musical personality." [32] In all of his enormous production made up of more than 1,400 compositions, from the most pungent, powerful and colorful pages of his *Bachianas* to the *Cirandas*–delicious rounds, original arrangements of popular melodies,–Villa-Lôbos is always a marvellous voice in which there are expressed with an unequalled intensity the characteristic joy in life of the Latin, the life of the country, the contact with the earth, and that intimate feeling for the tropics which is not only, as Rosenfeld says, "a consequence of the frequent use of barbaric melodies and rhythms and sonorities derived from the Negroes and Indians," but the very essence of his music,

[32] See Francisco Curt Lange, *Vila Lôbos, um pedagogo criador.* In "Boletim latino-americano de música, pp. 189-196, ano I. April 1935, Montevideo; Alfred Frankenstein. In "San Francisco Chronicle," San Francisco, Cal. December 1939; Paul Rosenfeld, *Current Chronicle.* In "The Musical Quarterly," Carl Engel, editor, New York, October, 1940; Eurico Nogueira França, *Vila Lôbos, pedagogo.* In "Música Viva," January-February, 1941, p. 6; Burle Marx, *Vila Lôbos.* In "Vogue," January 1, 1941, New York, p. 82.

or in other words, an essential part of his being which is extremely sensitive to the lyrical suggestions of the land and of the race in all its restlessness and in the vigor of its force and primitive passion.

In that magnificent effort to achieve a synthesis of popular music and artistic music, if Villa-Lôbos acquired an exceptional position, in the richness, the variety and above all the high quality of his production, he is not however a solitary figure, this most remarkable composer, whose fame has already passed beyond the frontiers of his own country, as formerly did that of Carlos Gomes. After the romantic flowering which ended with Glauco Velasquez, "a restless experiment with flashes of genius giving a precarious result," in the words of Mário de Andrade, others younger than Villa-Lôbos gave proof of possessing great force and originality in their production which was inspired in Brazilian popular music and songs. Folklore music, at whose fountain the best living composers came to drink and which constitutes through its richness of material a treasure that is still in large part to be exploited, continues to exercise a notable influence on modern music and to be one of the most important factors in its evolution. This is shown by the production of Lorenzo Fernandez (1898) with his *Reisado do pastoreio,* the delicious miniatures *Presentes de Noel* and the opera *Malazarte,* so strongly marked by its Brazilian character; of a Francisco Mignone (1897), not with his opera *L'innocente—*"one of the best and most strongly dramatic of all the Brazilian lyrical production"—but with *Congada,* from a celebration of Negro slaves in the second act of the *Contratador de diamantes* (The Diamond Contractor) and above all in his symphonic work and chamber music; and of a Camargo Guarnieri (1907) of São Paulo, the youngest of the three, whose music in the judgment of Luiz Heitor, "is one of the best constructed and most profound of the Brazilian school." But, although in this period [33] for musical production is really important, but which is more

---

[33] In a recent work in which he traces the evolution of Brazilian music, Mário de Andrade distinguishes three chief periods in that evolution: 1) essentially religious music, of the colonial period, at first popular, with a nativist flavor (the music of the first Jesuits), and later erudite, with pretension to nobility and stripped of Brazilian elements (the art of aristocratic chapels); 2) the phase of love (lyric music, amorous music) which announces the transition to profane art; the rise of the figure of Francisco Manuel da Silva, "the greatest that Brazil has produced," in the opinion of this leading critic; and 3) the period of open nationalism which began after and under the influence of the Great War (1914–1918) or, better, of the events which flowed from it. "First, God; then, love, and last, nationality." In the first phase of its development, music, which was "a liturgical means of socialization," became universal, in the European sense, employing the Catholic song of the Portuguese, with the first chants—the organ and Gregorian. But, by the efforts of the Jesuits, it came to attempt to make use of all the elements of an American Indian character (songs, words, dances), generalizing the caterete (Tupi song and dance) and even some parts of the Indian mystic ritual. Father José Maurício was the highest expression of religious music, the learned music which dominated until Independence. Then there began the secularization of music, with the *modinha,* impregnated with mestizo sensuality, and the melodrama, in which learned music of the Empire concentrated its expression. This stage, at the beginning of which there looms up the figure of Francisco Manuel, the author of the National Hymn, culminates in Carlos Gomes, who began a period of open internationalism. But the existence of a competent technique gave music in Brazil what it needed to make its own way and throw off foreign influences and their imitation. After the European war, of 1914, Brazilian music, which was embryonic with Francisco Braga and Barros Neto, but which had not yet surmounted its internationalism at the end of the nineteenth century, attained a new high point with Villa-Lôbos, Luciano Gallet, Lourenzo Fernandez, Francisco Mignone, Camargo Guarnieri, Frutuoso Viana, Radamés Gnatalli, and others. (See Mário de Andrade, *Música do Brasil.* Collection, "Caderno Azul." Guaira, Curitiba, 1941.)

important is vigorously related to the national spirit and temperament, it is not, however, only in this way that the history of music has taken on a new interest in the last phase of its evolution. In proportion that it rose in stature, musical culture has tended to expand since 1930, when Luciano Gallet founded in June the Brazilian Association of Music, and raised in December of that same year to be director of the National Institute of Music, succeeded in securing the greatest reform of that institution by the decree which, in 1931, increased its program of studies and created ten new chairs and connected it with the University of Rio de Janeiro. The artistic activities of the Teatro Municipal of Rio de Janeiro were reorganized and it came to maintain a permanent orchestra of eighty pieces, a choral group and a corps and school of ballet; and a musical creator like Villa-Lôbos became active in 1932, placing himself in Rio de Janeiro at the forefront of musical education of the masses and of the spread of group singing, with the most efficient pedagogical organization which has yet been attempted among us with the object of the musical initiation of children' in primary schools. There was founded, through the activity of Villa-Lôbos, a choral group of professors and under the influence of the educational work of the great composer, our choral repertory took on a notable development and choral groups were organized in various cities as in São Paulo, Pôrto Alegre and Recife, and the first attempts at children's orchestras were made. But, if on the one hand the campaign in favor of children's musical development and popular music begun by Villa-Lôbos was enlarged, and a more intense effort was made to improve our musical education, on the other hand, there worked enthusiastically to raise the cultural level, a number of artistic and musical reviews like the *Ilustração Musical*, the *Revista da Associação Brasileira de Música*, the *Revista Brasileira de Música*, founded in 1934 and published by the National School of Music, *Cultura Artística*, the *Música Viva*, all of Rio de Janeiro, and the *Resenha Musical* of São Paulo, which constitute not only symptoms but actual factors in our musical life through their critical work, their erudition and their research. The extraordinary material and technical development, of radio broadcasting in the last decade, with the growing number of stations and the receiving sets, and the growing industry of electrical recording, put at the service of the spread of musical taste through the people and the closer relations of the public and the artist, two of the most powerful educational instruments which radio broadcasting and recording are everywhere, when they are directed toward the improvement of culture.

Art, moreover, in all of its forms developed in Brazil more rapidly than the public, almost inexistent, at least considered as a "mass," when art took on new life in the past century, and which could not accompany the progress of its evolution in this period. Hence the divorce between the public and the artist which has grown less, doubtless, but which is still alive. In the Empire as in the Colony, the rural aristocracy of the big houses, the bourgeoisie of the city mansions which could make up, in the great uncultivated mass, its true "public," had not the slightest interest in the arts and could not become, on account of its own education, a "consumer" of its product. The interior of the Brazilian house, wrote Eduardo Prado in 1889, "offers in general the same bareness and the same bad taste as the Portuguese houses. Objects of art are rare. Pictures and statues coming from abroad pay enormous duties, *ad valorem*, like simple merchandise. Brazilian artists of merit apply themselves to grandiose paintings, make pictures vaster than apartments, and their prices are still higher than those of the living masters of European painting. Nothing is hung on the walls but portraits,—the only recourse of painters who, not daring to approach the monumental, wish in some way to sell their canvasses. Landscapes, water colors, genre painting, pictures of moderate size, meant to beautify homes, are given up." In the colony, artists,—painters, makers of statues, carvers and architects,—worked for cloisters and churches. All that period was dominated by religious art, in the development of which, as a function of the clergy and of the public of the churches, there was very evident that essential trait of art which makes of it a luxurious activity of a social character inseparable from the existence of the public, or from the idea of such a public which is always present in the mind of the artist. In the Empire, as there still had not been established a taste for the artistic ornamentation of interiors, artists devoted themselves to the monumental or, at the most, to busts and portraits. The government constituted the chief consumer of works of art,—historical pictures and monuments,—which were frequently done on commission. In the departments of the government and in public gardens, the busts which also adorned the palaces grew in number, and in the private dwellings of the nobility and of the bourgeoisie, paintings in oil were scattered. If the élite was not prepared to favor the arts and to consume their products, which were dispersed through museums and public picture galleries,[34] much less was the public from which they came, which remained uncultivated, without any artistic education; and

[34] The most important art museum we possess is the National Museum of Fine Arts, of Rio de Janeiro, made up of the old galleries which separated from the National School of Fine Arts, founded in the time of Dom João VI. The collection of the Museum which Félix Taunay, of the French art mission, was instructed to install, was composed at first of the more or less famous pictures brought in their baggage by the nobility who accompanied the Prince Regent to Brazil. Enriched by gifts of value, it already had a collection of more than five hundred pictures when the Republic was proclaimed in 1889, and in 1922 it exceeded a thousand, not counting marbles and bronzes, by Brazilian and foreign artists. Canvasses signed by Renaissance masters, like Rubens, Murillo, Velasquez, Tintoretto, Correggio and others, works of French masters and of Portuguese and Argentine painters, and names old and new among Brazilian artists, figure in its collections which are considered among the most precious of South America. Installed in the sumptuous mansion of Mariano Procópio Ferreira Laje, founder of Juiz de Fora, which was constructed in 1861 by the German architect Carlos Augusto Gambs—a building compared by Lomonaco to the famous Villa Pallavicini of Genoa—there stands in that city of Minas Gerais, the Mariano Procópio Museum, surrounded by the beautiful park laid out by Glaziou, which the naturalist Agassiz called "the paradise of the tropics." This museum, founded by Dr. Alfredo Ferreira Laje, in the historical property of his parents, and given to the city, in addition to its splendid sections of history, numismatics and ceramics, possesses one of fine arts in which one finds a valuable collection of pictures by foreign and Brazilian painters. It is a monument of history and art of which the largest industrial city of Minas Gerais is justly proud; Juiz de Fora is one of the great cultural centers of the country. Among the galleries which have the most valuable collections, we may mention that of the State of São Paulo, that of the Municipality of Belém, that of the Liceu de Artes e Ofícios of Recife, and that of the Academy of Fine Arts of Bahia. Beside these which are among the oldest, there were recently created by the Federal Government the Museum of the Missions, to preserve and study the monuments erected by the Jesuits in the Brazilian region of the Missions, and the Imperial Museum, which was installed in Petrópolis, in March, 1940, in the old palace of the Emperor, with the double object of bringing together objects of historic and artistic value from the reigns of Dom Pedro I and Dom Pedro II and documents concerning the historic growth of the State of Rio, and especially of the city of Petrópolis. If we add the religious museums and the old churches, with their magnificent interiors—relics of our colonial past—we have the complete picture of museums and monuments of art in Brazil, Brazil which during almost a century of neglect, allowed a large part of her artistic wealth to slip through her hands to foreign countries.

as public education comes from even the elite, the multitude cannot have a soul that is elevated and sensitive to things of art, if the former, whom fortune and chance have placed above them in the social scale, do not have these qualities. There were no relations between great works and the production of industrial art, which was extremely limited and still without any influence in its earlier stages. No fruitful movement existed to propagate works of art or tending to bring together, at least in the larger centers, in a working fraternity, the various classes of the Brazilian people. The public, certainly, grew with the progress of urban life, the development of wealth, of facilities of communication and the multiplication of environment tending to bring them in contact with the arts and to awaken their artistic sentiment; and there was spread ever more in the higher social strata a taste for creating in interiors an atmosphere of beauty and distinction due to the presence of works of art. But the aesthetic education of the people was not carried on in courses or in special schools as Eduardo Prado observes, but everywhere, in the street, in gardens, in public squares, in museums and in picture galleries, in individual and group expositions, and with the application on a large scale of art to industries, which during the Empire was no more than a dream of rare idealists; and it is only in these last years after the Great War (1914–1918) and the national revolution of 1930, that it began with a more intense and more widely diffused artistic life, although it was richer in promises than in reality. If one still does not see a multitude of attentive visitors passing through museums and exposition halls; if down to the present, no really fruitful effort has been made looking toward the industrial reproduction of the great pictures of art painting, and the more intimate collaboration between art and industry; if the Brazilian artist appears to fear to lower his art by applying it to objects of daily use and in the artistic decoration of the interiors, it is sure, however, that in architecture, in interior decoration, in furniture as well as in clothing, there are the signs, patent in some of the large cities,—of an ever growing interest in the arts in all their manifestations.

These symptoms will be less in the numerous accomplishments, rarely of high quality, of the major arts,—painting and sculpture—, than in the movement of artists in search of a greater contact with the public, in the reactions of that public and in the general cultural atmosphere of the country. Artistic associations, in fact, multiplied: The Brazilian Society of Fine Arts into which the Centro Artístico Juventas was transformed in 1919, was followed in turn among others, in Rio de Janeiro by the Association of Brazilian Artists, in São Paulo by the Association of Plastic Artists, to whose admirable efforts we owe the movement for expositions and, as a result of them, the popularity of works of a group of young artists. Far from growing less, the interest in industrial reproduction tended to take shape and plans were made for the reproduction of a limited number of samples of our best pictures and for art applied to industry.[35]

[35] Of the black and red clays that are found in Brazil, there were made, during the colonial and imperial periods, vases of various sizes and shapes, including original ones: *potes, talhas, quartinhas* and *moringues.* Ceramic products were practically limited to glazed and varnished ceramics. The makers of clay products, if they tried, as they probably did, did not leave us any work of artistic value in the field of sculptured objects, representing types, figures or scenes; and, in that of painted ceramics, the only ones known were those of Bahia, especially the great painted amphorae, painted "on a foundation of enamel in green or blue, with gilding on the designs," and, along the Amazon, "ceramics adorned with color designs which usually took the form of animals of the country (parrots, tortoises, etc.)." But the evolution of pottery took place without continuity,

The production in series of objects marked by the seal of the arts and accessible to another, larger public, will have in the field of the plastic arts, by diffusing artistic tastes, a function similar to that which has been exercised in the field of music by recordings and by radio transmission of good art music and popular music, both Brazilian and foreign. The work of the pioneers of decorative art, inspired by the flora and fauna of the country and by historical motifs, the ceramics of Marajó, is acquiring new life with the alliance of artists and industrial leaders, in order to make ceramics, porcelains and tiles. Public powers have taken part in this movement, favoring it and stimulating it in various ways and mounting guard over the artistic tradition of the country. The federal government after 1930 created, with a model piece of legislation, the Serviço do Patrimônio Histórico e Artístico which replaced the old Inspetoria de Monumentos Nacionais which formed part of the Historical Museum. It raised the historic city of Ouro Preto,—considered as a whole and with its whole urban environment—, to the category of a national monument. It promoted the inventory of the artistic heritage; separated from the School of Fine Arts the halls of its old picture galleries, in order to constitute with them the present National Museum of Fine Arts, officially inaugurated in May, 1938. It confided the decoration of the new building of the Ministry of Education and Health to the great painter, Cândido Portinari, and began a series of publications of high artistic interest and documentary value. Certainly the great mass of people remained alien to all these new activities either public or private; and,—like a young people still in process of formation—, Brazil continued, to employ the expression of A. Siegfried, "to give the appearance of a venerable country with some very ancient traditions and with an atmosphere of culture which goes back to the aristocracy," but the élite which shared these traditions became ever more numerous and more refined in its taste and in its capacity for appreciation. What was a pleasure acceptable to few became slowly one within the reach of a larger number due to the development of wealth and of construction and of the principal urban centers of the coast and of the plateau. The growing tendency to city life, manifest in the

---

with the abandonment by the industry of the old forms influenced by the Arabs (amphorae of Bahia) of Hindus (*quartinhas* and *moringues*), imported by the Portuguese. In the nineteenth century porcelain was made in Brazil only once. It was from Portugal that there came vases, faience lions and statues of enameled terra-cotta, which topped the great pillars of doorways with their gratings of forged iron, through which one entered the gardens of mansions and houses of the nobility. It was only in the twentieth century and especially in the last twenty years that a new movement started, inspired by the pottery of the natives, found in the island of Marajó; of this movement, Teodoro Braga of Para was a forerunner, famous for his work in decorative art, based on motifs of the art of Marajó and the fauna and flora of the country; Paim Vieira of São Paulo who also works at the stylization of flower and vegetable forms, and F. Correia Dias, a Portuguese artist, illustrator and ceramist, who came to Rio de Janeiro in 1915 and died in 1935, leaving excellent work in this field. There is also new interest in the faience which was applied to the exterior and interior of Brazilian houses: "the polychrome tiles which deflect the rays of the sun and preserve the agreeable coolness of the houses which they protect from the humidity of the rain," writes Eduardo Prado. Instead of interpretations which bear the stamp of individual imagination, we still prefer imitations of historic styles or authentic pieces which are appliqued to rich constructions in colonial style. Some artists, however, are on the search for a new decorative style, utilizing tiles based on regional motifs; the most interesting of these attempts is perhaps that of P. Rossi, under whose direction in São Paulo, A. Volpi and M. Zanini work, painting little pictures and preparing themselves for great decorative panels.

development of the great cities and the formation of new cities; the progress of means of communication which tend to bring together gradually the regions of the country with their different cultural and economic levels; the intensity of social life and the diversity of directions in which the various currents of urban influence move, not only contributed to bring art closer to its popular sources, but also to raise intellectuals to a high plane and to open ever faster fields to the exploitation of artists. Under the pressure of these phenomena, more than by individual efforts, the isolation in which artists lived became reduced. Formerly they had been condemned by the force of circumstances to a narrow, closed circle of glory or of lack of understanding, from which few succeeded in breaking out. These facts of urban concentration, of mobility and circulation both of individuals and of ideas, of the propagation of currents of thought, helped also to render our social and political unity a more living thing and to give to the cultural atmosphere of the country a sufficient pressure so there could arise in artists new means of expression and make of them centers in which modes of feeling characteristic of an epoch or the national life should become intensified or more effective. For what moves the artist, as E. Durkheim observes, "is not always a centrifugal effort to spread to others an intimate personal feeling; it is also the pressure exerted upon him by a collective emotional state which he feels with a greater acuteness and to which he is capable of giving expression."

This modern movement, derived in its origin from European art and influences, which were more powerful in proportion as Brazil entered fully into the civilization of which it forms a part, showed in fact a marked tendency to assert its Brazilian character, in the spirit and style appropriate to the national art and its search for new sources of inspiration. It is not only characterized, as we have seen and has been observed, by a concern to preserve old art, but also to come close to the living sources of popular art and to create a new art which shall be characteristically Brazilian. Examined more closely, what it reveals is less an effort at emancipation under the influence of intellectual theory than a process of maturing of the artistic activity and culture of the country. Art history and criticism, formerly almost entirely confided to journalists, whose hasty articles had no artistic value, is showing that same maturity manifest in the field of production and which is expressed in this other field by research, by a more keen awareness of what is national in the arts, and by a love of truth, reality and exactness. Under the double influence of new historic theories and of a more national definition of art, art history and criticism, in which at the end of the nineteenth century there stood out the names of Gonzaga Duque in painting, J. Rodrigues Barbosa and later Oscar Guanabarino in music, were renewing their methods and becoming more reflective, objective, better documented, and were prophesying in works of detail and in essays, the first rate general works on the history of art in the past of our country. The history of painting and sculpture, of recent development, among us could count upon only one writer, L. Gonzaga Duque Estrada, Rio de Janeiro (1863–1911), author of *Arte Brasileira* (1888), a purely literary book without critical spirit and without rigor in its documentation and written in the taste of the romantic critics and historians; and music had nothing to offer except the erudite and documented work (1908), without general ideas, of Pereira de Melo who wrote the history of music in Brazil in colonial times. Argeu de Guimarães, in his work, dominated by the facts instead of dominating them, and Laudelino Freire, motivated exclusively by the desire to inform, and both of them without general and artistic culture and without the taste of exact judgment, made no noted contribution to the study of the history of the plastic arts in Brazil. There is no broad grasp, either of the general line of evolution nor no original sure views of a part of the tradition in these fragmentary works, in which beloved adjectives and exaggerated praise take the place of taste and of the critical spirit which is practically always absent, and in which art and artists are confused on the same plane without historical perspective. . . . It is only in the last years that there appeared, in 1926, with the work of Renato de Almeida, a history of Brazilian music in which the sagacious method of the writer brings to life the rather dry documents which he found in the work of the scholars. Historians and musical critics arose, like Andrade Muricí and, after 1930, Luiz Heitor Correia de Azevedo, and Mário de Andrade began to attain the fullness of his force,—one of the most perspicacious minds in modern criticism, a musical historian thoroughly familiar with criticism and with musical folklore, he has brilliant and penetrating flashes of intuition. In painting, the history of which is still to be written, like that of the arts in general, we get clear and living impressions, with an attitude that reflects modern art, in a Sérgio Milliet, an Angelo Guido and a Luiz Martins while Marques dos Santos, Augusto de Lima Júnior and, above all, José Mariano Filho, whose works reveal a critic who is truly familiar with all of the phases of the evolution of colonial architecture, form the beginning of a new series of valuable studies of the arts of the first three centuries. In proportion as the area is extended and the level of culture of the country is raised,—that living and organic culture which is the substance of letters and arts—, the reaction against mediocre or improvised criticism grows, for it is far from bringing together artists and public and rendering works of art more comprehensible to all. Rather it tends to separate them, to corrupt the taste of both and to make the public suspicious of the sincerity of artists. All of these works of research and of scholarship not only contribute to change the methods of artistic criticism, by removing it from the changeability of individual opinions which may be ingenuous or tendentious and furnishing new elements to the objectivity of the critical judgment, and they also prepare with greater solidity the bases of our great history of the arts, studied not in isolation but in their relation with the general history of culture in Brazil and with the ideas of the time which had the greatest influence upon us, and in the deep roots which the arts thrust down into the life of the Brazilian people, who have in their manners and therefore in their souls, an extraordinary predisposition to art.

BIBLIOGRAPHY

Almeida, Renato, *História da música brasileira* (Rio: Briguiet, 1926).

Andrade, Almir de, *Aspectos da cultura brasileira* (Rio: Schmidt, 1939), especially "O Aleijadinho: O Estilo e a época," pp. 11–15.

Andrade, Mário de, *Compêndio de história da música* (São Paulo: Miranda, 3rd ed., 1936), especially Chaps. 11–12, "Música artística brasileira," "Música popular brasileira," pp. 151–177.

——, *Música do Brasil* (Curitiba: Guaíra, 1941—Coleção "Caderno Azul").

Araújo Viana, Ernesto da Cunha de, "Das artes plásticas no Brasil em geral e no cidade do Rio de Janeiro em particular," 5 lectures at the Instituto Histórico Brasileiro, begun Aug. 30, 1915, in *Revista do Instituto Histórico Brasileiro*.

Azevedo, Fernando de, "Arquitetura colonial," inquiry by *O Estado de São Paulo* with an introduction by Ricardo Severo, Alexandre Albuquerque, Wash Rodrigues, and José Mariano Filho, and conclusions, in *O Estado de São Paulo,* Apr. 13–17, 21, 24, 29–30, 1926.

Barleus, G., *Rerum per octennium in Brasilia, etc.* (Cleves, 1660), pp. 358–374.

——, *História dos feitos recentement praticados durante oito anos no Brasil e noutras partes sob o governo do ilustríssimo João Maurício de Nassau, etc.,* translated and annotated by Cláudio Brandão (Rio: Serviço gráfico do Ministério da Educação, 1940).

Bastide, Paul, "Estudos de sociologia estética brasileira," Pt. 2, "O Mito do Alejadinho." See "A Sociologia do Barroco," in *O Estado de São Paulo,* Sept. 11, 1940.

Correia de Azevedo, Luiz Heitor, "Um velho compositor brasileiro: José Maurício Nunes Garcia," in *Boletim Latino-American de Música,* Vol. 1, No. 1 (Apr., 1935), pp. 133–150.

——, *Dois pequenos estudos de folclore musical* (Rio, 1938).

——, *Escala, ritmo e melodia no música dos índios brasileiros* (Rio, 1938).

——, *Relação das óperas de autores brasileiros* (Rio: Serviço gráfico do Ministério da Educação e Saúdɜ, 1938).

Ferreira Bretas, Rodrigo J., *Traços biográficos relativos ao finado Antônio Francisco Lisboa* (1858).

Freire, Laudelino, *Um Século de pintura: Apontamentos para a história da pintura no Brasil (1816–1916)* (Rio: Röhe, 1916).

Freyre, Gilberto, "A Pintura no Nordeste," in *Diário de Pernambuco,* centennial number, 1925.

Gonzaga Duque, *A Arte brasileira: Pintura e escultura* (Rio: Lombaerts, 1888).

Guido, Angelo, "As Artes plásticas no Rio Grande do Sul," in *Anais do III Congresso Sul-riograndense de história e geografia* (Pôrto Alegre: Edição da Prefeitura Municipal, 1940), Vol. 4, pp. 2095–2121.

Guimarães, Argeu, "Historia das artes plásticas no Brasil," in *Revista do Instituto Histórico e Geográfico Brasileiro,* special vol., Vol. 9 (Rio: Imprensa Nacional, 1930), pp. 401–497.

Harnisch, Wolfgang Hoffmann, *Viagem às missões jesuíticas* (São Paulo: Martins).

——, "Arte antiga das missões brasileiras," in *Cultura política,* 2nd yr., No. 33 (Rio, 1943), pp. 215–218.

Jardim, Luiz, "A Pintura decorativa em algumas igrejas de Minas Gerais," in *Revista do Serviço do Patrimônio Histórico,* 1939.

Lange, F. C., "Vila Lôbos, um pedagogo criador," in *Boletim Latino-Americano de Música,* 1st yr., Vol. 1 (Apr., 1935), pp. 189–199.

Lima Júnior, Augusto de, "Evolução do barroco no Brasil," in *Estudos brasileiros,* 1st yr., No. 6 (May–June, 1939), pp. 72–84.

——, *A Capitania das "Minas Gerais": Suas origens e formação* (Lisbon, 1940), especially "A Casa, o mobiliário e as alfaias," "A Arte barroca em Minas Gerais," pp. 105–136.

Mariano Filho, José, "O Pseudo Estilo barroco-jesuítico e suas relações com a arquitetura tradicional brasileira," in *Estudos brasileiros,* 2nd yr., Vol. 3, No. 9 (Nov.–Dec., 1939), pp. 259–269.

——, "Evolução do mobiliário e da ornamentação litúrgica sob a influência dos jesuitas e de Dom João V," in *Revista do Brasil,* 3rd yr., 3rd fase, No. 22 (Apr., 1940), pp. 41–44.

Marques dos Santos, Francisco, "As Belas Artes no primeiro reinado (1822–1831)," in *Estudos brasileiros,* 2nd yr., Vol. 4, No. 11 (Mar.–Apr., 1940) pp. 471–509.

——, "A Ourivesaria no Brasil antigo," in *Estudos brasileiros,* 2nd yr., Vol. 4, No. 12 (May–June, 1940), pp. 625–651.

Martins, Luiz, *A Arte moderna no Brasil* (São Paulo, 1937).

——, "A Evolução social da pintura," *Coleção Departamento de Cultura* Vol. 27 (São Paulo, 1942).

Melo Franco, Afonso Arinos de, *Roteiro lírico de Ouro Preto* (Rio: Sociedade Filipe d'Oliveira, 1937).

Milliet, Sérgio, *Pintores e pinturas* (São Paulo: Martins, 1940).

Pereira de Melo, G. T., *A Música no Brasil desde os tempos coloniais até o primeiro decênio da República* (Bahia: Tip. de São Joaquim, 1908).

Querino, Manuel Raimundo, *Artistas baianos* (Rio, 1909).

Ribeiro de Lessa, Clado, "Mobiliário brasileiro dos tempos coloniais," in *Estudos brasileiros,* 1st yr., No. 6 (May–June, 1939), pp. 1–18.

Rodrigues, José Honorio, and Joaquim Ribeiro, *Civilização holandesa no Brasil* (São Paulo: Comp. Editora Nacional, 1940—Brasiliana, Vol. 180), especially Chap. XVI, "Meio urbano."

Rubens, Carlos, *Andersen: Pai da pintura paranaense* (São Paulo: Carvalho, n.d.).

——, *Pequena História das artes plásticas no Brasil* (São Paulo: Comp. Editora Nacional, 1941—Brasiliana).

Silva Prado, Eduardo, "L'Art," Chap. XVIII, pp. 519–562, in *Le Brésil en 1889* (Paris), prepared by a group of Brazilian writers under the direction of M. F.–J. de Sant'Ana Nery.

Smith, Robert C., "O Caráter da arquitetura colonial do Nordeste," in *Estudos brasileiros,* 3rd yr., Vol. 4, No. 10 (Jan.–Feb., 1940), pp. 419–430.

Sousa Leão, *Franz Post: Seus quadros brasileiros* (Rio, 1937).

Souto Maior, "Arte holandesa no Brasil," in *Revista do Instituto Histórico e Geográfico Brasileiro.*

Taunay, Afonso de E., "Missão artistica de 1816," in *Revista do Instituto Histórico e Geográfico Brasileiro,* 74th vol., Vol. 123 (1911).

Vasconcelos, Diogo de, *A Arte de Ouro Preto* (bicentennial ed., 1934).

Vieira, Hermes, *O Romance de Carlos Gomes* (São Paulo: Miranda).

——, *Guia de Ouro Preto* (Serviço do Patrimônio histórico e artístico, Ministerio de Educação, 1939).

——, *Portinari,* with a Preface by Manuel Bandeira and a study by Mário de Andrade (Serviço gráfico do Ministerio da Educação, 1939).

——, *Portinari: His Life and Art* (University of Chicago Press, 1940). With 100 full-page reproductions, 8 in color, and an Introduction by Rockwell Kent.

PART III

THE TRANSMISSION OF CULTURE

CHAPTER ONE

THE SIGNIFICANCE OF COLONIAL EDUCATION

The ecclesiastical origin of education in Brazil—The Jesuit Missions and catechism in the colonies—The first school master—Manuel da Nóbrega and Aspilcueta Navarro—Apostles and educators—José de Anchieta—In the patios of the colleges and in the villages of the catechumens—Schools of reading and writing—Popular literary education with a religious background—The expansion of the Portuguese language among the aborigines—The social landscape of the Colony—The patriarchal family—The situation of women—The three careers or directions followed by the sons—The chaplains and uncles who were priests—The ideals of the cultivated man in Portugal—Teaching and the Jesuits—The colleges of the Fathers—Bachelors and masters of arts—Higher studies in the home country—The role of the University of Coimbra in the training of the élite—Seminaries—The monopoly of teaching—Toward the training of clerics and men of letters—The system of teaching as an ally of the city against the country—The colleges of the Jesuits and the patriarchal regime of life— The process of urbanization of the élite—The work of the Jesuits and national unity—The Marques de Pombal and the expulsion of the Jesuits (1759)—The destruction of the colonial educational system—The reform of Pombal put into execution—The royal schools and the literary subsidy—The schoolmaster-priests and chaplains of the sugar mills—Colleges of the monastic orders—The period of decay and transition.

THE COMING of the Jesuit Fathers in 1549, not only marked the beginning of the history of education in Brazil, but inaugurated a first phase, the longest in our history and certainly the most important, if we consider the amount of the work carried on and, above all, the consequences which resulted from it for our culture and civilization. When in that year six Jesuits came to Bahia with the first Governor General, Tomé de Sousa, the Society of Jesus was not more than nine years old officially, its base having been laid down on August 15, 1534 in the chapel of Montmartre by Ignatius de Loyola and his six companions and, scarcely had it been confirmed in 1540 by Paul III, when it scattered over the continent of Europe in missions designed to combat heresy and, abroad, to propagate the faith among the unbelievers and to diffuse the gospel to all people. Animated by an apostolic zeal and bound together and to the Catholic church by rigorous, carefully thought out and universally accepted discipline, the disciples of Ignatius de Loyola, not slow in conquering a place of just preeminence in the hierarchy of religious orders and an immense moral authority, to which they gave the seal of martyrdom in their ceaseless combat to serve religion without compromise. An unshakable faith like that of the first apostles, and one disposed to make all sacrifices; a discipline which gave the appearance of a militia to the new order, founded during the stormy days of the Reformation by the intrepid soldier of Pomplona, and a literary culture both sacred and profane, which had reached a high level and which was used as an instrument of domination, made of these great missionaries the most efficacious and robust force in the fight against Protestantism and in the implantation of the power of the church among the infidels. It was a new order which was created in a sombre period of religious passion and struggles and with the fixed object of confronting them, and it was one which even at the beginning kept intact and living the flame of the evangelical spirit of its founder; and the Jesuit missions which arrived in Brazil in 1549 and in 1553 were among the first legions of missionaries who crossed the seas to convert the heathen in distant unknown lands. Everyone knows what these monks came to, sent on the advice of Diogo de Gouveia by Dom João III, who was beginning to be worried about the colonization of Brazil. The essential compromise of the Jesuit with the church, in the defense and propagation of the faith, had created with his arrival here as everywhere a clear and well defined situation in which his amazing missionary, political and educational activity presented itself as entirely subordinate to the ecumenical requirement of the church and the supreme interests of religion. The Jesuits laid out their settlements immediately upon disembarking. They founded their residences and convents which they called "colleges;" they installed their centers of action and of self-support, or if you wish, their quarters, for the conquest and rule of souls. They penetrated into the villages of the Indians, and multiplying along the coast their principal points of irradiation, they established themselves in the south, under the brilliant guidance of Father Manuel da Nóbrega, in the Captaincy of São Vicente, in which they recognized "the surest and safest port and road by which to enter the interior." For two centuries, or more exactly in two hundred and ten years, which extend from the arrival of the first Jesuit to the expulsion of the Order by the Marquês de Pombal in 1759, they were almost the only educators of Brazil. Priests of other Orders, Franciscans, Carmelites, Benedictines, did not establish themselves among us until later, in 1580, and also, being faithful to the monastic tradition, they maintained a more ascetic regime of life and a more separate one, and if they were then beginning to break with their early isolation and to devote themselves to preaching and to more practical tasks, they did not give the educational function the leading place which it assumed in the activities of the Jesuits. For when "the Portuguese soul, heroic and beautiful, cooped up in Europe between the walls of Castela and the walls of the sea, desired to spread out in kind and in genius," it was in the Jesuits that it found full support in its colonizing efforts and also, to restrain it in its adventurous impetus, one of the greatest and most powerful instruments of spiritual domination and one of the surest ways by which European culture penetrated the culture of the peoples of the new land who were conquered but still rebellious.

To speak of the first schools of Brazil is, in fact, as Serafim Leite writes, "to recall the epic of the Jesuits in the sixteenth century," in which they laid down, in the midst of perils and trials, the foundations of a whole vast system of education which went on progressively developing with the territorial expansion of Portuguese rule. To get an idea of the plan that they brought and of the rapidity with which they began to work, it is sufficient to recall with Serafim Leite that in Bahia, "while the city of Salvador was being founded, a fortnight after the Jesuits arrived, a school of reading and writing was already in operation,—and that this was the beginning of their policy of education which they were to maintain unchanged across the centuries, opening a school wherever they erected a church. The teacher of this first school was Vicente Rijo or Rodrigues . . . , historically the first school-master of Brazil, to which he dedicated more than fifty years of a lifetime full of labor and of sickness,—and of things worthy of the highest praise." At this time there began going out from Bahia, vigorously pushed in its first ten years (1549–1559) by Father Manuel da Nóbrega, and afterward by Luiz da Grã, his successor in the position of provincial (1559–1569), that encompassing movement which spread in the direction of the south, from Salvador to Pôrto Seguro, through Espírito Santo and São Vicente, where toward the end of 1549, Leonardo Nunes founded a seminary-school (middle school), transferred later on in 1554 to Piratininga,[1] restored to São Vicente in 1561, and finally and definitively located in Rio de Janeiro. The political genius of Nóbrega, "the great apostle of education," had conceived the plan of raising upon the foundations of education, the whole work of catechization and colonization, and he had struggled with all his might to carry out this plan, determining as early as 1550 that houses should be constructed, "to receive and teach the young of the heathen and also of the Christians," not only for the sake of catechization, but also "for the rest of the land and the profit of the Republic." When the leader of the Fathers of the Society of Jesus died in 1570 after twenty-one years in Brazil, the work which he inspired and had aided to build up had already acquired great height and breadth, embracing five schools of elementary instruction, established in Pôrto Seguro, in Ilhéus, in Espírito Santo, in São Vicente, and in São Paulo de Piratininga, and three colleges, in Rio de Janeiro, in Pernambuco and in Bahia, which, besides the preliminary class, had another of Latin and humanities. In the middle of the sixteenth century, when scarcely five years had passed since the death of the illustrious Jesuit, they were able to give degrees of bachelor of arts in the College of Bahia, in which in the following year, 1576, they conferred degrees of master of arts. Certainly that notable organization, planned and knowingly conducted by Nóbrega down to the end of his period of government, and constantly developed in later administrations, was in the first ten year period the result of the efforts of the two initial nuclei of the Jesuits, twelve in all, Fathers and lay brothers, hard at work in attacking the problem of catechization of the Colony from its foundation. But leading all of these efforts as a result of his position and authority, there was always Nóbrega,

---

[1] The foundation in 1554 of the College of São Paulo, on the plain of Piratininga, with the presence of Father José de Anchieta, who had just arrived from Portugal, was decided upon by Nóbrega, who chose the place,—the future center from which missionaries and bandeirantes spread, and appointed the young Jesuit to that house, making him the master of his colleagues. This was not, however, a new school for the Captaincy, but was the school of São Vicente which was moved to fields of Piratininga,—"because the climate was better and it was easier to get food,— and also out of love for the Indians." The seminary-school, "first set up in São Vicente by Leonardo Nunes," writes Serafim Leite, "moved and practically founded over again in Piratininga in 1554, raised to the rank of "colégio" by Nóbrega in 1556, when he endowed it with all the real estate and movable property belonging to the Society in the south, and again moved to São Vicente in 1561, was to be located for good in Rio de Janeiro, once it was perfected and made official." (Serafim Leite, *As primeiras escolas do Brasil.* In "Páginas da História do Brasil," pp. 35-62.) A school for elementary instruction, however, remained in São Paulo de Piratininga, bearing the same name which was extended to the whole region on the plain; thus the colleges or "houses" of the Captaincy of São Vicente were doubled: that of São Vicente and that of São Paulo, both of which, the latter in 1561 and the former in 1567, became once more elementary schools for children, the sons of Portuguese, mamelucos and Indians.

the founder and the provincial, a great man among the greatest who came with him in 1549, like João de Aspilcueta, or who came later with the second governor, Dom Duarte da Costa in 1553, like José de Anchieta, the former Navarrese in origin, who threw himself intrepidly into the apostolic work and died in 1557 defeated by his labors in only eight years of residence in Brazil, and the latter, whose family came from the Bay of Biscay and who with his sanctity and miracles dominated almost half a century of colonial life, which is inseparable from the forty-four years of his aposthood. It was Aspilcueta Navarro, among the Jesuits, who was the first to learn the language of the aborigines and used it from 1550 on in preaching to the savages and was the first teacher and missionary of the heathens and the first to make those extraordinary trips into the interior for evangelization, traversing it in 1553, writes Afrânio Peixoto, "from Pôrto Seguro, 350 leagues in all, to the headwaters of the Jequitinhonha, the valley of the São Francisco, returning to the coast by the river Pardo." If in this splendid trinity— Nóbrega, the politician, Navarro, the pioneer, and Anchieta, the saint,[2] the extraor-

---

[2] José de Anchieta, a great figure of the whole Church, and one of the greatest of Brazil, the apostle of the New World, was born in Tenerife on March 19, 1534, in the same year in which the Society of Jesus was created, and he became one of the most eminent figures of its whole history. In 1548 he was sent by his parents to Coimbra where he studied and entered the Society on March 1, 1551; two years later, still a novice, he left for Brazil with the second group of Jesuit missionaries. He was then little more than an adolescent, weak in constitution and with precarious health, made worse by an accident which he suffered in Portugal; his superiors thought to give him relief from his sufferings by sending him to a better climate. "Who, seeing him embark on March 8, 1553," writes Brasílio Machado, "could have dreamed that in time that nineteen year old invalid, would stir up a whole world of heathen with his tireless zeal, would be the apostle of this land and would support on his weak back the hegemony of Portugal in the land of the Holy Cross! A teacher in the college of Piratininga, to which Father Manuel da Nóbrega sent him in 1554; a missionary in São Vicente, in Piratininga, in Rio de Janeiro and in Espírito Santo; provincal of the Society of Jesus, from 1579 to 1586; rector of the college of Espírito Santo, he was in all the positions he occupied, in the teaching of children, the sons of Indians and colonists, in his spiritual ministry and in the propagation of the faith in the interior, an incomparable example of apostolic zeal, of the spirit of sacrifice and of heroic devotion. The companion or emissary of Nóbrega, in the most dangerous and responsible missions, in Iperoig (1563), the mission to pacify the Tamoyas, in Rio de Janeiro, where he was present at the founding of the city, as well as at that of São Paulo, rendering services in the matter of the expulsion of the French, or in Bahia, whither he was sent in 1566, to inform Mem de Sá of the fortunes of the war, no one was his superior in prudence or in self-sacrifice with which he carried out all missions, spreading on all sides the authority of the Church and the influence of religion. When he took holy orders in 1566, in Bahia, his labors and the fatigue he had undergone in the work of conversion, in which he was first "for his sacrifice which reached the level of heroism, saintliness, and the desire of martyrdom," had already made him in the eyes of all the minister of God and the missionary of the Gospel. The activities in which he busied himself, to conquer and rule the heathen, crossing deserts, going into Indian villages, building churches, preaching and teaching, helping everyone and looking after everything, still astonish us, not only for the variety they reveal in an extraordinarily endowed personality, but also for the intensity with which the flame of idealism burned in this great educator and missionary. As a linguist, he organized the *Arte da gramática da língua brasílica*—"the first monument of Brazilian linguistics"—in manuscript form in 1560 and published in 1595; as a poet and theatrical author, he wrote in Latin the *Poema da Virgem*, and in Portuguese and Tupi, sermons, poetry, songs and religious solemnities; as an historian, he wrote *Informações e fragmentos históricos* (1584–1586),—the lives of the fathers of the Society who had died in Brazil, and left us in his precious letters, one of the most reliable sources for the history of the first century of the colony. With his death, on June 9, 1597, in Reri-

dinary activity of the Jesuits in the sixteenth century is symbolized,—this being the fairest and most heroic page in the history of the Society of Jesus—, among all these apostles and educators, the magical figure of Anchieta stands out with singular relief. Anchieta had arrived in the reenforcements sent by Dom João III in 1553, a simple novice of fragile build and less than twenty years old.

In this period in which the desire to catechize was more important than any other concern and which was to continue down to the seventeenth century, José de Anchieta, from his arrival to his death, carried on an apostolic labor of such vast proportions and with such intensity that he became the central figure of this stupendous movement of the propagation of the faith among the heathen. Not that his admirable companions of the order were inferior to him in fervor and in self-sacrifice, for although they were so few in the first decade, they were not afraid of the task to be accomplished in the immense field of action which lay before the exploration of the missionaries. But the fact is that in none of them did there meet in so high a degree all the evangelical virtues and intellectual capacities which were combined in the surprising personality of Anchieta to give us the great apostle of the Indian. While still young, wearing "his hempen cassock dyed black which he himself had made from remnants of sails," he was already a teacher, appointed to teach Latin and humanities to his brothers in the College of Piratininga, a college which was in 1554 no more "than a little shack of cane and mud covered with straw, fourteen feet long and ten wide," in which as a letter to Ignatius de Loyola reported, at times more than twenty companions in the apostolate were compressed. But even in 1555, a year after the foundation of the college in Piratininga, which was the most advanced point in the movement of catechization and colonization on the plateau, Anchieta could pride himself on the fact that the Jesuits had there "a large school of Indian children who were being well educated in reading, writing and good manners." For this task of teaching in which all took part, but which lacked books and material, it was he who composed songs, wrote little theatrical pieces and organized text books which, copied and recopied, became of common use in practically all the colleges. The author of the first grammar of the difficult language of the aborigines, of which he became a master in order the better to instruct them, poet, inventor of solemnities, religious mysteries in dialogue and verse which the children gave in the patios of the colleges and in the villages of the catechumens, this eminent educator who had the secret of the art of teaching, utilized everything that might be useful or capable of working upon the mind of the heathen—the theater, music, songs and even dances, multiplying his resources to reach the intelligence of the children and to find a way to their hearts. In the really remarkable work of this bandeirante missionary, who for half a century passed his days, from São Paulo to Espírito Santo, preaching the Gospel to the Indians, making excursions into the interior, instructing the converts, assisting the sick and consoling the afflicted, not the smallest part is the uninterrupted series of efforts in catechization and in the education

---

tiba (the former Benevente, now called Anchieta), in the State of Espírito Santo, there came to an end 44 years of an apostolic life,—one of the longest and certainly the most fruitful and admirable that any missionary lived in America. (Cf. Simão de Vasconcelos, *Vida do Venerável Pe. José de Archieta*. Lisbon, 1672; *Cartas, informações, fragmentos históricos e sermões*. Brazilian Academy of Letters, Rio, 1933; Jônatas Serrano, *Anchieta educador*. In "Jornal do Comércio," September 29, 1940.)

of children to whose training he was able to make original contributions that had their foundations in his understanding of the child's soul, in his personal experience and in his observation on the mystic mentality of the Indians. If, to this work—an integral and fundamental part of his apostolate—the Jesuits were dedicated, scattered all over the Colony, none acquired a better right than Anchieta to the title of school-master, educator, protector, and apostle of the little Indians to whom he directed himself, certainly to convert them to his faith and thus to serve the triumph of his ideas, but with all his heart and with an admirable intelligence and clearness of view. Understanding, —a profoundly human understanding, sublimated by faith, that is what characterizes Anchieta, who therefore exercised an exceptional influence, directing himself not only to all but to each in particular, according to his nature and necessities, of which he revealed a truly intuitive understanding. It is in this work of popular education in the patios of their colleges and in the towns of catechization that the Jesuits laid the foundation of their system of education and that one has therefore to look for the profound significance of the mission of the Society whose role in the history of the progress of Christianity and of education in Brazil was to be for more than two centuries so central and indisputably superior to that of other orders. But if the facts are represented in their true light the work of catechization and that of teaching in the schools of reading and writing went beyond their immediate ends at which the Jesuits were aiming in their effect. Attracting the Indian boys to their houses and going to the villages where they were; bringing together in the same school community the children of natives and of Portuguese—whites, Indians and mestizos—and attempting through the education of the sons to conquer and reeducate the fathers, the Jesuits were not merely servants in the work of catechization but were laying the basis of popular education and spreading the same faith, the same language, and the same customs through the younger generation, they were beginning to shape through spiritual unity the political unity of a new country.

In the elementary schools which lay at the basis of the whole colonial system of education, which was still in its early stages, and which functioned not only in the colleges but "all over the country wherever there existed a house of the Society of Jesus," the children of the Indians learned to read, write, count and to speak Portuguese, and the sons of the colonists also received their earliest instruction. Not only in the colleges and in the lower schools, but in each one of the villages where the Fathers had "their little houses covered with straw, well equipped, and their capacious churches," beside instructing the Indians in things necessary to their salvation, they taught their children, as Anchieta informs us, "to read, write, count and speak Portuguese, which they learned and spoke with grace, to dance in the Portuguese style, to sing and to have their musical choruses and flutes for fiestas." If the Jesuits concentrated in the higher schools the great ambition of their educational policy—"the formation of a cultivated and religious élite which would accomplish the mystical and social objectives of Saint Ignatius," it is certain, as we may conclude from all of the ancient documents, that among their concerns with their neighbors, there was always during the sixteenth and seventeenth centuries, that of teaching the children of the Indians and the Portuguese to read and write in the villages of the neophytes, and in the schools of the Indian and white children. With all of this magnificent work of catechization and colonization, the Fathers utilized not only the influence of white children, orphans, or children of colonists upon the Indian children, placed in contact with the former in the same schools, but also the action of the Indian boys, who after being taught by the Fathers went out to the villages to teach their fathers in the very language of the Indians. It was there, in these schools of reading and writing, whether fixed or moving, wandering about among the towns and through the interior, that their great educational policy had to begin from the bottom up; and with them it was that there began in Brazil at the same time in Europe, that popular literary education, essentially religious, organized in consequence of and under the influence of the struggles of the Reformation and the Counter-Reformation, for the propagation of the faith. It was, moreover, in these primary schools,—a powerful instrument for affecting the country—and through the courses in grammar maintained in all the colleges, that the Portuguese language became the common language which the Indians learned, not only from the colonists but especially from the priests and from the boys who were sons of Portuguese or orphans brought from Lisbon by the Jesuits, and whose presence in the colleges (since "for children there is no distinction of races and they are by nature universalists") helped greatly, in the opinion of Serafim Leite, to attract the little Indians and to lead them along the pathway of instruction.[3] To be sure the Fathers from the sixteenth century had learned from the Indians, their language in which they had become distinguished masters and the grammar of which they wrote down, but they learned it only to instruct by means of it and more easily to win the savages over to their faith and religious and social ideas. "The facility which the aborigines of the East Indies had in learning Portuguese, the common language of Asia and Africa in the sixteenth century, was repeated in Brazil," as Pedro Calmon has noted. "The expansion of the language corresponded to the effective conquest of the territory." The culture of the aborigines not only as far as language is concerned, but in the spontaneity and variety of its forms, was slowly replaced within the sphere of influence of the missionaries by another type of culture in accordance with the ideals of the Jesuits and their conception of life and the world, which was identical for all peoples. It is for this reason that Gilberto Freyre, examining the question in this light of the contact and collision of two cultures and the attitude

[3] Serafim Leite, commenting on a letter dated from Bahia, "from this house of the Colégio dos Meninos de Jesús, today August 5, 1552," which gives us information on the common work of the Indian boys with the orphans, refers to the excursions into the interior which they made, going distances which were considerable for the time and their age. Among other bits of information, however, we note especially one which is given by "a note in another handwriting, perhaps that of someone who sent it from Portugal to Rome." It says that in Lisbon they received more letters of Indian boys, as many as eleven or twelve. These boys went through the villages surprising the men in their hammocks, and after a festive introduction of songs and dances, taught them "the Passion of Our Lord, the Commandments, the Lord's Prayer, the Creed, and the Salve-Regina, in the language of the Indians. So that the children in their own language teach their fathers, and the fathers, with their hands folded, go behind their sons, singing Holy Mary, and they answer *ora pro nobis.*" In what year was this? asks Serafim Leite. in 1552. The priests taught the children . . . and the children taught their parents! "But this cordial comradeship, which brought with it admirable virtues, and was so useful in various ways, would seem not always to have been exempt from vices and corruption. This is the opinion of Gilberto Freyre, who bases his findings on the information given by Arlindo Camilo Monteiro to the effect that in the books of offences they (these orphan children) were frequently listed: "a part of the Portuguese colonization in Brazil," writes Gilberto Freyre, "that was apparently pure, but really a corrupting agency, was the orphan boys brought by the Jesuits to their schools." (Casa grande e senzala, Rio, 1933, p. 360.)

of the Jesuits towards this conflict, considers the missionary as "the great destroyer of non-European cultures, from the sixteenth century down to the present," and their action as being "more dissolving than that of the layman." The Jesuits from this point of view were in fact "pure European agents for the disintegration of native values." But superimposing upon the natural situation of different regional languages a single one,—a common one; bringing to an end the customs of the aboriginal peoples within their reach, and raising Indian children to "abominate the usages of their ancestors," as Anchieta declares in one of his letters, attempting to destroy among the people of the interior, their dances, songs and festivals, which were "not in harmony with Catholic morality and European conventions," the missionaries as universalists evidently carried on a work of assimilation and of imposing uniformity which was not without its consequences for the life of the nation whose unity began to be shaped under its action, as a result of which we can appreciate the enormous value of catechization in the making of Brazil.

But this work undertaken by the Jesuits by means of a vast educational system which, growing up, was to attain at least the beginnings of higher education in the first century of the Colony, is not to be looked at merely from this point of view, that of the conquest of the Indian to a new civilization. At the same time that they attempted in their imperialist dream to replace by another the aboriginal culture which was decaying before the vigorous assaults of these new agents of colonization, they were giving themselves in their colleges and churches to a task no less difficult and complex,—that of restoring and maintaining in all its integrity the Iberian civilization, which was passing through profound transformation and tending to be dissolved in the Colony under the powerful influences of the aborigines and of the Africans, and the unity of which was twice in the sixteenth and seventeenth century menaced by foreign invasions. If it was inevitable, as everyone recognizes, that the greatest and deepest influence which was to be exercised in our country should be that of Portuguese civilization, brought by the colonists, merchants and adventurers, and the defense of which was a duty of the home country in its own economic and political interests, it is none the less certain that it was constantly worked upon in the course of its evolution by the interpenetration of cultures of different levels and aspects, and was upon the point of yielding to new European influences, those of the French and Dutch. If it had not been for the Jesuits who became the intellectual and social guides of the Colony during more than two centuries, it would have been perhaps impossible for the Portuguese conqueror to preserve the unity of his culture and civilization from the dangers which assaulted it. They were, in fact, the center of this Europeanizing reaction in colonial society. Organizing the first institutions of education and culture,—through which the clergy came to obtain the almost unlimited preponderance in the Colony which they had enjoyed in the home country—the Jesuits struggled to make their possession and unity of spiritual power more sure, with the same firmness which one of them, Manuel da Nóbrega, intervened in politics against the French (1564–1567), when indecision was causing the reins of government to lie weakly in the hands of the chiefs, or with another no less illustrious, Antônio Vieira, in his campaign against the Dutch, aroused the settlements and villages to raise the standard of the cross, hoisted above the bell towers, and led the Portuguese to close their ranks under the banner of faith which was unfurled in front of their soldiers and colonial troops. Whatever may be the point of view from which we consider the work accomplished by the Jesuits, it cannot do less than impress us, not only by the extension of the social area over which it went on from Bahia to Olinda and, toward the south, as far as São Vicente in the sixteenth century, and from Pernambuco to Pará in the seventeenth century, but also on account of the difficulties which they had to overcome in order to carry it on and maintain it in a heterogeneous society made up of whites, Negroes, Indians and mestizos, based upon a regime of slavery, broken up into scattered nuclei, separated by great distances and split by struggles and internal dissensions. If in the north in the seventeenth century, the social landscape of the Colony already presented, with the sugar cane plantations, an ethnic and economic stratification in which to a morality of slaves there was added the unrestrained morality of lords, social mobility in the south, intensified by the penetration of the interior and the bandeiras, was mixing populations and classes, leading to a long process of differentiation and to the rise, out of the tumult of unstable social life, of a new form of individualism, as despotic and uncontrolled as that of the lords of the sugar mills. The Jesuits, in order to impose the Catholic morality, had then to confront in the north the omnipotence of the slave-owning masters who were opposed in their plantations with their accustomed arrogance to all other outside authority, and to maintain in the south a struggle without truce in defense of the freedom of the Indians against violent and bold men, neglectful of the few laws which then ruled civil society and habituated to all those lawless types of activity and excesses with which pioneers and tamers of the interior were accustomed to make their way in their march toward the unknown. Everywhere, conflict between the colonizer and the natives; the influences of the Negroes and the Indians, or the two races and cultures, modifying the Portuguese language, infiltrating into religion and sapping the influence of the Portuguese; and everywhere the irrepressible explosion of the instincts of libertinism, favored and stimulated by the climate, by the race mixture practised on a large scale, by immorality and freedom of customs,[4] proper to a society "camping out," like the societies of the interior, or as a result of the voluptuous leisure of a slave owning class which made of each of the slave quarters in the sugar plantation or the mansions of the bourgeoisie "a great licentious seraglio." It was not only the big houses which allowed themselves to be contaminated by the slaves: in this "land so wide and of people so licentious," according to the picturesque expression of one of the Jesuits, who first arrived

---

[4] The descendants of the discoverers, born in Brazil, writes Humberto de Campos, "inherited with the blood of their fathers that violent process of multiplying the species, dictated by circumstances. The importation of the Negro, whose race brought to the libertine spirit of America the idea of a new pleasure, raised the libertinism of our ancestors to an even higher pitch, and it became thus one of the factors bringing about the mixture of those human elements, and not less one of the reasons for making an almost unpassable gulf between the incompatibility of blood between master and slave. Brazilian poetry and fiction of the nineteenth century reproduce, in practically all its shades, the various aspects of this depraved civilization. The white, owner or manager, was master of the virginity of all the Negro girls at puberty, crossing with them in complete irresponsibility; forming, without love, that is, without any feeling in his soul, any involvement of his heart, a mestizo race, the female part of which would later serve the lust of his legitimate sons. From this right, which the European or his direct descendant considered undeniable, came the great crimes, the deep revolts, the eternal rivalries. . . . The white man, in the meantime, was realizing his historic destiny, adventuring his life in the midst of all kinds of dangers, to establish as he did, the definite bases of a new race." (Humberto de Campos, *Carvalhos e roseiras*. 2nd ed., pp. 80-81, José Olímpio, São Paulo, 1934.)

in Brazil, corruption had in the sixteenth century already reached the very clergy themselves, among whom it had grown up under the complacent eyes of colonial society
without shaking ecclesiastical prestige nor constituting any obstacle to social rise of the
sons of priests, whether white or mestizos, which was generally so easy.

In the patriarchal family, the only force which was really opposed to the educational action of the Jesuits was that of the lord of the sugar mill, whose sovereign
authority dominated from above not only the slave group, but his wife and children,
who were kept at a distance, and added to the government of his plantation, the
administration of justice and the policing of his region. A rigid discipline under the
command of the pater-familias, whose interest it served, took refuge in the big houses
where the sentiment of authority and the principle of hierarchy emphasized differences of age, making the social distance between the child and the man, between
the fathers and the sons, enormous. The women,—the wife or lady with her court of
mucamas employed in domestic industry, and the daughters who did not leave the
skirts of the mothers until they were married, practically before the age of puberty,
or became nuns in convents, lived like prisoners behind the shutters and the doors, in
the melancholy solitude of their women's quarters, where no stranger could penetrate
and from which they never came out except for church celebrations. Submitted to
a cloistral regime, between parents of cruel severity and jealous and brutal husbands,
and dividing their time between caring for their children, religious practices in chapels
and in churches, and household work, they neither had nor could have in the Colony
an intellectual situation different from that which women knew in Portugal in the
three centuries of the colonial period. The traditional situation of inferiority in which
custom and law placed them, the absence of social and wordly life, and their almost
absolute lack of education (since they rarely learned to read and write), gave them
that habitual timidity of reserve which made them blush if they were caught by
strangers, or left them disconcerted in the presence of guests and strangers.[5] So in this

---

[5] The reserve, or even timidity and ignorance, the result of the system of seclusion to which
custom condemned women in the colonial period, were kept up down to the beginning of the
nineteenth century, as characteristic traits in women, which did not escape the notice of foreign
travellers. The tradition of the Portuguese family, the scarcity of white women, which was more
noticeable the farther you went from the coast, and the licentiousness of customs, explain this
attitude of defense with which men surrounded their women and kept them from contact with
strangers, cloistering them in the interior of their houses. "In the province of Minas Gerais ladies
are not accustomed to show themselves to men," writes A. de Saint-Hilaire, who rarely in his
long journeys through Brazil (1816–1822) had the pleasure of resting his eyes on a feminine
face in the houses where he was a guest. In Vila Rica, the party which the governor of the province, D. Manuel de Castro e Portugal, gave, led the French naturalist to suppose that he would
get to see the ladies he had caught a glimpse of in an evening affair at the palace on the day following his arrival. The illusion was short lived. "We frequently called upon their husbands, who
were the leading personages of the city; but," he adds in disappointment, "we did not see a single
woman." (*Viagem pelas Províncias do Rio de Janeiro e de Minas Gerais,* Vol. 1. Series Brasiliana,
Vol. 126, São Paulo, 1938, p. 142.) "During the whole time that I spent in the house of Captain
Verciani," the French scholar relates, "the lady of the house never appeared. However, while we
were eating, I could see a pleasant feminine figure softly come up to the half-open door. But as
soon as I turned my glance in that direction, the lady would disappear. It is through the satisfaction of this kind of curiosity that the ladies attempt somewhat to alleviate the scanty freedom they
enjoy." (*Viagem pelas Províncias do Rio de Janeiro e de Minas Gerais,* Vol. 2, Series Brasiliana,
Vol. 126-A, São Paulo, 1938, p. 287.) In the region of Rio Grande, and in general in the district

almost inviolable rule of the big house in which all authority was concentrated in the pater-familias, and both slaves and children and even the wife were kept at a distance of inferiority and subordination, which varied according to age and social condition, the Jesuit was not long in penetrating, breaking down for the profit of the church through the influence which he exercised over the wife and over the children, the arbitrary power of the masters. "In the first century of the colony," writes Gilberto Freyre, "the college of the Jesuits had succeeded in overshadowing the big house and the patriarchal mansions in its authority over children, wives and slaves. Through the college and through the confessional and even through the theater, the Jesuits attempted to subordinate to the church these same passive elements of the big house, the wife, the child and the slave. They attempted to take away from the big house two of its most important functions, that of school and that of church. They attempted to weaken the authority of the pater-familias in two of its most powerful roots." [6] But it was not only in the religious life of the family that the Jesuits met a favorable climate for their educational action, which was so much more efficacious in that atmosphere of servitude, when the slave, the wife and the son found in the support and strength of the church a counterweight to the excesses of domestic, patriarchal authority, with which no other power could contend unless it be that in the name of which the missionaries spoke—the power of religion. According to a tradition of Portuguese families, on the model of which the patriarchal family in the Colony was shaped, the sons took three roads or careers, "not rarely," as Pedro Calmon reminds us, "after many goings and comings ending in the same family house which was the inheritance of the oldest." He, the heir, followed the path of his father, the second the career of literary man, which he undertook by beginning his studies in the college, to go and conclude them in Europe afterwards; and the third entered the church taking his vows at fifteen in the convent, in a college or donning the cassock in a seminary. "His pious mother made him into a priest." All of them, then, who were destined in the patriarchal home to the career of letters or to ecclesiastic or monastic life,—and all well-to-do families were proud of having an educated son and a son who was a priest—, fell naturally under the influence of Jesuit education in their colleges in the Colony, or at the University of Coimbra, which was under the power of these religious teachers, beginning in 1555, and became the most useful instrument through which their ideas and their methods made their way. The tradition of the patriarchal family

of São Joao, "they show themselves a bit more than in other parts of the province of Minas Gerais, but," comments Saint-Hilaire, impressed by this lack of sociability on the part of the women, "as this is a usage not generally permitted and those who appear before guests only do so by trampling on prejudice, they often show a certain boldness which is rather disagreeable. Here, as in the rest of the Province, the ladies of the house and their daughters introduced their faces cautiously into the crack between the wall of the room where I was and the half-opened door, to see me write or examine plants, and if I turned quickly, I caught a glimpse of figures hastily withdrawing. A hundred times this comedy was played." (*Viagem às nascentes do rio São Francisco e pela Provincia de Goiaz*. Vol. 1, Series Brasiliana, Vol. 68, São Paulo, 1937, pp. 79-80.) Under the Empire, if we make an exception of the court, these customs did not undergo any noticeable change, either on the coast or the plateau. From the time of Saint-Hilaire, who travelled through Brazil at the end of the colonial period (1816-1822) to Max Leclerc, who visited us, sent by the *Journal des Débats*, when the Republic was proclaimed (1889–1890) all travellers make similar if not identical observations on the social status of women in Brazil.

[6] Gilberto Freyre, *Sobrados e mocambos*. Series Brasiliana, Vol. 64, pp. 92-93, São Paulo, 1933.

in two of the careers which it reserved to its sons, thus opened between the big house and the college channels of communication by which the influence of the Jesuits was to come, overshadowing that of the fathers and by which the flower of colonial youth was to flow towards the church and toward letters. "Hence the terrible strategy of the Jesuit educators, which was nevertheless very subtle," observes Gilberto Freyre, "that strategy of securing that the Indians should give them their young sons, or that the white colonists should confide their sons to them to be educated, all of them, in their boarding schools, so that they became more the sons of the priests and of the church than of the Indian chiefs and half-breed mothers, of the lords and ladies of the sugar mills." [7]

But the authority and cultural influence which the Jesuits had in the big houses by a kind of action from the outside toward the interior, that is a taking away of the education of the children whom they gathered into their colleges, afterwards was transformed into their attempts in the interior of the patriarchal family itself through the uncle-Fathers and chaplains of the sugar mills,[8] through the close meshes of that cultural network which they wove with their teaching institutions, few talented boys could escape in each of the generations which followed each other in the big houses and from which the majority of the boys had to stay in the colleges of the Fathers, while the education of the remainder from the seventeenth century on remained in charge of the chaplains and Fathers who were teachers. The church which at the beginning circled about the big house, disputing the authority of the pater-familias, who was arrogant and licentious, ended by installing itself in the big house, living with its chaplains under the same roof and sitting down at the very table of the lords of the sugar mills. It was by this joint and successive activity of the Jesuits in their colleges and of the chaplains and priestly tutors coming from Portugal or educated in the colony in large part by the Fathers of the Society of Jesus, that the rising tide of

---

[7] Gilberto Freyre, *Sobrados e mocambos*. Series Brasiliana, Vol. 64, pp. 92-93, São Paulo, 1933.

[8] The chapel, the mansion and the slave quarters—the essential elements of all big houses—made up the triangle within which the system of patriarchal economy was enclosed: the Church, the family, and slavery. In the mansions of the bourgeoisie, when there was no chapel, there was always at least an oratory, taking the place of the richer chapels of the noble houses, for the devotions of the family. This domestic practice of religious rites, installed in the big houses and the city mansions of the coast, as one of the most characteristic cultural traits of family life, spread over the plateau, even into the captaincy of Minas Gerais, which had not been touched by the work of the Jesuits, and where, during the whole of the eighteenth century, the religious orders got no foothold. "In almost all the great residences and in many of the middle-sized ones, in the corner of the verandas, at the back, opening on the dining room, there was," writes Augusto de Lima Júnior, "the chapel, where, on the cedar altar, beside the Crucifix of Our Suffering Lord or the Good Jesus, Christ in agony or dead on the cross, were to be seen images of the figure of Our Lady, in various styles, always in wood, with a feeling of life about them, that is, painted in a characteristic style. . . . In the houses without chapels, there was the 'saint's room,' an apartment set aside for pious practices, where there was an oratory set on a chest of drawers. . . . Here were arranged the various saints, as well as the obligatory Crucifix." (*A Capitania das "minas gerais:" Suas origens e formação.* Lisbon, 1940.) This old tradition, which so strongly expresses the religious sentiments of the Brazilian family, extended from the patriarchal house to the more important houses of city and country, and was kept up until the end of the nineteenth century, when, either because it became commoner for women to go out on the street, or because of the breakdown of traditional customs at that time, the whole practice of religions moved to churches and temples.

African influences coming up from the slave quarters to the big houses was defeated. "Mammies and slave girls," writes Gilberto Freyre, "in alliance with the boys and the girls, the white young women of the big houses, created a Portuguese different from that stiff and grammatical variety which the Jesuits were trying to teach the Indians and half-white children in their colleges, and from the Portuguese of the home country which the Fathers had the vain dream of conserving in Brazil. After them but without the same rigidity, the priestly tutors and chaplains endeavored to combat the influence of the slaves, opposing to it a Portuguese almost of the hot-house variety." [9] The action of the Jesuits and the chaplains who received from them and then transmitted to colonial youth the same spirit and ideals of culture, was not limited, of course, to the defense of Portuguese against Negro and aboriginal influence, which at the same time menaced the language of the fatherland, the authority of the church, morality and customs. They raised a barrier against the disintegration of the cultural heritage of which they were the depositories and of which they were, in the colony, the most authorized representatives, the most eager propagandists. The waters which they drew from the fountains of the church and the traditions of the home country and which they poured down from the tops of their colleges so to speak, led down by two slopes,— that of the slave quarters and that of the Indian villages. Although they had not succeeded with all their efforts in neutralizing the enormous influence of these two cultures,—the aboriginal culture and above all the African which was closest and most penetrating, it is sure that they did succeed in restraining them sufficiently so that cultural unity was not dissolved or broken under the permanent pressure of an extraordinary diversity of heterogeneous elements. They were the ones to transmit to the generations which were formed under their spiritual direction in more than two centuries, almost intact, the patrimony of a homogeneous culture, the same language, the same religion, the same conception of life and the same ideas, ideals of a "culti- vated man," bringing together through the higher levels of society all of these scattered nuclei which from south to north were breaking up under the assault of the powerful forces of dissolution. Humanists par excellence, and the greatest of their time, they concentrated all their efforts, from the intellectual point of view, on developing in their disciples literary and academic activities which corresponded for that matter, to ideals of the "cultivated man" in Portugal, where as in the whole Iberian peninsula, the spirit of the Middle Ages had taken refuge and an education dominated by the clergy at that time aimed at nothing but forming men of letters and scholars. The clinging to dogma and authority, scholastic and literary tradition, the almost total lack of interest in science, the repugnance to technical and artistic activities, were neces- sarily to characterize in the colony all the education which was modelled on that of the home country, which had remained closed and bitterly opposed to the critical, analytical spirit, to research and experimentation, and therefore to that "bold men- tality which in the sixteenth century broke out, to become stronger in the seventeenth, a century of light for the rest of Europe and a century of darkness for Portugal." [10] Not that the old scholastic mentality had entirely deserted the rest of Europe beyond the Pyrenees, that mentality which ruled without any opponent in the peninsula; but with it and in open struggle, there already existed a revolutionary mentality which

[9] Gilberto Freyre, *Casa grande e senzala*. Maia e Schmidt, Rio, 1934, p. 373.
[10] Antônio Sérgio, *Ensaios*. Lisbon, Seara Nova, 1929, p. 22.

flowed from the critical spirit of liberty of investigation and from experimental methods and was vigorously opening for itself a path through the still living forces of tradition.

The civilizing work which the Jesuits accomplished in Brazil in the two first centuries of colonization cannot then be understood unless it is situated in its time, in the framework of conditions of social life in the home country and in the colony, and of the spirit with which the Society of Jesus began and which it transported to its missions. In the face of the struggle which was breaking out in Europe between Catholicism and Protestantism, the spirit of the Reformation and of free examination, and of authority and discipline, the Society of Jesus from its very origin took a position in the vanguard in defense of the church against the Reformation and the modern spirit. From 1554, when Saint Ignatius adopted the plan of the campaign which was vigorously carried out after 1573 with the modifications introduced by Gregory XIII, the Society of Jesus took on the character of a militant, anti-Reformation Order and the educational function and the fight against Protestantism came definitely to the forefront of its activity. The differences of ideas and educational processes in North and South America come not only from the diversity of the temperaments of the two peoples who conquered and colonized those regions, but from the opposition between two concepts of Christianity—that which remained faithful to Catholic orthodoxy, and that which implanted the religious schism, establishing itself in the northern European countries, while those of the south, like Portugal and Spain, remained Catholic. Besides a conception of duty common to the two camps into which Christianity was divided, it is necessary to recognize greater independence of mind in the Englishman and to a certain extent in the Protestant of England and of other countries. In theology, as in politics and in science, the Englishman refuses to accept received opinions, tending to form his own opinions. Far from prohibiting free examination, Protestantism requires it. It is sufficiently broad to permit the use of reason and sufficiently simple to follow better the evolution of modern ideas, retaining nevertheless, the essence of faith—a fact which permits the religious sentiment to remain always alive among Anglo-Saxon people. The Jesuit, who did not have a strong belief in liberty was, on the contrary and par excellence, the restorer of dogma and authority, in which he found a means to impose civilization upon savages whose instincts had not yet been tamed and in which he recognized and proclaimed in spite of all the errors, which it was condemned to commit, one of the means which humanity had to rise gradually from low social stages to the various phases of civilization. His culture,—and none of the religious orders after the sixteenth century raised culture to so high a level—, is above all a "professional" culture, which is governed, oriented and measured according to the requirements of the ministries of the priesthood and of teaching; a culture which has as its object the formation of the humanist and the philosopher and only as a basis, for the training of the perfect theologian; a culture disciplined to achieve morality, broken up into parts for catechism and for teaching, equipped like a weapon of combat for religious struggle, flowering for the tourneys of the mind, splendidly ornate for the pulpit. With this spirit of authority and discipline and with that admirable intellectual instrument for domination and penetration which he had in his learned, systematic, measured, well proportioned system of teaching, clearly abstract and dogmatic, the Jesuit exercised in the colony, which was worked upon by the ferment of dissolution, an eminently conservative role, and teaching letters to youth, he led to the birth for the first time in the colony of a taste for things of the mind. Free examination, the spirit of analysis and criticism, passion for research and a love of adventure, which were barely dawning in Europe, would without doubt have enlarged our mental horizon and enriched our culture in the philosophic field, for it remained without thought and without substance, being almost exclusively limited to letters. But, beside the fact that surroundings favorable to the flourishing of the modern spirit were lacking in the colony, even the most elementary conditions of intellectual life, a freer culture more broken up, prematurely developed, without a ballast of tradition, might even have led to the extension to the spiritual plane of zones of disagreement and added religious struggles to the differences and discords which were operating in the heart of society. This mix-up, above all, was avoided with the cultural influence of the clergy and particularly with the Fathers of the Society of Jesus who erected authority and mental and moral discipline to be principles of action. With the solidity of their organization, fortified by their hierarchical scale, with their privileges and immunities built upon the church, with their clear and precise ideas and their uniform culture spread through all their colleges, the Jesuits were able to become perhaps the greatest nucleus of resistance and cohesion in colonial society, where social bonds, relaxed on account of the imperfection of institutions, became even weaker on account of internal struggles and dissensions.

If the Jesuits in the sixteenth century attacked the civilizing mission which they proposed for themselves, beginning, as was natural, in the condition where everything was lacking, with schools of reading and writing, they did not, however, stop with elementary education even in the first century, in which in the colleges of Rio de Janeiro and of Pernambuco there were classes in humanities and in which there were conferred, in their college in Bahia, the degree of bachelor of arts in 1575, and in 1578 the first degrees of master of arts. The elementary teaching which served them only as an instrument for catechization and as the basis for the organization of their system, which at the close of the sixteenth century had already attained in Bahia the level of a course of arts, with forty students in 1598 and which, less than a century after their arrival, had reached almost a maximum of expansion through the territory of the country. The first century was, then, one of adaptation and of building and the second, that of development and extension of the educational system which when it had attained the necessary height, went on extending progressively, its sphere of action adding new school units. According to the *Ratio studiorum* published in 1599 by Father Cláudio Aquaviva, General of the Order, and in which there were incorporated the pedagogical rules of Saint Ignatius and later experiences in the field of education, the complete plan of studies of the Society was to embrace a course in humane letters, one of philosophy and sciences and one of theology and sacred sciences. Of these three courses, which in the major European establishments of the Society were completed by a biennium of specialization reserved for the preparation of university teachers, the third, that of humane letters, divided into three classes (grammar, humanities and rhetoric) was meant to educate the student *in litteris humanioribus*, providing him with an eminently literary type of education based on the classics, and it therefore constituted, as the course of humanities, the true foundation of this whole solidly built structure of Jesuit education. It was this course, that of humane letters, which spread most in the colony in the colleges of the Fathers. The course of philosophy and sciences, also called arts, and divided into three years, had as its object the formation of the philosopher by means of study of logic, general metaphysics, elementary and higher mathematics, ethics, theodicy, and the physical and natural sciences, taken from the scholastic point of view and studied even at this time as "sciences once and for all constituted by the speculations of Aristotle." In Aristotle, according to the scholastics, there was everything. There was nothing to investigate or discuss, you had only to write commentaries. So, the whole intellectual life "in so far as it was concerned with the study of the external world," writes Antônio Sérgio, "was reduced to commentaries. Write commentaries on the books of antiquity,—to write commentaries, to split hairs, to write commentaries. It was a dream of formal subtlety, the play of aerial illusion. One was always chewing up the same food of no nutritive value; one was always going around in eternal circles like a horseman in the riding academy." [11] In Brazil, this course of arts was for the first time established in the College of Bahia in which at the end of the sixteenth century, as Serafim Leite says, "it was already flourishing and well attended." Once the humanist was formed in the course of humane letters, and the philosopher in that of arts, the pupil of the Jesuits who meant to go on to the priesthood was ready to undertake the third course, that of theology and sacred sciences which, with its four years, made up the crown of all the studies, and serving directly the ends of the Society, was only established in the larger seminaries and in houses designed for the intellectual training of the Jesuits. This was the plan adopted in Brazil after the publication of the *Ratio studiorum* in 1599, by the Fathers of the Society who made certain modifications in it, in the direction of adapting it to the peculiar necessities of the church and the colony, such as the substitution for Greek in the course of humanities of the Brazilian language, "a useful and even necessary instrument for catechization." In the seventeenth century the Jesuits possessed, besides schools for children and other lower colleges, eleven colleges properly so-called, namely, that of Todos os Santos in Bahia, founded in 1556, for the teaching of rhetoric, philosophy and theology; [12] that of São Sebastião, transferred

---

[11] Antônio Sérgio, *Ensaios*. Lisbon, Seara Nova, 1929, p. 23.

[12] The educational success of the Jesuits, who just a few years after the founding of the Order were considered the most skillful and practiced teachers of Europe, was not only due to the organization of their system and of their methods of teaching and of action. The fervor of the fathers of the Society and the great zeal with which they sprang to the defense of the Church, when the offensive of the Reformation was at its height, could not fail to win for them the sympathy and preference of Catholic families. In a society deeply rent by serious religious and political dissensions, they raised higher than ever before, on the foundation of dogma and faith, the principles of "catholicity," of universality, which allowed them to rise above national rivalries and antagonisms. It was a flag of war that they unfurled, but only to plant the standard of peace, in whose shade all peoples were to find shelter, when the dominion of the Church should be extended over them: fundamentally, this was a new expression of "ideological imperialism." This principle of universality and the wisdom with which they sought to establish it, linking intransigeance in doctrine to suavity of manners (*fortiter in re, suaviter in modo*) made it easy for them to extend their sphere of activity, in missions and education, over and above all frontiers. To the direct teaching of Latin, which was offered as the "general language," the international tongue of the educated man, and which, together with Greek, constituted the basis of the classical humanities, they were careful to add, for the sake of their intra-national work, the study of the language of the country,—"an indispensable instrument for the work of the priesthood and of teaching." Excellent teachers, they had a special care, moreover, for the education of the youth of the so-called "ruling classes" and the training of the clergy, and thus, for the preparation of cultural, social, political

from São Vicente in 1567, and installed with this name in the Morro do Castelo in Rio de Janeiro; that of Olinda which passed from being a simple residence and elementary school to being a college in 1568; that of Saint Ignatius, in São Paulo (1631); that of São Miguel in Santos (1652); that of São Tiago in Espírito Santo (1654); that of Our Lady of Light in Sao Luiz do Maranhão; and that of Saint Alexander in Pará, established in 1652 but only raised to the category of "complete colleges" in 1670; that of Our Lady of the O in Recife (1678); that of Paraíba (1683) and the Seminary of Belém of Cachoeira, the foundation of which was requested and obtained in 1687 by Father Alexandre do Gusmão. If we add to these establishments already flourishing in the seventeenth century, the seminaries founded the following century in Paraíba, in Paranaguá, in Bahia, in Pará and in Maranhão, the number of educational and cultural institutions being maintained by the Jesuits when they were expelled from Brazil would amount to seventeen.

Of all these colleges, the most important and those which had the greatest influence, were those of Todos os Santos in Bahia in which Father Antônio Vieira was educated, and of São Sebastião in Rio de Janeiro, both of which represented the organization of Jesuit teaching in its complete state from the course of humane letters of art to that of sacred theology and science. It was in them that the majority of Brazilians who took their vows in the Society of Jesus, or entered the priesthood, or became teachers in the colleges scattered over almost all of the colonial territory, had obtained their education. They were, so to speak, nurseries of religious leaders, the central houses of the Society, in which teaching for the formation of priests reached a high level, so much so, that there were carried out in Rio de Janeiro,—as we deduce from a document of 1747 still extant in the library of the ancient college of Anchieta in Nova Friburgo—the solemn defense of theses in philosophy which, according to the authoritative judgment of Father Manuel Madureira, "had no reason to envy the present programs of philosophical controversy of the great Catholic universities." A great number of the Fathers who were professors in our seventeen Jesuit colleges, writes Father Madureira, "had all of their studies in Brazil, as for example Father Vieira who was already the 'great Vieira,' when he went to Europe for the first time, returning later the astonishment of all who heard him and were able to admire in

---

and ecclesiastical élites, going about the reformation of society from the top downwards; they came in this way, with their special calling, to meet grave needs that were felt by all, needs created by the decay of the medieval universities and by the anarchy and corruption which were ravaging the countries of Europe, to the influence of which the clergy and prelates themselves were giving way. If we add the fact that they gave their education for nothing, we shall have, in this complex of factors, some of the principal reasons which contributed powerfully to the spread of the schools of the Jesuits. But of all the causes, perhaps the most important, the one which we can consider the key to the growth of Jesuit education, was certainly the principles and the pedagogical plan laid down in the regulation of Saint Ignatius, and later in the *Ratio studiorum*,—that famous scholastic constitution, with which, according to Francis Bacon, there was restored in the schools of the Jesuits, "the noblest part of ancient education." These rules, drawn up in 1599, by Father and General Cláudio Aquaviva, and remodeled in 1832, with modifications which did not fundamentally change in substance, the original plans and methods, still in their basic lines guide all the education given by these teachers; and, as far as the intellectual preparation of the Jesuits is concerned, they are still the "fundamental statute," not only in connection with methods, but also with reference to the structure of the system, with its three-fold division into courses meant to train the humanist, the philosopher, and the theologian.

colonial Brazil the splendid education which the Society of Jesus gave to its sons." But in these two colleges, like that of Bahia and that of Rio de Janeiro, and in all of the others which were established from the sixteenth century down to the expulsion of the Jesuits in 1759, the Fathers of the Society, teaching Latin and grammar to white and mestizo children, educated the first bachelors of art and men of letters in Brazil and prepared for their higher studies in Coimbra all of the young men who, preferring a career of law or of medicine, were forced to seek universities in Europe, above all that of the home country. To these students,—because there were no higher schools in Brazil—, the Jesuits gave the fundamental preparation in their colleges, where many students received from the colleges of Bahia or Rio de Janeiro the degree of bachelor or master of arts.[13] In the education meant for youth which did not aspire to the priesthood, either secular or regular, Portugal did not bother to erect on top of its system a higher faculty for any specialty (like civil law, canon law and medicine which were the exclusive property of Coimbra), nor did the Jesuits succeed in in-

[13] The degree of master of arts,—the highest which was conferred on completing the course in arts, corresponded, according to Canon Fernandes Pinheiro, to that of "the bachelor in letters." Pedro Calmon is also of this opinion, when, apparently deriving his opinion from this author, he classified masters of arts as a "colonial kind of bachelors of letters." (*História Social do Brasil*, 1st vol. 1937, p. 124.) On the contrary, Moreira de Azevedo assures us that this title, so much sought after in colonial society, was more esteemed than that of doctor in our institutions of higher learning. (*Instrução pública nos tempos coloniais no Brasil*. In "Revista" do Instituto Histórico, LV, 1892, p. 142.) Father Manuel Madureira, Rodrigo Otávio and Serafim Leite, all quoting Moreira de Azevedo, support this opinion that the ancient degree of master of arts was the same or better than that of doctor given by any university today. (Manuel Madureira, *A Companhia de Jesús. Sua pedagogia e seus resultados*. 2nd vol., 1929, p. 392; Serafim Leite, *Páginas de história do Brasil*. São Paulo, 1937, p. 25.) The truth, however, seems to be otherwise, and does not lie with either those who raise the degree too high nor with those who reduce it to the level of "bachelor of letters." The course in arts, in the Jesuit plan, was really one of higher level: on a foundation of the course in humane letters, and given in three years, it preceded the course in theology and sacred science. This organization was based on models from the medieval curriculum, but with the changes that had been made in the Arts Faculty in the University of Paris; according to this, one studied first rhetoric and dialectic (logic), once one had finished the study of Latin with the grammarians,—and these three disciplines made up the *trivium*, and later they became a real faculty of philosophy. On completing the course in arts (philosophy), three degrees were given,—that of bachelor, that of licentiate, and that of master of arts, all of which were being given, even in the sixteenth century, in Brazil, by the central college of Bahia: the degrees of bachelor of arts, in 1575, of the licentiate in 1576, and in 1578, "the first degrees of master of arts, with the presence of the governor general, the bishop and other people of quality." (Serafim Leite, *Páginas de história do Brasil*, pp. 25 and 59.) Of the three degrees, that of master of arts, which was given upon the defense of a thesis, was not, however, so highly regarded in the old school system, in which the Arts Faculty was on a lower plane than the others (theology, canon law, law and medicine), nor can it be considered equal to or better than that of doctor in present-day universities. In 1565 and even in 1572 there was a controversy between the Jesuits and the university authorities in Portugal over the carrying out of the new statutes approved by Cardinal Henrique, according to which the master of arts could preside over the jury in which an examiner was doctor in theology. It was considered wrong that a Jesuit, a simple master of arts, should have precedence over a doctor of theology in the jury for an examination in arts. . . . This degree scarcely corresponded to the "doctor of philosophy" given by modern universities. Neither more nor less, and rather less than more, if we take into account the fact that present faculties of philosophy, raised to university level, are on the same plane as other schools, while "the course of arts" was on a lower level than that of the university courses.

ducing the Portuguese government to recognize a course of philosophy and science (arts) in spite of various attempts, like that of the merchants of Bahia who in 1671 vainly solicited the king, Dom Pedro II, to put the College of Salvador on an equal basis with that of Evora, so they would not be obliged to send their sons to the home country to complete their studies. Excellent educational establishments for the humanities with a sketch of something higher for lay students, these colleges of the Fathers nevertheless had a capital importance in our formation, for they were, during the seventeenth and eighteenth centuries "the most important educational buildings in the first cities of Brazil." Luxurious mansions of stone and stucco like that of Bahia which Gilberto Freyre describes, basing his description on Gabriel Soares,—with its cubicles for eighty priests, its great dormitories, many of which "look out upon the sea with a great view," and with a capacity for two hundred boys, and with its landings "where they received what came to them by sea, and that was almost everything, seeds, tools, books." Through the cultural activity of these indefatigable educators, it came to pass that it was not only through landed property and number of slaves that one measured importance or esteemed the social situation of colonists; the degrees of bachelor or master of arts came to play the role of ladder or elevator in the social hierarchy of the colony for there grew up a little aristocracy of the lettered, of future theologians, priestly teachers, judges and magistrates. In the enormous houses of stone and stucco, the Jesuits established in fact not only the institutions to transmit the cultural heritage from one generation to another, but agencies of selection and distribution,—the only ones which existed in the colony, and with an importance as channels of vertical social mobility which can be estimated by the number of writers, poets and orators, clergymen, higher and lower judges who were educated in the colleges of the priests. Of the three social institutions which served as channels for rise in society, the patriarchal family, the church and the school, the last two which constituted a counterweight to the influence of the big house, were practically in the hands of the Society of Jesus. Almost all of the youth, whites and mestizos, had to pass through the mold of the Jesuit education, manipulated by the Fathers in their colleges and seminaries, according to the principle of their famous plan for education and then distributed to ecclesiastical functions, to magistracy and letters. The taste for studies and for academic degrees which were awakened (and here there were given to lay students only the degrees of bachelor and of master of arts), and the desire to rise in the social scale, which was as keen in mestizos as in the white sons of the lords of the sugar mills and of the bourgeoisie, early led to making the university a common ideal. "The magistracy, the position of canon," writes Pedro Calmon, "conferred honor on account of their privileges and raised a man to an uncommon level and gave him in the colony above all an eminent situation on a level with a government office."

The Jesuit teaching which was established in the colony for youth in general included, in nearly all of the colleges, the course in humane letters, the classical type of teaching, reaching in some houses, like the central college in Bahia and in that of Rio de Janeiro, the course of arts which was intermediate between the humanities and the higher courses. It was at this point, when he terminated his course of letters or of arts (philosophy and sciences) that the teaching, although it still aimed at an intellectual uniformity, divided into two different paths, one which led to the course of theology and sacred sciences (for an ecclesiastical career), and that which turned in the direction of courses of canon law, civil law and medicine. The former was given either by the Jesuits themselves in the Central College of Bahia or in the greater seminaries, or in the Faculty of Theology in Coimbra; the latter, which prepared for worldly careers (the liberal professions) were given only in European universities, especially in the University of Coimbra,—the only one, strictly speaking, which existed in the kingdom for Portugal and for its dominions. There were not, then, in the colony, higher university studies, except for the regular and secular clergy, the latter educated in Coimbra or by the Jesuits in the colony, especially in the eighteenth century; and for those who were not aiming at the priesthood but at other careers, the only long hard road that was open to them at this point of bifurcation led to the universities beyond the sea, to that of Coimbra, organized on the model of Bologna and most famous for its theological and juridical sciences, and to that of Montpellier in France, and which had received there in the basin of the Mediterranean, the medical traditions of the Greeks, developed and enriched by the Jews and the Arabs. The government of Portugal to which the council of Bahia had gone in 1671 to request the equality of the local school with that of Évora, had only permitted in its provision of July 16, 1675, "that the students of rhetoric and philosophy who had finished the course of the Jesuits in Bahia should be given credit in the University of Coimbra or that of Évora, for one year of arts." Practically with this provision, the general education of the Jesuits in the colony had been reduced to the course of humane letters, and all possibilities for the creation in colonial Brazil of higher courses destined for preparation for the liberal professions had been closed. The policy of the government had definitely traced the itinerary to be followed by Brazilian students and it was one that, begun in the colleges of the Fathers with the course in humanities, was generally to end in the University of Coimbra whose "college of arts," founded in 1548 in the Joanine reform and organized by André de Gouveia, its first director, was even in 1555 under the power and direction of the Jesuits. It was no longer possible for Portugal to prevent preliminary studies of grammar, Latin and rhetoric entrusted to the Fathers of the Society from being given in the colony, nor was it interested in doing so; but as for the higher studies, it always seemed to the policy of the home country fitting, if not necessary, that they should be kept centralized in its old universities to which Brazilian students as early as the seventeenth century were beginning to come. The University of Coimbra came to have then a role of great importance in the formation of our cultural elite. It was in it, in fact, that "almost all the educated men of Brazil," got their education in law, philosophy and medicine and that some of the greatest figures of our intellectual history in the first three centuries were started in the direction of medicine, letters and the magistracy. But, by forcing young Brazilians to complete their studies in Portugal, instead of accomplishing their desire to "uproot them," to break their desire for independence or that natural rebellion of the sons of colonists, to make them Portuguese, what the policy of the home country accomplished was to bring together students coming from the different captaincies, to make it possible for them to know each other better and thus to widen their vision of their home country, making it higher and broader than the frontiers of their own provinces. If, on the one hand, they were to become, as in fact they did, the prisoners of moral and intellectual habits contracted from the Portuguese university environment, their memories of their families, the diversities of customs and tendencies, their situation of inferiority in comparison with Portuguese students, tended on the other hand to unite them among themselves, to attract them all to Brazil, and to cause them to discover the awakening of a new feeling,—that of a country of their own, primitive and rude, with moving frontiers, still in process of formation, of which they were beginning to get a vision of the whole and of which they would never have been aware in the isolation of their several captaincies. For national sentiment does not develop only on account of community of race or of language, nor even through the free choice of the reflective will; it is an impulse of the whole being which, once it has been awakened, forbids us to think that we might belong to any other country except the land in which we have been born,—the tomb of our ancestors and the cradle of our sons.

But, in addition to the colleges established in the sixteenth and seventeenth centuries for colonial youth, of whom they were the first masters and to whom they taught letters, the Jesuits founded in the eighteenth century seminaries for the secular clergy to whose education they brought an invaluable contribution in the last phase of the Society in Brazil down to the time of the expulsion. The Order in all this period had practically exclusively in its hands not only the education of Brazilian boys, but also the formation of the clergy, that came to be recruited principally among local elements, prepared by the Jesuits, whereas in the earlier centuries, they had been made up largely of Portuguese clerics. The Catholic fervor of the Fathers of the Society, their culture and the professional skill with which they carried on their teaching, and the scarcity of priests in the secular clergy who could undertake the task of preparing candidates for careers in the church, led the bishops in the colony as well as in Portugal and to some extent all over Europe to entrust to the sons of Saint Ignatius the training of priests and the direction of the first seminaries. If the sixteenth century in which the magnificent work of catechization and the conversion of the heathen is so prominent and extends into the following century, was from the point of view of education that of the organization of the system of Jesuit education, and the seventeenth century that of the horizontal spread of this system, which had been almost entirely constructed in the first century, the latter century, the eighteenth, is the one of the organization of seminaries, of which only one had been established earlier, that of Belém, in Cachoeira (Bahia), founded in 1687 at the request or upon the initiative of Alexandre de Gusmão. In the eighteenth century, there were in fact created beside other smaller ones, the seminary of Paraíba in 1745, that of Pará in 1749, that of Maranhão in 1751, and that of Paranaguá in 1754, the two most important being those of Pará and of Maranhão, which together have constituted since 1725, a vice-province of the Society of Jesus with two great colleges and two seminaries.[14] We see that, materially speaking, in these

[14] Only the seminary of Belém, in Cachoeira, founded by the Jesuits in Bahia, in 1687, or, according to Pedro Calmon, in 1686, on the request of Alexandre de Gusmão, preceded the two seminaries of São José and São Pedro, established in 1739 in Rio de Janeiro, through the efforts of Bishop Antônio de Guadalupe, the Franciscan friar. The four seminaries founded by the Society in the eighteenth century, in Paranaguá, in Paraíba, in Pará and in Maranhão, were later than these two diocesan institutions, created by the Bishop of Rio de Janeiro and always kept under the direction of secular clergy. The orphans' seminary of São Pedro, so called because it was located next to the church of that name, and created by an act of June 8, 1939, came to have another name (Seminary of Saint Joaquim) when it was moved next to the São Joaquim Church, and it kept this name until it was converted into the Colégio Pedro II in 1837. The most important of the seminaries of Rio de Janeiro was certainly that of São José, created on September 5 of the

initiatives, one after the other, the circle which the Society of Jesus was drawing around education in colonial society drew ever closer, and upon it there converged all the forces and all of the resources of the Jesuits in their effort to extend their domination. Founders of seminaries for the training of the secular clergy, they contributed not only to raise the level of religious culture in Brazil, but by training priests who later became teachers and chaplains of the plantations, they were transmitting their spirit and their culture to those who after the expulsion of the Society, would become in a way the depositories of the tradition of Jesuit education and the principal people responsible for the education of Brazilian youth. If it had not been for the contribution made by the Jesuits to the preparation of the secular clergy in their seminaries, great and small, from which there came out a large proportion of the priestly teachers and chaplains of the great houses, the humanistic and literary tradition of Jesuit teaching would not have been conserved in such a living and intense form, that seventy years after the leaving of the Jesuits, it arose again in all the lay and confessional colleges, entirely victorious in the various struggles with opposing tendencies and currents. It is certain that to this end, there must have concurred, in the nineteenth century, the pressure of other similar influences on the old colonial culture which, having been dislocated from the orbit of the Jesuits fell in the following century under the domination of the French language and literature, which, becoming the most humane and universal of all Europe, carried on a process of intellectual penetration in the world, and whose ideas and tendencies entered into our minds more than those of any other nation. When it began to gravitate about this universal literature, didactic, impersonal and disinterested, more than about any other faithful to classic traditions, Brazilian culture did not have to deviate noticeably from the literary direction which the Jesuits had impressed upon it as the educators of colonial Brazil, and the principal educators of the French as well, from the foundation of the Society of Jesus down to its extinction by Clement XIV in 1773, that is, fourteen years after the expulsion of the Jesuits had been ordered by Pombal. But if we observe attentively what took place after the departure of the Fathers of the Society, it will be easy to assure ourselves, in spite of all the decay of teaching which resulted from it in the last period of the colony, of the persistence of the literary, classic and didactic heritage, which together with the Catholic inheritance forms part of the great body of tradition left by these religious leaders who had the exclusive direction of the education and mentality of the colony. The explanation of this fact is to be found not only in the pedagogical activity of the monastic orders, but also and above all in the direct influence which the Jesuits exercised from the end of the seventeenth century upon the training of the Brazilian clergy, educating in their seminaries seven generations of priestly teachers and chaplains, and

---

same year and in which, from its foundation in 1739, there were given courses in Latin, philosophy, moral and dogmatic theology, and plain chant. There arose later, as a result of efforts on the part of the church, other establishments of this character, like the seminary of Mariana (Minas Gerais), founded in 1750 by his first bishop, D. Manuel da Cruz, and closed in 1811, for lack of income, to reopen in 1820; the Episcopal Seminary, established in 1751 by Bishop Miguel de Bulhões, who entrusted the running of it to the Jesuits; the seminary of Pernambuco, in 1798, that of Maranhão, in 1805, and that of Bahia, in 1816, the last seminaries to be set up in the colonial period. With the departure of the Jesuits in 1759, five seminaries were closed, beside other smaller ones, and the training of priests to keep up the necessary supply was left exclusively in the hands of the secular clergy, in the diocesan seminaries.

making of the secular clergy, which was to survive them, the guardian of their pedagogical and literary traditions.

So then, "in that thick, deep darkness into which Portugal threw Brazil," as Viriato
Correia writes, "only in the neighborhood of the college of the Jesuits was there light." [15]
In the colleges and seminaries, they were the first and, during the sixteenth century,
the only teachers of Brazil; in their colleges and in their houses, they established the
first libraries and, on the initiative of the Academia dos Seletos and of its president,—
a Jesuit, Father Francisco de Faria, there was founded in Rio de Janeiro in the eighteenth century the first printing office, destroyed later by order of the Portuguese
government (Royal Letter of July 6, 1747), which "ordered the fonts to be taken and
sent to Portugal, prohibiting the books, works or separate papers should be printed
under penalty of imprisonment in the home country." [16] The almost complete absence
of attempts on the part of the colonists, who in contrast to the English and Protestant
colonists in North America, did not bring with their religious ideal that of instruction; the penury and ignorance of the clergy imported from Portugal and the lack of
external activity of the monastic orders, who down to the end of the eighteenth century lived withdrawn in their convents and faithful to ascetic traditions, joined, with
other causes associated with the negative and absolutistic policy of the home country,
to leave the field of colonial education entirely free and open to the pedagogical rule of
the Jesuits. Educators by vocation, notable teachers in every respect, they were able
to exercise in the colony, where they were favored by exceptional circumstances, a true
monopoly of education, which did not lack to characterize it, the official support which
the government of the home country gave them, supporting them in their civilizing
and pacific missions with large gifts of land and applications of royal revenues to the
endowment of their colleges. The government of a country like Portugal, "which was
exhausting itself in colonial attempts disproportionate to its resources in men and
material means," necessarily tended to concentrate all its thought and all its effort on
the exploitation and defense of the colonies. Education did not interest it except as
a means of securing submission and political domination which could be more easily
attained by the propagation of the faith with the authority of the church and the
restraining influence of religion. She entrusted it, in the colony as in the home country,
to the Society of Jesus, already well known for the superiority of its schools, and which
through its apostolic zeal was in a better situation than any other order to accomplish
an important type of penetration and of colonization in the lands of Portugal in the
New World. The government did not directly intervene in the plan of education and
culture except to create on the margin of the Jesuit system, schools in which one could
learn artillery, to aim and load guns, and to construct fortifications, at the school of
artillery and military architecture of Bahia (1699), and the course in artillery created
in 1738 in Rio de Janeiro, or by cutting at the root of institutions like the university
and the press which in the future might come to constitute centers or instruments for
the emancipation of the colonists. With the same mentality with which in the Royal
Letter of March 19, 1614 and the decree of February 21, 1620, it prohibited the gov-

[15] Viriato Correia, *A instrução colonial.* In "Correio da Manhã," Rio de Janeiro, December 17,
1920.

[16] M. A. Moreira de Azevedo, *Instrução pública nos tempos coloniais do Brasil.* In "Revista" do
Instituto Histórico, LV, 1892, p. 144.

ernor general from visiting the various captaincies without the express permission of the King (in order to rule, it was important to keep the captaincies, if not divided, at least separated and isolated), and refused in 1675 to put on a par the College of Bahia and that of Evora and ordered the first printing establishment set up in Brazil and destroyed in 1747 . . . The university and the circulation of printed books might constitute a threat to the unity of the cultural pattern and a peril for Portuguese despotism. With education handed over entirely to its skillful and firm hands, the Society of Jesus, which since 1555 had completely dominated public education in the whole of Portugal and on the continent alone, at the moment of its expulsion, had twenty-four colleges and seventeen houses, was able to organize colonial teaching in its seventeen colleges and seminaries as it wished, in accordance with the principles and fixed patterns of its pedagogical statutes. The thick, profound darkness into which, in the words of Viriato Correia, Portugal had thrown Brazil, was nevertheless the same which descended upon the Kingdom itself, now in a state of decay, closed and insensible to the new European currents and to the intellectual and scientific agitation which surrounded Portugal without bringing it into its sphere of activity. Luminous points in this vast zone of darkness, the schools of the Jesuits in Portugal as well as in the colony, marked with their uniform, semi-official teaching of a classic type, set up for the training of clergy and the men of letters, the greatest effort undertaken by a religious association to create a "cultural élite," without doubt artificial, universalist in its essence, but so intensely worked upon that it persisted in the following century as a residue in intellectual tradition of the two countries, balancing their internal forces and the peripheric pressure of outside, foreign influences. This culture which remained always that of an elite, which the people never assimilated nor could assimilate, and through which Brazil became for a long time in America, "a European country," had, nevertheless, an effect of the greatest importance in the creation of tendencies and characteristics of the directing classes, in the formation of the bourgeoisie and in the establishment of a tradition and continuity that was thoroughly Brazilian.

Of all the branches of activity of the Jesuits, it was the education of the elite and in this field an essentially classical literary education in which their influence was most profoundly felt and for the longest time, and it is through this education above all that the Society of Jesus was most richly and constantly represented in its colleges, scattered all over the country. It was this humanistic and literary culture which they attempted to spread among us, in a primitive and rude society, unorganized and heterogeneous, putting within the reach of boys, sons of the colonists, what was in the Middle Ages still an attribute of the clergy (hence the double sense of clerk, cleric of letters) and, later in the Renaissance, the privilege of professional scholars. To appreciate correctly this standardized culture with its universalist tendencies and classic type as it was transmitted by Jesuit teaching, it is necessary that it should be seen not in the light of present day civilization, but that going back to the sixteenth and seventeenth century, we examine it and measure it with the customs and ideals of that time, in accordance with which an effort was being made to maintain Latin still in the category of a universal language and to keep up in men the fascination for classic letters, even to servile copying of the ancient model. That the Society of Jesus, faithful to this tradition, educated in Brazil only clerics and men of letters can be demonstrated by the fact that in various generations of students which passed through its colleges, none of them became distinguished in the colony for any interest in the physical or natural sciences or any scientific, technical or artistic preoccupation. They were all literati, chroniclers and historians like Frei Vicente do Salvador, Rocha Pita and Pedro Taques; poets like Gregório de Matos, Cláudio Manuel da Costa and José Basílio da Gama, or sacred orators like Eusébio de Matos and many others whose names have been cast into the shade by the brilliant figure of Father Antônio Vieira, with the supremacy of his work and the incomparable strength of his genius. Vieira, who was the greatest of all of the disciples of the Jesuits in the colonial colleges,—a remarkable prose writer and an unrivalled preacher, with whom the greatest writers learned to polish and sharpen their phrases and with whom the eagles of sacred and political eloquence tried their first flight; a really great shaper of the Portuguese language which he made rich and extremely beautiful, he was with his virtues and defects, which are both enormous due to the exuberance of his talent, the highest expression of that intellectualistic, dialectic and formal education, concentrated upon the word, form, literary taste and imagination. But even in literature of a sterile formalism,—if we make an exception of Gregório de Matos and Basílio da Gama, poets, and Antônio Vieira, whose eloquence is a harp that possesses the whole gamut and in which all notes and vibrations are heard, —the classic spirit, reduced to form for form's sake, was diluted in stuffy, humanistic reminiscences, here as well as in Portugal, in a wave of mediocre, standardized production, of a poverty of style, imagination and thought rarely attained in the history of letters. The first scientific work, the *Historia Naturalis Brasiliae,* of Piso and Marggraf, in which important observations on medicine and the flora and fauna of the country were to be found, came out during the Dutch occupation of Pernambuco; in spite of being published in 1648 in Latin, a language taught in all the colleges of the Fathers, it did not succeed in awakening any interest in Brazil or leaving any vestige of its existence in a vague allusion in the whole of colonial literature. However excellent the organization of Jesuit teaching was and however sure and efficient were its methods, with which humanists everywhere covered themselves with glory, it is certain that practiced within a system of educational monopoly, excessively literary and rhetorical, without the stimulus of new influences, they tended toward uniformity and stagnation and were not without their efficacy in the eradication of all free and creative activity of the mind. There was not in fact a single door through which there could be introduced a new ferment into the mass of semi-official teaching, which, organized for the training of men of letters and casuists, necessarily had to lead the governing élite in the direction of letters and accentuate the opposition between them and the governed and thus constitute "a system of education which was the ally of the city against the country." Developing as it did before anything else literary and academic activities and "attaching an exaggerated importance to the intelligent child who took to letters," the Jesuits created very early with their literary tendency and their keenness, which became traditional, for the degree of bachelor of arts, a neglect of technical and productive work and they made of their colleges channels for horizontal mobility from the country to the city, and for rise in the social scale, and therefore became powerful elements in the process of urbanization. "In their enormous big stone houses," writes Gilberto Freyre, "there were trained in Brazil the first men of letters who were to be the first bachelors of arts, the first judges, Fathers and judges, men more of the city than of the country." [17]

Certainly the Jesuit also paid attention to agriculture and industry; and, organizing and exploiting his plantations, building his sugar mills, he was able to become, even in the seventeenth century and especially in the first half of the eighteenth, "the great colonial producer, the greatest plantation owner of the tropics." For the construction of his churches and schools,[18] as for the installation of his plantations and his experiments in cultivation, there could not be lacking workmen and capable foremen who came from Portugal or were recruited either among the mass of Negro slaves and catechized Indians and half-breeds, or among the lay brothers, who were specialized in some craft. In the novitiates of the Society, and more generally before taking the robe, those monks who were to rise to the ministry of the priesthood and of teaching were selected in accordance with their aptitudes, and also those who having finished the two year period of trials would be used in auxiliary services, in manual and me-

---

[17] Gilberto Freyre, *Sobrados e mócambos.* São Paulo, 1936, p. 96.

[18] The fathers, who at the beginning lived under the greatest difficulties and were supported by alms, as one learns from the letters of the first Jesuits, came in the sixteenth century and later to possess goods and land and to receive gifts which permitted them to keep their pupils in boarding schools. Both Father Manuel da Nóbrega and Father Luiz da Grã, who succeeded him as provincial, worried over the maintenance of the children, immediately understood the necessity of finding a way to "get food and other necessities from outside," so that parents should not be burdened with expenses beyond their means and so that the priests should not be left with "the task of seeking support for themselves and their pupils." From the correspondence exchanged between Bahia, Rome, and Lisbon, it was finally settled that "royal income in Brazil should be applied to the endowment of three great colleges in Bahia, Rio de Janeiro and Olinda." The first college to be endowed, writes Serafim Leite, was naturally that of the capital of the colony. We find in the "Provision of the King of Portugal that he ordered the captain of Bahia to find out how much is necessary sixty persons of the Society in the college of São Salvador (sic) and if the tithe which I gave them for foundation is not sufficient, to make up what is lacking from the Treasury of His Highness." The provision is of November 7, 1654. It is a date to remember in the annals of public instruction. It marks the founding of the first official college in Brazil. (Serafim Leite, *Páginas de história do Brasil.* São Paulo, 1937, p. 53). In 1568, Father Serafim Leite informs us, there came "an authorization for the founding in the captaincy of São Vicente of a college for fifty fathers, who should have the same maintenance as those of Bahia." The place chosen was Rio de Janeiro, which at this time was the Captaincy of El-rei (the King). Although the endowment is of the year 1568, it is certain that the college began to be established at the same time as the city, as one sees from a document or series of notarized documents, brought together under the title of "Lands which Estácio de Sá gave to the college of Rio de Janeiro." (Op. cit. p. 55). With these gifts which were the first, and others bestowed on the new schools; with the organization of the work of the Indians, in their settlements, and with the agricultural and pastoral development of their land, which were not lacking in Negro slaves, as on the fazenda of Santa Cruz, in Rio de Janeiro, the Society was able to attain great material prosperity, which permitted it to put up its enormous houses of stone and stucco and keep up its schools and seminaries, maintaining numerous fathers and hundreds of students. These resources were sufficiently varied and abundant for the sustenance and growth of the schools, and there was even money left over for charity in the villages and towns, like São Paulo de Piratininga, "where the college dispensary was the general reserve stock of all." Father Serafim Leite; from whom we take this information, refers, with the support of Fernão Cardim, to the cultivation "of native and Portuguese plants in the gardens of the Jesuits, from which they spread to others. Side by side with cultivation, there was cattle-raising. Their cattle ranches were models. They supplied the schools, professors, pupils and missionaries; and also the innumerable workers, slave and free, who lived in the shadow of the schools and the fathers." (Op. cit., p. 22).

chanical activities. The young lay brothers, living the same religious life and working side by side with the older ones, skillful and experienced masters, passed their apprenticeship in this or that craft, in conditions which would be useful to the interests and requirements of the houses, churches and schools. But all this, the exploitation of their fazendas, the product of which they sold; the use of slave or Indian labor, and the very professional training, under the pressure of circumstances, of a group of workmen and artisans, were nothing more than mere instruments means toward the accomplishment of the religious and educational ends which the Jesuit Fathers were undertaking. The elementary, utilitarian techniques, necessary to the civilizing mission of the Society as well as to colonial life, and sufficiently simple to require a special training, were transmitted directly from one generation to another and did not constitute an object of education for boys in the schools of the Fathers. The vocation of the Jesuits was another certainly, not popular primary or vocational education, but the education of the governing classes, an aristocratic education based upon the teaching of the classical humanities. That was true here as everywhere; it is true today as it was in the colonial period. Their schools were by preference located in the big cities of Brazil and in the shade of the big houses, in the plantation system of the coast where they recruited their disciples, and the stability of the patriarchal family offered a secure and necessary base for their system of teaching, a basis which it would be difficult to find in the molecular, fluctuating society of the mamelucos who hunted Indians and emeralds, or who raised cattle. Although, however, created for a society characterized by the big house, plantations and slave owning, this class education, far from contributing to strengthen it in the one hundred per cent Portuguese sense, of which Gilberto Freyre speaks, helped to further the development of a new governing class already in process of formation from the middle of the seventeenth century,—that of the urban bourgeoisie. This contribution of Jesuit teaching, Europeanizing, universalist as it was, to the process of the organization of our elites has been observed with clarity by Gilberto Freyre in several points of his fundamental works. It does not seem to me that the Fathers, as he thinks, were aiming at a social domination over the patriarchalism of the big houses, when "they tried to make men or adults out of boys as quickly as possible," and stimulated the literary precocity "which became so characteristic of the Brazilian child in the patriarchal regime of our history." But it is certain, as the great interpreter of our social life writes, that "the children in these seminaries and colleges were an element on which instead of there being marked traits and tendencies which were on the one hand creative but on the other tending to dissolve an excessively patriarchal formation, in the shade of heroic fathers, of extremely powerful individuals, lords of the big houses, almost independent of the world, there were developed on the contrary a spirit of conformity, a certain love of discipline, order and of universality which the Fathers, and especially the Jesuits, were able to communicate to their Brazilian pupils, as no one else could. These pupils of the schools of the Fathers, once they were graduated, were factors making for urbanization and universalization, in an environment strongly influenced by the autocrats of the big houses in the direction of rural stagnation and of extreme regional differentiation." [19]

One of the consequences, however, certainly the most far reaching and most important, of this urbanizing culture which was being developed by the pedagogical ac-

[19] Gilberto Freyre, *Sobrados e mocambos*. São Paulo, 1936, pp. 93, 99, 100.

tivities of the Jesuits, was the spiritual unity which it contributed notably to establish, by furnishing an ideologic, linguistic, religious and cultural basis for the unity and defense of the nation. The influence of Catholicism in general and, in particular, that of the Company of Jesus in the formation of Brazil was in this respect so powerful that it seemed to Joaquim Nabuco even "quite doubtful whether the unity of Brazil would have existed without the unity of the Society of Jesus," and even whether there would have been a Brazil "if in the lifetime of Loyola it had not been made a province of the Society," [20] almost at the same time at which there was being organized as a substitute for the regime of the captaincies, the first central government of the colony. It was, in fact, largely through the influence of the Fathers that the base of the national unity was prepared on the three-fold ground of community of language, religion and culture in the whole territory. No intellectual element was more powerful than the Jesuit teaching in the defense and conservation of the cultivated language, the unifying action of which was of prime importance and which constituted, together with the study of Latin, a central nucleus and the only "nationalistic" element of that teaching which was so preponderantly literary and rhetorical. In the propagation and defense of the faith,—another factor in the making of the nation—, the Jesuits did not merely put their missionary zeal into evangelical preaching and the catechizing of the heathen, but the whole organization of their teaching in the schools, some of which, like the Central School of Bahia, as Father Serafim Leite reminds us, rendered to Brazil during two centuries, "the highest services, not only within the framework of its specific object of instruction and education, but also as a defense and point of resistance against the foreign invader," against the Calvinist invader, French or Dutch, chased out in his attempts at conquest, which had threatened to break up the unity of the territory and of religion. The unity of culture was established by their "general education,"—the only really general education which we have had until today, organized with this character, in the double sense of an education that is not special and vocational and also in a sense which can be opposed to the "regional," or in other words both in its nature and in its extension. It was an education destined to form a free and disinterested basic culture without vocational concerns and equal and uniform over the whole extension of the territory. The "Brazilian" culture which was formed and spread through the élite of the colony by this education could certainly not be called "national" except in the quantitative sense of that word, since it tended to spread its European coloring over the whole of the territory and over all of the people; a culture imported en bloc from the west, internationalist in tendency, based upon a religious, Catholic ideology and at the base of which there lay the Latin humanities and the commentaries on the works of Aristotle taken in a Christian sense. Since it was a question of a culture that was neutral from a national point of view (even from the Portuguese point of view), closely related to European culture in the Middle Ages and unconcerned with political boundaries,—as had to be the case with a culture which was spread by "an essentially international association with the character of a true papal militia," it is certain that this very neutrality (if we place ourselves in a qualitative point of view) would prevent our seeing in this culture, in its origins and its products, a specific Brazilian culture, a national culture even in an incipient stage. But, by reason

---

[20] Joaquim Nabuco, *José de Anchieta*. A significação nacional do Centenário Anchietano. In "III Centenário do Venerável Pe. José de Anchieta," pp. 326-327, Paris-Lisbon, 1900.

of being a general and uniform culture, universalist in its essence and its manifestations, and by reason of the sphere of influence which it attained, accompanying the Portuguese advance in the geographic expansion of the country to the north as far as the Amazon and to the south to Desterro, it constituted without doubt, in a period in which there was not political unity, one of the most important factors making for the integration and unity of the nation. It exercised through the teaching of the colleges of the Fathers, a unifying function dissolving regional differences; and, in this way, it was not threatened by the progress of the Tupí language as a general language, taught also in the colleges, and by the concentration of the Indians in "townships" governed by the Fathers.[21] Although moved by the highest objectives, the Jesuits, segregating the converted Indians into great villages, would have constituted true cysts of ethnic and cultural differentiation if it had not been for the contrary action of the bandeirantes, who in their excursions through the interior, hunting for Indians, dispersed what the Fathers had brought together, contributing to dissolve into the general mass

[21] This question to which we have previously referred, of the settlements of the Indians, can be looked at in at least three different ways: what the Jesuits were aiming at in creating and organizing separate villages for the Indians; the consequences for the primitive populations and cultures segregated by the Jesuits, and the effects that resulted or might result from the isolation, for the growing colonial society. The idea of these great concentrations certainly came to the Jesuits in connection with their desire to serve the end of conversion more efficiently and they hoped by organizing the native population in the European manner and according to their own moral and religious ideas, to be able better to look after their spiritual and material necessities, and the defense of the converted Indians who were always being threatened with the prospect of enslavement. In these settlements ruled by the priests, the Indians, as Serafim Leite writes, "acquired habits of work, cultivated the soil, lived in marriage, educated their children, and carried on the most common and necessary industries, which the Jesuits personally taught them." (*Páginas de história do Brasil*, 1937, pp. 19 and 20.) There is no doubt that the Jesuits decided to bring them together in villages in order to make life easier and to protect them better, and that they tried hard to give these populations the best possible organization from the point of view of the Church and their social and pedagogical ideas. But, as Gilberto Freyre observes, examining the question from another point of view, "the whole rhythm of their social life was altered among the Indians. Peoples accustomed to scattered, nomadic life always are degraded when they are forced to live in congestion and in an absolutely sedentary fashion." Gilberto Freyre therefore considers the influence of the Fathers deleterious and concludes that they were "pure European agents for the disintegration of native values." (*Casa grande e senzala*, 2nd ed., 1936, pp. 76-77.) Father Serafim Leite himself, a member of the Society of Jesus and its illustrious historian, does not fail to recognize at least in part the legitimacy of this criticism, when he asserts that "the Indians, accustomed to living scattered in the woods, at first felt cramped by the towns. From time to time they were victims of malaria, of smallpox, and other diseases." (*Op. cit. p.* 20.) But the effort of the Jesuits may be looked at in another way, that is, in connection with the effects which settlements, forming real cysts, produced or might produce; they were the more dangerous to the nation, since the many-sided activity which the Fathers imparted to them tended to make these Indian villages almost autonomous. If the attitude of the Jesuits toward the pursuit of Indians and their exploitation will remain, as Father Serafim Leite writes, "one of the purest campaigns for human liberty in the whole history of humanity," the measure taken in the settlements, which for that matter was not very effective in defending the liberty of the Indian, constituted an obstacle to the mixture of the races and the interpenetration of cultures, and a threat to social unity itself, to linguistic and cultural unity, which was getting started, and which the Jesuits in other respects did much to further. By scattering what the Fathers had brought together, the *bandeiras* organized with the express object of capturing Indians, succeeded, without meaning to do so, in first neutralizing the effects of this segregation of the Indians in large villages, and later in totally destroying it.

of culture and population, the primitive societies and cultures that were insulated in their villages.

While in the first half of the eighteenth century the educational work of the Jesuits attained its maximum of expansion in Brazil, there were growing in Europe those struggles against the Society which were to end with extinction and in which the attacks arose from all sides, from universities and the parliaments, from civil and ecclesiastical authorities, and from the religious orders themselves. It was everywhere alleged that the Society of Jesus, having lost the ancient spirit of its founder, had entered upon a period of decadence and that, dominated by ambition for power and wealth, it was attempting to manipulate government as a political instrument for its own purposes and against national interests. Jesuit education, in the opinion of its adversaries, had grown old and had become petrified over the generations, and hardening into ancient forms, was proving incapable of adapting its methods to new necessities. In Portugal, two elements of propaganda against the Jesuits in addition came to make this tenacious campaign more obstinate, namely, the monopoly of education which they had exercised since 1555, when Dom João III entrusted to them the direction of the College of Arts, and the economic and intellectual poverty of the realm, for which these monks were pointed out as the principal responsible parties. The decadence of the kingdom had reached, in fact, such a point that in the testimony of Verney, some Portuguese "being more sensible, left Portugal," and when they found themselves in foreign countries, it seemed to them that they were in a new world, and if they had good judgment they were not slow in changing their opinions. "Dom Luiz da Cunha who passed through these places with praise, and who after long service in the ministry is now Ambassador in France, said to a friend of mine (writes Luiz Antônio Verney in 1746) that when he left Portugal and heard other people speak, the greatest task which he had had been to try to forget everything which he learned in Portugal in order to understand things aright and to speak to the point." The new philosophic and scientific conceptions which were spreading over almost all of Europe and were little by little winning over the best Portuguese minds, translated themselves from the time of Dom João V into various attempts at the reform of education; and the new ideals and pedagogical types which were opposed to those of the Jesuit school, threatening to dethrone it, achieved a vigorous expression in the sixteen letters of the *Verdadeiro método de estudar* of Luiz Verney which, published in 1746, had the greatest effect and came to be considered in various lights "the greatest work of thought which has been published in Portugal." All this criticism directed against the authoritarian pedagogy of the Jesuits found a favorable situation in the kingdom and in the countries where they had exercised a preponderant influence and whose intellectual backwardness and economic impoverishment, which had certainly been produced by a complex of causes, among them religious fanaticism and the persecutions of the holy office,[22] were laid at the door of the monks who had had the

22 "In 1668, freed from the war with Castela," writes Antônio Sérgio, "we were once more able to visit Europe with the calm necessary to intellectual occupations. The persecutions of the Holy Office drove out (of Portugal) the best minds: and these emigrants came gradually to compose that fine group of exiles that like a full moon gave light and hope to our intellectual night, in the second half of the eighteenth century. The exiles, as you know, had an influence on the mind of Dom João V, in whose reign there began the struggle to make us once more a part of cultured

240. The School of Mines of Ouro Preto, created in 1875 under the Ministry of Rio Branco, and located in the former Governors' Palace. Under the direction of Henri Gorceix this school became the leading center of higher studies during the last quarter of the nineteenth century.

241. Henri Gorceix, organizer and first rector of the School of Mines of Ouro Pre who inspired a remarkable generation of s cialists in mineralogy, geology, and mini

242. Eugênio Hussak (1858–1911), petrographer, who worked with Henri Gorceix and encouraged him in geological investigations and the study of the natural wealth of Brazil.

243. Joaquim Gomes de Sousa (1829–1863), born in Maranhão, Brazil's greatest mathematician.

244. The National Museum in Rio de Janeiro (formerly Royal, and later Imperial Museum), a great center of research and scientific work, located since 1892 in the former Imperial Palace of the Quinta da Boa Vista. Photo by the National Museum.

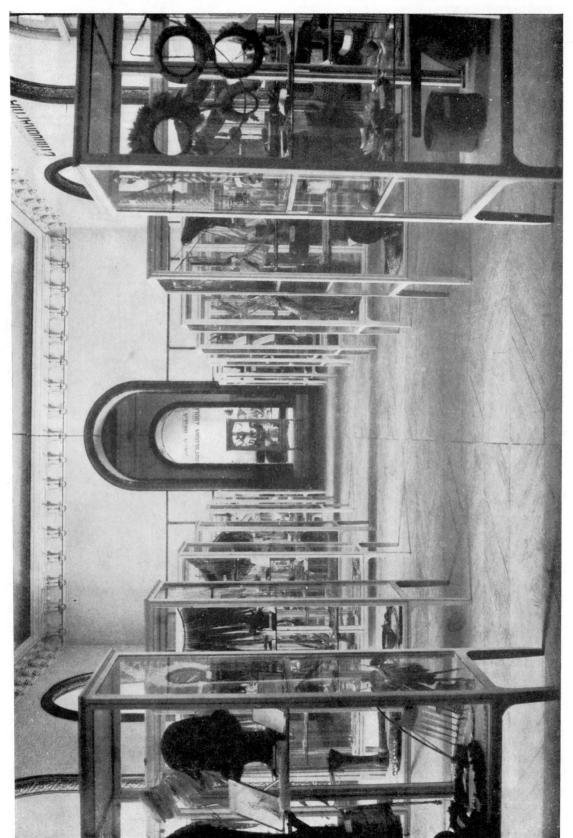

245. National Museum. Hall of Ethnography.
Photo by the National Museum.

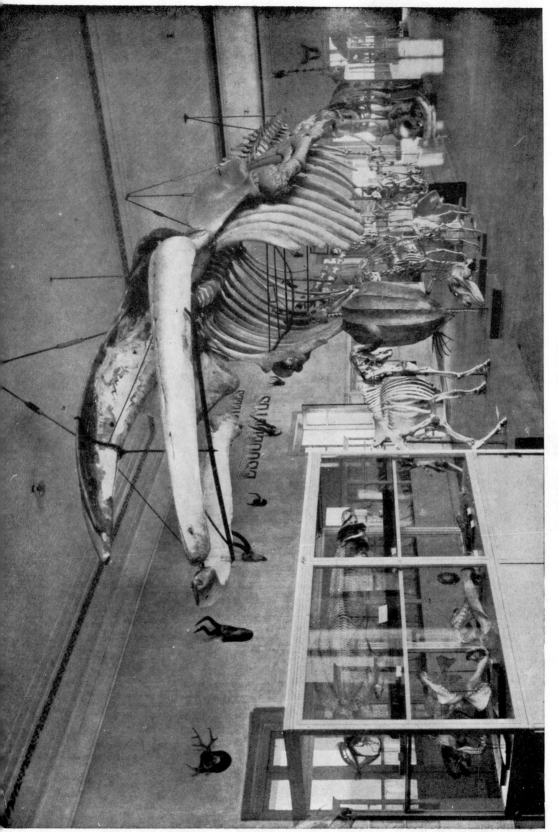

246. National Museum. Hall of Skeletons.
Photo by the National Museum.

247. Raimundo Nina Rodrigues, born in Maranhão, who marks a new phase in the scientific development of medicine in Brazil.

248. The Institute of Manguinhos, now called the Osvaldo Cruz Institute, founded in 1901, the greatest center of research in experimental pathology in the country. Photo by the Photographic Section of the Osvaldo Cruz Institute.

249. National Library in Rio de Janeiro, the richest and most important library in South America.

Photo by Vosylius, in collection of the Census Bureau.

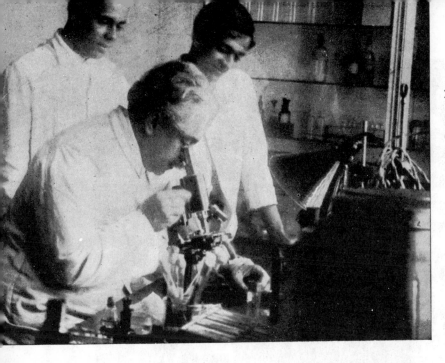

250. Osvaldo Cruz (1872–1916), in his laboratory at the Institute of Manguinhos, Rio de Janeiro. Photo by J. Pinto.

251. Carlos Chagas, pupil of Osvaldo Cruz, who in 1909 won for the Institute of Manguinhos its greatest triumph with his work on American trypanosomiasis and its propagating agent (Trypanosoma cruzi). Photo by J. Pinto.

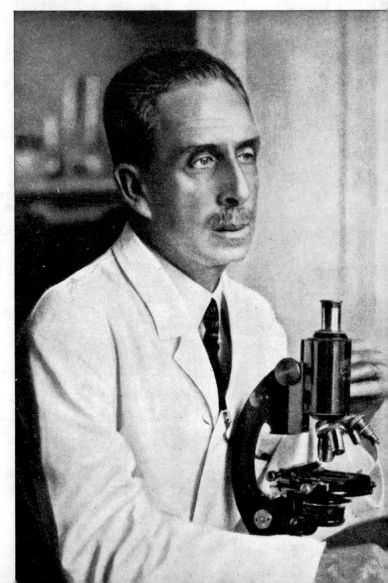

252. Butantã Institute, founded in 1899, the really scientific phase of which, begun between 1901 and 1902 by Vital Brasil, its Director from 1899 to 1919, and carried on in 1913 by J. Florêncio Gomes, took on new life after 1918, with Afrânio Amaral.

253. General José Vieira Couto de Magalhãe
(born in Minas, 1837, died at Rio, 1898), ex
plorer of the *sertão* and ethnographer, author o
Viagem ao Araguaia and of *O Selvagem*. Phot
from Ethnography Department of the College o
Philosophy of São Paulo.

254. General Cândido Mariano da Silva Rondon,
who opened up and civilized the *sertão* between
1892 and 1930, leader of Brazilian scientific expeditions (the Rondon Commission) which made
the greatest contribution to the development of
natural history in Brazil.

255. Church of the Third Order of St. Francis, Salvador, Bahia. Marvelous façade in carved stone, of baroque style.
Photo by Voltaire Fraga, in Brazilian Institute of Geography and Statistics.

256. Church of St. Francis, Salvador, Bahia. The interior.
Photo by Voltaire Fraga, in Brazilian Institute of Geography and Statistics.

257. Monastery of Carmel, Salvador, Bahia. Sacristy.
Photo by Voltaire Fraga, in Brazilian Institute of Geography and Statistics.

258. Church of St. Francis, Olinda. A view of the sacristy.
Photo by Stille, in collection of the College of Philosophy of São Paulo.

259. Church of St. Peter, Recife. Part of the magnificent doorway.
Photo by Stille, in collection of the College of Philosophy of São Paulo.

260. Monastery of St. Benedict, Rio de Janeiro. The majestic main altar.
Photo by Stille, in collection of the College of Philosophy of São Paulo.

261. Monastery of St. Benedict, Rio de Janeiro. View of a side altar and the choir.
Photo by Stille, in collection of the College of Philosophy of São Paulo.

262. Monastery of St. Benedict, Rio de Janeiro. Sacristy.
Photo by Stille, in collection of the College of Philosophy of São Paulo.

263. Church of Our Lady of Carmel, Rio de Janeiro. Principal façade.
Photo by Stille, in collection of the College of Philosophy of São Paulo.

264. Church of Our Lady of Carmel, Rio de Janeiro. View of the main altar.
Photo by Stille, in collection of the College of Philosophy of São Paulo.

265. Church of Our Lady of Carmel, Rio de Janeiro. View of an altar.
Photo by Stille, in collection of the College of Philosophy of São Paulo.

266. Church of Our Lady of Carmel, Rio de Janeiro. The magnificent baptismal font.
Photo by Stille, in collection of the College of Philosophy of São Paulo.

267. Church of St. Anthony, Rio de Janeiro. Sacristy.
Photo by Stille, in collection of the College of Philosophy of São Paulo.

268. Church of St. Anthony, Rio de Janeiro. Another view of the sacristy.
Photo by Stille, in collection of the College of Philosophy of São Paulo.

269. Church of Our Lady of Carmel, Ouro Preto. Portico.
Photo by Radio Inconfidência of Minas Gerais.

270. Church of Our Lady of Carmel, Ouro Preto. Detail from main chapel.
Photo by Radio Inconfidência of Minas Gerais.

271. Church of the Rosary, Ouro Preto. View of the exterior.
Photo by Radio Inconfidência of Minas Gerais.

272. Mother church, São João d'El Rei. Detail of the main chapel.
Photo by Radio Inconfidência of Minas Gerais.

273. Church of St. Francis, São João d'El Rei. View of exterior.
Photo by Stille, in collection of the College of Philosophy of São Paulo.

274. Mother church, Tiradentes. Retable of main altar.
Photo by Radio Inconfidência of Minas Gerais.

275. Mother church, Tiradentes. Columns and entablature of the main altar.
Photo by Radio Inconfidência of Minas Gerais.

276. Church of Our Lady of Carmel, Ouro Preto. Pulpit in sandstone by Aleijadinho.
Photo by Radio Inconfidência of Minas Gerais.

exclusive control of the character and education of the nation. The storm, raised by political and religious struggles, which on various occasions seemed about to disappear, its stay on the horizon prolonged, finally broke out in full force. The Marquês de Pombal in 1759 expelled the Jesuits from the kingdom and its dominions, beginning with this radical policy a series of similar measures taken by France (1763), Spain, Naples and Sicily (1767) and by other governments, and which culminated in 1773 in the total suppression of the Society of Jesus by Pope Clement XIV,—a center of convergence of the clamors which rose from all countries. Thus there ended in the colonial period, with the expulsion of the Society, the work of these missionaries, who for more than two centuries had educated Brazilian youth and had so efficiently aided the Portuguese to colonize Brazil, softening the asperity of the customs of an epoch of violence and rapine, reducing discord between the big houses, restricting the abuses of the government, strengthening faith, giving new life to charity, emphasizing the restraining power of religion and contributing to implant order and discipline where everything conspired to give roots to anarchy, the daughter of civil hate and of class and race struggle. The civilizing work of these men, who came up from the sea and the caravels to spread all over the coast and far into the interior, was such as in fact seems supernatural to the anemic, civilized pleasure-seeking men that we are today. Their apostolic ardor, their fearlessness of death, their almost impossible mobility over the whole land and their practical organization and discipline cannot be measured in its greatness except by the serenity and resignation with which they abandoned their schools and left for exile, silent like soldiers, who fold their tents . . .

In 1759, with the expulsion of the Jesuits, what Brazil suffered was not a reform of education, but purely and simply the destruction of the whole system of colonial education under the Jesuits. It was not that one system or type of education was transformed or replaced by another, but that a scholastic organization was extinguished without this destruction being accompanied by immediate measures, sufficiently efficacious to diminish its results or to reduce its extension. When the decree of the Marquês de Pombal dismissed the Fathers of the Society, expelling them from the colony and confiscating their goods, all their schools were closed with the stroke of a pen and there remained only the buildings, and the whole apparatus of education erected and directed by the Jesuits in the land of Brazil fell to pieces and was completely destroyed. To understand the full impact of this blow for Portugal and especially for Brazil, it will be sufficient to recall once more that at the time of their expulsion, the Jesuits possessed in the kingdom of Portugal twenty-four colleges, besides seventeen houses, and in the colony twenty-five residences, thirty-six missions and seventeen colleges and seminaries, without counting smaller seminaries and schools of reading and writing es-

Europe . . . Jacó de Castro, who was in London, was charged with the study of the problem. When he consulted the scholars of England, they told him that it was first of all necessary to modernize our mentality, replacing the medieval attitudes of our ruling classes with the experimental and critical spirit; and, to this end, to translate the *Novum organum* of Francis Bacon. And this was right: it was a question of destroying the peripatetic philosophy in which the Portuguese had imprisoned himself. It was also on the request of the government that Verney wrote his great book, *O verdadeiro método de estudar,* which provoked the first of the great debates, or rather the first high point of a single debate which has been going on in our country for two centuries." (Antônio Sérgio, *Ensaios.* Vol. 2. "O reino cadaveroso ou o problema da cultura em Portugal," pp. 44-45, Lisbon, Seara Nova, 1929).

tablished in practically all the villages and settlements where houses of the Society existed. In this landscape of the schools, which is uniform and without relief, there were found outside the spiritual rule of the Jesuits, only the school of art and some military buildings created in Bahia in 1699,—perhaps the first lay institution of education in Brazil, a course in artillery created in 1738 in Rio de Janeiro, beside the seminaries of Sao José and São Pedro, established in 1739, in the same city. We might add the episcopal seminary of Pará, which was founded by the bishop, Dom Frei Miguel de Bulhões, but the running of which had been handed over to the Jesuits. So that, with the possible exception of elementary studies of military art, two or three seminaries, some classes for the secular clergy, and some others of philosophy in the convents of the Carmelites and Franciscans, education in Brazil down to 1759 was almost totally in the hands of the Fathers of the Society whose system of education was the only one existing in the country. The education of Portuguese and colonial youth, monopolized by the Fathers, looked doubtless in the direction of intellectual uniformity; the program of its teaching, dogmatic and abstract, showed no plasticity capable of adjusting itself to new necessities; the methods were authoritarian and conservative even to the point of routine; and besides the fact that the teaching did not include the sciences, in this program of studies that were excessively literary and rhetorical, it gave no place to modern languages, keeping the élite in such an ignorance of these languages that it was a marvel if one could find in the colony a Brazilian who knew French . . . These were, from the pedagogical point of view, the principal accusations which in Portugal were raised against the Jesuits by their adversaries. Of the extension which Tupí as a general language won, to the point of being utilized even in the pulpits, that could not at this time be made an accusation against the Jesuits. As early as 1727, by a provision dated in that year, the government of the home country, alarmed at the abandonment of Portuguese, by the Portuguese themselves, had expressly proscribed Tupí, prohibiting the use of that Brazilian language; and if these religious leaders contributed in fact to the study and use of Tupí as an instrument of catechization, not only had they never wished to eliminate the Portuguese language from Brazil, but they had even been earlier, during the whole colonial period, its incomparable masters. But be that as it may, down to 1759, instruction had developed from the second half of the sixteenth century in a steady progress, within the point of view and method "perfectly adequate to the aim which the Jesuits had in mind," as José Veríssimo writes. The schools and colleges constantly grew in number; their endowment resources grew daily; their program, although already antiquated, both for Portugal and the colony, was considered sufficient by public opinion; their teachers, skilled and highly competent,—the beginners of education in Brazil, enjoyed for the most part, public esteem in colonial society. Instead of developing this organism, of enriching, enlarging and reforming this system, the Marquis de Pombal eliminated it and once this destruction was complete, he waited thirteen years to commence to rebuild, under the government, what the Jesuits had succeeded in doing in a period of two centuries with their notable work of penetration, evangelization and education, which had covered with the movement of their tentacles the whole coast from south to north and had extended the spiritual frontier in the same proportions as the explorers and bandeirantes penetrated into the interior, extending the geographic frontiers of the country.

But if the powerful minister of Dom José I destroyed, neither he nor the Portuguese government which followed him knew how or were able to restore. Where there had been a scholastic organization slowly and solidly built in a period of two centuries, he had to erect another, in an immense effort at reconstruction beginning from the very foundations. This was not what the minister did in the reform that he undertook, after he had obtained his fundamental object of freeing public education from the pedagogical influences of the Jesuits. What came down to us was not exactly reforms (nor was it possible to require immediately reforms which could be accomplished only over a long period), but an incoherent series of measures, belated and fragmentary, with which in 1759 and in 1772, the government of the home country set about carving in the inert mass of colonial society, a work which might give the illusion of taking the place of the dismantled organism. The expulsion of the Jesuits, followed only by resolutions (decree of June 28, 1759), tending to substitute courses and classes for those which had been suppressed, had opened too profound a breach both in the work of the mission and in the education of colonial youth, for any of these measures to be able to repair it. The beginning of classes of Latin grammar, of Greek and of rhetoric and the creation by the same decree of 1759 of the position of "director of studies," with which there was an attempt at an administrative organ in Portugal which should guide and inspect teaching, were in fact far from providing solutions for the problems which arose as a consequence of the expulsion of the Fathers of the Society, even on the hypothesis, which was not correct, that they would create as many classes in all of those disciplines as there were colleges destroyed in the kingdom and its dominions. With these emergency measures which the decree baptized "reforms" the king aimed "not only to rescue those studies (those of humane letters) so that they should not fall into total ruin to which they were near, but also to restore to them their former lustre which had made the Portuguese so famed in the republic of letters (sic) before the said religious order had taken upon itself to teach them their sinister intent and unhappy results." It is only in 1772, however, that is thirteen years after the expulsion of the Society of Jesus and after this decree which claimed to reorganize the study of humanities, that a royal order commanded the establishment of these classes of letters, of grammar, of Latin and of Greek in Rio de Janeiro and in the principal cities of the captaincies. It was in that year also by the order of November 10, 1772, that there was instituted the "literary subsidy,"—a tax created especially to maintain primary and middle education, and which, ordered collected in Brazil in the following year, never succeeded in bringing together either in Portugal or in the colony the necessary resources for education. Later, in 1774, a royal course of Latin was inaugurated in São João d'El-Rei in Minas Gerais, and one of philosophy in Rio de Janeiro, where two years later there were started on the initiative of the Franciscan friars, courses in Greek, Hebrew, philosophy and theology. There was created in the same city in 1783 by the Viceroy Luiz de Vasconcelos, a course of rhetoric and poetry for the poet Silva Alvarenga; a course of design and of the figure was opened in 1800 and classes in elementary arithmetic, geometry, French and design for the instruction of the military, and these were followed by other efforts of the same character in the principal cities of the coast and in some rare ones of the plateau and the interior. Although it had been ordered by the decree of 1759 which created in Portugal a general direction of studies, the inspection of royal courses and schools did not begin to be regularly carried out in Brazil except after 1799, that is to say the twilight of the eighteenth century, when the Portuguese government assigned to the Viceroy the general inspection of the colony, with a right to name annually a professor to visit the courses and to inform him on the state of instruction. So that when the Society of Jesus was suppressed and separated from education, both in Portugal and its dominions, the State, which did not intervene in the management of the elementary and secondary schools, undertook through the initiative of Pombal the educational function which it came to exercise in collaboration with the church, entering upon a far-extending plan to give official character to education. The scholastic landscape acquired without doubt a greater variety of appearance, with the introduction of the teaching of Greek and Hebrew and modern languages such as French and English and above all the mathematical, physical and natural sciences in the University of Coimbra, which in 1772 passed through a profound change,—the most important of the reforms of university studies in Portugal. But the general plan of education did not any longer present the least cohesion. In place of that enormous, homogeneous block which was the educational organization of the Fathers of the Society,—an association of such unity of directive point of view, the government instituted the regime of royal courses,—courses of isolated disciplines—, which in the colony were only later organized by the Franciscan friars in 1776, "in schools with graduated and systematized courses."

If, therefore, with the reform of the Marquês de Pombal, there did not occur in the colony a "real break-up of culture," because the union of the Chuch and the State and the very cultural tradition which still kept in a resistant and extremely alive state a kind of unity, fundamentally religious and humanistic in character, it is certain that from the formal point of view, that of organization, the "unity of system" was followed by fragmentation into a plurality of isolated and dispersed courses.[23] This break-up of structure became so much the more grave as the reforming government did not know

[23] In the opinion of Mílton Rodrigues, this break-up was not merely formal, but substantial: "it was," he writes, "substantial because at the time the encyclopedist tendencies of France had had a great influence; this school of thought was followed by Pombal who wanted to impress it upon the college of the Nobles, founded with this object in 1761; substantial also, in a negative sense, on account of the lack of any other principle of unification capable of replacing that of religion." (*Educação comparada*. 3rd part, O Brasil. Histórico e doutrinas, 1938, p. 251). However, it is not true that the tendencies of French encyclopedism succeeded in influencing us, in thè colony, at that time, nor was the religious principle lost or reduced in its power to bring unity. Those tendencies which, it is true, lay back of the plan of studies in the college of the Nobles, in Portugal, in 1761, and later, in 1772, of the reforms in the University of Coimbra, only reached the colony at the end of the eighteenth century, that is, forty years after the expulsion of the Jesuits, having a considerable influence upon the organization of the seminary of Olinda, founded in 1798, by Azeredo Coutinho. Through all this period, up to Dom João VI, not only did religious unity remain the unifying principle, but this was true of the very tradition of Jesuit teaching, literary and humanistic; this tradition was preserved in its essential values and methods, by the whole Church in Brazil, by the priestly teachers, the chaplains of sugar plantations and the schools of the monastic orders. There was not, then, a break-up of the essence of culture, the unity of which was maintained both by the pressure of religious unity and by the living, persistent tradition of literary studies based on the classics, and by the permanence of the medieval concept of culture, with its adoration of letters, its neglect of facts and the great importance which it attached, in education, to the acquisition of what the Germans call *Weltanschauung*, of a "view of the world as a whole," rather than to the acquisition of special techniques.

how to and was not able to recruit the teachers which it needed, to give them a fitting situation, nor to submit them to a discipline capable of introducing the necessary unity of views and of effort into the teaching staff. The education which was given, almost exclusively in confessional schools,—the colleges of the Fathers, came to be provided in royal courses and schools by teachers appointed in agreement with the bishops and by priestly Fathers and chaplains of the plantations, "who became after the Jesuits left the principal parties responsible for the education of Brazilian children." The lay teachers of these courses and schools, which did not succeed in assimilating the spirit of the reform of Pombal, showed generally, according to the testimony of the time, not only a dense ignorance of the subjects which they taught, but a complete absence of pedagogical sense. Although less rigid and disciplinary than that of the Jesuits, of whose traditions of teaching they were, as it were, depositories, the pedagogical activity of the Fathers and chaplains, directed toward the same objectives, played an important role in the conservation of Brazilian culture in the European sense and of its unity in a national sense. It is Gilberto Freyre who observes and emphasizes this influence of the chaplains and uncle-priests who, after collaborating in the activities of the Jesuits, became the principal or preponderant type of activity after the expulsion of the members of the Order. "The number of illustrious men of the colonial period and the first years of the Empire who received their primary and secondary education in the schools of the Fathers surpasses," writes Gilberto Freyre, "that of those educated at home by the chaplains and uncle-Fathers. Chaplains and uncle-Fathers, subordinated more to the *pater-familias* than to the church, did not fail, however, to represent, under the roof of the patriarchal mansions, something subtly urban, ecclesiastical and universal,—the Church, Latin, the classics, Europe, a sense of another life beyond that dominated by the watchful eye of the lords from the top of their big houses." Educated with lay teachers or secular clerics in the royal courses and schools or with chaplains at home in the country sugar mills, in the plantations or in the mansions of the bourgeoisie, "whence the bigger boys went almost directly to Coimbra" or to other universities, Brazilian boys continued to receive an instruction almost always inferior as to level but certainly in its ends and methods similar to that which had formerly been given to them by the Jesuits in their famous colleges. If to the instruction at home, in the case of well-to-do families and to these royal courses, which were not well attended, we add the activity carried on by the monastic orders of the Carmelites, Benedictines and Franciscans who opened new courses in their convents and monasteries for secular students, and the education designed to train priests which was furnished in the seminaries of São José and São Joaquim in Rio de Janeiro, in that of Pernambuco created in 1798 and in that of Maranhão, founded in 1805, little will be lacking to complete the picture of scholastic activities and institutions at the end of the colonial period from the expulsion of the Jesuits down to the arrival of Dom João VI in Brazil. But, over all this instruction, unorganized and fragmentary, the level of which had gone down notably, but which remained faithful to the tradition of Jesuit pedagogy and its essential values, the shadow of the Portuguese reformer was barely cast in the colony, although one cannot deny either breadth of view nor fidelity to the aims which guided his plans of reform, in which the tendencies of French encyclopedism were such a powerful influence. The new philosophic and scientific spirit which inspired the reorganization of higher studies in Coimbra, appears in the courses and colleges of the religious orders as a very weak solution and one singularly neutralized both by the ignorance of the new teachers and by the important residues of the old culture disseminated by the Jesuits.

The reform of Pombal, planned for Portugal, was not only a profound blow to basic general education in the colony breaking it up into classes in the separate disciplines (royal courses), without any systematic plan of study, but also cut off from its normal pedagogical evolution the development of education toward higher planes. Both the middle courses which broke up into the regime of "courses," and the higher teaching which was in an incipient stage in the development of the arts courses of the Jesuit plan, lost all possibilities of further development due to their lack of resources and the necessary organs to insure the continuity of teaching and its progress. The fundamental unity of thought which gave the Society of Jesus and its operating agencies the power and the preponderance which it had in the spiritual life of the Brazilian people, as indeed everywhere, was transmitted by a closed and admirably hierarchical organization which made it easy to organize all of its resources for action, furthering both the unity and the autonomy of its colleges. In the reform of Pombal on the other hand, in addition to the regime of courses, which weakened all efforts at organization, the distance between the general directorate of studies (in Brazil the Viceroy himself) and the teachers, who were not collected in colleges but dispersed, without any permanent intermediary organs, did not even permit any kind of efficient inspection nor create an environment favorable to larger initiatives. Everything, down to the details of the programs and the choice of books, had to come from above and from afar, from the supreme power of the realm, as if the latter had been organized to install routine, paralyze individual efforts and to stimulate, instead of absorbing them, those parasitic organisms which usually develop in the shade of distant governments which are naturally slow in intervening. This was one of the reasons for which the reforming activity of Pombal only indirectly affected school life in the colony. Of the body of reforms undertaken by the minister of Dom José, the most important was doubtless that of university studies, in which the vigorous hand of the reformer was most strongly felt. After reforming the lower schools (decree of November 6, 1772) and instituting the scholastic fund (decree of November 10, 1772) he ended by reaching the heart of the University of Coimbra, giving it new statutes and opening, with the creation of the faculty of philosophy and mathematics, new horizons to the culture of his country and to the study of the sciences of observation. But the Portuguese government created no institution of higher learning in Brazil like the Royal College of the Nobles founded in 1761 in Portugal or in the style of the new or old faculties of Coimbra. The only attempt which is interesting in this respect was the course of literary and theological studies created by the Franciscan friars in Rio de Janeiro and organized on the model of the faculty of theology of the Portuguese university. In its organization and its plan of study (Greek, Hebrew, philosophy, church history, dogmatic theology, morals and exegesis), this course, which was approved by the decree of July 11, 1776, was meant above all for the special and professional preparation of the priests and it cannot therefore be pointed out, as José Veríssimo thinks, "as the first and only attempt made in Brazil to start a university course of disinterested higher studies." Of the reform of the University of Coimbra [24] undertaken by Pombal, Brazil received only the benefits which were to result in the case of the young Brazilians who at this time went to Portugal to complete their studies. During this period and under the new regime established by the statutes of Pombal, there were educated the Paulista, Francisco José Lacerda e Almeida, who took his degree about 1776 and was a notable geographer; Azeredo Coutinho, born in the State of Rio, founder of the seminary of Olinda, who took courses in the University in the Faculty of Canon Law (1775–1780); the Bahiano, Alexandre Rodrigues Ferreira (1756–1815), a physician and splendid naturalist; and José Bonifácio de Andrada e Silva who, besides taking courses in the Faculty of Laws, where his parents sent him, frequented also the courses of philosophy and took his degree in both schools. In the University of Coimbra in which he studied (1784–1790) and of which he was to be later the professor of the chair of metallurgy, José Bonifácio acquired a taste for the sciences of observation and for studying nature which, perfected in travels through the principal scientific centers of Europe, permitted him to become a great mineralogist and one of the most cultivated Brazilians of his time. The history of our scientific culture can be said then, to have had its origin in the work carried on

[24] The University of Coimbra, which played so important a part in the training of the upper classes and the creation of Brazilian mentality, during the colonial period, down to the first quarter of the nineteenth century, is to this day the only university that exists in Portugal. Founded in Lisbon on March 1, 1290, by Dom Deniz and moved by the government of that poet-king to Coimbra, in 1308, it returned to Lisbon in 1338, to be restored to the old town in 1354 and moved to the capital once more in 1377; here it stayed until the major reform of Dom João III who in 1537 once and for all located it in Coimbra, making it the intellectual center of the nation. The reform of Dom João and the founding of the College of Arts, the direction of which was entrusted to André de Gouveia and later to the famous Diogo de Gouveia, "principal" of the College of Santa Barbara, professor of theology in the University of Paris and its former rector, opened the most brilliant period in the history of Portuguese learning. Later, in 1555, the College of Arts, to which the King had granted the exclusive right to teach publicly Latin studies and philosophy, in Coimbra, was handed over to the direction of the Jesuits, who, in the following century, obtained further concessions in the matter of degrees in theology. The University of Coimbra had the exclusive right to offer as disciplines, law and canon law (juridical science), theology, and medicine, which made up the different sections of university teaching. With the death of Dom João III in 1557, the university entered upon a period of decay which lasted until the reform of Pombal, through the constant struggles with the Jesuits and successive reforms of its statutes. It was in this period of open decay (1557–1772), of more than two centuries that the University of Coimbra served for the higher education of Brazilian youths, who, ever since the end of the sixteenth century, had been going to Portugal to finish the studies that they had begun in the colony. This fact suffices to explain the harm it did the formation of the mentality of our country, as well as the services which it rendered, as the only Portuguese center of higher learning, in the preparation of the colonial élite. The credit for the restoration of the University certainly belongs to the minister of Dom João; with the new statutes (1772) and the solemn visit of the Visiting Marquis, it entered upon the most important and fruitful period of its history. Not only were the old Faculties of Theology, Canon Law, Law and Medicine, reorganized on new bases by the Statutes of Pombal, but two other faculties were created, those of Mathematics and Philosophy; in these schools mathematics (integral and differential calculus), physico-mathematical sciences, experimental physics, chemistry and natural history won their place in the university program. In the University thus thoroughly changed,— and soon the target of the attacks of those who began to see in it "a center of dangerous doctrines, dangerous because new and seductive," were educated the first Brazilians who made an appreciable contribution to the development of science in Brazil. (Cf. *Mário Brandão* and M. Lopes de Almeida, *A Universidade de Coimbra: Esboço de sua história,* by order of the University, Lisbon, 1937.)

by the Marquis de Pombal in the University of Coimbra, which with its new statutes became a center of scientific studies, drawing into its enthusiastic advance toward modern culture a group of young Brazilians and training them in the new methods of studying and of investigation.

The reforms of Pombal, as we see, reached Brazil especially through the intermediacy of the University of Coimbra, which continued to be at once the creative center and the distribution center for Portugal and its dominions, but now with a new spirit, in which the Faculties of Philosophy and Mathematics became a center of irradiation. If the distant action of the University, reorganized according to new tendencies, was not sufficient either in breadth or in profundity to reduce the predominating concern of our education for literature, it served doubtless to infiltrate into the colonial elite the current of the modern spirit and to inaugurate in certain, selected figures, the scientific culture in Brazil. The scarcity of students of which the Marquis de Pombal complained in 1773 in the sections of natural and philosophic sciences and in the courses which later (1791) were created in the Faculty of Philosophy (botany and agriculture, zoology and mineralogy, physics, chemistry and metallurgy), and the very technical necessities of the realm and of the colony, led the Portuguese government to attract to the University Brazilian students. In 1800, writes José Veríssimo, "the King sent to the governor of Maranhão asking him to appoint four students to receive instruction in Portugal, taking their courses at Coimbra, two in mathematics, afterwards to be employed as hydraulic engineers, surveyors and accountants, one in medicine and the last in surgery. If in addition to the four, someone else might through his capacity merit it, the council might send him, allotting for this end, a special stipend." With the exception of these rare attempts which were without influence on colonial mentality, the whole period of almost half a century which extends from the expulsion of the Jesuits (1759) to the transfer of the Portuguese court to Brazil, was one of decay and transition. At bottom and behind the most varied forms of schooling, there is to be seen clearly in all its characteristic traits, the pedagogic and cultural tradition left behind by the Jesuits, continued by the priestly teachers, and resulting from an exclusively literary education, based upon the study of grammar, rhetoric and Latin, in the plans of which there was no place either for natural science nor for modern languages and literature. Although broken up and fragmentary, and declining in level, education although more varied in its aspects looked toward the same religious and literary objectives and was carried on with the same pedagogical methods, in which the appeal to authority and to strict discipline which take concrete form in the yardsticks of quince wood and in the rulers of sicupira wood, tended to stifle originality and initiative and the creative power of the individual, to put in their place submission, respect for the authority of the teacher and slavery to ancient models. This was, moreover, in its values and in its processes, the dominant education of Portugal and practically all over Europe, where it was beginning to be shaken by the assault of new ideas. Colonial Brazil, educated by the Jesuits, was one of the zones in this vast geographic extension of this type of education. Outside of this, there was no movement for different values. The ideals of man, which are transformed with changes in social and economic structure, remained the same in colonial society, rude and slave holding, which had no means and felt no necessity for a broader and more diversified type of education directed toward other careers. But in this dark atmosphere in which the Seminary of Olinda, founded in 1798, was to lead to a brusque and transitory movement toward the modern spirit, marking the watershed between Jesuit pedagogy and the new orientation of the molders of the statutes of Pombal in 1772, there appeared clear indications of the period which was to open in the nineteenth century and in which these two tendencies were to confront each other. Instead of a single system of teaching, the duality of schools, some lay, others confessional, all ruled, however, by the same principles. Instead of a purely literary, classical education, the development of scientific teaching which would begin slowly to make progress side by side with the literary education, which was preponderant in all the schools; instead of the exclusive teaching of Latin and Portuguese, a slow penetration of living languages and modern literatures (French and English); and finally, the ramification of tendencies which if they are not sufficient to lead to a break-down of unity of thought, do open the field to the first collisions between the old ideas embodied in Jesuit teaching and the new current of pedagogical thought, influenced by the ideals of the French encyclopedists, which were victorious after 1789 in the schools of the French Revolution.

BIBLIOGRAPHY

Azevedo, Lúcio de, *Os Jesuítas no Grão Pará: Suas missões e a colonização* (Lisbon, 1901).

Brandão, Mário, and M. Lopes d'Almeida, *A Universidade de Coimbra: Esboço de sua história* (Coimbra, 1937). Memorial published by order of the University on the fourth centenary of the definitive establishment of the University of Coimbra.

Cabral, Luiz Gonzaga, S.J., *Jesuítas no Brasil: Século XVI* (São Paulo, 1926).

Calógeras, J. Pandiá, *Os Jesuítas e o ensino* (Rio: Imprensa Nacional, 1912).

Calmon, Pedro, *História social do Brasil*, Vol. 1, *Espírito da sociedade colonial* (São Paulo: Comp. Editora Nacional, 2nd ed., 1937—Brasiliana, Vol. 40), Chap. VII, pp. 112–131.

Cardim, Fernão, S. J., *Tratados de terra e gente do Brasil,* with preface, introduction, and notes by Rodolfo Garcia, Batista Caetano, and Capistrano de Abreu (Rio, 1925). Containing the epistolary narrative of a Jesuit journey and mission from 1583 to 1590 and the two dissertations "Do clima e terra do Brasil" and "Do princípio e origem dos índios do Brasil e de seus costumes, etc."

Freyre, Gilberto, *Casa grande e senzala* (Rio: Maia & Schmidt, 1934). Transl. by Samuel Putnam as *The Masters and the Slaves* (New York, 1946).

———, *Sobrados e mocambos* (São Paulo: Comp. Editora Nacional, 1936—Brasiliana, Vol. 64).

Júlio Maria, Father, "A Religião: Ordens religiosas" (Chap. I, "No período colonial," II, pp. 5–63), in *Livro do Centenário* (Rio: Imprensa Nacional, 1900).

Leite, Father Serafim, S.J., *Páginas de história do Brasil* (São Paulo: Comp. Editora Nacional, 1937–Brasiliana, Vol. 93), Chap. II, pp. 35–62, "As Primeiras Escolas do Brasil."

———, *História da Companhia de Jesús no Brasil, século XVI* (Lisbon, 2 vols., 1938).

———, *Novas Cartas jesuíticas: De Nóbrega a Vieira* (São Paulo: Comp. Editora Nacional, 1940—Brasiliana, Vol. 194).

Madureira, J. M. de, S.J., *A Companhia de Jesús e o Brasil: 1549–1759 e 1841–1924* (Rio, 1924).

———, *A Liberdade dos índios: A Companhia de Jesús—A Sua Pedagogia e seus resultados* (Rio: Imprensa Nacional, 1927).

Mariz de Morais, José, *Nóbrega: O Primeiro Jesuíta do Brasil* (Rio: Imprensa Nacional, 1940). Separate reprinted from the *Revista do Instituto Histórico e Geográfico Brasileiro.*

Melo Morais, A. J., *História dos jesuítas e suas missões no América do Sul* (Rio, 2 vols., 1872).

Moreira de Azevedo, M. D., "A Instrução nos tempos coloniais," in *Revista do Instituto Histórico e Geográfico Brasileiro,* Vol. 55 (1892).

Pires, Father Heliodoro, "Azeredo Coutinho," in *Revista do Instituto Histórico,* pp. 783–810. 1st Congresso de História Nacional.

Pires de Almeida, J. R., *L'Instruction publique au Brésil: Histoire-Législation* (Rio: Leuzinger, 1889), pp. 1–146.

Rodrigues, Francisco, S. J., *A Formação intelectual do jesuíta: Leis e fatos* (Pôrto, 1917).

——, *História da Companhia de Jesús na assistência de Portugal,* Vol. 1 (Pôrto, 1931).

Santos Vilhena, Luiz dos, *Cartas soteropolitanas, ou Recapitulação de noticias soteropolitanas e brasílicas contidas em XX cartas,* annotated by Dr. Braz Amaral and published by Dr. J. J. Seabra (Bahia: Imprensa Oficial do Estado, 1922), especially "Carta oitava," pp. 281–302.

Serrano, Jônatas, "Anchieta educador," in *Jornal de Comércio,* Rio, Sept. 29, 1940. Lecture given in the Auditorium of the Brazilian Education Association.

Vasconcelos, Simão de, S.J., *Crônica da Companhia do Estado do Brasil e do que obraram seus filhos nesta parte do Novo Mundo, etc.* (Lisbon, 1663; 2nd ed., 2 vols., 1865).

Veríssimo de Matos, José, "A Instrução e a imprensa (1500–1900): A Instrução publica—I, Período colonial (1547–1822), IV," pp. 5–12 in *Livro do Centenário* (Rio: Imprensa Nacional, 1900).

Viana, Hélio, *Formação brasileira* (Rio: Olímpio, 1935), Chap. XV (a), "Síntese de uma história da educação no Brasil: Período colonial," pp. 223–230.

——, *A Educação do Brasil colonial* (Lisbon, 1938). Presented at first Congresso da Historia da Expansão Portuguesa no Mundo.

Vilhena de Morais, Eugênio, "Qual a influência dos jesuítas em nossas letras?" in *Revista do Instituto Histórico Brasileiro,* special vol. of the Congresso de História Nacional, Vol. 5 (1914), pp. 633–673.

CHAPTER TWO

THE ORIGINS OF SCHOLASTIC INSTITUTIONS

The revival of culture in Brazil—The influence of the ideas of the encyclopedists—Azeredo Coutinho and the Seminary of Olinda—The work of Dom João VI: the founder of institutions —The first schools for higher vocational training—The foundation of law courses in the first Empire—The Additional Act (1834) and decentralization—The absence of organized basic teaching and of general university teaching—The Colégio Pedro II—The patriarchal economy and the corresponding type of culture—Education for civilization based on slavery—Exaggerated tendency in the direction of the liberal careers—The predominance of a culture of professional character—Popular education and the first normal schools—Secondary education of a classical type—The almost exclusive cultivation of belles lettres—The splendor and decay of private secondary education—The great educators—The cooperation of the religious orders in secondary education—The activity of Dom Pedro II—The influence of the higher institutions of culture—The reforms of the Viscount of Rio Branco—The School of Mines in Ouro Preto—The opinion of Rui Barbosa in 1882—Tendencies of pedagogical thought—The last speech from the throne—A fruit which was not yet ripe . . .

BETWEEN THE EXPULSION of the Jesuits in 1759 and the removal of the Portuguese court to Brazil in 1808, there is a parenthesis of almost half a century, a long hiatus which is characterized by the lack of organization and decay of colonial education. No institutional organization, in fact, came to take the place of the powerful homogeneity of the Jesuit system, which had grown up all along the plantation owning coast, with branches in the wooded interior and on the plateau, and whose colleges and seminaries in the colony were the great centers for the spread of culture. In their places, we have seen, what arose under the pressure of circumstances were isolated classes in fragmentary and scattered subjects which hardly succeeded in taking on the appearance of systematic education in the rare, religious schools established in convents. But neither the mass departure of the Fathers of the Society of Jesus nor the reforms of Pombal with their belated effect upon the colony, succeeded in shaking the social and cultural unity which had been imparted by the religious idea and maintained by the same conception of life and culture and by the same social and economic regime. The type of teaching and education adopted by the Jesuits,—a system which was moreover useful for the ends of their principal consumer, the Church, and had formerly been organized by the Church—, appeared to satisfy entirely the elementary requirements of the society at that time with its agricultural and slave owning structure in which study, when it was not a mere luxury for the feudal and aristocratic group, was no more than a means of social classification for mestizos and the business bourgeoisie of the cities. Remaining almost entirely ecclesiastical, all of this traditional teaching which had been transferred from the hands of the Jesuits to those of the secular priests and to the Franciscan and Carmelite friars,—their natural continuers, as they were the most lettered part of colonial society—, did not catch in their meshes any more than the students who came in large part from the élite of rural and bourgeois society, and a few others recruited from the mass of mestizos who gravitated toward the towns and cities. The royal courses and the schools, still in an embryonic condition, which grew up in the convents, looked in the same direction, following the same methods and the same regime of discipline, under the influences of the Church and of agrarian feudalism; and transmitting what the collective soul still considered its most precious inheritance, they represented a sturdy instrument for unity and resistance to the course of events. The school then, although it did not enter into the framework of any system of education, continued like the family to live in its traditional form [1] and was for a long time still to maintain its prestige side by side with other forms of education, also showing European tendencies, which were slowly being worked out under foreign influence. It was under the pressure of these influences,—which did not reach us only by way of Portugal—, that there began in the early years of the nineteenth century a revival of culture in Brazil with from time to time a reflection in scholastic institutions. The importation of new liberal and democratic ideas which were already stirring the cultural atmosphere in the last days of the eighteenth century and were to have so marked an influence upon the play of political forces, took place then by means of books which succeeded in penetrating the colonial environment, and above all by young men who came from Edinburgh, Paris, Montpellier or had just left the University of Coimbra, now reformed by Pombal, and which they still preferred for law studies. But other factors, more efficacious than these individual and isolated courses, detaching themselves from the intellectual aristocracy, were to contribute later to the propagation of the new foreign ideas and to the establishment of the first contacts in the field of pol-

---

[1] "Education (in the family) was limited," writes Capistrano de Abreu, "to extinguishing the vivacity and spontaneity of the pupils. Boys and girls went about the house naked until the age of five years; during the five following years they wore only a shirt. But if they went to church or on a visit, they dressed with all the formality of grown-ups, with only a difference in the dimensions. Few of them learned to read." (Capistrano de Abreu, *Capítulos da história colonial*, pp. 209-210). In the schools of the priests and in the seminaries, they wore their cassocks, even when on the street, walked sad and silent in Indian file. The students, orphans, of the seminary of São Joaquim, in Rio de Janeiro, wore a white cassock: hence the nickname of "sheep" that the people gave them, and with which they liked to annoy them in the streets. As late as 1868, in his journey to the plateau of Minas, Captain Richard Burton, visiting Congonhas do Campo and its school founded by Father Leandro de Castro, a Portuguese Lazarist, observed the same custom, kept up in the famous college of Caraça and in other schools of the priests, in the time of the Empire: "the students, about sixty or seventy in number," he writes, "all wear the cassock." (*Viagens aos planaltos do Brasil*. Translation. 1st vol. Do Rio de Janeiro a Morro Velho. São Paulo, 1941, p. 280). In other schools, instead of the cassock, the boys wore a black topcoat, and exhibited in their appearance as well as in their manners the air of "precocious men." The uniformity of dress, although it was somber and aristocratic, contributed to a democratic leveling of whites and mulattos; the latter were now admitted without distinction to the seminaries and schools. Mestizos and Negroes "who appear to have been barred from the first Jesuit schools," from the seventeenth century began to enter, and in the nineteenth century in greater numbers flocked both to the royal courses and to lay or religious schools. Gilberto Freyre cites, reproducing it in its entirety, the Royal Letter of November 20, 1686 in which the King, astonished to find that the schools of the priests excluded or did not care to admit mulattos, lays down the rule that they shall be obliged not to exclude them, "these children of ours, because of their color, for schools of science must be common to all kinds of persons, without exception." (Cf. *Casa grande e senzala*, Rio, 1933, pp. 441-442).

itics between tradition and the new current which was to find in imported doctrines an ideological basis for independence and the organization of the nation.

These ideas, with their markedly revolutionary coloring and taken up especially in their social and political aspects, had already spread to Portugal under the successive influences of the reform of Pombal (1772) and the French Revolution of 1789 and especially, of the French Invasion of 1807 which, by breaking up the traditional forms, had opened a pathway for their propagation. In Brazil, the theories of the encyclopedists, stimulated by the recent example of the independence of the United States (1776), had exercised an influence upon the conspiracy of Minas of 1789, which aimed at the emancipation of the country under a government, republican in form, and of which there formed a part, among others, Alvares Maciel of Vila Rica who had arrived in 1788 from England, educated in natural and philosophical sciences, and Domingos Vidal Barbosa, who arrived in the same year from France, where he had taken a medical course and been one of the Brazilian students, who in Montpellier in 1785, were already dreaming of our freedom. The poet Silva Alvarenga, one of the conspirators, who had studied at Coimbra, at the full height of the agitation about the reform of Pombal, had published in Lisbon a satire on methods of teaching adopted in universities before the reform of Pombal. Returning to Brazil, the poet of Vila Rica, who had brought from the new university environment an interest in modern literatures and a taste for physical and natural sciences, founded in Rio de Janeiro a Scientific Society which, transformed in 1786 into a literary society, but still with scientific objects, was ordered closed by the Count of Resende under some pretext or for political motives. But only with the introduction of the Masonic lodges which, transplanted from Portugal in the nineteenth century, became the most important center of propaganda of the new tendencies dominating Europe and especially France, was it that the theory of the encyclopedists took form and gained in extension, just as they were inspiring the ideology of the French Revolution. The friars, however, as Pedro Calmon writes, "did not lose their faith in the direction of society with the enlightenment of the coast centers. They acquired greater importance because they spread universal enlightenment. Their virtues were weak, but in literature they were more influential. In the interest of combatting French philosophy, they studied it and many helped to spread it. They became tolerant and protectors of foreigners . . . Ideas crept in and insinuated themselves, thanks to the secret society, whose most useful members belonged to the Brazilian clergy." [2] And, concluding in his attempt to strike a balance with regard to the collaboration of the priests in political movements and in the inspiration of the new liberal and democratic tendencies, Pedro Calmon reminds us that "the Inconfidência of Minas had been a conspiracy of priests and poets; the revolution in Pernambuco in 1817 was a movement of churchmen and free masons. The agitation for independence found them in the vanguard. The revolution of 1824 was also made by them." But, if the theories of the encyclopedists came to constitute in Brazil the ideology of these political movements or contributed at least to give them the tonality of the time, they did not develop sufficiently to break down the unity of culture or to color very strongly the educational system with their tendencies, the culminating expression of which, in the field of schools, was the

[2] Pedro Calmon, *História social do Brasil*, 1st vol. São Paulo, 1937, pp. 283-284.

Seminary of Olinda created in 1798 and founded in 1800 by the Bishop Azeredo Coutinho. From the cultural point of view, absorbing much foreign material, the literati and the clergy became more European, although remaining faithful to the universalistic and literary tradition of colonial culture, which was sufficiently deeply rooted to resist the new influences. From the pedagogical point of view, these tendencies, with which there had barely begun a movement of subterranean agitation, were not much more than three significant, isolated facts: the structure of the seminary of Azeredo Coutinho,[3] which no other took as a model; the project for the organization of teaching of Garção Stockler, "directly and narrowly inspired by the encyclopedist ideas of which Pombal himself had already been a follower, and most closely resembling the project we owe to Condorcet," as Mílton Rodrigues has pointed out; and finally, the large part assigned in the early organization of the Colégio Pedro II

---

[3] Azeredo Coutinho (José Joaquim da Cunha de), son of a sugar magnate, was born in 1742 in the district of Campos de Goitacazes, now the city of Campos, in the State of Rio de Janeiro. He had his early education and his training in Latin, grammar, rhetoric and philosophy in Rio de Janeiro, to which city his family removed; and, having lost his father, in 1768, he, as the first born, came into the inheritance. In 1775, at thirty-three, and master of a sugar mill, he left for Portugal, to take work in the School of Canon Law of the University of Coimbra, shortly before reformed by the Marquês de Pombal. Dom Francisco de Lemos (de Faria Pereira Coutinho), his relative, was still rector of the University; Lemos had been appointed to this post in 1770 and to that of rector and reformer of the University in 1772; with his older brother, Azeredo Coutinho (Dr. João Pereira Ramos),—a leading collaborator in the reform of Pombal—, he was one of those who worked most actively in drawing up the new statutes. Azeredo Coutinho studied for five years in the School of Canon Law in the University restored by the Marquis de Pombal, continuing as a priest his favorite philosophical and scientific studies. Among the Brazilians who, at this time, underwent the new influence of the University, some of whom came to be outstanding in the sciences, such as Lacerda e Almeida, Rodrigues Ferreira, and José Bonifácio, he was the only one imbued with the new ideas who carried on direct pedagogical and cultural activity, with the creation of the Seminary of Olinda, where the new spirit and methods implanted by the reform of Pombal were later to appear, under the leadership of his relatives, the brothers Dom Francisco Lemos and J. P. Azeredo Coutinho. In fact, after having held various posts in Lisbon, among them, that of deputy of the Holy Office (1784–1794), he left in 1798 for Brazil, with the appointment of Bishop of Pernambuco; there he founded the famous seminary. He was fifty-six when he returned to his own country, after a long absence (1775–1798), and with a great reputation for learning and prudence, earned not only in the difficult post he occupied, but by his works published in Lisbon,—the *Memória sôbre o preço do açúcar*, which won him an invitation to be a member of the Royal Academy of Sciences, and his *Ensaio econômico sôbre o comércio de Portugal e suas colonias*. On February 22, 1800, the Seminary of Olinda was opened, in accordance with statutes prepared, while he was still in Portugal, by Azeredo Coutinho, and published in Lisbon in 1798, before his departure for Pernambuco. The new seminary created by Bishop Azeredo Coutinho was located in the old building of the Jesuit college, given in 1796, with the church and its belongings, to the cathedral of Pernambuco, "for a seminary to educate youth." (Decree of March 22, 1796, of Dr. Maria I). Bishop and interim governor of Pernambuco, President of the Committee of the Royal Treasury and Director General of Studies, the learned prelate, who was, together with the Viscount of Cairú, one of the founders of commercial and economic studies in the Kingdom and the Colony, rendered in a brief period (1799–1802) the highest services to Brazil; from Brazil, with his appointment to the diocese of Bragança and Miranda, he retired in 1802 to Portugal. Bishop of Elvas, from 1802 to 1818, and named, in the latter year, by Dom João VI, General Inquisitor of the Realm, Azeredo Coutinho died in Lisbon in 1821, scarcely having taken his seat in the Constituent Assembly, to which he had been elected deputy by the province of Rio de Janeiro.

(1837–1838) to scientific teaching, without detracting from the preponderance of the classical literary education.

It was in fact in the seminary of Pernambuco, created in the city of Olinda by Azeredo Coutinho, that there was the strongest manifestation in spirit and in methods of the principles which guided the reforms of Pombal, in great part based upon the ideas of the encyclopedists. This seminary was the first belated reflection in the colony of the great educational revival which took place in Portugal on the initiative of the minister of Dom José and with the leading collaboration of relatives of Azeredo Coutinho. A Brazilian born in Campos of an illustrious family of Paraíba do Sul, the founder of the seminary of Olinda, who had just arrived from Portugal appointed Bishop of Pernambuco, was "a spiritual son of the University of Coimbra, reformed under the auspices of his relative, the Bishop and Count Dom Francisco de Lemos." [4] A kind of college which was no longer the Jesuit type with its excessively rhetorical, religious and literary teaching, as Gilberto Freyre observed, the seminary of Olinda, almost immediately considered to be "the best school for secondary education in Brazil," in the opinion of Oliveira Lima, and compared by Tollenare [5] to a French lycee in the provinces, represents in its methods a "break with the Jesuit tradition of colonial education." The new pedagogical tendencies were expressed not only in the liberal environment which was created in it, in the gentler and more humane methods, in the greater respect for the personality of the child, in the profound transformation of the relation of adults to children, of teachers to students, but also in the importance given in the program of studies to the teaching of mathematics, the physical and natural sciences. Side by side with the subjects which constituted the traditional curriculum,—grammar, Latin, rhetoric, poetry, philosophy (but now according to new points of view) and theology—, there figured Greek, French, history, chronology, geometry, physics, natural history, and drawing, which were taught not only to those who wanted to take the course in humanities, but also to those who were destined for holy orders. According to Oliveira Lima, the learned bishop "aimed at forming in the seminary which he had founded with a certain abundance of teaching of the natural sciences—chairs of physics, chemistry, mineralogy, botany and drawing—generations of parish-priests and explorers, who at the same time, would undertake the cure of souls and would open up the vegetable and mineral wealth of their parishes, being able to understand the discoveries which they made and to derive profit from them." [6] In a general way, since it was not organized only for those who were meant for the priestly life, the seminary of Olinda, as Gilberto Freyre writes, "began to teach the useful sciences which would render the boy more able to meet the necessities of the Brazilian environment, whose transition from an agrarian patriarchalism to a more urban and more industrial type of life required leaders, well trained experts, and not only Negro and mulatto mechanics and artisans . . ." but also "the study of economic problems created by the mining industry, by industrialization, by the decline of an economy based simply upon the single crop system or monopoly." [7] The generation

[4] Muniz Tavares, *História da revolução de 1817.* Notes by Oliveira Lima. Recife, 1917, p. 36.

[5] Tollenare, *Notas domincais.* Trans. by Alfredo de Carvalho. In "Revista" of the Historical, Archaeological and Geographic Institute of Pernambuco, p. 477.

[6] Oliveira Lima, *Pernambuco e seu desenvolvimento histórico.* Leipzig, 1895, p. 320.

[7] Gilberto Freyre, *Sobrados e mucambos.* São Paulo, 1937, p. 105.

educated in the seminary of Olinda, which became the center of irradiation of liberal ideas, was the shock brigade of the new European order in Brazil and exercised such an influence upon the preparation and direction of the revolution of Pernambuco in 1817, that this may be considered socially connected in its roots with that institution, owing to the diffusion of liberal ideals. "Without Azeredo Coutinho," writes Capistrano de Abreu, "the idealistic generation of 1817 would not have arisen." Brazilian independence, according to Oliveira Lima, was still more directly served in its early stages by the institution founded in Pernambuco. To appreciate the work of intellectual revival undertaken by the illustrious prelate and interrupted later by the consequence of his retirement in 1802 to Portugal,—as it seemed, persecuted by the Court, which was systematically hostile to all attempts at progress in the colony—, it would be sufficient to remember that it was not limited to the foundation of the seminary, without doubt his most important creation. It was he who began wih the Retreat of Our Lady of the Gloria, founded in Recife, with the same spirit, the first college for girls from the big houses and city mansions.

But the scholastic landscape, without color and relief, in which the seminary of Olinda took on "an appearance that was almost scandalous for the times," according to Gilberto Freyre, was not changed to any noticeable degree in Rio de Janeiro or in Bahia, until the arrival of the Prince Regent, Dom João. Upon receiving the news of the invasion of Portugal by the troops of Bonaparte, Dom João de Bragança embarked hastily for Brazil, "in the remains of a fleet," convoyed by British ships. On January 22, 1808, upon his arrival at the city of Bahia, he decreed on the suggestion of José da Silva Lisboa, Viscount of Cairú, the opening of the ports of Brazil to foreign commerce, establishing this freedom in the Royal Letter of January 28 of the same year; he annulled in Rio de Janeiro, with that of the 1st of April, the decree of January 5, 1785, which had ordered the closing of all the factories; and besides these two decrees, "equivalent to the effect of two liberal revolutions," as Euclides da Cunha writes, he annulled also the decree of July 6, 1747 by founding the Royal Press [8] in which

[8] The Royal Printing Office, in which the present National Printing Office has its origin, was created by decree of May 13, 1808, and began to operate in 1809, at no. 41, Passeio Street, with a press made of wood and built for the Printing Office in Rio de Janeiro. The decree of Dom João VI marks "the introduction of a permanent printing office in Brazil." Before the creation of the Royal Printing Office, we know of only one printing establishment,—the first to be set up in the country, founded in 1747, in Rio de Janeiro, with the consent of Gomes Freire de Andrade, Count of Robadelea, and soon afterwards suppressed by order of the Portuguese government. The great engraver João Caetano Rivara and two others, Romão Elói Casado and Paulo dos Santos Ferreira, whom brother José Mariano da Conceição Veloso brought with him on his return from Portugal, in 1808, and who started work in the Royal Printing Office, are considered the first to introduce the graphic arts into Brazil. It was also in the Royal Printing Office,—the only one in Rio de Janeiro until 1821,—that the first newspaper that was published in Brazil was printed; this was the *Gazeta do Rio de Janeiro*, which lasted from 1808 to 1822: a kind of official newspaper which appeared twice a week. The second newspaper and the first daily that Rio de Janeiro had, the *Diário do Rio de Janeiro* (1821), began to appear at the Royal Printing Office, then called the Royal Typography, which was the cradle of Brazilian journalism. From the date of the founding of the Royal Printing Office down to 1822, there came from its presses 1,154 various printed works, among them some remarkable publications such as the *Marília de Dirceu*, of Tomaz Antônio Gonzaga, works of José da Silva Lisboa, later Viscount of Cairú, the first Brazilian edition of *Uruguai*, by Basílio da Gama (1811), the *História do Brasil*, by Southey, botanical works by Manuel de Arruda Câmara, and the *Dicionário da Língua Portuguesa* (facsimile edition of the

the first work published in Brazil was printed, and began the history of Brazilian journalism with the publication of *Gazeta do Rio de Janeiro* in 1808. With the coming of Dom João VI and about fifteen thousand persons who arrived with the royal family, the old city—"a great village of 45,000 souls," which sleeping in its weakness, awoke to a new life, shaken by the unexpected events and suddenly raised to the category of capital of the Portuguese Empire. The colonial city with its narrow, tortuous streets was transformed with the splendor of the Court and the movement of its commerce and, through the attraction of the new charms of city life, it became the center of the intellectual life of the country to which Brazilians converged from almost all of the provinces. The change in mentality and customs which went on slowly spread out through the new capital of the monarchy to distant cities, Vila Rica, Bahia, Recife, which following the example of Rio de Janeiro and, seized by a spirit of emulation, also commenced to change not only their appearance as cities but also their old colonial habits. The distance which separated them from the country, almost nil in the seventeenth century and beginning to be marked in the eighteenth, became constantly greater with the progress of cities and with urban freedom, to be followed timidly by small local cities. But of all the cities, it was the ancient capital of the colony which benefitted most by the movement of the Portuguese Court. By the degree which the intensity of urban life attained at the heart of the monarchy, we may measure social mobility,—the greatest which was ever recorded by the rhythmic variation of colonial society, oscillating between periods of stagnation and periods of movement—, and with which there developed the migration of people and of customs which was not only from one class to another, but also from one region to another.[9] In a country where, outside of the convents, there had practically been no collections of books, and those rare and small, there arose the first public library, created by Dom João VI in 1810 with his own books which he got rid of and which were installed and opened to the public in 1814 in the Hospital of the Third Order of Carmel. It was in this library, made up initially of the 60,000 volumes belonging to the Royal Library of the Palace of Ajuda and brought by Dom João VI, that our National Library has its origin, the library which today is one of the most important if not the most important of this part of the American continent. The productions of Brazilian literature which Martius had sought in vain in the rare bookshops of his time, began to circulate, published by

---

2nd), by Antônio Morais Silva (1822). Reorganized by a decree of February 17, 1815, with the name of Royal Typographic Workshop, it came to be called the National Printing Office in September, 1921, by virtue of the decree of the Portuguese congress in which it was laid down that all the property of the Crown belonged to the Nation and was to be called national property. With the rise of political journalism, from the time of the proclamation of Independence on, and the development of the printing industry (in 1860 Rio de Janeiro already had more than thirty printing shops), the role of the National Printing Office in the spread of culture became less important in comparison with its great importance during the last phase of the colonial period (1808–1822). The institution created by Dom João VI came to concern itself almost entirely with official publications (reports, annals, archives, legislation), the chief of which from 1862 on was the *Diário Oficial* of the Empire, and later of the Republic, created on October 1 of that year. In the building on May 13th Street, erected especially for it, and to which it moved in July, 1877, the National Printing Office remained with all its sections and shops until July, 1938, when its demolition was begun.

[9] Oliveira Lima, *Dom João VI no Brasil*, 2 vols. Rio, 1909.

the Royal Press, from whose printing shops from 1808 to 1822 there issued 1,154 printed works, among which are notable the lyric poems of Tomaz Antônio Gonzaga, the poem of Basílio da Gama, the works of the Viscount of Cairú and the dictionary of Morais. The flat surface of colonial culture which had barely begun to take on its monotonous beach, a fringe of literary spray, was for the first time roughened and took form with the spread of foreign works which now entering the ports of the country freely, with the actions and reactions of opposing principles and under the influence of the new ideas which found in Masonry one of their principal centers of irradiation. But it was not only with these movements and their first results that the city of Rio de Janeiro, now with its press, its newspaper, its library and museum, became the center of the intellectual life of the country. The higher schools, of which the great creator of institutions laid the foundation, remain at the base of the progress and transformation of national culture.

The work of Dom João VI, which was dictated rather by immediate necessity, than suggested by any model, recalls in certain ways the educational work of the French Revolution. The technical schools, both old and new, in France, had shown a marked growth in proportion as the influence of universities declined, and the ideology of the French Revolution taught everywhere an anti-university prejudice. All knowledge that was not utilitarian or included the entire personality of the individual, was suspect to it. "For medieval man," writes Stephen d'Irsay, "what was important was rather the acquisition of a solid *Weltanschauung*, of a view of the wholeness of the world; he did not have that adoration of facts that modern man has," an admiration which began to develop in modern times with English empiricism and under the influence of the encyclopedists. What was important, however, at the height of the European revolution, furthered by the development of the sciences and the decline of the prestige of the old universities, was the acquisition of a certain special technique, of a certain limited science, of a profession. It is not possible to say with precision to what point these tendencies in the direction of the professionalization of higher learning, favoring special schools and hostile to the university, may have influenced the orientation of Dom João VI or his advisers who, creating schools, aimed above all at specialized training and the preparation of a staff capable of serving the public. Upon the ruins of the old colonial system, Dom João VI limited himself to creating special schools, erected with the object of satisfying as quickly as possible and as inexpensively as possible this or that necessity of the environment to which the Portuguese Court had moved. It was necessary, before anything else, to provide for the military defense of the colony, and to train for this end officers and engineers, both civil and military. Two schools came to meet this fundamental necessity, when there were created the Naval Academy in 1808 and the Royal Military Academy in 1810, both with eight year courses.[10] Doctors and surgeons were necessary for the army

[10] The Naval Academy (1808) and the Royal Military Academy (1810), founded by Dom João VI, were united in 1832 into a single institution of military, naval, and civil engineering, with the following courses: a) mathematics, four years; b) military, two years; c) bridges and roads, two years; and d) naval architecture, two years. It was from this institution, that by a gradual process of dismemberment, there were split off, in 1833, 1858, and 1874 to form autonomous schools of higher grade, three great schools: the Military School, the Naval School, and the Engineering School of Rio de Janeiro. In 1833, the regulation of 1832 was revoked, and the Naval

and navy. There were created at this time, in 1808, in Bahia, a course in surgery which was installed in the Military Hospital and, in Rio de Janeiro, courses in anatomy and surgery to which were added, in 1809, courses in medicine and which, amplified in 1813, constituted together with those of Bahia or the model of the Rio courses, the beginnings of medical teaching in Brazil. Men trained and expert in economics, agriculture and industry were no less necessary. There were founded in Bahia the chair of economics in 1808, the course in agriculture in 1812, that of chemistry (including industrial chemistry, geology and mineralogy) in 1817, and of technical drawing in 1818, and in Rio de Janeiro the chemical laboratory (1812) and the agricultural course (1814), which were meant to supply the absolute lack of technicians who would meet the necessities of the Brazilian environment, which was in the period of transition toward a more urban and industrial type of life and a better organization of the agriculutral economy of the country. The Royal School of Sciences, Arts and Crafts, created on August 12, 1816 and transformed in October of 1820 into the Royal Academy of Painting, Sculpture and Civil Architecture, showed in a sketch of its early plan (1816) which, however, was never carried into execution, the same concern with technology. Named, however, the Academy of Arts by another decree—of November 23, 1820, it only began to function under this new and final orientation in 1826 in the first Empire, and ten years after the arrival of the mission of French artists in Rio de Janeiro. If we make an exception, then, of some chairs which were instituted to supply the gaps in traditional education and aiming at disinterested studies like that of higher mathematics in Pernambuco (1809), that of drawing and history in Vila Rica (1817), and that of rhetoric and philosophy in Paracatú in Minas Gerais (1821), almost all of the educational work of Dom João VI, motivated by his concern for practical and immediate utility, can be said to have been the complete rupture with the scholastic and literary program of the literary period. Circumscribed in space, limited practically entirely to Bahia and Rio de Janeiro, the field which it

---

Academy was separated from the Military Academy which was left with two courses (a three year military course and a six year course for engineering officers), down to 1839, when it took the name of Military School, with a new organization. In the reform through which the Military School passed in 1842, its two year course in infantry and cavalry was extended to three years, and that of artillery, military engineering and General Staff (which since 1839 had been a five year course), was split into two: that of artillery, in six years, and that of engineering, seven years. In 1855 the Applied School of the Army was created, consisting of the fifth and sixth years of the Military School, which separated from the Military School to form the school of Application. By the law of 1858, the School of Application took the name of Military and Applied School, and the Military School became the Central School, with two courses: a) that of mathematics and physical and natural sciences, in four years, and common in whole or in part to all the students looking forward to civil engineering or any of the military courses; and b) that of civil engineering, with two years (the first three of the other course being prerequisites). The Military School was left by the 1858 reform with three courses: a) the infantry course, in two years (or one year of the Central School followed by a year of the Military School); b) artillery and General Staff, in five years (the first three years of the Central School, plus two of the Military School); and c) military engineering, in six years (the first four of the Central School, plus two of the Military School.) The complete separation between the two schools took place only in 1874, when the Central School took the name Polytechnic School, with a new structure and the following courses, three general and three specialized: a) the general two year course; b) physical and natural sciences, three years; c) physical and mathematical sciences, three years; d) civil engineering, two years; e) mines, three years; and f) arts and manufactures, two years.

illuminated was certainly very limited, leaving outside of its influence all the remainder of the colony which continued sunk in the same backwardness. It represented, however, not only one of the most important phases of our cultural evolution, but the most fruitful period in which the seeds of numerous Brazilian institutions of culture and education were planted.

After Independence was proclaimed and the Empire of Brazil was founded in 1822, the victory of the liberals over the conservatives and the debates which went on in the Constituent Assembly of 1823 announced a new orientation for educational policy, under the influence of the ideals of the French Revolution, with which the liberals were imbued, and through the development of the national spirit which obliged people to face the great problems of the country from a new point of view. Ideas, as usually happens, in crises of political change, took another direction and for the first time the concern for popular education,—as the basis for the system of universal suffrage, came to occupy the minds of the cultural élite made up of priests, bachelors of law and literati. But out of this political movement in favor of popular education, which was manifested in the debates and in the petitions presented to the Constituent Assembly dissolved in 1823, there came nothing but the law of October 20, 1823, which abolished the privileges of the State to give instruction, laying down the principle of liberty of teaching without restriction, Article 179, No. XXXII of the Constitution given by the Crown on December 11, 1823, which guarantees "free primary schooling for all citizens," and finally the law of October 15, 1827,—the only one which was promulgated in more than a century on the subject for the whole country and which ordered the creation of primary schools in all cities, towns and places (Article I) and in Article XI, "grade schools in the cities and towns which were the most populous." The results of this law, however, never corresponded to the intent of the legislator, for it failed on account of various causes, economic, technical and political. The government proved incapable of organizing popular education in the country. Few were the schools which it created, especially those for girls, which did not amount to more than twenty in the whole land in 1832, according to the testimony of Lino Coutinho; and in the illusory hope of solving the problem by the spread of the Lancaster method of teaching by the students, which practically dispensed with the professor, fifteen years passed (1823–1838) before all illusions were lost . . .[11]

[11] The introduction of the Lancaster method of mutual teaching and the hopes which it aroused constitute one of the most curious and significant episodes illustrating the habit we have of accepting over-simple and elementary solutions for extremely complex problems. According to this method which was in vogue for more than twenty years, each group of students (decúria) was directed by one of the number (decurião), who acted as teacher of the group, and who was the least ignorant, or if you like the most skillful. By this method of having the teacher explain to the boys and the latter, divided into groups, teach each other, one teacher would be enough for a school with a great many pupils. In a primary school of five hundred pupils, for example, instead of twelve teachers, needed for twelve classes, each with forty pupils, more or less, one would not need more than one teacher, who would hand over to the fifty best pupils the teaching of the rest, divided into decúrias . . . "A lot, and fast, and cheap: an ideal system for Brazil," Afrânio Peixoto ironically remarks. So the imperial government endeavored to spread such a system, for years on end, until the most complete disappointment was reached, as was to have been expected; the surprising thing is that it took so long. The law of October 15, 1827, refers in three sections to the schools for mutual teaching; in article 4, in which it is stated that schools in the capitals of provinces and in cities, towns and populated places shall be schools for mutual teaching; no. 5, in

With regard to higher education, the debates in the Constituent Assembly seemed to mark a regression in the policy of Dom João VI. Instead of projects on the subject of special schools, there arose motions and proposals on university education and, among them, that of Fernandes Pinheiro, Viscount of São Leopoldo, who in the session of June 14 proposed that "there should be created immediately at least one university, for the seat of which it would seem that the city of São Paulo should be preferred on account of its natural advantages and reasons of general convenience." The project of the Constitution presented in the session of September 1, 1823, and signed by José Bonifácio, Antônio Carlos, Araújo Lima and others, adopted a measure calling in Article 250 for the creation of "primary schools in every township, secondary schools in every county, and universities in the most appropriate centers." The idea of unity and of the universality of teaching which appeared to prevail over that of special training, did not however succeed in leading to the slightest change in the form of policy, whose spirit of continuity was not broken for more than a century. During this century, higher learning remained almost entirely dominated by the professional and utilitarian spirit. No real effort was made to create a university; no institution of general culture and training appeared. To the schools of professional training instituted by Dom João VI, the first Empire added the two courses of juridical and social sciences, which, created by the law of August 11, 1827, were located, that of the city of São Paulo on March 1, in the Convent of São Francisco and that of Olinda on May 15, 1828, in the Monastery of São Bento. With the two faculties of law which were founded, one in the north and the other in the south and whose role was so important in the life of the country, the picture of schools destined for the preparation of the liberal professions was completed. Made up at the beginning, in the first half of the nineteenth century, of the two schools of medicine, into which in 1832 the Academies of Medicine and Surgery in Bahia and Rio were transformed, and of the Royal Military Academy, from which in 1833 the Naval School was separated and which took the name of Military School in 1839; and of those two new institutions,—a vigorous graft on the branch of higher professional training—, this group of schools, in which a whole élite of doctors, engineers and bachelors of law was prepared, was for a long time the most important center of professional and intellectual life in the nation.

But in 1834 the educational and cultural system, in process of formation from the time of Dom João VI and which was slowly being reorganized from the top downwards, was hit in its development by an act of the imperial policy which attacked its very basis and was to paralyze all later efforts at unification. Among the consequences of the movement which forced Pedro I to abdicate (April 7, 1831), one of the most important was, as Azevedo Amaral observes, "the impetus acquired by regional tendencies which were on the other side of the balance from the spirit of national unity

---

which measures are taken for their installation, and the professors "who do not have the necessary training in this system are told to go and learn it quickly and out of their own salaries in the schools of the capitals;" and no. 15, in which it is laid down that "punishments shall be those used in the Lancaster method." The system was set up as the "official method," imposed upon all the primary schools of the Empire. In 1833, the first serious doubts began to appear, and in 1838 a man of the eminence of Bernardo Pereira de Vasconcelos was still trying to find excuses for the failure of the Lancaster method in the time allotted and the imperfections of drill; the method was finally almost completely abandoned.

which the Constitution of 1824 attempted to consolidate. The ascendancy of the liberal current of thought, which characterized the whole period of the Regency, contributed powerfully to weaken the bonds of national cohesion. These centrifugal tendencies had their culminating legal expression in the so-called Additional Act of 1834, which was one of the major aberrations in the evolution of the imperial policy." [12] From the educational point of view, the Additional Act, approved August 6, 1834, and which resulted from the victory of the decentralizing tendencies dominating at the time, suppressed by one blow all possibilities of establishing the organic unity of the system then being formed, which on the best of hypotheses (that of the provinces being able to create them), would break up into a plurality of regional systems, functioning side by side,— and all necessarily incomplete—, with the school organization of the Union in the capital of the Empire and the national institutions of higher learning at various points in the territory. In fact, by No. 2 of Article 10 of the Additional Act with which important reforms were introduced into the Constitution of 1824, the task of regulating primary and secondary education was transferred to provincial assemblies, while higher education throughout the country and the school organization of the Neutral Township remained dependent on national control. The government of the Union, which as the coordinating center and the leader in the political life of the country, should have undertaken this task, was thus, according to the words of Tavares Bastos, exonerated from "the principal one of the public duties of a democracy," which is that of carrying general and common education to all the points of the territory and organizing it on a uniform and nationwide basis. If we consider that in the school system, primary education has the object of establishing this community of ideals and sentiments,—indispensable to the political unity of the nation and therefore to developing national feeling, and that the unity of secondary education, destined to enrich this common background of civilization and morality, is so much the more precious and useful as individuals entering later upon different careers tend to become differentiated by their special occupations, it will be easy to understand how important it was for the life of the nation that the Union gave up the task of organizing primary and secondary education throughout the country. The spiritual unity of a nation, if it does not only depend, as Liberato Barroso judged, on this unity and homogeneity of general and common education, has doubtless a powerful unifying agent in the primary schools, uniform, equal for all throughout the national territory. The decentralization of the fundamental education begun by the Additional Act and maintained throughout the period of the Republic as far as primary education is concerned, attacking one of the essential points of the structure of education, did not permit for a whole century the building on a solid, wide basis of common education, of a superstructure of higher education, either general or professional, nor did it permit the reduction of the intellectual distance between the lower social strata and the elite of the country. Public education was condemned not to have an organization, its links being broken and its central, directive force paralyzed, that center from which an educational policy should be spread to the school institutions of various grades and which should have coordinated in its system the civilizing forces and institutions scattered throughout the

[12] Azevedo Amaral, *Evolução da política imperial.* In "Cultura política," a monthly journal of Brazilian studies. Ano. I, no. II, April, 1941, pp. 45–46.

national territory. Neither were the provinces, under whose supervision there remained only primary and secondary education, able to complete their systems and raise them to the level of higher education, nor was the Imperial government able to raise upon a solid basis of elementary and middle education a national system of education. The very Constitution, reformed in 1834, consequently established the break down of education and the duality of systems; the federal and the provincial, both of them necessarily mutilated and incomplete; one without the necessary base, the other without the natural crown of a higher professional or disinterested education. The professionalization of higher education, begun by Dom João VI, and the fragmentation of education, instituted by the Additional Act, were to mark so profoundly for more than a century the characteristic physiognomy of our institutionalized education that all attempts to alter the course of its evolution would necessarily fail.

Certainly the absence in the education of the country of a common thought, of unity of guidance, was not more than one of the expressions of a fluctuating, molecular state of society, resulting from the fragmentary character of our social development and from the fundamental divergence of interest and ideals linked with differences in culture and economic level of the provinces and of the social classes. It was this state of social disorganization which placed obstacles in the way of political unification and hindered the educational consolidation of a system of public education which, if not uniform and centralized, would be at least subordinated to common principles. But the reform of 1834, instead of establishing measures tending to solve the problem, aggravated it, making its solution impossible within the framework of our Constitution. From then on, there was no chance for an educational policy of wide scope. Education was to drag on through the whole of the nineteenth century, disorganized, anarchical, constantly broken up. Between primary and secondary education, there were no bridges or connections. They were two worlds, each of which looked in its own direction. The primary schools, like the institutions of secondary grade, were in general anchored in routine. There was no connection not only in the vertical sense between the different levels of the hierarchy, but also in the horizontal sense between scholastic units on the same level functioning side by side. The faculties of higher education, at times located side by side in the same city (Bahia and Rio de Janeiro), were, as it were, invited to isolate themselves and to be completely ignorant, one of the other. We cannot infer, however, from the fact of there being no organization, that there was no basic general education and even some disinterested higher education. There certainly was. What did not exist (and on this point all testimony is unanimous) was a general plan of organization. One of the consequences of the movement imparted to higher professional education and to the regime of decentralization begun by the Additional Act, was the extraordinary development of private secondary education in almost all of the provinces, and especially in the capital cities. The Caraça college, founded in 1820 by Lazarist Fathers,—a typically traditional college organized on the model of Jesuit education, had a lively career, becoming one of the most important institutions of secondary education.[13] The Jesuits who in 1842 returned to Brazil,

[13] The school which took the name of the Serra do Caraça, in Minas Gerais, was founded in 1820 and officially opened in 1821, with fourteen students of Latin grammar, by Portuguese fathers of the Mission Congregation of St. Vincent de Paul. The Lazarist Fathers who came to Brazil, on

eighty-three years after their expulsion, in 1845 founded the first college in Destêrro (Santa Catarina), a college which acquired great fame but only lasted a short time (1845–1853), like the seminary and college of Pernambuco (1867–1873), created in the same year in which the great College of São Luiz was opened (1867–1917), in Itú in the State of São Paulo. On all sides, classes and secondary schools arose, some of them important as in the interior of Liceu Paraibano in 1842 and the Colégio Brandão in Cajazeiras (1866) in Paraíba, or in the principal cities like the Ginásio Bahiano of Abílio César Borges, the founder, later on, of secondary schools in Rio de Janeiro and Barbacena and the Meneses Vieira College in Rio de Janeiro. The idea of a university, which according to many should have preceded the Proclamation of Inde-

---

the request of Dom João VI, were legally given possession of the lands and inheritance of the famous Irmão Lourenço (1714–1819),—that "mysterious man," to use the expression of Saint Hilaire—, a Távora, who, according to the legend, fleeing from the persecution of the Marquês de Pombal, took refuge in the mountains of Caraça, founded the House of Our Lady the Mother of Men, and inhabited those solitary regions for almost half a century. The learned naturalist A. de Saint Hilaire, who was a guest of the pious hermit in 1816, when he was travelling through the province of Minas Gerais, describes in one of his books of travel, the marvellous scene which was the background of the old house of Caraça, situated on the slope of a hill, at an altitude of 1300 meters above sea level, and surrounded by a great chain of mountains. In the same year in which Irmão Lourenço died, in 1819, the Fathers of the Mission Congregation embarked in Portugal; they intended to go to Mato Grosso, and they had barely arrived in Brazil when they settled in Caraça on the house and lands which were given them by Dom João VI, and there they founded the famous college. From 1820 to 1835 the number of students reached a total of 1535; at this time they taught reading and writing, Latin, French, geometry, philosophy and music, and the Fathers of Caraça became famous throughout the province, and it was not long (1827) until they were called upon to found other important institutions in Congonhas and Campo Belo. With the removal in 1842 of their property, slaves, books and the school to Campo Belo, Caraça remained entirely abandoned until 1854, although it had been the cradle and central house of the Congregation and the center to which students came from all points of the Empire. In 1854, however, the Greater Seminary of Mariana was established in Caraça; it was to stay there for about forty years, and the ancient and celebrated college was reopened. One of the most brilliant periods, if not the golden one of the history of this educational establishment, was that of the direction of Father Jules José Clavelin (1867–1885), a French Lazarist, a man of great learning and virtue and one of the most cultivated of the missionaries of the province of the Congregation of the Mission in Brazil. In 1882, Pedro II and the Empress, who had left the Court to visit the province of Minas Gerais, arrived at the little city of Caete and from there reached Caraça, where they visited the classes of the seminary and the chief ones of the college. Side by side with the old college, which reached its peak under the direction of Father Júlio Clavelin and entered upon decay at the end of the past century, there grew up, contiguous with the House of Missions, an Apostolic School which in 1907 was just beginning to revive and which today has spread over the whole establishment: instead of the old college, which disappeared in 1912, after ninety one years of existence, there now flourish the Apostolic School and the Seminary, for the preparation of priests and Lazarist missionaries. Through this institution of secondary education,—one of the most important of the Empire and the most famous center of humanistic studies, in Minas Gerais, there had passed up to 1907 more than five thousand pupils, many of whom attained the highest positions in the church, in the magistracy, and in the political life of the country. (Father F.S., *Caraça. Apontamentos históricos e notas biográficas.* In "Revista" of the Public Archives of Minas, ano XII, 1907, Official Printing Office of Minas Gerais, Belo Horizonte, 1908; *O centenário de Caraça*, 1820–1920. By a Father of the Mission Congregation. Besnard Frères, rua Buenas Aires, 130, Rio de Janeiro, 1920).

pendence and the foundation of the Empire, but which Primitivo Moacir correctly denies arose in the time of Dom João VI,[14] did not go beyond debates in the Constituent Assembly with regard to the proposal presented in the Assembly by J. F. Fernandes Pinheiro, and beyond that Article 250 of the project of the Constitution of 1827 which, upon the dissolution of the Assembly did not secure approval. In 1843 and in 1870, this idea was to arise again to meet the same fate in the proposed law (1843) submitted to the examination of the Council of State and with which there was founded in the capital of the Empire a university with five faculties, and in the proposal formulated by the counsellor José Paulino Soares de Sousa, who proposed the creation of a university with four faculties, of theology, of law, of medicine and of natural and mathematical sciences. The only institution of general culture created from the time of Independence down to the Republic was the Colégio Pedro II, founded in 1837,— an excellent establishment of secondary education in which the students, having finished their seven year course, received the degree and diploma of bachelor of letters, after swearing an oath before the minister of the Empire, who put on their heads the white cap of the faculty of letters (Article 7 of the decree of December 20, 1943). The degree of bachelor in physical and mathematical sciences and later also in physical and natural sciences was given in the old Military School, in the Central School (1858) which was derived from it, and in the Polytechnical School into which the Central School was transformed in 1874 and in the organization of which, general courses without immediate application in the physical, mathematical and natural sciences were maintained.

In spite of the solemnity which the decree of December 20, 1843 gave to the ceremony of the granting of the degree of bachelor of letters, establishing the swearing upon the Gospel, the putting on of the white cap, and the signing of the parchment by a minister of the Empire, the College of Pedro II was far from being equal to a faculty of letters or a higher institution for disinterested studies. It was, from its origin, a great school of humanities,—the most important created by the government of the Empire, and in the field of literary studies, the only institution for culture and general training, although on a secondary level, as were also the only ones that existed in the country in the field of scientific studies without any idea of application, namely the courses in physical, mathematical and natural sciences introduced into the organization of the School of Military and Civil Engineering (Escola Militar, Escola Central and Escola Politécnica) of Rio de Janeiro. Only one official school, the Colégio Pedro II, represents literary, disinterested studies, always through all the changes which it passed through keeping its character of basic culture necessary to the governing elite

[14] According to a common opinion, repeated in books, parliamentary speeches and even in accounts of the reasons back of the laws passed during the Republic, the first idea of creating a university in Brazil belongs to Dom João VI, who is said to have thought of founding a university in Rio de Janeiro and entrusting its direction to José Bonifácio de Andrada e Silva, who, in 1819, had just returned from Europe and who came to have a decisive influence on the movement for National Independence. Of this university planned by Dom João VI and which seems to be no more than a legend, there is not, however, as Primitivo Moacir affirms, "the slightest trace in legislation, not the shadow of a governmental act." (Primitivo Moacir, *A universidade de Dom João VI*. Articles I and II. In "O Estado de São Paulo. December 1939 to January 1, 1940.)

of the country.[15] The variety of its chairs, which as enumerated in Article 3 of the decree of December 2, 1837, embraced practically the whole circuit of letters and sciences, revealed at the beginning along with the tendency to universalistic and encyclopedic teaching, a large concession to scientific studies. In fact, in the plan established in the statutes, approved by decree No. 8 of January 31, 1838, the part which was reserved to mathematics (arithmetic, algebra, geometry and general mathematics), taught in the six years of the course; and to physical sciences, the study of which was to be carried on in the last three years, and to geography and natural history, showed if not a victory of scientific studies over literary studies, at least a healthy effort to make them equal, breaking with the tradition of an exclusively literary and rhetorical education. But the predominance of literary education based on the classics, already notable in the original plan, was singularly marked in the plan of studies presented by the rector Joaquim Caetano da Silva and approved by Antônio Carlos in the new regula-

[15] The Colégio Pedro II, the origin of which goes back to the Orphans' Seminary of São Pedro, created by the provision of June 8, 1739, of Bishop Antônio de Guadalupe, and later called by the name of São Joaquim upon being moved to its new building, was founded in 1837, by a decree issued by Bernardo Pereira de Vasconcelos, interim regent. The Seminary of São Joaquim which, already converted into a house for artisans, had passed to the hands of the Municipal Chamber of the Court, was at this time in complete decay. The decree of 1837,—dated December 2, the birth day of the young Emperor—, changed it radically, transforming it into an institution of secondary education, with the name of the Colégio Pedro II. In this school,—article 3 of the decree above mentioned—, "there shall be taught the Latin, Greek, French and English languages, rhetoric and the principles of geography, history, philosophy, zoology, mineralogy, botany, chemistry, physics, algebra, geometry, and astronomy." Decree no. 8, of January 31, 1838, approved the studies ordered and set up a system of studies and made other rulings with regard to administration, discipline, and teaching. According to these statutes, the pupil who had completed the course received the degree of bachelor of letters, which exempted him from examinations to enter the academies. On February 5, 1838, its first rector was appointed; this was Brother Antônio de Arrabida, who on March 25, before the Emperor, who was still a minor, and in the presence of the Regent Araújo Lima and the cabinet, received from the hands of Minister Bernardo de Vasconcelos the rules of the school. Among its first professors, appointed on April 29, there figure Justiniano José da Rocha, Joaquim Caetano da Silva, Manuel Araújo Pôrto Alegre and Gonçalves de Magalhães. In 1840 the chair of German was created,—the first of that language in our country; it was held by the Baron of Planitz. Soon after, in 1841, the statutes of the school were changed for the first time; according to the new rules, the plan of studies was modified and the complete course was made a seven year one, with Latin in all seven years, and Greek in the last four. Of all the decrees which introduced changes in it, generally changes of minor importance (decrees of 1849, 1851, 1862, 1870, 1874, 1881, 1882, 1888), none during the Empire period so profoundly affected its structure and privileges as the two decrees of 1878 and 1879, submitted by Minister Leôncio de Carvalho; the latter of these was responsible for his retirement from the ministry. The decree no. 6,884, of April 20, 1878, which rearranged the curriculum and opened the day school as a free school, took away the compulsory character of religious instruction, permitting non-Catholic students to receive the degree of bachelor without taking religious intruction. By the decree no. 7,247, of April 19, 1879, the prerogatives which the Colégio Pedro II enjoyed were under certain conditions extended to establishments of secondary education which followed the same curriculum. The famous school still remains in the same building of the Seminary of São Joaquim in which it was installed and which, rebuilt, with new architectural lines, by Bethencourt da Silva (1877), was completely transformed in 1913–1914, although still not adapted to the needs of modern teaching. (Cf. Eugênio de Barros Raja Gabaglia, *O Colégio Pedro II*. Rio de Janeiro, 1914; Escragnolle Dória, *Memória histórica*, comemorativa do 1° Centenário do Colégio Pedro II. Ministry of Education, Rio de Janeiro, 1937).

tion (February 1, 1841), with which the statutes of the College were altered. In the four first years of the course, which came to be seven years, in addition to ancient and modern languages (Latin, Greek, French, English and German) nothing was taught except drawing, geography and music; the study of general and Brazilian grammar only figured in the first year; mathematics and physical sciences, chemistry and natural sciences were piled up in the last three, while Greek was taught in four years and Latin, French and English extended through seven years, Latin showing a larger number of hours than that of any other subject. This program of studies gave final form in the Colégio Pedro II to a secondary education of a classic type, with a predominance of literary studies and adapted less to the special conditions of the environment, than to the moral and intellectual traditions of the country. The teaching of the mother tongue reduced to one year of general and Brazilian grammar (first year) and to two of rhetoric and poetics, was not enough to give a national coloring to this strongly Europeanizing tendency; and the scientific studies piled up in the last part of the course, confusedly with those of classic and modern languages, could with difficulty pass the limits of mere "information," and bookish learning. The obsession with higher professional studies as a means of rendering individuals useful to the society of the time or raising them to the rank of the governing class and the utilitarian spirit which was developed, partly under the pressure of immediate necessities, partly on account of the predominance of professional culture, were necessarily to hinder the progress of scientific studies, already impeded to a certain extent by the character of the general basic teaching, so decidedly literary and rhetorical both in the Colégio Pedro II and in private secondary institutions. Although they were certainly capable of conceiving programs of studies based upon the conditions of the Brazilian environment which was then in process of transformation, the statesmen of the Empire, imbued with juridical formulas and full of the ideals of European culture, set up an institution of secondary education of the first order, but aristocratic and one which tended to separate the child from his environment, to separate man from useful technical and economic functions, and to have a powerful influence, along with the colleges and seminaries, as an instrument of social selection and of class formation.

This education of an aristocratic type, destined rather for the preparation of an élite than for the education of the people, was developed under the Empire, following without noticeable deviation the lines of its evolution, strongly marked by the intellectual traditions of the country, by the regime of patriarchal economy, and by the corresponding ideal of the man and citizen. The type of culture which it proposed to serve is not explained only by the colonial tradition, fundamentally European, which in a certain way led up to it, but is closely bound up with the forms and framework of the social structure which persisted throughout the Empire. In fact, with the change of the political state from colony to nation, and with the foundation in 1822 of the Constitutional monarchy, no modification in the structure of society took place, for it continued as in the colony to be organized on an agricultural, patriarchal economy with a slave base from the sugar mills of the north to the coffee plantations of the south, which were, by the middle of the nineteenth century, fully developed. In this regime of education at home and school, a regime calculated to create an anti-democratic culture of privileged classes and social distance between adults and children, rigor of authority, absence of collaboration on the part of women, the great difference

in the education of the two sexes and the almost absolute domination of purely intellectual activities over those basically manual and mechanical, showed to what an
extent a civilization based on slavery influenced the evolution of our education. The
boy, treated on the whole either "like a demon once he was past the phase of being
considered an angel, which was up to five or six" (in the words of Gilberto Freyre),
when he did not wear a gown in the schools, put on a black coat, or "with all the severity
of grown-up people except only in dimensions," would take his vengeance when he
was a big boy, in the absence of discipline of the higher school, on the regime of
authority in which fathers and teachers had asphyxiated his natural childish vivacity . . . It is this sad and bleak aspect with which boys and girls appeared, all with
the airs of adults, and it is this precocious, external maturity in clothes and manners
which led a foreign traveler to call Brazil at this time "a country without children." As
for the woman, generally treated with superiority by man who was almost a lord in
relation to his own wife (and she frequently called him so), cloistered in the big
houses, and suffocated in her personality, she devoted herself to household tasks, the
care of her children, in general having no more than a domestic education, surrounded
by slaves for all services, and occupied by her home, her piano and her needle "she
was content with the mediocre life which was reserved for her, not seeking to enlarge
her horizon nor improve her condition." [16] The slavery which cast dishonor upon
work in its rude forms, ennobled leisure and stimulated parasitism, contributed to
emphasize among us the repulsion for manual and mechanical activities and to make
us consider arts and crafts as vile occupations. According to the common opinion "to
work, to submit oneself to any rule was the occupation of slaves." In this society, with
its economy based upon the plantation and slavery, and which had therefore no interest
in popular education, it was to the secondary and higher schools that the boys of the
town flocked if they had any opportunity to study. Public activities, administrative
and political, which achieved a notable place on account of the life of the court and
the parliamentary regime, and the titles given by the Emperor, contributed still more
to give an exaggerated value to the man of letters, to the bachelor of laws and the
doctor, and the government along with the liberal professions became the principal
consumer of the intellectual élite who were formed in the higher schools of the
country. This contrast between the almost total absence of popular education and the
development of a training for the élite, was necessarily to establish, as it did, an
enormous lack of equality between the culture of the governed class with its extremely
low level and that of the governing class, rising above a great mass of the illiterate,—
"the human nebula separated out from the mass of the colonists"—, a little élite in
which there figured men of a very refined culture and which, as Max Leclerc observed
in 1890, would not be out of place among the elite of the most cultivated European
societies.

If one of the most valuable documents for the study of the evolution of a society
and the character of a civilization is to be found in its school legislation, in its plans
and programs of study and in the ensemble of its educational institutions, the analysis
of this material and of these institutions reveals to us precisely the continuity of the
social and economic structure and the development of the colonial type of culture

---

[16] Max Leclerc, *Lettres du Brésil.* Chapter XI. L'esprit public. L'état social les moeurs et les institutions. Pp. 203–236. Plon, Paris, 1890.

which was the product of a civilization founded upon slavery. Primary schooling, entrusted to the provinces and reduced almost entirely to the teaching of reading, writing and arithmetic, with no structure and without educational character, did not catch in its meshes more than a tenth part of the population of school age and showed itself to be badly directed not only with regard to the real necessities of the people, but also with regard to the interests of unity and cohesion in the nation. In 1867 Liberato Barroso, basing his opinion upon official data,[17] estimated at about 107,500 (or more exactly 107,483) total attendance at primary schools in all of the provinces out of a free population of 8,830,000. At this period of the Empire of about 1,200,000 individuals who were fit to receive instruction, only 120,000 or say a tenth of the population of school age, according to this estimate, were receiving such instruction, or about one individual for eighty inhabitants. Technical, agricultural and industrial teaching was no more than mere attempts and essays. The School of Arts and Crafts, privately motivated, founded by Bethencourt da Silva in 1856 in Rio de Janeiro, had not developed like a plant which grows in free air and in the sun, but like an artificial institution transplanted to a strange and hostile environment and barely comprehended by anyone. There was no other school of industrial education; there were two of commerce, the Instituto Comercial of Rio de Janeiro which had fifty-three students in 1864, and the commercial course at Pernambuco which had no more than twenty-five students in that same year; and only three of agriculture, one still in a stage of planning, which the Companhia União e Indústria was obliged to create in Rio de Janeiro in virtue of an agreement arrived at in 1864 with the imperial government, and two others with respectively twenty-four and fifteen pupils in 1864 in the Provinces of Pará and Maranhão. None of these schools or those which were afterwards created in the country prospered, and they ended by going out of existence for lack of resources, pupils and organization. The Imperial Instituto Fluminense de Agricultura and other similar institutes which were founded in Bahia, Pernambuco, Sergipe and Rio Grande, —associations created with the object of spreading, theoretically and practically, the best systems of agriculture and of exploitation of the land—, did not merely not succeed in accomplishing a useful and lasting work, but not even in rising from the swamp in which they were stagnating in apathetic and almost indifferent government. This picture, which is really discouraging, as Liberato Barroso defined it in 1864, showed in its neglect for popular and professional education the dominant literary and rhe- torical mentality as well as the slave-owning spirit, which was opposed or showed itself indifferent to every effort to direct general education in the direction of social and economic conditions or with more practical and utilitarian objects. The work of the land, like mechanical and industrial activity, seemed reserved to the ignorant and incapable and was hardly to be adjusted to that kind of nobility which passage through school conferred,—passage through secondary schools and the higher faculties destined to train for the liberal professions. The students who in Brazil, or for that matter everywhere, came from the elite of society—from the rural aristocracy or from that little bourgeoisie which was attempting to rise in the social sphere—, sought the classes and secondary schools and from there went to the professional schools and especially to the two law schools. This is what is revealed to us by the following significant contrast. For a little more than a hundred students scattered through small commercial

[17] J. Liberato Barroso, *A instrução pública no Brasil*. B. L. Garnier, Rio de Janeiro, 1867, p. 35.

and agricultural schools, the number of pupils that attended classes and public and private establishments of secondary education in that same year of 1864 attained about 8600 and there were enrolled in the, faculty of law of Recife, 396 boys, and in that of São Paulo 430, while during the period 1855–1864, according to official data, 8,036 pupils had been enrolled in the two law faculties of the Empire.[18] In this society governed by the material interests of an oligarchy of great rural proprietors, exploiters of slaves, and by the juridical idealism cultivated in the two law schools, continuing the traditions of Coimbra, there rose, superior to the social and economic structure,

[18] By the law of August 11, 1827, approved by Dom Pedro I and submitted by the Viscount of São Leopoldo (José Feliciano Fernandes Pinheiro) there were created two courses in juridical science and social science, one in the city of São Paulo, and the other in Olinda, the ancient seat of the Captaincy of Pernambuco. The two courses were started in 1828, the former in the Convent of São Francisco in São Paulo, and the second, that of Olinda, in the Monastery of São Bento. Authorized by the law no. 714, of September 19, 1853, to carry out the increase in expenditure necessary for the execution of the new Statutes handed down with the decree of March 30, 1853, and to make in these Statutes the changes he might deem expedient, Minister Pedreira do Couto Ferraz submitted decree no. 1,386, of April 28, 1854, which gave a new organization to the juridical courses. By dint of this decree, which gave them new statutes, the juridical courses changed their name to law schools. In this same year of 1854, the Faculty of Law of Olinda moved to Recife, by virtue of an express provision of the statutes handed down with the decree no. 1,134 of March 30, 1853, which was not put in force, and approved with changes by decree no. 1,386, authorized by legislative enactment no. 714, of 1853. It was this decree no. 1,386, of the government of the Marquis do Paraná (1853–1856) which was the most important administrative document referring to law courses since the time of their foundation. In 1879, the reform of Leôncio de Carvalho (decree no. 7,247, of April 19, 1879), which touched upon primary and secondary education in the district of the Court and upon higher education throughout the Empire, instituted the regime of liberty of teaching in Brazil. The chairs of legal medicine and history of Brazilian law created by decree no. 9,360, of January 17, 1885, which gave the law schools new statutes, did not come into force, and the very decree which created them was suspended, about eleven months later (decree 9,522 of November 28, 1885). Of all the reforms through which the law schools passed in the period of the Republic, from 1890 to 1930, the most important in its innovating character was certainly that of Benjamim Constant (decree no. 1,232 H, of January 2, 1891), which gave them a new structure, increasing the number of professorial chairs, creating the *Revista Académica* and setting up three special courses: of juridical sciences, of social sciences, and of training for notaries, abolished in 1895 by law no. 314, of October 30 of that year. Decree no. 8,650, of April 5, 1911, which approved the organic law of higher education and basic education in the Republic; and decree no. 11,530, of March 18, 1915, and no. 16,782 of January 13, 1925, which reorganized secondary and higher education, introduced new modifications in the law schools. "The evolution expressed in this legislative and administrative document," writes Clovis Bevilacqua, "can be represented graphically by an ascending line slightly off the horizontal, if we consider the progress of technique. There was a marked rise in 1854, and another in 1891. Some names are resplendent, like those of São Leopoldo, the instigator, Pedreira do Couto Ferraz (Bom Retiro), the organizer, and Benjamim Constant, the reformer. The other reforms, from this point of view, appear merely the keeping up of a movement imparted by the preceding reforms." In 1920 the Law School of Rio de Janeiro was added to the University of Rio de Janeiro, created by decree no. 14,343, of September 7, 1920, and organized, with the name of the University of Brazil, by law no. 452, of July 5, 1937. The old Law School of São Paulo, incorporated in the University of São Paulo, created January 25, 1934, was, in that year, transferred from the Union to the government of the State of São Paulo. There are now nineteen law schools in the country, of which seventeen are in the capitals and two in interior cities (that of Pelotas, in Rio Grande do Sul, and that of Campos, in the State of Rio de Janeiro).

the political structure directed by the men of law, and, instead of being reduced, the distance between the culture of the élite and the classes of the people grew greater, for the latter remained in relation to the former, like a "miserable reality of a poor man under a mantle of sequins" and precious stones . . .

So, then, with the exception of the mass of slaves and primitive peoples entirely neglected, within free society itself, in which there existed the most divergent stages in civilization, the governing class was excessively separated from the rest of the population of the country, not only from the point of view of its external aspects, the level and style of life and its essential interests, but above all of culture. A minority of literati and scholars and an enormous mass of illiterates. And if it is true that inequality of fortune (and of power), on the contrary from what the economists affirm, is more endurable than that of culture, this great inequality could not be without effect upon the evolution of culture and upon that of politics in the Empire. For in North America, in relation to culture, the population is more homogeneous, and the governing class is nearer the governed,—which explains in part the benign character of the class struggle and the greater solidity of democratic institutions in that country—, in Brazil cultural inequality between the elite and the rest of the population was extremely marked. This lack of equality, which is a normal effect of an agrarian, slave-holding civilization, was notably increased by the development in the growing school system, of schools destined to train for the liberal professions without a parallel development in education of the people. What lay at the base of their progress was not only, however, the necessity of providing for the revival of the personnel of the various intellectual professions (lawyers, doctors, engineers) and the public activities of the State. Nor could this movement be explained,—this exaggerated movement in the direction of the liberal careers—, by reasons of a more general character which were related to the characteristics of the society of that time and to the progress of the bourgeoisie and the modifications which were going on in their internal structure. The new social class which was developing with the growth of urban centers became in fact ever more open to the studies, which in the beginning interested it little and which came to exercise so great an attraction on the younger generation. Among the causes of this tendency is certainly the selective role which the higher professional schools were called upon to play, adding to their specific function of transmitting a certain part of the cultural heritage from one generation to another, that of being agencies of selection or distribution. The secondary school, preparing for the higher institutions, and the latter, training bachelors and doctors of law, had as their mission not to maintain the individual in the habitual occupations of his environment, but that of raising him in social dignity, giving him a title or including him among the intellectual professions, opening to him access to journalism and to letters, to administrative posts and political activity. These were possibilities which were open not only to the whites but also to the mestizos, who having risen in the period of the colony by means of art, letters and ecclesiastical functions, now found a new ladder for social ascension in the higher schools, where they entered in great numbers with the object of attaining the so-called liberal professions. The importance of these schools as channels of vertical social mobility is evident if we look at the growing percentage of youth that went to them from the time of their establishment, and of which a part dedicated themselves exclusively to their careers, and part rose from their professions to secondary and higher teaching, politics and to the higher ranks of the administration of the country, which recruited their best elements from the liberal professions. In the professional hierarchy, these professions occupied the highest step and above all the most sought out were the professions for which training was given in the law faculties. In fact in 1864, which we may take as an example, there were registered in the two law faculties 826 students, for 294 in the two medical schools; [19] 154 (of whom 15 were soldiers) in the Central School and 109 in the Military School, not counting the Naval School, data for which with regard to this year were impossible to find, but which in 1866 had a matriculation of 94 students. In the decade 1855–1864, in contrast with 8,036 students registered in the two courses of law, the number of students in the medical schools was 2,682 (excluding the 533

[19] The Medical Schools of Rio de Janeiro and Bahia originated in the courses of surgery created in 1808 by Dom João VI and enlarged into courses of medicine and surgery in 1813 and 1815, when the courses of Bahia were modelled on those of Rio de Janeiro. In 1832, by a decree of the Regency, of October 3, of that year, the two medico-chirurgical academies were reorganized and transformed into medical schools. Taking advantage of the legislative authorization contained in decree no. 714, of September 19, 1853, Minister Luiz Pedreira do Couto Ferraz submitted decree no. 1,386, of April 28, 1854, with which he gave a new organization to the two medical schools of the Empire. The statutes of 1854, with which teaching was deprived of its freedom and the schools of their autonomy, as Fernando de Magalhães observes, were inferior to the law of October 3, 1832, "notable for its foresight and liberalism." The initiative of the government of the Marquês de Paraná (1853–1856), born of an anti-liberal spirit, authoritarian, represents, however, from the technical point of view, the first important change in these schools. In relation to medical teaching, the reform instituted by Leôncio de Carvalho (decree no. 7,247, of April 19, 1879), founded practical courses, extended general clinics and created special ones, introducing other important innovations, which like the former ones, remained unexecuted. The setting up of a system of freedom of teaching, in which class attendance was not compulsory, partly modified by decree no. 8,918 of March 31, 1883, was not long in producing effects on the teaching in medical schools as well as in other institutions of higher learning in the Empire. Decree no. 8,024, of March 12, 1881, establishing measures to develop practical teaching, increasing the number of professorial chairs and creating new clinics, gave encouragement to medical instruction, which developed in a far-reaching manner in the following year, with the changes included in the Reform of Leôncio de Carvalho, which the decree of October 30, 1882, ordered carried out in the totality of the plan and its provisions. But, of all the reforms undertaken since 1854, the greatest, in its material and technical results, was that of October 25, 1884; led up to be a long campaign, in which eminent professors took part, among them, Sabóia, director of the Medical School of Rio de Janeiro (1881–1889), and showing the influence of the notable petition sent in 1880 by the Bahia Medical School to the Chamber of Deputies, the reform laid down in the decree of 1884, which gave new statutes to the medical schools, marks an ascending curve and begins a new epoch in the evolution of medical teaching in the country. After the reform movement which was expressed in decree no. 1,270, of January 10, 1891,—the first republican reform of the medical schools in accordance with the statutes of Benjamim Constant—, new alterations were introduced in the organization of medical teaching by the organic law of 1911, by the law of Carlos Maximiliano (decree no. 11,530, of March 18, 1915) and by decree no. 16,782 A, of January 13, 1925, which had as its principal supporter Professor Rocha Vaz, rector of the University of Rio de Janeiro and president of the Higher Council of Education. In the reorganization of the University of Rio de Janeiro by the law of Francisco Campos (1931) the medical schools of Brazil were once more reorganized, with the double object of "instructing the doctor in the knowledge that is indispensable to his noble profession, and of stimulating original scientific research, in all fields of applied biology." In 1940, beside twelve schools of pharmacy and odontology, there were eleven schools of medicine, two of which, that of São Paulo,—the best equipped of all, with its monumental Clinical Hospital, and that of Rio de Janeiro, formed part, respectively, of the Universities of São Paulo and Brazil.

278. Statue of the prophet Amos, carved in Brazilian stone by Antônio Francisco Lisboa, known as Aleijadinho (the little cripple), in the sanctuary of Congonhas do Campo, in Minas Gerais.
Photo by Stille, in collection of the College of Philosophy of São Paulo.

277. One of the prophets carved in sandstone by Aleijadinho for the chapel of Congonhas do Campo, in Minas Gerais.
Photo by Stille, in collection of the College of Philosophy of São Paulo.

279. "Father José Maurício at the Court of Dom João," painting by Henrique Bernardelli. Photo by *Vosylius*, in collection of the Census Bureau.

280. Central doorway of the Imperial Academy of Fine Arts. Planned by Grandjean de Montigny, architect of the French Mission.
Photo by Stille, in collection of the College of Philosophy of São Paulo.

281. Self-caricature, by Pedro Américo.
Photo by Carlos.

282. "Brazilian Woodcutter," painting by Almeida Júnior, the greatest Brazilian painter of the last century.
Photo by Rembrandt.

283. "Frontiersmen Stalking Game," oil painting by Almeida Júnior.
Photo by Rembrandt.

284. "Drawing of the Model," oil painting by Almeida Júnior.
Photo by Carlos.

285. "Sapucaia Trees in Their Glory," oil painting by J. Batista da Costa.
Photo by Rembrandt.

286. "The Return to the Corral," landscape by J. Batista da Costa.
Photo by Rembrandt.

287. "Still Life," oil painting by Pedro Alexandrino.
Photo by Rembrandt.

288. Carlos Gomes (born at Campinas, 1836, died at Belém do Pará, 1896), one of the great masters of melody of the nineteenth century, and one of the greatest artists Brazil has produced. Photo from the collection of the Companhia Melhoramentos of São Paulo.

289. Small model of the monument "The Flags," an outstanding work by the sculptor
Vítor Brecheret.

290. Detail from the monument "The Flags," by Vítor Brecheret.

291. "Coffee," oil painting by Cândido Portinari, one of the great Brazilian painters and the most vigorous of the moderns. Property of the Museum of Fine Arts of Rio de Janeiro.

292. "St. John," oil painting by Cândido Portinari.
Photo by Vosylius, property of Sr. Carlos Guinle.

293. "Composition," oil painting by Cândido Portinari.
Photo by Rembrandt, property of Sr. Mário de Andrade.

294. Heitor Villa-Lôbos (1890), the chief
ponent of modern music in Brazil; he base
work on folklore, and is one of the greatest
posers of the two Americas.

295. Gonzaga Duque Estrada, critic and art historian. Oil painting by Eliseu Visconte. Photo by
Carlos.

in pharmacy) and therefore only a third of the total matriculations of the two law schools. In 1876, the numbers were tending to become equal. In that year 78 students received the degree of bachelor of laws in the two schools of Recife and São Paulo, 102 that of doctor in the two medical schools and 58 the diploma of the engineer (civil 35, geographers 22, mining 1) in the Polytechnic School into which two years before the Central School of Rio de Janeiro had been transformed.

All the efforts and all the favor of the imperial power were naturally applied to develop higher education, not only because the Additional Act had removed to the provinces the center of primary and secondary education, but also because of the enormous importance which the schools of the liberal professions took on in the educational system. Numerous debates took place in Parliament over proposals and plans for reform, and the decrees that were approved on higher education and on the different types of these schools constitute an abundant source of information for the study of this chapter of the history of education of the country. Of all of the measures which under the imperial regime had to do with the legislation regulating higher education, there stand out for their significance of the far-reaching character of their innovations the decrees signed in the government of the Marquis do Paraná, by Minister Luiz Pedreira do Couto Ferraz, Baron of Bom Retiro (decrees no. 1,386 and 1,387, April 28, 1854), the reforms undertaken by the government of the Viscount of Rio Branco (1871–1875) and the celebrated decree 7,247 of April 19, 1879, with which Leôncio de Carvalho set up liberty of teaching and of class attendance and profoundly modified the plan of the official faculties. These reforms of a general character and others that were more specific, relating to each one of the great institutions, always revealed an effort in the direction of adapting them to the new necessities of the technique of these professions, and marked, above all in 1864, in 1874 and in 1884, notable progress in the evolution of higher education in the Empire. But all of this academic teaching to which there was added only that of fine arts was, as Max Leclerc justly observes, "façade that was too rich and heavy for the fragile and badly constructed edifice which was to support it. The student, insufficiently prepared, without a solid foundation, assimilated badly the science which the faculties poured out in front of him. He did not have for this reason any less pretension and the abundance of false doctors, of "bachelors" overflowed naturally from the crowded liberal professions into politics." [20] Nurseries of the aristocracies or at least establishments to which sons of rich families of the rural aristocracy and the bourgeoisie flocked by preference; nurseries of bachelors and doctors, of politicians and state functionaries, these schools contributed to popularize and spread in Brazil a taste for the rings symbolic of graduation from the professional school, and for honorifics, a taste which was as much alive as the love for titles and so widespread at the end of the Imperial period, that Max Leclerc was amazed in 1890 by the incalculable number of "distinguished" and "illustrious" persons in our country, which involved, therefore, "greater difficulties than elsewhere when an occasion for eulogy occurred, in finding a form of praise which had not already served a thousand times." This absence of a sense of measure and equilibrium and therefore of a true conception of the relative value of men and things, if on the one hand it is connected with the popularization and with the overuse of the title of bachelor and bachelor of law, be-

[20] Max Leclerc, *Lettres du Brésil.* Chapter XI. L'esprit public, l'état social, les moeurs et les institutions, p. 215. Plon, Paris, 1890.

cause of the grand percentage of individuals graduating, was on the other hand connected with the taste and habit of emphasis, cultivated in an education which was excessively rhetorical and with the lack of methods and standards of judgment. All our culture, for that matter, is marked in its most typical aspects by this purely literary and professional type of training under the influence of which, without the ballast of solid scientific and philosophical studies, a tendency toward brilliant generalizations was developed rather than one of fruitful specialization, a taste for rhetoric and bookish erudition, a superficiality barely concealed by verbal pomp, a one-sidedness of vision and a dilettantism which leads the individual to examine superficially all questions of doctrine without studying any of them deeply. The fact is that during the whole nineteenth century, at the root of this culture and at its source, there lay a system of education of the intellectual elite made up of a literary and rhetorical secondary education and a higher education that was exclusively professional and in which there were lacking those institutions destined to systematic, philosophic studies and scientific research, in which the critical and experimental spirit and a taste for observation and facts might be developed. This tendency to put quantity above quality, erudition above culture, the value of eloquence above the passion of ideas, the "more or less" instead of exactitude, if it did not have its origins in it, certainly was strengthened by the traditional type of teaching, utilitarian and informative, in which it was not so much a question of appreciation as of sheer accumulation, and in which the spirit of exactitude, profundity, penetration, critical and aesthetic maturity was (as it still is today) sacrificed to the acquisition of an encyclopedic learning. Thus, if we accept the substantial and solid literature of a Tavares Bastos, a Caetano da Silva, a Teixeira de Freitas, a Lafayette, a Joaquim Nabuco and a few others, in the most cultivated men of the time, in whom poverty of ideas is more apparent than real, the sumptuous form which they were accustomed on account of their education to give to their thought almost always reached such a point that it stifled that thought, just as a court mantle that is so rich and enriched by embroidery and gold can reduce in our eyes the most beautiful human figure to a mere insignificant detail. . . .

In an excellent essay on the evolution of imperial politics, Azevedo Amaral [21] attaches great importance, as a factor of political development, to the new social class made up of mestizos which had been in process of formation since the eighteenth century and which, becoming more and more numerous, acquired after the movement of April 7, 1831, "a growing influence in the play of political forces and in the determination of the course of the nation." Among the three elements of society,—the northeast group, aristocratic and feudal, the nucleus of Minas which was the society of a bourgeois, democratic type, and this city middle-class "made up of elements that were petit bourgeois in type," more consumers than producers, it is this last which exercised, in his opinion, the most persistent and harmful influence in the critical phases of the political evolution of the Empire. Product of a large scale miscegenation and composed of elements "that carried on in the cities the most varied professions, undergoing the effects of permanent economic instability," and which were characterized as much by fluctuations of character as by an extreme plasticity of temperament, it was destined in fact to play an important role in periods of crisis and transition. But

[21] Azevedo Amaral, *Evolução da política imperial*. In "Cultura Política," ano I, no. 2, April, 1941, Rio de Janeiro, pp. 21-53.

it was not only as a result of race mixture and economic instability that this class lived, "cut off from the deeper realities of economic life in Brazil" and ended by becoming a nursery for professional politicians and a center of demagogic activities. The higher schools, with their almost absolute domination in the system of education, and with the encyclopedic character of their teaching, contributed for their part to remove the individual from the habitual occupations of his environment, whether urban or rural, cutting him off from the economic realities of national life and drawing him through the door of the liberal professions, either to bureaucracy or to professional politics. Sought by all of those who desired or were able to acquire a higher culture which would be capable of indicating their social class or raising them in social level, they were not slow in transforming themselves into schools generating opposition, for there was a growing number of individuals, petite bourgeoisie and mesticos, who came to them looking for a ladder on which to rise in society, or by creating declasses—bachelors of law who gave up their professions, which were more and more saturated by the high rate of production in these schools. This is what, in part at least, Azevedo Amaral recognizes when he affirms that in the period of the regency "the intellectual level of a part of this class (the city middle-class) was relatively high and among its members not a few were noted for their abundant bookish learning, and not rarely were they included in the circles of the so-called liberal professions." Now, the schools destined for the training for these professions were all institutions tending to give to the student a theoretical education, to communicate to them the state of mind of diploma winners and to remove them from the atmosphere of their own environment, whether it was that of the rural aristocracy or of the merchant bourgeoisie of the cities. If we consider moreover that higher professional education did not take, unless it was with the creation of the School of Mines of Ouro Preto (1875), a special form more or less adapted to the conditions of the environment and that at the basis of this academic teaching one could not find a sufficient education of the mass nor specialized professional schools of various grades and adjusted to the different environments of agriculture, commerce or industry, it will be easy to understand that the higher schools of this type, erected on the sub-structure of literary education and dominating the whole system, could not contribute anything except to cut off the élite that they were training from the deeper realities of the economic life of the country, and to accentuate a whole mechanism of thought to which the rhetorical and bookish character of colonial education had accustomed us. Meanwhile, it is not possible nor just to underestimate the services, which were notable in certain respects, which the law schools, medical schools and engineering schools rendered, even though it was outside their specific functions of preparing professional men, of whom we had men of the first class in the liberal careers. They made a notable contribution to raising the intellectual level of Brazil and carrying everywhere an element of culture, urbanity and civilization; and besides functioning as true institutions of selection and social classification, they were factors of mobility in a horizontal sense and therefore of democratization, attracting from different social environments and bringing together in the same school society rich and poor, white and mestizos, and submitting them all to a common process of intellectual assimilation, which almost always led to a moral rapprochement of feelings and tendencies. Centers of cultural irradiation, of opposition and of political agitation, as a result of the interdependence of the political world and the academic world, these schools, situated at four points, in the North and South, in Recife and Bahia and Rio de Janeiro and São Paulo, played a worthy part, standing out as forgers of the national consciousness. To the two medical schools, the two law schools which were transformed into true *studia generalia,* and to the Central School, the Military School and the Naval School, there flocked Brazilians from all the provinces which thus came into contact with each other, and from them every year there were distributed over all the territory of the nation, not only lawyers, judges, doctors and engineers but also through letters, teaching, journalism and politics, those elements which spilled over from the professions or which were able to direct their activity in two or more directions at the same time.

Certainly, this élite, with its political and rhetorical mentality, imbued with general ideas, cut off by its very education from the realities of national life, and accustomed to examine concrete problems either from a single point of view, narrow because it was professional, or in their more general and theoretical aspects, was not prepared to solve the great technical and economic problems of the country. With these characteristics, so many times pointed out, this élite did not tend to march directly toward its object, the possession of which would by means of economic and pedagogical reforms insure a reform of education at its base and its progressive extension throughout the people. By their culture, fundamentally European, and the more abstract because it was less complex than that of western civilization, a culture with which they were saturated, they stood too far off from the masses to understand their necessities and from the essential local and specific problems of the country to confront them with decision. Their great merit was not that of uniting ideal to form, word to action, and to maintain each by the other. It seemed that the distance to be traversed from the word, which was always ready and exuberant, to the action which was slow and timid, appeared enormous; those who threw themselves into practical accomplishment remained generally halfway to their aim or took refuge anew in the verbal world, disappointed . . . This is what was already remarked upon at the beginning of the nineteenth century, by José Bonifácio when he said of the Brazilians that "they undertook everything and finished nothing;" and in 1865 by Louis Agassiz who found nothing to correct or to add in this respect to the sagacious observation of that eminent scientist and statesman: "No country," said this Swiss savant, "had more orators or better programs. Practice, however, is what is completely lacking." If in truth we took the trouble to trace on the one hand the history of ideas and planned pedagogical reforms, and on the other the history of educational institutions, we should see in the superiority of the former over the latter, the impressive contrast between the dreams of a mentality dominated by the charm of formulas and heated by political romanticism, and the incapacity to accomplish, which is obvious in the small size of the tasks undertaken and the lack of continuity in action.[22] But this mentality, which made the policy of

[22] The contrast between the little that was accomplished and the mass of decrees and planned legislation during the Empire is, indeed, striking. If we exclude sketches, proposals and plans of lesser importance, which were numerous, projects on public education presented to the Legislative Chambers during the first kingdom, the Regency and the second reign attain the number of forty. The decrees on secondary and higher education alone reach the number of thirty-two, including legislative decrees. In 1823 there were proposed to the Constituent Assembly not less than eight projects (June 4, 16, and 27; July 31; August 4, 5, 11, and 27), beside the memorial presented on June 16 by deputy Martim Francisco. In 1826 appeared the project of May 27, presented anew

the Empire hesitate between a Utopian idealism and a strict utilitarianism, is not the only nor even the principal mentality responsible for the backwardness in which popular education remained during almost the whole period of the Empire. This evil had deeper roots. What was lacking for a vigorous educational campaign on a high level and on a large scale was, above all, really favorable conditions in the environment which might lead to a change of mentality and to the progress of the culture of the country. The economic system which rested upon an exclusively agrarian foundation and a slave regime; the lack of a basic economic culture or a great source of wealth which might lead to a more rapid transformation from the agricultural phase to that of industrial exploitation; the consequent lack of an extensive network of communications which would permit a greater effect of cultures upon each other and a more intense activity on the part of the centers of intellectual development over the wide "zones of silence"—cultural zones "without resonance or vibration;" the loss of energy in personal competition and in party struggles which paralyzed governmental action in the moments of greatest domestic and foreign tension,—all this helped to neutralize the constructive efforts in this heterogeneous society broken up into social groups of the diverse economic levels, isolated and scattered at great distances from each other. It was not a society, a plastic mass, in which the government had to work, but an "aggregate" of many societies, some, those of the coast and of the plateau, under the more direct influences of western civilization, and others living for almost three centuries, so to speak, on their own substance, lost in the interior and walled up in an almost complete isolation. The Additional Act in which the decentralizing forces prevailed and which, handing over to the provinces the double charge of primary and

---

on June 16 with limitations made by Januário da Cunha Barbosa, José Cardoso Pereira de Melo and Antônio Ferreira França, and on July 5 by deputies Cunha Barbosa and Pereira de Melo. There followed in 1827 at short intervals, still in the period of the first Empire, the project presented on July 2 by deputy Feijó, and during the Regency, projects no. 82 and 179, in 1831; no. 122, in 1832; 66,104,108, and 135 in 1837; no. 37, in 1838; and no. 108, in 1839. In the second reign, this parliamentary literature is not less extensive; among the most important pieces of work on education, there are listed the projects A, F of the Senate, in 1843, on the creation of a university in the Court; nos. 35, 36 and 37, in 1846; 31 and 51, in 1847; 46, 64 and 93, in 1850; 74, in 1851; 5 and 6, in 1868; 183, in 1870; 290 and 463, in 1873; no. 92, in 1877; 158, in 1880; and on April 13, 1882, project no. 64, on secondary and higher education, presented by deputies Rui Barbosa, Uísses Viana and Bonfim Espinola, which, although it was the most important of all the bills, got nowhere in Parliament. Compare now the large number of bills with the movements and institutions created by the imperial government, in almost seventy years, and you will see in all its importance the contrast that is so striking between ideas and facts. To compare with this enormous mass of bills and decrees, in addition to other special ones, we have only seven new institutions in this long period: the two juridical courses, created in 1827, in the first reign; the Colegio Pedro II, in 1837, during the Regency; the Institute of the Blind, created in 1854, and that of Deaf Mutes, in 1856; the Imperial Observatory, of Rio de Janeiro, and the School of Mines, opened in 1877, in Ouro Preto. . . . The institutions which undertook the education of the blind and of deaf-mutes,—arising from the humanitarian spirit rather than aiming at the solution of serious problems, were no more than tentative, almost inoperative, in their limited sphere of action: the Institute for Blind Children, in 1874, had only thirty-five pupils (23 boys and 12 girls) out of a population of twelve thousand blind in the Empire, according to an official estimate; and the Institute of Deaf-Mutes, at the same time, had only seventeen pupils out of a population estimated at ten thousand deaf-mutes. Of the decrees of the imperial government, the major part were concerned with the organization and reform of the Colégio Pedro II, and of higher education in the Empire, looking toward the training of doctors, lawyers, and engineers, both civil and military.

secondary education, broke in two this system of education which was being formed, rose in 1834 to aggravate these difficulties like a permanent obstacle to any attempt at organization. The principle of autonomy of the provinces, the almost superstitious respect for juridical formulae, and the constitutional scruples, appeared more lively than the awareness of the national interest. Even those men,—a J. Liberato Barroso in 1867, a Tavares Bastos in 1870, a João Alfredo in 1874, among others, who perceived clearly that the Additional Act was one of the causes "of the anomalous and disorderly spectacle" which the education of the people presented—, did not have courage to suggest more than an action on the part of the central government in the form of cooperation or collaboration in some sectors and in favor of the less important provinces. Meanwhile, José Paulino de Sousa gàve his opinion in 1870 that, "the general assembly was not prevented from creating, maintaining and directing in the provinces, establish- ments of public education at the cost of the State," and with a bolder and more con- structive criticism, Minister Rodolfo Dantas in 1882 called for the need of "disseminating through the provinces, normal schools maintained in whole or in part by the national treasury, encouraging or carrying out in the same way, the founding of model primary schools, establishing gifts of public land for the sake of popular in- struction, and allotting to the development of general education, taxes appropriated in the national budget and distributed proportionately over all the country."

It is to this group of causes of different kinds, that there is related the sporadic character of the timid, fragmentary, inoperative measures that were taken rather by chance, without any general, over-all plan, and the extreme slowness of the develop- ment of popular education and technical teaching. Primary education, entrusted to the provinces, continued to be organized by a system of trial and error, in conformity with the limited resources of each one of them and with the influence of chance, depend- ing upon the domination of this or that partisan group, the personal inspiration of the president, in whom one can find the immediate cause of the periodic movement of variations in local policies of education. The teaching staff, almost all made up of im- provised teachers with no specific preparation, did not improve noticeably with the first normal schools which were created in the country, that of Niteroi in 1835, that of Bahia in 1836, that of Ceará in 1845, which were not to continue, that of São Paulo in 1846 and that of Rio de Janeiro in 1880, all with a rudimentary organization, mere attempts, like that of São Paulo which was founded with a single professor in 1846, disappeared in 1867, to rise again with a new plan and a two year course in 1874, to close anew in 1877 and finally to be reestablished in 1880, and only then with a more complete three year course.[23] In the Neutral Township, where the organization of

23 Primary education, which was under the control of the provinces, far from developing even in the most advanced of them, continued to move along with a slow and even irregular rhythm, marked by advances and retreats. What happened in the Province of São Paulo is a significant indication of this state of affairs. In 1836, there were only two teachers of reading and writing in the city, one for the parish of the Sé and the other for that of Santa Efigèna, Father Bento José Pereira and Carlos José da Silva Teles, both advocates of corporal punishment as a means of maintaining discipline. In a petition sent to the Municipal Council, they asked "permission to have certain physical punishments in their schools in order to improve teaching and to correct their pupils, since the pupils paid no attention to moral punishment, making fun of their teachers" (Nuto Sant'Ana, *O mestre-escola.* In "O Estado de São Paulo," November 21, 1926). In 1846, law no. 34, of March of that year, created the first normal school of São Paulo, meant only for

teaching on all grades fell on the lap of the central government, it was only in 1854, by decree no. 3,331-A which created the Central Council of Public Instruction, that more efficient measures were taken with the object of developing, raising and inspecting primary teaching, and only after 1870 that the first school buildings were constructed with the resources of a subscription made to erect a statue to Pedro II, and by the express will of the Emperor turned over "to the construction of a building appropriate for primary schooling." Thus in 1872, for a population estimated by the census at about 10,000,000 inhabitants, the general matriculation in the primary schools was not more than 150,000 pupils and the percentage of illiterates was calculated according to official data at 66.4 per cent. However, with all the slowness of this progress, the situation had been modified sufficiently even with regard to girls' schools (primary schools), which according to the testimony of Lino Coutinho had not exceeded twenty in the whole Empire in 1832, and already in 1852 reached 49, and in 1873, 174 in the province of São Paulo alone. Technical education, which was to furnish industry, commerce and agriculture with services indispensable to their prosperity, had not emerged from its embryonic forms. Neither industry which was rudimentary, almost non-existent, nor commerce, laid down according to empirical methods imposed by the Portuguese tradition, nor agriculture resting upon routine and slave labor was for the creation of these professional schools in which a personnel well qualified in all sectors and on all levels should be trained, and the progress of which is closely related to the transformation of technique and of economic structure and to the division and organization of labor. If the education of the people is deficient, badly oriented and if there exists no technical education, the prestige of secondary, literary education goes up, as it is a class of education and has a traditional value. It was not only the Colégio Pedro II—the most important official institution of the middle grade—, which developed, preserving through all the reforms the general lines of its organization, modified

---

males, and with a single teacher, Manuel José Chaves, professor of philosophy and morals in the course connected with the Law School; this school was carried on in a room of the Cabido, next to the Sé Cathedral, and was abolished in 1867, after training about forty teachers in almost twenty years (an average of two a year). Teachers for girls' schools came from the Educational Seminary, where orphans were recruited for teaching girls and "provided with the first chairs of reading and writing that fell vacant;" these were the orphans that upon reaching 18 failed to get married and were not employed as domestic servants (Regulation of January 7, 1845). By a law passed by the Assembly in 1868, a teacher was to be appointed by means of an examination before a committee, and in the presence of the President of the Province and the Inspector General of Education. Hence the name by which they were called: "palace professors." In the second half of the nineteenth century there was greater progress, especially from a quantitative point of view. In fact, from 1852 to 1873, in twenty years, the number of schools almost tripled, going up from 147 to 437, and the number of students enrolled in primary schools multiplied seven-fold (from 2,018 to 14,737). But, this movement which already put São Paulo in the vanguard of the provinces, in the matter of education, was not as rapid as the increase in free population, which, in 1852, was 333,000 and in 1873 had reached 825,000 inhabitants. The problem of training teachers moved slowly toward a solution, which came only with the change in political regime. In 1874, by law no. 9, of March 22 of that year, there was created in the capital of São Paulo a Normal School, with a two year course; it opened on February 16, 1875, with thirty-three students, in a room belonging to the extension course of the Law School. This too, for lack of appropriations for its installation and maintenance, was closed in 1878, to reopen, this time with a three year course, on August 2, 1880, by virtue of the educational reform passed by the Assembly on the suggestion of Laurindo Abelardo de Brito, then president of the Province.

in 1841 by Minister Antônio Carlos, in 1854 by Minister Couto Ferraz and, more profoundly in 1878, by Minister Leôncio de Carvalho. Although restricted to an insignificant part of the adolescent population and set up, above all, in the form of courses
preparing for higher institutions, secondary education took on considerable life, more
through private initiative than through the action of the imperial government and that
of the provinces. In 1832 the Seminary of Olinda—the admirable institution of Azeredo
Coutinho,—already a little falling off from its earlier prestige was transformed by the
legislative decree of August 7th of that year into a preparatory school of arts for the
law course, and whether through the strength of its example or through the growing
number of pupils that sought to enter, the great number of private schools which were
opened later were announced as separate preparatory courses for the law school. The
public classes in secondary education, separate and scattered, either came together in
colleges, as in 1836 in Ateneu of Rio Grande do Norte and in 1838 in the Liceu Provincial of Bahia, created by a law of March 19, 1836, or were suppressed like those of
Rio de Janeiro, in spite of having legislative authorization (decree of September 17,
1851) to group them into day schools with the same organization and the same subjects
taught in the Colégio Pedro II. This renaissance of preparatory studies almost a century after the expulsion of the Jesuits (1759), and under the influence of the higher
schools, even though its major evidence is quantitative expansion, does freely present
the first tendencies and signs of "organization." In fact, with the absorption of the
public classes in the colleges; with the progressive transformation into a series of courses
of the instruction which had been pulverized with the separate classes in the regime
of fragmentary studies without any connection, and with the creation of new colleges
not only private but official, like the schools of Taubaté and Curitiba, founded in 1846
in São Paulo, the secondary schools in which the traditional domination of letters was
maintained, clearly entered upon a period of organization with a highly individual
character of their own, if we except the residues, now of slight importance, of the old
system of royal classes and of separate preparatory courses.

But the efforts of the provinces in creating high schools like that of Rio Grande do
Norte and the Liceu Provincial of Bahia (1836), those of Taubaté and Curitiba in
São Paulo (1846), which immediately passed out of existence for lack of pupils or
professors, the Ateneu Cearense, the School of Maranhão and that of Pará, among
others, did not succeed in accompanying the evolution that was attained in the private
field by institutions of secondary education. In 1865, out of 439 pupils who were re·
ceiving secondary education in Ceará, 156 were attending public school and 283
private schools; in Pernambuco out of a total of 635 registered in classes and colleges,
only 99 were receiving public education; in Bahia, in whose Liceu Provincial, the
most sought after of the schools at that time, 337 pupils were studying humanities, 860
were studying in private colleges; and in the Neutral Township itself, with its model
Colégio Pedro II, founded by the imperial government in 1837, of the 2,550 pupils in
secondary schools, 327 were students of that official institute, and the other 2,223 were
distributed in numerous courses and colleges. Only in the province of Minas Gerais,
in which the most important establishments of learning of this grade were the College
of Caraça and the Seminary of Mariana, which dated from 1750 and was attended by
secular students, the number of students registered (638) in the 38 classes that existed,
was equivalent in 1865, if not superior, to that of the students registered in private

institutions.[24] The fact is that the Additional Act, handing over to the provinces primary and secondary instruction, involved, as Pedro Calmon observes, "sacrificing both to worry over their miserable local budgets, to the timid and routine spirit which persisted far from the court." [25] He adds, moreover, that the faculties, subordinated to the central government, would not accept the examinations of the provincial high schools, thus putting them on a foot of equality with private colleges and opening fruitful perspectives by means of the free rivalry between colleges, to the flourishing of private institutions of secondary education. In an epoch in which only the degree of bachelor of letters conferred by the Pedro II College opened the door to registration in the faculties of the Empire, all other students, candidates to a higher school, were obliged, in order to gain admission to these faculties, to take examinations before commissions organized by these institutions. This situation, evidently abnormal from the morphological point of view of the structure of the school system, inaugurated a brilliant period of preparatory studies, substituting for the rigid structure, dryly bureaucratic, which provincial teaching had, strangled by budgets and a spirit of routine, a real flowering of institutions outside the direct pressure of the state and, becoming rivals, they disputed first place in reputation through the efficiency of their teaching, and whose role was to assure the continuity and progress of the study of the humanities in the country. There arose then or developed in consequence, thus marking in the period from 1860 to 1890 the high water mark of private, secondary education, model institutions such as in Minas the famous Colegio do Caraça which had its most brilliant phase between 1865 and 1885 under the direction of Father Jules José Clavelin, and the Colleges of Campo Belo and of Congonhas do Campo; and that of Dr. Kopke, who in 1855 hired professors in Europe, and the College São Pedro de Alcântara of the Fathers Paiva, also founded in Petrópolis, the Ginásio Bahiano of the Baron de Macaúbas, the Colégio de São João of João Estanislau da Silva Lisboa and that of Ernesto Carneiro Ribeiro in Bahia; the Ateneu Sergipano, the number of whose pupils went up from 99 in 1871 to 334 in 1874; in Rio de Janeiro the Colleges Stall, Meneses Vieira, Abílio, the Aquino Day School,[26] and the Colégio Progresso, in which Rui Barbosa found inspiration and

[24] J. Liberato Barroso, *A instrução pública no Brasil.* B. L. Garnier, Rio de Janeiro, 1867, pp. 56-69.

[25] Pedro Calmon, *História social do Brasil.* 1st vol. Espírito da Sociedade Colonial. São Paulo, 1937, pp. 316-319.

[26] The Aquino Day School had its origin in a little tutoring course in mathematics, opened in March, 1864, in a room in the building at no. 43 Carioca St., and it was for students of the first year of the old Central School, now the National School of Engineering. The tutor of this group was their oldest fellow-student, João Pedro de Aquino, later founder of the day school; he continued his studies up to the fourth year of the Central School, in Rio de Janeiro. In 1867, this course of explanations of mathematics was changed into the Aquino Day School, of which Dr. João Pedro de Aquino, professor of mathematics, took charge; his courses began in May. Courses in this school were entrusted to men like Tomaz Alves, who was professor of Greek in the Colégio Pedro II, Alfredo d'Escragnolle Taunay, later Senator of the Empire and Viscount of Taunay, André Rebouças, Joaquim Murtinho and Councillor Nuno Ferreira de Andrade, among other famous Brazilians. In 1874, the School, to which a primary school had already been added, was with the latter moved to buildings at nos. 78 and 80, Lavradio St., where it operated with its three courses, the elementary (little day school), the middle, and that which prepared students for institutions of higher learning. The teaching, which was well equipped with teaching materials and laboratories, used both in the primary and secondary departments modern methods adopted in the best schools of North America. On June 5, 1875, this model establishment was honored for the

collected data for his reform plans in 1882; in Santa Catarina the College of the Jesuits in Destêrro, which acquired great fame in its short period of existence (1845–1853), and in São Paulo, the Colégio da São Luiz, founded in 1867 in Itú by the Jesuits, and that of Campinas established in 1874 by the Sociedade Culto à Ciência, and which became one of the best educational establishments. Never in the history of Brazilian education did private education have such importance or win such a position of authority as in these and other institutions which were the initial points of support upon which the secondary education of the country rested to acquire new life and which contributed to perfect its education in its organic make up, to develop it, in the lack of official effort, and to form it into a general system of education. Without the basis of preparatory studies, for the progress of which the self-sacrifice and the intelligence of private individuals made such a great contribution in this period, the faculties of law and medicine and the schools of engineering "would not have been," as Pedro Calmon writes, "the seminaries of literary vocation, of spiritual concern, of political philosophy, and of cultural action which they constituted." It is out of this period that the notable group of educators whose illustrious tradition has come down to the present generation, arose: a Baron of Tautphoeus, professor of the College Pedro II, a Freeze, a Kopke, a Pujol, and those three great fighters for the improvement of studies in Brazil and the reform of methods of teaching: Abílio César Borges (Bahia, 1824–1896), Baron of Macaúbas, who exchanged medical activity for those of an educator creating schools in Bahia, Rio de Janeiro and Minas Gerais (Barbacena) and putting his plan at the service of education in numerous published works during a campaign of about twenty-five years; Joaquim José Meneses de Vieira (Rio de Janeiro, 1851–1897), also a physician, founder of the college which bore his name and of the "Pedagogium" (1890) which he directed until his death, and João Pedro de Aquino, an engineer, who from the time when he was a student dedicated his entire life to educational work and had the good fortune to carry on for nearly half a century the college which he founded,—the most beautiful and fruitful creation of his mind.

The free competition and rivalry which grew up between colleges, furthering the flourishing of private institutions and causing the rise of a new constellation of values out of the nebula of education, contributed moreover to introduce into the educational life of the country new pedagogical forces taking refuge as it were in little fortresses of

---

first time by a visit of the Emperor: the great geologist, Charles Frederick Hartt, professor at Cornell University, in the United States, who had been present at examinations in the school, had passed on to Pedro II the deep impression which the work of the remarkable Brazilian educator had made on him. In 1884, the Aquino Day School closed, as a result of financial difficulties into which the maintenance of a boarding department, opened in 1876, had plunged it; since the middle of 1883, the school had been operating at Passeio St., no. 62, and it reopened only in 1892, under the direction of its founder, Dr. João Pedro de Aquino. Adopting in 1903 the curriculum of the National High School, it continued to render important services to the education of youth. This Day School was one of the most important educational establishments in the second half of the nineteenth century, not only because of the unity and efficiency of its direction and the moral atmosphere one breathed in it, but through its spreading of new methods and because of the group of professors, chosen from among the most skillful and experienced of the capital of the country. In the Aquino Day School, through which there passed in more than half a century, thousands of students, some of the Brazilians who achieved most distinction in politics, letters and the liberal professions got their education. (João Pedro de Aquino, *Breve notícia sôbre o Externato Aquino.* "Gazeta de Notícias," Rio de Janeiro, 1903).

reaction in the lay educational establishments which we owe to private initiative. The first movements of reform came, in fact, from the lay colleges which were more progressive and advanced, either under the direct inspiration of their founders or through the action of professors hired in Europe or recruited among the best elements of Brazilian education, or among the most cultivated men of the foreign "colonies." One feels passing through these colleges, stimulated by a noble spirit of emulation, a renovating breath of air which led to the abolition of corporal punishment, to a new encouragement given to studies of modern languages and sciences, to the adoption of new techniques of teaching and in the equipment of their laboratories. Meneses Vieira undertook trips to Europe in order to study the organization of similar institutes, and besides introducing improvements in his college, founded the "Sunday school," or course for workmen and later the "Pedagogium," and published didactic works which constituted, together with the school books of the Baron of Macaúbas, the most important pedagogical contribution of the epoch in the sense of improving methods of secondary teaching. Wherever the rivalry of the lay colleges and their renovating activity did not make itself so intensely felt, education retained its conservative character, faithful to the traditions of classic education. This was the case of the province of Minas Gerais, which became the greatest center of humanistic studies in the Empire, a kind of "Latin colony," according to Pedro Calmon, owing to the marked predominance of ecclesiastical education furnished in the two seminaries of Mariana and of Diamantina, and in the Colleges of the Fathers of the Congregation of São Vicente de Paulo. One of these, the College of Caraça, clinging to the lonely mountains of Minas, constituted, on account of its isolation, the rigor of its discipline, and its fidelity to tradition, "something sinister," writes Gilberto Freyre, "in the Brazilian social landscape of the first days of the Empire." But in addition to the fact that the influence of these fortresses of new thought was almost always local, this thought, strictly pedagogical, which was sought as a "value in itself" and not as a modification of technique related to new social and political objects, the activity of the clergy preserved its predominant position in the seminaries and in the religious orders, which were co-operating in secondary education with a great number of confessional institutions, essentially conservative in nature and scattered through the principal cities of the country. It was the Lazarists who had established themselves as early as 1820 with the College of Caraça and who spread out from their mother house into Campo Belo and Congonhas do Campo; the Jesuits,[27] great educators and humanists, who had returned to

[27] The first Jesuits who arrived in Brazil, 83 years after their expulsion by the Marquês de Pombal, and 28 years after the reestablishment of the Society of Jesus by Pius VII, were Spanish fathers. Founding their first religious house in Pôrto Alegre in 1842, they at first devoted themselves, as Father Manuel Madureira notes, exclusively to missionary work and the conversion of the Indians. The first school they established, in Destêrro, now Florianópolis, had in its first phase only a brief existence, although a fruitful one: in 1853, due to the rise of yellow fever in the south, the school created in 1845 by the Spanish fathers had closed, to reopen, under the direction of fathers of the Roman Province, in 1865, and to be closed anew in 1880, and later reopened, this time by fathers of the German Province. In 1867, the Spanish fathers,—the first to turn toward the south of Brazil in the nineteenth century—, "were completely replaced by fathers of the Province of Germania, to whom the Father General entrusted, in recent times, the mission of Rio Grande do Sul, joining to this, under the general designation of Southern Province of Brazil, Santa Catarina and Paraná." By decision of the Father General, as we see, German Jesuits settled in the south (1849) and in the center, fathers of the Italian Mission. This decision, with which in 1867 Spanish fathers were replaced by those of the Province of Germania, and the whole region of Rio Grande

Brazil 83 years after their expulsion, founding one college in Destêrro and another, with a seminary, in Pernambuco (1867–1873), both short lived, and later the three colleges which became remarkable, that of São Luiz in Itú, in the province of São Paulo (1867), that of Anchieta (1886) in Nova Friburgo, in the province of Rio de Janeiro, and that of Our Lady of the Conception (1870) in São Leopoldo in Rio Grande do Sul; the Benedictines, old guests of Brazil, who created primary and secondary courses; the Salesians, recently arrived in the country, in 1883, who specialized here as elsewhere in professional and secondary teaching. The ecclesiastical origins of education in Brazil, the interpenetration of the clerical world and the pedagogical world, still so close that the College of Pedro II itself had among its rectors, vice-directors and professors, many Fathers and Friars from Brother Antônio de Arrabida, Bishop of Anemúria, its first rector (1838), and finally the development which the collaboration of the religious orders acquired in the education of girls and boys, accentuated the religious, literary and rhetorical character of secondary education, whose high schools found their inspiration in the European models of a classic type. No new ferment was introduced into the dough of education, except that which was prepared in the lay colleges, or which was constituted at the end of the Empire by the appearance of the first Protestant schools like the Escola Americana, founded in 1870 in São Paulo, for elementary education, to which was added in 1880 the secondary school, both part of "Mackenzie College," or the Colégio Piracicabano (1881) for girls in São Paulo, and the Colégio Americano (1885) in Pôrto Alegre, both undertaken by the Methodists. In Brazil, which was only beginning to divide itself into two religious beliefs, both Christian, the Roman Church, closely bound up with the origins of our social and historic formations and united to the State, kept the influence of the Protestant at a distance, circumscribed to certain restricted circles. The Protestant influence had arrived recently and was still badly acclimated to the traditionally Catholic Brazilian environment. In the educational field only the first contact had taken place and the first struggles about concepts of education had barely broken

---

do Sul transferred to the latter, with the later addition of Santa Catarina and Paraná, was certainly motivated by the current of German immigration which, begun in the time of Dom João VI with the colonies of Leopoldina and Nova Friburgo and continued by Pedro I, with the founding of São Leopoldo, in the South, and by the government of Pedro II, in 1840, with that of Petrópolis, must, as Euclides da Cunha writes, have left from 1850 on, "with the coming of Hermann Blumenau, a continuous trail, of which the main points were Blumenau, Joinville, Mundo Novo, São Lourenço, Teutonia, and other settlements." (*A Margem da história,* Pôrto, 1922, p. 275). In 1870 the German Jesuits founded in São Leopoldo the Gymnasium of Our Lady of the Conception (1870–1912), and the Italian Jesuits, after having created in 1867 the Seminary and School of Pernambuco, which was closed in 1873, definitely settled in the central part of the country. It was about this time that they founded in Itú the Colégio da São Luiz (1867–1917), which moved to São Paulo in 1917, and in Friburgo the Colégio Anchieta (1886), which was closed in 1922, and in the buildings of which the Central House of the Society of Jesus installed itself; this house was meant for the novitiate and the training in humanities and philosophy of future Jesuits. These two schools, that of São Luiz and that of Anchieta, among the best known of their time, rendered inestimable services to the education of youth, the latter in about forty years, and the former in a half century of life. When the Colégio Anchieta closed, the fathers of the old Italian Mission, now the Brazilian Province, opened the Colégio de Santo Inácio, which is one of the best secondary schools and one of the most popular in Rio de Janeiro. When the Jesuit fathers of Portugal were expelled, on the proclamation of the republic in that country in 1910, Brazil was a refuge of the exiles,—the fathers of the Portuguese Province,—who settled in the North, in Pernambuco, in Ceará, and in Bahia, with their schools for the education of adolescents.

out, corresponding as they did to two religious beliefs and linked to the two cultures, the European and the North American, which were already differentiated. Protestant pedagogy, progressive and liberating, which tended to the emancipation of the mind rather than to intellectual domestication, and the Catholic point of view, more conservative and authoritarian, especially that of the Jesuits who in Macaulay's phrase, "appear to have found the point to which one can drive the cultivation of the mind without arriving at intellectual emancipation."

In all of this work of education and culture which developed irregularly under the influence of private initiative, the imperial government played the role rather of encourager than of actual undertaker, and showed something patriarchal in the assistance which it gave to educational institutions. Without doubt Pedro II always showed an extraordinary interest in things of the mind and a remarkable attraction for intelligence, surrounding himself with scholars, thinkers and artists in order to admire them and to hear their words. It is said that, asked by Frederick II about his relations with Louis XVI of France, the great D'Alembert replied to the King of Prussia, "I have seen him only once, when he was presented to me, according to the custom, after my election to the French Academy." "And what did he say to you?"—"He did not speak to me," replied D'Alembert. "But," replied Frederick, "to whom does he talk then?" The Emperor of Brazil, on the other hand, was not accustomed to wait in order to speak to them for a scholar, a philosopher or an artist to come to him. He frequently went to meet them, taking the initiative of visiting in Paris the poet Victor Hugo, or directing himself in Rio de Janeiro to the explorer Captain Richard Burton in order to converse with him cordially on the night of a reception at the Palace of São Cristóvão. He always contributed the stimulus of his word or his presence to all men who were working and to all institutions in which a great effort in favor of culture and education was being carried on. His visits to the college which took his name were frequent, and many others won the honor of the imperial presence like the Aquino Day School, which he visited in 1875 and the Colégio do Caraça which he endeavored to become acquainted with in his trip to Minas Gerais in 1882, attending the principal classes of the college and the seminary. He gave encouragement to letters, science and arts, not only with the catalytic action of his presence upon occasions of festivals of the arts or the mind, but having works published at his expense, paying the costs of traveling scholarships for artists of the Imperial Academy of Fine Arts or the Conservatory of Music and lending the prestige of his example to intellectual activity. The Brazilian Historical and Geographical Institute, founded on October 21, 1838, had no greater protector than Pedro II, who attended and presided over 506 of its sessions in 40 years, gave it valuable donations of his books and manuscripts, and even when exiled in 1891, a little before his death, bequeathed to it his private library and a precious collection of portraits, engravings and ancient maps. Certainly, the function of Maecenas has been exercised by no one with more naturalness and more elegance than by this illustrious and magnanimous monarch. It could count for much of the sciences, letters and arts to have the constant support with which the Emperor encouraged them, but it is less than the full responsibility of a man and a Chief of State. Nevertheless, it was in large part this warm stimulus that permitted the development throughout the Empire of the high cultural functions of great institutions such as the National Museum, the Astronomical Observatory, the Historical Institute and the National Library,—one of the most important if not the greatest on the American Continent.[28] The Brazilian Historical Institute, whose traditional house is inhabited by illustrious shades, and which today possesses a library of 80,000 volumes, 50,000 manuscripts and the best collection of maps in the country (3,000), made the publication of its review, which appeared regularly from its foundation in 1839, a work not only stimulating historical study, awakening and attracting talent, but also one for propagating the national culture within the country. The *Revista do Instituto* which published in 1889 numbers 79 and 80 (Volume 52) when the Republic was proclaimed and which in 1938, on the occasion of its hundredth anniversary, already could count 168 volumes, in addition to 28 special numbers, the *Arquivos do Museu Nacional*—a review created in 1876, the *Anais do Observatório Astronômico*, the first number of which came out in 1882 under the inspiration of E. Liais, and the *Anais da Biblioteca Nacional* publication of which was begun in 1876, and which was already in its XIII volume in 1890, constituted the best sources of Brazilian studies and were centers for spreading cultural activities in the time of the Empire. Under the influence of isolated but hard working talents, and with the warm support which Pedro

[28] The National Library, the origin of which goes back to 1814, when Prince Regent Dom João opened the Royal Library to the public, with the sixty thousand volumes which in 1808 he had brought from Portugal, was located in Rio de Janeiro, in the Hospital of the Third Order of Carmel. Made up at the beginning of this notable collection of works coming from the Royal Library of the Palace of Ajuda immediately incorporated in the new institution created by Dom João VI, the Royal Library went on improving constantly, through more than a century, with thousands of volumes being added to its original collection, by means of acquisition, legacies and gifts. In 1822 it bought the 6,322 volumes which belonged to the Count of Barca, and in 1838 there came to the Imperial Library almost five thousand volumes comprising the library of José Bonifácio, the Patriarch, which were given the library by his heirs. In a little more than sixty years, by 1876, the library reached the 120,000 volumes and large quantity of important manuscripts, which won the admiration of Herbert Smith, who visited Rio de Janeiro at that time. He says: "A library which would do honor to any city of the United States." (Herbert Smith, *Brazil: The Amazons and the Coast*. 1879). The Imperial Library, which at that time had received new regulations, by the decree of March 4, 1876, "open to the public day and night, always had its reading room full of students and research workers." In 1884 it was used by 9,234 readers. In 1889, when the Republic was proclaimed, the Imperial Library took the name National Library; it then possessed 179,631 volumes, this number including 28,806 duplicates and 1,746 copies of Spix and Martius' *Flora Brasiliensis;* 896 pieces of music, and 30,000 engravings and 12,000 manuscripts. Among its treasures, made up of ancient or famous works, first editions, there is to be found one of the Latin Bibles printed on parchment by Gutenberg, in 1462, on his first press, of which only three other copies are known. Its notable collection of works now exceeds 500,000 volumes, beside maps and manuscripts. Since 1876, *Anais da Biblioteca Nacional* have been published; sixty volumes have come out, the last, for the year 1938, was published in 1940; these constitute one of the most important official publications of the country. The National Library was even in the last century considered the best library of South America. Illustrious men have been its directors, among others, Brother Antônio de Arrabida (1822–1831), Canon Januário da Cunha Barbosa (1839–1846), one of the founders of the Historical Institute, J. de A. Alves Branco Muniz Barreto (1846–1853), Brother Camilo de Monserrate (1853–1870), Ramiz Galvão (1870–1882), Saldanha da Gama (1889), Teixeira de Melo, Manuel Cícero, Mário Behring, and Rodolfo Garcia. Its first directors who were librarians were Brother Gregório José Viegas and C. P. Joaquim Dâmaso. The National Library, today under the direction of the great historian Rodolfo Garcia, has for some thirty years been located at the southern end of the Avenue of Rio Branco, in a sumptuous edifice, already crowded for the deposit of such enormous and growing quantity of publications of all kinds, and inadequate for the cultural function which the library is called upon to exercise, as a center of research and of literary and scientific culture.

II gave them, creating a spiritual atmosphere, there developed in this period a flowering of culture which the history of the country has never known. It was also after 1876 that on the initiative of Ladislau Neto, its director (1874–1893), the Museu Nacional, opening courses in science and a series of published lectures on botany and zoology, anthropology and physiology, planted, with a group of collaborators, Lacerda, Niobey, Rodrigues Peixoto and Couty, the French physiologist, the seed from which an interest in pure science was later to flower into research. With the same zeal and the same solicitude with which he took part in 1856 in the meeting of the Sociedade Palestra Científica, and presided customarily over the sessions of the Historical Institute, opened art expositions, watched over educational institutions and paid for the expenses of publication and traveling fellowships, the Emperor accompanied closely by attending various conferences this attempt at cultural extension and in favor of disinterested scientific studies.

But not only is it true that around these gestures, frequently ridiculed, there existed a large area of indifference and disdain, but also (and hence the distrust which they aroused and which was exploited in political struggles) there was not shown in action a vigor corresponding to the keenness of intellectual interests that was revealed in every way. There was no harmony, in fact, between the personal attitudes of the Emperor and the imperial educational policy. There was no really fruitful effort that succeeded in winning the attention of the intellectual public over to the natural sciences and scientific work. There was no attempt on the part of the government to convert public opinion to the idea of the utility, of the necessity even, of directing the teaching of the schools in a different direction. The schools were developing with a particularly slow evolution and were continuing to prepare their students not for life in its various manifestations, but only for the liberal professions. Hindered by the Additional Act which paralyzed any decisive action with regard to the provinces; paralyzed by the struggles of the parties which alternated in power, leading to successive change in the ministries; dominated by pressing problems, such as the maintenance of order, the restraint of regional claims, the Paraguayan War, and finally the abolition campaign, which during the last decade excited all minds, the government could not really, for its constructive work, count upon anything except periods of "truce," which the difficulties of internal and external politics occasionally permitted the country. It was in one of these pauses, marked by the government of conciliation of the Marquês do Paraná—the "culminating point" of the Empire, as Euclides da Cunha calls it, or "the divider of the waters" to which Joaquim Nabuco used to refer, that it was possible to develop an intense activity of revision and reconstruction of the educational system. This effort took concrete form in the reforms of Luiz Pedreira de Couto Ferraz, Viscount of Bom Retiro, the organizer who by the decree no. 1,331-A of February 17, 1854, took measures with regard to primary and secondary education in the township of the court and gave a new structure to Pedro II College and to higher teaching under the Empire. But none of his efforts introduced into the system any innovation of importance nor served to deflect from its dominant literary and academic line the form of our education. It was by the openly progressive action of the Viscount of Rio Branco (1871–1876) that, without breaking the chain of tradition, there arose with the School of Mines in Ouro Preto a culminating point outside the main line of our development. Under the influence of the Counsellor

João Alfredo, who proposed in 1874 the creation of professional schools, as well as the foundation of popular libraries, education already appeared to be moving in the direction of our economic and social necessities, deviating in various aspects from the traditional direction.[29] The great statesman, the Viscount of Rio Branco who, according to Euclides da Cunha, did most to civilize us, an engineer, professor of the Central School of which he was director, reorganized that school in 1874, when it came to be called the Polytechnic, putting at the base of its three specialized courses, civil engineering, mining, and arts and manufactures, the general courses of physical and mathematical sciences and of physical and natural sciences; and finally created in 1875 the School of Mines, installed in Ouro Preto on October 12, 1876, and whose origins go back to the courses of metallurgy created by the decree of the Regency in 1832 and which remained inoperative for 45 years . . . When one considers these long delays, these "provisional" legislative acts, and the pettiness of the assignment of budgets for the development of our scientific teaching either pure or applied, one has a right to doubt that the political men of the Empire were fully aware of the high interest of institutions destined to favor scientific work and the teaching which is connected with this kind of intellectual activity. If the Polytechnic School, however, was really organized with the objective of making of it a great center not only of professional higher education but also of the spread "of the highest theoretical knowledge of the exact sciences," the point at which the hand of the reformer was most strongly felt was in the School of Mines which, handed over to a head like Henri Gorceix, was not slow in becoming transformed into a remarkable institute preparing specialists in mineralogy, geology and mines. With this reform,—the one which possesses most scientific interest among all those that were undertaken in the nineteenth century—, the circle of professional separation in which higher learning was enclosed was enlarged rather than broken. In that circle the liberal reforms of Leôncio de Carvalho were kept, although he was the boldest and most radical innovator in education during the period of the Empire. Liberalism, which felt a vigorous new movement in the regency and a decay, even in the educational field, with the decree of Couto Ferraz (1854), had a violent *reprise* with the decrees of April 20, 1878 and April 19, 1879, with which the obligatory character of religious teaching in the Colégio Pedro II was abolished, permitting non-Catholics to receive the degree of bachelor without the course of religious instruction and with which, under the inspiration of German and Anglo-Saxon practices, there was instituted in a country character-

[29] But the social environment was still hostile or indifferent to efforts of this kind, as is shown by the vicissitudes experienced by the Agricultural School of Bahia, founded by the Imperial Instituto Baiano de Agricultura and established in 1877 on a fazenda named S. Bento das Lajes, in the township of S. Francisco da Barra do Sergi do Conde. In 1880 the first class of agronomists graduated. The school, however, could not long resist the difficulties it had to face. It was closed in 1901 for lack of resources, reopened a few years later, completely reformed through the efforts of the State government, which when it later found itself forced by the failure of this new attempt to close it, transferred the school to the federal government, under whose administration it was reestablished in 1911, when Dr. Pedro Toledo was Minister of Agriculture. In 1913, a new crisis came; it was closed for several years, finally returned to the State Government, which ordered it reestablished and maintained it down to 1931 uninterruptedly; at that date it was handed over by the Interventor, Leopold Amaral, to the Immigrant Hospice of the Capital. In S. Bento das Lajes, once more under federal control, we now find the School for Agricultural Apprentices named for Sérgio de Carvalho.

ized by liberty to the point of license, liberty of teaching (primary and secondary in the Court Township) and also of class attendance in the official faculties.[30]

If, however, we take the trouble to examine these and other reforms from those of Couto Ferraz, the organizer, to those of Leôncio de Carvalho, the innovator, who departed most from the model of the University of Coimbra, it will not be possible to reconstitute by means of them the various phases or the variations of a definite educational policy. What they show generally in their more substantial part is the transitory influence of the cabinets of ministers which, with the possible exception of that of the Viscount of Rio Branco, did nothing more than to preserve and perfect the institutions founded by Dom João VI, or created in the first Empire, like the law courses or in the Regency like the College of Pedro II. There was no serious political program presupposing a complete and precise analysis, as far as possible, of the environment upon which one was to act and the knowledge of its laws of evolution. There was no project for a general reform with an organic unity of conception and plan. Solidity was lacking at the very basis of these official undertakings which, limited to higher education in the Empire and to primary and secondary education in the Court District, were as it were undertakings which proposed to erect a wide and heavy building on old foundations of little depth. With the Counsellor Rodolfo Dantas, who was the first, in his report of 1882, to attack with boldness and breadth of vision the very heart of the question, when he pointed out the necessity of a "cooperation of the general powers (a cooperation to which in his judgment the Additional Act offered no obstacle) in the many-sided and immense work of education for which the resources of the provinces are and long will remain insufficient." The reform project which he presented to Parliament, and which did not arrive at the point of open discussion, was studied by a commission especially appointed on September 12, 1882, by the Chamber of Deputies. As reporter for this Commission, Rui Barbosa wrote his famous opinion no. 64, with which he approved the project of the law, "a marvel of science and of conscience," in the opinion of Afrânio Peixoto, "a magnificent and

---

[30] The part concerned with the reform of medical schools, in the decree submitted by Leôncio de Carvalho, is due to the Viscount of Sabóia, professor and director of the Medical School of Rio de Janeiro and physician to the royal family. The Viscount of Sabóia, whose eight year administration (1880–1888) was the most brilliant period of the school, had been asked in 1871 to study the organization of medical schools in the most advanced countries of Europe. Returning from his journey, in 1872, he presented a report on the organization of medical instruction in France, Italy, Austria, Germany, Belgium and England. Other professors were sent to Europe, too, to study the teaching of their specialties, from a practical point of view. However, it was not until 1878 that Leôncio de Carvalho, Imperial Minister, requested the Viscount of Sabóia to present a plan for reform, "based upon the free teaching which he wished to establish." This project, writes the Viscount of Sabóia, "delivered and printed two months later, served as a basis for the decree of April 19, 1879; some thought it was the first step in the break-down of our higher education; in my opinion, it was the first blow directed at the ignorance and rhetoric of our scientific education. Since this decree brought out into the open the inadequacy of our higher education, Professor Pertence in a series of lectures given in 1880 proposed the creation of a university as a means to improve that education, and with that aim the government acquired land, worked out plans and began the work." (Baron de Sabóia, "Facultés de Médecine," pp. 568-579 of "Le Brésil en 1889," by Sant'Anna Neri, Paris, 1889.) But once more the idea of a university remained in the stage of planning; it was to come up in various proposals, and for the last time, still without effect, in the Speech from the Throne, which was the monarchy's farewell.

substantial document," which in the opinion of Raja Gabaglia, "would honor the intellectual capacity of the most erudite assembly of any country in the world." But, in this opinion, which from the point of view of form and erudition is really a master-piece, as in that of the following year, with regard to primary education, what is approved is not a plan of reform adjusted to the reality of Brazil but an ideal and theoretical plan in which there are brought together by a kind of eclecticism, dis-cordant elements in institutions which find their inspiration in the most diverse social environments, such as England, Germany and the United States. With his remark-able erudition, Rui Barbosa was able to bring together in this parliamentary work,— a quarto volume of 378 pages—, the most complete documentary information about educational institutions in some of the most advanced countries of the time and pre-sented with that elegance and purity of language which was peculiar to the great orator and constitutes one of his chief charms. Driven no doubt by his ardent and generous idealism, which did not permit him to keep his feet on the ground, and allowing himself to be dominated by his erudition and eloquence, which prevented the development of a critical spirit, and exalting the literary and informative value of his opinions above its ideological value, the eminent reporter preferred wide theo-retical schematization to the objective observation of facts and reflection upon them. He proposed a whole plan under the form of reorganization, after tracing a rapid sketch of the history of education in the Empire and presenting tables of statistics of the provinces, but without proceeding to an inventory of the material, social, eco-nomic and moral condition of the country and without establishing beforehand the pedagogical, social and political object to which the whole structure of the system should be directed and for which its educational institutions of various natures and levels should converge, coordinated and subordinated to a fundamental unity of prin-ciples. But one must recognize that in the working out of his opinion, in which he opened new perspectives to education in Brazil, widening its mental horizon in other directions, the vigorous fighter of the liberal campaigns, if he might have and should have sought in the Brazilian environment for the bases and suggestions of his con-struction, could not find in that environment a clearly formulated, pedagogical thought, upon which to take a firm stand nor a current of ideas by which to allow himself to be swept away. "In the whole period of the Empire of 67 years," Lourenço Filho tells us, relying on official data, "there were listed only 193 educational works" . . . and "down to 1882, when more than 70 years had transpired since the first publication (1812), the bibliography of education could be summed up almost entirely in official reports of scant doctrinal value and at times of little informative value or mere propa-ganda speeches." Even in the period from 1862 to 1886 in which we find the largest number of works published in a 25 year period in the Empire (147), a number almost four times as great as that of the books on education published in the 50 years before, and in which there appeared the first works on the creation of universities (1873), the idea of a national plan of education (1874), and professional education (1876), there does not stand out with clarity any current of pedagogical thought. They were all works more or less erudite, generally bookish, without general views, and without critical and constructive spirit. To study a subject, it was sufficient to go among the books, to handle them and to bring them together, oppose some of them to others, collect data and indicate ideal solutions and, after a more or less careful glance at the European countries, to saturate one's work with erudition and to accompany it by personal reflections.[31] The opinion of Rui is, in this way, a brilliant application, which reflects, together with the mentality of the period, the powerful force of his ideals and his talent. The contrast between the height of the ideal and the reality which rejected it and in which it was to be inserted after being deformed, was moreover, together with his combative temperament, the principal cause for the slightly ironical, almost always sarcastic, attitude which masked his bitterness in the fact of the resistance of the environment to the plan of a mind animated by a robust faith in life and in the spiritual values which transcend life and in the heat of which the arms for his best campaign were forged.

Thus, at the end of the monarchy, the vague and diffuse aspirations in the matter of education were concentrated, taking form in the project of Rodolfo Dantas and in the opinion with which in 1882 Rui Barbosa supported that project, transforming it almost into another project, and in the speech from the throne in the last opening session on May 3, 1889, of the last session of Parliament of the second Empire. In this last speech, the Emperor requested the creation of a ministry to undertake public instruction, the foundation of technical schools "adapted to local conditions and convenience," the beginning of two universities (one in the south, another in the north of the country), as well as faculties of science and letters in some provinces, tied up with the university system. All this system proposed by the Emperor and which would have at its peak the two universities, "centers of high scientific and literary organization, whence the vigorous and harmonious impulse which education so much needs would go out," according to the official word, would rest "freely and firmly on primary and secondary education," spread out widely over the territory of the nation. But the fruit into which the legislation of proposals and projects was to flower was not yet sufficiently ripe for the irresolute hand of the Emperor to pluck it with ease . . . It was to take still almost half a century to ripen and then not sufficiently to be picked until 1930 without the violence of a revolution. The broad and ambitious aspirations of that project of 1882 and of the last speech from the throne in 1889 did not find to support them either a new mentality or a social reality that was malleable and plastic, nor an economic rise which would permit profound changes in educational system. Culture was already "a Brazilian culture," in spite of all of its borrowings from the culture of the west, but the mentality remained the same, literary and rhetorical, as attracted by bookish learning as it was divorced from a critical and experimental spirit. We still preferred, together with grammar and

[31] As opposed to the general and political press, which played so important a part in the field of literature, didactic printing which rose after 1875 did not succeed in stimulating the flowering of pedagogical literature. It came in the last quarter of the century and never had sufficient importance nor a large enough public to arouse and channelize currents of thought in the field of education. The first periodical publication, due to the efforts of Alambari Luz, "founder, in Brazil, of the educational press," was the journal *A Instrução Pública*, which had as contributors, among others, the Baron of Macaúbas, Felisberto de Carvalho, and Councillor J. Liberato Barbosa. Among other publications, like *O Ensino* and the *Revista de Liga do Ensino*, both published in Rio de Janeiro, all of them short-lived, the one that had the most influence was this last, in which we find work by Rodolfo Dantas and Rui Barbosa. None of them, however, represented a definite tendency in pedagogy nor endeavored to distinguish among the mass of old and new ideas, the still indefinite currents of opinion.

Latin (and for a long time we were to continue to prefer) the mashed potatoes of convalescents and of old men rather than the diet of raw meat of young, strong peoples. If the system of education, erected to prepare man for a single task, put ahead of the ideal of a complete man that of the professional man or the group of special ideals,—those of the liberal professions, the predominance in the intellectual life of the country of literary, journalistic and political activity offered a safety valve or a way out to this type of specialization. The Brazilian, however, reacted against the professionalization of teaching and of culture, either falling, for lack of a philosophical or scientific base, into brilliant generalities, or giving himself over to that easy erudition to which Defoe referred "of barterers of Greek and Latin," or by running away into the literature of fiction. From the point of view of quantity, the cultural and pedagogical heritage of the Empire was not superior to its qualitative value. For a population of almost 14,000,000, the matriculation in the primary schools was little more than 250,000 pupils, not reaching 300,000 or even the seventh part of the population of school age registered in all of the schools of different types and grades in the whole country. Certainly this general picture of education in the Empire is not sufficient either in its extension or variety or level of teaching to lead to the intellectual movement which was produced in that period, or to produce the group of men who arose in it to mention only a few names, a Tôrres Homem, physician, a André Rebouças, engineer, a Teixeira de Freitas, jurist, a Gonçalves Dias in poetry, a José de Alencar in the novel or a Rui Barbosa in eloquence; a mathematician of the value of Gomes de Sousa, or a botanist of the capacity of Freire Alemão. But in the total picture of social life, which is so many-sided and complex, the education which is crystallized in institutions is only one of numerous factors which influence the formation of the individual and the development of society. In that continuous process which grows from the cradle to the grave and which is identified with life itself, the school,—one of the special agencies of education, cooperates not only with the family and the church but with cultural society, public lectures and libraries,[32]

[32] The libraries and reading centers, the activities of the bookstore business and the public lectures, which constitute a stimulant to intellectual activity, contributed largely to the appearance of new ideas and their diffusion and to the guidance of opinion. Educated Brazilians, who were generally rather receptive than creative, had a love, a passion for books. Private libraries were not rare, and some of them were excellent, in Rio de Janeiro and in various provincial capitals, like São Paulo, Ouro Preto, Bahia, Fortaleza, Recife, and São Luiz de Maranhão. The Emperor, who was one of the most luxurious bibliophiles of his time, had in the Palace of São Cristóvão, for his own literary and scientific pleasure, a magnificent private library, estimated at 150,000 volumes, and capable of being a rival, in certain ways, to the best public library of the capital of the Empire. In Rio de Janeiro,—the principal center of the intellectual life of the country, with its schools, its newspapers, its bookstores and printing shops—there were about thirteen libraries, some of them first-rate, open to the public, in addition to the Imperial Library with almost 171,000 volumes and a precious collection of bibliographical treasures, maps and manuscripts. These were the Library of the Imperial Museum, that of the Institute of History and Geography, that of the Medical School, which in 1882 had a collection of 32,575 volumes; the Municipal Library,—one of the most used—,founded in 1874 by the City Council of Rio de Janeiro, on the proposal of Councillor João Alfredo, and opened that same year with 12,000 volumes; that of the Benedictine Convent; that of the Retiro Literário Português de Leitura,—a literary association created in 1859 which had about 7,000 volumes; that of the Gabinete Português de Leitura, founded in 1837, and in 1884 in possession of a splendid collection of 60,000 volumes, located since 1887 in the society's own building in the street of Luiz de Camoes; and that of the Society for Promoting Teaching,

to form the individual, who is subject to the most diverse influences, including episodic ones such as the reading of a great book, a personal contact that proves fecund, or a journey for the purpose of study, all of these things being capable of hastening his intellectual development or of changing its direction. However, if the school which cannot be superior to the society which organizes it, tends to leave the deepest mark of its influences on mediocre personalities, the richest natures with a superior endowment tend to react against its moderating action, rising above the pedagogical and social environment in which they were formed, and at times openly opposing its ideals and tendencies. It is necessary to take into account the power of self-teaching which exceptional individuals have. Culture rises like a geyser for those who pierce through the rock of inertia and are stimulated by creative power and by the questioning attitude of a nature with great internal resources. The very movement which the physical and medical sciences had in Europe in the sixteenth and seventeenth centuries, if we except Italy, is not one which they received from the universities, "which showed little haste," writes Stephen D'Irsay, "in taking possession of scientific education, because they could not perceive its immediate utility,—that of the humanities was much more evident—and they did not grasp its importance." [33] These facts and reflections will help us to understand how a country was able during the nineteenth century to maintain its civilization and to have a prosperous culture without possessing what in most great countries of the world at that time was the very instrument for literary, philosophical and scientific progress: the universities.

---

founded by Councillor Manuel Francisco Correia, who in 1874 took the initiative in founding schools, of a library which came to have six thousand volumes, and of a series (1874–1886) of public lectures. If we add the specialized libraries, like that of the Academy of Fine Arts, of the Conservatory of Music, of the Polytechnic School, and that of the Military and Naval Schools, we shall have a total of fourteen libraries, with more than 500,000 volumes in all, which made Rio de Janeiro the bibliographical center of the country. The daily movement of readers was growing constantly: the Imperial Library in 1887 was visited by 15,000 readers, and the Naval Library, open to the public from 1881 on, by 1887 recorded an attendance of 3,624 readers. But this very significant movement, although it was greatest in Rio de Janeiro, extended also to various provinces. Beside the libraries of monastic orders, Brazil had those of the Law School of Recife; of the Medical School of Bahia; of the School of Mines, in Ouro Preto, which also had a public library of 2,871 volumes, and of the Law School of São Paulo, the first catalogue of which appeared in 1884. Some interior cities like Campinas, Itú, Lorena, and Bragança, in São Paulo, and Campanha da Princesa, and São João d'El Rei, in Minas Gerais, could boast of possessing public libraries; that of Campanha, with 2,664 volumes and that of São João d'El Rei with 2,444, the oldest of the Province of Minas Gerais, after that of Ouro Preto, the former Vila Rica.

[33] Stephen d'Irsay, *Histoire des universités françaises et étrangères*. Vol. 2. Du XVIme siècle à 1860. Paris, Auguste Picard, 1935.

BIBLIOGRAPHY

Aquino, João Pedro de, *Breve notícia sôbre o Externato Aquino (1864–1903)*. (Tip. da Gazeta de Notícias, 1903).

Barbosa, Rui, *Parecer sôbre a reforma do ensino secundário e superior* (Rio: Imprensa Nacional, 1882).

———, *Parecer sôbre a reforma do ensino primário* (Rio: Imprensa Nacional, 1882).

Calmon, Pedro, *História social do Brasil*, Vol. 2, *Espírito da sociedade imperial* (São Paulo: Comp. Editora Nacional, 1937—Brasiliana, Vol. 83), Chap. XXI, pp. 310–327.

Escragnolle Dória, *Memória histórica do Colégio Pedro II* (Rio: Ministério da Educação, 1937). From Dec. 2, 1837, to Dec. 2, 1937.

Freyre, Gilberto, *Sobrados e mocambos* (São Paulo: Comp. Editora Nacional, 1936—Brasiliana, Vol. 36).

Giomini, José, S.J., *O XXV aniversário do Colégio Anchieta* (Nova Friburgo, 1911).

Júlio Maria, Father, "A Religião: Ordens religiosas, Chap. II, "Durante o Império," pp. 63–107, in *Livro do Centenário* (Rio: Imprensa Nacional, 1900).

Liberato Barroso, José, *A Instrução pública no Brasil* (Rio: Garnier, 1867).

Moacir, Primitivo, *A Instrução e o Império: Subsídios para a história da educação no Brasil* (São Paulo: Comp. Editora Nacional, 3 vols., 1936–1938).

———, *A Instrução e as Províncias* (São Paulo: Comp. Editora Nacional, 1939–1940).

Oliveira Santos, M. P. de, "Instrução pública," *Dicionário histórico, geográfico e etnográfico do Brasil*, Vol. 1, Chap. XV, 381.

Peixoto, Afrânio, *Noções de história da educação* (São Paulo: Comp. Editora Nacional, 1933), Chaps. XVII–XIX ("Brasil"), pp. 211–249.

Pires de Almeida, J. R., *L'Instruction publique au Brésil depuis l'Indépendance jusqu'à nos jours: Histoire, Législation* (Rio: Leuzinger, 1889).

Raja Gabaglia, E. de Barros, *O Colégio Pedro II* (Rio, n.d.).

Sant'Anna Neri, Baron de Sabóia, L. Cruls, and Baron de Tefé, "Instruction publique," in *Le Brésil en 1889*, prepared by a group of Brazilian writers under the direction of M. F.–J. de Sant'Anna Nery (Paris), Chap. XIX, pp. 563–590.

Sousa Brasil, Tomaz Pompeu de, *O Ensino superior no Brasil e Relatório da Faculdade de Direito do Ceará nos anos de 1911 e 1912* (Ceará: Tip. Minerva de Assís Bezerra, 1913).

Teixeira Brandão, *A Educação nacional no regime republicano* (Rio: Imprensa Nacional, 1907).

Veríssimo de Matos, José, *A Educação nacional* (Belem, 1896; 2nd ed., Rio: Francisco Alves, 1906).

———, "A Instrução e a imprensa (1500–1900): A Instrução pública—II, O Império (1822–1889)," in *Livro do Centenário* (Rio: Imprensa Nacional, 1900), IV, pp. 5–30.

Viana, Hélio, *Formação brasileira* (Rio: Olímpio, 1935), p. 230, Chap. XXV (b), "Síntese de uma história da educação no Brasil: Período monárquico."

CHAPTER THREE

DECENTRALIZATION AND THE DUAL SYSTEM

The transformation of the social and economic structure—The first rise of industry and the abolition of slavery—The change in the political regime—The Republic and the triumph of the federative principle—The Military School and influence of Positivistic ideas—The reform of Benjamim Constant—The separation of Church and State—The competition of the Protestant Schools and the influence of American pedagogical theories—Decentralization and the dual system—The federal system made up of secondary and higher education—The Institute of Manguinhos as a center of scientific research—The successive reforms of secondary education—The parallel, irregular expansion of state systems—The development of primary and normal school education in the States—The progress of education in São Paulo, the new center of the economic life of the country—New higher schools for the liberal careers— Isolated movements in the field of technical and professional education—An analysis of the educational structure in process of formation—Duality in the vertical sense—The system of education for the people and that for the training of the élite—Bureaucracy and stratification in the school system—Reaction against the traditional school and the movement of reform— New tendencies of pedagogical thought—Toward a national educational policy

AT NO PERIOD of the nineteenth century after Independence were there prepared and produced so many important events for the life of the nation as in the last quarter of that century in which there took place the first rise in industry, there was established the policy of immigration, the regime of slavery was abolished, the organization of free labor was begun and, with the fall of the Empire, the experience of a new political regime was begun. It is in fact in 1885 that we find the first beginnings of the rise of industry and the period in which the industries of the country attracted the largest amount of capital of the whole nineteenth century was the decade 1885–1895. Of the capital invested in Brazilian industry down to 1920, as a census carried out in that year concludes, 23 per cent was invested in that decade, whereas before 1885 there had been invested only 10 per cent, and later, in 1895-1905, the percentage reached only 11, to go up again to 31 between 1905 and 1914, and to 25 between 1914 and 1920, from which dates the most important period in the industrial evolution of the country. This first rise of industry, beginning in 1885, followed immediately by a period of decline, was not sufficient to lead to a vigorous transformation of the economic structure and to introduce a new progress, but it did indicate that the population, growing, was moving toward the city and that the market for manufactured products whether Brazilian or foreign was tending to grow. The young country, bound to tradition and to the routine of agricultural work, was in the large centers for the first time expressing its desire to become industrial. The campaign which condemned slavery led, in turn, to the organization of free labor, favoring the immigration movement and allotting considerable sums to immigration. In 1876, immigration policy took on new life with the entry of 3,567 immigrants, of whom only 1,303 went to São Paulo; in 1881 that province began its immigration service, offering its subvention to the entrance of immigrants; in 1888, the year in which slave labor disappeared, 133,253 immigrants entered the country of whom 91,826 went to the province of São Paulo, while during the decade 1888–1898 the surge of European immigration into the southern provinces developed still further.

But as immigration attracts immigration, side by side with the immigration of agricultural workers receiving a subsidy from the central government and from that of the province of São Paulo, there came a larger, spontaneous movement of immigrants of different social levels and specialized in the most diverse occupations. Certainly upon the abolition of slavery, upon which it had been based for three centuries, Brazilian society found itself, as Max Leclerc observes, "without foundations attacked by evils which the subjection of man to man involved, and seeking for a new form and a new base of its life," and exchanging a barbarous regime for one that was unknown, without any serious previous preparation, it did not succeed in recovering from the chronic perturbation of the national economy which had been aggravated by difficulties growing from abolition and the replacement of slave labor by the activity of free men.[1] Meanwhile, the beginning of the industrial upsurge in 1885; the vigorous civilizing movement that we owe to immigration; the suppression of the slave regime which, even when carried on rapidly, as in the United States, coincided with a great increase in production, and the new economy of free labor, contributed to the transformation of the social and economic structure, which could not be without effect upon habits and mentalities, especially in the urban population. The rapid succession of these facts, of which we are gaining a different idea from the light which recent historians have thrown upon it; the reciprocal action and reaction and the importance of its effects upon the vital centers of the country were to impose upon the new political regime the necessity of making a great effort at adaptation, in order to find that equilibrium which instinctively it had to seek for, facing a series of situations suddenly created and poorly understood in the whole range of their consequences.

Among the facts, however, that had the greatest influence upon the atmosphere in which the coming of the Republic took place, Azevedo Amaral correctly points out that one of the most important was "the ascendancy which federalist ideas had won over the mind of the governing class of the country." The other two elements which are linked with this capital point were, in his judgment, the disorganization of the agricultural economy in many regions of the country, "as an effect of the abolition that was carried out in a demagogic atmosphere and without the public power having taken the measures which were necessary for the normal replacement of the slave by the free laborer," and the military question, which "bringing the Army against its will into the political arena, automatically gave the armed classes a decisive function in the shaping of the new national order." [2] The triumph of the federalist principle with the change of the political regime not only consecrated but widened the regime of decentralization established by the Additional Act of 1834, and throwing fundamental education (primary and secondary) from the national plane into the local plane, removed the organization of the bases on which the national system of educa-

[1] Max Leclerc, *Lettres du Brésil,* Chapter XI. L'esprit public. L'état social, les moeurs et les institutions, pp. 203-236. Plon, Paris, 1890.

[2] Azevedo Amaral, "Evolução da política republicana." In *Cultura Política,* I, no. 3. May, 1941, Rio de Janeiro, pp. 154-172.

tion should rest from the control of the federal government. In this respect, the Republic went farther, yielding to federalist aspirations which had almost been limited under the old regime "to the narrowly political orbit of regional life," and now in the Republican period extended to the fields of administration, which had been strongly centralized by the unitary policy of the Empire. The provinces which then enjoyed privileges of a political nature, observes Azevedo Amaral, "had their internal administration placed in the sphere of the government which from the center regulated the movement of the most domestic administrative and economic activities of each province." The idea already in progress, that of giving unity of direction to education [3] or at least of the intervention of the central government in primary and secondary education was paralyzed in its development by the victory obtained with the change of regime, by the claims of autonomy, of which São Paulo had become, by reason of its economic expansion, one of the principal centers.

From the point of departure,—the Convention of Itú and the Manifesto of Campinas, published on December 3, 1870—, to the definitive triumph in 1889, the march of the Republican idea, to which new life was given by the religious question, the

[3] The idea of unity in direction or orientation of education had already been broached during the Empire, in the second half of the nineteenth century, by some of the most eminent political figures that attacked problems of education. In 1849, Gonçalves Dias, the poet and ethnologist, concluded from the observations he had made in his inspection trip to the provinces of the North, from Pará to Bahia, that "it was necessary to create a center of unity of action and to make education uniform throughout the Empire." This question was taken up again and treated lucidly and at times even vehemently by Councillor Liberato Barroso in 1867, by João Alfredo, in 1874, and in 1882 by Councillor Rodolfo Dantas, Minister of the Empire. Tavares Bastos, who called for the complete autonomy of local powers, made an exception with regard to education, saying that he accepted "for certain ends the aid of the federal government itself, at least in the case of the smaller provinces and during the period of the beginnings." João Alfredo is not less decided, for he notes, in support of the doctrine of intervention opposing broadly decentralizing tendencies, the example of England, whose policy, in this respect, was not "to limit the sphere of the State by making public instruction a local or individual matter, but on the contrary to strengthen the central authority and achieve harmony in the direction of education through a unified administration." In the report presented to the General Legislative Assembly, in the second session of the 18th Legislature (1882), Councillor Rodolfo Dantas once more attacks the question, showing on the one hand that "the government cannot sit with crossed arms in the face of the backwardness and defective distribution of popular education in the provinces," and on the other, that "the frankly decentralizing tendencies of the Additional Act do not prevent the State from taking a step in this direction" (pp. 9-10). The minister of the Empire became the preacher and the proponent "of an active interference of the State in matters of popular education, not acting contrary to the useful prerogatives of local administration, but stimulating it by the power of example and by the advantages of working together in a positive sense." Rui Barbosa is of the same opinion, when, following the example of the United States and Argentina, two federal republics, he calls for national intervention, justifying, in his famous "opinion," the bill presented to the Chamber of Deputies in 1883, in his capacity as spokesman for the Commission on Public Instruction. This current of ideas favorable to a "national policy of education," which was to be achieved by direct intervention or through the collaboration of the federal government, broke up or died out, however, as a result of meeting the victorious federalist ideas, which finally imposed the complete decentralization which the federative system stands for, breaking up education into an artificial and complicated system of constitutional rights and duties with respect to Brazilian education. (See Pires de Almeida, *L'instruction publique au Brésil*, Rio de Janeiro, 1889, p. 533; Teixeira Brandão, *A educação nacional no regime republicano.* National Printing Office, Rio de Janeiro, 1907, pp. 94-103.)

abolition of slavery and the military question, developed at the same rate as federalist aspirations in the direction of an increase of political and administrative autonomy on the part of the provinces. Under the influence of these victorious ideas, the Constitution of February 24, 1891 instituted a federative form of the state and continued the traditions of Empire which came down through the Additional Act of 1834, transferring primary instruction to the States, which were assured the right to organize education in general, and reserving for itself, but not exclusively, the right to create institutions of secondary and higher education in the States and to provide for instruction in the Federal District, formerly called the Neutral Township.[4] Secondary and higher instruction in the Capital of the country was placed directly under the jurisdiction of the central government which transferred (law of November 20, 1892) to the orbit of the municipal powers of the district, the primary and professional education, which as far as the Neutral Township was concerned had been under the care of the Union in the Empire. Instead of removing the obstacles to the organization of a general system, the Republic did no more than aggravate them, sharing between the Union and the States the sphere of education and explicitly renouncing the duty which democratic institutions indicated belonged to it, to give leadership and to lay down the lines of Brazilian educational policy. With the decentralization imposed by the victory of federalist ideas; with the economic disorganization resulting from the

[4] The Republican Constitution of February 24, 1891 gave the Union exclusive competency to legislate on higher education in the capital of the Republic (art. 35, no. 30), and the right, but not exclusively, to create institutions of secondary and higher learning in the States and to provide for instruction in the Federal District (art. 35, nos. 3 and 4). Moreover it established the lay character of instruction given in public establishment (art. 72, no. 6), and guaranteed, in paragraph 24, of art. 72, "the free exercise of any moral, intellectual or industrial profession." By these few provisions, scattered through the Constitution of 1891, the rights of the government of the Union and of the state governments were divided as follows: a) the Union had the exclusive right to legislate on higher education in the capital of the Republic, and it was able, but shared this right, to set up institutions of secondary and higher character in the States and to provide for education in the Federal District; b) the States were permitted to organize their complete school systems; c) in the Federal District, higher education belonged to the jurisdiction of the government of the country, which was permitted, but not obliged to provide education of primary and middle grade. Hence came the possibility of simultaneous and parallel organization of three types of school systems: a) the federal system, made up, throughout the country, of secondary and higher education, and necessarily incomplete; b) complete state systems; c) and two types of public school organization in the Federal District, one belonging to municipal authorities, without higher education, and the other to the Union, which had the exclusive right to legislate on higher education and the option of organizing education of all levels in the Federal District. But, as primary, vocational and artistic education was transferred to the Municipal Chamber by the law of November 20, 1872, the school system in the Federal District was broken up into two parts, that of primary and vocational education which came to belong to municipal jurisdiction, and that of secondary and higher education, in the hands of the Union. As one sees, it was anarchy which was set up in the education of the country, with all this decentralization, which beside making a national system less possible, left primary education, which lies at the foundation of all democratic organization of education, at the mercy of local policies and budgets. The Constitution of February 24, as Teixeira Brandão rightly observes, "giving primary education to the States, and secondary and higher education jointly to the Union and the States, broke up the unity of public education and made it anarchical, by subordinating it to diverse and accidental interference, depending on the economic situation of the different regions of the Republic." (*A Educação nacional no regime republicano*, Rio de Janeiro, 1907.)

abolition of slavery, and with the struggles which followed to consolidate the new regime, the essential questions of a political and financial order tended to occupy the foreground, and education and culture, which only grew in the most important economic regions of the country like São Paulo, were able to follow without any profound change the lines of their traditional development, predetermined by the life of the colony and the regime of the Empire. "The most important elements of history (in cultural development) do not lie," writes Lamprecht, "in the political constitution, in social structure nor economic life, but in the field of morals, religion, art and science. Even if historic materialism were right, it would be necessary to classify the periods of culture not according to their root but according to their flower." [5]

If we were to classify the culture of Brazil during this period, not by its root but by its flower, not by economic and political transformations which were going on then, but by the governing class which had brought the Republic into existence and which came from the Empire, we would not be able to separate the phases of its cultural evolution into two, corresponding to these two regimes. In the Republican period, at least down to the European war of 1914–1918, the type of mentality and culture which had been formed in the colonial phase and during the Empire, was, in fact, continued with all of its characteristics. The same literary and bookish spirit; the same lack of boldness in construction, and the same excessive concern for juridical formulae, the formalism and "juridicism" in the words of José Maria Belo. It is this spirit which is reflected in the liberal Constitution of 1891 and which was to dominate all school legislation, with the exception of the first reform of Benjamim Constant, strongly influenced by certain Positivistic ideas. Side by side with the humanistic mentality of rhetoric and law, of the great majority of the governing class, educated in the old regime, there arose, with its scientific tendencies and its body of doctrines, the almost sectarian mentality of Positivism, which had been introduced into Brazil in the middle of the nineteenth century and which, through the discipline of mathematics, had won over the sympathy of the youngest generation of military men. These two types of mentality, so different and frequently in conflict, were incarnate, as it were, in two supreme beings, in Rui Barbosa, the principal figure of the First Republican Ministry and in Benjamim Constant, one of the first followers of the Positivistic philosophy of Brazil, who was proclaimed by the Constitutional Assembly the founder of the Republic because of his services. The influence of Positivism of the more orthodox type, that of Lafitte, represented by Miguel Lemos and Teixeira Mendes, or of the more heretical type, like that of Littré, which had penetrated by mathematical philosophy into the minds of the younger generation of officers, had extended beyond the orbit of debates over ideas in the civil and military academies, to attract into its range of action the political sphere in the initial phase of the Republican period.[6] If the fed-

[5] Karl Lamprecht, *Moderne Geschichtswissenchaft* (Modern Historical Science), 1905.

[6] Positivism, after the death of Auguste Comte in 1857, was divided, as we know, into two doctrines, both of which considered themselves equally orthodox, that of Pierre Lafitte, which accepted the theories on the political and religious organization of society, and became a sect with its worship (sacraments, feast days and pilgrimages) and that of E. Littré, which, rejecting the theories of Comte on the political and religious organization of society, retained some fundamental principles as absolutely fixed and invariable. Among these principles figure the suppression of all research which goes beyond phenomena, the law of the three stages, the division of the sciences into concrete and abstract, and the hierarchical classification of the abstract sciences, according to

erative Republic in Brazil did not owe its existence to Positivism, as Rui Barbosa observes, if it "is derived from the constitution of Hamilton, not from the catechism of Comte," it was not only the "*anima vilis* of Comtist empiricism," but with all the complications and the lack of popularity which it owed to it, it had in the definite ideology and severe morality of the Positivists, as well as in their tendency to certain forms of discipline reaching the point of oppression, one of the factors which most efficaciously contributed to break the forward march of demagogic power and to assure the stability of the new institutions.[7]

---

an order of growing complexity and decreasing generality. These two currents of thought into which the family of Auguste Comte was divided after the death of the founder, were represented at the time in Brazil by two groups, that of the Military School, in which the doctrine of E. Littré predominated, and the civilian group, for it was among civilians that the orthodox school recruited most disciples. The nucleus of the positivist élite formed in the Military School under the influence of Benjamim Constant, whose first contact with the philosophy of Comte, established through the mathematical disciplines, seems to go back to 1857, was almost entirely a branch of the school of E. Littré, while the group led by Miguel Lemos and Teixeira Mendes remained faithful to the current of Pierre Lafitte. "More than once," writes Rui Barbosa, referring to Benjamim Constant, "in the intimacy of confidences with which he honored me, he spoke of the excommunications which separated him from his coreligionists, protesting his orthodoxy and declared his impatience with the exigencies of the church's political intrigues." (Rui Barbosa, Lecture given on February 22, 1893, in the Theatre of São João, Salvador, Bahia. In "Discursos e Conferências," Pôrto, 1921, pp. 343-344).

[7] In 1893, in a lecture given in the city of Salvador, Rui Barbosa denied to Positivism "the predominant role attributed by it to itself, as a factor in the coming of the republic"; he affirmed the existence of "irreconcilable repugnancies," between Comtism and the sentiments of the country; and, with regard to what was therefore obvious enough, that is the impossibility of replacing a traditional religion, like the Catholic which was more than three centuries old in Brazil, by the religion of humanity, invented by Comte, which was beginning to have followers among us, declared timidly "that there was no indication that our race was about to exchange so soon the religion of charity incarnate in Christ for the religion of humanity." For him, the school of Comte in Brazil was no more than "a group of disciples, the cream if you like of our philosophical thought, but a cream . . . which was as isolated as a Utopian colony, representing in the eyes of the nation, a pugnacious, exclusivistic, intolerant group of fighters." From the political point of view, Positivism appeared in the eyes of the fighter for liberal ideas like a monstrosity, with its tendency "toward forms of iron oppression, not exceeded by theocracy," and with its practical tendencies,—"the perpetual dictatorship in the hands of its faithful." His political passions, his combative spirit, full of zeal and impetuosity, and his love for the principles of liberal democracy, did not permit him to see clearly nor appreciate with objectivity the role which Positivism had, in spite of all the intolerance of his sectarian spirit, in the establishment of republican institutions. Far from being "a dissolving ferment within the regime," as the great orator and politician thought, the influence of Positivism, to which the Republic certainly does not owe its existence, was "a conservative or consolidating element," with its cult of order, of authority, of hierarchy and of discipline. He did not see or was unwilling to recognize the moderating action of Positivism. The demagogic republicanism in which the new regime was struggling met, in fact, in the armed classes, in the church and in Positivism, some of the principal points of resistance to its expansive force, which was the more dangerous as the propagation of the ideals of liberty helped to aggravate the political and economic crisis, reducing the efficacy of the means by which the transformation of institutions established in the Constitution of 1891 was to take place. "It was the Positivists who encouraged in the young Republic," writes Azevedo Amaral, "the healthy ideals of an authoritarianism in harmony with the republican spirit, an authoritarianism which in the early years of the new political organization was a decisive factor in steadying the regime and repressing effectively all kinds of anarchical forces." (Azevedo Amaral, *Evolução da política republicana*, Cultura Política, Ano. 1, no. 3, May, 1941).

What gave the Comtist group "a disproportionate power in that historic moment," was not only the singular position in which the Positivistic current found itself "due to the absence of intellectual forces to counterbalance it," as Azevedo Amaral writes, but also the prestige and authority which the Army and, among the armed classes, the youngest generation of officers had attained. The sacrifices and glory of the Paraguayan War, "the separation of military studies in the Central School to form a specialized academy," and also the military question which brought the Army into the political arena, awakening its awareness of its historic role in the new national order, helped to develop not only the sentiment and pride of class, but also the desire to have an influence and to participate in politics outside the specific sphere of its own role. With the creation of the Military School in 1874, "military engineers," writes José Maria Belo, "acquired the best of rights to include themselves in the élite of official culture, in this country of doctors of law. The turquoise of their symbolic rings was worth as much or more than the ruby, the emerald and the sapphire of the lawyers, the doctors and the engineers." When, then, Positivist ideas entered the Military School and won the adhesion of a group of officers who had been subject to the influence of Benjamim Constant, military youth had already acquired a lively awareness of the important role of the armed classes and with this a new desire to act. The philosophy of Comte had only furnished this nucleus of the élite with one more element of cohesion, and the spiritual and political objectives of the young officers of the Army who were to be "the most ardent Republican conspirators." The generation of mathematicians educated under the Positivist influence in the Military School, like Benjamim Constant, Roberto Trompowsky and Samuel de Oliveira, was training in this center for the spread of Comtism a group of young men whose scientific culture, in strong contrast "to the superficial belletrism which characterized the great majority of the governing houses of the Empire," made them at the time, as Azevedo Amaral justly considers, "not only a spiritual power within the Army but also one of considerable influence in the whole of Brazilian life."

The influence of Positivist ideas and the influence of the Comtist group in the educational field, although superficial and temporary in their effect, became so much the easier as the first reform of education in the Republic was to be planned under the inspiration of Benjamim Constant, Minister of Education. On April 19, 1890, in fact, there was created by the government of the Republic, a strange Ministry of Instruction, Posts and Telegraphs, which besides involving an original error in organization by including in the same portfolio so different and separate a body of public services, appeared to be "a pure political expedient," utilized to keep out of the portfolio of War in the provisional government by this delicate means the great professor of the Military School who was the most influential personality among the younger officers of the Army. It was for this reason to last a short time and, in fact, the new ministry did last only a short time, ceasing to exist on December 26, 1892, when the business of education was transferred to the portfolio of Interior and Justice. The first Minister to hold the portfolio, Benjamim Constant Botelho de Magalhães, undertook in this period the reform of all public instruction, from primary and secondary of the Federal District up to higher education including artistic and technical education in the whole territory of the country. He instituted reforms of the Faculties of Law and Medicine, the Polytechnic School of

Rio de Janeiro, the School of Mines of Ouro Preto, the Military School, the Academy of Fine Arts, which took the name of Escola Nacional de Belas Artes, the Conservatory of Music which came to be called the Instituto Nacional de Música, the Imperial Institute of Blind Children, then named the Benjamim Constant, and the Institute of the Deaf and Dumb. As we see, there was not an institution which was not touched by the reforms of the first Minister of Education of the Republic; and if all of them show to a greater or lesser extent the influence of Positivistic ideas, it was in the reorganization of the Pedro II College—or National High School, according to the name with which the new regime rebaptized it—,and the Normal Schools of the Federal District, that some of the ideas of the French philosopher left the deepest marks. Although "a disciple refractory to the yoke of his school" and, certainly, far from orthodoxy, according to Rui Barbosa, the reformer of education gave to his innovations a strong Positivistic coloring, but it cannot be said that he directed them in the true sense of the philosophic and pedagogic ideas of Auguste Comte, which were frequently badly interpreted by his Brazilian followers.

According to the personal testimony of Rui Barbosa, Benjamim Constant did not know the politics of Comte; and his reforms of primary, normal and secondary education constitute the evident proof that the Minister of Education, "imbued rather than penetrated by the pedagogical and philosophical doctrines of Comtist Positivism," as José Veríssimo observed, had not reflected sufficiently upon the conceptions of education which were expressed in the treatises of philosophy and positive politics, or which can be deduced from that philosophical system. There is nothing, in fact, more contrary to the educational doctrines of Comte than to include any of the sciences of the Positivist classification in the plan of studies destined for children under fourteen years of age, an education which should be above all aesthetic and based on poetry, music, drawing and the study of languages. Now, in the program of studies organized in 1891, there figured in schools of the first grade (for pupils from 7 to 13) the physical and natural sciences, and in schools of the second grade (for those from 13 to 15) arithmetic, algebra, geometry and trigonometry, besides physical and natural sciences.[8] Introducing into normal and secondary education the whole hierarchical

---

[8] Neither purely scientific education, nor the control of education by the State, nor even the importance given, in the reform of Benjamim Constant, to professional specialization, find support in the pedagogical ideas of Auguste Comte, who dreamt of no exclusively scientific education for humanity and did not expect that the efforts or intervention of the government would bring about his plan of education. The great schools are not favorably judged by him; they, according to Comte, aim only at specialization and turn out only half-scholars, a species of intellectual monsters obtained by intensive specialization. In the system of education which is derived from his work, as Alexis Bertrand has shown, "education, exclusively domestic and quite spontaneous down to seven or eight years, must consist above all in the cultivation of the senses, the development of natural dexterity, by games, and in the acquisition of good habits." The mother must have charge of this period. From seven or eight until puberty, education, without ceasing to be domestic and directed by mothers, will become more systematic, "very free still, but no longer entirely spontaneous," and will be aesthetic, the basis of teaching being formed by poetry, music and drawing. During this period, to the predominantly artistic education of which it will be necessary to add the study of languages, the child should not hear anything about the seven sciences of the famous classification. Only then, when he has reached fourteen or fifteen, and after he has been initiated into the arts and languages, should scientific education begin: the seven fundamental sciences have until this time been unknown to him, except as he learns them through physical exercises, skills and also

series of abstract sciences, according to the classification of Comte, and overloading them with mathematics, elementary and higher, astronomy, physics, chemistry, biology, sociology and morals, the reformer broke with the tradition of literary and classical education and, aiming to establish the primacy of scientific studies, he did no more than install an encyclopedic type of teaching in secondary courses with the sacrifice of the study of ancient and modern languages and literature. Of all the reforms and creations of Benjamim Constant, the most important however "for the new regime of complete decentralization was," as José Veríssimo writes, "the Pedagogium, in the intent which he had of making it serve as a central source of ideas for reforms and improvements, which national education needed, and as a centralizing point for whatever was done in the matter of public education by Brazil. As it was founded and came to develop, this institution was to have had the same function as the Bureau of Education in the United States and was to be, as the latter actually was, an agent making for unity in the variety of public education in the nation and thus a powerful factor for national unity itself." [9]

But this excellent institution to which a role of major importance was assigned in the vast plan of reform of Benjamim Constant handed over to the Municipality, was not long in dying and with it there disappeared the only organ of coordination and control of pedagogical and cultural activities in the country. The other moves and reforms were no more successful and some of them did not succeed in being carried into practice, like that of the Polytechnic School of Rio de Janeiro and the School of Mines of Ouro Preto, or were abandoned, after undergoing alterations and mutilations, like those of the secondary and normal school education which showed a more marked trace of Positivistic influences. In spite of his moderation, Benjamim Constant was not able to resist the intellectual temptation of putting reforms of education in the framework of Comtist doctrine, and he fell into some of the snares which the systematic spirit delights in spreading before the steps of those who are intoxicated by its heady wine. The reforms, especially those of fundamental education, either primary or secondary, which moreover were bitterly criticized, as were those of normal and military education, by the orthodox Positivists of Brazil,[10] not only marked a rupture with the old tradition of humanistic, predominantly literary teaching, but also involved tendentious innovations, being suspected of closed plans or complete constructions with which the systematization of the schools was begun. and which

---

the arts, which necessarily take something from science. Education after fifteen "will not be domestic, but public; not spontaneous, but systematic; it will follow scrupulously the hierarchic scheme of positivism in the sciences and the logical order of the relation of the sciences." In the pedagogical system of Comte, who did no more than systematize the ideals of Plato, taking into account the progress of the sciences, this part of education is the only one that can immediately be carried out; "domestic education offers insuperable difficulties, for it presupposes an education in the woman of the people which we are far from having attained and a cooperation of the family environment which, in the present state of our manners, may pass for Utopian. Young women would receive the same instruction as boys, slightly tempered as far as science is concerned." (Alexis Bertrand, *Un réformateur d'éducation*. In "Nouvelle Revue," January 15, 1898.)

[9] José Veríssimo, *A instrução pública* (1500–1900.). III. República. Estado atual (1890–1900) p. 25. In "Livro do Centenário," National Printing Office, Rio de Janeiro, 1900.

[10] R. Teixeira Mendes, *A política positiva e o Regulamento das escolas do Exército*. Rio de Janeiro 1890.

either belonged or was supposed to belong to the imagination or to the spirit of the system. To these closed and rigid plans, tradition was opposed, for its continuity was menaced by the innovations inspired by the Positivists and the successive unexpected forms which economic, social and political evolution created in the country and which tended to transform and to overthrow the dreamed of conceptions, within the system at a given instant, and the reaction of the contrary theories, within or without the field of the Catholic church, which maintained in the face of Positivism an attitude of hostility or at least of defense. The Church, which had retired in the face of the humiliations which it suffered in the incident of the Bishops of Pernambuco and Pará, could not approach the imperial government because of the royal victory in the religious question, nor was it disposed to establish a closer contact with the republican government, accused of atheism and suspected of having fallen into the orbit of influence of the two Positivistic groups.

With the separation of Church and State and the growing lay character of the teaching provided in public establishments (article 72, no. 6 of the Constitution of 1891), and therefore with the agnosticism of the republican constitution, the school policy of the Church, which up until that time had exercised almost a monopoly of spiritual direction, suffered the first blows that the Comtist attitude in educational reform in the provisional government only served to accentuate, relegating the influence of the clergy to the background. The reaction against the lay ideology consecrated by the Constitution and the intervention of the Positivists in the shaping of the new educational order was to take some time yet to organize itself, and with regard to the suppression of the confessional public school, it did not become effective until about forty years later, when it obtained again the reestablishment of religious teaching in the schools. The fact is that Catholicism, as Rui Barbosa observes, had not become in Brazil, as it did in the United States, "due to the necessities of struggle, practically a new religion" and besides not being accustomed to struggle in a traditionally Catholic country, in which powerful resistance to the domination of the church did not arise, it did not have at this time a clergy with sufficient influence on consciences and with sufficient force in society to undertake an efficacious reaction of great scope. But, within the new regime in which the State instituted the system of educational neutrality, the school which before had been developing in the shade of the Church, the official religion in the Empire, continued to progress through private initiative and under the influence of various religious orders. In a country already divided between different beliefs, none of which as yet succeeded in disputing the primacy of the Church, there were clearly distinguished two confessional points of view,—the Catholic and the Protestant, developing side by side in the shade of the constitutional principle of freedom of thought and of belief, and having between them the interconfessional institution, the lay, neutral school of public education under the temporary influence of Positivistic ideas.[11]

The educational and cultural landscape tended from this time on to differentiate, not only in consequence of the separation of Church and State and the freedom of belief and teaching, but also as the result of the competition which was beginning

[11] P. Arbousse-Bastide, *A instrução pública e a República*. As reformas didáticas de Benjamim Constant e a crítica dos positivistas ortodoxos (1890–1892). In "O Estado de São Paulo," October 26, 1941.

on the part of the Protestant schools, with which two confessional points of view or two pedagogical systems, not antagonistic but different, had come into each other's presence and even into conflict. The struggle in the educational field was not to break out only between the agnostic State, which remained faithful to its affirmations of confessional neutrality, and the conception of Catholic pedagogy, but also in the religious field between the points of view of the two churches. We had the competition of the lay school and of the church school, on the one hand, and on the other, in the field of church schools, the competition between two school conceptions,—the Catholic and the Protestant. If we compare the mentality which came from the lay school with that which was formed in the church schools, we cannot fail to recognize with Pandiá Calógeras the importance which he pointed out in 1911, which the facts confirmed, of "the internal political problem created by the separation of Church and State and arising from the possible conflict between the theological concept of man and society and the mentality which presided over the republican organization and, which until today is maintained in its organic law; a conflict which may break out (and which in fact did break out, we may add) in the struggle for victory between the two ideals, when from the schools, some of them lay in character, others under the Church, there come and engage in struggle the directors of the national policy of tomorrow, reflecting the deeper strife between these two conceptions of life itself." [12] It did not seem to him, however, that such divergence was to be feared with regard to the schools affiliated with the innumerable variations of the Protestant church. Calógeras explains: "An open schism in the name of individual liberty in the interpretation of the sacred writings, its essential principle acts continually and perpetually as a ferment, ceaselessly favoring and encouraging new religious currents of thought and authorizing the change of dogma. It does not permit, therefore, the great ecclesiastical centralization which gives to Catholicism and its organs of action the power and the preponderance which they have in the spiritual life of peoples. Besides this, the analytical tendency of Protestantism and the austerity of its mental habits coincide so closely with the characteristics of the spirit of scientific investigation, that it is natural there should arise between the two a tacit alliance and mutual understanding. The moral concept which is constantly looking for progressive improvement corresponds to the dogma which is always open to individual correction."

It is for this reason, due to the friendly relations existing between the lay concept and the sects derived from the Reformation, that the Protestant schools during the republican regime made such rapid progress, which not only gave them an indisputable place in the history of education of the country, but opened up to them a period of fruitful renovating activities. It was in large part through the schools under the direct influence of Protestant ministers and educators from North America, that there took place in Brazil the first propagation of American pedagogical ideas, which commenced to spread in São Paulo, with the foundation of the Escola Americana in 1871 and of the Colégio Piracicabano in 1881 and which, before being reflected in the reform movement of Caetano de Campos, Cesário Mota and Gabriel Prestes in São Paulo (1891–1895), had inspired the reforms of Leôncio de Carvalho (1878–1879) and the opinion of Rui Barbosa (1882–1883), already modelled on American and

[12] J. Pandiá Calógeras, *Os jesuítas e o ensino*. National Printing Office. Rio de Janeiro, 1911, Chapter V, p. 53.

German ideals. Among the principal centers of Protestant and American influence,[13] there emerged then in Minas Gerais, the Colégio Granbery, founded in Juiz de Fora in 1889, and in São Paulo, the Escola Americana, which dates from 1871, and which gave rise to Mackenzie College by the successive additions of other courses such as the secondary in 1886, the Engineering School in 1896,—the time at which the establishment took its present name—, and in 1902, the School of Commerce. Founded above all by the Methodist and Presbyterian churches, these and other schools related to various currents of Protestant thought made a notable contribution to the education of girls; they introduced co-education, establishing mixed classes as early as 1871 in all the courses of Mackenzie and other institutions; they helped to change didactic processes, influenced by the imported ideas of North America pedagogical technique, and for a long time they were to be among the few innovating forces in education,— those living forces which keep the temperature of spiritual institutions from a kind of moral cooling off due to uniformity and routine.

But, apart from lay tendencies, the infiltration of Positivist ideas and the renovating movement of São Paulo, which was limited to primary and normal school education and was under the influence of American pedagogical technique, all of the other facts relative to education and culture showed in the last decade of the nineteenth century the survival of the traditions of the Imperial regime. There was no essential modification of the educational policy of the Empire, no creation of technical or professional schools to meet the specific needs of the national interest nor any

[13] The Protestant schools, begun in the last quarter of the nineteenth century, were able only in the present century to enlarge their sphere of activity and gain sufficiently in depth to produce their real effects and have a genuine influence on the modernization of educational thinking and the processes of teaching in the country. Still very limited in the orbit of their influence, the few schools founded by Protestants in the decade before the Republic (1880–1889), prepared the way for the progress of the movement of penetration in the first decade of the Republic. The separation of Church and State with its consequences,—freedom of worship and belief and the lay character of the public school, contributed toward this development, which beginning with the Republic has been notable, not only from the quantitative point of view—, the numerical growth of these schools, but also from the point of view of the quality of their buildings, pedagogical methods and educational work in general, on all levels of instruction. It was the Methodist Church which had the leading part in Brazil in the field of pedagogical and cultural activity. At the end of the Empire, the Methodist Church had founded two schools, the Piracicabano in São Paulo (1881), and, in Pôrto Alegre, the Colégio Americano (1885). In the first decade of the Republic there were set up, for girls, the Escola do Alto (1892–1895), in Santa Teresa, which afterwards functioned in the old Colégio Progresso, of Rio de Janeiro; the Colégio Mineiro (1891–1914), in Juiz de Fora; the Colégio Americano Fluminense (1892–1915); the Colégio Americano, in Petrópolis (1895–1920), which all closed on the dates indicated; and the Colégio Metodista (1899), in Riberião Preto. For boys, there were founded in that period, the Colégio Granbery (1889), which in 1917 had a complete organization with primary, secondary, commercial, theological and higher courses; and the Colégio Americano, of Taubaté, which lasted a short time (1890–1895). Later in the present century, there arose other institutions, due to the efforts of the Methodists, three for girls, the Colégio Isabela Hendrix, founded in 1904, in Belo Horizonte; the Colégio Bennett, located in Rio de Janeiro, in 1921, which united the Colégio Americano Fluminense and the school of Petrópolis, and the Colégio Centenário begun in 1922, in Santa Maria, in Rio Grande do Sul; and three for boys, all in Rio Grande do Sul, the Colégio União (1907), of Uruguaiana, the Instituto Ginasial (1910), of Passo Fundo, and the Pôrto Alegre College (1919), one of the most important educational institutions of that State. (Cf. James Kennedy, *Cinquenta anos de Metodismo no Brasil*. Methodist Press, São Paulo, 1928.)

serious attempt at the creation of courses of free and disinterested culture. In the shade of the government's policy of religious neutrality in education, schools directed according to Catholic concepts continued to flourish, for these concepts through the force of tradition continued to dominate even the public schools in spite of the suppression of religious teaching. The last vestiges of the ephemeral influence of Positivism which had marked the school legislation of Benjamim Constant were not slow in dying out under the demolishing or reconstructive action of successive reforms. The penetration of the Protestant schools, which became the principal center of the spread of American ideas, starting slowly in the last quarter of the century, continued to develop with more rapidity in the republic, although these elements coming from outside did not have sufficient time to incorporate themselves in the culture of the nation or to exercise upon it real influence in the sense of orienting it in a new direction. The continual migrations which went on in the south and which, in the sweep of ther current of immigration attracted foreign artists and professional men, either were concentrated on the fazendas or in little towns, like those of Santa Catarina, or were scattered through the cities where they were diluted in the mass of the Brazilian population. The mixture of peoples, the variety of origins in customs, and all these mixtures, not deeply rooted, of cultures and traditions, were to take a long time to modify the traditional type of culture, saturated as it was with the literary and juridical spirit which had been formed through more than three centuries into a compact and homogeneous whole capable of resisting the civilizing influence of other currents.

If, then, there was arising already the diversity of tendencies under the pressure of economic, political and cultural causes, it is certain that Brazil in 1891 preserved, as Azevedo Amaral remarked, and was to preserve for a long time, "the last vestiges of the defects of Coimbra," and was continuing "spiritually nourished only by the superficial culture which belletrism and philosophical and juridical archaism had maintained during the Empire and which was scarcely shaken by the blows of Tobias Barreto." With the victory of the centrifugal tendencies of regionalism, and the growing expansion of state autonomy, not only were there not created by the action of the States new cultural institutions outside the field of the liberal professions, but the development of professional higher schools even took on new life. This was above all true of the schools of law which were not slow in spreading throughout the country. For eight free law schools which were created during the first twenty years of the Republic,—two in Rio de Janeiro, and that of Bahia, founded in 1891, that of Minas Gerais which dates from 1892, that of Fortaleza (1907), that of Pará, Manaus and Pôrto Allegre,—there were founded only three schools of engineering: the Polytechnic School (1893), the School of Engineering of Mackenzie College created in 1896 in São Paulo, and another, due to private initiative, in Rio Grande do Sul, and beside a Higher School of Agriculture (1910), one of Veterinary Medicine and the Chemical Institute in Rio de Janeiro. Decentralization, consecrated in the Constitution, borrowed, as far as the parliamentary regime is concerned, from the English system and as far as the federative principle is concerned from the model of the United States, was to demonstrate in the organization of the two school systems which began to confront each other, the domination without any counterbalance of the same mentality which came down from the Empire and which marked these parallel, scholastic formations with the old characteristics. In fact, the duality of systems which decentralization produced,—the federal system made up of secondary and higher education and the State system with legal possibilities of establishing schools of all grades and types—, not only maintained and emphasized the line of demarcation between the liberal professions and manual and mechanical activities, but also facilitated the reproduction by the States of the traditional school organizations, multiplied in examples that were more or less evolved, but all imitating the old model of the Imperial period.

The tendency based upon academic traditions and the liberal professions continued to develop, now with the double backing and with the same spirit which came to it from the old federal schools founded under the Empire and the new institutions of the same type which were arising at various points in the land through private initiative or that of state governments. In this way, instead of a single action exercised by central power, which guided at a distance the whole school policy in the direction of the liberal careers on a basis of literary study, under this regime of decentralization there emerged a variety of regional actions, not divergent but harmonized: actions corresponding to each one of the States and dominated by the old Coimbra mentality and influencing strongly in the same direction a great variety of cultural centers. Only this education with a literary base,—classical and designed to prepare for the professions of lawyers, doctors and engineers, conferred upon Brazilians a title, raised them in social dignity, and continued to be the path to important occupations. The preeminence of literary studies over scientific studies remained so strongly marked in the cultural system of the country that the rare schools or institutes designed for scientific teaching, not applied, or for research in the field of the natural sciences, still constituted, and were to constitute for a long time, solitary institutions without influence. Reform of secondary and normal school education under the leadership of Benjamim Constant gave to preparatory education and to that for the professional training of the teacher a character that was more encyclopedic than scientific. Except for the field of mathematics, in which the Positivist philosophy had had an influence, helping to develop these studies in civil and military academies, Positivism did not bring to Brazil any weighty contribution to the progress of the sciences. The fact is that, as we have already observed, Positivism had entered the country not as a "method of investigation," but as a manner of thinking which could be called scientific or even empirical, and above all as a social, political and religious philosophy which had and still has its adherents. That Positivism which is a method and not a doctrine; which seems to repudiate the *a priori* and aims to proceed by the experimental method and not mere geometrics; and which was inspired, as Stuart Mill says, by a general doctrine which Comte had learned in the method of the physical sciences and in the writings of earlier philosophers; this trend of Positivism, if it had its followers in Brazil, did not penetrate their minds very profoundly nor was it extended sufficiently far to exercise a notable influence upon the development of the critical and experimental spirit and the liking for exact sciences.

No institution, in fact, was created in this long period for the cultivation of the various sciences without some idea of professional application; and in the field of the technical and special schools, the few scattered and isolated attempts did not show any over all plan conceived in accord with the new policy of education, nor did they express nor succeed in arousing any movement of interest for technical culture, for agriculture or industry, economic or social studies in the country. Between the two terms "literary-juridical" and "professional-utilitarian," dominant throughout the period of the Empire, there began to be inserted a whole range of intermediate terms, which still gravitated by preference around the middle term "literary-professional" which is the characteristic and most marked trait of our culture and our system of education. The School of Manguinhos itself, which was the name given to the Instituto Soroterápico Federal, created in 1901 and which was transformed in 1907 into the Institute of Experimental Pathology with the name of Osvaldo Cruz was, in its origins, an institution destined to prepare anti-plague serums and to combat the bubonic plague which had broken out in Santos and threatened to spread to other regions. This institute although it was to become the major center of research in Brazil was not born out of any deliberate plan of governmental policy with the object of promoting the progress of scientific studies. The necessity of confronting two terrible diseases in their height as epidemics necessitated the creation of an institution with an immediate and practical end, which Osvaldo Cruz transformed by expanding its field of activity into the most important institute of tropical diseases and research in the field of medical zoology and experimental medicine. The authority and prestige of Osvaldo Cruz, strengthened by his magnificent victory in the struggle which went on against the plague and yellow fever permitted him to acquire the means to support this extraordinary foundation, in which there was grouped a handful of eight disciples and collaborators of first rate ability, and which was not slow in becoming a school of research men and a center for the spread of scientific work and the methods of the experimental sciences.

But scientific activities in Brazil, although with the creation of the Institute of Manguinhos the field of scientific research had notably enlarged, continued to be dispersed in special institutions of various kinds,—museums, experimental stations and laboratories—, which did not serve the purpose of teaching nor fit into the educational system proper of the nation. They won, without doubt, under the splendid leadership and through the obstinate will of Osvaldo Cruz, one more field of application of the scientific attitude and method which the founder of the Institute of Manguinhos, returning to Brazil in 1899, had brought from his stay of three years in the Institut Pasteur in Paris. This movement of conquest on the part of the scientific spirit did not, however, reach the point of including in its sphere of influence higher education, which was developing within the traditional framework without any really fecund effort to enrich the cultural heritage and to transmit along with the cult of the sciences, a taste for observation and experimentation. In fact, while during this period only one higher school,—that of the Medical School of Bahia—, accomplished a vigorous piece of work in this direction with the scientific activity developed by Nina Rodrigues during the whole period in which he conducted the courses of legal medicine (1891–1905), it was in five institutions outside the system that investigations limited to the field of the natural sciences took shape. The illustrious professor from Maranhão, beginning a new phase in the evolution of legal medicine in Brazil and creating a so-called "Bahiana school" which gave us an Afrânio Peixoto, a Diógenes Sampaio, an Oscar Freire and their disciples, may be considered the creator of the only nucleus of research men which in this period was trained in the higher schools of the country. The fact is that it was in the cultural institutions of applied science that research activities, almost entirely limited to natural sciences, took on new life. They were done or guided by exceptional men, foreigners or Brazilians, and the latter almost entirely educated abroad; an Emílio Goeldi, a zoologist of universal renown, of the Museum Paraense, founded in 1885, which in 1900 took the name of its founder (Museu Goeldi); a F. W. Dafert, first director (1887–1898) of the Instituto Agronômico, created in 1887 by the imperial government in Campinas and transferred in the republican period to the State of São Paulo; a Hermann von Ihering in the Museu Paulista founded in 1893, of which the notable German zoologist was the first director; and among the Brazilians a Barbosa Rodrigues, the great botanist of *Sertum Palmarum,* in the Botanical Garden, which he came to direct in 1890, and Osvaldo Cruz and his group of collaborators in the Institute of Manguinhos.

Important as may have been,—and in many respects it was truly notable—, the work undertaken in this institution of research, and useful and fruitful as was the activity carried on in various cultural institutions,—centers of investigation embracing different sectors of the sciences of nature—, they did not show that progress which presupposes a change in mentality or cultural policy. Isolated and scattered products of individual efforts, they lived on the inspiration which those rare spirits attracted to research and original work gave to their precious activity turned in various directions. Some of them, like the Agronomical Institute at Campinas and the School of Manguinhos were in their origin and in their aim institutions meant to meet the need for the national health and economic life; and others owed their success in the field of the natural sciences so much to the personal effort of certain individuals that the loss of a Dafert, of a Goeldi or of a Von Ihering was enough to lead to a deviation from the line of their evolution, or an abrupt decrease in the progress of their work. These facts show evidently that at the beginning of the republican period nothing was done to change the mentality of the dominant elite by means of great schools created not only to form specialists highly qualified in the different branches of human knowledge, but also to promote the progress of the sciences by disinterested research. From a cultural and pedagogical point of view, the Republic was a revolution which aborted and which, contenting itself with a change of regime, did not have the thought nor the decision to accomplish a radical transformation in the system of education, to lead to an intellectual renovation of the cultural and political élite which were necessary to new, democratic institutions. Neither was the system of higher education, which kept its almost exclusively professional character, enriched by institutions of higher culture such as faculties of philosophy, of letters and sciences, in which theoretical research should be united to the function of teaching, nor was there begun at the base a penetration of the scientific spirit by means of the reorganization, on a new foundation and with a new purpose of secondary education, on which normally the superstructure of higher education, applied or not, professional or disinterested, is based.

If, in fact, there persisted in the school system that capital fault which is the absence of universities or those higher schools, the pedagogical role of which becomes the function of research, education, which lies at the base of the schools for professional training, continued to be reduced to the minor function of preparing students for the higher courses. We did not solve nor put in the way to be solved any of the fundamental problems related to the reorganization of our secondary education, such as a program of studies that should be regular and methodical, designed rather for training than for acquisition and destined to provide that general culture which is indispensable to later specialization. Without schools created for the uniform education of secondary school teachers, who were almost all self-taught or recruited, as in the Empire, from the ranks of the liberal professions, secondary education could not show, as indeed it did not, that educational power and cultural efficiency which come from the slow action of a course of study that is prolonged and disinterested, and the more efficacious as it is carried on by a group of professors prepared in a common environment and therefore bearers of the same ideals of life and education. None of the reforms down to 1930 faced or tried to solve this great problem; and precisely in the lack of a body of professors who made a career of teaching and were educated under a uniform system in schools of a high level, is it that one can seek the origins of many of the difficulties in which the most honest efforts at organizing secondary education bogged down in their execution. From the point of view of structure, our middle education, the heir and continuer of the colleges of the Jesuits, remained more or less faithful to its Latin and purely literary origins and kept, without essential modifications, if not the traditional plan of studies, at least the same spirit and the same character which the Empire had impressed upon it, without keeping the efficiency which constituted the prestige of the Colégio Pedro II in the old regime. The question which was discussed everywhere, that of the preeminence of literary studies over scientific studies, remained without any solution, through the plans of the various reformers, legislators or ministers of the State, who abstained from examining, in order to choose one of them, any of the solutions proposed for this century-old question and which consisted either in the creation of two types of teaching (system of bifurcation), one with a preponderance of letters and the other with a preponderance of sciences, the two branches growing off from a common trunk; or in the close association of literary and scientific studies, with which it was hoped to put the two parts of culture on the same basis of equality; or again by the penetration of the scientific spirit through all of education, including education in letters.

It certainly was not and could not be by means of our reform, in a country without scientific traditions, that this last solution would be tried, a solution which was the most logical and the most complete and was discussed at that time, with the object that "the triumph of the scientific spirit should assure the unity of education, which has been pushed about for a century between the traditional culture of the literary humanities and the new culture of the sciences." But whichever of the two first solutions had been for a long time tried in countries like, to cite only two, France, which adopted the system of ramification on a common base, and Germany, which attempted to secure the equilibrium of letters and sciences, not in a single type of school (unified education) but by various fixed categories of high schools corresponding to the divergent tendencies and equally powerful (classic letters, modern letters and science), which disputed the first place in the struggle for the conquest of secondary education. The fact is that in the Republic the successive remodelling of secondary education,— regimes characterized by arbitrary and partial plans,[14] almost all without breadth of

[14] If we examine the reforms in secondary education, in the first period of the Republic, we shall find that, unless it be the reform of Benjamim Constant, none of them made a substantial change in the internal structure nor attempted to eliminate from our schools their utilitarian character nor made provision for the training of secondary school teachers. All of them showed much hesitation, beside an absolute lack of a spirit of continuity, in the study and in the solutions proposed for the

view and of ideas and incapable of getting away from the most elementary questions of organization, oscillated between the regime of preparatory school and the graduated course, with a ladder made up of partial or subject examinations, and between the system of official education (with a pattern for education and with the schools following that pattern) and an entirely free system of education, such as that which was established by the Organic Law of 1911, which made education unofficial and instituted the regime of ample autonomy. Of all of these reforms the only two which corresponded to a system of ideas and which, as expressions of Positivism in Brazil, brought with them a philosophic content that was more or less defined,—the Reform of Benjamim Constant in 1890, the Organic Law of Rivadávia Correia in 1911, were however, through their systematic character both the most radical and the farthest from the environment for which they were meant. The former, aiming, under

---

fundamental problems of the organization of education. Differences of opinion began to appear as to the obligatory character itself of the course with its arrangement in series, and even as to the duration of the course, which, set at seven years in the time of the Empire and the reform of Benjamim Constant (1890), was reduced to six in the Código Epitácio Pessoa, which was in force from 1901 to 1910, and to five in the law of Carlos Maximiliano (1915), to be raised once more to seven years only by the reform of Francisco Campos (1931),—this last the most important reform of all that were undertaken under the republican regime. The obligatory series which reappeared, after various advances and retreats, in the reform of João Luiz Alves (1925), only won out then over the system of preparatory courses, with which secondary education had been struggling for about forty years. The reform of Benjamim Constant (decree of November 8, 1890), which introduced into the Ginásio Nacional, the former Colégio Pedro II, the whole hierarchical series of the abstract sciences, according to the classification of Comte, established, side by side with the course for the bachelor of letters, in seven years, in the Ginásio Nacional, the "maturity examination," as a proof of intellectual capacity on the part of the students at the end of their studies. But this measure was not put into practice or was badly carried out when it was, as José Veríssimo observed ten years later, and it existed simultaneously with the system of separate examinations, preferred by most people. In the Educational Code of 1901 (decree No. 3,890, of January 1, 1901), worked out by Minister Epitácio Pessoa, during the government of Campos Sales, we kept, side by side with the course arranged serially (with or without the bachelor's degree), the system of preparatory courses, which resisted successfully all attacks. With this code, we set up a system of "coordination" of private schools, modeled on the federal pattern and inspected by the government of the Republic. No radical change took place as a result of the reform in secondary education; nor was its structure changed, although it suffered a serious blow, with the law of Rivadávia Correia, so sectarian and radical in character. The so-called "organic law of education" (decree of April 5, 1911), reflecting the dominant positivistic outlook in Rio Grande do Sul, set up a system of free education, depriving the State of the right to interfere in the field of education, called for entrance examinations, suppressed diplomas, and asserting the autonomy of the religious Congregations, took from the government the right to concern itself with the internal economy of higher schools. Far from stopping it, this reform helped to accentuate the degradation into which secondary education had fallen, whether under the system of separate examinations or under that of maturity examinations, or under the system of "coordination." Therefore, reaction was not long in coming, with the law of Carlos Maximiliano (March 18, 1915), which restored the former situation and once more made secondary education official, with a five year course, keeping the preparatory examinations in private schools, to be taken in the presence of boards appointed by the Higher Education Council,—an institution created by the reform of Rivadávia Correia, to which art. 11 of this decree (April 5, 1911), assigned the inspecting function of the State. In the reform of João Luiz Alves, also called by the name of Rocha Vaz (January 13, 1925), which remained in force down to 1930, the arrangement of courses in an obligatory series finally won out, and the system of preparatory courses, resting on the strong support of almost a century of tradition, was no longer permitted, except in the cases of those who had licenses in it.

the influence of Positivist ideas, to give a scientific character to the plan of secondary studies, did no more than set up a type of encyclopedic teaching; and the latter, which did not succeed, like that of Benjamim Constant, in touching the structure of secondary education, took away its official seal, removing it from the interference of the State and restoring by law the regime of free competition or rivalry which had been established by the pressure of circumstances under the Empire.

Reduced, in the federal plan of education, to the National High School, which was again to come to be called the Colégio Pedro II, and submitted to trials and new trials of reform in every decade,—two of them separated only by five years—, middle education or that of general culture did not find in the Republic down to 1930 a legislator who, by putting order into confusion, could give it a solid and flexible structure at the same time, and one adopted as much to its ends as to the necessities and social aspirations of the time and place. The regime which lasted until 1925, one of preparatory schools and "partial examinations" held back for about forty years the definite replacement of fragmentary studies by systematic studies, which it was always possible to escape through the open door of the concession to students that they might take examinations in isolated subjects or groups of disciplines. Under the operation of the regime of preparatory courses or the system of making schools equivalent to the standard school, secondary education, which was provided by a single federal establishment and some few others maintained by the States, had to develop mostly as a result of the generous impulse of private initiatives, either religious or lay, whose effort was not sufficient to render this education accessible to any but a small part of society and a small fraction of adolescents. From the qualitative point of view, the schools which were created then or developed thanks to the efforts of private institutions, contributed very little to the reform of the spirit and methods of secondary education in the country. Obliged to subordinate themselves to the plans given and to systematic schemes that were excessively rigid, fixed by federal legislation which controlled not only the plans of study but even hours and programs, these schools could not organize themselves freely and serve as laboratories with their own system and methods, laboratories in which we might find inspiration or ideas which would guide future reforms. The education of girls on the secondary school level did take on new life in the normal schools, in the colleges of the nuns and in other private institutions which were opened to women at the end of the past century and especially in the present century, in which in 1907, as Francisco Venâncio Filho tells us, "the first two young women who ventured upon it completed the secondary course for the bachelor in letters." [15] The expansion of education and of culture took place, then, thanks not only to private initiative in the field of secondary education, but especially to the development of independent organisms,—state school systems which were established according to the model of the system of education in the Imperial period rather than according to an over all plan.

The formation of the state systems of education which began to be organized parallel with the federal system,—the latter being limited to secondary and higher education—, and whose evolution was particularly favored by the regime of autonomy and political and administrative decentralization, took place, however, irregularly, de-

[15] Francisco Venâncio Filho, *Educação*, III. In "Cultura Política," ano I, no. 3, May, 1941, pp. 281-284.

pending upon the great differences of economic and cultural level between the different States of the Union. Not only did it develop with evident irregularity, connected with this lack of economic and cultural equality in the various regions of the country, but still along the traditional lines and more notably in the field of primary normal school education, which entered on a new phase in certain states, like that of São Paulo in the administration of Cesário Mota, in the Federal District, formerly called the Neutral Township, under the initial influence of Medeiros e Albuquerque, and in Minas Gerais with João Pinheiro da Silva, as President of the State. What the Empire had left us in this respect was, in the harsh but exact words of Azevedo Sodré, "a primary education that was most deficient, weak and ragged in almost all the territory of the nation." [16] But with all the effort which was carried on in various States, the abnormal situation in which the Empire had left us and the Republic kept us, was not noticeably changed, to judge by the impressive data on the percentage of illiterates, which estimated at 66.4% in 1872, 67.2% in 1890, went down to only 58.8% in 1900, to rise to 60.1% in 1920, that is thirty years after the beginning of the republican regime. In some states, these appear even to have been a retrogression, as in Bahia and in Pernambuco, "notable parts of the Union, which during the Empire," Afrânio Peixoto tells us, "spent 25 and 15 per cent respectively of their income on education, and during the Republic came to spend only 3 and 5 per cent of their receipts for this purpose." The geographic extent of the country in which there were included populations walled up in an almost complete cultural isolation, the insufficiency of local communications and the extremely low density of population, which rendered necessary the creation of an enormous quantity of school establishments if we were to reduce notably the percentage of illiterates, constitute, together with the small budgets of the majority of the States, the principal reasons for the slowness with which popular education dragged on in most of the parts of the federation. With primary education handed over to the States and the central government in consequence stripped of any positive influence over this essential field of education, the primary and normal schools financed by the States naturally were conditioned, in amount of expansion and in their development, by the economic conditions of each region.

It was in São Paulo, to which the center of the economic life of the country was transferred, that education in its various ways and forms took on the most vigorous life. The policy adopted of financing immigration, which came to be subsidized by the State after 1886; the new possibilities that were opened to the work of the colonists with the abolition of the servile element, and the development of coffee growing, which attained in 1895 one of its culminating points with the great rise in the price of coffee, contributed powerfully to attract to this region of the country and to settle in it, the major currents of immigration. While in 1891 and in 1895, respectively, there were distributed to the other States of the Union 108,072 and 27,620 immigrants, to the State of São Paulo alone there flowed 108,688 foreigners in 1891 and 139,998 in 1895, or let us say in that last year an immigration five times greater than ʰhat which was spread out through the other States. This situation of prosperity which was prolonged to 1928 in the rural economy based upon coffee growing and to which the rise of

[16] A. A. de Azevedo Sodré, *O problema da educação nacional.* Rio de Janeiro, Printing office of the "Jornal do Comércio," 1926, p. 18.

industry, especially after 1918, was to impart more vigorous life, permitted the State of São Paulo to organize the system of education on a more solid, broad basis. After 1890, when the first reform of primary and normal school education emerged, the school for the training of primary teachers entered upon a new phase,—one of the most brilliant of its history—, under the guidance of Antônio Caetano de Campos, assisted in his reforming effort by Maria Guilhermina Loureiro de Andrade, who had spent four years studying in the United States, and Miss Marcia Browne, former principal of a normal school in St. Louis, head of a high school in Malden, near Boston in the United States. These two teachers,—one a Brazilian, who finished her studies in North America, and the other an educator from that country, had been suggested by Dr. Horace Lane of the American School to collaborate with Caetano de Campos, director of the Normal School, in the direction of the school annexes (model schools) which served as a field for practice teaching for the students and for experimentation in new methods. In 1892 when Bernardino de Campos was president of the State, a law was passed reorganizing public education (September 8, 1892) and it was regulated on November 23, 1893, under the leadership of Cesário Mota who on February 8th of that year had succeeded Vicente de Carvalho in the portfolio of the Interior.

There were then created by this reform, three more normal schools, besides the so-called complementary schools and high schools. Services of inspection were organized; various consolidated schools were started, and the Normal School of São Paulo, whose course came to be a four year one, was installed in 1894 in a new and magnificent building which even today remains after undergoing various additions and remodelling. This reform movement inspired by North American pedagogical ideas and techniques went on until the beginning of the present century as a result of the action of a group of educators like Gabriel Prestes, who followed Caetano de Campos in the direction of the Normal School, and Oscar Thompson who, having replaced Miss Browne in 1893, assumed in 1909 the general direction of education in São Paulo. If to this State, then, belongs the credit which Caetano de Campos claimed for "having created the public school with reformed education," and if in São Paulo the awareness became most vivid, that one must be the master of educators in order to be the master of youth and therefore must give attention to the training of teachers, this new spirit, limited to the pedagogical techniques, did not in its desire for reform get outside the ground of primary and normal school education, which it influenced for many years. However, the spirit of initiative and interest in culture, although in the old traditional sense, were manifested in other sectors. In 1892, there was created the Instituto Bacteriológico, the direction of which was entrusted to Felix Le Dantec, suggested by Pasteur, and in 1893 to Adolfo Lutz; in 1893, there were created the Escola Politécnica and the Museu Paulista, which opened its doors in 1895; the Agronomical Institute, established in Campinas by the imperial government in 1887 was transferred in 1892 to the control of the state; [17] in 1896 arose the Engineering School at Mackenzie College;

---

[17] The Agronomical Institute of the state of São Paulo has its origin in the Agronomical Station of Campinas which, on the request of Councillor Antônio Prado, then Minister of Agriculture, was created by decree of the Imperial government, on June 27, 1887, with the object of studying tropical agriculture. The government of the monarchy hired to organize and direct it Prof. F. W. Dafert, a great Austrian scientist, who rendered inestimable services during his admin-

in 1899 the Institute of Butantã was founded, and its scientific activities were begun under the direction of Vital Brasil; and in 1901 the Higher School of Agriculture in Paracicaba, and in the following year, 1902, the first two schools of commerce began,—that of Mackenzie College and the one which took the name of Alvares Penteado. The two first secular and professional schools, one for boys and the other for girls, created in Braz, date from 1911 and the first Medical School of São Paulo from 1913. In all of this cultural equipment, the Agronomic Institute, destined to the study of problems related to agriculture; the Luiz de Queiroz Higher School of Agriculture, meant for the training of agricultural administrators, technicians for agricultural services and agronomy, and the Biological Institute which, after its origin through a commission to fight the coffee blight, was transformed in 1928 into a permanent institution for the defense of agriculture and animal life, represent a truly notable effort to make a close connection between teaching and research and the agricultural production of the State and the economy of the nation.

But if these institutions destined to teaching and to scientific research relating

---

istration (1887–1897), and brought to completion scientific studies of great value, on coffee and its cultivation. The federal decree of February 8, 1892, transferred the Agricultural Station of Campinas to the jurisdiction of the State of São Paulo, with the name which it still bears, the Agronomical Institute, and an annual appropriation of $750 was voted for its upkeep. After Uchoa Cavalcanti, who succeeded F. W. Dafert, in the direction of the Institute, and occupied the post ad interim (1897–1898), we had at the head of the technical and scientific institution Gustavo d'Utra (1898–1906), Lourenço Granato (1906–1907), Max Passon (1907–1909), and Berthet (1909–1924). Its direction was taken over in 1924 by Teodureto de Camargo, an agricultural engineer, to whom we owe its continued progress during a long period of seventeen years; he gave the Institute some of the most vigorous leadership it had had since its founding. In December, 1927, by law no. 2,227-A, the Institute passed through one of the most important reforms of its history, which affected its whole structure, dividing its scientific and technical services into eight sections: 1) agricultural and technological chemistry; 2) agronomy; 3) horticulture; 4) genetics; 5) botany; 6) applied entomology; 7) agricultural bacteriology; 8) fermentation industries. Experimentation was being carried on, in 1930, in five farms of its property (experimental stations), in Campinas, Tieté, Sorocaba, Limeira and São Roque, which although they grew many crops, tended to specialize in certain types of farming. After the reform which it underwent with decree no. 5,447, of March 29, 1943, and which was more administrative than technical, the Institute passed through a profound remodeling by virtue of decree no. 7,312, of July 5, 1935, which endowed it with all the sections necessary to its full functioning, and with some of them grouped into services. The Agronomical Institute, which today has a network of a dozen experimental stations, embraces, in accordance with this reform, three services: 1) cotton, which includes experimental sections, control of seeds, and the technology of fibers; 2) horticulture, with the section of cultivation of citrus fruits, which was created in 1928–1929 and became an independent service and then returned to the Institute, and the sections of various fruits and vegetables; 3) genetics, divided into genetics proper and cytology; and the following sections: a) coffee; b) cereals and leguminosae; c) sugar cane; d) roots and tubers; e) tobacco; and f) oleaginous plants. There were created, and are still to be installed, sections of botany, bacteriology and fermentation, agricultural economics and mechanics, irrigation and drainage, which are to complete the organization. In order to appreciate the importance of the reforms undertaken at that time, we must note that the appropriation for the upkeep of the Institute almost tripled from 1934 to 1935, rising from about 1,500,000 cruzeiros ($75,000) to a little less than 4,400,000 cruzeiros (or exactly Cr. $4,331,474, equivalent to approximately $216,575.70 U.S.). The library of this Institute,—one of the most important in South America—, reorganized in July, 1935, included in 1937, 1,810 books in various languages, 4,091 volumes of journals, and 8,868 reprints of articles, coming from all parts of the world.

to vegetable and animal production began to enrich the cultural system of São Paulo, where agriculture, commerce and industry grew notably, the movement of specialization, corresponding to a greater complexity of structure, did not extend to the other States, which remained bound to the scholastic traditions of the country. In the State of São Paulo itself, which, under the inspiration of agriculture had acquired a more rapid rate of progress and in which new technical schools and scientific institutions were created to supply the gap in traditional teaching in the older faculties, very little was done to introduce a new spirit and to orient part of the youth that were going into the high schools toward technical instruction, especially agricultural and toward commercial schools. This State maintained, like the rest, a type of teaching which, viewed as a whole, was markedly traditional, although it was richer and more differentiated, which was in all its institutions singularly removed from the necessities of the environment and from the conditions of modern life which surrounded and modified its fundamental economic activities. The ideal of the "cultivated man" remained, at least down to the World War of 1914, the same that had predominated during the Empire; and the higher schools destined for the liberal careers, satisfied these dominant aspirations in the surroundings in general and especially in the families of the lords of the sugar mills, the fazendeiros, and the owners of cattle ranches, as well as the urban bourgeoisie who continued to see in the professions of lawyer, doctor and engineer, the noblest occupations, and in the higher professional schools a ladder for the social and political rise of their sons. In an environment in which the title of doctor was still an ornament for the rich, as well as one more recommendation for politics and high posts in public administration and an instrument of social rise for the families which aspired to rise in the social hierarchy, neither disinterested scientific research nor the study of technology could easily come to take first place in the thought of candidates for the higher schools.[18] In the little independent centers of intellectual

[18] The comparison between the number of research institutes created between 1890 and 1930, and that of the schools meant for the preparation of students for the liberal professions, in the same period, shows quite obviously the almost entire predominance of the latter over institutions in which first place is given to free research in the field of applied science. For nine institutes of this kind, founded between 1890 and 1940, of which five are in São Paulo, 33 higher professional schools were created, including 8 of medicine, 8 of engineering, and 17 of law. There were, in fact, established during this period the medical schools of Pôrto Alegre (1897); of Minas Gerais, in Belo Horizonte (1911); of Paraná, in Curitiba (1912), which was officially recognized in 1922; of São Paulo (1913); of Recife, of Niterói, and in the Federal District, the school of Medical Sciences and that of Medicine and Surgery of the Hahneman Institute. The Paulista Medical School of São Paulo dates from 1933. The engineering schools created from 1890 to 1930, are the Polytechnic of Bahia, which, founded in 1887, really only opened its courses in 1897 and was coordinated with its sister federal school in 1898; the Polytechnic of Recife, in Pernambuco (1896); that of Minas Gerais (1911); that of Paraná, in Curitiba (1912) and that of Juiz de Fora, in 1914, rounding out a total of eight, with the exclusion of the Engineering School of Rio de Janeiro and the School of Mines, in Ouro Preto. Among the fourteen law schools which were started in the first forty years of the republican regime, seven are still in operation, namely, that of the Federal District (1891), now the National Law School; that of Bahia (1891); that of Minas Gerais (1892); and that of Ceará (1903); that of Amazonas (1910), that of Paraná (1912), and that of Goiaz (1921), which, with the addition of schools founded after 1930,—that of Piauí and that of Alagoas (1931) and that of Campos, in the State of Rio (Clovis Bevilacqua Law School), brings the number of law schools up to ten new ones, or twelve if we include the traditional law schools of Recife and São Paulo.

life which were formed and which came to gravitate like satellites about the principal center of education and culture of the country, generally there was no question of enriching and rendering flexible the educational system and reforming it according to new necessities and a new conception of culture, but only of organizing it according to the model of higher learning which came down from the Empire and which was made up of the three traditional faculties.

To the two law schools created in 1827, there were added, after 1891, seventeen more institutions of juridical education, of which only three were posterior to 1930. To the two old medical schools, the origins of which go back to courses in medicine and surgery created in the time of Dom João VI, there were added new schools of this type, to round out a total of eleven in 1940; and eight schools of engineering between 1891 and 1914 were added to the two which the Imperial regime had bequeathed us,— the Polytechnic School of Rio de Janeiro and the School of Mines in Ouro Preto. This phenomenon of multiplication or of "mushrooming" of higher schools for the liberal careers and their geographic distribution, which was very uneven and which with rare exceptions (the School of Engineering of Juiz de Fora in Minas and the Law School in Campos, State of Rio) were concentrated in Rio de Janeiro or distributed through the capitals of the State, would be enough to prove the persistence of the mentality created in the time of the Empire which grew up and developed in the shade of the old faculties of the country. The preferences of youth and of their families all still turned toward the law and medical schools, while schools of engineering had a smaller registration of students, partly on account of the more "technical" character of these schools, partly on account of the few opportunities which were open due to the economic and industrial conditions of the country for the activities of the engineer, and partly also because they did not give the title of doctor, which was given by medical schools and which tradition extended to bachelors of law. The cultural élite, both political and administrative, made up in large part of doctors and bachelors of law, put its mark upon our culture, the traditions of which were centralized in the rural aristocracy and in the bourgeoisie of the city as nuclei of resistance to new ideas. The new ideas, the imported theories and the most ambitious reforms melted in the warmth of family life, since this was the social institution that was most stable and conservative in this society in process of formation, as well as from the older schools not all destined to create professional men from which the dominant élite came and around which gravitated the aspirations of youth and were grouped the nuclei of interest of the most elevated social classes. The older faculties continued, then, to be the principal centers through which the traditional culture penetrated as well as centers of study in which generation after generation, numerous mental workers were educated, men who were to give to Brazil an influence that at times was sufficiently great to pass its frontiers.

It is not, then, surprising that with this juridical and professional type of mentality, entirely directed toward the liberal careers and toward letters, politics and administration, technical education and scientific should continue relegated to the background. The abolition of slavery did not bring with it, as it could not indeed bring over night the transformation of the mentality that had grown up with it, the mentality of neglect of science and technology, and disdain for manual and mechanical activities. The industrial structure which was barely beginning to grow up in some regions like Rio de Janeiro and São Paulo, could not raise to the first plane of political concern in the organization of the school system, the various technical types of culture which aimed to put order into the economy of the nation by the practice of a professional point of view and a rational apprenticeship and by the fitting of men to material and to industrial tasks. There were too much lacking in Brazil the solid, disciplined traditions of the guilds, which by fixing the duration and the conditions of the apprenticeship for each craft, had maintained in Europe for generations the efficiency and prestige of some technical activities which penetrated as survivals into the system of standardized mechanism and of mass production characteristic of the industrial evolution of the world. Thus, the problems of technical education did not yet present themselves in a concrete form, at once more palpable and more efficacious, such as would cause a lively interest on the part of the cultivated classes. The bourgeoisie everywhere, with that keener awareness of reality which its habit of business bestows, and with its clinging to tradition and to values which correspond to its material interests, tended to link the problems of education to its necessities and dominant concerns, and although the élite which represented it turned them always into terms of general interest to hide their egoism, they never solved the problem in any other way except in the sense of their private interest. Nevertheless, there were not lacking isolated public and private efforts in the field of technical and professional education, in which São Paulo was also the State that opened the road, but without sufficient conviction and energy to continue in the work of which, at this time, barely the foundations were laid. The School of Arts and Crafts which, although created under the Empire in 1873, was consolidated, to enter upon its most fruitful phase of activity, after 1895 with the administration of Ramos de Azevedo; the School of Agriculture named for Luiz de Queiroz in Piracicaba (1901); the Alvares Penteado School of Commerce (1902) and the two first vocational schools for boys and girls, installed in São Paulo in 1911, are so many other efforts which promised to multiply and with time to impose the organization of an over all plan of wide scope with unity of orientation. But they remained in the State of São Paulo for many years just scattered and solitary institutions.

At this time, in 1911, in the Federal District, Alvaro Batista undertook the organization of technical and vocational education, creating various schools, among them the Sousa Aguiar School, under the direction of Corinto da Fonseca, which entered upon an active phase of new experiments. The School of Arts and Crafts named for Venceslau Braz, founded in 1919 by the municipal government to train master workmen and foremen, was later transferred to the government of the Union with the object of educating teachers for schools for apprentices, created by the government of Nilo Peçanha (1909–1910) in the captaincies of the State and destined to the vocational education of poor children. These schools of apprentices and of agriculture under the direction of the Ministry of Agriculture, like the Higher School of Agriculture founded in 1910 in Rio de Janeiro, were the most important, if not the only creations of the federal government, which was not able to develop and bring together the work which had been begun after 1910 in almost all the States of the Union. In Minas Gerais there were created later the model Escola Agrícola of Viçosa, under the direction of Rolfs, a North American specialist under contract, who planned the school and was succeeded in its direction by Belo Lisboa, and the Instituto Eletrotécnico of Itajubá, a private institution founded by Teodomiro Santiago. If we add to these institutions, the Escola Doméstica of Natal, in Rio Grande do Norte, which we owe to the generous impulse of Henrique Castriciano, and some dozens of commercial schools, almost all private, we will have the picture of technical and vocational education, which is deficient and precarious, not connected with the educational system as a whole and not bound up with industry. In fact, in this growing system, in which there predominated, as was natural, agricultural schools and institutes, among which we should remember the Instituto Borges de Medeiros (of agronomy and veterinary science) in Rio Grando do Sul, no effort was carried on to solve the problem of the relations between vocational education, treated in isolation, and other types of education, nor to establish a closer contact between industrial schools and interested professional groups, nor to unite in a rational fashion science and technology and to teach the place of each industry in the whole economic life, the *processus* of different types of production and their mutual dependence, and that general technology from which flow all particular technologies.

The dispersion of these and other institutions which arose, isolated, and did not succeed in fitting into any system, comes above all from the fragmentary character of the efforts and reforms and the complete absence of an educational policy. None of these reforms, which were at times preceded by consultation with representative figures of higher education, was established on the basis of objective data collected in questionnaires and direct investigation of the special conditions of the environment which the new institutions were to serve, or reorganized in accordance with an over all plan. An analysis, even a brief one, of the structure of the educational system which was growing up in the republican period down to 1930, shows clearly that on the one hand the lack of uniform direction in educational policy, and on the other the multiplicity of systems to which political and administrative autonomy in the States gave rise, ended by breaking down, not the fundamental unity of spirit which was closely tied up to tradition, but at least the unity of the national educational structure. This school system, both on the federal plane and in its regional diversifications, was an inheritance from the very complex traditions which were combined and fused, coming from the three centuries of experience of the colony and the cultural activity of the Empire. The line of resistance to innovations, more or less strong according to the order of education in question, is a faithful reflection of the strength of these social and religious, literary and professional traditions. It was not exactly a school policy, conscious, the outcome of reflection and clearly formulated, but rather the almost mechanical force of tradition which lay like a propulsive element at the base of the development of the higher schools created to train for the liberal professions and of which examples were multiplied through all of the States where instruction was beginning to take on new life. The stream of candidates to these institutions showed no signs of decreasing; and as the number of admissions, conditioned only by the material possibilities of each faculty, was not limited with a view to the necessities of the country and the placement of the graduates, it was not long until we could see an overcrowding of the liberal careers which soon became saturated, in spite of spilling over from the ranks of the professional men into other activities, especially those of politics, administration and journalism by a great number of bachelors and doctors of law.

If the doors of the normal schools had already been entirely open to women, who came to dominate primary education as their own element and began to figure in the secondary schools, although in an extremely limited percentage down to 1930, the doors of the higher schools remained still practically closed to them.[19] The fact is that the preparatory courses and high school courses, unconnected with the primary schools, continued in their utilitarian object of serving the higher schools in which candidates were prepared for the liberal professions, reserved at that time entirely to men and from which the cultural élite of the country were recruited. Thus if we examine the vertical organization of the school systems, both of the Union and of the States, it will be easy to verify the fact that in each of them there was a duality of systems superimposed, constituting two worlds which kept separate from the time of the Empire and between which the Republic had not attempted to lay down any connecting bridges: primary, normal and technical and vocational education on the one hand, and secondary and higher education on the other, or in other words a system of education of the people and that for training the élite. Certainly very little was done as a result of deliberate planning to bridge the abyss which separated the popular strata and the cultivated levels of the country, a country whose population was and still is characterized by extraordinary lack of equality and culture, according to regions and classes. While the élite of great cities took part very actively in the intellectual life of western Europe, the popular masses remained almost entirely without cultivation and their education received no development corresponding to their great demographic development. But, on the one hand, the plurality of centers of education which resulted from the centrifugal tendencies stimulated by the regime of autonomies, and on the other hand the growing entrance of women and their large and generous contribution in the field of primary education, which was entrusted to the States, and which men were already beginning to desert, contributed to reduce both the lack of cultural equality as between regions and also the divorce between the people and the cultivated classes of the nation.

The substitution of a single guiding center in the matter of education for a great variety of centers of influence, although it had the advantage of developing the extent of education and bringing together the people and the cultivated classes in various regions of the country, helped to retard the establishment of a national educational system and also to create new centers of resistance to the progress of the new ideas. The idea on its way since the time of the Empire, of national education, was in fact paralyzed by the victory of federalism in the Constitution of 1891 which gave to the States the

---

[19] It was only in 1907, as we have already had occasion to note, that the first two young ladies who finished secondary studies took bachelors' degrees. Education for girls was then given almost entirely in schools of the religious orders, made up for the most part of foreign teachers, especially French and Belgian women, and in a few Protestant schools, in short, in church schools. In the secular schools, whether official or private, women were rare, for they turned mostly to normal schools, designed to train for primary school teaching, and to vocational schools of the so-called "domestic arts." In Brazil, down to 1930, women had won their place in higher or university education. In European countries, for that matter, the number of women who attended higher schools was very small at the end of the past century. In France, for instance, in 1891, 10,518 students had entered higher schools in Paris, to whom 1,091 were in the Faculty of Letters, 668 in that of Sciences, and the rest divided among various other educational establishments. There were not, in these schools, more than 252 women, of whom 105 were French girls, and the rest foreigners. Women, who had won a place for themselves in the universities in France had not yet done so in Germany.

right to control primary education and recognized their right to organize their own school systems without the preliminary fixing of the general lines of an educational policy. Everything from that time on in the educational field would have to develop, as indeed it did develop, under the pressure of local circumstances which varied from one region to another, and went from demographic and economic conditions and differences in cultural level to the diversity of tendencies of the governing groups and the fluctuations of empirical, fragmentary reforms, in which the discontinuity of administration was so clearly expressed. After its tranference to the jurisdiction of the government of the Federal District, the *Pedagogium*—an institution created in 1890 by Benjamim Constant as a central organ for coordinating the pedagogical activities of the country, departed from its national ends, and it was not until 1911 that there arose, with the Organic Law, the Higher Council of Education to which the inspecting function of the State was returned (Articles 5 and 13) and which, transformed in 1925, by the reform of Rocha Vaz into the National Council of Education, did not enlarge its technical and fiscal attributes beyond the fields of higher and secondary education. In its early organization (Article 21 of Decree no. 8,659), the Higher Council of Education was composed of the directors of the federal schools of law, medicine, engineering, of the Colégio Pedro II and of a teacher from each of these establishments. No guiding and inspecting activity with respect to the State educational organisms was proposed, and in fact, there was conferred upon them an even more ample liberty by the Organic Law, imbued with the traditions of liberalism which it carried to the last possible point, in the age-old reaction against "the centralizing and retrograde" policy which dominated the country under the Empire and which was continued even in the Republic, with regard to federal institutions of learning or institutions recognized by the Union. The minister of the Interior, to whom were entrusted affairs of education, did not administer anything but secondary and higher education and had no influence whatever in the essential field,—that of primary education.

It might seem at first sight that the possibilities opened up by the Constitution of 1891 for organizing school systems in the States would give rise to the creation of new centers of culture and of education. As, however, the new school institutions were created on the initiative or under the inspiration of the élite who came from the old faculties and had the same mentality and cultural formation, these educational systems came to be so many other instruments, not of renovation, but of conservation and of the spread of traditional types of education and of the old culture. Tradition constituted an element not only in the sense of organizing but as a solidifier of structures, still weak in their foundations, which continued to conform as they developed to the dominant ideas and to the models of the federal system arrived at in the period of the Empire. Certainly the State systems, new, in progress of growth and formation, presented more plasticity and it was from the periphery to the center, from the Federal District and the States to the government of the Union that there came the first movements of reform and general reconstruction. But the identity of the conception of culture, the poverty of the local budgets and the pressure of the bureaucracy and of the treasury, hindering new initiatives and installing routine, accelerated the process of stratification and bureaucratization of these systems in which, instead of new forces, there were installed, as in the Federal System, conservative and at times reactionary forces. The old faculties, so many times reformed, reorganized themselves without losing their original physiognomy and their traditional organic constitutions, and the new types of schools, both those in which priority was given to research and the higher technical schools considered to be luxury institutions, counted upon indifference if they did not encounter the opposition of the élite, which for generations had been recruited in the faculties, created with the function of training professional men. It might be said that we considered that this school system would last forever, corresponding to an economic, social and political structure which is already openly changing. We almost considered it to be permanent, statutory. They had no other origin except the traditional mentality and the bureaucracy which, by smothering all reforming energy, established the preeminence of the political over the administrative, and of the administrative over the technical, the age-long resistance and the radical opposition to the creation of universities and higher schools which should receive and maintain before everything, the privileges of disinterested research.

This situation of stability and routine, however, could not last forever. The variations of population, the evolution of economic life in consequence of the industrial rise which took place after the war of 1914, had to be accompanied by a group of transformations and beliefs characteristic of Brazilian social life in our principal centers of human concentration such as São Paulo, Rio de Janeiro and others which were more accessible to the influences of Western civilization. The European War with all its economic, social and political consequences spread beyond the continent in which it broke out this state of restlessness and revolt, of hopes and aspirations, of the will to destroy and of an impulse to recreate which it provoked everywhere, releasing new forces and arousing new currents of thought. "The events which were unfolding in the Old World during the conflagration and in consequence of it,—the democracy of Wilson, and the socialism of Germany and Austria, the Bolshevism of Russia and the Fascism of Italy, were so important, violent and precipitate," (writes Mílton Rodrigues) "that they demanded the attention of the whole world and in Brazil public opinion was strongly shaken by them."[20] If public opinion, shaken and broken up by the successive shocks of these occurrences, did not yet arrive at the point of dividing itself into clearly differentiated currents of thought, it is certain that there began to spread an ever more lively feeling of distress with relation to the earlier state of affairs and established ideas and an aspiration, still vague as to content and as to the direction of reforms, but nonetheless vigorous as to its will to destroy and to bring about economic, social and political change. The revolts of 1922 and 1924, which occurred in this period and were accompanied by the people if not with a movement of solidarity at least with sympathy and interest, constituted extremely lively symptoms and marked the phases of development of this revolutionary mentality which was being formed in an atmosphere laden with electricity and was to break out in 1930 in a revolution of the broadest scope. The War of 1914 with the whole train of its devastations and tremendous consequences also must have contributed powerfully to raise to the first rank of social and political preoccupations those reforms of education with which it was hoped to forge a new humanity on which the last hopes for a better world, for the restoration of peace by means of the schools, and for the formation of a new spirit, better adjusted to conditions and necessities of a new type of civilization, were concentrated.

[20] Mílton da Silva Rodrigues, *Educação comparada*. Tendências e organizações escolares. Editora Nacional, São Paulo, 1938, p. 268.

In 1918, England started this movement of reform with the *Education Act* of Lord Fisher; in 1919–1920 there was begun, through the series of convergent measures, the progressive execution of the great task planned by Otto Gloeckel in Vienna; immediately afterwards, Prussia and the German States undertook between 1922 and 1925 the reorganization of their school systems, and an extraordinary activity in studies, research and pedagogical experiments took place under the liberal Constitution of Weimar; Léon Bérard in 1923 in the Chamber of Deputies, led the discussion of a new reform of education in France,[21] and in that same year, Gentile laid down a plan for the educational reconstruction of Fascist Italy and Lunascharski, aided by Krupskaya, attacked the same problem in Communist Russia with the boldest and most radical of all the reforms which were then carried out, and there arose everywhere similar plans for reorganizing education on all levels in accordance with the new ideas and new political regimes. But at the same time as the social, political and pedagogical questions, breaking the bonds in which they had been discussed in circles of philosophers, men of science, reformers and politicians, came to interest the public opinion of the world and to encompass Brazil in the orbit of their influence, our country entered upon an epoch of economic transformation, due not only to the extraordinary progress of agriculture and the great rise in the price of coffee, but to the greatest industrial boom which had taken place in the economic evolution of the nation. The intensity of economic and cultural interchange, the development of immigration of peoples of diverse origins, and the growth of cities, through which there was vigorous expression given to the impulse taken by Brazilian industry after the European conflict, created an environment more favorable to the fermentation of new ideas which were spreading out from all the principal centers of culture both of Europe and the United States. The tendency toward urbanization was clearly shown in Recife, and especially in the south, in Rio de Janeiro, in Belo Horizonte, Santos and Pôrto Alegre, without speaking of São Paulo, the growth of which is only equalled by that of Chicago and Sydney and attained unexpected proportions. The population of the greatest city of the plateau doubled in fact in less than ten years, rising from 380,000 inhabitants in 1920 to almost 800,000 in 1930 and attaining in 1934 more than a million (1,033,202) of which, in that year, about 200,000 (190,218) persons were employed in industry, 84,699 worked in commerce, and 26,543 in transportation.

It was in this atmosphere of agitation of ideas, of economic transformation, and of expansion of the cities that the reform movement in culture and education began on the plateau and along the coast, to spread through the principal cities of the country. The first sign of alarm which showed that we were clearly on the road to reform education was the reform undertaken in 1920 by Antônio de Sampaio Dória, who called upon to direct the public education of São Paulo, led a campaign against old methods of teaching and there were heard blows so vigorously applied to the front constituted by the traditional, that entire pieces of the wall of the old school began to fall down. But not only were resistances still so strong that the work begun and interrupted in its first year could hardly develop and produce all of its effects, but also while avoiding a purely administrative attitude, this reform, limited to primary education, concentrated its best efforts upon the transformation of the methods and techniques of teaching. In 1924, Lourenço Filho, in Ceará, to which he had been called to reorganize primary

[21] Léon Bérard, *Pour la réforme classique.* Paris, Colin, 1923.

teaching, and Anísio Teixeira in Bahia, where he was trying out the reforms which he was afterwards to develop in all their plenitude in the Federal District (1932–1935), after his return from his studies in the United States; Carneiro Leão in Rio de Janeiro and Lisímaco de Costa in Paraná, all were facing in the same direction, their activity varying in grade of intensity as in its content and objective, all looked toward the reform of the school system, sowing new ideas and pedagogical techniques, promoting new accomplishments and organizing plans of reform, partial or complete, but all limited to primary education and its fundamental problems. There were not lacking, here and there, private activities, as for instance to cite one of the first and one of the most coura-geously reformist, the Escola Regional of Meriti, founded in the State of Rio in 1921 by Armanda Alvaro Alberto, who took his place among the pioneers of the new edu-cation in Brazil. Reforming activities in the field of public education if they succeeded in constituting number of centers of renovation, did not succeed, most of them, in preventing problems of administrative architecture from hiding the most important problems of pedagogical reform, held up as it was by the governments in Paraná and Rio de Janeiro, and others did not succeed in establishing firmly the position of the reformers against the resistance put up by tradition and by the new attacks of the con-servative forces which were not slow in reconquering the terrain.

Moreover, these reforms did not show an organic policy laid down by the govern-ing élite, but rather the personal tendencies of certain educators, who were acting on their own, directing their energies in the direction of the new ideas, but being followed by counter reforms and the return to the past. These radical perplexities led in Rio de Janeiro and in various States, as in São Paulo, to a pendulum movement of education from 1920, from a reactionary policy to a reform policy, and from this to that again, the pendulum taking years to arrive anew at the dead point, that is at the moment at which the governments, being incapable of carrying out their own policy, with the support of the reformers, and refusing to adopt the policy of the latter, preferred to do nothing and to move in neither direction. There was evidently lacking, in the absence of an official school policy, a force of agglutination of these scattered groups of new educators who, when they had barely formed, already threatened to break up and whose successes in school administration were only a function of their personal author-ity and prestige and therefore of various factors which obliged them to adopt a very complex tactic in order to make their ideals prevail. The Brazilian Association of Edu-cation, founded in 1924 by the great idealist Heitor Lira, had this function, bringing together the educators of Rio de Janeiro, putting them in contact with each other, offer-ing opportunities for full debate of doctrines and reforms, frequently of a confused and contradictory intellectual content, and bringing educators together for congresses or conferences of education, three of which, that of Curitiba in 1927, that of Belo Horizonte in 1928 and that of São Paulo in 1929, took place before the advent of the revolution. After 1922, there was inaugurated the epoch of educational conferences. In contrast with one educational congress which was planned in 1883 and did not ever come to the point of meeting at the Court,—the only attempt of this kind in the whole period of the Empire—, since from that date down to 1922 not a single educa-tional conference was held, there met between 1922 and 1937, nine conferences, two of official origin, that of 1922 which met under the presidency of Alfredo Pinto during the government of Epitácio Pessoa, to study the relation of the federal government to primary education [22] and the Congress of Higher Education which met in 1927 in commemoration of the first century from the foundation of the law schools, and the other seven, called by the Brazilian Association of Education. This society of educators—the first in Brazil with a national character—was doubtless one of the most efficacious instruments in spreading European and North American pedagogical thought, and one of the most important if not the greatest center of coordination and of debate for the study and solution of educational problems which were discussed in every way, in questionnaires and communications to the press, in summer school courses, and in the conferences which it promoted in the State capitals.

The new currents of pedagogical thought which were beginning to appear in publications on special subjects, like the work of Carneiro Leão on rural education (1918) and Medeiros e Albuquerque on the question of tests (1924), of Antônio Monteiro de Sousa and José Augusto [23] tended to take on definite form in São Paulo, in the first poll which was taken on public education in general in that State. In fact in 1926 the author of this work, then editor of the *Estado de São Paulo*, organized and directed in that great newspaper, the greatest investigation which was carried on among teachers, on education of all grades, guiding the debates in his introductory articles and his questionnaires, commenting upon the testimony in his final articles, raising educational questions of the greatest interest, and looking at them not, as did some of the professors who were questioned, only from a pedagogical point of view, but also in their philosophical and social aspects.[24] In this great inquiry, which was guided and directed and is certainly, "one of the most important documents in the history of the reform of education which took shape in the various great reforms," such as those of Rio de Janeiro (1927–1930), of Minas Gerais (1927–1930), of São Paulo (1931–1932 and 1933), of Rio de Janeiro (1932–1935), Pernambuco (1932–1935), among others, there were separated then, as by a watershed, and clearly differentiated, the two great currents which were from then on to confront each other in the major campaign for national education and culture in the last fifteen years. It marked, indeed, as we have already observed, "an acute period in the fermentation of ideas with which, in the field of education, there was going on a frankly reformist movement like those which had been manifested in art and literature and which culminated in the Week of Modern Art in São Paulo. In other sectors of social life, the same atmosphere of battle could be breathed." [25] It was, however, in the reform of education undertaken in the Federal District from 1927–1930 by the author of this inquiry, that the great directive lines, then clearly defined, were emphasized with most precision and vigor. They had already been foretold in that ample sounding of public opinion and they led to the most important attempt at the reform and reconstruction of education in the country. At this same time, in 1927, Francisco Campos and Mário Casassanta, in Minas Gerais,

[22] V. *Anais da Conferência Inter-Estadual de Ensino Primário*, Rio, 1922.

[23] *A educação*, a monthly journal devoted to the defence of education in Brazil, was founded in 1922 in Rio de Janeiro and edited by José Augusto, journalist and politician, who was governor of Rio Grande do Norte and federal deputy for that State.

[24] Fernando de Azevedo, *A educação pública em São Paulo*. Problemas e discussões. Investigation for "O Estado de São Paulo," in 1926. Series Brasiliana, Vol. 98, Editora Nacional, São Paulo, 1937.

[25] Fernando de Azevedo, *A educação pública em São Paulo*. Problemas e discussões. In "introdução," p. XXIX, São Paulo, 1937.

resolutely joining the reform movement of which they had assumed the leadearship in that State, carried on one of the most far reaching education reforms,[26] with which a notable forward movement was given to the education of the people, the programs of primary teaching were reformed and the problem of training and improving the teachers of the primary schools was faced.

But certainly, on account of the tremendous moral force which it mobilized, the movement of ideas and of public opinion which it unloosed, and the rapidity with which it spread, and above all the boldness and breadth of its construction and the extent of the field that it covered,[27] the reform of education in the Federal District (1927–1930), was, of all those which have been accomplished in the country, the most vigorous, the most revolutionary, and the one with most effect, including in its sphere of influence almost all the States. It was by this reform—"a true revolution which took place in the country," in the opinion of Léon Walther of the Institut J. J. Rousseau or in the judgment of Ad. Ferrière, assistant director of the International Bureau of Education, "one of the most remarkable pieces of work of our time"—that there was awakened in Brazil an educational conscience and that there was begun a new policy of education. "The force of resistance and of expansion of the reform of 1927, it derived above all, as we have had occasion to write, from its clear ideology,

[26] Francisco Campos, *Educação e cultura*. José Olímpio, Rio de Janeiro, 1940.

[27] Lourenço Filho, who was one of the most attentive and sagacious observers, describes what the campaign was like; after referring to the moral and material situation in which scholastic institutions were, in the Federal District, when the professor from São Paulo assumed the direction of education and proposed to reorganize it, he goes on: "But the professor who went from São Paulo was not frightened by the extent of the demonstrable evil. With impetuous idealism, Sr. Fernando de Azevedo proposed an heroic remedy: the total reconstruction of the system, from the primary schools to the normal school, remodeling also the vocational institutes of the District. This proposal, which constituted a project for a law, personally explained and defended by him before the committees of the Municipal Council, made many smile at its audacity and the ingenuity of its very high pretentions . . . But the Council accepted the reform in principle, giving it, through the most authoritative voices of the majority and minority, the praise to which it had a right. The draft passed in the first discussions; on the third reading, however, the majority came out in open opposition to the ideals they had previously applauded. The fact is that Sr. Fernando de Azevedo, desiring to be an administrator, not a politician, had refused the offers which had been made to him for an exchange which would pay for the final approval. A very interesting phenomenon then took place: the minority began to fight for the government's proposal, the press began to support it, and public opinion, through professional organs and intellectual associations, began to exert pressure on the political majority of the District legislative body. Sr. Fernando de Azevedo published a note which was a challenge to the courage of the men who composed it: "If the reform was a good one, if it aimed at the public good, let them approve it; if it was defective, let them amend it; if it was no good, let them condemn it at once" . . . He for his part asked nothing for himself, claimed nothing, and therefore, was not going to be a party to any kind of bargain. The campaign in the press, without the exception of a single paper, was admirable. The Brazilian Education Association, the League of National Defense, the Rotary Club,—to name only the societies with greatest social prestige, came out for the approval of the principles of the draft. The National Conference of Education which was meeting for the first time in Curitiba, at the height of the campaign, gave its warm and enthusiastic vote in favor of the proposal, in which it saw nothing but the improvement of education in the capital of the country, and a new era in education which the proposed reform would inaugurate. Finally morality and culture won, and the Municipal Council as the lights went out made the proposal law." (Lourenço Filho, *O Ensino no Distrito Federal*. A reforma Fernando de Azevedo. In "O Estado de São Paulo," June 15, 1928).

which was firmly and frankly reformist. This code is a work of synthesis that is affirmative and constructive, entirely dominated by a new conception of life. The school system which the reform established comes from a philosophy which corresponds to it, giving it its unity of conception and of plan, and causing a breath of pedagogical and social renovation to blow over it as a whole and in all its details. It is in these new ideals of education that we must seek for the fundamental principles which presided over the organization of the school system, adjusted like a technical apparatus in its systematic ensemble of measures and institutions (scholastic, semi-scholastic and post-scholastic), to the clearly formulated pedagogical and social ends, which it proposed to serve. The radical transformation of processes which the reform involved came, then, from the new object (social, democratic, national) which was laid at the door of the system of education and therefore of the very philosophy from which it was derived." [28] It was not a reform "of the surface," of an administrative character or a mere change in techniques, but a radical reform made in depth and erected upon a basis of industrial civilization, and in which, by considering the direction of modern life and the necessities of the nation, an attempt was made to solve the questions of technique as a function of the new concept of life and culture and therefore of new principles and main lines of education.

Of a local character in their origin, but national in their objects and effects and limited to primary, normal and technical education, to which for that matter the Constitution of the Federal District limited the activities of the government in the field of public education, these reforms, however, that of Minas Gerais and especially that of Rio de Janeiro marked, on account of their significance and their effect, the most important phase in the development of a national educational policy. The new ideas which they adopted and which shook the school system to its base were to circulate in a vertical direction like a new sap, which went up from primary and normal school education to reach the superstructure of the school system, provoking movements of reaction,—teaching secondary and higher education which until then had remained rebellious and almost inaccessible to the current of new thought which was spreading through the country. But before this vertical circulation which was naturally slower, there had begun to develop in a horizontal direction, spreading through the country, especially from the principal center of irradiation, which was Rio de Janeiro, and enlarging their sphere of influence and action ever more through the different States. The national conferences which the Brazilian Association of Education promoted in the capitals, and which began with that of Curitiba in 1927, that is in the very same year in which the two major movements of scholastic reform which had taken place in the Empire and in the Republican period broke out in the Federal District and in Minas Gerais, aided the attainment of this end. The annual conferences called by this society of educators, bringing together professors of all grades and from all the States, creating an atmosphere favorable to the discussion of ideas, and promoting the spread of ideals of the reforms undertaken in some of the principal centers of culture, attained objects that were genuinely national, giving concrete form to the dream of its founder Heitor Lira, when he thought of making the seat of the Association movable and said in his original plan that it should meet annually in one of the States, "now

[28] Fernando de Azevedo, *Novos caminhos e novos fins.* A nova política de educação no Brasil. Editora Nacional, São Paulo, 1931, p. 19.

in the north, now in the south, now in the center, in such a manner as to achieve a true transfusion of ideas and of sentiments." [29]

To appreciate duly the almost unique function which the Brazilian Association of Education exercised by establishing mutual understanding and provoking everywhere an awakening of the mind and an awareness of political unity, it will suffice to recall that in the essential fields of popular education, the government of the Republic in forty years took only two actions, in 1918 ordering the German schools in the south closed and giving a subvention to primary education in Paraná, Santa Catarina and Rio Grande in order to combat the Germanic infiltration in the interest of national unity, and calling in 1922, under the government of Epitácio Pessoa, an official conference to study the relation of the Union to primary education. [30] These periodic, interstate meetings, "bringing together educators of all of the States and assembling them in different cultural centers of the country, evidently contributed, as we have observed, to the acquisition of new points of view, to reconstruction of opinions and the spread of the movement of reform in Brazilian educational thought. The idea of a new educational policy (I wrote in 1932) is daily developing further under the influence of these rapprochements and of local attempts at reorganization, with the speed and the force of a current which is digging its bed and carrying away in an irresistible drive all of the living forces of the national teachers' group. [31] We may have been and in fact we were far from a national policy of education, whose fundamental principles

[29] Francisco Venâncio Filho, *Educação,* IV. In "Cultura Política," ano I, no. 4, June, 1941.

[30] While the old constitutional question was being debated,—and it lasted through the whole period in which the Constitution of 1891 was in force,—German and Italian schools continued to flourish in various States of the south; their primary and secondary education was given in a foreign language by foreign teachers. The primary school, which is everywhere the great source of national unity, remained in various States not only subject to foreign influences but entirely under the control of other nations. The anomalous situation resulting from the progress of these schools, and from the almost total absence, in certain regions and cities, of Brazilian schools, became ever more serious and the solution of the problem ever more difficult and complex, while waiting for the jurists and interpreters of the Constitution to find a constitutional way of having the federal government intervene in the primary education of the States, even if it were to solve problems intimately bound up with the unity and defense of the nation. Lincoln, when during the war of secession he was worked upon by political partisans who wished him to reestablish the constitutional regime, is said to have replied, resisting their pressure: "The Union is older than the Constitution." The juridical fetishism of Brazil inverted the terms of the problem, putting its scruples about the defense of the Constitution of 1891 above the supreme interests of the Union . . . After referring to the policy of assimilation, so extensive and so intensive, carried out with abundant resources by the North Americans, not in the least important of their States, but in the least important of their territories, Hawaii,—a series of islands in the Pacific, which they took in 1898 and in which they were spending in 1920 more on primary schooling than does the State of São Paulo—, Afrânio Peixoto remarks bitterly upon the constitutional scruples by which republican parties allowed themselves to be swayed. In those little islands of Hawaii, for 1,000 Anglo-Saxon children, the statistics recorded 17,600 Japanese, 3,800 Chinese, 5,300 Portuguese, 3,300 Hawaiians, and 4,100 half-breeds. "Out of these people," concluded Afrânio Peixoto, the Americans make Americans; what a contrast with us, who are afraid to intervene in our States, and let Germany and Italy intervene in our nation, by supporting schools and making Germans and Italians out of children born in Brazil!" (Afrânio Peixoto, *História da Educação.* Brasil, Chapters XVII, XVIII, and XIX, p. 238. São Paulo, 1933.)

[31] Fernando de Azevedo, *A educação e seus problemas.* Editora Nacional, São Paulo, 1937, pp. 35-36.

should penetrate from above down the organization of all scholastic systems, and which should pay attention not only to the needs of a new industrial society, openly evolving toward social and economic democracy, but also to the specific conditions of the Brazilian social environment, still not deeply touched by the effects of the industrial revolution. But the great reforms and pedagogical conferences in which a new concept of life was stirring and which were attempting to break through the restricted circle of certain types of teaching or of certain regions to embrace the general educational system in all of its levels, indicated our resolute march through immense difficulties toward a national policy of education. The organic unity of this school policy either had to come from above and be imposed by revolution within the limits and according to the direction of a general policy, or it had to be worked out slowly under the pressure of the facts, when the spiritual fusion of the people should have attained a greater degree of intensity, uniting more intimately these scattered societies affiliated by language and religion, mixed by miscegenation and by internal migrations, but still not joined by intranational and international commerce and by those loans of new techniques which presuppose new habits of life and new ideals corresponding to a new type of civilization.

BIBLIOGRAPHY

Assís Ribeiro, Paulo, "A Evolução do ensino secundário," in *O Estado de São Paulo*, Sept. 1–3, 1937. Address at the Instituto de Educação de São Paulo, Aug. 26, 1937.

Azevedo, Fernando de, *A Reforma do ensino no Distrito Federal: Discursos e entrevistas* (São Paulo: Comp. de Melhoramentas, 1929).

———, *Novos caminhos e novos fins: A Nova Política de educaçáo no Brasil* (São Paulo: Comp. Editora Nacional, 1931).

———, *A Educação pública em São Paulo: Problemas e discussões* (São Paulo: Comp. Editora Nacional, 1937—Brasiliana, Vol. 98). Inquiry by *O Estado de São Paulo* in 1926.

Azevedo Sodré, A. A. de, *O Problema de educação nacional: Conferência realizada na Escola Politécnica do Rio de Janeiro no dia 1 de julho 1926* (Rio: Jornal do Comércio, 1926).

Belo Lisboa, J. C., *O Ensino agrícola no Brasil: Conferência pronunciada na 4ta Conferência Nacional de Educação* (Belo Horizonte: imprensa Oficial de Minas Gerais, 1932).

Bordeaux Rêgo, Oziel, "Introdução," in *Estatística da Instrução* (Primeira parte, Estatística escolar) Tip. da Estatística, 1916), Vol. 1 pp. ix–ccxxxii.

Calmon, Pedro, *História social do Brasil*, Vol. 3, *A Epoca republicana* (São Paulo: Comp. Editora Nacional, 1939—Brasiliana, Vol. 173).

Calógeras, J. Pandiá, *Os Jesuítas e o ensino* (Rio: Imprensa Nacional, 1911).

Escragnolle Dória, *Memória histórica do Colégio de Pedro II* (Rio: Ministerio do Educação, 1937). Period from Dec. 2, 1837, to Dec. 2, 1937.

Franca, Father Leonel, *Ensino religioso e ensino leigo* (Rio, 1931).

———, *O Protestantismo no Brasil* (Rio: Editora ABC, 1938).

Júlio Maria, Father, "A Religião: Ordens religiosas—Instituições pias e beneficentes" (Chap. III, "No regime republicano") pp. 107–123, in *Livro do Centenário* (Rio: Imprensa Nacional, 1900).

Kennedy, James, *Cinquenta anos de metodismo no Brasil* (São Paulo: Imprensa metodista, 1928).

Lourenço Filho, M. B., *Introdução ao estudo da escola nova* (São Paulo: Comp. de Melhoramentos, n.d.—Biblioteca de educação, Vol. 11).

———, *Tendência da educação brasileira* (São Paulo: Comp. de Melhoramentos, 1940—Biblioteca de Educação, Vol. 29).

Moacir, Primitivo, *A Instrução e a República*, Vol. 1, *Reforma Benjamim Constant (1890–1892)*, Vol. 2, *Código Fernando Lobo (1892–1899)* Rio: Imprensa Nacional, 1941). Publication of the Ministerio de Educação e Saude.

Peixoto, Afrânio, *História da Educação*, Chaps. XVII–XX ("Brasil"), pp. 211–265. Comp. Editora Nacional, São Paulo, 1933.

Pires de Almeida, J. R., *L'Instruction publique au Brésil depuis l'Indépendance jusqu'à nos jours: Histoire-Législation* (Rio: Leuzinger, 1889).

Raja Gabaglia, E. de Barros, *O Colégio Pedro II* (Rio: Foto-mecânica do Brasil).

Sant'Anna Neri, Baron de Sabóia, L. Cruls, and Baron de Tefé, "Instruction publique," in *Le Brésil en 1889,* prepared by a group of Brazilian writers under the direction of M. F.—J. de Sant'Anna Neri (Paris), Chap. XIX, pp. 563–590.

Serrano, Jônatas, *A Escola nova* (Rio: Schmidt, 1932).

Silva Rodrigues, Mílton, *Educação comparada* (São Paulo: Comp. Editora Nacional, 1938), Pt. 3, "O Brasil," pp. 233–290.

Sousa Brasil, T. Pompeu de, *O Ensino superior no Brasil: Relatório da Faculdade de Direito no anos de 1911 e 1912* (Ceará: Tip. Minerva de Assís Bezerra, 1913).

Teixeira, Anísio, *Educação pública, sua organização* (Rio, 1934).

———, *Educação para a democracia* (Rio, 1936).

Teixeira Brandão, *A Educação nacional no regime republicano* (Rio: Imprensa Nacional, 1907).

Veríssimo de Matos, José, *A Educação nacional* (Belém, 1896; 2nd ed., Rio, 1906).

———, "A Instrução e a imprensa (1500–1900): A Instrução pública—III, República, Estado atual (1890–1899), pp. 5–30 in *Livro do Centenário* (Rio: Imprensa Nacional, 1900).

Viana, Hélio, *Formação brasileira* (Rio: Olímpio, 1935), Chap. XV (c), "Síntese de uma histório da educação no Brasil: Período republicano."

1—*Lei Orgânica do ensino superior e do fundamental no República: Comentários precedidos de uma carta do Sr. Dr. Rivadávia Correia, Ministro do Interior* (Rio: Francisco Alves, 1912).

2—*Estatística da Instrução* (Primeira parte, "Estatística Escolar") Vol. 1 (Tip. da Estatística, 1916), with a 232-page introduction by Oziel Bordeaux Rêgo.

3—*Anais da Conferência Inter-Estadual do Ensino Primário* (Rio, 1922).

CHAPTER FOUR

THE REFORM AND UNIFICATION
OF THE EDUCATIONAL SYSTEM

The movement of educational reform and its effect in Brazil—The reform of 1928 in the Federal District—The revolution of 1930—The Ministry of Education is created—The reform of Francisco Campos—The reorganization of secondary and higher education—The question of religious teaching—The Church and the State—The Manifesto of the pioneers of the new education—The Fifth National Conference of Education—Toward educational reconstruction in Brazil—Conflict of tendencies—The educational policy of the Federal District (1932–1935)—New cultural and scientific institutions—The foundation of the University of São Paulo—The first Faculty of Philosophy, Science and Letters—The University of the Federal District—the Constitution of July 16, 1934—The quantitative expansion of secondary education—The process of democratization—The first professors of secondary education trained in Brazil—The regime implanted on November 10, 1937—Tendencies toward unification of the educational system—The renaissance of the nationalist spirit—The University of Brazil—The National Faculty of Philosophy—The new factors of expansion and cultural unity—The library movement—Radio broadcasting and educational motion pictures—The cultural activity of the Ministry of Education—Toward the defense of our artistic traditions—The organization of national statistical services

O BSERVERS HAVE CONSIDERED as the culminating point in the movement of educational reform in Brazil, the reform of 1928 in the Federal District, which became the most intense center of irradiation of the new ideas in pedagogical techniques. Some historians of education have not hesitated in affirming that with the reform substantiated in decree no. 3,281 of January 23, 1928, we entered resolutely upon a new phase of the history of Brazilian education.[1] Whatever may be, however, the point of view

[1] "In a visit made recently to various schools of the District, and renewed just now," writes Prof. Lourenço Filho at that time,—"I had the impression that not only is there prevalent a vigorous desire to make teaching more progressive, and free it from the routine of decades, but the conviction that the material transformation of the equipment of schools will be almost complete in the present administration. Preparations are being made to construct five large school buildings. The foundations of the normal school are being laid; according to the plans that have been approved, it will be the largest and will have the best plant of any institute of the kind in South America. Furniture and teaching materials are being replaced . . . If the reform did nothing else, it would be magnificent. But it is doing more, and doing it splendidly. As a result of an official decision, the teachers are coming together in courses of specialization. And in its extension courses, the Brazilian Education Association is patiently carrying out one of the university functions which the University of Rio de Janeiro has not yet started: that of passing on higher culture to primary school teachers, thus perfecting their culture, broadening their philosophic point of view, and trying out the new discoveries of scientific technique. . . . Sr. Fernando de Azevedo has acted in masterly fashion, and the gods have given him opportunities which never appear together; the firm decision of the District Government to engage in administration rather than in politics; fermentation of ideas among the teachers, who had been prepared by the Brazilian

446

which one adopts in estimating this reform, it is certain that according to the judgment of Brazilian and foreign authorities, it marked a revolutionary period in the field of education, revolutionary not only through the frankly reformist ideas which inspired it and which through it entered into circulation, but also through the fermentation of ideas which it provoked and through the social state which it led to, a state of indecision of mind, of impatient eagerness and of ardent aspiration. No other in fact, down to 1930, impressed upon our system of education a more vigorous social direction, as nationalist as possible, nor took more into account in the whole picture as well as in its details, the social function of the school; no other paid more attention to the internal enrichment of the school and to the enlargement of its sphere of action; no other attempted to connect more closely the activities of the school with the family and with interested professional circles, with national life and with the necessities and conditions of the modern world. Giving the system of education new objectives, national, social, and democratic, the reformer proceeded to the renovation of techniques and processes which as instruments had to vary in function of the objectives which one proposed to attain and which acted upon the whole, and he attempted to furnish through the reform, a concrete basis of technical and administrative services to schools of all types and grades to the end that they might have a more efficient education and that it should really be extended to all. Thus, relieving the school of the dead weight of traditional teaching, reacting against the purely individualistic objects of the old schools, raising to the first plane of its concerns the principles of action, solidarity and social cooperation, breaking down the barriers which separated the different types of teaching in order to relate them to each other and introducing new ideas in pedagogical technique, the reform of 1928 in the Federal District did in fact begin a new policy of education in Brazil.

What we were trying to attain in the capital of the country by means of this reform based upon a democratic conception of existence and respect for the human personality, was that "universal education" to which John Dewey refers, and which puts within the reach of all its advantages and satisfies the enormous variety of social requirements and individual necessities and aptitudes, or to employ his words, "the panorama of an ampler and richer life for man in general, a life of greater freedom and of equal opportunity for all, to the end that each may develop and may achieve all that is in him to be." The vigorous affirmation of fundamental principles by which this reform was oriented; the passion of polemics which arose about it, and the movement of ideas to which it gave rise, producing a break in the unity of pedagogical thought that had been dominant since the Empire, gave it such energy and such great power of development that it was able to have a strong effect upon the various States of the Union, bringing them into its sphere of influence. In the tempest of protest and

---

Education Association, a fermentation that had already been stirred up by the previous administration, up to a certain point . . . There is no doubt that what is being done will mark an epoch in the education of the people of Brazil. The conception which he preaches with regard to the primary school (which is not one of merely bookish or intellectual teaching), is appearing for the first time in official documents of the country. The "work school," the "community school," the vital significance of the new education,—are the main points of that extraordinary technical and social reform in education." (Cf. Lourenço Filho, *O ensino no Distrito Federal*. A reforma Fernando de Azevedo. In "O Estado de São Paulo," June 15, 1928.)

applause, in the current of enthusiasm and the avalanche of criticism which it aroused on every hand, we cannot fail to recognize rather the shock of ideological conflict than a simple reaction in the face of a reform by means of which Brazil entered the movement of the renovation of the school which had been developing in some countries of Europe and America.[2] With it, not only did we attack the position of reformers who clung to technical formulas and were at once dogmatic in their principles and purists in their action; it was the very traditional, scholastic systems which were shaken to their foundations. Certainly with the reform of education of one city, and constrained by its charter to keep within the limit of primary, normal school and vocational education, we did not break or could not break that unity which exists in every culture, giving it its own character, like the form and the spirit of one phase of that culture in which new acquisitions which arise or are imported take shape. Nor were its effects so very profound except in a few points of the national territory, more within the reach of its influence. But in the regions of denser population and the more industrial and urban civilization there were created by this and other subsequent movements of intellectual, artistic and pedagogical renovation, various cultural centers which had as a point of departure the Federal District, Minas Gerais and São Paulo (the center south) and from which there spread out over some cultural zones on the periphery these new ideas and tendencies, becoming weaker and less commonly adopted the farther they got from the principal centers of elaboration and diffusion of the national culture.

The movement of educational reforms which were undertaken in 1928 in the Federal District and about whose directive principles and accomplishments various works and documents [3] give us complete information, cannot be studied by itself but

[2] This is what was recognized by all who had a chance to analyze the work, which was at this time examined and discussed from all points of view by the great newspapers of Rio de Janeiro, by eminent men, both foreigners and Brazilians, and by some of the leading authorities in the field of education. (V. especially Lourenço Filho, *O ensino no Distrito Federal*. O reforma Fernando de Azevedo. In "O Estado de São Paulo," June 15, 1928; Everardo Backheuser, speech on December 21, 1929, in the name of the Pedagogical Crusade for the New School, on the occasion of the opening of the Pedagogical Exposition of the Federal District. In "Boletim de Educação Pública," April-June, 1930, Rio de Janeiro, pp. 256-257); Manuel Bernardes (ex-minister of Uruguay in Brazil), *Problemas de nosso tempo*. A nova política de educação no Brasil. Series of articles published in "O País" of Rio de Janeiro and in "La Razón" of Buenos Aires. In "Boletim de Educação Pública," July-September, 1930, Rio de Janeiro, pp. 299-346; Gerardo Seguel (of the Normal School of Santiago, Chile), *A reforma da educação no Distrito Federal* (Brazil). In "Revista Pedagógica," edited by Lorenzo Luzuriaga. April, 1931, Madrid: Ad. Ferrière (assistant director of the International Bureau of Education), *L'Education nouvelle au Brésil*. In "Pour l'ère nouvelle," May-April, 1931, 10e an., no. 67, Paris; and Anísio S. Teixeira, M.A. Teixeira de Freitas, J. G. Frota Pessoa and others, in Comemoração do 1° decênio da Reforma da Instrução Pública do Distrito Federal de 1928. Brazilian Education Association, Rio de Janeiro, 1938.

[3] Decree no. 3,281 of January 23, 1928, which reformed public education in the Federal District, and decree no. 2,940, of November 22, 1928, which regulated the basic law (Regulation of Teaching), foreseeing in its 764 articles, "all the details of a really organic piece of work, the structure of which makes it a genuine code of education;" Fernando de Azevedo, *A reforma do ensino no Distrito Federal*. Lectures and interviews. Comp. Melhoramentos de São Paulo, 1929; and, *Novos caminhos e novos fins*. A nova política de educação no Brasil. Editora Nacional São Paulo, 1931; Boletim de Educação Pública. Quarterly publication of the Directorate of Public Instruction of the Federal District. Ano I, nos. 1, 2, 3, and 4. Rio de Janeiro, Brazil, 1930; Comemoração de 1° decênio da Reforma da Instrução Pública do Distrito Federal de 1928. Brazilian Education Association, Rio de Janeiro, 1938.

only in the complex of its causes, relations and consequences, and therefore as one of the "aspects" and one of the phases of the revolutionary process which was going on in the country after 1922 and which was to break out in a revolution in 1930. It may be admitted that the reform of 1928 was, as has been written, "an ideological movement of great scope which opened entirely new perspectives for the country and for the problem of education in Brazil, placing Brazil in the current of ideas defended by the greatest philosophers and technicians of education." [4] But if it was "the generating center of a great reform movement of education in Brazil," it was also one of the manifestations or a "symptom" of the new state of affairs which had been established under the pressure of economic, social and political causes and of that fermentation of ideas which, after the War of 1914, spread through all fields of culture. The mobility and the variations of the population, due not only to the current of immigration, but to internal migration as well, especially toward the south; the rise of industrialism in the States of the south and especially São Paulo, to which the demographic center of gravity of the country had moved, and to which the population flowed attracted as it were by an irresistible magnet, polarized in the better standard of life and the high wages; the evolutions of economic life and the agitation of ideas which came from Europe and the United States involved transformations of mentality, such as were to lead to changes of institutions and the beliefs characteristic of Brazilian life, creating a frankly revolutionary atmosphere in the great urban centers. The Revolution of 1930 was, in this revolutionary process, one of the culminating and decisive phases. Prepared and unleashed, however, by an alliance of political groups with very divergent tendencies, which disputed among themselves the first place, and which, one after another, kept being annulled by the revolution itself and therefore not bringing, to impose and execute that revolution, a definite political program of educational and cultural action, the revolution did not have a uniform point of view, but had at the beginning two effects that were far reaching in the field of culture and education. Intensifying social mobility or, in other words, the migration of persons as well as of ideas and of culture traits from one group or social class to another, and raising to power "new men," not always with well established ideas but with fewer compromises, it had among other consequences that of a rapid social change, the disintegration of the traditional customs of the old cultural pattern and greater complexities in social relations; and breaking the lines of social cleavage between various groups and classes, it contributed powerfully not only to a deeper "democratization", but also to a greater intensity of economic and cultural exchange.

The new ideas already in circulation spread with greater rapidity, whether through the impulse which the very social mobility gave them, being favored by the revolution and its consequences, or by the slowness of the working out of the fundamental principles of a new national policy, entering into frequent contact which facilitated fusions and interpenetrations as well as culture conflicts and different tendencies. In this atmosphere of effervescence of ideas, Lourenço Filho, who had founded in 1929 in a publishing house of São Paulo, the excellent Educational Library, published his *Introdução ao estudo da Escola Nova* (1930),—the best essay in Portuguese on the bio-

---

[4] Cf. *Comemoração do 1° decênio da Reforma da Instrução Pública do Distrito Federal de 1928*, publication of the Brazilian Education Association, with a preface by its president, Dr. M. A. Teixeira de Freitas, p. 27, Rio de Janeiro, 1938.

logical and psychological bases of the new theories of education; and the author of this work, who in 1929 justified in one of his books the reform of education in which he had taken the initiative and borne the responsibility in the Federal District (1928), traced in *Novos caminhos e novos fins* (1931) the principles by which he had been guided in the new policy of education adopted in the scholastic reform of the capital of the country, and founded in 1931 a Library of Brazilian Pedagogy of which *Atualidades Pedagógicas* constitutes one of the principal series.[5] In this same year, three representatives of Catholic thought criticized bitterly the new tendencies in a pamphlet *Pedagogia da Escola Nova*, edited by the Dom Vital Center of São Paulo. In the field of accomplishment, the partial reforms undertaken in 1931 in São Paulo by Lourenço Filho are superior to all other State initiatives, for he reorganized and developed the technical services, handing them over to specialized assistants; he defined and related the administrative services better; installed the Central Pedagogical Library; had the monthly review which had been published under the name *Educação* published under the new title of *Escola Nova*, reserving each of its numbers for the specialized study of a limited subject-matter; he reformed normal school and vocational education; began the use of tests for the organization of selected classes and gave a vigorous impulse to educational motion pictures, statistical services and to associations on the fringe of the school.[6] Although the experiment remained very short (1930–1931), too short for us to be able to estimate with precision the total of its results, the reform of Lourenço Filho in São Paulo in the first year of the revolutionary government was certainly one of the most important movements that formed part of the great reform movement of education.

But, although this result,—that of facilitating and intensifying the circulation of ideas and cultural exchange—, was one of the immediate and most fruitful effects of the Revolution, which contributed to the propagation of all revolutionary ideas, it had another consequence which could not remain without profound effect upon the fields of cultural and pedagogical life in the country. The revolution which unfolded the standard of liberalism did not precisely bring a program of educational policy, although that plan was clearly formulated, even implicit in the form of national reorganization which it was supposed to execute when victorious arms had concentrated the power of the nation in the hands of the chiefs. Nor did there prevail, except in some of the revolutionary groups with more advanced tendencies, the idea that the seizure of power formed a sufficient condition for great social, economic and pedagogical transformations. However, there had already been created an educational conscience; and some cultural aspirations, like the creation of a Ministry of Education, the reorganization of secondary and higher education and the creation of universities, already formed part of the program, in a current so strong that it could not help working upon the revolutionary gov-

[5] V. *Biblioteca de Educação*, founded in 1928 and organized by Dr. Lourenço Filho. Now extends to thirty volumes. Publisher, Comp. Melhoramentos de São Paulo (Weiszflog Brothers Incorporated), São Paulo-Rio; *Atualidades Pedagógicas*, series III (now in thirty volumes) of the Biblioteca Pedagógica Brasileira (B.P.B.) founded in 1931 and edited by Fernando de Azevedo, made up of five series: I. Children's literature; II. Textbooks (manuals, text-books, and source-books); III. Present-day pedagogy (for the cultural and professional training of the teacher); IV. Introduction to science, and V. Brasiliana. Editora Nacional, São Paulo-Rio, 1931–1942.

[6] On the administration of Lourenço Filho (1930–1931), see *Anuário do Ensino do Estado de São Paulo*, organized by Prof. A. F. de Almeida Júnior, 1935–1936. São Paulo, pp. 288-307.

296. Map of the chief cultural centers of Brazil and their approximate spheres of influence.

298. Title page of the *Vocabulário na lingua brasílica*, one of the greatest repositories of Tupí terminology in the seventeenth century. The author is unknown; it bears the date 1621. It was published in 1938. Photocopy from the Department of Ethnography of the College of Philosophy of São Paulo.

297. Title page of the first edition of the *Arte de grammatica da lingoa mais usada na costa do Brasil*, by José de Anchieta, S.J., the first and most complete attempt at a systematic grammar of the Tupi language. Published in Coimbra in 1595. Photocopy from the Department of Ethnography of the College of Philosophy of São Paulo.

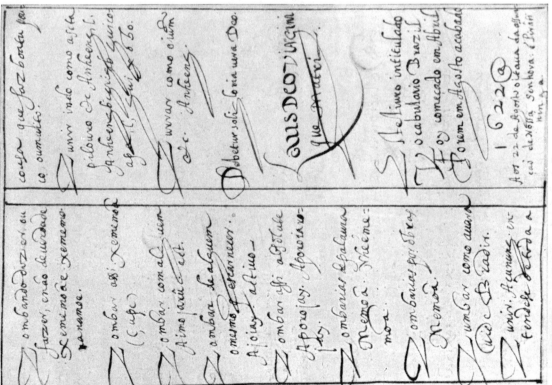

ARTE
DA LINGVA BRASILICA,

Composta pelo Padre Luis Figueira daCompanhia de
IESV, Theologo.

EM LISBOA.
Com licença dos Superiores.
Por Manoel da silva.

300. Front page of the first edition of the *Arte da lingua brasilica* of Father Luiz Figueira, 1576(?)–1643, a real contribution to the study of the Tupi spoken in the north of Brazil. Probably published in 1621. The copy in the National Library of Lisbon is unique in the whole world (cf. Serafim Leite). Photocopy from the Department of Ethnography of the College of Philosophy

299. Last page of the *Vocabulário na lingua brasilica*, of 1621, anonymous, written in Piratininga and published by Plinio Airosa in 1938. Photocopy from the Department of Ethnography of the College of Philosophy of

301. Church of the old College of the Jesuits, Salvador, Bahia. Photo by Voltaire Fraga, in Brazilian Institute of Geography and Statistics.

302. College of St. Ignatius in São Paulo, in the eighteenth century. In *Revista do Serviço do Patrimônio Histórico e Artístico Nacional*, no. 4, 1940.

303. "Old Mother Church and College of St. Michael of the Jesuits, in Santos," painting
by Benedito Calixto.

304. Old College of Our Lady of the Rosary, of the Jesuits, in Paranaguá.
Photo by Hess, from the Archives of the Serviço do Patrimônio Histórico e Artístico Nacional.

305. College of Our Lady of the Rosary, of the Jesuits, in Paranaguá. Arches of the cloister. Photo by Hess, from the Archives of the Serviço do Patrimônio Histórico e Artístico Nacional.

306. College of Our Lady of the Rosary, of the Jesuits, in Paranaguá. Cloister patio, seen from one of the archways. Photo supplied by Dr. Daví Carneiro, historian and director of the Colonel Daví Carneiro Museum, Curitiba, Paraná.

307. Church of St. Francis, Recife, built in 1606.
Photo by Stille, in collection of the College of Philosophy of São Paulo.

308. Church of St. Francis, Recife. Sacristy.
Photo by Stille, in collection of the College of Philosophy of São Paulo.

309. Church of St. Francis, Recife. A view of the interior.
Photo by Stille, in collection of the College of Philosophy of São Paulo.

310. Church of St. Peter, Recife. Principal façade.
Photo by Stille, in collection of the College of Philosophy of São Paulo.

311. Convent of St. Francis, Olinda. View of the cloister patio.
Photo by Stille, in collection of the College of Philosophy of São Paulo.

312. Convent of St. Francis, Olinda. The building as a whole.
Photo by Stille, in collection of the College of Philosophy of São Paulo.

313. Convent of St. Francis, Olinda. View of the sacristy.
Photo by Stille, in collection of the College of Philosophy of São Paulo.

314. Church of St. Francis of Assisi, São João d'El Rei.
Photo by Stille, in collection of the College of Philosophy of São Paulo.

315. University of Coimbra, in Portugal, which played so important a part in the education of the Brazilian élite. North façade.

Photo by Rasteiro. In *História de Portugal*, by Damião Peres, p. 605.

316. Seminary of Olinda, created by the Bishop Azeredo Coutinho and installed in 1800 in the old building of the College of the Jesuits.

317. Seminary of Our Lady of the Happy Death, at Mariana in Minas Gerais. Photocopy of a lithograph in the book "Viagem pelo Brasil," by H. Burmeister, Berlin, 1853.

318. Seminary of Our Lady of the Happy Death, Mariana. Present condition.
Photo by Hess, from the Archives of the Serviço do Patrimônio Histórico e Artístico Nacional.

319. Seminary of Mariana, in Minas. Another view showing its present condition.

320. Seminary of Mariana, which was, from the end of the eighteenth century and throughout the period of the Empire, the chief center of humanistic studies in Minas Gerais.

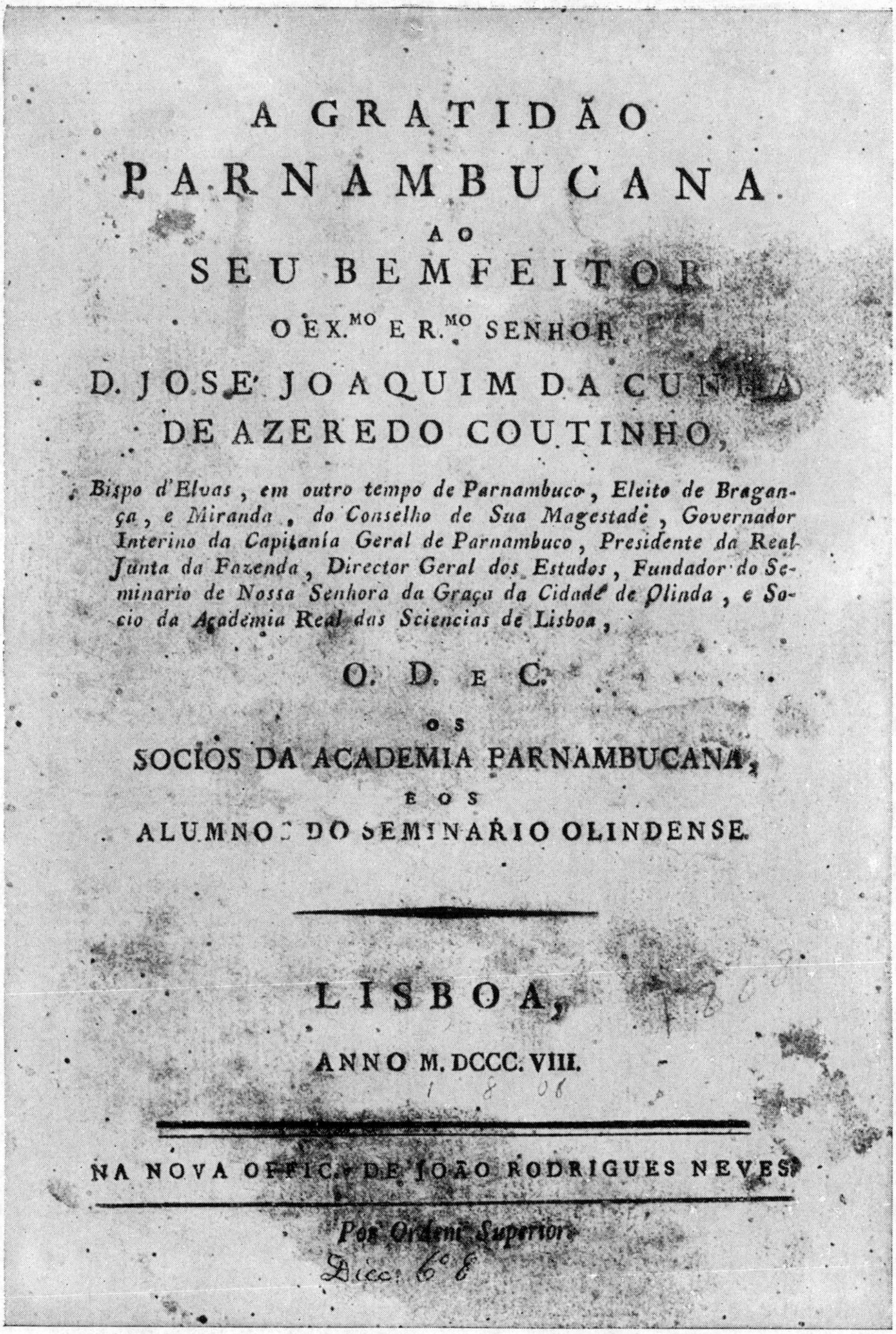

A GRATIDÃO

PARNAMBUCANA

AO

SEU BEMFEITOR

O EX.MO E R.MO SENHOR

D. JOSE JOAQUIM DA CUNHA

DE AZEREDO COUTINHO,

Bispo d'Elvas, em outro tempo de Parnambuco, Eleito de Bragança, e Miranda, do Conselho de Sua Magestade, Governador Interino da Capitania Geral de Parnambuco, Presidente da Real Junta da Fazenda, Director Geral dos Estudos, Fundador do Seminario de Nossa Senhora da Graça da Cidade de Olinda, e Socio da Academia Real das Sciencias de Lisboa,

O. D. E C.

OS

SOCIOS DA ACADEMIA PARNAMBUCANA,

E OS

ALUMNOS DO SEMINARIO OLINDENSE.

LISBOA,

ANNO M. DCCC. VIII.

NA NOVA OFFIC. DE JOÃO RODRIGUES NEVES.

Por Ordem Superior.

---

321. Facsimile of the title page of the book *A gratidão parnambucana ao seu bemfeitor o Exmo. Exmo. Senhor D. José Joaquim da Cunha de Azeredo Coutinho,* then Bishop of Elvas in Portugal, and earlier Bishop of Pernambuco, founder of the Episcopal Seminary of Olinda (1800), which became the center from which liberal ideas and the new European trends spread in Brazil. Lisbon, 1808 edition. From the copy in the possession of the Lamego Library, now incorporated in the Central Library of the College of Philosophy of São Paulo.

322. Dom João VI, the founder of institutions. Drawing by J. B. Debret, engraving by C. S.
Pradier, printed by Chardon, in collection of the Museu Paulista.

A N N A E[S]

DA

CAPITANIA DE S. PEDRO

PELO

DESEMBARGADOR

JOSÉ FELICIANO FERNANDES PINHEIRO.

Tomo I.

RIO DE JANEIRO: NA IMPRESSÃO REGIA.

1819.

Com Licença da Mesa do Dezembargo do Paço.

324. Facsimile reproduction of the title page of the book *Annaes da capitania de São Pedro*, by the appellate judge José Feliciano Fernandes Pinheiro, issued in 1819 by the Royal Printing Office, which came to be called the National Printing Office in 1821. From the copy belonging to the Lamego Library, now incorporated in the Central Library of the College of Philosophy of São Paulo.

ESPIRITO DE VIEIRA,

ou

S E L E C T A

DE

PENSAMENTOS ECONOMICOS, POLITICOS, MORAES, LITTERARIOS,

COM A BIOGRAPHIA

DESTE CELEBRADO ESCRIPTOR.

APPENDICE

AOS

ESTUDOS DO BEM-COMMUM.

POR

JOSÉ DA SILVA LISBOA.

O que unicamente desejo, he ver o Reino unido, fiel, e obediente; os meios de sua conservação promptos, e bem applicados; e para mim, acabaf o resto dos dias na minha Missão.

Vieir. Cart. Rom.

RIO DE JANEIRO. NA IMPRESSÃO REGIA.

1821.

Com Licença.

323. Facsimile of the title page of the book *Espirito de Vieira, ou Seleta, etc.*, by José da Silva Lisboa, issued in 1821 by the Royal Printing Office—the only establishment that existed in Rio up to 1821, created by a decree of Dom João VI, on May 13, 1808, which marked "the introduction of a permanent press in Brazil." From the copy in the possession of the Lamego Library, now incorporated in the Central Library of the College of Philosophy of São Paulo.

325. The old Military School of Rio de Janeiro, into which in 1858 was transformed the army School of Application, coming as the Central School from the Royal Military Academy, founded by Dom João VI, which, still located in Realengo, is to be moved to its new quarters in Resende, in the state of Rio.

326. The College of Caraça, which took its name from the Caraça mountain range in Minas Gerais, founded by Lazarist fathers in 1820, famous for the severity of its discipline and for its humanistic studies.

327. Dom Pedro II, patron of the Pedro II College, in 1837.
Drawing by Luís Aleixo Boulanger.
Collection of Francisco Marques dos Santos.
Photo by Manuel Pinto Gaspar.

328. Bernardo Pereira de Vasconcelos, minister of the Empire, who signed the decree of December 2, 1837, founding the Pedro II College. The decree was handed down by Pedro Araújo Lima, acting as regent, in the name of the Emperor, Dom Pedro II.

329. Antônio de Arrábida, Bishop of Anemúria, Rector of the Pedro II College until 1839, when he resigned and was succeeded by Joaquim Caetano da Silva, 1839–1851. Etching by Modesto Brocos, in collection of the National Library.

330. College of St. Louis, of the Jesuits, the first teachers of Brazil, founded in 1867 at Itu, State of São Paulo.

331. Imperial Academy of Fine Arts, at Rio de Janeiro, which now houses the Treasury Department. Plan by Grandjean de Montigny, architect of the French Mission which came to Brazil in 1816. Photo by Stille, in collection of the College of Philosophy of São Paulo.

332. Manuel de Araújo Pôrto Alegre, Baron of Santo Angelo (1806–1879), poet and painter, professor and first Brazilian director of the Imperial Academy of Fine Arts. Portrait by Pedro Américo. Photo by Carlos.

333. Abílio César Borges, Baron of Macaúbas (Bahia, 1824–1896), physician and great educator, who gave more than forty years' service to Brazilian education.

334. João Pedro de Aquino, engineer, founder of the Aquino Day School (1867), through which, during more than half a century, there passed thousands of students. This school inspired Rui Barbosa, and furnished data for his reform proposal in 1882.

335. Anchieta Academy, founded by Jesuit fathers in 1886 at Nova Friburgo, in the state of Rio, one of the most important secondary schools of the country.

336. Pedro II, who always showed an extraordinary interest in intellectual matters and was a great encourager of education and culture in general. A little known official portrait.

337. The Imperial (later known as National) Museum, founded by Dom João VI as the Royal Museum. Here, beginning in 1876, scientific courses and public lectures were given at the initiative of Ladislau Neto, who was its director from 1874 to 1893. Photograph of the building in which the Royal Museum was originally located, and which was occupied in 1892 by the National Archives, with the transference of the National Museum to the Imperial Palace of the Quinta da Boa Vista, Rio de Janeiro. Photographic copy from the National Archives.

Assignatura de D. PEDRO 4.º de Portugal e 1.º do Brasil
(Existente na Carta Constitucional)

Assignatura do Imperador D. PEDRO II. do Brasil

Assignatura de EL-REI D. JOÃO VI
Como Rei de Portugal e Imperador do Brasil

338. Facsimiles of the signatures of King João VI, the founder of institutions, of Pedro I, creator of law courses in Brazil, and of Pedro II, whose name is linked to all the scientific movements of the past century.

339. Viscount Rio Branco, under whose ministry (1871–1876) was established in 1875 the School of Mines of Ouro Preto, and reforms and movements took place that were of the greatest importance to Brazilian civilization.

340. Henri Gorceix (1842–1919), a Frenchman, who organized and was the first director of the School of Mines of Ouro Preto.

341. Joaquim Cândido da Costa Sena (1852–1919), mineralogist and third director of the School of Mines of Ouro Preto.

342. Counselor Rui Barbosa, author of the famous opinion no. 64, with which he supported, as reporter for the commission appointed on September 12, 1882, the plan for reform presented by Counselor Dantas, in the Chamber of Deputies. Photograph of the year 1918

343. Counselor Leôncio de Carvalho, mir.ister of the Empire, the innovator, author of reforms in 1878 of radical character based on liberal ideas.

344. Benjamim Constant Botelho de Magalhães, famous professor in the Military School, Minister of Instruction, Posts and Telegraphs, whose school reforms, undertaken between 1890 and 1892, all show to a greater or less degree the influence of positivist ideas.

345. A. Caetano de Campos, eminent physician and educator, one of the leaders of the reform movement of São Paulo, 1891–1895, a movement limited to primary and normal-school education, and strongly influenced by American pedagogical tendencies.

346. Colégio Granbery, at Juiz de Fora in Minas Gerais, created in 1889, one of many schools founded by Protestants in the last quarter of the nineteenth century. Such schools aided materially to spread American educational ideas in Brazil.

347. Cesário Mota, Secretary in the State Government, who, with the support of Caetano de Campos and Gabriel Prestes, promoted in São Paulo between 1891 and 1895 the most fruitful reform movement of the first decade of the Republic.

348. A view of the library of the oldest Normal School of São Paulo, still located in the building constructed in 1894 and enlarged in 1936–1938.

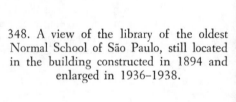

349. Another view of the library of the old Normal School, now known as Caetano de Campos Normal School.

ernment and find in the new environment more favorable conditions for its execution. The Provisional Government created in fact in 1930 a Ministry of Education and Health, which, as we have seen, was not more than an episodic and temporary accident in the beginning of the Republic and came to constitute with the solidity and progress of its organization, one of the most important ministries of the revolutionary government. In the eminent reformer of primary and normal school education of Minas Gerais, Sr. Francisco Campos—one of the leaders of the Revolution—the Chief of the Provisional Government Dr. Getúlio Vargas, found the man marked by his intelligence and cultivation as well as by his prestige in the new political groups as the proper one to assume the position of Minister of State in charge of Education and Public Health, of which he took possession on November 18, 1930, affirming in his incisive inaugural speech that to give sanitation and education to Brazil constituted "the first duty of a revolution which was made to liberate Brazilians." The first reform which the new Minister undertook, and without doubt the farthest reaching among all that were accomplished in this field, in more than forty years of the Republican regime, was that of higher education, which Francisco Campos reorganized on new bases with great sureness and breadth of view.

The central part of this reform, the lines of which are laid down in decree no. 19,851 of April 11, 1931, and a truly innovating part of our cultural apparatus, is the statute of Brazilian universities, in which "the university system was adopted as a rule of organization of higher education in the Republic," and it was required for the foundation of any university in the country that it should "incorporate at least three institutes of higher education, among which should be included those of Law, of Medicine and Engineering, or instead of one of them, the Faculty of Education, Sciences and Letters." This last particularly, wrote Francisco Campos, referring to the new organization of the University of Rio de Janeiro, "on account of the high function which it has in the national life, is the one which gives most markedly to the ensemble of institutions united into a university, the university character properly so-called, permitting university life to transcend the limits of purely professional interests, embracing in all its aspects the highest and most authentic values of culture which give the University its character and the attributes which define it and make it individual." In this way, they were giving attention to a lively aspiration a century old, and a little earlier clearly formulated and defended ardently in the articles and testimony of the inquiry on public instruction in São Paulo, organized and directed in 1926 by the author of this work, and in the inquiry promoted in 1928 and 1929 by the Brazilian Association of Education on the problem of the university in Brazil.[7] The Faculty of Sciences, Letters and Education which was created by that decree and which should have become the backbone of the University of Rio de Janeiro, limited up until that time to the teaching of law, medicine and engineering, was not begun; but with the first Statute of Brazilian Universities wider perspectives were opened not only to the training of the secondary school teacher, but also to the development of the national culture in

[7] Fernando de Azevedo, *A educação pública em São Paulo*. Problemas e discussões. Investigation for "O Estado de São Paulo," in 1926. Part III. Secondary and higher education. Pp. 287-448. Series Brasiliana, Vol. 98. Editora Nacional São Paulo, 1937; cf. *O problema universitário brasileiro*. Investigation undertaken by the Section on Technical and Higher Education, of the Brazilian Education Association. "A Encadernadora, S.A." São José St. Rio, 1929.

all of its aspects. The government which began university teaching in Brazil could not fail to face the problem of the reconstruction of secondary education on the solidity and efficiency of which all education of a higher level, whether professional or disinterested, rests. A week later, on April 18, 1931, the chief of the provisional government on the proposal of Francisco Campos, signed decree no. 19,890 which gave to secondary education the best organization it has yet had among us, raising it from being a simple "passageway" or tool for access to the higher courses, to being an eminently educational institution, increasing the duration of its course to seven years and dividing it into two parts,—the first, of five years, which is common and fundamental, and the second made up of the complementary course of two years, destined to fit students for their future professional specialization.[8]

The creation of a Ministry specializing in educational and health services and the change from the label "instruction" or "public instruction" with which the Ministry was organized at the beginning of the regime (1890) and occupied by Benjamim Constant, to the label "education" and which always turned up as the most appropriate denomination every time that the idea of the restoration of this Ministry of State arose, showed clearly a profounder consciousness of the problem of education and a more lively interest in the problems of national education. The reforms of secondary and higher education in which the Provisional Government took the initiative in its first months confirmed the hopes that the reconstruction of the Brazilian system of education would finally achieve first place among political concerns. The agitation of ideas which for almost ten years had been at work on cultural and pedagogical problems attained, however, its greatest degree of intensity, not with these reforms with which some old aspirations already clearly stated were satisfied, but with the rejection by the new government of the policy of neutrality in the matter of religious teaching, which had been confirmed by the Constitution of 1891, and the institution of religious teaching in public schools. The decree of the Provisional Government, instituting in the schools of the government optional religious teaching, which was an integral and fundamental part of the claims of the Catholics and of the educational policy of the Church, furnished matter for long and bitter debate, marking a deeper line between the larger group of the reformers in whose program the lay character of education formed a part, and the Catholic educators who took up positions in defense of the capital points of their school program and especially of religious teaching in public schools. The Catholic doctrines with regard to education had already been enunciated with vigor and precision in the Code of Canon Law promulgated in 1917 and even more recently in the encyclical of Pope Pius XI (1929), in which the principles already pointed out in that Code reappear, when Catholics are prohibited to attend not only schools that are hostile to their beliefs, but even those which include in their program the neutrality of the school on religious matters. The Church which had remained in an attitude of ex-

---

[8] V. *Organização do ensino secundário*. I. Summary of the motives, presented to the Chief of the Provisional Government by Minister Francisco Campos. II. Decree no. 19,890, of April 18, 1931. III. Programs of Education. Published by the Ministry of Education and Public Health. National Printing Office, Rio de Janeiro, 1931; *Organização do ensino superior*. I. Summary of the motives, presented to the Chief of the Provisional Government, by Minister Francisco Campos. II. Decree no. 19,851, of April 11, 1931; Francisco Campos, *Educação e cultura*, pp. 45-58; 58-104; 117-119. José Olímpio, Rio de Janeiro, 1930.

pectation if not of distrust with regard to the movement of pedagogical reforms, threw itself into the battle, launching an offensive against the last reformers, who for that matter never admitted "that it should be permitted to the professors to offend in any way the religious feelings of their pupils," but whose attitude with regard to the question of religious neutrality in the schools drew upon them the suspicion, rarely well founded, that they were defending materialist or extremist doctrines.

These two groups entered openly into conflict, not only with regard to doctrinal points of view, with respect to pedagogical problems and the relation between the State and education, but particularly with regard to the execution of the decree on religious education, which occurred at the beginning in an atmosphere laden with suspicion and prejudice. In 1931, the Center Dom Vital published in a little volume a series of polemics under the title of *Pedagogia da Escola Nova*; Tristão de Ataíde launched his book *Debates pedagógicos*; Father Leonel Franca, the illustrious Jesuit, took up in his fundamental work *Ensino religioso e ensino leigo* the question of religious teaching, studying it from all angles and with abundant documentation, and there was brought together in the Cúria Metropolitana in the capital of São Paulo, the first Catholic Congress of Education, promoted by the Center Dom Vital of São Paulo.[9] In most of the works which were then published, as in the theses defended in this Congress, the ideas most ardently fought by the Catholics, who defined their position with regard to the State and the official school, were those of the lay character of teaching, coeducation, and that of the monopoly of education by the State. The totalitarian pretensions of the State in the matter of education appeared, however, to meet the same resistance on the part of the Catholics as from various leaders and reformers who, even although they considered education an eminently public function, showed themselves little disposed to yield to the totalitarian and tentacular conceptions of certain regimes, among which all education of youth is grasped by the State and the human personality as well as the life of the spirit do not find favorable conditions for their natural development and their progress in all directions. The struggle which from then on took place about the new forms and new ideals of education and which was made up in part of real divergencies and in part of mutual lack of understanding was to be prolonged openly for almost seven years, assuming an extremely acute character in various phases of its development. In the petition which later, in 1933, was presented to the Constituent Commission, the Catholics summed up in a firm and serene exposition their principal claims, asking among other measures that religion should be considered as a subject of teaching in the public schools (Article 4) for those pupils whose fathers or guardians had manifested explicitly their wish in this respect (Section 1) and proclaiming (Article 2, Section 1), upon the basis that the family was anterior to the State, that parents should have the duty and the natural right to educate their children and that they

---

[9] *Pedagogia da Escola Nova*. Published by the Centro D. Vital, São Paulo, 1931; Congress of Education, called by the Centro D. Vital of São Paulo and meeting October 17, 1931, in the auditorium of the Curia Metropolitana. Published by the Centro D. Vital of São Paulo, 1933; Father Leonel Franca, *Ensino religioso e ensino leigo*. Rio de Janeiro, 1931; Tristão de Ataíde, *Debates pedagógicos*. Rio de Janeiro, 1931; cf. *Os problemas da educação na Constituição*. Memorial presented to the Constituent Commission and signed by many Catholic professors and intellectuals of the Federal District and the States. In "Jornal do Brasil," Rio de Janeiro, February 3, 1933.

may accomplish this in the public schools, in private establishments or in the home.[10]

It was, then, the question of the teaching of religion, repudiated by the reformers, which broke out or rendered most harsh the struggle which, if it did not have as its object, certainly had as one of its consequences, the creation of an almost insurmountable incompatibility between the idea of religion and the reform in education. At the beginning of the regime, when the Constitution of 1891 consecrated the principle of the lay character of teaching, the campaign against the policy of neutrality had produced similar effects. The struggle which then was undertaken appeared to have as its object in its efforts to create between the religious idea and the republican idea a gulf that was ever deeper and thus to ruin in the minds of the people the traditional beliefs of the nation through the competition of public power. So far, however, from combatting them were the reformers of 1928 in the Federal District and Minas Gerais that on various occasions they pointed out in speeches and interviews the necessity and the duty of the State to respect the sources of moral and religious life, in which so many men find the energy necessary to dedicate themselves better to the general interests and the public service. Taking up again the principle of the lay attitude in the period of operation of the regime which had begun it (when the Constitution of 1891 was still in force), they refused to confuse in any way or to seem to confuse, impartiality between the different religious sects in a nation in which there did not exist unity of belief with that laicism which makes of irreligion a kind of State religion. However that may be, the division grew more marked until it was impossible to establish a "zone of harmony" between the two groups in the Fourth National Conference of Education which met from December 13th to 20th, 1931, and which the head of the Provisional Government and the Minister of Education and Health entrusted the task of "defining the principles of education" and the "happiest formula" in which the educational policy of the Revolution could be expressed. The debates which arose about the fundamental questions posed by the Government of the Republic gave evidence of the difficulties that the Assembly had in solving them and which compelled them to leave them without an answer, as material for discussion in the new Congress. Now they could no longer nourish the illusory hope of having educators form an organization that would be not a "party" but a "national association," in which all would join without distinction of religion and of party, in order to trace an educational and cultural policy that would be the program of the government as far as education was concerned, for the work of reorganization of the country.

Out of this situation of perplexity and hesitation, of disagreements and divergencies, there was born in one of the groups into which the Assembly was divided the idea of entrusting to the author of this book, as the reformer and interpreter of the new current of pedagogical thought, the task of formulating into a manifesto these new ideas and in this way to establish the fundamental meaning of a Brazilian policy of education.[11] This resolution of the ideological current, whose principles and aspirations Nóbrega da Cunha and Frota Pessoa, among others, had defended with warmth and

---

10 V. *Os problemas da educação na Constituição*. Memorial presented to the Constituent Commission and signed by many Catholic professors and intellectuals of the Federal District and the States. In "Jornal do Brasil," Rio de Janeiro, February 3, 1933.

11 Nóbrega da Cunha, *A revolução e a educação*. Printing office of the "Diário de Notícias," Rio de Janeiro, 1932.

exactness, was communicated to the reformer of education in the Federal District who was then in São Paulo and accepted the mission with which he was entrusted and the task that the partisans reserved for him in that Assembly, of a new educational policy in Brazil.[12] In the manifesto of the pioneers of new education, presented to the people and to the government and published in 1932 in Rio de Janeiro and in São Paulo with the signature of numerous professors, were laid down the directives of an educational policy inspired by new pedagogical and social ideas and plans for an urban and industrial civilization, with the objective of breaking with the excessively individualistic traditions of the policy of the country, strengthening the bonds of national solidarity, maintaining the democratic ideals of our ancestors, and adapting education as well as life "to the social and economic transformations brought about by mechanical inventions which governed natural forces and had revolutionized our habits of work, of recreation, of communication and of exchange." [13] The defense of the principle of lay education, the nationalization of instruction, the organization of popular education, both urban and rural, the reorganization of the structure of secondary education and of technical and professional education, the creation of universities and of institutes of higher learning for the development of pure studies and of scientific research, constituted some of the most important points of this program of educational policy which aimed to fortify the work of lay teaching, to render compulsory education effective, to create or establish for children the right to a whole education according to their aptitudes, facilitating without privilege their entrance into secondary and higher education, and to enlarge by means of reorganization and enrichment of the school system, its scope and its means of action. And, as today more than ever teaching in general may be compared to a game of chess with which "the dislocation of one pawn brings about a general change in the situation on the entire board," they managed to establish a kind of "orchestration" of the school system, in the sense of articulating and harmonizing all the parts of the system and taking into account the mutual repercussions of the teaching of various grades and types and the reaction of the institutions upon each other.

Whatever may be the point of view that we hold, in order to appreciate this document, and which may lead us to oppose it or to support it, we cannot deny that in the manifesto of 1932—"Educational reconstruction in Brazil," the problem of national education is analyzed in all its aspects, principles are defined, and for the first time the directives of a general program of education are traced, whose pieces, all articulated in one systematic plan, are subordinated to definite ends which affect the whole. Certainly there had already arrived,—we wrote in 1932 in the introduction to this public document,—"the moment to define, limit and impose the program of the new educational policy by means of an organic and synthetic view of modern theories of education in

[12] V. Nóbrega da Cunha, *A revolução e a educação.* Printing office of the "Diário de Notícias," Rio de Janeiro, 1932, pp. 37-44; petition and explanation to the chair and the assembly of the IV National Conference of Education, in the sessions of December 19 and 20, 1931; and pages 5-6: letter, dated, December 24, 1931, in which the author of this book replied to Prof. C. Nóbrega da Cunha, in compliance with the request made to him, in the name of the vanguard of educators, to draw up the manifesto of the pioneers of the new education.

[13] *A reconstrução educacional no Brasil.* Ao povo e ao govêrno. Manifesto of the pioneers of the new education. With an introduction by Fernando de Azevedo (pp. 7-30). Appendix: A nova política educacional. Sketch of an educational program derived from the manifesto. Pp. 113-117. Editora Nacional, São Paulo, 1932.

which, when the essence of the doctrines has been extracted, there may be established a new system of aims superimposed on the means suited to the new aims and necessary for their realization." [14] The idea of a complete system of education with an organic structure and the construction in consequence of a system of teaching, flexible and as far as possible unified at all grades and in which theory and practice are closely united; the unity of a national policy controlling, by means of general principles and norms established by the Union, the variety of regional educational systems; the role which it assigns to the State as an organism truly capable, under present conditions, of carrying out educational work; the priority given to the principle of activity and free research; the penetration of all teaching by the scientific spirit and the rebuilding of secondary education with the aim of developing technical and professional education, give to this public document an importance which we can not fail to recognize, and which still was not properly appreciated in its true consequences, not only in the field of Brazilian thought in the field of education, but also in the field of concrete accomplishment under the direct influence, whether admitted or not, of many of its fundamental principles. "The group of educators that has just issued the manifesto containing the sketch of an educational policy opened up a new phase of constructive action in the domain of ideas," observed Azevedo Amaral in 1932, who recognized in this same article, that the manifesto had been "the first pronouncement of exponents of national culture in the sense of defining pure directives for the solution of the problems in this period of necessary reform of Brazilian life." [15] The manifesto was not merely a "declaration of principles," which had a great repercussion and aroused numerous debates; nor was it only a document by means of which a group of educators took positions with regard to the most serious problems of national education, but it was in addition a vigorous effort to constitute a new educational policy and to propose the carrying out of one of the broadest educational plans which had yet been traced in Brazil.

The Fourth Conference, during whose debates there arose the idea of a declaration of principles and of a program of educational policy; the manifesto of the pioneers of new education launched soon afterwards in 1932, and the Fifth National Conference of Education, which met in Niteroi in the last days of that year and which was the most notable of those that took place through the initiative of the Brazilian Educational Association, without doubt constituted a culminating point in the great campaign begun with the movement of 1928 for pedagogical reform and for an educational policy of national character, along the general lines of its plan and with its essential objectives. In this Conference, carried out under the auspices of the government of the State of Rio, when Celso Kelly was director general of instruction, there were reaped not only the benefits which are obtained from these periodic meetings and consist above all of a widening of mental horizons and closer relationship of men for mutual comprehension: "the direct personal acquaintance of people occupied in the same professions, who do not know each other, or scarcely know each other, tightening the bonds of sympathy, laying the foundation for friendship, uniting to further their common desires, and planting in the immensity of this distended Brazil," according to the vigorous expression of Francisco Venâncio Filho, "firm bases for a bridge of cooperation and solidarity in the

[14] *A reconstrução educacional no Brasil.* Ao povo e ao govêrno. Manifesto of the pioneers of the new education. Editora Nacional, São Paulo, 1932, p. 23.

[15] Azevedo Amaral, *O Estado e a Educação.* In "O Jornal," of Rio de Janeiro, March 27, 1932.

urgent work of the education of Brazilians." Having as its main if not its only objective the evaluation of suggestions for an educational policy and a plan of national education for the first draft of the Constitution, the Fifth Conference assembled in Niteroi, after a long study by the Committee of 32, discussed and approved the plan for national education, worked out by the Committee of 10, and aimed at the reconstruction, on new bases, of the system of education and culture of the country. The Committee of 32, to the chairmanship of which the author of this book was raised, who was already a member of the Committee of 10, had as its reporters, Lourenço Filho, the reformer of instruction in São Paulo in 1931, and Anísio Teixeira, who was already deeply involved in educational reform in the Federal District. The directives toward which the new educational program were directed, the initial debates that were aroused by the examination of a problem that is really as complex as that of education and the stubbornness shown in the defense of divergent if not opposed points of view, increased the division which soon was open in the second plenary session, and which transferred the leadership in the assembly to the new current of educational thought, with the resignation of the president, Fernando de Magalhães, and the unanimous acceptance of the name of Lourenço Filho to take his place in the direction of its work.

These two groups remained in open opposition down to 1937,—the year in which the coup d'état by its authority put an end to the conflict, tranquilizing the polemical spirit, calming passions and imposing as a line of conduct in the field of education, the policy of compromise, of adjustment and of balance. In spite of having attained its period of greatest acuity between 1928 and 1933, this conflict of tendencies did not fail to continue its development, the struggle varying according to the region, the degree of preparation of the professors and according to the nature and intensity of the resistance which they met. It is impossible, however, to limit the field of these struggles in the terrain of education, to a lack of harmony or opposition between the school policy of the Church and the new educational policy which adopted as planks in its platform certain principles that were rejected by the other group, such as coeducation, and the lay character of teaching. These struggles were complicated doubtless, and rendered more bitter and heated in the course of their development, by the conflict of ideologies of left and right, communist and fascist, which had founded in Europe upon the party regime and the name of a class ideal, or a race or national ideal, the totalitarian State destined to make war upon capitalism and Marxism, and which then had a more or less violent effect in Brazil through the organization and activities of extremist parties. But, unleashed by the reaction of the Church against some of the new ideas; shaken and perturbed by the shocks of extremist doctrine and of attempts at infiltration on the part of subversive parties, these campaigns to reform the school system had in their origin and kept during their whole life, the opposition which is a normal and constant fact in all societies, between the young and the old, between traditionalists and experimenters, a conflict which having remained latent or scarcely concealed at the beginning, became open when favorable circumstances for retaliation and resistance arose. In the book *O rejuvenescimento da política,* in which there was published in 1932 the inquiry made in France among intellectuals who could not be less than 30 nor more than 40 years old and among whom figured the names of Daniel Rops, André Wurmser, Pierre Cot, Marcel Déat, Robert Garric and others, one could feel in various replies, the resistance opposed to innovations by the old and the necessity of fighting the meddling of older men in politics because they prevent the reformation of all values.[16] "Revolutions are full of old men who have hindered the renovating work," observed one; "it is necessary, then, to give a youthful character to the revolution in order to give this character to politics. Young men who will accomplish something, take your positions," cried another. "We are facing a conflict between two mentalities, one which struggles because it is dying, the other which struggles because it is being born," concluded a third, in other words, all of which indicated the at times invincible obstacle opposed by the routine and the tradition of the old to the building of new ideas.

In this critical period, which was profoundly disturbed but at the same time fruitful in new things, which followed upon a long and deep rooted period of the dominion of tradition of established ideas, the educational and cultural life of the country was characterized by the breaking up of pedagogical thought at the beginning into two currents and afterwards into many, and the confusion of doctrines which scarcely fitted under the common denomination of "new education" or of "the new school," names which were capable of many different significances.[17] Thus the opposition of the educa-

[16] See *Le Rajeunissement de la politique* (R. A. Correia, Paris, 1932).

[17] In fact, people came to consider as "new education" all kinds of plans and experiments in which new ideas or techniques were introduced (such as active methods, the replacement of traditional examinations by objective tests, the adaptation of instruction to the phases of development and to individual differences) or which brought to the reorganization of structure or to a process of teaching, the stamp of novelty. The expression, which is vague enough, to be sure, and not precise in its content, might be taken to include all forms of education which took into account modern pedagogical thought and the needs of children. It is for that reason that one could see forming part of the same plan of reform, principles at times divergent if not contradictory, as for example the idea that everyone has a right to an education cut to his measure ("individualization" of education) and that of the organization of homogeneous classes, selected by objective means and intelligence tests and tests of advancement. Processes and new techniques were at times adopted or tried out, without due regard to the pedagogical and social ends which these new "instruments" or means of education were to serve. It seems to us, then, that if we wish to restore this confused and distorted expression, with its variable and contradictory content, to its more honest meanings, we shall have to distinguish between at least two forms of new education: one, inspired by the new bio-psychological idea of the child and the functional concept of education, and the other linked to the evolution of knowledge and of social ideas, and suggested by a clearer concept of the role of the school as a social institution, and a keener awareness of the need of relating the school to the environment and adapting it to the conditions of a new civilization. The former, with its individualistic tendencies, takes the individual as the point of departure for the reorganization of the school; the latter, socially minded, and at times even socialistic, starts with the community to arrive at the training of the individual; one aims rather at methods of teaching, that is, the processes of apprenticeship and methods of school work; the other directs its attention chiefly to the structure of the school and its better adaptation to the social environment. These are conceptions with different origins and bases, capable of leading to divergent tendencies, but which in a way complement each other, and in any case are not opposed in nature. The new education or the new school, in its first meaning (Bovet, Ed. Claparède, Ad. Ferrière, and among the Americans, John Dewey), is guided by the following fundamental principles: 1) greater freedom for the child, to whom one tries to give more favorable conditions for his natural development through free and spontaneous activity; 2) the principle of "an essentially active being, whose faculties are developed by exercising them;" and 3) respect for the personal originality of each child, and in consequence, the "individualization" of teaching, based on the idea that each of us has a right to the education that suits him (the "school that is custom made," of which Claparède speaks). But childhood is not merely a "development," as P. Fauconnet remarks; it is also an "imitation." It is necessary that the child should little by little become part of a civilization that he finds ready made. "This process

tional policy of the Church; the coincidence in time of the movements of pedagogical reform and of the propagation of extremist political doctrine; the very lack of exactness and the variety of conceptual content of the words "new education," and the reaction of the die-hard conservatives between whose ideas and those of the reformers, there was the same distance that exists between repose and movement, stagnation and progress, all of this helped to develop that state of mind which Thibaudet called "sinistrism," which is imminent in the sensibility of most men and the intimidation which the mere word "left" exercises upon their minds, together with its variant such as "new ideas," "advanced ideas," "broad-minded ideas," and a whole series of satellite formulas. Not only was there enlarged in this way the zone of "dangerous thought," but it became ever more sensitive. This zone exists in every society and, varying according to time and place, it always tends in critical periods of change and social transformation to enlarge. The zone of dangerous thought, extending, threatened now to embrace within its frontiers the aspirations of the "new school," and in a general way the new ideas in education. And even more, thought itself, the critical spirit and freedom of judgment. For as Louis Wirth observes, "the subjects marked with the danger signal are those which the society or the controlling elements in it believe to be so vital and hence so sacred that they will not tolerate their profanation by discussion. But what is not so easily recognized is the fact that thought, even in the absence of official censorship, is disturbing, and, under certain conditions, dangerous and subversive. For thought is a catalytic agent that is capable of unsettling routines, disorganizing habits, breaking up customs, undermining faiths, and generating scepticism." [18]

But in spite of this state of mind which developed, above all after 1932 with the publication of the manifesto, and the vigorous new offensive of the Fifth National Conference of Education, and with which it was hoped to disturb in every way the work of educational reconstruction in the country, the campaign begun with the reform of 1928 in the Federal District and in Minas Gerais and continued in 1931 in the State of São Paulo immediately after the revolution did not suffer defeat. Elements of the vanguard took their position in the press of the country and especially in Rio de Janeiro where in *Diário de Notícias* in 1931–1934, Cecília Meireles with her keen and mordant column, and Nóbrega da Cunha with his subtle activity and his great power of penetration, Azevedo Amaral in *O Jornal,* with his persuasive argument in the service of a

---

of penetration is a laborious one. In a way, the whole process of initiation does violence to the nature of the child or adolescent." The new education, in its second meaning, puts the accent exactly on the *initiation,* and not on the *development,* trying not only to understand the needs of the individual through those of the community, but also to organize the school like a living community (Paulsen's *Gemeinschaftsschule*), and steer it in the direction of the principles of solidarity and cooperation, and with a partial sacrifice of the individual to the common good. The individualistic ideals of a free and active school, which aims at liberating the child, by the combined efforts of the scientific method and of intuitive understanding, tend, if they are carried to their final consequences, to collide with the social ideals, and in some cases, socialistic ideals, of the work school or community school (*Schulgemeinde*) organized with the aim of bringing out in the child his cooperative and creative tendencies, and lead him to the culture and responsibilities of adult life.

[18] In Karl Mannheim, *Ideologia y utopia.* Introducción a la sociologia del conocimiento. Spanish version by Salvador Echavarría. Fondo de Cultura Económica, Mexico, 1941.

masterful thinker, and later J. G. Frota Pessoa, who beginning in 1933 made of his column in the *Jornal do Brasil* a front line trench, with his implacable lucidity and with the sureness of his blows, brought new stimuli and new accent to this campaign, the content of which was not limited to the cultural plane and in the development of which the modern spirit and the profoundly human wave of feeling vibrated forcefully. In the field of actual accomplishment, the reforming wave was not stopped for it found anew in the Federal District with Anísio Teixeira (1932–1935), and in São Paulo with the author of this work (1933) and with Professor A. F. Almeida Júnior (1935–1936), some of the most important phases of the process of evolution. In Rio de Janeiro, Anísio Teixeira, who had recently arrived from North America, and in São Paulo the author of this work sought with big plans of reform that were deep-rooted and strong, to inject into reality all which it could at that moment endure of the new doctrine and its principles. It was through the vigorous activity of Anísio Teixeira that in the educational policy of the Federal District, the influences of North American pedagogical ideas and techniques already enunciated in the reform of 1928 [19] were emphasized and educational services had a truly notable development through the creation of new and far-reaching institutions, through new methods of scholastic administration, and through the broader application of scientific methods to the problems of education. Upon taking possession of the post of director general of Education on October 15, 1931, he defined his attitude clearly in the speech which he then gave, declaring his allegiance to the new educational policy, the foundations of which had been laid down with the reform of 1928 in the Federal District, and announced his object as being that of developing in breadth and in profundity that naturally incomplete work which had been received by the capital of the country "like a fruit long awaited which is coming to meet a dynamic, modern educational consciousness which has been strengthened and fortified by the reform."

[19] The influence of pragmatism and North-American ideas on the most advanced current of educational thought was so great that it seemed to many that "the new education" was a specifically American thing or a product of the kind of civilization that was growing up in the United States. However, as P. Fauconnet concludes, "it would not be correct to think of the new education as purely American, nor even Anglo-Saxon, seeing that Germany stands at the head of the list (he is referring to the Second Conference of Locarno) and French Switzerland gives to the League (the International League of New Education) some of its leaders. Why is it that countries with civilizations so different as those of Germany, England, and the United States agree with this revolutionary pedagogy, while other countries like France seem rather resistant to it? Are they, in the last analysis and for the same reason, seeking the same thing? This would be a good object of research for competent sociologists. In any case, we cannot see in the new education just a manifestation of national temperament. The influence of the United States is undeniable, not only because they have so much to offer in experience and plans; it is necessary to keep in mind that the powerful thought of John Dewey was one of the sources of the movement. Shall we, then, have to say that the world is tending to become Americanized? There is some truth in this view. In France you will find easily enough enemies of the new education who consider their resistance legitimate, as a defense of the traditional Latin culture against the youthful pragmatism of the Americans. It remains to explain why countries with an old culture of their own, like England and Germany, are seduced by Americanism. The success of the new ideas does not, in my opinion, depend only on the leadership of the United States in the world; there are deeper reasons, more human ones; it is not a mere fad." (P. Fauconnet, *O Congresso da Educação Nova*. In "O Estado de São Paulo," May, 1928; Cf. Francisco Venâncio Filho, *Contribuição americana à educação*. Published in "Lições da vida americana," 2, Rio de Janeiro, 1941.)

Accepting, however, the new attitude in educational policy with its social and democratic ends formulated in 1928, Anísio Teixeira undertook between 1932 and 1935 a series of reforms and moves with which he gave a new life to the school system of the Federal District and by a series of measures gave it a breadth of action which it had not succeeded in acquiring up until then through earlier reforms. With the creative force of his enterprising spirit and his liberty of action, which was only possible as a result of the Revolution of 1930, and the abrogation of the Organic Law, he broadened and developed the school system in order to make it as complete as possible; he promoted the enrichment of the scholastic program, the specialization of primary school teachers in order better to accomplish the ends that had been formulated; he raised technical and vocational education to the level of secondary education (to the fourth year), relating it to general secondary education, with the end of permitting its equivalence on a cultural level and the transference of pupils from one course to another; he reorganized normal school training with the object of raising the professional training of the teacher to a higher level with a basis in preparatory studies or general culture; he created the University of the Federal District (1935), made up of five schools, and remodelled the technical equipment of the administrative services in education so as to fit them to fulfil their technical functions and those of scientific research and administration. While under the administration of Anísio Teixeira,[20] this vigorous transformation of the school system of Rio de Janeiro was going on, other reforms were being accomplished in Ceará with Moreira de Sousa, in Pernambuco under the leadership of Aníbal Bruno,[21] in Paraná, and above all in the State of São Paulo, in which the author of this work was once more called to the post of director general of Education in 1933 and undertook in six months the complete reform of the scholastic apparatus and handed down on April 21, 1933, within the broad general lines of the movement of scholastic reform, the *Code of Education of the State*. Among the reforms in which he took the lead and which included various degrees and types of teaching, there figured that which gave a new object to rural education by means of the creation of farm schools and technical and cultural missions; the remodelling of administrative and technical services, with the object of establishing scientific processes for the solution of problems of school administration; the reorganization of the structure of normal schools, raising the professional training of the primary school teacher in a two year course with a preparatory basis (fundamental course of five years), as a support for professional specialization with the philosophical attitude and the scientific spirit, and the creation of

[20] Anísio Teixeira, Speech upon taking office as director general of education, October 15, 1931; *As diretrizes da escola nova*. In "Boletim de Educação Pública," Ano II, nos. 1 and 2, January-June, 1932, pp. 1-24; *O sistema escolar de Rio de Janeiro*. In "Boletim de Educação Pública," Ano III, nos. 3, and 4, July-December, 1932, pp. 307-370; *Educação Pública, sua organização e administração*, Rio de Janeiro, 1934; *Em marcha para a democracia*. A margem dos Estados Unidos. Guanabara, Rio de Janeiro, 1934; *Educação para a democracia*, Rio de Janeiro, 1936; Cf. "Boletim de Educação Pública," Ano II, nos. 1 and 2, January-June, 1932; nos. 3 and 4, July-December, 1932; Ano III, nos. 5 and 6, January-June, 1933; Ano III, Nos. 7 and 8, June-December, 1933.

[21] V. Boletim de Educação, Ano III, nos. 3 and 4, March-June, 1933; Ano IV, nos. 5 and 6, June-December, 1934; Ano V, no. 7, December, 1936; Diretoria Técnica de Educação. Recife, Pernambuco.

the Instituto de Educação, for the further training and specialization of primary school teachers, the training of school administrators, technicians and curriculum specialists.[22]

The movement implanted in 1928 through the reformist campaign in education continued, as we see, and was to continue in spite of all the difficulties and lack of understanding and with sufficient force to extend the struggle from the field of ideas to that of practical activity in the field of primary, normal school and vocational education in various States. In the biennium 1935–1936, Professor A. F. Almeida Júnior carried on in the direction of education in São Paulo a fruitful activity entirely looking in the direction of the new educational policy of which he was one of the pioneers and whose fundamental line of action had been laid down, with his adherence, in the manifesto issued in 1932 by a group of Brazilian educators. Few even among the elements of the vanguard have put more objectively and analyzed more lucidly than he, the problem of rural education [23] and felt more profoundly the necessity for reacting against an education without vital relations with the requirements of the social environment and with the imperatives and conditions of the modern world. Acting within the lines of the *Code of Education* in which he had collaborated in 1933 and which expressed aspirations that were common to the whole new current in educational thought, he confronted the great problem of scholastic building; endeavored to give to the questions of the organization of the school system a scientific treatment looking upon them as technical problems and according to well defined principles. He promoted lectures and courses on school administration, and with the object of providing an education drawn from life and facing life, he reorganized intellectual programs, taking them from the realities of the environment and simplifying them for the sake of physical education, character formation and spiritual values.[24] After these and other moves, the campaign for the reform of education appeared to decline in Brazil. It had been developing with a growing intensity for more than ten years and, as we know, it came at the right moment, falling like a ripe fruit from the tree of the modern mind, a tree which in turn did not cease to give savory and bitter fruit and often contradictory results. Those who were at the front of the movement did not believe that the educational structure was so defective and archaic in its various grades that it was not possible to improve it definitively without so general and profound a reform as would mean a real revolution. Wherever it happened that they put their hands upon the levers of command, they threw themselves into the reforming work with a faith and a tenacity which could not fail to have an effect upon the whole educational system and cultural

22 V. *Código de Educação* do Estado de São Paulo. Decree no. 5,884, of April 21, 1933. Official Printing Office of the State. São Paulo, 1933; *Administração do Prof. Fernando de Azevedo* (from January 11 to July 27, 1933) in "Anuário do Ensino do Estado de São Paulo," organized by Prof. A. F. Almeida Júnior, Director of Education, 1935–36, São Paulo, pp. 327-345; *Arquivos do Instituto de Educação*, Ano I, no. 1, September, 1935; Ano II, no. 2, September, 1936; Ano III, no. 3, March, 1937; Ano III, no. 4, September, 1937.

23 A. F. Almeida Júnior, *A escola rural*. In "Anuário do Ensino do Estado de São Paulo," 1935–1936, organized by A. F. Almeida Júnior, Director General of Education, pp. 180-226; Fernando de Azevedo, *O problema da educação rural*. Lecture given in Rio de Janeiro, August 17, 1933, in "*A educação e seus problemas*." Editora Nacional, São Paulo, 1937, pp. 45-75.

24 V. on the activities of Prof. A. F. Almeida Júnior, in the superintendence of education in São Paulo, the "Anuário do Ensino do Estado de São Paulo," organized by A. F. Almeida Júnior, Director General of Education, 1935–1936. São Paulo, pp. 3-283.

life of the country. But, Brazilian in their spirit and in their objective and aiming always at the installation of a national system of education, these reforms, confined to the boundaries of one region, could not and did not exercise, on account of their local character, a direct and profound action except in certain school systems in the Federal District and the States.

In the field of education the revolutionary government of the Union, down to 1934, like the constitutional government from 1934–1937, being caught between antagonistic forces, although it felt the necessity, saw no opportunity to make a coordinated and general effort, with which it would be possible to transfer to a national plane the spirit of scholastic reform which had been shown by the reformers and which could not exhaust itself in isolated and fragmentary experiments. Besides, the reform movement, which, starting from below and working up, expressed itself in far-reaching reforms in the field of primary, normal school and vocational education, had not yet succeeded in penetrating with the same force the field of secondary and higher education, which remained almost impermeable or inaccessible to the movement of educational reform. Certainly the movement which shown by the old Instituto Agronômico de Campinas, the Instituto de Higiene and the Instituto Biológico of São Paulo, created under the inspiration of Artur Neiva, and which became under the direction of Rocha Lima one of the greatest scientific centers created in America for the investigation of problems of vegetable and animal biology,[25] like the creation of new cultural and scientific insti-

[25] The Biological Institute, created in 1928 in São Paulo, through the efforts of Artur Neiva, who was chairman of the technical committee formed to combat the coffee blight, had for its first director, hired to organize it, the former assistant chief of the Osvaldo Cruz Institute of Rio de Janeiro. Artur Neiva was followed in the post by Prof. Rocha Lima, who was also one of the helpers of Osvaldo Cruz, and having been professor in the Institute of Tropical Diseases, of Hamburg, was then exercising the functions of vice-director of the new institute, founded in São Paulo. Installed today in a magnificent edifice of vast proportions, constructed especially for this institute of study and scientific research, it extends its sphere of action, as the present director tells us, "from the investigation of the most general problems of biology to any disease which threatens to destroy, harm, or lower the value of the source of wealth based on farming and cattle raising. The heart of its activity is scientific investigation in the field of pathology of living beings, animal and vegetable, and especially of those that are of the greatest use or interest to man. Within the vast field of comparative pathology, the chief scientific activity of the Institute is centered on the study of communicable plagues and diseases." Its first and most important experimental station, obtained for the Institute in 1937,—the Fazenda "Mato Dentro," located near Campinas, is a great agricultural property, with an area of 112 Paulista alqueires, which is, as it were, its rural extension and serves all its sections and all its experts. In the Biological Institute there are functioning in connection with the training of technicians, the School of Comparative Pathology, that of Phytopathology, and the specialized school of Veterinary Pathology, all subordinated to this great scientific research institution. Its staff of scientists and technicians, made up of sixty-five specialists, the number of assistants being forty-two, includes names of world-wide reputation, and is recruited from the best centers of training in the country and abroad. By the investigations and experiments carried on in its two divisions, vegetable and animal, among which we note the demonstration of the efficacy of Valdemar's vaccine against hoof and mouth disease and the experimental verification of the poisoning with photo-sensibility by the bush Rosmarinus officinalis as the cause of the mortality of the cattle of the great herds of Andradina; by the value and volume of its scientific productivity, of more than a hundred works, like the "Treatise on the diseases of poultry," which is of international value, and by its accomplishments in the field of industry, established by more than forty products meant for fighting the plagues which attack farming and breeding, the Biological Institute is one of the great centers of research and technology in America,

tutions such as the Escola de Sociologia and Política (1932) in São Paulo and the
Escola Nacional de Química (1934) in Rio de Janeiro, were signs of the progress which
the penetration of the scientific spirit was making in the culture of Brazil. Higher education continued, however, to be limited to an education in "the interests of the profession," not in the intellectual interests of the individual nor for the sake of science, the
development of which took place rather in institutions of applied science, where the
necessity of confronting urgent problems related to the national economy directed work
toward an original scientific investigation in various fields. No attempt had been made
in the field of actual accomplishment to the end that this movement of the spread of
the scientific spirit should be marked in our pedagogy and should affect all teaching,
leading in higher education with the same spirit to the reforms which had been undertaken in fundamental and popular education which was entrusted then exclusively to
the States. The fact is that the intellectual classes, recruited for more than a century
from the professional schools (law, medicine and engineering), and which in a static
society enjoyed a monopoly in the formation both of the élite and also of the conception
of culture, showed a "scholastic," that is to say academic and lifeless, form of thinking
which was opposed in its indifference or hostility to profound transformations in the
system of culture and higher education in the country.

If these élites, recruited in social classes and situations which constantly varied,
did not constitute and could not constitute a closed and perfectly organized class of
intellectuals, it is nonetheless true that with their cultural formation directed towards
"the interest of the profession," they had acquired and preserved those modes and
forms of thought and experience linked to a traditionally professional training which
unfitted them to control from above and in all their aspects the problems of education
and culture. They therefore never had a keen awareness, much less a profound one,
of the necessity of creating universities in Brazil, founding them upon ancient forms
or modelling them according to new forms. When we say "university" we do not mean
anything but a certain way of organizing human knowledge, in institutions, to raise
it to the highest level, to coordinate investigation, to promote the progress of science,
to spread culture and to utilize all this for the benefit of the community. Add that, if
the organization of primary and normal school teaching, which was still recent,—since
rigorously speaking it was no more than forty years old—, and therefore was more
flexible and plastic, submitted with less opposition to the attacks of the reformers,
higher education of a professional type, which was more than a century old, and secondary and humanistic education with traditions three centuries old, were opposed in
their intellectual tradition, offering a stronger resistance to innovation. But this same
group which fought ardently for the educational reconstruction of the country insisted upon the necessity of a radical reform of teaching and upon the introduction
into the system of schools of free research and of higher studies. We all felt that if we
had begun to introduce scientific method, we were still far from having really introduced it into education in the degree which would match the role which it had in the

---

and it enjoys world-wide fame. Beside a monthly journal, *O Biológico*, written by experts and aiming
at bringing together the laboratory and the breeders, the Biological Institute maintains *Os Arquivos*,
a journal of great importance, in which the original work of scientific research carried on in the
various sections of this institution are published.

actual formation of our lives. Hence the move which was made by the government of Armando Sales de Oliveira in founding, by the decree of January 25, 1934, the University of São Paulo, made up of the existing higher professional schools of a Faculty of Economic Science, of a Faculty of Education, and a Faculty of Philosophy, Sciences and Letters, according to a plan worked out by a commission of which the author of this work was the reporter and of which, among others, Júlio Mesquita Filho formed a part, having been the most ardent proponent of the idea of the creation of a university in São Paulo. The Provisional Government under the proposal of Francisco Campos had already instituted the university regime and had given out in 1931 the first decree regulating Brazilian universities. This was doubtless a great step forward in the educational policy of the nation.

The University of São Paulo was, however, the first institution in which the restless current of men's thoughts was poured out, that restless spirit which men feel in the face of nature, of life and of its problems, and which was born like the Platonic Academy in Greece, and the University in the Middle Ages, from the conviction that men with cultural responsibilities must be awakened in their minds to speculation, research and the experimental method, or in a few words, "to live on truth and the search for it." [26] Eminent professors and some who were among the most notable in

[26] The first university to be created in Brazil was the University of Rio de Janeiro, which came into existence as a result of decree no. 14,343, of September 7, 1920, a decree of President Epitácio Pessoa, submitted by Minister Alfredo Pinto. But this University, the Statutes of which were approved by the decree no. 14,572, of December 23, 1920, was no more than a grouping of three institutions for training professional men,—the Law School, the Medical School, and the Polytechnic School of Rio de Janeiro, and it did not amount to any essential change in the structure and methods of higher education in the country. In Belo Horizonte, seven years later, there was founded through the efforts of Francisco Mendes Pimentel, the University of Minas Gerais, in which there were brought together Schools of Law, Medicine and Engineering, already in existence in the capital of that State. By decree of September 7, 1927, which set up that University, and which, signed by President Antônio Carlos, was submitted by Francisco Campos, no substantial change was made in the system of higher education, which continued, under the new university regime, in the traditional structure and methods. The most important measure which this decree introduced, when it created the University of Minas Gerais, was autonomy in teaching and administration, based upon an endowment made up of large real estate holdings and a fund of $1,500,000 in State bonds. We can, then, assert that if true university organization was begun by decree no. 19,851, of April 11, 1931, issued by the chief of the Provisional Government, Dr. Getúlio Vargas, and submitted by Francisco Campos, Minister of Education, the first university that Brazil had, created in the new spirit and organization, and under the system established by that decree, was the University of São Paulo. In comparison with earlier establishments, markedly traditional in character, even though with the new label, what shows the originality of this university system, created on January 25, 1934, in accordance with the federal decree, which only then really began to operate, was not only the addition to the organism of the university of a Faculty of Philosophy, Sciences and Letters, which became the heart of the system, but also the ruling interest in scientific research and disinterested study, which, for that matter, are quite within the spirit of the federal law which regulated Brazilian universities. The Provisional Government of the Republic started the university system in 1931, but it was São Paulo which in 1934 took the lead in putting it in execution in complete form. Before there was created, in 1937, the National Faculty of Philosophy, Anísio Teixeira founded the University of the Federal District, with a new structure, and just a year later than the founding of the University of São Paulo. We must recognize, however, that the initiative in this movement of reform and broadening of higher education, although with a closed system, belongs to the Benedictine Order, under whose auspices there was created in São Paulo, in 1908, through the efforts of D. Miguel Kruse, the

their fields of specialization were hired in France, Italy and Germany to give courses in the Faculty of Philosophy, Sciences and Letters, the direction of which the government of São Paulo entrusted to Teodoro Ramos, a professor of the Polytechnic School and one of the greatest Brazilian mathematicians. In 1935 Anísio Teixeira created the University of the Federal District, made up of the five schools,—the Faculty of Philosophy and Letters, that of Sciences, that of Political Economy and Law, the School of Education, and the Institute of Arts, having sent Afrânio Peixoto, who was named director, to Europe to hire a new mission of foreign professors. These two Universities,—that of São Paulo, whose Faculty of Education died in 1938 and in which the Faculty of Philosophy was on the point of perishing for lack of resources (1938–1940), and the University of the Federal District absorbed in 1938 into the University of Brazil—, had their evolution beset by difficulties, in part growing from the utilitarian and professional mentality which still dominated the system of higher education, and in part resulting from the very "historic climate" in which they were born. The advent of the universities in Brazil coincided in fact with the greatest crisis of the mind which is recorded by the history of human thought, with the crisis of western universities and of the very idea "of the university," and with the formation of totalitarian States and the development of aggressive forms of nationalism. "The pitching of the boat," in the beautiful image of Paul Valéry,[27] "was so extreme that the lamps, even the best hung, were finally knocked down." The profound restlessness of the mind, the origins of which went back to the break-down of the unity of thought and to the intellectual monopoly of the Church, attained their maximum with the scientific discoveries, the technical and economic transformations and the conflict of extremist ideologies. To the intellectual movement characterized by humanistic culture and by the humanistic attitude toward life, which was incorporated into the first occidental university in the twelfth century, and under the renewed impulse of which (the neo-humanism of 1800) the modern German university arose (nineteenth century), there now followed the reaction of specialized studies marked by a high degree of tenacity, the glorification of specialists and the effort to raise to the first plane technical knowledge and methods instead of culture and disinterested research. And, finally, the political struggles that went on in the western world about the universities fought over by different antagonistic groups who were trying to transform them into front line trenches or instruments of political power (*instrumentum regni*) tended to suppress the pure, high, free life of the spirit and the priority given to free research, and to include under the rubric of "dangerous thought," philosophical investigations and economic, political and social investigations and at times even biological ones, limiting more and more the field of original scientific investigation.

The social atmosphere in which the work of the Constituent Assembly was en-

---

Faculty of Philosophy of São Bento, connected in 1911 with the Catholic University of Louvain (Belgium) and recognized by the federal government in 1936, after it had been broadened and adapted in conformity with the federal decree regulating the organization of Faculties of this kind. (V. Barbosa Viana, *Organização universitária no Brasil*, I and II, in the "Jornal do Comércio," Rio de Janeiro, March 24 and 31, 1940).

[27] "L'oscillation du navire a été si forte que les lampes les mieux suspendues se sont a la fin renversées." (Paul Valéry—*La crise de l'esprit*).

compassed was not, and could not be, very different. There was going on a process of intellectual boiling over, made of all the philosophical, scientific, political and pedagogic ferments which were capable of influencing the Assembly. Between doubts and hopes, the Constituent Assembly met in 1933 to face its task of working out and promulgating the new constitution and reestablishing the constitutional order which the Revolution of 1930 had suppressed and for the restoration of which a revolution broke out in 1932 in São Paulo. A New Constitution!—was in fact the battle cry which the State of São Paulo raised against the Provisional Government. The heterogeneous composition of the Chamber, in which elements coming from the regime before 1930 won positions; the confusion of the debates, which were neither vigorous nor elevated, the attitude of the Assembly, which was unable to find a firm basis for its activity in the tumult of the divergencies and passions, helped, however, to develop in many a scepticism provoked by the multiplicity and opposition of the systems and to stimulate to a larger extent, as an heroic solution, the movements of that mysticism which characterizes vigorous and totalitarian epochs. The revolutionary process in this period, 1933 to 1934, continued its normal course, which went on below the surface at a less rapid pace but certainly in more powerful form, while on the surface problems of national organization were being discussed and also the solutions which should find their place in the future constitution . . . Intellectual and literary production at this period not only constituted one of the most lively symptoms of the dominant, critical and destructive spirit, but also contributed to develop that spirit, sharpening its sensibility and emphasizing its tendencies. What predominated in this production was in reality social criticism and novels of a dark and sordid kind in which the social landscape of the Northeast was studied, the life of the small bourgeoisie, the factory environment and aspects of life related to the cultivation of sugar cane, and with all of this revolutionary sensibility was heightened and men's hearts were prepared for revolution. The claims for autonomy on the part of the larger States, the conflicts between centralizing and decentralizing tendencies, and the collisions of extremist ideologies of left and right, were later on to have the task of causing the revolution to pass from this idyllic phase to its violent phase, in two successive movements separated by short intervals (1935–1938) and looking in different directions.

In the midst of this mental and political anarchy, the Constituent Assembly found, however, sure points of support in the matter of educational policy in the forces which had been working for the educational reconstruction of Brazil and had arrived at positive results in numerous studies which might serve as norms and inspiration for the future constitution that was being worked upon. The ground had been long prepared for this end in the campaign of pedagogical and cultural reform, by an almost uninterrupted series of debates, measures, conferences and projects in which the fundamental questions examined from every point of view had been put upon a way to solution and some of which constituted proposals especially formulated for the chapter with regard to the problem, in the Constitution of the country. In 1932, in the Fifth National Conference of Education which met in Niteroi, there were approved after long examination, the draft of the chapter "On national education" for the Brazilian Constitution, and the sketch of the national plan of education, and in February of 1933, in the petition presented to the Constituent Commission, the Catholics summed up in four articles and their respective paragraphs, their principal claims,[28] already ardently defended in the Congress that had been called with the intent of contributing to direct the conscience of the Catholic world in the field of education, and which actually met on October 17, 1931 in the Curia Metropolitana under the inspiration of the Centro Dom Vital of São Paulo. In the *symposium* of December 13 to 23, 1933, organized by the Department of Rio de Janeiro of the Brazilian Educational Association, the council also discussed the matter in various meetings, concluding with the final drawing up of the proposal which was based largely upon the drafts worked out in the Fifth Conference at Niteroi, and in which the unanimous desires of that society of educators were summarized. It was under these influences that Chapter II, "Of education and culture," of the Constitution of July 16th, 1934 was worked out. In this Constitution, side by side with "provisions not proper to a constitutional law, contradictory among themselves and not adapted to the educational system," there are to be found the fundamental points of the Catholic claims, such as religious teaching in the schools and many of the minimum desires for which the pioneers of the new education had been fighting in Brazil. The two most vigorous currents of educational thought, and above all that of the reformers, whose campaign encountered all the difficulties of new and vigorous types of work and met all types of misunderstanding, thus crossed, not only in the propositions presented in the Constituent Assembly, but also in the Magna Carta which resulted from their debates and in which there achieved definite form as great conquests of the movement, some of the capital theses proposed with the aim of instituting a national policy of education on modern principles and bases.

The Charter of 1934 in fact instituted measures which were to assure a national policy in the matter of education, giving to the Union the exclusive competency to lay down the directive lines of national education (Chap. I, art. 5, XIV) and of fixing the national plan of education (art. 151). It was to be the duty of the States, according to art. 151, to organize and maintain their educational systems, respecting the general lines laid down by the Union. Establishing that the central government should have the duty of "fixing upon a national plan of education, including education of all grades and branches, both common and specialized, and coordinating and supervising its execution in the whole territory of the country" (art. 159); creating the National Council and the State Councils of Education (art. 152); and calling for the appropriation of never less than 10 per cent of their revenue from taxes on the part of the townships and never less than 20 per cent on the part of the States "for the maintenance and development of educational systems," (art. 156), the Constitution of July 16, 1934 caused the country to enter upon a national policy of education in conformity with the postulates and aspirations that had been victorious in the Conference at Niteroi in 1932 and in the manifesto of the pioneers for educational reconstruction in Brazil. The state educational systems, according to this new educational policy which the Constitution adopted, would not be anything more than variations from the common background of the species; under all the dissimilarities of educational structure in these

---

[28] Cf. *Os problemas da educação na Constituição*. Memorial presented by the Catholics to the Constituent Commission. In "Jornal do Brasil," Rio de Janeiro, February 3, 1938; *O problema educacional e a nova Constituição*. Organized by the Brazilian Education Association. Editora Nacional, São Paulo, 1934.

systems, varying according to regional conditions, it would be possible to find not only a "certain fundamental tonality," but the unity of policy expressed in the general lines laid down by the Union. The tendencies for a rational organization themselves, but upon statistical inquiries and data, and those for selection by means of objective tests (art. 150 letter e),—one of the clearest desires manifested by the campaign for educational reform—, took definite form in the provisions of the Constitution in 1934 which, in nearly all of its articles, remained within the sphere of influence of the initiators of the reform movements in Brazilian education.

But, beside the beginning on a national policy capable of establishing a unity of aims and of general lines in the variety of school systems, and beside the principles to which it gave definite form, of "rationalization," of reorganization of educational systems on a scientific basis of studies, inquiries and objective data, the Constitution also established democratic ends in the school policy of the country, recognizing in education "a right of all" (art. 149), instituting liberty of teaching in all grades and branches (art. 150, only section, line 3), freedom of teaching, free education and compulsory attendance which were to be extended progressively from primary education as a whole to the highest forms of education, in order to render it more accessible (art. 150, only section a and b), and creating special educational funds, part of which (art. 157) would be allotted to needy pupils by means of various forms of social assistance and scholarships. These democratic tendencies, which were to be still more marked in the Constitution of 1937, did not only correspond to the clearly formulated aspirations of the movement for educational reform, but also to a real process of democratization, which reached above all secondary education, rendering the reorganization of its structure on a humanistic base extremely difficult. In fact, instead of a class education for a small faction of the adolescent population, generally recruited in the bourgeoisie, secondary education became through its extraordinary extension, if not "education for the people," at least an education of a more democratic character, for between 1930 and 1936 the number of pupils increased from 40,000 to about 160,000, or quadrupled, while the population rose from 34,000,000 to 38,000,000 in the same period. If the girls who managed to complete the course for the bachelor of letters down to 1930 were still few in number, their numbers came to be equal to that of the boys in many colleges and courses which were open throughout the country, and the number of which only in São Paulo alone, without counting private schools, rose from 5 in 1930 to 58 in 1940, among high schools maintained by the State and by Townships, and high school courses connected with normal schools, either State or Municipal. But, as this process of democratization, legitimate enough in itself, which initiates the masses into culture, presents a negative aspect, inasmuch as the quality of teaching is lowered, we remain face to face with a double movement in two directions: on the one hand, this phenomenon of democratization by which the masses not only acquire new intellectual necessities but also begin to exercise their domination upon culture and to adapt the latter to their own level; and on the other a movement of reaction in the direction of humanistic culture, which never was democratic and in favor of a regular and systematic separation on the university level of candidates for this type and grade of teaching, of whom the first group of professors ever to receive their diplomas in Brazil received their licenses for secondary teaching in 1937 at the University of São Paulo.

If, with the coup d'état which on November 10, 1937 established in Brazil a single authoritarian regime, the campaign which had been developing for educational reform entered upon decline, it is certain that some of its principles received definite form in the new Constitution promulgated by the President of the Republic and signed by the whole Cabinet. The state of siege or of war, as it was called, in which the country lived from 1935 to 1937 and the coup which put an end to the constitutional regime of public liberty, prevented effectively in the field of educational and cultural policy a balance sheet which would show the real weight of the contenders, and the policy adopted by the government of the Union deemed it possible to make an accounting in this and other fields by knowing and weighing the opposing forces. The new Constitution granted in 1937 did in effect reaffirm, carrying them much farther than the Constitution of 1934, the finalities and the democratic objects and bases of national education, not only establishing by article 128 that "art and science and their teaching are freely open to individual initiative and to associations or societies both public and private," but also maintaining the gratuitous and compulsory character of primary schooling, instituting as compulsory the teaching of manual work in all primary, normal and secondary schools, and above all giving a preponderance in the program of the educational policy to pre-vocational and vocational teaching, which is destined "for the less privileged classes and is the first duty of the State in the field of education" (art. 129). From this point of view the Constitution of 1937, breaking with the intellectualistic and academic traditions of the country and raising technical and vocational education to the category of the first duty of the State, may be considered the most revolutionary and democratic of the laws which have been promulgated in the field of education. Revolutionary not only in the objects which it had in view, of educating youth by means of work, but also by the means which it adopted to attain these ends, and which constituted a radical change in the structure of vocational education, by the close linking of theory and practice, assured by the immediate application of lessons to the laboratory, by the organization of work in the field and in shops, and by the compulsory collaboration of industries and the State in the training of well qualified workmen. The system of apprenticeship with a master,—a system which came down from the Middle Ages and was handed over to the traditional type of vocational school organized for the necessities of manufacture—, was, as it still is, the system of our few vocational schools that were extremely expensive and which here, as everywhere, offered conditions different from those of actual production and surroundings that are entirely different from those of the factories into which the pupils are meant to go.

The Constitution of 1937, without rejecting institutes for vocational education, but on the contrary establishing that it was the duty of the State to found them and to give a subsidy to those founded by the States, Townships and private associations, began the regime of cooperation between industries and the State with the statute (art. 129) that "it is the duty of industries and of syndicates to create in the sphere of their specialties, apprenticeship schools for the sons of their workmen or their associates." [29] The Constitution of 1937 was not less exact when, following in this respect

[29] By decree-law no. 1,238, of May 2, 1939, signed by President Getúlio Vargas and submitted by the ministers of Labor and Education, respectively Valdemar Falcão and Gustavo Capanema, it was further laid down that factories employing more than 500 employees "shall have courses of vocational training for adults and minors, in accordance with the regulation the working out

the tendencies already affirmed in the Charter of 1934, it determined that it was the exclusive right of the Union to "fix the bases and determine the framework of national education laying down the general lines which the physical, intellectual and moral training of youth must obey" (art. 15, no. IX). This provision with which the principles established in the Charter of 1934 (art. 5, XIV and art. 150) were reaffirmed and broadened, marks the definitive victory of an educational policy of a national character, which character is shown in its principles and in its fundamental objectives, which are established for all grades and types of education in such a manner as to favor in Brazil an education that is sufficiently free to respect diversity, but sufficiently strong to move forward with the common task in spite of these diversities. From this point of view, we find that the two Constitutions, that of 1934 and that of 1937, looked in a single direction, both deciding to break unreservedly with the traditional abstentionism of the Union in education, assigning to it the exclusive right to fix the bases and determine the framework, and trace the general lines of national education. After a long period of more than forty years in which the States, big and little, motivated by an excessive federalism, claimed a right to "live their own life," and in which local groups, usages, resistance and traits of character of each region were affirmed to the point of combatting the federal power, creating an "imperialism of the bell tower," we entered frankly upon a new experiment with the establishment of a regime of unity and centralization, which involved the sanction of a strong power, the abolition of barriers within the country, the interpenetration of customs, legislation, public business, and particularly of systems of culture and education. This policy, which was decidedly favored in a period in which science, with the inventions of the radio and airplanes, was knocking down the barriers which were opposed to communication and to transportation, doubtless met with local and individual resistance, resistance which would end by being conquered, not so much by force as by gentleness and by time and by cooperation between the administration of the States and that of the Union.

The reorganization of systems of education, both state and municipal, under the new authoritarian regime installed by the coup d'état in 1937, might go on doubtless either by "the imposition" of a school policy adopted by the Union, or more slowly "by a plan for the coordination of objectives, the standardization of processes, and cooperation in technical and financial resources," to which Lourenço Filho refers in

---

of which shall be left in the hands of the Ministries of Labor, Industry and Commerce and of Education and Health" (art. 4). Later, on May 17, 1939, an inter-ministerial committee was set up to regulate the operation of these vocational courses for industrial workers to which decree no. 1,238 refers. When this committee, composed of six members, of whom three were named by the Minister of Education and Health and three by the Minister of Labor, met, it began its activities, under the chairmanship of Dr. Saul de Gusmão, juvenile court judge of the Federal District, who appointed Dr. Joaquim Faria de Góis Filho to be the reporter of its deliberations. The draft of the regulation of decree-law no. 1,238, the working out of which had been entrusted to the committee, did not succeed in winning approval in the form of a decree-law. The study which precedes the draft, and which was presented by the inter-ministerial committee after its inquiries and investigations, constitutes a careful and objective analysis of the problem which it was called upon to examine in order to accomplish its mission. (See *Aprendizagem nos estabelecimentos industriais.* Inter-ministerial committee appointed to regulate the functioning of complementary courses in industry. Joaquim Faria Góis, reporter. Rio de Janeiro, 1939.)

his introduction to the study of the general situation of primary education. That it was not possible "to continue with the Union indifferent to the extension of the evil which afflicted us in that territory (that of primary education)," and that it was its duty to combat this evil by all possible means whether that of indirect intervention or, if it is convenient, by direct intervention, had already been recognized by Francisco Campos in the incisive oration which he pronounced on November 18, 1930, when he took over the Ministry of Education and Health,[30] and Minister Gustavo Capanema has on various occasions proclaimed the same doctrine in speeches and interviews. "A step that cannot be further postponed,"—observed that Minister in 1937—, "is the working out of a code of the general lines of national education . . . There will be established (in this single body of laws) the ideological guiding lines under the influence of which all education will be carried on, and also the general principles of organization and the functioning of the whole educational apparatus of the country."[31] The Minister of Education and Health at that time announced the intent of the federal government to submit the Code which was already being organized to the discussion of a National Conference, in which all federal units would be represented by their experts. The acts of the central government since 1934 have shown decidedly rather an adhesion to the idea of a plan of cooperation between administrations than the will to impose a certain educational policy, as can be inferred, according to the statement of Lourenço Filho,[32] from the text of the decree-law no. 24,787, of July 14, 1934, which authorized the calling and fixed the bases of the National Convention of Education; from the law no. 378 of January 13, 1937, which took measures with regard to the National Conferences of Education; from the decree-law no. 580 of January 31, 1938, which created the National Institute of Pedagogical Studies; from the measure of the decree-law no. 868 of November 18, 1938, which instituted the National Commission of Primary Education; and moreover,—we may add—, from the calling of the First National Conference of Education in conformity with the decree-law no. 6,788 of January 30, 1941, among the objects of which were listed the study of the bases of the organization of a program, a synthesis of the objectives of national education and of the means to attain them by common action on the part of the government and of private initiative.[33]

---

[30] Francisco Campos, *Educação e cultura*. On taking office as Minister of Education and Health. Speech given November 18, 1930, pp. 117-119. José Olímpio, Rio de Janeiro, 1940.

[31] Gustavo Capanema, *Panorama de educação nacional*. As realizações e os propósitos do govêrno federal. Speech given in commemoration of the Centenary of the Colégio Pedro II. In "Jornal do Comércio," Rio de Janeiro, December 13, 14, 1937.

[32] Lourenço Filho, *Introdução ao estudo sôbre a situação geral do ensino primário*, pp. 52-53. National Institute of Pedagogical Studies. "Boletim no. 13," Rio de Janeiro, 1941.

[33] The National Institute of Pedagogical Studies (I.N.E.P.), created by decree no. 580, of July 30, 1938, corresponds in certain respects to the old Pedagogium to which, in the early days of the Republic, decree no. 667, of August 16, 1890, assigned the function of "being the active center for the reforms and improvements that the education system of the country needs." The policy of decentralization which the Constitution of 1891 maintained, did not permit the institution of the Pedagogium to succeed, and in 1896 it passed with more limited prerogatives to the jurisdiction of the government of the Federal District, and it died in 1919, already stripped of its national objectives. The system of centralization, instituted on November 10, 1937, was one of the causes which contributed most to the flourishing of the new institution to which the task of research, carried on jointly with administration, by the National Directorate of Education, now passed. The

Cooperation between administrations, under the regime of political centralization, if it was not a "conquest of the revolution," marked a phase in the evolution of the idea of a national policy of education and culture and is certainly the natural sequence of that march toward unity which was the whole history of the Revolution of 1930 and which had its culminating point in the coup d'état and in the Constitution of 1937; to group, to bring together, to assimilate federated units in a spirit of national communion, such was the principal task of the government which was instituted with the new political system and began by fortifying the authority of the central power, enlarging its frontiers, abolishing local distinctions, and fusing the States and rural and urban communities into a nation. The unification of educational systems, not by identity of structure of education, but by a fundamental identity in aims, or in other words, public education organized in accordance with a general policy and an overall plan, is one of the means, certainly the most powerful and efficacious, which the new regime intended to utilize in order to accomplish its task of assimilation and reconstruction of the nation. Making the flag, the hymn, the national shield and coat of arms of compulsory use throughout the country at the same time that it suppressed the use of other flags, hymns, shields and arms (art. 2); assigning to the Union the exclusive right to establish the bases and lay down the general lines of an edu-

---

National Institute of Pedagogical Studies, which constitutes the "center for the study of all educational questions, related to the work of the Ministry of Education" (art. 1 of decree-law no. 580, of July 30, 1938). This Institute has as its object, in accordance with art. 2 of the above mentioned decree, "to build up factual material on the history and present study of pedagogical techniques and doctrines, as well as on different kinds of educational institutions; to maintain exchanges with foreign educational institutions; to promote investigations and research on all problems connected with the organization of education, as well as on methods and processes of education; to promote investigations in the field of psychology as applied to education, as well as to the problem of professional guidance and selection; to render technical assistance to state services, and municipal and private services as well, and to broadcast information on pedagogical theory and practice." Directly subordinated to the Ministry of Education and Health, the Institute has, in addition to a library and a museum of Pedagogy, two services and four technical sections, two of which, Documentation and Research and Investigation, make direct studies of education, and two others (that of Applied Psychology and that of Professional Selection and Guidance) are to cooperate with the D.A.S.P. (Administrative Department of Public Service, which since its inception has been presided over by Dr. Luiz Simões Lopes) for the analysis and solution of problems of the selection, adjustment and in-service training of state employees. The National Institute of Pedagogical Studies, which from its founding has been directed by Prof. Lourenço Filho, has already brought to completion studies of first-rate importance, with relation to material on pedagogical institutions and activities in the country, and consisting of manuals of national and state legislation on education and teaching, records of data which are constantly being collected and analyzed by the Statistical Service of the Ministry, and of the organization of a card catalogue of its material, already reaching a total of 13,623 cards, catalogued by chronological order and by subject. The bulletins which it has published, among which we find the series on "organization of primary and normal school education," in each State, constitute a proof of the efficiency of its services and the honesty and exactitude of its publications, which are of high value as information and as sources. In the field of pedagogical investigations, its activities, methodically carried out, show that the Institute, by its structure, the strength of the staff its superior leadership has brought together, will certainly be not only the central organ, but the most important institute of the country for the purpose of inquiries, studies and researches on educational problems in their various aspects. (V. *Instituto Nacional de Estudos Pedagógicos,* in the journal "Educação,"—organ of the Brazilian Association, no. 7, July, 1940, pp. 17-18, and 27).

cational policy (art. 15); putting under the protection of the Nation, the States and the Townships historic, artistic and national monuments, and placing attacks upon them in the same category as attacks on the national property (art. 134), the Constitution of 1937 vigorously aroused that national feeling which was its inspiration and established fundamental aspects of that sensibility through which we attain a sort of collective temperament and perhaps, further, a national mission, the content of which is not limited to the political plane. The government of the Union, resuming the policy timidly tried out in 1918, has developed since 1937 a campaign for the nationalization of the schools of the south of the country and especially in Santa Catarina and Rio Grande do Sul and, in the face of strong organizations which were receiving subvention and support from abroad, it undertook by a systematic series of measures the adjustment of immigrants and their descendants to the Brazilian environment. This task of nationalization on an even larger scale was undertaken by the federal government with vigor and was conducted methodically, both by supporting the efforts of the States, like Rio Grande do Sul, Santa Catarina, Paraná, São Paulo and Espírito Santo, where, from 1937 to 1941, 774 private schools were closed because they were considered "denationalizing" in tendency and replaced by 885 public schools opened in the same localities, or by giving in 1940 special aid to those States for the construction of school buildings in centers of foreign population, or by giving a new organization to the colonial centers, the foundation of which met the needs of the national interest.[34]

But, if in the field of education "the capital question whose importance demands efforts corresponding to the scope and proportions of its size," continued to be, according to the opinion and the wish of Francisco Campos in 1930, that of primary education, the activities of the Union and of the States were not within this period limited to the solution of the fundamental problem of the education of the masses. Certainly a brief analysis of the general situation of primary teaching in the last ten years demonstrates, as Lourenço Filho has pointed out,[35] a notable development of primary schools, which from 27,000 in 1932 increased to more than 40,000 in 1939, while in eight years the number of teachers in service in the 40,000 schools of the country with their three and a half million pupils increased from 56,000 to about 78,000. Nor, if we keep a sense of proportion, was the quantitative expansion of the secondary schools any less, for in ten years they enjoyed an increase greater than that which had taken place during the whole century of independence, and they showed in their progress the tendency of the high schools to be transformed from a course preparing for entry into the professional schools, into a college for the people. This numerical growth, which is certainly surprising, brought to the fore in an aggravated form the problems of the structure of secondary education, the object of which, now being as broad as the activities of our complex modern life, as John Dewey observes, cannot be the same as it was in the time when the academies existed only for the sons of those who received a classical education. Although it cannot be compared with

[34] Pedro Calheiros Bonfim, *As escolas estrangeiras e a nacionalização do ensino. Alguns aspectos do problema.* In "Formação," Brazilian journal of education, ano IV, September, 1941, no. 38, pp. 48-51.

[35] *Situação geral do ensino primário*—Introduction by Prof. Lourenço Filho, pp. 9-53. Instituto Nacional de Estudos Pedagógicos. "Boletim no. 13," Rio de Janeiro, 1941.

the growth which primary and secondary education acquired during this period, higher education, both professional and disinterested, had at that time a quantitative development which cannot be without effect, more upon the extension than upon the refinement of the culture of the country, for the quality of that culture is doubly menaced in our educational system by the rapid numerical growth of secondary schools and the consequent lowering of the level in preparatory studies, and by the proliferation of higher schools in general and especially of faculties of philosophy, grafted on to old educational organizations of private initiative.

That crisis in the quality of culture which is observable everywhere, is not a product only of the progressive limitation of the field of "liberty of the mind," under the pressure of the phenomena of concentration of power, of the advent of dictatorships of the left and of the right, and of the tendencies of the totalitarian State or the State conceived as an end in itself and endowed with the right to extend its influence even into the most intimate corners of the life of individuals and human societies. A university implies the idea of universality and calls for free examination, as it is a type of work whose creative impulse rests upon and is nourished by freedom, taken in its full sense as freedom of criticism and investigation. From the sociological point of view, this crisis is to be explained also according to Nikoloi Berdyaev, by the fact that an aristocratic principle,—a principle of quality, is inherent in all higher culture, and that this principle is gravely menaced by the process of democratization and of leveling through the rule of the masses. Now this extraordinary quantitative growth of secondary schools and the "mushrooming" of faculties of philosophy founded by private citizens in a country in which four or five schools of a high level could barely be maintained, although on the one hand these factors aid in bringing, if not the mass, at least a greater number of citizens into contact with culture, tend at the same time to lower culture, dragging it into the whirlpool of social mediocrity and adjusting it to the level of the masses, to their necessities and to their tastes. Perhaps, due to these new cultural conditions and to the difficulty of restraining the rush of this process of democratization, the official encouragement given to universities, which was slow and without vigor, did not live up to the hopes which the institution of the university regime in Brazil in 1931 had aroused. In fact, of the four universities that exist in the country,—that of São Paulo, created in 1934, that of Brazil, into which the University of Rio de Janeiro was transformed in 1937, that of Pôrto Alegre and that of Minas Gerais,—only the first two can show as part of their university system, a Faculty of Philosophy, Sciences and Letters, created with the double end of developing philosophical and scientific culture and training teachers for secondary schools.[36] The National Faculty of Philosophy, created by the decree no. 452 of July 5, 1937, which organized the University of Brazil, formerly that of Rio de Janeiro, opened its doors only in 1939 when, by the decree-law no. 1,063 of January 20th of that year, there were transferred to the University, various institutes and courses which composed the University of the Federal District, founded in 1935 and abolished by this decree. The creation of the National Faculty of Philosophy, for which foreign professors were contracted, the absorption of the University of the Federal District by that of Brazil, and

[36] Fernando de Azevedo, *O magistério secundário.* Speech given at the ceremony of graduation of the first class of secondary school teachers, on April 21, 1937, in the auditorium of the Medical School. "Boletim no. 13," Secretariat of Education and Public Health, São Paulo, 1937.

the foundation in 1940 of the Catholic University in Rio de Janeiro, were, together with the beginning of the University of São Paulo in 1934 and that of the Federal District in 1935, the most important facts with which in the evolution of the university idea, the extremely slow transformation of higher education directed toward higher studies without a utilitarian concern and with an interest in original scientific research was marked.

The tendency to the expansion of middle education, which has extended in proportion as the network of primary schools has extended, losing gradually its character as class education (high schools of a classic type), and the slowness of progress of university education in spite of the effort expanded to raise the level of culture, show the extreme difficulty of the task to which we have set ourselves in recent years: the adjustment of two epochs and of two opposed types of history. Certainly, the strength which this cultural expansion acquired, contributing to bring the masses closer to the sources of culture and to raise their level of knowledge, would not fail to make a contribution to reduce, if not with time to heal, the rupture between the creative factors and the people, and to prepare that culture needed by society which admits and presupposes a qualitative principle and, while it is an aristocratic type of work, is also the work of a whole people,—"a double character which is profoundly inherent in epochs of organic growth." But this extension of education and culture which is, as we have seen, a process of democratization, cannot be realized except at the price of the cultural level by a reduction of quality or a lowering of the level in which the old privilege of the élite, crystallized for their own use, will end by yielding and extending to the wider public of a democratic society. The development of culture in the vertical sense collides with this extraordinary tendency to cultural expansion, which was aided by the progress of old resources and techniques of publicity (the book, the magazine and the newspaper) in whose service, discoveries and inventions put new and powerful instruments for the spread and assimilation of ideas, sentiments and aspirations, or in a few words, of a common culture accessible to all. The publishing movement increased, in fact, considerably; [37] publishing houses multiplied and

[37] We have not yet collected in Brazil statistical data on the production of books by subject, in the different publishing houses, and on their circulation and distribution through the different regions of the country. Such statistics would be extremely useful not only for a correct estimate of various aspects of culture, such as for studies on the types of books which achieve the widest circulation, and therefore, the greatest popularity, the diversity of "publics" that exist and the consuming capacity and geographic distribution of consumption of our production of books, whether didactic, literary or scientific. There is not, however, any doubt that the publishing business in the country has increased notably in the last twenty, and especially the last ten years. It is sufficient to recall that, beside the old publishing houses, such as Francisco Alves, now Paulo Azevedo and Co., Garnier, now Briguiet-Garnier, seven more really important enterprises have been founded, the Company of Melhoramentos (Improvements), which devotes itself especially to textbooks, the Editora Nacional and the Acadêmica (Saraiva), in São Paulo; Freitas Bastos, which specializes in juridical books, Guanabara, best known for its medical books, and José Olímpio, in Rio de Janeiro, and Globo in Pôrto Alegre, not counting a large number of publishers scattered over the country. Production reached such proportions that the Editora Nacional alone attained 2,480,000 copies in 1936, and its annual production stayed between 2,300,000 and 2,500,000 during the five following years down to 1941, in spite of the serious consequences of World War II on the book industry and business. In that period, the Editora Nacional, among whose activities we must mention the *Brasiliana*,—a collection of Brazilian studies, with more than two hundred volumes, in a single decade (1931–1941), reached the point of publishing an edition of twenty thousand, and,

their number reached 177 in 1937; in that same year printing establishments rose to 2,044; printing increased to such a point in the capital of the country that in 1939 the number of works published rose to 797 and a single publishing house, after 1936, succeeded in reaching an annual production of about two and a half million copies; and the bookstore business attained in ten years a surprising growth, both in the sale of books published by Brazilian houses and in the placing of imported works, not only from Europe but from the United States.

The spread of printing and the flowering of magazines of various types aided not less than the business in the 1,179 bookshops listed in 1937 to bring about this movement of cultural expansion from one region to another and through all of the strata of society. If in 1912, according to statistics, there were 1,377 periodicals circulating in the country, of which 1,275 were founded since the proclamation of the Republic, this number had doubled in 1937, in which the capital alone had to show not less than 161 newspapers, of which 21 were dailies, and 14 with a circulation above 50,000 copies. The Federal District, the State of São Paulo with the *Diário* and *O Estado de São Paulo,* which came to have a circulation of 80,000, Pernambuco and Rio Grande do Sul continued to maintain their position in the vanguard of Brazilian journalism with newspapers of the first class whose effect and influence led beyond their boundaries at times.[38] The Brazilian Press Association, which is the principal organ of those who give their lives to press activities, today has its quarters, thanks to the progress of Brazilian journalism, in a magnificent building—the "House of the Journalists" especially constructed and installed in Rio de Janeiro, for all the technical and social functions of a central apparatus of this kind, destined to coordinate efforts and to examine problems which interest workers in the newspapers affiliated with this Association, which is one of national character and with national objects. If we add to these elements that help to diffuse culture, the action undertaken by literary societies, by numerous associations for cultural interchange and by expositions and congresses of all types, scientific, technical and educational,[39] which have seconded the efforts

---

in the case of another book that went through several editions, a circulation of more than forty-five thousand copies. When we compare these figures, which are still law, with those of editions before 1920, which oscillated between one and two thousand copies, it becomes impossible to deny the significance of the publishing business of the last ten years, which is unprecedented in the history of the book business in Brazil.

[38] It is hardly possible in a work of the present limits to cite all the outstanding figures of journalism during the republican period. Moreover, the number of men from other professions and from letters who were "episodically" journalists is not small; they felt the pressure of public life, which led them to enter or abandon journalism. But, among the great "professional" journalists, we cannot omit mention of the illustrious names of Quintino Bocaiuva (Rio, 1836–1912), who took an important part in the abolitionist and republican campaigns; Alcindo Guanabara (State of Rio, 1865–1918); José Carlos Rodrigues (State of Rio, 1844–1923), editor of the "Jornal de Comércio": Edouardo Salamonde and João Lage of "O Pais"; Edmundo Bittencourt, founder and director of the "Correio da Manha"; Júlio Mesquito, of "O Estado de São Paulo"; and more recently, José Eduardo Macedo Soares, founder and editor of the paper, "O Imparcial"; Costa Rêgo, of the "Correio da Manhã," and Assis Chateaubriand, one of the most important journalists of Brazilian history, founder of the chain Diários Associados,—the largest and most powerful Brazilian chain of newspapers, magazines, and radio stations, spread all over the country.

[39] Lourenço Filho, *Congressos e conferências de educação* (Rápida resenha histórica). In the journal "Formação," no. 41, Ano IV. December, 1941, pp. 5-17.

to simplify, coordinate and organize more logically and more economically our whole system of education and of culture, we will be able the better to appreciate what this constant effort at interpenetration of ideas and assimilation represents, that it is upon these efforts that the élites which society desires must rest as upon a wider base, and it is with their aid that they must prepare themselves for their great task. On the basis of this culture, which is becoming generalized and the level of which for that very reason is automatically being lowered, but from which there has already resulted a growth in strength and a more profound search for talent, the élites which have arisen, already more numerous, will receive support and help through the greater communion of the masses with culture, which will permit them to achieve a higher type of thought reflecting the whole life of the nation.

Certainly, one of the indications which best expressed this movement of cultural expansion with which our customs were broadened and our ways of thinking and of feeling were extended and which spread everywhere the love of reading, was the movement which the public libraries in the country took on. An analysis, even a brief one, of the movement of libraries, to which the new pedagogical theories and the more lively awareness of the role of libraries as an auxiliary element in education contributed with such efficacy, not only reveals to us the growing number of these institutions, but an effort, which was notable in some centers like São Paulo, to reorganize them and make them more useful and accessible to the public and to give a uniform guidance to their technical services of cataloguing and classification. From 456 that existed in Brazil in 1912,—of which the institutions founded before 1821 like that of Convento do Carme in Rio (1545), that of the Monasteries of São Bento of Rio, Bahia and Pernambuco, the origins of which go back to the sixteenth century, that of the Seminary of Mariana in Minas Gerais which dates from 1748 and the National Library created in 1810,—the number of libraries went up to 1,527 in 1929, with about 9,100,000 volumes, and in 1935 to 2,312, excluding the collections of the primary schools. In 1938, public and semi-public libraries existing in the capitals and maintained by government and private institutions rose to 192, recorded in statistics which did not include in their number either the libraries owned and used by individuals nor school libraries or those belonging to institutions of primary, secondary or higher education, whether official or private. Of these libraries, through which there passed 949,460, or almost a million consultants, 48 were located in Pôrto Alegre, which figured in first place; 47 in São Paulo; 17 in Recife; 14 in Florianópolis, where there was located the excellent Public Library of the State, almost a century old (since it was created in 1854) and with more than 30,000 volumes; 13 in Salvador, and the rest scattered through other capitals. The statistics of the works consulted show not only a notable growth of culture and a greater variety of intellectual tendencies and ambitions, but also the growing interest shown in North American works, especially in São Paulo and in Rio de Janeiro, thanks to the influence of North American ideas in the movement for educational reform and to the new life which was shown by Pan-American policy, especially after the War (1939), and to the coming of novels by Anglo-Saxon authors, accompanying great films, and to the creation in 1938 of institutions, like the Instituto Brasil-Estados Unidos founded in Rio de Janeiro and the São Paulo União Cultural Brasil-Estados Unidos, which was opened the same year in São Paulo, with the object of facilitating intellectual cooperation and promoting between the two countries a better mutual knowledge and understanding by means of lectures, expositions of American books and other cultural activities.

The place, however, in which the library movement had the largest development was in the city of São Paulo, the government of which created in 1935 in the Department of Culture, a Division of Libraries to which they subordinated the Public Municipal Library, the Children's Library and the School of Library Science. It reorganized the Public Municipal Library, which was founded in 1925 and whose collection of 67,277 was increased in 1938 by the addition of a collection of 40,000 volumes belonging to the old Public Library of the State. It installed the Children's Library and began the first library school in which candidates could prepare themselves for the various technical activities related to the profession and which, having begun its courses in 1937 with 215 students, was ready in 1939 to graduate 65 librarians. For the installation of the Public Municipal Library, to which that of the State was added by the decree no. 2,839, of January 5, 1937, the government of the city had constructed a magnificent edifice with a capacity for 500,000 volumes, and in accordance with all the hygienic and technical requirements of the best modern construction destined for use as libraries. The State law of 1937,—which is one of the major conquests of the movement which went on in São Paulo—, regulated the exercise of the profession of librarian, establishing among other requirements, taking a special course in the library school, and created the Library Council of the State, with the object of coordinating the work, of promoting the organization of the Union Catalogue of all state and municipal libraries, and even of private libraries existing in the State which were willing to collaborate in this common work of a complete local bibliography.[40] In its turn, the government of the Union, by law no. 378, which gave a new structure to the services of the Ministry of Education and Health, created in 1937, with the object of organizing the Brazilian Encyclopedia, the Institute of Cairú, which was afterwards transformed into the Instituto Nacional do Livro by decree-law no. 93, of December 21st of that year and which continued its task of stimulating the organization and of aiding the maintenance of public libraries throughout the territory of the nation. It has already aided the establishment of about one hundred of these institutions by means of the distribution of more than 20,000 volumes.

But, among the principal means for diffusing and conserving culture, those which in recent years have aided most in the transformation of the mentality and habits of life in Brazil have been, without doubt, the motion picture and the radio, which everywhere had a profound influence upon human relations. Of all the inventions we owe to the scientific spirit, the motion picture and the radio are not only the most beautiful, but the most laden with the poetic spirit and those which open new horizons to art and to thought. Powerful educational and cultural instruments, instruments of information, propaganda and teaching, factors in the education of the people of first rate importance, due to their extraordinary power of suggestion, they play a part so important that their influence may not only be compared but may be considered superior to that of the daily newspaper, especially in countries where the number of illiterates is still

[40] Dorothy M. Gropp, *Bibliotecas do Rio de Janeiro e de São Paulo e o movimento bibliotecário da capital paulista*. Lecture given in New Orleans, Louisiana, in 1939. Translated by Francisco de Azevedo. Off-print of the "Revista do Arquivo," no. LXVIII. Department of Culture, São Paulo, 1940.

great. A marvellous art which is a summary of all others, uniting sound and picture, beauty of line and of movement, and in addition color and relief, it may have in certain cases its educational power utilized in a direction which is not favorable to the mutual comprehension of peoples, but no other art tends to transmit, as the motion picture does, that feeling of universality and of the identity of the human species with which our conceptions of life are enlarged, tracing before our very eyes, brought from all over the world, reality present in the exciting succession of events, in the picturesque diversity of natural scenery and in the multiplicity of social types and landscapes, through the variety of whose forms we see the fundamental unity of the human spirit. This enlargement of mental horizons, above classes and frontiers, once it began to operate through the motion picture in which the American film had a position of preponderant importance, was to take place as historically it did, under the immediate influence of American thought and customs, both because of the dominant place of the United States in the motion picture industry, and on account of the technical and artistic superiority of its films, and the influence upon the masses of the people resulting from the "mass production" of American films. The spread of the radio and of the motion picture through almost all of the cities of the country could not fail to have considerable effect upon Brazilian culture and upon the customs of the nation, contributing notably not only to modify them but also to accelerate that process of assimilation in which for more than twenty years, these two means of expansion of thought and expansion of culture in all their forms have been active. Radio broadcasting which, in fact, was begun in Brazil in 1919 with the first station,—the Radio-Clube of Pernambuco, and acquired some new momentum in 1922, with the acqusition by the Federal government of two transmitters, given up later in 1924 to the Radio Clube and to the Radio Educadora of Brazil, was only developed in reality, and in a surprising manner, after the revolution of 1930, and, above all, after that of São Paulo in 1932, in which the radio played a prominent part in the propaganda of the revolution.

It was at this time that there were handed down the two most important decrees among those which regulated broadcasting services, one reforming the first law on the subject (1924), and the other concerned with the distribution of frequencies given to Brazil by the International Agreement of Radio Telegraphy. From then on, there arose big new transmitting stations which in December of 1939 had already increased to the number of 64 in Brazil, of which 39 were in São Paulo (10 in the capital and 29 in the interior); receiving sets grew in number, in 1939, 357,921 were registered in the country, 115,042 in São Paulo, or one-third of all of the sets in existence at the time. The National Service of Educational Radio was created, in which there reappeared the idea of applying radio to educational objects which had come up for the first time in Brazilian legislation with the reform of education in the Federal District in 1928.[41] New radio societies were founded; the "Hour of Brazil" was begun, and

[41] The first law promulgated in the country on radio and educational motion pictures was in effect in the decree no. 3,281, of January 23, 1928, which reformed education in the Federal District, and was regulated by decree no. 2,940, of November 22 of that same year. Title IV "on school motion pictures and radio," in the first decree, no. 3,281, has two articles and one paragraph: in art. 296 it is laid down that all schools "shall have rooms fit for the installation of projectors, for slides and film, for purely educational purposes, as well as for the installation of radio-telephonic apparatus and loud-speakers;" and, in art. 297, there is created a radio-school, with its broadcasting station, for daily broadcasting to schools and the public, of hymns and school songs, of an official

there was organized, in the Department of Press and Propaganda, the Division of Radio, under whose control and inspection all Brazilian radio stations were placed. The motion picture, which had been introduced into the country much before the radio, at the beginning of this century, took on an extraordinary development in the last ten years. In 1938, when we had 316 motion picture houses in the capitals alone, there were 195,647 shows for about 44,000,000 spectators. The development was so great that in 1932, by decree no. 21,240 of April 4th of that year, the federal government had to nationalize the censorship service of the films, creating a special tax and establishing other legislative measures tending to regularize the process of examining films and to promote the nationalization of their services. Although utilized officially in the Federal District, by means of the decree which reformed teaching in the capital of the country, —this was the first law which undertook to use motion pictures for scholastic purposes—, and in São Paulo, by means of the decree of April 21, 1933 which approved the Educational Code, educational motion pictures only became of real interest to the government of the Union in 1934, when it took measures concerning the use, distribution and greater development of school films (decree no. 24,651), and created by law no. 378 in 1937, the National Institute of Educational Films with the object of coordinating the application of educational films and providing for their spread by all means.[42]

---

hour, of the bulletin of acts and instructions of the Directorate, of all kinds of material related to teaching, lessons and artistic programs of educational character. In Title IV of decree no. 2,940, the use of motion pictures for educational ends is regulated (articles 633–635), the aims of the Radio-School are laid down and its organization given (articles 636–637); we refer to the school created by the decree which reformed education in the Federal District, which resulted from the efforts of the author of this book, and for which he is responsible.

[42] The utilization of the motion picture in teaching and scientific research began to be practiced in the National Museum, which, in 1910, began its film collection, enriched in 1912 by the first films of the Nambiquara Indians, which Roquete Pinto brought from Rondônia and the admirable films with which the Rondon Commission documented its geographic, botanical, zoological and ethnographic explorations. In other educational and cultural institutions later on, attempts were made to use the educational motion picture. It was only, however, in 1928, that there came the first law on the use of the cinema for school purposes: the author of this book, then director general of Public Instruction in the Federal District, laid down the principle and regulations for its utilization in all the schools of the capital of the country (Decree no. 3,281, of January 23, 1928, articles 296–297; and decree no. 2,940, of November 22, 1928, articles 633–635). In 1929, through the efforts of the General Directorate of Instruction, there was opened officially the first Exposition of Educational Cinematography, the organization of which was the work of Jônatas Serrano, one of the beginners of the movement. Under the leadership of Anísio Teixeira, there was created soon after, in 1932, (decree no. 3,763, of February 1, 1932) a Division of Education Cinema. In that same year, decree no, 21,240, of April 4, of the federal government, nationalized the censorship service for films. In the State of São Paulo there were set up Services of Radio and Educational Motion Pictures, by decree no. 5,884, of April 21, 1933, which instituted the *Código de Educação* (Educational Code) worked out by the efforts and under the guidance of Fernando de Azevedo. In decree no. 24,651, of July 10, 1934, which created the Department of Propaganda and Cultural Extension in the Ministry of Justice, measures were taken (art. 2, lines a, b, c), with reference to the use, circulation, and increased production of educational films. The creation, in 1937, of the National Institute of Educational Motion Pictures, by law no. 378, which gave a new organization to the Ministry of Education and Health, marks, in the evolution of this idea, one of the culminating phases. This Institute, the direction of which was entrusted to Roquete Pinto,—one of the pioneers of the movement for school films,—has as its aim to organize and edit

All these activities in the extension of culture, which were aided at unequal ratios and at different rates of development by the State and by private initiative, the central government and the various parts of the federation, if they did not all have their origin, at least all found support and favorable repercussion in the Ministry of Education and Health, which was, together with those of Labor and of Aviation, one of the three great ministries created by the government and implanted by the two revolutions. From 1930 to 1934, the new Ministry could not fulfill all of the role which had been reserved for it in the national policy of the revolutionary government, due to the fact that it still formed, in its primitive and rudimentary structure, more a juxtaposition of parts than a true connection in which each one of the services of education and culture, formed into a hierarchy, would have its place and its role in conformity with the importance and the variety of technical, administrative and cultural functions. The activities of teaching and of culture had acquired, moreover, such a development that they broke through the framework of the original organization requiring the reform of some services and the creation of others, so that the Ministry might extend its coordinating activity into all sectors of the national culture and education. This was exactly what was had in view by the law No. 378 of January 13, 1937, which, inspired by Minister Gustavo Capanema, gave a new organization, a more complete and broad one, to the Ministry of Education, opening out possibilities in the direction of a fruitful activity in the sense of studying and conducting research in the technical problems posed by the growing development of educational institutions, of coordinating the scattered and at times contradictory activities, and arousing cultural activity in all fields and making it both more exact and more rich. "In the documents which accompanied the government's project when sent to the legislature,"—writes Professor Lourenço Filho—"this new spirit is clearly defined. There are three fundamental points to be brought out: that of a tendency to rationalize administration; that of the greater national effect of the services of the Ministry; that of the broader understanding of the functions of education both in school and outside of school. The various organs and services were classified in distinct categories. The country was divided into regions for the administration of education. The supplementary activity of the Union in the field of teaching and education was defined, and an institute was created for the purpose of pedagogical research. Finally services were created to stimulate and develop educational institutions that were not simply schools . . . The new structure of the Ministry, in short, defined the educational policy to be developed on the wide plane of

---

Brazilian educational films: to exchange copies of films it has produced, or others; to produce and exchange records or sound films, together with classes, lectures and talks; to organize a library of educational films, to service educational institutions, and to publish a journal devoted to the cinema, to phonographs and radio, in the applications to research, to radio and to education. Although still recent,—for it is not more than five years old,—the National Institute of Educational Motion Pictures has already made about four hundred films; it has equipped itself to furnish information and explanations on school films, in all their applications; it has organized a library, specializing in works and magazines on cinematography and has brought together in its archives, and coordinated valuable contributions which were in a dispersed state. In the field of research, it has proceeded to the study of problems related to the series of school films of less than standard width, that is 16 mm., in natural colors, and research in experimental phonetics on the pronunciation of the national language in various regions of the country. (Cf. Jônatas Serrano and Francisco Venâncio Filho, *Cinema e educação*; Mendes de Almeida, *Cinema contra cinema*.)

350. The Polytechnic School of São Paulo, founded in 1893, three years before the Engineering School of Mackenzie College. Photo by Liberman.

351. The School of Manguinhos, created in 1901, which took the title in 1907 of Osvaldo Cruz Institute of Experimental Pathology, honoring its founder, who cleaned up Rio de Janeiro. Photo by Walter Sales, in *Travel in Brazil*, Vol. II, no. 2, p. 12.

352. The Institute of Manguinhos, which played an important part in the victory and spread of the scientific, experimental spirit. Reading room and library. Photo by the Photographic Section of the Osvaldo Cruz Institute.

353. The Institute of Manguinhos. Third floor gallery. Photo by the Photographic Section of the Osvaldo Cruz Institute.

354. Epitácio Pessoa, minister in the government of Campos Sales and author of the Educational Code of 1901, in force to 1910.

355. Rivadávia Correia, who was responsible for the "organic educational law" (decree of April 5, 1911). With its sectarian radicalism it reflected the positivist attitude then dominant in Rio Grande do Sul.

356. The Agronomical Institute of Campinas, which, created in 1887 by the Imperial Government, was transferred in 1892 to the state of São Paulo, and had Franz W. Dafert as its first director, 1887–1897. Old building (1920).

357. Luiz de Queiroz Higher School of Agriculture, at Piracicaba, created in 1901. Part of the grounds, with the principal building in the background.

358. Luiz de Queiroz Higher School of Agriculture. Laboratory, Department of Genetics, recently added to the equipment of the school.

359. Álvares Penteado School of Commerce, founded in 1902, one of the first commercial schools created in Brazil.

360. Nilo Peçanha, during whose government (1909–1910), schools for apprentices were created in the state capitals.

361. Paulo de Frontin Vocational School, in the Federal District, for domestic science and girls' vocational education, in its new quarters built during the administration of Antônio Prado Júnior (1926–1930).

362. Heitor Lira, a great idealist, who in 1924 founded the Brazilian Education Association. This has played a notable part in promoting and stimulating movements for the spread of culture and the improvement of schools in the country.

363. The United States School, in the Federal District, in traditional Brazilian style. One of the side views. Photo by Nicolas.

364. Uruguay School, in the Federal District, erected in various blocks between 1928 and 1930—one of the largest built during the administration of Antônio Prado Júnior. Side view from the patio of the school.

365. School for physically weak children, in the Quinta da Boa Vista (Federal District, 1926–1930). Gallery and fountain of one of the patios. Photo by Nicolas.

366. Father Correia de Almeida Consolidated School, at Belo Horizonte in Minas Gerais, where the new movement in education was especially strong under Francisco Campos and Mário Casassanta (1927–1930). Principal façade.

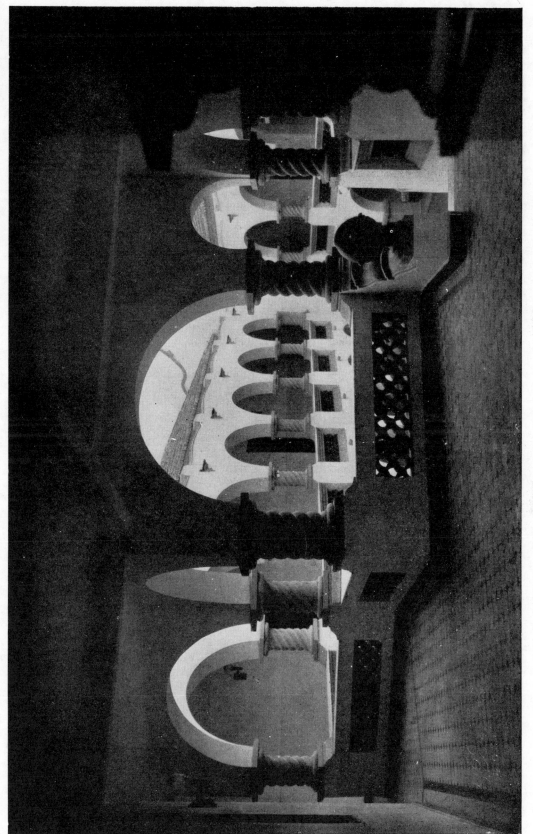

367. Pedro II Consolidated School, at Belo Horizonte, one of the most important school buildings erected during the administration of Francisco Campos, Secretary of State of Minas Gerais. Galleries and internal courtyard.

368. The Normal School of the Federal District. Building erected between 1928 and 1930, during the administration of Antônio Prado Júnior. Drawing by Cortez & Bruhns, architects.

369. The Normal School of the Federal District, which in 1933 was reorganized and named Institute of Education. A view of the courtyard. Drawing by Cortez & Bruhns, architects.

370. The new Normal School of the Federal District, reorganized by the reform movements of 1928 and 1933, and located in its new buildings constructed during the administration of Antônio Prado Júnior, 1926–1930. General view. Aerial photograph by S. H. Holland, Rio de Janeiro, 1930.

371. The new Normal School of the Federal District, known since its second reorganization in 1933 as Institute of Education, in its new buildings finished in 1930. Central court seen from a gallery of the ground floor. Photo by Nicolas, Rio, 1930.

372. Normal School of the Federal District, now Institute of Education. Gymnasium, magnificently equipped with apparatus, baths, dressing rooms, and galleries. Photo by Nicolas, Rio, 1930.

373. Francisco Luís da Silva Campos, one of the leaders of the 1930 revolution, and first Minister of Education and Health, author of the most important reform of secondary and higher education in the republican regime (1931).

374. The Biological Institute of São Paulo, created in 1928 as a result of the efforts of Artur Neiva, former assistant chief of the Osvaldo Cruz Institute, and reorganized by Professor Rocha Lima, its present director, who was also one of the colleagues of Osvaldo Cruz. General view.

375. The Biological Institute of São Paulo, for study and research in the pathology of all forms of life, animal and vegetable, and especially those that are of the greatest interest to man. Principal façade.

376. The Biological Institute of São Paulo. One of its experimental farms.

377. The Biological Institute of São Paulo, one of the greatest research centers in America—like the Osvaldo Cruz Institute, famed throughout the world. View of one of the laboratories.

378. The Agronomical Institute of Campinas, in the state of São Paulo, today one of the most important centers in Brazil for the investigation of plant life. One of the new buildings erected beside the old building.

379. The Agronomical Institute of Campinas. View of a greenhouse.

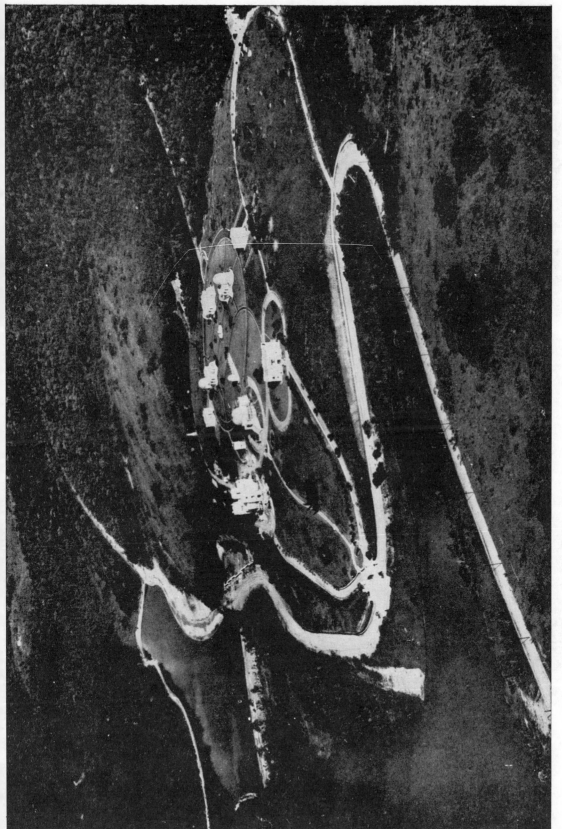

380. The Astronomical Observatory of São Paulo, in its new and excellent quarters. General view of the buildings. Photo by ENFA.

381. The College of Philosophy, Science, and Letters of the University of São Paulo—the first to be founded by government in Brazil. A view of one of its buildings, showing the greenhouses of the Botany Department. Photo by Liberman, São Paulo, 1942.

382. The first College of Philosophy, Science, and Letters—that of the University of São
Paulo, created in Brazil by the decree of January 25, 1934. A view of the Mineralogy Museum
of the Department of Mineralogy and Petrography.
Photo by Liberman, São Paulo, 1942.

383. College of Philosophy, Science, and Letters of the University of São Paulo, in which,
under the guidance of foreign and Brazilian professors, a group of first-rate research men
has been formed. One of the biology laboratories.
Photo by Liberman, São Paulo. 1942.

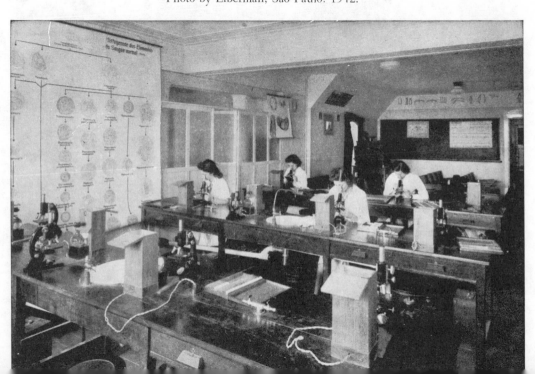

384. Principal façade of the Institute of Education of the University of São Paulo, which graduated in 1937 the first class of secondary-school teachers in Brazil. They had previously

385. Institute of Education of the University of São Paulo, which was created in 1933, and no longer existed in 1938. A view of the Ethnographic Museum of the Department of Educational Sociology.

386. The new and magnificent building of the São Paulo Public Library, to which was added in 1937 the State Library. Here the first course in library science in Brazil was given. General view.

387. Minister Gustavo Capanema, who was responsible for numerous reforms and cultural initiatives and accomplishments, among them the construction of the building of the Ministry of Education and Health and of various technical schools.

388. Model of the building of the Ministry of Education and Health, Rio de Janeiro.
Photo by the Documentation Service of the Ministry of Education and Health, 1942.

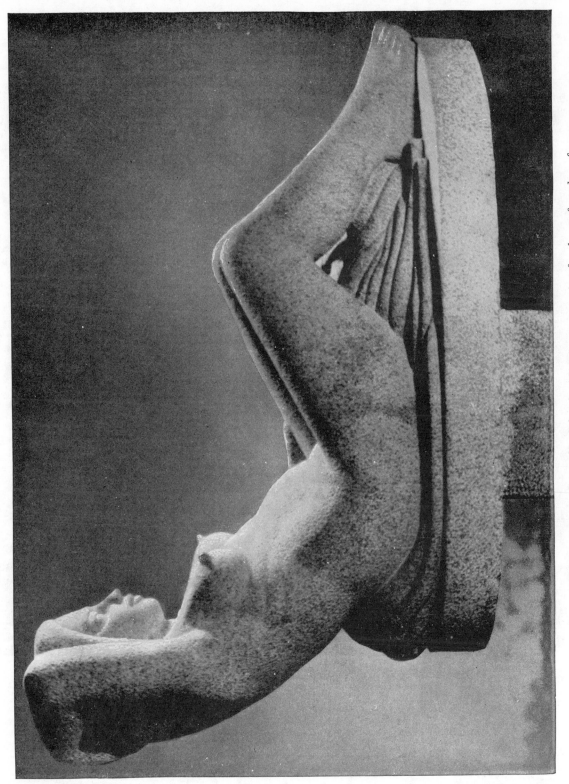

389. "Reclining Girl," sculpture by Celso António, in gray granite, for the roof garden of the new building of the Ministry of Education.

Photo by the Documentation Service of the Ministry of Education and Health, 1942.

390. Detail of the sculpture "Reclining Girl," by Celso Antônio.
Photo by the Documentation Service of the Ministry of Education and Health, 1942.

391. St. Louis College of the Jesuit fathers, which moved from Itu to São Paulo in 1918, after seventy-five years of service in the education of Brazilian youth.

392. Rio Branco National Academy at São Paulo, founded by Antônio de Sampaio Dória,
one of the principal private secondary schools of the country.

393. Rio Branco National Academy. A view of the library.

394. St. Ignatius College, of the Society of Jesus,
Rio de Janeiro. View of the courtyard.

395. Law School of São Paulo. View of the c[entral] patio, rebuilt in all the severe simplicity [of] the original lines of the old Convent of St. Fran[cis].

396. National Law School of Rio de Janeiro, now
located in the building once occupied by the Senate, originally the Palace of the Count dos Arcos.

397. Medical School of the University of São Paulo. General view of the building, before
the construction of the Clinical Hospital.

398. Clinical Hospital of the Medical School of the University of São Paulo. View from an airplane. Photo by ENFA.

a national coordination of educational services properly so-called and those of culture in their various forms." [43]

The Ministry of Education was preparing to be, after the reform of 1937, not only an organ for central research, for methodical investigation with the aim of studying and recording normal growth, thanks to which institutions carry on the plan from which they proceed, but also the center for coordinating the cultural activities in the magnificent development of all of the living forces of the nation. Its program, extremely broad in character, one of educational and cultural action, embracing teaching of all grades and types and extending through all of the forms which culture can take on was marked throughout by a national if not nationalistic character, which strikes us in the fundamental objects of all of its services, its plans of coordination of activities, the spirit with which it was organized, not only to further the continuity and progress of culture, but to safeguard, by putting them under the protection of the State, in accordance with the constitutional precept (Const. of 1937, art. 134), the elements of the historical and artistic tradition of the country. [44] There is nothing rigid

[43] Lourenço Filho, *Tendências da educação brasileira.* Biblioteca da Educação, Vol. 29. Companhia Melhoramentos de São Paulo, São Paulo-Rio de Janeiro (n.d.), p. 41.

[44] One of the important institutes created by the Federal Government in 1937 and put under the Ministry of Education and Health is, in fact, the Service of the National Historical and Artistic Property, into which the old Inspectorate of National Monuments was transformed, with a broadening of its objectives and its structure. It may be said that only then was the idea of the original project embodied in an efficient organization; this idea had been presented in 1923 to the Federal Chamber by Luiz Cedro, deputy from Pernambuco, and it dealt with the protection of the historic and artistic property of the country, and was closely followed, in 1925, 1927, and 1928 respectively by Minas, Bahia, and Pernambuco; their governments were concerned with the problem and proposed to study it and to work out laws with the same objective. In 1933, by decree no. 22,928, of July 12 of that year, the federal government began the work to which it was later to give larger proportions, by making the old mining city of Ouro Preto a National Monument. This city is a real open air museum, and deserves the name for the historic and artistic value of its urban landscape. With decree no. 24,735, of July 14, 1934, which created the Inspectorate of National Monuments, as a department of the Historical Museum, the bases were laid for the system of protecting the historic and artistic property of the Brazilian nation. This system was set up under the name of "Serviço do Patrimônio Histórico e Artístico Nacional." The draft for the law, submitted by the President of the Republic for the consideration of Congress, was never approved, because there intervened the coup d'état which in 1937 set up a new regime, dissolving the House and Senate. The Constitutional Charter of November 10, 1937, pushed the idea farther along, establishing in art. 134 the principle that "historic, artistic and natural monuments, as well as landscapes or places especially endowed by nature, enjoy the protection and special care of the Nation, the States and municipalities," and attacks upon these monuments "will be considered as if committed against the property of the Nation." The draft was reviewed by the Ministry of Education and Health, and this project which had been under consideration since 1936 finally became law in decree-law no. 25, of November 30, 1937, which wiped out the old Inspectorate and organized, under the Minister of Education and Health, the special service for the protection of the historic and artistic property of the nation. Among the accomplishments of the new Service, the importance of which we do not need to exaggerate, figure the inventory it began to make of all the historic and artistic treasures of the country; the recording, down to 1940, of about three hundred objects of historic and artistic value, from cities or parts of cities, to works of architecture, in a great variety of types and shapes; the repairing, restoration and conservation, depending upon the circumstances, of churches, chapels, convents, forts, private houses and other things to a total of eighty, by the end of 1940, and the preparatory study and planning of museums like that of the Inconfidência, created in 1938, to be installed in

in this organization, nothing static or fixed, but everything was established in the manner of experiments, as a constant appeal to carry on the work which had begun and to accelerate the rate of this process of expansion, which had opened up through many obscurities, as a result of this creative impulse, new perspectives not only to the assimilation into one of the Brazilian people, but also for the differentiation of cultural values. All of this movement of reform and of the extension of education and of culture in general leaves us in fact very far from the old imperial and republican society constituted, down to the first World War (1914–1918), according to a law of conformity, in which the then incipient nuances of ideas and sentiments did not succeed in achieving definition and acquiring prestige and great influence, even in the most advanced states. The diversity of fields of investigation which arouse curosity and call for talent, the richness of points of view, the abundance of different types of personalities, the variety of tastes, of dreams and of intellectual ambition, all of this bears witness, in a multitude of vague and incoherent elements, to the vitality of the nation which, under the influence of official and private initiative, was developing,— to employ a happy image—, "like a great river fed by numerous tributaries or like those trees which produce the more fruit the larger the number of their branches."

The political, social and economic transformation and the problems which arose, the development and growing complexity of public services which demanded a complete remodelling of the administrative apparatus, could not fail to arouse a consciousness of the necessity of statistical research as an objective base for the study and solution of national problems. The man of the government and the administrator, more than in any other period, felt moved to take a realistic attitude, one of positive polity, oriented by the observation of social facts which could be stated in numerical terms and therefore in a statistical, objective attitude toward Brazil and those public services destined to satisfy Brazil's fundamental needs in all the fields of human activity. It was necessary to be aware of the problems of the country to be able to solve them, reducing to the minimum failures and disillusions, disappointments and ruin, to which governments expose themselves as they are dreamers of great things but often poor calculators of the obstacles in their way and since their need of haste often drives them counter to their own objectives. In a period in which problems were becoming complicated and the appeal was made to men of action, whose major defect, one capable of causing their ruin, is exactly the lack of harmony between their imagination and reality, statistics appeared to the eyes of many, not only as a "process of research" and a "objective estimate of everything that interests society and can have qualitative or quantitative numerical expression," but also as the most efficacious means of directing study and the solutions of problems, restraining men's impatience and limiting to what

---

the old Palace of the Chamber and former jail of Vila Rica; that of the Missions, in São Miguel, in Rio Grande do Sul, created in 1940; that of Moldagem (molding) in Rio, and of Religious Art, in Bahia, still in the stage of studies and organization. The Service of the Historic and Artistic Property of the Nation publishes an excellent journal, the "Revista do Serviço," and has brought out works of real historical and documentary interest, such as the *Guia de Ouro Preto,* by Manuel Bandeira, the *Diário íntimo do engenheiro Vauthier,* by Gilberto Freyre, the *Arte indígena da Amazônia* by Heloisa Alberto Tôrres, and *Em torno da história de Sabará,* by Zoroastro Passos. (Cf. Afonso Arinos de Melo Franco, *Arte, tradição, e nacionalismo.* Lecture given in São Paulo, May 31, 1941. In "O Estado de São Paulo," January 8, 1941.)

is possible the constructive haste of men of action. Add moreover that the modifications which were taking place in economic life, especially in the density, distribution and movement of population, in the professions and social classes, and in the old educational structure, had given extraordinary breadth to the field of statistical investigation, demanding a great effort for the development, coordination and uniformity of the statistical services of the country.

This was the task, admirably accomplished in every way, of Teixeira de Freitas, who took up with notable vigor the great campaign begun by Bulhões Carvalho.[45] It

[45] Statistical services in Brazil took on new life with the reorganization, in 1907, of the old General Directorate of Statistics, which was created in 1871 and presided over the taking of the census in 1872 and 1890. Under the Imperial regime, the statistical activities of greatest importance were limited to the census of 1872,—the only one taken in this period—, when the law promulgated in 1870 prescribed the taking of decennial censuses; to the census of the population of the Neutral Município, in the year before, and to some attempts at organizing statistical tables, carried out in different provinces. After the census of 1890, the federal government did nothing, under the Republic, except the general census of 1900 and 1920, the latter including, in addition to population, minute inquiries on agriculture and industry. The General Directorate of Statistics was reorganized in 1907 and under the direction of José Luiz Salão de Bulhões Carvalho, "founder of general Brazilian statistics," it started a phase of intense activity, collecting by means of a vast questionnaire information on education throughout the national territory; publishing in 1916 the volume *Statistics of Education*, in which it brought together the results of the inquiry, preceded by a long and excellent introduction by Oziel Bordeaux Rêgo, and preparing for the taking of the population census of 1920, which was the most important taken either under the Empire or the Republic, down to the Revolution. (Cf. Bulhões Carvalho, *Estatística, método e aplicação*. Rio de Janeiro, 1933). It was, however, after 1930 that statistical services developed a really notable fashion, with the creation in 1931, of the National Department of Statistics, in which there were fused, in 1932, the old General Directorate of Statistics and the Directorate of Commercial Statistics, whose services had been set up in 1900, and the Directorate of Information, Statistics and Popularization, in the Ministry of Education and Health (decree no. 19,560, of January 5, 1931), and, in 1934, with the decrees which set up the Directorate of Statistics of Production, in the Ministry of Agriculture, and of Economic and Financial Statistics, in the Treasury, and of Statistics and Publicity, in the Ministry of Labor, Industry, and Commerce, and of General Statistics of the Ministry of Justice,—the last two resulting from the extinction in 1934 of the National Department, created in 1931, the duties of which were transferred to various Ministries. All this legislation, which reveals a growing interest in statistical services on the federal level, culminated in the creation, by decree no. 24,609, of July 6, 1934, of the National Institute of Statistics (now the Brazilian Institute of Statistics and Geography), the plan for which resulted from the studies of an interministerial committee called together and presided over by the then Minister Juarez Távora. This institution has as its object, "by means of the gradual articulation and cooperation of the three administrative orders of the political organization of the Republic, as well as of private initiative, to promote and cause to be carried out, or to give technical advice to, according to rational criteria, the systematic collection of all national statistics." Set up in 1936, under the presidency of J. C. de Macedo Soares, this Institute, whose origins are to be sought in the Statistical Agreement, signed in 1931, for making uniform and improving school and related statistics, within five years either solved or put on the way to be solved "all the basic problems of Brazilian statistics." It promoted the National Statistical Convention, which met in 1936 in Rio de Janeiro; it carried on municipal inquiries, and others of a regional or national character; it began the regular publication of the *Anuário Estatístico do Brasil* and of its twenty-two offprints for different regions; it started two first-rate reviews,—that of *Estatística* and that of *Geografia;* it encouraged the creation of the major part and the reorganization of practically all the twenty-two state departments of statistics, connected with the Institute; and it organized and directed, through the National Census Commission, presided over by J. Carneiro Felipe, the national census of

was in him that the revolutionary government found its most solid point of support and its most enlightened guide in the activities that it undertook in the direction of giving rational organization to the national system of statistics on the basis of a regime of cooperation between administrations laid down in the first year of the Revolution. The Revolution of 1930 marks, in fact, a new era of Brazilian statistics.[46] The Statistical Agreement consisting of 27 clauses signed in 1931 in Rio de Janeiro; the creation of the National Department and the various Services of Statistics in the Ministries of the Republic; the organization by decree no. 24,609 of July 6, 1934, of the National Institute of Statistics which became the Brazilian Institute of Geography and Statistics by decree law no. 208 of January 28, 1938; the creation or the reorganization of State Departments of Statistics which gradually joined this Institute, and the development of the teaching of statistics through the creation of chairs of that subject in the Faculties of Philosophy, constituted so many other conquests in the evolution of the idea and of the coordination of statistical activities, the results of which were recognized by the Eighth American Scientific Congress that met in Washington in 1940 as being "of great interest and great importance to the statistics of other American nations." The victory of the regime for which Teixeira de Freitas fought, that of "cooperation between administrations,"—the most adequate regime for federal States or those of a federative form like Brazil, took concrete form in the Instituto Brasileira de Geografia e Estatística, which is a central organ and an organic system, as complete as possible, established by the coming together of the efforts of the Union, the States, and the Municipalities, in the coordination and systematization of national, statistical services. For the success of this great undertaking, entrusted to the young institution, J. C. de Macedo Soares made a notable contribution. He was its president from the beginning and, even at the period of its foundation, he had as chancellor in the Ministry of Foreign Relations taken the initiative in solving the problem with regard to the agreement of the results of the Brazilian contribution with international statistics. The census which was carried on in 1940, directed by the National Census Commission under the chairmanship of J. Carneiro Filipe, gives us the measure of this preliminary work of organization in the amplitude of its census plan, in the sureness of its research methods: farseeing, mature, its preparations made over a long time by means of a constant union of efforts, it represents, in fact, the greatest and the most complete collection of data which has been carried on in Brazil, to reveal the nation to itself in a faithful image, in all of the aspects of its peculiar physiognomy and in the variety of its forms of life, culture and production.

1940,—the census operation of the broadest scope, and the most complete and perfect which has been carried out in Brazil. (Cf. *O Instituto Brasileiro de Geografia e Estatística e o Município.* Printing Office of the I.B.G.E. Avenida Pasteur, 404, Rio de Janeiro, 1941; *Educação e estatística.* Printing Office of the I.B.G.E., Rio de Janeiro, 1941.)

[46] Germano G. Jardim, *A administração pública e a estatística. O papel e a missão de um órgão central de estatística no quadro das realizações do govêrno Getúlio Vargas.* D.I.P. (Department of Press and Propaganda), Rio de Janeiro, 1941.

BIBLIOGRAPHY

Almeida Júnior, A. F., *A Escola pitoresca* (São Paulo: Comp. Editora Nacional, 1934).

——, *Anuário do ensino do Estado de São Paulo* (São Paulo, 1935–1936), pp. 13–283.

Arbousse–Bastide, P., "O Ensino secundário, chave de toda a reforma educacional," in *O Estado de São Paulo,* Oct. 30, 1935.

Assís Ribeiro, Paulo, "A Evolução do ensino secundário," in *O Estado de São Paulo,* Sept. 1–3, 1937. Address at the Instituto de Educação, São Paulo, Aug. 26, 1937.

Azevedo, Fernando de, *A Educação pública em São Paulo: Problemas e discussões* (São Paulo: Comp. Editora Nacional, 1937—Brasiliana, Vol. 98). Inquiry by *O Estado de São Paulo,* 1926.

——, *A Reforma do ensino no Distrito Federal: Discursos e entrevistas* (São Paulo: Comp. de Melhoramentos, 1929).

——, *Novos caminhos e novos fins: Uma Nova Política de educação no Brasil* (São Paulo: Comp. Editora Nacional, 1st ed., 1931, 2nd ed., 1935).

——, *A Educação e seus problemas* (São Paulo: Comp. Editora Nacional, 1937).

Barbosa Viana, "Organização universitária no Brasil," in *Jornal do Comércio,* Rio, Mar. 24, 1940. Address at the ceremonial opening of courses, 1940.

Campos, Francisco, *Educação e cultura* (Rio: olímpio, 1940).

Capanema, Gustavo, "Panorama de educação nacional: As realizações e os propósitos do govêrno federal," in *Jornal do Comércio,* Dec. 13–14, 1937. Discourse at the commemoration of the Centenary of the Colégio Pedro II.

Figueira de Almeida, A., *História do ensino secundário no Brasil* (Rio: Jacinto, 1936).

Frota Pessoa, J. G., *A Educação e a rotina* (Rio: Francisco Alves).

——, *A Realidade brasileira* (Rio: Francisco Alves, 1931). Labouriau, V., Roquette Pinto, Licínio Cardoso, and others, *O Problema universitário brasileiro* (Rio, 1929). Inquiry by the Associação Brasileira de Educação.

Licínio Cardoso, Vicente. *À Margem da história do Brasil: Instrução e educação* (São Paulo: Comp. Editora Nacional, 1933—Brasiliana, Vol. 13), pp. 188–193.

Lourenço Filho, M. B. *Tendências da educação brasileira* (São Paulo: Comp. de Melhoramentos, 1940—Biblioteca de Educação, Vol. 29).

Moacir, Primitivo, *A Instrução e a República: Subsídios para a história da educação no Brasil* (Rio: Imprensa Nacional, 3 vols., 1941). Publication of the Instituto Nacional de Estudos Pedagogicos.

Montojos, Francisco, "História e evolução do ensino industrial no Brasil," in *Jornal do Comércio,* Rio, Sept. 10, 1939. Exposition before the Comissão Interministerial charged with regulating vocational courses in factories.

Osório de Almeida, A., "A Organização universitária e as faculdades de ciências e letras," in *Jornal do Comércio,* Rio, Jan. 21, 1928.

Peixoto, Afrânio, *História da educação* (São Paulo: Comp. Editora Nacional, 1933), Chaps. XVII–XIX ("Brasil") and XX ("Escola Nova"), pp. 211–265.

Silva Rodrigues, Mílton, *Educação comparada* (São Paulo: Comp. Editora Nacional, 1938), Pt. 3, "O Brasil," pp. 233–290.

Sousa Campos, Ernesto, *Educação superior no Brasil* (Rio: Serviço Gráfico do Ministério da Educação, 1940).

——, *Instituições culturais e de educação superior no Brasil* (Rio: Imprensa Nacional, 1941). Publication of the Ministério da Educação.

Teixeira, Anísio, *Educação pública, sua organização e administração* (Rio, 1934).

——, *Educação para a democracia* (Rio, 1936).

Toledo Dodsworth, Henrique, "Cem anos de ensino secundário," in *Livro do Centenário da Câmara dos Deputados* (Rio: Emp. Brasil, 1926).

Tôrres, Alberto, *A Organização nacional* (São Paulo: Comp. Editora Nacional, 1933—Brasiliana, Vol. 17).

——, *O Problema nacional brasileiro: Introdução a um programa de organização nacional* (São Paulo: Comp. Editora Nacional, 1933—Brasiliana, Vol. 16).

Vargas, Getúlio, *A Nova Política do Brasil* (Rio: Olímpio, 8 vols., 1938–1941).

Veríssimo de Matos, José, *A Educação nacional* (Belém: 1896; 2nd ed., Rio, 1906).

——, "A Instrução e a imprensa" and "A instrução pública," pp. 5–30, in *Livro do Centenário* (Rio: Imprensa Nacional, 1900).

——, *Estatística escolar*, Vol.1, *Repartição federal de estatística* (Rio, 1916).

——, *Anais da Conferência Interestadual de Ensino Primário* (Rio, 1922).

——, *Anais da Terceira Conferência Nacional de Educação* (São Paulo, 1930).

——, *Congresso de Educação* (São Paulo: Edição do Centro D. Vital, 1933). Organized by Centro D. Vital de São Paulo and held Oct. 17, 1931.

——, *O Problema educacional e a nova Constituição* (São Paulo: Comp. Editora Nacional, 1934). Publication of the Associação Brasileira de Educação.

——, *Anuário do Ensino do Estado de São Paulo* (São Paulo, 1935–1936), compiled by Prof. A. F. de Almeida Júnior.

CHAPTER FIVE

GENERAL EDUCATION AND VARIOUS TYPES
OF SPECIAL EDUCATION

Education and culture in the light of their historic development—The cultural heritage of Brazil—The enlargement in the system of the general or common education—Primary education, according to statistics—The quantitative extension and the lowering of level in secondary education—Special types of education—The predominance of schools preparing for the liberal professions—Military and naval teaching—Industrial development and the new technical requirements of a society in the course of transformation—Vocational, agricultural, commercial and industrial schools—Industry and the training of technicians and vocational training—The cooperation of workshops and factories in vocational education—The hierarchy of vocational types—The universities and the formation of the cultural, technical and political elite—The mission of the schools of higher studies and of pure research—Professional specialization and scientific specialization—Aesthetic culture—The pedagogical training of teachers of all grades—From the unity of education to the intellectual unity of Brazil—A national policy of education and culture.

I N THE PAGES ABOVE, which are neither very difficult nor very technical, in which reflections and opinions have been mixed with an abundant source material, unfortunately of unequal merit and heterogeneous in character, we have traced in summary the picture of the cultural evolution of Brazil and of its educational institutions down to the point where they reach their present structure. But, if in this synthesis of culture and education in the country, the general picture is historical, it has not been constructed according to a chronological plan, the strict plan of pure historians, but on the contrary with a sociological attitude, one of analysis and of interpretation, which would permit us to detach from the complex network of facts, activities and reforms, the movement of ideas and the most significant phenomena which appeared to us to dominate education in the various phases of its development. In this study, which is at once analytic and genetic, in which we have attempted to go back to the origins of institutions and to establish through their evolution the tendencies of modern education, the character of Brazilian culture, its relations with the social state of each period, and the Europeanizing influences, generally so retarded, which the general currents of thought in the western world exercised upon it have all been set down. All Brazilian culture in the colonial period, as in the nineteenth century, is in the lines which the Jesuits drew of it with their notable teaching of the humanities, which had such profound and persistent effects that far from disappearing during their absence of more than eighty years (1759–1843), they made themselves strongly felt, seconded by the influence of the French, through the period of the Empire and took on new vigor during the part of the republican period. The culture which was attained by general or common education of the middle grade and without any ideas of specialization, constituted in fact the intellectual stratum that was most dense and rich in its literary aspects down to the end of the second Kingdom. Our sources on Jesuit teaching in colonial life, and later in the last quarter of the nineteenth century, permit us to reveal the first center which was lit up in the rude period of the colony, and to accompany through its irradiation that light which was never extinguished and which was handed on in the intellectual élite from one generation to another with a great intensity.

So powerful was the influence of this humanistic and literary type of culture, that the ecclesiastical career, from which it came, was sought out as one of the most effica-cious means for winning it, and the very liberal professions of lawyers, doctors and engineers deemed that they could find in it, not only support and the harmony indis-pensable to professional specialization, but one more ornament, the brilliance which would enhance their authority, the power which was capable of giving them greater influence. The ecclesiastical career, writes Vilhena de Morais, "was, in fact, in the convents almost the only one which was open to the sons of the people, some of whom entered it without the slightest religious spirit, at times forced by their fathers as a good method of learning science and acquiring honor and position." Even when, in the time of Dom João VI, the first schools of medicine and surgery and those for mili-tary engineers were created, and when in the first reign in 1827, the law courses were founded, our higher culture, which down to 1830 still depended upon Coimbra, did not lose on account of its more marked professional character this taste for general culture nor the literary spirit, nor that erudite gongorism, nor that broad curiosity which leads us to take an interest, even though it be a superficial one, in the most varied problems. The priests,—the great representatives of mentality down to the second reign, as Capistrano de Abreu tells us—, were then replaced upon the scene by the bachelors of law, educated in the Academies of São Paulo and Olinda, but these, as well as the doctors and engineers, rarely sacrificed letters to their concern to deepen their knowledge of their specialty, yielding less to the desire to limit themselves than to the ideal of being "complete" in the manner of the times, and to the necessity of placing their profession in a more general framework, amplified by literary study and the reading of books which formed the foundation of human culture.

All that more than a century of higher education produced in the field of juridical and medical specialization and wrote in that great page of the conquests of man in Brazil, "did not rub out from the human palimpsest its primitive legends," to employ an image of Rui Barbosa. Under what specialized culture produced, even with the precision of a Lafaiete Rodrigues Pereira or with the clarity of a Teixeira de Freitas, the essentially humanistic literary culture is hardly concealed. We got it from the Jesuits and we kept it for almost four centuries as the cultural inheritance of Brazil. The Brazilian might have what profession he wished (and those who could through nature or their own resources did not aspire to anything but the liberal professions), but he would not renounce that which Alfonso Reyes in his *Homilia por la cultura* called "the profession of man," that is the feeling of the human, of disinterested study and the love of general ideas, which constitute what is most truly human in us, and in us what is most truly social. If the analysis of Brazilian culture leads us to this affirmation when we judge it by the best products of the time (in the Colony and in the Empire), the conclusion at which we arrive is not other if we study the "table of values," which these same creators of culture applied to these products, and of which we get a precise idea which completes our understanding of that culture, if we examine criticism, that is to say, the reception and judgment of works of that time. In their general lines, in their structure and in their form, if not in their spirit, which varies according to the epoch, almost all of the works of the nineteenth century, if they do not belong to the specifically French tradition of Jesuit humanism, show the domination of literary culture and of general ideas in education, both coming from the colonial system of Jesuit education and from the influences of French thought and above all, French literature, under the Empire. Our intellectual, although judged "within his profession," was the opposite of a specialist; and the value of his works, even in his own field of specialization, was to be judged particularly by their literary qualities, by the richness of their quotations and by their erudition.

Certainly it is through our general ideas that we get out of ourselves, that we detach ourselves from our professional specialty and rise above our daily occupations. And this is one of the benefits which our traditional system of education brought us, with its less utilitarian character, its less professional, more general, if not truly human character, through the basis of secondary education and under the pressure of the conception of culture and ideas that spread in the cultural atmosphere of the country. The spiritual unity which the plurality of regional cultures, nourished by distance and isolation, never broke up, and which was favored by the interpenetration of the two worlds of education and religion, was also doubtless another effect of that general culture which was so successful in producing the uniformity and assimilation of the intellectual classes. But we cannot fail to recognize that some of the major defects of our culture are related to it,—our excessively literary tendency, our love for erudition for its own sake, our inclination or easy resignation to the superficial elegancies of the academic, our lack of interest in experimental science, our indifference to technical questions,[1] and also the divorce between the people and the intellectual creators in

---

[1] This cultural atmosphere which controls man in Brazil, this "paideuma," to use the expression of Frobenius to designate the "soul of culture," was obviously transmitted to us from Portugal, through the Jesuits and the Portuguese colonizers. The mentality which penetrated the man of the colony, having a powerful influence upon him, was the same which ruled the mother country. Portugal, which in the fifteenth century "kept pace with the best minds of Europe," saw the stagnation of its sources of new life in the sixteenth century, the history of which, in that country, as Antônio Sérgio writes, is "the spectacle of the loss of vigor on the part of the Portuguese mind." While in the seventeenth and eighteenth centuries the critical and experimental spirit was spreading through other countries of Europe, with its ideals of free examination and of investigation, the Iberian peninsula stayed outside the orbit of the new influences and was impenetrable to the critical and scientific humanism which put life and experience in first place, with the direct observation of reality, research and personal reflection, and under the influence of which a real cultural revolution took place in the old continent. (Cf. Antônio Sérgio—*Ensaios*. O problema da cultura em Portugal. Vol. 2. Seara Nova, Lisbon, 1929). With bitter vehemence, José Agostinho de Macedo referred, passing a keenly critical judgment upon it, "to that fatal century, the sixteenth," in which Portugal had already become "the barracks of fanaticism." The words of Antero de Quental are not less hard, in his criticism of the Portuguese mind of the seventeenth and eighteenth centuries, in which, in the Iberian peninsula, "a generation of philosophers, scholars and creative artists was followed by a vulgar tribe of learned men without a critical spirit, of academicians and imitators . . . In the last two centuries the Peninsula has not produced a single superior man that can be put side by side with the great creators of modern science; there has not come from the Peninsula a single one of the great intellectual discoveries which are the greatest honor of the modern mind." The revolutionary reforms of the Marquês de Pombal, with tardy

politics, literature and the arts. If the great representative figures of this type of culture made history precise by their erudition and gave life to erudition by literature and acquired forms of a notable harmony, clarity and precision, the dogmatic and oratorical development, which was almost always romantic, of the works of this time (I refer to the nineteenth century), from which there results more darkness than clarity, shows a tendency towards abstract discussion of the abstract, confusion of the real and the imaginary, the primacy of letters over science, the ideal over method, of the dogmatic spirit over the critical and investigating spirit. These élites found in the environment to which they directed themselves,—the highest classes of the urban and rural environment—, a setting which was exactly fitted to their tastes and their talents, and they felt in harmony with the little cultured public which was theirs—the only one really for which they were willing to write or to speak from the professor's chair, from the tribune of the parliament, in their books and daily newspapers. Although it fulfilled a social role and served society, serving the ecclesiastical career and afterwards public life in the first and second reigns, this culture, however, had no strength to bring about between the élite and the people that fusion which would be capable of transforming it from an expression of the higher classes without a social basis, into a collective culture with a double character of being an aristocratic work and the work of a whole people . . .

This type of general culture which had been developing since the dawn of colonial society and down to the twilight of the Empire, or more exactly, of the nineteenth century, corresponded not only to the ideal of a period (sixteenth and seventeenth centuries), but also to the very social and economic conditions of the environment to which it was transferred and which, if they did not give rise to it, at least prepared for its development a favorable climate. Humanistic culture, which never was democratic, satisfied the taste of a rural aristocracy and of the urban bourgeoisie which found in it exactly that principle of refinement or quality inherent in all superior culture, and with which the distinction between classes was more strongly marked. It flourished in the shade of the big house, in the primitive structure of the patriarchal family with its lords of the sugar mill and its sons, priests and doctors, and was installed in the mansion of the city, when there began, as a result of urbanization, as Gilberto Freyre remarks, the separation of the two types of family—the disintegrated patriarchal family (mansion) and the incipient working class family (hut), the latter kept in almost the

---

and slight effects in the colony, broke almost uselessly against the wall of the resistance of the medieval spirit which from the university and the schools in which it had dwelt for more than two centuries, spread among the élite of the country, setting up the man of Aristotle (and that in his lowest form) against the man who thought in Galilean terms, the medieval man against the modern mind. What was cultivated, under the influence of this teaching was vegetated in the routine of theology, was the love of stereotyped and abstract formulas, learned dilettantism, an apologetic and rhetorical tone which showed what was the favorite way of thinking,—i.e. deductive, a priori—and the culture that matched it, excessively verbal in character, without science to counterbalance it. Intelligence was not, for the élite, an adventure in creation and discovery, but a dialectical instrument, if not a mere apparatus for recording impressions and reading, for commentaries and scholarly works. No critical spirit, no creative impulse of doubt, unrest, or research; literary, grammatical and philological studies of a purely formal sort would end by taking first place in this "Appolinean" culture, of form for form's sake, crowding out Dionysian culture, which was suffocated by a rigid, dry, humanistic philosophy, which letters without science had stripped of its content of human experience.

same darkness in which the slave population of the slave quarters and the cities dragged out its existence. With the expulsion of the Jesuits in 1759, the reforms of Pombal, and the creation of higher professional education of a specialized kind in the beginning of the nineteenth century, the tradition of the humanistic education of the country threatened to enter upon a critical phase. But the influence of the priestly teachers and chaplains and of the religious orders, who conserved the inheritance of the Jesuit teaching; the belated effect of the reforms of Pombal in the colony; the institution, along with national independence, of the parliamentary regime, and the growing influence of French literature, contributed not only to maintain, but also to develop, in a "liberal" civilization based on slavery, that "class" education, which in addition to being a hierarchical and conservative force, gave to politics in its experiments in a parliamentary regime the brilliance of letters and of eloquence, and constituted the school to which the necessity of exercising argumentative functions attracted that class.

The professionalization of higher education, with the creation by Dom João VI of schools of medicine and military engineering and with the foundation of law courses in 1827, was counterbalanced in its influence making for "specialization" by various facts, among which was the persistence of the old ideal of the human type, the cultural function which academies of law were called upon to exercise, side by side with their specific professional function because of the lack of higher schools of free and disinterested culture, and also the circumstance that it was among the students graduated from these schools that men were recruited for the highest posts in teaching, politics or administration. Under the Empire, the great reforms of education aimed consequently at higher schools of a professional type and at the Pedro II College, raised to the category of a kind of faculty of letters; and it was exactly at this time that this college and the private institutions of secondary education had their epoch of greatest brilliance and flourishing. With the abolition of the regime of slavery and the coming of the Republic in 1889, the new institutions led to the wide expansion of general or common education of a primary grade, the history of which, so undistinguished in the Empire, began to develop in the States under the influence of democratic ideas, and is marked not only by a notable quantitative increase, but also by the introduction into elementary teaching of new forms and new methods of education. If, on the one hand, the greater diffusion of primary education entrusted to the States by the Constitution of 1891 was a notable step in liberal and democratic evolution, on the other, the federal Republican government, reserving for itself the right to legislate on secondary and higher education, finally abandoned to the States the education of the people, established in this distribution of functions the hierarchy of values contrary to the ideals in which the name of the government was constituted. At the same time, however, that starting from the political periphery, and above all from São Paulo, Minas and the federal District, this movement of reorganization of general teaching at the base grew more intense,—the preparatory stage of a democratization of culture—, secondary education, which is also in its nature an education in general culture, began slowly to lose, through successive reforms, its character of "class education" which still remained, however, without the same vigor, without the same brilliance during the forty years of the first phase of the Republican period.

After this situation, created in part by the educational policy adopted in the Charter of 1891, a double process which led straight to the democratization of culture had to develop, as it did develop: one under official leadership, the other outside the narrow bonds of organized public education. This spread, in the system of education, of common, fundamental education (primary education), promoted by the States, not only extended "a minimum of general culture" to an ever larger population, but also stimulated the quantitative development of secondary schools to meet the needs of the increasing number of candidates for schools that prepared for the liberal professions. In the lack of initiatives taken by the central government, which limited itself to promoting reforms of secondary education, without increasing the number of schools of this type, private cooperation either lay or religious, began to grow, in this field, through the volume of its foundation and made a contribution much superior to that of the official schools of the Union and the States. The growing number of candidates for the colleges and high schools formed, with their families, a mobile and restless element, which began to react and to counterbalance the scholastic reforms, tending to restore to secondary education the especially humanistic character which constituted its tradition in the colony with the Jesuits, and made its glory during the whole period of the Empire. Not only as a result of the general extension of the network of schools, but under the pressure of American ideas that had come in through Protestant schools, secondary education slowly asserted its utilitarian and pragmatic tendencies, which influenced both the objects and the structure of education and the duration of the course, obliging the federal government to make constant reforms, with the object of readapting secondary education to new conditions and to the requirements of present day civilization. But, one cannot deny the role which the numerical growth of school units had in this evolution. It was already marked in the first quarter of this century and grew so vigorously after 1930 that, in the five year period 1932–1936, it showed the greatest power of expansion that had taken place in the country in the system of common education, of primary and secondary grade.[2]

[2] Both primary schooling and secondary, which are meant to furnish general common culture, the former inculcating the basic ideas, and the latter giving humanistic culture, experienced between 1930 and 1940 the greatest development which has been recorded in our country in an equal period, in any epoch of the history of our education. To understand better the statistical data with regard to this period, we must keep in mind the distinction between "secondary education," properly so-called, and "education of the second grade," or middle grade, according to our statistical nomenclature; while the expression "secondary education" designates especially the education furnished in colégios and liceus, "especially humanistic studies," with the exclusion of vocational schools of the middle level, the expression "education of the second grade," or middle education, serves rather, as P. Arbousse-Bastide observes, "to distinguish the levels, and is based on the age of the pupils rather than the nature of the teaching." Designating both the intermediate education between primary and higher, meant for youths of twelve to eighteen years, the first expression (secondary education) has a limited meaning, pointing to a type of education of the second grade (humanistic education), and the second (education of the second or middle grade) "indicates the fusion or the intent to fuse in a single type all the varieties of education given to boys of that age." Having made this clear, we pass to the statistics. In the five year period, 1932–1936, primary education grew from 100 to 129 and secondary education from 100 to 149, that is, primary school units numbered 27,662 in 1932, and rose to 35,555 in 1936, while secondary schools increased from 394, in 1932, to 552, in 1936, or, in other words, an increase of 158 units in five years. In 1938 the matriculation in the primary schools, giving common or complementary education, reached a total of 3,110,000 pupils, or more exactly, 3,109,784, as compared with 2,860,000 in the year before, and therefore, an increase from one year to the other of 232,000 pupils, "or in percentage increase, 8.5%, a figure never before seen in two consecutive school years, in Brazilian educational

This process, legitimate in itself, of democratization which initiates the masses in culture, always presents, as we have noticed, a negative side, for it takes place at the cost of quality, which is consequently lowered. If the secondary schools in which "humanistic education" was provided, as taught in the colleges of the Fathers or in the high schools and liceus of the country, were still far from the classic literary ideal to which they were subordinate in the Empire, by dint of the tradition of Jesuit teaching and the conception of culture that was still dominant in the nineteenth century, they did not become sufficiently democratic so that one can consider them "schools for the people," either through their quantitative expansion (552 secondary schools in 1936 as compared with 35,555 primary schools in the same year) nor in their objects and their organization. Blocked by their own growth, which did not permit them to equip themselves efficiently nor to recruit their professors with assurance and led them to pick them generally from a great variety of professional groups, worked upon in their internal structure by new tendencies and the introduction of new cultural elements, they certainly entered upon a critical period of transition, one of whose consequences was the lowering of the level of teaching and a lack of "quality" in the culture which they were called upon to provide within the framework of their specific objects in our system of education. Between two different ideals, not opposed, our educational reform oscillated, hesitating, generally forgetful of the fact that it is not by their content,—by the subjects which they teach,—but rather by their objects, that is the spirit in which they are taught, that one must define humanistic education, which is capable of taking on new forms. Without losing their original character, what constitutes their proper function and confers upon them their profound organic unity,—"to form the spirit of youth, to give them a general culture and to make of them men who cultivate everything which exalts man,"—the secondary schools will find new forms of humanism, as yet barely sketched, which will arise within the spirit of the time and in which —if the content of culture is amplified and the concept of it is transformed—present day civilization will be reflected as in a living image.

But modern civilization of a profoundly industrial and technical character, is the epoch of specialization, and specialization in Brazil, restricted in the field of education to higher professional education during the Empire, began in the field of the liberal professions. Thence, at least in part, the conflict between the present tendencies of secondary education and the three hundred year old tradition which made of it in the colony an education in the humanities as an end in themselves and in the Empire linking it exclusively to the liberal professions to which it gave access, conserved the humanistic character and accentuated it, and by that character as by that bond, provided all the appearance of an anti-democratic culture, one of the privileged classes. In contrast to North America, in which the history of higher education is closely con-

---

statistics, and rarely in those of other countries." The number of students registered went up from a little more than two million in 1932 to almost 3,110,000 in the school year 1938, revealing a growth of 50% in comparison with the first figure, or 40%, if we take into account the growth (10%) in total population in the same period. Out of a thousand inhabitants in 1932, we had only fifty pupils registered; in 1937, this number went up to 62, and in 1938 it reached 70,—which represents a considerable growth in the network of schools of the primary level, whether common or completion in type, and it is the greatest growth known in an equal period in the last fifty years. (Cf. *O ensino no Brasil no quinquênio 1932–1936*. Instituto Nacional de Estudos Pedagógicos. "Boletim no. 1", Rio de Janeiro, 1939.)

nected with that of religion and the organization of churches, under the influence of different religious sects, it is the history of secondary education and not that of higher education which in Brazil, from the beginning of the colony, was bound up with the history of religion and especially with that of the Jesuits. From this point of view, the organization of higher professional education, in the time of Dom João VI, may be considered as a reaction against the Jesuit education in general culture, or a "pedagogical revolution," probably inspired by the school policy of the French revolution. Certainly the schools of medicine and surgery and the school of military engineering, as well as those of economics and agriculture, which did not take root, were instituted by the State with the object of recruiting the personnel to direct various public services: surgeons, military engineers and colonial administrators. However, the absence in the government of Dom João VI of the idea of creating the university, the foundation of isolated higher schools outside of organized universities, and narrowly specialized, and the lack of interest in law courses which were only founded in 1827, in the first reign, show the retarding influence of the men of the Revolution, the child of the Encyclopedia which issued from the philosophy of the seventeenth century, men who abolished universities, suppressing even their names and who, although they had a broad conception of higher education, as Jaques Cavalier observes, "had neither the time nor the means to work it out and on the other hand, worked toward a conception that was very different, that of restricted establishments, each one dedicated to a particular subject matter and without any relation between one and another." [3]

Of all the faculties created at the beginning of the nineteenth century and administered entirely or directly by the State, those which grew most were the law schools in Recife and Olinda, either on account of the closer relation which their plan of studies had to the *studia generalia,* based on Latin, Greek and rhetoric, or because of the opportunities which law courses, destined for the professional preparation of lawyers, opened up upon other careers such as teaching and journalism, politics and administration. But if these schools shone with a more intense brilliance, all of them— the law, medical and engineering schools, developed their influence and their intellectual activity, which in some respects was notable, but due to their very narrow professional specialization, it was not easy for them to open their doors "to the new disciplines which the progress of science causes to be born and to extend their field of action." The absence, in a system of higher education, of faculties of philosophy and letters and of sciences, created to promote teaching and scientific research, left our culture, during the whole period of the Empire and during more than forty years of Republican regime, almost completely outside the movement of scientific renewal which was at work in the western world. There was no school for intellectual and scientific specialization in the whole period of the Empire, nor was there any technical specialization of real importance, for it was scarcely begun in the schools of arts and crafts, privately established, and did not succeed in being more than isolated and fragmentary essays. If, then, to the schools of higher professional education,—law, medicine, pharmacy and engineering, we add those for the teaching of art,—the Academy of Fine Arts and the Conservatory of Music, we shall have the complete picture

[3] Jacques Cavalier, *L'organisation de l'enseignement supérieur en France.* In "L'organisation de l'enseignement supérieur," I., pp. 103-167. Institut International de Coopération Intellectuelle. League of Nations, Paris, 1936.

of the organization of special education in a society based on conformity and servile labor, without industrial life, and with only elementary necessities, in which education was beginning to be diversified according to the liberal professions and could not become complicated until much later by virtue of the greater complexity of social life.[4]

In a society of economic and industrial structure so rudimentary down to the time in which the first great rise in industries took place in the country, it cannot surprise us then to find the domination which the liberal careers and consequently the schools that prepared for these professions maintained down through the Republic. Even in 1932 in São Paulo,—the greatest agricultural center and the most industrialized of all the States of the Union—while 147 professional men graduated from the Faculty of Law; 72 from the Polytechnic School and the Engineering School of Mackenzie College; 49 from the Faculty of Medicine; and 127 from the School of Pharmacy and Odontology, the number of graduates from the Higher School of Agriculture reached only 22, and those who completed the course of Veterinary Medicine in São Paulo were only 7. There was still no school for higher technical and industrial education; there was no official school, down to 1934, destined to intellectual and scientific specialization, to teaching and research at the same time. The schools meant for the preparation of primary school teachers (normal schools), the technical and vocational schools and those of commerce, which existed in great numbers, remained on the secondary level in their plan of studies. If we take the data collected by the general censuses of 1872, 1900 and 1920, with reference to the occupations of the population of Brazil, we find that from 1872 to 1920 the figure per thousand inhabitants which represents the liberal professions kept increasing; and this increase is further affected in an emphatic and undeniable way, by the statistics on the schools destined to prepare men for these professions, according to which in 1900 there existed 19 law schools, 11 medical schools, 12 of pharmacy and odontology, and 11 of engineering, for 5 of agriculture or agronomy, 2 of veterinary medicine, one of chemistry and three faculties of philosophy, sciences and letters in the whole country. But this marked preponderance of the liberal professions is not to be explained only by the social and

[4] In fact, in the capital of the Empire, in 1874, among establishments of special education, beside the Medical School, Central School, and the Military School, there were no others except a Commercial Institute, with thirty-eight students, and, in the field of the arts, the School of Arts and Crafts, founded in 1856, which, born amid disdain, for many years was a pilgrim, struggling and begging, the Imperial Academy of Fine Arts, with a hundred and twenty students and fifty-seven auditors, and the Conservatory of Music, with seventy students and thirty-one auditors. We do not mention the diocesan seminaries, for they belong to the two types of education, general and special, the latter marked only by the ecclesiastical disciplines clearly aiming at preparation for the priesthood. All the schools preparing for professions come under the head of "special education,"—an expression used in contrast to "general or common education," or education without the idea of specialization, that is, primary and secondary education. This type of education, however, is called in present-day statistics, "specialized education," while the expression "special education" is reserved for schools for the abnormal, feebleminded, or those with a physical defect, and the backward. In relation to schools of this last type, there were under the Empire only the Institute for the Blind and that for Deaf-Mutes, which in 1874 had respectively thirty-five and seventeen pupils, out of a population of more than twelve thousand blind and ten thousand deaf-mutes, to judge by the statistics given by Pires de Almeida in a work to which we have already referred more than once. (*L'instruction publique au Brésil.* Histoire-Legislation. G. Leuzinger e Filhos, Ouvidor, 31, Rio de Janeiro, 1889).

economic conditions of the environment, which particularly favored it and by the age-old traditions which imprisoned within the framework of professional teaching, meant for the liberal professions, the whole higher education of the country, keeping it as indifferent to intellectual specialization and scientific research as it was hostile to the idea of bringing together the faculties in a university body.

If, during the Empire and in part of the Republican period, these schools had a supplementary function—that of nourishing our spiritual needs, maintaining culture on a high level, and broadening our horizons—which explains their intellectual and social influence, the function of professional men, far from diminishing, really increased in modern civilization; the schools were organized to train these men, and the professional role was ever more important within the narrowly defined limits of their fields of specialization and their technical work. With the appearance after 1932, of new types of higher schools destined for research and high studies, that supplementary function could no longer be so marked, that function which for more than a century they had been called upon to exercise within the limits of their specific object and which came as much from the atmosphere of general culture in which they were bathed, constantly renewed by humanistic studies in the colleges of the Fathers during the Empire, as from a process of "compensation" with which they supplied the deficiencies of our higher culture, and also by the very nature of the professions for which they prepared,—especially those of medicine and law. The members of the liberal professions, obliged to undertake longer studies, which still were not too much specialized, not only had time to cultivate themselves and extend their general knowledge, but also (and this is true especially for the men of law and the doctors) were more in contact with life, being called upon as they were professionally to examine more complex problems, to see suffering close to, and to consider man in his whole personality. Hence, perhaps, the smaller contribution in this respect of the engineer, who is struggling for the most part only with matter and tends more easily to confine himself to his specialization, to the narrow field in which he works, and to forget the human, to see only technical returns. But, if this supplementary cultural function was reduced in our traditional higher schools, the importance of their specific functions grew. The man of law found opening to him in a period of profound political, juridical and social transformation, vaster fields of study, of exploration and of constructive work. The doctor was called upon by the thousands to undertake a rude effort in the urgent organization of the struggle for health and life in rural populations as well as in cities, in the fields as well as in the cities, that have been brutally built on the basis of enormous industrial growth; and as to the engineer, the field which was offered to his various technical specialties, in the mechanical and industrial civilization which arose from the progress of science and its application to human activities, was ever larger.

But, among the special types of education created in the time of Dom João VI, who promoted the "professionalization" of higher education, it was military instruction for the army and the navy which exercised the least influence and had, during the Empire, the slowest progress. We were not and we are not a people of conquerors, struggling with a hostile environment and moved to an imperialistic policy of expansion, and therefore with a historical geographic predestination for the career of arms. If we had no vocations nor warlike traditions, our concern with military and naval education, conducted on a systematic basis, on a plane which should meet the needs of national defense, dated only from the first quarter of the nineteenth century, with Dom João VI and, more especially, from Independence. From Portugal we had received no inheritance of military culture; neither the conditions of the time nor our formation imposed upon us the necessity of constructing such a culture, nor did economic resources permit us the organization of a great warlike machine with the industry and education that belonged to it. It must be for this reason, above all, that the education preparing officers and military engineers inserted into schools of general and special culture, at once civil and military, took more than sixty years to acquire autonomy and a physiognomy of its own in a system of national education. The Royal Military Academy,[5] founded

[5] Founded in 1810 by Dom João VI (Law of December 4, 1810), the Royal Military Academy installed itself in the following year (April 23, 1811) in the Academia do Trem, whence it moved in 1812, to the building on the São Francisco Square which is still the seat of the Polytechnic School of Rio de Janeiro. In 1822, when Independence had been proclaimed, it took the name of Imperial Military Academy; in 1832, that of Military and Naval Academy, and the Imperial Naval Academy became a part of it (1832–1833), and in 1839, that of Military School. In the organization of the Military School there appeared for the first time the General Staff course, and it was from this course that in 1835 (decree no. 1536, of January 23, 1855) that the last two years were taken to make the School of Application. The Staff course, writes Tasso Fragoso, "may be said to be limited to the fundamental preparation, and the latter to professional training." In 1858 the Military School was reorganized, and called the Central School (decree no. 2,116, of March 1, 1858), and the General Staff course moved to the Military School of Application, from which it returned in 1863 to the Central School, together with the courses of artillery and engineering, as a result of the new reforms. The separation of civil and military engineering, which began in 1858, was only completed after the Paraguayan War, in 1874, when the Central School was changed to the Polytechnic School (decree no. 5,600, of April 25, 1874) and when there arose, with its annex,—the Preparatory School of the Court,—the Military School, with a five year course, the first four years of which made up the General Staff course, and all five, the course of Military Engineering. By decree no. 330, of April 12, 1890, under the leadership of Benjamim Constant, the Military Schools of Rio de Janeiro and Pôrto Alegre were reorganized, and came to have a four year course, to give the basic scientific preparation to future officers, and an extra complementary year for each branch of the service (Infantry, Cavalry, and Artillery). The Higher War College, created in 1889, continued with three courses (Artillery, Engineering, and General Staff), each two years in duration. After the reforms introduced in 1898, with which military education took a step backwards, there came for the first time, in the reorganization of 1905, the School of the General Staff, and "with it a decided step in the direction of progress was taken." In the structural changes in military education, made in 1914, 1918, and 1919, "the General Staff School kept its general lines." It was, however, with the coming of the French Mission that there began, according to the observation of Tasso Fragoso, a new era in the history of military institutions. In his words, "there was at once created a School of Administration; the Veterinary School was further developed; an attempt was made to complete and improve the teaching in other services, such as Health and Communications, and above all, it may be said that the General Staff School was really created." After the revolution of 1930 military education in Brazil took on new life: the Military School in Realengo was reorganized, now ready to move to Resende,—a school of higher professional character, with a four year course, for the training of officers of all four branches (infantry, artillery, cavalry, and engineering), on top of which were added the School of Arms (one year), which prepared for promotion up to the rank of colonel, the General Staff School (three years), whose course is indispensable for promotion to the rank of general, and the High Command Course (one year), for the advanced training of colonels and generals; the Technical School started a new phase in its history of training of specialized military engineers; the School of Geography enlarged its plans; the Aviation School developed notably, now under the Ministry of Aeronautics, created in 1940; the schools for health, veterinary medicine and administration were

by Prince Regent Dom João VI, on the model of the French schools which exercised a marked influence on our military teaching for more than a century was meant, in fact, above all, to train officers and military engineers and also, after 1839, in which year the course of civil engineering was created, to train the personnel of military engineers and those of public services. In the slow evolution of this type of professional higher education, we may distinguish four separate phases: (1) from the beginning of the Royal Military Academy in 1810 down to the separation of the two courses, civil and military, in 1874, with the splitting of the old Central School into the Polytechnic School and the Military School as autonomous institutions; (2) from this time down to the definitive creation of the School of the General Staff in 1905; (3) from 1905–1930, a period which marks a new era in the history of military institutions with the coming of the French mission; and (4) from 1930 on, in which military education acquires the greatest development which the history of the country records and which is characterized by the enrichment and greater complexity of institutions as well as by a growing tendency toward specialization and mechanization.

The course of the General Staff which arose for the first time in 1839, side by side with the courses of the different arms (infantry, cavalry, artillery, engineering), when the Imperial Military Academy was transformed into a Military School, had as its object, writes Tasso Fragoso, "to form not officials skillful in the knowledge of tactics and strategy capable of aiding their chief in the command of the armies in operation, but versed principally in topography and geodesy, and consequently capable of carrying on reconnaissance and organizing the cartography necessary in peace and in war." Although in 1858, with the decree no. 2,116 of March 1st of that year, the two schools,— the Central School into which the Military School was transformed and the School of Applied Military Art created in 1855 (School of Application) both under the Ministry of War,—"began to move toward their new destinies," it was only in 1874 that the two fields of study, civil and military, were definitely separated, the Central School being transformed into the Polytechnical School and the Military School being reorganized independently of this as a school for the preparation of officers. Since it is a question of the reform that was undertaken immediately after the war with Paraguay was terminated, a war that had been going on for five years, "in a foreign country to which we took more than 100,000 men and a powerful squadron," it is surprising that military instruction had profited nothing from the war, unless it be through the dissociation of the two schools, which was rather the product of a normal evolution than a consequence of this great event. General Tasso Fragoso explains the fact not only by the circumstance that the teaching in the schools continued to be conducted by officers who had not taken part in the fighting, but also by the political tendency of the great republican movement in running down that war as it did all of the work of the Empire.

reformed, and schools or centers for advanced training and specialization of officers were either created or enlarged (Coast Artillery School, Motors and Mechanization). This was the period of most rapid and fruitful technical progress and specialization in all fields. (Cf. Lt. Colonel Joaquim Marquês da Cunha, *A evolução do ensino militar no Brasil.* In "Anuário da Escola Militar," no. 1, 1914, pp. 9-58; J. Carlos Martins, *Origem da Escola Militar.* In "Revista da Escola Militar," Ano XIV, no. 27, August, 1934, pp. 60-62; A Sampaio Pirassununga, *O ensino militar no Brasil.* In "Revista Militar," 1936; Tasso Fragoso, *O ensino militar e a Escola de Estado Maior.* Lecture given in 1931 in the General Staff School. In the review "Nação Armada," no. 5, April, 1940).

This is, however—this fact of the separation of the two schools in 1874—the culminating moment in the nineteenth century in the evolution of military education, which in 1889 took a decided step with the creation of the Higher School of War. It was further developed, with the reform of Benjamim Constant, who, according to the correct observation of Tasso Fragoso foresaw "a solid theoretical preparation," but without the complement of a perfect, practical education, and it entered finally in 1905 upon a new phase of its progress with the creation of the General Staff School, with a new plan of studies more adequate to the special object of that institution.

The difficulties and vicissitudes through which the naval academy passed were certainly not the same. They did not have a less profound effect upon its evolution. This school was founded by the initiative of Dom João VI, the first institution of its kind in Brazil meant for the formation of naval officers. The Royal Naval Academy, the origins of which go back to 1808, and which functioned for more than thirty years in the guest houses of the Monastery of São Bento, changed its name various times on various occasions without any great alteration in the character of its teaching. In 1832 the Imperial Naval School was incorporated in the Military School, from which it was again separated in 1833, undergoing in 1832 and 1839 the most important reforms through which it passed during the Empire, and down to the modifications introduced in 1891, at the beginning of the Republican regime. The organization of naval education in an autonomous institution from the beginning of its foundation and throughout its history for more than one hundred years, if we except the brief critical period of 1832–1833; the practical and more specialized character which these studies took on, especially after 1839; the voyages of instruction on board an armed naval ship, with which the teaching was completed, and which opened to the future officers wider horizons and greater possibilities of contact with different cultures, and the role which the Navy, from the period of Independence, was called upon to play, contributed in large part to maintain naval education on the higher level and to break down the resistance and to overcome the difficulties which the conditions of the environment still opposed to its reform and development.[6] In the Republican period,

---

[6] The Royal Naval Academy, founded in 1808 by Dom João VI, was installed in that year, along with the company of Marines, in the hospice of the Monastery of São Bento. It was in that building that the Naval Academy functioned from 1808 until 1832, when this School, uniting with the Military Academy, moved to the Square of São Francisco de Paula, from which it returned once more, almost two years later, to the Monastery of São Bento (1833–1839). In 1821 this establishment for naval education came to be called the National and Royal Academy of the Navy, and after the proclamation of Independence, the National and Imperial Naval Academy. The decree of March 9, 1832, signed by the Regency, reformed the Military Academy of the Court, adding to the school of Marines and giving it new statutes. In the Military and Naval Academy which resulted from this union, in 1832, there were taught "mathematical and military sciences, as well as the design which is proper for Army officers, Naval officers, and engineers, and in its four essential classes." The Academy, divided by the new organization into four scientific courses, 1) the mathematical courses, four years, 2) the military course, 3) the courses in bridges and roads, and 4) naval architecture, the last three being two year courses, came to operate with fifteen professors and seventeen substitutes, "with the same salaries and prerogatives as those which the professors of the law courses of Olinda and São Paulo receive," (art. 10). By the decree of December 19, 1833, it was ordered that the Naval Academy and the Company of Marines should be reestablished "on the footing they used to have," before the union decreed by the above mentioned law of March 9, 1832, and the Naval Academy, as an autonomous institution, returned

beginning in 1891,—the date of the first reform of naval education in that regime,—down to 1930, naval education, which in 1916 was still limited to the Naval School, more than one hundred years old, and to the schools of apprentice seamen, took on a new life, not only because of various reforms, of which one of the most important was that of the administration of Alexandrino de Alencar, but also through the influence of the American naval missions. Military education and naval education entered upon a new phase, respectively, with the French mission to the Army and the American mission to the Navy, to whose already illustrious traditions, in spite of the fact that they were recent,[7] there had been lacking, up until that time, the experience of great foreign teachers to enrich them.

Doubtless the Military School, writes Tasso Fragoso, "already existed with an acceptable plan of studies, but it lacked the essential thing; competent and authoritative professors to teach us the art of command. . . . Its old professors, truly self-taught, hunted in their books with laudable energy for the lessons which they should transmit to their pupils, but they spoke of operations which they had never taken part in. We must confess (concludes the illustrious military leader) that we only really learned the important service of the General Staff, that is the art of directing troops and provisioning them, after the mission had taught it to us." The military and naval mission, after the first World War; the experience of the revolution of 1930; the high point which militarism reached in the world, and the imperative needs of national defense imposed a total renovation of military technics and of their teaching which grew more complicated in proportion as the cultivation and art of war grew complicated. At that

---

to its original home in the Monastery of São Bento. The regulations handed down by decree no. 27, of January 31, 1839, moved the Naval Academy on board a warship (the ship Pedro II), where, according to the terms of the decree, the students taking the course were quartered as boarding students. No great reform took place in naval education during the second reign. In 1866, the Naval School, whose courses were attended by 94 students (71 candidates and 23 civilians), kept up a theoretical and practical general course, four years long, consisting of basic subjects and special disciplines (astronomy and its application to navigation, ballistics, naval tactics, hydrography, topography, steam engines applied to navigation and naval architecture), the instruction of the last year being given in an armed warship on a long voyage. There was also the Practical School of Naval Artillery. In 1886, with the name which it still bears, of Naval School, the Naval School (Escola de Marinha) and the Naval College (Colégio Naval) were united. By decree no. 1256, of January 10, 1891, the Naval School was reorganized; it was still operating in its buildings on the Island of Enxadas, and its educational structure was divided into two courses: 1) the preliminary course of one year; and 2) the higher course, of four years, or three for candidates, and one for marines. This course was completed by training voyages, three months long. "In spite of the reforms through which we have passed in recent years," the Ministerial report of 1891 asserted, the school has not "yet reached the level of other such schools in other countries." It was in the first quarter of the present century in the two administrations of Alexandrino de Alencar, and especially in the last decade, 1930–1940, that naval education became more complex in structure and made more rapid progress, to which the American naval mission made an important contribution. The Naval School is today installed in the magnificent buildings which the government of Getúlio Vargas had constructed, on Villegaignon Island, connected with the mainland by a causeway. (Cf. A. Z. Fonseca Costa, *Esboço histórico da Academia de Marinha*, 1873; Ernesto Sena, *Escola Naval. Seu centenário*, 1908; Lucas Alexandre Boiteux, *A Escola Naval. Seu histórico* (1761–1937). 1st part—from the founding to the majority of Pedro II. National Printing Office, Rio de Janeiro, 1940).

[7] Henrique Boiteux, *Os nossos almirantes*. 8 volumes; Lucas A. Boiteux, *Ministros da Marinha*, 2 vols.

time, after the revolution of 1930 and the government of President Getúlio Vargas, there began the period which was certainly the most brilliant and fruitful in the history of our military and naval education, which improved and developed in the various schools of their specialization. To remedy their early rigidity, to supply their gaps, and to follow the evolution of the science and technique which tend to grow more specialized and also to extend their field of action, the institutions of military and naval education were led to reform themselves into new organisms, more malleable, perhaps more restricted, but certainly better adapted to modern necessities. It is not only the organization of teaching which was enriched and broadened in the growing complexity of their institutes, either new or reorganized, destined to train officers of the various arms in their higher training and specialization, as in the field of the art of commanding (General Staff School), in the knowledge of sanitary tactics, and in the mechanism of administration. Not less was the progress made in the field of material accomplishments. Schools of aeronautics were created; the first factories making airplanes were installed; the navy yard entered upon a period of activity; and there rose in Resende and on the Island of Villegaignon magnificent buildings that were to be the homes of the traditional schools destined to train officers of the national Army and Navy.

During more than a century, since the Empire had been founded, these two military careers and the liberal professions were the only ones which were within reach of Brazilians by means of higher education. Technical activities, routine in character and still undeveloped, required no special preparation and did not exert the slightest attraction upon youth. When Independence was proclaimed, the forms of a still semifeudal Brazil built on the regime of slavery had still not been restored by the industrial revolution which was beginning slowly to develop at the end of the past century. However, from the moment at which Brazilian society attained a certain degree of differentiation, the education founded essentially upon class distinction and with an extremely limited base of common education also began to be diversified according to classes and professions with a marked tendency toward the liberal careers. Professional specialization in these careers was not, however, dictated by the social necessities of the environment, but at the same time corresponded to the manner in which work was divided and organized at that historic moment (we refer to the beginning of the nineteenth century), in which sciences were not sufficiently developed nor their applications to industry sufficiently extensive, and therefore the programs of the higher schools could embrace the whole of knowledge. The type of instruction and culture based upon humanities and looking toward the liberal professions was what was called for by that society which a trip through Brazil of a hundred years ago reveals to us— a society worked upon by political differences, but consisting of a population, mentality and customs that were uniform, with an elementary economic system similar in its external characteristics and in its domestic organization, with its litters and stage coaches, with its herds and its oxcarts, and without very marked differences between the life of the country, of the fazendas, and of the sugar mills, and that of the great villages that its cities of mansions, quiet and somnolent, really were.

Activities in the field of industry, almost entirely dominated by slaves and mestizos, continued still to be limited to the sugar mills, the extraction of gold in Minas Gerais, and to little industries with their small groups of artisans. Industry which had arisen, resting upon slave labor in the sugar mills in the seventeenth century, and upon the exploitation of gold in the eighteenth century, undertaken on a large scale, but according to old processes brought in by the Portuguese, may be said to have been still, in the nineteenth century, in its twilight period, less than in the period before the dawn, vegetating in routine and tradition. From the system of labor based upon slavery and from the domination, in consequence, of the slave element in manual and mechanical activities, that society which had barely emerged from the colony, had inherited a lack of interest, if not a repugnance, for technical occupations and physical labor. The arts and crafts, generally relegated to slaves, mestizos and aliens, were, moreover, in the whole colonial period, as Francisco Montojos observes, "the privilege of immigrants who transmitted their knowledge only stingily, often denying their true technique to apprentices—the technique to which they gave the name of 'secrets of the craft.' In the shops with incompetent masters, apprenticeship was carried on empirically and without educational ends." The force of prejudice with relation to manual and mechanical work, which enjoyed little social esteem because they were considered to be proper to slaves, could not fail in this society of academic élites to be opposed to the spread of technical, agricultural, commercial or industrial education, which, in the development of industries, found no element upon which to rely to conquer that prejudice inherited from the colonial system of education and culture and powerfully supported by the economic, agricultural and slave-holding system that was dominant during the whole period of the Empire.

In the face of social necessities and the current mentality which reigned in that liberal society of agricultural economy and colonial habits, organized upon the basis of conformity and preoccupied with its literary and juridical creations, no truly efficacious reaction in favor of crafts and industrial occupations was possible. Certainly, in the second half of the nineteenth century, the development of sciences became so considerable in Europe and North America and the field of its applications was so extended that there began to arise new schools of a specialized character, and teaching in the technical field tended to be diversified, taking as its base one industry or group of industries. This specialization of education which was less closely related to class distinction than to the growing occupational diversification, corresponded to the extraordinary development of industries, to the improvement and growing specialization of technique and to the favor which these careers began to enjoy in various countries such as Germany, England and the United States. But in Brazil, slavery constituted as yet an insuperable barrier to the development of agriculture and of industrial arts and occupations. During the whole period of the Empire and for a large part of the Republican period, economic organization, before and even after the abolition of slavery, offered no basis of industrial action whence there could begin that movement that was stirring the society of several nations, leading them through the development of their industries, to diversify their education, not only from one class to another, but within the same class, according to the variety of careers and occupations. It was this state of affairs, more than the lack of foresight of the government, which explained the odyssey of that "sublime madness" as Rui Barbosa called it in his emphatic words on the institution of the School of Arts and Crafts founded in 1856. "Born mid disdain" (writes Rui Barbosa, drawing a somber picture which remained without effect), "it wandered, struggled and begged during long years; it climbed the stair of indifferent power, harder, more avaricious and more humiliating than that, the remembrance of which makes

Dante so bitter; it came down, many times dismissed with the neglected indigence of lazy or useless mendicity. Budgets and ministers there were, who had for it only the poverty of three contos of reis—a ridiculous amount, a bonus for a secretary. Thanks to this shameful situation, the fault of citizens without enlightenment and to government without foresight, its light came to be extinguished temporarily for the people." [8]

The imperial society was rolling along and appeared to be in equilibrium, when two elements came to disturb this equilibrium—immigration and the abolition of slavery —but almost indifferent to technique, the progress of which in other countries only excited its imagination. In the Republic, during about thirty years, Brazilian society, with industry barely being formed, could not, and did not try to assimilate, except perhaps in the field of agriculture, modern technique which was in a period of rapid and constant progress, while society appeared to be fixed within limits and a framework which it judged immutable. And everyone still told stories of his childhood, his first trip on the railroad, his amazement when electricity came to replace oil and gas, his fear when for the first time he heard at the end of a wire a human voice. Scientific culture and technical culture were still very little spread among the bourgeoisie, as well as among the intellectual and governing élite, which were content in general to admire en bloc in a literary manner the "marvels" of science and technique with no real concern for enlarging the field of their application in the country. Youth itself, amazed by techniques—which it imagined through the romances of Jules Verne as marvellous, poetic and human—but still strongly attracted by the liberal careers, did not feel either melancholy or restlessness before such changes, in its romantic admiration for the surprising transformations from which industrial civilization had arisen, as if it had not the slightest awareness of the threat which weighed upon old things—traditions and institutions—nor of the problems of a moral or political order which were already arising everywhere as a result of the industrial revolution.

The preponderance of the agrarian economy which still constituted the backbone of our whole economic system; the insufficiency of organization of industrial labor, scarcely in its beginning, and the introduction of new techniques, which was still recent did not in fact justify the specialization of technical education, of the creation of new special schools. A professional differentiation in the field of technology would have to commence, as it actually did, in agricultural schools, in the beginning by tentative moves which aimed at the establishment of this type of teaching, as in Minas Gerais the creation of the Agricultural School in Juiz de Fora, owing to the efforts of Mariano Procópio, and the institutes of Itabira and of Uberaba "which for some time enjoyed the inspection of Henri Gorceix" and, later, with the installation of great agricultural schools in Minas Gerais and in São Paulo. There were created at that time, in 1901, in Piracicaba, the Luiz de Queiroz Higher School of Agriculture, the foundation of which in São Paulo was authorized in 1892 (law no. 26 of May 11, 1892), with ten experimental stations, and then the School of Agronomy and Veterinary Science of Pôrto Alegre and, in 1917, in Viçosa, the Higher School of Agriculture and Veterinary Science of Minas Gerais. Commercial schools for elementary and middle teaching and rare higher schools, like that of Pôrto Alegre, followed closely upon the agricultural

[8] Rui Barbosa, *Discurso pronunciada no Liceu de Artes e Ofícios*, November 23, 1882. In "Orações do Apóstolo," pp. 69-113. Published by "Revista de Língua Portuguesa," Rio de Janeiro, 1923.

schools.[9] In the field of industry and of technical education, besides the schools, the necessity for which was still not felt and which for that reason were short lived, there were created schools for artisan apprentices, begun by Nilo Peçanha in 1909 (decree no. 7,566 of September 23, 1909), to the number of 19, one in each State, with the exception of Rio Grande do Sul, where there was maintained, as an institution of this character, the Instituto de Parobé, founded in 1908, and connected with the Technical University and duly supported by the Union; the Institutes of Montauri (of electricity and mechanics), of Industrial Chemistry and Borges de Medeiros (of Agronomy and Veterinary Science), which made up the Technical University of Rio Grande do Sul, and the Instituto Electrotécnico of Itajubá—a move we owe to the eager enthusiasm of Teodomiro Santiago. In this field, however, we have not yet passed beyond the limits of the vocational schools of a traditional type and of primary or middle grade, which besides having an archaic type of organization, did not show, even in São Paulo, a quantitative growth which would demonstrate any real deviation from the normal lines followed for more than a century by the educational policy of the country.

The great changes did not come until after 1930. In 1918–1920, after the first

[9] Certainly the oldest of all, the present Higher School of Agriculture, of Piracicaba, was founded only in 1901, under the name of Luiz de Queiroz Practical Agricultural School; the law which created it (no. 678), however, dated from 1899, and went back to 1892, the first law of the State of São Paulo on agricultural education, which authorized "the founding of a Higher School of Agriculture" in the State. The Luiz de Queiroz Agricultural School, which two years later underwent a complete reformation with the regulation approved by decree no. 1266, of February 18, 1905, in accordance with the legislative authorization of 1903 (art. 24 of law no. 896), included elementary, middle and higher courses, the last of which was for the training of professors of agriculture, industrial managers, experts for agricultural services and agronomists. Reorganized in 1912 by law no. 1,536, which suppressed its elementary and middle courses; in 1919, by decree no. 3,070 which gave it a new organization; in 1925, by law no. 2,111, which authorized the conferring of the degree of agricultural engineer to its graduates, and in 1931 by decree no. 5,206, it was joined, in 1934, to the University of São Paulo. In Rio Grande do Sul, the Borges de Medeiros Institute,—a higher school of agriculture and veterinary science, also reacted at the beginning of this century,—forms, together with the Montauri Institute (of electricity and mechanics) and that of Industrial Chemistry, the Technical University of Rio Grande do Sul. The Higher School of Agriculture and Veterinary Science, of Rio de Janeiro, is the most recently created one: in 1933, with the reorganization of the Ministry of Agriculture, under Minister Juarez Távora, it split into two schools,—the National School of Agriculture and the National Veterinary School, while the course in industrial chemistry, which in 1920 had been included in its course of study, was made into the institute of Chemistry, set up at this time; this course had been taken out of the internal structure of the School in 1926, and considered as an extension course. The present National School of Agriculture which resulted by the split of the Higher School of Agriculture and Veterinary Science, will be located, with a new organization, in buildings which rose under the administration of Fernando Costa, Minister of Agriculture (1937–1941), at kilometer 47 on the Rio-São Paulo Highway, in the Fluminense Swamp; here it will operate, in the most splendid agricultural property of the country, and in addition branches of the National Center of Agricultural Education and Research will function, too. In 1917, through the efforts of Artur Bernardes, the Higher School of Agriculture and Veterinary Science of Minas Gerais was founded in Viçosa: recognized as an official school by the government of the Republic, this school, entirely devoted to agriculture, with its three courses, elementary, middle, and higher, is one of the model institutions for agricultural training in the country. The bi-monthly review *Ceres*, which is published in the Higher School of Agriculture, of Viçosa, is kept up by the Ceres Club—a scientific and cultural association in the school, and aims to spread both theoretical and practical teaching on agriculture, veterinary science and rural industries.

World War, which brought, with its effects upon Brazil, as everywhere, a greater variety of points of view and a division of the intellectual élites who took different positions, the first upsurge of industry contributed to enlarge our ways of thinking and of feeling and to modify in various ways the character of the nation. Among the different factors which aided in bringing about the transformations which then took place, there figured the rise of industry, which resulted in part from the necessities imposed by the war and its consequences; the phenomenon of urban concentration which was observed to be most intense in the center south (Rio, São Paulo and Minas), as also in Rio Grande do Sul and Pernambuco, and the move toward São Paulo, not only of the currents of immigration which flowed especially in the direction of that State, but also of the internal movement of migration. In fact, if in the first five year period (1920–1925) 279,540 persons arrived at São Paulo, of whom 204,950 came from Europe and 74,590 were Brazilians, who came by the hundreds from almost all of the States of Brazil through stations of the North and of the Sorocabana railway, in the following five year period (1925–1929) São Paulo received 461,668 immigrants, of whom 171,-727 were Brazilians. It was in this period and under the pressure of its industrial development, and not in 1909, as Rui Barbosa proclaimed, with more prophetic vision than sense of reality, that "a stupendous metamorphosis in the *Yankee* fashion transformed into a magnificent capital" the city of São Paulo in which, only then, did one begin to feel "the growth of force, the exuberance of the sap, the flow of the milk of life in the tumescence of those mysterious breasts which bend over the cradle of pre-destined races." [10] But it was in the decade of 1931–1941, with the growing development of industry and the improvement of techniques that there began to flow vigorously, in the direction of a new civilization, new economic forces, now coordinated by the direction of captains of industry and sufficiently powerful to raise in the to and fro movement of economic and industrial life, technical, social and political problems that had scarcely been felt by earlier generations.

It is not only the social and economic landscape which was transformed in this last decade. With the beginning of restrictions upon immigration after 1930, the movement of internal migration, which had grown after 1920, took on the proportions of an impressive movement of human masses from all of the States of Brazil toward the agriculture of the south, and especially of São Paulo. The population density of some States, consequently, decreased, as for example Pará and especially Alagoas, which in 1920 was one of the most densely populated States, and in which the census of 1940 found about 20,000 inhabitants less than in the previous census, owing in large part to the movement of families from Alagoas to São Paulo in the last twenty years. The phenomenon of urbanization took on a growth without precedent in the history of the country and the populations of Pôrto Alegre, Curitiba, Belo Horizonte, Recife and, more than all, those of Rio de Janeiro and São Paulo grew notably. If we compare the results of the census of 1920 with the preliminary data which are revealed by that of 1940, we find that while in 1920, 648,153 agricultural units were listed, the total of the returns of this investigation in 1940 rose to 1,898,200, or almost triple, and as to industry, the number of units listed by the census rose from 13,336 in 1920 to 44,359 in 1940, beside 3,788 in the field of transportation and communication. If we take,

[10] Rui Barbosa, *Discurso pronunciado na Faculdade de Direito.* In "Excursão eleitoral ao Estado de São Paulo," Garraux, 1909, São Paulo, pp. 117-133.

for example, a State as progressive as São Paulo, which contributes more than 44 % of the value of industrial production of Brazil, and another, still in the early phases of its industry, like Goiaz, we find in figures of the census, two aspects of this extraordinary development. In São Paulo, in whose industries there were already working in 1941 more than 800,000 specialized workmen, the number of factories in the capital alone rose to 8,016 in that year, and one alone of the cities of Goiaz shows today a greater industrial movement than the whole State in 1920, when there were in Goiaz 16 manufacturing establishments in which 244 workmen were employed. On the other hand, the successes of socialism after the World War and the new ideologies of the right and left, came to change completely the character of our political struggles and to bring about between 1930 and 1937 new groupings of parties.

The problem of education which remains central since 1920 came to concern all; and the reforms and currents of thought in education were colored by new social and political ideas which represented a variety of points of view and the diversity if not the conflict of doctrines. But, of all the problems which become acute and the study and solution of which began to be imperative under the pressure of affairs, the one which acquired most importance was that of industry and of technical training by means of professional schools of the primary, middle and higher grades, and of specialized schools (mechanics, chemistry and electricity, for instance) in which theoretical instruction in these sciences should be given and technical instruction on the industries to which these principles would be applied. It was at this time that there were created institutions of the type of the Technical School (of chemical and electrical techniques) of Mackenzie College, founded in 1932, and that vocational education took on new life, especially in the Federal District and in São Paulo; this, in the five year period 1932–1936, reached in its various forms (commercial, technical-industrial, domestic and artistic) a growth represented in index numbers from 100 to 174, "which really shows a new tendency on the part of youth to seek the studies preparing them for work.[11] In the federal field, various acts clearly indicate the new tendencies, which were sketched in local reforms and activities of a private character, and of which one of the most characteristic symptoms was the financial outlay of the States and of the Federal District, and the growing concern with vocational education, which in 1940 went from 4% to 8% of the total appropriation for the schools. The government of the Union which, from 1910, had been giving a subsidy to commercial education, the development of which was owing to private initiative, established in 1931, for this type of teaching, entirely reorganized, an inspection upon the model of the inspection of secondary education;[12] organized in 1934, in the reform of the Ministry

[11] *O ensino no Brasil no quinquênio de 1932–1936*. National Institute of Pedagogical Studies, "Boletim no. 1," 1939.

[12] Commercial education, of which we find no important traces during the Empire (the only news we have being of a "commercial course," created by law, and a Commercial Institute which had 38 students in 1874), really began to develop in the present century. In fact, it was not until 1902 that the first two schools of commerce were founded,—the Academy of Commerce, of Rio de Janeiro, by Dr. Cândido Mendes de Almeida, and the Practical School of Commerce, in São Paulo, which took the name of the Alvares Penteado School. In 1905, Counselor Rodrigues Alves, then President of the Republic, sanctioned the first federal law on commercial education, declaring these two schools to be of public utility and recognizing as official the diplomas which they conferred. Stimulated by this decree, there followed other private undertakings in this field. In 1926 the original program of studies in commercial schools officially recognized was modified

of Education and Health, the Superintendency of Industrial Education, into which the Inspectorate of Professional and Technical Education begun in 1932 was transformed; created in that same year, the Federal Technical University (decree no. 24,-738 of July 14, 1934), of which the National School of Chemistry came to form a part. This school, organized in 1933 by decree no. 23,172 and passing out of existence in 1937, added its institutes to the University of Brazil; and the government attempted in other ways, not always the safest, to find the new road which the industrial concentration in cities and the growing tendency toward specialization and occupational differentiation pointed out to it.

It is above all after 1937, however, that the federal government resolutely entered upon this new road, giving educational policy a new course and inaugurating its most brilliant and fruitful phase in the field of professional education in all of its different grades and forms. The speeches of President Getúlio Vargas showed clearly in various incisive passages of a far reaching character which it is not necessary to exaggerate, these tendencies, as well as his own personal attitude, which is frankly directed toward technical and professional education in the country. The Constitution of November 10, 1937, establishes in art. 129 the new attitude toward educational policy. This article is of capital importance, not only because it is a vigorous expression of this new tendency, but also because of the means which it establishes for the organization of professional teaching and its development. "Prevocational and vocational education, destined to the less privileged classes, is in the educational field the first duty of the State. It must execute this duty by founding institutes of professional education and giving subsidies to those established by States, Townships and private individuals, and private or professional associations. It is the duty of industries and of labor unions to create in their specialties apprenticeship schools for their members. The law will regulate the carrying out of this duty and the powers which belong to the State with regard to these schools, as well as the aids, facilities and subsidies which will be given them by the government." (Art. 129). In the Constitution, there were, then, traced in this way, the general lines of educational policy which opened up new perspec-

---

by decree no. 17,329. The law which reorganized the public education of the Federal District in 1928, under the leadership of Fernando de Azevedo, gave new structure and quarters to the Amaro Cavalcante School of Commerce, which, reformed once more, under the administration of Anísio Teixeira, in 1933, became one of the best business schools in Rio de Janeiro. The most important of the changes through which business education in this country has passed was, however, that of Minister Francisco Campos, who reorganized it in 1931, by decree no. 20,158, giving it a new outlook and structure; this law looked forward to a vocational guidance service and established the system of inspection for business schools. By this decree of 1931, commercial education was divided into two courses: 1) the preparatory, three years; and 2) the technical, made up of five courses: the secretarial course, one year; courses of bookkeeping and sales manager, two years, and the last two, for actuaries and expert accountants, three years. This system of the technical teaching of commerce, based on the preparatory course, is completed by a higher course of administration and finance, in three years, for admission to which a diploma as expert accountant or actuary is required. The diploma of bachelor in economic science is conferred upon the student who finishes this course. The schools and courses of commerce are subject to inspection by the Ministry of Education, which has a Division of Commercial Education which is the central organ for control and guidance of all technical commercial education in the country. (Cf. Josué Montuelo, *Considerações sôbre o passado e o presente do ensino comercial brasileiro*. In "Ilustração Brasileira," no. 81, ano XX, January, 1924, pp. 46-47.)

tives both in the enlargement of the field of professional education and in its *processus* of adjustment to social changes coming from the development of industry, the division and rationalization of labor, the multiplication of occupations, the organization of unions, and therefore, the new necessities of individuals. The modifications of industrial conditions, such as the improvement and extension of work with machines and the employment of scientific processes of manufacture, changed occupational necessities, which could not be met by professional schools of the old type without a close relation to industry.

Hence, the resolution of the State, in accordance with the constitution, to reorganize on a new basis the whole apparatus of technical and occupational education, to adjust it to the necessities of agriculture, commerce and industry and to insist upon the cooperation of the unions and factories in vocational education by creating and maintaining in the factories themselves, schools for apprentices and courses of industrial advancement for adults and minors.[13] The systematic plan of industrial education laid down by the government of the Union,—and the program for agricultural education is not less comprehensive and efficacious,[14]—includes schools with brief or

[13] Joaquim Faria Góis Filho (Reporter), *A aprendizagem nos estabelecimentos industriais.* Interministerial committee appointed to regulate the functioning of completion courses for workers in industry. Rio de Janeiro, 1939.

[14] Vocational courses in agriculture, the development of which had begun in the early years of this century, with the founding, in 1901, of the Higher School of Agriculture, of Piricicaba, in São Paulo, and had spread later, with the creation of the Borges de Medeiros Institute (of Agriculture and Veterinary Science), in Rio Grande do Sul, of the Higher School of Agriculture and Veterinary Science, of Viçosa, in Minas Gerais, and of the Agricultural Institute of Tapera in Pernambuco, also received, in this decade, the vigorous support of the government of the Union. The old Higher School of Agriculture, of Rio de Janeiro, was divided, in 1933, into the National School of Veterinary Science and the National School of Agriculture. Through the activity of Fernando Costa, in the Ministry of Agriculture (1937–1941), there rose in the Fluminense Swamp, at kilometer 47, on the Rio-São Paulo Road, the buildings destined to house not only the National School of Agriculture, but also branches of the National Center of Agricultural Study and Research. These notable structures, remarkable in every way, were constructed according to "a landscaping and architectural plan for the construction of a great Brazilian agricultural property that was really impressive." There was made at the time a plan for the thorough reorganization of agricultural education, including schools of various levels and types, beside extensive teaching of the illiterate or those who had not finished primary school, as well as boys under 18, with regular primary schooling, to be given by agronomists, rural administrators and agricultural experts. According to this plan, there were to be installed: a) at least one middle school in each State of the Union, for vocational education of middle grade in agriculture, given in two year courses, for rural administrators, and three year for agricultural specialists; b) and five regional schools of agriculture, for higher education, given in four year courses. This structure, the foundations of which would be laid for extensive education on a big scale, given by services for encouraging agriculture, and would develop in a vertical direction, with the regional agricultural schools of middle and higher level, was to have as the keystone of the arch the National School of Agriculture with its various levels of teaching in agriculture and agronomy and courses for advanced training and specialization. The National School of Agriculture, a center for spreading agricultural teaching and research, would be organized as a model institution to serve as a pattern for others. These initiatives and accomplishments on a large scale, like the breadth of this plan, embracing agricultural education of all grades, and having Rio de Janeiro as its center, and peripheral branches in all the States, indicate clearly the way in which the government of Getúlio Vargas was moving with regard to technical professional education, and especially, agricultural education (Cf. Fernando Costa, Lecture given on the commemoration of the first decade of the government of Getúlio Vargas. Ministry of Agriculture, Official Printing Office, Rio de Janeiro, 1941).

complete courses destined to train artisans in the various sectors of industry, or industrial high schools into which the schools of apprentices created in 1909 will be transformed, schools destined to prepare master workmen, and also technical schools which have as their object the formation of technicians as intermediaries between artisans and engineers. Industrial schools will receive, according to this plan, already decreed by the federal government (decree law no. 4,073 of January 30, 1942), pupils who have finished their primary course and who, when they have finished the industrial high school, will be able to enter technical schools which will also be open to students coming from the secondary schools. To carry out the plan approved by the organic law of industrial education, there had already been hired in Switzerland in 1941, 44 specialists who would be joined, to complete the staff of foreign technicians, by 25 engineers or experts hired in the United States with the special object of directing industrial education in the industries themselves and directing sections or taking charge of courses in the first federal technical school to be installed in the capital of the country. In 1939, work upon the Industrial High School of Manaus was already concluded, with an area of more than 20,000 square meters and almost 6,000 of the area already constructed, with a capacity for 400 pupils; and others to be concluded with equal plants and according to the same type as the High School of Manaus, for the use of Industrial High Schools of Pelotas in Rio Grande do Sul, of Goiânia in Goiaz, of Vitória in Espírito Santo and of São Luiz in Maranhão. In addition to the Technical-Industrial School which would be located in Rio de Janeiro, the federal government decided to create and maintain another in São Paulo with two courses, one a fundamental course of four years and a higher course of three years, meant respectively to educate industrial technicians in various sectors and to promote higher specialization, preparing specialists in various branches of industry and in industrial teaching.

But, however great may have been the progress made by occupational specialization as a consequence of the division of labor and the modifications which took place through the phenomena of urbanization and industrialization, it cannot be claimed that marked variations in the hierarchy of occupational types have resulted from them. If it is true that education was becoming a "specialized function," in proportion as society was divided into classes and professional groups, it is not less certain that these "special types of education," divergent only after a certain point up to which they were the same—that is common education—were erected in our school system upon the basis of a collective mentality which remained essentially the same, under its various appearances. Under this variety and wealth of types of special education, at the base of which lies the process of the break-up of general society into a greater number of functional groups, with different occupations, tendencies and modes of life, there subsisted, although it was changing, but still resistant, that old ideal which came down from a century-old tradition and which society was trying to carry out in its members by way of education. Now this system of education which was being transformed, or better was being enriched by specialized schools of a technical character superimposed upon common education which was also a function of the condition of society, was guided basically, in primary and secondary education, almost according to the same conception which the country had of man in the time of the Empire and the Republic, and which reflected its necessities, its special mentality and its historic past. Down to the World War of 1914–1918, no profession, in fact, appeared to have greater attraction and to offer more to youth than those of the law, medicine and engineering. The professions which were chosen, not according to the degree and type of intelligence which they required, but according to the social setting and dominant mentality, differed according to the environment, varying from one class to another, and the liberal careers served as ladders for social mobility, while manual and mechanical activities were reserved for individuals of a lower social category. It was still believed that it was necessary to carry on a liberal profession, to have not a "different type" of education so much as a greater degree of education than for the crafts or industrial profession.

Certainly, men have in the liberal professions, as Léon Walther observed, "more liberty in choosing the means which will lead to professional success—which does not happen in industrialized occupations where the worker is more controlled by fixed technique in which nothing can be modified." [15] But it was less by the more intellectual character of the work which they required, than because they were "socially" more reputable that these professions continued to exercise a great power of attraction. Moreover, as during almost a century the only higher schools that existed in the country were those which prepared for the liberal professions, no other opportunities were open to young men except these careers and activities purely and preponderantly intellectual. For a father, a fazendeiro or businessman or merchant to make of his son a bachelor or doctor of laws was to rise in society. Young men, educated in these schools, brought with them all the promise of the future, and mothers dreamed of nothing for their daughters except these husbands who were bachelors of law, doctors or engineers. In the commercial or rural hierarchy, even if he did not carry on his profession, the bachelor or doctor of law took a higher place. If the majority were ambitious to exercise their profession, all desired the title. Being a civil, military or naval engineer never succeeded at any time in our history in becoming the dominant ambition, as one may see in the contrast year by year between 1828 and 1930, in the number of polytechnical schools with relation to those of law and medicine, or in the number of students graduated by the different schools training for the liberal professions. [16] The engineers, who

15 Léon Walther, *Orientation professionelle et carrières libérales. Etude psychologique.* Delachaux-Niestle, Neuchatel-Paris VIIᵉ. 1936.

16 If we take as a sample the statistics on the University of Minas Gerais, made up of the three traditional schools of higher learning,—the Law School, founded in 1892, and the Engineering School and Medical School, founded in 1911, and coordinated respectively in 1916, 1917 and 1918, we shall find a clear proof of the preponderance of the two schools of law and medicine over engineering. The three higher schools making up the whole were united in the University of Minas Gerais by state decree no. 22,579, of March 27, 1933. All of them had professors of distinction, like Tito Fulgêncio, Alves Pereira, Estêvão Pinto, Mendes Pimentel, Orosimbo Nonato, Francisco Brant, and Mário Casassanta, in the Law School; Borges da Costa, Baeta Viana, Alfredo Balena, and Otávio Magalhães, in the Medical School; and Alvaro Silveira, Baeta Neves, Lúcio José dos Santos, among others, in the Engineering School. The number of students graduating from the Law School, between 1935 and 1940, was 735, the number from the Medical School 458, while the graduates of the Engineering School in the same period were no more than 94. The traditional preponderance of graduates of law or medicine over those of polytechnic or engineering schools was thus maintained during this five year period, in which it can be demonstrated that the preferences of young students in the Universities of Rio de Janeiro, São Paulo, and Pôrto Alegre did not alter or change direction.

from the time of imperial society had always enjoyed social esteem, were now able in the hierarchy of the professions to dispute the primacy with bachelors of law and physicians; and if scientific and technological ideas were still not triumphant, one could not only perceive greater enthusiasm for the application of science, but also agricultural and industrial studies tended gradually to gain in esteem, in an epoch in which the field of their activities was constantly being enlarged the sciences were finding every day new applications, industry was developing and new wealth was being created. Side by side with the intellectual professions with their deep-rooted traditions, which presented no evidence of decline, technical professions and schools began to exercise a greater attraction over youth and to enjoy greater social prestige, coming from the activity and perfection of technical services in all the fields of agricultural, commercial and industrial activity.

Although intellectual and scientific specialization had taken on a new movement after 1930 with the creation of the Brazilian universities, it did not in that decade (1931–1941) reach the development and public favor which technology and technical schools won. The fact is that the first universities of Brazil, organized according to the regime instituted in 1931 by the reform of Francisco Campos, but actually founded in 1934, 1935 and 1939, were born or were formed in an unfavorable atmosphere laden with hostility and prejudice. In a time characterized by the predominance of material civilization and in which the basis of our whole system tends to be ever more one of technique, special and technical schools commenced everywhere to acquire greater influence, if not domination, while, at least in western Europe, the prestige of the universities, still modelled on traditional types, was declining. Beside this, democracy, which is founded upon knowledge and reason, and which in the political field was, as Francisco Campos observes, "the form taken by the spirit which presided over the development of science and the industrial revolution," had entered after the first World War upon a grave crisis which had its effects in Brazil and was marked in the last ten years. Now, between democracy, which, being relativistic, pluralistic and sceptical, "excludes absolute points of view and all monisms," and the universities which, destined to further the progress of the sciences, can only develop in a climate, not of belief in a truth, but of research for truths and therefore of a spirit of restlessness, doubt and relativity, there exist so intimate a dependence and so essential a relation that the development and crises of a democratic process are accompanied always by progress or decadence of university institutions. If we add, moreover, that the process of leveling brought about by the rule of the masses which commenced among us to enter into closer relation with human knowledge, everywhere generated a crisis in culture, gravely menacing the principle of aristocracy or quality "which is inherent in all higher culture," we shall have almost the complete social picture of the epoch in which the first Brazilian universities were created.

Moreover, we had on various occasions already noted the contrast between the enthusiasm with which nations, opening their doors to the currents of influence of the west, accepted European technical knowledge and methods and the careful and reserved way in which they came to cultivate philosophy and scientific research, above all in the field of the social, political and economic sciences. However, with the first

official faculties of philosophy, sciences and letters that were created,[17]—that of São
Paulo in 1934, that of the Federal District in 1935, and that of the University of Brazil
in 1939, we not only differentiated and complicated our system of higher education,
up until then limited exclusively to the professional schools, but we also began a
transformation of mentality and opened new opportunities to the higher culture of
the country. It was not only that new fields were opened up for intellectual and scientific
specialization, but a new spirit came into our system of culture and education. Philosophical and scientific culture up until this time had been carried on only by great
efforts and with all of the disadvantages of self-teaching, or in the higher professional
schools under the direct influence of professors who had an extraordinary value due
to the breadth and clearness of their points of view. Rarely sought out, philosophical
speculation and scientific activity, when they were reduced to pure dilettantism, constituted no more than a temporary "departure" from the professional line laid down
by the strength of an irresistible calling, or suggested and assured in this or that career
by purely chance support. Intellectual, philosophical, scientific activity was not considered in this way a work discipline methodically conducted, beginning at the school
bench, but an "adventure of talent," in its expeditions, at times brilliant but always

[17] The first university founded in Brazil was that of Rio de Janeiro, created by decree no. 14,343,
of September 7, 1920, and organized in that same year by decree no. 14,572, which approved its
statutes. In 1927, through the efforts of Mendes Pimentel the University of Minas Gerais was
founded in Belo Horizonte. The decree which set it up was signed on September 7, by President
Antônio Carlos and submitted by Francisco Campos. But both the University of Rio de Janeiro
and that of Minas Gerais were made up by simply uniting the three traditional institutions for
professional training, the Schools of Medicine, Law, and Engineering (or Polytechnic Institute),
which already existed. No institution for higher intellectual or scientific specialization was made
part of these universities organisms. It is from 1931 that the first real university organization of
Brazil dates; it was set up by decree no. 19,851, of April 11, 1931, signed by the Chief of the
Provisional Government, Dr. Getúlio Vargas, and submitted by Dr. Francisco Campos, Minister
of Education and Health. Although the University of Rio de Janeiro had, as a result of decree
no. 19,852, which gave it a new organization, added a Faculty of Education, Sciences and Letters,
among other schools, this new institution was not set up until 1939. The University of Minas
Gerais, created in 1928, and reorganized in accordance with the federal law in 1933 united in
that year, by state decree, no. 22,579, of March 23, the schools of Medicine, Law and Engineering, which still are the only component parts of that university system. The first Faculty of Philosophy, Sciences and Letters founded in the country, by official action, was that of the State of
São Paulo, created and installed during the government of Armando Sales, and made part of
the University of São Paulo set up by state decree no. 6,283, of January 25, 1934; its statutes were
approved by the federal government, by decree no. 39, of September 3 of that same year. State
decree no. 5,758, of November 28, 1934, which created the University of Pôrto Alegre, includes
among the establishments which go to make it up, a Faculty of Education, Sciences and Letters
(art. 2) which is still to be set up. So the fact is that only the University of São Paulo, created
in 1934, and that of Brazil,—into which the University of Rio de Janeiro was transformed in 1937,
and which absorbed the University of the Federal District, founded in 1935,—have in their systems institutes of higher studies and disinterested research in the various fields of pure science.
In addition to the Faculty of Philosophy of São Bento, founded in 1908, when only courses of
philosophy and classics were functioning, and the Free School of Sociology and Politics, created
in 1932, also in São Paulo, there have been founded since 1939, through private efforts, the
Instituto Santa Ursula (Faculty of Education, Sciences, and Letters) in Rio de Janeiro, the
Instituto Sedes Sapientiae (Higher Institute of Pedagogy, Sciences, and Letters), of the Sisters
of Saint Augustine, and in 1940, the Faculty of Philosophy, Sciences, and Letters, of the Catholic
University of Brazil.

399. Medical School of the University of Minas Gerais, at Belo Horizonte. Principal façade. Photo by Leonar.

400. Engineering School of Pôrto Alegre, Rio Grande do Sul. Principal façade of the Institute of Engineering.

401. Engineering School of Pôrto Alegre. Astronomical Institute. Section of Meteorology and grounds.

402. Building of the Military School of Rio de Janeiro, at Realengo in the Federal District.

403. General Staff College, housed in a magnificent building on the Praia Vermelha in Rio de Janeiro. Photo by Vosylius, in collection of the National Census Bureau.

404. Technical School of the Army, on the Praia Vermelha, Rio de Janeiro, for the training of specialists in military engineering. Photo by Rosenbauer.

405. The old Naval School, the origins of which go back to the Royal Naval Academy, founded in 1808 by Dom João VI. General view of the buildings on the Island of Enxadas.
Photo by the Naval School.

406. Naval School of Rio de Janeiro. Central court of the new and sumptuous building on the island of Villegaignon, now linked to the mainland.
Photo by the Naval School.

407. The National School of Fine Arts, in its new building put up after the transformation of Rio de Janeiro and the opening of the Rio Branco Avenue, according to the city plans of Pereira Passos.

408. Luiz de Queiroz Higher School of Agriculture, at Piracicaba in the state of São Paulo. Principal building.

409. National Technical School, in the Federal District. One of the great technical schools of the systematic plan of industrial training drawn up by the central government and established by the decree-law of January 30, 1942.

Photo by the Documentation Service of the Ministry of Education and Health.

410. National Technical School of the Federal District. One of the galleries of the central courtyard.
Photo by the Documentation Service of the Ministry of Education and Health.

411. Technical School of Vitória, in Espírito Santo. General view.
Photo by the Documentation Service of the Ministry of Education and Health.

412. Technical School of Curitiba, in Paraná. One of the schools which, according to the plan of the central government, will train artisans and master craftsmen in various types of industries. Photo by the Documentation Service of the Ministry of Education and Health.

413. College of Philosophy, Science, and Letters of the University of São Paulo. One of the laboratories of the Department of Zoology. Photo by Liberman, São Paulo, 1942.

414. Institute of Education of Rio de Janeiro, built in 1928–1930, reorganized in 1933.
It trains primary-school teachers and school administrators and councilors.
Photo by Nicolas Pie, 1939.

415. Institute of Education of the Federal District. One of the wide galleries of the third floor, opening on the sumptuous central court. Photo by Nicolas, Rio, 1930.

416. Institute of Education at Salvador, Bahia, with its excellent modern equipment. Photo by Voltaire Fraga, in Brazilian Institute of Geography and Statistics.

417. Army School of Physical Education, the most important center and leading influence in Brazilian physical education, near Fort St. John, Rio de Janeiro. Principal building. Photo from the Archives of the Army School of Physical Education.

418. Army School of Physical Education, beside Fort St. John—a school that has done pioneering work for physical education in Brazil. View of the porticoes and the Hebert tower.

superficial, along unknown ways. There was no consciousness acquired in the schools of that fact that just as spiritual life requires a perpetual effort to enable the soul to know and control itself, so the scientific career imposes an almost ascetic discipline in its habitual practice of objective methods of investigation, knowledge and experimental verification. What among us almost never was more than an adventure of the intelligence should have become under the pressure of a new cultural environment, a severe but fruitful discipline, looking to the development of the critical spirit and with it of scientific methods.

That the absence of these schools of higher studies and of pure research representeted one of the gravest lacks in our cultural system was demonstrated once more by two facts, each extremely significant, when there were created in 1934 and 1935 the first two faculties of philosophy, sciences and letters maintained by the State. We never were so keenly aware of the scarcity in the country of really eminent men in the various fields of intellectual and scientific specialization, men who would be capable with the solidity of their culture and the efficiency of their methods of inaugurating courses in the new universities. It was necessary to have recourse for the teaching of almost all the subjects to missions of foreign professors—French, Italian and German,— hired in their own countries for the Faculty of Philosophy, Sciences and Letters of the University of São Paulo and for the Faculty of Philosophy and Letters, and that of Sciences of the University of the Federal District, created in 1935, whose insitutes were incorporated by decree no. 1,063, of January 20, 1939, in the University of Brazil. These professors, some of whom were truly remarkable, like a Gleb Wataghin and a Luigi Fantappié, among the Italians, a Henrich Rheimboldt and an Ernst Breslau, among the Germans, a Robert Garric and an Emile Coornaert, among the Frenchmen, to cite only names among the first specialists who were hired, brought, in fact, more than the contribution of their culture, a new spirit and new methods of work destined to perfect and revolutionize processes of teaching and the common techniques of research and investigation. This was not a fact which should surprise us,— since it had been on various occasions pointed out, even in the decade prior to the creation of the universities, in the investigations which were promoted by the *Estado de São Paulo* in 1926, under the direction of the author of this book, and in 1929 by the Brazilian Education Association.[18] But, with this fact, we confirmed on all points the analysis, severe only in appearance, of the few who had studied the problems of higher education from all points of view and who, from the time of the Empire, had been pointing out the grave lack of universities in our cultural system. If, in the field of applied sciences, there had already been developed before the advent of the universities in 1934, sections of research and experimentation in different institutes, and if in the Institute of Manguinhos research activities had already transformed that school of experimental pathology into the greatest center of training and of the spread of scientific culture in the country, almost everything remained yet to be done in the dif-

18 Cf. Fernando de Azevedo, *A educação pública em São Paulo*. Problemas e discussões. Investigation for "O Estado de São Paulo," in 1926. Part III. *O ensino secundário e superior*, pp. 287-457. Series Brasiliana, Vol. 98. Editora Nacional, São Paulo, 1937; *O problema universitário brasileiro*. Investigation made by the Section of Technical and Higher Education of the Brazilian Education Association. "A Encadernadora S.A.," Rio de Janeiro, 1929.

ferent branches of pure science in which, with the exception of the natural sciences, the original contributions of Brazilians were extremely rare.

In this regime in which the problems raised by society were "continually handed over to practical men without technique and to technicians without science," and in which the practical and utilitarian interest of "professionalism" was dominant, as that professionalism had been cultivated for more than a century by higher professional schools, people did not easily come to understand that the study and use of applied sciences depended upon the knowledge and upon the progress of the pure sciences. Hence the resistance which the faculties of philosophy had to meet from the beginning (and this is one of the facts to which I referred), and which contributed extraordinarily to retard their development and disturbed them in the exercise of their essential functions. All those who struggled for their creation or made efforts to maintain them, attacking with their critical spirit a tradition that had been established in higher education, drew upon themselves a coalition of the systems already in existence, of preconceived ideas and hidden inertia, and spent their lives in fighting as innovators for those institutions whose pedagogic role should be that of research and of the discovery of new truths. The traditional professionalism of higher education, raising applied science to the first plane, and accustomed to train its clients for the careers of practical life, received with distrust and prejudice the new faculties to which the priority given to free research and the absence of an immediate practical end gave the appearance of luxury institutions in the eyes of professional men. As we had not up until that time had those great schools to which the inheritance of scientific research is transmitted generation after generation, we had not yet become aware of the fact that research is the characteristic of universities and that it is not possible to create the scientific spirit except by study and the investigation of pure science, that is to say, a type of investigation that is completely objective and free from any considerations whatever except the investigation and the discovery of truth.[19]

Meanwhile, in spite of these and other resistances, the Faculty of Philosophy of São Paulo, the oldest of all, could show in 1942, eight years after its foundation, the characteristics of a life of its own and vigorous signs of vitality to such an extent that we no longer talked of giving it a solid base, but of promoting its progress in accordance with its specific functions in the university system. In 1941, the number of students registered in its various sections reached 530, beside 350 who were preparing for its courses in the University College; and the registration of candidates for its entrance

[19] "Although recognizing the practical value of truth," writes Francisco Campos, "it should not be for the sake of that value that the university investigates and searches for truth. In the investigation of truth, any interest other than that of the pure truth, instead of leading to its discovery, only serves to cover it with a thick veil, to disfigure it or twist and distort the face of truth. Chemistry did not develop when the interest which presided over research was one of a purely practical order, such as the desire to transmute other metals into gold; medicine in its turn remained stationary as long as the pre-clinical sciences did not free themselves from the practical interest and establish themselves as independent disciplines of a theoretical character. The social sciences, if they are still in a rudimentary and embryonic stage, owe the fact exclusively to practical interests of all sorts which in their investigation and by the very nature of their object, interfere with the purely theoretical interest in truth as truth and in its value as truth." (Francisco Campos, Speech given in 1933 at the opening exercises of the university. In *Jornal do Comércio*, Rio de Janeiro, March 9, 1933.)

examinations in 1942 reached 408, an extraordinary number that up until that time had only been found in the principal law schools. Although the proportion between the students who sought out matters of general culture and those who gave themselves to the study of applied sciences had remained frankly favorable to the latter, being about in the proportion of 3 to 1, it is certain that the situation improved somewhat, as can be inferred from the matriculation in 1941 and 1942 in the various faculties of philosophy, sciences and letters, and especially in that of São Paulo. Side by side with professional specialization, there was beginning to develop and to take on new life, a specialization of an intellectual and scientific character, especially in the field of physical and chemical sciences, in which there arose, graduated by the Faculty of Philosophy of São Paulo, physicists like Marcelo Damy dos Santos and Mário Schenberg, whose works on experimental physics and mathematical physics had a great effect in international scientific circles.[20] The first, graduated in 1936, in the following

[20] In more than a century since the teaching of physics was begun with the creation in 1832 of a chair of that subject in the medical schools of Rio and Bahia, that science has been cultivated among us only as "a subject to be taught." The first professor of the chair created by the reform of October 3, 1832, was Vicente Ferreira de Magalhães, a surgeon trained by the Bahia Medical School, graduated in 1829, and appointed in 1833 as the result of public competition. The Military Academy had as its first professor of physics and chemistry Brother Custódio Alves Serrão. Among those who achieved most distinction in the teaching of this subject in the Medical School of Rio de Janeiro, there figure Francisco de Paula Cândido (1805–1864), of Minas Gerais, who took his doctorate in the Medical School of Paris and left various works; Antônio Sattamini and F. Lafaiete Rodrigues Pereira (1887–1936), who under other circumstances, "with his solid mathematical culture and rare experimental ability, would have been (writes Francisco Venâncio Filho) one of our physicists, in the exact meaning of that word." It was Lafaiete Rodrigues Pereira who set up, in that School, the most modern physical laboratory in Brazil, which was enlarged and enriched later by Carlos Chagas Filho. Other educational institutions had illustrious teachers; among them, the old Military School, which was changed into the Central School; the Polytechnic School, created in 1875; the School of Mines, in Ouro Preto, the origin of which goes back to 1875; the Naval School and the various Medical schools and engineering schools which were founded after the setting up of the republican regime. Counsellor Sousa Pitanga (Epifânio Cândido de), the first professor of the Polytechnic School (1875), coming from the Central School, was the beginner of experimental physics in Brazil. Henrique Morize (1860–1930), a fine meteorologist, who held the chair of physics in the Polytechnic School, which today has a laboratory of physics considered one of the best in the country; Augusto Barbosa da Silva (1860–1939), who taught for more than forty years in the School of Mines; Oscar Nerval de Gouveia, one of our greatest teachers, in the Colégio Pedro II; Pedro Barreto Galvão, an esteemed teacher in his time; Adolfo de Vecchio, of the Naval School, professor from 1891 to 1915; these were professors who helped to develop the teaching of this science in its various aspects and raised it to a higher level. Among our contemporaries who are teachers with solid reputations we note Dulcídio Pereira, of the Polytechnic School of Rio de Janeiro; Adalberto Meneses de Oliveira, of the Naval School, and among younger men, Luiz Cintra do Prado, of the Polytechnic School of São Paulo. We do not know, however, in this whole period down to 1936, of a single original contribution in the field of mathematical and experimental physics. With the creation of the Faculty of Philosophy of São Paulo, in 1934, a new phase in history of these studies began, and Brazil for the first time was represented by its physicists in the greatest scientific centers of the world. In 1937 two Brazilians, Marcelo Damy dos Sousa Santos, of Campinas, in São Paulo, and Mário Schenberg, of Pernambuco, both born in 1914, who had studied in this Faculty, under the guidance of the Italian scholar, Professor Gleb Wataghin, undertook in Brazil the first scientific work which achieved great influence in international circles. All the works of Marcelo Damy dos Santos, about forty in all, show, in the opinion of Gleb Wathagin, a remarkable creative spirit and a deep knowledge

year attained the Wanderley Physics prize for his work "A Thermoionic Electrometer With Methods of Compensation," and for his studies on radiation and the techniques employed in these studies, and earned the important fellowship of the British Council for one year of study in Cambridge, where he conducted notable research and a new method of registering the passage of cosmic corpuscles (The Method of the Multivibrator), adopted already by some physicists in England and the United States. The second, Mário Schenberg, owed to his first publications in 1936 and 1937 an invitation to work with Dirac in Cambridge, and Fermi in Rome, both winners of the Nobel prize. He received a fellowship of the Guggenheim Foundation, and carried on among other researches, which already number more than forty, a study on the function of Dirac, the function of Green, the applications of spinor calculus to physics, ultramolecular cosmic radiation and mesotronic radiation, and an important contribution to the theory of new stars.

But, if the most notable progress was made in the field of physics, in which at least two students educated under the direction of Gleb Wataghin were judged by that great teacher to be capable of following him in the professorship and in the laboratory, the influence of the new attitude was also felt in other sectors of studies. In all the other departments of chemical and of natural sciences, as in the section of social science, geography and history, and in those of classic and modern literature, there were being formed, under the influence of the faculties of philosophy and of some eminent foreign professors who created schools, a group of new talents in fields that up until a short time ago had been almost unexplored in the country. In spite of the prudence and reserve with which we turned to the investigation of economics and social conditions, attitudes which were imposed by political factors, the social sciences themselves, in which through their very nature the zone of "dangerous thought" is broad, acquired in the last decade a development that is unprecedented in our cultural history. Everywhere, for that matter, especially in a period of violent political passions, as Louis Wirth observed, one can find examples of the difference that exists "between the effects of knowledge of the physical sciences and of the techniques and attitudes which are assumed with respect to them, on the one hand, and the effects of social science and the attitude we have toward it, on the other." In any case, whatever may be the restrictions which were imposed by circumstances upon the development of this or that field of study, philosophical or social, the number of specialists has grown a great deal in the various sectors of intellectual and scientific specialization developed and intensified by the rare schools of higher studies and of free research. If variety of individuals is necessary to the progress of human activity and if the work of the nation is more fruitful in accordance as more individuals aid it, the Brazilian universities which were instituted after 1934 had already begun to render an inestimable service to Brazil, meeting the ever growing need for men of science and technicians, not only preparing a greater number of these specialists, but also by perfecting their equipment and their teaching staff, so as to educate men equipped with better scientific and technical knowledge.

---

of physics, beside a rare skill in experimentation, and the very important scientific publications of Mario Schenberg have made him known as "a penetrating investigator and a man of uncommon knowledge in the various branches of mathematics and physics."

Of all of the higher professions, those which experienced the most growth with the creation of universities in Brazil were certainly the "gnostic professions," if we may thus define, according to the classification of Lipmann,[21] the professions of scientific research, that is, those in which the intellectual activity which consists in observing, comparing and distinguishing, is directed by a knowledge of the objective world. Training for the so-called "liberal professions," preponderantly intellectual, remains, however, in quantity and in the domination of schools of this type, the center of education and of resistance of the university system. In two universities like that of Belo Horizonte, which is exclusively professional and that of Pôrto Alegre, in which the schools which prepare for the liberal careers and for higher technical teaching form part of the same organism, no faculty of philosophy, sciences and letters was installed, and such faculties exist only in the University of Brazil and in that of São Paulo. Schools created for the "symbolizing professions" or artistic activities in which "the psychic task consists of projecting into the external world, by means of symbols, what the artist feels," were added to the field of the university, in the University of Pôrto Alegre, in which there figures a School of Fine Arts, and in that of Brazil—the richest and most complex university system of the country—to which were added in 1939 the National School of Music and that of Fine Arts. In the University of São Paulo, as in that of Belo Horizonte, the benefits and advantages of the university regime were not extended to these sectors of aesthetic culture, which remained outside the sphere of its influence. The technical professions,—those which aim at modifications and transformations of the external world—, are not strongly represented except in the University of Pôrto Alegre in which, in addition to the Engineering School which figures in each of the four official universities, there were incorporated the higher establishments for technical education belonging to the former Technical University of that State. The first Brazilian universities were made up as we see, according to the western European pattern and made up by means of coordination and subordination in a single system, of the existing higher institutes, varying according to the regions and among which a constant is the presence and the grouping together of the three schools destined to prepare for the liberal careers.

In this period of transition between the deep-rooted and traditional forms of universities and the "embryonic sketch of new structures which are being formed by means of essays and experiments that are more or less contradictory," the Brazilian universities, initially adjusted to the European pattern and subject to a direct and uniformizing influence of the central government, hesitated in their search for new forms, better adapted not only to the necessities of the time, but also to the economic and cultural peculiarities of each region. It is not that the conception of higher learning which presided over the formation of the university was not a broad one, especially in the first law signed by President Getúlio Vargas, which instituted the university regime in Brazil in 1931. Theoretically for the legislator, as for those who fought for their creation, the university was looked upon as "an organism including the whole of the sciences and their application, embracing all that can be the object of study, of research and of teaching,—letters, sciences and technical arts,—with as many departments as there are separate disciplines, departments not separated, but on the contrary, united in the

[21] Lipmann, *Psychologie der Berufe*, p. 483.

general unity of science." But, in the first place, there had necessarily to be organized about the existing nuclei, invariably made up of schools destined to train for the basic and indispensable professions, and whose solidity, assured by the constant flow of candidates, rested upon a century old tradition with regard to the liberal careers. They brought together and directed everything that could be found in their field of attraction and they still constitute, with the exception of two, mere groups of vocational schools destined to the training of students for the exercise of these professions. In the second place, modelled from the beginning on the European type, their tendency shown in the form which they assumed was one of adding to the schools of the professional type the faculties of philosophy and letters and those of science, in accordance with the standards on which they were based, and in consequence of proving more or less resistant to schools of other types, like those destined to aesthetic or technical cultivation, the progress of which, only possible when the industry of a country becomes more strongly equipped and achieves a hierarchy, did not justify the creation and incorporation of higher technical schools. We may add—to explain the slowness of progress and the hesitation of universities in their search for new structures—not only the tendency of the central power to impose uniformity, but also the fact that the effect of ideas corresponding to a new conception of life and of culture are first manifest in the culture of the vanguard before they descend to the politician to be carried out in a great work of reconstruction.

But it is not only in the various fields of philosophical, scientific and literary knowledge that specialization began to develop in the last decade under the influence of the universities or outside the orbit of their influence. Also in the pedagogical field or that of the professional training of teachers, this movement toward specialization had effects. Schools of preparation for teaching there were none in the country, except for some isolated experiments, outside the so-called "normal schools," destined to train primary school teachers and the progress of which really began after 1889 under the influence and in the warmth of republican ideals. These institutions which existed in all States and received, after 1928 in the Federal District, the first attacks upon their traditional structure were reorganized by the reform which they underwent in 1933 in Rio de Janeiro with Anísio Teixeira, and in São Paulo under the leadership of the author of this work, both aiming at the separation of the two courses, the preparatory and the professional, and putting at the basis of the training of the primary school teacher, the high school course required for admission to the higher schools. For teaching in the high schools, on a higher level and with greater responsibility, there was not required, however, that special preparation which for more than fifty years had been claimed and imposed upon the primary school teacher. From the time of the Empire down to the foundation in 1934 of the Faculty of Philosophy, Sciences and Letters of São Paulo—the first which was installed in the country on State initiative—the secondary schools, as we have had occasion to point out, "either were a field of apprenticeship and experiment for men who had left other professions and for the self-taught,—later often illustrious professors through their own efforts; or had to be—which is worse—a campaign spot for young men hunting for jobs to enable them to continue their studies and for professional men at the beginning of their career before they had established themselves in their profession." [22] After a regular and systematic preparation in the Faculty of Philosophy of São Paulo, which remained within the limits of its strictly cultural and scientific purposes, and in the Institute of Education, where they got their pedagogical training, the first teachers licensed for secondary education in Brazil won in 1937 their permission to teach.

With this event there began, in fact, a new era in secondary school education, the personnel of which up until that time, made up of men who had left other professions, or self-taught, or practical men with some experience in teaching, began to be renewed and to grow richer, although slowly with the addition of specialists educated in the faculties of philosophy, who in addition to their cultural and scientific preparations, received moreover the pedagogical training of candidates for secondary school teaching. A little later, the task that had begun in the preparation of teachers of physical education by the School of Physical Education of the Army created in 1929 and reorganized after the Revolution of 1930 under the administration of General Leite de Castro, took on new life and was transferred to the buildings which the government set aside for this school beside the Fortress of São João in Rio de Janeiro. Two other schools,— that of Physical Education created in São Paulo in 1933 and installed in 1937 and the National School of Physical Education and Sport, incorporated in the University of Brazil, were founded to extend to the civil field the activity which had been developed in the military field by the School of Physical Education of the Army, a pioneer in this movement in Brazil and for several years the principal center and focus of irradiation of physical education in the country. We did not, however, limit to the cultural and professional training of secondary school teachers and physical education teachers the efforts of the governments of the Union and of the States in the direction of training specialized teachers in various domains of teaching. Of all of the activities undertaken, looking toward the formation of master workmen,—of which before 1930 the most important was the old School of Arts and Crafts named for Venceslau Braz, soon transferred from the Union to the government of the Federal District and turned away from its object—none is more important than that of the government of President Getúlio Vargas which, in decree no. 4,073 signed January 30, 1942 established in its 80 articles the bases and the regime of industrial teaching destined to the preparation of industrial workers and workers in transportation, giving to the technical schools among other functions that of forming master workmen and specialized teachers for the industrial high schools.

All this diversity of interest, tendencies and ambitions, this constant search for new ways and this fascination of the broad horizon, or in other words, this growing differentiation in the fields of science, literature, technology and pedagogy could not fail to modify noticeably the cultural landscape of the country, breaking its monotony and enriching it with new aspects. Instead of a very homogeneous society with the same conceptions of life, the same mentality, and the same high occupations, there began to arise, although slowly, and limited to the principal urban centers, a society that was more differentiated by division of labor; instead of the bicephalism of a literary and professional culture (juridical and medical), of social prestige, which

---

[22] Fernando de Azevedo, *O magistério secundário.* Speech given at the graduation exercises of the first class of secondary school teachers, April 21, 1937, in the auditorium of the Medical School. Secretariat of Education and Health. Directorate of Education. "Boletim no. 13," São Paulo, 1937.

had been developed since the time of the first Empire and down to the Revolution of 1930—a culture with a more scientific basis and of élites that were more varied in their make up; instead of a uniform culture that was brilliant but excessively romantic, crystallized around the torches which had been lit with the higher schools of a professional type, and above all the law schools, a culture which is attempting to assert itself and to become differentiated in important variations of the basic type and of distinct types of personality, achieving new forms adapted to the environment and to historic climate. We know to what an extent the missions of foreign professors and scholarships and travelling fellowships to Europe and North America contributed to enlarge our horizon, to open up new perspectives, to indicate roads which lead to higher specialization, and to open the whole zone of culture in which new generations found their nourishment not only in letters, but also in mathematics and the sciences, not only in the past, but also in the life of the present which is the raw material of the future.[23] It is largely through these influences of eminent professors from various countries, hired abroad, and by the action at a distance of European and American universities on our young graduates sent abroad for advanced work, that Brazilian intelligence has been able to extend its field and to broaden the radius of its adventures. Already, in fact, it is not rarely that we find publications and monographs in which there appear with original points of view and even original contributions and in different degrees a fundamental individualism, a critical and scientific spirit, even a certain

[23] The courses of the Faculty of Philosophy, Sciences and Letters, of São Paulo, founded in 1934, were inaugurated in that year by foreign professors hired in France, Italy and Germany. There were altogether thirteen professors, of whom six were French, four, Italians, and three, Germans. In 1935 Etienne Borne, contracted to teach philosophy, was replaced by Jean Maugüe, who occupies this chair down to the present day; P. Arbousse-Bastide, professor of sociology since 1934, was joined by Claude Lévi-Strauss in 1935. Lévi-Strauss, a French ethnologist, was followed by Roger Bastide, in 1938; he is at the present time professor and one of the directors of the Ecole Libre des Hautes Etudes, in New York. Professor Ernst Marcus, in zoology, was contracted in 1936, to replace Ernst Breslau, who died in May, 1935; Pierre Monbeig was put in charge, in 1935, of the course in physical and human geography, instead of Pierre Deffontaines, who went back to Europe, after a year's stay in São Paulo; and Robert Garric was followed in 1935 by Prof. Pierre Hourcade, replaced three years later by Alfred Bonzon, the present professor of French language and literature. Among the professors under contract in the first two years of the Faculty, we find great names such as Luigi Fantappié, an Italian, in mathematical analysis; Gleb Wataghin, Russian by birth, a naturalized Italian, and a great physicist; Heinrich Rheimboldt, German, in chemistry, and Ernst Breslau, in zoology, Félix Rawitscher, also German, in botany and Robert Garric, a Frenchman, in literature, among others. In 1935, Francisco Rebêlo Gonçalves (1935–1936) was hired in Portugal for the chair of Portuguese philology; he was succeeded in 1938 by Professor Fidelino Figueiredo. The history of American Civilization was, from 1936 to 1940, in the hands of Professor Paul Van Orden Shaw, a North American. In 1942 there were still twenty-two foreign professors teaching in the Faculty of Philosophy of São Paulo; six of them had been there since the second year of its existence. From 1934 there passed through this Faculty,—without counting laboratory assistants,—forty-five foreign professors from various countries. Although the movement of Brazilian professors and students to other countries for advanced work and specialization was less important, there was constant interest in scholarships and trips for purposes of study. From 1937 to 1942, eleven graduates obtained scholarships, three of which were renewed. Two students did work in France, one in England, one in Italy, and seven in the United States, where various graduates are still in residence; students have turned to the United States since the second world war has made studying in European countries extremely difficult.

perhaps morbid negativism, a profounder respect for clear ideas, a love of objectivity and of analysis and even of subtlety, sharpened by a more penetrating sense of the complexity of things.

This tendency to specialization in all fields, from which we have begun to receive the first results, was, however, accompanied by the greatest effort made in the history of education in Brazil to achieve moral and spiritual unity by unity of education in its essential lines. For the first time, the central government, the influence of which went out over all the regional organization, paid serious attention to the problem of the education of the people and the training of Brazilian primary teachers, by means of a uniform organization of the normal schools, which would permit the horizontal movement of students by transferring from one institution to another, and of primary teachers from one State to another. Secondary education, both official and private, was reorganized on the same bases in the whole country and is directly inspected by the federal government. Its teaching staff is being gradually renewed by the addition of professors trained with a common point of view and licensed by the faculties of philosophy, sciences and letters. The extinction of the military colleges,—of which there remains that of Rio, created on March 9, 1889 and reorganized by decree no. 371 of May 2, 1890, but, as everything indicates, ready to pass into the hands of the Ministry of Education,—tends to complete this work of unification of secondary education in Brazil. It is not only by these and other measures put in practice on the plane of educational policy that we feel the force, not to say impetuosity, of that wave of uniformity which took shape and rose, above all since the coup d'état of 1937 and with the regime instituted by the new Constitution. Certainly all the provisions of the federal laws and decrees, aiming at the coordination of education, at the continuity and interpenetration of forms of education both scholastic and post-scholastic, and at the development of auxiliary mechanisms put at the service of national ideals, have given notable aid to bring about the institution of a national policy of education looking toward the spiritual and moral unity of the country. But, if we follow closely these pulsations of the national consciousness which proceed everywhere from economic and social events, deeper in their effects than the surface play of political forces, we shall find as elements of the support and encouragement of all the tendencies in the direction of uniformity, the greater facilities of communication and of transportation, the lines of aerial navigation which already cross the country in almost all directions, and the extraordinary progress of radio broadcasting, which permits us to bring, in fractions of seconds, the voice of the government of the Union to the most distant regions, which were formerly entirely isolated.

Science and industry, submitting to nature, dominating space and reducing distances, are in fact seconding the work of political and spiritual unification undertaken by the government in all its sectors. In the field of administration, by the Departamento Administrativo do Serviço Público (Administration of Public Service); in the field of statistics by the initiative and under the inspiration of the Instituto Brasileiro de Geografia e Estatística (Brazilian Institute of Geography and Statistics); and in the pedagogical and cultural field by the organs of guidance, culture and research of the Ministry of Education. The radio and the airplane, of all modern discoveries and inventions, are those which have most contributed to bring together and to make one the Brazilian people, constituting without doubt the most powerful instruments of which Brazil disposes to conquer its principal enemy—space. The white or red ribbons of the roads which cut the plain and go around the circle of our mountains and in which almost everywhere there is circulating, together with the automobile, the freed velocity of the rails; the broadcasting stations, whose progress was notable in this decade and especially after 1932, on account of the important role which they had in the Revolution of São Paulo, and the aviation fields which arise everywhere, lead to a higher level of social mobility, of mobility of values and of persons, bringing our cities and our interior closer to the principal centers of civilization in the country. The campaign of unification, strongly supported by the introduction of modern techniques of industry and transportation, thus preceded and is accompanied by legislation; and before entering into the laws which favor, regulate and discipline it, the idea of national unity had already entered our minds and our customs. So, then, while individual evolution is moving in the direction of specialization and there is taking place in the regions of urban and industrial civilization an ever greater diversification of functions, individual variations, which are spreading and multiplying, find a counterbalance in social democratization, and the community is evolving in the direction of growing equality and uniformity of all of its members. The idea on the march, in the last fifteen years, of the national policy of education and culture never had more favorable conditions for its development, as well as for the extension of educational services in which in 1940, 20.03% of the receipts of all the units of the Federation was being spent.

But, if it is in a progressive movement toward unity and a ever more comprehensive generalization, in an incessant effort toward oneness that the work of intelligence consists, this enormous task accomplished by the central government has been, in the political field if not also in the play of cultural forces, one of the most fruitful and appropriate to maintain, without failing to enrich it at the same time, the sacred inheritance of our history and our traditions, an inheritance which must be immortal. In contrast to what has happened in countries with an older civilization, the replacement of the tool by the machine, the revolution in consequence of methods of production, the conflict between the economic and the political, the rivalry of liberal democracy and of socialism, and the profound effects of industrialization and of urban life upon the organization of the family and of property, have not made Brazil return to the communal forms of primitive times. The economic and social transformations have taken place without the sacrifice of universal values, perhaps not specifically Christian, but at least in a broad sense, human, the persistence of which authorizes the belief to which Gilberto Freyre refers, "in the reform of culture on a basis that is at once personalist and socialist, universalist and regionalist." Certainly the whole economic, political and social structure in this new phase of humanity is being transformed also among us by a bloodless revolution; and the change which we witness in our country from a stratified social system to another with a higher grade of mobility is being accomplished without the least system of degeneracy of the higher social instincts and of those human values which constitute one of the fundamental characteristics of our culture and civilization. No doctrine which pays no attention to one half of man, or which, exaggerating the technical aspect of civilization, stimulates old gregarious instincts and prepares hordes of mechanized barbarians, has yet been written into the plans of national policy or into any of the programs of our policy of culture and education. Both, and they are intimately connected,—because every educational policy varies in function of a general policy,—have not entered into the heart of the movement except to find there, to arouse and to develop both personal and community aspirations, which no temporary deformation would be able entirely to stifle, to search for a type of socialism which would be able to combine the person and the community and to lay down at the base of education and of culture, freedom of conscience and respect for the rights and dignities of the human personality.

BIBLIOGRAPHY

Almeida, M. O., *A Alta Cultura e sua organização* (1927).

Almeida Prado, A., "Algumas necessidades do ensino médico," in *Estudos brasileiros*, Rio, July–Aug., 1939.

Arbousse-Bastide, P., "O Ensino secundário, chave de toda a reforma educacional," in *O Estado de São Paulo*, Oct. 30, 1935.

Azevedo, Fernando de, *A Educação pública em São Paulo: Problemas e discussões* (São Paulo: Comp. Editora Nacional, 1937—Brasiliana, Vol. 98). Inquiry by *O Estado de São Paulo*, 1926.

——, *Novos caminhos e novos fins: Uma Nova Política de educação no Brasil* (São Paulo: Comp. Editora Nacional, 1st ed., 1931; 2nd ed., 1935).

——, *A Educação e seus problemas* (São Paulo: Comp. Editora Nacional, 1937).

——, *A Reconstrução educacional do Brasil: Manifesto dos pioneiros da educação nova* (São Paulo: Comp. Editora Nacional, 1932), especially the introduction, "Ao povo e ao govêrno."

Barbosa, Rui, *Reforma do ensino primário* (Rio: Imprensa Nacional, 1883).

——, *Reforma do ensino secundário e superior* (Rio, 1882).

Belo Lisboa, J. C., *O Ensina agrícola no Brasil: Conferência pronunciada na IV Conferência Nacional de Educação* (Belo Horizonte: Imprensa Oficial de Minas Gerais, 1932).

Boiteux, Lucas Alexandre, *A Escola Naval: Seu histórico, 1761–1937* (Rio: Imprensa Naval, 1940), Pt. 1, "Da fundação à maioridade de Pedro II."

Calógeras, J. Pandiá, "O Problema universitário brasileiro," in *Res Nostra* (São Paulo: Irmãos Ferraz, 1930), pp. 248–252.

Campos, Francisco, *Educação e cultura* (Rio: Olímpio, 1940).

Coarací, Vivaldo, *Problemas nacionais* (Rio, 1930), Chaps. XII, XIV.

Dreyfus, André, "Ensino humanístico e científico no ensino secundário," in *Folha da Noite*, São Paulo, Apr. 30, 1937.

——, "O Valor da Faculdade de Filosofia e a ciência pura," in *O Estado de São Paulo*, Apr. 14–17, 1938.

Frota Pessoa, J. G., *A Educação e a rotina* (Rio: Francisco Alves, 1928).

——, *A Realidade brasileira* (Rio: Francisco Alves, 1931). Lourenço Filho, M. B., *Tendências da educação brasileira* (São Paulo: Comp. de Melhoramentos, n.d.—Biblioteca de Educação, Vol. 29).

Pinto, Estêvão, *A Escola e a formação da mentalidade popular brasileira* (São Paulo: Comp. de Melhoramentos, n.d.).

Simonsen, Roberto, "Objectivos da engenharia nacional," in *Boletim do Instituto de Engenharia*, São Paulo, Sept., 1939.

Silva Freire, V. da, *Engenharia e seu ensino superior* (1931).

——, "As Escolas de engenharia e o plano nacional de educação," in *Jornal do Comércio*, Rio, Aug. 22, 1937.

Silva Melo, A. da, *Problemas do ensino médico e de educação* (Rio: Ariel, 1937), with Preface by Gilberto Freyre.

Silva Rodrigues, Mílton, *Educação comparada* (São Paulo: Comp. Editora Nacional, 1938), Pt. 3, "O Brasil," pp. 233–290.

Sousa Campos, E., and I. Azevedo Amaral, "O Problema educativo," in *O Estado de São Paulo*, Apr. 8–9, 1937.

Tasso Fragoso, "O Ensino militar e a Escola de Estado Maior," in *Nação Armada*, No. 5 (Apr., 1940). Address, in 1931, at the Escola de Estado Maior.

Teixeira de Freitas, M. A., *O Ensino primário no Brasil* (Biblioteca de Educação, Vol. 21).

———, *O que dizem os números sôbre o ensino primário* (São Paulo: Comp. de Melhoramentos, n.d.—Biblioteca de Educação, Vol. 27).

Vargas, Getúlio, *A Nova Política do Brasil* (Rio: Olímpio, 8 vols., 1938–1941).

Willems, Emílio, *Mobilidade e flutuação das profissões no Brasil e o problema educacional* (São Paulo: Escolas Profissionais Salesianas, 1937).

———, *Relatório do Primeiro Congresso de Instrução Secundária* (1911).

———, *Anais do Quarto Congresso Brasileiro de Instrução Superior e Secundária, realizado em 1922* (Rio, 1926).

———, *Livro do Centenário dos cursos jurídicos* (Rio, 1928), II.

———, *O Problema universitário brasileiro* (Rio: A Encadernadora S.A., 1929). Inquiry by Secção de Ensino Técnino e Superior da Associação Brasileira de Educação.

GENERAL BIBLIOGRAPHY

Agassiz, Louis and Elizabeth Cary, *A Journey in Brazil* (Boston, 1868). Transl. as *Viagem ao Brasil (1865–1866)* (São Paulo: Comp. Editora Nacional, 1940—Brasiliana).

Antonil, André João, *Cultura e opulência do Brasil por suas drogas e minas*, with a bio-bibliographical study by Afonso de E. Taunay (São Paulo: Comp. Melhoramentos, 1923).

Armitage, John, *História do Brasil, desde a chegada da família de Bragança até a abdicação de Dom Pedro I em 1931* (São Paulo, 1914).

Buarque de Holanda, Sérgio, *Raízes do Brasil* (Rio: Olímpio, 1935—Coleção Documentos Brasileiros, vol. 1).

Burton, Richard, *The Exploration of the Highlands of Brazil* (London, 1869).

Calmon, Pedro, *História da Civilização brasileira* (São Paulo: Comp. Editora Nacional, 1933).

Calógeras, J. Pandiá, *Formação histórica do Brasil* (Rio: Pimenta de Melo, 1931; 3rd ed., São Paulo: Comp. Editora Nacional, 1938—Brasiliana, Vol. 14).

Capistrano de Abreu, João, *Caminhos antigos e povoamento do Brasil* (Rio: Briguiet, 1931—Edição da Sociedade Capistrano de Abreu).

———, *Capítulos de história colonial, 1500–1800* (Rio: Briguiet, 1934—Edição da Sociedade Capistrano de Abreu).

Cardim, Father Fernão, *Tratados da terra e gente do Brasil* (São Paulo: Comp. Editora Nacional, 1939). With introduction and notes by Batista Caetano, Capistrano de Abreu, and Rodolfo Garcia.

Castelnau, François de, *Expédition dans les parties centrales de l'Amérique du Sud* (Paris, 1850).

Denis, Ferdinand, *Résumé de l'histoire du Brésil, suivi du résumé de l'histoire de la Guyane* (Paris: Lecointe & Durey, 1825).

Denis, Maurice, *Resumo da historia do Brasil até 1828*, transl., rev., and expanded by H. L. Niemeyer (Rio: Gaufrier, 1931).

Fleiuss, Max, *Elementos de história contemporânea, 1815–1897* (Rio: Laemmert, 1900).

———, *História da administração do Brasil* (São Paulo: Comp. Melhoramentos, 2nd ed., n.d.).

Freire, Felisbelo, *Os Portugueses no Brasil* (Rio: Economista Brasileiro, 1907). Historical and critical study, from the 16th to the 19th century.

Freyre, Gilberto, *Casa Grande e Senzala* (Rio: Schmidt, 2nd ed., 1936. Transl. by Samuel Putnam as *The Masters and the Slaves* (New York, 1946).

———, *Sobrados e Mocambos* (São Paulo: Comp. Editora Nacional, 1936).

———, *Nordeste: Aspectos da influência da cana sôbre a vida e a paisagem do nordeste do Brasil* (Rio: Olímpio, 1937—Coleção Documentos Brasileiros, Vol. 4).

Galenti, Father Rafael Maria, *História do Brasil* (São Paulo: Dupart, 5 vols., 1911).

Gandavo, Pero de Magalhães, *Tratado da terra e da gente do Brasil*, and *História da Província de Santa Cruz* (Rio: Anuario do Brasil, n.d.).

Gardner, George, *Travels in the Interior of Brazil, Principally Through the Northern Provinces* (London, 1824).

Graham, Maria, *Journal of a Voyage to Brazil and Residence There During the Years 1821, 1822, 1823* (London, 1824).

Handelman, Heinrich, *Geschichte von Brasilien* (Berlin: Springer, 1860).

Homem de Melo, Francisco Inácio Marcondes, *Estudos de história brasileira* (São Paulo: Tip. 2 de dezembro, 1858).

Kidder, D. P. and J. C. Fletcher, *Brazil and the Brazilians* (Philadelphia, 1857). Transl. by Elias Dolianti as *O Brasil e os Brasileiros: Escoço histórico e descritivo*, rev. with notes by Edgar Süssekind de Mendonça (São Paulo: Comp. Editora Nacional, 1941—Brasiliana, Vols. 205, 206).

Koster, Henry, *Travels in Brazil* (London, 1816).

Leite, Serafim, *História da Companhia de Jesús no Brasil* (Rio: Livraria Portugalia, Lisboa e Civilização Brasileira, 1939).

Licínio Cardoso, Vicente, *A Margem da história do Brasil* (São Paulo: Comp. Editora Nacional, 1933).

Luccock, John, *Notes on Rio de Janeiro and Southern Parts of Brazil* (London, 1820)

Mawe, John, *Travels in the Interior of Brazil* (Philadelphia, 1816).

Melo Morais, A. J. de, *Brasil histórico* (Rio: Fauchon & Dupont, 1867).

——, *Crônica geral e minuciosa do Império do Brasil* (Rio: Dias da Silva Jr., 1879).

——, *A Independência e o Imperio do Brasil* (Rio: Globo, 1817).

——, *História do Brasil Reino e do Brasil Império* (Rio: Pinheiro, 1871).

Nash, Roy, *The Conquest of Brazil* (New York, 1926). Transl. by Moacir de N. Vasconcelos as *A Conquista do Brasil* (São Paulo: Comp. Editora Nacional, 1939—Brasiliana, Vol. 150).

Normano, J. F., *Brazil: A Study of Economic Types* (Chapel Hill: Univ. of North Carolina Press, 1935). Transl. by T. Quartim Barbosa, P. Peake Rodrigues, and L. Brandão Teixeira as *Evolução econômica do Brasil* (São Paulo: Comp. Editora Nacional, 1939—Brasiliana, Vol. 152).

Oliveira Lima, Manuel de, *O Império Brasileiro (1822–1889)* (São Paulo: Comp. Melhoramentos, 1927).

——, *Dom João VI no Brasil* (Rio: Jornal do Comércio, 2 vols., 1908).

Peixoto, Júlio Afrânio, *História do Brasil* (Porto: Lelo, 1940).

Pereira da Silva, J. M., *História do Brasil durante e menoridade de Dom Pedro II, 1831–1840* (Rio: Garnier, 2nd ed., rev. and enlarged, 1878).

——, *História da fundação do Império brasileiro* (Rio: Garnier, 2nd ed., rev. and enlarged, 3 vols., 1877).

Prado Junior, Caio, *Evolução política do Brasil* (São Paulo: Empresa Gráfica da Revista dos Tribunais, 1933).

Reybaud, Charles, *Le Brésil* (Paris: Guillaumin, 1856).

Ribeiro, João, *História do Brasil: Curso superior* (Rio: Jacinto, 2nd ed., 1901).

Rocha Pita, Sebastião, *História da America Portuguesa* (Lisbon: Antero da Silva, 2nd ed., rev. and annotated by J. Gois, 1880).

Rocha Pombo, J. F., *História do Brasil* (Rio: Fonseca & Saraiva, 10 vols., n.d.).

Saint-Hilaire, Auguste de, *Voyages dans l'intérieur du Brésil* (Paris, 1852).

Serrano, Jônatas, *História do Brasil* (Rio: Briguiet, 1931).

Simonsen, Roberto, *História econômica do Brasil* (São Paulo: Comp. Editora Nacional, 1933).

Soares e Sousa, Gabriel, *Tratado descritivo do Brasil em 1587*, ed. corrected after examination of many old MSS. in Brazil, Portugal, Spain, Holland, and France by Francisco Adolfo de Varnhagen (São Paulo: Comp. Editora Nacional, 3rd ed., 1938).

Southey, Robert, *History of Brazil* (London, 2nd ed., 3 vols., 1822).

Steinen, Karl von den, *Entre os aborígenes do Brasil Central,* transl. by Egon Shaden—separate of the *Revista do Arquivo Municipal* (São Paulo: Departamento de Cultura, 1940).

———, *O Brasil Central: Expedição em 1884 para a exploração do rio Xingú,* transl. by Catarina B. Canabrava (São Paulo: Comp. Editora Nacional, 1942—Brasiliana, Grande Formato, No. 3).

Taunay, Afonso d'Escragnolle, *História geral das bandeiras paulistas* (São Paulo, 1924–1929).

Tavares de Lira, A., *Organização política e administrativa do Brasil: Colonia, Imperio, Republica* (São Paulo: Comp. Editora Nacional, 1941).

Varnhagen, F. A. de, *História geral do Brasil, antes da sua separação e independéncia de Portugal* (Rio: Laemmert, 2nd ed., rev. and enlarged, 2 vols., n.d.) 3rd ed., São Paulo: Comp. Melhoramentos, n.d.).

Viana, F. J. de Oliveira, *Evolução do povo brasileiro* (São Paulo: Comp. Editora Nacional, 3rd ed., 1933—Brasiliana, Vol. 10).

———, *Populacões meridionais do Brasil* (São Paulo: Comp. Editora Nacional, 2nd ed., 1933 —Brasiliana, Vol. 8).

Warden, Davi B., *Histoire de l'Empire du Brésil* (Paris: Moreau, 2 vols., 1932).

Wied-Neuwied, Maximilian, Prince of, *Viagem ao Brasil,* transl. by Edgar Süssekind de Mendonça and Flávio Poppe de Figueiredo, and annotated by Oliverio Pinto (São Paulo: Comp. Editora Nacional, 1940—Brasiliana, Grande Formato, No. 1).

NAME INDEX

SUBJECT INDEX

ABOLITION, 410, 412, 428, 432
consequences of, 106
growth of primary education and, 493, 494
romanticism and the abolitionist ideal, 209
slaveholding mentality and technical education, 383
ACADEMY
Brazilian Academy of Letters, 215
Brazilian Academy of Sciences, 233
of Fine Arts, 298, 301n., 416
Imperial Naval, 499n.
Medico-Chirurgical, 236
Military, 236
Military of the Court, 499n.
Military and Naval, 499n.
National and Imperial Naval, 499n.
National, of medicine, 185n., 233
Naval, 175n.
Royal Military, 174, 174n.
Royal Naval, 175n.
Royal, of Painting, Sculpture, and Architecture, 373
of Sciences of Paris, 253, 253n.
Scientific, 233
AFRICANS
African population in Brazil, 31-33
Catholicism and, 147-148
popular Brazilian music and, 285-286
slavery. See ABOLITION, NEGRO
SLAVERY
See ASSIMILATION
AGRICULTURE
agricultural properties. See PROPERTY
agricultural schools. See under SCHOOLS
coffee. See COFFEE
coivara, destruction of forests by fire, 54
monoculture. See MONOCULTURE
National Center of Agricultural Education and Research, 506n.
polyculture, 58-62, 430
Royal Garden, 238, 239
sugar cane. See SUGAR
sugar mills. See SUGAR MILLS
tilling of the soil and the Jesuits, 350-351
See also BOTANY, ECONOMY, SCHOOL,
STATISTICS
AGRONOMY. See AGRICULTURE
AMERICAN INDIANS. See ASSIMILA-
TION, NATIVES
American Naval Mission, 502
ANTHROPOLOGY, 257, 258
ARCHITECTURE
campaign for traditional architecture, 310

churches and convents of Bahia, 151
cloisters of the Northeast, 278, 279
colonial houses, 283, 284
colonial renaissance, as a function of its architectural elements, 310, 311
landscape architecture and, 311, 312
modern, 311
religious and civil, 276, 284
urban developments in the twentieth century, 309, 310, 311
See also ACADEMY, ART, LICEU, MU-
SEUM, SCHOOL, SOCIETY
ARISTOCRACY
aristocratic education, 381
landed, a conservative force in the Republic, 106, 107
rural, in colonial society, 94, 95; and the monarchical regime, 101, 102
ART
aesthetic education of the peole, 318, 319
appearance of, in Brazil, 276, 277
applied, 299; applied to industry, 317, 318
architecture, See ARCHITECTURE
artistic expansion, 304, 305
artistic maturity of the country, 319
Baroque style. See BAROQUE
caricature. See CARICATURE
carving, 306n., 307n.
centers of artistic life, 298, 305, 306
ceramics, 305n., 317, 318
criticism of, 318-320
development of, under Dutch rule, 274-276
drawing. See DRAWING
factor in cultural documentation, 273-274
French influence and colonial art, 289-298
gardens and architecture, 311, 312
goldsmithing, 282-283, 307n.
modern movement in, 319
music. See MUSIC
painting. See PAINTING
political decentralization and, 304, 305
popular and native arts, 304, 305
public and the artist, 315-318
Republic and the development of art in Brazil, 273-274
sculpture. See SCULPTURE
Servico do Patrimonio Historico e Artistico Nacional, 484n.
zenith of, and of economic life, 279
See also ART INSTITUTIONS
Art Institutions: See ACADEMY, ART, AS-
SOCIATION, CENTER, CONSERVA-
TORY, INSTITUTE, LICEU, MU-
SEUM, SCHOOL, SOCIETY

CULTURE—(*Cont'd.*)

Catholicism and Brazilian, 145-152, 162-163

Centers of artistic, 298, 304-306

colonial, 145-148, 233-234, 351-354; obscurantism of Brazil in the colonial period, 233

concept of, 1-10

Constituent Assembly of 1933 and the cultural renaissance, 467-468

cultural level and school systems, 427-428

cultural unity of the country. *See* UNITY

"cultural type," 6 and n.

Departmento de Propaganda e Difusão Cultural do Ministério da Justica, 481

Dom João VI and specialized, 174, 372; and general culture, 204

Dutch and Portuguese, 276-278

economic organization and the type of, 503
  of the élite and the rest of the population, 383-385
  of an encyclopedic character, 185

evolution of Brazilian, the Empire and the Republic, 413-414 and n.

historical roots of the development of, 489-491

humanistic. *See* HUMANISM

Jesuits and Brazilian. *See* JESUITS

juridical, 171

Kultur, 5-6 and n.

Kulturkreise, 4

Kulturschichten, 4

liberalism and the Brazilian cultural scene, 366-367

national educational policy and, 523-524

native, 39

November 10, 1937, and cultural policy, 469-470

private initiative in Brazilian, 372-373 and n.

Protestantism and Brazilian, 157-158 and n.

qualitative, 474-475

religion and Brazilian, 141-143

Republic, from the cultural point of view, 424

scientific culture in Brazil and the reform of the University of Coimbra, 360-361; and social transformation, 504-505

Seminary of Olinda and its cultural influence. *See* SEMINARY OF OLINDA

Society for Artistic Culture, 305

universities and the training of the cultural élite, 513; their role in our cultural life, 514-515 and n. *See also* ASSIMILATION, CIVILIZATION, EDUCATION, MENTALITY, PROFESSIONS

DEGREE

of bachelor of arts, and rise in the social scale, 168-169, 342n., 511-512; and the political direction of the country, 180-181

of master of arts, and rise in the social scale, 342-343

DEMOCRACY

decentralization of education and narrowing of the distance between social classes, 435

democratization of education, 469-470, 475, 493

humanistic culture and the democratic spirit, 492-493

Demography. *See* POPULATION

DEPARTMENT

Departamento Administrativo do Serviço Publico (D.A.S.P.), 473n., 523

Departamento Municipal de Cultura de São Paulo, 264

Departamento de Propaganda e Difusão Cultural do Ministério da Justica, 481

DIAMONDS. *See* MINES

DRAWING

caricaturists, 300n.

humorous and caricature, 300 n.

School of Drawing and Painting of Curitiba, 304

See also ART

ECONOMY

Attraction of European immigrants and economic life, 57

colonial society: its structure and the sugar economy, 91-97

division of labor and hierarchy of professional types, 511

economic classes and literature, 193-200

economic frontiers, 51-53

economic organization and educational diversification, 503, and professional diversification, 504, and type of culture, 503

educational system and the evolution of economic life, 437; and the economic and cultural level, 448-449

evolution of educational ideals and change in economic life, 438-439

Faculty of Economics, Politics and Law of the Federal District, 465n.

lack of interest in economics, 125-126

Negro slavery and free labor, 58-59

relations between the high point of economic life and of art, 278

rise of industry and new problems, 109-111, 409-410, 507-508

small properties and economic life, 111-112

social classes, and the economic life of the country, 58-60

technological development and sugar, 46-48

See also AGRICULTURE, CATTLE, COMMERCE, INDUSTRY, STATISTICS

EDUCATION

aesthetic, 317-319

Brazilian Association of, 439-440, 441n., 442, 448n., 449n.

Brazilian Pedagogical Library (published by the Editora Nacional), 450

EDUCATION–(*Cont'd.*)
centralization and decentralization in education. *See* UNITY
Church, its educational policy, 452-453; and educational reform, 454, 457, 458-459. *See* CATHOLICISM, PROTESTANTISM
congresses and conferences of. *See* CONFERENCES, CONGRESSES
debates on educational questions, 440, 442-444
degrees of bachelor of arts and master of arts, and rise in the social scale, 168-169, 343
diversity of education in different social classes, 381-382, 387-388, 434-436, 502
"Education Act" of Lord Fisher, 438
  and cultural life under the Empire, 405-406
  and cultural policy, 523-525; conditions of organic unity, 443-444; as a function of politics in general, 523
Education Library (published by the Improvement Co. of São Paulo), 449
educational cinema. *See* CINEMA
educational policy and Independence, 373-375
educational radio. *See* RADIO
excess of bachelors and doctors, 180
expansion of urban centers and the reform movement in education, 438-439
Federal and State school system, 435-436; and political transformations in postwar Europe, 437; and the economic and cultural level, 427-428
Foreign professors, missions, 265-266, 515, 522n.
great Brazilian educations, 389-390, 428-429
humanistic. *See* HUMANISM
imperial educational policy and the personal attitude of the emperor, 400-401
interpenetration of the clerical and pedagogical spheres, 398-399
Jesuit. *See* JESUITS
manifesto of the pioneers of the new education, 454-455
Ministry of Education and Health, 450, 454, 472, 479, 482, 483 and n., 509n.
Ministry of Instruction, Posts and Telegraph, 415
national legislation and, *See* CONSTITUTION, LEGISLATION
nationalization of schools of the south of the country, 471
new educational ideas, 440, 441
new educational ideas in Portugal, 356
Pedagogium, 436; and the unity of Brazilian education, 416-417
Portuguese policy and education in Brazil, 344-345
private initiative and, 399
private institutions of secondary education, 394-399

Protestant educators and American pedagogical ideas, 419-420
reform of education and the Constituent Assembly of 1933, 467; and the Pan-American policy, 478; and the Seminary of Olinda, 368n. *See* EDUCATIONAL REFORM
reform projects. *See* EDUCATIONAL REFORM
religion. *See* CATHOLICISM, PROTESTANTISM, RELIGION
Revolution of 1930 and, 450-454, 456-460, 522
scholarships for study in North America and Europe, 522; for the University of Coimbra, 361 and n.
social function of the schools, 405-406
statistics of. *See* STATISTICS
universities, their role. *See* UNIVERSITY
of women, 427, 434-435
See also CULTURE, INSTITUTES, LEGISLATION, PROFESSIONS, SCHOOL, TEACHING, UNIVERSITY
EDUCATIONAL REFORM
churches and pedagogical reform, 452-454, 457-459
manifesto of the pioneers of the new education, 455-457
projects for, 415-416
  of Anísio Teixeira, 439
  of Gustavo Capanema (Jan., 1937), 470 n., 472
  of Benjamim Constant, 413, 416-418, 421, 425n., 426-427
  of Carneiro Leão, in Rio de Janeiro, 439
  in Ceará, 438
  in the Federal District, 439
  of Councilor Dantas and the mentality of the period, 404; and the opinion of Rui Barbosa, 403-405, 411n.
  of Lisímaco da Costa, in Paraná, 439
  of Fernando de Azevedo, in the Federal District (1928), 441n., 446-448, 480-510; critical analysis of, 441-443
  of Pombal, and humanistic education, 493; and middle and higher education, 360; the Franciscans and education after, 360-361; effect in Brazil, 234-235; and pedagogical unity, 360
  in São Paulo (1920), 438; and American educational ideas, 419-421
of Carlos Maximiliano, 426n.
of 1928, its effect in Brazil, 448-449
of higher and secondary education, 435, of industrial education, 461; and new pedagogical techniques, 438-439, 440-443
in Minas Gerais, 440
of Francisco Campos, 426n.
of Rocha Vaz, 436
ELITES
assimilation of, 169

MENTALITY—(*Cont'd.*)
Portuguese, 491n.
 professional juridical, 432
 Protestant, 338
 rhetorical, in the imperial regime and the
  problems of national life, 390-391
 scholastic, in the Iberian Peninsula, 337
 slaveholding, and technical education,
  383
lack of interest in economics, 124-125
objectivity, 126
patriotism, 132-133, 169
persistence, 127
political romanticism and the Brazilian, 390
Positivism and the Brazilian, 420-421
psychological traits of races that formed the
 Brazilian people, 115-117
relation between individual and State, 131-132
sensibility, 126
spirit of cooperation, 129
transformation of the Brazilian, 135
verbalism, 249
MESTIZOS
industrial activity and slaves and, 503-504
social structure in the colony and miscegenation, 91-95
sugar mills, centers of race mixture, 71
MILITARY
French military mission, 500
General Staff course, 500
military education, 498-503. *See also* ACAD-
 EMY, LEGISLATION, SCHOOL
philosophy of Comte and the military class,
 413n.-414 and n.
See also ACADEMY, LEGISLATION,
 NAVY, SCHOOL
MINERALOGY
exploration of the grottoes of Maquiné and
 Sumidouro, 244
School of Mines and the specialists in, 252-
 253
See also MINES
MINES
cities of the region of, 74-78
diamonds, statistics of production, 49
dislocation of the political axis and, 49
gold, statistics of production, 49
incentive to occupy the soil, 48-49
mining in the colonial period and its consequences, 48-49; and equalitarianism, 97-
 98; and Brazilian individualism, 48; and
 movements of internal migration, 48-49
republican nativistic sentiment and mining,
 201
School of Mines, 175, 182, 252, 253
School of Mines of Ouro Prêto, 417, 431n.;
 and objective teaching, 389, 401
tax of the "Fifth," 49n.
MINING. *See* MINES
MISSION OF FRENCH ARTISTS, 289-
 291

MISSIONS OF FOREIGN PROFESSORS,
 265, 267, 515, 522 and n.
MODERNISM
 in architecture, 311
 in the artistic movement in general, 319-
  320
 in literature, 222-227
 in music, 312-315
 in painting, 307-308
 in sculpture, 306-308
MONASTERIES
 and convents, 150-152
 and schools, 150-152
 of São Bento, 501 and n.
MONOCULTURE
 replaced by diversified agriculture, 58-59
 sugar and complementary industry, 56;
  and the small property, 111 and n.
 and technology, 167-168
MUSEUM
American Museum of Natural History, 3
Cologne Ethnographic, 4
Copenhagen Museum, 244
Museu de Arte Religiosa, 420n.
Museu Histórico Nacional, 263 and n.
 Imperial, 253, 316n.
 da Inconfidência, 483n.
 Mariano Procópio de Juiz de Fora, 316n.
 das Missões, 316n.
 de Moldagem, 484n.
 National, 399
 do Ouro, 483n.
 Paraense (Goldi) 424
 Paulista, 263n., 424
 Real, 236, 238
Oxford University Museum, 2
MUSIC
Brazilian art music and the religious spirit,
 285-288
Brazilian Association of Music, 315
evolution of Brazilian, 300-305
Father José Muarício, 287
modern, 312-315
musical activities, 315
popular Brazilian, 285-286, 312-313 and n.;
 and art, 312; Portuguese and Afro-Indian
 influence on, 286
reviews of art music, 314-315
sacred, 285-288, 301
Society of Artistic Culture, 305
Society of Symphonic Concerts, 305
symphonic and chamber, 313-315
See also ART, CONSERVATORY, INSTI-
 TUTE, RADIO, SCHOOL

NATIVES
and Catholicism, 147-149
defense of, and the Jesuits, 144 and n.-145
native civilization, 39-40
native population, 31-36
native themes and romanticism, 207-208

TEACHING—(*Cont'd.*)

character, 393-394. *See also* EDUCATIONAL REFORM

secondary education for women, 427, 435 and n., 469; higher education for women, 435 and n.

secularization of, 417-419, 420-422, 453-455

social change and the development of technical, 503-507; and specialization of, 511-512

special education, 415, 497; Imperial Institute of Blind Children, 415; Institute of the Blind, 497n.; Institute for Deaf Mutes, 416, 497n.

specialization of, and the development of industry, 503, 508-510; and the transformation of social life, 511-512

technical and professional, 432-436, 463-464, 470-471, 508-511; and the bourgeoisie, 433; commercial, 505-506, 508-510; and the Constitution of 1837, 509; cooperation of factories and workshops in, 509-511; statistics of, 511-512; in the Empire, 384n.; industrial, 511-513; and slaveholding mentality, 385; in São Paulo, 505-506 and n.; higher, and the French Revolution, 496

type of instruction and the organization of Brazilian society, 502-504

See also CULTURE, EDUCATION, LEGISLATION, PROFESSIONS, SCHOOL, UNIVERSITY

TEMPLES

Catholic, 148 and n.

statistics, 158n.

THEATER

evolution of the, in Brazil, 200

Municipal Theater of Rio de Janeiro, 315

THEORY OF THE CONTINENTAL DRIFT, 19-23

THEOSOPHY, 159

TRANSPORTATION

coastwise navigation, 21, 60

commerce, 59-62, 65, 66

increase of, and national unity, 524

railroads, 56, 59, 61n., 62; first plans and accomplishments, 175, 176-177

renewal of, 83

river navigation, 60-61

river ports, 60, 61

roads, 60, 61 and n., 62

TREASURY

literary subsidies, 357

tax of the "Fifth," 49n.

TREATY

of Madrid, 89

of Santo Ildefonso, 99

of Tordesillas, 98

UNITY

cultural, and the chaplains, 359; and the Church, 358; and the Jesuits, 351-354; and books, newspapers, and magazines, 476-478

and educational decentralization, 377, 410-412, 434, 438-439, 470-474; and the rapprochement of the social classes, 435; and the Additional Act, 376-378, 387, 391, 411-413; and the Constitution of 1891, 412, 435; during the 19th century, 377-379; and the "Pedagogium," 417; and the Reform of Pombal, 360; and the intellectual unity of Brazil, 523-524

national, the spirit of, 98-104, 219-222; and the bandeiras, 98-99; and humanistic and literary culture, 491-493; and federalism, 101-108, 410-412; and liberal ideals, 376; and the Jesuits, 351-353; and means of communication, 523-524; and mining, 201; and the nationalization of the schools of the south of the country, 473-475; and the vernacular, 149

and political decentralization, 107-108, 111-112; and the Jesuit mission work, 330-332; and art, 304; and equalitarianism, 113; and the beginning of colonization, 90-97; and the second Empire, 103-104

UNIVERSITY

of Belo Horizonte, 519

of Brazil, 465-466 and n., 475, 509, 514n., 521

Brazilian universities, 451, 455, 464-466, 519-520

Catholic, of Rio de Janeiro, 476

of Coimbra, 146n., 169n., 233, 344, 358, 360-361 and n.

of the Federal District, 461, 466, 476, 514

of Minas Gerais, 465n., 475, 514n.

of Pôrte Alegre, 265, 514n., 519

of Rio de Janeiro, 265, 379n., 465n., 514n.

of São Paulo, 237, 265, 465, 475, 506n., 514-517, 520-522

Technical Federal, 509

Technical, of Pôrte Alegre, 519

Technical, of Rio Grande do Sul, 506

universities and the formation of cultural élites, 513

universities and their role in our cultural system, 511-513, 515-516

occidental universities, 466-467

WAR

European, and the Brazilian educational system, 437

of the Farrapos, 102-103

Paraguayan, 499n.

WOMAN

attendance by women at normal schools, 434-